The **Rough Guide** to

Poland

written and researched by

Jonathan Bousfield and Mark Salter

with additional contributions by

Thomas Brown, Taissa Csáky and Gordon McLachlan

ROUGH
GUIDES

NEW YORK • LONDON • DELHI

www.roughguides.com

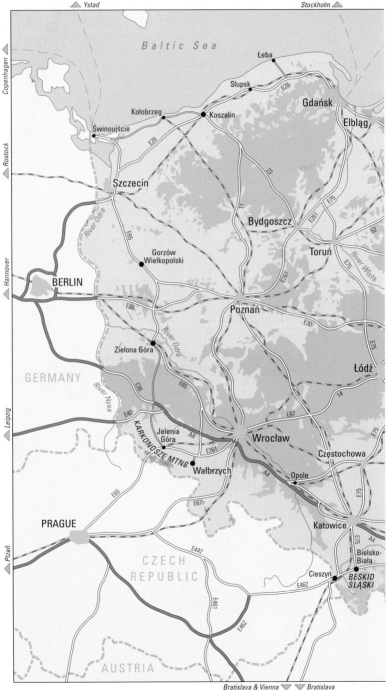

Ystad ▲   Stockholm ▲

Baltic Sea

Łeba

Słupsk   E28

◁ Copenhagen

Kołobrzeg   Koszalin   Gdańsk

Świnoujście   Elbląg

E28

◁ Rostock

Szczecin   73

Bydgoszcz   E261   E75

◁ Hannover

Gorzów   Toruń   *River Wisła*   52
Wielkopolski   E75

BERLIN   E261

E65

Poznań

E30   E30   E75

River Odra

Zielona Góra   Łódź

◁ Leipzig   *River Nysa*   E36   E65   14

GERMANY   E40

E67   E75

KARKONOSZE MTNS   Jelenia   A4   Wrocław
Góra

E261   Częstochowa

Wałbrzych   A4   Opole

E65   E67   E75

PRAGUE   Katowice   A4

◁ Plzeň   E442   Bielsko-
Biała

CZECH   Cieszyn   BESKID
REPUBLIC   E462   ŚLĄSKI

E461

E462

AUSTRIA

2

Bratislava & Vienna ▽▽   ▽ Bratislava

3

SLOVAKIA

UKRAINE

BELARUS

RUSSIAN FEDERATION

LITHUANIA

Budapest

Košice & Budapest

Helsinki

Kaunas & Vilnius

Vilnius

Minsk

Minsk

Kovel

Lviv

100 km
0

N

Metres
below sea level
0
100
200
500
1000
1500
2000

Zakopane

TATRA MOUNTAINS

BIESZCZADY MOUNTAINS

Nowy Sącz

Krosno

Sanok

Kraków

Tarnów

Rzeszów

Przemyśl

River San

A259

A256

Zamość

Kielce

Lublin

Chełm

A255

Radom

River Wisła

River Bug

Terespol

WARSAW

Płock

BIAŁOWIEŻA FOREST

River Narew

PISKA FOREST

Białystok

A237

AUGUSTÓW FOREST

A236

Augustów

Suwałki

Giżycko

Mrągowo

Mazurian Lakes

Olsztyn

Kaliningrad

A231

A235

E30

E77

E40

E71

E75

17

19

7

73

83

19

18

10

16

51

Contents

Front section   1–24

Introduction 6
Where to go 10
When to go 14
Things not to miss 16

Basics   25–74

Getting there............................. 27
Visas and red tape 36
Insurance................................. 37
Health 38
Costs, money and banks 39
Information, websites
    and maps............................. 40
Getting around......................... 43
Accommodation 49
Eating and drinking................. 54
Communication and
    the media............................ 58
Opening hours and holidays 62
Festivals, entertainment
    and sports........................... 63
Outdoor activities 69
Police and trouble.................... 70
Work and study........................ 71
Travellers with disabilities 71
Directory 73

Guide   75–656

❶ Warsaw and Mazovia 77
❷ Northeastern Poland 165
❸ Southeastern Poland 285
❹ Kraków, Małopolska
    and the Tatras 379
❺ Silesia 503
❻ Wielkopolska and
    Pomerania...................... 579

Contexts   657–704

History 659
Polish music 683
Books 692

Language   705–723

Pronunciation......................... 707
Useful words and phrases 708
Food and drink 712
Glossaries.............................. 714

Advertisers   725–730

Small print & Index   731–744

Introduction to
Poland

In many ways, Poland is one of the success stories of the new Europe, transforming itself from communist-bloc one-party state to parliamentary democracy and European Union member in a remarkably short period of time. More than a decade and a half of non-communist governments have wrought profound changes on the country, unleashing entrepreneurial energies and widening cultural horizons in a way that pre-1989 generations would have scarcely thought possible. Gleaming corporate skyscrapers have taken root in Warsaw, and private shops and cafés have established themselves in even the most provincial of rural towns. The country has a radically different look about it, having exchanged the greyish tinge of a state-regulated society for the anything-goes attitude of private enterprise – and all the billboards and window displays that go with it.

All this may come as a shock to those who recall the Poland of the 1980s, when images of industrial unrest and anti-communist protest were beamed around the world. Strikes at the Lenin shipyards of Gdańsk and other industrial centres were the harbingers of the disintegration of communism in Eastern Europe, and, throughout the years of martial law and beyond, Poland retained a near-mythical status among outside observers as the country that had done most to retain its dignity in the face of communist oppression.

For many Poles, the most important events in the movement towards a post-communist society were the visits in 1979 and 1983 of Pope John Paul II, the former archbishop of Krakow, for whose funeral in April 2005, televised live on huge video screens, crowds of almost a million massed in the city. Poland was never a typical communist state: Stalin's verdict was that imposing communism on the nation was like trying to saddle a cow. Polish society in the postwar decades remained fundamentally traditional, maintaining beliefs, peasant life and a sense of nationhood to which the **Catholic Church** was integral. During periods of foreign oppression – oppression so severe that Poland as a political entity has sometimes vanished altogether from the maps of Europe – the Church was always the principal defender of the nation's identity, so that the Catholic faith and the struggle for independence have become fused in the Polish consciousness. The physical presence of the Church is inescapable – in Baroque buildings, roadside shrines and images of the national icon, the **Black Madonna of Częstochowa** – and the determination to preserve the memories of an often traumatic past finds expression in religious rituals that can both attract and repel onlookers.

World War II and its aftermath profoundly influenced the character of Poland: the country suffered at the

> The sense of social fluidity, of a country still in the throes of major transitions, remains a primary source of Poland's fascination

Fact file

• **Poland** occupies a vast swathe of territory in north-central Europe, bordered by Germany to the west, the Czech Republic and Slovakia to the south, and Ukraine, Belarus, Lithuania and Russia to the east.

• Much of northern and central Poland is made up of agricultural plainland and gently rolling country-side, although the Sudeten and Tatra mountains in the south provide a dramatic contrast.

• Its population of 38.6 million is predominantly both Polish and devoutly Catholic, although, unsurprisingly for a country which has changed its borders many times in the past, significant pockets of Ukrainians, Belarusians, Bojks and Łemks exist in the east of the country.

• Traditionally, Poland is known for its shipbuilding, coal and steel industries, although these days cosmetics, medicines and textile products – often made under licence for Western conglomerates – are increasingly important sources of foreign earnings.

• The vast bulk of foreign visitors head for splendid old cities like Kraków, or the ski resorts of the Tatras, although Baltic beaches and inland lake resorts – both much patronized by the Poles themselves – help to complete a varied tourist picture.

hands of the **Nazis** as no other in Europe, losing nearly twenty percent of its population and virtually its entire **Jewish** community. In 1945 the **Soviet**-dominated nation was once again given new borders, losing its eastern lands to the USSR and gaining tracts of formerly German territory in the west. The resulting make-up of the population is far more uniformly "Polish" than at any time in the past, in terms of both language and religion, though there are still **ethnic minorities** of Belarusians, Germans, Lithuanians, Slovaks, Ukrainians and even Muslim Tatars.

To a great extent, the sense of social fluidity, of a country still in the throes of major transitions, remains a primary source of Poland's fascination. A decisive attempt to break with the communist past as well as tenacious adherence to the path of radical market **economic reforms** adopted in the late 1980s have remained the guiding tenets of Poland's new political leadership – a course seemingly unaltered by the changing political complexion of successive governments. Few would question the economic and human toll reaped by Poland's attempt to reach the El Dorado of capitalist prosperity – not least among the most vulnerable sectors of society: public sector employees, farmers, pensioners and the semi- or unemployed. Paradoxically, many of those who made the country's democratic revolution possible – militant industrial workers and anti-communist intellectuals – have found themselves marginalized in a society in which street-smart businessmen and computer-literate youth are far better poised to take advantage of the brave new Poland's burgeoning opportunities.

Dramatically changed geopolitical circumstances have seen Poland join **NATO**, the US-led military alliance of which it was – officially at least – a sworn enemy only ten years previously. Perhaps even more significantly, Poland, along with neighbours the Czech Republic and Hungary, is now a fully-fledged member of the **EU** – a status which promises to transform the country more profoundly than anything since the advent of communism.

Tourism is proving no exception to Poland's general "all change" rule, but despite the continuing state of flux in the country's tourist infrastructure, it is now easier to explore the country than anyone could have imagined only a few years back. This sea change is reflected in continuing and significant increases in the numbers of people visiting the country.

Encounters with the **people** are at the core of any experience of Poland. On trains and buses, on the streets or in the village bar, you'll never be stuck for opportunities for contact: Polish hospitality is legendary, and there's a natural progression from a chance meeting to an introduction to the extended family.

Folk music in Poland

Polish **folk music** may hold a significant position in the general national consciousness, but it's especially vibrant in the folk cultures found chiefly among the country's minorities and in its southern and eastern parts. Thanks to Chopin, whose inspiration came in large part from his native **Mazovia**, music from here is probably the best known but there are other equally worthwhile traditions in **Silesia**, the **Tatras** and the **Beskid Niski**. The festivals in **Zakopane** and **Kazimierz Dolny** offer excellent opportunities for getting to grips with many of these rootsy rural styles, while along the **Baltic coast** the popularity of sea shanties is demonstrated in many an annual festival. For a more detailed look at Polish music see p.64 and p.683.

Where to go

Poles delineate their country's attractions as "the mountains, the sea and the lakes", their emphasis firmly slanted to the traditional, rural heartlands. To get the most out of your time, it's perhaps best to follow their preferences. The **mountains** – above all the Carpathian range of the Tatras – are a delight, with a well-established network of hiking trails; the **lakes** provide opportunities for canoeing and a host of other outdoor pursuits; and the dozen or so **national parks** retain areas of Europe's last primeval forests, still inhabited by bison, elks, wolves, bears and eagles. Yet you will not want to miss the best of the **cities** – Kraków, especially – nor a ramble down rivers like the Wisła for visits to Teutonic **castles**, ancient waterside towns and grand, Polish **country mansions**, redolent of a vanished aristocratic order. Regions inhabited by **ethnic minorities** offer insights into cultures quite distinct from the Catholicism of the majority, while the former centres of the **Jewish community**, and the concentration camps in which the Nazis carried out their extermination, are the most moving testimony to the complexity and tragedy of the nation's past.

Unless you're driving to Poland, you're likely to begin your travels in one of the three major cities: Warsaw, Kraków or Gdańsk. Each provides an immediate immersion in the fast-paced changes of the last decade or so and a backdrop of monuments that reveal the twists and turns of

◄ Willow trees at sunset

the nation's history. **Warsaw**, the capital, had to be rebuilt from scratch after World War II, and much of the city conforms to the stereotype of Eastern European greyness, but the reconstructed Baroque palaces, churches and public buildings of the historic centre, the burgeoning street markets and the bright shopfronts of Poland's new enterprise culture are diverting-enough. **Kraków**, however, the ancient royal capital, is the real crowd puller for Poles and foreign visitors alike, rivalling the central European elegance of Prague and Vienna. This is the city where history hits you most power-fully, in the royal Wawel complex, in the fabulous open space of the Rynek, in the one-time Jewish quarter of Kazimierz, and in the chilling necropolis of nearby Auschwitz-Birkenau, the bloodiest killing field of the Third Reich. **Gdańsk**, formerly Danzig, the largest of the Baltic

> **The real crowd puller for Poles and foreign visitors alike, Kraków rivals the central European elegance of Prague and Vienna**

ports and home of the legendary shipyards, presents a dynamic brew of politics and commerce against a townscape reminiscent of mercantile towns in the Netherlands.

German and Prussian influences abound in the **north** of the country, most notably in the austere castles and fortified settlements constructed by the Teutonic Knights at **Malbork**, **Chełmno** and other strategic points

11

Seeing Poland's Jewish heritage

The history of Poland is inexorably linked to that of its **Jewish** population which, before World War II, comprised roughly ten percent (three million) of the country's total, Europe's largest Jewish community and the world's second largest. Of the current world population of fifteen million, over half are thought to be related to Polish Jewry, but up until the late 1980s those travelling to their ancestral home remained few in number due largely to fear of anti-Semitism and apprehension about travelling in communist Eastern Europe.

Nowadays, **organized tours**, particularly from Israel and the US, are common, visiting the traditional focal points of Polish-Jewish life and culture. Every effort has been made in the Guide to cover sites of interest to Jews, and many of the organizations on p.42 can provide further information. For more on Jewish heritage, see the "Books" section of Contexts, p.692.

along the **River Wisła** – as the Vistula is known in Poland. **Toruń** is one of the most atmospheric and beautiful of the old Hanseatic towns here.

Over in the **east**, numerous minority communities embody the complexities of national boundaries in central Europe. The one-time Jewish centre of **Białystok**, with its Belarusian minority, is a springboard for the eastern borderlands, where onion-domed Orthodox churches stand close to Tatar mosques. Further south, beyond **Lublin**, a famous centre of Hassidic Jewry, and **Zamość**, with its magnificent Renaissance centre, lie the homelands of Ukrainians, Łemks and Boyks – and a chance to see some of Poland's extraordinary wooden churches.

In the **west**, ethnic Germans populate regions of the divided province of **Silesia**, where **Wrocław** sustains the dual cultures of the former

▲ Near Mikołajki, Mazurian lakes

German city of Breslau and the Ukrainian city of L'viv, whose displaced citizens were moved here at the end of World War II. The other main city in western Poland is the quintessentially Polish **Poznań**, a vibrant and increasingly prosperous university town.

Despite its much-publicized pollution problems – problems it is now finally making a serious attempt to address – Poland has many regions of unspoilt natural beauty, of which none is more pristine than the **Białowieża Forest**, straddling the Belarusian border; the last virgin forest of the European mainland, it is the habitat of the largest surviving herd of European bison. Along the southern borders of the country lie the wild **Bieszczady** mountains and the alpine **Tatras** and, further west, the bleak **Karkonosze** mountains – all of them excellent walking country – interspersed with less demanding terrain. North of the central Polish plain, the wooded lakelands of **Mazury** and **Pomerania** are

Polish vodka

The tipple most associated with Poland, **vodka** is actually in danger of being eclipsed in popularity by beer among young Poles, so it's well worth seeking out the varieties you can't find abroad before they disappear from Polish shops and bars completely. Traditionally served chilled and neat – although increasingly mixed with fruit juice – vodka can be **clear** or **flavoured** with anything from bison grass to mountain herbs to juniper berries or honey. There's even been a revival of **kosher** vodkas – although whether their rabbinic stamps of approval are kosher themselves or just a marketing gimmick isn't always obvious.

13

as tranquil as any lowland region on the continent, while the Baltic coast can boast not just the domesticated pleasures of its beach resorts, but also the extraordinary desert-like dunes of the **Słowiński national park** – one of a dozen such parks.

◀ Wawel

When to go

S**pring** is arguably the ideal season for some serious hiking in Poland's mountainous border regions, as the days tend to be bright – if showery – and the distinctive flowers are at their most profuse. **Summer**, the tourist high season, sees plenty of sun, particularly on the Baltic coast, where the resorts are crowded from June to August and temperatures are consistently around 24°C (75°F).

Autumn is the best time to come if you're planning to sample the whole spread of the country's attractions: in the cities the cultural seasons are beginning at this time, and the pressure on hotel rooms is lifting. In the countryside, the golden Polish October is especially memorable, the

◀ Stall at Easter fair

rich colours of the forests heightened by brilliantly crisp sunshine, and it's often warm enough for T-shirts.

In **winter** the temperatures drop rapidly, icy Siberian winds blanketing many parts of the country with snow for anything from one to three months. Though the central Polish plain is bleak and unappealing at the end of the year, in

the south of the country skiers and other wintersports enthusiasts will find themselves in their element. By mid-December the slopes of the Tatras and the other border ranges are thronged with holiday-makers, straining the established facilities to the limit.

Average maximum temperatures (°F/°C) and rainfall

	Jan	March	May	July	Sept	Dec
Kraków						
max (°F)	32	45	67	76	67	38
max (°C)	0	7.2	19.4	24.4	19.4	3.3
Rainfall (mm)	28	35	46	111	62	36
Gdynia						
max (°F)	35	40	59	70	64	38
max (°C)	1.7	4.4	15	21.1	17.8	3.3
Rainfall (mm)	33	27	42	84	59	46
Poznań						
max (°F)	33	45	67	76	67	38
max (°C)	0.6	7.2	19.4	24.4	19.4	3.3
Rainfall (mm)	24	26	47	82	45	39
Przemyśl						
max (°F)	32	43	67	76	67	38
max (°C)	0	6.1	19.4	24.4	19.4	3.3
Rainfall (mm)	27	25	57	105	58	43
Warsaw						
max (°F)	32	41	67	76	67	36
max (°C)	0	5	19.4	24.4	19.4	2.2
Rainfall (mm)	27	27	46	96	43	44

28

things not to miss

It's not possible to see everything that Poland has to offer in one trip – and we don't suggest you try. What follows is a selective taste of the country's highlights: outstanding buildings and historic sites, natural wonders and vibrant festivals. They're arranged in five colour-coded categories, which you can browse through to find the very best things to see and experience. All highlights have a page reference to take you straight into the guide, where you can find out more.

01 The Tatras Page **479** • Poland's prime highland playground is a paradise for hikers of all abilities, with relaxing rambles in subalpine meadows for the easy-going, or hair-raising mountain-ridge walks for the more experienced.

02 Słowiński national park Page **630** • Trek across Sahara-like dunes just outside the seaside town of Łeba, pausing to sunbathe, bird-watch or explore World War II rocket installations along the way.

04 Lublin Page **290** • A jewel of an old town and a large student population make Lublin the liveliest and most rewarding of Poland's eastern cities – and one that's relatively undiscovered by tourists.

05 Vodka Pages **13** & **57** • The essential accompaniment to any social occasion. It has to be drunk neat and downed in one go if you want to do things properly.

03 Gdańsk's ulica Długa Page **176** • A stroll down one of Poland's most beautiful set-piece streets will take you past a string of wonderfully restored town houses, recalling the mercantile dynasties that made Gdańsk one of the great trading centres of northern Europe.

17

06 Wooden churches Page **360** • An age-old form of folk architecture still preserved in rural corners of the country. Visit some of the best examples in Jaszczurówka near Zakopane, or in the remote villages of the Bieszczady.

07 Malbork Castle Page **203** • The Teutonic Knights lorded it over northern Poland for more than 200 years, and this – a rambling complex of fortifications on the banks of the Wisła – is their most imposing monument.

08 Markets Pages **138** & **443** • In order to investigate the changes wrought by free-market economics in Poland, savour the street-level commerce of the country's outdoor markets – often frequented by small-time traders from Poland's eastern neighbours – where you'll find everything from fresh fruit and veg, fake designer tracksuits and car parts to traditional smoked cheeses.

09 Zamość Page **323** • A model Renaissance town located deep in the countryside of eastern Poland, and stuffed with the palaces and churches built by the Zamoyskis, one of the country's leading aristocratic families.

10 Baltic beaches Page **70** • Experience the bracing sea breezes and mile upon mile of unspoilt sands in laid-back, old-fashioned seaside resorts like Hel (p.198), Międzyzdroje (p.642) and Mielno (p.636).

11 Palace of Culture, Warsaw Page **115** • Love it or hate it, this soaring Art Deco monument to Stalinist ideology is still the outstanding feature of the downtown skyline.

12 Milk bars Page **54** • A particularly Polish institution in which you can scoff heartily and cheaply on staples like *bigos* (sauerkraut stew), *pierogi* (dumplings stuffed with meat) and *placki* (potato pancakes) in unpretentious, canteen-style surroundings.

13 Catholic festivals

Page **63** • As well as understanding Poland's politics it's essential to appreciate the religious backdrop. Attending one of the big Church festivals like Easter, Corpus Christi or the Annunciation will give you a flavour of this deeply religious country.

14 Białowieża national park

Page **277** • One of the most extensive areas of primeval forest in Europe, which you can explore on foot or by horse-drawn cart. Also famous for being home to a beast indigenous to Poland: the European bison.

15 Open-air museums

Pages **349**, **372** & **619** • Poland's rich tradition of folk crafts has been preserved in the open-air museums (or *skansen*) that gather together examples of vernacular architecture from around the country – often featuring the kind of timber-built farmhouses which have all but disappeared in the rest of Europe. Those in Nowy Sącz, Sanok and Lednica are particularly worth a visit.

16 Wawel

Page **409** • One of the most striking royal residences in Europe and a potent source of national and spiritual pride, Wawel is to Poles what Westminster Abbey, the Tower of London, Windsor Castle and Canterbury Cathedral are to the British – only all rolled into one.

17 Auschwitz-Birkenau Page **445** • Poland was once home to one of the most vibrant Jewish communities in Europe, a presence that was all but snuffed out by the Nazis during World War II. The most notorious extermination camp of them all, Auschwitz-Birkenau, offers the profoundest of insights into the nature of human evil, and demands to be visited – few who come here will be unchanged by the experience.

18 Kazimierz Dolny Page **312** • One of the best-preserved small towns of Poland's rural heartland, and an age-old centre of Jewish culture, now popular with the Warsaw arts-and-media set, who descend on Kazimierz en masse on summer weekends.

19 Folk festivals Page **685** • July and August are the busiest months in Poland's considerable calendar of traditional festivals. The International Festival of Highland Folklore in Zakopane is the main event to aim for, although there are numerous other regional events worth considering.

21 Poznań Page **585** • Recharge your urban batteries in the down-to-earth, work-hard-and-play-hard city that epitomizes the invigorating mercantile bustle of the new Poland.

20 Młoda Polska Page **405** • Get to grips with the *belle époque* art movement that transformed Polish culture by visiting the Wyspiański Museum in Kraków.

22 Zalipie Page **478** • For an insight into the riches of Polish folk culture, visit the village whose householders are famous for their distinctive taste in interior design.

22

23 Wrocław Page **528** • Wrocław's historic core is an exhilarating mixture of architectural influences, from Flemish-style Renaissance mansions to the late Gothic monstrosity of its town hall. At its heart stands a typically vibrant, café-splashed Rynek.

24 **Rynek Główny, Kraków** Page **384** • A spectacular medieval market square, packed with fine architecture, in a country that's famous for them. Settle down in one of the numerous pavement cafés and soak up the atmosphere.

26 **The Mazurian Lakes** Page **233** • The central Mazurian Lakes are a hugely popular destination for Polish tourists in summer, but the further east you head into the lakeland, the closer you can get to the lakes' essence as discovered by the first visitors here – beauty and solitude.

25 **Toruń** Page **209** • Birthplace of the astronomer Copernicus, and famous for the local gingerbread, Toruń is a medieval university town with a satisfying jumble of historical monuments, and a laid-back, easy-going charm.

27 Warsaw's Old Town Page **94** • Lively pavement cafés, fine restaurants and exuberant street life in a historic town centre that was faithfully reconstructed after its almost total destruction by the Nazis. As strong a symbol as any of Poland's struggle to rebuild in the aftermath of World War II.

28 The Black Madonna of Częstochowa Page **456** • The world-famous Black Madonna should not be missed, although what you actually do get to see of the painting is limited as the figures of the Madonna and Child are always "dressed" in sets of richly decorated clothes. More impressive, perhaps, is the sense of wonder, excitement and devotion the icon inspires in the pilgrims who come here.

Basics

Basics

Getting there 27

Visas and red tape 36

Insurance 37

Health.. 38

Costs, money and banks.. 39

Information, websites and maps... 40

Getting around 43

Accommodation 49

Eating and drinking... 54

Communications and the media... 58

Opening hours and holidays.. 62

Festivals, entertainment and sports....................................... 63

Outdoor activities... 69

Police and trouble 70

Work and study... 71

Travellers with disabilities 71

Directory 73

Getting there

The easiest way to get to Poland from Britain and Ireland is by air, with a number of airlines offering cheap flights to Polish cities. Trains are unlikely to be any better value, although you might save a few pennies by travelling by bus. Driving involves a long haul of 1000km or more, best attempted over two days. Coming from the US and Canada, there are direct flights to Warsaw and, less commonly, Kraków. Alternatively, you can fly to London, or another good-value Western European destination, and continue by plane or overland. There are no direct flights to Poland from Australia or New Zealand, but as well as catching one- or two-stop flights you again have the option of flying into another European country and then going overland.

When it comes to buying flights, it's worth bearing in mind that while some **airlines** have fixed return fares which don't change from one month to the next, others depend very much on the **season**, with high season being from early June to September, when the weather is best. Fares drop during the "shoulder" seasons – April to May and October to November – and you'll get the best prices during the low season, December to March (excluding Christmas, New Year and Easter when prices are hiked up and seats are at a premium). Note also that flying at weekends is generally more expensive; price ranges quoted below assume midweek travel, and are subject to availability and change.

You can often cut costs by going through a specialist **flight agent** – either a consolidator, who buys up blocks of tickets from the airlines and sells them at a discount, or a discount agent, who in addition to dealing with discounted flights may also offer special **student and youth fares** and a range of other travel-related services such as travel insurance, rail passes, car rentals, tours and the like.

Finally, it's worth noting that an increasing number of international travel companies are offering city breaks to Polish cities such as Warsaw and Kraków – taking advantage of their **flight-plus-accommodation deals** may work out cheaper than organizing your trip independently (see p.29). Specialist travel agencies are listed on the following pages.

Online booking

Many airlines and discount travel websites offer you the opportunity to book your tickets **online**, cutting out the costs of agents and middlemen. Good deals can often be found through discount or auction sites, as well as through the airlines' own websites.

Online booking agents

Ⓦ **www.cheapflights.co.uk** (UK and Ireland), Ⓦ **www.cheapflights.com** (USA), Ⓦ **www.cheapflights.ca** (Canada), Ⓦ **www.cheapflights.com.au** (Australia and New Zealand). Flight deals, travel agents, plus links to other travel sites.

Ⓦ **www.cheaptickets.com** US and UK discount flight specialists.

Ⓦ **www.expedia.co.uk** (UK), Ⓦ **www.expedia.com** (US), Ⓦ **www.expedia.ca** (Canada). Discount air fares, all-airline search engine and daily deals.

Ⓦ **www.flyaow.com** Online air travel info and reservations site.

Ⓦ **www.hotwire.com** Bookings from the US only. Last-minute savings of up to forty percent on regular published fares.

Ⓦ **www.lastminute.com** (UK), Ⓦ **www.au.lastminute.com** (Australia and New Zealand). Offers good last-minute holiday package and flight-only deals.

Ⓦ **www.priceline.co.uk** (UK), Ⓦ **www.priceline .com** (US). Name-your-own-price website that has deals at around forty percent off standard fares. You cannot specify flight times (although you do specify dates) and the tickets are non-refundable, non-transferable and non-changeable.

@ **www.skyauction.com** (bookings from the US only). Auctions tickets and travel packages using a "second bid" scheme. The best strategy is to bid the maximum you're willing to pay, since if you win you'll pay just enough to beat the runner-up regardless of your maximum bid.

@ **www.travelocity.co.uk** (UK),
@ **www.travelocity.com** (US),
@ **www.travelocity.ca** (Canada). Destination guides, hot web fares and best deals for car hire, accommodation and lodging as well as fares.

@ **www.travelshop.com.au** Australian website offering discounted flights, packages, insurance, online bookings.

From Britain and Ireland

With a flying time of 2hr 30min and plenty of airlines to choose from, getting to Poland **from the UK** by air is relatively problem-free. The cheapest way of flying from the UK is with one of the **budget airlines** such as **Centralwings**, **easyJet**, **Ryanair**, **Sky-Europe** or **Wizzair**. Most of these companies fly to the two cities most popular with tourists, Warsaw and Kraków (note that some use the airport at Kraków's near-neighbour Katowice), although other destinations like Gdańsk (Wizzair) and Wrocław (Ryanair) are also accessible. The majority of UK budget departures are from airports in southeastern England such as Stansted or Luton, although Wizzair's use of Liverpool suggests that other UK airports may be joining the fray. For full details of which routes are offered by which company see "Airlines", below – although be aware that the cheap-flight market is in a state of constant fluidity, and there may be changes in operators and routes in the future. The best way to secure low-price tickets is to book well in advance, be flexible about your departure and return dates (midweek seats are often the cheapest) and avoid major holidays. Above all, beware that budget airline tickets booked at the last minute may work out just as expensive as their major airline counterparts. Bear in mind too that prices advertised on budget airline websites often fail to include **airport tax** – which may well amount to an additional £20/€28 in each direction.

Most useful of the mainstream airlines is Poland's national carrier **LOT**, which operates daily flights from London Heathrow to Warsaw, Kraków and Gdańsk, and also fly to Warsaw from Manchester. Kraków is also served from London Gatwick by **British Airways**. Both airlines offer return tickets from around £150, rising to about £250 in busy periods such as Christmas, Easter and midsummer – special cheaper deals are occasionally offered. If you don't live near London or Manchester, **BritishMidland** can get you from Edinburgh, Glasgow or Leeds/Bradford to connect with a LOT flight from Heathrow for a very reasonable add-on fare.

If you're aiming for a Polish city not served by direct flights, LOT can get you to most provincial centres with a change of plane in Warsaw, with the combined return fare hovering around the £200–250 mark.

Flight agents may occasionally come up with cheaper deals if you're prepared to change planes in a European hub: flights with **Malev** (changing in Budapest), **CSA** (via Prague) and **Lufthansa** (via Frankfurt or Munich) often undercut LOT and British Airways prices by a few pounds.

From Ireland, LOT flies daily from Dublin to Warsaw for about €200, depending on season, with occasional much cheaper deals available. Slightly cheaper fares are sometimes available from European airlines such as Lufthansa or **Alitalia** who will get you to Poland with a change of plane en route. Best option coming from Belfast is provided by British Midland, which will connect you with one of the LOT flights out of Heathrow.

Airlines

Aer Lingus in Ireland ☎ 0818 365 000; @ www .aerlingus.ie. Flights from Dublin to Warsaw involving a change of plane (and airline) in London or another European hub.
Air Berlin ☎ 0870 7388 880, @ www.airberlin .com. London Stansted to Warsaw weekly.
Alitalia in Ireland ☎ 01/677 5171, @ www.alitalia .com. Dublin to Warsaw via Milan.
British Airways ☎ 0870 850 9850; in Ireland ☎ 1800 626 747; @ www.ba.com. London Gatwick to Kraków daily.
British Midland ☎ 0870 607 0555; in Ireland ☎ 01/283 8833; @ www.flybmi.com. Flights from Belfast, Edinburgh, Glasgow and Leeds/Bradford into London, and onwards to Poland with LOT.
Centralwings ☎ 0801 454545, @ www .centralwings.com. Budget flights from London Gatwick to Kraków and Warsaw.

CSA ☎0870 444 3747, ⓦwww.csa.cz/en. London Gatwick to Kraków via Prague.

easyJet ☎0870 600 0000, ⓦwww.easyjet.com. Flights from Luton to Warsaw and Kraków.

LOT (Polish Airlines) ☎0870 414 0088, in Ireland ☎1890 200 514; ⓦwww.lot.com. Daily direct flights from London Heathrow to Warsaw, Kraków and Gdańsk, and from Dublin to Warsaw. Connecting flights from Warsaw to most other Polish cities.

Lufthansa ☎0845 773 7747; in Ireland ☎01/844 5544; ⓦwww.lufthansa.com. Flights from various British and Irish airports to Warsaw, Kraków and Gdańsk, with a connection in Frankfurt or Munich.

Malev ☎020/7439 0577, ⓦwww.malev.hu. London Stansted to Kraków via Budapest.

Ryanair ☎0870 156 9569; in Ireland ☎01/609 7800; ⓦwww.ryanair.com. From London Stansted to Wrocław.

SkyEurope ☎020/7365 0365, ⓦwww.skyeurope .com. Flights from London Stansted to Warsaw and Kraków.

Wizzair ☎00 48 22 351 9499, ⓦwww.wizzair .com. Daily flights from Luton to Gdańsk, Warsaw and Katowice; several times weekly from Liverpool to Warsaw and Katowice.

Flight and travel agents

Bogdan Travel ☎020/8992 8866. Poland specialist dealing in flights and bus tickets.

Bridge the World ☎0870 444 7474, ⓦwww .bridgetheworld.com. Specializing in round-the-world tickets, with good deals aimed at the backpacker market.

ebookers ☎0870 010 7000, ⓦwww.ebookers .com. Low fares on an extensive selection of scheduled flights.

Gem Tazab ☎020/7963 1700. Budget flights and bus tickets to Poland.

Gosia ☎020/7581 5154, ⓦwww.gosiatravel.com. Cheap flight and bus tickets to Poland.

Joe Walsh Tours Ireland ☎01/241 0800, ⓦwww .joewalshtours.ie. General budget fares agent.

Lee Travel Ireland ☎021/277 111, ⓦwww .leetravel.ie. Flights and holidays worldwide.

McCarthy's Travel Ireland ☎021/270 127, ⓦwww.mccarthystravel.ie. General flight agent.

North South Travel ☎01245/608 291, ⓦwww .northsouthtravel.co.uk. Friendly, competitive travel agency, offering discounted fares worldwide – profits are used to support projects in the developing world, especially the promotion of sustainable tourism.

Poland Street Agency ☎020/7381 6966. General budget fares agent.

Polish Travel Centre ☎020/8741 5541. Specialist in discounted flights and buses to Poland.

Poltours ☎020/8810 8625. Polish flight specialist.

Premier Travel ☎028/7126 3333, ⓦwww .premiertravel.uk.com. Discount flight specialists based in Northern Ireland.

STA Travel ☎0870 160 0599, ⓦwww.statravel .co.uk. Worldwide specialists in low-cost flights and tours for students and under 26s, though other customers welcome.

Top Deck ☎020/7244 8000, ⓦwww .topdecktravel.co.uk. Long-established agent dealing in discount flights.

Trailfinders ☎020/7938 3939, ⓦwww .trailfinders.com; in Ireland ☎01/677 7888, ⓦwww.trailfinders.ie. One of the best-informed and most efficient agents for independent travellers.

USIT Northern Ireland ☎028/9032 7111, Republic of Ireland ☎01/602 1904, ⓦwww.usit.ie. Student and youth specialists for flights and trains.

Packages and organized tours

An increasing number of **tour operators** are offering city breaks in Warsaw, Kraków and Gdańsk, thereby providing an excellent way of picking up a **flight-plus-accommodation package** at a reasonable price – the comfortable three- to four-star hotels used by tour operators would probably work out more expensive if you tried to book them independently. A typical three-night city break in a Polish city costs somewhere in the region of £280–350 in low season (Oct–March), rising to £380–450 in high season (July–Aug), with additional nights costing £35–55 depending on the hotel. Prices assume that you're departing from London or Manchester – add-on fares from other UK airports can be pretty hefty.

In addition, several specialist travel operators offer **guided-tour packages** to Poland. The bulk of these are one- or two-week trips taking in Warsaw, Kraków and a clutch of other places of cultural or historical interest. Seven-day trips can cost anything from £600 to £1000, depending on the standard of accommodation you'll be staying in; two-week trips are fifty to sixty percent more expensive. Special interests are catered for by companies such as Explore, which offers hiking tours of the Tatra mountains; and Naturetrek and Wildlife Worldwide, which will bring you up close to Poland's flora and fauna.

Specialist tour operators

Adventures Abroad ☎0114/247 3400, ⓦwww
.adventuresabroad.com. Seven-day tours taking in
Warsaw and other historic cities.
Bridge Travel ☎0870 191 4065, ⓦwww
.bridgetravel.co.uk. City breaks in Kraków.
Exodus ☎0870 240 5550, ⓦwww.exodus
.co.uk. Two-week tour mixing culture and nature;
also combined holidays featuring Poland, Slovakia
and Hungary.
Explore ☎01252/760 000, ⓦwww
.exploreworldwide.com. Eight-day hiking tours in
the Tatras, and two-week tours of Poland's natural
beauty spots.
Fregata ☎020/7420 7305, ⓦwww.fregatatravel
.co.uk. Tailor-made trips to Kraków, Warsaw and
Gdańsk.
Martin Randall ☎020/8742 3355, ⓦwww
.martinrandall.com. History-and-culture tour through
the erstwhile province of Galicia (southeastern Poland
and western Ukraine).
Naturetrek ☎01962/733 051, ⓦwww.naturetrek
.co.uk. Expertly led wildlife treks concentrating on
seasonal fauna (there's one tour each in winter, spring
and autumn).
Polish Regency Tours ☎020/8992 8866,
ⓦwww.polish-travel.com. Flights, city breaks and
two-centre holidays combining Warsaw, Kraków or
Gdańsk.
Polorbis ☎020/7636 2217, ⓦwww.polorbis
.co.uk. Weekend breaks, in Warsaw, Kraków and
Gdańsk, seven- and fourteen-day tours of the
country's top sights.
Regent Holidays ☎0117/921 1711, ⓦwww
.regent-holidays.co.uk. Tailor-made itineraries in
Poland and neighbouring countries.
Travelsphere ☎0870 240 2426, ⓦwww
.travelsphere.co.uk. Eight-day Kraków-plus-mountains
combinations, plus some Tatra holidays for singles.
Wildlife Worldwide ☎020/8667 9158, ⓦwww
.wildlifeworldwide.com. Nine-day wolf-tracking tours
in south and eastern Poland, taking in a lot of other
wildlife along the way.

By rail

Travelling by **train** to Poland is a relaxing and
leisurely way to travel for those who don't
like flying, although it can't compare price-
wise with taking the plane. The fastest option
from London involves taking the **Eurostar**
from London Waterloo to Brussels, and then
continuing across Belgium and Germany,
either with a direct Brussels–Warsaw train
or with a change in Berlin (where you can

pick up expresses to Warsaw, Wrocław or
Kraków). None of these options take longer
than 24 hours. A return ticket for the whole
journey will set you back around £220, more
if you book a couchette or sleeper for the
overnight part of the journey.

Rail passes

If you're planning to visit Poland as part of
a more extensive trip around Europe, it may
be worth buying a **rail pass**. There are no
individual passes covering Poland itself,
although Poland is covered in the Inter Rail
pass scheme, which is available to European residents. Non-European residents
can make of the Eurail Pass (which doesn't
cover Poland but does include most of the
countries which you might travel through en
route) and the European East Pass (which
covers Poland and neighbouring countries).

Inter Rail

Inter Rail passes are available from any
major UK train station or youth/student travel
office; the only restriction is that you must
have been resident in a European country for
at least six months. They come in over-26
and (cheaper) under-26 versions, and cover
29 European countries (including Turkey and
Morocco), grouped together in zones:

A Republic of Ireland/Britain
B Norway, Sweden, Finland
C Germany, Austria, Switzerland, Denmark
D Czech and Slovak Republics, Poland,
Hungary, Croatia
E France, Belgium, Netherlands, Luxem-
bourg
F Spain, Portugal, Morocco
G Italy, Greece, Turkey, Slovenia plus some
ferry services between Italy and Greece
H Bulgaria, Romania, Serbia and Montene-
gro, Macedonia.

The passes are available for 12 or 22 days
(one zone only) or 1 month, and you can
purchase up to three zones or a global pass
covering all zones. As Poland is in zone D
(and you'll need to pass through zones C
and E en route), you'll need a three-zone
pass (£320, £225 for under 26s) to get there
from Britain or Ireland. Inter Rail passes do
not include travel between Britain and the

continent, although Inter Rail pass holders are eligible for discounts on rail travel in the UK and on cross-channel ferries.

Other rail passes

Non-European residents qualify for the **Eurail Pass** (see p.33), which must be purchased before arrival in Europe (or from Rail Europe in London if you were unable to get it at home). Note however that it is only likely to pay for itself if you plan to travel widely before reaching Poland, since travel within Poland itself is not included in the pass. Non-European residents might also consider the **European East Pass**, which covers rail travel in Poland, Austria, Hungary, the Czech Republic and Slovakia (see p.34).

Rail contacts

ⓦ **www.interrailnet.com** Official Inter Rail website, with full details of passes, prices and discounts available with Inter Rail.

ⓦ **www.seat61.com** Compendious guide to rail travel in Europe compiled by committed enthusiasts. You can't book tickets online but the information provided is usually more reliable than that of the official sites.

Deutsche Bahn UK ☏ 08702 435 363, ⓦ www .deutsche-bahn.co.uk. International arm of the German rail network selling through tickets on London–Poland routes.

Rail Europe UK ☏ 08705 848 848, ⓦ www .raileurope.co.uk. Through ticketing on most European routes; also agents for Inter Rail and Eurostar.

Trainseurope UK ☏ 0900 195 0101, ⓦ www .trainseurope.co.uk. Tickets from the UK to Poland, plus Inter Rail and other individual country passes.

By bus

Bus travel is an attractively cheap way of getting to Poland as an alternative to a budget airline flight, although the journey itself is relatively dull unless you have a penchant for north European motorway landscapes. Numerous Polish cities are served from several UK departure points, with the most reliable services being operated by **Eurolines**, a division of the National Express bus company. They run regular services from London to Warsaw, Kraków, Rzeszów, Olsztyn and a whole host of other Polish cities. Return tickets for Warsaw, for example, start

at £90 (with minimal reductions for under 26s, senior citizens and children), but attract a thirty percent discount if you book a fixed return one month in advance. Tickets can be bought at any National Express office in the UK, and will include connecting fares from anywhere outside London. There's a ten-percent discount on all fares booked via the Eurolines website.

In addition, a number of other **Polish-run companies** run buses from London to an array of Polish destinations, with tickets handled by a number of UK-based travel agents (see "Bus contacts" below). Prices hover around the £75 mark for a London–Poland return, with pick-ups from major northern English cities adding £10–20 to the price of the ticket.

Bus contacts

Bogdan Travel See p.29.
Eurolines ☏ 0870 514 3219; Republic of Ireland ☏ 01/836 6111; ⓦ www.eurolines.co.uk.
Fregata See p.30.
Gem Tazab See p.29.
Gosia See p.29.
Interlink ☏ 020/8748 4420. Agent for several London–Poland operators.
Poland Street Agency See p.29.
Polish Travel Centre See p.29.

By car

Driving to Poland means a long haul of 1000km from Calais or Ostend to the Polish border – and another 450–500km from there to Warsaw or Kraków. Flat out, and using the Channel Tunnel, you could do the journey to the border in eighteen hours, but it makes more sense to allow longer, breaking the journey in central Germany.

The most convenient **Channel crossings** are on **SpeedFerries.com** from Dover to Boulogne (from £50 return per car with up to six passengers), the **P&O Stena** services from Dover or Folkestone to Calais, **Hoverspeed** to Ostend (around £129–189 return for up to five adults and a car depending on season), or **Le Shuttle**'s Channel Tunnel option from Folkestone to Calais (£180–299 for two adults and a car depending on season, with a fifty-percent cancellation charge, although there are frequent special offers). From any of these ports, the most popular and direct route is on toll-free motorways all the way, bypassing Brussels, Düsseldorf, Hannover and Berlin.

A more relaxing alternative, which halves the driving distance, is to catch the thrice-weekly **DFDS Seaways** ferry from Harwich to Cuxhaven in Germany (19hr) and then drive east past Berlin, getting to the Polish border in another six hours. This costs £232–292 per passenger, depending on season (including a comfortable cabin with shower and toilet) and £80–96 for a car, plus an extra £10 or so if you travel at the weekend. The most convenient ferry route from the north of England is the nightly **P&O North Sea Ferries** service from Hull to Rotterdam (14hr), costing £240–298 with reclining seats, or £292–350 for a cabin – again, prices are for two adults and a car depending on season.

Ferry contacts

DFDS Seaways ☎ 0870 5333 000, ⊛ www .dfdsseaways.co.uk. Harwich to Cuxhaven; Newcastle to Amsterdam.
Hoverspeed ☎ 0870 240 8070, ⊛ www .hoverspeed.co.uk. Dover to Calais and Ostend.
P&O North Sea Ferries ☎ 08701 129 6002, ⊛ www.ponorthseaferries.com. Hull to Rotterdam and Zeebrugge.
P&O Stena Line ☎ 0870 600 0600, ⊛ www.posl .com. Dover to Calais.
Sea France ☎ 0870 571 1711, ⊛ www.seafrance .com. Dover to Calais.
SpeedFerries.com ☎ 0870 220 0570, ⊛ www .speedferries.com. Calais to Boulogne.
Stena Line ☎ 0870 570 7070, ⊛ www.stenaline .co.uk. Harwich to Hook of Holland.

From the US and Canada

The easiest way to get to Poland from the US and Canada is to **fly** direct to Warsaw or Kraków. Alternatively, you might consider flying to London, Frankfurt or elsewhere and continuing by a combination of bus, train and ferry, though this won't necessarily work out to be cheaper.

Flights

From the US, **LOT** (Polish Airlines) offers daily flights to Warsaw from New York and Chicago. It also flies once a week from New York and Chicago to Kraków. Approximate fares are: New York–Warsaw US$900 (high

season) or US$700 (low); Chicago–Warsaw US$1000 (high), US$800 (low). If you're coming from another part of the USA, LOT will connect you with a domestic carrier – **United Airlines** being their favoured partner. Typical fares from LA to Warsaw, flying with United and LOT, are roughly US$1100 (high season), US$750 (low). Several other carriers, including **British Airways**, **Austrian Airlines**, **Swiss Airlines**, **Northwest/KLM** and **Lufthansa** have daily flights from the US to Warsaw via their European hub cities. **Delta** has flights connecting via Paris.

From Canada, LOT operates a direct service to Warsaw from Toronto (twice a week in the winter months, five flights a week in the summer). Fares weigh in at around CAN$1350 in high season, CAN$750 in low. Starting from another Canadian airport, **Air Canada** will connect you with LOT's Toronto flight for a reasonable add-on fare. Discount agents sometimes come up with cheaper deals involving other major airlines which fly daily to Warsaw, but require a change of plane in Western Europe – **British Airways** flies to Warsaw via London, **Lufthansa** via Frankfurt, **Northwest/KLM** via Amsterdam and **Swiss** via Zürich. The cost of most of these, however, will be significantly higher than LOT. BA for instance quotes a Toronto–Warsaw fare of roughly CAN$1500 (high season) or CAN$1050 (low), and a Vancouver–Warsaw fare of CAN$1800 (high) or CAN$1400 (low). **Austrian** has flights from Toronto to Kraków, via Vienna, from CAN$1200 (low) to CAN$1550 (high).

One further option is to book a flight to London on a major airline and then connect to Warsaw or Kraków using Ryanair, easyJet or one of the other **budget carriers**, with one-way flights starting from around US$30 (see pp.28–29 or check ⊛ www.whichbudget .com, which has comprehensive listings of airlines and destinations). This is cheaper, and will give you the option of a stop in London, but as the budget flights leave from smaller airports you'll need to cross the city to catch your second flight: plan carefully. National Express (⊛ www.nationalexpress .com) is a British bus company that runs inter-airport shuttles.

Airlines

Air Canada ☎1-888-247-2262, ⊛www
.aircanada.com. Flights from most Canadian airports
to Warsaw, with a change of plane and airline in
Toronto.

Austrian Airlines US ☎1-800-843-0002, Canada
☎1-888-817-6666, ⊛www.aua.com. Flights to
Warsaw and Kraków via Vienna.

British Airways US ☎1-800-247-9297, Canada
☎1-800-668-1059, ⊛www.ba.com. Flights
to Warsaw and Kraków from a number of North
American cities, via London.

British Midland ☎1-800-788-0555, ⊛www
.flybmi.com. Flights from Washington and Chicago to
Manchester, followed by connections to Warsaw.

Czech Airlines US ☎1-877-359-6629, Canada
☎416/363-3174, ⊛www.czechairlines.com.
Flights to Warsaw from New York, Washington and
Toronto, changing planes in Prague.

Delta Airlines ☎1-800-221-4141 (domestic
flights), ☎1-800-241-4141 (international flights),
⊛www.delta.com. Flights to Paris and other
European hubs with onward connections to Warsaw.

KLM/Northwest Airlines ☎1-800-225-2525
(domestic flights), ☎1-800-447-4747 (international
flights), ⊛www.nwa.com, ⊛www.klm.com. Flights
from several North American cities to Poland, with a
stop-off in Europe.

LOT US ☎1-800-223-0593, Canada ☎1-800-668-
5928, ⊛www.lot.com. Direct flights from New York
to Warsaw, from Chicago to Warsaw and Kraków, and
from Toronto to Warsaw.

Lufthansa US ☎1-800-645-3880, Canada
☎1-800-563-5954, ⊛www.lufthansa-usa.com.
Flights from Montréal and various other North
American cities to Frankfurt, with onward connections
to Warsaw and other Polish cities.

Swiss Airlines ☎1-877-359-7947, ⊛www
.swiss.com. Flights to Warsaw via Zurich.

United Airlines ☎1-800-241-6522 (domestic
flights), ☎1-800-538-2929 (international flights),
⊛www.united.com. Flights from most American
cities to Poland via New York or Chicago.

Virgin Atlantic Airways ☎1-800-862-8621,
⊛www.virgin-atlantic.com. Flights from Los
Angeles, Miami, New York and Washington to London,
followed by onward connections to Poland.

Flight and travel agents

Airtech ☎212/219-7000, ⊛www.airtech.com.
Standby seat broker; also deals in consolidator fares
and courier flights.

Educational Travel Centre ☎608/256-5551 or
1-800-747-5551, ⊛www.edtrav.com. Student/
youth discount agent.

Pekao International Travel and Tours
☎416/588-1988 or 1-800-387-0325, ⊛www
.pekao-canada.com. Flight agent and tour company
operating charter flights from Toronto and Edmonton
to Poland.

SkyLink US ☎1-800-AIR-ONLY or 212/573-8980,
Canada ☎1-800-SKY-LINK, ⊛www.skylinkus.com.
Consolidator.

STA Travel US ☎ 1-800-781-4040, Canada
1-888-427-5639, ⊛www.statravel.com. Worldwide
specialists in independent travel; also student IDs,
travel insurance, car rental, train passes and so on.

Student Flights ☎1-800-255-8000 or 480/951-
1177, ⊛www.isecard.com. Student/youth fares,
student IDs.

TFI Tours ☎212/736-1140 or 1-800-745-8000,
⊛tfitours.com. Consolidator.

Travel Avenue ☎1-800-333-3335, ⊛www
.travelavenue.com. Full service travel agent that
offers discounts in the form of rebates.

Travel Cuts Canada ☎1-800-667-2887, US
☎1-866-246-9762, ⊛www.travelcuts.com.
Canadian student travel organization with branches
nationwide.

Traveler's Advantage ☎1-877-259-2691,
⊛www.travelersadvantage.com. Discount travel
club; annual membership fee required (currently $1
for three months' trial).

Travelling via Europe

If you have the time, travelling to another
European capital and continuing your journey
overland can be an excellent way to reach
Poland, allowing stopovers en route and
enabling you to see much more of Europe
along the way. See pp.28–32 for details of
the options from London.

There are a variety of **rail passes** available
which must be purchased before you arrive
in Europe, but a **Eurail Pass** is only likely to
pay for itself if you're planning to travel widely
before reaching Poland. Allowing unlimited
free train travel in seventeen countries, not
including Poland, it will get you there from
other European destinations, but does not
allow travel within Poland itself. The **Eurail
Youthpass** (for under 26s) costs US$382
for fifteen consecutive days, US$495 for 21
days and US$615 for one month; if you're
26 or over you'll have to buy a first-class
pass, available in fifteen-day (US$558), 21-
day (US$762) and one-month increments
(US$946). A **Eurail Flexipass** allows you to
stagger your rail travel over a longer period:

ten days of travel over a two-month period costs US$451 (under 26) or US$694 (over 26); fifteen days of travel over two months weighs in at US$594 (under 26) or US$914 (over 26).

The excellent-value **European East Pass**, covering Poland, Austria, Hungary, the Czech Republic and Slovakia, has no age restrictions, allowing five days' first class (US$228) or second class (US$162) rail travel within the space of a month, with the option of buying extra days for US$28/21.

To buy Eurail passes and most single-country passes, contact **Rail Europe** (US ℡1-877-257-2887, Canada ℡1-800-361-RAIL, ⓦwww.raileurope.com), or **Europrail International** (Canada ℡1-888-667-9734, ⓦwww.europrail.net). More information on Eurail passes and ticket agents can be found on ⓦ**www.eurail.net**.

Packages and organized tours

Booking a **flights-plus-accommodation** deal through a specialist travel agent can often work out cheaper than organizing things yourself. Luckily, there's a number of companies operating **organized tours** to Poland, ranging from city breaks to two- or three-week cultural tours of the whole country. Beware however that prices vary a great deal according to which part of North America you're flying from.

A good place to start shopping around would be **Orbis**, the biggest of the Polish travel companies. It has an extensive selection of tours, ranging from eight to fifteen days, including flights, accommodation and two daily meals. A fifteen-day excursion called Panorama of Poland, which takes in the main sights of the country, will cost from US$1969 (low season) or US$2399 (high season) if travelling from New York; you'd need to add US$80 (from Chicago) or $310 (from LA) for the airfare if coming from another city. Southern delight is a ten-day tour of the country's southern provinces, starting in Warsaw and visiting Kraków, Zakopane and Auschwitz before returning to Warsaw. From New York, this will cost you between US$1429 and US$1899, depending on the time of year. Another option is the twelve-day Castles and Palaces trip, starting at US$1799 (low season from New York)

or US$2079 (high). Orbis will also help you customize specialist tours, such as explorations of Warsaw's Jewish heritage or visits to Kraków, Lublin, Auschwitz and Treblinka.

Another major operator to Poland is **PAT Tours** (Polish American Tours), whose specialist packages are similar to Orbis' but include Grandeur of Poland, a luxury eighteen-day trip starting at $2250 from New York, exclusive of airfare. **Tradesco Tours** also offers several options, such as the seven-day Scenic Poland tour, with four-star accommodation, starting at US$1098 (excluding airfare). Otherwise, **General Tours**, which operates the Eastern European division of Delta Vacations, has air-inclusive packages to Warsaw (3 nights from US$899) and Kraków (3 nights from US$780).

All prices are calculated for single person/ double occupancy, are exclusive of applicable taxes and are subject to availability and change. If you're considering travelling independently, bear in mind that rail tickets for journeys within Poland should, whenever possible, be purchased inside the country, as prices for tickets reserved abroad can be up to fifty percent higher; see "Getting Around", p.43. If you're willing to make your own flight arrangements, it's also possible to book a tour with one of the Europe-based agencies (see "Getting there from Britain and Ireland", p.28).

Specialist tour operators

Adventures Abroad ℡604/303-1099 or 1-800-665-3998, ⓦwww.adventures-abroad.com. Exclusive Poland tours plus Poland/Baltics/Russia combinations.

American Travel Abroad ℡1-800-228-0877, ⓦwww.amta.com. Poland specialists offering flights, hotels, car rental and escorted tours.

Canadian Travel Abroad ℡416/364-2738 or 1-800-387-1876, ⓦwww.cantrav.ca. General interest, churches, pilgrimages, museums and Jewish-oriented tours to Poland.

Chopin Tours Canada ℡416/537-9202. City breaks and a big choice of escorted tours covering folklore, history and culture.

Elderhostel ℡877/426-8056, ⓦwww.elderhostel .org. Specialists in educational and activity programmes for senior travellers, offering general Central European art-and-culture tours and Polish Jewish heritage tours.

General Tours ℡603/357-5033 or 1-800-221-2216, ⓦwww.generaltours.com. City packages including Warsaw and Kraków, two-week tours including Kraków and other Central European cities.

Kollander World Travel ☎1-800-800-5981, ⊛www.kollander-travel.com. Escorted tours in Poland and Central Europe.

Kompas ☎1-800-233-6422, ⊛www.kompas .net. Warsaw and Kraków city packages and escorted tours.

Orbis ☎212/867-5011 or 1-800-TO-POLAND, ⊛www.orbistravel.com. Big choice of city breaks and escorted one- or two-week tours, as well as flight bookings, car hire and tailor-made arrangements for individual travellers.

PAT Tours ☎413/747-7702 or 1-800-388-0988, ⊛www.polandtours.com. Hotel bookings, car rental, and a range of escorted tours with historical or folklore themes.

Pekao International Travel and Tours Canada ☎416/588-1988 or 1-800-387-0325, ⊛www .pekao-canada.com. Flight agent and tour company operating charter flights from Toronto and Edmonton to Poland.

Pilgrim Tours ☎1-800-322-0788, ⊛www .pilgrimtours.com. Escorted tours focusing on history, culture and folklore.

Polish Travel Center ☎215/533-1294. Flights, tailor-made itineraries and escorted tours.

Saint Thomas Tours ☎1-877-456-9327, ⊛www.saintthomastours.com. Runs an Easter-week trip to Kraków, the Tatras and sites connected with the life of Pope John Paul II.

Smolka Tours ☎1-800-722-0057, ⊛www .smolkatours.com. Has a week-long tour of Kraków, Warsaw and Zakopane and a separate trip to northern Poland, both with high-quality accommodation.

Stay Poland ☎+48 22/829 4072, ⊛www .staypoland.,com. Warsaw-based firm with a series of airfare-exclusive guided trips, including "Jewish Heritage" and "Off the Beaten Path", as well as custom-designed tours.

Tradesco Tours ☎310/649-5808 or 1-800-448-4321, ⊛www.tradescotours.com. Tailor-made arrangements, city breaks and escorted tours to Central and Eastern Europe.

Unique World Cruises ☎516/627-2636 or 1-800-669-0757, ⊛www.uniqueworldcruises.com. Eight-day tours of Poland and the Czech Republic, visiting Warsaw, Kraków and Prague.

From Australia and New Zealand

Although there are no direct **flights** to Poland from Australia or New Zealand, there are plenty of one- or two-stop alternatives. **From Australia**, typical one-stop routings (involving European hubs such as London, Frankfurt or Vienna) tend to be expensive, with the average return fare from Sydney, Melbourne or Perth to Warsaw or Kraków hovering around the AUS\$3000 mark. Cheaper deals involve a combination of airlines and two stops en route – Sydney–Kuala Lumpur–Vienna–Warsaw or Sydney–Bangkok–Frankfurt–Warsaw being typical examples. Fares on these routes range from AUS\$1750 in low season to AUS\$2200 in high season.

From New Zealand, Air New Zealand operates daily flights from Auckland to London and Frankfurt, where you can pick up connecting flights to Warsaw and other Polish cities. All other flights from New Zealand involve at least two stops. Return fares start at around NZ\$2100 in low season, rising to NZ\$2600 in high season.

Airlines

Air New Zealand Australia ☎13 24 76, ⊛www .airnz.com.au; New Zealand ☎0800 737 000, ⊛www.airnz.co.nz. Daily flights from Auckland to London via Los Angeles, then onward connections to Warsaw or Kraków.

Austrian Airlines Australia ☎1800 642 438, ⊛www.aua.com. From Melbourne and Sydney to Warsaw via Vienna.

British Airways Australia ☎02/8904 8800, New Zealand ☎09/356 8690, ⊛www.ba.com. Daily flights to London from Sydney, Melbourne or Perth, with onward connections to Poland.

Cathay Pacific Australia ☎13 17 47, ⊛www .cathaypacific.com/au; New Zealand ☎09/379 0861, ⊛www.cathaypacific.com/nz. Flights from Australia and New Zealand to Hong Kong, with onward connections to major European hubs then Poland.

LOT Polish Airlines Australia ☎02/9244 2466, New Zealand ☎02/632 5134, ⊛www.lot.com. One- or two-stop flights to Poland involving at least one other airline.

Lufthansa Australia ☎1300 655 727, ⊛www .lufthansa-australia.com. Flights from Australia to Frankfurt with onward connections to Warsaw and other Polish cities.

Malaysia Airlines Australia ☎13 26 27, New Zealand ☎0800 777 747. ⊛www.malaysiaairlines .com.my. Flights from Melbourne to a European hub via Kuala Lumpur, with onward connections to Warsaw.

Qantas Australia ☎13 13 13, New Zealand ☎0800 808 767, ⊛www.qantas.com.au. Flights from Sydney to a European hub with onward connections to Warsaw.

Thai Australia ☎ 02/9251 1922, local-call rate 1300 651 960; New Zealand ☎ 09/377 3886; Ⓦ www.thaiair.com. Flights from Auckland to Bangkok, with onward connections to Polish destinations via Copenhagen, London or Frankfurt.

Flight and travel agents

Flight Centre Australia ☎ 133 133, Ⓦ www .flightcentre.com.au, New Zealand ☎ 0800 243 544, Ⓦ www.flightcentre.co.nz.
Passport Travel Australia ☎ 03/9867 3888, Ⓦ www.travelcentre.com.au.
STA Travel Australia ☎ 1300 733 035, Ⓦ www .statravel.com.au; New Zealand ☎ 0508 782 872, Ⓦ www.statravel.co.nz.
Trailfinders Australia ☎ 1300 780 212, Ⓦ www .trailfinders.com.au.
travel.com.au and **travel.co.nz** Australia ☎ 1300/130 482, Ⓦ www.travel.com.au; New Zealand ☎ 0800 468 332, Ⓦ www.travel.co.nz.

Travelling via Europe

You might save money by flying to a Western European city and continuing **overland** to Poland from there (see p.33); if you want to see the country as part of a wider trip across Europe, it might be worth your while considering a **European rail pass** (see p.33 for details). In Australia, Eurail and other passes are available from **Cit World Travel** (☎ 02/9267 1255 or 03/9650 5510, Ⓦ www.cittravel.com.au); **Rail Plus Australia**

(☎ 1300/555 003 or 03/9642 8644, Ⓦ www .railplus.com.au); and **Trailfinders** (see above).

Packages and organized tours

There's a small number of package-tour operators offering holidays in Poland from Australia and New Zealand, including accommodation, sightseeing packages and rail passes.

Specialist agents and tour operators

Adventures Abroad Australia ☎ 1800 147 827; New Zealand ☎ 0800 800 434; Ⓦ www .adventures-abroad.com. Escorted tours covering Poland's cultural and historical highlights.
Eastern Eurotours Australia ☎ 07/5526 2855 or 1800 242 353, Ⓦ www.easterneurotours.com .au. Flights, hotel accommodation, city breaks and guided tours.
Explore Holidays (bookable through STA; see "Flight and travel agents" above), Ⓦ www .exploreholidays.com.au. City breaks in Warsaw and Kraków.
Gateway Travel Australia ☎ 02/9745 3333, Ⓦ www.russian-gateway.com.au. Eastern European specialists offering flights and packages.
Orbis Express Travel Australia ☎ 02/9891 6133, Ⓦ www.orbisexpress.com.au. Air tickets, big choice of packages.
Passport Travel See "Flight and travel agents" above. Includes a Tatra hiking tour.

Visas and red tape

Citizens of EU countries, the USA, Canada, Australia and New Zealand can stay in Poland for up to ninety days without a visa. Once the ninety days are up, you have to leave the country or apply for a residence permit. Nationals of other countries should check current visa regulations with the nearest Polish consulate before setting out.

Polish embassies and consulates abroad

Australia 7 Turrana St, Yarralumla, Canberra, ACT ☎ 02/6272 1000, Ⓦ www.poland.org.au. Also consulate at 10 Trelawney St, Woollahra, NSW 2025 ☎ 02/9363 9816.

Canada 443 Daly Ave, Ottawa, Ontario K1N 6H3 ☎ 613/789-0468, Ⓦ www.polishembassy.ca. Additional consulates at 2603 Lakeshore Blvd W, Toronto, Ontario MBV 1G5 ☎ 416/252-5471; 1500 Ave des Pins Ouest, Montréal, Québec H3G 1B4 ☎ 514/937-9481; and 1177 W Hastings St, Suite 1600, Vancouver, BC V6E 2K3 ☎ 604/688-3530.

Ireland 5 Ailesbury Rd, Ballsbridge, Dublin 4
℡ 01/283 0855, ⓦ www.polishembassy.ie.
New Zealand 17 Upland Rd, Kelburn, Wellington
℡ 04/475 9453, ⓦ www.poland.org.nz.
UK 47 Portland Place, London W1B 1JH
℡ 020/7580 4324, ⓦ www.polishembassy.org.uk.
US 2640 16th Street NW, Washington, DC 20009
℡ 202/234-3800, ⓦ www.polandembassy.org.

Additional consulates at 223 Madison Ave, New
York, NY 10016 ℡ 212/686-1541, ⓦ www
.polandconsulateny.com; 1530 North Lake Shore
Drive, Chicago, IL 60610 ℡ 312/337-8166, ⓦ www
.polishconsulatechicago.org; and 12400 Wilshire
Blvd, Suite 555, Los Angeles, CA 90025 ℡ 310/442-
8500, ⓦ www.polishconsulatela.com.

Insurance

Even though EU health care privileges apply in Poland, you'd do well to take out an insurance policy before travelling to cover against theft, loss and illness or injury. Before paying for a new policy, however, it's worth checking whether you are already covered: some all-risks home insurance policies may cover your possessions when overseas, and many private medical schemes include cover when abroad.

In Canada, provincial health plans usually provide partial cover for medical mishaps overseas, while holders of official student/ teacher/youth cards in Canada and the US are entitled to meagre accident coverage and hospital inpatient benefits. Students will often find that their student health coverage extends during the vacations and for one term beyond the date of last enrolment.

After exhausting the possibilities above, you might want to contact a specialist travel insurance company, or consider the **Rough**

Guides travel insurance deal we offer (see box below). A typical travel insurance policy usually provides cover for the loss of baggage, tickets and – up to a certain limit – cash or cheques, as well as cancellation or curtailment of your journey. Most of them exclude so-called dangerous sports unless an extra premium is paid. Many policies can be chopped and changed to exclude coverage you don't need – for example, sickness and accident benefits can often be excluded or included at will. If you do take

Rough Guides Travel Insurance

Rough Guides has teamed up with **Columbus Direct** to offer you travel insurance that can be tailored to suit your needs.

Readers can choose from many different travel insurance products, including a low-cost backpacker option for long stays; a short break option for city getaways; a typical holiday package option; and many others. There are also annual multi-trip policies for those who travel regularly, with variable levels of cover available. Different sports and activities (trekking, skiing, etc) can be covered if required on most policies.

Rough Guides travel insurance is available to the residents of 36 different countries with different language options to choose from via our website – ⓦ www .roughguidesinsurance.com – where you can also purchase the insurance.

Alternatively, UK residents should call ℡ 0800 083 9507; US citizens should call ℡ 1-800-749-4922; Australians should call ℡ 1300 669 999. All other nationalities should call ℡ +44 870 890 2843.

al cover, ascertain whether benefits paid as treatment proceeds or only ̨turn home, and whether there is a ̨4-hour medical emergency number. When securing baggage cover, make sure that the per-article limit – typically under £500 – will cover your most valuable possession. If you need to make a claim, you should keep receipts for medicines and medical treatment, and in the event you have anything stolen, you must obtain an official statement from the police.

Health

Citizens of the EU are entitled to free emergency health care in Poland providing they have a copy of form E111 (obtainable from most post offices), which has to be filled in and stamped at the post office before leaving home. Lengthy courses of treatment (as well as any prescribed drugs) must be paid for, however, so it's sensible to take out adequate health insurance. North Americans, Canadians, Australians and New Zealanders must arrange full insurance before leaving home.

Inoculations are not required for a trip to Poland. Tap water is officially classified as safe, at least in the major cities, but most people prefer to drink bottled mineral water (*woda mineralna*).

Pharmacies and hospitals

Simple complaints can normally be dealt with at a regular **pharmacy** (*apteka*), where basic medicines are dispensed by qualified pharmacists. In the cities, many of the staff will speak at least some English or German. Even in places where the staff speak only Polish, it should be easy enough to obtain repeat prescriptions if you bring along the empty container or remaining pills. In every town there's always at least one *apteka* open 24 hours; addresses are printed in local newspapers and guides.

For more serious problems, or anything the pharmacist can't work out, you'll be directed to a **public hospital** (*szpital*), where conditions will probably be cramped, with more patients than beds, a lack of resources and occasionally insanitary conditions. Health service staff are heavily overworked and scandalously underpaid. Hospital patients may be required to pay for the better-quality medicines, and will probably need friends to bring food in for them. If you are required to pay for any medical treatment or medication, remember to keep the receipts for your insurance claim when you get home.

In the larger cities you can opt for **private health care**. Kraków and Warsaw now have a considerable Western expatriate population, with health centres run on Western lines. In a crisis, it may even be best to ring the 24-hour emergency service of one of these clinics rather than an ambulance; the ethics of private versus public health care aside, there are advantages to being able to talk to someone in English. See the relevant city listings – or check the local press – for details.

Costs, money and banks

BASICS | Costs, money and banks

Despite the gradual rise in prices that has accompanied the transition to a market economy, travel in Poland is still relatively cheap. Many of the essentials, such as food and drink, public transport and entrance fees, remain well below their Western equivalents. Accommodation is priced on a different scale, but is still inexpensive as a rule. Note that prices are often much higher in Warsaw than in the rest of the country, and are similarly increased in places which see a lot of foreign visitors, such as Kraków, Gdańsk and Poznań.

The Polish unit of currency is the złoty (abbreviated to zł). It comes in notes of 10zł, 20zł, 50zł, 100zł and 200zł; and coins in 1, 2 and 5zł denominations, subdivided into groszy (1, 2, 5, 10, 20 and 50). Currently the exchange rate is around 6zł to the pound sterling, 4.30zł to the euro and 3.40zł to the US dollar, and looks set to remain reasonably stable – minor fluctuations aside.

Prices of hotels and other tourist services are often quoted in euros, although payment is made in złoty.

Average costs

Poland remains a relatively cheap country for Western visitors. You can **eat and drink** well for £15/€21/US$27 or less even at some of the country's best restaurants, though it's becoming increasingly easy to spend £20/€28/US$36 or more for a meal, especially if you want to move beyond home cuisine. In a more basic restaurant, a meal can be had for not much more than £5/€7/US$9, and substantial hot meals are available at milk and snack bars for even less than this – £1.50/€2.10/US$2.70 will often buy a main course. Coffee or tea with cakes in a café costs a similarly nominal amount.

Prices for **public transport** are relatively low – even travelling across half the length of the country by train or bus only costs around £20/€28/US$36. Similarly, you never have to fork out much more than £2/€2.80/US$3.60 to visit even the most popular **tourist sights**, with half that the normal asking price.

Only if you go for expensive **accommodation** will your costs start to rise. Here at least there's plenty of opportunity to spend money, with international hotels in the main

cities charging up to £180/€250/US$320 per night. On the other hand, if you stick to campsites, youth and tourist hostels, you'll seldom spend much more than £5/€7/US$9 on a bed. Budget on about twice as much for a room in a private house or in the cheapest hotels.

Exchange

The easiest place to change money is at a **kantor** or exchange bureau. Very often little more than a simple booth with a single cashier sitting behind a thick plate of glass, these can be found on the main streets of virtually every Polish town. They tend to work longer hours than regular banks (in big cities some kantors are open 24 hours a day), usually offer competitive exchange rates and rarely charge any commission. Be aware, however, that it pays to shop around in well-touristed parts of Warsaw and Kraków, where a kantor on the main street will offer a substantially less advantageous rate than a similar establishment in a side alley nearby.

Exchange rates at Polish **banks** (usually Mon–Fri 7.30am–5pm, Sat 7.30am–2pm) tend to be the same from one establishment to the next, although banks are much more subject to long queues and usually deduct a commission. It's wise to avoid changing money in **hotels**: they tend to offer poor rates and charge hefty commissions.

Travellers' cheques, credit cards and ATMs

Although **travellers' cheques** are the safest way of carrying your money, they're also the least convenient way of getting local currency, with only main banks, Orbis offices and hotels accepting them. American Express, which now has offices in Warsaw, is a useful alternative and will cash most brands of travellers' cheques, in addition to their own. Cashing a travellers' cheque can often be a lengthy process, with cashiers so unfamiliar with the procedure that you can be kept waiting for hours. Hotels usually charge a hefty commission of five percent, banks around one percent, while American Express will cash cheques free of charge (into local currency only).

Major **credit** and **debit cards** are accepted by an increasing number of travel agents, hotels, restaurants and shops. You can also arrange a cash advance on most of these cards in big banks. **ATMs** are now ubiquitous in urban areas: you'll find them dotted around the main squares, outside banks and in hotel lobbies. It is now perfectly viable to arrive in the country with a plastic card and a PIN number and pull out złotys wherever you go.

Information, websites and maps

Poland has a National Tourist Office with branches in a number of European countries and the US (see below for addresses). Within the country, however, tourist information centres of the Western European kind are a relatively new phenomenon, and the level of help you will get from them remains unpredictable. Often you'll have to resort to other sources of information – commercial travel agencies or the reception staff at your hotel – in order to get a full picture of what tourist sights and facilities are on offer.

Most towns and cities now have a **tourist information centre** (known as *informator turystyczny* or IT). Sometimes these are run by the local municipality and are rather effective, offering full hotel listings, accommodation bookings and a range of brochures and maps (which are usually for sale rather than given away free). More often than not, however, IT offices are privately run travel agencies that are using the IT label to attract tourists, in order to sell them tours and travel tickets. Some of these privately run IT offices do an admirable job in finding you a bed for the night and answering your queries; others show a distinct lack of commitment to their information-giving task. Many provincial towns, especially those that see few tourists, have yet to establish an IT office of any kind.

Tourist offices abroad

UK Level 3, Westec House, West Gate, London W5 1YY ☎ 08700 675 010, ⓦ www.visitpoland.org.

US 5 Marine View Plaza, Hoboken, NJ 07030 ☎ 201/420 9910, ⓦ www.polandtour.org.

Travel agents in Poland

You'll find a range of travel agents on Polish high streets – most of which concentrate on selling foreign holidays to Poles, although several (especially in Warsaw and Kraków) arrange sightseeing tours and hotel bookings for incoming tourists. One chain which has offices all over the country is **Orbis** (ⓦ www.orbis.pl), a former state-run concern that controlled all incoming travel to the country until its privatization in the 1990s. Its offices can still be useful, selling air, rail, bus and ferry tickets, changing money, arranging car rental and handling hotel reservations – especially in the hotels belonging to the Orbis chain (see "Accommodation", p.49).

Another useful name to look out for is **PTTK** (ⓦ www.pttk.com.pl) – which translates literally as "The Polish Country Lovers'

Association" – an organization responsible for maintaining hiking routes and administering mountain huts, hostels and hotels. PTTK offices can be found throughout the country, providing bookings in PTTK-run accommodation and selling hiking maps. Despite signs of change, however, PTTK remains a remarkably old-fashioned organization: with a few exceptions, its offices are dingy, underfunded affairs whose resolutely monolingual staff feign bemused indifference to queries launched at them by foreigners.

Almatur is a student and youth travel bureau which sells ISIC cards, books discounted travel tickets for the under 26s, and sometimes arranges accommodation in student hostels during July and August. Almatur's head office is at ul. Kopernika 23, Warsaw (☎022/826 3512, ⓦwww.almatur .pl); other addresses can be found in the Guide under the appropriate section.

Polish cultural organizations abroad

An estimated fifteen million Poles, or people of Polish origin, live outside Poland itself. Many of these are relatively recent migrants, although the vast majority comprise the descendants of those Poles who fled the country for economic or political reasons over the last century and a half. Of these, by far the largest group are **Polish-Americans**, thought to number anywhere from seven to ten million, with a particularly strong base in Chicago, which is still said to have the largest Polish population in the world after Warsaw. In Europe, the largest populations are in **Germany** and **France** (around one million each). Despite its smaller size, the Polish community in **Britain** (around 200,000), the majority of whom originally came during World War II as refugees or with the Polish armed forces, held a symbolically significant position as the home of the Polish Government-in-Exile which moved to London in 1939.

All the major English-speaking countries have **Polish cultural organizations** that are worth contacting if you want to learn more about the country or if you have Polish heritage yourself. They organize cultural events, run language classes and disseminate information about Polish arts, literature and folk traditions. The Internet is an invaluable tool in finding out what they offer: Polonia, the organization which looks after the interests of expatriate Poles worldwide, has a useful website (ⓦwww.polonia.org) with numerous links to affiliated organizations. Some of the more active groups around the globe include the Polish Cultural Institute in London (ⓦwww .polishculture.org.uk), the Polish Cultural Institute in New York (ⓦwww.polishculture -nyc.org) and the Polish Community of Australia (ⓦwww.polish.org.au).

Jewish tourism

Jews and **Jewish heritage** loom large in the history of Poland. Prior to the outbreak of World War II, Jews comprised roughly ten percent (three million) of the country's population, the largest Jewish community in Europe and the second largest in the world at the time. Of a current world population of fifteen million Jews, more than half are reckoned to have historical connections to Polish Jewry.

Cities such as **Warsaw, Łódź** and **Lublin** had particularly large pre-Holocaust Jewish populations, and are increasingly receptive to the needs of organized heritage tours and individuals seeking out family roots. **Kraków** – site of the thriving Jewish suburb of Kazimierz and within visiting distance of Holocaust memorials such as **Auschwitz-Birkenau** – is particularly well organized in this regard. If you find yourself hunting around the back streets of a town in search of Jewish buildings and monuments – a common experience in the further flung reaches of the country – the basic words and phrases to know when asking for directions are *bóżnica* or *synagoga* (synagogue) and *cmentarz żydowski* (Jewish cemetery). However, you can't bank on everyone knowing where to find what you're looking for: generally speaking, the older the person the more likely they are to be able to point you in the right direction. Bear in mind too that many former synagogues are now used for something totally different, and all too often don't have any signs indicating their original use. Many of the Polish-Jewish organizations (see p.42) can be extremely helpful in providing further information and contacts. For more on Jewish heritage, see the "Books" section of Contexts.

Polish-Jewish organizations

Jewish Communities Federation (Związek Religijny Wyznania Mojzeszowego) ul. Twarda 6, Warsaw ☎022/620 4324, ⓦwww.jewish.org.pl. Headquarters of religious congregations throughout Poland.

Jewish Historical Institute ul. Tlomackie 3/5, Warsaw ☎022/827 9221, ⓦwww.jewishinstitute .org.pl. Archives, exhibitions, library and irregularly open bookshop.

Judaica Cultural Centre ul. Meiselsa 17, Kraków ☎012/430 6449, ⓦwww.judaica.pl. Ambitious new cultural centre in the heart of the Kazimierz district, with a library, reading room, gallery, café and bookshop.

Our Roots ul. Twarda 6, Warsaw ☎022/620 0556, ⓦour-roots.jewish.org.pl. Jewish travel agency that provides general information and local guides, produces guidebooks and helps with tracing family ancestry in Poland. See also p.106.

Ronald Lauder Foundation ul. Twarda 6, Warsaw ☎022/652 2150, ⓦwww.lauder.pl. US-based foundation supporting Polish cultural and religious initiatives within Poland.

Useful websites

ⓦ**www.gopoland.com** General travel guide and resource for Poland. Also train schedules, Internet café locations, hotel discounts.

ⓦ**www.inyourpocket.com** Independent online travel guides to Warsaw, Wrocław, Kraków, Poznań and Gdańsk, as well as a host of other Central and Eastern European cities.

ⓦ**www.krakow.pl** Official Kraków city home page. Lots of useful tips and city information.

ⓦ**www.pgsa.org** Site of the Polish Genealogical Society of America; invaluable if you're researching family roots.

ⓦ**www.polandtour.org** Good National Tourist Office site, maintained by the New York office. Also contact details for NTO offices around the world.

ⓦ**www.polishworld.com** Useful all-round resource: discount hotel bookings, travel information, arts and entertainment, politics, news and media, plus plenty of links to other Poland-related sites.

ⓦ**www.polishwriting.net** Excellent guide to Polish literature, with fragments of prose in English translation, and author biographies.

ⓦ**www.polonianet.com** General portal with lots of links to sites dealing with history and culture.

ⓦ**www.visit.pl** General travel information, and a hotel booking service.

ⓦ**www.warsawtour.pl** Official Warsaw tourist information site. Plenty of useful practical information, city listings and public services.

ⓦ**www.warsawvoice.com.pl** Warsaw's leading English-language magazine online, with business and cultural information.

ⓦ**www.zem.co.uk/polish** British-based site boasting tons of Polish links, covering all aspects of society and culture, often covered in lively style.

Maps

Best of the **general maps** available outside the country are Freytag & Berndt's 1:750 000 map; and the 1:800 000 GeoCenter Euro map. GeoCenter Euro also produces a useful set of 1:300 000 **regional maps**, covering northeast, northwest, southeast and southwest Poland respectively.

More easily available once you're inside the country are the series of national and regional maps produced by local publishers Demart and Copernicus. Demart's spiral-bound 1:250 000 **road atlas** (*atlas samochodowy*) is particularly useful if you're touring the country by car.

Both companies produce detailed and up-to-date **city maps** (*plan miasta*) of almost every urban area in Poland, invariably with public transport routes clearly marked and an A–Z street index on the back – which one you prefer will probably depend on price and visual appearance.

Hiking maps (*mapa turystyczna*) of the National Parks and other rural areas are produced by an array of small companies. They're universally clear and simple to use, although it's wise to choose a larger-scale map – 1:25 000 or greater – if you want to walk a particular route.

The best places to buy maps are the EMPiK multimedia stores found in big city centres – although most other bookshops and newspaper kiosks will carry a small selection.

Map and guide outlets

In the UK and Ireland

Stanfords 12–14 Long Acre, London WC2E 9LP ☎020/7836 1321; 29 Corn St, Bristol BS1 1HT ☎0117/929 9966; 39 Spring Gardens, Manchester M2 2BG ☎0161/831 0250; ⓦwww.stanfords .co.uk.

Blackwell's Map and Travel Shop 53 Broad St, Oxford OX1 3BQ ☎01865/793 550, ⓦwww .blackwell.co.uk

Easons Bookshop 40 O'Connell St, Dublin 1 ☎01/858 3811, ⓦwww.eason.ie.

Hodges Figgis Bookshop 56–58 Dawson St, Dublin 2 ☎ 01/677 4754.

The Map Shop 30a Belvoir St, Leicester LE1 6QH ☎ 0116/247 1400, ⊕ www.mapshopsleicester .co.uk.

National Map Centre 22–24 Caxton St, London SW1H 0QU ☎ 020/7222 2466, ⊕ www.mapsnmc .co.uk.

Newcastle Map Centre 55 Grey St, Newcastle upon Tyne NE1 6EF ☎ 0191/261 5622.

The Travel Bookshop 13–15 Blenheim Crescent, London W11 2EE ☎ 020/7229 5260, ⊕ www .thetravelbookshop.co.uk.

USA and Canada

Book Passage 51 Tamal Vista Blvd, Corte Madera, CA 94925 ☎ 1-800-999-7909, ⊕ www .bookpassage.com.

Distant Lands 56 S Raymond Ave, Pasadena CA 91105 ☎ 1-800-310-3220.

Elliot Bay Book Company 101 S Main St, Seattle, WA 98104 ☎ 1-800-962-5311, ⊕ www .elliotbaybook.com.

Globe Corner Bookstore 28 Church St, Cambridge, MA 02138 ☎ 1-800-358-6013, ⊕ www.globercorner.com.

Map Link Inc 30 S La Patera Lane, Unit 5, Santa Barbara, CA 93117 ☎ 1-800-962-1394, ⊕ www .maplink.com.

Rand McNally US ☎ 1-800-333-0136, ⊕ www .randmcnally.com. Around thirty stores across the US; dial ext ☎ 2111 or check the website for the nearest location.

World of Maps 1235 Wellington St, Ottawa, Ontario K1Y 3A3 ☎ 1-800-214-8524, ⊕ www .worldofmaps.com.

In Australia and New Zealand

Mapland 372 Little Bourke St, Melbourne ☎ 03/9670 4383, ⊕ www.mapland.com.au.

The Map Shop 6 Peel St, Adelaide ☎ 08/8231 2033, ⊕ www.mapshop.net.au.

Map World (Australia) 371 Pitt St, Sydney ☎ 02/9261 3601, ⊕ www.mapworld.net.au. Also at 900 Hay St, Perth ☎ 08/9322 5733, Jolimont Centre, Canberra ☎ 02/6230 4097 and 1981 Logan Road, Brisbane ☎ 07/3349 6633.

Mapworld (New Zealand) 173 Gloucester St, Christchurch ☎ 0800/627 967, ⊕ www.mapworld .co.nz.

Getting around

Poland has comprehensive and cheap public transport services, though they can often be overcrowded and excruciatingly slow. As a general rule, trains are the best means of moving across the country, as all but the most rural areas are still crisscrossed by passenger lines. Buses come into their own in the more remote regions of the country, where you'll find that even the smallest of villages are served by at least one bus a day. For information on major train and bus connections, consult the "Travel details" section at the end of each chapter. Car rental prices are fairly reasonable, and taxis are cheap enough to be considered for the occasional inter-town journey, especially if you can split costs three or four ways.

Trains

Polish State Railways (PKP) is a reasonably efficient organization, though its services, particularly on rural routes, have been heavily cut since the fall of communism and continue to be reduced at frequent intervals. PKP runs four main types of train (*pociąg*).

Intercity services (IC; marked in red on timetables) run on premium routes (such as Warsaw–Kraków or Kraków–Berlin) and only stop at major cities. They're by far the fastest and most comfortable means of getting around, but are more expensive than other trains and reservations (20zł) are obligatory. **Express** services (*ekspresowy*; marked in red as "Ex") link Poland's main cities, are only slightly slower than IC trains, and often operate long cross-country routes which allow you to traverse Poland from north to south or east to west without changing trains. Again, reservations (10zł) are compulsory. **Fast** trains (*pospieszny*; marked in red as "posp.") have far more stops than express trains, are correspondingly slower, and come much cheaper than expresses – which is why they're often overcrowded. Cheapest of all are the **normal** services (*osobowy*; marked in black), which travel at snail-like speeds stopping at every wayside halt, and often feature outdated carriages with uncomfortable seats. Unless you're looking to save money they're well worth avoiding, although in rural areas they may be the only option available.

Fares shouldn't burn too big a hole in your pocket: using *pospieszny* trains, cross-country journeys such as Warsaw to Wrocław, Kraków or Gdańsk shouldn't set you back much more than £15/€21/US$27. Travelling with an express or intercity train will be 30–50 percent more expensive. At these prices, it's well worth paying the fifty percent extra to travel first class (*pierwsza klasa*), in order to avoid the sardine-like conditions that sometimes occur in second-class coaches – especially at weekends or during holidays.

Many long intercity journeys can be made overnight, with trains conveniently timed to leave around 10 or 11pm and arrive between 6 and 9am. For these, it's advisable to book either a **sleeper** (*sypialny*) or **couchette** (*kuszetka*) in advance; the total cost will probably be little more than a room in a cheap hotel. Sleepers cost about 120zł (£20/€28/US$36) per head in a three-bunk compartment (though it's rare that all three beds are used), complete with washbasin, towels, sheets, blankets and a snack. At about 90zł (£15/€21/US$27), couchettes have six bunks and also come with sheets, a blanket and a pillow. Finally, a reminder about **theft** on trains: overnight sleepers on the principal lines are prime targets for robberies. One major hazard to watch out for is night-time stops at Warsaw's Central station en route to elsewhere – thieves regularly hop on, steal what they can, and hop off again. The best advice is to keep your compartment locked and your valuables well hidden at all times.

Tickets and passes

Buying **tickets** in the main city train stations can be a time-consuming process, with a bewildering array of counters and long queues. Make sure you join the line at least 45 minutes before your train is due to leave, though usually the absolute maximum you'll have to wait is half an hour. Booking a sleeper or couchette is often done at a separate counter (look for the bed logo). Since most officials don't speak any English, a good way to get the precise ticket you want is to write all the details down and show them at the counter: include destination, time of departure, class (first is *pierwsza*, second is *druga*) and whether you want a seat reservation (*miejscówka*).

As an alternative to the station queues, you can buy tickets for journeys of over 100km at **Orbis** offices. The main branches of these are also a good way of booking for international journeys.

Discounted tickets (*ulgowy*) are available for pensioners and for children aged between 4 and 10 years; those under 4 travel free, though they're not supposed to occupy a seat. For students, ISIC cards no longer entitle you to discounted travel within Poland.

Inter Rail passes are valid in Poland (see p.30), but not Eurail.

Station practicalities

In train stations, the **departures** are normally listed on yellow posters marked *odjazdy*, with **arrivals** on white posters headed *przyjazdy*. Fast trains are marked in red and normal services in black. An "R" in a square means that seat reservations are obligatory. Additionally, there may be figures at the bottom indicating the dates between which a particular train does (*kursuje*) or doesn't run (*nie kursuje*) – the latter usually underlined by a warning wiggly line. The platform (*peron*) is also indicated.

Information counters, if they exist, are usually heralded by long queues and manned by non-English-speaking staff. If you're intending to do a lot of travelling in Poland, it makes sense to invest in the six-monthly **network timetable** (*rozkład jazdy*), which can, in theory, be bought at all main stations, although it usually sells out soon after publication.

Each **platform** has two tracks which often have different numbers allotted to them, so take care that you board the right train; electronic departure boards are yet to be installed in many Polish stations, and trains don't always display boards stating their route, so it pays to ask before boarding.

The main station in a city is identified by the name Główny or Centralny. These are open round the clock and usually have such **facilities** as waiting rooms, toilets, kiosks, restaurants, snack bars, cafés, a left-luggage office (*przechowalnia bagażu*) – or, in the largest cities, lockers – and a 24-hour post office.

Facilities on the trains are much poorer, though IC and express trains have a buffet car, and light refreshments are available on all overnight journeys. **Ticket control** is rather haphazard, particularly on crowded services, but it does happen more often than not. If you've boarded a train without the proper ticket, you should seek out the conductor, who will issue the right one on payment of a small supplement.

Buses

The extent to which you'll need to make use of the services of PKS, the Polish national bus company, depends very much on the nature of your trip. If you're concentrating on journeys between major cities, then the trains are faster and more numerous. As soon as you start visiting provincial towns and villages, however, buses are likely to be your best bet.

The **PKS** network is extraordinarily comprehensive, and buses provide an excellent means of getting around in those areas not well served by rail – especially in the mountains, along the coast, and in the Mazurian lake district. The main disadvantages of bus travel are the slow speed (in some rural areas, buses rarely exceed an average of 30km per hour) and the discomfort: buses are likely to be crammed with local schoolchildren on weekdays, and many of the older vehicles feature broken seats and bad ventilation – avoid the temptation to sit at the back; the fumes rising from the engine will have you retching within minutes.

Private bus companies like Polski Express (Ⓦwww.polskiexpress.pl) and Komfort Bus (Ⓦwww.komfortbus.pl) run fast and cheap intercity services, although these only operate on radial routes linking Warsaw with the major provincial capitals.

Tickets

In towns and cities, the **main bus station** (*dworzec autobusowy*) is usually alongside the train station. **Tickets** can be bought in the terminal building; in larger places there are several counters, each dealing with clearly displayed destinations. In a few places the terminal is shared with the train station, so make sure you go to the right counter. **Booking** in the departure terminal ensures a seat, as a number will be allocated to you on your ticket. However, the lack of computerized systems means that many stations cannot allocate seats for services starting out from another town. In such cases, you have to wait until the bus arrives and buy a ticket – which may be for standing room only – from the driver. The same procedure can also be followed, provided the bus isn't already full to overflowing, if you arrive too late to buy a ticket at the counter. With a few exceptions, it isn't possible to buy tickets for return journeys on board. Note too that routes run by private companies like Polski Express generally leave from outside the bus station and use travel agents such as **Orbis** (see p.40) to handle their tickets. There are no student discounts on buses.

Timetables

Noticeboards show **departures** (*odjazdy*) and **arrivals** (*przyjazdy*) not only in the bus stations, but on all official stopping places along the route. "Fast" (*pospieszny*) buses (which carry a small supplement) are marked in red, slow in black. As at the train stations, departures and arrivals are marked on different boards, so make sure you're looking at the right one. If in doubt, ask at the information counter, which may – if you're lucky – be equipped with the multi-volume set of timetables listing all PKS routes. It's very rare to find an English speaker in the average Polish bus station, so it's best to write your destination down to avoid any confusion.

City transport

Trams are the basis of the public transport system in nearly all Polish cities. They usually run from about 5am to 11pm, and departure times are clearly posted at the stops. **Tickets** can be bought from a Ruch kiosk (just ask at any kiosk selling newspapers). They can only be used in the city where they were bought. On boarding, you should immediately cancel your ticket in one of the machines; checks by inspectors are rare, but they do happen from time to time. Note that some tickets have to be **cancelled** at both ends (arrows will indicate if this is so); this is for the benefit of children and pensioners, who travel half-price and thus have to cancel only one end per journey. In some cities (like Gdańsk) you pay for the time you spend on the tram, and have to keep cancelling tickets (if you're making a long journey) as if feeding a meter. In other cities (like Warsaw) you pay a flat fare for each single journey – and if you transfer from one tram to another you'll need a second ticket.

Tram tickets are valid on **municipal buses**, and the same system for validating them applies. The routes of the municipal buses go beyond the city boundaries into the outlying countryside, so many nearby villages have several connections during peak times of the day. Note that on both buses and trams, **night services** require two or three tickets.

The price of **taxis** is cheap enough to make them a viable proposition for regular use during your visit. In the new free-market economy, plenty of people have turned to taxi driving, and outside hotels, stations and major tourist attractions you often have to run the gauntlet of cabbies. Make sure you choose a taxi with an illuminated sign on its roof bearing the company name and phone number.

If you pick up a taxi in the street, you're more likely to pay above-average prices; the safest and cheapest option is to ring a quoted taxi number and order one. Generally speaking, you should pay 15–25zł for a cross-city journey, depending on your time of travel (prices are fifty percent higher after 11pm). Prices are also raised by fifty percent for journeys outside the city limits. However, costs are always negotiable for longer journeys – between towns, for example – and can work out very reasonable if split among a group. For more advice on travelling by taxi, see the Warsaw account (p.90).

Flights

The domestic network of **LOT**, the Polish national airline, operates regular flights from Warsaw to Gdańsk, Katowice, Kraków, Poznań, Rzeszów, Szczecin and Wrocław – each of which take about an hour. Some routes are covered several times a day, but services are reduced during the winter months (end Oct to mid-April). Most of the cities mentioned are also linked directly to some of the others, but Warsaw is very much the lynchpin of the system. As a general rule, **airports** are located just outside the cities, and can be reached either by a special LOT bus or by a municipal service.

Tickets can be purchased at the airport itself or from LOT and Orbis offices, where you can also pick up free timetables (ask for *rozkład lotów*). Prices are currently in the region of £100–140/€140–195/US$180–250 one-way (the cost of returns is not much higher), though advance booking and occasional promotional offers can reduce the cost substantially. Children up to the age of 2 travel for free, provided they do not occupy a separate seat; under 12s go for half-price.

Driving

Although access to a **car** will save you a lot of time in exploring the country, **traffic** is heavy on Poland's main roads. There's a dearth of multi-lane highways on the trunk routes, ensuring that you'll spend much of your time trailing behind a stream of slow-moving cars and lorries. Poland's rural backroads are quiet and hassle-free by comparison, and – providing you have a decent map – present the perfect terrain for unhurried touring.

If you're **bringing your own car**, you'll need to carry your vehicle's registration document. If the car is not in your name, you must have a letter of permission signed by the owner and authorized by your national motoring organization. You'll also need your **driving licence** (international driving licences aren't officially required, though they can be a help in tricky situations), and you may

need an **international insurance green
card** to extend your insurance cover – check
with your insurers to see whether you're
covered or not. You're also required to carry
a red warning triangle, a first-aid kit, a set
of replacement bulbs and display a national
identification sticker. Note that rear-wheel
mud flaps are obligatory in Poland.

Car rental

Car rental in Poland works out at about £45/
€60/US$80 a day and £225/€300/US$400
a week for a Fiat Punto or equivalent with
unlimited mileage. An Opel Vectra, Nissan
Primera or equivalent will cost fifty percent
more. Cars can be booked through the usual
agents in the West (see below) or in Poland
itself: all the four major operators now
have their own agents in all or most of the
big Polish cities. Alternatively you can rent
through the main Orbis offices in large cities
(see the Guide for addresses). **Payment** can
be made with cash or any major credit card,
and you can drop a car at a different office
from the one where you rented it.

Cars will only be rented to people over 21
(or for some types of vehicle, over 25) who
have held a full **licence** for more than a year.
If you're planning on renting a car outside
Poland and bringing it into the country you
should be aware that rising levels of **car
theft** (see p.48) have led several of the major
rental companies to slap severe restrictions
on taking their cars east.

Check the conditions carefully before renting anything – if you do take a rental car into
Poland without permission it means you
effectively accept the financial risk for the
car's full value if it's damaged in an accident or stolen. Of the major companies,
Hertz currently seems to operate the least
restrictive policies, but since it (like the other
majors) has agents in Poland, you're better
off renting inside the country.

Car rental agencies

UK

Avis ☎08700 100 287, ⓦwww.avis.co.uk.
Budget ☎08701 539 170, ⓦwww.budget.co.uk.
Europcar ☎0870 607 5000, ⓦwww.europcar
.co.uk.
Hertz ☎0870 844 8844, ⓦwww.hertz.com.

Holiday Autos ☎0870 400 0099, ⓦwww
.holidayautos.co.uk.

Ireland

Avis Northern Ireland ☎028/9024 0404, Republic
of Ireland ☎01/605 7500, ⓦwww.avis.ie.
Budget Republic of Ireland ☎0906/627711,
ⓦwww.budget.ie.
Europcar Northern Ireland ☎028/9442 3444,
Republic of Ireland ☎01/614 2800, ⓦwww
.europcar.ie.
Hertz Republic of Ireland 01/676 7467, ⓦwww
.hertz.com.
Holiday Autos Republic of Ireland ☎01/872 9366,
ⓦwww.holidayautos.ie.

US and Canada

Avis US ☎1-800-331-1084, Canada ☎1-800
-272-5871, ⓦwww.avis.com.
Budget ☎1-800-527-0700, ⓦwww.budget.com.
Europcar ☎1-877-940-6900, ⓦwww.europcar
.com.
Hertz US ☎1-800-654-3001, Canada ☎1-800-
263-0600, ⓦwww.hertz.com.

Australia

Avis ☎136 333, ⓦwww.avis.com.au.
Budget ☎1300 362 848, ⓦwww.budget.com.au.
Europcar ☎1300 131 390, ⓦwww.deltaeuropcar
.com.au.
Hertz ☎133 039, ⓦwww.hertz.com.

New Zealand

Avis ☎09/526 5231 or 0800 655 111, ⓦwww
.avis.co.nz.
Budget ☎0800 283 438, ⓦwww.budget.co.nz.
Hertz ☎0800 654 321, ⓦwww.hertz.com.

Rules of the road

The main rules of the road are pretty clear,
though there are some particularly Polish
twists liable to catch out the unwary. The
basic rules are: traffic drives on the right;
it is compulsory to wear seat belts outside
built-up areas; children under 12 years of age
must sit in the back; seat belts must be worn
in the back if fitted; right of way must be given
to public transport vehicles (including trams).
Driving with more than 0.2 promile of alcohol
in the bloodstream (about equivalent to one
glass of beer or wine) is strictly prohibited
– anyone with a foreign numberplate driving around after 11pm, however innocently,

has a strong chance of being stopped and breathalyzed. Talking on hand-held mobile phones while driving is also against the law. From November through to March, headlights must be switched on at all times.

Speed limits are 60kph in built-up areas (white signs with the place name mark the start of a built-up area; the same sign with a diagonal red line through it marks the end), 90kph on country roads, 110kph on main highways, 120kph on dual carriageways, 130kph on motorways, and 80kph if you're pulling a caravan or trailer. **Fines**, administered on the spot, range from the negligible up to around £20/€28/US$36. Speed traps are common, particularly on major trunk roads such as the Gdańsk–Warsaw route, so caution is strongly advised, especially on the approach to, and when travelling through, small towns and villages.

Other problems occur chiefly at night, especially on country roads, where potential disasters include horses and carts, mopeds without lights and staggering inebriated peasants. In cities, beware of a casual attitude towards traffic lights and road signs by local drivers and pedestrians.

Road conditions are varied: on the one hand, backroads Poland still features large stretches of near-deserted, idyllic countryside routes; on the other, the rapidly expanding volume of traffic is putting an increasing strain on the country's major roads, and with few resources devoted to their upkeep, a number of routes – particularly those used by lorries – are quite simply beginning to fall apart. Motorways are still confined to a couple of stretches in the south (between Katowice and Kraków, for example), and major new projects remain the subject of much discussion.

Fuel

With car ownership increasing rapidly, and operators of all kinds waking up to the economic potential of the Polish market, the old problems with finding **fuel** have largely faded away. A growing number of small-scale operators, privatized CPN fuel depots and brand new multinational outlets have added substantially to the number of service stations around. Many stations in cities and along the main routes are open 24 hours a day, others

from around 6am to 10pm; almost all out-of-town stations close on Sunday. Unleaded fuel is *benzyna bezołowiowa*. Carrying at least one fuel can permanently topped up will help to offset worries in rural areas.

Car crime

With car-related **crime** – both simple break-ins and outright theft – one of the biggest criminal growth areas in Poland today, and foreign-registered vehicles one of the major targets, it pays to take note of some simple precautions. In big towns especially, always park your vehicle in a guarded parking lot (*parking strzeżony*), never in an open street – even daylight break-ins occur with depressing frequency. Never leave anything of importance, including vehicle documents, in the car. **Guarded lots** are not too expensive (about £5/US$7 a day, more in major city centres) and in most towns and cities you can usually find one located centrally – the major hotels almost always have their own nearby. If you have a break-in, report it to the police immediately. They'll probably shrug their shoulders over the prospects of getting anything back, but you'll need their signed report for insurance claim purposes back home.

Breakdowns and spares

The Polish motoring association (Polski związek motorowy or PZMot) runs a 24-hour car **breakdown service**. The national HQ, which can provide some English-language pamphlets on their services, is at ul. Kazimierzowska 66, Warsaw (☎022/849 9361, ⓦwww.pzm.pl). Anywhere else dial the national breakdown **emergency number** – ☎9637 – and you'll eventually be towed to a garage. If you have insurance against breakdowns, the tow will be free; otherwise it will cost you 2.5zł per kilometre.

The wide range of cars now available in Poland means that you will not have problems finding **spares** for major Western makes like Volvo, Renault and Volkswagen. If it's simply a case of a flat tyre, head for the nearest sizeable garage.

Cycling

Cycling is often regarded as an ideal way to see a predominantly rural country like

Poland. Particularly on the back roads, surfaces are generally in good shape, and there isn't much traffic around – anyone used to cycling in Western traffic is in for a treat. An additional plus is the mercifully flat nature of much of the terrain, which allows you to cycle quite long distances without great effort. You'll need to bring your own machine and a supply of **spare parts**: except in a few major cities like Warsaw and Kraków, and a number of southern mountain areas like the Bieszczady, **bike rental** and spare part facilities are still a comparative rarity. In rural areas, though, bikes are fairly common, and with a bit of ingenuity you can pick up basic spares like inner tubes and puncture repair kits.

Taking your bike on **trains** isn't a problem as long as there's a luggage van on board: if there isn't you usually have to sit with it in the last carriage of the train, where if you're lucky there'll be fewer passengers; either way there's a nominal fee. Hotels will usually put your machine either in a locked luggage room or a guarded parking lot. You need to exercise at least as much caution concerning security as you would in any city at home: strong locks and chaining your bike to immobile objects are the order of the day, and always try and take your bike indoors at night.

Accommodation

Accommodation will probably account for most of your essential expenditure in Poland. The hotel market has witnessed a considerable shake-up in recent years, with the construction of new business-oriented international franchises and the privatization and refurbishment of old state-run establishments.

The overall effect of these developments has been to force prices upwards, although accommodation bargains are still easy to come by in Poland – especially in the rural resort areas favoured by the Poles themselves. Listings in the Guide have been made as wide-ranging as possible to reflect the immense diversity on offer: privately run hotels, pensions, hostels, youth hostels, upmarket B&Bs, rooms in private houses and a good range of campsites.

Booking hotels online before you travel may save you a few pennies, with the websites listed below offering attractive deals on accommodation across the country – beware, however, that they only deal with mid-range hotels and upwards, and are unlikely to be a source of bargains for budget travellers.

Accommodation booking websites

Ⓦ **www.discover-poland.pl** Discount hotel reservations covering pretty much everywhere you might want to go in Poland.

Ⓦ **www.hotelspoland.com** Plenty of good discounts on selected hotels all over the country. Also cut-price air fares from the USA.

Ⓦ **www.polhotels.com** Another site specializing in discount hotel bookings only available via the Internet. Prices are similar to the above site, although this one usually has a wider selection of places and towns.

Ⓦ **www.travellingpoland.com** Another big range of accommodation.

Hotels

There's a growing range and diversity of hotel accommodation in Poland, although standards of service and value for money vary widely from place to place. The international five-star **grading system** is in use but is yet to be applied universally – and even in those cases where star ratings are in use, they aren't always an accurate guide to quality. As a general rule however, one-star hotels provide rooms with a bed and not much else; two-star hotels offer rooms with at least an en-suite shower; while three-star hotels are likely to provide you with a telephone

Accommodation price codes

All accommodation listed in the Guide (apart from youth hostels) is **price graded** according to the scale below. Unless specified otherwise, prices given are for the **cheapest** double room.

In the cheapest places (categories ❶–❷), rooms generally come without their own private bath/shower, breakfast is often not included, and in some instances (specified in the text) beds are in dorms only. In categories ❸–❺ you can normally expect breakfast and an en-suite shower/bath. Overall, room quality in the **middle ranges** is affected by the age of the building (generally speaking the newer the place, especially post-1990, the better) and its geographical location – the more popular tourist centres are improving room quality faster than the rest, and the east of the country still lags noticeably behind western regions. Into the **top bracket** hotels (categories ❽–❾), it's another story: high prices are generally matched by consistently high standards.

The majority of places will expect you to pay in złoty, though prices are often quoted in euros.

❶ under 60zł (under £10/€14/US$18)
❷ 60–90zł (£10–15/€14–21/US$18–27)
❸ 90–120zł (£15–20/€21–28/US$27–36)
❹ 120–160zł (£20–27/€28–38/US$36–49)
❺ 160–220zł (£27–37/€38–52/US$49–67)
❻ 220–300zł (£37–50/€52–70/US$67–90)
❼ 300–400zł (£50–67/€70–93/US$90–120)
❽ 400–600zł (£67–100/€93–140/US$120–180)
❾ over 600zł (over £100/€140/US$180)

and a TV. Anything four-star or five-star is in the international business league.

Most Polish towns and cities still retain one or two (usually unclassified) **budget hotels** offering sparsely furnished rooms in old, unrenovated buildings, customarily with shared bathroom facilities located in the hallway. Despite an outward air of shabbiness these places are usually clean and well run, and shouldn't be discounted if all you need is a bed for the night. They rarely cost more than £10/€14/US$18 per person per night, although they're decreasing in number – largely because of the temptation to refurbish and upgrade these establishments as soon as investment becomes available.

Another traditional source of cheap rooms is the **sports hotel** (*Dom Sportowy*; sometimes known by the acronym OSiR or MOSiR), usually built adjacent to the town stadium (often located in a park way out from the centre) and intended for the use of visiting sporting teams – which means they're likely to be fully booked for at least part of the weekend. Sports hotels often have a mixture of en-suite rooms and rooms with shared facilities, and are likely to provide

several triples and quads as well as doubles – although single travellers may be asked to share a room with a stranger.

Occupying a similar price range are the hotels run by the **PTTK** organization (see p.40), which are found in many city centres and usually go by the name of *Dom Turysty* or *Hotel PTTK*. These usually contain a mixture of dorm rooms, rooms with shared facilities and simple en suites, with beds costing anything from £10/€14/US$18 to £15/€21/US$27 per person. Although the majority of PTTK places are budget-oriented establishments patronized by international and Polish youth, a few of them are being modernized and turned into mid-price hotels.

Long lacking in Poland, there are now plenty of competitively priced **mid-range hotels** which would fit comfortably into the international two- and three-star brackets. Prices and quality vary considerably in this category (see box above), but for a standard medium-range double room expect to pay anything from £30/€42/US$54 to £50/€70/US$90 a night – more in Warsaw and Kraków. Breakfast is usually included in the room price. The older of these mid-range hotels often have a few cheap rooms with shared facilities as well as the standard en suites which are invariably offered to new arrivals – there will be a substantial difference in price, so always ask.

Five-star hotels are still something of a rarity outside Warsaw and Kraków, but four-star establishments are mushrooming all over the place, largely thanks to the booming numbers of business travellers roaming around post-communist Poland. Double-room prices at this level can be anything from £55/€77/US$100 to £120/€170/US$215, although you may well find significant reductions at weekends.

The biggest hotel chain in Poland is **Orbis** (@www.orbis.pl), the former state-owned tourist company privatized in the 1990s. Once a byword for shoddiness, their hotels (mostly in the three- and four-star brackets) are now more or less up to international standards, especially those run in conjunction with Western chains such as Novotel and Mercure.

Apartments

An increasing number of establishments in Warsaw (and to a lesser extent Kraków) are offering serviced **apartments** in modern blocks. These usually offer the same comforts as a three-star hotel or above, but come with the added advantage of a small kitchenette (breakfast won't be provided) and – depending on what size of apartment is available – the chance to spread yourself out a bit more than you would do in a hotel room. A range of apartments from simple studios to one- and two-bedroom affairs are on offer from outfits such as Old Town Apartments in Warsaw and Kraków (see the accommodation sections of the relevant chapters for details). Prices depend on how many of you are sharing, but are usually slightly cheaper than the equivalent level of accommodation in a hotel. Always enquire about the dimensions of an apartment before committing yourself: some are generously proportioned, others are little more than glorified cupboards.

Pensions

Some of Poland's best accommodation deals can be found in the growing stock of **pensions** (*pensjonaty*) situated in major holiday areas – especially in the mountains, the Mazurian lake district, and along the coast. There's no hard and fast rule governing what constitutes a pension in Poland. Some are small hotels that used to cater for workers taking rural rest cures and are now open to all; others are private houses transformed into family-run B&Bs. In all cases they tend to be cosy, informal affairs offering simple en-suite rooms, often equipped with the additional comforts of a fridge and an electric kettle. Rates hover between £16/€22/US$29 and £25/€35/US$45 per double. Breakfast is sometimes available at an extra cost.

Private rooms

You can get a room in a **private house** (*kwatera prywatna*) almost anywhere in the country. In urban areas these tend to be located in shabby flats, which may be situated some way from the centre of town. You will be sharing your hosts' bathroom, and breakfast will not be included. In lake, mountain and seaside resorts, however, hosts are often more attuned to the needs of tourists and may provide rooms with an en-suite bathroom, electric kettle, and even TV. Staying in private rooms doesn't necessarily constitute a great way of meeting the locals: some hosts will brew you a welcome glass of tea and show a willingness to talk; most will simply give you a set of house keys and leave you to get on with it.

In big cities such as Warsaw, Kraków, Gdańsk and Poznań, a **private-room bureau** (*biuro zakwaterowania*) or one of the local travel agencies undertakes the job of allocating rooms – details of these are given in the relevant sections of the guide. In the lakes, mountains and on the coast, the local IT office will usually find you a place. Expect to pay around £6–10/€8.50–14/US$11–18 per person per night, slightly more in Kraków and Warsaw. In case you don't like the place you're sent to, it makes sense not to register for too many nights ahead, as it's easy enough to extend your stay by going back to the agency, or paying your host directly.

At the unofficial level, many houses in the main holiday areas hang out signs saying *Noclegi* (lodging) or *Pokoje* (rooms). It's up to you to bargain over the price; £5/€7/US$9 per person is the least you can expect to pay. In the cities, you won't see any signs advertising rooms, but you may well be approached outside stations and other obvious places. Before accepting, establish the price and check that the location is suitable.

Rural homestays

An increasing number of Polish farmers are offering **B&B-style accommodation** in order to augment their income. As well as being ideal for those seeking rural tranquillity, they also offer the chance to observe a working farm and sample locally produced food and drink.

The accommodation on offer is cheap though not as basic as you might imagine, and includes easy access to some of the most beautiful parts of the Polish countryside, plenty of scope for outdoor activities (for example, many farms keep horses that guests are welcome to use) and the knowledge that you're doing something to support the local rural economy.

In most places, the local IT office will have a list of farms offering accommodation. A yearly handbook of farms throughout Poland offering holiday stays, *Gospodarstwa Gościnne*, written in English despite the title, is available from the Polska Federacja Turystyki Wiejskiej, ul. Wspólna 30, Warsaw (☎022/623 2350, ☎623 2352). Another useful source of information is the European Centre for Eco-Agro Tourism (ECEAT), a Netherlands-based foundation dedicated to supporting practical initiatives in the field of ecofriendly tourism; it produces *Green Holiday Guides* to all its properties in Poland (call ☎+31/20 668 1030 or check out ⓦwww.eceat.nl).

Hostels and refuges

Cities like Kraków and Warsaw are increasingly well served by small, privately run **backpacker-oriented hostels** providing neat and tidy dormitory accommodation and a friendly atmosphere. They're invariably equipped with kitchen, washing machine and common room, and aren't subject to curfews. Prices hover around the £10/€14/US$18 mark.

Elsewhere in Poland the picture is less encouraging, with an ageing network of some 600 **official youth hostels** (*schroniska młodzieżowe*) offering somewhat more spartan conditions – accommodation usually consists of rickety beds in sparsely furnished dorms. Preference is supposedly given to those under 26, though there's no upper age restriction. Finding a place is often a problem: many hostels serve as digs for Polish high-school students who are studying away from their home town, while others seem to be constantly booked up by Polish school groups. Two plus points are the prices (rarely more than £5/€7/US$9 a head) and the locations, with many hostels close to town centres. Against that, there's the fact that dormitories are closed between 10am and 5pm, you must check in by 9pm, and a 10pm curfew is often enforced (though usually negotiable in large cities). You will probably be able to rent a sheet or sleeping bag for a nominal fee. Cooking facilities are usually available.

The most useful hostel addresses are given in the Guide, but if you need a complete list, either buy the official *International Handbook* or contact the head office of the **Polish Youth Hostel Federation** (PTSM) at ul. Chocimska 28, Warsaw (☎022/849 8128) for their own comprehensive handbook (*Informator*). Though you can buy a Hostelling International (HI) membership card before you go (see below for addresses), it's best to get a national card once you're in Poland (7Ozł).

In mountain areas, a reasonably generous number of **refuges** (*schroniska*), many of them PTTK-run, enable you to make long-distance treks without having to make detours down into the villages for the night; they are clearly marked on hiking maps. Accommodation is in very basic dormitories but costs are nominal and you can often get cheap and filling hot meals; in summer the more popular refuges can be very crowded indeed, as they are obliged to accept all comers. As a rule, the refuges are open all year round but it's always worth checking for closures or renovations in progress before setting out.

Youth hostel associations

Youth Hostel Association UK (YHA) ☎0870 770 8868, ⓦwww.yha.org.uk. Annual membership

£13; under 18s £6.50; lifetime £190 (or five annual payments of £40).

Scottish Youth Hostel Association ☎ 0870 155 3255, ⓦ www.syha.org.uk. Annual membership £6; under 18s £2.50.

Hostelling International Northern Ireland ☎ 028/9032 4733, ⓦ www.hini.org.uk. Adult membership £10; under 18s £6; family £20; lifetime £75.

Irish Youth Hostel Association ☎ 01/830 4555, ⓦ www.irelandyha.org. Adult membership €15; under 18s €7.50; family €31.50; lifetime €75.

Hostelling International/American Youth Hostels ☎ 202/783-6161, ⓦ www.hiayh.org. Annual membership for adults (18–55) is US$25, for seniors (55 or over) is US$15, and for under 18s is free. Lifetime memberships are US$250.

Hostelling International Canada ☎ 1-800-663 5777 or 613/237-7884, ⓦ www.hostellingintl.ca. Rather than sell the traditional one- or two-year memberships, the association now sells one Individual Adult membership with a 16- to 28-month term. The length of the term depends on when the membership is sold, but a member can receive up to 28 months of membership for just CAN$35. Membership is free for under 18s and you can become a lifetime member for CAN$175.

Australia Youth Hostels Association ☎ 02/9261 1111, ⓦ www.yha.com.au. Adult membership rate AUS$52 (under 18s AUS$52) for the first twelve months and then AUS$32 each year thereafter.

Youth Hostelling Association New Zealand ☎ 0800 278 299 or 03/379 9970, ⓦ www.yha .co.nz. Adult membership NZ$40 for one year, NZ$60 for two and NZ$80 for three; under 18s free; lifetime NZ$300.

Campsites

There are some 500 **campsites** throughout the country classified in three categories: **category 1** sites usually have amenities such as a restaurant and showers, while **category 3** sites amount to little more than poorly lit, run-down expanses of grass; **category 2** sites could be anywhere in between. The most useful are listed in the text; for a complete list, get hold of the *Camping w Polsce* map, available from bookshops (particularly EMPiK stores) and some tourist offices. Apart from a predictably dense concentration in the main holiday areas, sites can also be found in most cities: the ones on the outskirts are almost invariably linked by bus to the centre and often have the benefit of a peaceful location and swimming pool. The major drawback is that most are open **May to September** only, though a few do operate all year round. Charges usually work out at a little under £3/€4.20/US$5.40 per tent/caravan space, £3/€4.20/US$5.40 per person, and £3/€4.20/US$5.40 per car.

One specifically Polish feature is that you don't necessarily have to bring a tent to stay at many campsites, as there are often **bungalows** or **chalets** for rent, generally complete with toilet and shower. Though decidedly spartan in appearance, these are good value at around £5/€7/US$9 per head. In summer, however, they are invariably booked long in advance.

Eating and drinking

Poles take their food seriously, providing snacks of feast-like proportions for the most casual visitors, and maintaining networks of country relatives or local shops for especially treasured ingredients – smoked meats and sausages, cheeses, fruits and vegetables. The cuisine itself is a complex mix of influences: Russian, Lithuanian, Ukrainian, German and Jewish traditions all leaving their mark. To go with the food, there is excellent beer and a score of wonderful vodkas.

Once, if you wanted a really good meal in Poland, you had to hope for an invitation to someone's house. Now, however, with the moves towards a market economy, the country's fast-growing number of **restaurants** – most of which specialized in ungarnished slabs of meat during the communist era – are looking up. In the cities at least, there's now a distinctly Western spread of places to eat and a cosmopolitan range of cuisines. What is undeniable still is that eating out is a bargain, with splendid meals available for under £10/US$14 a head.

Drinking habits are changing, too. Poles for years drank mainly at home, while visitors stuck to the hotels, with such other bars as existed being alcoholic-frequented dives. In recent years, though, something of a café-bar culture has been emerging in the cities, and though the old drinking dens survive, you'll find plenty of choice for a relaxing, unthreatening night out.

Food

Like their Central and Eastern European neighbours, Poles are insatiable **meat** eaters: throughout the austerities of the past decade, meat consumption here remained among the highest in Europe. Beef and pork in different guises are the mainstays of most meals, while hams and sausages are consumed at all times of the day, as snacks and sandwich-fillers. Game is also common, and lamb is a speciality in the mountain regions where sheep-rearing is practised. In the coastal and mountain regions, you can also expect **fish** – particularly carp and freshwater trout – to feature prominently on the menus, with lots of seafood in the Baltic region.

A meal without meat is a contradiction in terms for most Poles, and **vegetarians** will often be forced to find solace in customary stand-bys like omelettes, cheese-based dishes and salads. Thankfully there are now a few vegetarian restaurants starting to appear in the larger cities, while an ever-increasing number of mainstream restaurants offer vegetarian dishes (*potrawy jarskie*), albeit largely unimaginative ones. The word *wegetariański* is useful, as are the phrases *bez mięsa* (without meat) and *bez ryby* (without fish). The Ⓦ www.wegetarian .com.pl site has details of vegetarian restaurants throughout the country, although it's currently in Polish only.

Breakfasts, snacks and fast foods

For most Poles, the first meal of the day, eaten at home at around 7am, is little more than a sandwich with a glass of tea or cup of coffee. A more leisurely **breakfast** might include fried eggs with ham, mild frankfurters, a selection of cold meats and cheese, rolls and jam, and this is what you are liable to encounter in hotels, but for most people this full spread is more likely to be taken as a second breakfast (*drugie śniadanie*) at around midday. This is often eaten in the workplace, but a common alternative is to stop at a milk bar or self-service snack bar (*samoobsługa*).

Open from early morning till 5 or 6pm (later in the city centres), **snack bars** are works-canteen-type places, serving very cheap but generally uninspiring food: small plates of salted herring in oil (*śledź w oleju*), sandwiches, tired-looking meat or cheese, sometimes enlivened by some Russian salad (*sałatka jarzynowa*). **Milk bars** (*bar mleczny*; often called *jadłodajnia* in Kraków) are a little more wholesome, offering a selection of solid meals with the emphasis on quantity. Milk bars and snack bars both operate as self-service cafeterias: the menu is displayed over the counter, but if you don't recognize the names of the dishes, you can just point.

Although the classic milk bar is something of a threatened institution, with many closing down in the face of fast-food competition, the style of food they offer remains enduringly popular, and looks set to remain part of the Polish snack-eating scene for some time to come. Two national specialities you'll find everywhere are *bigos* (cabbage stewed with meat and spices) and *pierogi* (dumplings stuffed with meat and mushrooms – or with cottage cheese, onion and spices in the non-meat variation, *pierogi ruskie*). Potato pancakes (*placki ziemniaczane*) – either in sour cream or covered in goulash (*gulasz*) – are another filling milk-bar favourite.

Takeaways and fast food

Traditional Polish **takeaway stands** usually sell *zapiekanki*, baguette-like pieces of bread topped with melted cheese; a less common but enjoyable version of the same thing comes with fried mushrooms. You'll also find hotdog stalls, doling out frankfurter sausages in white rolls, and stalls and shops selling French fries; the latter are generally skinny and oily, sold by weight, and accompanied by sausage or chicken in the tourist resorts and some city stands, or by fish in the northern seaside resorts and lakeland areas.

Western-style **fast food**, the totemic symbol of transformation towards a market economy all over Eastern Europe, has been seized on with eager enthusiasm in Poland. Many of the major international burger/pizza chains are now established in the big cities. Stalls selling grilled chicken (*kurczak z rożna*) have long been a local favourite, and no self-respecting high street is likely to be without one. Perhaps more appetizing are the new crop of oriental fast-food stands you'll find in the bigger cities, particularly Warsaw, often equipped with a few plastic chairs for instant eating convenience.

Do-it-yourself snacks

If the snacks on offer fail to appeal, you can always stock up on your own provisions.

Most people buy their bread in **supermarkets** (*samoobsługowe*) or from market traders; **bakeries** (*piekarnia*) are mostly small private shops and still something of a rarity, but when you do find them they tend to be very good, as the queues indicate. The standard loaf (*chleb zakopiański*) is a long piece of dense rye bread, often flavoured with caraway seeds. Also common is *razowy*, a solid brown bread sometimes flavoured with honey, and *mazowiecki*, a white, sour rye bread. Rolls come in two basic varieties: the more common is the plain, light white roll called a *kajzerka*, the other is the *grahamka*, a round roll of rougher and denser brown bread.

Supermarkets are again a useful source for fillers, with basic **delicatessen counters** for cooked meats and sausages, and fridge units holding a standard array of hard and soft cheeses. **Street markets** will be cheaper for fruit and vegetables. Few market stalls supply bags, so bring your own.

Cakes, sweets and ice cream

Cakes, pastries and other **sweets** are an integral ingredient of most Poles' daily consumption, and the cake shops (*cukiernia*) – which you'll find even in small villages – are as good as any in Central Europe. *Sernik* (cheesecake) is a national favourite, as are *makowiec* (poppyseed cake), *drożdżówka* (a sponge cake, often topped with plums) and *babka marmurkowa* (marble cake). In the larger places you can also expect to find *torcik wiedeński*, an Austrian-style *schlagtort* with coffee and chocolate filling, as well as a selection of eclairs, profiteroles and cupcakes.

Poles eat **ice cream** (*lody*) at all times of the year, queueing up for cones at street-side kiosks or in *cukiernia*. The standard kiosk cone is watery and pretty tasteless, but elsewhere the selection is better: decent cafés offer a mouthwatering selection of ices.

Restaurant meals

The average **restaurant** (*restauracja*) is open from late morning through to mid-evening. Until recently, all but the smartest closed early, winding down around 9pm in cities, earlier in the country, although these days there's more variety and most cities now boast several late-opening options (particularly at weekends). Bear in mind that the total shutdown principle, applied around religious festivals and public holidays, often applies to restaurants. In smaller towns, the big hotels may be the only places open.

Although many restaurant **menus**, particularly in the bigger cities, are in both Polish and English, those in smaller, rural places will usually be in Polish only. Menus are broken up into courses with separate headings: *zupy* (soups); *przekąski* (starters/hors d'oeuvres); *dania drugie* (main courses); *dodatki* (side dishes); *desery* (desserts); and *napoje* (drinks). The language section on p.712 should provide most of the cues you'll need. While the list of dishes apparently on offer may be long, in reality only things with a price marked next to them will be available, which will normally reduce the choice by fifty percent or more. If you arrive near closing time or late lunchtime, the waiter may inform you there's only one thing left.

There are no hard and fast rules about **tipping**, although it's increasingly common to leave an additional ten to fifteen percent, or round the bill up to the nearest convenient figure.

Soups and starters

First on the menu in most places are **soups**, definitely one of Polish cuisine's strongest points, varying from light and delicate dishes to concoctions that are virtually meals in themselves.

Best known is *barszcz*, a spicy beetroot broth that's ideally accompanied by a small pastry. Other soups worth looking out for are *żurek*, a malty soup made from fermented rye and often flavoured with sausage; *botwinka*, a seasonal soup made from the leaves of baby beetroots; *krupnik*, a thick barley and potato soup with chunks of meat, carrots and celeriac; and *chłodnik*, a cold Lithuanian beetroot soup with sour milk, served in summer.

In less expensive establishments, you'll be lucky to have more than a couple of soups and a plate of cold meats, or herring with cream or oil to choose from as a **starter**. In better restaurants, though, the hors d'oeuvres selection might include Jewish-style gefilte fish, jellied ham (*szynka w galarecie*), steak tartare (*stek tatarski*), wild rabbit paté (*pasztet z zająca*), or hard-boiled eggs in mayonnaise, which sometimes come stuffed with vegetables (*jajka faszerowanie*).

Main courses and side dishes

Snack-bar favourites such as *bigos*, *pierogi* and *placki* also form a large part of the average restaurant menu, although here they're served in larger portions and with slightly more style. Otherwise, the basis of most **main courses** is a fried or grilled cut of meat in a thick sauce, commonest of which is the *kotlet schabowy*, a pork cutlet which is often fried in batter. Another favourite is *flaczki* (tripe cooked in a spiced bouillon stock with vegetables – usually very spicy), while also worth trying are *gołąbki* (cabbage leaves stuffed with meat, rice and occasionally mushrooms) and *golonka* (pig's leg with horseradish). Duck is usually the most satisfying poultry, particularly with apples, while carp, eel and trout are generally reliable fish dishes, usually grilled or sautéed, occasionally poached. Pancakes (*naleśniki*) often come as a main course, too, stuffed with cottage cheese (*ze serem*).

Main dishes come with some kind of vegetables, normally boiled or mashed potatoes and/or cabbage, either boiled or as sauerkraut. Wild forest mushrooms (*grzyby*), another Polish favourite, are served in any number of forms, the commonest being fried or sautéed. Salads are generally a regulation issue plate of lettuce, cucumber and tomato in a watery dressing. If available, it's better to go for an individual salad dish like *mizeria* (cucumber in cream), *buraczki* (grated beetroot) or the rarer *ćwikła* (beetroot with horseradish).

Desserts

Desserts are usually restricted to a selection of cakes and ice creams. If it's available try *kompot*, fruit compote in a glass – in season you may chance upon fresh strawberries, raspberries or blueberries. Pancakes are also served as a dessert, with jam and sugar or with *powidła*, a delicious plum spread.

Tea and coffee

Poles are inveterate tea and coffee drinkers, their daily round punctuated by endless cups or glasses, generally with heaps of sugar.

Tea (*herbata*), which is cheaper and so marginally more popular, is drunk Russian-style in the glass, without milk and often with lemon. In most places, you'll get hot water and a tea bag, though occasionally it will come *naturalna*-style – a spoonful of tea leaves with the water poured on top. Drinking tea with milk (*z mlekiem*) is not common in Poland, but you might find it offered in the more touristy places, where it appears on café menus as *herbata angielska*.

The quality of **coffee** (*kawa*) varies considerably from place to place, with international-style coffee bars in city centres serving up espresso, cappuccino and other Italian-inspired brews; while provincial cafés and train-station snack bars offer a dispiriting brown liquid made by dumping grounds (or instant powder) in a cup and pouring water over them. If you're anything of a coffee connoisseur, it's best to stick to the classier-looking places. In the cheaper cafés, coffee is served black unless you ask otherwise, in which case specify with milk (*z mlekiem*) or with cream (*ze śmietanką*). In cafés and bars alike a shot or two of vodka or *winiak* (locally produced cheap brandy) with the morning cup of coffee is still frequent practice.

Alcoholic drinks

Poles' capacity for alcohol has never been in doubt, and **drinking** is a national pursuit. In the cities and larger towns, there's an ever-expanding range of atmospheric and pleasant drinking holes, with a convivial crop of **bars** (*bary*) and **café-bars**, plus the odd faux-Irish, Scottish or English pub. In the provinces you'll still come across traditional drink bars – basic and functional, these are almost exclusively male terrain.

Beer

The Poles can't compete with their Czech neighbours in the production and consumption of **beer**, but there are nevertheless a number of highly drinkable, and in a few cases really excellent, Polish brands.

Most beer is sold on draught – ask for *jedno duże* ("a big one") if you want the full half-litre; *jedno małe* ("a small one") will get you a 33cl glass. The biggest Polish breweries are all owned by multinational companies now, and produce a palatable lager-style beer. Żywiec is by far the most widespread brand, although Okocim, Tyskie and EB (long considered the Trabant among Polish beers, but now improving) are also fairly ubiquitous. There's also an assortment of regional beers you'll only find in the locality, Dojlidy (Białystok) being one of the most highly rated.

Vodka and other spirits

It's with **vodka** that Poles really get into their stride. Such is its place in the national culture that for years the black-market value of the dollar was supposed to be directly pegged to the price of a bottle. If you thought vodka was just a cocktail mixer you're in for some surprises: clear, peppered, honeyed – reams could be written about the varieties on offer. And although younger Poles are increasingly adopting the Western habit of mixing it with fruit juice (apple juice is a particular favourite), traditionally – and ideally – vodka is served neat, well chilled, in measures of 50 or 100 grams and knocked back in one go. A couple of these will be enough to put most people well on the way, though the capacities of seasoned Polish drinkers are prodigious – a half-litre bottle between two or three over lunch is nothing unusual.

Best of the **clear vodkas** is Wyborowa, although there are plenty of other brands to choose from. Many of the **flavoured vodkas** are now exceedingly hard to get hold of, having been forced off bar counters and supermarket shelves by imported spirits. One that you won't have any trouble in finding is Żubrówka, a legendary vodka infused with the taste of bison grass from the eastern Białowieża forest – there's a stem in every bottle. Some say the bison have urinated on the grass first, but don't let that put you off. Tatrzańska, the Tatra mountain equivalent, flavoured with mountain herbs is harder to find, but excellent. Also worth seeking out are Pieprzówka, which has a sharp, peppery flavour, and is supposed to be good at warding off colds. The juniper-flavoured Myśliwska tastes a bit like gin, while the whisky-coloured Jarzębiak is flavoured with rowanberries. Others to look out for are Wiśniówka, a sweetish, strong cherry concoction; Krupnik, which is akin to whisky liqueur; Cytrynó wka, a lemon vodka; and Miodówka, a rare honey vodka. Last but by no means least on any basic list comes Pejsachówka, which, at 75 percent proof, is by far the strongest vodka on the market and is rivalled in strength only by home-produced *bimber*, the Polish version of moonshine.

Other popular *digestifs* are *śliwowica*, the powerful plum brandy that is mostly produced in the south of the country, and *miód pitny*, a heady mead-like wine. Commonest of all in this category however is *winiak*, a fiery Polish brandy you'll find in many cafés and restaurants (see p.57).

Soft drinks

The range of soft drinks on offer in Poland is pretty much the same as in any other European country, with international brands widely available – alongside locally produced equivalents.

Poland's own sparkling **mineral water** (*mineralna*) from the spas of the south is highly palatable and available throughout the country; the commonest brand name is Nałęczówianka. Well water, taken from different levels underground, is available in shops, together with a few Western brands like Perrier. If you order mineral water in a pub, it usually comes with ice and a twist of lemon.

Communications and the media

Post offices and the mail

Big-city post offices (*Poczta*) are usually open Monday to Friday from 7/8am until 8pm, with some open on Saturday mornings. Smaller branches usually close at 6pm, often earlier in rural areas. A restricted range of services is available 24 hours a day, seven days a week, from post offices in or outside the main train stations of major cities.

Each bears a number, with the head office in each city being no. 1. Theoretically, each head office has a poste restante (general delivery) facility: make sure, therefore, that anyone addressing mail to you includes the no. 1 after the city's name. This service works reasonably well, but don't expect

complete reliability. Mail to the UK currently takes four days, a week to the US, and is a day or so quicker in the other direction. It currently costs 1.90zł to send a card or letter to the UK, 2.10zł to the USA and 2zł to Australia or New Zealand. Always mark your letters "Par avion", or better still "Lotnicza", or pick up the blue stickers with both on from post offices; if you don't, they may take longer. Post boxes are red.

Telephones

The antiquated **telephone** system bequeathed by the communist system was long one of the biggest obstacles to Poland's economic development. Fortunately, things have improved immeasurably in recent years, though the omnipresence of mobile phones implies that many Poles have found their own solutions to the communication problem.

Making calls

Public payphones are operated by a card (*karta telefoniczna*), bought at post offices and Ruch kiosks, the latter usually marginally more expensive. Cards come in

Time

Poland is one hour ahead of GMT, nine hours ahead of US Pacific Standard Time and six hours ahead of Eastern Standard Time. Clocks go forward one hour at the end of March and an hour back at the end of October.

Phone codes

Phoning Poland from abroad

Dial the international access code (given below) + 48 (country code) + area code (minus initial 0) + number.
UK ☎00
Ireland ☎010
USA ☎011
Canada ☎011
Australia ☎0011
New Zealand ☎00

Phoning abroad from Poland

Dial the country code (given below) + area code (minus initial 0) + number
UK ☎0044
Ireland ☎00353
USA ☎001
Canada ☎001
Australia ☎0061
New Zealand ☎0064

Polish phone codes

Białystok ☎085
Bielsko-Biała ☎033
Bydgoszcz ☎052
Częstochowa ☎034
Elbląg ☎055
Gdańsk/Gdynia/Sopot ☎058
Katowice ☎032
Kielce ☎041
Kraków ☎012
Lublin ☎081
Łódź ☎042
Olsztyn ☎089
Opole ☎077
Poznań ☎061
Rzeszów ☎017
Szczecin ☎091
Tarnów ☎014
Toruń ☎056
Warsaw ☎022
Wrocław ☎071
Zakopane ☎018
Zamość ☎084

---

denominations of 25, 50 or 100 units, and cost 10, 18 and 37zł respectively. Trim off the top corner of the card before you insert it into the machine.

Local calls, and dialling from one city to another, should present few problems, and the recent standardization of the country's area codes has helped a great deal (see the codes in the box above); these usually apply to the surrounding area as well as the cities themselves. You can also make **long-distance calls** from the main post offices in large cities, phoning from a booth with the time monitored and paying the cashier after you've made your call.

Making **international calls**, at least within Europe, is far less of a problem these days than it was. Use cards rather than tokens, and buy those with the maximum number of credits. Though local calls are cheap, international calls are not – 50 units will buy just a three-minute connection to the UK.

Emergency calls (police ☎997, fire ☎998, ambulance ☎999) are free. To make a **collect call**, go to a post office, write down the number you want and "Rozmówa R" and show it to the clerk – persistence and, above

all, patience will eventually pay off. Remember, too, that calls from hotels are usually far more expensive than calls from a payphone.

Travellers with GSM **mobile phones** will find that almost all of Poland enjoys coverage – apart from the odd remote mountain valley. Before using your mobile phone abroad you will need to ask your phone company to switch on your international access, and you'll probably have to pay a sizeable deposit against future bills.

One way of avoiding hefty call charges while you're away is to buy a **pre-paid SIM card** from local operators like Era, Idea and Simplus on your arrival in Poland (starter packs can be purchased from street kiosks), and inserting it into your phone.

Calling home from abroad

One of the most convenient ways of phoning home from abroad is via a **telephone charge card**. Using access codes for the particular country you are in and a PIN number, you can make calls from most hotel, public and private phones that will be charged to your own account. Since most major charge cards are free to obtain, it's certainly worth getting one, at least for emergencies; enquire first though whether Poland is covered, and bear in mind that rates aren't necessarily cheaper than calling from a public phone.

In the **UK and Ireland**, British Telecom (☎0800 345 144, ⓦwww.payphones.bt.com/callingcards) will issue the BT Charge Card free to all BT customers, which can be used in 116 countries; AT&T (Dial ☎0800 890 011, then 888 641 6123 when you hear the AT&T prompt to be transferred to the Florida Call Centre, free 24 hours) has the Global Calling Card; while NTL (☎0500 100 505) issues its own Global Calling Card, which can be used in more than sixty countries abroad, though the fees cannot be charged to a normal phone bill.

In the **USA and Canada**, AT&T, MCI, Sprint, Canada Direct and other North American long-distance companies all enable their customers to make credit-card calls while overseas. Call your company's customer service line to find out if they provide service from Poland and, if so, what the toll-free access code is. Calls made from overseas will automatically be billed to your home number.

To call **Australia and New Zealand** from overseas, telephone charge cards such as Telstra Telecard or Optus Calling Card in Australia, and Telecom NZ's Calling Card, can be used to make calls abroad, which are charged back to a domestic account or credit card. Apply to Telstra (☎1 800 038 000), Optus (☎1 300 300 937), or Telecom NZ (☎04/801 9000).

Email and the Internet

One of the best ways to keep in touch while travelling is to sign up for a free Internet **email** address that can be accessed from anywhere, for example Yahoo! or Hotmail – accessible through ⓦwww.yahoo.com and ⓦwww.hotmail.com.

Internet cafés are springing up all over Poland, and are listed in the Guide where relevant. Outside Warsaw and Kraków, however, connections tend to be slow – making the sending and receiving of emails a patience-sapping process. ⓦwww.kropla.com is a useful website giving details of how

to plug your laptop in when abroad, phone country codes around the world, and information about electrical systems in different countries.

The media

The Polish **media** scene has long been one of the most lively in Eastern Europe, not least because of the popularity enjoyed by semi-official and dissident publications during the communist period.

Newspapers and magazines

Among Polish-language **daily newspapers**, most popular is the tabloid-sized *Gazeta Wyborcza* (ⓦwww.gazeta.pl), Eastern Europe's first independent daily. With a circulation of around 500,000 (750,000 at weekends), it's one of the top-ten-selling European dailies. *Gazeta* is strong on investigative journalism, has a liberal political stance and, in a bid to further enhance its popularity, now comes with regional supplements and colour magazines. Even if you don't read Polish it's worth getting for its cultural listings – especially on Fridays, when the week's attractions are previewed in the *Co jest Grane?* supplement.

Other national daily papers include *Rzeczpospolita*, originally the official voice of the communist government, now a highbrow independent paper with a strong following among business people and government officials because of its good economic coverage. *Trybuna*, once the official newspaper of the communist party, is still pursuing a leftist agenda and supports the post-communist-led SLD. However, local rather than national papers are what most of the population reads: though generally pretty unexciting, they're often useful for current events and cultural listings.

Best of the **weekly news magazines** is *Polityka*, although *Wprost*, *Przekrój* and the Polish-language edition of *Newsweek* all cover similar ground. More sensationalist fare can be found in *Skandale*, which features the usual diet of sex, violence and pure invention; and *Nie*, edited by the flamboyant and outspoken Jerzy Urban, spokesman for the communist government throughout most of the 1980s.

Glossy **monthly magazines** are devoured as eagerly in Poland as anywhere else in the developed world. Home-grown women's magazines like *Ewa* and *Twój Styl* have been joined by Polish-language versions of *Cosmopolitan*, *Marie-Claire* and others; the worldwide explosion in men's lifestyle magazines has been mirrored here too.

There's a mind-boggling number of periodicals dealing with cultural, social and intellectual concerns, including *Midrasz* (Ⓦwww.midrasz.home.pl), a lively monthly devoted to Polish-Jewish issues.

English language publications

There are a number of **English-language publications**. Longest established is the *Warsaw Voice* (Ⓦwww.warsawvoice.com .pl), a Warsaw-based weekly that's widely available throughout the country. It's readable and informative, with good listings, though noticeably slanted towards the business community. The increasingly ubiquitous *In Your Pocket* people publish useful A5-format guides to Warsaw, Kraków, Gdańsk, Poznań and Wrocław (Ⓦwww.inyourpocket .com). The best choice in this genre though is probably the monthly *Warsaw Insider* (Ⓦwww.warsawinsider.pl), written for the capital's 20,000-strong expatriate community and invaluable for the visitor.

Western newspapers and magazines are now available the same day as publication in the big cities. Most common are the *Guardian International Edition*, the *Financial Times*, *The Times* and the *Herald Tribune*, plus magazines like *Newsweek*, *Time* and *The Economist*.

Ruch and other **kiosks** are the main outlets for papers and magazines, with a wide selection also available in EMPiK stores. The latter usually stock a reasonable choice of international, English-language glossies – especially the leading fashion, lifestyle and pop music titles.

TV and radio

Poland's **TV network** has improved by leaps and bounds in recent years, with the previously rather staid state-run channels now competing for viewers with a plethora of private stations. The regular diet of game shows, soap operas and American films doesn't differ that much from anywhere else in Europe, although Polish TV has managed to preserve a few quirks of its own – notably the tendency for foreign imports to be dubbed by a single *lektor*, who reads all the parts in the same voice. For increasing numbers of Poles, satellite and, in the big cities, cable TV are popular additions to the range of viewing options. Most hotels now carry a selection of international cable/satellite channels, although German-language stations tend to be more common than English.

Most popular Polish **radio stations** are Warsaw-based Zet, and Kraków's RMF FM (both of which now broadcast to other cities on a variety of different frequencies), offering a varied and often rather imaginative diet of pop, rock and other contemporary musical styles. A number of local stations broadcast occasional English-language news bulletins, although for a full English-language service you'll have to track down BBC World Service, for which you'll need a shortwave radio; Ⓦwww.bbc.co.uk/worldservice lists all the World Service frequencies around the globe.

Opening hours and holidays

Most shops are open on weekdays from approximately 10am to 6pm. Exceptions are grocers and food stores, which may open as early as 6am and close by mid-afternoon – something to watch out for in rural areas in particular. On Saturdays, most shops will have shut by 2 or 3pm, while there's a minority trade on Sunday afternoons.

Street **kiosks**, where you can buy newspapers and municipal transport tickets, are generally open from about 6am to 5pm, although many remain open for several hours longer. Increasing numbers of **street traders** and makeshift kiosks also do business well into the evening, while you can usually find one or two food shops in most towns offering late-night opening throughout the week.

As a rule, **tourist information offices** are open from 9 or 10am until 5pm (later in major cities) during the week; hours are shorter on Saturdays and Sundays.

Tourist sites

Visiting **churches** seldom presents any problems: the ones you're most likely to want to see are open from early morning until mid-evening without interruption. However, a large number of less famous churches are fenced off beyond the entrance porch by a grille or glass window for much of the day; to see them properly, you'll need to turn up around the times for Mass – first thing in the morning and between 6 and 8pm. Otherwise it's a case of seeking out the local priest (*ksiądz*) and persuading him to let you in.

Visiting times for **museums** and **historic monuments** are listed in the text of the Guide. They are almost invariably closed one day per week (usually Mon) and many are closed two days. The rest of the week, some open for only about five hours, often closing at 3pm, though 4pm or later is more normal.

Public holidays

The following are national **public holidays**, on which you can expect some shops, restaurants and most sights to be closed. It's well worth checking if your visit is going to coincide with one of these to avoid frustrations and disappointments. It's particularly worth noting that because Labour Day and Constitution Day are so close together, most businesses (including the majority of banks and shops) give their employees a full four days of holiday.

January 1 New Year's Day
March/April Easter Monday
May 1 Labour Day
May 3 Constitution Day
May/June Corpus Christi
August 15 Feast of the Assumption
November 1 All Saints' Day
November 11 Independence Day
December 25 & 26 Christmas

Festivals, entertainment and sports

One manifestation of Poland's intense commitment to Roman Catholicism is that all the great feast days of the Church calendar are celebrated with wholehearted devotion, many of the participants donning the colourful traditional costumes for which the country is celebrated.

This is most notable in the mountain areas in the south of the country, where the **annual festivities** play a key role in maintaining a vital sense of community. As a supplement to these, Poland has many more recently established **cultural festivals**, particularly in the fields of music and drama. As well as a strong ethnic/folk **music** scene, contemporary music in Poland is intriguing, if a little inaccessible to outsiders.

Religious and traditional festivals

The highlight of the Catholic year is **Easter** (Wielkanoc), which is heralded by a glut of spring fairs, offering the best of the early livestock and agricultural produce. **Holy Week** (Wielki Tydzień) kicks off in earnest on **Palm Sunday** (Niedziela Palmowa), when palms are brought to church and paraded in processions. Often the painted and decorated "palms" are handmade, sometimes with competitions for the largest or most beautiful. The most famous procession takes place at Kalwaria Zebrzydowska near Kraków, inaugurating a spectacular week-long series of mystery plays, re-enacting Christ's Passion.

On **Maundy Thursday** (Wielki Czwartek) many communities take symbolic revenge on Judas Iscariot: his effigy is hanged, dragged outside the village, flogged, burned or thrown into a river. **Good Friday** (Wielki Piątek) sees visits to mock-ups of the Holy Sepulchre – whether permanent structures such as at Kalwaria Zebrzydowska and Wambierzyce in Silesia, or ad hoc creations, as is traditional in Warsaw. In some places, notably the Rzeszów region, this is fused with a celebration of King Jan Sobieski's victory in the Siege of Vienna, with "Turks" placed in charge of the tomb. **Holy Saturday** (Wielka Sobota) is when baskets of painted eggs, sausages, bread and salt are taken along to church to be blessed and sprinkled with holy water. The consecrated food is eaten at breakfast on **Easter Day** (Niedziela Wielkanocna), when the most solemn Masses of the year are celebrated. On **Easter Monday** (Lany Poniedziałek), girls are doused with water by boys to "make them fertile" (a marginally better procedure than in the neighbouring Czech Republic where they're beaten with sticks). Even in the cosmopolitan cities you'll see gangs of boys waiting in the streets or leaning out of first-floor windows waiting to throw water bombs at passing girls.

Seven weeks later, at **Pentecost**, irises are traditionally laid out on the floors of the house, while in the Kraków region bonfires are lit on hilltop sites. A further eleven days on comes the most Catholic of festivals, **Corpus Christi** (Boże Ciało), marked by colourful processions everywhere and elaborate floral displays, notably in Łowicz. Exactly a week later, the story of the Tatar siege is re-enacted as the starting point of one of the country's few notable festivals of secular folklore, the **Days of Kraków**.

St John's Day on June 24 is celebrated with particular gusto in Warsaw, Kraków and Poznań; on the night of June 23/24 at around midnight, wreaths with burning candles are cast into the river, and there are boat parades, dancing and fireworks. July 26, **St Anne's Day**, is the time of the main annual pilgrimage to Góra Świętej Anny in Silesia.

The first of two major Marian festivals on consecutive weeks comes with the **Feast of the Holy Virgin of Sowing** on August 8 in farming areas, particularly in the southeast of the country. By then, many of the great pilgrimages to the Jasna Góra shrine in Częstochowa have already set out, arriving for the **Feast of the Assumption** (Święto Wniebowzięcia NMP) on August 15. This is also the occasion for the enactment of a mystery play at Kalwaria Pacławska near Przemyśl.

All Saints' Day (Dzień Wszystkich Świętych), November 1, is the day of national remembrance, with flowers, wreaths and candles laid on tombstones. In contrast, **St Andrew's Day**, November 30, is a time for fortune-telling, with dancing to accompany superstitious practices such as the pouring of melted wax or lead on paper. **St Barbara's Day**, December 4, is the traditional holiday of the miners, with special Masses held for their safety as a counterweight to the jollity of their galas.

During **Advent** (Advent), the nation's handicraft tradition comes to the fore, with the making of cribs to adorn every church. In Kraków, a competition is held on a Sunday between December 3 and 10, the winning entries being displayed in the city's Historical Museum. On **Christmas Eve** (Wigilia) families gather for an evening banquet, traditionally of twelve courses to symbolize the number of the Apostles; this is also the time when children receive their gifts. **Christmas Day** (Boże Narodzenie) begins with the midnight Mass; later, small round breads decorated with the silhouettes of domestic animals are consumed. **New Year's Eve** (Sylwester) is the time for magnificent formal balls, particularly in Warsaw, while in country areas of southern Poland it's the day for practical jokes – which must go unpunished. The Christmas period winds up with **Epiphany** (Dzień Trzech Króli) on January 6, when groups of carol singers move from house to house, chalking the letters K, M and B (symbolizing the Three Kings Kaspar, Melchior and Balthazar) on each doorway as a record of their visit. The chalk marks are usually left untouched throughout the coming year, thereby ensuring good fortune for the household.

Folk music

Though less dynamic than some of its Eastern European neighbours, Polish **folk music** nevertheless plays a noteworthy role in national cultural life. Traditional folk comes in (at least) two varieties: a bland, sanitized version promoted by successive communist governments and still peddled, with varying degrees of success, principally for foreign consumption: and a rootsier, rural vein of genuine and vibrant folk culture, which you chiefly find among the country's minorities and in the southern and eastern parts of the country. Thanks in part to Chopin, who was profoundly influenced by the music of his native **Mazovia** (Mazowsze), Mazovian folk music is probably the best known in the country, traditional forms like the mazurka and polonaise offering a rich vein of tuneful melodies and vibrant dance rhythms. Other regions with strong traditional folk music cultures include **Silesia**, the **Tatras**, whose music-loving *górale* (highlanders) have developed a rousing polyphonically inclined song tradition over the centuries, and the Lemks of the **Beskid Niski**, whose music bears a tangled imprint of Ukrainian, Slovak and Hungarian influences. Among the notable showcases for Polish folk music of all descriptions are the triennial Festival of Polonia Music and Dance in **Rzeszów**, which draws a welter of ensembles from the worldwide Polish diaspora, and the annual summer folk festival bash in **Kazimierz Dolny**.

In the north of the country along the **Baltic coast** the popularity of sea shanties is a surprising discovery, with annual festivals during the summer in many towns.

For a detailed account of Polish folk music, see Contexts, p.683.

Classical music

The nation's wealth of folk tunes have found their way into some of the best of the country's **classical** music, of which Poles are justifiably proud, the roster of Polish composers containing a number of world-ranking figures, including Chopin, Moniuszko, Szymanowski, Penderecki, Panufnik, Lutoslawski and the 1990s runaway best-seller Henryk Górecki. The country has also produced a wealth of classical musicians, mostly in the first half of the twentieth century when pianists Artur Rubinstein and musician-premier Ignacy Paderewski gained worldwide prominence. A cluster of Polish **orchestras**, notably the

Polish Chamber Orchestra, the Warsaw and Kraków Philharmonics, and the Katowice-based Radio and TV Symphony Orchestra, have made it into the world league and are regularly in demand on the international touring circuit.

All the big cities have music **festivals** of one sort or another, which generally give plenty of space to national composers, the international Chopin Piano Competition in Warsaw (held every five years) being the best known and most prestigious of the events. Throughout the year it's easy to catch works by Polish composers since the repertoires of many regional companies tend to be oriented towards national music.

Jazz

Jazz has had a well-established pedigree in Poland ever since the 1950s, when bebop broke through in a country hungry for Western forms of free expression. This explosion of interest in jazz brought forth a wealth of local talent, most notably **Krzystof Komeda**, who wrote edgy, experimental scores for Roman Polański's early movies during the 1960s. Other home-grown musicians who made it into the international big league include tenorist **Zbigniew Namysłowski**, singer **Urszula Dudziak**, violinist **Michał Urbaniak** and trumpeter **Tomas Stanko**. The late Krzystof Komeda excepted, all of the above are still very much around on the gig circuit, and CD reissues of their oeuvre can be picked up in most Polish record shops. Poland's considerable jazz heritage is increasingly attracting the attention of sample-hungry hip-hop producers – most notably Polish DJ duo Skalpel, who record for hip UK label Ninja Tune.

As far as major jazz events are concerned, the annual **Warsaw Jazz Jamboree** in October always attracts a roster of big names from abroad. There's a reasonably healthy jazz **club** scene in the major cities – especially Kraków, which regards itself as the spiritual home of Polish jazz.

Rock and pop

There was a time when Poland was the Liverpool of Eastern Europe, producing a stream of guitar-wielding mop-tops and warbling starlets whose music was then exported all over the Soviet bloc. It started in the early 1960s, when a whole raft of groups emerged to cover the skiffle, rock-and-roll and rhythm-and-blues hits that had entered the country via the long-wave radio transmissions of Radio Luxembourg. Aided by the emergence of a nightclub scene in Gdańsk and Sopot, and the inauguration of the Festival of Polish Song in Opole (see p.524), Poland developed a home-grown version of Western pop which went under the name of **Bigbeat** – with groups like **Czerwone Gitary** and **Skaldowie** providing the local answer to the Beatles and the Rolling Stones. However the biggest name to emerge from the Sixties was **Czesław Niemen**, a national institution who is still regularly voted the best Polish singer-songwriter of all time. Moving from saccharine pop to earthy rhythm-and-blues, psychedelia, then prog-rock, Niemen introduced a new breadth of vision to Polish pop, although his voice – a cross between Otis Redding and a castrated wildebeest – is very much an acquired taste. In the 1970s intellectual art-rock held sway (**Marek Grechuta** and his group **Anawa** are the names to look out for if you're shopping for CDs), while in the 1980s punk and reggae came to the fore, the popularity of both due in part to their latent espousal of political protest – anything gobbing at authority or chanting down Babylon went down particularly well in post-martial-law Poland. Nowadays the Polish pop scene resembles that of any other European country, with hardcore, rap, reggae and death-metal subcultures coexisting with a mainstream diet of techno.

There's a regular **gig circuit** in the major cities, and an underground scene in most places with a large student population. **Clubs** that host regular live music are listed in the relevant sections of the guide. Fly posters, or the Friday edition of Gazeta Wyborcza, are the best sources of information about up-and-coming events. In summer, **open-air concerts** (often featuring Western acts) take place in parks or sports grounds – again, posters advertising these events are plastered up just about everywhere.

Cinema

Cinemas (kino) can be found in almost every town in Poland, however small, with big

Arts festivals

The list below is not exhaustive, so contact the Polish National Tourist Office (see p.40) for a list of upcoming events before you leave home. The listings in *Gazeta Wyborcza* or the *Warsaw Insider* will provide an idea of what's on once you arrive.

January
Warsaw Traditional jazz
Wrocław Solo plays

February
Poznań Boys' choirs
Wrocław Polish contemporary music

March
Częstochowa Violin music
Łódź Opera; student theatre

April
Kraków Organ music
Kraków Student song

May
Bielsko-Biała International puppet theatre (every even-numbered year)
Gdańsk "Neptunalia" (student festival)
Hajnówka Orthodox choirs
Katowice Festival of cult films (Festiwal Filmów Kultowych)
Kraków "Juvenalia" (student festival)
Łącko (near Nowy Sącz) Regional folk festival
Łańcut Chamber music

Warsaw Festival of sacred songs
Wrocław Contemporary Polish plays (May/June)
Wrocław Jazz on the Odra

June
Brzeg Classical music
Kamień Pomorski Organ and chamber music (June/July)
Kazimierz Dolny Folk bands and singers (June/July)
Krynica Arias and songs
Kudowa-Zdrój Music of Stanislaw Moniuszko
Opole Polish pop songs
Poznań Festival of contemporary theatre
Płock Folk ensembles
Toruń Contact Festival. Prestigious review of modern drama from around Europe
Warsaw Summer jazz days

July
Gdańsk-Oliwa Organ music (July/Aug)
Gdynia Summer jazz days

multiplexes springing up on the outskirts of major cities. International films arrive as soon as they're released elsewhere in Europe, and are usually shown in the original language with Polish subtitles. The month's listings are usually fly-posted up around town or outside each cinema with the titles translated into Polish (the *Warsaw Insider* has a useful, regularly updated list of the original titles next to the Polish translations).

Based around the famous Łódź film school, postwar Polish cinema has produced a string of important directors, the best known being **Andrzej Wajda** (see also p.103), whose Cannes Palme d'Or-winning *Człowiek z żelaza* ("Man of Iron") did much to popularize the cause of Solidarity abroad in the early 1980s. As in all the ex-communist countries the key issue for Polish film-makers used to be getting their work past the censors: for years they responded to the task of "saying

without saying" with an imaginative blend of satire, metaphor and historically based parallelism whose subtle twists tend to leave even the informed Western viewer feeling a little perplexed. In the case of Wajda and other notables like **Agnieszka Holland, Krzysztof Zanussi** and **Krzysztof Kieślowski**, though, a combination of strong scripting, characterization and a subtle dramatic sense carries the day, and all these directors enjoy high prestige in international film circles.

State funding for film withered away after 1990, but domestic cinema production remains strong. Post-communist efforts like Kieślowski's award-winning The *Double Life of Véronique*, his masterful *Red*, *White* and *Blue* trilogy, and Wajda's *Korczak* point towards an artistically productive future for Polish cinema, although the local public have shown more enthusiasm for the kind of home-grown historical blockbusters that

Jelenia Góra Street theatre (July/Aug)
Koszalin World Polonia Festival of
Polish Songs (every 5 years – next 2006)
Kraków Jewish culture
Międzyzdroje Choral music
Międzyzdroje "Stars on Holiday"
Film Festival
Mrągowo Country Picnic (Country
and Western music)
Nowy Sącz Festival of ethnic/
electronic crossover music
Rzeszów Festival of Polonia Music
and Dance Ensembles Groups (every
3 years – next in 2005 & 2008)
Sanok Festival of Alternative and
Art Films
Świnoujście Fama Student Artistic
Festival

August
Duszniki-Zdrój Music of Frédéric Chopin
Gdańsk Dominican fair
Jarocin Rock festival
Kazimierz Dolny Film festival
Kraków Classical music
Sopot International songs
Zakopane Highland folklore
Zielona Góra International song and
dance troupes
Żywiec Beskid culture

September
Bydgoszcz Classical music
Gdańsk Polish feature films
Słupsk Polish piano competition
Toruń International old music festival
Warsaw Contemporary music
Wrocław "Wratislavia Cantans"
(choral music)
Zamość Jazz festival

October
Kraków Jazz music
Warsaw Baroque opera festival
Warsaw Chopin Piano Competition
(every 5 years – next 2005)
Warsaw International film festival
Warsaw Jazz jamboree

November
Gdynia Film festival
Poznań International violin competi-
tion (every 5 years – next 2006)
Warsaw Ancient music festival

December
Łódź Camerimage international film
festival (specializing in camerawork)
Warsaw Theatre festival
Wrocław Old music

rarely win international prizes. The outstanding example of this was **Jerzy Hoffman**'s
1999 adaptation of Henryk Sienkiewicz's
patriotic novel *With Fire and Sword*, an
extravagant costume drama that soon
became the most successful Polish film of
all time – but sank without trace outside the
country.

Theatre

Theatre in Poland is popular and relatively
cheap (with seats starting at around £4/
US$6), and most towns with a decent-sized
population have at least one permanent
venue with the month's programme pinned
up outside and elsewhere in the town. Aside
from the odd British or US touring company,
there's little in English, though the generally
high quality of Polish stagecraft combined
with the interest of the venues themselves – Poles go as much for the interval

promenade as the show itself – usually
makes for an enjoyable experience.

Theatre's special role in Polish cultural life
dates from the Partition era, when it played
a significant role in the maintenance of both
the language and national consciousness,
although in recent decades the country has
become associated with the kind of avant-
garde contemporary theatre that relies as
much on movement and ritual as the spoken
word. The tone was set in the early 1960s
by **Tadeusz Kantor**, who mesmerized awestruck Polish beatniks with a series of now
legendary performance art-happenings in
the cellars of Kraków. Another trailblazer
was **Jerzy Grotowski**, whose experimental
Laboratory Theatre in Wrocław (disbanded
in 1982 when he emigrated to Italy) was
regarded as one of the most exciting and
innovative trends in drama to emerge since
Stanislavski's work in Moscow in the early

part of last century. Other companies like the excellent **Teatr Ósmego Dnia** (Theatre of the Eighth Day) from Poznań, carried the torch through the trials of martial law in the early 1980s, developing a probing, politically engaged theatre that closely reflected the struggles of the period. Among a handful of companies currently in demand internationally is **Gardziennice**, a consistently innovative group based in a village near Lublin of the same name, which specialize in field trips to villages throughout Eastern Europe where oral cultural traditions are kept alive; and the experimental **Wierszalin** group from Białystok, recent prize-baggers at Edinburgh and other international festivals.

Sport

The Polish media devote a vast amount of coverage to team games as diverse as **basketball** (*koszykówka*), **handball** (*piłka ręczna*) and **volleyball** (*siatkówka*). One sport that enjoys major popularity in Poland is **speedway** (*żużel*). Most major cities boast a team and a stadium, although it's in the industrial conurbations of the southwest that the sport arouses the greatest passions. Events usually take place on Saturdays; street posters advertise times and venues.

Football (*piłka nożna*) remains the only sport that commands a genuine mass following nationwide. Franz Beckenbauer described the Polish national side as "the best team in the world" in 1974's World Cup, when they were unlucky to finish only in third place. The Poles remained a major

force in the world game for the next decade, with players such as Grzegorz Lato, Kazimierz Deyna and Zbigniew Boniek becoming household names.

Despite receiving blanket coverage from the country's private TV stations, Polish **league football** is currently in the doldrums: few clubs are rich enough to pay the wages of top players, and the country's best talents ply their trade in Germany, Italy or elsewhere. Kraków club Wisła currently enjoys the biggest countrywide following, with Warsaw's Legia running them a close second. Other teams with proud historical pedigrees are the Silesian trio of GKS Katowice, Ruch Chorzów and Górnik Zabrze; and the two Łódź sides, LKS and Widzew. The season lasts from August to November, then resumes in March until June. Some of the top teams have equipped their stadia with plastic seating in order to comply with UEFA safety guidelines; elsewhere wooden benches, or uncovered concrete terraces, remain the rule. Inside, grilled sausages and beer are the order of the day. Regular league fixtures suffer from pitifully low attendance figures, not least because the emergence of a serious hooligan problem has scared many stadium-goers away. Unsurprisingly, you shouldn't have trouble buying tickets (£4/€5.50/US$7) on the gate for most games, although you may be asked to show ID before being subjected to a spot of vigorous security frisking. For details of results and fixtures, check out the Polish Football Federation's website, ⓦwww.pzpn.pl.

Outdoor activities

For a growing number of visitors, it's the wide range of outdoor pursuits Poland has to offer, as well as its better-known cultural and architectural attractions, that constitute the country's chief lure. Most obvious of these are the hiking opportunities provided by the extensive national (and regional) parks, several of which incorporate authentic wilderness areas of great beauty.

Equally attractive for **skiers** are the slopes of the Tatra mountains – long the country's most developed, but by no means its only, ski resort area. Lakes and rivers offer generous opportunities for water-based activities. **Anglers** can sample Poland's significant collection of pristine fishing areas, notably in the outlying eastern regions of the country.

Hiking

Poland has some of the best **hiking** country in Europe, especially in the mountainous regions on the country's southern and western borders. There's a full network of marked **trails**, the best of which are detailed in the Guide. Many of these take several days, passing through remote areas served by *schroniska* (refuges; see "Accommodation" p.52). However, much of the best scenery can be seen by covering sections of these routes on one-day walks.

Unless you're in the High Tatras (see p.492 for some important tips), few of the one-day trails are especially strenuous and although specialist **footwear** is recommended, well-worn-in sturdy shoes are usually enough.

Skiing

Poland's mountainous southern rim provides some good **skiing** opportunities, seized on, in season, by what can often seem like the country's entire population. The best and, not surprisingly, most popular ski slopes are in the Tatras, the highest section of the Polish Carpathians, where the skiing season runs from December through into March.

Although still in the shadow of the Alps and other well-known European resorts, Zakopane, the resort centre of the **Tatras**, has acquired a strong and growing international following, not least in the UK, where a variety of travel operators specialize in cheap, popular skiing packages. Though the skiing facilities in and around Zakopane may still leave a little to be desired, both in volume and quality, they have improved considerably over the last few years, not least in the provision of ski lifts. Certainly, you shouldn't have any problems renting skiing gear in Zakopane itself.

Less dramatic alternatives to the Tatras include the **Beskid Sudety**, notably the resorts at Karpacz and Szklarska Poręba; the Beskid Śląski resort of Szczyrk; and the **Bieszczady** (a favourite with cross-country skiers). One great advantage with all these is that they are relatively unknown outside Poland, although, consequently, facilities are fairly undeveloped – usually involving a single ski lift and a limited range of descents. As yet relatively free from package hotels, these smaller resorts are perhaps better suited to individual tourists than Zakopane, which can be jam-packed with groups throughout the season.

Kayaking, sailing and windsurfing

Large stretches of lowland Poland are dotted with lakes, especially Mazuria (see p.233) in the northeast of the country, and it's relatively easy for travellers to rent a variety of **watercraft** – from simple kayaks to luxury yachts – once they arrive. Most people content themselves with a day or two on the water, although the number of navigable waterways in Mazuria ensures there's a host of lengthy **canoeing and kayaking** itineraries to choose from, often involving overnight stops at campsites or hostels en route. The most popular of these are the nine-day traverse of the Mazurian lakes (see p.236), and the three-day journey down the Czarna Hańcza river (see p.252). Well-equipped marinas at Mikołajki (see p.242), Giżycko (p.247) and Ruciane-Nida (p.245) are packed with **sailing** folk in the summer months. Simple sailing boats are easy enough to rent at these places; although at least one member of your party will have to have sailing experience if you want to rent out a bigger craft.

Given the short duration of the Baltic summer, Poland's northern coast doesn't offer the kind of watersports opportunities that you'll find in the Mediterranean. However there's an established **windsurfing** scene in Łeba (see p.629), and in the resorts on the southern side of the Hel peninsula (p.197).

Fishing

Especially in the outlying regions of the country, where the rivers are generally less polluted, **fishing** is a popular pastime. The season effectively runs all year in one form or another, with winter fishing through holes in the ice and on the major Mazurian lakes, and fishing for lavaret with artificial spinners in summer.

The best fishing areas include the Mazurian lakes (pike and perch), the Bieszczady, notably the River San and its tributaries (trout), and the southeast in general. For details on how to buy compulsory fishing licences, contact The Polish Fishing Association (Polski Związek Wędkarski), ul. Twarda 42, Warsaw (☎022/620 8966, ⓦwww.fishing.pl), or the National Tourist Office (see p.40).

Police and trouble

The biggest potential hassles for visitors to Poland come from petty crime – notably hotel-room thefts and pickpocketing in crowded places such as train stations (especially in Warsaw) and markets. A few common-sense precautions should help you avoid trouble: display cameras, fancy mobile phones and other signs of affluence as little as possible; never leave valuables in your room; and keep large sums of cash in a (well-hidden) money-belt. Guard against opportunistic thefts on overnight trains by booking a couchette or sleeper and keeping it well locked. If you're travelling in the regular carriages, try not to fall asleep. Theft of Western cars and/or their contents is something of a national sport in Poland – see p.48 for further details and advice.

Your best protection against crime is to take out **travel insurance** before you go (see p.37). If you do have anything stolen, report the loss to the police as soon as possible, and be patient – the Polish police rarely speak English, and filling out a report can take ages. The chances of getting your gear back are virtually zero.

Poles are obliged to carry some form of ID with them at all times: you should always

keep your **passport** with you, even though you're unlikely to get stopped unless you're in a car; Western numberplates provide the excuse for occasional unprovoked spot checks. It's a good idea to carry a photocopy of the final, information-bearing page of your passport. This will help your consulate to issue a replacement document if you're unlucky enough to have it stolen.

Work and study

Despite the booming international business scene in cities like Warsaw, Gdańsk and Poznań, it's extremely unlikely that you'll want to pick up casual work in Poland, given that the average monthly wage is still below US$400.

The popularity of learning **English** has mushroomed in recent years, leading to a constant demand for native-language English teachers both in the state education system and in the private language schools that seem to have sprung up all over the country. However, you'll probably need a TEFL certificate or equivalent in order to secure a job at any but the most fly-by-night organizations. Some of the bigger English-teaching organizations actually organize TEFL courses in Polish cities, and may well help you get a job there once you've qualified. Otherwise, vacancies are sometimes advertised in the education supplements of Western newspapers; otherwise it's a question of touting your CV around the language schools and making use of local contacts once you arrive.

Study

Summer language courses are run by the universites of Kraków, Poznań, Lublin (KUL),

Toruń and Łódź. Courses last from two to six weeks, covering all levels from beginners to advanced; a six-week course with full board and lodging will cost in the region of £500/€700/US$900. Information on these courses can be obtained from the Polish Cultural Institute in London (see p.41) or Polish consulates abroad.

In addition, many private language schools in Poland are beginning to offer language courses to the growing army of expatriate Westerners keen to learn Polish. A typical two-week course will cost something in the region of £185–215/€260–300/US$340–390 for tuition, £360–430/€500–600/US$640–770 if accommodation is included. Well-established schools include the Institute of Polish Language for Foreigners (ⓦwww.iko.com.pl) in Warsaw, and Prolog (ⓦwww.polishcourses.com) and Glossa (ⓦwww.glossa.pl), both in Kraków.

Travellers with disabilities

In the past, very little attention was paid to the needs of the disabled (*niepiełnosprawni*) in Poland. Attitudes are slowly changing – the 1997 Constitution included provision banning discrimination against people with disabilities – but there is still a long way to go and there is not a lot of money available for improvements.

The State Fund for the Rehabilitation of the Disabled, established in 1991, now sponsors a number of programmes designed to make buildings and other **public facilities** wheel-chair-accessible. **Lifts** and **escalators** are gradually becoming more common in public places, although the majority of set-piece museums in Warsaw and Kraków remain difficult to get in and out of. An increasing number of **hotels**, mainly in Warsaw and Kraków, have access and rooms designed for the disabled. The downside is that the majority of these places are expensive, meaning that such provision is still, by and large, a luxury. The **Orbis** hotel chain (ⓦwww.orbis.pl) offers special facilities in its hotels in over fifteen cities including Poznań, Częstochowa and Zakopane. A handful of **youth hostels** also offer facilities suitable for wheelchair users; contact the Polish Youth Hostel Federation (PTSM; see p.52) for further details.

Public transport remains a major problem. The newer buses in Warsaw and Kraków are equipped with hydraulic platforms to ease wheelchair access, although only a couple of these run on each route and English-language timetable information is difficult to come by. The Warsaw metro boasts lifts at each station, although they're badly signed from the surface. Polish Railways claims that seats in each carriage are designated for disabled passengers, this can't be relied on. Taxi drivers in Eastern Europe in general are also very reluctant to lift passengers to and from their wheelchairs.

If you can read Polish, the ⓦwww .niepielnosprawni.info website is an invaluable source of news, views and links. Otherwise, the organizations listed below may be able to provide help and advice.

Contacts for disabled travellers

Britain and Ireland

Tripscope ☎0845 758 5641, ⓦwww.tripscope .org.uk. This registered charity provides a national telephone information service offering free advice on UK and international transport for those with a mobility problem.
Irish Wheelchair Association ☎01/818 6400, ⓦwww.iwa.ie. Information and advice.

USA and Canada

Society for the Advancement of Travelers with Handicaps (SATH) ☎212/447-7284, ⓦwww.sath.org. Non-profit educational organization with some useful online information.
Wheels Up! ☎1-888-38-WHEELS, ⓦwww .wheelsup.com. Provides discount airfare and tour and prices.

Australia and New Zealand

ACROD (Australian Council for Rehabilitation of the Disabled) National Branch ☎02/6282 4333, ⓦwww.acrod.org.au. Provides lists of travel agencies and tour operators.
Disabled Persons Assembly ☎04/801 9100, ⓦwww.dpa.org.nz. Resource centre with details of travel agencies.

Poland

State Fund for the Rehabilitation of the Disabled (Państwowy Fundusz Rehabilitacji Osób Niepełnosprawnych) ul. Jana Pawła II 13, Warsaw ☎022/620-0351, ⓦwww.pfron.org.pl.

Directory

Addresses The street name is always written before the number. The word for street (ulica, abbreviated to ul.) or avenue (aleja, abbreviated al.) is often missed out – for example ulica Senatorska is simply known as Senatorska. The other frequent abbreviation is pl., short for plac (square). See Contexts (p.719) for details on the most common street names.

Cigarettes Most Western cigarette brands – alongside innumerable Polish brands – are available from street kiosks. Matches are *zapałki*. Smoking is banned in all public buildings and on all public transport within towns.

Contraceptives Condoms (*prezerwatywy*) are purchased from street kiosks or high-street pharmacies, with familiar Western brand names widely available.

Drugs Hard drug abuse – principally amphetamines, *kompot*, a locally produced opium derivative, and heroin – is on the rise. Marijuana and hashish are fairly common, and possession of small quantities of soft drugs is currently legal, though selling or trading in them is not.

Electricity is the standard Continental 220 volts. Round two-pin plugs are used, so UK residents will need to bring an adaptor.

Embassies and consulates All foreign embassies are in Warsaw, though a number of countries maintain consulates in Gdańsk and Kraków. See respective listings for addresses.

Emergencies Police ☎997; fire ☎998; ambulance ☎999. There are private ambulance services in Warsaw and other big cities; see listings in the Guide.

Film With photo printing shops springing up on virtually every Polish high street, print film and memory cards for digital cameras are easy to get hold of. Outside major cities, the choice of transparency and black-and-white film is limited, so stock up before leaving home.

Gay and lesbian Although homosexuality is legal in Poland, it remains something of an underground phenomenon, and public displays of affection between members of the same sex may provoke outrage and hostility, especially outside the big cities. Warsaw has a small gay scene, and Kraków and Gdańsk are beginning to develop one. Details of pubs and clubs are given in the Guide where relevant; otherwise the ⓦ www .gay.pl website is a good source of info.

Jaywalking is illegal but everyone does it, since you can grow old waiting for some of the lights to turn green. If caught you'll be fined on the spot.

Laundry Self-service facilities are virtually non-existent in Poland – although most towns do boast a *pralnia* (laundry), these tend to concentrate exclusively on dry-cleaning. Some of them offer service washes, too, although this might take up to three days. You can get things service-washed in the more upmarket hotels within 24 hours, but at a cost.

Left luggage Most train and bus stations of any size have a left-luggage office (*przechowalnia bagażu*). In big-city train stations these are often open 24 hours; elsewhere, take note of opening and closing times.

Student cards Carrying an ISIC card will save you about 50 percent in admission fees to museums and galleries, and also qualifies you for cut-price city transport tickets in Warsaw and Kraków.

Tampons Polish shops supply all the main international brands of sanitary towels (*podpaski*) and tampons (*tampony*).

Toilets Public toilets (*toalety, ubikacja* or WC) can be found at most bus and train stations, and usually cost something in the order of 1–2zł. The days when you had to buy toilet paper by the sheet are numbered, but there may be a rural toilet somewhere in Poland where it still happens. Gents are marked ▼, ladies ● or ▲.

Guide

Guide

1 Warsaw and Mazovia 77–164

2 Northeastern Poland 165–284

3 Southeastern Poland 285–378

4 Kraków, Małopolska and the Tatras 379–501

5 Silesia 503–577

6 Wielkopolska and Pomerania 579–655

Warsaw and Mazovia

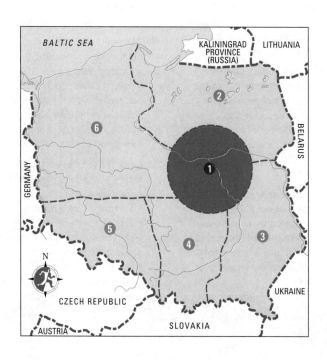

CHAPTER 1 # Highlights

✳ **Warsaw's Stare Miasto** A testament to Poland's postwar efforts to reconstruct itself after World War II, this historic town centre was re-created from almost nothing after being razed by the Nazis. See p.94

✳ **Zamek Królewski** The sumptuous palace of Poland's seventeenth- and eighteenth-century kings is a treasure-trove of Baroque overstatement. See p.96

✳ **Pałac Kultury i Nauki** A colossal monument to the ideological certainties of the Stalinist period, this imposing neo-Baroque monolith is still the defining feature of downtown Warsaw's skyline. See p.115

✳ **Park Łazienkowski** The most elegant of Poland's urban parks, crisscrossed with oak-lined promenades and a favourite with strollers whatever the time of year. See p.121

✳ **Wilanów** Warsaw's grandest palace, tucked away in the almost rural surroundings of the southern outskirts of the city. See p.123

✳ **Warsaw nightlife** The drinking and dining scene in the Polish capital keeps getting better, and can now stand comparison with any other city in Central Europe. See p.134

✳ **Żelazowa Wola** Chopin's birthplace, and nowadays a national shrine; there's a museum dedicated to the composer and you can even attend summertime piano recitals in the surrounding park. See p.142

✳ **Łódź** The Art-Nouveau villas and red-brick factories and warehouses of the "Polish Manchester" are a must for lovers of nineteenth-century architecture, while its cultural scene boasts some of the country's most important festivals. See p.146

△ View over Warsaw

Warsaw and Mazovia

Warsaw has two enduring points of definition: the Wisła River, running south to north across the Mazovian plains, and the Moscow–Berlin road, stretching across this terrain – and through the city – east to west. Such a location, and four hundred years of capital status, have ensured a history writ large with occupations and uprisings, intrigues and heroism. Warsaw's sufferings, above all the World War II uprising which led to the city's near-total obliteration, have lodged it in the national consciousness, although in the most recent era of political struggle Warsaw was at times overshadowed by events in Gdańsk and the industrial centres of the south. Its role has always been a key one nonetheless, as a focus of popular and intellectual opposition and the site of past and future power, and today, as memories of the communist Poland recede into the distance, the city is again pre-eminent economically, politically and culturally.

The extensive renovation and development that has come in tandem with Poland's 2004 accession to the European Union have left Warsaw looking better than at any time in the last sixty years – though all the same no one is likely to confuse it with Prague or Vienna: communist planning left the city awash with concrete, and there's sometimes a hollowness to the faithful reconstructions of what was destroyed in the war. The pace of social change, however, is tangible and fascinating, and in the city centre, mixed in with Western commercial brashness and the remnants of the Polish People's Republic, you'll find a new generation of restaurants and nightspots with genuine style.

You're less likely to find outward manifestations of modernity in the villages of **Mazovia** – **Mazowsze** in Polish – the plain which surrounds the capital. Mazovia is historically one of the poorer regions of Poland, its peasant population eking a precarious existence from the notoriously infertile sandy soil. It is not the most arresting of landscapes, but contains a half-dozen or so rewarding day-trips to ease your passage into the rural Polish experience. The **Park Narodowy Puszcza Kampinoska** (Kampinoski Forest National Park), spreading northwest of Warsaw, is a remnant of the primeval forests that once covered this region, with tranquil villages dotted along its southern rim. Nearby is **Żelazowa Wola**, the much-visited birthplace of Chopin, and, on the opposite side of the river, the historic church complex at **Czerwińsk nad Wisłą**. **Łowicz** is well known for its folk culture, while the palace at **Nieborów** is one of the finest aristocratic mansions in the country. A hundred kilometres southwest of the capital lies industrial **Łódź**, the country's second city and an important cultural centre, while to the north there are historic old Mazovian centres, notably the market town of **Pułtusk**. Finally, fans of Secessionist art won't want to miss the outstanding museum at **Płock**, west along the river.

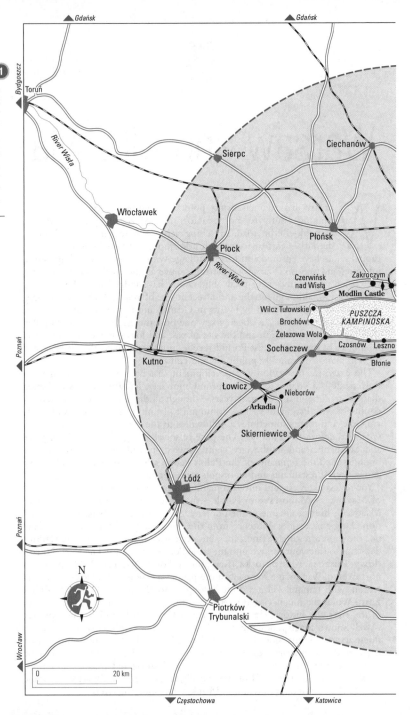

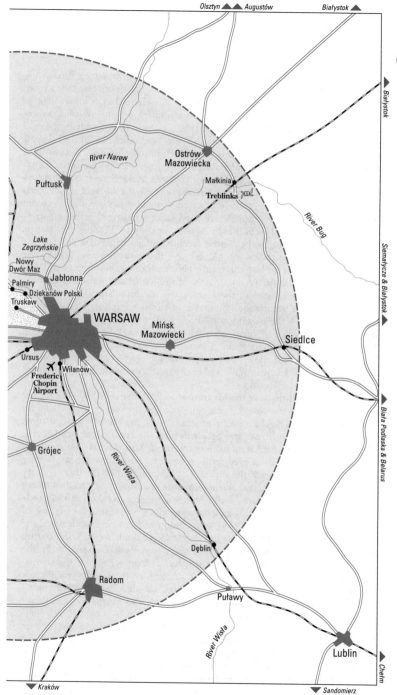

Olsztyn ▲▲ Augustów ▲▲ Białystok ▲

► Białystok

River Narew

Ostrów Mazowiecka

Pułtusk

Małkinia

Treblinka 爪

River Bug

► Siemiatycze & Białystok

Lake Zegrzyńskie

Nowy Dwór Maz

Jabłonna

Palmiry

Dziekanów Polski

Truskaw

WARSAW

Mińsk Mazowiecki

Siedlce

Ursus

Frederic Chopin Airport

Wilanów

► Biała Podlaska & Belarus

Grójec

River Wisła

Dęblin

Radom

Puławy

River Wisła

Lublin

► Chełm

Kraków ▼

Sandomierz ▼

Warsaw

Travelling through the grey, faceless housing estates surrounding **WARSAW** (**WARSZAWA**) or crossing the windswept avenues that punctuate the centre, you could be forgiven for wishing yourself elsewhere. But a knowledge of Warsaw's rich and often tragic history can transform the city, revealing voices from the past in even the plainest quarters: a pockmarked wall becomes a precious prewar relic, a housing estate the one-time centre of Europe's largest ghetto, the whole city a living book of modern history. Amongst the concrete, there are reconstructed traces of Poland's royal past, including a castle, a scattering of palaces and parks, and the restored streets of the historic Stare Miasto, while fifteen years of democracy and capitalism have left a different architectural legacy, some of it familiar – towering skyscrapers and plush shopfronts – some more original – Party headquarters turned stock exchanges, Stalinist palaces housing restaurants and cafés. Public squares, notably pl. Piłsudskiego and pl. Trzech Krzyży, have received extensive facelifts and attractive new buildings.

Wending its way north towards Gdańsk and the Baltic Sea, the **Wisła** river divides Warsaw neatly in half: the main sights are located on the western bank, while the eastern consists predominantly of residential and industrial districts. Marking the northern end of the city centre, the busy **Stare Miasto** (Old Town) provides the historic focal point. Rebuilt from scratch after World War II like most of Warsaw, the magnificent Zamek Królewski (Royal Castle), ancient Archikatedra św. Jana (St John's Cathedral) and the Rynek Starego Miasta (Old Town Square) are the most striking examples of the capital's reconstruction. Baroque churches and the former palaces of the aristocracy line the streets west of the ring of defensive walls, and to the north, in the quietly atmospheric **Nowe Miasto** (New Town).

West of the Stare Miasto, in the **Muranów** and **Mirów** districts, is the former **ghetto** area, where the Nożyk Synagogue and the cemetery on ul. Okopowa (**Cmentarz Żydowski**) bear poignant testimony to the lost Jewish population. South from the Stare Miasto lies **Śródmieście**, the city's commercial centre, which was rebuilt in a haphazard manner following World War II, leaving plenty of empty spaces that have proved fertile ground for new office blocks. In spite of recent additions, however, the skyline is still dominated by the Pałac Kultury i Nauki (Palace of Culture and Science), Stalin's enduring legacy to the citizens of Warsaw. Linking the Stare Miasto and Śródmieście, **Krakowskie Przedmieście** is dotted with palaces and Baroque spires, and forms the first leg of the **Trakt Królewski** (Royal Way), a procession of open boulevards stretching all the way from pl. Zamkowy to the stately king's residence at **Wilanów** on the southern outskirts of the city. Along the way is **Park Łazienkowski**, the most delightful of Warsaw's many green spaces and the setting for the charming Pałac Łazienkowski (Łazienki Palace), surrounded by waterways and lakes. Further out, the city becomes a welter of high-rise developments, but among them, historic suburbs like **Żoliborz** to the north and **Praga** across the river give an authentic flavour of contemporary Warsaw life.

Warsaw is much livelier and more cosmopolitan than it's often given credit for, and the postwar dearth of nightlife and entertainment is now a complaint of the past. A constantly growing range of inviting bars, restaurants and clubs has appeared to cater for the new consumer classes and the thousands of resident expatriates, and if prices are high by Polish standards they still compare favourably to those in the West. If you're arriving without personal connections or contacts, the city can seem forbidding, with much of the place still shutting down within a few hours of darkness, but Varsovians are generous and highly hospitable people: no social call, even to an office, is complete without a glass of *herbata* and a plate of cakes. Postwar austerity strengthened the tradition of home-based socializing, and if you strike up a friendship here (and friendships in Warsaw are quickly formed) you'll find much to enrich your experience of the city.

Some history

For a capital city, Warsaw entered history late. Although there are records of a settlement here from the tenth century, the first references to anything resembling a town at this point on the Wisła date from around the mid-fourteenth century. It owes its initial rise to power to the Mazovian ruler **Janusz the Elder**, who made Warsaw his main residence in 1413 and developed it as the capital of the Duchy of Mazovia. Following the death of the last Mazovian prince in 1526, Mazovia and its now greatly enlarged capital were incorporated into **Polish** royal territory. The city's fortunes now improved rapidly. Following the Act of Union with Lithuania, the Sejm – the Polish parliament – voted to transfer to Warsaw in 1569. The first election of a Polish king took place here four years later, and then in 1596 came the crowning glory, when **King Sigismund III** moved his capital two hundred miles from Kraków to its current location – a decision chiefly compelled by the shift in Poland's geographical centre after the union with Lithuania.

Capital status inevitably brought prosperity, but along with new wealth came new perils. The city was badly damaged by the **Swedes** during the invasion of 1655 – the first of several assaults – and was then extensively reconstructed by the **Saxon** kings in the late seventeenth century. The lovely Ogród Saski (Saxon Gardens), in the centre of Warsaw, date from this period, for example. Poles tend to remember the **eighteenth century** in a nostalgic haze as the golden age of Warsaw, when its concert halls, theatres and salons were prominent in European cultural life.

The **Partitions** abruptly terminated this era, as Warsaw was absorbed into Prussia in 1795. Napoleon's arrival in 1806 gave Varsovians brief hopes of liberation, but the collapse of his Moscow campaign spelled the end of those hopes, and, following the 1815 Congress of Vienna, Warsaw was integrated into the Russian-controlled **Congress Kingdom of Poland**. The failure of the **1830 uprising** brought severe reprisals: Warsaw was relegated to the status of "provincial town" and all Polish institutes and places of learning were closed. Its position as the westernmost major city in the Tsar's domain brought commercial prosperity towards the turn of the century, but it was only with the outbreak of **World War I** that Russian control began to crumble, and late in 1914 the **Germans** occupied the city, remaining until the end of the war.

Following the return of Polish independence, Warsaw reverted to its position as capital; but then, with the outbreak of **World War II**, came the progressive annihilation of the city. The Nazi assault in September 1939 was followed by round-ups, executions and deportations – savagery directed above all at the Jewish community, who were crammed into a ghetto area and forced to live on a near-starvation diet. It was the Jews who instigated the first open revolt, the **Ghetto Uprising** of April 1943, which resulted in the wholesale destruction of Warsaw's six-centuries-old Jewish community.

As the war progressed and the wave of German defeats on the eastern front provoked a tightening of the Nazi grip on Warsaw, **resistance** stiffened in the city. In August 1944, virtually the whole civilian population participated in the **Warsaw Uprising**, an attempt both to liberate the city and to ensure the emergence of an independent Poland. It failed on both counts. Hitler, infuriated by the resistance, ordered the total elimination of Warsaw and, with the surviving populace driven out of the city, the SS systematically destroyed the remaining buildings. In one of his final speeches to the Reichstag, Hitler was able to claim with satisfaction that Warsaw was now no more than a name on the map of Europe. By the end of the war, 850,000 Varsovians – two-thirds of the city's 1939 population – were dead or missing. Photographs taken immediately after the **liberation** in January 1945 show a scene not unlike Hiroshima: General Eisenhower described Warsaw as the most tragic thing he'd ever seen.

The momentous task of **rebuilding** the city took ten years. Aesthetically the results were mixed, with acres of socialist functionalism spread between the Baroque palaces, but it was a tremendous feat of national reconstruction nonetheless. The recovery that has brought the population up to 1.7 million, exceeding its prewar level, is, however, marred by a silence: that of the exterminated Jewish community.

Arrival and orientation

The wide, open expanse of the Wisła River is the most obvious aid to **orientation**. Almost everything you will want to see lies on the western bank, with the **Stare Miasto** (Old Town) squatting on high ground to the north, and the modern commercial heart of Warsaw, the **Śródmieście** district, stretching out to the south. Linking the two is the two-kilometre-long street known as **Krakowskie Przedmieście** (which changes name to **Nowy Świat** in its lower reaches), the city's main artery of tourist traffic, which cuts through the centre from north to south. The main points of arrival are all within easy reach of the city centre.

By plane

Frederic Chopin airport (flight information ☎022/650 4220, ⓦwww .lotnisko-chopina.pl; locals still use the old name, Okęcie), handling both international and domestic flights, is 8km southwest of the city. Budget carriers arrive at Etiuda terminal, a short walk south of the main terminal. From either, **bus** #175 runs every ten to fifteen minutes and takes you to the old town in about half an hour, passing Warszawa Centralna train station (see below) and Krakowskie Przedmieście on the way. Twice an hour from about 11pm to 5am, night bus #611 heads from the airport to Warszawa Centralna. Buy your tickets (2.40zł day, 4.80zł night) from the Ruch kiosk inside the terminal building, or from the driver; watch out for **pickpockets** on the bus to the centre. **Taxis** are better regulated than they used to be, but drivers may still try to overcharge foreigners, and you should go to one of the taxi stands outside the terminal rather than with a driver waiting in the building. If the meter is running properly the trip to the centre will cost 25–35zł, or fifty percent more at night.

By train

Warszawa Centralna, the main train station (information ☎022/9436 is just west of the central shopping area, a ten-minute bus ride (#175; wait across from the station, in front of the *Marriott* hotel) or a thirty-minute walk from the Stare

Miasto. There are always reliable taxis waiting outside on **ulica Emilii Plater**, east of the station.

A confusing, cacophonous hive serving all international routes and the major national ones, the station is much cleaner than it used to be but is still definitely not a place in which to hang around: keep a close eye on your luggage. With the opening of the new Zlote Tarasy shopping complex, surrounding the station, the atmosphere should continue to improve here, but the layout will remain confusing. To get your bearings, head for the tourist office inside the main ticket hall. Just downstairs from here you'll find coin-operated **lockers** of varying sizes, where you can store luggage for up to ten days.

Most trains also stop at **Warszawa Wschodnia** (East) station, out in the Praga suburb, or **Warszawa Zachodnia** (West), in the Ochota district – the latter is also the site of the main bus station (see below). Both stations have regular connections to Centralna. **Warszawa Śródmieście** station, just east of Warszawa Centralna, handles local traffic to and from Łowicz and other regional destinations.

By bus

Warsaw's **main bus station** (information ☎022/9433) 3km west of the centre on al. Jerozolimskie, handles all international services from Western Europe and the Baltic States, as well as those from major domestic destinations in the south and west. Although officially known as Dworzec Centralny PKS, this bus station is usually referred to as **Warszawa Zachodnia** (Warsaw West), because it's housed in the same building as the Warszawa Zachodnia train station (see above). From here, a short train ride will take you in to Warszawa Centralna – virtually every eastbound municipal bus will take you to Warszawa Centralna too; #127 continues on to pl. Bankowy on the fringes of the Stare Miasto. Some buses from eastern Poland terminate at **Dworzec Stadion** on the east bank of the Wisła, next to the enormous Stadion market; from here either tram #12 or a suburban train will take you to Warszawa Centralna. Intercity buses run by private companies like Polski Express and Komfort Bus drop off on **aleja Jana Pawła II**, just behind Warszawa Centralna train station.

Information

Warsaw's municipal **tourist office** (☎022/9431, ⓦ www.warsawtour.pl) operates several **tourist information centres** (Informacja Turystyczna, or IT) in the city, with English-speaking staff who can provide information on accommodation throughout Warsaw, handle hotel bookings, have plenty of brochures to give away and sell maps and guidebooks. There are branches at Warszawa Centralna train station (in the main ticket hall; daily: May–Sept 8am–8pm; Oct–April 9am–6pm); at Warszawa Zachodnia bus and train station (daily 9am–5pm); and in the airport's arrivals hall (daily: May–Sept 8am–8pm; Oct–April 9am–6pm). A new Stare Miasto branch may open soon – check the website or at the other branches for information.

The growing influx of Western tourists and the large number of English-speaking expatriates has resulted in a number of English-language publications in the city. Most useful of these is *Warsaw in Your Pocket* (5zł; ⓦ www.inyourpocket .com), a bimonthly, A5-format **listings** magazine that gives critical coverage of hotels, restaurants and bars as well as addresses of all kinds of useful services. It's available at the IT office and from bookshops and a few newspaper kiosks. Less

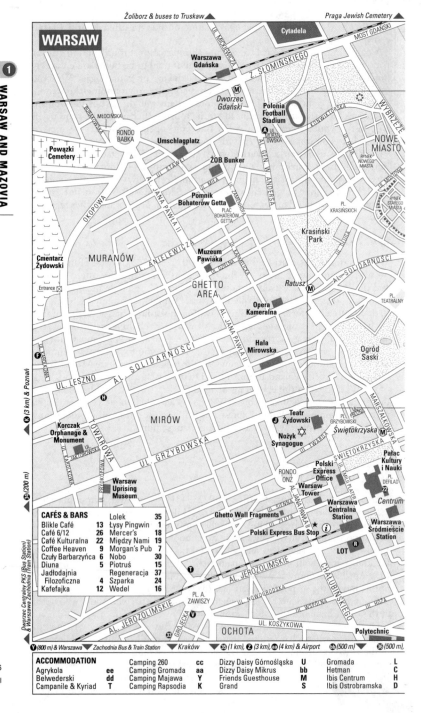

WARSAW

Żoliborz & buses to Truskaw ▲

Praga Jewish Cemetery ▲

Cytadela

MOST GDAŃSKI

UL. MICKIEWICZA

Warszawa Gdańska

Z. SŁOMIŃSKIEGO

WYBRZEŻE

Dworzec Gdański Ⓜ

Polonia Football Stadium Ⓐ

KONWIKTORSKA

NOWE MIASTO

MŁOCIŃSKA

RONDO BABKA

Umschlagplatz

UL. MURAN- OWSKA

RYNEK NOWEGO MIASTA

Powązki Cemetery

AL. JANA PAWŁA II

UL. STAWKI

ŻOB Bunker

UL. MIŁA

AL. GEN. W. ANDERSA

UL. MOSTOWA

OKOPOWA

Pomnik Bohaterów Getta

UL. ZAMENHOFA

PLAC BOHATERÓW GETTA

RYNEK STAREGO MIASTA

Cmentarz Żydowski

MURANÓW

UL. ANIELEWICZA

Muzeum Pawiaka

UL. KARMELICKA

PL. KRASIŃSKICH

Krasiński Park

Entrance ⊠

GHETTO AREA

Ratusz Ⓜ

PL. TEATRALNY

Ⓕ

Opera Kameralna

AL. JANA PAWŁA II

Ⓚ (3 km) & Poznań ▲

UL. LESZNO

AL. SOLIDARNOŚCI

Hala Mirowska

Ogród Saski

Ⓗ

MIRÓW

AL. SOLIDARNOŚCI

Teatr Żydowski Ⓙ

PL. GRZYBOWSKI

Świętokrzyska Ⓜ

MARSZAŁKOWSKA

Korczak Orphanage & Monument

UL. JAKTOROWSKA

TOWAROWA

UL. GRZYBOWSKA

Nożyk Synagogue

UL. TWARDA

ŚWIĘTOKRZYSKA

Pałac Kultury i Nauki

Ⓝ (200 m) ▲

UL. CHŁODNA

Warsaw Uprising Museum

RONDO ONZ

Polski Express Office

Warsaw Tower

PL. DEFILAD

Centrum

CAFÉS & BARS

Blikle Café	13	Lolek	35
Café 6/12	26	Łysy Pingwin	1
Café Kulturalna	22	Mercer's	18
Coffee Heaven	9	Między Nami	19
Czuły Barbarzyńca	6	Morgan's Pub	7
Diuna	5	Nobo	30
Jadłodajnia		Piotruś	15
Filozoficzna	4	Regeneracja	37
Kafefajka	12	Szparka	24
		Wedel	16

Ghetto Wall Fragments ■

Polski Express Bus Stop ★ ⓘ

UL. ZŁOTA

UL. SIENNA

Warszawa Centralna Station

Warszawa Śródmieście Station

LOT Ⓡ

Ⓣ

Dworzec Centralny PKS (Bus Station) & Warszawa Zachodnia (Train Station)

Ⓨ (800 m) & Warszawa ▼ Zachodnia Bus & Train Station

Ⓥ

PL. A. ZAWISZY

UL. GRÓJECKA

AL. JEROZOLIMSKIE

UL. NOWOGRODZKA

UL. WSPÓLNA

UL. HOŻA

AL. JEROZOLIMSKIE

OCHOTA

UL. KOSZYKOWA

CHAŁUBIŃSKIEGO

Polytechnic

◄ Kraków ▼ Ⓑ (1 km), Ⓩ (3 km), ⓐⓑ (4 km) & Airport ⓑⓑ (500 m) ▼ Ⓑ (500 m),

ACCOMMODATION

Agrykola	ee	Camping 260	cc	Dizzy Daisy Górnośląska	U	Gromada	L
Belwederski	dd	Camping Gromada	aa	Dizzy Daisy Mikrus	bb	Hetman	C
Campanile & Kyriad	T	Camping Majawa	Y	Friends Guesthouse	M	Ibis Centrum	H
		Camping Rapsodia	K	Grand	S	Ibis Ostrobramska	D

86

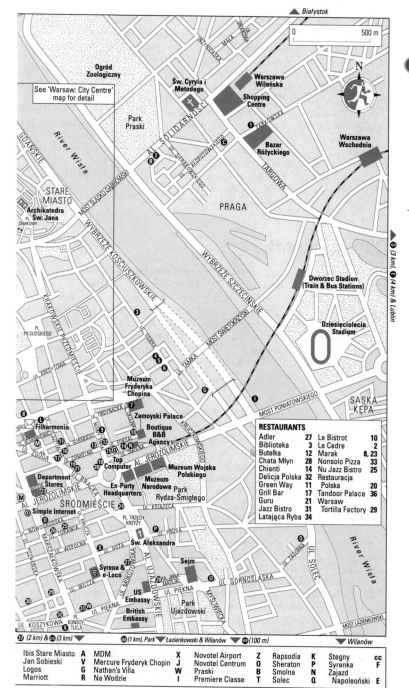

Białystok

0   500 m

N

See 'Warsaw: City Centre'
map for detail

Ogród
Zoologiczny

Św. Cyryla i
Metodego

Park
Praski

Warszawa
Wileńska

Shopping
Centre

Warszawa
Wschodnia

Bazar
Różyckiego

STARE
MIASTO

Archikatedra
Św. Jana

PRAGA

River Wisła

Dworzec Stadion
(Train & Bus Stations)

Dziesięciolecia
Stadium

Muzeum
Fryderyka
Chopina

SASKA
KĘPA

Zamoyski Palace

Boutique
B&B
Agency

Filharmonia

Top
Computer

Muzeum Wojska
Polskiego

Department
Stores

Ex-Party
Headquarters

Muzeum
Narodowe

Park
Rydza-Śmigłego

ŚRÓDMIEŚCIE

Simple Internet

Św. Aleksandra

Sejm

Syrena &
e-Loco

US
Embassy

British
Embassy

Park
Ujazdowski

River Wisła

RESTAURANTS

Adler	27	Le Bistrot	10
Biblioteka	3	Le Cedre	2
Butelka	12	Marak	8, 23
Chata Młyn	28	Nonsolo Pizza	33
Chianti	14	Nu Jazz Bistro	25
Delicja Polska	32	Restauracja	
Green Way	11	Polska	20
Grill Bar	17	Tandoor Palace	36
Guru	21	Warsaw	
Jazz Bistro	31	Tortilla Factory	29
Latająca Ryba	34		

(3 km) & (4 km) & Lublin

(2 km) & (3 km) ▼   (1 km), Park ▼ Łazienkowski & Wilanów ▼ (100 m)   ▼ Wilanów

Ibis Stare Miasto	A	MDM	X	Novotel Airport	Z	Rapsodia	K	Stegny	cc
Jan Sobieski	V	Mercure Fryderyk Chopin	J	Novotel Centrum	O	Sheraton	P	Syrenka	F
Logos	G	Nathan's Villa	W	Praski	B	Smolna	N	Zajazd	
Marriott	R	Na Wodzie	I	Premiere Classe	T	Solec	Q	Napoleoński	E

info-packed but with more feature-based content is the booklet-sized monthly *Warsaw Insider* (10zł; Ⓦ www.warsawinsider.pl), available from the IT offices and bigger bookshops around town. The weekly **newspaper** *Warsaw Voice* (Ⓦ www .warsawvoice.com) is good on local politics and business news but not so strong on listings. Even if you can't read Polish, it's worth buying the Warsaw edition of the national daily *Gazeta Wyborcza* for news of what's on in town, especially on Fridays, when the *Co jest grane* entertainment supplement covers cinema, concerts and clubs – the listings are fairly straightforward, and you'll just need to translate the days of the week. Also in Polish, the monthly *City Magazine*, given away in bars and restaurants, is a more youth-oriented source of listings.

The tourist office gives away an excellent **map** of the central area with sights and hotels marked; good plans of the whole city include those printed by Demart and Copernicus, both of which cost under 10zł and are widely available. Otherwise, your needs will be adequately met by the maps in *Warsaw in Your Pocket*, the *Warsaw Insider*, or this guide.

City transport

Warsaw can boast a reliable and well-integrated **bus**, **tram** and **metro** network (☎ 022/9484, Ⓦ www.ztm.waw.pl for timetable information). Buses and trams cover most of the city, while the relatively new – if not especially useful to tourists – Warsaw metro consists of a single fifteen-stop line running from Dworzec Gdański in the north to suburban Kabaty 14km to the south. The major points where overground and underground public transport lines meet are **plac Bankowy** itself, and **Centrum** in the modern commercial centre, a loosely defined area around the Pałac Kultury i Nauki, 400m east of the Warszawa Centralna train station.

All services get very crowded at peak hours but are by and large punctual. Regular bus, tram and metro routes close down around 11–11.30pm; from 11.15pm to 4.45am a confusing array of **night buses** leaves from behind the Pałac Kultury i Nauki on ul. Emilii Plater at 15 and 45 minutes past the hour Also note that on weekends, when Nowy Świat is pedestrianized, buses running between the old town and the modern centre and Wilanów are shunted west to ul. Zgoda and ul. Krucza. One especially useful bus is #180, the **Warszawa Linia Turystyczna** (Warsaw Sightseeing Route), which runs along the Trakt Królewski from the Stare Miasto to Wilanów and also stops at the Jewish Cemetery.

Tickets (*bilety*) for trams, buses and the metro are bought from any newspaper or tobacco kiosk sporting the "MZK" logo, or from ticket machines at some of the central stops. They can also be bought from drivers, but with an added surcharge. A single flat-fare ticket (changing trams or buses requires a new ticket) costs 2.40zł (1.25zł for students) – two single tickets (or one 4.80zł ticket) are required for a journey on a night bus. It's more economical to buy a **day pass** (*bilet jednodniowy*; 7.20zł; students 3.70zł), **three-day pass** (*bilet trzydniowy*; 12zł; students 6.20zł) or **week pass** (*bilet tygodniowy*; 26zł; students 12.40zł): the day and three-day passes are available from most kiosks, but for a week pass you may need to go to a post office students under 26 (with valid ISIC card) can use 48 percent reduced tickets, but not the slightly cheaper 50 percent reduced tickets, which are only for Polish students.

Punch your ticket in the machines on board or at the metro entrance – pleas of ignorance don't cut much ice with inspectors, who'll fine you 120zł on the

△ Tram, Warsaw

spot if they catch you without a validated ticket. It's no longer necessary to stamp an extra ticket for luggage.

Taxis

Warsaw **taxi** drivers have a better reputation than they used to but foreigners may still be overcharged, especially at the airport and train station. As a guide to **fares**, there's an initial charge of 5–6zł, followed by, depending on the firm, 1.5–2zł per kilometre. There's a fifty-percent mark-up at weekends and after 10pm. All reputable taxis bear a driver number and the taxi company's name, logo and telephone number: avoid any vehicles that are less clearly marked. Checking in advance what you ought to be paying by asking hotel receptions or IT points is always a good idea, but the best way to ensure a fair price is to call for a pick-up: try MPT (☎022/919), Radio Taxi (☎022/9621) or Super Taxi (☎022/9622). Switchboard operators at these firms usually speak English. Many drivers, however, do not, and it helps if you can pronounce the street you want and the place you're going to.

Accommodation

There's an ever-growing number of accommodation options in Warsaw, but the city's newfound importance as a European commercial centre has ensured that most of the new places are aimed squarely at expense-account visitors from the West (or East), rather than budget-minded tourists. These **upmarket** establishments, which have altered the skyline dramatically, are on a par with anything in Western Europe in both price and quality. For **low-** and **mid-range** travellers, however, the number of good-value places is limited, and new arrivals without reservations often find themselves paying over the odds for substandard accommodation.

For those who haven't booked in advance, the IT offices at the airport, train and bus stations (see "Information", p.85) will arrange hotel and hostel rooms, although they're beset by queues in summer and may not be well informed about the places they're recommending.

Warsaw's stock of **youth hostels** has improved, but demand still outstrips supply: again, booking is essential. There's also a choice of **private accommodation** in Warsaw, ranging from basic spare bedrooms let out by pensioners – tolerable budget accommodation for a day or two – to furnished apartments or bed-and-breakfast suites, excellent value at the price of a hotel room or less. **Camping** in Warsaw's suburbs is a reasonable option if you don't mind being a lengthy public-transport ride away from the centre.

Hotels

Warsaw's **hotel** scene represents both the best and worst of post-communist Poland. While there's no shortage of new, Western-financed hotels offering high standards for high prices, there are still a large number of communist-era hotels peddling overpriced, unrenovated rooms, coupled with old-fashioned ideas of customer service.

It's difficult – though not impossible – to find a double room in central Warsaw for anything below the 200zł mark, and most establishments charge considerably more than this, regardless of whether their rooms are up to scratch. You may find yourself paying 300zł or more for international standards of comfort, although the entry of the Ibis and Premiere Class **chains** into the Warsaw market have made things easier for mid-range travellers. Bargains are still to be had, though: nearly every hotel offers **weekend reductions** of twenty percent or more – be sure to ask when you phone. Many of the top places also offer substantial discounts for **Internet reservations**.

In the handful of inexpensive options in the **centre**, you'll have to book in advance in order to secure a bed – a task made all the more difficult by the fact that reception staff in the cheaper places rarely speak English. Otherwise finding a budget place to stay involves settling for something some way from the centre. The up-and-coming suburb of **Praga**, just east over the Wisła, is a good place to look, although it has a reputation for being unsafe at night. There's a scattering of hotels in the **southern** and **western suburbs** too.

The Stare Miasto and around

Europejski Krakowskie Przedmieście 13 ☎022/826 5051, ⓦwww.orbis.pl. One of Warsaw's oldest and most storied hotels, but the smallish, functional rooms don't live up to the *belle époque* exterior. Still, it's a fair value given the professional service and central location. See also p.113. **❽**

Harenda Krakowskie Przedmieście 4/6 ☎022/826 0071, ⓦwww.hotelharenda.com.pl. International-standard rooms furnished in a pleasing, beige colour-scheme; this is one of the best places in Warsaw that's not run by a global chain. Friendly staff, and location right in the centre of things. Especially good value at weekends, when your second night is free. **❼**

Ibis Stare Miasto ul. Muranowska 2 ☎022/310 1000, ⓦwww.ibishotel.com. Warsaw's three Ibis branches offer quality, if anonymous, modern rooms and facilities at a realistic price (breakfast 26zł extra) and should be booked ahead. All offer big weekend reductions. This one is 500m north-west of the Stare Miasto. Bus #175 from the train station. **❼**

Le Meridien Bristol Krakowskie Przedmieście 42/44 ☎022/551 1000, ⓦwarsaw.lemeridien.com. Warsaw's first luxury hotel, the legendary prewar *Bristol* is looking better than ever (see p.113). Completely modernized and right in the centre, this is also the finest Art-Nouveau building in the city. The double rooms are tasteful and superbly comfortable, and not more expensive than those at the city's other top hotels. **❾**

Le Regina ul. Kościelna 12 ☎022/531 6000, ⓦwww.leregina.com. A new entry into the luxury market, this boutique hotel in a restored eighteenth-century palace boasts individually designed rooms, crisp service and a lovely courtyard. In the Nowe Miasto. **❾**

Mazowiecki ul. Mazowiecka 10 ☎022/827 2365, ⓦwww.mazowiecki.com.pl. Recently renovated mid-range hotel on a quiet side street in the centre. A dozen or so very comfortable but somewhat dark

en suites (often booked) and a larger number of rooms with shared bath. Good location for nightlife. With the excellent *Kuźnia Smaku* restaurant on-site (see p.130). **❺–❻**.

Metalowcy ul. Długa 29 ☎022/831 4021, ⒺÞsekretariat.op.pl. Spartan and shabby but more or less clean former workers' hostel, with unwelcoming and generally monoglot staff, and a brilliant location just a few steps west of the Stare Miasto. A mixture of rooms with shared facilities and one en-suite double. Advance reservations essential; you might find an English speaker on Fridays. **❸–❹**.

Sofitel Victoria ul. Królewska 11 ☎022/657 8011, ⓦwww.orbis.pl. International-class business hotel on pl. Piłsudskiego, in a glorified communist-style block that has been wired and furnished to meet contemporary standards. Quite comfortable, with spacious, attractive rooms and good views of the Ogród Saski. Just a few minutes' walk from old town. **❽**

Śródmieście

Campanile ul. Towarowa 2 ☎022/582 7200, ⓦwww.campanile.com.pl. Similar to but more expensive than the attached *Premiere Classe* (see p.92), but still excellent value. Rooms at the *Campanile* (**❻**) have air conditioning and are slightly larger and better furnished. The third hotel at the same address, the *Kyriad* (☎022/582 7500; **❼**), is a fairly good, but not especially interesting, luxury option.

Grand ul. Krucza 28 ☎022/583 2100, ⓦwww .orbis.pl. Hulking grey Orbis-owned hotel that has been completely revamped inside and is popular with upscale tour groups, and especially package tourists from the Polish diaspora. Within walking distance of the central train station. **❽**

Gromada pl. Powstanców Warszawy 2 ☎022/582 9900, ⓦwww.gromada.pl. Comfortable mid-range provision in a large modern building; the rooms are reliable but numbingly dull. Fair value though if you're looking for something central and not too pricey. **❻–❼**

Ibis Centrum al. Solidarności 165 ☎022/520 3000, 🌐www.ibishotel.com. Warsaw's second Ibis hotel, though not quite as central as the name would indicate, has the same trustworthy standards as the branch north of the Stare Miasto. Three trams stops west of Stare Miasto. From Warszawa Centralna take trams #12, #22 or #24 to "Okopowa". ❼

Jan Sobieski pl. Artura Zawiszy 1 ☎022/579 1000, 🌐www.sobieski.com.pl. Expensive hotel in Ochota, 800m west of Warszawa Centralna. The wacky exterior, with brash yellows and pinks, sets it apart from other luxury choices; inside, the swish, classy rooms are among the best in the city. ❽

Logos ul. Wybrzeże Kościuszkowskie 31/33 ☎022/625 5185, 🌐hotellogos.pl. By the river, downhill from the centre. Basic place with care-worn, dusty feel and communist-era brown colour schemes. Sometimes there's an English speaker on duty. En suites and rooms with shared facilities. ❹–❻

Marriott al. Jerozolimskie 65/79 ☎022/630 6306, 🌐www.marriott.com/wawpl. This looming glass monstrosity is one of the city's top hotels, right opposite Warszawa Centralna, and in the heart of the modern business district. Blandly luxurious rooms, many with outstanding views, and more amenities than any other hotel in Poland. ❾

MDM pl. Konstytucji 1 ☎022/621 6211, 🌐www.syrena.com.pl. Pleasant and quiet rooms overlooking the vast socialist-realist expanse of pl. Konstytucji – the next best thing to staying in the Palace of Culture. Popular with tour groups but not especially good value for independent travellers. Students, however, can stay for half-price at weekends. Handy location for the main business and shopping districts and Park Łazienkowski. ❽

Mercure Fryderyk Chopin ul. Jana Pawła II 22 ☎022/528 0300, 🌐www.mercure.com. Brash, modern and stylish four-star place that's one of the most appealing of the main business hotels. The rooms have nice views, and the unusual colour scheme of yellow, maroon and brown provides added interest. Part of a French chain, with a couple of good restaurants. ❽

Na Wodzie Wybrzeże Kościuszkowskie ☎022/628 5883, 🌐www.hostel-warsaw.pl. A central "boatel" with small but clean single and double cabins with shared bath, and a nice café on the deck with a stereo playing Polish sea shanties. Moored just north of the Poniatowskiego bridge; take any tram from Centralna station towards Praga and get off at the fourth stop, on the bridge. Closed Nov–April. ❷

Novotel Centrum ul. Nowogrodzka 24/26 ☎022/621 0271, 🌐www.orbis.pl. Unmissable yellow-brick skyscraper, popular for business conferences, on the corner of busy Marszałkowska and al. Jerozolimskie. Comfortable, with high standards of service. Upper rooms come with stunning views over the city. ❽

Premiere Classe ul. Towarowa 2 ☎022/624 0800, 🌐www.premiereclasse.com.pl. The cheapest of three high-quality new hotels in the same building of pl. Zawiszy, two tram stops west of the station; the small but pleasant en-suite doubles here are the best bargain in town, cleaner and more comfortable than anything else close to this price range. The *Campanile* and *Kyriad* hotels (see p.91) are in the same building. ❹

Sheraton ul. Prusa 2 ☎022/657 6100, 🌐www.sheraton.com/warsaw. The best located of the Western chain hotels, on the east side of the attractive and fashionable pl. Trzech Krzyży. Standards are impeccable, though some of the rooms are rather dark. ❽–❾

Solec ul. Zagórna 1 ☎022/625 4400, 🌐www.orbis.pl. Cheaper than the other Orbis hotels due to its out-of-the-way location on a gloomy street near the river. English-speaking staff and reliable, good-quality rooms, but you'll spend a fair amount of time in buses or taxis. ❻

Praga and the other suburbs

Belwederski ul. Sulkiewicza 11 ☎022/840 4011, 🌐www.hotelbelwederski.pl. Boxy mid-range hotel right by the southern reaches of Park Łazienkowski. Rooms are clean and well lit, but drab, and the beds are rather small. Buses #131 from Centrum and #180 from Nowy Świat pass right by. ❼

Hetman ul. Kłopotowskiego 36. ☎022/511 9800, 🌐www.hotelhetman.pl. Friendly, completely renovated place down a quiet side street in the Praga quarter, with attractive, very well-furnished cream-coloured rooms and a small health club. Tram #25 from Warszawa Centralna to "Ząbkowska" or any tram two stops east from below the Stare Miasto. ❼

Ibis Ostrobramska ul. Ostrobramska 36 ☎022/515 7800, 🌐www.ibishotel.com. Rooms and service identical to the other Ibis hotels but cheaper because it's across the river, in the far fringes of the Praga district. From Warszawa Centralna trams #24 or #44 to the last stop. ❻

Novotel Airport ul. 1 Sierpnia 1 ☎022/575 6000, 🌐www.orbis.pl. Smart, modern, business-oriented place with a swimming pool, 6km southwest of the centre, and 1km short of the airport. Bus #175 stops right by it. ❼–❽

Praski al. Solidarności 61 ☎022/818 4989, 🌐www.praski.pl. Decent two-star hotel in the

Praga district, only one tram stop from the heart of the Stare Miasto. Pleasantly situated opposite the Praski park, with a great Lebanese restaurant next door (see p.131). Rooms fairly comfortable, and are good value for the price and location. Shared and en-suite facilities. Tram #4 from Centrum. ⑤–⑦
Rapsodia ul. Fort Wola 22, off ul. Wolska. ☎022/634 4165, ⓦwww.rapsodia.com.pl. Hotel/campground several kilometres west of the centre in the suburb of Wola. Modest en-suite rooms with new but flimsy beds and furniture. Passably comfortable for the price. Tram #8 from the station. ④

Stegny ul. Inspektowa 1 ☎022/842 2768. Simple sports hotel next to stadium, well south of the centre, with an impressive range of athletics equipment. Basic rooms with shared facilities, and there's also a campground here (see "Campsites", p.94). ②
Zajazd Napoleoński ul. Płowiecka 83 ☎022/815 3068, ⓦwww.napoleon.waw.pl. 8km east of the centre, a small luxury inn dating from the sixteenth century and reputedly visited by Napoleon on his way to Moscow. Genuinely elegant, understated rooms with furnishings of a superior quality, and a good restaurant. Bus #525 from Warszawa Centralna. ⑦

Hostels

Warsaw has two good **private hostels**, a handful of **summer-only hostels**, and two old-fashioned **HI hostels** with curfews, though you should always book, especially in summer. Some of the hostels listed below also have affordable double rooms, though these again need to be booked well in advance.

Agrykola ul. Myśliwiecka 9 ☎022/622 9110, ⓦwww.hotelagrykola.pl. Bright, modern rooms in a youth athletic facility. Just east of Łazienki park; bus #151 from the station to the "Rozbrat" stop before the bridge. Dorms 47zł; rooms ❸
Dizzy Daisy Górnośląska ul. Górnośląska 14 ☎022/660 6712, ⓦwww.dizzydaisy.pl. Clean and friendly summer hostel in a student residence north of the Łazienki park. From Warszawa Centralna walk three blocks south to ul. Koszykowa, then take bus #159 east to stop "Wiejska". Open early July to late August. Two- and three-bed dorms (45–50zł) and en suites ❸
Dizzy Daisy Mikrus ul. Waryńskiego 10 ☎022/660 9859, ⓦwww.dizzydaisy.pl. The chain's second location, in university housing just south of the "Politechnika" metro station, one stop from "Centrum". Two- and three-bed dorms (40–50zł) and en suites ❸
Nathan's Villa ul. Piękna 24/26 ☎022/622 2946, ⓦwww.nathansvilla.com. Warsaw branch of the excellent Kraków hostel, with Ikea furniture, free laundry service and Internet access. Very popular with backpackers. Off Marszałkowska, two tram stops south of the main station. A few doubles ❹; dorms 50–60zł.

Oki Doki pl. Dąbrowskiego 3 ☎022/826 5112, ⓦwww.okidoki.pl. The most original hostel in Poland, with individually designed rooms in the communist-era Agricultural Ministry building. Internet access, on-site café/bar and well-informed staff. A 10min walk northeast from the main station. Rooms with bath ❺ and without ❹; dorms 45zł.
Przy Rynku ul. Rynek Nowego Miasta 4 ☎022/831 5033, ⓦwww.cityhostel.net. The best of the summer hostels, in a private school residence right on the Rynek Nowego Miasta; friendly and helpful staff. July–Aug only. No curfew; lockout 10am–5pm. Two doubles ❸; otherwise dorms 45zł.
Smolna ul. Smolna 30 ☎022/827 8952. Barrack-like conditions but central location; HI member reductions. Take any tram three stops east of the main station. June–Sept curfew 2am, Oct–May 11pm. En suites ❸; dorms 36zł.
Syrenka ul. Karolkowa 53a ☎022/632 8829, ⓦwww.ptsm.com.pl/ssmnr6. Old-fashioned, with basic dorms, garish but decent doubles and a midnight curfew. English-speaking staff. Tram #12 or #24 west of the main station to "DT Wola". En suites ❹; dorms 36zł. HI card reductions.

Private rooms, apartments and B&Bs

The main source of inexpensive **private rooms** in Warsaw is the Syrena travel agency at ul. Krucza 17, a fifteen-minute walk east from Warszawa Centralna (☎022/629 0537, ⓦwww.kwatery-prywatne.pl; May–Sept Mon–Fri 9am–6pm, Sat 10am–2pm; Oct–April Mon–Fri 9am–6pm); the adjacent e-Loco Internet café (daily 10am–midnight) is under the same management and offers the same service. They will fix you up with a single (**❷**) or double (**❸**) room in a private flat, usually shared with an elderly woman augmenting her pension. Some of these are superbly situated in the city centre, while others are in the suburbs, so check the location carefully. Conditions vary, but are usually at least up to the standard of youth hostels.

A more upmarket option – and one with considerably more privacy – is Old Town Apartments, at Rynek Starego Miasta 12/14 (☎022/887 9800, ⓦwww .warsawshotel.com), which offers well-furnished **apartments** in the Stare Miasto and other good locations starting at around 250zł for up to four people, very good value for the standard and location, especially if you're travelling in a small group.

The excellent Boutique Bed & Breakfast agency at ul. Smolna 14, apt. 7 (☎022/829 4801, ⓦwww.bedandbreakfast.pl), run by a returned Chicago émigré who is very knowledgeable and happy to give advice about the city, has impeccably furnished apartments and en-suite rooms (**❺**). The breakfast is better than anything you're likely to find at a hotel, and office and self-catering facilities are available. There's also a very central **gay**-run guesthouse, *Friends* (☎601 243 444, ⓦwww.gay.pl/friendswarsaw), with three comfortable rooms (**❻**) on ul. Sienkiewicza that come with complimentary mobile phone rental.

Campsites

Even in Warsaw, **camping** is extremely cheap and popular with Poles and foreigners alike. On the whole, facilities are reasonable and several offer bungalows (around 20zł per person per night). In all cases expect small extra charges for linen, tent, parking and so on.

Camping 260 ul. Inspektowa 1 ☎022/842 2768, ⓦwww.camping260.pl. In the same sports complex as the *Hotel Stegny* (see p.93), with clean but very basic facilities. May–Sept.

Camping Gromada ul. Zwirki i Wigury 32 ☎022/825 4391. Best and most popular of the Warsaw campsites, 7km southwest of the centre on the way out to the airport – bus #175 will get you there. As well as tent space the site has a number of cheap bungalows **❷**. May–Sept.

Camping Majawa ul. Bitwy Warszawskiej 1920 15/17 ☎022/823 3748. Closest campsite to the centre, about 600m south of the Warszawa Zachodnia bus and train station. Less crowded than the *Gromada* site, with some bungalows **❷**. May–Sept.

Rapsodia ul. Fort Wola 22. ☎022/634 4165, ⓦwww.rapsodia.com.pl. Respectable place with simple but decent amenities; popular with Polish families. Attached to the hotel of the same name (see p.93).

The Stare Miasto

The term **Stare Miasto** (Old Town) is in some respects a misnomer for the historic nucleus of Warsaw. Sixty years ago, this compact network of streets and alleyways lay in rubble – even the cobblestones are replacements. Yet surveying the tiered houses of the main square, for example, it's hard to believe they've been here only decades. Some older residents even claim that the restored version is in some respects an improvement, perhaps because the postwar builders worked from Baroque-era drawings by Bellotto, nephew of Canaletto, rather than prewar photographs showing nineteenth- and early twentieth-century alterations. Today, although the streets of the Stare Miasto are thronged with tourists, Varsovians themselves can be in short supply here, at least on weekdays; with the shift of Warsaw's centre of gravity south to Śródmieście, the small streets and market square of the Stare Miasto – not really on the way to anything – are now more historical cul-de-sac than heart of the modern city.

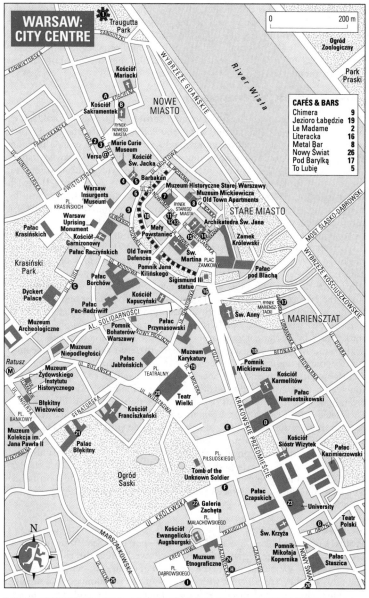

WARSAW: CITY CENTRE

0 ___ 200 m

CAFÉS & BARS

Chimera	9
Jezioro Łabędzie	19
Le Madame	2
Literacka	16
Metal Bar	8
Nowy Świat	26
Pod Barylką	17
To Lubię	5

ACCOMMODATION				**RESTAURANTS**						
Europejski	E	Przy Rynku	B	Artibus	22	Karczma Gessler	13	Puszkin	14
Harenda	G	Sofitel Victoria	F	Bar pod Barbakan	6	La Boheme	20	Qllinarnia	25
Le Meridien Bristol	D			Forteca	1	Maharaja Thai	10	St Antonio	21
Le Regina	A			Freta 33	3	Na Prowincji	7	Uniwersytecki	23
Mazowiecki	H			Fukier	11	Pewne Miejsce	15	Varna	24
Metalowcy	C			Jazz Bistro		Pierogarnia	18		
Oki Doki	I			Gwiazdeczka	12	Pod Samsonem	4		

95

Plac Zamkowy (Castle Square), on the south side of Stare Miasto, is the obvious place to start a tour. Here the first thing to catch your eye is the bronze **statue of Sigismund III**, the king who made Warsaw his capital. Installed on his column in 1640, Sigismund suffered a direct hit from a tank in September 1944, but has now been replaced on his lookout; the base is a popular and convenient rendezvous point.

The Zamek Królewski

On the east side of the square is the former **Zamek Królewski** (Royal Castle), once home of the royal family and seat of the Polish parliament, much of which is now occupied by a **museum** with two separate sections (last entry 1hr before closing, opening hours vary according to route – see below; Ⓦwww.zamek -krolewski.art.pl). What you can see in the castle is divided into two separate "routes" – **Route I**, which covers the bulk of the castle, and **Route II**, which includes only the Royal Apartments. On Sundays you can follow the **Sunday route** (11am–6pm; free), which includes highlights from both circuits. All rooms contain clear explanations in English of what's on display.

Dynamited by German troops in the aftermath of the Warsaw Uprising, the seventeenth-century castle stood in ruins until 1971, when reconstruction began. In July 1974 a huge crowd gathered to witness the clock of the domed Sigismund Tower being started up again – the hands set exactly where they were stopped by the first Luftwaffe attack. A crucial symbol of independent nation-hood, the project was funded by personal donations from home and abroad, and hundreds of volunteers helped with the labour, which was completed in 1984. Though the structure is a replica, many of its furnishings are originals, scooted into hiding by percipient employees during the first bombing raids. Parallel with its tourist role these days, the castle regularly serves as a glorified reception hall for foreign dignitaries.

For now, **entry** is through the Senatorial Gate and a vaulted hallway; the early nineteenth-century **Kubicki gardens** running behind the palace down to the river, however, are coming out of a long restoration, and when the project is completed, set for late 2005, the entrance will be through the garden. Attached to the castle on the south side is the graceful **Pałac pod Blachą** (Tin-roofed Palace), one of the most beautiful buildings in Warsaw. Built in 1720, the palace was the home of Józef Poniatowski, nephew of the last king of Poland and a die-hard patriot who fought in the 1794 insurrection. There are plans to recon-struct his apartments, but for now the palace's interior holds the worthwhile Sahakian collection of oriental carpets (same hours as Route I; either ticket is valid for entrance).

Route I

Route I (coloured blue on maps; Mon 11am–4pm, Tues–Sat 10am–4pm; 10zł) takes you through the **Jagiellonian Rooms**, overlooking the river from the northeast wing. Originally part of the residence of eighteenth-century monarch Augustus III, they are adorned with portraits of the Jagiellonian royal families and some outstanding Flemish tapestries, including the ominously titled *Tragedy of the Jewish People*.

Next are the chambers where the Sejm (parliament) used to meet. Beyond the chancellery, which features more tapestries and portraits of the last dukes of Mazovia, comes the **Old Chamber of Deputies**, formerly the debating chamber. Democracy as practised here was something of a mixed blessing. On the one hand, the founding decree of the Polish Commonwealth, hammered out here in 1573, demonstrated an exceptionally tolerant attitude to religious differences; on the other, it was also here that the *liberum veto* – unanimity as a prerequisite for the passing of new laws – was established in 1652, marking the beginning of the end of effective government in Poland. Under this principle, a single cry of *nie pozwalam* – "I do not permit" – spelt the end of even the most sensible proposals. Arguably the Sejm's finest hour, however, came precisely at the moment when political developments threatened its – and the country's – very existence: the famous **Third of May Constitution**, passed here in 1791, being one of the radical highpoints of European constitutional history (see "Contexts", p.665). The painted pillars and heraldic emblems adorning the chamber are recently completed reconstructions of the original decorations by Baptista Quadro (of Poznań Town Hall fame – see p.592) in the Italianate style typical of much Polish architecture of the period.

The first route culminates in the **Matejko rooms** in the north wing, crammed with paintings by the doyen of nineteenth-century Polish painters, Jan Matejko. A romantic visionary consumed by a sense of patriotic mission, Matejko specialized in grandiose historical paintings commemorating key moments in Poland's past. *Rejtan* shows a bare-chested deputy blocking the path of a group of deputies preparing to accept the First Partition, imploring them to kill him rather than Poland, while *The Third of May Constitution* (see above) celebrates the moment of enlightenment in a similarly intense vein.

Route II

Route II (yellow on maps; Mon 11am–6pm, Tues–Sat 10am–6pm; 18zł) can only be visited in the company of an official guide – so you may have to wait for enough people (usually 25) to gather. Alternatively, it's possible to hire a guide in English (call ahead ☎022/657 2170; 70zł plus ticket price). This part takes you to the most lavish section of the castle, the **Royal Apartments** of King Stanisław August Poniatowski. Amid all the pomp and circumstance, it can be hard to remember that this is all a reconstruction of the eighteenth-century original – in this case, postwar architects had to rely on archival sources from Dresden to rebuild the rooms from scratch.

Through two smaller rooms you come eventually to the magnificent **Canaletto Room**, with its views of Warsaw by Bernardo Bellotto, a nephew of the famous Canaletto – whose name he appropriated to enhance his reputation. Marvellous in their detail, these cityscapes provided invaluable information for the architects involved in rebuilding the city after the war. Unfortunately, only a few of the paintings are currently on display, with the majority undergoing conservation work until 2006. Next door is the richly decorated **Royal Chapel**, designed and decorated by Domenico Merlini in the 1770s, where an urn contains the heart of Tadeusz Kościuszko, the swashbuckling leader of the 1794 insurrection, and hero of the American War of Independence (see box, p.428–429). Like many other rooms on this floor, the **Audience Chamber** has a beautiful parquet floor as well as several original furnishings. The four pictures on display here are by Bacciarelli, court painter to Stanisław August, and symbolize the cardinal virtues of Courage, Wisdom, Piety and Justice, while the room itself was again designed by Merlini, a good example of solid Polish Neoclassicism.

The **King's Bedroom**, another lavishly decorated set up, is followed by the **Study Room**, decorated with paintings by the last Polish king's court artists. Napoleon is supposed to have slept here during his short stay – apparently he had Stanisław's bed moved in here, not wishing to sleep in the bedroom occupied so recently by a deposed ruler.

From here you proceed through to the reception rooms, where the sumptuous **Marble Room** is dominated by portraits of the 22 Polish monarchs, including a much reproduced portrait of Stanisław August in his coronation robes. Highlight of the parade of royal splendour is the **Ballroom**, the largest room in the castle, with its dual-titled ceiling allegory by Bacciarelli, *The Dissolution of Chaos or The Apotheosis of the Genius of Poland*. Napoleon met the elite of Warsaw society here in 1806, the occasion on which he made his comments (legendary in Poland) about the beauty of Polish women – his mistress-to-be Countess Maria Walewska included, presumably.

North of the Zamek Królewski

Souvenir shops, bars and restaurants line **ulica Piwna** and **ulica Świętojańska**, the two narrow cobbled streets leading northwards from pl. Zamkowy. Both streets have churches worthy of a stop off. On ul. Piwna there's the fourteenth-century **Kościół św. Martina** (St Martin's Church), with a Baroque facade and completely modern interior. Among those buried here is Adam Jarzibski, king's musician and author of the first guide to Warsaw, written in verse. You should take the opportunity to nip down to **plac Kanonia** at this point (lodged behind ul. Jezuitska, just north of the castle), where the narrowest house in Warsaw puts even the equivalents in Amsterdam to shame.

On ul. Świętojańska is the entrance to **Archikatedra św. Jana** (St John's Cathedral), the main city church, an early fourteenth-century structure built in the Mazovian Gothic style on the site of an earlier wooden shrine. Some of the bitterest fighting of the 1944 Warsaw Uprising took place around here. German tanks entered the church after destroying its southern side, and you can see sections of their caterpillar tracks built into the wall along **ulica Dziekania**. The church standing today reflects the original Gothic style rather than the many alterations undertaken in later centuries.

Next to the cathedral is the **Kościół Jezuitski** (Jesuit Church), a popular shrine dedicated to Our Lady of Charity, the city's patron saint. Its high belfry is the tallest in the Stare Miasto area, standing out for miles around.

Rynek Starego Miasta and around

The compact Old Town Square, **Rynek Starego Miasta**, is one of the most remarkable bits of postwar reconstruction anywhere in Europe. Flattened during the Warsaw Uprising, the three-storey merchants' houses surrounding the square have been scrupulously rebuilt to their seventeenth- and eighteenth-century designs, multicoloured facades included. Natives of the city of Szczecin in western Poland (formerly Stettin in Germany) may have mixed feelings on beholding the main square, as it was reassembled in part using bricks taken from the city's historic quarter. By day the buzzing Rynek teems with visitors, who are catered for by buskers, artists, cafés, moneychangers and *doroski*, horse-drawn carts that clatter tourists around for a sizeable fee. Plumb in the centre are two nineteenth-century pumps; for years the only creatures capable of stomaching their water were the horses, but now, following the installation of a filter system, the one that works is a good alternative to the overpriced drinks in the square's cafés.

The **Muzeum Historyczne Starej Warszawy** (Warsaw Historical Museum; Tues & Thurs 11am–6pm, Wed & Fri 10am–3.30pm, Sat & Sun 10.30am–4.30pm; 5zł, free on Sun) takes up a large part of Strona Dekerta, the north side of the square; entrance is through a house called the Pod Murzynkiem ("Under the Negro"), a reference to the inn sign that used to hang above the doorway.

Adam Mickiewicz (1789–1855)

If one person can be said to personify the Polish literary Romantic tradition it is **Adam Mickiewicz**. A passionate, mystically inclined writer, Mickiewicz's unabashedly patriotic writings have served as a central literary (and, in times of crisis, political) reference point for generations of Poles. Quotations from and references to Mickiewicz's considerable volume of writings litter subsequent Polish literature and politics – even the avowedly unacademic Lech Wałęsa has been known to quote the national epic poem, *Pan Tadeusz* – and performances of his plays are still among the most popular in the country. More controversially, there's a muted discussion of the man's "ethnic" origins, with several scholars now claiming that at least one of Mickiewicz's parents was **Jewish**, a view that might go some way, it is argued, to accounting for the sympathetic portrayal of Jews – notably the musical innkeeper, Jankiel – in a work like *Pan Tadeusz*. Despite the fact that the best of Mickiewicz's writings rank among the finest outpourings of Romanticism, he's still relatively unknown in the West, a situation not helped by the general lack of decent, readily available translations of his works.

Born in Lithuania of an impoverished Polish *szlachta* (gentry) family, Mickiewicz studied at **Vilnius University** where, like many of his generation, he was drawn into conspiratorial anti-Russian plotting. Already a budding writer (*Poezje*, his first collection of ballads and romances based on Lithuanian folklore, appeared in 1822), Mickiewicz was arrested along with fellow members of a secret student organization on suspicion of "spreading Polish nationalism" and was deported to Russia in 1823, where he remained, mostly in **Moscow**, for the rest of the decade, befriending – and sometimes quarrelling with – Russian writers such as Pushkin. Notable works of this period include *Dziady* ("Forefather's Eve"), the innovative patriotic drama whose Warsaw performance in spring 1968 sparked student protests, and *Konrad Wallenrod*, an epic poem depicting the medieval struggle between Teutonic Knights and Lithuanians, in reality an allegory of the age-old Polish–German conflict.

Following the failure of the **November 1830 uprising**, Mickiewicz moved in exile to **Paris**, like many Polish intellectuals, and quickly immersed himself in émigré politics. It was here too that he wrote *Pan Tadeusz* (1834), his greatest work. Modelled on the novels of Walter Scott, it is a masterful, richly lyrical depiction of traditional gentry life in his native Polish–Lithuanian homeland, a region dear to many Polish writers – Miłosz and Konwicki are two contemporary examples – both for its outstanding natural beauty and powerful historical associations.

The remaining years of Mickiewicz's life read like a litany of personal and political disappointments. Appointed to a professorship in Lausanne in 1839, he resigned the following year to teach Slavonic literature at the Collège de France. With the outbreak of the **1848 revolutions** in central Europe, the "Springtime of the Nations" that briefly appeared to herald a new dawn for the oppressed nations of the region, Mickiewicz travelled to Rome to try and persuade the new pope, Pius IX, to come out in support of the cause of Polish independence. Later the impassioned Mickiewicz also organized a small Polish military unit to fight with Garibaldi's forces – the nucleus, he hoped, of a future Polish national liberation army – and assumed editorship of the radical agitprop newspaper *Tribune des Peuples* ("Tribune of the Peoples"), a move which led to dismissal from his tenure at the Collège de France by Napoleon III.

The writer's life came abruptly to an end in 1855 when Prince Adam Czartoryski, a leader of the Paris exile community, sent Mickiewicz on a mission to Turkey to try and resolve the factional quarrels bedevilling the Polish military forces that had volunteered to fight against Russia in the approaching Crimean War; having contracted typhus soon after his arrival, Mickiewicz died in November 1855 in **Istanbul**, and is commemorated in a museum there. He was already a national hero of almost mythic proportions, and his remains were eventually brought back to Poland and placed in the crypt of Kraków's cathedral on Wawel Hill.

Exhibitions here cover every aspect of Warsaw's life from its beginnings to the present day, crammed tightly into a warren of rooms on three floors – there are excellent views over the parasol-crowded Rynek from the upper storeys. The early history of the city is told in a didactic words-and-pictures style (in Polish), but things improve with an evocative display of old photographs, theatre posters and fashion magazines, and there's a particularly moving chronicle of everyday resistance to the Nazis – an uplifting complement to the wartime horrors documented in the film shown in the cinema at the entrance (English version plays Tues–Sat at noon).

On the square's east side, Strona Barssa, the **Muzeum Mickiewicza** (Mickiewicz Museum; Mon, Tues & Fri 10am–3pm, Wed & Thurs 11am–6pm, Sun 11am–5pm, closed one varying Sun every month; 5zł, free Sun) is a temple to the national Romantic poet, with a stack of first editions, contemporary newspapers and family memorabilia, as well as temporary exhibitions devoted to other Polish authors.

The west side of the Rynek, **Strona Hugo-Kołłątaja**, named after the co-author of the 1791 Constitution, features a number of fine reconstructed residences, notably the Dom Fukiera (Fukier House) at no. 27, longtime home of one of the city's best-known *winiarnia* (wine cellar; see "Restaurants" p.129) and still going strong, and the Klucznikowska mansion at no. 21, which has a carefully reconstructed Gothic doorway.

West of the Rynek, the narrow cobbled streets and alleyways bring you out to a long section of the old **city walls**, split-level fortifications with ramparts, rebuilt watchtowers and apple trees lining their grassy approaches. Along Podwale, the open path surrounding the walls and a favourite with evening strollers, an array of plaques commemorates foreigners who supported the Polish cause, including the French poet Alfred de Vigny. Here, as in many places around the city, the fresh flowers laid on the ground mark places where the Nazis carried out wartime executions. The most poignant of the memorials, however, is the **Mały Powstaniec** (Little Insurgent), a bronze figure of a small boy with an oversized helmet carrying an automatic rifle – a solitary figure commemorating the children and young people killed fighting in the Warsaw Uprising, personifying all that was heroic and tragic in the city's resistance to the Nazis (see box, pp.104–105). During term-time it is usually thronged by schoolchildren on class outings.

From the Rynek, **ulica Nowomiejska** runs north towards the sixteenth-century **Barbakan**, 200m beyond, which formerly guarded the Nowomiejska Gate, the northern entrance to the city. The fortress is part of the Stare Miasto defences, running all the way round from pl. Zamkowy to the northeastern edge of the district. In summer, the Barbakan attracts street artists, buskers and hawkers of kitsch souvenirs. Walk east along the walls to the Marshal's Tower, and you have a good view over the river to the Praga district (see p.127). Conversely, some of the best views of Stare Miasto itself are from the **Praga waterfront**: take any tram over Most Śląsko-Dąbrowski, the bridge immediately south of Stare Miasto, get off at the first stop and cross into **Praski Park**, then down to the riverbank.

The Nowe Miasto

Across the ramparts from the Barbakan is the **Nowe Miasto** (New Town) district, which, despite its name, dates from the early fifteenth century, although it wasn't formally joined to Warsaw until the end of the eighteenth. At that time, the wooden buildings of the artisan settlement were replaced by brick houses, and it's in this style that the area has been rebuilt.

Along ulica Freta to the Rynek Nowego Miasta

From the Barbakan, **ulica Freta** – the continuation of ul. Nowomiejska – runs north through the heart of the Nowe Miasto. On the right is **Kościół św. Jacka** (St Jacek's Church), a Dominican foundation, which is an effective blend of Renaissance and early Baroque. The adjoining monastery, the largest in Warsaw, was a field hospital and was heavily bombed as a consequence; hundreds died here when the Nazis regained control in October 1944. Today there's a pleasant café in the church belltower, while the **Asian Gallery**, across the street at no. 5 (Galeria Aziatycka; Tues & Fri–Sun 1–7pm, Wed & Thurs 11am–5pm; 5zł) holds changing exhibitions of Asian and Pacific art. For a

Marie Curie (1867–1934)

One of many Poles to rise to fame abroad rather than at home, the Nobel Prize-winning scientist **Marie Curie** (née **Maria Skłodowska**) was born during the Partition era into a scientifically oriented Warsaw family. The young Maria showed academic promise from the start, and after completing her secondary education at the city's Russian lyceum, Curie travelled to Paris in early 1890 to follow the lectures of the prominent French physicists of the day at the Sorbonne.

The intellectually voracious Curie threw herself into the Parisian scientific milieu, landing a job in the laboratory of the noted physicist Gabriel Lipmann and meeting fellow researcher Pierre Curie, whom she married in 1895. Thus began a partnership that was to result in a number of spectacular scientific achievements, first the discovery of **polonium** – so named in honour of her native country – in summer 1898, and soon afterwards, **radium**. Following her colleague Henri Becquerel's discovery of the phenomenon she eventually dubbed "radioactivity", Curie set to work on systematic research into the revolutionary new wonder, which eventually gained worldwide recognition in the **Nobel Prize for Physics** which she, Pierre Curie and Becquerel were awarded jointly in 1903. Pierre's sudden death in 1906 was a heavy emotional blow, but led to Curie's appointment to his professorship, making her the first woman ever to teach at the Sorbonne. A **second Nobel Prize**, this time in chemistry, came in 1911 for the isolation of pure radium.

Despite the upheavals of World War I, with the assistance of one of her two daughters Curie worked on developing the use of **X-rays** and was a prime mover in the founding of the famous **Institut de Radium** in 1918, which rapidly developed into a worldwide centre for chemistry and nuclear physics. By now known internationally, and deeply committed to developing the medical applications of the new radiological science, Curie and her daughters visited the US in 1921, receiving a symbolic gram of prized radium from the president, Warren G. Harding, in the course of the visit. During the rest of the 1920s Curie travelled and lectured widely, founding her own **Curie Foundation** in Paris and eventually realizing a long-standing ambition, the setting up of a Radium Institute in her native Warsaw in 1932, to which her sister Bronia was appointed director. Constant exposure to radiation began to have its effect, however, and in early 1934 it was discovered that Curie had **leukaemia**, of which she died later that year. The scientific community in particular mourned the loss of one of its outstanding figures, a woman whose research into the effects of radioactivity pioneered both its medical and research-oriented applications, simultaneously paving the way for subsequent developments in nuclear physics.

time, the German Romantic writer E.T.A. Hoffmann lived at ul. Freta no. 5, and no. 16 was the birthplace of one of Poland's most famous women, **Marie Skłodowska-Curie**, the double Nobel Prize-winning discoverer of radium (see box, p.101). Inside there's a small but fascinating **museum** (Tues–Sat 10am–4pm, Sun 10am–3pm; 6zł) dedicated to her life and work, where photographs of her with other scientists are reminders of the male preserve she managed to break into.

Ul. Freta leads to the **Rynek Nowego Miasta** (New Town Square) – once the commercial hub of the district. Surrounded by elegantly reconstructed eighteenth-century facades, this pleasant square makes a soothing change from the bustle of Stare Miasto. Tucked into the eastern corner is the **Kościół Sakramentek** (Church of the Holy Sacrament), commissioned by Queen Maria Sobieska in memory of her husband Jan's victory over the Turks at Vienna in 1683 (see "Contexts", p.664); as you might expect, the highlight of the calm, white interior is the Sobieski funeral chapel. The architect of the church, Tylman of Gameren, was the most important figure in the rebuilding of Warsaw after the destruction of the Swedish wars in the 1660s. Invited to Poland from Utrecht by Count Jerzy Lubomirski, he went on to redesign what seems like half the city in his distinctive, rather austere Palladian style. Photographs of the church in its ruined postwar state hang in a side chapel.

Just off the northern edge of the square, the early fifteenth-century **Kościół Mariacki** or **N.M.P.** (Church of the Virgin Mary), one of the oldest churches in Warsaw and once the Nowe Miasto parish church, has retained something of its Gothic character despite later remodellings. The adjoining belfry is a Nowe Miasto landmark, easily identifiable from the other side of the river. Staggered rows of benches provide a wonderful viewing point across the water.

Plac Krasińskich

The streets west of the square lead past ul. Bonifraterska toward the Muranów district (see p.106). Heading south on ul. Bonifraterska brings you to the large **plac Krasińskich**, augmented by one of Warsaw's several **Uprising monuments**, this one a controversial piece commissioned by the communist authorities and viewed with mixed feelings by many Varsovians. Now dwarfed by the glass and concrete monstrosity built to house the National Court, the monument was built on the spot where AK (Home Army) battalions launched their assault on the Nazis on August 1, 1944. The large metal sculpture depicts AK insurgents surfacing from manholes on to the street to begin their attack on the Germans, as well as their final forlorn retreat into the sewers of the city. Just beyond the monument, on the corner of ul. Długa, is the **Union of Warsaw Insurgents Museum** (Mon–Thurs 11am–4pm; free), a one-room display arranged by surviving combatants from the Uprising, with black-and-white photos and a scale model of the main battleground.

Immediately opposite the Uprising monument is the **Kościół Garnizonowy** (Garrison Church), the soldiers' main place of worship, with the key Uprising symbol, a large anchor, and a tablet on the facade with a roll call of World War II battles in which Polish units participated. Overlooking the west side of the square is the huge and majestic **Pałac Krasińskich** (Krasiński Palace), built for regional governor Jan Krasiński by Tylman of Gameren, its facade bearing fine sculptures by Andreas Schlüter. As a branch of the National Library, most of the palace's documents – forty thousand in all – were destroyed in the war, so today's collection comes from a whole host of sources. Theoretically the building is only open to official visitors, but enquiries at the door should get you in to see at least some of the library. The interior is splendid, the Neoclassical decorations being restored versions of the designs executed by Merlini in the 1780s. Behind the palace are **gardens**, now a public park, and beyond that the ghetto area. If you've got the stomach for it you could visit the **Muzeum Pawiaka** (Pawiak Prison Museum; Wed 9am–5pm, Thurs & Sat 9am–4pm, Fri 10am–5pm, Sun 10am–4pm; free), ten minutes' walk west at ul. Dzielna 24/26, which tells the grim story of Warsaw's most notorious prison from tsarist times to the Nazi occupation.

Ulica Długa and around

Back on pl. Krasińskich, at the corner of **ulica Długa** and ul. Miodowa, is a small streetside **plaque**, one of the least conspicuous yet most poignant memorials in the city. It commemorates the thousands of half-starved Varsovians who attempted to escape from the besieged Stare Miasto through the sewer network during the Warsaw Uprising. Many drowned in the filthy passageways, were killed by grenades thrown into the tunnels, or were shot upon emerging, but a hundred or so did make it to freedom. The bitter saga was the subject of Andrzej Wajda's film *Kanał*, the second in his brilliant war trilogy. The first film, *A Generation*, was also about the Uprising; the last, *Ashes and Diamonds*, is an adaptation of Jerzy Andrzejewski's thrilling novel of the postwar chaos and communist takeover (see "Books", p.699). Made during the cultural thaw that followed Gomułka's rise to power in 1956, all three are available on video and DVD with English subtitles.

A number of old patrician residences can be seen west along ul. Długa, which leads to the **Muzeum Archeologiczne** (Archeological Museum; Mon–Thurs 9am–4pm, Fri 11am–6pm, Sun 10am–4pm, closed third Sun every month; 8zł, Sun free), housed in the seventeenth-century arsenal. Starting with Neolithic, Paleolithic and Bronze Age sites, the museum continues through to early medieval Polish settlements, the highlight being a reconstruction of the early Slav settlements in Wielkopolska and records of other excavations from around the country, notably the Jacwingian cemetery site at Jegleniec near Suwałki (see p.255).

A little way east from the museum, at 62 al. Solidarności, on the traffic island, is the **Muzeum Niepodległości** (Museum of Independence; Tues–Fri 10am–5pm, Sat & Sun 10am–4pm; 5zł, Sun free), in a charming old Neoclassical pile. The museum, popular with elderly Poles, features changing displays on the theme of the national struggle for independence, generally with interesting old photographs.

Ulica Miodowa and around

South from pl. Krasińskich, along **ulica Miodowa**, you find yourself in the heart of aristocratic old Warsaw. The palaces lining Miodowa mainly date from the prosperous pre-Partition era, when this section of the city hummed with the life of European high society. Next door to the **Pałac Borchów** (Borch Palace) – now the residence of the Catholic Primate, Cardinal Glemp – stands the **Pałac Radziwiłłów** (Radziwiłł Palace), designed by Tylman of Gameren, and adjoined by the later **Pałac Paca** (Pac Palace; the resulting agglomeration is sometimes known as the Pac-Radziwiłł Palace), with its distinctive frieze-topped entrance. Across the street is the Basilan church and monastery, the city's only Greek Catholic (Uniate) church, designed with an octagonal interior by Merlini in the 1780s.

The 1944 Warsaw Uprising

Of the many acts of resistance to the savage Nazi occupation of Poland, the **1944 Warsaw Uprising** was the biggest. Over sixty years on, the heroic, yet ultimately tragic, events of the autumn of 1944 remain firmly lodged in the national memory, at once a piece of history whose interpretation remains controversial, and a potent source of national self-definition.

The immediate circumstances of the Uprising were dramatic. With Nazi forces reeling under the impact of the determined push west launched by the Red Army in mid-1944, a German withdrawal from Warsaw began to seem a possibility. The **Armia Krajowa** (Polish Home Army) or AK as they were commonly known, the largest of the Polish resistance forces (indeed, with over 400,000 soldiers, the largest resistance force anywhere in Europe) were thereby confronted by an agonizing dilemma. On one side, they were being strongly urged by the Allies to cooperate actively with advancing Soviet forces in driving back the Nazis. On the other, news of the treatment being meted out to AK units in areas of eastern Poland already liberated by the Red Army served to confirm the long-held suspicion that there was little, if any, room for the AK or its political backing – the Polish government-in-exile in London – in the Soviet scheme of things to come, a fact chillingly symbolized in news of the Soviet detention of AK units in the ex-Nazi concentration camp at Majdanek.

Throughout the second half of July, AK Commander **Tadeusz Komorowski**, known as **Bór**, hesitated over which course of action to take. With the arrival of the first Soviet tanks across the Wisła in the Praga district, the decision to launch a single-handed attack on the Germans was taken and, on August 1, the main Warsaw AK corps of around 50,000 poorly armed troops sprang an assault on the city centre. For the first few days the element of surprise meant AK forces were able to capture large tracts of the city centre. By August 5, however, the tide was already beginning to turn against them. Supported by dive bombers and hastily drafted reinforcements, Nazi troops under the command of ruthless General von dem Bach-Zelewski began the task of clearing out the insurgents. Partisans and civilians alike were treated as legitimate targets for reprisals by the fearsome collection of SS and Wehrmacht units – including three battalions of half-starved Soviet POWs, an "anti-partisan" brigade made up of pardoned criminals and the notorious RONA Red Army deserters brigade – assembled for the task. The Nazi recapture of the **Wola district**, the first to be retaken on August 11, was followed by the massacre of over 8000 civilians. Even worse followed in **Ochota**, where over 40,000 more civilians were murdered. Hospitals were burned to the ground with all their staff and patients; during the initial attack, women and children were tied to the front of German tanks to deter ambushes, and rows of civilians were marched in front of infantry units to ward off AK snipers.

With German troops and tanks systematically driving the beleaguered partisans into an ever diminishing pocket of the city centre, the decision was made to abandon the by now devastated Stare Miasto. On September 2, around 1500 of the surviving AK troops, along with over 500 other wounded, headed down into the city sewers through a single manhole near pl. Krasiński – an event imprinted firmly on the national consciousness as much thanks to Wajda's legendary film *Kanał*, a stirring 1950s rendition of the Uprising, as to its symbolic depiction in the contemporary Warsaw Uprising monument. Fighting continued for another month in the suburbs and

A few steps down ul. Miodowa to the southwest is the late seventeenth-century **Kościół Kapucyński** (Capuchin Church) repository of the heart of Jan Sobieski, while off to the left, at the bottom of ul. Kapitulna on ul. Podwale, the **Pomnik Jana Kilińskiego** (Jan Kiliński Monument) commemorates another stirring figure in the country's history. During the 1794 insurrection, it was the shoemaker Kiliński who led the citizens of pockets of the city centre until October 2, when General Bór and his troops finally surrendered to the Germans, 63 days after fighting had begun. Heavy AK casualties – around 20,000 dead – were overshadowed by the huge losses sustained by the city's civilian population, with over 225,000 killed during the fighting.

With the AK and eventually almost the entire population of Warsaw out of the way, Nazi demolition squads set about the task of fulfilling an enraged Hitler's order to wipe the city off the face of the map, dynamiting and razing building after building until the city centre had to all intents and purposes ceased to exist, as confirmed in the photos taken when the Soviets arrived in January 1945.

Of the many controversial aspects of the Uprising, the most explosive, in Polish eyes at least, remains that of the **Soviet role**. Could the Red Army have intervened decisively to assist or save the Uprising from defeat? Throughout the postwar years, the official Soviet line combined the arguable claim that the Uprising was a mistimed and strategically flawed diversion from the goal of driving the Germans west in 1944 with absurd ideological denigrations of the AK as reactionary, anti-Soviet nationalists whose actions were a betrayal of the anti-Nazi cause. Certainly the lack of Soviet action during August 1944 was fertile ground for subsequent Polish misgivings about Stalin's real intentions. The Soviet tanks that had reached Praga, for example, sat idly by throughout September 1944 as the Germans pounded the city across the river. Equally significantly, on several occasions the Soviet authorities refused Allied access to Soviet airbases for airlifts of supplies to the beleaguered insurgents, and the secret telegram correspondence between Stalin, Roosevelt and Churchill at the time reveals a Stalin contemptuous of the whole operation, arguing on one occasion that sooner or later "the truth about the handful of criminals who started the Warsaw disturbance to take over power will become known to all".

The essence of the Polish interpretation of all this was that Stalin had simply allowed the Germans to do what his future plans for Poland would have anyway necessitated – systematically to annihilate of the sections of Polish society that formed the core of the AK forces with their uncompromising commitment to a free, independent postwar Poland. With sentiments like these around, it's not surprising that the Warsaw Uprising has remained an area of disagreement in Polish–Russian relations.

Tensions surfaced visibly during the solemn **fiftieth anniversary commemorations** of the start of the Uprising, held in the city throughout August 1994. In a move widely criticized in Poland, particularly among older sections of Polish society, President Wałęsa invited his Russian and German counterparts to participate at the opening ceremony held in Warsaw on August 1. While the German President **Roman Herzog** accepted the invitation (reportedly under the mistaken impression that the 1943 Ghetto Uprising was being commemorated) and made a speech asking Polish forgiveness for the country's treatment at the hands of the Nazis, Russian President **Boris Yeltsin** declined the invitation, sending a lower-level aide instead, giving rise to the wry popular quip that the Russians had accepted the invitation but decided to stay in Praga instead. The **sixtieth anniversary** in 2004 was celebrated with less controversy but even more avidly, and saw the release of the new history of the Uprising by Norman Davies (published simultaneously in English and Polish; see "Books", p.694) and the opening of the new Uprising Museum (see p.109).

Warsaw in their assault on the tsarist ambassador's residence on this street. His special place in local consciousness was amply demonstrated during World War II after the Nazi governor took down the uncomfortably defiant-looking monument and locked it up in the Muzeum Narodowe – the next day this message was scrawled on the museum wall: "People of Warsaw, here I am! Jan Kiliński."

Muranów and Mirów

Like Lublin, Białystok and Kraków, Warsaw was for centuries one of the great Jewish centres of Poland. In 1939 there were an estimated 380,000 Jews living here, one-third of the city's total population. By May 1945, around 300 were left. Most of **Jewish** Warsaw was destroyed after the Ghetto Uprising (see box opposite), to be replaced by the sprawling housing estates and tree-lined thoroughfares of the **Muranów** and **Mirów** districts, a little to the west of the city centre. However, a few traces of the Jewish presence in Warsaw do remain, along with a growing number of newly erected monuments to the notable personalities of the city's historic Jewish community. Equally important, there's a small but increasingly visible Jewish community here – well supported by its exiled diaspora. Today, Mirów is also the home to the new **Warsaw Uprising Museum**.

Virtually all the Jewish monuments and memorials you will find here are enclosed within the confines of the wartime ghetto area, sealed off from the city's "Aryan" population by the Nazis in November 1940. Warsaw Jews actually lived in a considerably larger part of the city before World War II. Following the wholesale obliteration of the area both during and after the 1943 Ghetto Uprising, streets like ul. Grzybowska, the centre of Jewish life in Isaac Bashevis Singer's panoramic Warsaw novel *The Family Moskat* (see "Books", p.701), lack even the slightest resemblance to their former selves. Other streets changed their name or course, or simply disappeared altogether after the war, making it difficult to gain an impression of what the ghetto area looked like.

The Nożyk Synagogue

First stop on any itinerary of Jewish Warsaw is the **Nożyk Synagogue**, a stately ochre structure hidden behind a white office block on ul. Twarda, the only one of the ghetto's three synagogues still standing. The majestic Great Synagogue on ul. Tłomackie – which held up to three thousand people – was blown up by the Nazis and, in a gesture of crass insensitivity, the Polish authorities decided to build a flashy skyscraper on the site, now the Peugeot building.

The Nożyk, a more modest affair built in the early 1900s, was used as a stable, a food store and then gutted during the war, reopening in 1983 after a complete restoration. To see the refined interior you have to ring the buzzer on the opposite side of the building from the main entrance (Mon–Fri 11am–7pm; 5zł). The **Jewish Theatre**, just east of the synagogue on pl. Grzybowski, continues the theatrical and musical traditions of the ghetto.

Before you leave the area, walk across pl. Grzybowski to **ulica Próżna**. This street has somehow survived the ravages of war and reconstruction, and stands scaffolded but surviving as a testimony to prewar red-bricked Warsaw.

The Warsaw Ghetto and the Ghetto Uprising

In 1940, on the order of Ludwig Fisher, the governor of the Warsaw district, 450,000 Jews from Warsaw and the surrounding area were sealed behind the walls of the Nazi-designated ghetto area, creating the largest **ghetto** in Nazi-occupied Europe. By 1941, nearly one and a half million Jews from all over Poland had been crammed into this unsanitary zone, with starvation and epidemics the predictable and intended consequence. By mid-1942, nearly a quarter of the ghetto population had died, a plight communicated to the Allied command by a series of searingly forthright reports from the budding Polish underground.

Deportations to the death camps from Umschlagplatz began in summer 1942, with 250,000 or more taken to Treblinka by mid-September. After further mass round-ups, the Nazis moved in to "clean out" the ghetto in January 1943, by which time there were only 60,000 people left. Sporadic resistance forced them to retreat, but only until April, when a full-scale Nazi assault provoked the **Ghetto Uprising** under the leadership of the Jewish Combat Organization (ŻOB). For nearly a month, Jewish partisans battled against overwhelming Nazi firepower, before ŻOB's bunker headquarters, on the corner of ul. Miła and ul. Zamenhofa, was finally surrounded and breached on May 9, following the suicide of the legendary Mordechai Anieliewicz and his entire staff. A few combatants survived and escaped to join up with the Polish resistance in the "Aryan" sector of the city, as did the pianist Władysław Szpilman, subject of Roman Polański's recent Oscar-winning movie. Of those remaining in the ghetto, 7000 were shot immediately, the rest dispatched to the camps. On May 15, Jürgen Stroop, commander-in-chief of the German forces, reported to Himmler, "The Jewish quarter in Warsaw no longer exists."

The Ghetto Uprising has remained a potent symbol both of the plight of Jews under Nazi tyranny and – contrary to the dominant received images – of the absolute will to resist under conditions of systematic terror manifested by a small but significant minority of the Jewish community. The dual nature of the Uprising's legacy was amply attested to in the fiftieth anniversary commemorations held in Warsaw in May 1993, attended by a broad assembly of Jewish and Gentile dignitaries from around the world. including a handful of survivors of the Uprising, notably Marek Edelman, the only ŻOB commander still alive today.

Plac Bohaterów Getta and the Path of Remembrance

Fifteen minutes' walk north of the synagogue is the **Pomnik Bohaterów Getta** (Ghetto Heroes Monument), actually built from blocks ordered from Sweden by Hitler in 1942 to construct a monument to the Third Reich's anticipated victory. Unveiled in 1948 on the fifth anniversary of the Ghetto Uprising, the stark monument recalls both the immense courage of the Jewish resistance and the helplessness of the deportees to moving effect. Once at the heart of the ghetto area, the pl. Bohaterów Getta itself is a wide-open green expanse surrounded by drab apartment buildings, with only the occasional rubble-filled bump disturbing the surface to remind you of the ghetto that used to be there. Plans to build a major new museum complex dedicated to the history of Polish Jewry in the nearby district were announced in spring 1995 but have yet to come to anything.

The decline of communism enabled local Jewish groups to commemorate their history actively in a way that had been officially discouraged before, and beginning in the late 1980s a series of memorial plaques known as the **Path of Remembrance** was laid out, starting from pl. Bohaterów Getta, then north along ul. Zamenhofa and up to the Umschlagplatz on ul. Stawki. The plaques, nineteen simple granite blocks engraved in Polish and Hebrew, honour important individuals and events of the ghetto. Along the way the route takes you past the grass-covered memorial mound covering the site of the **ŻOB Bunker** at ul. Miła 18 (see box, p.107) – the mound's height representing the level of rubble left after the area's destruction. In many of the surrounding streets you'll find houses built on a similar level, as the postwar communist authorities simply went ahead and constructed new housing blocks on the flattened remains of the ghetto. Continuing on up ul. Zamenhofa soon brings you to the junction with ul. Stawki.

A short walk west on the edge of a housing estate is the **Umschlagplatz**, where Jews were loaded onto cattle wagons bound for Treblinka and the other death camps. The simple white marble monument standing here, raised in the late 1980s and designed to resemble the cattle trucks used in the transportations, is covered inside with a list of four hundred Jewish first names, the way chosen to symbolize the estimated 300,000 Jews deported from here to the death camps. A stone stands at the exact point from which the trains departed, while across the road, one of the few surviving prewar buildings (no. 5/7) was the house of the SS commander supervising operations at the Umschlagplatz. It now houses a university psychology department.

The Cmentarz Żydowski and the Korczak orphanage

West along ul. Stawki and down ul. Okopowa (about fifteen minutes' walk in all, or take tram #22 west from Warszawa Centralna, or bus #175 north along Krakowskie Przedmieście), the large **Cmentarz Żydowski** (Jewish Cemetery; Mon–Thurs 10am–5pm, Fri 9am–1pm, Sun 9am–4pm, closed Sat; 4zł; men should cover their heads – skullcaps are provided) established in 1806, contains the graves of more than 250,000 people, and is one of the very few Jewish cemeteries still in use in Poland today. This site was left almost untouched during the war, the reason being that, unlike in smaller Polish towns, the Nazis didn't need the materials for building new roads. The tombs range from colossal Gothic follies to simple engraved stones.

Scattered among the plots are the graves of eminent Polish Jews like **Ludwig Zamenhof**, the inventor of Esperanto (see p.265), early socialist activist **Stanisław Mendelson** and writer **D.H. Nomberg**. Also worth seeking out is a powerful sculpted monument to Janusz Korczak (see below), erected in his honour in the 1980s. The caretaker at the entrance lodge has detailed guidebooks to the tombstones for anyone wanting to know more (information is also available from the Jewish Historical Institute and the Our Roots Foundation offices; see box, p.106).

From the cemetery entrance, a twenty-minute walk south down ul. Towarowa and then west along ul. Jaktorowska brings you to the site of the prewar **orphanage** set up by **Janusz Korczak**, the focus of one of Andrzej Wajda's better films of the 1990s, *Korczak*. Set back from the road and still functioning as an orphanage, the original building, which survived the war, has a Korczak memorial plaque on the outside and a monument to him in the main hall. The caretaker will let you have a look inside, and there's also a small selection of souvenirs on sale at the reception. Most powerful of all, though, is the simple statue of Korczak in front of the building – here at least, the city's Jewish past has been done justice.

The Warsaw Uprising Museum

In the southern reaches of Mirów, a few blocks south of the orphanage at ul. Przy-okopowa 28, a century-old former tramway power station has been converted into the new **Warsaw Uprising Museum** (Ⓦ www.1944.pl). Coming from the train station, take tram #12, #22 or #24 west to "Grzybowska". An Uprising museum, for decades a political impossibility due to the light in which it would by necessity shed the Soviet Union's role, had at least been in planning stages since 1981, but various financial and logistical difficulties prevented anything concrete happening until the site of today's museum was chosen in 2002. Two years later, the building was opened to the public, incomplete but with great fanfare, for the sixtieth anniversary of the Uprising in August 2004.

The centrepiece of the collection is a series of **photographs** by former PE teacher, Olympic javelin thrower and Polish officer **Eugeniusz Lokajski**, who after being taken prisoner in 1939 by the Soviet army escaped to Nazi-occupied Warsaw and opened a photography studio. He remained in the city throughout the occupation, commanded a platoon in the Uprising and died in a house on Marszałkowska in September 1944, leaving a legacy of over one thousand photos depicting everyday life both before and during the Uprising. Other exhibits focus on the role – or lack of one – played by Soviet and Allied forces at the time, while there's also a reconstruction of part of the sewer system through which combatants fled the destroyed city (see box, p.104). Outside is a new park with a 156-metre wall inscribed with the names of several thousands soldiers who died in the struggle.

The Muzeum Żydowskiego Instytutu Historycznego and the Ghetto Wall

The **Muzeum Żydowskiego Instytutu Historycznego** (Jewish Historical Institute), near the site of the former Great Synagogue at ul. Tłomackie 3/5, stands on the site of the prewar Judaic Library, and is part museum (Mon–Wed & Fri 9am–4pm, Thurs 11am–6pm; 10zł; Ⓦ www.jhi.pl), part library and research archive. The first section of the museum details life in the wartime ghetto, a fasci-nating and moving corrective to the familiar images of passive victims; the rest is devoted to ritual objects (some displayed in a re-created synagogue interior), folk art and secular paintings. The library includes a large collection of books rescued from Lublin at the outset of World War II and documents of Jewish life in Poland going back to the seventeenth century, along with an extensive collection of over thirty thousand photos. There's also a small bookshop at the entrance, where you might be able to find the invaluable *Guide to Jewish Warsaw* (12zł).

Finally, make your way downtown to ul. Złota at the southern edge of the wartime ghetto area. Wedged between ul. Sienna 55/59 and ul. Złota 62 are two of the few surviving fragments of the three-metre-high wartime **ghetto wall** (to reach it enter the courtyard from ul. Złota 62; if the gate is locked ring the buzzer of apartment #24 or #38 and say you're a tourist). Tucked away in a large court-yard between communist-era blocks of flats, the two short sections of brick wall stand as a poignant testimony to the rude separation of the ghetto – so close, and yet so far from life (and death) on the other side. The isolation was never absolute – post and phone communication with the Aryan sector continued long into the Nazi occupation, and food was continually smuggled into the starving ghetto, despite the threat of instant execution for anyone, Pole or Jew, caught doing so. In the first section a small commemorative plaque records former Israeli president Chaim Herzog's official unveiling of the monument in 1992, along with a helpful map showing you just how much of Warsaw the ghetto covered. At the second section, further north in the courtyard, another plaque records the removal of two bricks from the wall to the Holocaust Museum in Washington, DC.

Śródmieście

Śródmieście, the large area that stretches from the Stare Miasto down towards Park Łazienkowski, is the increasingly fast-paced heart of Warsaw. However, in keeping with the Polish spirit of reverence for the past, the sector immediately below the Stare Miasto contains an impressive number of reconstructed palaces, parks, churches and museums, all contributing to the distinctive atmosphere of faded grandeur spruced up. The broad boulevard known as **Krakowskie Przedmieście** (which becomes **Nowy Świat** in its southerly reaches) is the main artery of the Śródmieście, a popular promenading route lined with cafés, boutiques and private galleries. To the west, the brash shopfronts, office blocks and fast-food stands around **ul. Marszałkowska** are overshadowed by the looming form of the **Pałac Kultury i Nauki**, an architectural monument to Stalinist megalomania. Further west still, beyond the Warszawa Centralna train station, a modest collection of post-communist **skyscrapers** epitomizes the changing face of Warsaw city life. The broad expanse of **aleja Jerozolimskie**, a chaotic strip of trams and traffic, cuts a wide swath through the centre of this area, running west to east just below the Pałac Kultury i Nauki and providing access to the impressive collections of the **Muzeum Narodowe**.

Plac Teatralny and around

Running west from pl. Zamkowy is ul. Senatorska, once one of Warsaw's smartest shopping streets, now studded with wall plaques recording the civilian victims of Nazi street executions. The pseudo-classical giant dominating the nearby **plac Teatralny** is the **Teatr Wielki** (Grand Theatre), Warsaw's main venue for serious drama, opera and ballet. Dating from the 1820s, it boasts a fine classicist facade decorated with Greek sculptures. Rebuilt and enlarged after wartime destruction, the main theatre now holds almost two thousand people. Inside, the elegant entrance hall has a sumptuous rotunda overhead and an intricate parquet floor – worth a look even if you're not planning to attend one of the lavish productions staged here (see "Nightlife and entertainment", p.136).

The north side of pl. Teatralny looks fantastic, having just come out of a major facelift. Citibank hides its business concerns behind the facade of the Neoclassical **Pałac Jabłońskich** (Jabłoński Palace), city hall from 1817 until World War II. The building was torn down after being damaged in the war; what you see today was built from scratch in 1997. The redoubtable sword-waving goddess who once rose from the stone plinth on the other side of the square, Nike, otherwise known as the **Pomnik Bohaterów Warszawy** (Warsaw Heroes Monument), a state tribute to the war dead, has been moved a few blocks north and now stands directing traffic on the highway under the Stare Miasto – walk down Nowy Przejazd from pl. Teatralny and she's on the right. At the west end of pl. Teatralny, just north along ul. Bielańska stands the ruins of the **Bank of Poland**. Originally built as the Russian Imperial Bank in 1911, the building was used as a fortress by Polish soldiers during the 1944 Uprising and then bombed by the Nazis, one of the only such buildings in the city centre that was neither restored nor demolished. Continuing west along Senatorska, the Baroque **Kościół Franciszkański** (Franciscan Church) – a quiet place with restful cloisters – is followed by the

Pałac Błękitny (Blue Palace), where Chopin gave one of his earliest concerts at the age of six. Tragically, the palace's destruction in 1944 engulfed the fabulous Zamoyski library of over 250,000 books and manuscripts.

Plac Bankowy

Senatorska ends at **plac Bankowy**, formerly pl. Dzierżyńskiego; the giant statue of its former namesake Felix Dzierżyński, the unloved Polish Bolshevik and founder of the NKVD, was removed in 1990 to public rejoicing, and his place has been taken by the Romantic poet **Juliusz Słowacki**. On the northeast corner of the square is a tower known locally as the Blue Skyscraper, or **Błękitny Wieżowiec**, that's long been a talking point: built on the former site of the Great Synagogue (see p.106) – and cursed, according to local legend, as a consequence – from its inception in the early 1970s it took over twenty years to complete this lumbering Yugoslav-financed giant of a project, now the Peugeot building. The west edge of the busy square is taken up by a palatial early nineteenth-century complex designed by Antoni Corazzi, and originally housing Congress Kingdom-era government offices (see p.666). This grand building has been the seat of the city's administrative authorities since the destruction of the original town hall in 1944. On the southwest corner of the square is the old **National Bank** building, long the official Museum of the Workers' Movement but now taken over by the Muzeum Kolekcji im. Jana Pawła II.

The Muzeum Kolekcji im. Jana Pawła II

Entered from ul. Elektoralna, just off the square, the **Muzeum Kolekcji im. Jana Pawła II** (John Paul II Museum; Tues–Sun 10am–5pm; 11zł) comprises a large art collection assembled by the wealthy émigré Carroll-Porczyński family in the early 1980s and donated to the Polish Catholic church a few years later. The museum has proved controversial: sections of the academic world are dubious about the authenticity of some works, and while its artistic aspiration is unquestionably high, the galleries are musty and poorly lit, and there's also a catechistic tone to the place, the portraits of the pope and current Catholic Primate at the entrance reminding you whom the museum is supposed to honour. The paintings are hung in seven rooms, arranged by theme rather than chronology, and the whole collection is a hit-and-miss affair, with lovely works mixed in among the kind of daubs available in disreputable souvenir shops. Labels are in Polish only, but a free one-page guide in English is available at the entrance.

The first room, hidden behind the cloakroom, displays **Impressionist** and other modern paintings, including the early and typically brooding *Farm in Hoogeveen* by Van Gogh, a *Still Life with Cauliflower* by Renoir and, anachronistically, a small *Woman Carrying Water* by Goya. The second room is devoted to **Mythology and Allegory**, with mostly Baroque canvases on themes such as the labours of Hercules. Next is the Rotunda, a large, domed auditorium once occupied by the Warsaw Bourse and now doubling as a concert recital hall – hence the chairs. The theme here is **portraits**, with over eighty works including some by well-known artists (or, more often, their workshops), including Velázquez, Rembrandt, Titian and Tintoretto, as well as Sir Joshua Reynolds' penetrating *Miss Nelly O'Brian*, one of his three portraits of Irish women.

Going upstairs, you'll come to the **Still Life and Landscape** hallway, where there are several works by Abraham Breughel (1631–80), great-grandson of Pieter Breughel the Elder. This leads into the **Mother and Child** room and then the **Gerson** room, which features a monumental *Baptism of Lithuania* painted in 1889 by nineteenth-century Polish artist Wojciech Gerson, in which

Władysław Jagiełło leads the Lithuanian knights to the cross while a crowd of awestruck peasants look on. The last two rooms are devoted to the **Virgin Mary** and **Biblical Scenes**, many of the paintings here acknowledged to be copies of works hanging in other museums.

Plac Piłsudskiego, the Ogród Saski and around

Returning to pl. Teatralny, the way south leads onto an even larger square, **plac Piłsudskiego**. This was the site of Warsaw's largest Russian Orthodox church in the time of the partitions, a beautiful building, but one seen as a symbol of oppression and torn down once Poland regained independence in the 1920s. Following the imposition of martial law in the 1980s, a huge flower cross was laid here by Varsovians in protest. After the authorities had cleared the cross away, the whole area was closed off for public works for years, presumably to prevent embarrassing demonstrations happening in full view of the tourists staying in the *Victoria* and *Europejski* hotels. These days the military guard in front of the **Tomb of the Unknown Soldier** here is the only permanent security presence, and bollards keep the centre of the spacious square traffic-free. The north end of the square is the site of Sir Norman Foster's love-it-or-hate-it **Metropolitan Building**, resembling an enormous glass Mobius strip.

Beyond the tomb stretch the handsome and well-used promenades of the **Ogród Saski** (Saxon Gardens), laid out for August II by the tireless Tylman of Gameren in the early 1700s and landscaped as a public garden in the following century. The **royal palace** built in the gardens by August II was blown up by the Nazis in 1944 and never rebuilt; the Tomb of the Unknown Soldier is the only surviving part of the building. Other sections of the park were luckier, notably the scattering of Baroque sculptures symbolizing the Virtues, Sciences and Elements, an elegant nineteenth-century fountain pool above the main pathway, the old **water tower** (Warsaw's first) built by Marconi in the 1850s and the park's fine crop of **trees**, over a hundred species in all.

Immediately south of the gardens on pl. Małachowskiego, to the west of the plush *Victoria* hotel, is the **Galeria Zachęta** (Tues–Sun noon–8pm; 10zł, Thurs free; Ⓦwww.zacheta.art.pl), built at the turn of the twentieth century as the headquarters of the Warsaw Fine Arts Society, and one of the few buildings in central Warsaw left standing at the end of World War II. The stucco decoration in the entrance gives a taste of the building's original qualities. The gallery's considerable original art collection (Matejko's *Battle of Grunwald* included) was packed off into hiding in the Muzeum Narodowe at the start of the war, subsequently forming part of that museum's permanent collection. The Zachęta is now a leading contemporary art gallery, hosting a wealth of high-quality exhibitions by international artists.

Krakowskie Przedmieście

Of all the long thoroughfares bisecting central Warsaw from north to south, the most important is the one often known as the **Trakt Królewski** (Royal Way), which runs almost uninterrupted from pl. Zamkowy to the palace of Wilanów. **Krakowskie Przedmieście**, the first part of the Trakt Królewski, is lined with historic buildings. **Kościół św. Anny** (St Anne's Church), directly below pl. Zamkowy, is where Polish princes used to swear homage to the king; founded in 1454, the church was destroyed in 1656 by the besieging Swedes, then rebuilt in Baroque style in the following century. All that remains of the original church is the Gothic brick presbytery adjacent to the nave and Baroque chapel dome. There's a fine view over the Wisła from the courtyard next to the church, though your enjoyment of it is somewhat marred by the traffic thundering through the tunnel below. By 1983, the second year of martial law, resourceful oppositionists had assembled a new flower cross on this courtyard after the authorities removed the huge one from pl. Piłsudskiego (see opposite). For an even better view, you can climb the **belfry** on the northern side of the courtyard (May–Sept daily 10am–5pm; 3zł).

Behind the belfry a pedestrian path leads through a sloping park to the quiet district of **Mariensztat**. An important market area before World War II, the quarter was redesigned in the 1950s as a neo-Baroque housing project, and the interceding decades have given its streets something close to an eighteenth-century feel. The bar on the Rynek Mariensztacki, *Pod Barylką* (see p.133), is good for an afternoon beer.

South of St Anne's the bus-congested street broadens to incorporate a small green. The **Pomnik Mickiewicza** (Mickiewicz Monument; see box, p.99) stuck in the middle of it is one of many you'll see if you travel round the country. It was unveiled on the centenary of the poet's birth in 1889, before a twelve-thousand-strong crowd (the Russians were enforcing a ban on rallies and speeches at the time).

Just south of the statue stands the seventeenth-century **Kościół Karmelitów** (Carmelite Church) whose finely wrought facade, capped by a distinctive globe, is one of the first examples of genuine classicism in Poland. Next door is the **Pałac Namiestnikowski**, a Neoclassical pile dating from 1819, built on the site of the seventeenth-century palace where the Constitution of 3 May 1791 was passed. The present building was witness to the signing of the Warsaw Pact in 1955, at the height of the Cold War, and 34 years later, in spring 1989, it hosted the "Round Table" talks between the country's communist authorities and the Solidarity-led opposition. In 1995 the palace became the official presidential residence, following Lech Wałęsa's decision to move here from the Belweder (see p.122). In front of the large courtyard is a statue of another favourite son, Józef Poniatowski (see p.666).

West of the main street on ul. Kozia, a quiet, atmospheric cobbled backstreet, is the **Muzeum Karykatury** (Museum of Caricatures; Tues–Sun 11am–5pm; 4zł, free on Sat) at no. 11, a quirky but enjoyable set up featuring changing exhibitions of work by Polish cartoonists.

Back on Krakowskie Przedmieście, two grand old hotels face each other a little further down the street: the **Europejski**, Warsaw's oldest hotel, and the **Bristol**. Begun in the 1850s, the *Europejski* was badly hit in World War II, and though the exterior has been restored well enough to preserve at least a hint of *fin-de-siècle* grandeur, the rooms inside have been eviscerated and lack character. After years out of action, the *Bristol*, a neo-Renaissance pile that was one of Europe's top hotels when completed in 1901, is now back in business as part of the Meridien chain. Originally owned by musician-premier Ignacy Paderewski, and a legendary prewar journalist's hangout, the building somehow survived World War II but was neglected by communist authorities, invaded by cockroaches and rats and eventually closed in 1981. It's now been transformed into a luxury hotel possibly even more opulent than the original. Both hotels are listed in "Accommodation", p.91. The spectacled figure in the park opposite the hotel is **Bolesław Prus**, author of the nineteenth-century Warsaw saga *The Doll* (see "Books", p.700), whose works covered extensively the social life of the *fin-de-siècle* period.

Even in a city not lacking in Baroque churches, the triple-naved **Kościół Sióstr Wizytek** (Nuns of the Visitation) stands out, with its columned, statue-topped facade; it's also one of the very few buildings in central Warsaw to have come through World War II unscathed. The most curious feature of the richly decorated interior is a boat-shaped pulpit dating from the nineteenth century. The church's main claim to fame is that Chopin used to play the church organ here, mainly during services for schoolchildren.

The university

Most of the rest of Krakowskie Przedmieście is taken up by Warsaw's **university**. Established in 1818, it was closed by the tsar in 1832 as part of the punishment for the 1831 Insurrection, and remained closed till 1915. During the Nazi occupation, educational activity of any sort was made a capital offence, and thousands of academics and students were murdered. However, clandestine university courses continued throughout the war – a tradition revived in the 1970s with the "Flying University", when opposition figures travelled around the city giving open lectures on politically controversial issues. The cafés, restaurants and milk bars in this area are established student hangouts.

On the main campus courtyard, the old **library** stands in front of the seventeenth-century **Pałac Kazimierzowski** (Kazimierz Palace), once a royal summer residence and now home to the rector and associated bureaucrats, while across the street from the gates is the former **Pałac Czapskich** (Czapski Palace), now home of the Academy of Fine Arts. The building was Chopin's last Polish residence before he went into exile, and one room on the second floor of the southern wing has been appointed with period lithographs and furniture as a recreation of the **Salonik Chopina** (Chopin Family Salon; Mon–Fri 10am–2pm; 3zł). Just south is the twin-towered Baroque **Kościół św. Krzyża** (Holy Cross Church), which was ruined by a two-week battle inside the building during the Warsaw Uprising. Photographs of the distinctive stone figure of Christ left standing among the ruins became poignant emblems of Warsaw's suffering and now hang in the first chapel to the right of the altar. Outside, a statue of a broken Christ with a crown of thorns exhorts *Sursum Corda* ("Lift up your Hearts"). The church is also known for containing **Chopin's heart** – it's in an urn standing within a column on the left side of the nave.

Biggest among Warsaw's consistently large palaces is the early nineteenth-century **Pałac Staszica** (Staszic Palace), which virtually blocks the end of Krakowskie Przedmieście. Once a Russian boys' grammar school, it's now the headquarters of the Polish Academy of Sciences. In front of the palace is the august **Pomnik Mikołaja Kopernika** (Copernicus Monument), designed by the Danish sculptor Bertel Thorvaldsen in the 1830s and showing the great astronomer holding one of his revolutionary heliocentric models.

Ulica Marszałkowska, the Pałac Kultury i Nauki and around

The area below the Ogród Saski and west of Krakowskie Przedmieście is the city's busiest commercial zone. **Marszałkowska**, the main road running south from the western tip of the gardens, is lined with department stores and clothes shops, while smaller streets to the east like **Zgoda** and the pedestrianized **Chmielna** are good for bars and restaurants as well as shopping.

North of ul. Świętokrzyska, on ul. Kreditowa, the eighteenth-century **Ewangelicko–Augsburgski** (Lutheran) church is topped with Warsaw's largest dome. The building's excellent acoustics have long made it popular with musicians – Chopin played a concert here at the age of fourteen, and the church still holds regular choral and chamber concerts (see "Nightlife and entertainment", p.136). Opposite stands the **Muzeum Etnograficzne** (Ethnographic Museum; Tues, Thurs & Fri 10am–4pm, Wed 11am–6pm, Sat & Sun 10am–5pm, closed first Sun of the month; 8zł, free on Wed), whose collections were virtually destroyed in the war. Today the first two floors hold temporary exhibitions, while the top level displays an array of traditional costumes from all over Poland, before moving on to arcane, often bizarre, rural customs, with a host of decades-old photographs as well as masks and effigies used in parades with pagan roots – fascinating if you happen to have someone to explain it all to you. The final room has a fairly good collection of naive art, including some inventive drawings by Nikifor, the folk artist from Krynica (see p.375).

Towering over everything in this part of the city is the **Pałac Kultury i Nauki** (Palace of Culture and Sciences, or PKiN for short; ⓦ www.pkin.pl), a gift from Stalin to the Polish people, and not one that could be refused. Officially dubbed "an unshakeable monument to Polish-Soviet friendship" and in fact representing a kind of Soviet-style Marshall Plan, the palace was completed in 1955 after three years of work by 3500 construction workers brought specially from Russia for the job. Long popularly known as "the Russian cake", this neo-Baroque leviathan provokes intense feelings from Varsovians. Some residents invoke Maupassant's comment on the Eiffel Tower, maintaining that the best **views** of Warsaw are from the palace's top floor – the only viewpoint from which one can't see the building itself – while others are willing to grant it a sinister kind of elegance, especially when compared to the glass skyscrapers that have sprouted up nearby. Few dispute, however, that the building's sheer size and breadth creates a vacuum at the centre of the Warsaw, helping to make this among the least pedestrian-friendly of cities. The question of what to do with the area is often debated but unlikely to be answered in the near future. One popular idea is simply to demolish the whole thing, but the winning proposal of a recent international design competition called for surrounding it with small-scale buildings, while leaving the palace essentially untouched.

The entrance to the palace, now shorn of admonitions from Marx and Lenin, is up the steps from the expansive **plac Defilad**. Inside, a lift whisks visitors up to the thirtieth-floor platform (daily 9am–6pm; 18zł), from which, on a good day, you can see out into the plains of Mazovia. The cavernous interior, which is all marble and chandeliers, can be visited on a guided tour (July–Aug, by appointment only; 40zł per person, minimum 4 people; ☏022/656 6345), which takes in among other sights, Brezhnev's favourite lounge, the opulent Gagarin Hall and the famous **Sala Kongresowa** (Congress Hall), today used by visiting pop stars as well as for the prestigious Jazz Jamboree (see p.134). One truly epoch-defining gig to take place here was the appearance of the Rolling Stones in 1967 (a time when Western groups hardly ever made the trip to Eastern Europe), an event that kick-started the Polish beat boom of the Sixties. Three-dozen cats are reputed to keep the basement rodent-free, while the rest of the building contains offices, a multiplex cinema, a swimming pool, a youth centre and a lively bar (see p.133). The complete story is told in Agata Passent's wry account, *Long Live the Palace!* (see "Books", p.693).

South and west of the palace lie the areas of Warsaw that have experienced the most intense development in the years following the introduction of the free market. High-rise office blocks seem to be shooting up everywhere along the main westbound highway **Aleja Jerozolimskie** (Jerusalem Avenue) and in the streets surrounding Warszawa Centralna train station. The gleaming chrome and glass of the LOT building has long been the major landmark here, although its supremacy has recently been challenged by the **Warsaw Tower** (known as the Daewoo Tower when the Korean conglomerate first built it in 1997) a little further west along ul. Sienna – second only to the Pałac Kultury i Nauki in height, it's a curious structure whose combination of smooth curves and angular lines ensures that it has a different profile from whichever direction you look at it.

South of the Pałac Kultury i Nauki, the busy tramlined strip of ul. Marszałkowska leads south towards **plac Konstitucji**, another massive Stalinist ensemble, where buildings are decorated with outsized workers and other proletarian heroes. Cross-streets such as Hoża and Wilcza comprise a residential area whose discreetly well-heeled inhabitants are served by increasing numbers of chic stores and snazzy café-bars.

Nowy Świat and around

South of the university, Krakowskie Przedmieście becomes **Nowy Świat** (New World), an area first settled in the mid-seventeenth century. This wide boulevard, closed to traffic at weekends, has plenty of restaurants and shops but is known especially for its cafés, such as the *Nowy Świat* and the *Blikle* (see "Cafés and bars", p.132).

This street has been home to several cultural luminaries, including Joseph Conrad, who once lived at no. 45. A left turn down ul. Ordynacka brings you to the **Muzeum Fryderyka Chopina** (Chopin Museum; Mon, Wed & Fri 10am–5pm, Thurs noon–6pm, Sat & Sun 10am–2pm; 10zł), housed in the late-seventeenth-century Pałac Ostrogski on ul. Okólnik, which also forms the headquarters of the Towarzystwo im. Fryderyka Chopina (Chopin Society; Ⓦwww .tifc.chopin.pl). Memorabilia on display include the last piano he played, now used for occasional concerts, as well as sheet music, personal letters and a few sketches by the pianist. The museum also puts on summertime Sunday concerts in Park Łazienkowski (see p.121) and at Żelazowa Wola (see p.142). The Society organizes the International Chopin Piano Competition, held every five years.

The neo-Renaissance **Zamoyski Palace**, off to the left of Nowy Świat at the end of ul. Foksal (a Polonization of "Vauxhall"), is one of the few Warsaw palaces where you are permitted to see inside. In 1863, an abortive attempt to assassinate the tsarist governor was made here; as a consequence the palace was confiscated and ransacked by Cossacks, who hurled a grand piano used by Chopin out of the window of his sister's flat here. These days it's a suitably elegant setting for an architectural institute, boasting an expensive restaurant with terrace seating in the summer (see p.131). Round one side of the palace, an outwardly unassuming building houses the **Galeria Foksal** (Mon–Fri noon–5pm; free), one of the better contemporary galleries in the city, with a regular programme of temporary exhibitions by artists both Polish and foreign. It's been something of a cult place for avant-gardists ever since the 1960s, when it became the first Warsaw gallery to host happenings arranged by renowned Cracovian performance artist and theatre director Tadeusz Kantor.

Further down Nowy Świat, the concrete monster on the southern side of the junction with al. Jerozolimskie was for decades the headquarters of the now defunct Polish **communist party**. After a pleasingly ironic stint as the new Warsaw Stock Exchange (now relocated to premises nearby), today it houses the Centrum Bankowo-Finansowe.

The Muzeum Narodowe

Immediately east along al. Jerozolimskie from the old communist HQ is the **Muzeum Narodowe** (National Museum; Tues, Wed & Fri–Sun 10am–4pm, Thurs 10am–6pm; 11zł or 15zł with temporary exhibitions, permanent collection free Sat), a daunting grey-brown building that was considered a masterpiece

△ Street vendor, Nowy Świat

of modern functionalism when first built in the 1930s, and which managed to survive World War II intact.

The displays begin to the right of the entrance with the department of ancient art – assorted **Egyptian**, **Greek** and **Roman** finds. These, however, are overshadowed by the stunning array in the corresponding wing to the left of art from Faras, a town in **Nubia** (present-day Sudan), excavated by Polish archeologists in the early 1960s. There are capitals, friezes, columns and other architectural fragments, together with 69 murals dating from between the eighth and thirteenth centuries. The earliest paintings – notably *St Anne*, *The Archangels Michael and Gabriel* and *SS Peter and John Enthroned* – are direct and powerful images comparable in quality with later European Romanesque works, and prove the vibrancy of African culture at this period. No less striking are the later portraits such as the tenth-century *Bishop Petros with St Peter* and the eleventh-century *Bishop Marianos*.

In the rooms off the central hall is another star collection, that of **medieval art**, which is dominated by a kaleidoscopic array of carved and painted altar-pieces. Although most of the objects come from within the modern borders of Poland, the predominance of works from Silesia and the Gdańsk area suggests that most were created by German or Bohemian craftsmen, though there are also some fine, genuinely Polish works from Małopolska. Highlights include a lovely late-fourteenth-century "Soft Style" polyptych from the castle chapel in Grudziądz; the monumental fifteenth-century canopied altar from St Mary's in Gdańsk; and the altar from Pławno depicting the life of St Stanisław, painted by Hans Süss von Kulmbach, a pupil of Dürer who spent part of his career in Poland.

Much of the first floor is given over to **Polish painting**, beginning with a number of examples of what is a quintessential national art form, the coffin portrait. Important works here include the original sixteenth-century portrait of Queen Anna Jagiellońka, wife of Stefan Batory, the famed king of Poland and Transylvania, copies of which hang in palaces and museums around the country; and the *Battle of Orsza*, painted in the 1520s by a follower of Lucas Cranach the Elder and depicting the Polish-Lithuanian rout of the Muscovite army on the banks of the River Dnieper in 1514. Nearby, hangs an early sixteenth-century boyhood portrait of Tomasz Zamoyski, son of the great Renaissance figure and founder of Zamość, Jan Zamoyski (see p.323). Through the rather dull eighteenth-century Polish gallery you'll come to a room devoted to Jan Matejko, the centrepiece of which is the huge *Battle of Grunwald*, showing one of the momentous clashes of the Middle Ages, the defeat of the Teutonic Knights by Polish-Lithuanian forces in 1410.

The second wing of the Polish section is devoted to late-nineteenth-century artists, especially those from the turn-of-the-twentieth-century Młoda Polska school, little known outside the country. Stanisław Wyspiań-ski's intense self-portraits stand out, as do his 1905 views of the Kościuszko Mound in Kraków. Other interesting paintings include Józef Mehoffer's symbolist *Strange Garden* and Jacek Malczewski's haunting images of Death disguised as an angel. Most charming, though, is Józef Chełmoński's 1891 *Partridges*.

The left wing of the first floor, plus all of the second floor, are given over to the extensive but patchy department of foreign paintings, many "inherited" from museums in Wrocław and other formerly German cities following World War II. In the **Italian section**, look for some lovely Florentine primitives, as well as the tondo *The Madonna and Child with St John* from the workshop of Botticelli and *A Venetian Admiral* by Tintoretto. Among the **French paintings** in the following rooms is Jean-Marc Nattier's portrait of Queen Maria Leszczyńska, Louis XV's Polish wife. Upstairs, the **German Renaissance** is represented by a fine group of works by Cranach, including a gruesome *Massacre of the Innocents*. The most noteworthy piece from the **Low Countries** is the sculpted altarpiece commissioned in Antwerp in 1516 for the Church of Our Lady in Gdańsk. The final galleries, devoted to **Decorative Arts**, are little visited but hold curiosities such as Gothic chalices and seventeenth-century table clocks. Temporary exhibitions are held on the first floor, while there's a good café in the basement.

The Muzeum Wojska Polskiego

The **Muzeum Wojska Polskiego** (Army Museum; Wed–Sun 10am–4pm; 11zł, free on Wed), next door to the Muzeum Narodowe, was established in the 1920s and is devoted to an institution that has long played a pivotal role in the national consciousness, as much for its role in preserving national identity during periods of foreign occupation as for militaristic self-glorification. Greeting you outside the museum is an intimidating collection of heavy combat equipment, from sixteenth-century cannons through to modern tanks and planes. A unique item is Kubuś (Little Jakob), as it's affectionately known, an improvised truck-cum-armoured car cobbled together by Home Army forces and used to notable effect during the Warsaw Uprising. Inside there's a wide array of guns, swords and armour from over the centuries. Exhibits include an eleventh-century Piast-era helmet (the oldest exhibit); early cannon prototypes produced by the Teutonic Knights; fearsome Hussar "whistling" feather headgear; and scythes of the type used in combat by Polish peasants during the Partition-era struggles. The museum is a must for amateur military historians, a common breed in Poland, but to laymen (and women) the appeal may wear thin well before the end of the exhibits.

Plac Trzech Krzyży, the Sejm, the Senat and around

South of the museum, the fashionable **plac Trzech Krzyży** (Three Crosses), with the Pantheon-style **Kościół św. Aleksandra** (St Alexander's Church) in the centre, leads to the tree-lined pavements and magisterial embassy buildings of al. Ujazdowskie. Past the unattractive US embassy and off to the left, down ul. Jana Matejki, is the squat 1920s **Sejm** (Parliament) and **Senat** (Senate) building. A feeble institution stuffed with government-approved yes-men until the epoch-making elections of July 1989, these days sober debate is intermingled with the headline-making stunts of peasant leader Andrzej Lepper and his populist and Euro-sceptic Samoobrona (Self-defence) party.

Many of the streets in this area are lined with dull postwar frontages plastered over the pockmarks of World War II gunfire. However, these unprepossessing edifices often mask red-brick or stone buildings a century or more old, some also featuring elaborate shrines to the Virgin Mary; step through the archways ul. Mokotowska nos. 65 or 73, just south of pl. Trzech Krzyży, for good examples.

Further south along al. Ujazdowskie and over the junction with al. Armii Ludowej is the grim **Muzeum Walki i Męczeństwa** (Museum of Struggle and Martyrdom; Wed–Sun 10am–4pm; free), al. Szucha 25. Housed in the former Gestapo headquarters, now occupied by government ministries, the basement museum commemorates the thousands tortured and murdered here during World War II.

Ujazdowski and Łazienki parks

The old royal parks south of the city centre are one of Warsaw's most attractive features. The most popular and well-kept stretch of greenery begins with **Park Ujazdowski** (Ujazdowski Park), a half-kilometre south of the Muzeum Narodowe (see p.116), and continues beyond a highway overpass to the grounds of the **Zamek Ujazdowski** (Ujazdowski Castle) and then the **Ogród Botaniczny** (Botanical Gardens), before arriving at the most luxuriant public space of them all, **Park Łazienkowski** (Łazienki Park). If you haven't got the time to walk the whole distance, the numerous buses running along al. Ujazdowskie on the parks' western fringes provide a good way of getting around.

Park Ujazdowski

Aleja Ujazdowskie itself is one of the city's more elegant thoroughfares, with opulent nineteenth-century villas (most occupied by foreign embassies) lining its western side, and the regimented flowerbeds and duck pond of **Park Ujazdowski** on the other. Lurking on the far side of the highway overpass at Park Ujazdowski's southern edge is the **Zamek Ujazdowski**, a Renaissance structure with its own grounds separate from the park proper. Once inhabited by King Sigismund August's Italian-born mother Bona Sforza, it's now home to the **Centrum Sztuki Współczesnej** (Contemporary Art Centre; Tues–Thurs & Sat–Sun 11am–5pm, Fri 11am–9pm; 12zł, free on Thurs; Ⓦwww.csw.art .pl), the city's leading venue for modern art shows along with the Galeria Zachęta (see p.138). As well as organizing themed exhibitions, the centre mounts innovative theatre, film and video events. The building also contains an

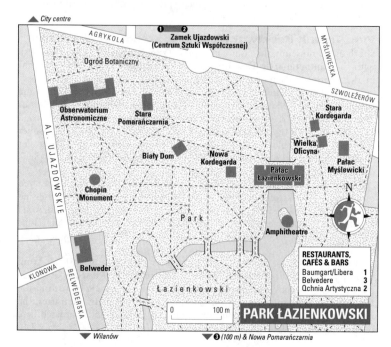

excellent café-restaurant, a student-oriented café and one of Warsaw's best clubs (see p.131, p.133 & p.135).

South of the palace across ul. Agrykola, the **Ogród Botaniczny** (Botanical Gardens; April–Oct Mon–Fri 9am–8pm, Sat–Sun 10am–8pm; 4.5zł) boast an impressive collection of carefully landscaped shrubs and trees, with a sizeable rose garden, and a knot garden crammed full of fragrant medicinal herbs. At weekends there's an entrance on al. Ujazdowskie, while the main gate is at the southern end of the gardens, opposite the Obserwatorium Astronomiczne (Astronomical Observatory).

Park Łazienkowski

South and east of here lie several entrances to the main body of **Park Łazienkowski** (Łazienki Park; open daily 8am–sunset). Once a hunting ground on the periphery of town, the area was bought by King Stanisław August in the 1760s and turned into an English-style park with formal gardens. A few years later the slender Neoclassical **Pałac Łazienkowski** was built across the park lake. Designed for the king by the Italian architect Domenico Merlini, in collaboration with teams of sculptors and other architects, it's the best memorial to the country's last and most cultured monarch. Before this summer residence was commissioned, a **bathhouse** built by Tylman of Gameren for Prince Stanisław Lubomirski stood here – hence the name, "Łazienki" meaning simply "baths".

The oak-lined promenades and pathways leading from the park entrance to the palace are a favourite with tourists and Varsovians, many of the latter coming prepared to feed the park's resident fauna, which include peacocks, squirrels and mandarin ducks. On summer Sundays at 11am and 3pm, **concerts** and other events take place under the watchful eye of the ponderous Chopin Monument, just beyond the entrance. On the way down to the lake you'll pass a couple of the many buildings designed for King Stanisław by Merlini; the **Nowa Kordegarda** (New Guardhouse), just before the palace, is now a pleasant and fairly moderately priced terrace **café** serving great ice cream. There's another café, less atmospheric but with a similar menu, next to the amphitheatre.

Pałac Łazienkowski

Often referred to as the Pałac na Wyspie (Island Palace) due to its location, the **Pałac Łazienkowski** (Łazienki Palace; Tues–Sun 9am–4pm; 12zł) is the smallest of Warsaw's royal palaces and the only one that can be visited without a guided tour. Nazi damage to the building itself was fairly severe, with all but three of the rooms destroyed, but many of the lavish furnishings, paintings and sculptures survived, having been hidden during the occupation. Curiously, only a few of the palace rooms have ever been electrified, and on cloudy days the rest are shrouded in darkness.

On the ground floor are three rooms incorporated from the earlier bathhouse, the only ones in the building to survive the war in anything like their original condition. The baths themselves are long gone, but the bas-reliefs decorating the walls in the **Bacchus Room** and **Bathing Suite** serve as a reminder of their original function. In the main section of the palace, entirely reconstructed, the stuccoed **ballroom**, the largest ground-floor room, is a fine example of Stanisław's classicist predilections, lined with a tasteful collection of busts and sculptures. As the adjoining **picture galleries** demonstrate, Stanisław was a discerning art collector. The Nazis got hold of some of the best pieces – three Rembrandts included – but a large collection drawn from all over Europe remains, with an accent on Dutch and Flemish artists. The view onto the lake from these rooms is at least as captivating as the pictures.

Upstairs are the **king's private apartments**, most of them entirely recon-structed since the war. Again, period art and furniture dominate these handsome chambers: a stately and uncomfortable-looking four-poster bed fills the royal bedroom, while in the study a Bellotto canvas accurately depicts the original Łazienki bathhouse. The back rooms, which in Stanisław's times belonged to Ryx, the royal valet, are furnished with fine examples of Polish Baroque furniture from Warsaw, Kraków and Gdańsk. An exhibition devoted to the history of Łazienki, with pictures illustrating the extent of wartime damage, completes the tour.

The rest of the park

The buildings scattered round the park are all in some way connected with King Stanisław. Across the lake from the palace, and north along the water's edge, is the **Stara Kordegarda** (Old Guardhouse; Tues–Sun 9am–4pm; free), built in the 1780s in a style matching the north facade of the main palace, which features regular exhibitions of contemporary art. Immediately next to it is the so-called **Wielka Oficyna** (Great Outbuilding), another Merlini construction, the former officers' training school where young cadets hatched the anti-tsar-ist conspiracy that resulted in the November 1830 Uprising. The building now houses the **Muzeum J. Paderewskiego i Wychodźstwa Polskiego** (Ignacy Jan Paderewski and Polish Expatriates in America Museum; Tues–Sun 10am–3pm; 6zł, free on Thurs), inaugurated during the summer 1992 celebra-tions surrounding the return of the composer's body to Warsaw from the US. Much of what's here was bequeathed to the country by the exile Paderewski in his will, with pride of place going to the grand piano he used at his longtime home on the shores of Lake Geneva. Standing on it, as during the man's lifetime, are the improbably paired autographed photos of fellow composer Saint-Saëns and Queen Victoria, while the walls are decorated with Paderewski's personal art collection. Adjoining rooms contain the dazzling array of prizes, medals and other honours awarded to him during his distinguished musical and political career, as well as his fine personal collection of assorted Chinese porcelain and enamelware. To finish off, there's a section devoted to mementoes of the Polish *emigracja*, detailing the Polish experience of America.

Immediately next to the museum is the **Pałac Myślewicki** (closed for reno-vation at the time of writing), a present from the king to his nephew Prince Józef Poniatowski, which imitates the studied decorum of the main palace. In summer the Greek-inspired **amphitheatre**, constructed for the king on an islet on the other side of the palace, still stages the occasional open-air performance (check with the tourist office for details, see p.85).

Back up towards the main park entrance, past the Nowa Kordegarda, is the **Biały Dom** (White House; Tues–Sun 9am–4pm; 5zł) built in the 1770s by Merlini for King Stanisław August's favourite mistress. It retains the majority of its original eighteenth-century interiors, including a dining room decorated with a wealth of grotesque animal frescoes, and an octagonal-shaped study which features enjoyable trompe l'oeil floral decoration.

Just beyond it, the **Stara Pomarańczarnia** (closed for renovation at the time of writing) contains a well-preserved wooden theatre (one of the few in Europe to retain its original eighteenth-century decor) with royal boxes and seating for over two hundred. To complete the classical pose, pieces from King Stanisław's extensive sculpture collection fill the long galleries behind the auditorium.

The path leading south up the hill from here ends back at al. Ujazdowskie, south from the Chopin monument and next to the **Belweder** (Belvedere), another eighteenth-century royal residence redesigned in the 1820s for the governor of Warsaw, the tsar's brother Konstantine. Official residence of Polish heads of state since the end of World War I (with a brief interlude as home of the Nazi governor Hans Frank), it was used for ten years by General Jaruzelski, in turn supplanted by Lech Wałęsa, the country's first freely elected president in over fifty years. In 1995, Wałęsa moved the presidential residence to the Namiestnikowski Palace on Krakowskie Przedmieście (see p.113). The Belweder is now used to host foreign dignitaries, and houses a small museum dedicated to **Józef Piłsudski**, the country's venerated president for much of the interwar period, and a former resident (visits by appointment only ☎022/849 4839). Back down the hill, a path through one of the wilder sections of the park leads to the **Nowa Pomarańczarnia**, where you'll find the *Belvedere* restaurant (see p.131), among the finest in Warsaw.

The **Trakt Królewski** (Royal Way) slopes gently down from here towards the Mokotów district, passing the **Russian embassy** building, huge if less influential these days. The route then continues a few kilometres south to Wilanów, its ultimate destination.

Wilanów

The grandest of Warsaw's palaces, **Wilanów** (mid-May to mid-Sept: Mon & Thurs–Sat 9.30am–4pm, Wed 9.30am–6pm, Sun 9.30am–7pm; mid-Sept to

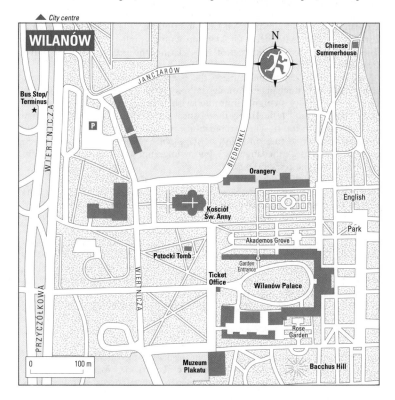

▲ *City centre*

WILANÓW

N

Chinese Summerhouse

JANCZARÓW

Bus Stop/ Terminus ★

WIERNICZA

P

BIEDRONKI

Orangery

English

Kościół Św. Anny

Park

Akademos Grove

Potocki Tomb

Garden Entrance

Ticket Office

WIERNICZA

Wilanów Palace

PRZYCZÓŁKOWA

Rose Garden

0   100 m

Muzeum Plakatu

Bacchus Hill

mid-May: daily except Tues 9.30am–4pm; last entry ninety minutes before closing; 20zł; ☎022/842 8101, ⓦwww.wilanow-palac.art.pl) is tucked away in almost rural surroundings on the outskirts of Warsaw, and makes an easy excursion from the city centre: it's the final stop of several bus routes, including #116 and #180 from pl. Zamkowy, and #130 and #522 from the Centralna station. Sometimes called the Polish Versailles, it was originally the brainchild of King Jan Sobieski, who purchased the existing manor house and estate in 1677. He spent nearly twenty years turning it into his ideal country residence, which was later extended by a succession of monarchs and aristocratic families. Predictably, Wilanów was badly damaged during World War II, when the Nazis stole the cream of the art collection and tore up the park and surrounding buildings. In 1945 the palace became state property and for eleven years was extensively renovated. It's now a tourist favourite, visitable only by **guided tour** (Polish-language tours usually start hourly; English-language tours, which need to be booked in advance, cost 135zł for a group of up to five.

The approach to the palace takes you past former outhouses, including the smithy, the butcher's and an inn. Also close at hand are some decent cafés, welcome refuges after the palace tour. The **entrance gates**, where you buy your tickets, are just beyond the domed eighteenth-century **Kościół św. Anny** (St Anne's Church) and ornate neo-Gothic Potocki mausoleum across the road.

The palace

Laid out in a horseshoe plan with a central core flanked by a pair of projecting wings, the classical grandeur of the **facade**, complete with Corinthian columns, Roman statuary and intermingled Latin inscriptions, reflects Sobieski's original conception. The centrepiece, a golden sun with rays reflecting from decorated shields bearing the Sobieski coat of arms, clarifies the essential idea: the glorification of Sobieski himself.

Despite extensive wartime damage, the essentials of the interior design have remained largely unchanged. Among the sixty or so rooms of Wilanów's **interior** you'll find styles ranging from the lavish early Baroque of the apartments of Jan Sobieski and John III, to the classical grace of the nineteenth-century Potocki museum rooms. The combination of all this pomp and glory with the ceaseless, didactic lecture on Polish heritage can be deadening – perhaps even more so if you speak the language – but by lingering a bit you can stay a room or two behind the rest of the group.

The tour starts with a basement exhibit on the palace's **history**, ending with photos of objects taken by the Nazis and never recovered. Several flights of stairs lead to the **portrait galleries**, containing a number of casket images, intended to be interred with the subject but sometimes removed from the coffin before burial. They are part of a total collection of over 250 portraits, most of which are hung in long corridor galleries – an intriguing introduction to the development of Polish Sarmatian fashion, with its peculiar synthesis of Western *haute couture* and Eastern influences such as shaved heads and wide sashes (see box, p.474). If you've already visited other museums, the portrait of Jan Sobieski in the **Sobieski Family Room** will probably look familiar – the portly military hero most often crops up charging Lone Ranger-like towards a smouldering Vienna, trampling a few Turks on the way. One of the undoubted highlights of the collection is the great masterpiece of Neoclassical portraiture, *Stanisław Kostka Potocki on Horseback* by Jacques-Louis David.

After Sobieski's **Library**, with its beautiful marble-tiled floor and allegorical ceiling paintings, you come to the **Faience Room**, clad in blue with white Delft tiles and topped by an elegant copper-domed cupola surrounded by delicate period stucco mouldings, the centrepiece an eagle raising aloft the ubiquitous Sobieski coat of arms. The **August Locci Room**, named after the architect who designed most of the early interiors, is one of several where the original seventeenth-century wooden beams have been uncovered. Many of the rooms on this floor offer excellent views over the palace gardens. The **Painted Cabinet Room**, next door, features recently uncovered eighteenth-century frescoes, notably a turbaned black man holding a caged parrot. In contrast, restoration work in the **Quiet Room** has uncovered seventeenth-century frescoes of preening Greek goddesses.

Next comes another series of long **portrait galleries**, mostly from the Enlightenment era, including Kościuszko (see box, pp.428–429), the architects of the Third May Constitution, and a benign looking Stanisław Poniatowski, Poland's last king. Another flight of stairs takes you up into the nineteenth-century portrait galleries, with a suitably demure Maria Walewska, Napoleon's mistress, next to a bust of the general himself, and a portrait of the Romantic poet Cyprian Norwid, who resembled Rasputin.

Downstairs again you come the other main set of apartments. First is the grand **Great Crimson Room**, as colourful as its name suggests, replete with a fabulously ornate ceiling and lashings of period art and furniture, including a massive dining table big enough to seat at least fifty people. Continuing on, you pass through the **Etruscan Study**, filled with third- and fourth-century BC vases collected in Naples by nineteenth-century palace owner Stanisław Potocki. The **Lower North Gallery** further on links the two wings to the main building. Converted into a mini-museum of antiquities by Potocki in the 1805 to show off his archeological finds, it's now been restored to its original early eighteenth-century state, murals included, though the classical sculptures have remained. The inscription on the floor, *Cuncti Patet Ingressus* ("Admittance free to all"), attests to the democratic ideals of the time.

The end of the gallery brings you into the **Queen's Apartments** originally used by Maria Kazimierza, Sobieski's wife, the most impressive of which are the **Antechamber**, containing two cabinets of fine late-seventeenth-century porcelain, an inevitably sumptuous Bedchamber, and the **Great Vestibule**, a three-storeyed affair of marble pillars and classicist mouldings connecting the royal apartments. The **King's Bedchamber** sports a great four-poster bed surrounded by period military trappings – precisely the kind of things the indefatigably warfaring Sobieski probably dreamed about – while his rooms are lined with eighteenth-century Genoan velvet and topped with banderols with quotations from Virgil. Past the **Chapel**, a simple shrine built by Potocki to commemorate his royal predecessor, you pass through further galleries containing more of Potocki's collection of classical sculpture, including some Roman sarcophagi, and a prize plaster **Sobieski Monument** of the corpulent king striking his customary equestrian pose over the hapless Turks.

Last, but by no means least, comes the **Grand Hall of August II**, also known as the White Hall. Designed in the 1730s for King August II and thoroughly renovated after 1945, the mirrors on the walls combine to create a feeling of immense space. The balconies standing above the fireplaces at both ends, originally for the royal musicians, were rediscovered during the postwar renovation.

The palace gardens

If your energy hasn't flagged after the palace tour, there are a couple of other places of interest within the grounds. The gate on the left side beyond the main entrance opens onto the stately **palace gardens** (daily 9.30am–dusk; 4.5zł, Thurs free). Overlooking the garden terrace, the palace's graceful rear facade is topped by statuary featuring a golden sundial on the southern side. Designed by Gdańsk astronomer Jan Hevelius, whose relief sits on the front section of the facade, the dial has Saturn, god of time, holding out the mantle of the heavens, on which both the time and the season's astrological sign are displayed. The fresco sequence punctuating the facade shows scenes from classical literature, notably the *Aeneid* and *Odyssey*. Strolling along the back terrace, it's easy to appreciate the fine synthesis between regal residence and country mansion achieved by the palace.

The gardens reach down to the waterside, continuing rather less tidily along the lakeside to the north and south; in autumn this is a fine place for a Sunday afternoon scuffle through the fallen oak leaves. Beyond the **Orangery**, which holds temporary exhibitions (daily 10am–6pm; 6zł, Thurs free), is the **English Park** – so-called because it was modelled on the landscaped gardens beloved of eighteenth-century British aristocrats – whose main feature is a Chinese summerhouse exhibiting pottery and other pieces of decorative art. Back outside and just below the main gates, the **Muzeum Plakatu** (Poster Museum; Tues–Sun 10am–3.30pm; 8zł, free Wed afternoon; Ⓦ www.postermuseum -wilanow.pl) is a mishmash of the inspired and the bizarre and is well worth a visit. The art form has long had major currency in Poland, but the changing exhibitions generally display posters from around the world.

The suburbs

For most visitors anything outside the city centre and Trakt Królewski remains an unknown quantity. While not visually attractive, some of the Warsaw **suburbs** – notably **Żoliborz** and **Praga** – are worth visiting both for their atmosphere and for their historic resonance, while at its furthest limits the city merges into the villages of the Mazovian countryside, with head-scarved peasants and horse-drawn carriages replacing the bustle of city life.

Żoliborz

Until the last century, the **Żoliborz** district (whose name comes from a corruption of the French *joli bord* – "pretty edge"), due north of the centre, was an extension of the Kampinoski forest (the Bielany reserve in the northern reaches of the city today is a remnant), but then evolved into a working-class stronghold. The district's heart is the large square near the top of **ulica Mickiewicza** – the northern extension of Marszałkowska and Gen. Andersa. Officially restored to its prewar name, **plac Wilsona** (reached on trams #4 and #36 from Centrum) was the stage for a fiercely fought campaign by local resident and veteran oppositionist-turned-government-minister Jacek Kuroń in the 1989 elections, who debated with his political opponents before packed audiences at the old Wisła cinema on the square. Kuroń was given a state funeral following his death in 2004; his son Maciej, almost equally beloved by Poles, hosts a television cooking show.

The **Church of St Stanisław Kostka**, off to the west side of pl. Wilsona, was Solidarity priest Jerzy Popiełuszko's parish church until he was murdered by militant security police in 1984 – a major event in Polish political life of the 1980s – which ensured his popular canonization. After Popiełuszko's funeral, attended by over half a million people, his church developed into a major Solidarity sanctuary and focus for opposition. Although Western politicians no longer troop here, the custom of newlyweds dropping by to pay their respects at Father Jerzy's shrine continues.

East of pl. Wilsona, just uphill from the Wisła, is an altogether more sinister place, the fearsome **cytadela** (Citadel). These decaying fortifications are the remains of the massive fortress built here by Tsar Nicholas I in the wake of the 1831 Uprising. Houses were demolished to make way for it, and Varsovians even had to pay the costs of the intended instrument of their punishment, whose function was to control and terrorize the city, not to guard it. For the next eighty years or so, suspected activists, including the later president Józef Piłsudski, were brought here for interrogation and eventual imprisonment, execution or exile.

The large steps up the hill lead to the grim **Gate of Executions**, where partisans were shot and hanged with particular regularity after the 1863 uprising. Uneasy with so obvious a symbol of Russian oppression and Polish nationalist aspirations, the postwar communist party attempted to present the Cytadela as a "mausoleum of the Polish revolutionary, socialist and workers' movement": thus, alongside the plaque commemorating the leaders of 1863, there are memorials to the tsarist-era Socialist Party, the Polish Communist Party and "the proletariat". Part of the prison is now a **historical museum** (Tues–Sun 9am–4pm; free), with a few preserved cells and some harrowing pictures depicting the agonies of Siberia by former inmate Aleksander Sochaczewski. The wagon in the courtyard is a reconstruction of the vehicles used to transport the condemned to their bleak exile.

Praga

Across the river from the Stare Miasto, the large **Praga** suburb – so named not after the Czech capital but after the fires set here long ago: the Polish verb *prażyć* means "to roast"– was the main residential area for the legions of tsarist bureaucrats throughout the nineteenth century – particularly the Saska Kępa district, south of al. Waszyngtona. Out of range of the main World War II battles and destruction, Praga still has some of its prewar architecture and atmosphere, and an increasingly bohemian reputation.

Immediately across from the Stare Miasto is the **Ogród Zoologiczny** (Warsaw Zoo; daily 9am–sunset; 12zł), whose run-down yet attractive park-like expanse houses, among others, elephants, hippos and bears, the latter kept in an enclosure visible from the road. The **Cerkiew św. Cyryla i Metodego** (Orthodox Church of SS Cyril and Methodius; Mon–Sat 11am–4pm, Sun 1–4pm; free; services daily at 9am & 5pm) just beyond al. Solidarności, is one remaining sign of the former Russian presence. A large neo-Byzantine structure topped by a succession of onion domes, its original mid-nineteenth-century interior decoration remains intact. If you visit during services you might hear the excellent **choir** in action. Continuing one block east you'll come to the heart of modern Praga, the multi-level shopping centre built above the Warszawa Wileńska train station.

Praga's most notorious connection with Russia stems from the time of the Warsaw Uprising (see box, pp.104–105). At the beginning of September 1944, Soviet forces reached the outer reaches of Praga. Insurrectionists from the besieged city centre were dispatched to plead with them to intervene against the Nazis, to no avail. Throughout the Uprising Soviet tanks sat and waited on the edges, moving in to flush out the Nazis only when the city had been virtually eradicated. For the next forty years, the official account gave "insufficient Soviet forces" as the reason for the nonintervention; as with the Katyń massacre, every Pole knew otherwise. A **monument** to the Soviet arrival, alongside the highway behind the Orthodox church, features four somnolent-looking Red Army soldiers known locally as the "Four Sleepies".

On a lighter note, Warsaw's best-known and longest-running flea and black market – the **Bazar Różyckiego** – is five minutes' walk south from the Orthodox church on ul. Ząbkowska, though now it's little more than another place to buy cheap clothes and fake leather bags. If you do go, watch out for pickpockets. Further south along the river, close to the Poniatowski bridge, is an equally dubious but more interesting venue, the **Dziesięciolecia** stadium, once the city's largest sports stadium and now taken over by a sprawling outdoor market (see "Markets and bazaars", p.138).

Praga was once home to a significant proportion of the city's Jewish population. Directly over the Śląsko-Dąbrowski bridge, south of the leafy Park Praski, there are a number of streets, notably **ulica Kłopotowskiego** and **ulica Sierakowskiego** where you can still see some typical old Jewish residences. As elsewhere in the city there are archways leading to red-brick buildings from an earlier age, often bearing signs of wartime shrapnel. Also worth exploring are the streets north of the Wileńska station, such as **ulica Środkowa**. A number of artists have moved their studios to the nearby **ulica Inżynierska**, and it was here and on the badly beaten **ulica Mała** that Roman Polański's shot street scenes for his movie *The Pianist*. This impoverished area is said to be dangerous, and most Varsovians from across the river wouldn't dream of coming here, but during the day there's no need to worry.

A little further out, in the Brodno district, is the **Cmentarz Żydowski** (Jewish Cemetery; entrance at the corner of ul. Odrowąża and ul. Wincentego; take tram #3 or #25 north from the Wileńska station), founded in the 1780s. It was badly damaged by the Nazis, who used many of the stones for paving. Restoration work is in progress on the thousand or so graves remaining.

Eating and drinking

Warsaw is one of the best places to eat in central Europe. Alongside **restaurants** specializing in traditional Polish cuisine, which range from homely to sumptuous, there's a welcome range of culinary variety; modern European, Italian and Japanese are some of the more widespread choices, but you'll find many others. With a few exceptions, the restaurants in the Stare Miasto are geared towards tourists, offering a conventional range of Polish staples, while more adventurous and fashionable places can be found further south.

Cafés range from upscale and old-fashioned to modern minimalist, while there are also plenty of down-to-earth student hangouts. Cakes and pastries worthy of the best of Central Europe are easy to come by, and if you follow the locals you'll spend half your time in the city musing over a cup of coffee or tea and a slice of apple pie.

There's a good variety of **bars** of all sorts. The ambience-free "drink bars", which served hard spirits to heavy-drinking locals in communist times, have mostly disappeared now that beer has surpassed vodka as the national drink of choice, but their place has been taken by dives of varying appeal, many serving European brands alongside local brews. Moving up the scale there's a range of upmarket places, from flashy bars aimed at expats and Warsaw's upwardly mobile to unmarked Bohemian clubs. There are also "ethnic" pubs, bars in wooden ranch-type shacks in the city's parkland, theme bars and unpretentious local haunts. In short, everything you need.

The distinction between Warsaw's eating and drinking venues is inevitably blurred, with many of the latter offering both snacks and full meals as well as booze – so bear in mind that many of the places listed under "Cafés and bars" below are also good places for a bite to eat.

Places to eat

All the central areas are packed with restaurants, many of which invitingly offer outdoor chairs and tables during the summer months. Snack bars may open as early as 8–9am for the benefit of those seeking breakfast, but some smaller places close early and at weekends. Mainstream restaurants are open daily, usually from around 11am until 11pm; closing times (and days) for those shutting earlier or later than that are listed below. English-language **menus** are available in better restaurants and even some low-end places; if you need help refer to pp.712–714.

Warsaw is the most expensive city in Poland, and restaurant prices are slowly edging towards those charged in the West. A number of the famously cheap **milk bars** – canteen-style places doling out filling Polish staples for well under 10zł a head – still survive, and we've listed two central ones with English menus, but there's also a new generation of places, some excellent, where it's easy to eat well for 15–20zł. Otherwise, the price of a main course and drink at a proper restaurant can range in price from as little as 20–30zł in casual establishments to 100zł or more at the most upmarket ones. Wherever you choose to eat, however, traditional Polish dishes like *barszcz* (beetroot soup), *placki* (potato pancakes) and *kotlet schabowy* (pork chop) invariably work out cheaper than the fancier items on the menu. In late summer and autumn you'll find *kurki* (chanterelles) and other forest mushrooms on the menus at most upscale restaurants and also a few of the cheaper ones. We've included telephone numbers for those restaurants where **reservations** – especially at weekends – are a good idea.

Fast-food joints – big Western names and Polish imitators – are firmly established. As well as burgers and hot dogs you'll find pizza, both genuinely Italian and the Polish pickled vegetable variety, *zapiekanka*. Numerous kiosks dole out sandwiches and salads, while kebab stands and Vietnamese/Chinese outfits are also widespread.

The Stare Miasto and the Nowe Miasto

Bar Pod Barbakan ul. Mostowa 27/29. Milk bar on the edge of the old town serving the standard range of *pierogi*, soups and potato pancakes; convenient for cash-strapped tourists, and with an English-language menu. Daily 9am–5pm.

Forteca Park Traugutta. Some of Warsaw's best and most unusual outdoor dining, this summer-only grill (late-May to mid-Sept) is set inside a nineteenth-century Russian fort and serves "slow food" dishes such as barbecued ribs (22zł) and spinach salad with smoked bacon and soft sheep's cheese (19zł). Resident goats up on the fort walls add a pastoral touch. Mon–Fri from 5.30pm, Sat & Sun from 1pm.

Freta 33 ul. Freta 33/35. Fresh and moderately priced Mediterranean food on the Rynek Nowego Miasta, with a popular terrace and small, stylish dining room. The tagliatelle with cream sauce and Parma ham (24zł) is the best of the pastas; salads and appetizers are also recommended.

Fukier Rynek Starego Miasta 27 ☎022/831 1013. Top-notch, lavishly decorated and suitably pricey Stare Miasto restaurant with a strong line in imaginatively reinterpreted traditional Polish cuisine, and candlelight after dark. Open noon until midnight. Reservations advised.

Jazz Bistro Gwiazdeczka ul. Piwna 40. The most elegant of the *Jazz Bistro* branches (see also p.131), and with its ensemble of whitewash, steel and glass, the only modern restaurant interior in the Stare Miasto. The carrot soup with mint leaves (14zł) is superb, and the salads (18–30zł) and meat dishes (24–36zł) are also recommended.

Karczma Gessler Rynek Starego Miasta 21/21A ☎022/831 4427. Outstanding, rustic-themed place with endless labyrinthine cellars and a range of Polish dishes, including game and Jewish specialities. Alcohol is not sold, but the house wine is served as part of the meal. Very expensive, but there are affordable lunch specials at weekends, and upstairs a posh café with tantalizing cakes and windows overlooking the Rynek. Reservations advised.

Maharaja Thai ul. Szeroki Dunaj 13. Undistinguished atmosphere but dependable Thai food, surprisingly piquant and with plenty of vegetarian options, served until midnight in the Stare Miasto. Main courses 20–28zł.

Na Prowincji ul.Nowomiejska 10. Classic and well-prepared range of pizza (20–30zł) and pasta (17–24zł) in simple surroundings; a nice change from nearby tourist-only venues stuffed with faux-heirlooms and offering dubious "Old Polish" cuisine.

Pewne Miejsce ul. Świętojańska 13. Small, pleasant outfit in the old town, one of the few in the area catering to locals as much as tourists. Serving pasta, salads and Polish food, with most of the menu under 20zł. Also a good place for a quiet beer.

Pod Samsonem ul. Freta 3/5. Among the best of the many tourist-oriented restaurants in the Nowe Miasto, with good-quality Polish dishes and a sprinkling of Jewish choices. Low to moderate prices, and set meals at around 20zł. Open till 10pm.

Puszkin ul. Świętojańska 2 ☏ 022/635 3535. Plush and well-respected Russian restaurant with an impressive vision of tsarist-era extravagance: red velvet, samovars and costumed waiters, and specialities like sturgeon and blinis with caviar. Costly by Polish standards, but would be cheap in Moscow.

Krakowskie Przedmieście and around

Artibus pl. Małachowskiego 3 ☏ 022/828 0584. Grandly decadent, bordello-like interior in the basement of the Galeria Zachęta, popular with an arty, international crowd for its fine French food and long wine list. Strong on meat dishes such as veal medallions with tarragon sauce (54zł) and baked chicken stuffed with crabs (48zł).

Kuźnia Smaku ul. Mazowiecka 10 ☏ 022/826 3024. Deservedly popular restaurant with an unassuming location in the one-star *Mazowiecki* hotel (see p.91). In spite of service that's anything but attentive, this was the talk of Warsaw foodies when it opened a few years ago. Modern interpretations of classic European, Polish and Russian dishes like blinis with salmon and steak with garlic butter. Main courses 35–45zł.

La Boheme pl. Teatralny 1 ☏ 022/692 0681. Excellent, modern European food in the Teatr Wielki, popular with a well-dressed and prosperous crowd for inventive dishes such as venison with juniper sauce, as well as French and Italian classics. Main courses around 40zł.

Pierogarnia ul. Bednarska 28/30. *Pierogi*-only place just below the old town, with a country-cottage atmosphere and portions for 12zł. Try *pierogi* with lentils (*z soczewicą*) or with buckwheat (*wrocławskie*). Till 10pm.

St Antonio ul. Senatorska 39 ☏ 022/826 3008. Upmarket but moderately priced Italian/Polish restaurant with a perfect location on the northwest edge of the Ogród Saski. The menu nicely balances homemade pastas like ravioli with ricotta (21zł) with traditional Polish dishes, including trout with wild mushroom sauce (25zł). Also daily specials, with fresh mussels (39zł) Thurs & Fri.

Uniwersytecki Krakowskie Przedmieście 20. Classic, typically cheap milk bar with an English menu by the university and convenient for a quick break from sightseeing. Much frequented by students. Mon–Fri till 8pm, Sat & Sun till 5pm.

Varna ul. Mazowiecka 12. Communist-style Bulgarian restaurant offering a nice line in mid-priced Balkan dishes – from *kebapcheta* (grilled mincemeat patties) and *kavarma* (meat braised in a pot) through to roast lamb. Stuffed peppers (22zł) a speciality. Folk music some evenings.

Nowy Świat and around

Butelka In the pavilion behind Nowy Świat 22. Tiny, pleasantly furnished Italian place serving tasty and affordable pasta dishes (12–16zł), including *penne z kurkami* (penne with chanterelles) in season. Good for a light meal and glass of wine, with lunch specials under 20zł.

Chianti ul. Foksal 17 ☏ 022/828 0222. Candle-lit cellar restaurant with intimate feel and great Italian food. The fresh pasta dishes, such as red tagliatelle with truffles and prosciutto (34zł), are recommended.

Green Way ul. Szpitalna 6. Crowded Warsaw branch of the national chain vegetarian restaurant, with a range of Polonized international dishes such as Mexican goulash, lasagne and samosas (9–13zł), as well as dark wheat pancakes with fruit toppings (7zł) and fresh fruit drinks. Take out service available. Daily 10am–9pm.

Grill Bar ul. Zgoda 4. Classy and comfortable, with country-style decor that's not overbearing. Good Polish dishes at low prices – grilled meats, all under 20zł, are a speciality. Till 10pm.

Guru ul. Bracka 18. One block down from *Green Way*, this slightly more refined vegetarian choice serves fresh and well-prepared Asian dishes for 12–20zł, as well as a panoply of teas and fruit shakes and an enormous 24zł lunch special. Tables and chairs on the main floor, or sit cross-legged upstairs.

Le Bistrot ul. Foksal 2. ☎ 022/827 8707. French cuisine in unimpeachably formal surroundings, and a standard of cooking that justifies the high prices on the menu. Located in one of the Zamoyski palaces, with a terrace overlooking the garden in summer. Sometimes closed for private parties.

Restauracja Polska In a separate building in the courtyard behind Nowy Świat 21 ☎ 022/826 3877. Despite the unassuming basement location, this is one of the best Polish restaurants in Warsaw, with sumptuous surroundings, impeccable service and a first-rate kitchen. Specialities include *pierogi* with veal (23zł), pike-perch with leek sauce (42.50zł) and duck with sour berry *confit* (42zł).

The rest of Śródmieście

Adler ul. Mokotowska 69 ☎ 022/628 7384. Folksy but professional Bavarian restaurant, with Polish/German dishes such as pork loin stuffed with prunes with potato dumplings (39.50zł). Atmospheric and popular, and with a nice summer garden – you should reserve.

Belvedere Park Łazienkowski's Nowa Pomarańczarnia (see p.123) ☎ 022/841 4806. One of Warsaw's best and most expensive eateries, with fresh oysters and other seafood a speciality, in a restored orangery at the southern end of the Park Łazienkowski. Tasteful, understated decor, and popular with politicians.

Biblioteka University of Warsaw Library, ul. Dobra 56/66 ☎ 022/552 7195. Imaginative, modern European menu in swish, modernist surroundings, with such specialities as marinated duck with caraway seeds (65zł) and, for dessert, pineapple carpaccio with pomegranate ice cream (29zł). Favoured by prosperous art and media types.

Chata Młyn al. Ujazdowskie 6a. Modest and pleasant little Polish restaurant with a selection of conventional meat-and-potatoes dishes (15–25zł), good salads and a relaxing terrace. Convenient for *Park Łazienkowski*.

Delicja Polska ul. Koszykowa 54 ☎ 022/630 8850. An outstanding and very traditional Polish restaurant, with sumptuous decor, polished service and prices to match. Specialities include lamb cutlets marinated in bison grass and caramelized apple (48zł), and roasted goose with red cabbage and dumplings (45zł). The desserts are also recommended.

Jazz Bistro/Nu Jazz Bistro ul. Piękna 20, ul. Żurawia 6/12. Café-restaurant chain with several addresses. The one on ul. Piękna is less formal, with a reliable, good-value menu (sandwiches 14zł; pasta 20–25zł), and is the only branch with regular live piano jazz (Tues–Sat 7–10pm). The artfully sparse and marginally pricier ul. Żurawia branch

has an adventurous fusion menu, with emphasis on wholewheat pasta (25–35zł), coconut curry and fresh vegetables.

Latająca Ryba ul. Kasprzaka 7. Engaging and affordable little sushi bar near the new Warsaw Uprising Museum, with set meals from around 25zł.

Marak ul. Świętokrzyska 18 and ul. Widok 19, among others. Smart soup kitchen serving up a range of Polish soups such as *ogórkowa* (pickle soup) and more exotic flavours like *tajska* (Thai chicken curry), as well as seasonal choices, including an outstanding *chłodnik* (chilled summer borscht). Large bowls 8–13zł.

Nonsolo Pizza ul. Grójecka 20c. Unpretentious Italian-owned pizzeria using high-quality ingredients and a brick oven; pizzas and pastas – made on site – from 18zł. Trams #7, #9, #25 or #44 three stops west from Warszawa Centralna.

Qchnia Artystyczna al. Ujazdowski 6. Wonderful location in the Ujazdowski Castle, just north of Park Łazienkowski, with excellent views down towards the river, quirky decor (it shares premises with the Centrum Sztuki Współczesnej, see p.120) and a great outdoor terrace. Well-chosen but limited menu, with a handful of meat (40–50zł), pasta (25–35zł) and potato pancake (20–25zł) dishes, some of which are vegetarian.

Qllinarnia ul. Zielna 5, Pavilion 59 (entrance on Marszałkowska). A cheerful nouveau milk bar with English-speaking staff. Wide range of vegetable soups (3–5zł), ten kinds of *pierogi* (with unusual choices like chicken with walnuts; 1.50zł per *pieróg*), Austrian pasta (*spezel*) from 9zł and chanterelles (*kurki*) in season. The best cheap lunch in Warsaw. Mon–Fri 11am–7pm.

Tandoor Palace ul. Marszałkowska 21/25. Award-winning Indian food, with curries from around 28zł and some interesting "Balti" dishes from Kashmiri Pakistan. Warsaw's expat curry club eats here Wednesdays, after meeting in the *Marriott* hotel bar (see p.92) at 7.30pm (visitors welcome).

Warsaw Tortilla Factory ul. Wilcza 46. An expat institution, lively Tex-Mex place serving large, well-spiced burritos (around 22zł), and plenty of less expensive bar snacks. Tequila shot specials, and brunch at weekends. Till 1am.

Praga

Le Cedre al. Solidarności 61 ☎ 022/670 1166. Great Lebanese restaurant next to the *Hotel Praski*, with belly dancing in the evening and grilled meats at around 30zł. The hot and cold *mezze* plates (31zł) are especially recommended.

Cafés and bars

Warsaw can boast a vivacious **café** life, though interest is as much social as gastronomic. Establishments vary between cosy haunts serving cakes and ice cream to trendier modern joints offering a range of fancy coffees and an international menu of snacks. Many of the latter stay open well into the night, competing for custom with the mushrooming number of **bars**, which range in style from hip designer joints to raucous beer halls with live bands and dancing. With a few exceptions, **pubs** are bland affairs that have little in common with their British or Irish namesakes. The cost of drinks in Warsaw are significantly higher than elsewhere in Poland, but still compare favourably with Western Europe as long as you stick to domestic beer and spirits.

Most cafés and bars are concentrated in the Stare Miasto and the modern centre to the south, but there are few obvious strolling areas where you'll find one establishment after another – it's best to plan your evening's itinerary before setting out. In summer, head for the fair-weather alfresco bars along Wybrzeże Gdańskie, just below the Stare Miasto on the western bank of the Wisła; or in Pole Mokotowskie, an area of parkland southwest of the centre (easily reached from the Pole Mokotowskie metro station), which is bustling with Varsovians on balmy evenings.

Cafés

Stare Miasto and around

Literacka ul. Krakowskie Przedmieście 87/89. Atmospheric, romantic place with quiet jazz at weekends. Serves toothsome snacks and shuts shortly after midnight.

To Lubię ul. Freta 10. Coffee, wine and tasty desserts in the bell tower of the Kościół św. Jacka (see p.101). Till 10pm.

Śródmieście

Blikle Café Nowy Świat 33. Open since 1869, this is the oldest cake shop in the city and an elegant place in which to enjoy coffee and desserts on the main drag. Famous for its doughnuts (*pączki*), it also does excellent but pricey breakfasts. Till 11pm.

Café 6/12 ul. Żurawia 6/12. Deserves mention as café, bar and restaurant, with smallish portions but boasting one of Warsaw's most eclectic menus – the emphasis is on Asian and Mediterranean dishes (20–35zł), but homely choices like hamburger with *rucola* and mashed potatoes (26zł) fare just as well. There's also a long list of fruit and vegetable shakes, and foreign newspapers to read. The house wine is surprisingly cheap. Till 11pm.

Coffee Heaven Nowy Świat 46; also Warszawa Centralna and other locations. Western-style coffee chain. Till 10pm.

Czuły Barbarzyńca ul. Dobra 31. Interesting bookstore/café buzzing with students; serves excellent cappuccino. Till 10pm, or midnight Fri & Sat.

Kafefajka In the pavilion behind Nowy Świat 26. Small Turkish-themed place specializing in tea and hookahs but also serving beer. Attracts a good crowd in evenings. Till 11pm.

Mercer's Nowy Świat 31. The best in a line of chic places on Nowy Świat, with long windows for watching passers-by and great coffee. Food options, though, are unimpressive. Till 11pm.

Między Nami ul. Bracka 20. Hip but relaxed place with two levels of seating, hosting an easy-going gay and straight clientele. Full food menu includes excellent salads, while in-house DJs spin discs some evenings. No sign outside, so look for the pale grey awnings. Till 11pm/ midnight.

Nowy Świat Nowy Świat 63, on the corner with Świętokrzyska. Sumptuous, roomy café that's long been a favourite with the cream of Warsaw's cultural elite. With formal service and officious cloakroom staff, it still feels like a wondrous relic from another era. Till 11pm.

Wedel ul. Górskiego 9. Poland's top *chocolaterie*, with a stunning range of cocoa products. Try hot chocolate *ekstra gorskie* (extra bitter). Till 10pm.

Bars

Stare Miasto and around

Chimera ul. Podwale 29. Kraków-style basement café, strong on unmatched furniture, amateurish abstract art and brightly painted walls. Serves beer to a mix of backpackers and local students, and also does a good line in crepes. Till 1am.

Diuna ul. Dobra 33/35. Relaxed, student-oriented bar down towards the river, with cheap beer, artificial fur on the walls and live music (of highly varying quality) almost every evening. Usually no cover. Till 1am or later.

Harenda Krakowskie Przedmieście 4/5. Roomy ranch-style bar behind the hotel of the same name, with a big open-air beer garden in summer. Occasional live rock, jazz or DJs – when there may be a cover charge. Till 3am.

Jadłodajnia Filozoficzna ul. Dobra 33/35. Next to *Diuna* and a bit more artsy and pretentious, with frequent DJs. Till 1am or later.

Jezioro Łabędzie ul. J. Moliera 4/6. Late night hedonism by the Wielki Teatr, drawing a well-heeled crowd with its vodka list, Polish/Russian food and an ambience that's part opera box and part techno club. The name means "Swan Lake". Till 2am or later.

Le Madame ul. Koźla 12. Bizarre, gay-friendly nightspot in an old industrial warehouse behind the Nowe Miasto that's furnished with not just ragged armchairs and sofas but also four-poster beds and odd machinery. DJs and performance art at night, Björk and Portishead in daytime. Occasional cover charges. Till 3am weekdays; weekend after-parties as late as noon.

Metal Bar Rynek Starego Miasta 8. One of the few establishments to bring nightlife to the heart of the Stare Miasto, all metal and glass and with cocktails and bar snacks. Till midnight, 2am at weekends.

Morgan's Pub ul. Okólnik 1. Irish joint that has built its reputation on friendly atmosphere and good service rather than its faux-pub decor. Popular with expat sports fans, and Tues is curry night. Till midnight.

Pod Baryłką ul. Garbarska 5/7. Down from pl. Zamkowy on the Rynek Mariensztacki, with outdoor seating in a pleasantly shady arcade and a smoky interior. For those who go to a pub to savour beer, with 14 draught varieties on offer. Till midnight.

Śródmieście

Baumgart/Libera al. Ujazdowskie 6. Cliquey but not unfriendly café-bar in the Zamek Ujazdowski, patronized by bohemian intellectuals and hosting occasional themed DJ nights. Till midnight or later depending on what's going on. Not to be confused with *Miejsce*, the club in the basement.

Café Kulturalna pl. Defilad 1. In the southeast wing of the Pałac Kultury i Nauki, this is one of the city's success stories. It's an airy student hangout with bizarre plastic chandeliers and DJs at weekends. Open late.

Champions Sport Bar al. Jerozolimskie 65/79. Large and garish, on the ground floor of the *Marriott* hotel (see p.92). Best place in town to catch football and other sporting events on TV, but beer prices are on the expensive side. Till midnight.

Nobo ul. Wilcza 58a. A cut above other bars, with first-rate cocktails, professional staff and good if pricey food. Packed with well-heeled Varsovians and expats. Cover charge (10–20zł) only when there's live music or a visiting DJ. Open late.

Piotruś Nowy Świat 18. Old-fashioned "drink bar", attracting a mix of ageing locals and students looking for communist kitsch. Till 11pm.

Szparka pl. Trzech Krzyży 18. A favourite with yuppies, models and the like on Warsaw's most fashionable square; pricey and open late.

Praga and the other suburbs

Lolek Rokitnica 20. The best of several watering holes in the middle of Pole Mokotowskie. Barbecue-style food, beer and daily live music (Mon–Sat 8pm; Sun 2pm) in and around a log cabin overgrown with foliage. Pole Mokotowskie metro station. Till dawn.

Łysy Pingwin ul. Ząbkowska 12. Run by transplant from Stockholm, a Seventies lounge with Czech beer, Spanish tapas and crates of old records for sale. Well worth the trip across the river to Praga. Mon–Thurs & Sat till midnight, Fri till 2am, Sun till 10pm.

Regeneracja ul. Puławska 61. A laid-back student favourite several kilometres south of the centre, with a good range of vegetarian dishes and live music or DJs some nights. Until 2am.

Nightlife and entertainment

After decades in the wilderness, there's a quality **club** scene in Warsaw now, with a fair spread that should cater for most tastes. If a Chopin **concert** or avant-garde **drama** (sometimes in English) is your idea of a good night out, you're unlikely to be disappointed. In summer, especially, high-quality theatre productions, operas and recitals abound, many of them as popular with tourists as with Varsovians themselves. They are also affordable, particularly if you buy tickets that entail taking whatever seats are available after the third and final call (it sounds risky, but there are always places).

For up-to-date information about what's on, check the current **listings** sections of the *Warsaw Insider* or *Gazeta Wyborcza* (see p.88) or look for posters around the city. The main **jazz festivals** are the excellent Warsaw Summer Jazz Days, a summer-long event featuring big western names with many of the concerts free; the related Jazz na Starówce (Jazz in the Old Town), with high-quality free concerts on the Rynek Starego Miasta at 7pm every Saturday in July and August; and the October Jazz Jamboree, a longstanding bash which has over the years attracted luminaries such as Duke Ellington and Miles Davis. The most important **film festivals** are the Warsaw Film Festival (ⓦ www.wff.pl), held in mid-October; and in May the Warsaw International Jewish Film Festival (ⓦ www.warsawjff.ant.pl). **Classical music festivals** include the five-yearly Chopin Piano Competition, always a launch pad for a major international career and to be held next in September 2005; the Festival of Contemporary Music (ⓦ www.warsaw-autumn.art.pl) held every September; the Easter week Beethoven Festival (ⓦ www.beethoven.org.pl); and the prestigious Mozart Festival, held in early summer at the Opera Kameralna. The tourist office will have details of these and other upcoming events.

Clubs and gigs

In addition to the numerous late-night bars boasting in-house DJs, there's a reasonable range of **clubbing** opportunities in Warsaw, with new venues opening all the time – *Warsaw in Your Pocket* and the *Warsaw Insider* will have details (see p.85). The accent is on commercial techno, although you'll find that there's always something else going on on any given night of the week – be it a reggae, hip-hop, Latin or golden oldies night.

Decent **live music** can be hard to find, but there are a number of alternative-leaning clubs which put on irregular concerts, while established bands (whether Polish or foreign) play in the larger discotheques, or in venues such as the Sala Kongresowa in the Pałac Kultury i Nauki. In summer, big Western pop-rock acts may play outdoor gigs in sports stadiums – if so, the posters announcing their arrival will be hard to avoid. In addition to the places mentioned here, several of the bars listed above (such as *Café Kulturalna*, *Diuna* and *Nobo*) may also have live music. The two big EMPiK stores (see p.137), both of which generally employ English speakers, have counters that sell tickets to rock and jazz concerts.

As for **opening hours**, while gigs often start quite early (typically 7–8pm), there's not much point in turning up to clubs before 10pm, and things may not really get going until after midnight. **Admission** to gigs and club nights costs between 5zł and 30zł depending on the prestige of the club and the night of the week. Tickets to see visiting western DJs or bands often cost much more. Gleaning what's on from Polish-language fly posters is easy enough: otherwise your best sources of information are the free monthly *City Magazine* and the

Friday edition of *Gazeta Wyborcza* (see p.88), which also tells you which places have *selekcja* (where you'll have to be attractive and/or dressed stylishly enough to get past a doorman).

Apetyt Architektów/Punkt ul. Koszykowa 55. Roomy cellar venue next to the restaurant of the same name, specializing in reggae, world music and offbeat music nights featuring DJs and occasional live performers. From 8pm.

Barbados ul. Wierzbowa 9. Warsaw's ultimate yuppie nightclub experience, playing conventional dance music and filled with beautiful people and an attendant cast of expats. Fancy food restaurant upstairs. It's not easy to get past the *selekcja* at the door, but eating in the restaurant first will gain you admittance to the club. Thurs–Sat till 5am.

Fabryka Trzciny ul. Otwocka 14 ☏022/619 0513, ⓦwww.fabrykatrzciny.pl. Concert hall/gallery in a 1916 rubber factory in the Praga district, on a run-down street that's best reached by taxi. Hosts visiting indie-rock bands, avant-garde classical music concerts and the like. An on-site restaurant serving modern European cuisine in post-industrial surroundings is planned for the near future.

Miejsce al. Ujazdowskie 6. Bright colours and DJs spinning electronic, jazz and reggae sounds in the basement of the Zamek Ujazdowski. Usually no cover. Till 11pm Mon–Fri, 1am weekends.

Piekarnia ul. Młocińska 11, Żoliborz ⓦwww .piekarnia.org.pl. Excellent club in an old bakery, generally considered the best in Warsaw and attracting frequent foreign DJs and a young and hip crowd. Just northwest of the centre, near to Rondo Babka. Fri & Sat only, from 10pm.

Proxima ul. Żwirki i Wigury 99a ☏022/822 8702. Very cheap, very spacious, and usually full of students as it's close to the big dormitories southwest of the centre. Sometimes hosts Western bands; otherwise expect mainstream dance music and throngs of youth drinking beer from plastic cups. Bus #175 from "Centrum". Wed & Thurs till 3am, Fri & Sat till 4am.

Spawarka ul. Mokotowska 59. New nightclub playing techno and house for a glamorous, moneyed crowd in a carefully designed faux-industrial setting. Open late.

Stodoła ul. Batorego 10 ☏022/825 6031. Student disco and gig venue of many years' standing (Western bands are likely to play here), with a large dance floor. One block northeast of the Pole Mokotowskie metro station. Open till 4am.

Tygmont ul. Mazowiecka 6/8, ⓦwww.tygmont .com.pl. The city's top jazz club, with a regular gig roster and a stylish, upmarket clientele. Open till 4am – or till the last customer leaves.

Underground Music Café Marszałkowska 126/134. Roomy drinking and dancing venue offering mainstream house, soul and funk, sometimes with big-name DJs. There's usually something going on here every night of the week. Open till 4am.

Utopia ul. Jasna 1. Fashionable house/techno club with a mostly gay crowd; it's notoriously difficult to get past the *selekcja*. Open late.

Gay and lesbian bars and clubs

The iron hand of Catholicism, strong as it may be in the Polish hinterlands, has little grip over Warsaw, and the **gay scene** is thriving. For **information** check sites ⓦwarsaw.gayguide.net or ⓦwww.gay.pl.

Like anywhere else, the scene changes rapidly in Warsaw. Though there are **gay pubs** (*Kokon*, downhill from the old town at ul. Brzozowa 37, and *Lodi Dodi*, ul. Wilcza 23, are two of the best known), most people meet in gay-friendly bars with a mixed clientele. *Między Nami*, ul. Bracka 20 (see p.132) and *Le Madame*, ul. Koźla (see p.133) are perennial favourites. *Bastylia*, ul. Mokotowska 17 (at pl. Zbawiciela – take any tram south on Marszałkowska), is a creperie popular with lesbians.

A couple of **clubs** stand out: *Paradise*, Skra stadium, ul. Wawelska 5 (bus #175 or #512 from the Centralna station), which has a friendly all-night disco (Fri–Sun) with a great combination of acts – lesbian George Michael impersonators, drag queens and so on – with a few self-conscious straights snogging in the corner; and the chic *Utopia* (see above).

Opera and classical music

Opera is a big favourite in Warsaw, and **classical** concerts, especially piano music, tend to attract big audiences, but despite this concerts are rarely sold out and they

airly inexpensive. **Tickets** for many concerts are available from the theatre
t office, Kasy ZASP (Mon–Fri 11am–6.30pm; ℡022/621 9454 or 621 9383),
l. Jerozolimskie 25, just along from the *Novotel Centrum*. Mazurkas Travel,
where good English is spoken, in the *Novotel Centrum* lobby (Mon–Sat 8am–6pm;
℡022/629 1878), sells theatre tickets but charges a commission. Tickets for some
theatre events are available at the EMPiK ticket counters (see opposite).

Akademia Muzyczna ul. Okólnik 2 ℡022/827 7241. Regular concerts by talented students. Free entry.

Filharmonia ul. Jasna 5 ℡022/551 7128, ☜www.filharmonia.pl. The main concert venue, with regular performances by the excellent National Philharmonic as well as visiting ensembles. This is also the venue for the International Chopin Piano Competition (see p.134). Tickets from the box office at ul. Sienkiewicza 10 (Mon–Sat 10am–2pm & 3–7pm), though you can always get cheap stand-by tickets just before the performance. An ISIC card gets you a thirty percent discount.

Kościół Ewangelicko-Augsburgski (Evangelical Church) pl. Małachowskiego 3. Focuses on organ and choral music, often with visiting choirs. Excellent acoustics.

Muzeum Fryderyka Chopina see p.116 ℡022/827 5441, ☜www.chopin.pl. Summer piano recitals and other occasional performances

organized by the Towarzystwo im. Fryderyka Chopina (Chopin Society).

Opera Kameralna al. Solidarności 76b ℡022/831 2240, ☜www.wok.pol.pl. Chamber opera performances in a magnificent white and gold stucco auditorium. Also a key venue during the Mozart Festival. Box office Mon–Fri 10am–7pm.

Park Łazienkowski see p.121. Varied summer programme of orchestral, choral and chamber concerts at the weekend, often held beside the Chopin monument, in the Orangery, or inside the Palace.

Teatr Wielki (National Theatre) pl. Teatralny 1 ℡022/692 0208, ☜www.teatrwielki.pl. The big opera, ballet and musical performances – everything from Mozart to contemporary Polish composers – in suitably grandiose surroundings. Box office Mon–Sat 9am–7pm, Sun 10am–7pm.

Towarzystwo Muzyczne Warszawskie (Warsaw Music Society) ul. Morskie Oko 2 ℡022/849 6858. Frequent piano and guitar recitals.

Theatre and cinema

Theatre is one of the most popular highbrow forms of entertainment in Warsaw, and still receives generous state subsidies. Not speaking Polish is, of course, an obstacle, but the all-round quality of performance and set design ensures that it's still worth considering a performance at one of the major theatres. Tickets start at about 20zł.

Warsaw's **cinemas** offer a mixture of mainstream Western pictures, global arthouse movies and homegrown hits. Films are shown in the original language with Polish subtitles (though child-oriented features are dubbed. The best place to find listings is the "Kino" page of the *Gazeta Wyborcza* (see p.88), in the paper every day but most extensive on Fridays. Cinema tickets cost about 10–20zł, usually with reductions on Mondays.

Theatres

Centrum Sztuki Współczesnej Pałac Ujazdowski ℡022/628 1271, ☜www.csw.art.pl. Plays host to many international theatre and dance performances.

Syrena ul. Waryńskiego 12 ℡022/660 9875, ☜www.teatrsyrena.art.pl. Modern drama in Polish.

Teatr Buffo ul. Konopnickiej 6 ℡022/625 4709, ☜www.studiobuffo.com.pl. Concerts, musicals, avant-garde plays. Has performances in English at times.

Teatr Dramatyczny Pałac Kultury i Nauki ℡022/620 2102 or ℡022/656 6844 respectively

☜www.teatrdramat yczny.pl. Two venues – one for big productions, another for intimate studio performances – in this huge arts complex, both staging plays in Polish, with the studio more avant-garde. In October each even-numbered year, it hosts the prestigious Festival of Festivals, with plenty of performances in English.

Teatr Powszechny ul. Zamoyskiego 20 ℡022/818 2516, ☜www.powszechny.art.pl. Lots of foreign plays, but always in Polish.

Teatr Żydowski pl. Grzybowski 12/16 ℡022/620 7025. Warsaw's Jewish theatre, with most performances in Polish or Yiddish.

Cinemas

Atlantik ul. Chmielna 33 ☏ 022/827 0894, ⓦ www.kinoatlantic.pl. Modern multiplex showing first-run films and the odd arty choice.

Iluzjon ul. Narbutta 50a ☏ 022/646 1260. National Film Archives venue, screening cinema classics from all over the world.

Kino Lab al. Ujazdowskie 6 ☏ 022/628 1271, ⓦ www.kinolab.independent.pl. Art movies and assorted cinematic weirdness in the Centrum Sztuki Wspólczesnej.

Kinoteka Pałac Kultury i Nauki ☏ 022/826 1961, ⓦ www.kinoteka.pl. Multiple screens showing commercial films in this extraordinary Stalinist building (see p.115).

Kultura/Rejs Krakowskie Przedmieście 21/3 ☏ 022/826 3335. Mostly specialist films. Late-night screenings at weekends and good Dolby sound system.

Luna ul. Marszałkowska 28. ☏ 022/621 7828, ⓦ www.kinoluna.pl. Student-oriented place with cheap tickets.

Relax ul. Złota 8 ☏ 022/828 3888, ⓦ www .kinoplex.pl. Comfy downtown cinema showing the latest releases.

Wars Rynek Nowego Miasta 5/7 ☏ 022/831 4488, ⓦ www.wars.gutekfilm.com.pl. Non-mainstream films right above the Stare Miasto. Big screen but uncomfortable seats.

Shopping

The old sparsely stocked state-run establishments are a distant memory in Warsaw, and **shopping** here today is not very different from shopping in any other major European city, with a variety of department and specialist stores catering to most consumer whims. Biggest of the central department stores is the **Galeria Centrum** on Marszałkowska, opposite the Pałac Kultury i Nauki. The pedestrianized **ul. Chmielna**, running east from here, has its fair share of clothes shops and boutiques.

Bookshops, newsagents and record stores

Thanks to the sizeable English-speaking community you won't find yourself lost for a newspaper or book in English. As well as the "new" bookshops listed below, **antykwariats** (second-hand booksellers) invariably have a few curiosities in English, sometimes including out-of-print works on Poland, and are always good for cut-rate, communist-era art albums. Try Troszkiewiczów at ul. Wspólna 51 and ul. Piękna 54, or Zaścianek, ul. Wilcza 5. Atticus, ul. Krakowskie Przedmieście 20/22, and Kosmos, al. Ujazdowskie 16, also sell prints and old maps.

American Bookstore ul. Koszykowa 55, Nowy Świat 61 and others ⓦ www.americanbookstore .pl. Poorly organized but excellent range of fiction, guidebooks and Poland-related titles. Stocks the *Warsaw Insider*.

Centrum Sztuki Współczesnej al. Ujazdowskie 6a. Shop at the entrance to the Zamek Ujazdowski, selling a wide array of new art albums and post-modern titles in Polish and English, and also some non-mainstream CDs.

EMPiK junction of Nowy Świat and al. Jerozolimskie (☏ 022/625 1219), and ul. Marszałkowska 116/122 (☏ 022/551 4437). Chain store with lots of books and CDs and a good selection of foreign press. The Marszałkowska branch is also well stocked with

Polish folk music. Both stores open Mon–Sat 9am–9pm, Sun 11am–7pm.

Pelta Świętokrzyska 16. A haven for boys of all ages, with books on cars, bikes, trains and planes and militaria – good for Polish military history. Plastic model kits upstairs.

Relay Warszawa Centralna. A good source of international press in the train station.

Traffic Club ul. Bracka 25. Warsaw's largest bookstore, with a good music section, a fair number of English titles and major newspapers. Nice on-site café, and plenty of armchairs.

Zachęta ul. Malachowskiego 3. Shop inside the art gallery of the same name, selling books on the whole gamut of Polish art and architecture, as well as arty cards and gifts.

Art, crafts and antiques

Ambra ul. Piwna 15. One of the better amber jewellery stores on a street that's stuffed full with them.

Bolesławiec ul. Prosta 2/14, ⊛www.ceramicboleslawiec.com.pl. Poland's favourite stoneware: bowls, mugs and the like with distinctive blue-and-white patterns.

Cepelia central branches at Nowy Świat 35, Krucza 23/31 and Marszałkowska 99/101. Chain of handicraft shops specializing in Polish ceramics, textiles and woodcarving – as well as more tacky souvenirs.

Desa Galeria Rynek Starego Miasta 4/6 and Nowy Świat 51. Upmarket antiques and paintings.

Galeria Zapiecek Rynek Starego Miasta 8. Cutting-edge jewellery, with an emphasis on minimalist silver pieces.

Metal Gallery ul. Zapiecek 1. Contemporary Polish art for the serious enthusiast.

Warsztat Woni ul. Bednarska 28. Flowers and decorative arts by Marta Gesller, owner of *the Qchnia Artystyczna* restaurant (see p.131).

Food

Shopping for food in Warsaw has improved dramatically in recent years. For a wide range of imported food and wines you should head to the outstanding Piotr i Paweł **supermarket**, on the bottom level of the Blue City shopping centre, 3km west of the centre at al. Jerozolimskie 179 (bus #517 from the main station); or Carrefour, one tram stop across the river from the old town, in the Wileński shopping centre.

Batida ul. Nowogrodzka 1/3. Just off pl. Trzech Krzyży, the only place in Warsaw for a perfect chocolate croissant or baguette. Also a small café with good espresso. Mon–Fri till 8pm, Sat till 4pm, Sun till 3pm.

Blikle The famous café/sweet shop now has an adjacent delicatessen, serving luxury meats, cheeses, breads and wines. Domestic products are affordable; imports less so.

Hala Mirowska pl. Mirowski, west of the Ogród Saski. The two Art Nouveau market halls contain grim supermarkets, but the surrounding outdoor

stalls are excellent for fresh produce, meats and flowers.

Marcpol In one of the "temporary" pavilions in the shadow of the Pałac Kultury i Nauki, this is the only central 24-hour supermarket.

Pawłowicz ul. Chmielna 13. Locals queue for doughnuts, usually just out of the oven, at this tiny kiosk.

Sezam ul. Marszałkowska 140. The best of the supermarkets in the *Centrum* area, just down from the intersection with Świętokrzyska. Mon–Fri 8am–8pm, Sat 9am–5pm, Sun 10am–4pm.

Markets and bazaars

Outdoor markets have lost ground to shopping centres in recent years, but there are still some interesting places to go.

Dziesięciolecia stadium Praga district, near Poniatowski bridge. Held in a sports stadium and reckoned to be Europe's largest outdoor market, this is probably your only chance to hear Vietnamese and Nigerians speak Polish. The brisk trade in bootleg DVDs and smuggled cigarettes has gone underground, but among the cheap cosmetics and sunglasses you'll find a fair amount of Soviet bric-a-brac and a few Orthodox

icons. Take any tram east from Warszawa Centralna.

Koło Bazaar ul. Obozowa, in the Wola district (trams #12, #13, #23 or #24 to Koło). Held on Sundays, this is the main antiques and bric-a-brac market, with everything from sofas and old Russian samovars to genuine Iron Crosses on offer. On Monday mornings, there's a pets market selling hamsters, carnivorous turtles and more.

Activities and sports

If you fancy **ice-skating**, then you could try your luck with the blink-and-you-miss-them hours at year-round Torwar rink, ul. Łazienkowska 6a (usually

Moving on

Warszawa Zachodnia (see p.85) handles all international **bus** departures to Western Europe and the Baltic States, as well as major domestic destinations to the south and west. Dworzec Stadion (see p.85) is the departure point for buses to eastern Poland, Belarus and Ukraine. International tickets can be purchased through Orbis offices (see "Travel agents", p.140) and international counters at bus stations. Domestic intercity buses run by the private Polski Express (☎022/620 0326, ⓦ www .polskiexpress.pl) are fast and comfortable, though slightly more expensive than state-run PKS buses (and you'll have to listen to the radio); they operate from a stop on al. Jana Pawła II, west of Warszawa Centralna. Note that there's little in the way of food or drink buying opportunities, so come prepared. From the same stop you can catch HaloBus (☎050 924 0999) services to Kazimierz Dolny, which stop at Puławy. For information on routes operated by the state-run PKS bus company call ☎022/9433.

Warszawa Centralna (see p.84) **train** station serves all international routes and the major national ones. For Sochaczew, Łowicz, Arkadia and Nieborów you'll need to use the adjacent Śródmieście station, while trains to Małkinia, near the site of the Treblinka concentration camp monument, leave from the Wileńska station in the Praga district, across the river from the Stare Miasto. An alternative to queuing for tickets is to book at Orbis offices (see "Travel agents", p.140), or online (www .pkp.pl; domestic trains only). Tickets purchased on the Internet should be picked up at Warszawa Centralna's Counter 21 one day before departure or on the train itself, though in the latter case you'll have to pay a fee. For train information call ☎022/9436 or 9431.

Thurs 8–9.30pm; otherwise check ⓦ www.torwar.pl; 9zł). In winter months the ice rink in front of the Palace of Culture is a more convenient option (daily 8am–8pm; free). You can rent skates at both places for a nominal fee.

The best of the city's **swimming** centres is the Wodny Park Warszawianka, ul. Merliniego 4, where there's an Olympic-sized pool as well as water slides and children's areas, and squash, archery and a fitness club (Mon–Fri 6.30am–10pm, Sat & Sun 8am–10pm; 15zł/hr; ⓦ www.wodnypark.com.pl; from the centre trams #4 or #18, or #35 4km south to Malczewskiego). In summer, there's an open-air pool at WOW Wisła, in the Praga suburb at Namysłowska 8 (July & Aug daily 9am–7pm; tram #32 from pl. Zamkowy). You can also use the pools at the better hotels, but this is expensive (80zł and up).

As for spectator sports, your best bet is **football**. Legia Warszawa, the army club with a nationwide following, plays at Stadion Wojska Polskiego, just southeast of the centre at ul. Łazienkowska (buses #155, #159 and #166). Their biggest rivals, Polonia, play at ul. Konwiktorska 6, a ten-minute walk north of Stare Miasto (or tram #2 from Centrum).

Listings

Airlines Air France, Nowy Świat 64 ☎022/556 5400, ⓦ www.airfrance.com; American Airlines, al. Ujazdowskie 20 ☎022/625 3002, ⓦ www .aa.com; British Airways, ul. Krucza 49 ☎022/529 9000, ⓦ www.ba.com; LOT, al. Jerozolimskie 65/79 ☎022/9572, ⓦ www.lot.pl; Lufthansa, Warsaw Towers, ul. Sienna 39 ☎022/338 1300, ⓦ www.lufthansa.pl; SkyEurope ☎022/433 0733,

ⓦ www.skyeurope.com; Wizzair ☎022/500 9499, ⓦ www.wizzair.com. See p.84 for airport information.

American Express In the *Marriott* hotel. Mon–Fri 9am–7pm, Sat 10am–6pm.

Banks and exchange There are exchange *kantors* and ATMs all over the city. Note that the rate posted in the window is often for $100 or €100; you may get a lower rate if changing smaller notes.

British Council al. Jerozolimskie 59 ⓣ022/695 5900. Small café upstairs with British newspapers and free Internet access; library for members only but visitors usually allowed to browse. Mon–Fri 8.30am–7pm, Sat 8.30am–1pm.

Camera repairs Foto and Video Service, ul. Marszałkowska 84/92.

Car rental Avis (ⓦwww.avis.pl), at the airport (ⓣ022/650 4872), and at the *Marriott* (see p.92; ⓣ022/630 7316); Budget (ⓦwww.budget.pl), at the airport (ⓣ022/650 4062) and the *Marriott* (ⓣ022/630 7280); Hertz (ⓦwww.hertz.com.pl), at the airport (ⓣ022/650 2896) and ul. Nowogrodzka 27 (ⓣ022/621 1360); Speed, a slightly cheaper local firm, al. Witosa 31 (Panorama shopping centre), ⓣ022/640 1362, ⓦwww.speedcar.com.pl.

Children Smyk, Warsaw's best-known toys emporium, has several branches, including ul. Krucza 50, at the corner of al. Jerozolimskie. The Railway Museum (Muzeum Kolejnictwa) at ul. Towarowa 1 (in the old Warszawa Główna station, two tram stops west of Warszawa Centralna; Tues–Sun 9.30am–3.30pm; 5zł, Fri free) is a child-friendly destination, as is the zoo in Park Praski (see p.127).

Embassies Australia, ul. Nowogrodzka 11 ⓣ022/521 3444, ⓦwww.australia.pl; Belarus, ul. Ateńska 67 ⓣ022/617 8441; Canada, al. Jerozolimskie 123 ⓣ022/584 3100, ⓦwww.canada.pl; Czech Republic, ul. Koszykowa 18 ⓣ022/628 7221; Germany, ul. Dąbrowiecka 30 ⓣ022/617 3011, ⓦwww.ambasadaniemiec.pl; Ireland, ul. Humanska 10 ⓣ022/849 6633, ⓦwww.irlandia.pl; Lithuania, al. Szucha 5 ⓣ022/625 3368; New Zealand, ul. Grecka 3 ⓣ022/672 8069; Russia, ul. Belwederska 49 ⓣ022/621 3453, ⓔambrus@poczta.fm; UK, al. Róż 1 ⓣ022/311 0000, ⓦwww.britishembassy.pl; Ukraine, al. Szucha 7 ⓣ022/625 0127, ⓦwww.ukraine-emb.pl; USA, al. Ujazdowskie 29 ⓣ022/5040 2000, ⓦwww.usinfo.pl.

Hospitals and emergencies The English-speaking American Medical Centre, ul. Wilcza 23/29 (Mon–Fri 8am–6pm, Sat 9am–3pm; ⓣ022/622 0489) is expensive but good, and has a 24-hour emergency service (ⓣ060 224 3024); Medicover, the C.M. Medical Centre, 3rd floor of the *Marriott* hotel (see p.92; Mon–Fri 7am–9pm, Sat 8am–8pm, Sun 9am–6pm; ⓣ022/458 7000), offers a similar service. Most central of the main hospitals is the State Clinical Hospital, ul. Marszałkowska 24 (ⓣ022/522 7333). The

emergency ambulance number is ⓣ022/999, but the private Falck ambulance service (ⓣ022/9675) will also respond, and you've more chance of being understood in English.

Internet cafés Good, central places include Simple Internet, ul. Marszałkowska 99/101 (24hrs); Verso, ul. Freta 17 (Mon–Fri 9am–5pm, Sat 9am–5pm, Sun 10am–4pm); e-Loco, ul. Krucza 17 (daily 10am–midnight); and Top Computer, Nowy Świat 18/20 (Mon–Fri 9am–11pm, Sat–Sun 10am–10pm). Expect to pay about 5zł per hr.

Laundry ul. Karmelicka 17. Mon–Fri 9am–5pm, Sat 9am–3pm.

Left luggage There are left-luggage facilities at Warszawa Centralna train station (see p.84).

Lost property If you've lost something on city transport, ul. Floriańska 10a ⓣ022/619 5668; 7am–3pm.

Pharmacies There are 24-hour *aptekas* on the top floor of Warszawa Centralna train station and at al. Solidarności 149. In the Nowe Miasto there's a good pharmacy at ul. Freta 13 (Mon–Fri 8am–8pm, Sat 8am–7pm, Sun 11am–7pm).

Police Report crimes at the police office at ul. Wilcza 21; include a full list of stolen items and their value.

Post offices The main office is at ul. Swiętokrzyska 31/33. It handles fax, poste restante (at window no. 12: postcode 00-001) and is open 24hr. Also at Rynek Starego Miasta 15 (Mon–Fri 8am–8pm, Sat 11am–8pm); and Warszawa Centralna station behind main train information board (Mon–Fri 8am–8pm, Sat 8am–2pm; phones 24hr).

Telephone and fax facilities In main post offices; some Internet cafés have fax facilities and cheap international calling (see "Internet Cafés", above).

Travel agents STA Travel, ul. Krucza 41/43 (ⓣ022/626 0800, ⓦwww.statravel.pl). Mazurkas, inside the *Novotel Centrum* at ul. Nowogrodzka 24/26 (ⓣ022/629 1878, ⓦwww.polhotels.com/tours/mazurkas), organizes Warsaw sightseeing trips and excursions to outlying attractions, notably Chopin's birthplace at Żelazowa Wola (see p.142). Orbis (ⓦwww.orbis.com.pl) at ul. Bracka 16 (ⓣ022/827 7603; Mon–Fri 9am–6pm, Sat 9am–3pm) sells all train tickets and international bus tickets. Intourist, ul. Nowogrodzka 10 (ⓣ022/625 0852, ⓦwww.intourist.ru), can arrange visas to Russia, Ukraine, Belarus and the CIS.

Western Union There are agents in the IT offices (see p.85) and at the *Marriott* hotel (see p.92).

Mazovia

Mazovia – the sandy plain surrounding Warsaw – is not the most attractive of landscapes, but it does have several rewarding day-trips to ease your passage into the rural Polish experience. If time is limited, then at least take a break outside the city in the beautiful forest of the **Puszcza Kampinoska** national park, or to Chopin's birthplace at **Żelazowa Wola**. Southwest of the capital, the great manufacturing city of **Łódź** offers a rich cultural scene and, unusually for Poland, a wealth of nineteenth-century architecture. Other towns south of Warsaw are less inviting, and industrial centres such as **Skierniewice** and **Radom** are likely to be low on most people's itineraries. **Płock**, under two hours by train west of the city, is more enticing, with a historic Stare Miasto complex and a couple of notable museums. Passing through the northern stretches of Mazovia, there are worthy detours to the market town of **Pułtusk** and the castle at **Ciechanów**, while the solemn monument to the vanished concentration camp at **Treblinka** lies to the east.

Just about everywhere covered in the following section can be reached from Warsaw on local **buses** and **trains**. Łódź is particularly well served by regular fast trains, making a day's outing from Warsaw an easy option.

The Park Narodowy Puszcza Kampinoska

With its boundaries touching the edge of Warsaw's Żoliborz suburb, **Park Narodowy Puszcza Kampinoska** – Kampinoski Forest National Park – stretches some 30km west of the capital, a rare example of an extensive woodland coexisting with a major city. Originally submerged under the waters of the Wisła, which now flows north of the forest, the picturesque landscape intersperses dense tracts of woodland – pine, hornbeam, birch and oak are the most common trees – with a patchwork terrain of swamp-like marshes and belts of sand dune. Protected as a national park, this open forest harbours the summer houses of numerous Varsovians, and in autumn draws legions of mushroom-pickers. Elk, wild boar, beaver and lynx (the latter two recently reintroduced) are sighted from time to time, and the park is rich in bird life – watch out for storks, cranes and buzzards. Access for walkers and cross-country skiers is pretty much unrestricted, though it's all too easy to get lost in the woods: stick to marked routes (good maps are available in the major Warsaw bookstores).

Truskaw and around

Buses from pl. Wilson in the Warsaw suburb of Żoliborz (#708 or #714; to get to pl. Wilson from the centre, take tram #4 or #36 north) take you 10km out to **TRUSKAW**, a rapidly developing village on the eastern edge of the forest. From the bus stop (there are no shops nearby, so bring food and water) you can follow ul. Skibińskiego into the forest, where, after 4km, you'll come to a small museum (Tues–Sun 9am–3pm; free) detailing the area's often bloody history – its proximity to town made it a centre of resistance activity during the 1863 uprising and World War II, and also a killing ground for the Nazis. The war cemetery next to the museum contains the bodies of about 2000 prisoners and civilians, herded out to the forest, shot and hurled into pits. From the museum there's a second path leading back to Truskaw, or you could press on a further 5km to the quiet hamlet of **PALMIRY**, though be warned that the path runs alongside a mosquito-ridden swamp. From the highway, one kilometre north of Palmiry, there are hourly buses back to the capital, though it's not an especially pleasant place to wait.

A few kilometres northeast of here, on the banks of the Wisła, the area around the village of **DZIEKANÓW POLSKI** is a noted bird-watchers' haunt. Among species regularly sighted is the **white stork**, whose nests can be seen on special platforms atop telegraph poles around the village. You're also likely to find **lapwings** and several kinds of **raptors** in the surrounding fields, while closer to the water you can spot brilliantly coloured **kingfishers** and **blue-throats** as well as a variety of gulls, terns and ducks.

Żelazowa Wola

Fifty kilometres west of Warsaw, just beyond the western edge of the Park Narodowy Puszcza Kampinoska, is the little village of **ŻELAZOWA**

Frédéric Chopin (1810–49)

Of all the major Polish artists, **Frédéric Chopin** – Fryderyk Szopen as he was baptized in Polish – is the one whose work has achieved the greatest international recognition. He is, to all intents and purposes, the national composer, a fact attested to in the wealth of festivals, concerts and, most importantly, the famous international piano competition held in his name. Like other Polish creative spirits of the nineteenth century, the life of this brilliantly talented composer and performer reflects the political upheavals of Partition-era Poland. Born of mixed Polish–French parentage in the Mazovian village of Żelazowa Wola, where his French father was a tutor to a local aristocratic family, Frédéric spent his early years in and around Warsaw, holidays in the surrounding countryside giving him an early introduction to the Mazovian folk tunes that permeate his compositions. Musical talent began to show from an early age: at six Chopin was already making up tunes; a year later he started to play the piano, and his first concert performance came at the age of eight. After a couple of years' schooling at the Warsaw lyceum, the budding composer – his first polonaises and *mazurkas* had already been written and performed – was enrolled at the newly created Warsaw Music Conservatory.

Chopin's first journey abroad was in August 1829, to Vienna, where he gave a couple of concert performances to finance the publication of some recent compositions, a set of Mozart variations. Returning to Warsaw soon afterwards, Chopin made his official **public debut**, performing the virtuoso Second Piano Concerto (F Minor), its melancholic slow movement inspired by an (unrequited) love affair with a fellow Conservatory student and aspiring opera singer. In the autumn of 1830 he travelled again to Vienna, only to hear news of the **November uprising** against the Russians at home. Already set upon moving to Paris, the heartbroken Chopin was inspired by the stirring yet tragic events in Poland to write the famous *Revolutionary Étude*, among a string of other works. As it turned out, he was never to return to Poland, a fate shared by many of the fellow exiles whose Parisian enclave he entered in 1831. He rapidly befriended them and the host of other young composers (including Berlioz, Bellini, Liszt and Mendelssohn) who lived in the city. The elegantly dressed, artistically sensitive Chopin soon became a high society favourite, earning his living teaching and giving the occasional recital. Some relatively problem-free years followed, during which he produced a welter of new compositions, notably the rhapsodic *Fantaisie-Impromptu*, a book of études and a stream of nationalistically inspired polonaises and mazurkas.

WOLA, the birthplace of composer and national hero, **Frédéric Chopin**. The journey through the rolling Mazovian countryside makes an enjoyable day out from the city; unless you've got a car, you'll need to take a **bus** from Warszawa Zachodnia (direction "Sochaczew" or "Kamion") or take a train from Warszawa Śródmieście or Warszawa Zachodnia to the town of Sochaczew, from where bus #6 trundles to Żelazowa Wola. Alternatively, book up on one of the many excursions offered by Orbis, Mazurkas and others (see "Travel agents", p.140).

The house where Chopin was born is now a **museum** (Tues–Sun: April 9.30am–4.30pm; May–Sept 9.30am–5.30pm; Oct–March 9.30am–3.30pm; 12zł) surrounded by a large, tranquil garden. The Chopin family lived here for only a year after their son's birth in 1810, but young Frédéric returned frequently to what became his favourite place – it gave him contact with the Polish countryside and, most importantly, the folk musical traditions of Mazovia. Bought by public subscription in 1929, the Chopin family residence was subsequently restored and turned into a museum to the composer run by the Warsaw-based Chopin Society. The Society also organizes **piano recitals** here throughout the summer (May–Sept 11am & 3pm;

Chopin's life changed dramatically in 1836 following his encounter with the radical novelist **George Sand**, who promptly fell in love with him and suggested she become his mistress. After over a year spent hesitating over the proposal in the winter of 1838, Chopin – by now ill – travelled with her and her two children to Majorca. Though musically productive – the B Flat Minor Sonata and its famous funeral march date from this period – the stay was not a success, Chopin's rapidly deteriorating health forcing a return to France to seek the help of a doctor in Marseille. Thereafter Chopin was forced to give up composing for a while, earning his living giving piano lessons to rich Parisians and spending the summers with an increasingly maternal Sand at her country house at **Nohant**, south of Paris. The rural environment temporarily did wonders for Chopin's health, and it was in Nohant that he produced some of his most powerful music, including the sublime *Polonaise Fantasie*, the Third Sonata and several of the major ballades. Increasingly strained relations with Sand, however, finally snapped when she broke with him in 1847. Miserable and almost penniless, Chopin accepted an invitation from an admiring Scottish pupil Jane Stirling to visit **Britain**. Despite mounting illness, Chopin gave numerous concerts and recitals in London, also making friends with Carlyle, Dickens and other luminaries of English artistic life. Increasingly weak, and unable either to compose or return Stirling's devoted affections, a depressed Chopin returned to Paris in November 1848.

Just a few months later he finally succumbed to the tuberculosis that had dogged him for years, dying in his apartment on place de Vendôme in central Paris; in accordance with his deathbed wish Mozart's *Requiem* was sung at the funeral, and his body was buried in the **Père-Lachaise Cemetery**, the grave topped, a year later, with a monument of a weeping muse sprinkled with earth from his native Mazovia. Admired by his friends, yet also criticized by many of his peers, the music Chopin created during his short life achieved a synthesis few other Polish artists have matched – a distinctive Polishness combined with a universality of emotional and aesthetic appeal. For fellow Poles, as for many foreigners, the emotive Polish content is particularly significant: many, indeed, feel his music expresses the essence of the national psyche, alternating wistful romanticism with storms of turbulent, restless protest – "guns hidden in flowerbeds", in fellow composer Schumann's memorable description.

free with museum ticket) – check Warsaw listings sources (see p.85) or with the Chopin Society (based at Warsaw's Chopin Museum; see p.116) for the current programme details.

The house itself is a typical *dwór*, the traditional country residence of the *szlachta* (gentlefolk) class, numerous examples of which can be found all over rural Poland – Mazovia and Małopolska in particular. Reconstructed frequently in the last century, all the rooms have now been restored to period perfection and contain a collection of family portraits and other Chopin memorabilia (though none of it was actually here during his own lifetime). Through the main entrance way the old **kitchen**, the first room on your right, has an attractively painted characteristic nineteenth-century Mazovian ceiling.

Next along is the **music room**; the exhibits here including a case full of manuscripts of early Chopin piano works as well as a plaster cast of the virtuoso pianist's left hand. If you've come for the popular weekend piano recitals – often by noted international performers – this is where they're held, performed on a luxury Steinway grand donated by wealthy Polish-Americans. On fine days, the audience sits outside, the music wafting through the open windows.

The **dining room** walls sport some original Canaletto copper-worked views of Warsaw (see p.97), while upstairs is the **bedroom** where Frédéric was born, now something of a shrine. Back outside it's worth taking a leisurely stroll through the magnificent house grounds, turned into a sort of **botanical park** (closes at 7pm in summer, dusk in winter; 4zł) following the place's conversion into a museum. In spring or autumn you'll catch the scented blossoms of the trees and bushes donated from botanical gardens around the world. The moderately priced *Pod Wierzbami* **restaurant**, on the corner of the main road, will fix you up with anything from simple soups to roast duck.

If you're travelling by car (although many of the bus tours also stop here), you could consider making a brief detour 11km north into the countryside to the village of **BROCHÓW**. The imposing brick parish **church**, a fortified sixteenth-century structure, became the Chopin family place of Sunday worship following his parents' marriage here in the early 1800s. The original of young Frédéric's birth certificate is proudly displayed in the sacristy, along with other family records. Just down the road from the church, a Chopin "complex" in a renovated nineteenth-century manor house holds a concert hall, studios and teaching centre.

The Sochaczew–Wilcz Tułowskie railway

Ten kilometres southwest of Żelazowa Wola, the unremarkable town of **Sochaczew** (reached by local train from Warsaw's Śródmieście station) is the starting point for steam-hauled narrow-gauge railway excursions to the tiny village of **Wilcz Tułowskie**, a scenic, eighteen-kilometre journey which takes you through the forests on the western fringes of Kampinoski national park. Services run every Saturday from June to September, departing at 9.40am and arriving just over an hour later, giving you time for a short walk in the forest before the train leaves for Sochaczew at noon. The narrow-gauge train station in Sochaczew has a museum (May–Oct Tues–Sun 10am–3pm; 6zł) devoted to the line – formerly used to transport logs out of the forest – which features an impressive line-up of narrow-gauge rolling stock. Further details about train running times are available from the Muzeum Kolej Wąskotorowy (Sochaczew Narrow-Gauge Railway Museum; ☎046/862 5976), ul. Towarowa 7, 95-500 Sochaczew.

Łowicz and around

At first sight **ŁOWICZ**, 30km southwest of Żelazowa Wola, looks just like any other small, concrete-ridden central Polish town, but this apparently drab place is, in fact, a well-established centre of folk art and crafts. Locally produced handwoven materials, carved wood ornaments and *wycinanki* – coloured paper cutouts – are popular throughout the country, the brilliantly coloured local Mazowsze costumes (*pasiaki*) being the town's best-known product. Historically Łowicz has not been without importance, for several centuries providing the main residence of the archbishops of Gniezno, normally the Catholic primates of all Poland, who endowed the town with its historic **churches**.

The ideal time to come here is at **Corpus Christi** (late May/early June) – or, failing that, during one of the other major Church **festivals** – when many of the women turn out in beautiful handmade traditional costumes for the two-hour procession to the collegiate church here. Wearing full skirts, embroidered cotton blouses and colourful headscarves, they are followed by neat lines of young girls preparing for first Communion.

The Town

The old **Rynek**, ten minutes from the train station, is the pivot of the town, along with the vast **collegiate church**, a brick fifteenth-century construction, remodelled to its present form in the mid-seventeenth century. Size apart, its most striking features are the richly decorated tombstones of the archbishops of Gniezno and former Polish primates, and the ornate series of Baroque chapels.

The other attraction is the local **museum** across the square (Tues–Sun 10am–4pm; 5zł, free Sat), housed in a Baroque missionary college designed by Tylman of Gameren and rebuilt following wartime destruction. The upstairs floor contains an extensive and carefully presented collection of regional folk artefacts, including furniture, pottery, tools and costumes resembling those still worn on feast days. Downstairs, as well as a section devoted to local history, the former seminary **chapel** houses a notable collection of Baroque art from all over the country, the vault of the chapel itself adorned with frescoes by Michelangelo Palloni, court painter to King Jan Sobieski. Many houses around the square contain examples of the distinctive coloured cutout decorations on display in the museum too. The back of the museum is a kind of mini-*skansen*, containing two old cottages complete with their original furnishings. If you're intrigued by the local craftwork, go to the Cepelia shop on the main square, where there's a reasonable selection on sale. Of the clutch of historic buildings dotted around the centre, most notable are the Baroque former **Piarist church**, with some enjoyable ceiling paintings, and the remains of the **castle** on ul. Zamkowa, originally the bishop's residence until it was razed by marauding Swedes in the mid-seventeenth century.

Practicalities

Łowicz is a ninety-minute **train** journey from Warsaw, with regular services from the Śródmieście station (see p.85). The best place to **stay** is the atmospheric *Zajazd Łowicki* hotel at ul. Blich 36 (☎046/837 4164, ⓦwww.zajazdlowicki .ta.pl; ❸), on the Poznań road on the west side of town, which also has a decent **restaurant**. Short of this, the food at *Polonia*, on the main square, is serviceable.

Arkadia and Nieborów

A short distance east of Łowicz are a couple of sights redolent of the bygone Polish aristocracy: the landscaped park of **Arkadia**, and seventeenth-century palace at **Nieborów**. They combine for an easy and enjoyable day-trip from Warsaw: Arkadia is an easy ten-minute walk from **Mysłaków**, a minor train station served by Warsaw–Łowicz **trains**; while Nieborów can be accessed by **bus** from either Mysłaków or Łowicz.

Arkadia

Ten kilometres southeast of Łowicz, the eighteenth-century **Arkadia** park (daily 10am–dusk; 5zł) is as wistfully romantic a spot as you could wish for an afternoon stroll. Conceived by Princess Helen Radziwiłł as an "ancient monument to beautiful Greece", the classical park is dotted with lakes and walkways, a jumble of reproduction classical temples and pavilions, a sphinx and a mock-Gothic building that wouldn't look out of place in a Hammer House film production. Many of the pieces were collected by the princess on her exhaustive foreign travels, and the air of decay – the place hasn't been touched since World War II – only adds to the evocation of times long past consciously created by the princess, who was caught up in the cult of the classical that swept through the Polish aristocracy in the latter half of the eighteenth century.

Nieborów

Five kilometres further east lies the village of **NIEBORÓW**, whose country **palace** was designed by the ever-present Tylman of Gameren and owned for most of its history, like the park, by the powerful Radziwiłł clan – just one of dozens this family possessed right up until World War II, when much of the family was deported to Siberia. Now a branch of Warsaw's Muzeum Narodowe, the Pałac Nieborów (Ⓦwww.nieborow.art.pl) is one of the handsomest and best maintained in the country, surrounded by outbuildings and a manicured **park** and **gardens** (same hours as palace; 5zł park and gardens only).

The palace **interior** (March & April daily 10am–4pm; May & June daily 10am–6pm; July–Sept Mon–Fri 10am–4pm, Sat & Sun 10am–6pm; Oct Tues–Sun 10am–3.30pm; 10zł), restored after the war, is furnished on the basis of the original eighteenth- and nineteenth-century contents of the main rooms – a lavish restoration that makes you wonder whether Polish communists suffered from a kind of ideological schizophrenia. Roman tombstones and sculptural fragments fill a lot of space downstairs, gathered about the palace's prize exhibit, a classical-era sculpture known as the **Nieborów Niobe**. The grandest apartments (including a library with a fine collection of globes) are on the first floor, reached by a staircase clad in finely decorated Delft tiles. It all has an air, these days, of studied aristocratic respectability, somewhat belying Radziwiłł history. Karol Radziwiłł, for example, head of the dynasty in the late eighteenth century, used to hold vast banquets in the course of which he'd drink himself into a stupor, and, as often as not, kill someone in a brawl. He would then, as historian Adam Zamoyski puts it in his book *The Polish Way* (see "Books", p.694), "stumble into his private chapel and bawl himself back to sobriety by singing hymns". A far cry from today's genteel environment, which, in the spring, is host to a much publicized series of **classical concerts** by international artists – the tourist office in Warsaw will be your most likely source of information on these. There's a **café-restaurant** in the palace itself, while Nieborów village offers a couple of regional-style restaurants.

Łódź

Mention **ŁÓDŹ** (pronounced "Woodge") to many Poles and all you'll get is a grimace, but Poland's second city, 110km southwest of Warsaw, is fascinating in its own way, with a significant place in the country's development and a unique and authentic atmosphere that grows on you the longer you stay. Essentially a creation of the Industrial Revolution and appropriately nicknamed the Polish Manchester, the nineteenth-century core has largely survived – you'll find tall chimneys (no longer smoking) atop castellated red-brick factories; grand historicist and Secessionist villas; dark slum quarters; and theatres, art galleries and philanthropic societies. With much of the the whole ensemble still caked in a century and a half of soot and grime, the city served as the ready-made location for Andrzej Wajda's film *The Promised Land*, based on the novel depicting life in Industrial Revolution-era Poland by Nobel laureate Władysław Reymont.

Today Łódź is in the process of reinventing itself as a cultural destination. The pedestrianized **ulica Piotrkowska** is at the heart of things, lined with restaurants and bars and teeming with life night and day. One of the old factories is being converted into a major entertainment complex, and the city now plays host to several important **festivals**. Łódź also boasts one of the best **orchestras** in the country, as well as an impressive array of galleries, theatres and museums. The **film school** here is also internationally renowned, attracting aspiring movie-makers aiming to follow in the footsteps of alumni such as Wajda, Polański, Kieślowski and Zanussi.

Some history

Missionaries came to the site of Łódź in the twelfth century, but at the end of the 1700s it was still an obscure village with fewer than two hundred inhabitants. Impulse towards its development came during the Partition period, with the **1820 edict** of the Russian-ruled Congress Kingdom of Poland, which designated Łódź as a new industrial centre and encouraged foreign weavers and manufacturers to come and settle. The city, on the westernmost edge of the Tsar's domain, was uniquely poised to use European skills and technology to supply the vast Russian and Chinese markets with cheap fabrics.

People poured in by the thousand each year, and within twenty years Łódź had become the nation's second largest city, a position it has maintained ever since. Despite being the imperial rulers, the Russians played little more than an administrative role, though they adopted a higher profile following the failed nationalist insurrection of 1863. The true political elite consisted in the main of **German entrepreneurs**, most of them Protestant, who founded large textile factories which made vast fortunes within a very short period of time. These were operated principally by **Polish peasants** enticed by the prospect of a better standard of living than they could claw from their meagre patches of land. By the end of the century, the urban proletariat had swelled to over 300,000. Industrialization brought politicization, and Łódź, like other new cities such as Białystok, had become a centre for working-class and anti-tsarist agitation.

The **Jews** were another highly significant community. When they first arrived, they functioned mainly as artisans and traders, but a number managed to rise to the status of great industrial magnates, notably the Poznańskis, whose luxurious homes now house many of the city's institutions. The Jewish contribution to the cultural life of Łódź was immense, two of the city's most famous sons being the pianist Artur Rubinstein and the poet Julian Tuwim.

Łódź's prosperity declined following World War I when, no longer part of the Russian Empire, the city lost its privileged access to the eastern market; but it remained a melting-pot of peoples and religions until **World War II**. At first, the Nazis aimed to make it the capital of the rump Polish protectorate, the so-called Générale Gouvernement, but, incensed by the largely hostile stance adopted by the powerful local German community, soon incorporated it into the Reich. In the process, they renamed it "Litzmannstadt" in honour of a somewhat obscure general who had made a breakthrough against the nearby Russian line in 1914, and established the first and longest-lasting of their notorious urban ghettos (see box, pp.150–151).

Although there was little fighting here, and the centre remains virtually as it was a century ago, today's Łódź is, in an important sense, a spectre of its former self; nearly all the Jews were wiped out, while most of the Germans fled west after the war, leaving only a tiny minority behind.

Arrival and information

The main **train station**, Łódź Fabryczna, on the eastern fringes of the town centre, handles trains terminating in the city, notably the regular services to and from Warsaw. Trains passing through Łódź en route to other destinations stop at Łódź Kaliska, 2km west of the city centre and connected by tram #12. The main **bus station** is right next to Łódź Fabryczna. The best way to get around the ul. Piotrkowska area is by rickshaw (see p.150), but for less central destinations there's a good **tram** network (tickets 1.50/2.20/3.30/4.40zł for

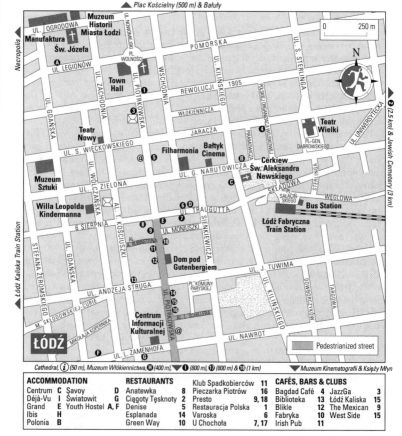

ACCOMMODATION			RESTAURANTS		Klub Spadkobierców	11	CAFÉS, BARS & CLUBS			
Centrum	**C**	Savoy	**D**	Anatewka	8	Pieczarka Piotrów	16	Bagdad Café	4	JazzGa	3
Déjà-Vu	**I**	Światowit	**G**	Ciągoty Tęsknoty	2	Presto	9, 18	Biblioteka	13	Łódź Kaliska	15
Grand	**E**	Youth Hostel	**A, F**	Denise	5	Restauracja Polska	1	Blikle	12	The Mexican	9
Ibis	**H**			Esplanada	14	Varoska	6	Fabryka	10	West Side	15
Polonia	**B**			Green Way	10	U Chochoła	7, 17	Irish Pub	11		

10/30/60/120min, or 8.80zł for a day pass). **Taxis** are also widely available, and those with company name and driver number printed on the car have standardized rates.

The English-speaking **tourist information** office at al. Kościuszki 88 (Mon–Fri 8.30am–4.30pm, Sat 9am–1pm; ☎042/638 5955, ⓦwww.uml.lodz .pl) has an excellent range of free maps and publications. Another office, the **Centrum Informacji Kulturalnej** at ul. Zamenhofa 1/3 (Cultural Information Centre; Mon–Fri 10am–6pm, Sat 10am–2pm; ⓦwww.cik.lodz.pl) has details on concerts, movies and events. The bimonthly pocket-sized publication *Kalejdoskop* (2.5zł, although some hotels give it away for free) is a good source of **listings**. There are **Internet cafés** on ul. Piotrkowska nos. 53 (24hr) and 118 (Mon–Sat 10am–6pm). For **books** about Łódź in English, try the newsagent in the *Hotel Grand* lobby or EMPiK, ul. Piotrkowska 87.

Accommodation

Łódź has a reasonable range of hotels (though too many fall into the bland communist-era category), and the only time it will be difficult to a room is during the film festival (see p.155). Most of the places listed below offer substantial weekend reductions.

Hotels

Centrum ul. Kilińskiego 59/63 ☎042/632 8640, ⓦwww.hotelspt.com.pl. Unatmospheric concrete pile next to the train station, with modern rooms and friendly staff. ❺

Déjà Vu ul. Wigury 4/6 ☎042/636 5656. Exclusive pension that aims to re-create the living quarters of a Łódź entrepreneur in the 1920s, with six double rooms furnished with a combination of antique and antique-looking furniture. Service can be uneven, but rooms are comfortable and good value. ❻

Grand ul. Piotrkowska 72 ☎042/633 9920, ⓦwww.orbis.pl. A *belle époque* establishment that lives up to its name, with high quality rooms and, unusually for this kind of place, well-furnished doubles without bath, which provide the best bargain in town. ❸–❼

Ibis al. Piłsudskiego 11 ☎042/638 6700, ⓦwww .ibishotel.com. Modern, reliable business hotel with good service. Breakfast 25zł extra. ❻

Polonia ul. Gabriela Narutowicza 38 ☎042/632 8773, ⓦwww.hotelspt.com.pl. Though there's a century of grime on the outside, it's more pleasant within, with a choice of reasonably priced en suites or rooms with shared facilities. ❸–❺

Savoy ul. Traugutta 6 ☎042/632 93 60, ⓦwww .hotelspt.com.pl. Clean, central and well-run place in an attractive nineteenth-century building. Cheaper standard rooms available as well as "retro" rooms with faux antiques ❻–❼.

Światowit al. Kościuszki 68 ☎042/636 3637, ⓦwww.hotelspt.com.pl. Dull but central pre-fab communist block with renovated rooms and agreeable, English-speaking staff. ❻

Hostel and campsite

Youth Hostel ul. Legionów 27 ☎042/630 6680, ⓦwww.ptsm.pl/lodz, and ul. Zamenhofa 13, ☎042/636 6599. Łódź's youth hostel has two central branches, the main one being at ul. Legionów. Both have dorms (18–30zł) and a number of simple singles and doubles with (❷) and without bath (❶). No curfew but you need to let the staff know if you'll be returning after 10pm.

Na Rogach ul. Łupkowa 10/16, 5km northeast of the centre ☎042/630 6111, ⓦwww .campingnarogach.hotel.lodz.pl. Camping and decent-quality bungalows, including some with television and bath (❷–❸). Take bus #60 from ul. Narutowicza.

The City

The first sight for visitors arriving at the central train station is the **Cerkiew św. Aleksandra Newskiego** (Orthodox Church of Alexander Nevsky) in the park across the road. Once used by the city's Russian rulers, it's a compact example of nineteenth-century Orthodox architecture, something of a rarity in central Poland. The church is opened only for services (Wed & Sat 9am, Sun 10am). A couple of blocks west of here is the pedestrianized **ulica Piotrkowska**, a three-kilometre-long boulevard that bisects the city from north to south. Extensive renovation projects have created a thoroughfare that bustles with activity day and night and forms the clear heart of the city's life, boasting plenty of sights and a wide range of places to eat, drink and relax. **Rickshaws** – a relatively new addition to the urban transport scene – will whisk you from one end of Piotrkowska to the other for a few złotys. All around the Piotrkowska area you'll come across the mansions and tenements of the city's former *haute bourgeoisie*, some still peeling with age and neglect, others restored to their former splendour.

Plac Kościelny and around

Plac Kościelny, the old market square on ul. Nowomiejska, the northern extension of Piotrkowska, is dominated by the twin brick towers of the

---

The Łódź Ghetto

The fate of the **Jews** of Łódź, who numbered just under a quarter of a million in 1939, is undoubtedly one of the most poignant and tragic episodes of World War II, particularly as a pivotal role was played by one of their own number, **Chaim Rumkowski**. One of the most controversial figures in modern Jewish history, he has been widely denounced as the worst sort of collaborator, yet seen by others as a man who worked heroically to save at least some vestiges of the doomed community to which he belonged.

Within two days of the Nazi occupation of the city on September 8, the first definite anti-Semitic measures were taken, with Jews hauled at random off the streets and forced to undertake pointless manual tasks. The following month, Rumkowski, a former velvet manufacturer who had made and lost fortunes in both Łódź and Russia before turning his attentions towards charitable activities, was selected by the Nazis as the "Ältesten der Juden" (Eldest of the Jews), giving him absolute power over the internal affairs of his community and the sole right to be their spokesman and nego-tiator. Plans were made to turn the entire Jewish community into a vast pool of slave labour for the Nazi war machine, and the rundown suburb of **Bałuty** to the north of the centre was earmarked for this **ghetto**, partly because this was where the bulk of the Jews lived. Those who resided elsewhere were rounded up into barracks or else chosen for the first transportations to the death camps. By the following spring, the ghetto had been sealed off from the rest of the city, and anyone who dared come near either side of its perimeter fences was shot dead.

Rumkowski soon made the ghetto a self-sufficient and highly profitable enterprise, which pleased his Nazi masters no end, even though this conclusively disproved a key tenet of their racist ideology, namely that Jews were inherently lazy and parasiti-cal. He ruled his domain as a ruthless petty **despot**, attended by a court of syco-phants and protected by his own police force and network of informers; his vanity extended to the printing of stamps bearing his own image (though the Nazis never allowed these into circulation), while his power is demonstrated by the fact that the currency specially minted for the ghetto was nicknamed *rumki*. Those who crossed him did so at their peril, as his omnipotence extended to the distribution of the meagre food supplies and to selecting those who had to make up the regular quotas demanded by the Nazis for deportation to the concentration camps. He cultivated a variation on the oratorical style of Hitler for his frequent addresses to the community. The most notorious and shocking of these was his "Give me your children" speech of 1942, in which he made an emotional appeal to his subjects to send their children off to the camps, in order that able-bodied adults could be spared.

Whether or not Rumkowski knew that he was sending people to their deaths is unclear. There is no doubt that he saw the ghetto as at least the embryonic neo-Gothic **Kościół Wniebozięcia** (Church of the Assumption). Two blocks south of here is the rather forlorn Stary Rynek, which lost its role as the hub of everyday life when the city rapidly expanded southwards. During World War II, the square formed the southern border of the **Łódź ghetto** (see box below) but ul. Nowomiejska itself (and its tramway) remained in the "Aryan" part of the city, dividing the ghetto into sections which were connected by wooden footbridges of the type seen in Roman Polański's film *The Pianist*, and by gates opened only at certain hours. Several blocks north, the **Rynek Bałucki** was at the heart of the ghetto, where Eldest of the Jews Chaim Rumkowski had offices in wooden barracks. Today the square holds a chaotic outdoor **market**.

South again, two blocks below the Stary Rynek, and marking the top of the pedestrianized ul. Piotrkowska, is the circular **plac Wolności**, with the

fulfilment of the **Zionist** ideal and believed that, after the Nazis had won the war, they would establish a Jewish protectorate in central Europe, with himself as its head. He also seems to have had few qualms about his role, insisting he would be prepared to submit himself for trial to a Jewish court of law once the war was over. Records suggest his repeated claims to have cut the numbers demanded for each quota were true, and it's also the case that the ghetto was far from being a place with no hope. On the contrary, there was a rich communal life of schooling, concerts and theatre, and many inhabitants kept detailed diaries. The most thorough (if also suspect) source of information on the ghetto, and a further testimony to Rumkowski's megalomania, is the *Chronicle of the Łódź Ghetto*, a work he sanctioned to record the minutiae of daily life, some two thousand pages of which survived the war.

Another chapter in the ghetto story relates to the camp which was established for some five thousand **Gypsies** from the Austrian province of Burgenland, over half of them children, on a separate twenty square-metre plot on the ghetto's eastern edge in November 1941, Rumkowski having used his influence to keep them out of the ghetto proper. The tiny space lacked even basic sanitary facilities such as running water and toilets, and within two months seven hundred had died of typhus. Fearing the spread of the disease, the Nazis sent those still alive to the Chełmno death camp early in January 1942.

The Łódź ghetto was **liquidated** in the autumn of 1944, following a virulent dispute at the top of the Nazi hierarchy between Speer, who was keen to preserve it as a valuable contributor to the war effort, and Himmler, who was determined to enforce the "Final Solution". Some one thousand Jews were allowed to remain in Łódź to dismantle the valuable plant and machinery; Rumkowski voluntarily chose to go with the others to Auschwitz, albeit armed with an official letter confirming his special status. He died there soon afterwards, though there are three versions of how he met his end: that he was lynched by incensed fellow Jews; that he was immediately selected for the gas chambers on account of his age; and that he was taken on a tour of the camp as a supposedly honoured guest, and thrown into the ovens without being gassed first. Had he remained in Łódź, he would have been among those who were **liberated** by the Red Army soon afterwards. Perhaps not surprisingly, the staunchest apologists for Rumkowski's policies have come from this group of survivors.

A large and fascinating collection of extracts from ghetto diaries, along with transcriptions of Rumkowski's speeches and many photographs, including some in colour, can be found in *The Łódź Ghetto*, edited by Alan Adelson and Robert Lapides, while *Traces of the Litzmannstadt-Getto*, by Łódź resident Joanna Podolska, is a richly detailed, well-written guide to what remains today (for both see "Books" in Contexts, p.694).

Neoclassical town hall, regulation Kościuszko statue, and a lovely domed Greek cross-plan Uniate church.

One block northwest of pl. Wolności, at the junction of ul. Zachodnia and ul. Ogrodowa, you'll find one of the most complete Industrial Revolution-era complexes anywhere in Europe, with monumental neo-Gothic warehouses. These are in the process of conversion into the **Manufaktura** centre (Ⓦwww .manufaktura.lodz.pl), a vast cultural and entertainment complex that will contain museums, shops, restaurants, a cinema and a hotel, all set for completion late in 2005. These warehouses were once the property of the Poznańskis, the celebrated Jewish manufacturing family, who lived in the haughty stone bulk of the adjacent Pałac Poznański. Their factory workers resided in the tenements across ul. Ogrodowa, while behind the flats stands Łódź's oldest church, the large wooden **św. Józefa**. Built in 1765 and moved to its present location in 1888, the church is open only for Mass (Mon–Sat 8am & 6pm, regularly on Sun).

The Pałac Poznański, now the **Muzeum Historii Miasta Łodzi** (City Historical Museum; Tues & Thurs 10am–4pm, Wed 2–6pm, Fri–Sun 10am–2pm; 6zł, free on Sun), is an excellent example of the way Łódź's nouveaux riches aped the tastes of the aristocracy, transferring, both inside and out, the chief elements of a Baroque stately home to an urban setting. Downstairs are temporary exhibitions of modern art and photography, while up the heavily grand staircase are the showpiece chambers, the dining room and the ballroom, along with others of more modest size which are now devoted to displays on different aspects of the city's history. Archive photographs show the appearance of prewar Łódź, including the now-demolished synagogues, while there's an extensive collection of memorabilia of **Artur Rubinstein**, one of the greatest pianists of the last century, and a quintessential hedonist. He was particularly celebrated for his performances of Chopin, and his recordings remain the interpretive touchstone for the composer.

The Muzeum Sztuki and around

A couple of blocks further south is the **Muzeum Sztuki** (Modern Art Gallery; Tues 10am–5pm, Wed & Fri 11am–5pm, Thurs noon–7pm, Sat & Sun 10am–4pm; 5zł, free on Thurs; Ⓦwww.muzeumsztuki.lodz.pl), at ul. Więckowskiego 36, installed in a mock-Renaissance palace with lovely stained-glass windows, which once belonged to the Poznański clan (though much, if not all, of the museum's collection will soon be moved to the new Manufaktura centre; see above). Founded in 1925, when it was one of the world's first museums devoted to the avant-garde, it is the finest modern art collection in the country. Artists represented include Chagall, Mondrian, Max Ernst and Ferdinand Léger, but there's also an excellent selection of work by modern Polish painters such as Strzeminski (quite a revelation if you've not come upon his work before), Wojciechowski, Witkowski, Witkiewicz and the Jewish artist Jakiel Adler. Further displays move on to the 1960s and 1970s, where, for some reason, British artists are strongly represented. At times some or all of the permanent collection is packed away and replaced by a temporary loan exhibition.

Just south of the Muzeum Sztuki, at ul. Wólczańska 31, you'll find Łódź's finest Secession building, the **Willa Leopolda Kindermanna** (Leopold Kindermann Villa). An eclectic palace with a floral-motif facade and fine chandeliers and woodwork inside, it was completed in 1903 for the industrialist whose name it bears and today houses the **Municipal Art Gallery**, which displays temporary exhibitions (Tues, Wed & Fri noon–5pm, Thurs noon–6pm, Sat & Sun noon–4pm; 4zł, Thurs free).

Lower Ulica Piotrkowska and around

Back on ul. Piotrkowska, behind the *Grand* hotel, it's worth taking a detour along **ulica Moniuszki**, an uninterrupted row of plush neo-Renaissance family houses. The best buildings on Piotrkowska itself include the extravagant **Dom pod Gutenbergiem** at no. 86, built by the printer Jan Petersilge in 1896 and sporting a statue of Gutenberg on the facade; the **Art Nouveau store** at no. 100, now the *Esplanada* restaurant (see p.154); and the **Pałac Juliusza Kindermanna** at no. 137/139, austere but for its frieze, a colourful neo-Byzantine mosaic of the unloading of cotton at a Russian port.

About 2km south of here, still on Piotrkowska and past several more fine villas, the neo-Gothic **cathedral**, dedicated to St Stanisław Kosta, looks rather unprepossessing from the outside, mainly because of the cheap yellow bricks used in its construction. The interior, with its spacious feel and bright stained-glass windows, is altogether more impressive. A little further south is the Lutheran **Kościół św. Macieja** (St Matthew's Church), a ponderous mid-nineteenth-century temple used by the descendants of the old German oligarchy. Frequent recitals are given on its Romantic-style organ, one of the best of its kind in Poland. Ask at the Centrum Informacji Kulturalnej (see p.149) for more information.

Across from the Lutheran church, the huge **Biała Fabryka** (White Factory), at no. 282, is the oldest mechanically operated mill in the city. Part of it is now given over to the **Muzeum Włókiennictwa** (Textile Museum; Tues–Fri 9am–4pm, Sat–Sun 11am–4pm; 5zł, Fri free), which features a large number of historic looms, documentary material on the history of the industry in Łódź and an impressive exhibition of contemporary examples of the weaver's art.

East of the centre

Walking east from the cathedral for fifteen minutes along ul. Tymienieckiego, you'll come to the **Księży Młyn** district; from the centre of town walk east (or take any eastbound tram for two stops) along al. Piłsudskiego and then turn right onto ul. Przędzalniana. Up to the nineteenth century, the parish priests who owned the surrounding land leased it to millers, and the name, which means "Priest's Mill", stayed even after one of Europe's largest cotton mills was built here mid-century. Almost a city in itself, the complex had its own residential quarter, schools, shops and train station. The mills have long since shut down, but the area remains a fascinating place to explore: most of the gorgeous red-brick buildings survive, including rows of workers' tenements and the main two-hundred-metre-long structure, which begs to be converted into artists' lofts. German magnate Karl Scheiber developed the area, but it was his son-in-law and factory director Edward Herbst who lived in the **Rezydencja Księży Młyn** (Priest's Mill Residence; Tues 10am–5pm, Wed & Fri noon–5pm, Thurs noon–7pm, Sat & Sun 11am–4pm; 6zł, Wed free). The building, which dates from 1875, outwardly resembles the Renaissance villas built by Palladio in northern Italy. Its interiors – with the grand public rooms downstairs, the intimate family ones above – are evidence of decidedly catholic tastes, with influences ranging from ancient Rome via the Orient to Młoda Polska Art Nouveau. The ballroom, which was added as an afterthought, is an effective pastiche of the English Tudor style.

North of here, past the Księży Młyn tenements and through Park Źródliska, you'll come to the fortress-like Pałac Scheiblera, the former home of the Karl Scheiber and now the **Muzeum Kinematografii** (Cinematography Museum; Tues noon–5pm, Wed & Fri–Sun 9am–4pm; 4zł, free on Tues), which celebrates Łódź's status as one of Europe's major training grounds for film-makers with

Łódź's cemeteries

Perhaps appropriately, the most potent reminders of the cultural diversity of Łódź's past are its **cemeteries**. The two most worthwhile are some way from the centre of town, but are worth the effort of visiting. Easiest to get to is the Christian **Necropolis**, a ten-minute walk west from the Poznański factory along ul. Ogrodowa. Of its three interconnected plots, by far the largest is the Catholic cemetery, whose monuments, with rare exceptions, are fairly simple. Even less ostentatious is its Orthodox counterpart, containing the graves of civil servants, soldiers and policemen from the tsarist period. In contrast, the Protestant cemetery is full of appropriately grandiose memorials to deceased captains of industry. Towering over all the other graves, though now crumbling and boarded up, is the **Scheibler family mausoleum**, a miniaturized Gothic cathedral with a soaring Germanic openwork spire.

Łódź's **Jewish Cemetery** (May–Sept Mon–Thurs & Sun 9am–5pm, Fri 9am–3pm; Oct–April Mon–Fri 8am–3pm; 4zł; skullcaps provided) is just west of the terminus of trams #1 and #6 (walk north from the tram stop and turn left onto ul. Zmienna). Although it only dates from 1892, this is the largest Jewish cemetery in Europe, with some 180,000 tombstones (and twice as many graves), including the spectacular domed mausoleum of Israel Poznański (died 1900), with fine Art-Nouveau mosaics inside. The cemetery is well kept, thanks to restoration funds from abroad, and near the entrance there's a pavilion that holds temporary exhibitions. Going back outside the cemetery walls and north to ul. Stalowa, you'll come to Radegoszcz Station, from where ghetto residents – over 140,000 Jews all told, as well as 5000 Gypsies – were deported to the Chełmno and Auschwitz death camps. The building has stood empty for years, but there are plans to convert it into a Łódź Ghetto Museum. For details, contact the local Jewish community centre on ul. Pomorska 18 (☎042/633 5156; Mon–Fri 9am–3pm).

changing exhibitions on the history of Polish film, though the sumptuous interior is at least as much a draw as the museum itself.

Eating and drinking

Łódź's **restaurant**, **bar** and **café** scene can compete with almost any city in Poland. By night, ul. Piotrkowska in the centre of town is the heart of the action, a two-kilometre-long strip of dining, drinking and dancing emporia.

Restaurants and snack bars

Anatewka ul. 6 Sierpna 2/4 ☎042/630 3635. High-quality Jewish restaurant, popular with local elite and well-heeled tourists.

Ciągoty Tęsknoty ul. Wojska Polskiego 144. Café-restaurant close to the Jewish cemetery, with good and affordable French-influenced food and occasional live music. Popular with students from the nearby fine arts academy. Tram #1 or #6 to "Sporna".

Denise ul. Piotrkowska 60. Łódź's most appealing Italian restaurant, with well-prepared pasta and live piano music, and not overly expensive.

Esplanada ul. Piotrkowska 100 ☎042/630 5989. Fine seafood in an elegant Art-Nouveau interior.

Green Way ul. Piotrkowska 80. Branch of the affordable vegetarian chain, in a spacious building right in the centre.

Klub Spadkobierców ul. Piotrkowska 77 ☎042/633 7670. Behind the stained-glass windows, a Wall Street atmosphere in the impeccably furnished former banking house of *fin-de-siècle* tycoon Maximilian Goldfeder. The name means "Inheritors' Club". Strong on fresh fish and steaks.

Pieczarka Piotrów ul. Piotrkowska 106. Traditional milk bar specializing in tasty mushroom dishes. Extremely cheap and well run.

Presto ul. Piotrkowska 67 and 142. With two branches, the best choice for inexpensive Italian food, with a fairly extensive menu and good-quality pizza and pasta in a comfortable, unpretentious setting.

Restauracja Polska ul. Piotrkowska 12. Upscale traditional Polish restaurant serving everything from *golonka* to rabbit. Fine decor and polished service.

U Chochoła ul. Traugutta 3 and ul. Piotrkowska 200. Folklore-themed restaurant with wooden-bench seating, bunches of dried herbs hanging from the rafters and traditional, reasonably priced Polish dishes, including fish and game.

Varoska ul. Traugutta 4. Pleasant, mid-priced Hungarian place with a nice line in *bigos*, goulash and potato pancakes and a good selection of Hungarian wines and spirits.

Ziemia Obiecana ul. Wigury 4/6 ☎ 042/636 7081. Atmospheric 1920s palace restaurant attached to the *Déjà Vu* pension. Serving a mix of Polish, German and Jewish dishes, including an excellent lamb *chulent* (stew) for 26zł. Reservations recommended.

Cafés, bars and clubs

Bagdad Café ul. Jaracza 45. Tucked between two chemists not far from the Teatr Wielki, this is the legendary home of Łódź bohemians – although nowadays a laid-back studenty hangout, good for billiards. DJ nights at the weekend.

Biblioteka ul. Kościuszki 36. Relaxed pub favoured by a mix of students and middle-aged idlers.

Blikle ul. Piotrkowska 89. Not up to the Warsaw original, but fine for coffee and dessert.

Cube ul. Kilińskiego 123. Currently the city's trendiest nightclub, playing a mix of techno and hip hop, around 500m south of the train station. Open Tues, Fri & Sat.

Espresso Inside the *Grand*, see p.149. Unpretentious coffee bar (not to be confused with the

hotel's posh *kawiarnia* on the other side) offering up good, cheap brews and excellent cakes and ice cream.

Fabryka ul. Piotrkowska 80. Legendary pub in a former textile factory, with the longest bar in Europe, if not the world. Live rock and open late, so a good place in the early hours. Go through the archway at ul. Piotrkowska 80 and turn left at the end of the alley. From 8pm Fri & Sat only.

Irish Pub ul. Piotrkowska 77. Bar posters in Ireland don't normally have Cyrillic lettering, but this is nonetheless an attractive upscale drinking spot.

JazzGa ul. Piotrkowska 17. Homely dive in an off-street courtyard. Jam sessions on Tues and concerts at weekends.

Łódź Kaliska ul. Piotrkowska 102. Hidden down an alley, a wonderful and very popular pub full of mirrors and curios, with a rooftop section that's open in good weather.

The Mexican ul. Piotrkowska 67. Raucous Mexican bar and restaurant hidden in a passage, serving margaritas and tequila specials.

West Side ul. Piotrkowska 102. Mainstream disco with commercial techno and themed party nights, right next to the *Łódź Kaliska* bar (see above).

Entertainment

Łódź can hold its own when it comes to culture. In early December the city plays host to Poland's most prestigious film event, the **Camerimage Festival** (Ⓦ www.camerimage.pl) attracting cinema luminaries from around the world. Equally interesting is the new annual **Festiwal Dialogu Czterech Kultur** (Four Cultures Festival; Ⓦ www.4kultury.pl), held in September and featuring films, concerts and discussions of and between the city's traditional residents – Poles, Jews, Germans and Russians. Other regular events are the **Meeting of Styles** graffiti festival, held in July, which features hip-hop concerts as well as the redecoration of a section of the Kaliska train station; and the **ballet festival** (Łódzkie Spotkania Baletowe) in May and June every odd-numbered year.

For **theatre** there's the highly rated Teatr Nowy at ul. Więckowskiego 15 (☎ 042/633 4494, Ⓦ www.nowy.pl) and the Teatr Wielki on pl. Dąbrowskiego 1 (☎ 042/633 9960, Ⓦ www.teatr-wielki.lodz.pl), which also presents **opera**; visiting foreign companies regularly perform at both venues. The **concert** programmes of the Philharmonic orchestra at ul. Piotrkowska 243 (☎ 042/637 2653, Ⓦ www.filharmonia.lodz.pl) feature soloists of international renown, while the Teatr Muzyczny, ul. Połnocna 47/51 (☎ 042/678 3511, Ⓦ www.teatr-muzyczny.lodz.pl), is the main venue for operetta and musicals.

Of numerous **cinemas**, the Bałtyk at ul. Narutowicza is central and plays alternative films, while there's a Silver Screen multiplex next to the Ibis Hotel on al. Piłsudskiego.

Along the Wisła

Northwest of Warsaw, the Mazovian countryside is dominated by the meander-ing expanse of the **Wisła** as it continues its trek towards the Baltic Sea. Many of the towns ranged along its banks still bear the imprint of the river-bound trade they once thrived on. Of these, the most important is **Płock**, one-time capital of Mazovia, and a thriving industrial centre. With a major museum and an enjoyable historic complex, it makes an eminently worthwhile outing from Warsaw. Closer to the capital is the ancient church complex at **Czerwińsk nad Wisłą**.

Modlin Castle

Some 36km northwest of Warsaw, at the intersection of the Wisła and the Narew rivers, stand the eerie ruins of **Modlin Castle** – you can see them from the northbound E81 road to Gdańsk. A huge earth and brick fortress raised in the early nineteenth century on Napoleon's orders, the already large complex was restored and extended by Russian forces in the 1830s and 1840s; at its height, the huge complex accommodated a garrison of some 26,000 people. It was devastated during the early part of World War II, but you can still wander through the atmospheric ruins of the castle, which offer a pleasant view over the river below.

Czerwińsk nad Wisłą

CZERWIŃSK NAD WISŁĄ, around 70km from Warsaw along the Płock road, is a placid village on the north bank of the Wisła. What pulls the crowds (and there can be plenty of them in summer) to this idyllic, out-of-the-way setting is the Romanesque church and monastery complex, one of the oldest, and finest, historic ensembles in the Mazovia region.

Sitting atop the hill above the village is the ancient **church complex**. Founded by the monks who were brought here in the early twelfth century by the dukes of Mazovia to hasten along the conversion of the region, it retains much of its original Romanesque structure, still visible amid the later Gothic and Baroque additions. The entrance, flanked by high twin towers, is through a delicately carved, brick Romanesque **portal** inside the brick facade added onto the building in the seventeenth century, its original ceiling decorated with geometric frescoes featuring plant motifs and representations of the Virgin Mary. Inside the building, a couple of fine Romanesque stone columns have survived, as has a remarkable selection of early polychromy, notably in the **chapel** off the east aisle – its luminous Romanesque frescoes were uncovered during renovation in the 1950s. The late Gothic **bell tower** near the church, whose powerful bells are among the oldest in the country, was once the gateway to the town. If you're here during the summer season, you should be able to climb this, or one of the church towers, for a view over the flat pastoral surroundings. Round the back of the church is the **monastery complex**, now occupied by a Salesian Fathers seminary, whose members act as guides in summer, some of whom speak English. You might also ask to see the **cloisters**, which contain a fine Gothic refectory and a small **museum** of local ethnography and church art (10am–dusk; 4zł). There is also a parochial museum (same hours) containing sculpture, painting and craftwork.

It's worth taking a stroll down the hill into the tumbledown **village** on the riverbank, which has a notable predominance of wooden houses. Non-express **buses** to Płock from Warszawa Zachodnia call at Czerwińsk (8 daily), a ninety-minute journey. The selection of food in the village **shop** is adequate for a picnic.

Płock

PŁOCK, the major town of western Mazovia, located some 115km west of Warsaw, is outwardly a nondescript industrial conurbation spread along the banks of the Wisła. In the midst of the town, however, lies a charming **Stare Miasto**, its predominantly low-rise centre characterized by spruced-up nineteenth-century facades and quiet, flower-bedded squares.

The oldest urban settlement in Mazovia, Płock became the seat of the Polish kings in the eleventh century, and remained so for nearly a hundred years. An important bishopric, and one of the number of strategically located riverside towns that grew fat on the medieval Wisła-bound commercial boom, Płock felt the full weight of mid-seventeenth-century Swedish invasions – much of the Płock bishopric's valuable library was purloined and taken to Uppsala, where it remains.

Arrival, information and accommodation

The most convenient way of getting to Płock by public transport is to use the Warsaw–Bydgoszcz bus services run by Komfort Bus and Polski Express – both companies pick up and drop off on the Nowy Rynek, just north of the Stare Miasto. Otherwise, the regular **bus and train stations** are next to each other on the northeastern side of town, a twenty-minute walk (or a short ride on bus #20) from the centre. The **tourist office** at Stary Rynek 8 (May–Sept

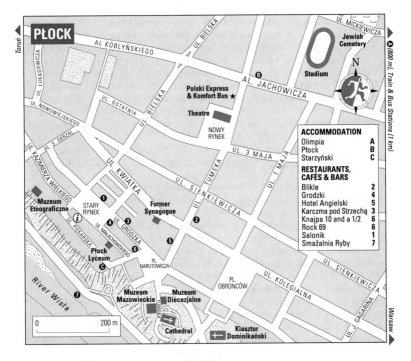

Mon–Fri 9am–5pm, Sat–Sun 10am–2pm; Oct–April Mon–Fri 8am–4pm; ☎024/369 1944, ⓦump.pl) is a fine source of maps and accommodation information.

Although Płock makes an easy day trip from Warsaw, there is a good choice of **accommodation** in town, beginning with the well-placed *Starzyński*, overlooking the river at ul. Piekarska 1 (☎024/366 0200, ⓦwww.starzynski .com.pl; ❻), a functional block, not much to look at from outside, but with very comfortable, fairly tastefully furnished rooms, including some with outstanding views. Other options include the basic but friendly *Płock*, quite good for the price but a step down from the *Starzyński*, just north of the centre at al. S. Jachowicza 38 (☎024/262 9393, ⓦwww.hplock.plocman.pl; ❹); and, northeast of the centre towards the stations at ul. Dworcowa 26, *Olimpia* (☎024/262 0407, ⓦwww.motelik-olimpia.pl), a pension with passable, decent value rooms with or without bath (❷–❸).

The Stare Miasto

On a clifftop overlooking the wide expanses of the Wisła, the **Stare Miasto** area provides the main point of interest. Known locally as "little Kraków", because the important buildings are grouped together at the top of a hill, the area has recently undergone excavations which have unearthed an ancient (c.400 BC) stone altar and pillar, indicating the presence of pagan cults. Walking down to the Stare Miasto from either the bus or the train station leads you eventually to the pedestrianized **ulica Tumska**, a busy shopping area. Crossing ul. Kolegialna, Tumska leads into the ancient core of the town.

The cathedral

At the end of ul. Tumska is the medieval **cathedral** (Mon–Sat 10am–5.30pm, Sun 2–5.30pm; sightseeing discouraged outside these hours), a Romanesque building begun after the installation of the Płock bishopric in 1075 and completed in the following century. Successive rebuildings have left few traces of the building's original character; what you see today reflects the classicist remodelling of the Italian architect Merlini in the mid-eighteenth century.

Inside, the **royal chapel** contains the Romanesque sarcophagi of Polish princes **Władysław Herman** (1040–1102) and his son, **Bolesław the Wrymouth** (Krzywousty; 1086–1138), while Secessionist frescoes decorate the nave. The sculptured **bronze doors**, the cathedral's most famous feature, were the subject of a major piece of architectural detective work. The Romanesque originals commissioned by the bishop of Płock from the Magdeburg artist Riquin in the mid-twelfth century went missing for over six centuries, when King Władysław Jagiełło gave them to his Russian counterpart as a present, around the time his own brother became Prince of Novgorod. Subsequently hung in the entrance to the Orthodox church of St Sophia in Novgorod, and adorned with fake Cyrillic inscriptions identifying them as booty from a twelfth-century Russian expedition to Sweden, the doors were located in 1970 by a Polish academic, who had noticed the Latin inscriptions mentioning Płock on a late-nineteenth-century gypsum copy of the doors hanging in the Historical Museum in Moscow. A further bronze copy of the originals (still in Novgorod) was made for the cathedral after the discovery, and it's these you see today, two dozen **panels** filled with a magnificent series of **reliefs** depicting scenes from the Old Testament and the Gospels as well as a number of allegorical pieces. Back from the building, the skyline is dominated by the twin brick Gothic **Zegarowa** and **Szlachecka towers** beside the cathedral, the best-preserved fragments of the fourteenth-century castle that once stood here. The former tower is the cathedral belfry.

The Muzeum Mazowieckie and the Muzeum Diecezjalne

A short way from the cathedral is Płock's other major monument, the Gothic former Mazovian dukes' castle, home of the **Muzeum Mazowieckie** (Regional Museum; mid-May to Sept Tues–Thurs & Sun 9am–4pm, Fri & Sat 10am–5pm; Oct to mid-May Wed–Fri 9am–3pm, Sat & Sun 9am–4pm; 8zł, Thurs free). One of the oldest such exhibitions in Europe, established here by the local Historical Society in 1820, the museum features a superb selection of **Secessionist** work; Art Nouveau is represented in all its various forms, including old photos of some of Poland's finest *fin-de-siècle* buildings. The museum starts with **period rooms**, showing how the style was applied to the ordinary everyday business of living; much of the furniture and decorative art is Austrian or Belgian, while in the last room there's a shaving set from Japan and a lovely desk from Kraków. Młoda Polska-school paintings are hung in the next rooms, with desolate landscapes by Julian Fałat and memorable portraits by Wyspiański and Alfons Karpiński. The rest of the floor displays stained glass and a bewildering array of silverware, while upstairs there's a section on local military history and some older period rooms with Biedermeier-type furniture.

Directly across from the cathedral entrance is the **Muzeum Diecezjalne** (Diocesan Museum; May–Sept Tues–Sat 10am–3pm, Sun 11am–4pm; Oct–April Wed–Sat 10am–1pm, Sun 11am–2pm; 4zł), in its own way just as interesting as the main museum. The highlight is the extraordinary collection of antiquarian books, starting with the Biblia Płocka (Płock Bible), an enormous twelfth-century tome that sits beside an even larger thirteenth-century choir book. There's also a gorgeous, Renaissance-era edition of St Augustine's *City of God*; a first edition of Mickiewicz's *Pan Tadeusz* (very much a treasure in Poland); and, most unusual of all, an Arabic translation of the works of Thomas à Kempis, printed in Rome in 1653. In addition there's a good collection of Gothic sculpture, taken from churches around the region; a case of mammoth tusks, trilobites and other fossils; some attractive nineteenth-century folk art; and, upstairs, what must be one of the world's worst displays of old master-era paintings, with one ghastly still life or allegorical landscape following another.

Back up along ul. Tumska and west past the former bishop's palace, halfway down ul. Małachowskiego, is the **Płock Lyceum**, the oldest school in the country, founded in the 1180s and still going strong more than eight hundred years years later. Next to it is a gallery sitting on the foundations of two recently uncovered Romanesque pillars located in the west wing of the school.

Continuing to the end of ul. Małachowskiego you'll come to the very quiet **Rynek**, lined with eighteenth- and nineteenth-century houses, including several with decent outdoor cafés. One block further west, on ul. Kazimierza Wielkiego, is the **Muzeum Etnograficzne** (Ethnographic Museum; same hours as Muzeum Mazowieckie, see above; 3zł), in an attractive nineteenth-century granary, housing temporary exhibitions related to Mazovian folk culture.

The waterfront

As you turn back towards the cathedral you'll see the **terrace** to the left of the building, overlooking the Wisła waterfront. An open, blustery spot on a fine day, it offers huge panoramas over the wide expanse of the river below, at its widest around Płock. A wooded path leads off in both directions along the clifftop, the Wisła spread below you along with the sandy promontories running out into the mainstream of the river. Walking west, expensive refreshments can be taken at the *Hotel Starzyński*, with its terrace offering a marvellous view of the river. If you're here in summer, you'll see townsfolk stretched out on the expansive sandy **beach** just down the hill from here. Walking east from the cathedral terrace and down through the park brings you to the **Klasztor Dominikań-ski** (Dominican church and monastery), a thirteenth-century edifice originally built for Duke Konrad of Mazovia, later given a predictably ornate classicist treatment. A Protestant church up until 1945, it sits isolated from the town in the middle of a park, part of the rolling woodland that covers much of the waterfront below the Stare Miasto.

Finally, there are reminders of the city's vanished Jewish population in the former **synagogue** at ul. Kwiatka 7, west of ul. Tumska, built in 1810 but now boarded up, peeling and left to go to ruin, and the untended, overgrown **Jewish cemetery** on ul. Mickiewicza, fifteen minutes' walk northeast of the centre, where there's a monument honouring local Jews who perished in the concentration camps.

Eating and drinking

The *Starzyński* hotel (see p.158) has a luxury **restaurant** with outstanding views over the Wisła, while if you descend to the river you'll be rewarded with excellent fish and chips at *Smażalnia Ryby* (April–Oct only). Otherwise, there's good, country-style food at the *Karczma pod Strzechą*, ul. Grodzka 5; meat-and-potatoes repertoire in provincial bourgeois surroundings at *Salonik*, Stary Rynek 19; and pizza and grills at *Knajpka 10 and a 1/2*, pl. Narutowicza 2. The curiously named *Hotel Angielski*, ul. Tumska 9, offers good, cheap Polish food, but no accommodation. *Blikle*, Tumska 14, is the place for cakes, ice cream and coffee.

Drinking venues include *Rock 69*, in the same courtyard as *Knajpka 10 and a 1/2* (see above), a friendly bar that has regular live music; and *Grodzki*, an appealingly seedy local at the eastern edge of the Rynek. There are also beer-oriented outdoor bars on the banks of the Wisła.

Northeastern Mazovia

North of Warsaw, the main routes whisk you through the suburbs and out into the flat Mazovian countryside, its windswept farmland divided by the Wisła from the west and by the smaller and less polluted Rivers Narew and Bug to the east. The old centres of **Pułtusk** and **Ciechanów** retain the rustic feel of a traditional Mazovian market town, while to the east the monument on the site of the **Treblinka** concentration camp is a more sober destination. **Transport** from Warsaw to Pułtusk and Ciechanów, by bus and train respectively, is straight-forward, but getting to Treblinka is more difficult without your own transport.

Pułtusk

Sixty kilometres north of Warsaw along the west bank of the River Narew stands **PUŁTUSK**, a lively Mazovian market town that was long a grain-trading centre on the river route to Gdańsk. Pułtusk twice hit the headlines in the nineteenth century, first in 1806 when Napoleonic and Russian forces fought a major battle here – a victory recorded alongside Bonaparte's other triumphs on the walls of the Arc de Triomphe in Paris – and later, in 1868, when a huge meteorite fell near the town. Badly damaged, like much of northern Mazovia, during the Soviet advance of winter 1944–45 when eighty percent of the buildings were destroyed, the town has nevertheless managed to retain its old-time market-town feel, thanks in part to a major postwar reconstruction programme.

The Town

The **Rynek** provides the main focus of the town. In the large cobbled area – nearly 400m long – a number of the original eighteenth- and nineteenth-century burghers' houses are still in evidence. These apart, the square mostly consists of tasteful postwar reconstruction.

The imposing Gothic brick tower tacked onto the town hall, in the middle of the square, houses the enjoyable regional **museum** (Tues–Sun 10am–4pm; 5zł). Erected in the 1400s, the tower was originally part of the town's defences, subsequently serving as a storehouse, Jesuit boarding-school house and prison. Inside, the first-floor exhibitions cover archeological finds uncovered here in the 1970s. The mostly medieval objects on display include reconstructed early wooden sailing vessels, military paraphernalia, silver and metalwork, and fine decorated tiles. The collection of folk art on other floors comes mostly from the forested Kurpie region to the east, an area noted for strong craft traditions. It's worth climbing the full six floors of the tower for the panoramic view over the town and surroundings from the top of the building – binoculars are available at the entrance.

The monumental collegiate **church** at the north end of the square is a Gothic brick basilica, remodelled in the sixteenth century by the Venetian architect Giovanni Battista. A striking feature is the arched vault of the nave, the design motif of circles connected by belts being a characteristic ornamental element of Renaissance-era churches in the region. The Renaissance Noskowski chapel modelled on the Wawel Kaplica Zygmuntowska (see p.412), is a beauty, featuring a Renaissance copy of Michelangelo's *Pietà*, and some delicate original polychromy. More eccentric is the main rear chapel, stuffed with local Catholic standards for use on Holy Day processions and lined from floor to ceiling with blue Dordrecht tiles.

Off the southern end of the square is the **castle**, one-time residence of the bishops of Płock, an oft-rebuilt semicircular brick structure straddled across a raised mound overlooking the Narew. The original fourteenth-century (perhaps earlier) wooden fortification was destroyed by marauding Lithuanians, and the castle was rebuilt from scratch in the 1520s. The arcaded bridge leading up to the brick castle was added a century later, only to be pummelled by the Swedes in the 1650s. The castle's claim to historical fame is as the site of the first public theatre in Poland, opened by the Jesuits in 1565. As with many towns in Mazovia, there's a Napoleonic connection too: Bonaparte stayed here with his brother Jérôme in 1806 prior to the nearby battle against Russian forces, and again in 1812 during the disastrous retreat from Moscow. It's also one of several places where he is supposed to have first met his lover-to-be, Maria Walewska.

In the 1970s, the castle was taken over by Polonia, the state-sponsored organization dedicated to maintaining links between émigré Poles and their home country. As a result the **Dom Polonii**, the official seat for all expatriate Poles, has now been converted into a luxury hotel and holiday/conference centre for the huge Polish diaspora, with émigrés young and old from all over the world – the USA and Germany in particular – taking part in events here throughout the year.

The **gardens**, laid out when the moat was drained and covered in the sixteenth century, lead down to the water's edge – a pleasant, tranquil place for a stroll, with sailing and other activities possible in good weather. In summer there's also a café open by the water. Back out towards the main square is the old castle **chapel**, a Renaissance structure largely rebuilt after wartime destruction.

Practicalities

The **bus station**, on the Nowy Rynek, is a ten-minute walk from the Rynek. For anyone tempted by a stay out in the country, the Dom Polonii's **hotel**, the *Zamek* (☎023/692 9000, ⓦwww.dompolonii.pultusk.pl; ❻), in the castle, is an obvious option. The castle **restaurant**, housed in a magisterial dining room, though quite pricey is worth trying, especially for the traditionally prepared duck dishes. There are some cheaper restaurants and cafés around the main square.

Ciechanów

Continuing northwest for 40km brings you to **CIECHANÓW**, a largish, dowdy-looking Mazovian town on the main rail line to Gdańsk, where life passes slowly. If you happen to be passing through it's worth stopping off to see the remains of the imposing fourteenth-century **Mazovian dukes' castle** stuck out on a limb on the eastern edge of town, one of a scattering of fortifications around the region originally occupied by the medieval rulers of Mazovia. A solid brick structure (the walls are over 55m high), the interior houses a museum of weaponry (Tues–Sun 10am–4pm; 5zł), the main point of going being for the chance to look around the castle itself. Totally unlike the Teutonic castles of the Gdańsk region, the castle has only two towers of the original building still standing.

The **Kościół św. Jozefa** (St Joseph's), off what passes for the main square, is a good example of Mazovian Gothic, a high brick structure with a tiered facade arranged in thin pointed layers. Immediately north of town, the countryside is scattered with **military cemeteries**, a reminder of the major battle fought here in September 1939, where German forces attempting to push straight to Warsaw encountered stiff resistance from the retreating Polish Army.

Ciechanów is on the main rail line north from Warsaw. The best bet for **accommodation** is the central and perfectly comfortable *Zacisze* hotel, ul. Mikołaczyka 8A (☎023/672 2046, ⓦwww.hotelzacisze.pl; ❸), which also has a good restaurant.

Treblinka

The site of the **TREBLINKA** concentration camp, one of the largest and most notorious the Nazis constructed, and one which saw the murder of an estimated 800,000 Jews between 1942 and 1943, stands some 80km northeast of Warsaw, just south of the main rail line towards Białystok. Liquidated by the Nazis, fearing a Soviet advance, in 1943, nothing of the camp itself remains and the site today is a **museum** (daily 9am–7pm; 2zł), comprising a series of **stone memorials.** Placed here under the auspices of the Polish authorities in 1959–63, these trace the outline and principal features of the camp: one set represents railway tracks, leading to a platform and cremation pit; another series marks the camp boundaries and gates; and a third, a symbolic graveyard, is dedicated to the victims and the countries they came from. The main monuments are on the site of Treblinka II, from which a path leads to Treblinka I, where there are more symbolic tombs. Little has changed at the museum since it was set up forty years ago, and information in English is scant: in spite of the gravity of the memorial it can be hard to get a feeling for what took place here, especially in good weather, when the surrounding forest is as pleasantly serene as any other.

The only way to get to Treblinka without your own transportation or a **guided tour** (which can be arranged by the Our Roots agency in Warsaw;

Treblinka

The **Treblinka I** labour camp, opened in an isolated tract of forest in 1941, held up to 2000 prisoners at a time, mostly Poles and Jews from Warsaw. Over half of the 20,000 held here between 1941 and 1944 were either shot or worked to death in the adjacent gravel pit. In April 1942, construction on the larger **Treblinka II** was started two kilometres to the east, a death camp nearly identical to the one in the Lublin suburb of Majdanek (see p.301), but without crematoria, and with the addition of an artificial train station, used to convince victims they were merely in transit. By July it was complete, and by mid-September 300,000 Jews from the evacuated Warsaw ghetto had already been gassed. The vast majority of those killed at Treblinka during the next year were Polish Jews, but thousands of Jews from Greece, Slovakia and elsewhere were also sent here, as well as 2000 Gypsies. The camp was run by two to three dozen Germans and Austrians, as well as around one hundred Ukrainian guards, including the infamously sadistic Ivan the Terrible, who wielded a sword at the camp and was responsible for the torture and murder of thousands. In 1943, following an uprising in which two hundred inmates escaped (sixty of whom survived the war), the Nazis, fearing a Soviet advance, liquidated the camp and transferred the remaining Jews to Sobibor. Every trace of the camp's existence was erased – an enormous task which involved the exhumation and incineration of over three-quarters of a million bodies – at the conclusion of which one of the guards was settled on the site to pose as a farmer.

see box, p.106) is by taking a **train** to Małkinia (there are frequent connections from Dworzec Wileński in Warsaw's Praga district and a few daily services from Warszawa Centralna), 8km north of the camp. There are usually **taxis** waiting outside the Małkinia station, and hiring one to take you to Treblinka and back shouldn't cost more than 35zł. The drive takes you across a creaking, old-fashioned bridge over the River Bug, and through several pretty villages, including Treblinka village itself, halfway to the camp, where there's a small grocery store. No buses run along this route, but hitching is a possibility.

Travel details

Trains

Warsaw to: Białystok (8 daily; 2hr 45min); Bydgoszcz (5 daily; 4hr); Częstochowa (5 daily; 3hr); Gdańsk/Gdynia (12–20 daily; 4–5hr); Jelenia Góra (1 overnight; 10hr); Katowice (12 daily; 2hr 30min–4hr); Kielce (9 daily; 3hr); Kraków (16 daily; 2hr 45min–5hr); Krynica (1–2 daily; 7–10hr); Lublin (12 daily; 2hr 15min–3hr); Łódź (Mon–Fri hourly; Sat & Sun every 2hrs; 2hr); Olsztyn (4 daily; 3hr 30min); Poznań (19 daily; 2hr 45min–4hr); Przemyśl (3 daily; 6–8hr); Rzeszów (3 daily; 5–7hr); Sandomierz (2 daily; 4hr 30min); Sanok (1 overnight; 11hr); Suwałki (3 daily; 5–6hr); Świnoujście (1 overnight; 10hr); Szczecin (6 daily; 5–7hr); Toruń (4–5 daily; 3hr); Wrocław (11 daily; 5–6hr); Zamość (1 daily; 5hr 30min); Zakopane (1–2 daily; 6hr–8hr 30min).

Łódź Fabryczna to: Częstochowa (2 daily; 2hr 30min–3hr 30min); Katowice (1 daily; 4hr); Kraków (2 daily; 5hr); Warsaw (Mon–Fri hourly, Sat & Sun every 2hr; 1hr 30min–2hr 30min).

Łódź Kaliska to: Gdańsk (3 daily; 6hr); Poznań (2 daily; 3hr 30min–5hr); Warsaw (3 daily; 2hr); Wrocław (5 daily; 4hr).

Buses

Łódź to: Bydgoszcz (3 daily; 4hr); Ciechocinek (5 daily; 3hr); Częstochowa (10 daily; 2hr 30min–3hr); Gdańsk (1 daily; 6hr 15min); Kraków (7 daily; 5hr); Płock (10 daily; 2hr 30min); Toruń (3 daily; 3hr–4hr); Warsaw (21 daily; 2–3hr).

Płock to: Bydgoszcz (7 daily; 2hr 30min); Łódź (17 daily; 2hr 30min); Toruń (10 daily; 1hr 45min); Warszawa Zachodnia (hourly; 2–3hr).

Warsaw Stadion to: Białystok (5 daily; 4hr); Kazimierz Dolny (5 daily; 2hr 30min); Lublin (6 daily; 4hr); Przemyśl (4 daily; 8hr); Suwałki (4 daily; 6hr); Zamość (2 daily; 7hr).

Warsaw Zachodnia to: Kazimierz Dolny (2 daily; 2hr 30min); Krosno (1 daily; 7hr); Mrągowo (1 daily; 5hr); Olsztyn (3 daily; 5hr); Rzeszów (1 daily; 8hr); Toruń (2 daily; 3hr 30min); Zakopane (2 daily; 9hr); Zamość (4 daily; 5hr); Żelazowa Wola (5 daily; 1hr 40min).

Warsaw Polski Express/HaloBus stop on al. Jana Pawła II to: Białystok (3 daily; 3hr 30min); Bydgoszcz (hourly; 4hr 30min); Ciechocinek (2 daily; 3hr 30min); Częstochowa (2 daily; 4hr); Gdańsk (2 daily; 5hr); Gdynia (2 daily; 5hr 40min); Kazimierz Dolny (3 daily; 2hr); Lublin (7 daily; 3hr); Łódź (7 daily; 2hr); Płock (hourly; 1hr 45min); Puławy (3 daily; 1hr 40min); Szczecin (2 daily; 8hr); Toruń (hourly; 3hr 40min).

Flights

Warsaw to: Bydgoszcz (1 daily; 45min); Gdańsk (5–6 daily; 1hr); Katowice (3 daily; 1hr); Kraków (5–6 daily; 1hr); Poznań (4 daily; 1hr), Wrocław (5–6 daily; 1hr).

International trains

Warsaw to: Berlin (4–5 daily; 6hr 30min); Brussels (1 overnight; 16hr); Budapest (2 daily; 10–12hr); Dresden (1 overnight; 12hr); Kiev (2 daily; 16hr); Minsk (2–3 daily; 10hr); Moscow (2 daily; 18hr); Prague (3 daily; 9–12hr); St Petersburg (1 daily; 27hr); Vienna (3 daily; 7hr 30min); Vilnius (3 weekly; 11hr).

International buses

Warsaw Zachodnia to: Amsterdam (1–2 daily; 20hr 30min); Frankfurt (daily; 19hr); London (2–4 daily; 27hr); L'viv (4–5 daily; 8hr); Paris (6 weekly; 24hr); Prague (3 weekly; 10hr 30min); Riga (1 daily; 13hr 30min); Rome (1–2 daily; 28hr); Tallinn (daily; 18hr 30min); Vilnius (3 daily; 9hr).

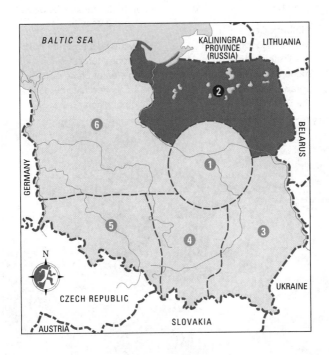

Northeastern Poland

BALTIC SEA

KALININGRAD PROVINCE (RUSSIA)

LITHUANIA

GERMANY

BELARUS

UKRAINE

CZECH REPUBLIC

SLOVAKIA

AUSTRIA

N

CHAPTER 2 # Highlights

* **Gdańsk** An archetypal north European maritime city, full of Gothic architecture, fog-bound quays and buzzing nightlife. See p.170

* **Hel** This quaint fishing village provides easy access to mile upon mile of pristine white-sand beaches. See p.198

* **Malbork Castle** For centuries the headquarters of the Teutonic Knights, this monumental medieval castle sprawls along the banks of the Wisła. See p.203

* **Toruń** A lively university town packed with a jumble of exquisite medieval buildings. See p.209

* **Mikołajki** Poland's prime venue for yachting, kayaking and generally messing about in boats, situated in the heart of the Mazurian lake district. See p.242

* **Białowieża national park** Europe's largest surviving area of primeval forest, famous for its large population of bison. See p.277

△ Gdańsk crane

Northeastern Poland

E ven in a country accustomed to shifts in its borders, northeastern Poland presents an unusually tortuous historical puzzle. Successively the domain of a Germanic crusading order, of the Hansa merchants and of the Prussians, it's only in the last forty years that the region has really become Polish. Right up until the end of World War II, large parts of the area belonged to the territories of East Prussia, and although you won't see the old place names displayed any more, even the most patriotic Pole would have to acknowledge that Gdańsk, Olsztyn and Toruń made their mark on history under the German names of Danzig, Allenstein and Thorn. Twentieth-century Germany has left terrible scars: it was here that the first shots of World War II were fired, and the bitter fighting during the Nazi retreat in 1945 left many historic towns as sad shadows of their former selves.

Gdańsk, **Sopot** and **Gdynia** – the **Trójmiasto** (Tri-City) as they are collectively known – dominate the area from their coastal vantage point. Like Warsaw, historic Gdańsk was obliterated in World War II but it now boasts many reconstructed quarters, a booming economy and a place in history as the cradle of Solidarity. It makes an enjoyable base for exploring neighbouring **Kashubia**, to the west, with its rolling hills, lakeside forests and distinctive communities of Prussianized Slavs. While waters around the Trójmiasto are a dubious (if ever-improving) proposition, the **Hel Peninsula** and the coast further west make a pleasant seaside option. On the other side of the Trójmiasto, **Frombork**, chief of many towns in the region associated with the astronomer Nicolaus Copernicus, is an attractive and historic lagoon-side town across the water from the **Wiślana Peninsula**, a beachside holiday-makers' favourite.

South from Gdańsk, a collection of Teutonic castles and Hanseatic centres dot the banks of the Wisła and its tributaries. Highlights include the huge medieval fortress at **Malbork**, once the headquarters of the Teutonic Knights, and **Toruń**, with its spectacular medieval ensemble. Eastwards stretches **Mazury**, Poland's biggest lakeland district, long popular with Polish holiday-makers and now with Germans. Canoeing and yachting are the main attractions of its resorts, but for anyone wanting to get away from the crowds, there are much less frequented patches of water and nature to explore, both in Mazury and in the neighbouring **Suwalszczyzna** and **Augustów** region.

South again, lakes give way to the forests, open plains and Orthodox villages of **Podlasie**, the border region with Belarus, centred on the city of **Białystok**. This is the obvious jumping-off point for journeys into the **Białowieża national park**, a unique area of virgin forest and home to a famous bison reserve. The Podlasie region maintains one of Poland's most fascinating ethnic

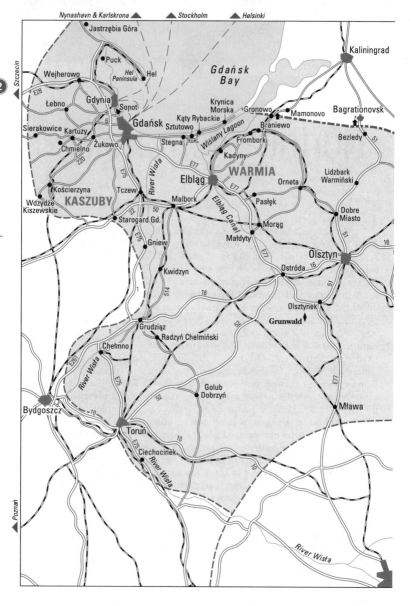

mixes, with a significant **Belarusian** population and smaller communities of **Tatars**. The Nazis wiped out the **Jewish** population, but their history is important in these parts, too, with one of Poland's finest synagogues well restored at **Tykocin**.

The area is covered with an extensive **public transport** network, although progress can be painfully slow once you get beyond the Gdańsk region – so

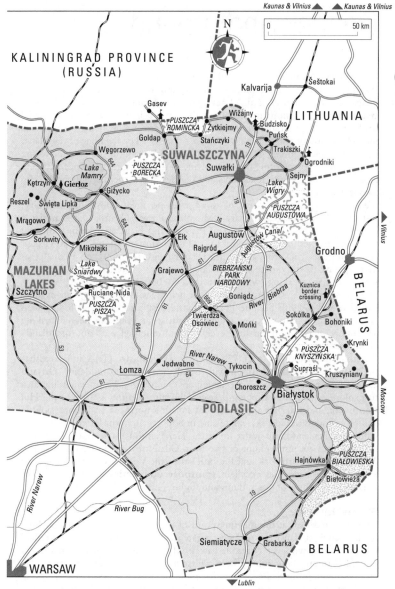

you should allow plenty of time if you're keen on exploring the rural northeast. Gdańsk itself offers generous bus and train links with most places in this chapter, while Olsztyn (and to a lesser extent Mrągowo) serves as the main gateway to Mazury. Białystok offers services to almost everywhere you'll want to visit in the east.

Gdańsk and around

To outsiders, **GDAŃSK** was until recently perhaps the most familiar city in Poland. The home of Lech Wałęsa, Solidarity and the former Lenin Shipyards, its images flashed across a decade of news bulletins during the 1980s. The harbour area fulfills expectations formed from the newsreels with its harsh industrial landscape; by contrast, the streets of the town centre are lined with tall, narrow merchants' houses dating back to Gdańsk's days as a key member of the Hansa League. As the economy grows – with a helping hand from the ever-increasing numbers of tourists visiting the city – many of these historic buildings are being restored and new shops, restaurants and businesses are opening, giving the city a confident, lively feel.

What is surprising, at least for those with no great knowledge of Polish history, is the cultural complexity of the place. Prewar Gdańsk – or **Danzig** as it then was – was forged by years of Prussian and Hanseatic domination, and the reconstructed city centre looks not unlike Amsterdam, making an elegant and bourgeois backdrop. What has changed entirely, however, is the city's demography. At the outbreak of the last war, nearly all of the 400,000 citizens were German-speaking, with fewer than 16,000 Poles. The postwar years marked a radical shift from all that went before, as the ethnic Germans were expelled and Gdańsk became Polish for the first time since 1308. Germans are returning in numbers now, chiefly as tourists and business people, making an important contribution to the city's rapid emergence as one of Poland's economic powerhouses.

With a population of over 750,000, the **Trójmiasto** (Tri-City) conurbation comprising **Gdańsk** (itself with more than 470,000 residents), **Gdynia** and **Sopot**, ranks as one of the largest in the country. It's an enjoyable area to explore, with ferries tripping between the three centres and up to the **Hel Peninsula**, and offering a good mix of Poland's northern attractions: politics and monuments in Gdańsk, seaside chic in Sopot, gritty port life in Gdynia and sandy beaches and clean water up at the Hel Peninsula. The lakes and forests of **Kashubia** are just an hour or two from Gdańsk by bus, as are the castles of **Malbork** and **Frombork** and the beaches of the Wiślana Peninsula. As you'd expect, Gdańsk also has excellent **transport connections** with the rest of Poland, with a host of buses, trains and flights.

Some history

The city's position at the meeting point of the Wisła and the Baltic has long made Danzig/Gdańsk an immense strategic asset: in the words of Frederick the Great, whoever controlled it could be considered "more master of Poland than any king ruling there". First settled in the **tenth century**, the city assumed prominence when the Teutonic Knights arrived in 1308, at the invitation of a population constantly threatened from the west by the Margraves of Brandenburg. The knights established themselves in their accustomed style, massacring the locals and installing a colony of German settlers in their place.

The city's economy flourished, and with the end of the knights' rule in the **mid-fifteenth century** – accompanied by the brick-by-brick dismantling of their castle by the city's inhabitants – Danzig, by now an established member of the mercantile Hanseatic League, became to all intents and purposes an independent city-state. It had its own legislature, judiciary and monopolies on the Wisła trade routes, restricted only by the necessity of paying homage and an annual tax to the Polish monarch. The key elements of Danzig/Gdańsk history were thus emerging: autonomy, economic power, cultural cosmopolitanism and German–Polish rivalry for control of the city.

The city's main period of development occurred between the **sixteenth century** and the Partitions of the **late eighteenth century**. The scale of its trading empire at this time is illustrated by the fact that the Danzig East-land Company had a bigger turnover than even London's mighty East India Company. (One of their major exports was wood, specifically spruce, the very name of which derives from the Polish *Z Prus*, meaning "from Prussia".) Most of the important building took place at this time, as the burghers brought in Dutch and Flemish architects to design buildings that would express the city's self-confidence. From the Renaissance period also dates a tradition of religious toleration, a pluralism that combined with trade to forge strong connections with Britain: a sizeable contingent of foreign Protestant merchants included a significant Scottish population, many of them refugees from religious persecution at home, who were granted land and rights and who lived in the city districts still known as Stare and Nowe Szkoty – Old and New Scotland. The following century, a time of continuing economic development, yielded two of Gdańsk's most famous sons – astonomer Jan Heweliusz (Johannes Hevelius), who spent most of his life here, and Daniel Fahrenheit, inventor of the mercury thermometer.

Prussian annexation of the city, following the Partitions, abruptly severed the connection with Poland. Despite the German origins of much of the population, resistance to Prussianization and support for Polish independence were as strong in early nineteenth-century Danzig as elsewhere in Prussian-ruled Poland. In 1807, a Prussian campaign to recruit soldiers to fight Napoleon yielded precisely 47 volunteers in the city. Even as German a native of Danzig as the philosopher Schopenhauer was castigated by the Prussian authorities for his "unpatriotic" attitudes. The biggest impact of Prussian annexation, however, was economic: with its links to Poland severed, Gdańsk lost its main source of trading wealth, Polish wheat.

Territorial status changed again after **World War I** and the recovery of Polish independence. The Treaty of Versailles created the semi-autonomous Free City of Danzig, terminus of the so-called Polish Corridor that sliced through West Prussia (an area heavily dominated by Germans during the nineteenth century) and connected Poland to the sea. This strip of land gave Hitler one of his major propaganda themes in the 1930s and a pretext for attacking Poland: the German assault unleashed on the Polish garrison at Westerplatte on September 1, 1939 – memorably described by Günter Grass in *The Tin Drum* – was the first engagement of **World War II**. It was not until March 1945 that Danzig was liberated, after massive Soviet bombardment; what little remained was almost as ruined as Warsaw.

The **postwar era** brought communist rule, the expulsion of the ethnic German majority, and the formal renaming of the city as Gdańsk. The remains of the old centre were meticulously reconstructed and the traditional shipping industries revitalized. As the **communist era** began to crack at the edges, however, the shipyards became the harbingers of a new reality. Riots in Gdańsk and neighbouring Gdynia in 1970 and the strikes of 1976 were important precursors to the historic 1980 Lenin Shipyards strike, which led to the creation of **Solidarity**. The shipyards remained at the centre of resistance to General Jaruzelski's government, the last major strike wave in January 1989 precipitating the Round Table negotiations that heralded the end of communist rule. Following the traumas of "shock therapy", the reform programme pursued with vigour in the **early 1990s**, Gdańsk blossomed economically until it ranked second only to Warsaw in terms of foreign investment. Such new-found economic optimism didn't extend to the famous shipyards, however, which were on the verge of bankruptcy in 1997, when a wave of workers' protests prevented a "post-communist" government from closing down the yards altogether. This time popular sympathy for the unions didn't extend to all-out support, and the Polish prime minister felt able to admonish the workers publicly for trying to turn the country into "a new Albania" rather than a "a new Japan". The shipyards remain a powerful emotional symbol of today's Poland, but their significance as the driving force of the local economy and major employer is diminishing, as new industries like communications and information technology come to the fore.

Arrival and information

Gdańsk's **airport** (Gdańsk Lech Wałęsa; information ☎058/348 1111), at ul. Słowackiego 200, is about 15km west of the city. Bus #B runs to the main train station between 5am and 10pm twice hourly on weekdays, and hourly at weekends. You'll need two 1.20zł tickets – buy these at the news kiosk and punch them when you get on the bus. A taxi into town from the rank outside the airport will set you back 40–45zł.

The main **train station** (Gdańsk Główny) is a ten-minute walk west of the core of the old city. The traffic speeding along Wały Jagiellońskie, the wide main road running immediately in front of the station is lethal, so be sure to take the pedestrian underpass on your way into the centre and to get to the island tram stops in the middle of the same road. The **bus station** (Dworzec PKS) is located behind the train station across ul. 3 Maja.

If you are coming **by car**, signposting into the city centre is reasonably clear, although the last leg of the journey in from Warsaw takes you along a rather tortuous approach road which gets heavy with lorries and buses. If you're arriving **by boat** from Scandinavia, you'll find yourself disembarking at the Nowy Port ferry terminal, 6km north of the city centre. Ignore the unscrupulous taxi drivers congregating outside and walk 500m to Brzeźno train station where you can take one of the regular local trains into town.

Information

The helpful **tourist information** centre at ul. Heweliusza 27 (Mon–Fri 9am–4pm; ☎058/301 4355), a five-minute walk from the train station, has a good supply of maps and brochures and can make hotel reservations. The **PTTK office** at ul. Długa 45, bang in the centre of the Główne Miasto (Mon–Sat 9am–6pm; ☎058/301 1761), is very helpful between May and September when it drafts in English-speakers, though for the rest of the year it is of little use. **Online information** is available at Ⓦ www.gdansk.pl.

The small-format English-language **listings** guide *Gdańsk In Your Pocket* (6zł; Ⓦ www.inyourpocket.com), available from newsstands, offers good up-to-the-minute information on hotels, restaurants and bars throughout the Trójmiasto area. More detailed entertainment and clubbing listings appear in Polish-language publications such as the monthly *City Magazine* (given away free in bars) or the Friday edition of the daily newspaper *Gazeta Wyborcza*.

Orientation and getting around

Orientation is fairly straightforward, the main sites of interest being located in three historic districts: Główne Miasto, Stare Miasto and Stare Przedmieście. **Główne Miasto** (Main Town), the central area, is within easy walking distance of the main station. The main pedestrianized avenues, ul. Długa and its continuation Długi Targ, form the heart of the district, which backs east onto the attractive and, in summer, very lively waterfront of the Motława Canal and the island of Spichlerze. To the north is the **Stare Miasto** (Old Town), bounded by the towering cranes of the shipyards, beyond which the suburbs of Wrzeszcz, Zaspa and Oliwa sprawl towards Sopot. South of the centre stands the quieter **Stare Przedmieście** (Old Suburb).

Travelling within the city area is also pretty straightforward. A regular local **train** service, Szybka Kolej Miejska (SKM; colloquially known as the Kolejka), between Gdańsk Główny (the SKM platforms are immediately north of the mainline platforms), Sopot and Gdynia, with plenty of stops in between, runs roughly every ten minutes in the middle of the day, with services thinning out to once every hour or so in the early hours. **Tickets**, which must be validated before you get on the train, can be bought in the passage beneath the main station or at any local station. Total journey time from Gdańsk to Gdynia is 35 minutes.

Trams run within all districts of Gdańsk, and **trolleybuses** in Sopot and Gdynia, but services do not connect between the districts. **Buses**, however, operate right across the conurbation – #117, #122 and #143 connect with Sopot, #171 connects with Gdynia, while #181 connects Gdynia with Sopot. The large-scale map of Gdańsk available from kiosks and bookshops gives all bus and tram **routes**. Tickets for both trams and buses can be bought from any kiosk, street vendor or from the driver and must be validated upon entry. A full fare ticket costs 1.20zł: punch one for a ten-minute ride, two for a thirty-minute ride and three for a sixty-minute ride – timetables at bus and tram stops tell you how long your journey should take. You can change between buses and trams during the life of your ticket. Alternatively, a 24-hour pass costs 7.80zł.

Ferry services, chiefly aimed at tourists, operate between Gdańsk and a number of local destinations, notably Westerplatte, Sopot, Gdynia and Hel (see p.198). The Gdańsk landing stage is on the main waterfront (Długie Pobrzeże), close to the Green Gate, below the waterfront promenade. In Sopot and Gdynia, it's on the pier. Current timetables (adjusted seasonally) are posted at all landing stages. **Tickets** are sold at the landing stages or, occasionally on the boats themselves; as an example of price, the current run between Gdańsk and Westerplatte is 35zł return, with children under four travelling free. Further **information** is available on ☎058/301 4926 and at Ⓦwww.zegluga.gda.pl.

Accommodation

As in the other big tourist cities, **accommodation** in Gdańsk ranges from the ultra-plush to the ultra-basic – and rooms in the centre are at a premium in summer. At the top end of the scale, Orbis runs a string of **hotels** aimed very firmly at Western tourists and business people. Lower down the price scale, hotels in the centre are thicker on the ground than they used to be but

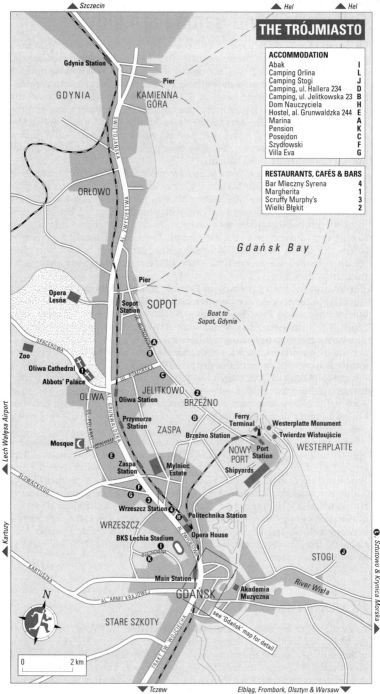

THE TRÓJMIASTO

ACCOMMODATION

Abak	I
Camping Orlina	L
Camping Stogi	J
Camping, ul. Hallera 234	D
Camping, ul. Jelitkowska 23	B
Dom Nauczyciela	H
Hostel, al. Grunwaldzka 244	E
Marina	A
Pension	K
Posejdon	C
Szydłowski	F
Villa Eva	G

RESTAURANTS, CAFÉS & BARS

Bar Mleczny Syrena	4
Margherita	1
Scruffy Murphy's	3
Wielki Błękit	2

Szczecin

Hel

Hel

Gdynia Station

Pier

GDYNIA

KAMIENNA GÓRA

ORŁOWO

Gdańsk Bay

Pier

Opera Leśna

Sopot Station

SOPOT

Boat to Sopot, Gdynia

SPACEROWA

Zoo

Oliwa Cathedral

Abbots' Palace

OLIWA

Oliwa Station

JELITKOWO

BRZEŹNO

Przymorze Station

ZASPA

Ferry Terminal

Westerplatte Monument

Twierdze Wisłoujście

Brzeźno Station

Mosque

NOWY PORT

Port Station

WESTERPLATTE

Zaspa Station

Mylniec Estate

Shipyards

Wrzeszcz Station

Politechnika Station

WRZESZCZ

Opera House

BKS Lechia Stadium

BEETHOVENA

STOGI

Main Station

Akademia Muzyczna

River Wisła

GDAŃSK

STARE SZKOTY

see 'Gdańsk' map for detail

Lech Wałęsa Airport

Kartuzy

SŁOWACKIEGO

KARTUSKA

KARTUZSKA

AL. ARMII KRAJOWEJ

TRAKT ŚW. WOJCIECHA

N

0   2 km

Tczew

Elbląg, Frombork, Olsztyn & Warsaw

Sztutowo & Krynica Morska

if you're prepared to stay a little further out, the range of options increases considerably.

Private rooms (❸) can be booked through Grand-Tourist in the mall at the end of the underpass leading from the station (Podwale Grodzkie 8; Mon–Fri 9am–6pm, Sat 10am–2pm). In July and August, if you find the year-round **hostels** are full, you can turn to **student dormitories** booked through Almatur, on the first floor at Długi Targ 11 (Mon–Fri 9am–5pm, Sat 10am–2pm; ☎058/301 2931). The city's **campsites** are open from May to September.

Hotels and pensions

Abak ul. Beethovena 8 ☎058/302 4170. Friendly pension with comfortable rooms, with or without bathroom, in a quiet suburb 2km west of the centre. Easily reached on buses #115, #130 and #184. ❹

Dom Aktora ul. Straganiarska 55/56 ☎058/301 5901. Simple but cosy pension in good central location. Rooms are en suite and come with TV. ❻

Dom Harcerza ul. Za Murami 2/10 ☎058/301 4936, ⓦ www.domharcerza.prv.pl. Simple but clean rooms just a few minutes' walk from Długa. Has dormitory-style accommodation (25zł), frugal doubles with shared bathrooms and a small number of en-suite doubles with kitchenettes. ❸

Dom Nauczyciela ul. Upenhaga 28 ☎058/341 9116. Nice location out in Wrzeszcz in a quiet side street ten minutes walk north of Gdańsk-Politechnika station. Basic singles and three- to four-person rooms, as well as en-suite doubles and doubles with shared facilities. Convenient car park next door. ❹

Hanza ul. Tokarska 6 ☎058/305 3427, ⓦ www .hanza-hotel.com.pl. Luxury hotel with lots of atmosphere right by the Motława canal. Some rooms come with dockside views. ❾

Hewelius ul. Heweliusza 22 ☎058/321 0000, ⓦ www.orbis.pl. Big modern Orbis showpiece five minutes from the central station, with tastefully decorated rooms; some have great views of the Stare Miasto. ❽

Holiday Inn Podwale Grodzkie 9 ☎058/300 6000. As comfortable and well run as you would expect from the international chain and bang opposite the station. ❽

Marina ul. Jelitkowska 20 ☎058/558 9100, ⓦ www.orbis.pl. Nine-storey white cube right on the administrative border between Gdańsk and Sopot. Rooms are bland but comfortable – and the beach is a mere 200m away. Swimming pool, tennis courts and kiddies' play area are on site. Take tram #2, #6 or #8 from the train station to the Jelitkowo terminus (a 40min ride). ❽

Novotel ul. Pszenna 1 ☎058/300 2750, ⓦ www .orbis.pl. A typical mid-range business hotel, within easy walking distance of the Główne Miasto, although the hotel itself is oddly stranded between a busy highway and scruffy parking lots. ❼

Pension ul. Beethovena 69 ☎058/301 5901. No-frills *pensjon* but rooms are clean and very good value. See *Abak* for directions. ❸

Posejdon ul. Kapliczna 30 ☎058/511 3000, ⓦ www.orbis.pl. Eight kilometres northwest of the centre in the seaside suburb of Jelitkowo, this is arguably the nicest Orbis hotel in town. Balconied rooms, some with a sea view, others looking onto the woods. Indoor swimming pool and fitness centre. It's near a pleasant stretch of beach, along which you can walk to Sopot. Take tram #2, #6 or #8 from the train station to the Jelitkowo terminus (a 40min ride). ❼

Szydłowski al. Grunwaldzka 114 ☎058/345 7040, ⓦ www.szydlowski.pl. Newish upmarket choice with plush rooms and attentive staff on the bustling main street of the Wrzeszcz suburb. Tram #6 or #12 from the main train station or SKM train to Gdańsk-Wrzeszcz. ❽

Villa Eva ul. Batorego 28 ☎058/341 6785, ⓦ www.villaeva.pl. Upmarket bed and breakfast in a quiet suburban street in Wrzeszcz. ❻

Hostels

Dizzy Daisy ul. Gnilna 3 ☎058/301 3919, ⓦ www.hostel.pl. Cheery hostel open July and August only. Dorm beds are 35zł per person, and there are some doubles and triples ❸.

Hostel, al. Grunwaldzka 244 ☎058/341 1660. Near Oliwa in the northern Wrzeszcz suburb; take tram #6 or #12 from the central station or the SKM train to Gdańsk-Zaspa. A decent-quality hostel inside a sports centre, with a restaurant and conference centre, which means it tends to get booked up by schools. Mostly quads (26zł per person) and doubles ❷.

Hostel Przy Targu Rybnym ul. Grodzka 21 ☎058/301 5627, ⓦ www.gdanskhostel.com. Relaxed place, close to waterfront, offering free bike and canoe rental and a laundry service. Some doubles ❹ as well as dorm beds at 40zł. Open year-round.

Hostel, ul. Wałowa 21 ☎058/301 2313. YHA place close to city centre, with prices from 19zł a night in ten-person dorms. Also some doubles and triples ❶. Often overrun with groups, so ring ahead.

Campsites

Camping Orlina ul. Lazurowa 5 ☎058/307 3915. On a lonely beach in the middle of woods, this is definitely the campsite with the nicest location, though some way out of town (about 15km east). Can be reached by bus #112. 12zł per person.

Camping Stogi ul. Wydmy 9 ☎058/307 3915, ⓦwww.kemping-gdansk.pl. Close to the sea in the Stogi district. Can be reached by tram #13 from town. About 10zł per person.

Camping, ul. Hallera 234 ☎058/343 5531. In the suburb of Brzeźno, due north of the town centre; trams #13 and #15 pass nearby from the central station. Sites cost 10zł each, and there are a few bungalows for 20zł. There's a small charge to keep cars or motorbikes overnight.

Camping, ul. Jelitkowska 23 ☎058/553 2731. Near the beach at Jelitkowo. Regular camping facilities plus bungalows – at around 20zł a bed, a bargain if you can get one. It's a short walk from the terminus of trams #2, #4 and #6, which run from the central station.

The City

The **Główne Miasto**, the largest of the historic quarters, is the obvious starting point for an exploration of the city; the **Stare Miasto**, across the thin ribbon of the Raduna Canal, is the natural progression. The third, southern quarter, **Stare Przedmieście,** cut off by the Podwale Przedmiejskie, has its main focus for visitors in the National Museum.

North along the canal, **Westerplatte** – and its monument commemorating the outbreak of World War II – can be reached by **boat** from the central waterfront (as can Gdynia, Sopot and the Hel Peninsula), a trip that allows good views of the famous **shipyards**. Moving north, out towards Sopot, is the **Oliwa** suburb, with its cathedral – one of the city's most distinctive landmarks – and botanical gardens.

The Główne Miasto

Entering the **Główne Miasto** (Main Town) is like walking straight into a Hansa merchants' settlement. The layout, typical of a medieval port, comprises a tight network of streets, bounded on four sides by water and main roads – the Raduna and Motława canals to the north and east, Podwale Przedmiejskie and Wały Jagiellońskie to the south and west. The ancient appearance of this quarter's buildings is deceptive: by May 1945 the fighting between German and Russian forces had reduced the core of Gdańsk to smouldering ruins. A glance at the photos in the town hall brings home the scale of the destruction and of its reversal.

Ulica Długa and Długi Targ

Ulica Długa, the main thoroughfare, and **Długi Targ**, the wide open square on the eastern part of it, form the natural focus of attention. As with all the main streets, huge gateways guard both entrances. Before the western entrance to Długa stands the outer **Brama Wyżynna** (Upland Gate) and the Gothic **prison tower** which once housed the city's torture chambers. The gate itself, built in the late sixteenth century as part of the town's outer fortifications, used to be the main entrance to Gdańsk. The three coats of arms emblazoned across the archway – Poland, Prussia and Gdańsk – encapsulate the city's history.

This gate was also the starting point of the "royal route" used by Polish monarchs on their annual state visits. After the Upland Gate they would pass

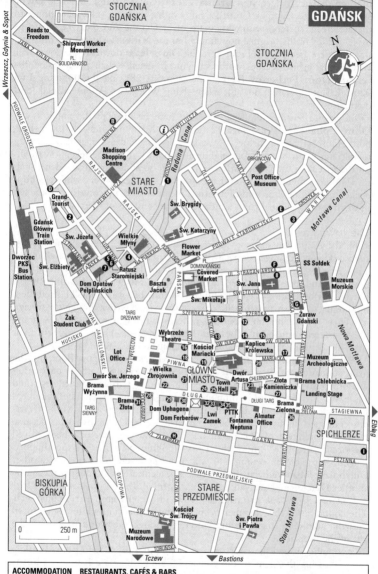

STOCZNIA
GDAŃSKA

GDAŃSK

N

Wrzeszcz, Gdynia & Sopot

JANA Z KOLNA

Roads to
Freedom

Shipyard Worker
Monument

PL.
SOLIDARNOŚCI

STOCZNIA
GDAŃSKA

PODWALE GRODZKIE

WAŁOWA

HEWELIUSZA

Raduna Canal

PL.
OBROŃCÓW

WARTKA

Mottawa Canal

ONILNA

Madison
Shopping
Centre

RAJSKA

STARE
MIASTO

HEWELIUSZA

RAJSKA

Raduna Canal

Św. Brygidy

Św. Katarzyny

PODWALE STAROMIEJSKIE

Post Office
Museum

GRODZKA

Grand-
Tourist

Gdańsk
Główny
Train Station

Św. Józefa

Św. Elżbiety

Dworzec
PKS
Bus
Station

Wielkie
Młyny

Ratusz
Staromiejski

Dom Opatów
Pelplińskich

Flower
Market

PANSKA

Baszta
Jacek

Św. Mikołaja

PL.
DOMINIKAŃSKI

Covered
Market

Św. Jana

SW. TROJAŃSKA

ŚWIĘTOJAŃSKA

SS Sołdek

Muzeum
Morskie

RYBACKIE POBRZEŻE

Mottawa Canal

Nowa Mottawa

Żak
Student Club

HUCISKO

TARG
DRZEWNY

WAŁY JAGIELLOŃSKIE

Wybrzeże
Theatre

Lot
Office

Dwór Św. Jerzego

Brama
Wyżynna

TARG
SIENNY

MODRA PARK

KOŻ

SZEROKA

Kościół
Mariacki

Wielka
Zbrojownia

PIWNA

GŁÓWNE
MIASTO

Brama
Złota

Dom Uphagena

Dom Ferberów

SW. DUCHA

Kaplice
Królewska

SW. DUCHA

MARIACKA

Dwór
Artusa

CHLEBNICKA

Town
Hall

D Ł U G A

Lwi
Zamek

Fontanna
Neptuna

SZEROKA

GRZELA

Złota
Kamieniczka

PTTK

DŁUGI TARG

Almatur
Office

Żuraw
Gdański

TKACKA

Muzeum
Archeologiczne

Brama Chlebnicka

Landing Stage

Brama
Zielona

MOST
ZIELONA

STAGIEWNA

Elbląg

SPICHLERZE

OGARNA

PODWALE PRZEDMIEJSKIE

OGARNA

UL. ZA MURAMI

OKOPOWA

BISKUPIA
GÓRKA

0   250 m

RZEŻNICKA

Stara Mottawa

STARE
PRZEDMIEŚCIE

Kościół
Św. Trójcy

Muzeum
Narodowe

SW. TRÓJCY

TOBIAŃSKA

Św. Piotra
i Pawła

PSZENNA

CHMIELNA

Tczew

Bastions

ACCOMMODATION		RESTAURANTS, CAFÉS & BARS							
Dizzy Daisy	B	Akademia Café	14	Gospoda pod		Lezzetli	2	Sphinx	27
Dom Aktora	F	Bar Mleczny Neptun	33	Wielkim Młynem	4	Mestwin	8	Tawerna	36
Dom Harcerza	H	Blue Café	37	Ha Long	10	Napoli	25	Towarzystwo	
Hanza	G	Caraska	32	Irish Pub	7	Palowa	26	Gastronomiczne	6
Hewelius	C	Celtic Pub	21	Jazz Club	34	Pierogarnia		Trattoria	
Holiday Inn	D	Cocktail Bar Capri	24	Kamienica	17	u Dzika	18	La Primavera	12
Hostel Przy		Cotton Club	13	Karczma	30	Pijalnia Sokow	29	Vinifera	1
Targu Rybnym	E	Cukierna Pellowska	35	Klub Aktora	20	Piwnica Pub	31	Złoty Kur	28
Hostel,		Czerwone Drzwi	19	Kubicki	3	Pod Łososiem	9		
ul. Wałowa 21	A	Euro	22	Kultu Kultu	5	Punkt	23		
Novotel	I	Gdańska	16	La Pasta	11	Puss and Rose	15		

through the richly decorated **Brama Złota** (Golden Gate) alongside **Dwór św. Jerzego** (St George's Court), a fine Gothic mansion (nowadays home to the architects' society) with a statuette of St George and the Dragon on its roof – a copy of the original now housed in the National Museum in the Stare Przedmieście (see p.184). From here, ul. Długa leads down to the town hall, with several gabled facades worth studying in detail – such as the sixteenth-century **Dom Ferberów** (Ferber Mansion; no. 28), and the imposing **Lwi Zamek** (Lion's Castle; no. 35), where King Władysław IV entertained local dignitaries.

One of the few houses along this stretch to be open to the public is the **Dom Uphagena** at ul. Długa 12 (Uphagen Mansion; Tues–Sat 10am–4pm, Sun 11am–4pm; 6zł), former home of a leading Gdańsk merchant dynasty, rebuilt and refurnished in late-eighteenth-century style. The reception rooms on the first floor are particularly elegant, each boasting carved wooden panels on a different theme: one room has butterflies, another flowers, while a third is decked out with exotic birds. Furniture, paintings and a reconstructed kitchen in the basement all help paint a picture of the comforts of merchant life.

The town hall

Topped by a golden statue of King Sigismund August, which dominates the central skyline, the huge and well-proportioned tower of the **town hall** makes a powerful impact. Originally constructed in the late fourteenth century, with the tower and spire added later, the building was totally ruined during the last war, but the restoration was so skilful you'd hardly believe it. "In all Poland there is no other, so Polish a town hall," observed one local writer, though the foreign influences on the interior rooms might lead you to disagree. They now house the **historical museum** (Tues–Sat 10am–4pm, Sun 11am–4pm; 8zł), their lavish decorations almost upstaging the exhibits on display.

From the entrance hall an ornate staircase leads to the upper floor and the main council chamber, the **Red Room** (Sala Czerwona). Interior decoration was obviously one thing that seventeenth-century Gdańsk councillors could agree on: the colour red completely dominates the room. The chamber's sumptuous decor, mostly from the late sixteenth century, is the work of various craftsmen: its furniture was designed by a Dutch fugitive who became municipal architect of Gdańsk in the 1590s; Willem Bart of Ghent carved the ornate fireplace – note the Polish-looking Neptunes in the supports – while most of the ceiling and wall paintings were produced by another Dutchman, Johan Verberman de Vries. The central oval ceiling painting, by another Dutchman, Isaac van den Block, is titled *The Glorification of the Unity of Gdańsk with Poland*, an imaginary view of the city atop a triumphal arch. The council used this chamber in spring and summer; in winter they moved into the adjoining smaller room, entered through the wooden door to the left of the fireplace.

Continuing around the courtyard you come to a room with painted ceiling vaults showing the signs of the zodiac. Exhibited here are haunting **photographs** of the city in 1945 after it had been almost completely flattened by a combination of Allied and Soviet bombing.

One floor up are the **archive rooms**, where you'll find a mixture of paintings, engravings and precious religious and ceremonial objects. In the former **treasury** there's a display of coins minted at Gdańsk over the centuries. After all the ornate carving and painting, the top floors provide a complete contrast, with reconstructions of ordinary shops and homes in the Free City of Danzig in the 1920s and 1930s.

Dwór Artusa

Immediately east of the town hall is **Dwór Artusa** (Arthur's Court; Tues–Sat 10am–4pm, Sun 11am–4pm, sometimes closed for functions; 6zł): even in a street lined with many fine mansions, this one is impressive. Recently opened to the public following extensive renovation work, the building encapsulates some fascinating aspects of the history of the city. Its origins date back to the early fourteenth century, a period marked by a widespread awakening of interest in British Arthurian legends among the European mercantile class. Attracted by the ideals of King Arthur's fabled court at Camelot, merchants began establishing their own latter-day courts, where they could entertain in the chivalrous and egalitarian spirit of their knightly forebears. Founded in 1350, the Gdańsk Court grew rapidly to become one of the most fabulous and wealthy in Europe. Initially occupied by the Brotherhood of St George, by the 1500s it had become a focal point of the city, with a growing array of guild- and trade-based brotherhoods establishing their own meeting benches in the main hall. The court's development was encouraged (and financed) by the city authorities, creating what was effectively northern Europe's first nonsectarian, nonpolitical meeting place, combining the functions of guild house, civic hall, judicial court and reception centre for foreign guests.

Rebuilt in the 1480s, with the main facade reworked by the ever-present Abraham van den Block in the early seventeenth century, the building was almost completely destroyed during the Nazi retreat in spring 1945. Mercifully, however, much of the court's rich interior was spirited away in advance of the Soviet bombardment and thus saved. Original features in the cavernous, reconstructed main hall and adjoining chamber include sections of the original ceiling, including the starred vaulting, supported on graceful columns, and the Renaissance ceramic heating oven used to keep the assembled burghers of Gdańsk from freezing during the winter.

Immediately outside Arthur's Court is the wonderful **Fontanna Neptuna** (Neptune Fountain), with water trickling from the very tips of the god's trident. Continuing just to the south, you'll come to the **Złota Kamieniczka** (Golden House), an impressive Renaissance mansion named after the luminous gilding that covers its elegant four-storeyed facade.

The waterfront and the Muzeum Morskie

The archways of the **Brama Zielona** (Green Gate), a former royal residence for the annual visit, open directly onto the **waterfront**. From the bridge over the Motława canal you get a good view to the right of the old granaries on Spichlerze island (there used to be over 300 of them), and to the left of the old harbour quay, now a tourist hang-out and local promenade.

Halfway down the waterfront is the massive and largely original fifteenth-century **Żuraw Gdański** (Gdańsk Crane), the biggest in medieval Europe. It's part of the **Muzeum Morskie** (Maritime Museum; May–Sept daily 10am–6pm; Oct–April Tues–Sun 10am–4pm; 6zł per section or 14zł for all) which sprawls across both sides of the river Motława. Inside the fifteenth-century **crane** (Europe's oldest), as well as the massive lifting gear used to unload goods at the harbourside, is an exhibition describing port life in the prosperous sixteenth to eighteenth centuries. Just across the road is a packed display of **boats** from all over the world, including an English coracle, Native American birch bark canoes, Vietnamese basket boats and Polynesian outriggers.

Across the Motława – the short boat ride is included in the all-in ticket – the main section of the museum is housed in three Renaissance **granaries**, known as the "Panna" (Virgin), "Miedź" (Copper) and "Oliwski" (Oliwa).

Here there are extensive displays on Poland's history as a seafaring nation, sweeping right through from the earliest Slav settlements along the Wisła to the late twentieth century, taking in the seventeenth-century power struggles around the Baltic, an exhibit on underwater archeology and numerous astonishingly detailed models of ships along the way. On the ground floor you'll also find a haul of Swedish cannons recovered by museum divers and on the top floor there's a display of maritime paintings – some of which are outstanding, others pretty ropey.

Back out on the quayside is the sturdy-looking *Sołdek*, the first **steamship** built in Gdańsk after World War II. You can investigate just about every part of the ship, including the boiler room and bridge.

All the streets back into the town from the waterfront are worth exploring. Next up from Brama Zielona is **ulica Chlebnicka**, reached through the fifteenth-century **Brama Chlebnicka** (Bread Gate), built during the era of Teutonic rule. The **Dom Angielski** (English House), built in 1569 and the largest house in the city at the time, is a reminder of the strong Reformation-era trading connections with Britain. It's the ornate grey building on the left, a few houses down as you walk away from the waterfront, and now converted into student halls.

Kościół Mariacki and around

Running parallel to ul. Chlebnicka to the north is **ulica Mariacka**, a charmingly atmospheric and meticulously reconstructed street of spindly iron railings and dragon-faced gutter spouts, its gabled terraced houses now occupied by expensive clothes and amber jewellery shops and stylish cafés. At its western end stands the gigantic **Kościół Mariacki** (St Mary's Church), reputedly the biggest brick church in the world. Estimates that it could fit 20,000 people inside were substantiated during the early days of martial law, when huge crowds crammed the cold whitewashed interior. Overall, the building is beginning to lose some of its austerity thanks to the gradual return of elements of original decoration removed to the National Museum in Warsaw after the war. The south aisle is dominated by a copy of the miraculous **Madonna of the Gates of Dawn** from Wilno (now Vilnius in Lithuania), a city whose Polish inhabitants were encouraged to emigrate in 1945 – many of them ending up in Gdańsk, where they replaced the departing German population. Beside it, there's a memorial to the Polish Home Army fighters who liberated Wilno in 1944 – only to be rounded up and deported by the Red Army. The **high altar**, totally reconstructed after the war, is a powerful sixteenth-century triptych featuring a *Coronation of the Virgin*. Of the chapels scattered round the church, two of the most striking are the **Chapel of 11,000 Virgins**, with a tortured Gothic crucifix – apparently the artist apparently nailed his son-in-law to a cross as a model – and **St Anne's Chapel**, containing the wooden *Beautiful Madonna of Gdańsk* from around 1415. A curiosity is the reconstructed fifteenth-century **astronomical clock**, which tells not only the day, month and year but the whole saints' calendar and the phases of the moon; when completed in 1470 it was the world's tallest clock.

If you're feeling fit, make sure you climb up the church **tower** (Mon–Sat 9am–5pm, Sun 9am–1pm; 3zł). The 402 steps are graphically described in the Polish guide (on sale at the church), which warns against anyone with claustrophobia or heart problems attempting this "cold spell of hell" as "after 130 steps you'll wish you'd given up smoking, after 150 that you'd visited the crypt instead . . .", it warns. On a good day the view over Gdańsk and the plains is excellent; for 0.5zł per minute you can hire binoculars.

After the bareness of the church, the Baroque exuberance of the domed late-seventeenth-century **Kaplica Królewska** (Royal Chapel), directly opposite on ul. św. Ducha, and designed by Tylman of Gameren for use by the city's then minority Catholic population, makes a refreshing change, though it's often shut. The **Muzeum Archeologiczne** (Archeological Museum; Tues–Fri 9am–4pm, Sat & Sun 10am–4pm; 4zł) describes the prehistory of Gdańsk and the surrounding areas. Though the displays are rather dry and academic there are some interesting exhibits: those with ghoulish tastes will enjoy the display of ancient skulls and bones showing evidence of battle scars, injury and disease.

From the Wielka Zbrojownia to the flower market

Ulica Piwna, another street of high terraced houses west of the church entrance, ends at the monumental **Wielka Zbrojownia** (Great Arsenal), an early seventeenth-century armoury facing the **Targ Węglowy** (Coal Market), whose appearance underscores its Flemish ancestry. Now a busy shopping centre, the coal market leads north to the Targ Drzewny (Wood Market), and on to the Stare Miasto over the other side of the canal. Ul. Szeroka, first off to the right, is another charming old street with a nice view of St Mary's from the corner with ul. Grobla Furty.

The Dominican-run **Kościół św. Mikołaja** (St Nicholas' Church) on ul. Świętojańska is another fourteenth-century brick structure, the only city centre church to come through the war relatively unscathed. The interior houses a rich array of furnishings, in particular some panelled early Baroque choir stalls, a massive high altar and a fine Gothic pietà in one of the nave bays, while the **Kościół św. Jana** (St John's Church), further down the same street, is a reputedly beautiful Gothic building badly damaged during World War II and still closed for restoration.

Continuing north towards the canal, at the edge of pl. Obrońców Poczty Polskiej, stands the **old post office** building immortalized by Günter Grass in *The Tin Drum*. Rebuilt after the war, it's here that a small contingent of employees of the Free City's Poczta Polska (Polish Post Office) battled it out with German forces in September 1939. As at Westerplatte, the Germans clearly weren't anticipating such spirited resistance; despite the overwhelmingly superior firepower ranged against them the Poles held out for nine hours, finally surrendering when the Nazis sent in flame-throwers. Official postwar accounts maintained that the survivors were taken to the nearby Zaspa cemetery and summarily shot. At least two appear to have survived, in fact, surfacing in recent years to tell their own story.

The spiky-looking **monument** on the square in front of the building commemorates the event that has played an important role in the city's post-war communist mythology, the Poles' heroic resistance presented as a further vindication of the claimed "Polishness" of the city. Inside the post office there's a small **museum** (Tue–Fri 10am–4pm, Sat–Sun 10.30am–2pm; 3zł), mainly devoted to the events of 1939, including copies of Nazi photos of the attack on the building, and, most preciously, an urn full of soil soaked in the defenders' blood. Additionally there's an exhibition of local postal history underscoring the importance of postal communications to the city ever since its early trading days.

The terraced houses and shops tail off as you approach the outer limits of the main town, marked by several towers and other remnants of the **town wall**. **Baszta Jacek**, the tower nearest the canal, stands guard over ul. Podmłyńska, the main route over the canal into the Stare Miasto. The area around the tower provides the focus of the annual Dominican fair (Jarmark) in August (see

△ Street market trader, Gdańsk

"Entertainment", p.190). The **market** opposite sells flowers and a fine selection of fruits and vegetables. As well as the regular traders at the stalls, along the pavement you'll see wizened old ladies in from the countryside to sell a few mushrooms or bunches of herbs.

The Stare Miasto and the Stocznia Gdańska

Crossing the canal bridge brings you into the **Stare Miasto** (Old Town), altogether a patchier and less reconstructed part of town characterized by a jumbled mix of old and new buildings. Dominating the waterside is the seven-storey **Wielki Mlyn** (Great Mill), built in the mid-fourteenth century by the Teutonic Knights and another Gdańsk "largest" – in this case the biggest mill in medieval Europe. Its eighteen races milled corn for 600 years; even in the 1930s it was still grinding out 200 tons of flour a day. The building has been converted into a fairly tacky shopping centre, but traces of the original building are still in evidence, notably the old foundations.

The **Kościół św. Katarzyny** (Church of St Catherine), the former parish church of the Stare Miasto, to the right of the crossway, is one of the nicest in the city. Fourteenth-century – and built in brick like almost all churches in the region – it has a well-preserved and luminous interior. The astronomer Jan Hevelius and his family are buried here in a tomb in the choir. Nearby **Kościół św. Brygidy** (St Bridget's Church) became a local Solidarity stronghold in the 1980s, and was the local church of Lech Wałęsa, the Solidarity leader. Although the political importance of the Church has diminished in recent years, it's still worth visiting places like this – ideally on a Sunday – to experience the specifically Polish mixture of religion and politics that is personified in the man whose statue watches over the church, Karol Wojtyła, aka John Paul II.

Moving further into the Stare Miasto, the merchants' mansions give way to postwar housing, the tattier bits looking like something off the set of *1984*. The most interesting part of the district is just west along the canal from the mill, centred on the **Ratusz Staromiejski** (Old Town Hall), on the corner of ul. Bielanska and ul. Korzenna. Built by the architect of the main town hall, this delicate Renaissance construction, until recently occupied by local government offices, has now been smartened up and converted into the new **Nadbałtyckie Centrum Kultury** (Upper Baltic Cultural Centre; daily 10am–6pm). The main ground-floor room houses a changing series of lively exhibitions, devoted to local and regional cultural and historical themes. There's also a pleasant café (see p.189) and bookshop, again with a historical bent. When it's not being used for receptions and other events, the place is fully open to the public – all in all, an inspired venue fully deserving of the support it has already garnered. The bronze figure in the entrance hall is of Jan Hevelius, the Polish astronomer after whom Orbis has named its nearby hotel (see p.175).

Continuing west from the town hall, the Gothic churches of **Kościół św. Józefa** (St Joseph's Church) and **Kościół św. Elżbiety** (St Elizabeth's Church) – facing each other across ul. Elżbietańska – and the Renaissance **Dom Opatów Pelplińskich** (House of the Abbots of Pelplin) make a fine historic assemblage. From here you're only a short walk through the tunnels under the main road (Podwale Grodzkie) from the train station.

The Stocznia Gdańska

Looming over the city from most angles you'll see the cranes of the famous **Stocznia Gdańska** (Gdańsk Shipyards), once known as the Lenin Shipyards.

With the Nowa Huta steelworks outside Kraków, this was the crucible of the political struggles of the 1980s.

Ten minutes' walk or one tram stop north from the railway station brings you to the shipyard gates on pl. Solidarności. In front of them stands a set of towering steel crosses, a **monument** to workers killed during the 1970 shipyard riots; it was inaugurated in 1980 in the presence of Party, Church and opposition leaders. A precursor to the organized strikes of the 1980s, the 1970 riots erupted when workers took to the streets in protest at price rises, setting fire to the Party headquarters after police opened fire. Riots erupted again in 1976, once more in protest at price rises on basic foodstuffs, and in August 1980 Gdańsk came to the forefront of world attention when a protest at the sacking of workers rapidly developed into a national strike.

The formation of **Solidarity**, the first independent trade union in the Soviet bloc, was a direct result of the Gdańsk strike, instigated by the Lenin Shipyards workers and their charismatic leader **Lech Wałęsa**. Throughout the 1980s the Gdańsk workers remained in the vanguard of political protest. Strikes here in 1988 and 1989 led to the Round Table Talks that forced the Communist party into power-sharing and, ultimately, democratic elections.

Standing at the gates today, you may find it hard to experience this as the place where, in a sense, contemporary Poland began to take shape. Yet ironically the shipyards remain at the leading edge of political developments: unlike those at nearby Gdynia, the sprawling Gdańsk yards have always been unprofitable, and it was a post-communist government that attempted to modernize them, bitterly opposed by President Wałęsa (as he had by then become). Attempts to interest foreign investors collapsed because of the insistence that the full local workforce must be retained by any buyer. When the post-communists went ahead with "downsizing" in 1997, protests and even riots followed. Successive Polish governments have been faced by a quandary: they cannot appear hostile to Solidarity, yet they are left supporting a shipyard which, from a capitalist point of view, is a lame duck.

The story of Solidarity's pivotal role in Poland's recent history is told in the **Roads to Freedom** exhibition (Tue–Sun 10am–5pm; 5zł). The path to the exhibition building starts from beside the main gates and leads you through two massive conceptual sculptures. The first resembles a rusting hulk; the second recalls the work of the Soviet constructivist Vladimir Tatlin (or a lopsided helter-skelter). The exhibition itself is an impressionistic but moving portrayal of the events of the Solidarity era, illustrated using news clips, black and white stills and crackly recordings of strikers' songs, and it is located in the very room – the BHP hall – where the communist government accepted the existence of Solidarity in 1981.

If you want to get a look at the working end of the yards, the best way is to take a cruise to Westerplatte (see opposite).

The Stare Przedmieście

Stare Przedmieście (Old Suburb) – the lower part of old Gdańsk – was the limit of the original town, as testified by the ring of seventeenth-century bastions running east from pl. Wałowy over the Motława.

The main attraction today is the **Muzeum Narodowe** (National Museum; Tues–Sun 10am–8pm; ⓦ www.muzeum.narodowe.gda.pl; 15zł), housed in a former Franciscan monastery at ul. Toruńska 1. There's a wealth of Gothic art and sculpture here, all redolent of the town's former wealth. The range of Dutch and Flemish art – Memling, the younger Brueghel, Cuyp and van Dyck are the best-known names – attests to the city's strong links with the Netherlands.

The museum's most famous work is Hans Memling's colossal *Last Judgement* (1473), the painter's earliest known work – though he was already in his thirties and a mature artist. The painting has had a more than usually chequered past, having been commissioned by the Medici in Florence, then diverted to Gdańsk, looted by Napoleon, moved to Berlin, returned to Gdańsk, stolen by the Nazis and finally, after being discovered by the Red Army, hidden in the Thuringian hills, to be returned to Gdańsk by the Russians in 1956.

Adjoining the museum is the old monastery, **Kościół św. Trójcy** (Holy Trinity Church), a towering brick Gothic structure with characteristic period net vaulting. The interior features a fine high altar, an assemblage of triptych pieces cobbled together following the wartime destruction of Isaac van Blocke's original, a delicately carved pulpit (the only Gothic original left in the city) and an array of other period furnishings, notably a pair of winged altar pieces. The church is currently closed for restoration but it's still worth going through the gates on ul. św. Trójcy to have a peep into the courtyard.

Westerplatte

It was at **Westerplatte**, the promontory guarding the harbour entrance, that the German battleship *Schleswig-Holstein* fired the first salvo of World War II on September 1, 1939. For a full week the garrison of 170 badly equipped Poles held off the combined assault of aircraft, heavy guns and over 3000 German troops, setting the tone for the Poles' response to the subsequent Nazi–Soviet invasion. The ruined army guardhouse and barracks are still there, one of the surviving buildings housing a small **museum** (May–Oct daily 9am–4pm; 3zł) chronicling the momentous events of September 1939. Beyond the museum it's a fifteen-minute walk to the main **Westerplatte Monument**, a grim, ugly-looking 1960s slab in the best Socialist Realist traditions, whose symbolism conveys a tangible sense of history. The green surroundings of the exposed peninsula make a nice, if generally blustery, walk to the coast, with good views out onto the Baltic.

There are a number of ways of getting to Westerplatte. Bus #106 from outside the train station runs all the way here, passing the huge local sulphur factory. More fun is a trip on one of the tour boats departing from near the Brama Zielona. Taking about thirty minutes each way, the trip provides an excellent view of the **shipyards** and the array of international vessels anchored there. Finally, tram #10 will take you to Nowy Port from where you can cross the Wisła by chain ferry (every 30min). While in Nowy Port another short hop on tram #15 will bring you to the elegant red-brick nineteenth-century **lighthouse** at ul. Przemysłowa 6a (daily 10am–7pm; 5zł). From the top there's a great view over Westerplatte and the Baltic and back over the shipyards to the city.

Twierdza Wisłoujście

If you take the boat out to Westerplatte, you'll pass the sturdy brick walls of the **Twierdza Wisłoujście** (Wisła Fortress). The fortress has guarded the harbour approaches since the fourteenth century and for many years was manned by a mercenary force called the *kaper* (see box, p.186).

Designed by Dutch architects using the octagonal zigzag defence plan popular at the time, the first fortifications for the two-storey fortress were put up in the 1480s, with additions built on throughout the following century. Doubling as the main port lighthouse, the whole construction was enlarged to its current size in the mid-eighteenth century, and reinforced by Napoleon's forces in the early nineteenth. Napoleon himself visited the place on his way to Moscow. The

The kaper of Gdańsk

In a city with a tradition of cosmopolitan and independent-minded attitudes the story of Gdańsk's one-time mercenary naval defence force is instructive. Right from the city's early days, the citizen merchants of Gdańsk appreciated the need for some form of sea-based protection to keep potential invaders out. The first Polish king to try and establish a proper navy was Kazimierz Jagiellończyk (1444–92), during his thirteen-year-long war with the Teutonic Knights. A significant portion of his navy actually consisted of local mercenaries – **kaper**, as they came to be known, after *kaap*, the Old Dutch for "ship" – who agreed to work on contract for the king, but not officially as his representatives.

The **crews** on the *kaper* vessels were a mixed bunch, the contingent of locals from the Gdańsk and Elbląg regions supplemented by an assortment of Swedish, Flemish, Scottish and Kashubian adventurers. Skilled sailors keen on risk, the *kaper* were ostensibly employed to guard the Gdańsk merchant fleet, which by the late fifteenth century was already nearly 100 vessels strong. In 1482 the newly constructed fortress at Wisłoujście became the base of their operations. Protecting the harbour aside, the *kaper* clearly weren't averse to a bit of adventuring-cum-piracy. Under the designation "the king's maritime military", King Sigismund Stary employed a *kaper* force for his assault on Moscow in 1517; their main interest, however, was actually in the Baltic port of Memling, which the *kaper* captured single-handedly under the leadership of one Adrian Flint, an English adventurer.

By the mid-sixteenth century, with their own base, ships and uniforms, the increasingly ill-disciplined *kaper* appear to have developed into a fully-fledged paramilitary naval outfit, capturing twenty vessels in one year (1568) alone. Recognizing that the Gdańsk *kaper* were flourishing in the vacuum left by the absence of a proper navy, King Sigismund Wasa set about creating a standing force and in 1600 asked *kaper* to work for him. It was left to King Jan Sobieski, however, to rein the *kaper* in fully, and finally to integrate them into an official Polish navy.

city's Partition-era Prussian masters used the fortress as a jail, notably for Polish political prisoners – Jósef Piłsudski included – which probably explains why they didn't dismantle it along with all the other port fortifications in the 1870s.

At present the fortress is closed to the public as it's being thoroughly renovated and restored – it's a massive project and as yet there's no firm date for reopening.

Oliwa

The modern Oliwa suburb, the northernmost area of Gdańsk, has one of the best-known buildings in the city – its cathedral. To get here, take the local train to Gdańsk-Oliwa station, walk west across the main Sopot road and carry on through the park.

The cathedral

Originally part of the monastery founded by the Danish Cistercians who settled here in the mid-twelfth century at the invitation of a local Pomeranian prince, the **cathedral** has seen its fair share of action over the years. First in a long line of plunderers were the Teutonic Knights, who repeatedly ransacked the place in the 1240s and 1250s. A fire in the 1350s led to a major Gothic-style overhaul, the structural essence of which remains to this day. The wars of the seventeenth century had a marked impact on Oliwa, the Swedish army carrying off much of the cathedral's sumptuous collection of furnishings as booty in 1626, the church bells and main altarpiece included. The second major Swedish assault of 1655–60 eventually led to the Oliwa Peace Treaty (1660), signed in the abbey hall: the following century brought lavish refurbishment of the building (notably the organ, begun in 1755), most of which you can still see today. The Prussian Partition-era takeover of Gdańsk spelled the end of the fabulously wealthy abbey's glory days, the monastery finally being officially abolished in 1831. Unlike most of its surroundings, the cathedral miraculously came through the end of World War II largely unscathed, though the retreating Nazis torched the abbey complex. Today the complex is a remarkable sight, both the cathedral and the abbey having been thoroughly renovated and restored.

Approached from the square in front of the building, the towering main **facade** combines twin Gothic brick towers peaked with Renaissance spires and dazzling white Rococo stucco work to unusually striking effect. The fine late-seventeenth-century portal brings you into the lofty central **nave**, a dazzlingly exuberant structure topped by a star-spangled vaulted ceiling supported on arched pillars. Past the side chapels filling the two side aisles, the eye is immediately drawn to the **high altar**, a sumptuous Baroque piece from the 1680s containing several pictures from the Gdańsk workshops of the period, including one ascribed to Andreas Schlüter the Younger. Above the altar rises a deliciously over-the-top decorative ensemble, a swirling mass of beatific-look herubs being sucked into a heavenly whirlpool, surrounded by angels, gilded sun rays breaking out in all directions, the whole thing leading towards a central stained-glass window.

Apart from some fine Baroque choir stalls and the old Renaissance high altarpiece, now in the northern transept, the building's finest – and most famous – feature is the exuberantly decorated eighteenth-century **organ**, which completely fills the back of the nave. In its day the largest instrument in Europe – seven men were needed to operate the bellows – the dark heavy oak of the organ is ornamented with a mass of sumptuous Rococo woodcarving, the whole instrument framing a stained-glass window of Mary and Child, a mass of supporting angels and cherubs again filling out the picture. It's a beautiful instrument with a rich, sonorous tone and a wealth of moving parts, trumpet-blowing angels included. The 110 registers of the organ allow for an extraordinary range of pitch, and there are frequent ribcage-rippling recitals to show it off (Mon–Sat 10am, 11am, noon & 1pm; free).

Passing through the gateway down the lane running alongside the cathedral brings you to the stately Abbots' Palace, which now houses the **Wystawa Sztuki Współczesnej** (Modern Art Museum; Tues–Sat 9am–4pm, Sun 10am–4pm; 9zł, free Sat). Upstairs is an enjoyable gallery of twentieth-century Polish art – the centrepiece being a large selection of 1960s Pop Art and conceptual sculptures – all going to show how postwar Polish art succesfully escaped the ideological fetters of communist cultural policy. The museum also hosts temporary exhibitions, mainly retrospectives of contemporary Polish artists.

Across the courtyard from the palace, an old granary contains an **ethnographic museum** (same hours; 7zł), a collection of furniture, handicrafts and fishing and farmyard tools, which paints a vivid picture of Kashubian country life.

Surrounding the complex is the old palace **park**, an appealing, shaded spot with an enjoyable collection of exotic trees, hanging willows and a stream meandering through the middle – a pleasant place for an afternoon stroll.

If you happen to be here on **All Souls' Day** (Nov 1), the large **cemetery** over the road is an amazing sight, illuminated by thousands of candles placed on the gravestones. Whole families come to visit the individual graves and communal memorials to the unknown dead, in a powerful display of remembrance which says much about the intertwining of Catholicism and the collective memory of national sufferings.

Around the cathedral

Like several Polish cities, Gdańsk has a small, low-profile **Tatar** community (see also "Białystok", p.262). They've recently put the finishing touches to a new **mosque** south of the cathedral; already in use by local Muslims, including the Arab student population, the mosque is at the south end of ul. Polanki, on the corner with ul. Abrahama (nearest station Gdańsk-Zaspa; trams #6, #12 and #15 also run nearby). Further up the same road, the attractive, late-eighteenth-century mansion at number 122 is where **Arthur Schopenhauer** (1788–1860), the Danzig/Gdańsk-born philosopher, grew up.

North of the cathedral is the **Trójmiejskie Park Krajobrazowy**, a hilly patch of forest behind the city, with trails and, when there's a break in the trees, refreshing views.

Eating, drinking and nightlife

Finding a place to eat is relatively straightforward and though tourist numbers are increasing, supply more than keeps up with demand: there's a good range of **cafés** and **snack bars**, as well as local Western fast-food lookalikes, and some genuinely recommendable **restaurants**. For a quick lunch in summer you could do a lot worse than visit the cluster of fried fish stalls at the northern end of Rybackie Pobrzeże. Fish dishes are obviously a local speciality and are well worth sampling.

Drinking in the city tends to centre on a number of bars and cafés on ul. Długa and parallel streets to the north. In summer the attractive terrace cafés of ul. Chlebnicka and Mariacka make the ideal place to sit out and enjoy the sun – and more often than not a decent espresso. The waterfront is the centre of activity, however, with a few good spots (and plenty of tackier ones) to sit.

The **clubbing** scene in Gdańsk is constantly growing, thanks in large part to the Trójmiasto's large student population. Several of the places listed as bars below also offer live music and/or dancing at weekends; while official closing times for clubs are given below, in practice they tend to stay open till the last person leaves. Dedicated clubbers should note that there's also a good range of nightlife opportunities in the **Sopot** area (see p.193).

Restaurants

Czerwone Drzwi ul. Piwna 52/53. Imaginative Polish- and Western European-style dishes, all beautifully presented in relaxed and stylish surroundings.

Euro ul. Długa 79/80 (℡058/305 2383). Vaguely Rococo-style place serving traditional European classics, like veal escalopes with fettucine in a cream sauce and *crème brûlée*. Worth splashing out on.

Gdańska ul. św. Ducha 16 (℡058/301 0322). Another fairly expensive option for a good meal out. The decor reflects the traditional Polish menu with mock-rustic heavy wooden furnishings.

Ha Long ul. Szeroka 37/39. One of the better Chinese places in town.

Karczma ul. Długa 18. Great-value Polish food served in folksy, wooden-bench surroundings.

Kubicki ul. Wartka 5. Slightly stolid versions of traditional dishes, but the fish is good and the over-the-top antique shop-style decor is worth a look.

Margherita ul. Cysterstów 11, Oliwa. Worth the trip to this northern suburb for fine pizzas from a brick oven. Handy if you've just been to visit Oliwa cathedral. Till 10pm.

Mestwin ul. Straganiarska 21/22. Serves delicious traditional Kashubian peasant food – mainly variations on meat, cabbage and potatoes, but that's what makes it authentic.

Napoli ul. Długa 62/63. Central pizzeria with plenty of room and fast service.

Palowa ul. Długa 47. Situated underneath the town hall, handsome rather than cosy, and with a suitably municipal atmosphere. Polish dishes as solid as the furnishings.

Pierogarnia u Dzika ul. Piwna 59/60. Perfect *pierogi* of every conceivable variety from mushroom to cherry in comfortable surroundings.

Pod Łososiem ul. Szeroka 52/3 (☎058/301 7652). One of the most luxurious restaurants in town, so you may have to book, though it's not as pricey as you might think. Specializing in seafood, it's also known locally as originator of Goldwasser vodka liqueur, a thick yellow concoction with flakes of real gold that's as Prussian as its name suggests.

Sphinx Długi Targ 31/32. One of the ever-growing chain of Egyptian-themed restaurants, offering hearty portions of grill food, including a few Middle Eastern specialities. Also takeaway kebab fare served from a hole in the wall. Till midnight.

Tawerna ul. Powroźnicza 19/20. Widely trumpeted as Gdańsk's best seafood restaurant, with an imaginative and luxurious menu including smoked eel, caviar and fish soufflé.

Towarzystwo Gastronomiczne ul. Korzenna 33/35. Imaginative range of modern European cuisine served up in the basement of the Ratusz Staromiejski, catering for an arty local clientele. Diners usually linger for a spot of late-night drinking and dancing at weekends.

Trattoria La Primavera ul. Grobla I/13 Skilfully cooked Italian dishes make this a definite step up from the average pizzeria.

Snack bars and cafés

Akademia Café ul. Grobla I/13. Stylish, airy café serving coffee and cakes across the street from Kościoł Mariacki.

Bar Mleczny Neptun ul. Długa 33. Reliable milk bar with a wide range of cheap Polish meals on the menu, though not all are available every day.

Bar Mleczny Syrena al. Grunwaldzka 73, Wrzeszcz. Not in the centre, but the best place to stock your tray with wholesome Polish food.

Caraska ul. Długa 31/32. Cosy café with a wide and delicious range of teas, coffees and desserts.

Cocktail Bar Capri ul. Długa 59/60. Outdoor seating in summer, good coffee and the best place in town for ice cream. Till 10pm.

Cukierna Pellowska ul. Długa 44. Bright, modern self-service café with excellent coffee, cakes and pastries. Look out for other branches around town.

Kamienica ul. Mariacka 37/39. Cosy intimate café on two floors in an old town house with quiet nooks and a terrace overlooking Mariacka. Good for a daytime coffee break or evening drinks.

Kultu Kultu inside the Baltic Cultural Centre, ul.

Korzenna 33/5. An artsy place where you can sip your cappuccino on a chaise longue while admiring the latest café exhibition.

La Pasta ul. Szeroka 32. Unpretentious order-at-the-counter restaurant with cheap and tasty pizza and pasta dishes. Till 10pm.

Lezzetli Podwale Grodzkie 8. Convenient fuelling point near train station for cheap kebabs and pizzas.

Pijalnia Sokow ul. Długa 11. Small, unpretentious takeaway serving kebabs, waffles and delicious fresh juices.

Puss and Rose ul. św. Ducha 87/89. Pleasantly kitsch tearoom with over 70 varieties of tea.

Wielki Błękit ul. Jantarowa 8, at the Brzeźno pier between Gdańsk and Sopot. Spacious seafood café, with self-service counter and pleasant decor. The perfect stop-off on a beach walk from Brzeźno to Sopot.

Złoty Kur ul. Długa 4. A fairly ordinary milk bar, but serves some of the cheapest food you'll find in such a central spot.

Bars and pubs

Blue Café ul. Chmielna 103/104. Spacious modern café-bar featuring live jazz and blues, and DJ nights at weekends (anything from acid jazz to golden oldies), when there's a cover charge. Open till midnight.

Celtic Pub ul. Lektykarska (off ul. Długa). Big basement pub with homely wooden benches, giant screen for music videos, and live music and dancing at weekends. Open till 3am at weekends.

Cotton Club ul. Złotników 25/29. Spacious bar/nightclub playing cheesy chart music. Good for billiards, and with room to sit and drink or to dance. Open till 1am.

Klub Aktora ul. Mariacka 3. Small atmospheric bar, decorated with modern good taste. Open till 11pm.

Gospoda pod Wielkim Młynem ul. Na Piaskach 1. Outdoor summer pub behind the Great Mill, on an island between two canals. Good on warm nights.

Irish Pub ul. Korzenna 33/35. Cavernous venue underneath the Ratusz Staromiejski, lined with church pews and full of students. Frequent live music, and discos at weekends. Open till 4am at weekends.

Jazz Club ul. Długa 39/40. All-ages jazz haunt with great live jazz at weekends, tacky cocktail-bar piano music and golden oldies disco on other nights. Open till 1am.

Piwnica Pub ul. Podgarbary 1. Relaxed bar in a lovely barrel-vaulted cellar just off ul. Długa – one of the few pub-style places that actually feels like a real pub. Open till midnight.

Punkt ul. Chlebnicka 2. Trendy drinking den with cutting edge dance music and electronica.

Scruffy Murphy's al. Grunwaldzka 76/78, Wrzeszcz. Decent pub grub, decent beer. Useful place to know about if you're in the Wrzeszcz district, but not worth a special trip. Open till midnight.

Vinifera ul. Wodopój 7. A nice canal-side bar-cum-café in a doll-size house (this is the little doll's house referred to in Günter Grass's *The Call of the Toad*). Open till midnight.

Clubs

Forty ul. 3 Maja 9a. Student disco and gig venue behind the main train station. Monthly Goth nights if that's your bag. Fri & Sat till 4am.

Gazeta Rock Café ul. Tkacka 7/8. Friendly and fashionable basement bar decked out with pop memorabilia – styles itself as the "Museum of Polish rock". DJs and dancing at weekends when it's open till 4am.

Iks ul. Polanki 66. Student club beneath the dorms, a little way out of town in the Oliwa district. Thurs–Sat till 4am. Gdańsk-Przymorze SKM station.

Klub Muzyczny Parlament ul. św. Ducha 2 (entrance on ul. Kołodziejska). Popular and unpretentious place for mainstream dance music and a lot of beer. Thurs–Sat till 4am.

Olimp ul. Czyzewskiego 29. Spacious student disco in Oliwa (nearest station Gdańsk-Zabianka) concentrating on techno and chart hits. Occasional live acts. Wed–Sat till 5am.

Piękni, Młodzi i Bogaci ul. Teatralna 1. Posey place – the name means "young, rich and beautiful" – with a lively dance floor. Open till 1am Sun–Thurs, till 5am Fri & Sat.

Yesterday ul. Piwna 50. 1960s-style decor; current dance music. Open every day but best on Fri and Sat when it stays open till 4am.

Entertainment

The National Philharmonic and Opera House, al. Zwycięstwa 15 (nearest station Gdańsk-Politechnika) is one of the best **classical venues** in the country, with a varied programme of classical performances and occasional ballet productions. Information and ticket reservations are available from the box office (☎058/320 6262). In addition, there are frequent chamber music recitals at the Akademia Muzyczna, ul. Łąkowa 1/2 (☎058/300 9200); and in the Nadbałtyckie Centrum Kultury, ul. Korzenna 33/35 (☎058/301 1051), which is also the venue for small-scale drama productions. The main city centre **theatre** is the Wybrzeże, just behind the Wielka Zbrojownia at ul. św. Ducha 2 (☎058/301 1328).

The **cinema**'s a valid option as foreign films are shown with subtitles, not dubbed. There are two city centre choices for mainstream cinema. Opposite the main train station there's a new multiplex, Cinema City Krewetka (☎058/769 3000); or, if you prefer the old-fashioned, sticky-floored type of place, there are three screens at ul. Długa 57: the Neptune (☎058/301 8256), the Kameralne and the Helikon (both ☎058/301 5221).

The Trójmiasto boasts a variety of **festivals** and other major cultural get-togethers. The Jarmark Dominikański (Dominican Fair), held annually in the first three weeks of August, is an important local event, with artists and craftspeople setting up shop in the centre of town, accompanied by street theatre and a wealth of other cultural events. Jarmark Mikołaja (St Nicholas's Fair) in the first three weeks of December is a pre-Christmas variation on the same theme. Musically there's the annual international Chamber Music Festival timed to coincide with the Jarmark Dominikański, an International Choral Festival, held in the town hall, or *ratusz* (June–Aug), and the Festival of Organ Music in Oliwa's cathedral during July and August. In early October, Gdańsk hosts the Sergei Diaghilev Choreography Festival. For Polish-speaking film buffs, the Gdańsk Film Festival takes place in late September.

The main city **football** team, Lechia Gdańsk, have plummeted down the divisions in recent years, although they still command a hard core of local support.

They play at the BKS Lechia stadium at ul. Traugutta 29; nearest station is Gdańsk-Politechnika.

There are some worthwhile diversions and entertainments for **children** in town. The Miniatura **puppet theatre**, ul. Grunwaldzka 16 (℡058/341 0123), is excellent: performances are every Saturday and Sunday at noon. There's a nice theatre interior, and children love the performances. The **zoo** in Oliwa at Karwińska 3 is set in enjoyably forested, hilly surroundings and can be reached by bus #122 (Aug 9am–7pm; Sept–July 9am–dusk).

Listings

Airline offices LOT, ul. Wały Jagiellońskie 2/4 ℡058/331 2827.

Airport information ℡058/348 1111.

Ambulance For emergency medical help call 999.

Banks and exchange ATMs are everywhere. *Kantor* shops are fine for regular foreign exchange and charge no commission. Regular banks, such as the Bank Polski at ul. Chlebnicka 52, will handle major credit cards and travellers' cheques.

Books, maps and newspapers For maps, guidebooks and English-language papers and periodicals try the EMPiK stores on Podwale Grodzkie (opposite the central station) and at Długi Targ 25/27.

Car rental Avis, ul. Długa 76 ℡058/301 8818; Budget, at the airport, see p.172 (℡058/348 1298); Hertz, ul. Brygidki 14B ℡058/301 4045.

Consulates Finland, ul. Jana z Kolna 25, Gdynia ℡058/621 6852; Germany, al. Zwycięstwa 23 ℡058/341 4366; Netherlands, al. Jana Pawła II 20 ℡058/346 9878; Norway, ul. Jana z Kolna 25, Gdynia ℡058/621 6216; Russia, ul. Batorego 15 ℡058/341 1088; Sweden, ul. Jana z Kolna 25 ℡058/621 6216; UK, al. Grunwaldzka 102 ℡058/341 4365. No US consulate – the embassy in Warsaw is the nearest (see p.140).

Ferries Ferries to and from Nynashavn in Sweden use the Nowy Port terminal, opposite Westerplatte (see p.185), and are operated by Polish Baltic Shipping, ul. Przemysłowa 1 ℡058/343 1887, ⊛www .polferries.com.pl. Ferries to and from Karlskrona, Sweden, use the ferry terminal in Gdynia and are operated by Stena Line, ul. Kwiatkowskiego, Gdynia

℡058/660 9200, ⊛www.stenaline.pl. Ferry tickets are also available from Orbis at ul. Podmłynska 95 ℡058/301 4544.

Internet Internet Café Trinity is upstairs at the train station.

Left luggage At the train station. Open 24 hours.

Parking Guarded parking is available at the main Orbis hotels (*Hewliusz, Marina, Novotel* and *Posejdon*) and is available to non-guests for a fee.

Pharmacy There's a 24hr pharmacy at the main train station.

Police City headquarters are at ul. Okopowa 15. In an emergency call 997.

Post office The main office, Poczta Główna, with poste restante (general delivery) available, is at ul. Długa 23/28 (Mon–Fri 8am–8pm, Sat 9am–3pm).

Shopping If you want to browse round a market, then try the Hala Targowa on ul. Pańska, which has vegetables and fruit, brought in fresh each day from the countryside, outside, loads of small stalls inside. Madison, on ul. Rajska near the train station, is the best of the modern shopping malls; ul. Długa is the place to browse for (admittedly expensive) antiques and souvenirs; and ul. Mariacka is good for amber and other jewellery.

Taxi Avoid taxi stands and order your cab by phone. Reliable firms include MTP (℡058/9633) and Hallo (℡058/9666).

Train tickets International train tickets are available from Orbis, ul. Podmłynska 95, and from the main stations in Gdańsk and Gdynia.

Sopot

One-time stamping ground for the rich and famous, who came from all over the world to sample its casinos and high life in the 1920s and 1930s, the beach resort at **SOPOT** is still popular with landlocked Poles, and is increasingly attractive to Westerners – Germans and Swedes in particular. It has an altogether different atmosphere from its neighbour: the fashionable clothes shops and bars scattered round ul. Bohaterów Monte Cassino, the main street, seem light years away from both historic central Gdańsk and the industrial grimness of the shipyards. Sopot has always enjoyed a special position in Polish popular culture, not least because it's the place where media personalities traditionally come to see and be seen. In the early 1960s Sopot witnessed the birth of Polish beat music, with most of the era's top names beginning their careers in the *Non Stop* discotheque – Poland's answer to Liverpool's *Cavern Club*. Today, Sopot's position slap in the middle of the Trójmiasto ensures that it's more than just a summertime seaside resort. It's a year-round nightlife centre servicing the big-city populations of both Gdynia and Gdańsk, as well as a growing business centre and an enduringly fashionable place in which to live. In terms of local affluence and outside investment, it's probably been the fastest growing town in Poland since the end of the communist era.

Arrival, information and accommodation

The simplest way to get to Sopot is by SKM **train** from Gdańsk, a twenty-minute journey. The **tourist office**, diagonally opposite the train station at ul. Dworcowa 4 (summer daily 10am–6pm; winter Mon–Fri 8am–4pm; ☎058/550 3783, ⓦwww.sopot.pl), will guide you towards private rooms (❸) in July and August, as well as advising on pensions and hotels. Sopot's holiday popularity means that rooms can be scarce, and during July and August prices are often considerably increased. Best of the **campsites** are *Kamienny Potok*, at the northern end of the resort near the Kamienny Potok SKM station (☎058/550 0445), and *Przy Plaży* (☎058/551 6523), close to the beach at Bitwy Pod Płowcami 67, about a kilometre south of the pier.

There's an **Internet** café, the Net Cave, in a courtyard off ul. Bohaterów at ul. Pulaskiego 7a (daily noon–9pm).

Hotels

Amber ul. Grunwaldzka 45 ☎058/550 0042. Plush, modern hotel that's small enough to feel intimate, cosy and characterful. Only 100m south of the main street. ❼

Chemik ul. Bitwy pod Płowcami 61 ☎058/551 6314. Supremely ugly concrete box with simple, spick-and-span rooms. Set back slightly from the beach, some 2km south of the pier. Bus #143 (direction "Gdańsk-Oliwa") from ul. Kosciuszki to the Złoty Kłos stop. A choice between en-suite rooms or those with shared facilities. ❸

Eden ul. Kordeckiego 4/6 ☎058/551 1503, ⓦwww.hotel-eden.com.pl. Nicely located pension in a park just south of the pier. Rooms not exceptional but many have balconies and original parquet floors. Smallish, so arrive early or ring ahead. ❻

Grand ul. Powstańców Warszawy 12/14 ☎058/551 0041, ⓦwww.orbis.com. Built in the 1920s in regal period style, the *Grand* was a favourite with President de Gaulle, Giscard d'Estaing and the Persian Shah. Tarted up to suit the demands of an increasingly prominent local nouveau-riche clientele, it retains some of its former magnificence, with huge old rooms making this an enjoyable indulgence. ❽

Irena ul. Chopina 36 ☎058/551 2073. A small, reasonably priced and well-kept *pensjonat* a short way down the hill from Sopot station. All rooms are en suite. ❻

Maryla ul. Sępia 22 ☎058/551 0034. A converted country villa with beautiful views of trees and the sea. Near Kamienny Potok SKM station; otherwise walk north along ul. Powstancóv Warszawy, then bear left onto Sępia, or catch bus #122 (direction "Kamienny Potok") from outside the *Grand Hotel*. Book early. ❻

Sopot ul. Bitwy pod Płowcami 62 ☎058/551 3201, ⓦwww.hotel-sopot.pl. Sprawling concrete buildings, 2km south of the pier, but despite an unprepossesing outside, the rooms are clean and all have a balcony. Directions as for the *Chemik* (see above). ❺

Wanda ul. Poniatowskiego 7 ☎058/550 3037. Lovely old villa right on the beach, 800m south of the pier, slightly let down by tacky Seventies decor inside. ❻

WDW (Wojskowy Dom Wypoczynkowy) ul. Kilińskiego 12 ☎058/551 0685. Big, army-owned

hotel, once a rest home for soldiers but now open to all-comers. Near the beach, about 1km south of the pier. En-suite rooms or shared facilities. ⑤
Zatoka ul. Emilii Plater 7/9/11 ☎058/551 2367. Reasonably priced B&B in a quiet street, right on the seaside walkway 1.2km south of the pier. All rooms are en suite. ⑤

Zhong Hua al. Wojska Polskiego 1 ☎058/550 2020, ✆www.zhonghua.com.pl. Well-located upmarket hotel, right on the beach just south of the pier. Housed in a spectacular wooden building which used to be used as a bathhouse for spa tourists. Good views from spacious rooms and worth the extra expense. ⑧

The Town

Most life in Sopot revolves around **ul. Bohaterów Monte Cassino**, the largely pedestrianized strip which slopes down towards the sea, and acts as both the main venue for daytime strolling and the centre of the summer nightlife scene. The street culminates in a supremely well-manicured stretch of seaside gardens which mark the entrance to Sopot's famous **pier** (*molo*). Constructed in 1928 but later rebuilt, at just over 500m it's by far the longest in the whole Baltic area, and a walk to the end is considered an essential part of the Sopot experience for visitors (3.30zł). Long sandy beaches stretch away on both sides. On the northern section you'll find ranks of bathing huts, some with marvellous 1920s wicker beach chairs for rent. On the southern side, a foot- and bike path leads all the way back to the northern suburbs of Gdańsk, passing endless sands and fried fish stalls on the way – a relaxing one-hour stroll if you're so inclined.

Upper Sopot, as the western part of town is known, is a wealthy suburb of entrepreneurs, architects and artists. Here, and in other residential areas of Sopot, many of the houses have a touch of Art Nouveau style to them – look out for the turrets built for sunrise viewing. The **park** in upper Sopot offers lovely walks in the wooded hills around Łysa Góra, where there's a ski track in winter.

You can rent crewed **sailing boats** out on the pier, by the hour or by the day. For **windsurfing** go to the Sopot Sailing Club down the seaside bike path just past the *Chemik*. **Biking** along the shoreline is very pleasant; rental operations alongside the bike path in Sopot or Jelitkowo will provide cycles for a substantial deposit. Back in town there are **tennis** courts at the Klub Tenisowy, ul. Haffnera 57.

Eating, drinking and entertainment

There's a pleasing spread of **restaurants** in Sopot, both Polish and international. In summer, especially, the pier area is full of bars and coffee shops, with Western-style fast-food joints making noticeable inroads of late. With the student halls not far away in the Oliwa district, and most of the pubs and cafés conveniently concentrated in the ul. Bohaterów Monte Cassino, Sopot scores over Gdańsk and Gdynia for a buzzing **nightlife**.

The open-air **Opera Leśna**, in the peaceful hilly park in the west of Sopot, hosts large-scale productions throughout the summer, including an **International Song Festival** in August which includes big names from the Western rock scene alongside homegrown performers; for tickets and current details of what's on, check with the Orbis office. The "Friends of Sopot" hold **chamber music** concerts every Thursday in the Dworek Sierakowskich, ul. Czyaewskiego 12 (off al. Bohaterów), in a room where Chopin is said to have played.

Restaurants

Bar Elita ul. Podjazd 3. Cheap and stodgy Polish favourites served up milk-bar-style in unassuming surroundings just behind the train station.

Bar Przystań al. Wojska Polskiego 11. Sopot's finest seafood café in a lovely spot about 1.5km along the beach path to Gdańsk. The fish is very good value, though expect queues of eager Poles at the weekend.

Greenway ul. Powstańców Warszawy 2/4/6. Cosy cafeteria serving a wide range of veggie food.
Pizzeria Brawa ul. Grunwaldzka 18. Cheap and reliable pizzeria – the place for a quick refuelling stop rather than a dinner date.
Rozmaryn ul. Ogrodowa 8 ☎058/551 1104. Mediterranean decor and a good, if pricey, pasta-based menu. Reservations recommended.
Secesja ul. Grunwaldzka 8/10. Polish-style food served by attentive old-school waiters in Art Nouveau surroundings.
Villa Sedan ul. Pilaskiego 18/20. In the conservatory of a fine old villa, this place is traditional and classy without being stuffy. French cooking with a definite Polish influence.
Wieloryb ul. Podjazd 2. Experimental French-style cooking served in surreal underwater grotto-style surroundings.
Zhong Hua al. Wojska Polskiego 1 ☎058/550 2019. Excellent Chinese cooking with outdoor seating and views of the sea. Not cheap, but well worth splashing out on.

Cafés and bars

Błękitny Pudel ul. Bohaterów Monte Cassino 44. Kitsch but cosy café-pub on the main strip which also does decent food. Always full in the evenings.
Daily Blues ul. Władysława IV 1a. Atmospheric little bar with gigs or jam sessions most nights.
Dworek Sierakowskich ul. Czyżewskiego 12. Refined daytime café housed in an art gallery just off ul. Bohaterów Monte Cassino. Best place in town for tea and cakes.
Galeria Kińsky ul. Kościuszki 10. Bar with antique clutter, intimate atmosphere and good coffee. Something of a shrine to crazed German actor Klaus Kinski, who was born on the premises.
Kawiaret ul. Bohaterów Monte Cassino 57/59. Café by day, bar by night. Live jazz and blues at weekends.

Language Pub ul. Pulaskiego 8. Cosy home-from-home pub with a Scottish theme in the side streets just south of ul. Bohaterów Monte Cassino. Decent international beers, good *craic*.
Lili Marlene ul. Powstańców Warszawy 6. Open till 2am and quieter than the other bars; as there's nothing beyond it but the pier, this makes a good choice for a nightcap.
Pubkin ul. Grunwaldzka 55. Eccentrically decorated little pub with cosy intimate feel – ring the bell for entrance.

Clubs

Enzym ul. Mamuszki 21. In the Park Pólnocny, about 500m north of the *Grand Hotel*. The place to go for a taste of alternative-leaning, studenty dance culture. Reggae nights, rap nights and rave nights. Open Fri & Sat till 5am.
Galaxy Lazienki Pólnocne. In the Park Pólnocny, just before you get to *Enzym* (see above). A hedonistic weekend disco venue catering for the commercial end of the spectrum. Fri & Sat till 5am.
Sfinks ul. Powstańców Warszawy 18. Art gallery-cum-club located in a pavilion in the park just beyond the *Grand*. Superbly atmospheric bar that's a magnet for bohemians and arty types. Live gigs and top DJ nights (cutting-edge dance music rather than the mainstream stuff) feature regularly. Sometimes operates a private-club-style door policy: ring the bell and charm the bouncer with your perfect English. Open daily till 4am.
Viva Club ul. Mamuszki 2. Big, brash and very popular place on the beach near the *Grand*, with five bars and two dance floors. Hosts innovative live shows including acrobats and theatre as well as the usual rave-style club nights. Thurs–Sat till 6am.

Gdynia

The northernmost section of the Trójmiasto, **GDYNIA** was originally a small Kashubian village, and the property of the Cistercian monks of Oliwa from the fourteenth to the eighteenth century. Boom time came after World War I when Gdynia, unlike Gdańsk, returned to Polish jurisdiction. The limited coastline ceded to the new Poland – a thirty-two-kilometre strip of land stretching north from Gdynia and known as the "Polish Corridor" – left the country strapped for coastal outlets, so the Polish authorities embarked on a massive port-building programme. By the mid-1930s Gdynia had been transformed from a small village into a bustling harbour, which by 1937 boasted the largest volume of naval traffic in the Baltic region. Hitler's propaganda portrayed the very existence of the corridor as an injustice, and after Gdynia was captured in 1939 the Germans deported most of the Polish population, established a naval base and, to add insult to injury, renamed the town Gotenhafen. Their retreat in 1945 was accompanied by wholesale destruction of the harbour installations, which were subsequently rebuilt from scratch by the postwar authorities. The endearingly run-down, almost seedy atmosphere of today's port makes an interesting contrast to the more cultured Gdańsk. In the 1990s the city centre saw major changes as the state-owned shops were privatized; thanks to Gdynia's historical position within Polish territory it was a much easier business than in the old Free City, where establishing retroactive property rights is still proving a tricky business. In the centre of town shopping streets like ul. Starowiejska have received a brash facelift and are helping to develop Gdynia's position at the forefront of the country's burgeoning economic transformation and development.

Arrival, information and accommodation

By **train** (every 10min), Gdynia Główna station is a thirty-minute journey from central Gdańsk. You can also get there by **ferry**, calling at Sopot on the way from the Motława waterfront (2 daily, 1hr 30min; return ticket 56zł) in Gdańsk. Tickets for boat trips around the harbour and to Hel can be bought at the ferry embarkation point in Gdynia. The city's **tourist office**, lurking in a corner of the main train station (May–Sept Mon–Fri 8am–6pm, Sat 9am–4pm, Sun 9am–3pm; Oct–April Mon–Fri 10am–5pm, Sat 10am–2pm; ☎058/628 5466), can fill you in on local accommodation and sightseeing possibilities. There's an **Internet café** at ul. Świętojańska 135 (daily 8am–10pm), across the main road from the Gdynia Wgórze SKM station.

Accommodation

There's a fair spread of beds in town, most of them acceptable if not outstanding. You can book **private rooms** (❸) through the tourist office at the railway station (see above). The main **youth hostel**, open all year, is near the shipyards at ul. Energetykow 13a (☎058/627 1005; 25zł); from Gdynia Główna take any bus going away from town (that's left as you come out of the station) along ul. Wiśniewskiego and get off at the second stop.

Hotels

Antracyt ul. Korzeniowskiego 19 ☎058/620 1239, ⓦ www.antracyt.home.pl. Modern medium-rise place on a bluff above the beach, in a quiet residential area 1500m south of the centre. Simple en suites with TV on the lower floors, roomier accommodation with balconies and sea views higher up. ❺

China Town ul. Dworcowa 11 ☎058/620 9221. In a convenient spot just across from the railway station. Simply furnished, very clean rooms, all with shower but some with shared lavatories. ❹

Dom Marynarza al. Piłsudskiego 1 ☎058/622 0025. Former Polish navy hostel across the road

from the *Antracyt*. The en-suite rooms are a bit sparsely furnished for the price, although Seventies nostalgia buffs will like the green/brown colour-clash interiors. ❺

Gdynia ul. Armii Krajowej 22 ☎058/666 3040, ⓦ www.orbis.pl. Big grey lump on the outside but comfortable on the inside, with an excellent swimming pool. The hangout for visiting yachting folk in summer. ❼

Nadmorski ul. Ejsmonda 2 ☎058/622 1542, ⓦ www.nadmorski.pl. Smart ultra-modern place with tennis courts and spa. Terrace café overlooks the sea. ❽

The City

Betraying its 1930s origins, sections of the **city centre** are pure Bauhaus, with curved balconies and huge window fronts: the contrast with the faceless postwar concrete jungle that envelops much of the rest of the centre couldn't be more striking. The place to head for is the **port area**, directly east across town from the main station. From the train and bus stations walk down bustling ul. 10 Lutego and through the park, where there's a small funfair, and you'll find yourself at the foot of the southernmost **pier**. Moored on the northern side is the **Błyskawica**, a World War II destroyer (Tues–Sun 10am–1pm, 2pm–5pm; 4zł). The sailors manning the ship are quick to point out to British visitors the desktop plaque commemorating the vessel's year-long wartime sojourn in Cowes on the Isle of Wight, where it helped to defend the port against a major German attack in May 1942. Further along is another proudly Polish vessel, the three-masted frigate **Dar Pomorza** (May–Sept daily 10am–6pm; Oct & Nov Tues–Sun 10am–4pm; 5zł), built in Hamburg in 1909 and used as a Polish Navy training ship during the 1930s and again after World War II. At the very end of the pier, a lumpy monument to Polish seafarer and novelist Joseph Conrad stands near the **aquarium** (Tues–Sun: May–Sept 9am–7pm; Oct–April 10am–5pm; 10zł), where amongst other sealife you can see piranhas, sturgeon and sea turtles.

For more local maritime history, the **naval museum** at ul. Sedzickiego 3, a short walk through the park south of the pier, was being completely renovated at the time of writing but should be open by the time you read this; it will no doubt retain its impressive collection of cannons, anchors and other hardware. To complete the tour, join the locals on a stroll along the Bulwar Nadmorski or climb the hill, Kamienna Góra, for a great view over the harbour.

Eating, drinking and entertainment

Gdynia is the least affluent part of the Trójmiasto, with a more run-down air than its neighbours. As a consequence it lacks the range of **eating and drinking** venues enjoyed by Sopot and Gdańsk, though there are a few places worth seeking out.

The **Teatr Muzyczny** (Musical Theatre), pl. Grunwaldzki 1, near the *Gdynia Hotel*, is a favourite venue with Poles and tourists alike, featuring quality Polish musicals as well as all-too-frequent productions of the Andrew Lloyd Webber oeuvre. Tickets (hard to find in the summer season) are available from the box office (☎058/621 7816) or the Orbis bureau in the *Gdynia Hotel*. Emphasizing the naval connection there's also an annual Sea Shanty **festival** held here in August. Silver Screen, Waszyngtona 21 (☎058/628 1800, ⓦwww.silverscreen .com.pl), is the main multiplex **cinema**.

Restaurants

Anker al. Piłsudskiego 50. Busy budget restaurant, usually packed at lunchtimes, serving up simple but satisfying dishes like pizza, crêpes and fried chicken.

Kwadrans ul. Kościuszki 20. Simple restaurant serving filling breakfasts and a straightforward selection of pizzas, salads and toasted sandwiches the rest of the day.

La Gondola ul. Portowa 8 ☎058/620 5923. High-quality Italian food, served in elegant surroundings. Reservations recommended. Open till midnight.

Monte ul. Świętojańska 50. No-nonsense pizzeria on the main shopping street.

Santorini ul. Świętojańska 61. Rather good Greek restaurant with soothing decor, good service, and satisfying eats.

Smok al. Piłsudskiego 36/38. Well-regarded Vietnamese place; though the decor is nothing special, the set lunches are good value. Closes at 9pm.

Thai Hut ul. Abrahama 11. Plenty of pot plants and bamboo furniture, as well as tasty Thai and Japanese food.

Cafés and bars

Café Rybacka al. Zjednoczenia 1, on the terrace at the aquarium. Tea, coffee, ice cream and snacks with great views out to sea and a sheltered area for blustery days.

Cyganeria ul. 3 Maja 27. Large wooden tables and deep, relaxing sofas make this a great place for daytime coffee or evening beers.

Delicje ul. 10 Lutego 27. Daytime café just east of Gdynia Główna station. The 1960s interior makes this feel a little like a coffee shop from outer space. Good pastries.

Donegal ul. Zgoda 10. Pretty authentic-feeling Irish pub based around a cosy suite of dark, woody rooms. Packed at weekends.

Dziupla al. Piłsudskiego 56. Lively café and late-night bar with occasional live music. Snacks and sandwiches from breakfast onwards.

Tygiel ul. Abrahama 86 (entrance on ul. Władysława IV). Absinthe helps wash down the eccentric decoration, including a life-sized winged horse. Open till midnight or the last customers leave.

Clubs

Babaloo ul. Świętojańska 46. Another of Gdynia's resolutely weird-looking places, perhaps inspired by Austin Powers. Hip-hop, disco and student nights for a youngish crowd.

Mandragora ul. Hryniewickiego 10/50, ❷www .mandragora.art.pl. Alternative-leaning club with lively weekend dance nights.

Ucho ul. św. Piotra 2, ❷www.ucho.com.pl. Big warehouse on the edge of the docklands that sees the best of the live acts coming to Gdynia, as well as hosting a retro indie night.

North of the Trójmiasto

If the prospect of escaping from the rigours of the city appeals, head for the **Hel Peninsula**, a long thin strip of woods and sand dunes sticking out into the Baltic Sea some 35km north of Gdańsk, as the crow flies. As in several places along the Polish section of the Baltic coast, a peninsula was formed over the centuries by the combined action of current and wind. The sandy beaches dotted along the north side are well away from the once poisonous Wisła outlet, making the water around here as clean as you'll get on the Baltic coast; what's more, they are easily accessible and, away from the main resorts, never overcrowded. Of all the settlements along the peninsula, the most rewarding is the fishing village of **Hel** itself.

A convenient place to stop off on the way to Hel, and well worth a visit in its own right, is the fishing town of **Puck**, a world away from the hustle and bustle of the Trójmiasto and home to a fine medieval church.

Travelling along the coast to the west will bring you to the leafy resort town of **Jastrzębia Góra**, perched on crumbling sandstone cliffs at the most northerly point in Poland.

Puck

Sheltered by the Hel Peninsula, **PUCK** is a small Kashubian fishing port with a smattering of elegant merchants' homes and a tremendous Gothic church. Back in the sixteenth century this was the base for Gdańsk's mercenary navy, the *kaper* (see box, p.186), and the sailing tradition continues with yacht and dinghy racing most weekends. Unlike many of the smaller resort towns along the Baltic coast, where the only business is the summer tourist trade, Puck is a bustling local centre worth visiting all year round.

Trains and buses from Gdynia stop at ul. Dworcowa. From there, a right turn down ul. Nowy Świat and a left onto ul. Woi. Polskiego bring you to the old town square, **plac Wolności**. Here, there's a pleasant variety of houses, some plastered and painted in pastel colours, some in the local warm red brick. The **town hall**, set into the east side of the square has a relatively plain brick facade and dates back to the fourteenth century. On the north side at pl. Wolności 28 is a small town **museum** (Mon–Fri 8am–3pm, Sat 9am–2pm, Sun 10am–2pm; 3zł). One street to the north of the square stands Puck's Gothic parish **church**, Kościoł św. Piotra i Paula. It's a magnificent building, small compared to the enormous edifices to be seen in Gdańsk, but beautifully proportioned; it enjoys a superb setting on a hillock above the **fishing harbour**. From the harbour there's a pleasant walk east along the sea front, past the sailing school and beach volleyball courts, to two wooden **piers**, the second of which serves the bustling marina. Beyond the piers lies a small sandy **beach**.

You could easily look round Puck in an hour or so and continue to Hel (by bus or train) or Jastrzębia Góra (bus only), or, if you want **accommodation** there's a good supply of private rooms (❶), which can be arranged through the **tourist office** at pl. Wolności 2 (☎058/673 2403; Mon–Fri 9am–4pm). Alternatively, the *Delphin* at Lipowa 4 (☎058/673 2210; ❸) is set in a pleasant park near the pier and offers comfortable, functional rooms in a refurbished seaside villa. For a quick coffee you could try *Café Mistral* down by the yacht club but the best place to **eat** is back in town at the Kashubian fish restaurant *Budyszowa Maszoporeya* at ul. Morska 13, with outdoor seating overlooking the harbour where the fish is landed.

Jastrzębia Góra

JASTRZĘBIA GÓRA was once the playground of the interwar Polish elite, Józef Piłsudski included. It's a reposeful and leafy place and despite the soulless strip of rest homes and hotels at the eastern entrance to the resort makes a pleasant stop for a few days on the beach.

Buses stop near the intersection of Rozewska, the main east–west thoroughfare, and Promenada Światowida, the pedestrianized street which runs down to the sea. **Private rooms** (❶–❷) can be obtained by hunting around for *pokoje* signs or by calling in at *Pensjonat Damian*, Rybacka 53 (☎058/774 4426; ❹), which maintains a list of vacancies as well as offering simple en-suite rooms of its own. Elsewhere, the popularity of the resort with well-heeled Trójmiasto folk is reflected in the quality and price of accommodation. *Willa Jasna*, Bałtycka 24 (☎058/674 9698; ❺), is a lovely house hard up against the woods in the western part of town, with cosy en-suite rooms with TV, a sizeable garden and a restaurant in the basement. Closer to what passes for the centre is the *Onyks*, Słowackiego 5 (☎058/674 9746; ❼), offering snazzy apartments with sitting room and kitchenette. Most **eating** and **drinking** takes place in the inevitable line of fried-fish huts along Rozewska and Promenada Światowida. For a bit more style, try *Café Kredens* on Promenada Światowida, which serves up T-bone steaks, salads, pasta dishes and drinks in an interior liberally strewn with driftwood and fishing nets.

Hel

HEL, the small fishing port at the tip of the peninsula, is the main destination and a day-trippers' favourite. Despite heavy fighting – a German army of 100,000 men was rounded up on the peninsula in 1945 – the town retains some nineteenth-century fishermen's cottages, sturdy one-storey brick-built affairs which add character to the resort's compact centre. It's a fast-developing place, with souvenir shops and amber jewellery stores aplenty, but it retains enough old-world appeal to distinguish it from the majority of Baltic holiday spots, and access to miles of beach is a major plus.

From the train station (where buses from Gdynia also stop), walk down ul. Dworska to reach the northwestern end of Wiejska, the pedestrianized main street on which most of the town's amenities are located. It's here that you'll find Hel's **Muzeum Rybołówstwa** (Fishing Museum; daily 9am–4pm; 5zł), housed in the fifteenth-century Gothic Kościół św. Piotra (St Peter's Church). Inside are plenty of model ships and fishing tackle displaying the history of the fishing industry in this area, as well as some local folk art. There's a good view of the bay from the observation deck. As on the adjoining mainland, the people of the peninsula are predominantly Kashubian, as evidenced in the local dialect and the distinctive **embroidery** styles on show in the museum.

A firm favourite with younger visitors is the **Fokarium** (Seal Enclosure; daily 9am–7pm; 2zł), about 50m west of the Fishing Museum along the seashore. Here five or six seals spend their days eating (feeding at 9am & 3pm), swimming and lazing about – much like the average human visitor to Hel. There's a strong emphasis on conservation with lots of information on sea life posted alongside the tanks. A small museum (same times; 2zł) within the enclosure has further displays, though the captions are in Polish.

At the eastern end of ul. Wiejska, the main drag, ul. Leśna continues northwards towards the open sea, passing a graceful lighthouse. A fifteen-minute walk through the woods will bring you to Hel's biggest attraction, the **beach** – a luxurious, semolina-coloured ribbon of sand that extends as far as the eye can see.

Practicalities

In summer, direct **trains** run to Hel from Gdańsk train station, but there's a wider range of year-round train and **bus** services from Gdynia, as well as faster minibuses (departing when full), which leave from the northern side of Gdynia bus station. In summer, tourist **boats** run to Hel several times a day from both Gdynia and Gdańsk (the latter providing excellent views of the Gdańsk shipyards). For times and fares check with the local tourist offices or call Żegluga Gdańska on ☏058/301 6355 (ⓦwww.zegluga.gda.pl). There are a couple of places to hire **bicycles** on ul. Leśna.

There are numerous **private rooms** (❷–❹) in Hel, and you may well be propositioned by prospective landladies upon arrival at the train station. If not, the area around Sikorskiego (just south of the station, at the northwestern end of Wiejska) is the place to look for *wolne pokoje* signs. Of the **hotels**, the sparsely furnished rooms (en suite or with shared facilities) at the impersonal *Riviera*, ul. Wiejska 130 (☏058/675 0528; ❸) will suffice, although you'd be better off shelling out a little more to stay in smaller family-run establishments such as the *Helios*, Lipowa 2 (☏058/675 0103; ❸); *Captain Morgan*, Wiejska 21 (☏058/675 0091; ❸); or *Gwiazda Morza*, Leśna 7 (☏058/675 0859; ❸), all of which offer cosy en suites. Alternatively, there are **campsites** tucked away under the trees all along the peninsula, most of them offering bungalows for around 40zł per person.

There are any number of snack food joints along Wiejska doling out fried fish at reasonable prices: the local halibut is particularly good. In addition, there are a growing number of more formal **eating** places, most of which are beginning to resemble each other in terms of ambience: chunky wooden furniture and ceilings hung with fishing nets are very much the order of the day. *Chërz*, in a charming red-brick building at Wiejska 109, stands out for the care it takes over cooking and presentation and the relative lack of maritime clutter, while *Maszoperia*, across the road at Wiejska 110, offers an intimate candle-lit interior. *Fiszeria*, Wiejska 100, is a fancy place with the full range of fish and meat dishes. The most convivial place for **drinking** is the *Captain Morgan*, a popular pub-style meeting place crammed with antique maritime junk.

Kashubia

The area of lakes and hills stretching west of Gdańsk – **Kashubia** (Kaszuby) – is the homeland of one of Poland's lesser-known ethnic minorities, the

Kashubians. "Not German enough for the Germans, nor Polish enough for the Poles" – Grandma Koljaiczek's wry observation in *The Tin Drum* – sums up the historic predicament of this group.

Originally a western Slav people linked ethnically to Poles, and historically spared the ravages of invasion and war thanks to their relative geographical isolation, the Kashubians were subjected to a German cultural onslaught during the Partition period, when the area was incorporated into Prussia. The process was resisted fiercely: in the 1910 regional census, only six out of the 455 inhabitants of one typical village gave their nationality as German, a pattern of resistance continued during World War II.

However, the Kashubians' treatment by the Poles has not always been better, and it's often argued that Gdańsk's domination of the region has kept the development of a Kashubian national identity in check. Certainly the local museums are sometimes guilty of consigning the Kashubians to the realm of quaint historical phenomena, denying the reality of what is still a living culture. You can hear the distinctive Kashubian language (supposedly derived from the original Pomeranian tongue) spoken all over the region, particularly by older people, and many villages still produce such Kashubian handicrafts as embroidered cloths and tapestries.

Żukowo and Kartuzy

The old capital of the region, Kartuzy, is tucked away among the lakes and woods 30km west of Gdańsk. From the main Gdańsk station a bus climbs up through **ŻUKOWO**, the first Kashubian village. The fourteenth-century Norbertine **church** and **convent** here has a rich Baroque interior and organ, resembling a country version of St Nicholas' in Gdańsk (see p.181). The arrangement of buildings – church, convent, vicarage and adjoining barns – has a distinctly medieval feel.

Though it can be reached in just under an hour on the same bus, the dusty, rather run-down market town of **KARTUZY** feels a long way from Gdańsk. The **Muzeum Kaszubskie** on ul. Kościerska (Kashubian Museum; May–Sept Tues–Fri 8am–4pm, Sat 8am–3pm, Sun 10am–2pm; Oct–April Tues–Sat 8am–3pm; 7.50zł) has some nice examples of Kashubian arts and crafts. The Gothic **church**, part of a group of buildings erected in 1380 on the northern edge of town by Carthusian monks from Bohemia, is a sombre sort of place. The building itself is coffin-shaped – the original monks actually used to sleep in coffins – while the pendulum of the clock hanging below the organ sports a skull-like angel swinging the Grim Reaper's scythe and bears the cheery inscription "Each passing second brings you closer to death." Apart from the church, nothing much remains of the original monastery. More appealing are the paths leading through the beech groves which surround nearby **Lake Klasztorne**, a nice place to cool off on a hot summer's day.

If you decide to make a night of it, the **tourist office**, Rynek 2 (Mon–Fri 9am–4pm, Sat 9am–3pm; ☎058/684 0201), will point you in the direction of **private rooms** (❶), although most of these are in the surrounding countryside and you'll need your own transport. The *Korman*, ul. 3 Maja 36 (☎058/685 3400; ❹), is the only **hotel** in town, and its **restaurant** is the best source of passable sit-down food. *Be-mol*, just off the Rynek at Kościuszki 19, offers cheap pasta and pizza dishes named after different styles of music (a dub reggae pizza comes with tuna and peas, if you were wondering).

In the postwar years, Kashubia has gathered some wealth through the development of strawberry production: if you want to sample the crop, the June

strawberry festival, held on a hill 2km out of Kartuzy (anyone will direct you), provides an ideal opportunity. The occasion is part market, part fair – a little like a German *Jahrmarkt* – with the local farmers bringing baskets of strawberries to the church at nearby Wygoda.

Around Kashubia

Behind Kartuzy the heartland of Kashubia opens out into a high plateau of low hills and tranquil woodland dotted with villages and the occasional small town. Running round the whole area is the **Ostrzydkie Circle**, an Ice Age hill formation that folds itself around several picturesque **lakes**. The lake resort of **Chmielno**, just west of Kartuzy, is one of the more obvious tourist targets, while the open-air museum at **Wdzydze Kiszewskie** is the place to aim for if you're at all interested in Kashubian folk culture. Being an intensely religious region, Kashubia is especially worth visiting during any of the major Catholic **festivals** – Corpus Christi for example, or Marian festivals such as the Assumption of the Virgin (Aug 15).

If you've got your own **transport** it's worth considering doing a round trip, taking in Chmielno and Wdzydze before heading back to Gdańsk, passing through some wonderful hilly countryside on the way. Travelling by bus, a day each for both destinations seems more reasonable. In summer, bus excursions are usually on offer from Gdańsk to Wdzydze Kiszewskie and elsewhere; ask at Orbis or the Gdańsk tourist offices for details of current offers.

Chmielno and Sierakowice

CHMIELNO, at the western edge of the Ostrzydkie Circle, is the most idyllic of several holiday centres around the area, and also the easiest to get to, lying some 12km west of Kartuzy and easily reachable by bus. Set in tranquil, beautiful surroundings overlooking the shores of three lakes – Białe, Rekowo and Kłodno – the waterside nearest the village is dotted with former workers' rest homes, many of them now holiday homes and *pensjonaty*. Chmielno is a centre of traditional Kashubian ceramics, and the **Muzeum Ceramyky Kaszubskiej** at ul. Fr. Necla 1 (Museum of Kashubian Ceramics; Mon–Sat 9am–4pm; 2zł) has a working pottery on site. Despite the village's holidaytime popularity, you shouldn't have any trouble finding somewhere to stay. The **tourist office**, right by the **bus** stop in the village cultural centre (Mon–Fri 9am–5pm; ☏058/684 2205), will fix you up with a **private room** (❶). Up from the museum at ul. Gryfa Pomorskiego 68, *U Czorlińskiego* (☏058/684 2278; ❹) is a homely **hotel** with a restaurant serving local food, while of the **pensions** the *Dorota*, at ul. Grździckiego 10 (☏058/684 2237; ❸), has en suites available. Walking east from the village centre, between lakes Białe and Rekowo, will bring you round to the far shore of Lake Kłodno, where there are a couple of **campsites** renting out boats and kayaks. Back in the centre, *U Świętopełka*, downhill from the bus stop on ul. Świętopełka, is another good **restaurant** serving traditional Kashubian fare (potatoes with everything).

Moving west, the town of **SIERAKOWICE**, 15km further on, borders on a large expanse of rolling forestland, some of the prettiest in the region, and deservedly popular hiking country. **MIRACHOWO**, a ten-kilometre bus journey northeast across the forest, is a good base for walkers. The village has several traditional half-timbered Kashubian houses similar to those featured at the *skansen* at Wdzydze Kiszewskie (see p.202). The same holds for **ŁEBNO**, some 15km north, and many of the surrounding villages, a firm indication that you're in the heart of traditional Kashubian territory.

Kościerzyna and Wdzydze Kiszewskie

Continuing south through the region, **KOŚCIERZYNA**, the other main regional centre, some 40km south of Kartuzy, is an undistinguished market town – bus change or a bite to eat on the way to Wdzydze aside, there's no particular reason for stopping over here.

Sixteen kilometres on through the sandy forests south of Kościerzyna brings you to **WDZYDZE KISZEWSKIE**: if your tongue has trouble getting round this tongue-twister of a name, simple "*skansen*" will probably do the trick when asking for the right bus. Feasible as a day-trip from Gdańsk (72km) – in summer **buses** travel direct, at other times you have to change in Kościerzyna – the *skansen* here (April–Oct Tues–Sun 9am–4pm; Nov–March Mon–Fri 10am–3pm; 8.50zł) is one of the best of its kind, bringing together a large and carefully preserved set of traditional Kashubian **wooden buildings** collected from around the region. Established at the beginning of the twentieth century, it was the first such museum in Poland. Spread out in a field overlooking the nearby Lake Goluń, the *skansen*'s location couldn't be more peaceful. After the real towns and villages of the region there's a slightly artificial "reservation" feel to the place – buildings without the people – but the *skansen* is clearly a labour of love, an expression of local determination to preserve and popularize traditional Kashubian folk culture. Most people join the hourly **guided tours** round the site (English- and German-speaking guides are available in summer) since most of the buildings are kept locked when a guide's not present.

The panoply of buildings, most culled from local farms, range from old windmills and peasant cottages to barns, wells, furnaces, a pigsty and a working sawmill. The early eighteenth-century **wooden church** from the village of Swornegacie in the southwest of the region, renovated on the *skansen* grounds, is a treat: topped by a traditional wood-shingled roof, the interior is covered with regional folk-baroque designs and biblical motifs, with the patron St Barbara and a ubiquitous all-seeing Eye of God peering down from the centre of the ceiling. The thatched cottage interiors are immaculately restored with original beds and furniture to reflect the typical domestic setup of the mostly extremely poor Kashubian peasantry of a century ago. Even the old-style front gardens have been laid out exactly as they used to be. Finances permitting, there are plans to expand the collection of buildings to reflect a broader selection of regional architectural styles.

Skansen aside, lakeside Wdzydze Kiszewskie is another popular local holiday spot. In summer, **private rooms** are on offer in the houses by the lake, and there's a seasonal **youth hostel** and a number of **camping sites**.

The Wisła delta

Following the **Wisła** south from Gdańsk takes you into the heart of the territory once ruled by the **Teutonic Knights**. Physically, the river delta is a flat plain of isolated villages, narrow roads and drained farmland, while the river itself is wide, slow-moving and dirty, the landscape all open vistas under frequently sullen skies. Towns are an occasional and imposing presence, mostly comprising a string of fortresses overlooking the river from which the religio-militaristic Teutonic order controlled the lucrative medieval grain trade – it was under their protection that merchant colonists from the northern Hanseatic League cities established themselves down the Wisła as far south as Toruń. The knights' architectural legacies are distinctive red-brick constructions: tower-churches, sturdy granaries and solid burghers' mansions surrounded by rings of defensive walls and protected by castles. **Malbork**, the knights' headquarters, is the prime example – a town settled within and below one of the largest fortresses of medieval Europe. Continuing downriver a string of lesser-fortified towns – **Kwidzyn**, **Gniew** and **Chełmno** – lead to the ancient city of **Toruń**.

During the Partition era – from the late eighteenth century up until World War I – this upper stretch of the Wisła was **Prussian** territory, an ownership that has left its own mark on the neat towns and cities. After 1918, part of the territory returned to Poland, while part remained in East Prussia. During World War II, as throughout this region, much was destroyed during the German retreat.

Travel connections aren't too bad in the area, with buses and trains between the main towns (and cross-river ferries at several points along the Wisła), all of which are within reasonable striking distance of Gdańsk.

Malbork

For Poles brought up on the novels of Henryk Sienkiewicz, the massive riverside fortress of **MALBORK** conjures up the epic medieval struggles between Poles and Germans that he so vividly described in *The Teutonic Knights*. Approached from any angle, the intimidating stronghold dominates the town, imparting the threatening atmosphere of an ancient military headquarters to an otherwise quiet, undistinguished and, following war damage, predominantly modern town.

The history of the town and castle is intimately connected with that of the **Teutonic Knights** (see box, p.204), who established themselves here in the late thirteenth century and proceeded to turn a modest fortress into the labyrinthine monster whose remains you can see today. After two centuries of Teutonic domination, the town returned to Polish control in 1457, and the Knights, in dire financial difficulties, were forced to sell the castle to the Czechs, who in turn sold it to the Polish Crown. For the next three hundred years the castle was a royal residence, used by Polish monarchs as a stopover en route between Warsaw and Gdańsk. Following the Partitions, the **Prussians** turned it into a barracks and set about dismantling large sections of the masonry – a process halted only by public outcry in Berlin. The eastern wings aside, the castle came through World War II (when it was used as a POW camp) largely unharmed until 1945, when a Soviet assault caused serious damage to the eastern wings and destroyed most of the old town. The damaged sections have been painstakingly restored to something resembling their original state and Malbork is now on the UNESCO World Heritage list.

Other than the castle, there is little to say about Malbork, whose Stare Miasto was virtually razed in World War II. Evidence of the intense fighting which took place in these parts can be seen in the **Commonwealth War Graves** on the edge of the town.

The fortress

The approach to the main **fortress** (Tues–Sun: May–Sept 9am–7pm; Oct–April 9am–3pm; 23zł) is through the old outer castle, a zone of utility buildings that

The Teutonic Knights

The Templars, the Hospitallers and the **Teutonic Knights** were the three major military-religious orders to emerge from the Crusades. Founded in 1190 as a fraternity serving the sick, the order combined the ascetic ideals of monasticism with the military training of a knight. Eclipsed by their rivals in the Holy Land, the Knights – the **Teutonic Order of the Hospital of St Mary**, to give them their full title – established their first base in Poland at Chełmno in 1225, following an appeal from Duke Konrad of Mazovia for protection against the pagan Lithuanians, Jacwingians and Prussians. The Knights proceeded to annihilate the Prussian population, establishing German colonies in their place. It's ironic that the people known as Prussians in modern European history are not descendants of these original Slavic populations, but the Germanic settlers who annihilated them.

With the loss of their last base in Palestine in 1271, the Teutonic Knights started looking around for a European site for their headquarters. Three years later they began the construction of Malbork Castle – **Marienburg**, "the fortress of Mary", as they named it – and in 1309 the Grand Master transferred here from Venice.

Economically the Knights' chief targets were control of the Hanseatic cities and of the trade in Baltic amber, over which they gained a virtual monopoly. **Politically** their main aim was territorial conquest, especially to the east – which, with their **religious zealotry** established in Palestine, they saw as a crusade to set up a theocratic political order. Although the Polish kings soon began to realize the mistake of inviting the Knights in, until the start of the fifteenth century most European monarchs were still convinced by the Order's religious ideology; their cause was aided by the fact that the Lithuanians, Europe's last pagan population, remained unconverted until well into the fourteenth century.

The showdown with Poland came in 1410 at the **Battle of Grunwald**, one of the most momentous clashes of medieval Europe. Recognizing a common enemy, an allied force of Poles and Lithuanians inflicted the first really decisive defeat on the Knights, yet failed to follow up the victory and allowed them to retreat to Malbork unchallenged. It wasn't until 1457 that they were driven out of their Malbork stronghold by King Kazimierz Jagiełło. The Grand Master of the Order fled eastward to Königsberg.

In 1525, the Grand Master, Albrecht von Hohenzollern, having converted to Lutheranism, decided to dissolve the Order and transform its holdings into a **secular duchy**, with himself as its head. Initially, political considerations meant he was obliged to accept the Polish king as his overlord, and thus he paid homage before King Sigismund in the marketplace at Kraków in 1525. But the duchy had full jurisdiction over its internal affairs, which allowed for the adoption of Protestantism as its religion. This turned out to be a crucially important step in the history of Europe, as it gave the ambitious Hohenzollern family a power base outside the structures of the Holy Roman Empire, an autonomy that was later to be of vital importance to them in their ultimately successful drive to weld the German nation into a united state.

was never rebuilt after the war. Entrance is technically by Polish-language guided tour only, but in practice it's fine to wander round the castle at your own pace. English-language guides are also available (150zł), though you'll need to contact the ticket office at least a day in advance (☎055/647 0802).

Passing over the moat and through the daunting main gate, you come to the **Middle Castle**, built following the Knights' decision to move their headquarters to Malbork in 1309. The right-hand side of the spacious **courtyard** is taken up by the **Grand Master's palace**. The fourteenth-century chambers are wonderfully elegant, with slender pillars leading up to delicately traced vaulting. The design is based upon a palm tree – a link with the Order's crusading past in the Middle East. Leading off from the courtyard are a host of dark, cavernous chambers, many of which house temporary exhibitions on the history of the castle and the Teutonic Knights. If you're visiting in summer, the main courtyard provides the spectacular backdrop for the castle's son et lumière shows.

From the Middle Castle a drawbridge leads under a portcullis into the smaller courtyard of the **High Castle**, the oldest part of the fortress. At the centre of the courtyard is the castle well – in the safest possible position to avoid the danger of besieging armies poisoning the water supply – and all along one side are the kitchens, with an enormous chimney over the stove running straight through five storeys to the roof.

The stairs just to the right as you enter the smaller courtyard lead to a first-floor balcony that runs its perimeter. From here you can enter the beautiful **Chapter House** with further palm leaf vaulting and wall paintings of Grand Masters of the Order. The balcony also gives access to the the knights' and monks' dormitories and to the **Church of Our Lady**, currently undergoing extensive restoration but nonetheless an impressive space.

A long, narrow corridor leads away from the courtyard to the *dansker*, positioned over the old moat. This tower had a dual purpose – the knights' final refuge in times of war, in peacetime it functioned as the castle lavatory. From the second floor above the courtyard you can climb the castle's central tower (6zł) for fantastic views over the plains. Back down at the drawbridge, a path leads round the outer walls of the High Castle to the **Chapel of St Anne**, where eleven former Grand Masters were buried, and the castle mill, which has been reconstructed on the east wall.

When you've finished looking around inside, head over the newly built wooden **footbridge** leading from the castle to the other side of the river (technically the Nogat – a tributary of the Wisła), where the view allows you to appreciate what a Babylonian project the fortress must have seemed to medieval visitors and the people of the surrounding country.

Practicalities

The **train station** and **bus station** are sited next to each other about ten minutes' walk south of the castle. Malbork is on the main Gdańsk–Warsaw line: the plethora of trains from Gdańsk (1hr–1hr 30min), as well as a regular bus service, ensures that it's easy to treat Malbork as a day-trip. There's a **tourist office** (Mon–Fri 10am–6pm, Sat & Sun 10am–2pm; ☎055/272 5599) at the southeastern side of the castle at Piastowska 15 – you'll pass it if approaching the castle from the train and bus stations – which will direct you towards the small number of **private rooms** (❷) in town.

The best located of the **hotels** is without doubt the *Zamek* (☎055/272 8400; ❼), right at the castle gates in the Knights' hospital. The decor here is brown and heavy but the en-suite rooms are very comfortable; as it's already an established tourist favourite, it's best to book ahead. Competing with the *Zamek* for comfort is the *Stary Malbork* at ul. 17 Marca 16–17 (☎055/647 2400; ❻) in a tastefully renovated Art Nouveau apartment building. Of the other places in town, the *Zbyszko*, between castle and stations at ul. Kościuszki 43 (☎055/272 2640; ❺), is a more modern affair with plain but respectable en suites with TV; while the *Parkowy*, 1.5km north of the castle at ul. Portowa 3 (☎055/272 2413; ❸), offers exceedingly neat and cosy en suites (loud carpets notwithstanding) with TV. The *Szarotka*, near the bus and train stations at ul. Dworcowa 1 (☎055/270 1444; ❶) offers careworn but clean rooms with shared facilities; and there's a basic **youth hostel**, 500m south of the castle at ul. Żeromskiego 45 (☎055/272 2408). There's a decent **campsite** at ul. Portowa 3 (June–Sept; ☎055/272 2413), next to the *Parkowy*; expect to pay around 15zł per person.

For a quick meal there are several **snack stalls** around the castle entrance, including a couple of floating bar-restaurants moored on the riverbank below. The **restaurant** of the *Hotel Zamek* is a very good source of traditional Polish fare, as is the *Restauracja Piwniczka*, entered through the river-facing side of the castle walls. The self-explanatory *Pizza*, on ul. Kościuszki diagonally opposite the *Zbyszko Hotel*, offers simple and filling pizza pies, pasta dishes, and truly excellent *pierogi*.

Kwidzyn and around

Set in the loop of a tributary a few kilometres east of the Wisła, **KWIDZYN** is a smallish fortified town ringed by a sprawling, dirty industrial belt. The first stronghold established by the Teutonic Knights – in the 1230s, some forty years before the move to Malbork – its original fortress was rapidly joined by a bishop's residence and cathedral. Three hundred years on, the castle was pulled down and rebuilt but the cathedral and bishop's chapterhouse were left untouched. Unlike the rest of the Stare Miasto area, the entire complex survived 1945 unscathed.

Most of the **castle** is poised on a hilltop over the River Liwa, but the immediately striking feature is the tower, stranded out in what used to be the river-bed and connected to the main building by means of a precarious roofed walkway – it looks more like the remains of a bridge-builder's folly than a solid defensive structure. Originally the castle toilet, the best views of it and the castle as a whole are from the other side of the river. Ranged around a large open courtyard, the castle houses a rather run-down local **museum** (Tues–Sun 9am–3pm; 6zł). Despite later reconstructions, the large, moody **cathedral** adjoining the castle retains several original Gothic features, the most noteworthy being a beautiful late-fourteenth-century mosaic in the southern vestibule.

Cathedral and castle apart, Kwidzyn is a pretty undistinguished place which doesn't demand an overnight stop. If you do need to stay, the most convenient **hotels** are the *Kaskada* opposite the train station (ul. Chopina 42, ☎055/279 3731; ❹); or the *Miłosna*, on route 55, 3km south of the centre (ul. Miłosna 5, ☎055/279 4052; ❺). The town has regular **bus** services to Malbork and **trains** run to Gdańsk twice daily (1hr 45min).

West from Kwidzyn

If you're travelling by car, it's worth continuing west from Kwidzyn some 20km through the lush farmland of the Wisła delta to the riverbanks just beyond the village of Janowo and the **ferry** crossing over to **Gniew**. "Ferry" (*prom*) in this case means an amazingly dilapidated old contraption operated by an extraordinary mechanical chain system. It's one of three similarly archaic-looking vessels in operation along the northern stretches of the Wisła. All run from 7am to 5.30pm. The trip costs nothing, since by law the local authorities are obliged to provide free transportation wherever a river "breaks" a road. The boats aren't large – the maximum car load at Janowo is four at a time – so in summer especially, car passengers may face a bit of a wait for the blustery ten-minute boat trip. It's an experience not to be missed though, giving you a unique chance to see the river from close up.

Gniew

Sixty-five kilometres south of Gdańsk, the little town of **GNIEW** is one of the most attractive and least known of the former Teutonic strongholds studding the northern shores of the Wisła, an out-of-the-way place that's worth a stopover. Clearly visible from the ferry thanks to the Wisła's changes of course, the town has been left stranded on the top of a hill a kilometre back from the river. Gniew's original strategic location overlooking the river led the Teutonic Knights to set themselves up here in the 1280s, taking the place over from the Cistercian Order and completing the requisite castle within a few years. Untouched by wars, it's a quiet and by Polish standards remarkably well-preserved country town, one of those places which modern history seems simply to have passed by. It's also a curiously unknown spot – the standard tourist literature barely mentions the town – so you're unlikely to encounter many other visitors, the odd German tour group excepted. However, the place's popularity is gradually increasing thanks to the activities of the enthusiastic group of locals who have now started organizing medieval jousting tournaments and costume battle re-enactments during the summer months – check with the Gdańsk tourist offices for current details.

At the centre of the Stare Miasto the solid-looking brick **town hall** provides the focus of such action as the deserted surrounding square sees – mostly kids kicking their footballs against the building. The atmosphere is enhanced however by the many original sixteenth- and eighteenth-century dwellings lining the square. West of here, the Gothic **parish church** is a typically dark, moody building, filled with wizened old characters reciting their rosaries. A short walk east of the square brings you to the battered remains of the **castle** (May–Oct Tues–Sun 10am–5pm; 8zł), a huge deserted ruin of a place that would make an ideal Gothic horror movie set, its cavernous heights dimly hinting at its past glories. A little way behind the castle, perched on the spur overlooking the river, the **Pałac Marysienkich** (Marysieńki Palace) – added on by King Jan Sobieski in the late seventeenth century for his wife – is a real find: a reasonably priced and scenically situated **hotel** (☎058/535 4949; ❺) with an excellent restaurant and one of the best views over the Wisła in the region. There's also a summer-only **hostel**, the *Dormitorium*, occupying a wing of the castle (☎058/535 2162).

Reasonably regular **buses** to and from Gdańsk (1hr 10min) stop off at Gniew from the shelter on the western edge of the town centre.

Chełmno

The hilltop town of **CHEŁMNO**, another important old Prussian centre, escaped World War II undamaged and has remained untouched by postwar industrial development. Perhaps the most memorable thing about the place is its atmosphere – an archetypal quiet rural town, steeped in the powerful mixture of the Polish and Prussian that characterizes the region as a whole.

Although a Polish stronghold is known to have existed here as early as the eleventh century, Chełmno really came to life in 1225 with the arrival of the Teutonic Knights. They made the town their first political and administrative centre, which led to rapid and impressive development. An academy was founded in 1386 on the model of the famed University of Bologna and, despite the damage inflicted by the Swedes in the 1650s, the town continued to thrive right up to the time of the Partitions, when it lapsed into provincial Prussian obscurity.

The Stare Miasto

On foot, the best way to enter the Stare Miasto is via the **Grudziądz Gate**, a well-proportioned fourteenth-century Gothic construction topped by fine

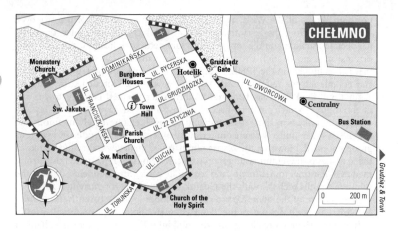

Renaissance gables that leads to the pedestrianized ul. Grudziądzka: if you're travelling by car enter by ul. Ducha. Grudziądzka continues to the Prussian ensemble of the **Rynek**, a grand open space at the heart of the grid-like network of streets. Gracing the centre of the square is the brilliant-white **town hall**, with an exuberantly decorated facade. Rebuilt in the 1560s on the basis of an earlier Gothic hall, its elegant exterior, decorated attic and soaring tower are one of the great examples of Polish Renaissance architecture. Inside there's a fine old courtroom and an appealing local **museum** (Tues–Fri 10am–4pm, Sat 10am–3pm, Sun 11am–2pm; 5zł), whose exhibits include an intriguing section devoted to brick production – traditionally the main building material in this part of Poland – with examples of how each individual brick was painstakingly smoothed down to the required size by hand. At the back of the town hall is the old Chełmno measure, the **pręt**, used up until the nineteenth century. Employed in the original building of the town, it explains why all the streets are the same width. Clearly a town of individual predisposition, it also used to have its own unique system of weights.

Most of Chełmno's seven churches are Gothic, their red-brick towers and facades punctuating the streets of the Stare Miasto at regular intervals. Best of the lot is the **parish church** standing just west of the Rynek, an imposing thirteenth-century building with a fine carved doorway. The interior retains sculpted pillars, a Romanesque stone font and fragmentary frescoes. Further west, past St James's Church (Św. Jakuba), is an early fourteenth-century **monastery**, former home to a succession of Cistercian and Benedictine orders, and now to Catholic sisters, who run a handicapped children's hostel here. Its church, whose Baroque altar is reputed to be the tallest in the country, features some original Gothic painting and a curious twin-level nave. The church backs onto the western corner of the town walls, crumbling but complete – and walkable for excellent views over the Wisła and low-lying plains.

Practicalities

The **bus station** is on ul. Dworcowa, a fifteen-minute walk from the Stare Miasto. The **tourist office** is inside the town hall (Mon–Fri 9am–5pm; ☎056/686 2104; ⓦwww.chelmno.pl). Central accommodation options boil down to the *Centralny*, just up from the bus station at ul. Dworcowa 23 (☎056/686 0212; ❸), and the small, family-run *Hotelik*, just inside the

Grudziądz Gate at Podmurna 3 (☎056/676 2030; ❹), both of which offer cosy en suites. Both hotels have restaurants; otherwise there's the usual selection of cafés and pizza bars ranged around the Rynek.

Toruń and around

Poles are apt to wax lyrical on the glories of their ancient cities, and with **TORUŃ** – the biggest and most important of the Hanseatic trading centres along the Wisła – it's more than justified. Miraculously surviving the recurrent wars afflicting the region, the historic centre remains one of the country's most evocative, bringing together a rich assembly of architectural styles. The city's main claim to fame is as the birthplace of **Nicolaus Copernicus** (see box, p.222), whose house still stands. Today, it is a university city: large, reasonably prosperous and – once you're through the standard postwar suburbs – one with a definitely cultured air.

Some history

The pattern of Toruń's early history is similar to that of other towns along the northern Wisła. Starting out as a Polish settlement, it was overrun by Prussian tribes from the east towards the end of the twelfth century, and soon afterwards the Teutonic Knights moved in. The Knights rapidly developed the town, thanks to its access to the burgeoning river-borne grain trade, a position further consolidated with its entry to the **Hanseatic League**. As in rival Gdańsk, economic prosperity was expressed in a mass of building projects through the thirteenth century; together these make up the majority of the historic sites in the city.

Growing disenchantment with the Teutonic Knights' rule and heavy taxation in the fifteenth century, especially among the merchants, led to the formation of the **Prussian Union** in 1440, based in Toruń. In 1454, as war broke out between the Knights and Poland, the townspeople destroyed the castle in Toruń and chased the Order out of town. The 1466 **Treaty of Toruń** finally terminated the Knights' control of the area.

The sixteenth and seventeeth centuries brought even greater wealth as the town thrived on extensive royal privileges and increased access to goods from all over Poland. The Swedish invasion of the 1650s was the first significant setback, but the really decisive blow to the city's fortunes came a century later with the Partitions, when Toruń was annexed to Prussia and thus severed from its hinterlands, which by now were under Russian control. Like much of the region, Toruń was subjected to systematic Germanization, but as in many other cities a strongly Polish identity remained, clearly manifested in the cultural associations that flourished in the latter part of the nineteenth century. The twentieth century saw Toruń returned to Poland (under the terms of the 1919 Versailles Treaty as part of the "Polish Corridor" that so enraged Hitler), captured by the Nazis during World War II and liberated in 1945.

Arrival, information and accommodation

The main stations are on opposite sides of the Stare Miasto. Toruń Główny, the main **train station**, is south of the river. It's only about 1km to the city centre but walking's not much fun as you'll need to use a busy road bridge to cross the Wisła. A better option is to take bus #22 or #27 (every 20min) from the stop outside the main station entrance and get off at pl. Rapackiego, just to the west of the Stare Miasto. Some slow trains stop at Toruń Miasto station, about 1km east of the centre. The **bus station** is on ul. Dąbrowskiego, a short walk north of the centre.

The well-organized municipal **tourist office**, at Rynek Staromiejski 25 (Mon & Sat 9am–4pm, Tues–Fri 9am–6pm, plus Sun 9am–1pm in July & Aug only; ☎056/621 0931), doles out free brochures and maps and is a useful source of information for the whole region.

Hotels

Heban ul. Małe Garbary 7 ☎056/652 1555, ⓦwww.hotel-heban.com.pl. Historic town house in the centre with plush rooms, the larger ones decorated in lavish Second Empire style. ❼

Helios ul. Kraszewskiego 1/3 ☎056/619 6550, ⓦwww.orbis.pl. Orbis joint in a modern building recently renovated to high standards. ❼

Kopernik ul. Wola Zamkowa 16 ☎056/616 2490 ⓦwww.kopernik.torun.pl. Army-owned and very well-run place, 5 minutes' walk from the Stare Miasto. Modern, civilized rooms with TV and shower. ❺

Kosmos ul. Ks. Popiełuszki 2 ☎056/622 8900, ⓦwww.orbis.pl. The second-string Orbis joint in

town; slightly less plush than the *Helios*, but enjoys a pleasant site near the river. ❻

Petite Fleur ul. Piekary 25 ☎056/663 4400 ⓦwww.hotel.torun.com.pl. Small hotel with an intimate feel a stone's throw from the Rynek. Rooms are simple and bright with pine floors and furnishings and modern bathrooms. ❻

Pod Czarną Różą ul. Rabiańska 11 ☎056/621 9637. Another small and cosy Stare Miasto choice. All rooms come with TV and shower; most come with reasonably plush furnishings and warm colours. ❺

Pod Orłem ul. Mostowa 17 ☎056/622 5024, ⓦwww.hotel.torun.pl. Good-value en suites with TV, in a central location. The walls and ceilings are paper-thin, however. ❹

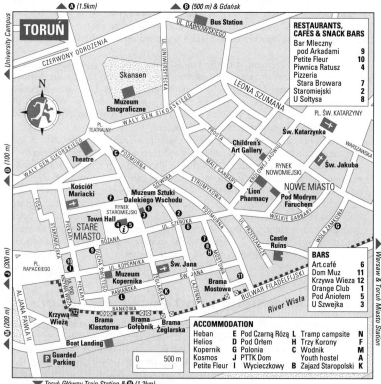

RESTAURANTS, CAFÉS & SNACK BARS

Bar Mleczny pod Arkadami	9
Petite Fleur	10
Piwnica Ratusz	4
Pizzeria Stara Browara	7
Staromiejski	2
U Sołtysa	8

BARS

Art.café	6
Dom Muz	11
Krzywa Wieza	12
Orange Club	1
Pod Aniołem	5
U Szwejka	3

ACCOMMODATION

Heban	E	Pod Czarną Różą L	Tramp campsite N
Helios	D	Pod Orłem H	Trzy Korony F
Kopernik	G	Polonia C	Wodnik M
Kosmos	J	PTTK Dom A	Youth hostel A
Petite Fleur	I	Wycieczkowy B	Zajazd Staropolski K

Polonia pl. Teatralny 5 ☏ 056/622 3028. Some rooms are on the small side, but all are comfortable and reasonably tastefully decorated and most have views of the elegant theatre across the road. ❺

PTTK Dom Wycieczkowy ul. Legionów 24 ☏ 056/622 3855. Basic but clean and well-run place just north of the bus station. Cramped 4- or 5-person dorms for 35zł per person, or simple doubles. Bathrooms in the hallway. Popular with students and school groups during the academic year. ❸

Trzy Korony Rynek Staromiejski 21 ☏ 056/622 6031. Ageing, slightly gloomy establishment, but it's clean and enjoys an enviable location on the edge of the main square. En-suite rooms with TV, those with shared facilities without. ❸

Wodnik ul. Bulwar Filadelfijski 12 ☏ 056/655 4672, ⓦ www.hotelwodnik.com.pl. Whitewashed concrete building that looks a bit like a Mediter-ranean package hotel, right by the river just west of the centre. Rooms are tired but functional and all have shower and TV. Hotel residents can use the outdoor swimming pool next door in summer. ❹

Zajazd Staropolski ul. Żeglarska 10/14 ☏ 056/622 6060. Comfortable place conveniently situated just down from the Rynek. Some rooms retain 1970s brown colour schemes, although most are bright and modern in style. ❻

Youth hostel and campsite

Youth Hostel ul. Józefa 22/24 ☏ 056/654 4107. Two kilometres northwest of the Stare Miasto – bus #11 from the stop opposite the train station access road passes by. ❶

Tramp ul. Kujawska 14 ☏ 056/654 7187. Campsite a short walk west of the train station, with some bungalows for rent (❶) as well as tent space, and a partly wooded setting near the river.

The City

The historic core of Toruń is divided into Stare Miasto and Nowe Miasto areas, both established in the early years of Teutonic rule. Traditional economic divisions are apparent here, the Stare Miasto quarter being home for the merchants, the Nowe Miasto for the artisans; each had its own square, market area and town hall.

Overlooking the river from a gentle rise, the medieval centre constitutes a relatively small section of the modern city and is clearly separated from it by a ring of signs pointing to the centre: ask for the way to the Stare Miasto. For motorists, the Stare Miasto centre's impenetrable one-way system is pretty much a case of "abandon hope all ye who enter here" – you're better off walking.

The Stare Miasto

The **Stare Miasto** (Old Town) area is the obvious place to start looking around – and as usual it's the **Rynek**, in particular the **town hall**, that provides the focal point. Town halls don't come much bigger or more striking than this: raised in the late fourteenth century on the site of earlier cloth halls and trading stalls, it's a tremendous, if rather austere, statement of civic pride. A three-storey brick structure topped by a sturdy tower, its outer walls are punctuated by indented windows, framed by a rhythmic succession of high arches peaking just beneath the roof, and complemented by graceful Renaissance turrets and high gables.

The south side entrance leads to an inner courtyard surrounded by fine brick doorways, the main one leading to the **town museum** (Tues–Sun: May–Sept 10am–6pm; Oct–April 10am–4pm; 7.50zł), which now occupies much of the building. Over the centuries Toruń's wealth attracted artists and craftsmen of every type, and it's their work that features strongest here. Most of the ground floor – once the wine cellar – is devoted to medieval artefacts, with a gorgeous collection of the **stained glass** for which the city was famed and some fine **sculptures**, especially the celebrated "Beautiful Madonnas" – in which the Virgin is portrayed swooning in an S-shaped posture of grace. Also housed on this floor is a collection of material relating to the guilds founded by the city's craftsmen, including massive ceremonial drinking cups and wrought-iron street signs. On the first floor, **paintings** take over, with rooms covered in portraits of Polish kings and wealthy Toruń citizens. A small portrait of the most famous city burgher, Copernicus, basks in the limelight of a Baroque gallery. Before leaving, it's worth the additional 6.50zł to climb the **tower** for the view of the city and the course of the Wisła, stretching into the plain on the southern horizon.

Lining the square itself are the stately mansions of the Hansa merchants, many of whose high parapets and decorated facades are preserved intact. The finest houses flank the east side of the square. No. 35, next to one of the Copernicus family houses, is the fifteenth-century **Pod Gwiazdą**, with a finely modelled late Baroque facade; inside, a superbly carved wooden staircase ends with a statue of Minerva, spear in hand. The house is now the small **Muzeum Sztuki Dalekiego Wschodu** (Museum of Far Eastern Art; Tues–Sun: May–Sept 10am–6pm; Oct–April 10am–4pm; 6.50zł), based on a private collection of art from China, India and other Far Eastern countries. There is a separate gallery in the basement belonging to the "U Kalimacha" cultural society.

Off to the west of the square stands the **Kościół Mariacki** (St Mary's Church), a large fourteenth-century building with elements of its early decoration retained in the sombre interior. There's no tower to the building, apparently because the church's Franciscan founders didn't permit such things; monastic modesty may also help to explain the high wall separating the church from the street. Back across the square, on the other side of the town hall, a noble bronze **statue** of Copernicus watches over the crowds scurrying round the building.

South of the square, on the dusty, narrow and atmospheric ul. Żeglarska, is **Kościół św. Jana** (St John's Church), another large, magnificent Gothic structure, whose clockface served as a reference point for loggers piloting their way downstream. The presbytery, the oldest part of the building, dates from the 1260s, but the main nave and aisles were not completed till the mid-fifteenth century. Entering from the heat of the summer sun, you're immediately enveloped in an ancient calm, heightened by the damp, chilly air rising from the flagstones and by the imposing rose window. The tower, completed late in the church's life, houses a magnificent fifteenth-century *Tuba Dei*, the largest bell in Poland outside Kraków, which can be heard all over town. Opening hours depend on when a service is being held. Check the notice board outside for current details, which will include at least one daily service.

West from the church runs ul. Kopernika, halfway down which you'll find the **Muzeum Kopernika** (Copernicus Museum; Tues–Sun: May–Sept 10am–6pm; Oct–April 10am–4pm; 7.50zł), installed in the high brick house where the great man was born. Restored in recent decades to something resembling its original layout, this Gothic mansion contains a studiously assembled collection of Copernicus artefacts: facsimiles of the momentous *De Revolutionibus*, models of gyroscopes and other astronomical instruments, original household furniture and early portraits. There's also a son et lumière display (performance times posted at the ticket desk; 6.50zł) on the city's evolution, worth seeing for the fascinating model of medieval Toruń.

Ulica Kopernika and its atmospheric side streets, lined with crumbling Gothic mansions and granaries, blend past glory and shabbier contemporary reality. Further down towards the river, the high, narrow streets meet the old defensive **walls**, now separating the Stare Miasto from the main road. These fortifications survived virtually intact right up to the late nineteenth century, only for some enterprising Prussian town planners to knock them down, sparing only a small section near the river's edge. This short fragment remains today, the walls interspersed by the old gates and towers at the ends of the streets.

To the west, at the bottom of ul. Pod Krzywą Wieżą, stands the mid-fourteenth-century **Krzywa Wieża** (Crooked Tower), followed in quick succession by the **Brama Klasztorna** (Monastery Gate), **Brama Gołębnik** (Dovecote Tower) and **Brama Żeglarska** (Sailors' Gate), all from the same period, the last originally leading to the main harbour. Head through Brama Klasztorna down to the riverbank to find a landing stage, from which in summer you can take a ninety-minute **boat trip** downriver and back.

Heading east, past the large **Brama Mostowa** (Bridge Gate), brings you to the ruins of the Teutonic Knights' **castle**, sandwiched between the two halves of the medieval city. While the castle here was nowhere near as massive as the later Malbork fortress, the scale of what's left is enough to leave you impressed by the Toruń citizenry's efforts in laying waste to it. For a złoty you can wander through the ruins (during daylight hours) and get some idea of the scale of the place. The castle grounds are the location for occasional summertime concerts (folk and classical) – check with the tourist offices for details – and there is an open-air café during the warmer months.

The Nowe Miasto

Following ul. Przedzamcze north from the castle brings you onto ul. Szeroka, the main thoroughfare linking the Stare and Nowe Miasto districts. Less grand than its mercantile neighbour, the **Nowe Miasto** still boasts a number of illustrious commercial residences, most of them grouped around the **Rynek Nowomiejski**. On the west side of this square, the fifteenth-century *Pod Modrym Faruchem* inn (no. 8) and the Gothic pharmacy with a golden lion as its shop sign at no. 13 are particularly striking, while the old *Murarska* inn at no. 17, on the north side, houses a children's art gallery (closed Sunday) with work from all around Poland and further afield.

The fourteenth-century **Kościół św. Jakuba** (St James's Church), south of the market area of the Rynek, completes the city's collection of Gothic churches. Unusual features of this brick basilica are its flying buttresses – a common enough sight in Western Europe but extremely rare in Poland. Inside, mainly Baroque decoration is relieved by occasional Gothic frescoes, panel paintings and sculpture – most notably a large fourteenth-century crucifix.

North of the square, ul. Prosta leads onto Wały Sikorskego, a ring road which more or less marks the line of the old fortifications. Across it there's a small park, in the middle of which stands the former arsenal, now the **Muzeum Etnograficzne** (Ethnographic Museum; Tues–Fri 9am–4pm, Sat & Sun 10am–4pm; 7.50zł), dealing with the customs and crafts of northern Poland. The displays covering historical traditions are enhanced by imaginative attention to contemporary folk artists, musicians and writers, whose work is actively collected and promoted by the museum. The surrounding park houses an enchanting *skansen* containing an enjoyable and expanding collection of traditional wooden buildings from nearby regions, including a blacksmith's shop, windmill, water mill and two complete sets of farm buildings from Kashubia.

West of the centre

If you're feeling the need for a bit of tranquillity, there's a pleasant **park** along the water's edge west of the city centre, reached by tram #3 or #4 from pl. Rapackiego. At weekends you'll be joined at the waterside by picnickers and the odd group of horse-riders, and there's a riverbank walk that's very enjoyable, particularly the section between the two great bridges straddling the mighty Wisła.

North of the park, the **Bielany** district houses the main section of the university campus, largely unmemorable in itself but it's the location of several of the really lively student clubs and discos (see below). To get here, take bus #11 or #15.

Eating, drinking and entertainment

There's an excellent choice of **places to eat** in Toruń. Pizza is particularly popular – it's impossible to walk the streets of the Stare Miasto without bumping into a cheap pizza joint every 100m or so. **Cafés** and **bars** are in plentiful supply, with daytime pavement-café places on streets such as ul. Szeroka providing an opportunity to enjoy the atmosphere of the Stare Miasto. The riverbank also provides good outdoor café spots on warm summer nights.

Restaurants and snack bars

Bar Mleczny pod Arkadami On the corner of Różana and św. Ducha. Traditional fast food, including filling *barszcz*, bean soups, pancakes and takeaway waffles (*gofry*).

Petite Fleur ul. Piekary 25 ☎ 056/663 4400. More formal and expensive than most in Toruń, this hotel restaurant is a great place for classic Polish and European meat dishes.

Piwnica Ratusz Rynek Staromiejski. A steep flight of brick stairs on the west side of the hall leads down to this medieval cellar with whitewashed vaulted ceilings and heavy wooden tables. A good place for a solid Polish meat-and-potatoes meal, washed down with a glass of beer.

Pizzeria Stara Browara ul. Mostowa 17. A student favourite and one of the best of the sit-down pizza places.

Staromiejski ul. Szczytna 2/4. Plusher than the *Stara Browara* and serves a bigger range of pasta dishes.

U Sołtysa ul. Mostowa 17. More atmosphere than the *Piwnica Ratusz*, with dried herbs and mushrooms and various animal skins hanging from the

rafters, and a range of traditional dishes served up with folk staples such as *kasza* (buckwheat) instead of the usual fries.

Bars

Art.café Szeroka 35. Disco-bar specializing in techno and house. Open 5pm–2am, later on Fri & Sat nights.

Dom Muz Podmurna 1/3. Towards the southern end of the street, a basement bar hosting gigs by an eclectic variety of local musicians.

Krzywa Wieza Pod Krzywą Wieżą 1/3. Cosy little bar that feels unchanged since medieval times, nestling in the Stare Miasto battlements.

Orange Club 33 Rynek Staromiejski. Bright and stylish cocktail bar just off the old town square in a grassy courtyard.

Pod Aniołem Rynek Staromiejski. Best of the evening haunts, a wonderfully atmospheric vaulted cellar under the town hall. Often features live music, cabaret performances or DJs at weekends.

U Szwejka 34/38 Rynek Staromiejski. Another roomy cellar bar catering for boisterous pleasure-seekers at weekends.

Nightlife and entertainment

Some of the best **nightlife** in town happens in the university district, clustered on and around ul. Gagarina. The *Imperial*, Gagarina 17, is a cult student club of many years' standing that currently serves as a weekend disco and live

---

Toruń gingerbread

Don't leave town without picking up some **gingerbread** (*piernik*), a local speciality already popular here by the fourteenth century – as attested by the moulds in the town museum. It comes in ornate shapes: stagecoaches, eighteenth-century figures and Copernicus are among the most popular. Numerous shops round the Stare Miasto sell the stuff, notably the one at ul. Żeglarska 25. Watch your teeth, though: the traditional type intended for display is rock hard, while the edible variety usually comes shaped in small cakes or biscuits.

music venue, while *Od Nowa*, Gagarina 37a, is a theatre and rock/jazz venue (☎058/611 4593).

The grand old Toruń **theatre**, pl. Teatralny 1 (box office ☎056/622 5021), is home to one of the country's most highly regarded repertory companies. It's also worth checking the listings in the local newspaper for occasional classical **concerts** in the town hall and regular ones given by the Town Chamber Orchestra in the Dwór Artusa at Rynek Staromiejski 6 (☎056/622 8805, ⓦwww.artus.torun.pl).

The city has a number of regular **festivals**, notably the International Theatre Festival (May), which is the most prestigious theatrical event in Poland; a folk festival (June); and an international festival of cinematographers (late Nov/early Dec). Contact the tourist office for details.

Golub-Dobrzyń

About 35km east of Toruń, the elegant facades of the **castle** at **GOLUB-DOBRZYŃ** are a traditional Orbis poster favourite. While the town itself is nothing to write home about, the castle, located high up on a hill overlooking the town, is an impressive sight. Coming in on the long, straight approach road from Toruń, it is signposted off to the right just before you enter the town – if you're coming by bus ask the driver to drop you off near the castle (*zamek*). There's a regular **bus** service from Toruń (hourly on weekdays, somewhat less frequent at weekends).

A Teutonic stronghold, raised in the early 1300s on the site of an early Slav settlement overlooking the River Drwęca, the original castle was built on the square ground-plan with an arcaded central courtyard that survives today. Following the conclusion of the Treaty of Toruń (1466) the place fell into Polish hands; the real changes to the building came in the early 1600s, when acquired by Anna Waza, sister of King Sigismund III. The king's redoubtable sister, a polyglot and botanist reputed to have imported the first tobacco to Poland and planted it on the hills near the castle, had the whole place remodelled in Polish Renaissance style, adding the elegantly sculptured facades and Italianate courtyard you see today. After taking a severe battering during the Swedish wars of the 1650s the abandoned castle was left to crumble away, restoration work beginning following the town's final return to Polish territory in the postwar era.

The castle buildings

Entrance to the castle **museum** (Tues–Sun: June–Sept 9am–7pm; Oct–May 9am–4pm; 10zł) is by Polish-language guided tour only. Tours start every half an hour, though, given that they only last half an hour, are overpriced. The tour begins with a routine collection of straw shoes, local costumes and assorted wooden objects, many of them related to the river economy – and with no direct connection to the castle itself.

On the next floor, you'll be taken into the **banqueting hall** and former castle **chapel**. There's little original material here – even the walls themselves have been restored to the point of characterless sterility. The banqueting hall currently displays some atrociously bad local marquetry work (which your guide will inform you is all for sale): subjects include Winnie the Pooh and Harley Davidsons. The chapel is anything but religious in atmosphere, being filled to the brim with contemporary replicas of Polish battle standards from the Battle of Grunwald. The one redeeming feature of the tour is the array of old cannon on display here, with tiny fourteenth-century pieces, monster seventeenth-century contraptions and just about everything in between.

The rest of the rooms on this floor (which you won't get to see) once comprised the knights' living quarters: apparently everyone used to ride their horses straight up the stairs to their rooms, the resulting local legend holding that anyone who merely walks up the stairs is liable to break out in unexpected public fits of neighing. Out of the castle it's worth strolling to the viewpoint at the edge of the field next to the building for the view over the surroundings.

The upper rooms of the castle are now a fairly basic **hotel** (☎056/683 2455) run by PTTK with dorms and a couple of doubles (**❸**). This is often booked solid with groups so it's best to phone ahead. Down in the town the *Kaprys* at ul. Kilińskiego 7 (☎056/683 2447; **❷**) is very basic, though again it's worth ringing ahead if you can as there are only a few rooms. It has a reasonable Polish **restaurant**.

Every July (usually around the middle of the month) the field here is the scene of a major international **chivalry tournament**, with national teams of jousters battling it out on horseback: a spectacular event by all accounts, it's worth trying to catch the event if you're in the area at the time.

Ciechocinek

Twenty kilometres southeast of Toruń, and reached by frequent buses, **CIECHOCINEK** has rather more life about it than the normal run of Polish spas. The main feature is the **Park Zdrojowy** (Spa Park), just down from the bus station, which features floral gardens, tree-lined avenues and the usual spa buildings – pump room, a wooden open-air concert hall and bandstand. Far more intriguing, however, is the chance to stroll around **Park Tężniówy** (dawn–dusk; 2zł) immediately to the west. Here, in three separate sections stretching for over 1.5km, is the massive wall of wooden poles and twigs which makes up the **saltworks** (*tężnie*), begun in 1824 but not completed until several decades later. It's an extraordinary sight and all the more remarkable in that it can still be seen functioning as originally intended. The technology behind it is very simple: water from the town's saline springs is pumped to the top of the structure, from where it trickles back down through the twigs. This not only concentrates the salt, it also creates a reputedly recuperative atmosphere in the covered space below. Formerly, patients would walk through the interior of the structure, breathing in deeply as they went, though for conservation reasons this is unfortunately no longer permitted. You can climb onto the top of the saltworks for an extra 3zł, but somehow this seems a poor substitute.

East of the spa gardens, about 1km out along Wojska Polskiego, lies a dainty, turquoise-painted **Orthodox church**, erected in wood by carpenters from the Urals in the nineteenth century. A bold ochre bell tower was added in the 1990s. Unfortunately the interior is usually only accessible at service times (Sun 8.45am; Wed 4pm).

Once you've pottered around the parks and paused at one of the numerous ice cream/grilled sausage/beer huts, you'll probably be ready to head back to Toruń. However there's plenty of **accommodation** on hand if you want to stick around; the tourist office on ul. Zdrojowa (Biuro promocja Ciechocinka; Mon–Fri 8am–5pm) will find you a place to stay in a private room (**❷**) or a pension (**❸**). Of hotels, the *Amazonka*, in a peaceful spot at the end of ul. Traugatta 5 (☎054/283 1274; **❹**), is slightly run down but still good value and has its own stables. The *Pałac Targon* at ul. Raczyńskich 3 (☎054/416 6000; **❼**) is a luxurious set-up in a thoroughly renovated early twentieth-century villa. There are a number of **restaurants** in the town centre: *Przy Grzybie*, on the corner of Zdrojowa and Kościuszki, serves up simple meat-and-potatoes standards on the verandah of a rickety half-timbered building; while the *Targon* restaurant is the best place for fine dining.

East of Gdańsk

East from Gdańsk a short stretch of Baltic coastline leads up to the Russian border and, beyond, to Kaliningrad. An attractive and largely unspoilt region, the beaches of the **Wiślana Peninsula** and its approaches are deservedly popular seaside holiday country with Poles and, increasingly, returnee Germans – **Krynica Morska** is the resort to aim for if the idea of a few days on the beach appeals. Inland, the lush rural terrain, well watered by countless little tributaries of the Wisła, boasts a host of quiet, sturdy-looking old Prussian villages and, more chillingly, the Nazi concentration camp at **Sztutowo (Stutthof)**. This is the region most closely associated with astronomer **Nicolaus Copernicus**, and several towns, notably the medieval coastal centre of **Frombork**, bear his imprint. Of the other urban sites, **Elbląg** is a major former Prussian centre which has lost much of its old character, but remains an important transport hub.

As for **transport**, cross-country bus links are generally good in this part of the country, with the additional option of a scenic coastal train route along the southern shore of the Wiślany Lagoon and short-hop ferry services in several places.

Stutthof (Sztutowo) concentration camp

May our fate be a warning to you – not a legend. Should man grow silent, the very stones will scream.

Franciszek Fenikowski, Requiem Mass, quoted in camp guidebook

A few kilometres before the main road reaches the Wiślany Peninsula you will come to a sign announcing the Nazi concentration camp site at **Stutthof (Sztutowo)** – a rude awakening after passing through so much idyllic countryside. The first camp to be built inside what is now Poland (construction began in August 1939, before the German invasion), it started as an internment camp for Poles from the Free City of Danzig area but eventually became a Nazi extermination centre for the whole of northern Europe. The first Polish prisoners arrived at Stutthof early in September 1939, their numbers rapidly swelled by legions of other locals deemed "undesirables" by the Nazis. The decision to transform Stutthof into an international camp came in 1942, and eventually, in June 1944, the camp was incorporated into the Nazi scheme for the "Final Solution", the whole place being considerably enlarged and gas ovens installed. Although not on the same scale as other death camps, the toll in human lives speaks for itself: by the time the Red Army liberated the camp less than a year later in May 1945, an estimated 65,000–85,000 people had disappeared here.

Gdańsk–Krynica Morska and Elbląg–Krynica Morska **buses** pass by the short access road to the camp, which is at the western end of Sztutowo village.

The camp

In a large forest clearing surrounded by a wire fence and watchtowers, the peaceful, completely isolated setting of the **camp** (May to mid-Sept 8am–6pm; mid-Sept to April 8am–3pm; no guides Mondays, children under 13 not allowed) makes the whole idea of what went on here seem unreal at first. In through the entrance gate, though, like all the Nazi concentration camps, it's a shocking place to visit. Rows of stark wooden barrack blocks are interspersed with empty sites with nothing but the bare foundations left; much of the camp was torn down in 1945 and used as firewood. The narrow-gauge rail line still crisscrossing the site reminds you of the methodical planning that went into the policy of mass murder carried out here.

A **museum** housed in the barracks details life and death in the camp, the crude wooden bunks and threadbare mats indicating the "living" conditions the inmates had to endure. A harrowing gallery of photographs of gaunt-looking inmates brings home the human reality of what happened here: name, date of birth, country of origin and "offence" are listed below each of the faces staring down from the walls, the victims, of 25 different nationalities, including political prisoners, communists and gays. Over in the far corner of the camp stand the gas ovens and crematoria; flowers lie at the foot of the ovens, as well as a large monument to the murdered close by. "Offer them a rose from the warmth of your heart and leave – here lies infamy": the words from Polish poet Jan Górec-Rosiński's elegy on visiting the camp, quoted in the official guidebook, seem an appropriate response. During the summer, the museum cinema provides further evidence of the atrocities.

The Wiślana Peninsula

East from Sztutowo, the coast road leads onto the **Wiślana Peninsula** (Mierzeja Wiślana), a long, thin promontory dividing the sea from the Wiślana Lagoon (Zalew Wiślany), a landlocked tract of water known as the Frische Haff in Prussian times, which continues some 60km up towards Kaliningrad. On the northern side of the peninsula a dense covering of mixed beech and birch forest suddenly gives way to a luxuriant strip of sandy shore, while to the south the marshy shore beyond the road looks out over the tranquil lagoon – 15km across at its widest – and beyond that to Frombork and the mainland. A naturalist's paradise, the peninsula forest is idyllic walking country, while the northern coastline offers some of the best and most unspoilt beaches on the Baltic coast. The main resort, **Krynica Morska**, is full of hotels and pensions, and camping sites dotted along the peninsula provide an alternative source of local accommodation.

Kąty Rybackie

Four kilometres beyond Sztutowo, **KĄTY RYBACKIE** is an uneventful little resort town and fishing port with long sandy beaches stretching out as far as the eye can see along the coast. It's an easy place to get to, with Gdańsk–Krynica **buses** dropping off at a number of stops along Kąty's main street.

An information board at the western entrance to the village points the way towards Europe's largest **cormorant sanctuary**, which can be reached in 25 minutes by taking the path into the forest immediately opposite. Beautifully situated in the middle of thick woodland and sandy scrub, the sanctuary is a bird-watchers' delight, with excellent views of the colony. Trails head round the reserve before continuing northwards to hit the western end of Kąty's beach.

Krynica Morska

Twenty-five kilometres on, the road brings you to **KRYNICA MORSKA**, a few kilometres short of the Russian border and the main holiday resort on the peninsula. A relatively small-scale, uncommercialized resort, patronized by Poles and a smattering of Germans, Krynica straggles along a single main street, Gdańska, with a cluster of factory-owned rest homes on the wooded spine of the peninsula just above, beyond which lies an alluring white-sand beach.

Buses from Gdańsk come to a halt at the eastern end of Gdańska, just below the agglomeration of cafés and knick-knack shops that passes for the village centre on ul. Portowa. The beach is 15 minutes' walk north of here. Numerous houses in town offer **private rooms** (**❷**–**❸**), and the **tourist office**, at ul. Żeromskiego 6 (Mon–Sat 9am–8pm, Sun 10am–8pm; ☎055/247 6444, ⓦwww.mierzeja.pl), will make reservations both here and in other villages along the peninsula. Of the many **pensjonaty** in town, the *Polonia*, ul. Świerczewskiego 19 (☎055/247 6097; **❺**, including a superb breakfast and dinner), is friendly and comfortable, while the *Pod Lwem*, at the eastern end of the village at ul. Wodna 10 (☎055/247 6141; **❺**), is plusher, but still intimate in feel. The *Kahlberg*, at ul. Bosmańska 1 (☎055/247 6017, ⓦwww.kahlberg.mierzeja.pl; **❻**), is probably the town's most comfortable **hotel** and has its own tennis court.

As in most Polish seaside resorts, **eating** out in Krynica revolves around unpretentious snack-food outlets rather than snazzy sit-down restaurants. There's a knot of fish-and-chip stalls around the central streets of Portowa and Świerczewskiego, although one of the best places to try local fish from the Wiślany lagoon is the homely *Tawerna Yachtowa*, by the yachting harbour on the lagoon side of town. Cheap meals are also available from *Koga*, a bar on Gdańska built in the shape of a beached sailing ship, which is also one of the best places in town to **drink**.

Elbląg

The ancient settlement of **ELBLĄG**, after Gdańsk the region's most important town, was severely damaged at the end of World War II: its Stare Miasto centre, reputed to have been Gdańsk's equal in beauty, was totally flattened in the bitter fighting that followed the Nazi retreat in 1945. After languishing for decades in a postwar architectural limbo, at the beginning of the 1990s Elbląg finally started to get the regenerative pick-me-up it badly needed, and the Stare Miasto area is now being sympathetically and imaginatively rebuilt on the principle that investors copy the feel, if not necessarily the precise architectural details, of the city's prewar architecture. Though still not complete, enough is in place for you to judge the results.

The Town

The **Stare Miasto** is a small section at the heart of modern Elbląg. Some parts of the old city walls remain, most notably around the old **Brama Targowa** (Market Gate) at the northern entrance to the area. Elbląg played an important role in Hitler's wartime plans, specifically as a centre of U-boat production – the city's easy access to the sea, via the Wiślana Lagoon, made it a perfect spot. The empty area between the Brama Targowa and the cathedral hides the ruins of the dry docks where scores of newly produced submarines were launched into wartime action – no wonder the Soviets hammered the place.

Rising dramatically out of the old market place, the **cathedral**, rebuilt after the war, is another massive brick Gothic structure, its huge tower the biggest in the region. Despite the restorers' efforts to give the building back some of its former character, the job was clearly a bit of an uphill struggle. A couple of fine original Gothic triptychs and statues and some traces of the original ornamentation aside, the interior is mostly rather vapid postwar decoration, leaving the place with a sad, empty feel to it. The area immediately surrounding the cathedral is a combination of old Prussian-style mansions and new restaurants, bars and cafés, mostly catering for the busloads of (principally German) day-trippers piling in throughout the summer season.

Not far from the cathedral is the Gothic St Mary's Church: no longer conse-crated, the building houses a small **modern art gallery** (Mon–Fri 10am–5pm, Sat & Sun 10am–4pm; 4zł). The art on display is not desperately exciting but makes for an interesting contrast with the crumbling red-brick surroundings. The English merchant Samuel Butler was buried here – one of many English traders who settled in Elbląg, headquarters for the Eastland Company, in the Reformation era.

South along the river, the local **museum** is located at ul. Bulwar Zygmunta Augusta 11 (Tues, Wed & Fri 8am–4pm, Thurs, Sat & Sun 10am–6pm; 5zł), featuring the usual displays dedicated to local history and archeology, as well as an absorbing collection of photos of the German city from the prewar era and beyond.

Practicalities

Elbląg's **bus** and **train stations** are close together, a fifteen-minute walk east of the Stare Miasto centre or a short ride on trams #1 or #2. Decent onward bus connections to the Wiślana peninsula and Frombork ensure that you're unlikely to need to stay in town, though if you do get stuck here there's a fair range of **accommodation**. The cheapest option lies outside the centre: bus #10 from the stations will take you to the plain but serviceable rooms at the *Stadion*, ul. Brzeska 41 (☎055/641 1105; ❸). In the centre of town, the plush *Elzam Gromada*, pl. Słowiański 2 (☎055/230 6191; ❼), is close to the cathedral and has facilities for the disabled; equally comfortable is the more contemporary *Vivaldi*,

Kaliningrad

Kaliningrad – formerly Königsberg – the longtime capital of East Prussia, annexed by the Soviet Union at the end of World War II, was left cut off from the rest of the Russian Federation following the collapse of the Soviet Union. Although the Kaliningrad territory's continued political status as an integral part of Russia is beyond question, its geographical position – squeezed between Poland and Lithuania – is decidedly problematic.

A heavily **militarized area** often referred to as Russia's "western aircraft-carrier", Kaliningrad occupied an important place in Soviet strategic military thinking. A key air-defence centre, the region also houses the main base of the Russian Baltic Fleet at Baltysk, as well as a number of infantry divisions. A drive through the Kaliningrad *oblast* (region) confirms the weight of local military presence: in between the crumbling Prussian villages you can easily spot a welter of air-defence installations, some camouflaged, some not. Estimates of current force levels vary widely – there were thought to be at least 150,000 troops remaining in the mid-1990s, though this has certainly been reduced since.

The former threat of military confrontation may have subsided, but while agreeing that troop levels should be reduced to "reasonable" levels, the Russian authorities have so far stopped short of accepting Polish and Lithuanian calls to demilitarize the region completely. As with earlier negotiations on troop withdrawals in Eastern Europe, behind this stance lurks the genuine and difficult issue of what to do with returning soldiers in a country already deep in the throes of a serious economic crisis, not least suffering from a chronic lack of employment and housing opportunities. **NATO** and Russia carried out joint exercises in Kaliningrad in 2004 but now that Lithuania and Poland are full NATO members Kaliningrad looks even more isolated from the Russian mainland.

The problematic position of Kaliningrad has also been thrown into sharp relief by the growth of the **European Union** (EU) to include both Poland and Lithuania. The territory's one-million-strong population is already far poorer than that of its neighbours, with an average wage of just $115 a month. The Kaliningrad region was declared a special economic zone in 1996 in the hope of encouraging Western

Stary Rynek 16 (☎055/236 2542; ❼). *Boss*, ul. św. Ducha 30 (☎055/239 3730, ⓔboss@elblag.com.pl; ❺), is an upmarket pension lying between the cathedral and the river, whose bijou rooms come with sparkling WCs.

For **eating** you can savour cheap and filling fare at *Pizzeria Monte Cristo*, near the cathedral on the Stary Rynek, or indulge in faux-Mexican eats in the rather fun *Pod Aniolami*, also on the Stary Rynek. For a quality Polish meal, the *Rattanowa* restaurant inside the *Elzam Gromada* hotel is probably your best bet.

East of Elbląg

Continuing east towards the Russian border, the high morainic inclines of the Elbląg plateau (Wzniesienie Elbląskie) stretch east along the high ridge overlooking the coast. Most traffic (including the vast majority of eastbound buses) follow the main road inland before rejoining the lagoon at the cathedral town of Frombork, some 30km from Elbląg. An alternative route involves following the minor road that loops northeast along the coast, passing through some stunningly beautiful scenery on the way. Twenty kilometres out of Elbląg, the village of **KADYNY** (Cadinen) conceals one of the region's real surprises: German Kaiser Wilhelm II's personal stables and **stud farm**. Established in 1898 as part of the Kaiser's summer residence here, the stables are still going strong,

investment by giving tax breaks to foreign importers, but while some international companies such as BMW and Hitachi have set up factories here to take advantage of cheap labour costs, there has not been enough outside investment to have a significant effect on the daily lives of the majority of the population.

It's estimated that fifty percent of Kaliningrad's income is derived from **black market** activities. Many Kaliningrad Russians make ends meet by travelling to Poland to sell cigarettes or vodka on local markets, returning home with a few dollars' profit. While EU bigwigs in Brussels, who tend to view Kaliningrad as a reservoir of potential economic migrants, would like to see frontier regulations toughened up, Poles and Lithuanians are keen to retain a lenient system of border controls with Kaliningrad.

Visiting Kaliningrad

There's actually not a great deal worth seeing in Kaliningrad, since most of the city was first flattened by Allied bombing raids, then by the fighting around the city in 1945, and afterwards rebuilt in what seems like the crassest and ugliest way the Soviets could come up with. In the old city only the ruins of the medieval **cathedral** survive, with a special stone marking the grave of **Immanuel Kant**, the city's most famous philosopher and about the only one deemed acceptable by the postwar Soviet authorities. Moving out into the suburbs, however, the uniform concrete blocks begin to give way to sections of old Prussian houses characteristic of those found throughout the former East Prussia.

In order to visit Kaliningrad you'll need a Russian **visa**, which can only be obtained from Russian embassies or consulates in your home country; applying to Russian consulates in Poland won't do much good.

Regular **buses** run from Warsaw, Gdańsk and Kętrzyn to Kaliningrad, crossing the border at Bezledy–Bagrationovsk, about 40km north of Lidzbark Warmiński. There are also border crossings at Gronowo–Mamonovo and Goldap–Gasev. The journey takes about 10 hours from Warsaw and 5 hours from Gdańsk or Kętrzyn.

In summer, tourist **hydrofoils** operated by Żegluga Gdańska (ⓦwww.zegluga.gda .pl) run to Kaliningrad from Hel (twice weekly) and Elbląg (daily).

with 170 high-quality horses kept in trim for use by a predominantly German tourist clientele. The half-timbered buildings of the Kaiser's country pad have recently been restored to their former Prussian opulence and converted into a luxury **hotel** (℡055/231 6120, ⓦwww.kadyny.com; ❼). The rooms are small but well equipped, and the grounds hold tennis courts, sun lounges and a swimming pool. The excellent but pricey hotel **restaurant**, the *Stara Gorzelnia*, housed inside the old stable brewery, still has its old cast-iron staircases and large windows. The hotel is very popular, with plenty of group bookings in summer, so if you want to stay you'll need to book in advance. The Kaiser's private **chapel** lies in the hotel grounds: it's kept locked but ask at reception and they'll organize entry.

Across the courtyard from the hotel lie the magnificent **stables**. Lessons and cross-country hacks along the coast or up onto the plateau are on offer but it's best to phone well in advance (℡055/231 6133) to make arrangements – though you're more likely to get through to a Polish- or German-speaker than an English-speaker. The village is also famous for **Jan Bażyński's Oak**, one of the oldest trees in Poland, 25m high and 10m in circumference.

To get to Kadyny, take the **bus** from Elbląg (25min) or the local **train** on the coastal line between Elbląg and Braniewo – although the latter boasts a meagre two departures per day.

Frombork

A little seaside town 90km east along the Baltic coast from Gdańsk, **FROM-BORK** was the home of **Nicolaus Copernicus** (see box below), the Renaissance astronomer whose ideas overturned Church-approved scientific notions, specifically the earth-centred model of the universe. Most of the research for his famous *De Revolutionibus* was carried out around this town, and it was here that he died and was buried in 1543. Just over a century later, Frombork was badly mauled by marauding Swedes, who carted off most of Copernicus' belongings, including his library, in World War II. The town was wrecked in World War II, after which virtually none of the Stare Miasto was left standing. Today it's an out-of-the-way place, as peaceful as it probably was in Copernicus' time, though of late the town has been rocked over land ownership – the Church, which owned much of the town centre before World War II, is now claiming the whole place back.

Nicolaus Copernicus

Nicolaus Copernicus – Mikołaj Kopernik as he's known to Poles – was born in Toruń in 1473. The son of a wealthy merchant family with strong Church connections, he entered Kraków's Jagiellonian University in 1491 and subsequently joined the priest-hood. Like most educated Poles of his time, he travelled abroad to continue his studies, spending time at the famous Renaissance universities of Bologna and Padua.

On his return home in 1497 he became administrator for the northern bishopric of Warmia, developing a wide field of interests, working as a doctor, lawyer, architect and soldier (he supervised the defence of nearby Olsztyn against the Teutonic Knights) – the archetypal Renaissance man. He spent some fifteen years as canon of the **Frombork** chapterhouse and constructed an observatory here, where he undertook the research that provided the empirical substance for the *De Revolutionibus Orbium Caelestium*, whose revolutionary contention was that the sun, not the earth, was at the centre of the planetary system. The work was published by the Church authorities in Nuremberg in the year of Copernicus' death in 1543; it was later banned by the papacy.

Around the cathedral

The only part of Frombork to escape unscathed from the last war was the **Wzgórze Katedralne** (Cathedral Hill), up from the old market square in the centre of town. A compact unit surrounded by high defensive walls, its main element is the dramatic fourteenth-century Gothic **cathedral** (Mon–Sat: May–Sept 9.30am–5pm; Oct–April 9am–4pm; 3zł), with its huge red-tiled and turreted roof. Inside, the lofty expanses of brick rise above a series of lavish Baroque altars – the High Altar is a copy of the Wawel altarpiece in Kraków. The wealth of tombstones, many lavishly decorated, provide a snapshot of Warmian life in past centuries; Copernicus himself is also buried here. The seventeenth-century Baroque **organ** towering over the nave is one of the best in the country, and the Sunday afternoon and occasional weekday recitals in summer are an established feature: check the concert programme at the tourist office in Gdańsk. If you like organ music but can't make it to a concert, you can obtain recordings (and much else) from the ticket office at the entrance.

To the west of the cathedral, the **Wieża Kopernika** (Copernicus Tower; May–Sept: Tues–Sat 9.30am–5pm; 4zł), the oldest part of the complex, is supposed to have been the great man's workshop and observatory. Doubting that the local authorities would have let him make use of a part of the town defences, some maintain that he's more likely to have studied at his home, just north of the cathedral complex. The **Belfry Tower** (daily: May–Sept 9.30am–5pm; Oct–April 9am–4pm; 4zł), in the southwest corner of the walls, displays a fairly ordinary selection of modern paintings. Hanging right down the centre of the tower is a large pendulum, based on the one used by the French scientist Jean Foucault to prove conclusively that the Earth rotates. There's an excellent view from the top of the tower of Wiślana Lagoon stretching 70km north towards Kaliningrad. Across the tree-lined cathedral courtyard in the Warmia Bishops' Palace is the **Muzeum Kopernika** (Copernicus Museum; Tues–Sun: May–Sept 9am–4.30pm; Oct–April 9am–4pm; 3zł). Exhibits include early editions of Copernicus' astronomical treatises, along with a number of his lesser-known works on medical, political and economic questions, a collection of astrolabes, sextants and other instruments, plus pictures and portraits.

Practicalities

Frombork's **bus** and **train stations** are located next to each other not far from the seafront. The Elbląg–Frombork train service has been cut to just two trains a day, but plenty of Elbląg–Braniewo buses pass through here. It's perfectly feasible to treat Frombork as a day-trip from Gdańsk; if there's no direct bus back, take one to Elbląg and change there.

The small IT **information office** in the souvenir shop just above the bus stop will help with public transport information and direct you towards the town's stock of **private rooms** (❸) – otherwise look out for signs advertising *pokoje* on and around the main street. Other than private rooms the main options are the *Rheticus* at ul. Kopernika 10 (☎055/243 7800; ❹), a charming **pension** boasting neat modern en suites and some family rooms with kitchenette; and the larger **hotel**, the *Kopernik*, ul. Kościelna 2 (☎055/243 7285; ❺), with spic-and-span en-suite doubles, all with excellent views up to the cathedral. On the road in from Elbląg there's the summer-only *Copernicus* **youth hostel**, at ul. Elbląska 11 (☎055/243 7453), and PTTK **camping** (May 15–Sept 15), some way from the centre on the Braniewo road at ul. Braniewska 14.

Apart from some summer takeaway bars and hotel restaurants, the best **place to eat** is *Akcent*, ul. Rybecka 4, which serves up traditional treats like *żurek*.

The Kanał Ostrodzko–Elblaski

Part of the network of canals stretching east to Augustów and over the Belarus border, the 81-kilometre-long **Kanał Ostrodzko–Elblaski** (Elbląg–Ostróda Canal) was constructed in the mid-nineteenth century as part of the Prussian scheme to improve the region's economic infrastructure. Building the canal presented significant technical difficulties (it took over thirty years to complete the project), in particular the large difference in water level (over 100m) between the beginning and end points. To deal with this problem, Prussian engineers devised an intricate and often ingenious system of locks, choke-points and slipways: the **slipways**, the canal's best-known feature, are serviced by large rail-bound carriages that haul the boats overland along the sections of rail tracks that cover stretches of the route where there's no water. Five of these amazing *Fitzcarraldo*-like constructions operate over a ten-kilometre stretch of the northern section of the canal, located roughly halfway between Elbląg and Małdyty (see below).

If you feel like travelling on the canal, **day-trips** along the whole stretch of the route operate daily from mid-May to the end of September, although departures are sometimes cancelled if fewer than twenty people turn up; incidentally, bird fanciers should note that the first leg of the cruise on the Drużno Lake is a nature reserve rich in waterfowl. Bear in mind, too, that you'll need to bring your own food – only drinks are served on board. Boats start at 8am from Elbląg, arriving in **OSTRÓDA**, at the southern tip of the canal, in the early evening (a total journey time of 11–12 hours): alternatively you can travel in the other direction on the boat leaving Ostróda at the same time and finishing up in Elbląg in the evening. If you don't feel like trekking the whole distance, you can at least follow a section of the canal from **MAŁDYTY**, a village just east of the main Elbląg–Ostróda road, some 40km south of Elbląg. If you're travelling by car and want to glance at the slipways, turn west off the main road at **Marzewo**, a few kilometres north of Małdyty, and you'll meet the canal 5km down the road.

At certain times of the year, the canal becomes a tourist attraction for other reasons – if you're here in July watch out for the "Canal Trophy" when world records are set for inner-tube racing, and the "Canal Blues", a waterside blues festival.

The lakes

The woodlands that open up to the east of the Elbląg plateau signal the advent of **Mazury**, or **Mazuria**, the "land of a thousand lakes" that occupies the northeast corner of the country, stretching for some 300km towards the Lithuanian border. The region's current form was determined by the last Ice Age, the myriad lakes a product of the retreat of the last great Scandinavian glacier. A sparsely populated area of thick forests and innumerable lakes and rivers, Mazury is one of the country's main holiday districts – and rightfully so. It's a wonderful haunt for walkers, campers, water sports enthusiasts or just for taking it easy.

Ostpreussen

Present-day Warmia and Mazuria make up the heartlands of what until fifty years ago was known as **Ostpreussen** (East Prussia). Essentially the domains ruled by the Teutonic Knights at the height of their power, the whole area was originally populated by pagan Baltic and Borussian (later known as Prussian) tribes, most of whom were wiped out by the Teutonic colonizers. **Warmia** (Royal Prussia), the main part of the territory, whose name derives from the Prussian tribe of the Warms that once lived here, passed into Polish control following the Treaty of Toruń (1466), after which Polish settlers began moving into the area in numbers. It remained part of Poland until the First Partition (1772), when it was annexed by Prussia.

Mazuria proper, the eastern part of the territory – Ducal Prussia as it eventually became known – has been **German**-ruled for most of its modern history. Following the secularization of the Teutonic Knights' lands in 1525, the Brandenberg Hohenzollern family acquired the region as a hereditary duchy, though they were still obliged to pay homage to the Polish king.

This was not the end of the original "German question", however, for in 1657, under the pressure of the Swedish wars, King Jan Kazimierz released the branch of the powerful Hohenzollern family ruling Ducal Prussia from any form of Polish jurisdiction, allowing them to merge the province with their own German territories. By 1701 Elector Frederick III was able to proclaim himself king of an independent Ducal Prussia, and impose limits on Polish settlement in the region; the way was now cleared for the disastrous – from the Polish point of view – slide to Frederick the Great and Partition-era Prussia.

From the German point of view, Prussia's first real setback in centuries came at the end of **World War I**, when the region was reduced to the status of a *Land within* the Weimar Republic and subjected to a series of plebiscites to determine whether Germany or Poland should have control of certain parts of the territory. As it turned out, both the Warmian and Mazurian provinces voted to remain in Germany, with the easternmost area around Suwałki going to Poland. Heavily militarized during the course of **World War II**, in 1945 East Prussia was sliced across the middle, the northern half, including the capital Königsberg, designated a new province of the Russian Federation (though separated from it by Lithuania), the southern half becoming part of Poland.

Prusso-German culture had a strong impact on the character of the area, as evidenced by the many Protestant churches and German-looking towns dotted around – Olsztyn was once known as Allenstein, Elbąg as Elbling, Ełk as Lyck. Today the most obvious sign of Prussian influence is the influx of Germans who flock to the major lakeside holiday resorts in the summer. Many of the older visitors had family roots here until 1945, when – as in other areas of newly liberated Poland – everybody of German origin was ordered to leave. Most fled to West Germany, joining the millions of other displaced or uprooted peoples moving across Europe in the immediate postwar period.

A particularly sad example of the Polish government's rigid displacement policy occurred with the peasant minority from the villages around **Olsztyn**. Like the other historic peoples of Warmia, they were of Baltic origin, but unlike the original Baltic Prussians they survived the onslaughts of the Teutonic Knights, only to be strongly Germanized, then Polonized during the Polish rule of Ducal Prussia. Yet after centuries of tending the forests, they were pressurized into leaving the Olsztyn area for good on account of the German taint in their history.

Coming from Gdańsk, **Olsztyn** is the first major town and provides a base for exploring the lesser-known western parts of Mazury, a landscape of rolling woodland interspersed with farming villages. Enjoyable as this area is, though, most holiday-makers head east to the area around lakes **Mamry** and **Śniardwy** – the two largest of the region – and to more developed tourist towns like **Giżycko**, **Mrągowo** and **Mikołajki**. Further east still is the **Suwalszczyna**, an area of mixed forest and undulating pastureland tucked away by the border, in many ways the most enchanting part of the region. As with other border areas there is a large non-Polish population, in this case Lithuanians.

Transport links within the region are reasonably well developed, if slow. Local trains and/or buses run between all the main destinations but further afield, notably in the Suwalszczyna, the bus service becomes more unpredictable, so you may have to rely on hitching – which is not too much of a problem in the holiday season. Approaching Mazury from the south can be tricky, however, as the lakelands were in a different country until 45 years ago. Olsztyn and Augustów are on main rail lines from Warsaw; anything in between may involve a couple of changes, so the (summer only) bus from Warsaw to Mikołajki may be a better idea if you're heading direct to the central lakes.

For **trekking** or **canoeing**, a tent, a sleeping roll, food supplies and the right clothing are essential – and are available for hire if you don't want to lug your own over. Canoe, kayak and yacht rental can usually be organized by the local offices of Almatur, PTTK and Orbis.

Olsztyn

Of several possible stepping-off points for the lakes, **OLSZTYN** is the biggest and the easiest to reach, and owing to the summertime tourist influx it's well kitted out to deal with visitors, most of whom stop here en route for points further east. The town is surrounded by pleasant woodland, but as a result of wartime destruction – Soviet troops burnt the place down in 1945 after the fighting had ceased – much of the old centre has the usual residential postwar greyness. Among the concrete blocks and dusty main thoroughfares, however, quiet streets of neat brick houses built by the city's former German inhabitants remain, and there are relaxing tree-lined riverside walks around the main Stare Miasto area.

Olsztyn was something of a latecomer, gaining municipal status in 1353, twenty years after its castle was begun. Following the 1466 Toruń Treaty, the town was reintegrated into Polish territory, finally escaping the clutches of the Teutonic Knights. Half a century later, Nicolaus Copernicus took up residence as an administrator of the province of Warmia, and in 1521 helped organize the defence of the town against the Knights.

Coming under Prussian control after the First Partition, it remained part of East Prussia until 1945. Resistance to Germanization during this period was symbolized by the establishment here, in 1921, of the Association of Poles in Germany, an organization dedicated to keeping Polish culture alive. With Hitler's accession, the Association became a target for Nazi terror, and most of its members perished in the concentration camps. The town also suffered, roughly forty percent being demolished by 1945.

Nonetheless, postwar development has established Olsztyn as the region's major industrial centre, with a population of 160,000. Ethnically they are quite a mixed bunch: the majority of the German-speaking population, expelled from the town after World War II, was replaced by settlers from all over Poland, particularly the eastern provinces annexed by the Soviet Union, and from even further afield – such as a small community of Latvians.

Arrival, information and accommodation

The Stare Miasto is fifteen minutes' walk to the west of the **bus** and **train stations**; as an alternative to walking, just about any bus heading down al. Partyzantów will drop you at pl. Jana Pawła II. The **tourist office** (Mon–Fri 8am–4pm, Sat 10am–2pm, plus Sun in July & Aug 10am–2pm; ☎089/535 3565), beside the High Gate on pl. Jedności Słowianskiej, will fill you in on most aspects of tourism in the region. In the same building, PTTK/Mazury (Mon–Fri 8am–4pm, Sat 10am–2pm; ☎089/527 4058) organizes boat rental and accommodation for the Krutynia kayaking route (see box, p.236). There's a reasonable choice of cheap to moderate **hotels**, while the all-year **youth hostel** is about ten minutes' walk from the town centre in a pleasant red-brick house at ul. Kosciuszki 72/74 (☎089/527 6650; 20zł).

Hotels

Gromada Kormoran pl. Konstytucji 3 Maja 4 ☎089/534 5864, ℗534 6195. Right opposite the train and bus stations, this hotel offers smart, comfortable rooms and guarded parking. ❻

Jantar ul. Kętrzyńskiego 5 ☎089/553 5452. A former workers' hotel, with rooms that are simple but clean. In a handy spot near the train station. ❸

Pod Zamkiem ul. Nowowiejskiego 10 ☎089/535 1287. Right under the castle walls, this is a small and welcoming place in a carefully renovated old villa. ❺

Relaks ul. Żołnierska 13A ☎089/527 7336. A slightly tatty medium-rise block 1km south of the train and bus stations, but there's a choice of clean and comfortable doubles with shared bathroom or en suites. ❷

Villa Pallas ul. Żołnierska 4 ☎ & ℗089/535 0115. Comfortable hotel in pleasant leafy grounds, within walking distance of the centre. ❻

Warmiński Głowackiego 8 ☎089/522 1400, ⓦwww.hotel-warminski.com.pl. Large, recently refurbished modern hotel aimed at the business market with correspondingly efficient service. ❻

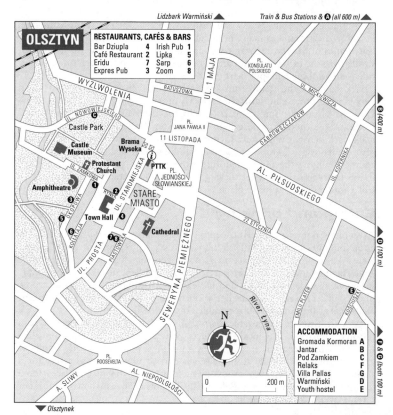

RESTAURANTS, CAFÉS & BARS
Bar Dziupla 4   Irish Pub 1
Café Restaurant 2   Lipka 5
Eridu 7   Sarp 6
Expres Pub 3   Zoom 8

ACCOMMODATION
Gromada Kormoran A
Jantar B
Pod Zamkiem C
Relaks F
Villa Pallas G
Warmiński D
Youth hostel E

The Town

The main places to see are concentrated in the **Stare Miasto**, and you won't need more than a couple of hours to take in the main sights. **Plac Jana Pawła II** is the modern town's central square, with the Gothic **Brama Wysoka** (High Gate) – the entrance to the Stare Miasto – a short walk away at the end of ul. 11 Listopada. Once through the gate, ul. Staromiejska brings you to the **Rynek**. At the centre stands the former town hall, the older half of which is red-brick – the more recent eighteenth-century part is lemon yellow. Surrounding the square are houses with an extraordinary variety of gables, taking the form of pediments, peaks and coronets.

Over to the west is the **castle**, fourteenth century but extensively rebuilt, surveying the steep little valley of the River Łyna. Its **museum** (Tues–Sun: June–Sept 9am–5pm; Oct–May 10am–4pm; 6zł) is an institution with an ideological mission – defining the region's historical record from an unashamedly Polish perspective. The ethnography section contains a good selection of folk costumes, art and furniture, while the historical section stresses the Warmians' general resistance to all things German. **Copernicus'** living quarters, on the first floor of the southwest wing, are the castle's other main feature; along with a wistful portrait by Matejko and several of the astronomer's instruments the rooms contain a sundial supposed to have been designed by Copernicus himself. It's also worth making the climb up the **castle tower** (same ticket, June–Sept only) for the view over the town and surroundings. Directly below the castle is a large open-air **amphitheatre**, used for theatre and concert performances in summertime, nestled on the leafy banks of the River Łyna. Coming out of the back of the castle you can stroll across the bridge over the gently coursing river to the park on the other side – an atmospheric spot, particularly at sunset.

Back towards the centre, up from the castle entrance, there's a stern neo-Gothic Protestant **church**, formerly used by the predominantly non-Catholic German population. To get to the early fifteenth-century – and Catholic – **cathedral**, whose high brick tower dominates the surroundings, walk back across the Rynek. Originally a grand parish church, this retains some of its original Gothic features, including an intricately patterned brick ceiling – among the most beautiful in the region – and a powerful Cruci-fixion triptych hanging over the high altar; despite extensive renovations it's still a moodily atmospheric place.

Eating and drinking

As so often in provincial Poland, central Olsztyn boasts several places which are good for a quick bite, but little in the way of slap-up **restaurants**. *Bar Dziupla*, Stare Miasto 9/10, is the place to go for a generous plateful of *pierogi*; while *Eridu*, slightly downhill at ul. Prosta 3/4, offers excellent sit-down or take-away *shawarma*, shish kebabs, *kibbeh* and falafel. *Lipka*, Okopowa 21, is an unatmos-pheric but serviceable pizzeria. For a touch more class there's the pleasant *Café Restaurant* at the corner of ul. Staromiejska and the Rynek.

For **drinking**, the enjoyable *Sarp* café at ul. Kołłątaja 14, housed in a restored granary, is the local Architects' Society hangout; *Zoom*, a pub-like bar with small beer garden at Piastowska 44, is a popular meeting point for Olsztyn youth. *Irish Pub*, at the eastern end of ul. Zamkowa, caters for a slightly older and less boisterous clientele. One of the nicest places for a daytime drink is the *Expres Pub* at ul. Okopowa 24, which has a summer terrace overlooking the castle.

North of Olsztyn

If you're not eager to press straight on to the lakes, it's worth considering a day-trip to one of the historical towns in the attractive countryside north of Olsztyn. **Morąg**, site of an impressive regional museum, is easily accessible by train, while the churches and castles of **Orneta** and **Lidzbark Warmiński** lie an easy bus ride away from Olsztyn.

The forty-kilometre journey to Lidzbark Warmiński takes you through the open woodlands and undulating farmland characteristic of western Mazury, and if you've caught an early bus there should be time for a stopoff en route at **DOBRE MIASTO**, a small town with a vast Gothic **church** – the largest in the region after Frombork cathedral – rising majestically from the edge of the main road. Baroque ornamentation overlays much of the interior, and there's a florid late-Gothic replica of Kraków's Mariacki altar; the collegiate buildings round the back house a minor local museum.

Lidzbark Warmiński

Set amid open pastureland watered by the River Łyna, **LIDZBARK WARMIŃSKI** started out as one of the numerous outposts of the Teutonic Knights. When they'd finished conquering the region, they handed the town over to the bishops of Warmia, who used it as their main residence from 1350 until the late eighteenth century. Following the Toruń Treaty, Lidzbark came under Polish rule, becoming an important centre of culture and learning – Copernicus lived here, just one member of a community of artists and scientists. A later luminary of the intellectual scene in Lidzbark was **Ignacy Krasicki** (1735–1801), a staunch defender of all things Polish; after Prussian rule had done him out of his job as archbishop, he turned his attention to writing, producing a string of translations, social satires and one of the first Polish novels.

Sadly, much of the old town centre was wiped out in 1945, only the parish church, town gate and a few sections of the fortifications managing to survive the fighting. Lidzbark's impressive Teutonic **castle**, however, came through unscathed, a stylish, well-preserved, riverside fortress which ranks as one of the architectural gems of the region. Used as a fortified residence for the Warmian bishops, it has the familiar regional look to it: the square brick structure echoes Frombork cathedral in its tiled roof, Malbork in the turreted towers rising from the corners.

Moving through the main gate you find yourself in a courtyard, with arcaded galleries rising dreamily above, while at ground level dark doorways lead down to Gothic cellars with delicate ribbed vaulting. Inside the main structure, fragments of fifteenth-century frescoes are visible in places, and the **chapel** retains its sumptuous Rococo decorations. But the chief interest comes from the exhibits in the **regional museum** (Tues–Sun: June–Sept 9am–5pm; Oct–May 9am–4pm; 6zł) that now occupies much of the building. The display begins with portraits of former Lidzbark luminaries, including Copernicus, then moves on to the **Great Refectory** where there's a display of Gothic sculpture. On the second floor are a collection of modern Polish art (not very riveting) and an exquisite exhibition of **icons**. These come from the convent at Wojnowo (see p.246), where the nuns are members of the strongly traditionalist Starowiercy (Old Believers) sect, a grouping which broke away from official Orthodoxy in protest at the religious reforms instigated by Peter the Great.

The east wing of the castle was demolished in the mid-eighteenth century to make way for a bishop's palace and gardens. The **winter garden** opposite the approach to the castle is the most attractive bit left, with a Neoclassical orangery that wouldn't be out of place in a royal residence. Into the town centre the tall **parish church** is another Gothic brick hall structure, similar in style to Dobre Miasto: the aisles off the vaulted nave reveal some fine Renaissance side altars and old tombstones. The old Protestant church in town is now an **Orthodox church** used by the Eastern settlers who moved here following the postwar border shifts.

The *Przy Brame* **pension**, (☎089/767 2099; ❸), located on the northern side of the town centre at ul. Konstitucji 18, is a cheaper, cosier alternative to the more upmarket *Pod Kłobukiem* **hotel**, 2km southwest of town at ul. Olsztyńska 4 (☎089/767 3292; ❺), where there's a small outdoor swimming pool and a reasonable restaurant.

Orneta

Just under 50km northwest of Olsztyn lies **ORNETA**, a small market town that boasts one of the finest and most satisfying of the many Gothic brick churches scattered around Warmia. It's well worth the detour to get here, and the journey itself is a real pleasure, passing through numerous attractive villages. Arriving in town by bus brings you almost immediately into the attractive old market square, at the centre of which stands the Gothic brick **town hall**, with a *kawiarnia* and billiard hall tucked away in its dimly lit medieval cellars.

Set slightly back from the square in one corner stands the magnificent, robust-looking Gothic **Kościół św. Jana** (St John's Church). Here, for once, the austere brick facade customary in the Gothic churches of northern Poland is transformed by some imaginative and exuberant decoration. A welter of tall slender parapets rises up on all sides of the building, while close inspection of the carved walls reveals sequences of grotesquely contorted faces leering out at the world – the masons obviously retained their sense of humour. Above them, a set of five menacing-looking dragon heads jut out from the roof edge, jaws agape and spitting fire down on the onlooker. Surmounting the church is a characteristic high brick tower, thicker and stockier than usual, lending solidity to the ensemble.

After the fabulous exterior, the interior lives up to expectations, the highlight being the complex geometrically patterned decorations on the brick vault soaring above the high nave. An even more than usually ornate high altarpiece and pulpit are matched by the large, solid-looking Baroque organ astride the entrance portal. A fine Gothic triptych stands in the right-hand aisle and Gothic and Renaissance murals decorate several of the side chapels, one sporting a colourful portrait of Renaissance-era Warmian cardinal Stanislaus Hosius.

By **bus**, Orneta is a one-and-a-half-hour journey from Olsztyn, making it a feasible day-trip. Like Dobre Miasto, it's also on the Olsztyn–Braniewo rail line, with services running a couple of times a day in each direction.

Morąg

Fifty kilometres west of Olsztyn, **MORĄG** is another notable old Prussian settlement. Historically its chief claim to fame is as birthplace of the German Enlightenment poet and philosopher **Johann Gottfried Herder** (1744–1803), a thinker known for his generally pro-Slav sympathies, a fact which explains German President Richard von Weizsäcker's decision to stop off at the town during his first state visit to post-communist Poland, specifically to inspect the great man's birthplace.

Ten minutes' east of the train and bus stations, the **Stare Miasto**, in slightly better shape than many neighbouring places, provides the focus of interest of an otherwise unmemorable postwar sprawl. Here, the entrance to the empty-looking Gothic **town hall** in the middle of the main square sports a pair of French cannon captured by German forces during the 1870 Franco-Prussian War. The brick-vaulted Gothic parish **church** immediately south of the square received the usual heavy-duty Rococo-Baroque treatment, though overall there's a distinctly Protestant feel to the building – which is what it was until 1945. Later additions aside, some sections of Renaissance polychromy are still visible in the presbytery, and there's a memorial tablet to Herder at the back. Just outside, a newish-looking **statue** of him – it hasn't always been exactly kosher to commemorate famous Germans born inside the borders of modern Poland – stands opposite the house where he was born. Behind the church the ruins of the Teutonic Knights' **castle**, embedded in the Stare Miasto walls, afford a fine view over the surrounding countryside, nearby Lake Skiertąg included.

Continuing the Herder theme, the elegant seventeenth-century **Dohna Palace** off the southwestern side of the square, destroyed during the war and rebuilt to the original design, is now a branch of the Warmia and Mazury **regional museum** (Tues–Sun 9am–4pm; 6zł). The first room contains an exhibition of the **life of Herder**: first editions of his work, manuscripts, paintings, busts and other contemporary memorabilia place the man firmly in his historical context, emphasizing Herder's extensive network of contacts with other Enlightenment thinkers around Europe – a testament to the eminent sanity and level-headedness of an internationalist-minded philosopher. Herder devoted much of his life to collecting and publishing the folk songs of the Baltic and Slav peoples in an attempt to demonstrate that they possessed a deep and dignified culture that had been artificially hidden by the feudal social order. Paradoxically, his discovery and promotion of folk-based national cultures provided the intellectual underpinning for the extreme right-wing ideologies of the twentieth century – something that would have horrified the man himself. A large chunk of the rest of the museum is devoted to some impressive and well-displayed collections of art, furniture and handicrafts including porcelain, glass and metalwork culled from four artistic schools – Baroque, Biedermeier, Secessionist and Second-Empire style. Last but by no means least comes the museum's artistic showpiece, a large collection of Dutch seventeenth-century portraits and landscapes by, among others, the Honthorst brothers, Pieter Nason and Caspar Netscher. The historical connection with Warmia is underlined by the portraits of the Dohna family, a branch of which moved to Warmia in the seventeenth century and built the palace here. The current exhibition, it turns out, substantially reassembles the palace's own prewar family portrait collection, carefully restored in the 1970s and 1980s at the castle museum in Olsztyn.

The town is easy enough to get to by **train**, lying on the main Olsztyn–Elbląg–Malbork–Gdańsk line. In addition, there are infrequent **bus** connections to Elbląg, Gdańsk and Olsztyn. The **tourist information** office on the main square, pl. Jana Pawła II, (☎089/757 3826) will sort you out with a **private room**. Most central of the **pensions** in town is the *Gościniec Herder*, just off the main square at ul. Sierakowskiego 9 (☎089/757 4212; ❸). The *Adria* **restaurant**, near the museum at ul. Dąbrowskiego 52, is a reliable source of decent Polish food.

South from Olsztyn

Heading south from Olsztyn takes you into more of the attractive rolling countryside for which the approaches to Mazuria are known. For most people, however, the main reason for heading this way is the battlefield at **Grunwald**, the well-kept *skansen* at **Olsztynek** providing an additional worthwhile stopoff.

Olsztynek and around

OLSZTYNEK, 26km south of Olsztyn, is home to an excellent **skansen** dating from 1941 (Tues–Sun: April & Oct 9am–3pm; May–Aug 9am–5.30pm; Sept 9am–4.30pm; 7zł). Located on the northern edge of the small town, the park is devoted to eighteenth- and nineteenth-century folk architecture from Warmia, Mazuria and Lithuania. Many fine examples of sturdy regional architecture have been gathered here: take a close look at the joints on some of the half-timbered cottages and you'll appreciate the superb workmanship that went into these buildings. Alongside the assorted farm buildings, barns, workshops and a water mill, there's a fine, early eighteenth-century wooden Protestant church with a thatched roof. The highlight of the lot, though, is undoubtedly the group of old windmills, two of them over two hundred years old. With its huge coloured blades and sturdy plank frame, the **Lithuanian mill** at the edge of the park, known as Paltrak, is a picture-postcard favourite.

For an **overnight stop** in Olsztynek – the town makes a good base if you're going on to Grunwald – the *Mazurski*, ul. Park 1 (☎089/519 2885, ℱ519 2926; ❹), is convenient of you're travelling by car: it's signposted off the main Gdańsk–Warsaw road. There's a good **restaurant** here, with local fish dishes a house speciality. The *Karczma* at the *skansen* gates is another good spot for traditional Polish cooking.

The Mauzoleum Hindenburga

About a kilometre west of the *skansen* close to the village of Sudwa lie the ruins of the notorious **Mauzoleum Hindenburga** (Hindenburg Mausoleum). The original monument was built here by the German army after World War I to commemorate victory under the command of Field Marshal Paul von Hindenburg over Russian forces at the battle of Tannenberg in August 1914. After Hindenburg's death in 1934, Hitler ordered the monument's transformation into a huge mausoleum for one of the nation's favourite Prussian military figures. With defeat in sight the retreating Nazis moved his remains to Worms Cathedral in Germany in 1945. The mausoleum was obliterated by Soviet forces soon afterwards, the stones eventually being used for a Soviet war monument near Olsztyn. The site isn't marked on the road, but you'll find it in the forest behind the village, a large enclosure marking the site of what was by all accounts a massive structure.

Grunwald

If there's one historical event every Polish schoolchild can give you a date for it's the **Battle of Grunwald** (1410). One of the most important European battles of the medieval era, the victory at Grunwald came to assume the mythological status of a symbol of the nation's resistance to – and on this occasion triumph over – German militarism. Predictably, the reality of the battle was rather more complicated. Commanded by King Władysław Jagiełło, the combined Polish-Lithuanian army opposing Grand Master Ulrich von Jungingen and his Knights included plenty of other nationalities among its ranks – Czechs, Hungarians, Ruthenians, Russians and Tatars. In an era when the modern concept of the nation-state was far from established the straight Polish–German struggle proposed in latterday nationalist interpretations of the event seems something of an oversimplification. What is certain is the fact that Grunwald was one of the biggest – over 30,000 men on each side – and bloodiest of medieval battles. The eventual rout of the Knights left the Grand Master and 11,000 of his men dead, with another 14,000 taken prisoner. The defeat at Grunwald finally broke the back of the Knights' hitherto boundless expansionist ambitions and paved the way for the first of a succession of peace treaties (1411) with Poland-Lithuania that decisively weakened their control over the northern and eastern territories.

The battlefield

The **battle site** lies 20km southwest of Olsztynek. It's not easy to get here without your own vehicle – by public transport local buses run from Olsztynek and, less frequently, Olsztyn. Stuck out in the middle of the pleasant, tranquil Warmian countryside, it's hard to square the surroundings with your idea of a major battle site. The odd modern farmhouse apart, though, the battlefield probably doesn't look that different today from the site that greeted the opposing armies nearly six hundred years ago. Walking up from the bus stop past the souvenir kiosk brings you to the centrepiece of the site, an imposing thirty-metre-high steel monument that looks uncannily like the Gdańsk Shipyard memorial, set on a hilltop overlooking the battlefield. To help you visualize the whole thing in context, just beyond the monument there's a large stone diagram set out on the ground illustrating the battle positions of the two armies and their movements throughout the fighting.

Back behind the monument the Grunwald **museum** (May to mid-Oct daily 10am–6pm; 6zł) contains a few bits and pieces of armour and weaponry, some original, most later copies; unless you're able to read the Polish wall displays there's little of interest on show. Much more interesting is the extraordinary 1960s building housing the museum, which looks like a granite spaceship half-buried in the battlefield.

The Mazurian lakes

East of Olsztyn, the central Mazury lakeland opens out amid thickening forests. In summer the biggest lakes – **Mamry** and **Śniardwy** – are real crowd-pullers, with all the advantages and disadvantages that brings. On the plus side, tourist facilities are well developed in many places, and you can rent sailing and canoeing equipment in all the major resorts. If the weather's good, Mazury can however get pretty busy on summer weekends, and accommodation can be hard to find in the main centres. If solitude and clean water are what you're after, the best advice is to get a detailed map and head for the smaller lakes: as a general principle, tranquillity increases as you travel east. In almost every village you'll find a house or two offering private rooms.

Among highlights, **Mikołajki**, commanding the approaches to Lake Śniardwy in the centre of the region, is arguably the most pleasant and most attractively located of the major-league lakeside resorts; while **Giżycko** and **Węgorzewo**, both perched on the rim of Lake Mamry to the north, attract yachters and canoeists and are useful bases for exploring the lakes. **Ruciane-Nida** provides access to the lakes and waterways of southern Mazury, and has a pleasantly laid-back, forest-shrouded feel. **Mrągowo**, the most westerly of the major towns and a useful transport hub, is nowadays best known for its Country and Western Festival. As well as lakeside pursuits, Mazury also boasts a wealth of historic

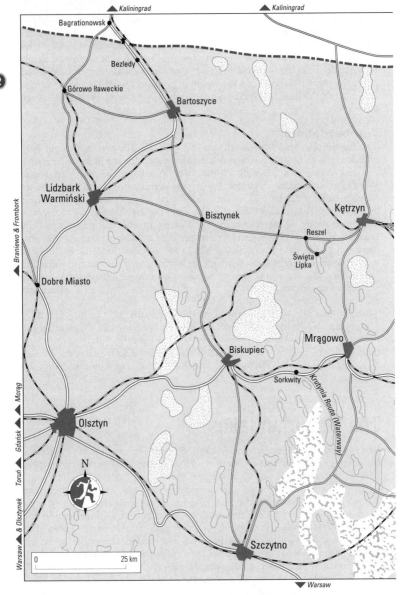

churches and castles, including the famous monastery complex at **Święta Lipka** and the Gothic ensemble at **Reszel**. A detour into the region's tangled ethnic history is provided by the Orthodox nunnery at **Wojnowo**. In addition, Mazury hides one of the strangest and most chilling of all World War II relics, Hitler's wartime base at **Gierłoz** – a short bus ride away from the pleasant small town of **Kętrzyn**.

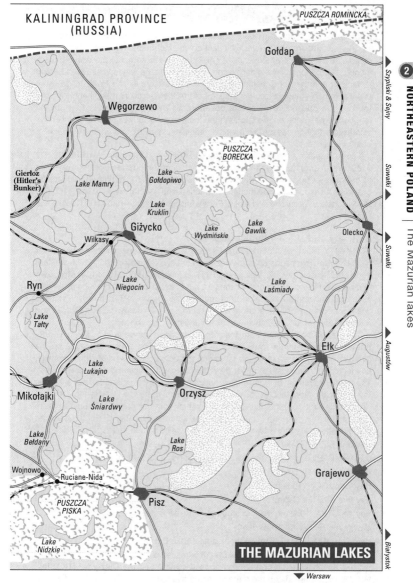

KALININGRAD PROVINCE
(RUSSIA)

2

NORTHEASTERN POLAND | The Mazurian lakes

Szypliski & Sejny

Suwałki

Suwałki

Augustów

Białystok

PUSZCZA ROMINCKA

Gołdap

Węgorzewo

PUSZCZA
BORECKA

Gierłoz
(Hitler's
Bunker)

Lake Mamry

Lake
Gołdopiwo

Lake
Kruklin

Giżycko

Wilkasy

Lake
Wydmińskie

Lake
Gawlik

Olecko

Ryn

Lake
Niegocin

Lake
Laśmiady

Lake
Tałty

Lake
Łukajno

Ełk

Mikołajki

Lake
Śniardwy

Orzysz

Lake
Bełdany

Lake
Ros

Wojnowo

Ruciane-Nida

Grajewo

PUSZCZA
PISKA

Pisz

Lake
Nidzkie

THE MAZURIAN LAKES

▼ Warsaw

On the whole, **transport** around the lakes isn't too problematic. While a car is a definite advantage for venturing into the further-flung reaches, **bus** connections between the main centres are more than adequate. Olsztyn is the usual jumping-off point if you're heading this way, while Mrągowo and Giżycko offer most in the way of onward connections to smaller resorts once you arrive. In addition, a number of **railway lines** run east from towards the lakes: one goes

Canoeing in the lakes

If you like messing about in boats, one of the best and most exciting ways of exploring the region is from the water. The vast complex of **lakes**, **rivers** and **waterways**
means there are literally thousands of options to choose from. For those who haven't
lugged their canoes, kayaks and yachts on trailers all the way across Poland – and
increasing numbers of Scandinavians and Germans are joining Poles in doing so
every summer – the key issue is getting hold of the necessary equipment. With the
tourist trade opened up to private operators it's becoming easier to turn up and
rent yourself a canoe on the spot. On the more popular routes, however, demand is
increasingly high in season, so it would definitely pay to try and organize yourself a
boat in advance.

A good resource here is the **PTTK office** in Olsztyn, ul. Staromiejska 1 (☎089/527
5156), which arranges **kayak hire** and advance **accommodation** bookings on some
of the more popular routes. Plenty of detailed **maps** of the region appropriate for
canoeists have come on the market: the most useful general ones are the 1:120,000
Wielkie Jezioro Mazurskie and a new Polish–English language 1:300,000 *Warmia and
Masuria*.

Sorkwity and the Krutynia route
SORKWITY, 12km west of Mrągowo, is the starting point for a beautiful and popular
canoeing run which ends 90km downstream at Lake Bełdany, adjoining the western
edge of Lake Sniardwy. As well as the PTTK in Olsztyn, the Orbis hotel in **Mrągowo**
can help sort out canoe rental for the trip, but in summer advance notice is virtually
essential. Accommodation along the route is provided by PTTK-run river stations
(*stanica wodna*; usually open from mid-April to Sept); basically these are kayak and
canoe depots which also have bungalows and camping space.

Canoeists generally start from the *stanica wodna* at the edge of Sorkwity village.
Known as the **Krutynia route**, after the narrow, winding river that makes up the
last part of the journey, the route takes you through a succession of eighteen lakes,
connected by narrow stretches of river, the banks often covered with dense forest.
The journey takes anything from nine days upwards, with Ruciane-Nida or Mikołajki
the final destination, though you can also shorten the route to a five-day trip ending at
Krutyń. The Krutynia route is very popular in high summer, so the best time to make
the trip is either in spring (April–May) or late summer (late Aug to Sept). Overnight
stops are generally in the following places (in *stanice wodne* unless specified):

day one BIEŃKI (15km)

day two BABIĘTA (12km); there's also a youth hostel (July–Aug) here

day three SPYCHOWO (12.5km)

day four ZGON (10.5km)

day five KRUTYŃ(14km)

day six UTKA (18.5km), the first stop on the Krutynia river itself

day seven NOWY MOST (6.5km)

day eight KAMIEŃ (10.5km) on the beautiful Lake Bełdany

day nine ending up at RUCIANE-NIDA (13.5km; see p.245)

If this ambitious excursion sounds appealing, note that the **Olsztyn PTTK** offers
ten-day kayak trips along the route including overnight stops for around 850zł. You
will need to provide your own gear for the trip, though, including a sleeping bag. For
advance booking (strongly recommended in summer) write or call – if you do there's
usually someone there who speaks English or, more likely, German. Other popular
routes are the **Czarna Hańcza** kayak route (see box, p.252), which starts in Stary
Folwark on Lake Wigry leading to the Augustowski Canal (100km), or the **Biebrza**
route starting in Lipsk and passing through the Biebrzański National Park.

through Kętrzyn and Giżycko, another through Mrągowo and Mikołajki, and a third through Ruciane-Nida – though services on these lines tend to be less frequent than buses.

As well as the usual spread of hotels, there's an expanding range of private rooms and B&B-style pensions in Mazury, especially in burgeoning resorts like Mikołajki. Bear in mind that the accommodation rates quoted in this guide are for the high season (July & Aug): prices drop by about twenty percent in spring and autumn and thirty–forty percent in winter. The tourism-oriented website Ⓦwww.mazury.com.pl is a useful resource if you're wanting to book accommodation in advance.

Mrągowo

MRĄGOWO, situated on the main Olsztyn–Augustów road, is one of the principal centres of the district, a busy town ranged around the shores of Lake Czos – a small expanse of water that can't really compete in terms of either natural beauty or holiday activities with the bigger lakes further east. It's best to pick up onward buses to Mikołajki, Ruciane-Nida or Kętrzyn rather than stick around, although there's a pleasant town centre just up from the edge of the lake if you've an hour or two to spare. Here the local **museum** (Tues–Sun 10am–4pm), housed in the old town hall on the Rynek, features an extensive collection of local wooden chests and cabinets alongside some elegant eighteenth-century furniture from around Prussia. A display centring on **Krzysztof Mrongoviusz** fills you in on the locally born priest and nineteenth-century champion of Polish culture after whom the town – originally Sensburg – was renamed in 1945.

The one event that really brings Mrągowo to life is the acclaimed Piknik **Country Festival**, held during the last weekend in July in an amphitheatre on the opposite side of the lake from the town centre. The festival, which has been running since 1983, attracts country music fans from all over Poland, and is an opportunity for aspiring Slav Hank Williamses and Dolly Partons to croon their hearts out in front of large, appreciative audiences. Alongside the local bands, there are always at least a couple of big-name stars from the US – for advance info try Ⓦwww.polcountry.medianet.pl.

Practicalities

Mrągowo's **train station** is on the western fringes of town: walk downhill from here for ten minutes to find the **bus station**, where you turn left to reach the town centre (another 10min). There's a **tourist information** office on the main road through town at ul. Królewiecka 60a (Mon–Fri 8am–4pm; ☏089/741 0150), where you can get information on **private rooms** (❸) and **pensjonats** (❹–❺); the *Edyta*, at ul. Laskowa 10 (☏ & ℗089/741 4366; ❸) on the far side of the lake from the town centre, is one of the nicer pensions. Not far away at ul. Jaszczurcza Góra 28 the **hotel** *Mazuria* (☏089/741 2975; ❺) is a good medium-range choice with rooms overlooking the lake. The plush *Mercure Mrongovia*, on the eastern edge of town at ul. Giżycka 6 (☏089/741 3221, Ⓦwww.orbis.pl; ❼), offers just about every facility imaginable, including two swimming pools, tennis and spa treatments. **Camping** *Cezar*, just below the *Mrongovia* at ul. Jaszczurcza Góra 1 (☏089/741 2533), has bungalows (❶).

Best of the **restaurants** is the *Staromiejski* at ul. Mały Rynek 4, which offers a range of reasonably priced Polish specialities, while *La Stalla*, almost opposite at ul. Mały Rynek 1, does a respectable line in pizza, pasta and classic Italian meat dishes.

Święta Lipka

Twenty kilometres north and a forty-minute bus ride from Mrągowo is the **church** at **ŚWIĘTA LIPKA**, probably the country's most famous Baroque shrine. Lodged on a thin strip of land in between two lakes, the magnificent church is stuck out in the middle of nowhere. As an approach area stuffed with souvenir stalls and locals peddling "folk art" at inflated prices suggests, the out-of-the-way location doesn't stop the tourists turning up in droves, though. As often in Poland, the draw of the church isn't purely its architectural qualities; Święta Lipka is also an important centre of pilgrimage and Marian devotion, and during religious festivals the church is absolutely jammed with pilgrims, creating an intense atmosphere of fervent Catholic devotion.

The name Święta Lipka – literally "holy lime tree" – derives from a local medieval legend according to which a Prussian tribal leader, released from imprisonment by the Teutonic Knights, is supposed to have placed a statue of the Virgin in a lime tree as a token of thanks. Within a few years healing miracles were being reported at the place, and a chapel was eventually built on the site by the Knights in 1320. The fame and supposed curative powers of the shrine increased by leaps and bounds, to such an extent that by the end of the fifteenth century it had become an important centre of pilgrimage. Following their conversion to Lutheranism, the Teutonic Knights destroyed the chapel in 1526, in characteristically brutal fashion placing gallows in front of the site in a bid to deter pilgrims. In 1620 Poles managed to purchase the ruins, and another chapel was constructed under the direction of Stefan Sadorski, King Sigismund II's private secretary, and handed over to Jesuits from the Lithuanian section of the Order in the 1630s. With pilgrims turning up in ever-increasing numbers the Jesuits decided to build a new and more ambitious sanctuary. Work on the Baroque edifice you see today was begun in 1687 under the direction of Jerzy Ertly, an architect from Vilnius, so to anyone familiar with the churches of the Lithuanian capital and its surroundings, the "Eastern" Baroque of Święta Lipka will come as no surprise.

The church

In a country with a major predilection for Baroque richness, the Święta Lipka complex is unquestionably one of the most exuberant of them all. Approached from a country road, the low cloisters, tapering twin towers of the church **facade** and plain yellow and white stucco covering the exterior are quintessential eastern Polish Baroque. **Entrance** to the complex (Mon–Sat 8am–6pm, Sundays in between Masses) is through a magnificent early eighteenth-century wrought-iron gate designed by Johann Schwartz, a local from Reszel, the surrounding cloisters topped by 44 stone statues representing the genealogy of Christ.

Through the main door you enter the body of the building, a rectangular structure with a long central nave, side aisles divided from the nave on each side by four sets of pillars supporting overhanging galleries and a presbytery. The first thing to catch the eye is the superb **fresco** work covering every inch of the ceiling, the work of one Maciej Meyer from nearby Lidzbark Warmiński, which draws on a wide range of themes ranging from the lives of Christ and Mary and Old Testament stories to depictions of Jesuit missions and the Marian cult of Święta Lipka itself. Young Meyer was sent off to Rome in the early 1700s to improve his craft, in particular the execution of three-dimensional and trompe l'oeil effects. He clearly learned a thing or two: particularly in the central nave's vaulted ceiling the polychromy is a triumph, several of the frescoes employing the newly acquired trompe l'oeil techniques to powerful effect.

Towering above the nave the lofty main **altarpiece**, an imposing wooden structure completed in 1714, has three levels: the upper two contain pictures on biblical themes, the lowest a seventeenth-century icon of the Madonna and Child – the *Holy Mother of God of Święta Lipka* as it's known locally – based on an original kept at Santa Maria Maggiore in Rome. Much revered by Polish pilgrims, the Madonna figure was adorned with its crown in the 1960s by the then Polish Catholic primate Cardinal Wyszyński, with a certain Karol Wojtyła (the future Pope John Paul II) in attendance. Imitating the original medieval shrine, a rather grubby-looking eighteenth-century lime tree stands to the left of the altar, topped by a silver statue of the Virgin and Child, the base smothered in pennants pinned there by virtuous pilgrims.

Filling virtually the entire west end of the building is the church's famous Baroque **organ**. Built in 1720 by Johann Mozengel, a Jew from Königsberg – many of the church artists and sculptors came from the old East Prussian capital – it's a huge, fantastically ornate creation, decked with two layers of blue gilded turrets topped by figures of the saints. Renovated by one of the Jesuit brothers during the 1960s, the instrument is in fine shape, producing a marvellously rich sound. When enough people are around, short concerts are given by one of the brothers, the real show-stopper being the exhibition pieces when the instrument's celestial assortment of moving parts are brought into action: the whole organ appears to come alive, gyrating angels blowing their horns, cherubs waving, stars jingling and cymbals crashing – Bach fugues with a heavenly back-up group in accompaniment. It's certainly an extraordinary sight and sound, worth capturing on one of the tapes or CDs you can pick up from the kiosk outside the church. Additionally there are special evening organ concerts every second and fourth Friday of the month from June to August, the second Friday of the month only in September.

Back out of the main building, the **cloisters** are a nice calm spot to recuperate in after the exertions of the church, the ceilings featuring more sumptuous polychromy by Meyer, most notably in the domed cupolas ornamenting the four corners of the structure.

Practicalities

There are a couple of daily buses to Święta Lipka from Mrągowo; otherwise head for Kętrzyn and change there – about fifteen daily Kętrzyn–Reszel services call in at Święta Lipka on the way. If you plan to **stay overnight**, the *Dom Pielgrzyma* in the monastery (℡089/755 1481; ❷) is where pilgrims usually lodge. Accommodation is frugal, with simple rooms (seven doubles and several dorms), and shared facilities and around the time of any major festivals – and for much of the summer – it's generally full. Considerably more comfortable is the *Hotel 500* over the road from the church (℡089/755 3737, ⓦwww.hotel500.pl; ❻). There's a **restaurant** here, with a terrace overlooking the church.

Reszel

Four kilometres northwest of Święta Lipka is the historic Warmian centre of **RESZEL**. Seat of the bishops of Warmia for over five centuries, from the establishment of Christianity in the region (1254) until the First Partition (1772), Reszel is another of Copernicus' many old regional haunts. These days the town is another quiet end-of-the-world provincial hangout, the main attraction being the small old town area that sits atop a plateau overlooking the surroundings.

Served by numerous daily buses from Kętrzyn, it's also easily accessible by bus from Mrągowo or Olsztyn.

Of the many Gothic country churches in Warmia, Reszel's **Kościół św. Piotra i Pawła** is one of the most immediately striking. Hardly the most elegant of buildings from the exterior, what the church lacks in delicacy it certainly makes up for in sheer size – perhaps that's how those bishops preferred things on their home patch. The monster **church tower** is visible for miles around, and from close up you feel almost as dwarfed as in Kościół Mariacki in Gdańsk (see p.180). The **altarpiece** is a fine piece of Neoclassical elegance, the nave vaulting displaying some of the intricate geometric brick patternwork common throughout the region. On a more delicate note, early Renaissance polychromy using enjoyable plant and animal motifs is still in evidence on the pillars and arches of the nave.

Bulk is also the name of the game in the fourteenth-century **bishop's castle**, just up from the church, an impressive hulk surrounded by the ruins of the old town walls. The castle now houses a rather superior **art gallery** (Tues–Sun: mid-May to mid-Sept 10am–5pm; mid-Sept to mid-May 10am–4pm; 5zł) featuring regular exhibitions by well-known contemporary artists, both Polish and foreign. Painters and sculptors are regularly invited to live and work in the castle for a few months, so in summer particularly the place is a mine of creative activity. To enjoy the views over the surrounding countryside you can climb the castle tower (same hours as the gallery). The chic **café** inside the castle court-yard is exactly what you'd expect of an artists' centre – more *quartier Latin* than back-of-the-woods Warmia.

There's a rather stylish **hotel** in the castle, the *Zamek Reszel*, whose rooms are equipped with wooden furniture handmade by the castle's curator (℡089/755 0109, ⓦwww.zamek-reszel.com; ❹, reductions for students). Down in the town a cheaper option is the simple *Pension Krysia* at ul. Wyspianskiego 8 (℡089/755 2279; ❷), and the summer-only **youth hostel** at ul. Krasick-iego 7 (℡089/755 0012), close to the bus station, a short walk north of the Old Town.

Kętrzyn and around

Known as Rastenburg until its return to Polish rule in 1945, **KĘTRZYN**, 15km east of Święta Lipka, is a quiet, unexceptional town whose main interest lies in its proximity to Gierłoz – Hitler's **Wilczy Szaniec** (Wolf's Lair).

A short walk up the hill from the bus and train stations stands the old Teutonic town complex, itself built on the site of an earlier Prussian settlement. Badly destroyed in 1945, the well-restored **Teutonic Knights' castle** is home to a regional **museum** (May–Sept Mon–Sat 11am–6pm, Sun 10am–5pm; Oct–April Mon 9am–3pm, Tues–Sat 9am–4pm; 4zł) housing an exhibition combining local archeology and wildlife. If you don't get to see boars, beavers or badgers in the Mazurian wild you'll find plenty of stuffed ones here, alongside a selection of similarly preserved eagles, owls, cormorants and other birds. The second floor is largely devoted to **Wojciech Kętrzyński**, a nineteenth-century local historian and patriot, the epitome of the sort of character after whom the postwar Polish authorities renamed Mazurian towns.

Just uphill from the castle the Gothic **Kościół św. Jerzego** (St George's Church), also rebuilt after 1945, is a rather barren, sorry-looking place, a couple of old Prussian memorial tablets all that's left of the original interior decoration. The small fourteenth-century chapel next door, rebuilt in the seventeenth century, and a small house down the hill are both Protestant chapels. North of here the town centre gathers itself around pl. Grunwaldzki, while on ul. Mickiewicza there's an early nineteenth-century freemasons' lodge, now a Polish-German Cultural Centre (Polsko-Niemeckie Dom Kultury)

With Święta Lipka, the Wolf's Lair and Giżycko well within striking distance, Kętrzyn makes for a convenient – if somewhat laid-back – touring base. The IT **information office**, sharing premises with Orbis at pl. Piłsudskiego 1 (Mon–Fri 8.30am–4pm; ☎089/751 2040, ⊛www.ketrzyn.com.pl), will fill you in on **private room** possibilities (❷–❸), although most of these are in outlying farms. Kętrzyn's **hotels** include the *Zajazd pod Zamkiem*, in a pretty old house at the castle gates at ul. Struga 3a (☎089/752 3117; ❹); and the *Wanda*, about 500m north of the centre at al. Wojska Polskiego 27 (☎089/751 8584; ❻), which features uninspiring but habitable en suites. *Koch*, bang in the centre of town at ul. Traugutta 3 (☎089/752 2058, ✉koch@post.pl; ❻), is a touch plusher, with smart and comfortable en suites firmly geared towards the predominantly German clientele. It also hires out bikes. The *Zajazd pod Zamkiem* has a good **restaurant** with an outdoor terrace and serves up trusty Polish fare.

Gierłoz

GIERŁOZ lies 8km east of Kętrzyn and can be reached from there by a regular municipal bus service (#1; June–Sept only), or by Kętrzyn–Węgorzewo buses, some (but not all) of which pass the site. Be careful to check return times, and allow two hours for a tour.

Here, deep in the Mazurian forests, Hitler established his military headquarters in the so-called **Wilczy Szaniec** (Wolf's Lair; Tues–Sun 8am–6pm; 8zł plus 16zł for parking), a huge underground complex from which the Germans' eastward advance was conducted. Other satellite bunker complexes were built for the army and Luftwaffe and are spread out in a forty-kilometre radius round the site, mostly now overgrown ruins.

Encased in several metres of concrete were private bunkers for Göring, Bormann, Himmler and Hitler himself, alongside offices, SS quarters and operations rooms. The 27-acre complex was camouflaged by a suspended screen of vegetation that was altered to match the changing seasons, and was permanently mined "in case of necessity". In 1945 the retreating army fired the detonator, but it merely cracked the bunkers, throwing out flailing tentacles of steel reinforcement rods. Most of today's visitors come in tourist groups – an English-speaking guide is generally on hand to take you round for a fee (call ☎089/751 4467, any day after 6pm, to make sure).

Peering into the cavernous underground bunkers today is an eerie experience. You can see the place, for example, where the assassination attempt on Hitler failed in July 1944 (see box, pp.242–243), the SS living quarters, the staff cinema and other ancillaries of domestic Nazi life. Gruesome photographs and films remind visitors of the scale of German atrocities but, as so often with such material, there's a tendency to resort to horrifying images at the expense of information and critical explanation.

The **airstrip** from which von Stauffenberg departed after his abortive assassination attempt is a couple of kilometres east from the main site, a lone runway in the middle of some heathland – you'll need a guide to show you the way.

For anybody wanting to **stay**, there's a simple hotel at the bunker site, *Wilcze Gniazdo* (☎ & ☎089/752 4429; ❷), which also has a reasonable **restaurant** open during the day.

The July Bomb Plot

In the summer of 1944, the Wolf's Lair was the scene of the assassination attempt on Adolf Hitler that came closest to success – the **July Bomb Plot**. Its leader, **Count Claus Schenk von Stauffenberg**, an aristocratic officer and member of the General Staff, had gained the support of several high-ranking members of the German army. Sickened by atrocities on the eastern front, and rapidly realizing that the Wehrmacht was fighting a war that could not possibly be won, von Stauffenberg and his fellow conspirators decided to kill the Führer, seize control of army headquarters in Berlin and sue for peace with the Allies. Germany was on the precipice of total destruction by the Allies and the Soviet Army: only such a desperate act, reasoned the plotters, could save the Fatherland.

On July 20, Stauffenberg was summoned to the Wolf's Lair to brief Hitler on troop movements on the eastern front. In his briefcase was a small bomb, packed with high explosive: once triggered, it would explode in under ten minutes. As Stauffenberg approached the specially built conference hut, he triggered the device. Taking his place a few feet from Hitler, Stauffenberg positioned the briefcase under the table, leaning it against one of the table's stout legs no more than six feet away from the Führer. Five minutes before the bomb exploded, Stauffenberg slipped from the room unnoticed by the generals and advisers, who were listening to a report on the central Russian front. One of the officers moved closer to the table to get a better look at the campaign maps and, finding the briefcase in the way under the table, picked it up and moved it to the other side of the table leg. Now, the very solid support of the table leg lay between the briefcase and Hitler.

At 12.42 the bomb went off. Stauffenberg, watching the hut from a few hundred yards away, was shocked by the force of the explosion. It was, he said, as if the hut had been hit by a 155mm shell; there was no doubt that the Führer, along with everyone else in the room, was dead.

Stauffenberg hurried off to a waiting plane and made his way to Berlin to join the other conspirators. Meanwhile, back in the wreckage of the hut, Hitler and the survivors staggered out into the daylight: four people had been killed or were dying of their wounds, including Colonel Brandt, who had moved Stauffenberg's briefcase and thus unwittingly saved the Führer's life. Hitler himself, despite being badly shaken, suffered no more than a perforated eardrum and minor injuries. After being attended to, he prepared himself for a meeting with Mussolini later that afternoon.

It did not take long to work out what had happened and the hunt for Stauffenberg was on. Hitler issued orders to the SS in Berlin to summarily execute anyone who

Mikołajki

Hyped in the brochures as the Mazurian Venice, **MIKOŁAJKI** is unquestionably the most attractive of the top Mazurian resorts. Straddled across the meeting point of two attractive small lakes – the Tałty and Mikołajskie – the small town has long provided a base for yachting enthusiasts on popular nearby Lake Śniardwy. Legend associates the town's name with a monster creature, known as the King of the Whitefish, that terrorized the local fishermen and destroyed their nets. The beast finally met its match in a young local called Mikołajek who caught the huge fish in a steel fishing net. Despite being the most popular resort in Mazury among well-heeled Varsovians, present-day Mikołajki has succeeded in retaining its low-rise, fishing village appearance. There's been a rash of new construction work in recent years – mostly in the form of luxury flats and shops – but new buildings have by and large blended in with their surroundings, aping the half-timbered styles of the past. Although there's an was slightly suspect, and dispatched Himmler to the city to quell the rebellion. Back in the military Supreme Command headquarters in Berlin, the conspiracy was in chaos. Word reached Stauffenberg and the two main army conspirators, generals Beck and Witzleben, that the Führer was still alive; they had already lost hours of essential time by failing to issue the carefully planned order to mobilize their sympathizers in the city and elsewhere, and had even failed to carry out the obvious precaution of severing all communications out of the city. After a few hours of tragicomic scenes as the conspirators tried to persuade high-ranking officials to join them, the Supreme Command HQ was surrounded by SS troops, and it was announced that the Führer would broadcast to the nation later that evening. The coup was over.

The conspirators were gathered together, given paper to write farewell messages to their wives, taken to the courtyard of the HQ and, under the orders of **General Fromm**, shot by firing squad. Stauffenberg's last words were "Long live our sacred Germany!" Fromm had known about the plot almost from the beginning, but had refused to join it. By executing the leaders he hoped to save his own skin – and, it must be added, knowingly saved them from the torturers of the SS.

Hitler's ruthless revenge on the conspirators was without parallel even in the bloody annals of the Third Reich. All the colleagues, friends and immediate relatives of Stauffenberg and the other conspirators were rounded up, tortured and taken before the "People's Court", where they were humiliated and given more-or-less automatic death sentences. Many of those executed knew nothing of the plot and were found guilty merely by association. As the blood lust grew, the Nazi Party used the plot as a pretext for settling old scores, and eradicated anyone who had the slightest hint of anything less than total dedication to the Führer. General Fromm, who had ordered the execution of the conspirators, was among those tried, found guilty of cowardice and shot by firing squad. Those whose names were blurted under torture were quickly arrested, the most notable being **Field Marshal Rommel**, who, because of his popularity, was given the choice of a trial in the People's Court or suicide and a state funeral.

The July Bomb Plot caused the deaths of at least five thousand people, including some of Germany's most brilliant military thinkers and almost all of those who would have been best qualified to run the postwar German government. Within six months the country lay in ruins as the Allies and Soviet Army advanced; had events been only a little different, the entire course of the war – and European history – would have been altered incalculably.

abundance of decent accommodation, it can be hard work finding a place to stay on summer weekends.

The Town

Most activity centres on the waterfront, just downhill from the main Rynek. Here you'll find an extensive **marina**, thronging with yachting types over the summer, and a generous collection of outdoor cafés and bars. Working your way west along the waterfront towards the three bridges (foot, road and rail) brings you to the passenger jetty used by the **excursion boats** operated by Żegluga Mazurska (see "Boat trips on the main lakes" box, p.244). There's also a **beach** of sorts on the other side of the lake (basically a grassy area with a couple of wooden piers), reached by crossing the footbridge and bearing left.

Unusually for modern Poland, the main church in town is the Protestant **Kościół św. Trójcy** (Holy Trinity Church), overlooking the shores of Lake Tałty. Designed by German architect Franz Schinkel, this solid-looking early

Boat trips on the main lakes

From mid-April to October the Żegluga Mazurska boat company (ⓦ www.zegluga
.gda.pl) runs regular **ferry services** on the main lakes. Numerous itineraries are
on offer, ranging from short circuits around a particular lake, to longer trips linking
Mazuria's main towns. They're intended as tourist excursions rather than as a means
of public transport, but they represent a scenic and leisurely way of getting around.
Prices are about 25zł per person for the shorter trips, rising to about 70zł per person
for a long trip through the whole lake system. Some of the more important routes
are as follows:

Giżycko–Mikołajki (3hr–4hr 30min)
Węgorzewo–Giżycko–Mikołajki (7hr 30min)
Mikołajki–Ruciane (2hr 30min)
Giżycko–Węgorzewo (2hr 30min)

During peak season (June–Aug) boats depart daily; otherwise, depending on
demand, it's likely to be weekends and national holidays only. Often packed, the
boats are mostly large, open-deck steamers with a basic snack bar on board for
refreshments. **Tickets** are purchased at the passenger jetties at each stop, or on the
boats themselves. **Timetables** (*rozkłady*) for departures are posted by the jetties at
all the major lakeside stopoff points, and should also be available from the tourist
offices in both Mikołajki and Giżycko. Otherwise contact Żegluga Mazurska's main
office in Giżycko at al. Wojska Polskiego 8 (ⓣ 087/428 5332).

nineteenth-century structure is the centre of worship for the region's Protestant
community. Portraits of two early pastors apart, it's a fairly spartan place, light
years away in feel from the usual Catholic churches.

Prime out-of-town attraction is the nature reserve round **Lake Łukajno**, 4km
east of town, the home of one of Europe's largest remaining colonies of wild
swans. It's an easy walk across rolling countryside, following the signed road
which heads eastwards just uphill from Mikołajki bus station. The best viewing
point is the **Wieża Widokowa** tower, signposted off the road and located at
the lake's edge, though even here whether you get to see the birds is a matter
of luck and timing. The best months to be here are July and August, when the
birds change their feathers – from a distance, the surface of the lake can look
like a downy bed.

Practicalities

The **train station** is twenty minutes' walk northeast of the centre, while the
bus station lies just west of the centre next door to the Protestant church. From
here, a five-minute walk down ul. 3 Maja will bring you to the main square, pl.
Wolności. At no. 3, you'll find the **tourist office** (May–Sept: Mon–Fri 9am–5pm;
ⓣ 087/421 9062, ⓦ www.mikolajki.pl), where you can enquire about **kayak** and
boat rental. Most of the lakeside hotels also have their own stock of canoes and
watersports equipment for use by guests, some also extending to bicycles.

The tourist office will direct you towards private rooms (❸) and **pensjonaty**
(❹–❻). Otherwise it's a question of looking for the numerous *wolne pokoje* signs
hanging outside private houses: ul. Kajki, the main street running east from
the square, is a good place to start looking. Among the pensions worth trying
are the *Mikołajki*, ul. Kajki 18 (ⓣ 087/421 6437, ⓔ pens.mik@pro.onet.pl; ❺),
a creaky but comfortable house that backs right onto the lakeside promenade;
and *Na Skarpie* at ul. Kajki 96 (ⓣ 087/421 6418; ❺), a slightly more modern
building that enjoys a similar lakeside position. There's an increasing number
of **hotels** to choose from: the *Mazur*, pl. Wolności 6 (ⓣ 087/421 6941; ❻), has

stylish if petite en suites right on the main square. The mammoth *Gołębiewski*, northwest of town at ul. Mrągowska 34 (☎087/429 0700, ⓦwww.golebiewski .pl; ❸), is a resort in itself, fully equipped for family holidays, with indoor pools, ice rink, riding stables, golf course and tennis courts. The main **campsite** is the *Wagabunda*, perched on a hill above town at ul. Leśna 2 (☎087/421 6018), a large tree-shaded site with bungalows and plenty of space for tents and caravans. In addition, numerous private gardens across the footbridge from the town centre accept tent-campers in summer (look for "*Pole namiotowe*" signs).

For **eating**, the *Cukiernia* at ul. 3 Maja 6 is the best place to stock up on bread and pastries, and also does a roaring trade in waffles (*gofry*) piled high with fruit and cream. *Café Mocca*, between pl. Wolności and the lakefront at Kowalska 4, does a decent set breakfast, alongside cheap lunches and good ice cream. There are any number of stalls along the lakefront offering cheap fried fish: *Okoń*, just beneath the main road bridge into town, is one of the more stylish of the fry-up joints. Slightly inland, *Cinema Quick Wojtek*, pl. Wolności 10, serves up a good-quality meat-and-fish menu in a movie-themed interior, and has a terrace from which you can observe goings-on on the square, while *Pizzeria Fenix* on the waterside near the footbridge is a good spot for pizza. **Drinking** takes place in the impromptu fish-fry stalls along the lakefront until about midnight, when people gravitate towards the unpretentious *ABC* **disco** in the Dom Kultury on ul. Kolejowa.

South from Mikołajki

Travelling south from Mikołajki you're soon into the depths of the **Puszcza Piska** (Pisz Forest), a characteristic Mazurian mix of woodlands and water. A huge tangle of crystal-clear lakes, lazy winding rivers and dense forest thickets, it's the largest *puszcza* in the region, one of the surviving remnants of the prime-val forest that once covered much of northeastern Europe. The forest is mainly pine, many of the trees reaching thirty to forty metres in height, with some magnificent pockets of mixed oak, beech and spruce in between. A favourite with both canoers – the Krutynia River (see box, p.236) runs south through the middle of the forest – and walkers, who use the area's developed network of hiking trails, the Puszcza Piska is a delightful area well worth exploring. The forest lakeside resort of **Ruciane-Nida** provides the obvious base.

Ruciane-Nida

Twenty-five kilometres south of Mikołajki along a scenic forest road is the lakeside resort of **RUCIANE-NIDA**. Actually two towns connected by a short stretch of road, it's an understandably popular holiday centre, offering a combi-nation of forest and lakeland, though Ruciane, the resort end of town, provides the main focus of interest – Nida is home to some postwar concrete housing blocks, a deserted factory and little else. Despite its forest location, the town is fairly accessible, with regular **trains** from Olsztyn, and **buses** from Mrągowo and (less frequently) Mikołajki.

Arriving by train from the Olsztyn direction, Ruciane is the first stopoff point – although buses sometimes drop off at Nida first before terminating at Ruciane train station. Walk just south of the station and you're at the water's edge, in this case the narrow canal connecting the two lakes nearest the town: the jetty with the sign marked "Żegluga Mazurska" is the boarding point for excursion boats on the Giżycko–Mikołajki–Ruciane line, the boats travelling through the connecting series of lakes culminating in Lake Nidzkie running south from the town. If you're staying in town, there are also daily summertime excursions round the lake itself.

The Old Believers

In a country characterized by a proliferation of historic religious groups, the Orthodox sect of **Old Believers** – *Starowiercy or Staroobrzędowcy* as they are known in Polish – are among the smallest and most archaic. The origins of the group lie in the liturgical reforms introduced into the Russian Orthodox Church by Nikon, the mid-seventeenth-century patriarch of Moscow. Faced with the task of systematizing the divergent liturgical texts and practices by then in use in the national church, Nikon opted to comply with the dominant contemporary Greek practices of the time, such as the use of three fingers instead of two when making the sign of the cross and the use of Greek ecclesiastical dress.

Widespread opposition to the **reforms** focused around a group of Muscovite priests led by archpriest Avvakum Petrovich, for which he and a number of others were eventually executed. In many instances, opponents of the reforms were motivated not so much by opposition to the substance of the changes as by the underlying assumption that the contemporary Greek church represented the "correct" mode of liturgical practice.

The stern attitude of the church authorities, who swiftly moved to endorse Nikon's reforms, anathematize dissenters and pronounce acceptance of the changes "necessary for salvation", ensured that compromise was out of the question, and for the next two centuries, dissenters, appropriately dubbed "Old Believers", were subjected to often rigorous persecution by the tsarist authorities. Initially strongest in the northern and eastern regions of the Russian empire (they also eventually gained a significant following in Moscow itself), the dissenters or **Raskolniki**, already divided into numerous, often opposing sects, strenuously opposed all attempts at change. This included the **Westernizing reforms** introduced in the early 1700s by Peter the Great, whom they regarded as the Antichrist. Under constant pressure from the authorities, groups of Old Believers began to move west, establishing themselves in the Suwałki region around Sejny (then on the borders of the Russian empire) around the time of the late-eighteenth-century **Polish Partitions** – as far as possible from

Much of the **accommodation** is located on ul. Wczasów, the forest-fringed main road that links the two towns: it's here that you'll find the lakeside *Perła Jezior* at no. 17 (☏ & ⓕ087/423 1044), which has holiday bungalows (❶) as well as camping space. On the wooded ul. Nadbrzeźna is the *Hotel Nidzki* (☏087/423 6401; ❻), with lovely lake views from the terrace and comfortable rooms with balcony.

The Wojnowo Nunnery

For much of the last two centuries the area round Ruciane-Nida has been populated by communities of Orthodox **Old Believers** (see box above). The quiet seclusion of the forests made the area an obvious choice for a habitually shy and retiring people. Slowly but surely the local Old Believers are dwindling in numbers, but you'll still find some of them living in the villages round the town.

One of these villages is **WOJNOWO**, some 6km west of Ruciane, which has a number of traditional low-slung wooden houses and is set in lush meadows on the banks of the Krutynia waterway; the **nunnery** here is one of the best-known monuments to the presence of the Old Believers. Established in the mid-nineteenth century as a centre for promoting and preserving the old-style Orthodox faith in Mazuria, the nunnery has had its ups and downs. Dwindling numbers forced it to close down in 1884, after which an energetic young nun was sent from the community in Moscow to revive the place. Her efforts led to

Moscow's reach. A few of these early settlements, including their original *molenna* (places of worship), survive in the region, notably in Suwałki, Wodziłki, Pogorzelec and Gabowe Grądy.

In the 1820s, a new wave of emigration saw the Old Believers moving further west into Prussian-ruled Mazuria, establishing the convent at Wojnowo (see opposite), which became the spiritual focal point of Old Believers in the surrounding regions. Life became easier for members of the sect following the tsar's April 1905 **Edict of Toleration**, and they were able to continue their religious practices relatively undisturbed in the Soviet Union, newly independent Poland and Prussia. The advent of World War II, however, dealt a severe blow to the Old Believer community within Poland. Under the pressure of Nazi persecution – the habitually long-bearded male members of the sect were often mistakenly identified as rabbis, for example, and subjected to all sorts of humiliations as a consequence – most of the rest fled to Lithuania, where they remain to this day in the Klaipeda region. Following the end of World War II, a few returned to their old settlements, but the soul had effectively been ripped out of the community. Today, it's estimated that no more than 2000 remain in Poland, a number that continues to diminish year by year, and at this rate the long-term future of the community definitely looks to be in doubt.

Despite the numerical decline, the rudiments of Old Believer faith and practice remain as they have long been. In liturgical matters, the sect is egalitarian, rejecting the ecclesiastical hierarchy of conventional Orthodoxy, electing their clergy and sticking firmly to the use of Old Church Slavonic for services. Strict social rules are also (at least theoretically) applied – no alcohol, tobacco, tea or coffee; many families still live in unmodernized wooden rural houses; the older people speak a curious mixture of Polish and old-fashioned Russian; and the community as a whole tends towards the shy and retiring. Outwardly, at least, the one place where they really come into their own is during their services, characterized by the use of distinctive and hauntingly beautiful trance-like hymns and chants.

a revival that continued until World War I, after which another lengthy period of decline set in.

The original convent buildings are now occupied by a farmhouse B&B (☎087/423 6401; ❸) but the church is still functional and worth a look. If it's locked ask at the farmhouse. The **interior** is not particularly grand but does have a very impressive collection of old icons – unfortunately mounted in an iconostasis made of cheap laminate. These are just some of the convent's collection, the remainder of which is displayed at Lidzbark Warmiński's castle museum (see p.229).

The remaining nuns live in quiet seclusion at the other end of the village where's there's also a charming **parish church** made of white-painted wood and crowned with a blue onion dome (Mon–Sat 9am–noon & 1–6pm); if the church is locked go down the path past the cemetery and through the flower garden to the house and ask for the key. There's no entry fee as such but you should certainly make a donation of a few złoty.

Giżycko and around

Forty kilometres north of Mikołajki, and squeezed between Lake Niegocin and the marshy backwaters of Lake Mamry, **GIŻYCKO** is one of the main lakeland centres. It was flattened in 1945, however, and the rebuilding didn't create a lot of character: if greyish holiday-resort architecture lowers your spirits, don't plan to stay for long before heading out for the lakes. Wilkasy (see below) is a much more pleasant base.

From the adjacent train and bus stations, head uphill to reach the modern town centre around ul. Warszawska, or head west to reach an attractive waterside area on the shores of Lake Niegocin, characterized by grassy open spaces and occasional stands of trees. Here you'll find the passenger jetty for **boat trips** (see box, p.244), and a swanky yachting marina. Carry on westwards for about a kilometre and you'll reach Giżycko's only real historical sight, **Twierdza Boyen** (Boyen Fortress), an enormous star-shaped affair built by the Prussians in the mid-nineteenth century to shore up their defences against the tsarist empire. During daylight hours you can ramble around the slightly unkempt, park-like interior.

The **tourist office**, ul. Warszawska 7 (Mon–Fri 9am–4pm; ☎087/428 5265, Ⓦwww.gizycko.turystyka.pl), will point you in the direction of private rooms (❸); otherwise the cheapest option is the **youth hostel** near the bus and train stations at ul. Kolejowa 10 (☎087/428 2244). Of the **hotels**, the *Jantar*, ul. Warszawska 10 (☎087/428 5415; ❺), is an unexceptional downtown place on the main street; while the *Zamek*, between the centre and the fortress at ul. Moniuszki 1 (☎087/428 2419; ❹), offers tidy little rooms in an attractive wooded area near the lake. Plushest of the lot is the *Wodnik*, ul. 3 Maja 2 (☎087/428 3872, Ⓦwww .cmazur.pl; ❺), a big concrete affair just off ul. Warszawska. There's a **campsite** next to the *Hotel Zamek* (May–Sept; ☎087/428 2419).

For **eating**, there's a basic pizzeria, *Nicola*, at ul. Warszawska 14; Polish fare at the restaurant attached to the *Hotel Wodnik*; and, best of all, a range of fish dishes at *Pod Złotą Rybką*, ul. Olsztyńska 15, the most expensive option but still a bargain.

Giżycko is one of the main bases for **yacht charter** companies, with craft being rented out between May and September – bear in mind that in peak periods (July & Aug), yachts often cannot be chartered for anything less than a seven-day period. Places at which to make enquiries include Marina Bełbot, ul. Smętka 20a (☎087/428 0385, Ⓦwww.marina.com.pl), and Wiking, ul. Królowej Jadwigi 10/9 (☎087/428 9602, Ⓦwww.wiking.mazury.info.pl). Depending on whether you're looking for a 4- or 6-person craft, you'll be paying 240–440zł per day in high season, 100zł less in May and September.

Wilkasy

Five kilometres west of Giżycko, and served by Giżycko–Mikołajki buses, **WILKASY** is a pleasingly laid-back holiday resort sprawled around the north-western shoulder of Lake Niegocin. If you want to experience how Poles (who flood the place in summer) take their Mazurian holidays, this is the place to head for, with its assortment of lakeside rest homes, holiday cabins and hostels – and may make for a more restful base than Giżycko itself. Apart from some nice enclosed swimming areas by the lake, the other attraction of Wilkasy is that it's easy to **rent canoes** or **kayaks** here. Before they are allowed to set oar to water, Poles have to produce an official card proving they can swim, but you should be able to persuade the attendants to let you aboard. It makes for a pleasant day, paddling round the lake, hiving off into reed beds or canals as the fancy takes you.

Best place to **stay** for an activity-based holiday is the *Country Club Wilkasy*, ul. Niegocińska 7 (☎087/428 0072, Ⓦwww.azs-wilkasy.com.pl), a sizeable settlement of simple chalets (❶) and well-appointed hotel blocks (❹), complete with tennis courts and boat-rental. Other alternatives include the *Tajty*, ul. Przemysłowa 17 (☎087/428 0194, Ⓦwww.hoteltajty.com.pl; ❺), a medium-sized, family-oriented hotel with respectable en suites; and the *Fregata*, a cosy pension in the south-western part of the resort beside the Mrągowo road at Olsztyńska 86

(☎087/428 0202; ❹). Plenty of fish-and-chip stalls sprout up during the summer, and both the *Country Club* and the *Tajty* have solid **restaurants**.

Węgorzewo

Twenty-five kilometres north of Giżycko on the furthest edge of Lake Mamry is **WĘGORZEWO**, another former Teutonic stronghold established on the site of an earlier Prussian settlement, and one of the major holiday centres for the northern Mazurian lakelands. Despite the enjoyable rural setting, however, like its bigger cousin Giżycko the town itself is a formless, unprepossessing sort of place, the only real reason to come here being the access it offers to Lake Mamry, the second largest in the region. The town is set back 2km from the lakefront: to get down to the water on foot take the path which heads south from the town centre, following the channel which connects Węgorzewo to the open water – you'll pass the passenger jetty for Żegluga Mazurska boats and a small yachting marina on the way.

The **tourist office** at pl. Wolności 11 (☎087/427 4009; Mon–Fri 9am–6pm, Sat & Sun 10am–2pm) will help you find a **private room** (❷) and arrange **bike** or **boat rental**. There's a very comfortable **pension**, the *Nautic*, down by the yachting marina at ul. Słowackiego 14 (☎087/427 2080; ❺), which offers en suites with TV. For **campers** there's the *Rusałka* (May–Sept), a good site with a restaurant nicely situated on the shores of Lake Święcajty, signed off the Giżycko road 4km south of the town (☎087/427 2049). Best of a basically undistinguished selection of **restaurants** is that of the *Nautic*, with some Italian and French dishes as well as Polish.

Augustów, Suwałki and the Suwalszczyna

The region around the towns of **Augustów** and **Suwałki** is one of the least visited parts of Poland; even for Poles, anything beyond Mazury is still pretty much *terra incognita*. An area of peasant farmers and tortuous ethnic and religious loyalties, as with most parts of eastern Poland, the region north of Suwałki – the **Suwalszczyna** – is little developed economically. Like the Bieszczady Mountains (see p.351), its counterpart in obscurity, the Suwalszczyna is also one of the most beautiful, unspoilt territories in Europe. Once a part of the tsarist empire, much of the region's older architecture – most notably in the regional capital, **Suwałki** – has a decidely Russian feel to it. **Jews** were long a major element of the region's fluid ethnic mix, almost the only surviving sign of this being the **cemeteries** you find crumbling away at the edge of numerous towns and villages throughout the area. The region's proximity to Lithuania is reflected, too, in the sizeable **Lithuanian** minority concentrated in its north-eastern corner.

Visually the striking feature of the northern part of the Suwalszczyna is a pleasing landscape of rolling hills and fields interspersed with crystal-clear lakes – often small, but extremely deep – the end product of the final retreat of the Scandinavian glacier that once covered the area. Much of the southern stretch of this region is covered by the **Puszcza Augustowska**, the remains of the vast forest that once extended well into Lithuania. In the north, by contrast, wonderfully open countryside is interspersed with villages and lakes – some reasonably well known, like **Lake Hańcza** (the deepest in Poland);

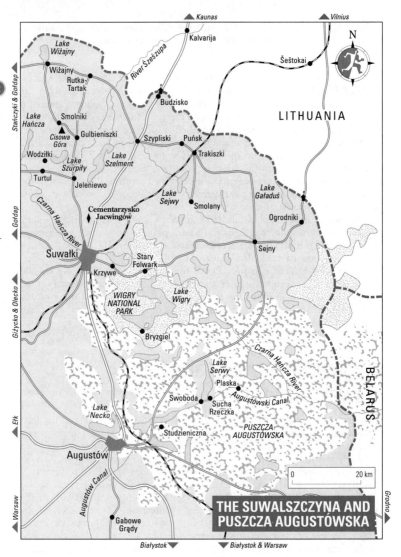

others, often the most beautiful, rarely visited. Wandering through the fields and woodland thickets you'll find storks, swallows, brilliantly coloured butterflies and wild flowers in abundance, while in the villages modern life often seems to have made only modest incursions, leaving plenty of time to sit on the porch and talk.

Getting around isn't exactly straightforward: buses operate across most of the region, but frequency declines the closer you get to the Lithuanian border. Suwałki and Augustów both have mainline train connections to Warsaw, and, slowly but surely, a fledgling network of rail and bus connections on into Lithuania is developing.

Augustów and around

The region around **AUGUSTÓW** was settled at some indistinct time in the early Middle Ages by Jacwingians, a pagan Baltic Slav tribe. The evidence suggests that the Jacwingians had a fairly advanced social structure; what's sure is that they posed a major threat to the early Mazovian rulers, persistently harrying at the edges of Mazovia from their northern domain. By the end of the thirteenth century, however, they had been effectively wiped out by the colonizing Teutonic Knights, leaving as testimony only a few sites such as the burial mound near Suwałki (see p.255) and a scattering of place names. The area remained almost deserted for the next two centuries or so, until the town's establishment in 1557 by King Sigismund August (hence the name) as a supply stopoff on the eastern trade routes from Gdańsk, though it only really developed after the construction of the **Augustów Canal** in the nineteenth century. Creating a hundred-kilometre network of rivers, lakes and artificial channels, this waterway was cut to connect the town to the River Niemen in the east, providing a transport route for the region's most important natural commodity, wood. Still in use today, the canal offers the most convenient approach to the heart of the forest (see p.253).

Thanks to its location on the edge of the *puszcza* and the surrounding abundance of water, Augustów is an increasingly popular holiday centre. As a town it's no great shakes, but it does allow immediate access to **Lake Necko**, which lies immediately north of the centre. Heading west from the Rynek along ul. Nadrzeczna leads after fifteen minutes or so to a small beach and boat rental facilities. However the best of the lakeside terrain lies north of the centre: head east from the Rynek and north across the bridge to find a small tourist **port** on ul. 29 Listopada, the departure point for sightseeing **boats** in the summer, and a pleasant spot from which to admire the swan- and duck-filled waterscapes of the lake. Beyond here, a network of woodland **walks** lead round the shore of the lake, passing several stretches of beach (the shore itself is grassy, but the lake bottom itself is quite sandy), and a waterskiing centre.

Practicalities

Augustów's **bus** station is right in the middle of town on Rynek Zygmunta Augusta. The main **train** station is 3km to the northeast: regular buses run into town. Some slower *osobowy* (local train) services also stop at Augustów Port (not to be confused with the tourist port as mentioned above), a small halt 1km west of the main train station. Augustów Port is slightly closer to the centre, although there's not much in it. Online **information** is available from Ⓦ www.augustow .pl, while the tourist information centre, in a shiny modern glass building at the southwest corner of the Rynek (July & Aug: Mon–Sat 9am–5pm; Sept–June Mon–Fri 9am–3pm; ☎087/643 2883), is reasonably well organized, and can help sort you out with a private room (❷), many of which are in the nicest part of town towards the lake, or point you towards the summer-only **youth hostel**. Other **places to stay**, most of which are concentrated in the northern part of town, midway between the centre and the train station, include the *Dom Nauczyciela* at ul. 29 Listopada 9 (☎087/643 2021; ❸), a medium-sized place offering neat and tidy en suites next to the tourist port; the *Hetman*, a rather functional hotel right by the lake at ul. Sportowa 1 (☎087/644 5345; ❸), designed in the late 1930s by Maciej Nowicki, one of the architects responsible for the UN building in New York – although you'd never be able to tell from the old-fashioned barrack-like building on display here; and the *Krechowiak*, ul. I Pułku Ułanów Krechowieckich 2 (☎087/643 2033; Ⓔ krechowiak@home.pl; ❷), a modern block with prim

Canoeing along the Czarna Hańcza River

Along with the Krutynia (see box, p.236) the **Czarna Hańcza River** is one of the most beautiful – and popular – **canoeing routes** in the northeast Polish lakelands, and part of the five percent of Polish rivers still designated as grade 1 (the cleanest) water. If you've ever had a hankering for a backwater canoeing expedition this is as good a chance as any to satisfy it.

Rising in Belarus, the 140-kilometre-long river, a tributary of the Niemen, flows into the Puszcza Augustówska, winding its way through the Wigry National Park up to Lake Hańcza, 15km northwest of Suwałki. On the usual canoe route, the first leg of the journey starts from **Augustów**, following the Augustów Canal (see p.251) east to the point where it meets the Czarna Hańcza, a few kilometres short of the Belarusian border; from there the route continues on up the river to **Suwałki** and, stamina allowing, beyond to **Lake Hańcza**.

An alternative route involves exploring **Lake Wigry** and the surrounding national park. This trip heads east from Augustów along the canal, turning north at **Swoboda** and continuing 12km into **Lake Serwy**, an attractive forest-bound tributary. From here the canoes are transported across land to the village of **Bryzgiel**, on the southern shores of Lake Wigry. Three days are given over to exploring the peaceful and unspoilt lake and its protected surroundings. Overnight camps are on the island of **Kamien**, one of several on the lake, and by the lakeside at **Stary Folwark** (see p.255), with a trip up to the monastery included. Leaving Wigry near the **Klasztorny peninsula**, canoeists re-enter the Czarna Hańcza, heading south through a spectacular forest-bound section of the river before rejoining the Augustów Canal and making their way back to Augustów.

Both the above trips can be organized through agencies in Augustów and take ten or eleven days, with accommodation – mostly in *stanice wodne* (waterside hostels) – and meals provided throughout: you'll need to provide your own sleeping bag and appropriate clothing, ideally including rubber boots. The current cost for both trips is around £170/US$270 – a bargain. Contact the **PTTK** office, ul. Nadrzeczna 70a (⌕087/644 3850), the **Sirocco** agency, ul. Zarzecze 5a (⌕087/643 0084, ⓦwww .siroccokajaki.pl), **Necko**, ul. Chreptowicza 3/39 (⌕087/644 5639) or **Solarsky**, ul. Nadrzeczna 70a (⌕087/643 6727, ⓦwww.solarsky.com.pl).

en suites a short walk east of the lake. Up several comfort zones is the upmarket *Warszawa*, ul. Zdrojowa 1 (⌕087/643 2805, ⓦwww.hotelwarszawa.pl; ⓞ), offering snazzy en suites in a prime location, with the lake on one side and dense woodland on the other. There's a **campsite** at ul. Sportowa 1, next to the *Hetman*.

Eating out in Augustów revolves around the kind of fish-fry stalls common to all of Poland's lake resorts. You'll find a couple next to the tourist port, as well as several along ul. Mostowa, which heads north from the main Rynek. *Best*, on the corner of Nadrzeczna and Mostowa is a pleasant, unpretentious pizza and kebab place, while the café-restaurant of the *Dom Nauczyciela* hotel offers up meat- and fish-based staples in simple surroundings. Best of the restaurants is the *Kolumnowa*, inside the *Hotel Warszawa*, where you'll find a mixture of Polish and modern European cuisine, a few vegetarian choices, and bearable prices.

You can also get snacks at the al fresco cafés that sprout up around the Rynek in summer, and serve as handy daytime **drinking** venues. *Hades Rock Café*, Mostowa 12a, is a basement bar with guitar-based noise on the sound system and is a lot friendlier than the bats-and-skulls decor suggests, while *Pub Bab*, Rynek 7, is an animated, welcoming cellar pub which also does substantial food.

There are numerous agencies in Augustów renting out **kayaks** and **canoes** by the day, which can also arrange longer trips down the Czarna Hańcza river: see box above.

The forest and the canal

The combination of wild forest, lakes and narrow winding rivers around Augustów has made the *puszcza* a favourite with canoeists, walkers, cyclists and naturalists alike. Following in the footsteps of their partisan ancestors, whose anti-tsarist forces found shelter here during the nineteenth-century insurrections, adventurous Poles spend days and sometimes weeks paddling or trekking through the forest. Such expeditions require substantial preparation, so for most people the practical way to sample the mysteries of the forest is to take a **day trip** from Augustów along the **canal system**. Boats leave from the tourist port on ul. 29 Listopada (see p.251) – *żegluga* (meaning, very loosely, "boats") is the key word when asking the way. There are usually about seven different excursions per day in the height of the season (July & Aug), falling to a couple per day in May, June and September. First departure is at 9.30am, and you should get there early to queue for tickets. It's also a good idea to take some food: most boats don't carry any, and restaurant stops on the way are unpredictable.

The shortest trips – a couple of hours – go east through the **Necko**, **Białe** and **Studzieniczne** lakes to **Swoboda** or **Sucha Rzeczka**, giving at least a taste of the beauty of the forest. Other boats go onward to **Płaska** and the lock at **Perkuc**, returning in the evening. Beyond this point, the canal is for canoeists only, and even they can only go another twenty or so kilometres to the Belarusian border.

The **forest** is mainly coniferous, but with impressive sections of elm, larch, hornbeam and ancient oak creating a slightly sombre atmosphere, particularly along the alley-like section of the canal between Swoboda and Sucha Rzeczka – the tallest trees blot out the sun, billowing reeds brush the boat, and the silence is suddenly broken by echoing bird calls. Among the varied wildlife of the forest, cranes, grey herons and even the occasional beaver can be spotted on the banks of the canal, while deeper into the *puszcza* you might glimpse wild boar or elk.

If exploring the highways and byways on wheels appeals, the Puszcza Augustowska makes for some enticing **cycling** territory. There are plenty of decent paths and roads, although they're not always particularly clearly marked. The *Puszcza Augustowska* **map** (1:70,000) shows all the main routes through the forest, right up to the Belarusian border. Several places in town rent out bikes – ask the tourist office (see p.251) for details.

Gabowe Grądy

Six kilometres south of Augustów down a track through woods (the nearest bus stop is a kilometre east), the village of **GABOWE GRĄDY** is populated by a sizeable number of Russian Orthodox **Old Believer** or *Starowierców* families (see box, pp.246–247). The wizened old characters with flowing white beards sitting by their front gates indicate you've arrived in the right place. People apart, the main interest here is the church (*molenna*) at the north end of the village, one of three remaining places of Orthodox worship in the region. The Gabowe Grądy *molenna* boasts a superb all-women **choir**, the only such group in the country: you can usually hear them at the Sunday morning service, the only time you're guaranteed to be able to get into the place anyway. For anyone interested in Orthodox music this is a must, the sonorous harmonies of the old liturgical chants intermeshing with the full-throated exuberance of the melodizing.

Suwałki and around

Founded as late as the 1720s, **SUWAŁKI** is another slow-paced provincial town with a decidedly Eastern ambience. For all its distance from the country's centre – less pronounced in previous Polish geographical configurations, it should be remembered – it and the surrounding region occupy an important place in contemporary Polish cultural consciousness. Nobel Laureate **Czesław Miłosz** spent his childhood holidays in Krasnogruda, hard up by the Lithuanian border; film director Andrzej Wajda stood for election in Suwałki in the landmark 1989 elections, and continues to take an active interest in the region; and the novelist Tadeusz Konwicki filmed his wonderful adaptation of Miłosz's *Dolina Issa* (The Issa Valley) around Smolniki. The town itself isn't much more than a stepping stone to the surrounding countryside – few people stop off here for long, and the cross-border traffic between Poland and nearby Lithuania has had little appreciable effect on the place.

A rambling, unfocused sort of place, Suwałki presents a mix of fine Neoclassical architecture and Russian-looking nineteenth-century buildings, with the usual postwar buildings around the outskirts. Religion is a mixed business here as well: the majority Catholic population uses the stately Neoclassical Parish Church of St Alexandra on pl. Wolności, but there's also an Evangelical church further down on the main ul. Kościuszki, and the **molenna**, a small wooden building serving the town's Old Believer population and retaining some fine original icons. It is tucked away on a side street off al. Sejneńska close to the train station; the only reliable time to gain entry is during the Sunday morning service.

The jumbled ethnic mix that characterized Suwałki up until the outbreak of World War II is clearly illustrated in the town **cemetery** on the west side of town, on the corner of ul. Bakałarzewska and ul. Zarzecze, overlooking the Czarna Hańcza River. As in Lublin and other eastern Polish towns, the cemetery is divided up into religious sections – Catholic, Orthodox, Protestant, Tatar and Jewish, the Orthodox section housing a special part for Old Believers. The Tatar gravestones have almost disappeared with the passage of time, while the Jewish cemetery was predictably devastated by the Nazis – a lone memorial tablet now stands in the middle of the area.

Back in the town centre, the local **museum** at ul. Kościuszki 81 (Tues–Fri 8am–4pm, Sat & Sun 9am–5pm; 5zł) contains a number of archeological finds relating to the Jacwingians and paintings by local artist Alfred Wierusz-Kowalski.

Practicalities

The **train station** lies east of the centre – take bus #1, #8 or #12 into town. The **bus station**, on ul. Utrata, is also on the east side of town, but closer to the centre. The helpful **tourist office** is on the main road through town at ul. Kościuszki 45 (June–Aug Mon–Fri 8am–6pm, Sat & Sun 9am–2pm; Sept–May Mon–Fri 8am–4pm; ☎087/566 5494, ⓦwww.suwalki-turystyka.info.pl). The management is particularly keen on promoting agro- and eco-tourism in the region, and can book you into **farmhouse B&Bs** (❷–❸) in the surrounding countryside – you'll need your own transport to get there though. Best of the **hotels** are the *Dom Nauczyciela* (ZNP), ul. Kościuszki 120 (☎087/566 6900, ⓦwww.domnauczyciela.suwalki.pl; ❺); and the *Suwalszczyzna*, ul. Noniewicza 71a (☎087/565 1929; ❺), both of which are central and offer comfy en suites with TV. Slightly more basic is the *Hańcza*, ul. Wojska Polskiego 2 (☎087/566 6644; ❹), near the river on the southern edge of town; while the nearby small *Motel Private*, ul. Polna 9 (☎087/566 5362; ❹), is well furnished and overlooks the river. There's a summer only (June–Aug) **youth hostel** at ul. Klonowa 51 (☎087/566 5140), 2km northeast of the town centre.

There's no great range of **places to eat**: the restaurant of the *Dom Nauczyciela* is the most comfortable place for a good-quality Polish meal with all the trimmings. *Pub Kuźnia*, just off ul. Kościuszki at Chłodna 9, is one of the few decent **places to drink** in the centre, and also does food.

The Cementarzysko Jacwingów and Soviet War Cemetery

The ancient Jacwingian burial ground, 4km north of Suwałki, which is dated from between the third and fifth centuries AD, is one of the few sites left by these ancient people, and a must for lovers of mystic sites. To reach it take bus #7 to the nearby village of Szwajcaria, or the Jeleniewo road by car; in both cases you'll see a sign at the roadside pointing you to the **Cementarzysko Jacwingów** (Jacwingian Cemetery). A short walk through the fields and over an overgrown ridge brings you to the round, variably sized burial mounds (the largest is 20m wide), discernible through a tangled mass of trees and undergrowth, just beyond the large Soviet war cemetery on the right-hand side of the road. Excavations around the sites have revealed a little about the Jacwingians – burying horses with their masters seems to have been a common practice. In general, though, little is known of this pagan people, but stay long enough in this beautiful and peaceful spot and you conjure up your own images of how they might once have lived.

The **Soviet War Cemetery**, established close to the site of the POW camp, Stalag 68, set up by the Nazis in 1941, contains the graves of over 45,000 inmates who died here in appalling conditions, as well as several thousand Soviet troops killed in the fighting that raged around Suwałki in the latter stages of World War II. The shoddy, unkempt state of the place says much about the enduring tension between Poland and its erstwhile Soviet/Russian neighbour.

Lake Wigry and the national park

Lake Wigry, the district's largest, lies 11km southeast of Suwałki. The lake and a large part of the surrounding area were designated a **national park** in 1989, an unspoilt area of nearly 15,000 hectares comprising a mixture of lake, river, forest and agricultural territory. The lake in particular is a stunningly beautiful spot, a peaceful haven of creeks, marshes and woods, with the occasional village in between. A wealth of wildlife shelters largely undisturbed in and around its waters, the lake itself harbouring over twenty species of fish – lavaret, whitefish, smelt and river trout included – while in the shoreland woods you can find stag, wild boar, elk, martens and badgers. Wigry's most characteristic animal, however, is the **beaver**, and particularly round the lake's southern and western shores you'll find plenty of evidence of their presence in the reservations set aside for the creatures. The park is also a rambler's paradise, with a good network of **marked trails** running through much of the area. For anyone tempted by the idea of exploring the region on foot the *Wigierski Park Narodowy* **map** (1:46,000), which shows all the main trails, is a must. The longest route, marked green, takes you round the entire lake – nearly 50km in total – but there are also plenty of good shorter routes. **Cycling** is another more challenging option: the trails take in narrow forest paths and sandy roads, which can make the going hard. Bike rental is theoretically possible from the PTTK (see p.252) or via the tourist office in Suwałki. Finally, the lake itself is a magnet for anglers. To cast your rod you'll need a local **fishing licence**; the Suwałki tourist office will put you onto the local branch of the Polish Angling Association – Polski Związek Wędkarski (PZW) – which issues the requisite papers.

The park's headquarters (May–Sept daily 7am–7pm; Oct–April Mon–Fri 7am–3pm) at the village of **KRZYWE**, 5km from Suwałki on the border of the park, is the best source of detailed information and has a small natural history **museum**. Buses to and from Suwałki, and on to Stary Folwark, run roughly every hour.

A few kilometres further down the road, **STARY FOLWARK** is a quiet spot on the lakeshore. The main **places to stay** here are the pension *Nad Wigrami*

(☎087/563 7546; ❸), in a family house right in the village; the *Holiday Hotel* (☎087/563 7120; ❸), which looks like a bland motel from the road but has comfortable rooms and friendly staff; and a **campsite** near the water. For a bite to **eat** you can choose between the restaurant of the *Holiday Hotel* and the *Pod Siejǫ*, both of which serve freshwater fish from the lake. You can **rent canoes** from a couple of outlets down by the water.

A short drive or walk round the lake – or a quick paddle across it – is the tiny village of Wigry, dwarfed by a former **Camadolese monastery** (see p.431), founded here by King Władysław Waza in the 1660s. Originally the monastery stood on an island but this is now linked to the shore. The monks were thrown out by the Prussians following the Third Partition and their sizeable possessions – 300 square kilometres of land and several dozen villages – sequestered. The church is a typical piece of Polish Baroque, with exuberant frescoes in the main church and monks' skeletons in the catacombs (guided visits only), standard practice for the death-fixated Camadolese. The monastery itself has been turned into a popular conference centre and **hotel**, the *Dom Pracy Twórcej* (☎087/563 7000; ❺), with a good **restaurant** and modern art gallery. You can also find **private rooms** and **boat hire** in the village.

The Suwalszczyzna

North of Suwałki the forests give way to the lush, rolling hills of the **Suwalszczyzna**. Two roads take you through the heart of the region: the first heads due north then veers west through sporadic villages towards the Russian border, while the other runs some way to the east, covering the 30km to **Puńsk**. Infrequent buses run between Suwałki, Puńsk and **Sejny**, to the east of Suwałki.

North from Suwałki

The great appeal of this route lies in getting right off the beaten track – and tracks don't get much less beaten than that to **WODZIŁKI**, tucked away in a quiet wooded valley, around 10km north of Suwałki. The hamlet is home to a small community of Orthodox **Old Believers**, whose original wooden *molenna* is still in use, along with a nearby *bania* (sauna); for more on the Old Believers, see the box, pp.246–247.

Life in this rural settlement seems to have changed little since the first settlers moved here in the 1750s: the houses are simple, earth-floored buildings with few concessions to modernity, the old men grow long white beards, the women don't appear to cut their hair, the children run barefoot. If you're lucky enough to get invited into one of their homes, you'll see amazing collections of icons, rosaries, Bibles and other precious relics. There's no access to the village for cars so the best way to get there is drive or get a bus (via Jeleniewo) to Turtul, from where it's thirty minutes' walk north to Wodziłki. Alternatively you could take a longer (roughly 7km) walk or bike ride from Jeleniewo around the shores of **Lake Szurpiły**. The lake itself is great for swimming and an ideal camping spot, provided the mosquitoes aren't out in force.

North of Jeleniewo along the main road is **GULBIENISZKI**, the point of access for **Cisowa Góra** (258m), the hill known as the Polish Fujiyama. It was the site of pre-Christian religious rituals, and it's rumoured that rites connected with Perkunas, the Lithuanian firegod, are still observed here; bear in mind that the Lithuanians, who still make up a small percentage of the population of this region, were the last Europeans to be converted to Christianity, in the late fourteenth century – Czesław Miłosz's semi-autobiographical novel *The Issa Valley*, set in neighbouring Lithuania, bears witness to the durability of pre-Christian beliefs here. Whatever the historical reality of the hill, it's a powerful place.

North of Gulbieniski the road divides: Wiżajny to the left, Rutka-Tartak to the right. Continuing along the Wiżajny route, the next village is **SMOLNIKI**, just before which there's a wonderful **panorama** of the surrounding lakes; if you're on the bus ask the driver to let you off at the *punkt wyściowy* (viewpoint). If you happen to have a compass with you, don't be surprised if it starts to go haywire around here – the area has large deposits of iron-rich ore, as discovered by disoriented German pilots based at Luftwaffe installations here during World War II. Despite the obvious commercial potential, the seams haven't been exploited to date owing to the high levels of uranium in the ore and the risks from direct exposure to it.

A couple of kilometres west of Smolniki, along a bumpy track through woods, is **Lake Hańcza**, the deepest in Poland at 108m; it's quiet, clean and unspoilt. The Czarna Hańcza River (see the box on p.252) joins the lake on its southern shore. There's a **youth hostel** at the southeastern edge at Błaskowizna (June–Aug; ☎087/566 1769) and several houses offer **private rooms**. To get to the village take the Wiżajny bus from Suwałki and get off at Bachanowo, a kilometre past Turtul Rutka; it's a short walk from here. Note that camping isn't allowed in the Suwałki Park, of which this area is part.

Stańczyki

Stańczyki, west of Lake Hańcza close up by the Russian border on the edge of the Puszcza Romincka, is a must for lovers of the bizarre, and can be reached by car if you follow the main route west of Wiżajny, turning left off the road about 4km past Żytkiejmy. The reason for coming is to admire the huge deserted twin **viaduct** straddling the Błędzianka River valley, seemingly lost out in the middle of nowhere. Before World War II this hamlet was right on the East Prussian–Polish border: in 1910 the Germans built a mammoth double viaduct here as part of a new rail line, one side scheduled to carry timber trains leaving Prussia, the other, trains entering the country from Poland. The viaduct was duly completed, the only problem being that the promised rail track never materialized. The crumbling viaducts have stood ever since, a towering monument to an architect and engineer's folly, no one apparently having the heart – or cash – to pull them down. These days a stroll on and around the viaducts is a favourite Sunday outing for local people. You could also take a more adventurous walk into the forests of the Romincka nature reserve – signs in the car park detail possible routes.

Camping is possible here as the viaducts lie just outside the reserve. In summer there's also the *Biały Dwór* pension (☎087/615 8172), which has a small restaurant.

Suwałki to Puńsk

Lithuanians are one of Poland's minorities, most of the 40,000-odd community living in a little enclave of towns and villages north and east of Suwałki. The further you go into the countryside the more common it becomes to catch the unfamiliar lilt of their language in bars and at bus stops.

The village of **Puńsk**, close to the border, has the highest proportion of Lithuanians in the area and is surrounded by some of the loveliest countryside. There are two ways of covering the 30km from Suwałki. The first is to take the **train** to **Trakiszki** (one daily at 12.30pm) and walk the last couple of kilometres. The journey takes you through ancient meadows – their hedgerows a brilliant mass of flora – and fields tilled by horse-drawn ploughs. The other option is to travel by **bus**. There are five or six services a day from Suwałki and Sejny.

With cross-border **travel between Poland and Lithuania** easier than at any time in the postwar period, a trip over the border to the Lithuanian capital, Vilnius, is now a straightforward option.

Situated around 160km east of Suwałki, along with Ukrainian L'viv, **VILNIUS** (in Polish, Wilno) is one of the great former Polish cities of the east – not a point to emphasize when you're there, incidentally – with a large old-town complex that ranks among the finest in Europe. Anyone expecting an orderly Protestant Hansa town on the lines of Baltic neighbours Riga, Tallinn or even Helsinki, though, will be disappointed. Vilnius is unmistakeably central European and Catholic in feel and atmosphere, a jumbled mix of cobbled alleyways, high spires, Catholic shrines and Orthodox churches. Originating as the medieval capital of the Lithuanian grand dukes, Vilnius was for centuries a multinational city which served as an important cultural centre for many different peoples – Lithuanians, Poles and Belarusians included. On the eve of World War II, the Jews made up the biggest ethnic group in the city – a fact that is skated over by present-day Lithuanian and Polish historians.

Largely unscarred by World War II, Vilnius's best-known monuments include the so-called **Gates of Dawn** (known to Polish pilgrims as Ostra Brama or the "pointed gate"), a street gallery shrine housing Eastern Catholicism's most venerated icon of the Madonna; and the fabulous **St Anne's Church**, an extraordinarily exuberant Gothic masterpiece which Napoleon is supposed to have contemplated dismantling and moving to Paris.

Vilnius is very tourist-friendly, and recent years have witnessed an explosion in the number of cafés, bars, restaurants and hotels. There's a **tourist information** centre bang in the middle of the old town at Vilniaus 22 (Mon–Fri 9am–7pm, plus Sat & Sun 9am–7pm in summer; ☎+370 5 262 9660 from Poland); while bimonthly listings publications like *Vilnius in Your Pocket* (⊛www.inyourpocket.com) and *City Paper* (which also covers Riga and Tallinn; ⊛www.balticsworldwide.com), both available from news kiosks, will fill you in on just about everything else you need to know. Lithuanians are a friendly and hospitable lot on the whole, and anyone tempted by the prospect of making the journey east will find it's well worth the effort.

Practicalities

Citizens of the EU, USA, Canada, New Zealand, Australia and the Nordic countries can enter Lithuania without a **visa** – nationals of other countries should contact the Lithuanian embassy or consulate in their home country for current requirements – or head for the Lithuanian embassy in Warsaw, al. Szucha 5 (☎022/625 3368).

There are several options for overland **travel** to Vilnius. There are border crossings at Budzisko (for Kalwarija) and Ogrodniki if you're travelling **by car**, while **by rail** there are three direct trains a week from Warsaw to Vilnius. Finally, going **by bus** is also a reasonable option, with direct Eurolines services from Warsaw (daily; 12hr), via Białystok and Suwałki, and Olsztyn (weekly; 8hr).

Puńsk

Tucked away a few kilometres from the Lithuanian border is the population of **PUŃSK**, with a seventy percent **Lithuanian** population. The community has a Lithuanian cultural centre, choir and weekly newspaper.

Puńsk's neo-Gothic parish **church** might look nothing special as a building, but turn up on a Sunday at 11am and you'll find the place packed for Mass in Lithuanian. If it's a major feast day, you may also see a procession afterwards, for which the women, especially, don the curiously Inca-like national costume. On ul. Szklona at the edge of the village you'll find the local **Zbiory Etnograficzne** (Lithuanian Ethnographical Museum). Inside there's an interesting collection of local ethnography, including wonderful decorative fabrics and crafts, bizarre-looking farm implements, and prewar Lithuanian books and magazines, as well as maps that illuminate the tangled question of the Polish–Lithuanian border. As well as Lithuanians, Puńsk was for centuries home to another minority – Jews. Almost every Jew from this region was either slaughtered or uprooted, but a few signs of the past are still left. The Dom Handlowy on the main street in Puńsk used to be the rabbi's house, and the older locals can point you in the direction of the abandoned **Jewish cemetery**, on the northern edge of the village, where a few Hebrew inscriptions are still visible among the grass and trees.

There's no regular accommodation in the village. The *Sodas* **café**, at ul. Mickiewicza 17, handles food-and-drink duties, including excellent *blynai* (Lithuanian pancakes).

Sejny

Instead of returning directly to Suwałki, you might try the bus trip via the market town of **SEJNY**, 25km south of Puńsk, a cross-country journey that's a treat in itself. Sejny is dominated by the **basilica** at the top of town. The grandiose church was originally built in the late Renaissance as part of a Dominican monastery and refurbished in Rococo style in the mid-eighteenth century. The fourteenth-century Madonna carved from lime-wood, located in the main side chapel on the right, is a long-standing object of popular veneration: on feast days the body of the statue is opened to reveal an intricately carved Crucifixion scene inside. The crown on the Madonna's head was put in place by the then bishop of Kraków, **Karol Wojtyła**, in 1975.

At the other end of the short main street, ul. Piłsudskiego, is the **former synagogue**, dwarfed by the basilica but nonetheless a substantial building, indicating the importance of the former Jewish population here. Built in the 1860s and devastated by the Nazis who turned it into a fire station, it has since been carefully restored and turned into a **museum** and cultural centre (Mon–Fri 9am–5pm; free) run by the Borderland Foundation (Fundacja Pogranicze), dedicated to promoting the culture, music and art of "the borderland nations". Started in the early 1990s, the Foundation organizes cultural events aimed at bringing together the peoples of the region – Poles, Lithuanians, Belarusians, Ukrainians and Russians – publishes books relating to intercultural tolerance and understanding, and also runs a Klezmer band in honour of Sejny's Jewish heritage. It's no accident that the Foundation was chosen by Polish-Jewish historian Jan Tomasz Gross to be the publisher of his controversial book *Neighbours* (see box on the Jedwabne pogrom, pp.270–271). For more information on the foundation's activities, contact its office – directly opposite the museum at ul. Piłsudskiego 37 (℡087/516 2765, ⓦwww.pogranicze.sejny.pl). Its highly knowledgeable staff can fill you in on local history, particularly issues relating to the history of the Lithuanian, Jewish and Old Believer minorities.

The main **hotel** in town is the slightly grotty *Skarpa* at ul. Piłsudskiego 13 (℡087/516 2187), which has rooms with shower but no WC or fully equipped en suites (❷), and also boasts a restaurant. You can also stay at the Lithuanian cultural centre, the *Lietuviu Namai* (or *Dom Litewski* in Polish), ul. 22 Lipca 9 (℡087/516 2908, ⓦwww.seinai.punskas.pl; ❸), which has well-appointed en suites, and a café-bar serving Lithuanian snacks.

Poles and Lithuanians

In Poland's relations with its eastern neighbours, none are as fraught with paradox and misunderstanding as those with **Lithuania**. This is almost entirely due to the fact that the two countries have large chunks of history and culture in common, but can rarely agree on which bits of the Polish-Lithuanian heritage belong to whom.

Dynastically linked by the marriage of Polish Queen Jadwiga to the Lithuanian Grand Duke Jogaila (or Jagiełło, as he is known in Polish) in 1386, the two countries coexisted in curious tandem, and embarked on mutual conquests, until the **Union of Lublin** finally bound them together in a single state – the so-called **Commonwealth** – in 1569. They were to stay together until the **Partitions** of Poland brought the Commonwealth to an end at the close of the eighteenth century. However, the precise nature of the Polish-Lithuanian state has always been a source of disagreement to both sides: the Lithuanians tend to regard it as a mutual enterprise undertaken by equal partners, while the Poles reserve for themselves the leading role.

One of the reasons why the Poles traditionally looked upon Lithuania as a constituent part of a Polish-dominated state was that the Lithuanian aristocracy had become almost wholly Polish-speaking by the sixteenth century, and increasingly identified with the courtly culture of Warsaw and Kraków rather than their own native ways. Lithuanian language and culture was reduced to the status of quaint folklore, spoken of rapturously by nineteenth-century romantic poets like Adam Mickiewicz (see p.99), but hardly ever taken seriously by the educated elite. This left Lithuanians with an inferiority complex vis-à-vis their overbearing Polish neighbours, an outlook that was transformed into outright hostility by the national struggles of the twentieth century.

When the end of **World War I** put the resurrection of the Polish state back on the political agenda, Polish leaders (Marshal Piłsudski, himself a Polish-Lithuanian aristocrat, included) were consumed by dreams of resuscitating the Polish-Lithuanian Commonwealth of old. However the Lithuanians, eager to escape from Polish tutelage, rushed to declare an independent state of their own. The two sides came to blows over the status of **Vilnius** which, as the medieval capital of Lithuania, was regarded by the Lithuanians as a natural part of their heritage. The Poles pointed to the city's large Polish-speaking population, and annexed it by force in 1920. The Lithuanians broke off diplomatic relations, and the border between the two countries remained closed throughout the 1920s and 1930s. Lithuania's forced incorporation into the **Soviet Union** in 1940 and the postwar imposition of communism in Poland enforced a new type of isolation between the two countries, with official Party-based relations about the only sanctioned source of contact right up into the mid-1980s.

The **glasnost** era, the collapse of communist power in Poland and the Lithuanian achievement of independence in 1991 opened the way for a new era in relations

Białystok and the Belarusian borderlands

As you head south from the lakes or east from Warsaw, you find yourself in a region of complex ethnicity, situated right up against the borders of Belarus. The Poles call the area **Podlasie** – literally "Under the Trees" – a name that only hints at the landscape of wide, open plains, tracts of primeval forest and between the countries, although they were almost immediately soured by conflicts regarding the national minorities residing in both countries.

Mostly located in the border area between Sejny and Puńsk, Poland's 40,000-strong **Lithuanian minority** has secured better educational and cultural resources for the community, including native-tongue teaching in primary and secondary schools in the region. With the notable exception of the 1989–91 struggle for Lithuanian independence, when local demonstrations in Puńsk were regular news on Polish TV, the Lithuanian community tends to keep itself to itself and is happy to remain in Poland.

Lithuania's **Polish minority** is a different story. Numbering around a quarter of a million – some seven percent of the total population – Poles are the largest minority grouping after Russians, the majority of them living in the east of Lithuania, in particular in the rural districts surrounding Vilnius. Lithuanian Poles initially saw Lithuanian independence as a threat to their own identity, and as a result, prompted by evidence that local Polish officials had actively collaborated in the old guard's Moscow coup in 1991, the Lithuanian authorities suspended Polish-run councils in the early 1990s. Polish-Lithuanian relations suffered, and didn't really recover until a **Friendship and Co-operation Treaty** was signed by Lech Wałęsa and his Lithuanian counterpart, Algirdas Brazauskas, in April 1994. The treaty has brought progress on several issues, notably the situation of the Polish minority in Lithuania.

Currently the relations between the two countries are as good, if not better, than at any point since the days of the Commonwealth, and the fact that Poland is Lithuania's most important trading partner has not gone unnoticed by either side. Top-level governmental contacts are cordial and frequent: each newly appointed Lithuanian prime minister usually jets off to see his Polish counterpart before meeting any other foreign leader. Poland lobbied succesfully for Lithuanian inclusion in NATO-led peacekeeping missions in the Balkans, and a combined Polish-Lithuanian infantry batallion – which rejoices in the rather predictably prosaic name of Litpolbat – has been formed in order to drive home the message that the two states have common defence interests. Most significantly of all Poland lent strong support to Lithuania's application to become a full member of **NATO** and both countries joined the **EU** in May 2004.

On a personal level individual Poles and Lithuanians continue to display a staggering ignorance and indifference towards each others' cultures, and yet frequently make use of the new freedom of travel to visit each others' countries to sightsee or shop – proof, of a sort, that they are well on the way to becoming normal European neighbours.

dark skies. Even without the increasing presence of onion-domed Orthodox churches, it would feel Eastern, more like Russia than Poland. The whole area also feels extremely poor, and is one of the most neglected regions of the country, with an overwhelmingly peasant population. On the long potholed country roads horsecarts and horse-drawn ploughs are a common sight. In the **Białowieża Forest** the isolation has ensured the survival of continental Europe's last belt of virgin forest – the haunt of bison, elk and hundreds of varieties of flora and fauna, and home, too, of the wondrous Żubrówka "bison grass" vodka.

Belarusians are the principal ethnic minority, numbering some 200,000 in all. Before World War II, Polish territory stretched far across the current Belarusian border, and today communities on either side are scarcely distinguishable, save that those on the eastern side are, if anything, poorer still. Another historic, but declining, minority are the **Tatars**, who settled here centuries ago and whose wooden mosques at **Bohoniki** and **Kruszyniany** are one of the sights of the Polish east: there are several more over the border. Long a melting-pot of cultures, **Białystok** and the surrounding region were also one of the main areas of **Jewish** settlement in Poland. Before the war almost every town in the region boasted at least one synagogue, often more; many of these were wooden structures, whose exuberant design clearly reflected the influence of the indigenous folk architecture. Sadly, all the wooden synagogues – pictures suggest many of them were spectacular – were burned down by the Nazis. A wealth of brick and stone **Jewish monuments** survive, though, and on any journey through the outlying towns and villages, you'll encounter former synagogue buildings and crumbling Jewish cemeteries. Of these, the restored synagogue complex at **Tykocin** is one of the most evocative Jewish monuments in the country – as in the rest of the region, the community itself was wiped out by the Nazis.

Once again, local **transport** consists mainly of buses, with services diminishing the nearer the border you get.

Białystok

Even the habitually enthusiastic official Polish guidebooks are mute on the glories of **BIAŁYSTOK**, industrial centre of northeast Poland; it's not a beautiful place and its main development occurred during the industrialization of the nineteenth century. Uniquely among major Polish cities today, however, it has kept the healthy ethnic and religious mix – Poles, Belarusians and Ukrainians, Catholic and Orthodox – characteristic of the country before the war, though the Jews, of course, are absent. And for all the industry, it's curiously one of the country's least polluted cities.

Despite the heavy wartime destruction, a number of characteristic examples of the regional **wooden architecture** have survived in parts of the city, most notably in the houses along streets such as ul. Grunwaldzka, Żelazna and Mazowiecka down from the train station in the southern section of the centre, and in the ramshackle old Bojary and Skorupy districts in the eastern part of the city.

Some history

According to legend, Białystok was founded in 1320 by the Lithuanian Grand Duke Gediminas (or **Gedymin** as he's known in Polish), but its emergence really began in the 1740s when local aristocrat Jan Branicki built a palace in the town centre. Partitioned off to Prussia and then to Russia, Białystok rapidly developed as a textile city, in competition with Prussian-dominated Łódź. In both cities, industrialization fostered the growth of a sizeable urban proletariat and a large and influential **Jewish community**. Factory strikes in the 1880s demonstrated the potency of working-class protest, as did the anti-tsarist demonstrations which broke out here in 1905. Echoing protests in other parts of the Russian empire, they elicited a similar response – an officially instigated pogrom, during which many Białystok Jews lost their lives. Fifteen years later, anticipating a victory that never came against Piłsudski's apparently demoralized forces, Lenin's troops installed a provisional government in Białystok led by **Felix Dzierżyński**, the notorious Polish Bolshevik and creator of the first ever Soviet secret police force – forerunner of the KGB.

World War II brought destruction and slaughter to Białystok. Hitler seized the town in 1939, then handed it over to Stalin before reoccupying it in 1941 – which is when the Jewish population was herded into a ghetto area and deported to the death camps. The heroic Białystok **Ghetto Uprising** of August 1943 (the first within the Reich) presaged the extinction of the city's Jewry. Nor was the killing confined to Jews. By 1945, over half the city's population was dead, with three-quarters of the town centre destroyed.

Following the end of the war, the authorities set about rebuilding the town and its industrial base. From a strictly utilitarian point of view they succeeded: today Białystok is a developed economic centre for textiles, metals and timber, with a population of over 250,000. The aesthetic cost has been high, though – the usual billowing smokestacks, ugly tower blocks and faceless open streets of postwar development. But Białystok has its share of sights – mostly associated with the Orthodox Belarusian community – and it makes an ideal base for exploring the border region to the east.

Arrival and information

The main **train station** is a five-minute bus ride (#2, #4 or #21) west of the city centre – supposedly it was built outside the centre as a punishment for anti-tsarist protests in the city. Somewhat confusingly the main exit also faces away from the town centre. On foot turn left out of the front door then left again over the footbridge and you'll be heading in the right direction. Close by, on ul. Bohaterów Monte Cassino, is the large, modern **bus station**.

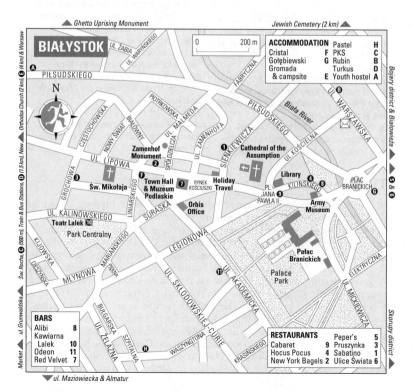

In the absence of a regular IT office, Holiday Travel, upstairs at ul. Sienk-iewicza 3 (℡085/653 7950), offers limited **tourist information**. You could also try Orbis, Rynek Kościuszki 13 (Mon–Fri 9am–5pm; ℡085/742 3047); or Almatur, ul. Zwierzyniecka 12 (Mon–Fri 9am–4pm; ℡085/742 8943), on the southern side of the centre (bus #10 from the train station), which may help with accommodation in **student hostels** (open June–Aug), whose venues change year by year. Otherwise, try going online for information at ⓦwww .city.bialystok.pl.

Accommodation

As with other major cities, the supply of hotels in Białystok is slowly but surely growing to include reasonable options in all price brackets, with the emphasis on the upper – read "business" – range. In addition there are dorm beds (25zł per person) in the all-year **youth hostel**, al. Piłsudskiego 7b (reception open 8am–8pm; ℡085/652 4250), a quaint wooden house squeezed between apart-ment blocks a fifteen-minute walk east of the train station – buses #1, #9, #12, #18 and #20 pass by. **Campers** have only one real option – the site next to the *Hotel Gromada* on ul. Jana Pawła II – bus #4 will take you there.

Hotels

Cristal ul. Lipowa 3 ℡085/742 5061, ⓦwww .cristal.com.pl. Slick and efficient upmarket hotel in a central location. The pricey restaurant is open till late. ❻

Gołębiewski ul. Pałacowa 7 ℡085/743 5435, ⓦwww.golebiewski.pl. Big, well-run place aimed at business travellers and the upper tourist bracket. Located close to the Pałac Branickich. Big weekend discounts. ❻

Gromada ul. Jana Pawła II 77 ℡085/651 1641, ⓦwww.gromada.pl. Motel-like concrete building but in a nice woodland setting on the edge of town (bus #4 from the station). ❺

Pastel ul. Waszyngtona 24a ℡085/748 6060, ⓦwww.kasol.com.pl. Smallish modern hotel offer-ing all the creature comforts, including a restaurant which does excellent game dishes. Surrounded by somewhat severe university and hospital buildings but within easy walking distance of the centre. ❺

PKS ul. Bohaterów Monte Cassino 10 ℡085/742 7614. Budget place in a gloomy block next to the bus station. Rooms (all with shared facilities) are sparsely furnished but bright and clean. No breakfast. ❷

Rubin ul. Warszawska 7 ℡085/677 2335. Old-fashioned but friendly overnighter in a fine Neoclassical building 10min walk east of the Rynek. Popular with "trade tourists" from across the border. Rooms with showers and TV or shared facilities. No breakfast. ❸

Turkus ul. Jana Pawła II 54 ℡085/662 8100. Simple en suites with TV, 1km west of the train station. Nothing special but perfectly adequate for the price. ❸

The Town

Białystok's main sights are situated on and around **ulica Lipowa**, the main thoroughfare cutting east–west across the city centre. Lipowa forms the north side of Białystok's historic centrepoint, the triangular **Rynek Kościuszki**, at the centre of which sits the **town hall**. A small, squat, eighteenth-century building, it was reconstructed from scratch after the war; these days it houses the **Muzeum Podlaskie** (Podlasie Museum; Tues–Sun 10am–5pm; 4zł). A good selection of works by some of the better-known nineteenth- and twentieth-century artists – Malczewski, Witkiewicz, Krzyzanowski and the like – is complemented by an enjoyable collection of local art, the portraits and landscapes displaying a strong feeling for the distinctive character of the region. In addition, the museum has an imaginative program of temporary shows.

A further 300m to the west along ul. Lipowa, the **Cerkiew św. Mikołaja** (St Nicholas's Church) was built in the 1840s to serve the swelling ranks of Russian settlers. A typically dark, icon-filled place of Orthodox devotion, its ornate

Ludwik Zamenhof and the Esperanto movement

Białystok's most famous son is probably **Ludwik Zamenhof** (1859–1917), the creator of **Esperanto**, the artificial language invented as an instrument of international
communication. Born in what was then a colonial outpost of the tsarist empire,
Zamenhof grew up in an environment coloured by the continuing struggle between
the indigenous Polish population and its Russian rulers – both of whom were apt to
turn on the Jews as and when the occasion suited them.

Perhaps because of this experience, from an early stage Zamenhof, an eye doctor
by training, dedicated himself to the cause of racial tolerance and understanding.
Zamenhof's attention focused on the fruits of the mythical Tower of Babel, the profusion of human languages; if a new, easily learnable **international language** could be
devised it would, he believed, remove a key obstacle not only to people's ability to
communicate directly with each other, but also to their ability to live together peace-
ably. On the basis of extensive studies of the major Western classical and modern
languages, Zamenhof – Doktoro Esperanto or "Doctor Hopeful" as he came to be
known – set himself the task of inventing just such a language, the key source being
root words common to European, and in particular Romance, languages.

The first primer, *Dr Esperanto's International Language*, was published in 1887, but
Zamenhof continued to develop his language by translating a whole range of major
literary works, *Hamlet*, Goethe's and Molière's plays and the entire Old Testament
included. The new language rapidly gained international attention, and the world's
first **Esperanto congress** was held in France in 1905. In the same year Zamenhof
completed *Fundamento de Esperanto*, his main work, which soon became the basic
Esperanto textbook and the one still most commonly in use today.

Even if it has never quite realized Zamenhof's dreams of universal acceptance,
Esperanto – **Linguo Internacia** as it calls itself – has proved considerably more
successful than any other "invented" language. With a worldwide membership of
over 100,000 and national associations in around fifty countries, the *Universala Esperanto Associo* represents a significant international movement of people attracted to
the universalist ideals as much as the linguistic practice of Esperanto. In Białystok
itself there's a thriving **Esperanto-speaking community**, with an office just southwest of the Rynek at ul. Piękna 3 (☎085/745 4600).

frescoes are careful copies of those in the Orthodox cathedral in Kiev. It is filled
to capacity for the Sunday services – worth coinciding with to hear the choir.
A kiosk inside the entrance sells replica icons while the one outside sells books,
cassettes and CDs of Orthodox music. Further down ul. Lipowa the **Orthodox
cemetery** contains another enchanting *cerkiew* – though your only chance of
getting in to look around is during the Sunday morning service.

Catholic competition comes from the huge **Cathedral of the Assumption**
at the east end of Lipowa and the imposing 1920s **Kościół św. Rocha** (St
Roch's Church) at the western end of the street. With its high spaceship-like
towers, the Cathedral of the Assumption is something of a historical curio: next
to it is a small seventeenth-century church built by the Branicki family, while
the main structure is a vast 1900 neo-Gothic building, completely dwarfing the
older church and only permitted by the tsarist authorities because the official
request billed it as an "addition".

The streets south of ul. Lipowa comprise part of the old **ghetto area**. A tablet
in Polish and Hebrew on the side of a building opposite the local courthouse
on ul. Suraska commemorates the one thousand Jews burned to death in June
1941 when the Nazis set fire to the Great Synagogue, reputedly one of the
finest in Poland, which used to stand on this site.

For a town whose population was roughly seventy percent Jewish at the turn of the twentieth century there are precious few other Jewish monuments left. Though you'd hardly guess so from today's uniform housing blocks, the streets leading north of ul. Lipowa were all mainly Jewish-inhabited before the war. Across the road from the town hall, in the leafy little park on the edge of ul. Malmeda, a **statue** commemorates the town's most famous Jewish citizen, **Ludwik Zamenhof**, the creator of Esperanto (see box, p.265), as does a plaque at the southern end of the same street. Continuing northwest over busy ul. Piłsudskiego and through streets of high concrete buildings brings you to another small park, off ul. Żabia. Tucked amongst the housing blocks, the monument to the **Białystok Ghetto Uprising** (August 16, 1943) recalls an important moment in the wartime history of the town.

The most striking building in the town centre is the **Pałac Branickich** (Branicki Palace), destroyed by the Nazis in 1944 but rebuilt on the lines of the eighteenth-century building commissioned by Jan Branicki – itself a reconstruction of an earlier palace. The main building is now a medical academy, whose classical grandeur you can wander in and admire without much trouble if you look the student part. The main front balcony, the so-called **Dzierżyński balcony**, is where Felix Dzierżyński and associates proclaimed the creation of the Polish Soviet Socialist Republic in 1920. There's a pleasant outdoor café in the inner courtyard. The **park** and formal gardens surrounding the palace are very pleasant and popular with the locals for Sunday promenading.

East of the palace across the busy main road is the **army museum** at Kilińskiego 7 (Tues–Sun 9.30am–5pm; 4zł). Among the usual collection of military items there's an interesting set of photos, newspapers and other documents from the wartime era of Soviet occupation (1939–41) and the original proclamation of the 1943 Białystok Ghetto Uprising. You can also see a Nazi "Enigma" code machine – the Polish resistance successfully cracked the code, much to the Allies' benefit. Opposite the museum is a **monument** to the AK (Home Army) – one of a number you can find spread around the city now – this time to the AK forces in the former Eastern Polish borderlands, now within Lithuania and Belarus.

Białystok's proximity to the Belarusian border ensures it a key place among the growing number of Polish towns heavily involved in "trade tourism". On Sunday mornings the open-air **market** – located on ul. Kawaleryjska, 2km south of the centre – is thronged with Belarusians, Ukrainians and others from across the border plying a strange assortment of consumer goods: gold, clothes, hi-fis, antiques, cosmetics – anything that Poles are prepared to buy. If you want **caviar**, this is the place to buy it, as the nearer the border you get, the lower the price: Gdańsk is fifty percent higher, Warsaw seventy-five. Pay in dollars only if you have to, be prepared to haggle, buy glass containers (not metal), and bear in mind that taking caviar out of Poland is illegal. Keep in mind, too, that the crowds are a haven for **pickpockets**.

Perhaps the saddest reminder of the city's one-time Jewish population is the **Jewish cemetery**, off ul. Wschodnia on the northeast edge of the city. Starting from Rynek Kościuszki in the centre of town, bus #3 stops right by the cemetery, just after the junction of ul. Władysława Wysockiego and ul. Władysława Raginisa, a 10–15-minute journey. The Jewish section of the cemetery makes for a sad contrast with the Catholic sections on either side – while the Catholic graves are without exception pristine and immaculately cared for, graves in the Jewish section have had no one to look after them since the war. The few surviving gravestones are scattered around in the undergrowth, some of them still legible, but if things carry on this way there may not be anything left in the not-too-distant future.

There's no bigger contrast imaginable than the massive new **Orthodox church** on ul. Antoniuk Fabryczny, 3km out of the centre in the northwest outskirts of the city (bus #5 will take you there). It's the largest Orthodox building in the country and a vivid testament to the new-found confidence of the Orthodox Church in Poland's eastern borderlands. The exterior attempts a blend of tradition and innovation and is impressive for size alone but it's the interior that's really worth seeing. Every available surface is decorated with murals and mosaic tiling and icons hang everywhere from ground level to the base of the lofty dome. Sunday Mass is the best time to get inside; otherwise the priest living behind the church may unlock the doors for you.

Eating, drinking and entertainment

Białystok doesn't have a huge number of **restaurants** but given its size it does offer some fairly imaginative options. Not surprisingly, most of the best places to eat are in the centre, on or around ul. Lipowa.

Restaurants and snack-bars

Cabaret Kilińskiego 15. A classy bar-restaurant, serving up modern European food. Live cabaret performances at weekends.
Hocus Pocus Kilińskiego 12. Serves decent pizza, salads and pancakes in a rather painfully trendy setting – fake sheepskin seat backs and rubber tubing dangling from the walls.
New York Bagels ul. Lipowa 12. A good option for something quick, with a range of bagel and sandwich snacks.
Peper's ul. Warszawska 30. A self-styled "eco-restaurant" and "eco-bar", serving a wide range of organic vegetarian dishes.
Pruszynka ul. Grochowa 9. Offers Polish basics like *bigos* in a cheap and cheerful cellar bar.
Sabatino ul. Sienkiewicza 3. Specializes in Mediterranean cuisine, including scrumptious seafood, served up in an interior that looks like something out of a design magazine.

Ulice Świata ul. Warszawska 30b. Located round the corner from the Gołębiewski hotel, this place has different rooms devoted to different national cuisines – Polish, Italian, Mexican and Chinese. None of the food's exceptional of its kind but it's a relaxed and friendly place.

Bars

Alibi Kilińskiego 8. A relaxed and cosy cocktail bar which livens up considerably on weekend evenings.
Kawiarna Lalek ul. Kalinowskiego 1. Inside the puppet theatre (see below), this is a lively place for an evening drink and has an outdoor patio in summer.
Odeon ul. Akademicka 10. A popular bar in an octagonal glass pavilion, with occasional live jazz or blues.
Red Velvet Rynek Kościuszki. In the courtyard of the town hall, this is the best place for alfresco daytime drinking. Summer only.

Nightlife and entertainment

Central **nightlife** options revolve around *Fama*, ul. Legionowa 5, a teen disco-bar which hosts occasonal live gigs; and *Metro*, ul. Białówny 9A, which offers mainstream dance music at the weekends, and more specialized styles (reggae, jungle) on week-nights. For **classical music** the Filharmonia, ul. Podleśna 2 (box office Mon–Fri 8am–3.30pm), runs concerts usually at least once a week. If you can cope with the language barrier, Wierszalin is an internationally known Białystok-based **theatre** group that sometimes puts on performances in town (check local listings). The Teatr Lalek at ul. Kalinowksiego 1 (☏058/742 5031, ⊛www.btl.bialystok.pl) is a popular puppet theatre, while the city theatre, Teatr Dramatyczny, is at ul. Elektryczna 12 (☏058/749 9175, ⊛www.teatrdramatyczny.bialystok.pl). The Pokój, ul. Lipowa 14, is the most central **cinema**.

Around Białystok

A handful of trips into the city's immediate surroundings are worth considering, notably the Orthodox monastery at **Supraśl**, north of the city, the Branicki Summer Palace at **Choroszcz** and the synagogue of **Tykocin**. The countryside offers some decent walking country, too, chiefly the tranquil **Puszcza Knyszyńska** stretching east of the town, a popular weekend haunt with city folk. All of these are accessible using local bus connections. Further afield is the **Biebrza National Park**, a rural idyll that's particularly popular with bird-watchers.

Supraśl and the Puszcza Knyszyńska

A sixteen-kilometre bus journey northeast of Białystok is **SUPRAŚL**, a sleepy provincial eastern hangout on the edge of the Puszcza Knyszyńska. The chief attraction here is the **Basilian Monastery** (Mon–Fri 9am–1pm & 3.30–5pm, Sat 10am–1pm, Sun 4–5pm), a complex of grand seventeenth-century buildings surrounding an impressive Orthodox church. Having seen several years' service as a local school the dilapidated monastery is once again occupied by bearded, black-robed Orthodox monks, who are carrying out thorough renovation works.

The **church** totally dominates the central courtyard. It was originally built in the sixteenth century by Grand Hetman of Lithuania, Aleksander Chodkiewicz, for the Orthodox order of St Basil, and was one of the spiritual centres of Orthodoxy in the Polish-Lithuanian Commonwealth. In 1944 Nazi bombing almost destroyed the church but the exterior, with its four defensive towers, has now been rebuilt. The interior, which was lavishly decorated with frescoes of the Serbian school, will take many years to re-create.

A small **museum** (open same hours as the monastery; 4zł) in the **Pałac Opatów** (Abbots' Palace) on the far side of the courtyard displays fragments of the original murals. The works gathered here encompass a range of themes and images: scenes from the lives of Mary and Jesus, benign-looking early church fathers and saints, ethereal archangels and cherubim – a wonderful panorama of Orthodox art and spirituality. The rooms that house the museum – the former refectory and chapel – are lavishly decorated in true baroque style. The fact that they are run down, with great swathes of paint peeling off the walls, makes them all the more atmospheric.

The Puszcza Knyszyńska

If you've come by bus from Białystok you could consider hiking back through the **Puszcza Knyszyńska**, a popular walking area with Białystok residents. The sandy local terrain is pretty easy-going underfoot, but the lack of signs once you get into the forest makes a local map, such as *Okolice Białegostoku* 1:150,000, readily available in Białystok, essential.

On a good day it's attractive and enjoyable walking country, the silence of the forest broken at intervals by cackling crows overhead or startled deer breaking for cover. Starting from the southern edge of Supraśl, a marked path takes you south through the lofty expanses of forest to the village of **Ciasne**, ending up by the bus stop near **Grabówka** at the edge of the main road back into Białystok – a twelve-kilometre hike in total.

Choroszcz

The highways and byways of eastern Poland hide a wealth of neglected old aristocratic piles, most of them relics of a not-so-distant period when a small group of fabulously wealthy families owned most of the eastern part of the country.

The eighteenth-century **Lietna Rezydencja Branickiego** (Branicki Summer Palace) at **CHOROSZCZ**, located 10km west of Białystok off the main Warsaw road, is a fine example of this phenomenon, the key difference being that the palace here has been completely renovated and converted into a **museum** (Tues–Sun 10am–3pm; 4zł, free on Sun). To get here, catch a local **bus** from Białystok; the palace is on the west side of town, just a short walk from the main stop.

The summer palace

After Białystok, the elegant statue-topped **summer palace** makes for quite a contrast with the architectural rigours of the city, with its tranquil country location on the edge of the grounds of the local hospital another agreeable feature. Few of the building's original furnishings remain; instead the house is arranged as a **museum** (Tues–Sun 10am–3pm; 4zł) of furniture and interior decoration from the time of the Branickis. The main ground-floor room is the **salon**, its sedate parquet floor complemented by a choice collection of period furniture. A portrait of the original master of the house, Jan Branicki, along with a number of other family portraits, hangs in the hallway, the finely wrought iron balustrades of the staircase illuminated by a lamp held aloft by a rather tortured-looking classical figure. The **second floor** is equally ornate, featuring a number of meticulously decorated apartment rooms, a dining room with a fine set of mid-eighteenth-century Meissen porcelain and a **Chippendale room**.

Back outside, it's worth taking a stroll along the canal running from beneath the salon windows at the back of the palace, its overgrown **grounds** stretching out in all directions. From the bridge over the canal you have a good view of the house along with the old lodge and manor farm.

Tykocin

Forty kilometres west of Białystok, north of the main Warsaw road (E18), is the quaint, sleepy little town of **TYKOCIN**, set in the open vistas of the Podlasie countryside. Tykocin's size belies its historical significance: as well as the former site of the national arsenal, it also has one of the best-restored **synagogues** in Poland today, much visited by Jewish tourist groups, a reminder that this was once home to an important Jewish community. It's a forty-minute journey from the main bus station in Białystok; services depart roughly hourly throughout the day.

The bus deposits you in the enchanting **town square**, bordered by well-preserved nineteenth-century wooden houses. The **statue** of Stefan Czarnecki in the centre of the square was put up by his grandson Jan Branicki in 1770, while he was busy rebuilding the town and his adopted home of Białystok.

The Baroque **parish church**, commissioned by the energetic Branicki in 1741, and recently restored, has a beautiful polychrome ceiling, a finely ornamented side chapel of the Virgin and a functioning Baroque organ. The portraits of Branicki and his wife, Izabella Poniatowska, are by Silvester de Mirys, a Scot who became the resident artist at the Branicki palace in Białystok. Also founded by Branicki was the nearby Bernardine convent, now a Catholic seminary. Next to the church looking onto the river bridge is the **Alumnat**, a hospice for war veterans founded in 1633 – a world first. Continue out of town over the River Narew and you'll come to the ruins of the sixteenth-century **Pałac Radziwiłłów** (Radziwiłł Palace), where the national arsenal was once kept; it was destroyed by the Swedes in 1657.

Jews first came to Tykocin in 1522, and by the early nineteenth century seventy percent of the population was Jewish, the figure declining to around

The Jedwabne Pogrom

The village of **Jedwabne**, 35km west of Tykocin, would have remained an insignificant rural backwater were it not for the recently rediscovered fact that a major anti-Jewish **pogrom** took place here on July 10, 1941. The dark secrets of Jedwabne came to light as a result of Jan Tomasz Gross's account of the pogrom in his book *Sąsiedzi* ("Neighbours"), a work that shocked the Polish public on its publication in 2000, and has remained the cause of controversy ever since.

It had long been known that something unpleasant had happened in Jedwabne in the summer of 1941. With the Red Army in full retreat and German forces moving in to take control, Jewish communities throughout eastern Poland were being faced with forced expulsions, beatings and arbitrary murder – the Jews of Jedwabne were no exception. However, it had always been assumed that crimes against the Jews had been committed by German soldiers, or local Poles acting under German duress. By talking to survivors of the Jedwabne pogrom, and piecing together a detailed chronology of events, Gross came to the disturbing conclusion that the local Poles had killed their Jewish neighbours without waiting for Nazi orders.

Relations between Poles and Jews had become strained as a result of the **Soviet occupation** of eastern Poland in 1939, with many Poles accusing the Jews of collaboration with the communist authorities. It's true that many younger Jews were attracted to communism, not least because it seemed to promise racial equality and an end to the anti-Semitic measures enacted by the Polish government in the late 1930s. The Soviet security forces recruited a higher proportion of Jews than Poles, strengthening the popular belief that the Jews were essentially pro-Bolshevik and felt little loyalty towards Poland. When Nazi Germany declared war on the Soviet Union in June 1941, Soviet power in eastern Poland melted away, leaving Jews to be scapegoated by a Polish population humiliated by two years of communist occupation.

A massacre of Jews by Poles certainly took place in **Radziłów**, a small town 20km north of Jedwabne, on July 7. Whether the locals did this on their own initiative, or because they feared German reprisals if they left the Jews alone, remains the subject of much conjecture. The Poles of Jedwabne, meanwhile, decided to take action against their Jewish fellow citizens on July 10 – according to Gross there were no German troops in town at the time. The Jews were forced from their homes and driven to the Rynek, where they were forced to demolish a statue of Lenin erected by the Soviets. They were then led along the road towards the Jewish cemetery on the outskirts of the village, with the majority being herded into a nearby stable – which was then set alight. Gross estimates that as many as 1500 died in the stable. Only a handful of Jedwabne's Jews survived, mostly by hiding out in the fields as the round-ups began.

Gross's account came as a profound shock to Polish society, not least because it suggested that Poles in wartime were just as capable of cruelty as the German occupiers. The concept of Poland as a heroic victim of Nazism had been an important plank of the country's identity in the half-century following 1945, and the idea that Poles could at the same time be the perpetrators of Nazi-style crimes was simply

fifty percent by 1900. The original wooden **synagogue** in the town centre was replaced in 1642 by the Baroque building still standing today. Carefully restored in the 1970s following the usual severe wartime damage by the Nazis, it now houses an excellent **museum** (Tues–Sun 10am–5pm; 5zł, free on Sun), where background recordings of Jewish music and prayers add to a mournfully evocative atmosphere. Information sheets in English and German give detailed background on both the building and the history of Tykocin Jewry. Beautifully illustrated Hebrew inscriptions, mostly prayers, adorn sections of the interior walls, as do some lively colourful frescoes.

incomprehensible to many. The effect of Gross's book was to split Polish society down the middle, with conservative opinion claiming that the historian's writings constituted a grotesque slur on the Polish nation, and left-liberal circles countering that the Jedwabne controversy offered a golden opportunity to face up to the past in a spirit of tolerance and forgiveness.

The response of the Polish establishment was measured and dignified. President Kwaśniewski made it clear that he would mark the sixtieth anniversary of the tragedy, scheduled for July 10, 2001, by issuing an **apology** on behalf of the Polish nation – a position supported by almost all major politicians. However, the idea that Polish honour had been besmirched retained a strong hold over the popular imagination. In Jedwabne itself, Poles who had spoken out about the pogrom were ostracized by the local community, and the local priest encouraged the distribution of anti-Semitic pamphlets. The Catholic hierarchy struggled to appease all factions in the dispute. A **remembrance service** for the victims of the pogrom was organized at All Saints' Church in Warsaw – a venue chosen because it was sited next to the wall of the wartime Warsaw ghetto – but was scheduled for May 27, 2001, in order to distance the service from President Kwaśniewski's official "apology", due to be delivered some weeks later. When the service at All Saints' took place, the Rabbi of Warsaw made his excuses and stayed away. At around the same time, Cardinal Glemp made comments in a widely distributed interview that seemed to reinforce many of the prejudices directed against Poland's Jews – namely that the Jews took a leading role in communist security forces (and should therefore apologize to the Poles rather than the other way round), and that world Jewry was leading a campaign against Poland in an attempt to make Poles admit guilt for the Holocaust.

In the lead-up to the July 10 commemoration, the site of the pogrom was subjected to intense examination, with investigators concluding that no more than 300 victims could have died at the stable, and that ammunition found at the site pointed to German involvement. While slightly diminishing the effect of Gross's book, these investigations nevertheless served to confirm that a mass murder had indeed taken place here. A new **memorial** was planned for the site, but the precise wording of the inscription caused inevitable disagreements. Ultimately it was decided to specify that the victims were indeed Jews, but the identity of the killers was skated over. A planned sentence referring to hatreds generated by "German Nazism" was omitted after complaints from the German community.

The memorial was unveiled on 10 July 2001, at a commemoration attended by a host of Polish and Jewish dignitaries – although the Polish Catholic Church declined to send a representative. Kwaśniewski delivered the kind of statesmanlike performance that was expected of him, declaring that "as a citizen and as President of Poland, I beg pardon. I beg pardon in my own name, and in the name of those Poles whose conscience is shattered by this crime." Officially, at least, the Jedwabne controversy was brought to an end, although the vexed question of Polish–Jewish relations looks set to remain the subject of debate for a long time to come.

Most striking of all is the large Baroque bimah, and there's a fine, ornate Aron Kodesh in the east wall. Valuable religious artefacts are on display, as well as historical documents relating to the now-lost community. Over the square in the old Talmud house there's a well-kept local history **museum** (same hours and ticket), featuring an intact apothecary's shop. The **Jewish cemetery** on the edge of town is gradually blending into the surrounding meadow – as so often, there's no one able or willing to take care of it. Among the eroded, weather-beaten gravestones, however, a few preserve their fine original carvings.

There's a basic **youth hostel** on ul. Kochanowskiego (July & Aug only; ☎085/718 1685) and a **hotel** inside the Alumnat at ul. Poświętne 1 (☎085/718 1649, ⓦwww.alumnat.pl; ❹). The *Tejsza* **restaurant**, behind the musuem at ul. Kozia 2, is pretty unexceptional, despite admirable attempts to reproduce some traditional Jewish dishes. The restaurant at the Alumnat is the only other option for a sit-down meal.

Biebrzański Park Narodowy

North and west of Tykocin lies one of Poland's unique natural paradises, a large area of low-lying marshland encompassed within the **Biebrzański Park Narodowy** (Biebrza National Park), added to the country's stock of officially protected areas in 1993, and, at around 600 square kilometres, its largest. Running through the area is the Biebrza River, which has its source southeast of Augustów close to the Belarusian border. It is the mainstay of an extensive network of bogs and marshes that constitutes one of Europe's most extensive and unspoilt **wetland** complexes. The scenic river basin landscape is home to richly varied flora and fauna. Important animal residents include otters, a large beaver population, wild boar, wolves and several hundred elk. The plant community includes just about every kind of marshland and forest species to be found in the country, including a rich assortment of rare mosses. The park's bird life – of which over 260 species have been recorded to date, many of them with local breeding habitats – is proving a major attraction with bird-watchers from all over Europe. **Spring** is the time to come, when floodwaters extend for miles along the river valley, making an ideal habitat for a large number of waterfowl, including the pintail, shoveler and teal, as well as such rarities as the black tern and, most prized of all, the aquatic warbler.

The park is divided into three sections corresponding to portions of the river. The **Northern Basin**, the smallest, and least easily accessible, lies in the upper part of the river, and is not much visited. The **Middle Basin** encompasses a scenic section of marshland and river forest, notably the **Red Marsh** (*Czerwone Bagno*) area, a stretch of strictly protected peatbog located some distance from the river valley floodlands that is home to a large group of elk as well as smaller populations of golden and white-tailed eagles. The area is off-limits to anyone not accompanied by an official guide (see below). The **Southern Basin**, coursed by the broad, lower stretches of the river, consists of a combination of peatbogs and marshland, and is the most popular bird-watching territory on account of the large number of species to be found here. It's relatively easy to spot elk browsing amongst the shrubs from the viewing towers in this area.

Park practicalities

The obvious starting point for any visit to the area is the national park (BPN) **headquarters** (May–Sept daily 7.30am–7pm; Oct–April Mon–Fri 7am–3pm; ☎086/272 0620, ⓦwww.biebrza.org.pl) in **TWIERDZA OSOWIEC**, a couple of hundred metres off the main Ełk–Białystok road from the train station – trains run every couple of hours in both directions. As well as selling the nominally priced **ticket** required for entrance to the park area, the helpful office staff, some of whom speak English, can arrange guides (150zł flat fee per group) and rowing boats – popular with bird-watchers.

If you want to stay in the area for a few days, **GONIĄDZ**, about 5km east of the park headquarters, is a pleasant little village and an increasingly popular base. A number of houses offer **private rooms** – there's no tourist information office here so just knock where you see a sign. The *Bartlowizna* on ul. Nadbrzeżańska 32

(☎088/272 0630; ❹) is a largish **hotel** on the edge of the village with its own tennis courts and stables. For wildlife enthusiasts and others planning to explore less accessible sections of the park, the network of basic but inexpensive **forester's lodges** (*leśniczówki*) dotted around the area are a vital resource – the BPN office in Twierdza Osowiec has the details and can also advise on other local accommodation including **campsites**. They also have a good stock of books, brochures and **maps**, of which the *Biebrzański Park Narodowy* (1:120,000), produced with support from the Worldwide Fund for Nature, is particularly useful for bird-watchers.

If you've only limited time, Twierdza Osowiec and its surroundings make a good starting point for exploration. Back up to the main road, the twisted ruin of a concrete bunker just over the other side of the railway is a reminder of a fierce World War II battle between German and Russian forces. A ring of fortifications, remnants of a tsarist-era fortress, covers the area, many of them used these days as nesting platforms for the park's bird population. Just beyond the bunker there's an observation point that provides a good panorama over the marshes beyond.

A good deal of the park can be explored **on foot**, easily accomplished thanks to an extensive network of maintained and signposted trails, taking you through areas rich in natural attractions. Alternatively, and more adventurously, you can go **by boat**, especially worthwhile if you want to head beyond the immediate vicinity of Twierdza Osowiec. The most ambitious locally organized excursion takes you along the Biebrza and Narew rivers all the way from Rajgród in the north down as far as Łomza – a five- to seven-day trip involving stopovers at campsites and forester's lodges along the river route. Check with the BPN office for current details or contact any of the Augustów agencies listed in the box on p.252.

Kruszyniany and Bohoniki

Hard up against the Belarusian frontier, the old Tatar villages of **Kruszyniany** and **Bohoniki** are an intriguing ethnic component of Poland's eastern borderlands, with their wooden mosques and Muslim graveyards. The story of how these people came to be here is fascinating in itself (see box, p.274), and a visit to the villages is an instructive and impressive experience.

Getting to them is no mean feat. Direct **buses to Kruszyniamy** from Białystok are scarce: the alternative is to take the bus to **Krynki** (about 40km) and wait for a connection to Kruszyniamy. If there aren't any of these, the only thing left to do is hitch. The only **buses to Bohoniki** are from **Sokołka** an hour's train journey north of Białystok. If you're trying to visit both villages in the same day, the best advice is to go to Kruszyniamy first, return to Krynki (probably by hitching) then take a bus towards Sokołka. Ask the driver to let you off at **Stara Kamionka**, and walk the remaining 4km east along the final stretch of the Szlak Tartarski ("Tatar Way"), which runs between the two villages. To get back to Białystok, take the late afternoon bus to Sokołka, then a train back to the city – they depart regularly up until around 10pm.

When visiting, bear in mind that to visit the mosques men and women should be appropriately dressed, with arms and legs demurely covered.

The villages

Walking through **KRUSZYNIAMY** is like moving back a century or two: the painted wooden houses, cobbled road and wizened old peasants staring at you from their front porches are like something out of Tolstoy. Surrounded by trees and set back from the road is the eighteenth-century **mosque**, recognizable by

The Tatars

Early in the thirteenth century, the nomadic Mongol people of Central Asia were welded into a confederation of tribes under the rule of Genghis Khan. In 1241 the most ferocious of these tribes, the **Tatars**, came charging out of the steppes and divided into two armies, one of which swept towards Poland, the other through Hungary. Lightly armoured, these superlative horsemen moved with a speed that no European soldiery could match, and fought with cruel and brutal efficiency, fuelled by a diet of raw meat and horse's milk thickened with blood. On Easter Day they destroyed Kraków, and in April came up against the forces of the Silesian ruler, Duke Henryk the Pious, at Legnica. Henryk's troops were annihilated, and a contemporary journal records that "terror and doubt took hold of every mind" throughout the Christian West. Before the eventual withdrawal of the Tatar hordes, all of southern Poland was ravaged repeatedly – Kraków, for example, was devastated in 1259 and again in 1287.

Within a generation, however, the Tatars had withdrawn into central Russia and the Crimea, ceasing to pose a threat to the powers of central Europe. By the late fourteenth century the Tatars of the Crimea had come under the sway of the Grand Duchy of Lithuania – a vast east-European empire which became dynastically linked to Poland after 1386. Lithuanian ruler Vytautas the Great drafted Tatar units into his armies, and a contingent of Tatars helped the Polish-Lithuanian army defeat the Teutonic Knights at the Battle of Grunwald in 1410 (see box, p.204 & pp.232–233). Over the next few centuries communities of Tatars continued to migrate into the Grand Duchy of Lithuania (which at the time covered most of Belarus and parts of present-day eastern Poland). In time, Poland effectively absorbed Lithuania and its peoples (for more on which, see box, pp.260–261). In the late seventeenth century, King Jan Sobieski granted additional lands in eastern Poland to Tatars who had taken part in his military campaigns, creating further pockets of Tatar settlement in the region, many of which – Kruszyniamy and Bohoniki included – have remained up to this day.

Today some six thousand descendants of these first Muslim citizens of Poland are spread all over the country, particularly in the Szczecin, Gdańsk and Białystok areas. Though thoroughly integrated into Polish society, they are distinctive both for their Asiatic appearance and for their faith – the Tatars of Gdańsk, for example, have recently completed a mosque. Apart from the mosques and graveyards at Bohoniki and Kruszyniamy, little is left of the old settlements in the region east of Białystok, but there are a number of mosques still standing over the border in Belarus.

the Islamic crescent hanging over the entrance gate, though the architecture is strongly reminiscent of the wooden churches of eastern Poland. A notice on the door of the mosque will tell you who the current keyholder is and where you can find them. You'll be expected to leave a few złoty as an offering.

Though the Tatar population is dwindling – currently the village musters only a handful of people for the monthly services conducted by the visiting imam from Białystok – the mosque's predominantly wooden interior is well maintained. A glance at the list of Arab diplomats in the visitor's book explains where the money comes from. The building is divided into two sections, the smaller one for women, the larger and carpeted one for men, containing the *mihrab*, the customary recess pointing in the direction of Mecca, and a *mimber* (pulpit) from which the prayers are directed by the imam.

The **Muslim cemetery**, five minutes' walk beyond the mosque, contains a mixture of well-tended modern gravestones and, in the wood behind, old stones from the tsarist era. Despite the Tatar presence, the population of the village is predominantly Belarusian, a fact reflected in the presence of an Orthodox church, an uninspiring concrete structure that replaced the wooden original, which was destroyed by fire. In summer you'll find **food** at the *Tatarska Jurta* across the road from the mosque or at *Pod Lipami*, a comfortable pension at no. 51 (☏085/722 7554; ❸).

The mosque in remoter **BOHONIKI** is a similar, though smaller, building, colourwashed in bright green on the outside, and stuffed with cosy-looking carpets within. Again you'll need to find the keyholder to let you in – the noticeboard will tell you where to go – and you should donate a few złoty for your visit.

In the **Tatar cemetery**, hidden in a copse half a kilometre south of the village, gravestones are inscribed in both Polish and Arabic with characteristic Tatar names like Ibrahimowicz – in other words, Muslim names with a Polish ending tacked on. Search through the undergrowth right at the back of the cemetery and you'll find older, tumbledown gravestones inscribed in Russian from the days when Bohoniki was an outpost of the tsarist empire. Tatars from all over Poland are still buried here, as they have been since Sobieski's time.

South from Białystok

Moving south of Białystok you're soon into the villages and fields of **Podlasie**, the heartland of the country's Belarusian population – you'll see the Cyrillic lettering of their language on posters (though not as yet on street signs) throughout the area. It's a poor, predominantly rural region that retains a distinctively Eastern feel. For visitors the best-known attraction is the ancient **Puszcza Białowieska** (Białowieża Forest) straddling the border with neighbouring Belarus. **Hajnówka**, a regional focus of Orthodox worship provides an intriguing gateway to the area. **Siemiatycze**, near the extraordinary convent at **Grabarka**, the focal point of Orthodox pilgrimage in Poland, is also worth investigating.

Buses represent the best way of getting round the region. A plenitude of services trundle south from Białystok to Hajnówka and Siemiatycze: change in Hajnówka for the Białowieża Forest and in Siemiatycze for Grabarka. On the way through the flat, wooded greenery of the Podlasie countryside you'll see more Orthodox onion domes than Catholic spires, a sure indication of the strength of the Belarusian population in the surrounding region.

Hajnówka

For most visitors to these parts, **HAJNÓWKA**, some 70km southeast of Białystok, only registers as an entry point to the enticing Białowieża forest stretching east of the town. If you have the time, however, there's good enough reason to stop off in this unhurried spot in the form of a significant Belarusian presence. As in other Belarusian-dominated parts of the region, Hajnówka has been the focus of a significant revival of Orthodox traditions and spirituality. The prime testimony to this is the **Cerkiew Świętej Trójcy** (Church of the Holy Trinity), a magnificent church begun in the early 1970s and completed amid much fanfare in 1992. An imposing, unconventionally shaped structure with a curving roof punctured by a pair of onion-domed towers topped by Orthodox crucifixes, the interior boasts a fine iconostasis, a series of luminous frescoes, and a fine set of stained-glass windows from Kraków. As usual in Orthodox churches the place is generally only open during services, which in this case is quite often. Failing that, during regular daylight hours you should be able to persuade one of the priests living in the presbytery opposite the main entrance to open up the church for you.

Poles and Belarusians

Poles and Belarusians have a long history of living together, but also one of long-suppressed cultural and political antagonisms, which began to surface with the collapse of communism. Under the old regime, minorities were actively recruited into the party and state security apparatus, and their Orthodox faith was given active state backing – so long as the community kept its separatist or nationalist impulses in check. Use of the Belarusian language was forbidden in public, and there were no concessions to the culture in schools or cultural institutions. Despite this, a handful of illicit Belarusian publications circulated during the communist years.

The result of these years of active state co-option, inevitably, was to reinforce Catholic Polish suspicion of their neighbours. With the state controls off, this suspicion has on occasion surfaced as openly expressed hostility. Meanwhile, Belarusians have reawakened their own search for a meaningful national identity. The **Polish-Belarusian community**, currently 250,000–300,000 strong, forms under one percent of the population of Poland but is still one of the largest minority groups after Germans and Ukrainians. Cultural, political and religious associations are flourishing, Belarusian newspapers, magazines and books are published in abundance, and there is a Belarusian radio station in Białystok.

Inevitably, a key concern for Polish-Belarusians is the question of cross-border ties with Belarus itself, a concern echoed by the substantial Polish minority in Belarus, an estimated 420,000-strong and likewise concentrated in the border regions. At the official political level, relations were long complicated by Belarusian demands that Białystok and its surroundings be declared an ethnic Belarusian region – a demand rejected by the Polish side on the grounds that its acceptance would undermine the territorial cohesion of the country. Relations improved visibly in the wake of the breakup of the USSR and the emergence of an independent Belarus in 1991. As with Poland's other eastern neighbours things progressed reasonably smoothly over the next few years, especially following the signing of an economic and trade agreement in October 1991, followed by a further official Friendship and Co-operation Treaty in June 1992. A number of new **border-crossing points** were established, the most important being the crossing at Sławatycze–Damachava, an old military bridge opened to civilian traffic.

As in other borderlands, the key underlying issue for the Belarusian community is how far government policy on minorities will go beyond rhetorical declarations towards active support for their development. At the political level, **relations** between Belarus and Poland have been severely strained by the behaviour of President Alyaksandr Lukashenka, whose increasingly confrontational and authoritarian style has won him few friends either at home or abroad. Lukashenka's Soviet-style treatment of political dissent and opposition has led to vocal Polish campaigns in support of the Belarusian opposition reminiscent of the Solidarity era. Hardly helping matters is a foreign policy that emphasizes a new customs union with the Russian Federation, while his general revival of ties with Moscow runs firmly against Poland's preoccupations with NATO and European integration. With Belarus increasingly following Putin's lead, and a 2004 referendum that did away with time limits on the presidential term suggesting that Lukashenka will be around for some time to come, Polish suspicions about its neighbour are on the rise.

Symbolizing the church's standing in the world of Polish Orthodoxy, once a year in early May it plays joint host, along with the nearby Dom Kultury at ul. Białostocka 2 (☏085/682 3203), to a week-long **festival** of Orthodox choral music, attracting top-notch Orthodox choirs from around the world and broadcast on national radio. There's also a small **museum** of Belarusian culture at ul. 3 Maja 42 (Tues–Sun: June–Sept 9am–4pm; Oct–May 10am–3pm; 4zł), housing a modest but informative collection.

Having seen the church and the museum, your best bet is to continue east-wards towards the Białowieża forest. Before you set out, the helpful **tourist information** office at ul. 3 Maja 45 (Mon–Fri 9am–5pm, Sat 9am–1pm; ☎085/682 5141) can sell you maps and give you information on the park, as well as on Hajnówka and the surrounding area. If you need a **place to stay**, the *Orzechowski*, ul. Piłsudskiego 14 (☎085/682 2758; ❹), has comfortable en suites, while the *Dom Nauczyciela*, ul. Piłsudskiego 6 (☎085/682 2585; ❷), has simple rooms with shared facilities, but is pretty small – don't bank on getting a place. The main **eating** options are *Leśny Dworek*, in the same building as the museum, offering Belarusian dishes (such as pork chops stuffed with ham and peas), and the restaurant of the *Orzechowski*.

The Puszcza Białowieska

One hundred kilometres southeast of Białystok, the **Puszcza Białowieska** (Białowieża Forest) is the last major tract of primeval forest left in Europe. Covering 1260 square kilometres and spreading way over the border into Bela-rus, a large part of the forest is included in the **Białowieski Park Narodowy** (Białowieża National Park), the first national park to be established in Poland and the only one currently numbered among UNESCO's World Natural Heritage sites. As well as being an area of inestimable beauty, the forest is also famous for harbouring a large population of **European bison** – captive speci-mens can be seen in a special reserve.

For centuries Białowieża was a private hunting ground for a succession of Lithuanian and Belarusian princes, Polish kings, Russian tsars and other poten-tates – patronage which ensured the forest survived largely intact. Recognizing its environmental importance, the Polish government turned large sections of the *puszcza* into a national park in 1921, not least to protect its bison herds, which had been hunted and eaten to extinction by famished soldiers during World War I. Like most *puszcza*, Białowieża has hidden its fair share of partisan armies, most notably during the 1863 uprising and World War II; monuments scatter the area, as no doubt do the bones of countless unknown dead.

Nearly forty percent of the forest located on the Polish side of the border belongs to a so-called **strict reserve** (*rezerwat ścisły*), a tightly controlled area clearly marked on the maps that can only be visited accompanied by a guide. Although subject to the usual national park regulations the rest of the area is open for visits, with or without guides, on the signed walking, cycling and horse-riding **trails**. If you're planning on spending any time in this part of the country, the extraordinary, primeval feel of the forest makes even a day-trip an experience not to be missed.

The place to aim for is **Białowieża** village, starting point for guided tours of the strict forest reserve, and also within walking distance of the bison reserve. There's one daily **bus** from Białystok to the village; if you miss this, catch one of the (roughly hourly) buses to Hajnówka, where you can pick up one of the frequent PKS buses or privately run Oktobus minibuses to Białowieża. If you start early in the day, you can treat the forest as a day-trip and be back in Białystok by nightfall. However there's plenty of **accommodation** in Białowieża, and the idea of a reposeful night or two in this beautiful landscape has undoubted appeal.

Białowieża and the Palace Park
BIAŁOWIEŻA, a mere 2km from the Belarusian border, is a sleepy agri-cultural village full of the single-storey wooden farmhouses that characterize

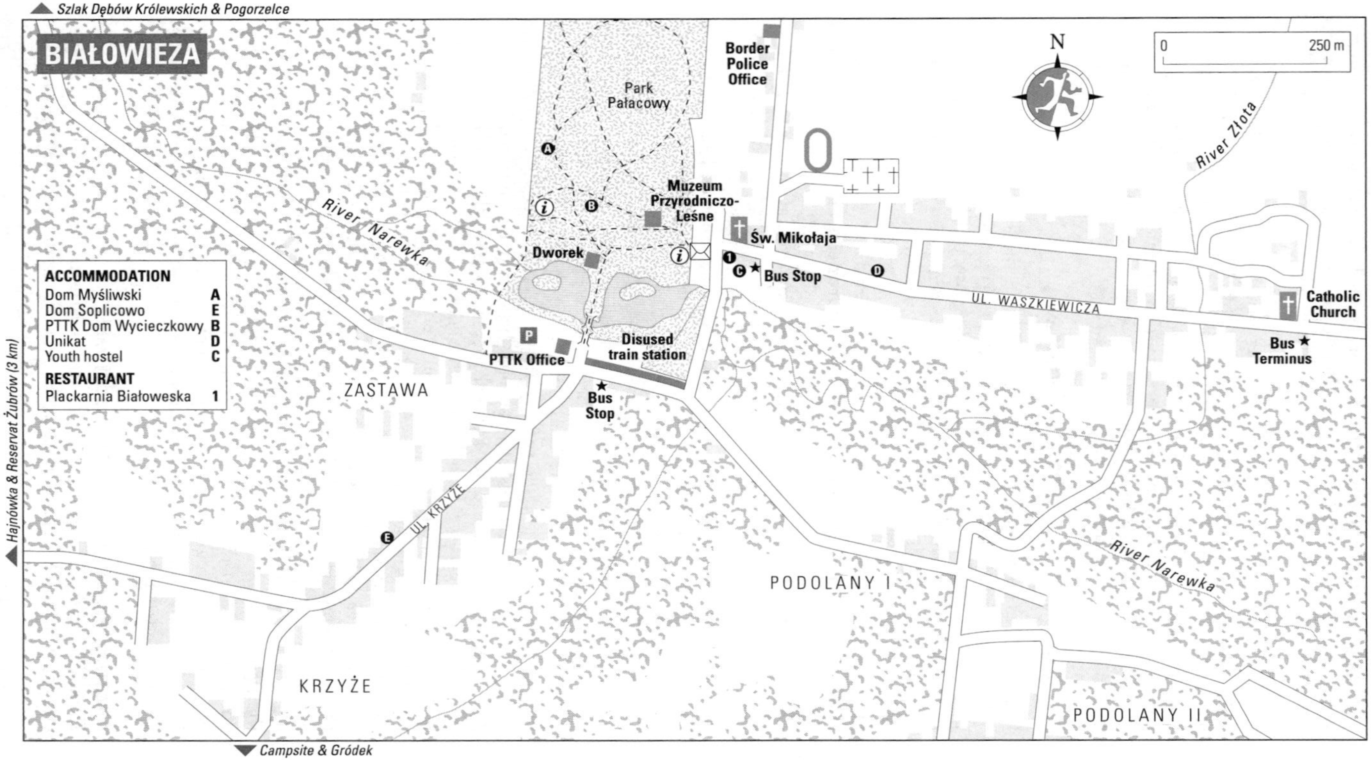

BIAŁOWIEŻA

250 m

N

River Złota

Catholic Church

Bus Terminus

Bus Stop

Św. Mikołaja

UL. WASZKIEWICZA

River Narewka

PODOLANY II

PODOLANY I

Border Police Office

Park Pałacowy

Muzeum Przyrodniczo-Leśne

Disused train station

Bus Stop

Dworek

PTTK Office

P

River Narewka

ZASTAWA

UL. KRZYŻE

KRZYŻE

Szlak Dębów Królewskich & Pogorzelce ◄

Hajnówka & Rezerwat Żubrów (3 km) ▼

Campsite & Gródek ▼

ACCOMMODATION
Dom Myśliwski — A
Dom Soplicowo — E
PTTK Dom Wycieczkowy — B
Unikat — D
Youth hostel — C

RESTAURANT
Piekarnia Białowieska — 1

Poland's eastern borderlands. Colourwashed in a variety of ochres, maroons and greens, with neatly stacked woodpiles in every yard, they're a picture of domestic tidiness. As the sprinkling of satellite dishes and gleaming new red roofs shows, tourism has made the village relatively prosperous compared with other parts of Podlasie.

Buses terminate at the eastern end of the village, opposite a red-brick Catholic church, although you'll save time by getting off earlier – either at the southern gate of the **Park Pałacowy** (Palace Park), near the disused train station; or at the eastern entrance to the Park, opposite a typical late-nineteenth-century Orthodox **Cerkiew św. Mikołaja** (Church of St Nicholas), which boasts a unique and very attractive tiled iconostasis.

The Palace Park is not part of the strict reserve so you're free to wander round it at your leisure. It was laid out in the 1890s to accompany an impressive palace, built at Tsar Alexander III's behest and destroyed by the retreating Nazis in 1944. Containing a brace of ornamental lakes and an agreeably strollable collection of tree-lined walkways, the park also harbours the **Muzeum Przyrodniczo-Leśne** (Forest Museum; June–Sept Mon–Fri 9am–4.30pm, Sat & Sun 9am–5pm; Oct–May Tues–Sun 9am–4pm; 20zł). The hefty entrance fee (which includes an English-speaking guide) is justified by an impressively detailed and well-presented introduction to the forest, including examples of the amazingly diverse flora and fauna. The tour lasts about an hour and includes a climb up the viewing tower to look out over the park and forest. Just downhill from the museum to the west is the deep blue-green **Dworek** (Little House; Mon–Fri 8am–4pm; 4zł), a timber-built former hunting lodge which now hosts art and photography exhibitions, usually with an ecological theme.

Visiting the forest

The parts of the forest most people want to see belong to the "strict reserve" to the north and west of the village, which can only be visited in the company of an **official guide**, although "non-strict" parts, including the **Rezervat Żubrów** and the **Szlak Dębów Królewskich** (see p.280), can be freely accessed whether you have a guide or not. To arrange a guide, ask at the PTTK office at the southern entrance to the Palace Park (Mon–Fri 8am–4pm, Sat & Sun 8am–3pm; ☏085/681 2295).

Most people choose to enter the forest as part of a **horse–drawn cart tour**. Only eleven carts are permitted in a day, which makes booking a day ahead a sound policy in summer. For a standard (2–3hr) trip to the bison reserve, reckon on paying about 145zł for the cart; for a five-hour trip going into the strict reserve it's 170zł. The cost of a Polish-speaking guide is included in the price; an English-speaking guide will cost an additional 100zł.

Dedicated enthusiasts maintain that exploring the forest **on foot** is the best way to experience its charms, especially if you want a chance of seeing wild animals. Licensed guides are allowed to take groups of up to 25 people on walking tours (2–3hr) including the strict reserve. Here your only costs will be for the guide (165zł per group) and the **ticket** (6zł) that everyone entering the strict reserve, by whatever means of transport, is required to purchase.

However you decide to enter the strict reserve, it's likely to be a magical experience. At times the serenity of the forest's seemingly endless depths is exhilarating, the trunks of oak, spruce and hornbeam swell threateningly to a dense canopy, momentarily pierced by shafts of sunlight that sparkle briefly before subsiding into gloom. Along with the larger animals, such as wolves, elk and beavers, the forest supports an astounding profusion of **flora and fauna**:

over twenty species of tree, twenty of rodents, thirteen varieties of bat, 228 of birds and around 8000 different insect species.

The Rezervat Żubrów

Situated some 4km west of the village on the road to Hajnówka, and accessible on foot along the green and yellow marked trails that start at the museum, the **Rezervat Pokazowy Zwierząt** (Tues–Sun 9am–5pm; 6zł) is a large fenced area where some of the most impressive species living in the forest are on display, including a few representatives of the 250-strong population of bison. Don't be fooled by their docile demeanour: when threatened, the bison – *żubr* in Polish – can charge at over 50km an hour, which makes for a force to be reckoned with when you bear in mind that the largest weigh in excess of 1000kg. The stout, sandy-coloured horses with a dark stripe on their backs that are also on show are **tarpans**, relations of the original steppe horses that died out in the last century. The tarpans are gradually being bred back to their original genetic stock after centuries of interbreeding with village horses. In other enclosures round the reserve you can see wolves, elk, wild boar, red deer and the *żubroń*, a vast and improbable-looking cross between bison and cow that's been specially bred here.

The Szlak Dębów Królewskich

One of the most memorable parts of the forest lying outside the strict reserve is the **Szlak Dębów Królewskich** (Royal Oaks Way; 4zł at busy times), located 3km north of the bison reserve along a yellow marked trail. It consists of a group of forty-metre-high oaks, the oldest of which are over four hundred years old. Each of the brooding, venerable specimens ranged along the forest path is named after one of the monarchs of the Polish-Lithuanian Commonwealth.

Park practicalities

The park **information centre**, just inside the eastern entrance to the Park Pałacowy (June–Sept 9am–4pm; ☎085/681 2901), gives away English-language leaflets detailing the attractions of the forest, sells local maps, and keeps a list of **private rooms** (reckon on 40–50zł per person) in the village. There are a couple of **hotels** within the palace park itself: the *PTTK Dom Wycieczkowy*, just west of the museum (☎085/681 2505; ❶), is a basic place located in the former palace stable, with a rudimentary café but no restaurant. Marginally better is the *Dom Myśliwski* (☎085/681 2584; ❷), a short walk north of the *PTTK*, which offers large rooms in a tranquil setting, again without a restaurant, though kitchen facilities are available. Alternative options are spread around the village. The *Unikat* at ul. Waszkiewicza 39 (☎085/681 2774; ❸), a short walk east of the palace park, is a good-quality, family-run *pensjonat*; while the *Dom Soplicowo*, ul. Krzyże 2a (☎085/681 2840, ⓦwww.dwor-soplicowo.pl; ❻), is extremely comfortable, though the full-on theming with thatch, animal skins and rustic furniture is a little over-the-top. The all-year **youth hostel**, just opposite the Orthodox church at ul. Waszkiewicza 6 (☎085/681 2560, ⓦwww.paprotka .com.pl), has dorm rooms at 20zł per bed and some doubles (❶). *U Michała* at ul. Krzyże 11 (☎085/681 2703) is the best-organized **campsite** but many villagers also allow more informal camping in their gardens in summer – look for *Pole namiotowe* signs.

For **eating**, the *Plackarnia Białoweska* by the park's east gate is good for a quick snack. The *Unikat* has a bar and restaurant in the basement offering fine Polish staples including a choice of game dishes, but for a top-quality meal you

△ Bison, Białowieża forest

should visit the restaurant at the *Soplicowo* – it's pricey by Polish standards but well worth it.

Siemiatycze and Grabarka

Lying about halfway between Białowieża and Warsaw, **SIEMIATYCZE** is a scruffy-looking market town serving the local farming communities, though it's not a bad place to break your journey and is just a short hop from **Grabarka** (see below). As usual the main square forms the focal point of the town. The **Catholic parish church** is ornate early Baroque with a triumphal-looking altarpiece and characteristic yellow and white stucco decoration. Following the Red Army's invasion of eastern Poland at the outbreak of World War II, the people of Siemiatycze found themselves inside Soviet territory, a fact recalled in the plaque inside the church commemorating Operation Bursa ("Akcja Bursa"), in the course of which Soviet forces attacked and liquidated AK (Home Army) bases in the forests east of the town, rounded up many local people and deported them to Siberia, most of them never to return. Just down the hill is the main local Orthodox **Cerkiew św. Piotra i Pawła** (Church of SS Peter and Paul), a typical nineteenth-century *cerkiew* that's looking much the better for a recently completed restoration.

Orthodox aside, the other main religious community here used to be **Jews**; typically, for the region before the war Jews comprised some forty percent of the town's population. South of the square off ul. Pałacowa is the former town **synagogue**, an eighteenth-century brick building that somehow survived the depredations of the Nazis. Following wartime use as an arsenal, the synagogue was restored in the 1960s though is starting to look run down again. The synagogue now houses the local Dom Kultury and local **museum** (Tues–Fri 10am–6pm, Sat 10am–2pm, Sun 2–6pm; 3zł), which has a presentable collection of local exhibits enhanced by some displays devoted to local Jewish themes. As often, the **Jewish cemetery**, east past the bus station on ul. Polna, is run down and wildly overgrown.

For a **place to stay**, the *Cezar* (☎085/656 4060; ❹), not far from the bus station at ul. 11 Mickiewicza 10, has neat and tidy doubles. Back in town, the *Oleńka*, just off the main square at ul. Grodzieńska 7, is the most central **restaurant**.

The Grabarka convent

Hidden away in the woods round Siemiatycze, the **convent** near the village of **GRABARKA**, 10km east of town, is the spiritual centre of contemporary Polish Orthodoxy; primarily a site of pilgrimage, it occupies a place in Polish Orthodox devotions similar to that of Częstochowa (see p.456) for Catholics. The contrast between the two religious centres couldn't be more striking, however: where the Jasna Góra monastery is all urban pomp and majesty, the Grabarka site is steeped in a powerful aura of rural mystery. If you've become accustomed to processions of Catholic sisters on the streets of Polish cities, the sight of the twenty or so Orthodox-robed nuns making their way to the church in Grabarka comes as quite a surprise. Sisters of the convent established here in 1947 to bring together all Orthodox women's religious communities within the country, they carefully – and understandably – guard their privacy from the hordes of pilgrims who descend for the major festivals of the Orthodox calendar.

Approached by a quiet forest road, the **church** stands at the top of a small wooded hill. Whether by accident or design – local opinion is divided on the issue – the church was burnt to the ground in 1991, a cause of great sadness among the Belarusian and Orthodox communities for whom it has long been a treasured shrine. Workmen set to work rebuilding it – judging by the brass plating used on the onion-domed roof, no expense was spared, either – and a new but very traditional-looking building is now fully functional. The best-known and certainly most striking feature, however, is the thicket of **wooden crosses**, the oldest dating back to the early eighteenth century, when pilgrims drawn by stories of miracles said to have occurred during a local epidemic of cholera first began coming here, packing the slopes below the church. A traditional gesture of piety carried by pilgrims and placed here on completing their journey, the thousands of characteristic Orthodox crucifixes clustered together in all shapes and sizes are an extraordinarily powerful sight; with all this wood around, the "no lighting-up" signs sprinkled among the crosses come as no surprise.

Despite the convent's backwoods location, groups of devotees can be found visiting the place at most times of the year. The biggest pilgrimages, however, centre round major Orthodox feast and holy days, notably August 19, the **Przemienienia Panskiego (Spasa)** – Feast of the Transfiguration of the Saviour – when thousands of Orthodox faithful from around the country flock to Grabarka, many by foot, for several days of celebrations beginning with an all-night vigil in the immediate run-up to the main feast day. As much celebrations of cultural identity as their Catholic counterparts are for Poles, the festivals at Grabarka offer a powerful insight into the roots of traditional, predominantly peasant Orthodox devotion.

If you don't have your own transport, note that **buses** run to Grabarka village – roughly half a kilometre from the convent – two or three times a day from Siemiatycze, more often in summer. Alternatively you can take a **train** from Hajnówka or Białystok to the village of Sycze, and walk the approximately 1km distance remaining though the woods up to the convent.

Travel details

Trains

Białystok to: Augustów (5 daily; 2hr); Gdańsk (3 daily; 7hr 30min; couchettes); Kraków (1 daily; 5hr); Olsztyn (5 daily; 5–6hr); Suwałki (5 daily; 3hr); Warsaw (9 daily; 2hr 15min).

Gdańsk to: Białystok (3 daily; 7hr 30min; couchettes); Bydgoszcz (hourly; 2hr); Częstochowa (2 daily; 8hr); Elbląg (hourly; 1hr 20min); Hel (July & Aug only: 3 daily; 3hr 15min); Katowice (3 daily; 9–10hr; couchettes); Kołobrzeg (3 daily; 2hr 30min); Koszalin (5 daily; 3hr); Kraków (4 daily; 7hr); Łódź (4 daily; 5hr 30min–6hr); Malbork (every 30 min; 1hr–1hr 30min); Olsztyn (6 daily; 2hr 30min); Poznań (6 daily; 4hr 30min); Przemyśl (1 daily; 10hr); Rzeszów (1 daily; 9hr); Szczecin (5 daily; 5hr 20min); Toruń (4 daily; 3hr); Warsaw (12 daily; 4hr); Wrocław (3 daily; 7hr).

Gdynia to: Hel via Puck (7 daily; 2hr).

Hel to: Gdynia (7 daily; 2hr).

Mikołajki to: Mrągowo (2 daily; 50min); Olsztyn (2 daily; 2hr 15min).

Mrągowo to: Mikołajki (2 daily; 50min); Olsztyn (2 daily; 1hr 20min).

Olsztyn to: Białystok (5 daily; 5–6 hr); Elbląg (11 daily; 1hr 30min–2hr); Gdańsk (6 daily; 2hr 30min); Kraków (1 daily; 8hr 30min); Mikołajki (2 daily; 2hr 15min); Mrągowo (2 daily; 1hr 20min); Poznań (2 daily; 4hr 45min); Szczecin (4 daily; 8hr 30min; couchettes); Toruń (6 daily; 2hr 30min–3hr); Warsaw (4 daily; 3hr 30min); Wrocław (2 daily; 7hr); Zakopane (1 daily; 13hr 30min).

Suwałki to: Białystok (5 daily; 2–3hr); Kraków (June–Sept only: 1 daily; 12hr); Warsaw (3–5 daily; 5hr).

Toruń to: Bydgoszcz (hourly; 1hr); Gdańsk (4 daily; 3hr); Kraków (1 daily; 7hr); Łódź (4 daily; 2hr 30min–3hr 30min); Olsztyn (5 daily; 2hr 30min–3hr); Poznań (5 daily; 2hr 15min); Warsaw (5 daily; 2hr 45min); Wrocław (2 daily; 4hr 45min).

Buses

Augustów to: Białystok (7 daily; 1hr 40min); Giżycko (1 daily; 2hr 40min); Sejny (4 daily; 1hr); Suwałki (20 daily; 45min); Warsaw (4 daily; 4hr 20min).

Białystok to: Augustów (7 daily; 1hr 40min); Białowieża (1 daily; 2hr 30min); Choroszcz (hourly; 30min); Hajnówka (4 daily; 1hr 10min); Lublin (2 daily; 6hr); Olsztyn (3 daily; 5hr); Suwałki (6 daily; 2hr 20min); Tykocin (8 daily; 40min); Warsaw (1 daily; 6hr).

Chełmno to: Bydgoszcz (6 daily; 1hr); Toruń (4 daily; 1hr).

Elbląg to: Frombork (every 30min; 45min); Kadyny (1 daily; 35 min); Krynica Morska (16 daily; 1hr 30min).

Gdańsk to: Białystok (1 daily; 9hr); Chmielno (5 daily; 1hr 20min); Elbląg (every 30min; 1hr 30min); Frombork (5 daily; 2hr 30min); Gniew (6 daily; 1hr 10min); Giżycko (4 daily; 5hr 20min); Hel (June–Sept only: 1 daily; 2hr 30min); Kamień Pomorski (1 daily; 7hr 30min); Kartuzy (every 30min; 1hr); Kętrzyn (4 daily; 5hr 30min); Kołobrzeg (1 daily; 6hr); Koszalin (1 daily; 5hr); Krynica Morska (hourly; 1hr 40min); Lębork (15 daily; 1hr 30min); Lidzbark Warmiński (4 daily; 5hr 30min); Malbork (7 daily; 1hr 20min); Olsztyn (6 daily; 3hr 20min); Sztutowo (hourly; 1hr 15min); Świnoujście (1 daily; 7hr 30min); Toruń (2 daily; 4hr 30min); Warsaw (4 daily; 6hr).

Gdynia to: Hel (16 daily; 2hr); Jastrzębia Gora (every 30min; 1hr 15min); Łeba (3 daily; 2hr 10min); Puck (16 daily; 35min); Warsaw (4 daily; 7hr).

Giżycko to Gdańsk (4 daily; 5hr 20min); Kętrzyn (9 daily; 50min); Mikołajki (4 daily; 50min); Mrągowo (every 20min; 1hr 20min).

Hajnówka to: Białowieża (10 daily; 45min); Białystok (4 daily; 1hr 10min).

Hel to: Gdynia (16 daily; 2hr); Jastrzębia Góra (4 daily; 1hr); Puck (20 daily; 1hr 20min).

Kartuzy to: Chmielno (10 daily; 15min).

Kętrzyn to: Gdańsk (4 daily; 5hr 30min); Giżycko (9 daily; 50min); Mrągowo (20 daily; 40min); Olsztyn (2 daily; 2hr 20min); Reszel (20 daily; 25min); Węgorzewo (18 daily; 1hr 5min).

Mikołajki to: Giżycko (4 daily; 50min); Mrągowo (2 daily; 30min); Olsztyn (1 daily; 2hr 15min); Warsaw (4 daily in summer; 5hr 40min).

Mrągowo to: Białystok (2 daily; 4hr); Gdańsk (1 daily; 5hr 30min); Giżycko (16 daily; 1hr 40min); Kętrzyn (20 daily; 45min); Olsztyn (24 daily; 1hr 30min); Pisz (8 daily; 1hr); Ruciane-Nida (8 daily; 40min); Suwałki (4 daily; 3hr 50min); Warsaw (1 daily; 5hr).

Olsztyn to: Białystok (2 daily; 4hr); Gdańsk (3 daily; 4hr); Kętrzyn (20 daily; 1hr 30min); Lidzbark Warmiński (8 daily; 1hr 10min); Mikołajki (3 daily; 2hr); Mrągowo (24 daily; 1hr 30min); Warsaw (3 daily; 5hr).

Puck to: Gdynia (16 daily; 35min); Hel (20 daily; 1hr 20min); Jastrzębia Gora (every 30min; 45min).

Sejny to Puńsk (7 daily; 45min).

Suwałki to: Augustów (20 daily; 45min); Mrągowo (5 daily; 3hr); Puńsk (7 daily; 50min); Sejny (every 30min; 50min); Warsaw (4 daily; 5hr).

Toruń to: Bydgoszcz (hourly; 50min); Chełmno (4 daily; 1hr); Ciechocinek (12 daily; 35min); Łódź (2 daily; 3hr 20min); Warsaw (8 daily; 4hr 30min).

Ferries

Gdańsk to: Hel (May to mid-June & Sept 1 daily; mid-June to end Aug 4 daily).
Gdynia to: Hel (May to mid-June & Sept 2 daily; mid-June to end Aug 8 daily).

International Trains

Gdańsk to: Berlin (1 daily; 9hr).
Suwałki to: Šeštokai (2 daily; 2hr).

International Buses

Białystok to: Minsk (1 daily; 7hr), Vilnius (1 daily; 9hr).
Gdańsk to: Kaliningrad (2 daily; 7hr); Vilnius (daily; 11hr).
Kętrzyn to: Kaliningrad (1 daily; 4hr).
Mrągowo to: Vilnius (1 weekly; 9hr).
Olsztyn to: Vilnius (1 weekly; 8hr).
Suwałki to: Vilnius (1 daily; 6hr).

3

Southeastern Poland

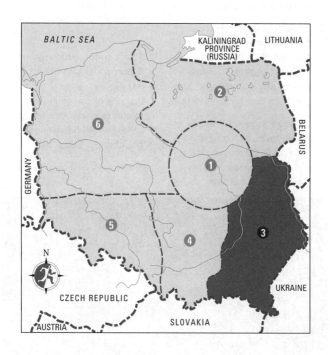

CHAPTER 3 # Highlights

✳ **Lublin** Youthful and vibrant city with a wonderfully atmospheric old centre. See p.290

✳ **Kozłówka** A stunning Baroque palace with lavish interiors, some of which have been given over to a mesmerizing museum of communist-era art and propaganda. See p.303

✳ **Kazimierz Dolny** The best-preserved medieval town in this part of Poland, long the favoured weekend destination for arty Warsaw folk. See p.312

✳ **Zamość** Sixteenth-century model town, built as a showcase for Renaissance ideals and with a pronounced Italianate feel. See p.323

✳ **The Icon Museum, Sanok** A treasure-trove of Orthodox art that's also a monument to the cultural diversity of the region. See p.348

✳ **The Bieszczady** This remote area of bare hills in the far southeastern corner of Poland is one of the most attractive expanses of wilderness in the country. See p.351

✳ **The wooden church in Binarowa** The interior of this late-Gothic village church, just one of scores in the region, is a splendid jumble of centuries-old furnishings and polychromy. See p.368

△ Castle, Kazimierz Dolny

Southeastern Poland

The **southeast** is the least populated and least known part of Poland: a great swath of border country, its agricultural plains punctuated by remote, backwoods villages and a few market towns. It is peasant land, the remnants of the great European *latifundia* – the feudal grain estates – whose legacy was massive emigration, from the late 1800s until World War II, to France, Germany and, above all, the USA.

Borders have played an equally disruptive role in recent history. Today's **eastern frontier**, established after the last war, sliced through the middle of prewar Poland, leaving towns like Lublin (and L'viv, formerly an important Polish city but now inside the Ukraine) deprived of their historic links. Border restrictions were eased in the 1990s, bringing a flood of ex-Soviet "trade tourists" – small-time merchants who gave a international touch to the region's street markets – but the tighter controls mandated by Poland's EU accession have stemmed this flow. Long-distance traffic, however, is still on the rise, especially on the main international roads. In the genuine wilderness of the **highland areas** you come upon a more extreme political repercussion of the War, with the minority **Łemks** and **Boyks** just beginning to re-establish themselves, having been expelled in the wake of the civil war that raged here from 1945 to 1947. In addition, this area's ethnic diversity is further complicated by divisions between Catholic, Uniate and Orthodox communities.

None of this may inspire a visit, yet the east can be a highlight of any Polish trip. Main town of the region is bustling, self-confident **Lublin**, a major industrial centre that also boasts one of Poland's most magical Stare Miasto areas. The smaller towns, particularly the old trading centres of **Kazimierz Dolny** and **Sandomierz** along the Wisła River, are among the country's most beautiful, long favoured by artists and retaining fine historic centres. A cherished weekend retreat of the Warsaw artistic set, Kazimierz in particular is one of the liveliest summertime destinations that Poland has to offer. Over to the east, **Zamość** has a superb Renaissance centre, miraculously preserved through wars and well worth a detour, while in the south there's the stately **Łańcut Castle**, an extraordinary reminder of prewar, aristocratic Poland. Each summer the castle hosts a chamber music festival, one of the most prestigious Polish music events. Other towns of note in the region include **Biecz** and **Krosno**, both of which long ago grew wealthy from trade with Hungary. Beer and nature lovers will probably want to make a beeline for **Zwierzyniec**, where an excellent local brewery lies adjacent to the deep forests of **Roztoczański national park**. The mountains of the far southeast, though not as high or as dramatic as the Tatras to the west, are much more isolated. A week or so hiking in the **Bieszczady** is time well spent, the pleasures of the landscapes reinforced by easy contact

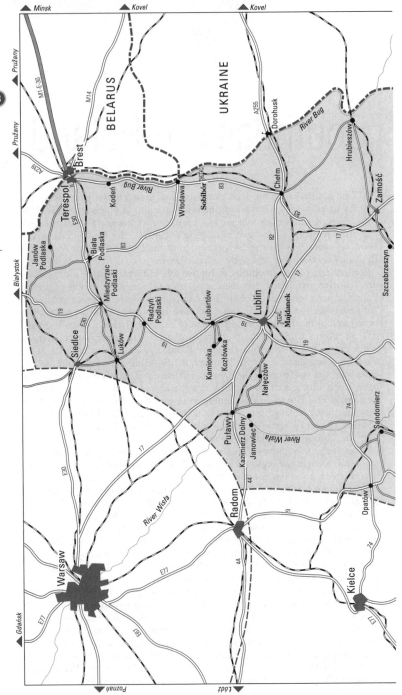

Iwaniska
Ujazd
Klimontów
Stalowa Wola
Bełzec
Tarnobrzeg
Baranów Sandomierski
Zwierzyniec
River Wisła
River San
ROZTOCZAŃSKI NATIONAL PARK
Hrebenne
Leżajsk
Łańcut
Tarnów
Rzeszów
Jarosław
Korczowa
UKRAINE
L'viv
Chotyniec
River Dunajec
River San
Przemyśl
Krasiczyn
Medyka
A259
A256
Bobowa
Biecz
Jasło
Krosno
Ulucz
Kalwaria Pacławska
Nowy Sącz
Gorlice
Bóbrka
Czerteż
Sanok
Dukla
Stary Sącz
BESKID NISKI MTS
Ustrzyki Dolne
Lesko
M17 - E471
Piwniczna
Krynica
Barwinek
Komańcza
A262
BIESZCZADY MTS
Cisna
Wetlina
Ustrzyki Górne
River Poprad
E371
SLOVAKIA
0
50 km
N
Kraków
Kraków
Prešov, Košice & Budapest

with the welcoming locals. The **Beskid Niski**, to the west, has some great rewards too: in particular its amazing *cerkwie*, **wooden churches** with pagoda-like domes and colourful interiors that are among the most spectacular folk architecture of Europe.

This region of Poland is rich in **Jewish heritage** too, although historical sites and synagogues are not always maintained or accessible. Kazimierz Dolny, Sandomierz and **Jarosław** form a procession of formerly Jewish-dominated towns situated along the old East–West trading routes, and the names of various obscure hamlets will be familiar to readers of Isaac Bashevis Singer, himself born in Biłgoraj, ninety kilometres south of Lublin. Lublin was one of the most important Jewish centres in Poland before World War II, which probably explains why its suburb **Majdanek** was chosen by the Nazis as the site of one of their most notorious death camps – a chilling place that demands to be visited.

Lublin

In the shops, oil lamps and candles were lit. Bearded Jews dressed in long cloaks and wearing wide boots moved through the streets on the way to evening prayers. The world beyond was in turmoil. Jews everywhere were being driven from their villages. But here in Lublin one felt only the stability of a long established community.

Isaac Bashevis Singer, *The Magician of Lublin*

The city of **LUBLIN**, the largest in eastern Poland, is one of the most alluring urban centres in the whole country, thanks in large part to the evocative hive of alleys that constitute its magnificent Stare Miasto. New arrivals are sometimes put off by the sprawling high-rise buildings and smokestacks of the suburbs, but once you're in the heart of the place, it's all cobbled streets and dilapidated mansions – a wistful reminder of past glories. The fabric of this old quarter came through World War II relatively undamaged, and although years of postwar neglect left it in shambles, recent restoration has made the city centre ripe for tourism, though as yet Lublin sees nothing like the crowds flowing into Kraków, Warsaw or Gdańsk. In among the numerous churches you'll find reminders that for centuries Lublin was home to a large and vibrant **Jewish community**, a population exterminated in the Nazi concentration camp at **Majdanek**, 6km from the city centre.

Some history

Like many eastern towns, Lublin started as a **medieval** trade settlement and guard post, in this case on the trade route linking the Baltic ports with Kiev and the Black Sea. Somehow managing to survive numerous depredations and invasions – the fearsome Tatar onslaughts in particular – Lublin was well established by the **sixteenth century** as a commercial and cultural centre.

The city's finest hour came in 1569 when the Polish and Lithuanian nobility met here to set a seal on the formal union of the two countries, initiated two centuries earlier by the marriage of Lithuanian grand duke Jagiełło and Polish queen Jadwiga (see "History", p.661). This so-called **Union of Lublin** created the largest mainland empire in Europe, stretching from the Baltic to the Black Sea. Over a century of prosperity followed, during which the arts flourished and many fine buildings were added to the city. The **Partitions** rudely interrupted this process, leaving Lublin to languish on the edge of the Russian-ruled Duchy of Warsaw for the next hundred years or so.

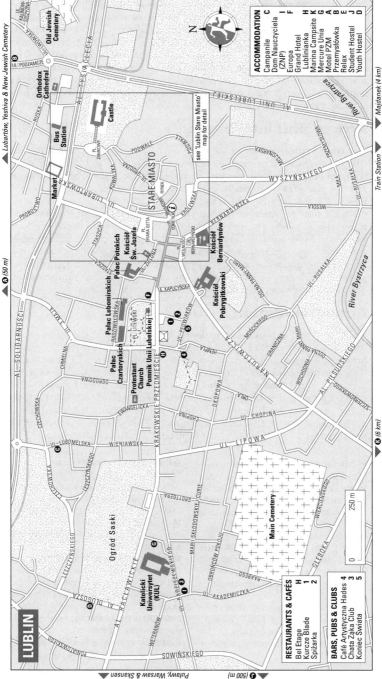

LUBLIN

▲ Zamość, Chełm & **Ε** (1.5 km)

◄ Lubartów, Yashiva & New Jewish Cemetery

▲ **Β** (50 m)

▼ Majdanek (4 km)

▼ Train Station ▼

▼ **Ξ** (6 km)

◄ Puławy, Warsaw & Skansen

▼ **Θ** (500 m) ▲

N

Old Jewish Cemetery

Orthodox Cathedral

UL PODZAMCZE

Bus Station

Castle

Market

STARE MIASTO

see 'Lublin Stare Miasto' map for detail

WYSZYŃSKIEGO

PODWALE

PL ZAMKOWY

RYNEK

i

Kościół Św. Józefa

Pałac Potockich

PL OFIAR GETTA

Kościół Bernardynów

PL WOLNOŚCI

Pałac Lubomirskich

F

UL KAPUCYŃSKA

Kościół Pobrygitkowski

Pałac Czartoryskich

Pomnik Unii Lubelskiej

Protestant Church

PL LITEWSKI

Η

Katolicki Uniwersytet (KUL)

D

Ogród Saski

C

G

Main Cemetery

River Bystrzyca

River Bystrzyca

UL LIPOWA

UL CHOPINA

ACCOMMODATION

Campanile	C
Dom Nauczyciela (ZNP)	I
Europa	F
Grand Hotel	H
Lublinianka	K
Marina Campsite	G
Mercure Unia	A
Motel PZM	B
Przemysłówka	J
Relax	E
Student Hostel	J
Youth Hostel	D

RESTAURANTS & CAFÉS

Bel Etage	H
Kurcze Blade	1
Spiżarka	2

BARS, PUBS & CLUBS

Café Artystyczna Hades	4
Chata Żąka Club	3
Koniec Świata	5

0 — 250 m

Following **World War I** and the regaining of national independence in 1918, a Catholic university – the only one in eastern Europe – was established, which grew to become a cradle of the Polish Catholic intelligentsia, most notably during the communist era. It was to Lublin, too, that a group of Polish communists known as the Committee of National Liberation (PKWN) returned in **1944** from their wartime refuge in the Soviet Union to set up a new communist-dominated government. Since the end of the war, the town's industrial and commercial importance has grown considerably, with a belt of factories mushrooming around the town centre.

Arrival and information

The **train station** is 2km to the south of the centre; from here bus #1 will take you to the edge of the Stare Miasto, while bus #13 and trolleybus #150 both run to Krakowskie Przedmieście, just east of the centre. The **bus station** (ⓦwww.pks.lublin.pl) is much more conveniently located, lying just beyond the castle at the northern end of the Stare Miasto.

Lublin's **tourist office**, in the Stare Miasto on the corner of Bramowa and ul. Jezuicka (May–Aug Mon–Fri 10am–6pm, Sat 10am–4pm, Sun 10am–3pm; Sept–April Mon–Fri 9am–5pm, Sat 10am–4pm; ⓣ081/532 4412), has helpful staff and comprehensive accommodation listings. They also sell maps and a few English books about the city, and can provide the telephone numbers of guides expert in the history of Jewish Lublin. You can get (Polish only) **information online** at ⓦwww.turystyka.lubelskie.pl and ⓦwww.lsi.lublin.pl.

Accommodation

The city's supply of **hotels and pensions** has improved over the last few years, but the selection of good central budget places is still inadequate. The **youth hostel**, al. Długosza 6 (10pm curfew; ⓣ081/533 0628; bus #13 or trolleybus #150 from the train station), offers space in dorms or in triples (25–38zł per person) and is 1.5km west of the city centre, off the street behind a high school. The all-year **student hostel**, ul. Sowińskiego 17 (ⓣ081/525 1081; ❷) in the university area, is another cheap alternative. Lublin's best **campsite** is the *Marina*, at the edge of Lake Zemborzycki, 7km south of the centre at ul. Krężnicka 6 (ⓣ081/744 1070; May–Sept; bus #8 from ul. Narutowicza).

Hotels and pensions

Campanile ul. Lubomelska 14 ⓣ081/531 8400, ⓦwww.campanile.com.pl. Just opened branch of the reliable French chain. High standards, attractive wood furnishings and spacious rooms. Just over a kilometre northeast of the Stare Miasto. ❻

Dom Nauczyciela (ZNP) ul. Akademiczka ⓣ081/533 8285. A basic but not especially cheap teachers' hotel near the university; often full, so try to ring in advance. Trolleybus #150 or bus #13 from the train station. En suites and rooms with shared facilities. ❸–❹

Europa Krakowskie Przedmieście 29 ⓣ081/535 0303, ⓦwww.hoteleuropa.pl. Brand-new and very central place that's aimed squarely at business travellers. Forty percent discount at weekends. ❼

Grand Hotel Lublinianka Krakowskie Przedmieście 56 ⓣ081/446 6100, ⓦwww.lublinianka.com. Recently renovated luxury hotel in a stately *belle époque* pile, with polished service, Turkish bath and a rooftop café. Rooms are discounted heavily at weekends and even more during July and August. There are also a few economy rooms. ❼–❾

Mercure Unia al. Racławickie 12 ⓣ081/533 2061, ⓦwww.orbis.pl. Respectable and modern Orbis hotel, with a reliable but unexceptional restaurant. Popular with well-heeled tour groups. ❽

Motel PZM ul. Prusa 8 ⓣ081/533 4232. Though unattractively set on a main highway, this is within walking distance of the city centre and bus station and is a good base for sightseeing in or around

Lublin. Neat and fairly modern en suites, breakfast included. **❺**
Przemysłówka ul. Podzamcze 7 ☎ 081/747 4407, Ⓦ www.hotel.przemyslowka.futuro.net.pl. Tall concrete block north of the castle, with basic but clean en-suite rooms (**❷**), dusty rooms with shared facilities (**❶**) and dorms (20zł) favoured by ex-Soviet trade tourists. The curtains are thin, so try to get a room with western exposure if you don't want to get up with the sun. No breakfast. **❶–❷**
Relax ul. Przyjaźni 17 ☎ 081/748 8500, Ⓦ www .hotelrelax.lublin.pl. Small, high-quality pension adjacent to the former Daewoo car plant, 1.5km

southeast of the centre, with a decent restaurant. The best budget accommodation in Lublin, in spite of the location. Bus #9 or #34 from the centre, #45 from the train station. **❸**
Waksman ul. Grodzka 19 ☎ 081/532 5454, Ⓦ www.waksman.pl. Upmarket but good-value "retro" pension in the heart of the Stare Miasto, with four doubles and two suites furnished with faux-antiques in styles ranging from Louis XVI to Victorian. Comfortable and generally tasteful, although one room does have a water bed. The helpful staff can arrange day-trips around the region. Breakfast included. **❺–❻**

The Stare Miasto and around

The busy pl. Łokietka forms the main approach to the **Stare Miasto** (Old Town), with an imposing nineteenth-century **Nowy Ratusz** (New Town Hall) on one side. Straight across the square is the fourteenth-century **Brama Krakowska** (Kraków Gate), one of three gateways to the Stare Miasto. Originally a key point in the city's defences against Tatar invaders, this now houses the **Muzeum Historyczne** (Historical Museum; Wed–Sat 9am–4pm, Sun 9am–5pm; 5zł); the contents aren't greatly inspiring, but the view of the new town from the top floor makes it worth a visit to orient yourself.

The Stare Miasto

A short walk round to the right along ul. Królewska brings you to the **Wieża Trinitarska** (Trinity Tower), home of the **Muzeum Diecezjalne** (Diocesan Museum; March 15–Nov 15 Tues–Sun 10am–5pm; 5zł), where there's an even better top-floor view, this time over the Stare Miasto, and an unremarkable but cleverly arranged collection of Baroque sculpture to divert you on the way up. Opposite is the **cathedral**, a large sixteenth-century basilica with an entrance framed by ornate neoclassical pillars. The interior decoration features a series of Baroque trompe l'oeil frescoes by the Moravian artist Joseph Meyer. The peculiar acoustic properties of the **Whispering Room** (Tues–Sun 10am–4pm; 4zł) – part of the former sacristy adjoining the Treasury, with ebullient frescoes by Meyer depicting the "triumph of faith over heresy" – allow you to hear even the quietest voices perfectly from the other side of the chapel.

Both Trinity Tower and Kraków Gate lead into the Rynek, dominated by the outsized **Stary Ratusz** (Old Town Hall), the subject of a complete overhaul several years ago. Built in 1389, it later became the seat of a royal tribunal and was given a Neoclassical remodelling in 1781 by Merlini, the man who designed Warsaw's Łazienki Palace. The well-restored cellars underneath the building house the **Muzeum Trybunału Koronnego** (Crown Tribunal Museum; Wed–Sat 9am–4pm, Sun 10am–5pm; 4zł), devoted to the history of the city, including a selection of ceramics and decorative objects unearthed in the course of the renovation of the houses around the Rynek.

Of the surrounding burghers' houses, the **Konopnica House** (no. 12) – where Charles XII of Sweden and Peter the Great were both guests – has Renaissance sculptures and medallions of the original owners decorating its facade, currently being restored, while the **Lubomelski House** (no. 8) – now housing the *Piwnica Pod Fortuną* restaurant – hides some racy fourteenth-century frescoes in its large triple-tiered wine cellars. The **Cholewiński**

House (no. 9), on the northeast corner of the square, features further lively Renaissance decoration on the facade, with a faded but fierce-looking pair of lions.

North of the Rynek, ul. Grodzka leads past **plac Po Farze**, a square created early in the nineteenth century when the Gothic St Michael's Church was demolished, to the **Brama Grodzka** (Grodzka Gate), which marked the entrance to the **Jewish Quarter** until 1862, when Jews were permitted to settle in the Old Town and elsewhere. Several of the buildings on the street bear memorials in Polish and Yiddish to their former inhabitants. The narrow, winding streets east and west of the Rynek are all worth exploring, as are the various alleys and courtyards, some of which are lined with elegant wooden balconies. East of the Rynek, at the end of ul. Złota, stands the fine **Dominican Church and Monastery**, founded in the fourteenth century and reconstructed in the seventeenth. The church suffers from the familiar Baroque additions, but don't let that deflect you from the Renaissance Firlej family **chapel** at the end of the southern aisle, built for one of Lublin's leading aristocratic families, nor from the endearingly out-of-scale eighteenth-century panorama of the city in the first chapel to the right of the entrance. Round the back of the monastery is a popular puppet theatre, the **Teatr im. Andersen**, one of the oldest theatres in the country, offering a good view over the town from the square in front.

LUBLIN STARE MIASTO

ACCOMMODATION

Waksman	A

RESTAURANTS & CAFÉS

Espresso Bar	10
Gospoda Sielsko Anielsko	12
Piwnica pod Fortuną	9
Przez Kresy	11
Pueblo Desperados	8
Szeroka 28	1
Zadora	7

BARS, PUBS & CLUBS

Magma	3
Old Pub	4
4 Pokoje	5
U Szewca	2
Złoty Osioł	6

The castle

On a hill just east of the Stare Miasto is the **castle**, an offbeat 1820s neo-Gothic edifice built on the site of Kazimierz the Great's fourteenth-century fortress, and linked by a raised pathway from the gate at the end of ul. Grodzka.

The castle houses a sizeable **museum** (Wed, Thurs & Sun 9am–5pm, Fri 9am–2pm, Sat 10am–5pm; ⓦ www.zamek.lublin.pl; 6.50zł), the high points of which are the **ethnography** section, including a delightful collection of contemporary folk art and woodcarving, and the **art gallery**, where moody nineteenth-century landscapes and scenes of peasant life mingle with portraits and historical pieces to form a virtual textbook of modern Polish history – helpfully, most of the pictures have English labels. Among the historical works, look out for two famous and characteristically operatic works by Matejko: the massive *Lublin Union* portrays Polish and Lithuanian noblemen debating the union of the two countries in 1569; the somewhat smaller *Admission of the Jews to Poland* depicts the Jews' arrival in Poland in the early Middle Ages, the two sides eyeing each other suspiciously. The section of the museum devoted to World War II recalls the castle's use by the Nazis as a prison and interrogation centre. Civilian prisoners were shot in the courtyard and thousands more, including many Jews, were detained here before being sent to Majdanek or other concentration camps.

The castle chapel

Among the best reasons for visiting Lublin is the **Kaplica św. Trójcy** (Chapel of the Holy Trinity), an elegant two-storey Gothic structure located at the back of the castle complex behind one of its two remaining towers (one of them thirteenth-century Romanesque). Entrance to the chapel is via the castle museum (same hours, plus Mon & Tues 10am–5pm; 6.50zł). The reason is the stunning set of **medieval frescoes** covering cross-ribbed vaulting supported on a single octagonal pillar – a striking architectural device similar to that used in the Holy Cross Church in Kraków (see p.403). Commissioned by King Władysław Jagiełło, who inherited a taste for Eastern art from his Russian mother, Julianna, the frescoes were painted by a group of Ruthenian artists from the Ukraine – exceptionally for the time, the main artist, Master Andrew, signed his name and the date of completion, August 10, 1418, in the dedication to his royal patron. One of the outstanding examples of Slavic-Byzantine church art, the frescoes are also unique for being the only known case where Eastern painters decorated a Western-style Gothic structure. Accidentally uncovered by builders at the end of the nineteenth century, they were subject to sporadic bursts of restoration over the next hundred years, but it wasn't until 1995 that the project was finally completed with the help of EU funding.

The frescoes are composed of panels, each painted in a single day. These, in keeping with the principles of Byzantine iconography, form sections illustrating a progression of themes, beginning with depictions of God the Father and moving on through the cosmic hierarchy to scenes from the life of Jesus and the saints, images of the archangels and other spiritual entities and ending with the risen Christ. There's an engrossing wealth of detail to take in here, which the well-produced English-language guide sheet available at the museum entrance (3zł) will help you through. Highlights include the vivid sequence of scenes from the life of Christ and the Virgin Mary covering the upper section of the nave and choir, in particular a powerful Passion cycle, along with an intriguing pair of frescoes involving King Jagiełło, the first depicting him kneeling in humble supplication before the Virgin, the second showing the king mounted on a galloping horse while receiving a crown and crucifix from an angel – a reference to the man's legendary missionary zeal. These are the only surviving likenesses of King Jagiełło painted during his lifetime. Overlooking the whole ensemble from the choir vaulting is a triumphal depiction of Christus Pantocrator.

Restoring the frescoes to something approaching their original state has been a taxing business. Certain sections have been lost irrevocably and the chapel has to be kept inside a narrow temperature band to preserve the extant frescoes. Entrance is limited to 25 viewers at a time, and the chapel is closed for ten minutes in every hour to ensure that the ventilation system does its job.

West of the Stare Miasto

West of pl. Łokietka stretches **Krakowskie Przedmieście**, a busy shop-lined thoroughfare pedestrianized for several blocks and with a number of worthwhile sites in its vicinity. Immediately west of the Nowy Ratusz is the **Kościół św. Ducha** (Church of the Holy Spirit), a small, early fifteenth-century structure with the familiar Baroque overlay and a quiet, restful feel to it.

Immediately opposite the church, a turn to the south takes you onto pl. Bernardyński, a car-jammed square surrounded by building activity. The fifteenth-century **Kościół Bernardynów** (Bernardine church) on the south side of the square, a large Gothic construction with a sumptuously ornate Baroque interior, has a good view over the southern rim of the city from the platform at the back of the building. On the eastern edge of another square, southwest along ul. Narutowicza, the **Kościół Pobrygitkowski** (Brigittine church), raised in the early fifteenth century by King Władysław Jagiełło as a gesture of thanks for victory at the battle of Grunwald, is another Gothic structure with the customary high brick period facade.

Back onto Krakowskie Przedmieście, north of the main street on ul. Zielona, a narrow side passage contains the tiny **Kościół św. Jozefa** (St Joseph's Church), founded by Greek Catholic merchants in the 1790s and used by the local Uniates into this century. Just beyond, on the corner of ul. św. Staszica, is the crumbling eighteenth-century **Pałac Potocki** (Potocki Palace), one of several patrician mansions in this part of the city.

Krakowskie Przedmieście runs along the southern edge of **plac Litewski**, a large open square with lots of people milling about and, in summer, a host of chess games in progress. On its eastern edge, the cast-iron 1826 **Pomnik Unii Lubelskiej** (Monument of the Union of Lublin) commemorates the Polish–Lithuanian concordat established here in 1569. The north side features two old aristocratic palaces: the former **Pałac Czartoryskich** (Czartoryski Palace) in the northeast corner, and the fading seventeenth-century **Pałac Lubomirskich** (Lubomirski Palace), with a Neoclassicist facade dating from the 1830s. The imperial-looking building to its left is the old tsarist-era city governor's residence, built in the 1850s.

The eighteenth-century Protestant **church** on Ewangelicka, further along to the north of Krakowskie Przedmieście, is also worth a look. An austere, Huguenot-style temple with classicist stylings, it has memorial tablets ranged around the walls, mostly to the church's former German-speaking congregation.

Continuing west along Krakowskie Przedmieście and turning south on ul. Lipowa, a five-minute walk brings you to the gates of the **main cemetery**. The peaceful, wooded graveyard is separated into confessional sections; to the north the predictably large **Catholic section** is flanked by Protestant and Orthodox cemeteries. The **Orthodox section**, with its own mock-Byzantine chapel, contains wartime graves as well as a sprinkling of older, tsarist-era Cyrillic tablets, including many of the city's imperial administrators and rulers. The graves in the **Protestant section** are mainly German, and many of the stones date from before and during World War I, when the city was occupied for several years by the Kaiser's forces. Finally, inspection of the group of plain tombstones without crucifixes in the western section of the graveyard reveals them to belong to those local Party members committed enough to the atheist cause to refuse Catholic burial.

Back to Krakowskie Przedmieście and a short distance west along its continuation, al. Racławickie, stands the **Katolicki Uniwersytet** or KUL (Catholic University), a compact campus housed on the site of an old Dominican monastery. The KUL's most famous professor was **Karol Wojtyła**, who taught part-time here from the 1950s up until his election as pope in 1978. He is commemorated in a bronze statue in the main courtyard, accompanied by his predecessor as primate of Poland, Cardinal Wyszyński.

Directly opposite the University building lie the **Ogród Saski** (Saxon Gardens), Lublin's principal open space, with fastidiously tended flowerbeds sloping down towards wilder, densely wooded sections in the park's northern reaches.

The skansen

Three kilometres northwest of the Ogród Saski, out along al. Warszawska (bus #5, #18 or #20 from al. Racławickie), an attractive jumble of rural buildings from surrounding villages have been reassembled to form the **Muzeum Wsi Lubelskiej**, usually referred to by the generic name for such collections, **skansen** (April & Oct daily 9am–5pm; May–Sept daily 10am–6pm; Nov to mid-Dec Mon, Sat & Sun 9am–3pm; Jan–March by appointment ☏081/533 8513; ⓦ www.skansen.lublin.pl; 6zł), providing a wonderfully rustic contrast to the downtown area. The interiors of the buildings are only open if you pay for the hour-long guided tour (25zł in Polish, 35zł in English, though there's not always an English speaker on duty), but a visit here will be rewarding either way. The entrance is marked by a massive, 1939 windmill from the village of Zygmuntów, while other highlights include a gate from Łańcuchów, carved in the Zakopane style by Stanisław Witkiewicz; a manor house from the village of Zyrzyna, crouching beneath an organic-looking mansard roof covered in wooden shingles; and a *cerkiew* from Tarnoszyna, which sports an exotic trio of bulbous domes.

Jewish Lublin

For anyone interested in Lublin's **Jewish history**, a scattering of monuments around the city's former Jewish quarters are worth visiting, most marked by tablets in Polish and English. Starting in the **Stare Miasto**, much of which was settled by Jews after they were emancipated from the traditional ghetto in 1862, there are a couple of buildings with wartime Jewish connections: on the corner of ul. Noworybna, east of the square, is the small house where the first **Committee of Jewish War Survivors** was set up in November 1944. Further east, to ul. Grodzka, at no. 11, is a plaque commemorating the Jewish **orphanage** in operation here from 1862 until March 1942, when the Nazis removed about two hundred staff and children and shot them in the fields behind the Majdanek camp.

Continuing along Grodzka to pl. Zamkowy, a plaque on a raised pedestal at the foot of the stairs up to the castle shows a detailed plan of the surrounding **Podzamcze** district, the main Jewish quarter destroyed by the Nazis in 1942 (see box below). The Nazi devastation was so thorough that it's hard to visualize the densely packed network of houses, shops and synagogues that used to exist in the streets around what's now a noisy main road (al. Tysiąclecia), a tatty square, the adjoining main bus station and the Orthodox **cathedral** – a dark, icon-filled structure built in 1633 on the site of an older wooden building and containing a late Renaissance iconostasis – originally a Uniate building, it is the sole active Orthodox place of worship in town, and is open only on Sundays.

The old Jewish cemetery

Continue east along al. Tysiąclecia and opposite the bus station, on the approaches to the castle, you'll find another plaque marking the prewar site of the main **Maharszal and Maharam synagogue**, originally constructed in the 1560s and razed along with all the surrounding buildings in 1942.

The Jews of Lublin

Along with Kraków, L'viv and Vilnius, Lublin ranked as one of the major – if not *the* most important – Jewish centres in Poland: at its peak in the sixteenth century the Lublin Jewry exerted a Europe-wide influence, dispatching locally trained rabbis to serve communities as far away as Spain and Portugal.

The **first recorded account** of Jews in Lublin dates from 1316, though it's quite possible that merchants established themselves here considerably earlier. King Kazimierz's extension of the **Statute of Privilege** for Jews to the whole territory of Poland in the mid-fourteenth century paved the way for the development of the first major Jewish settlement in the **Podzamcze** district, located below the castle walls. Originally a marshy river delta, the area was bought up by Jewish merchants, who drained the waters and established a community. The first brick **synagogue** and **yeshiva** (Talmudic school) were built in the mid-sixteenth century: from then on synagogues and other religious buildings proliferated – by the 1930s there were more than a hundred synagogues in operation inside the city area. Lublin's increasingly important position on trade routes resulted in its choice as one of two locations (Jarosław was the other) for meetings of the **Council of the Four Lands**, traditionally the main consultative body of Polish Jewry, a position it retained up to the 1760s.

Occasional outbreaks of Church-inspired ritual-murder accusations apart, local Jewish–Christian relations seem to have been fairly tolerant at this stage, the main blows coming in the form of outside assaults, notably the **Chmielnicki Insurrection** (1648), when Cossacks slaughtered thousands of Jews throughout eastern Poland, and the Russian siege of the city in 1655, when much of the Podzamcze district was razed. The whole area was subsequently rebuilt, this time with an emphasis on solid, brick buildings.

In the 1790s Lublin emerged as an important centre of **Hassidism**, the ecstatic revivalist movement that swept through Eastern Jewry in the latter part of the eighteenth century. The charismatic Hassidic leader **Yaakov Yitzchak Horovitz** settled in town during this period, drawing crowds of followers from all over Poland (by all accounts, the Hassids were no respecters of Poland's Partitions-era borders) to his "court" in the Podzamcze district. Always a controversial figure – contemporary opponents, for example, claimed that Horovitz died of excessive alcohol consumption – Jews from all over the world continue to make the pilgrimage to his grave in the old Jewish Cemetery.

In 1862, with the town's Jewish population increasing rapidly, Jews were first permitted to move into the Stare Miasto area, also occupying much of the new district that developed around ul. Lubartowska, to the north of the Stare Miasto. At the close of the century Jews numbered around 24,000, a little over half of the town's population.

Cross the main road, walk north along ul. Podzamcze and, bearing right on ul. Lwowska and then turning right onto cobbled ul. Kalinowszczyzna, you'll find yourself at the **old Jewish cemetery**, a small walled area which covers a ramshackle, overgrown hill, set in almost rural surroundings.

Unless a group happens to be there at the time, you'll have to contact the **caretaker**, Pani (Mrs) Honig, at ul. Dembowskiego 4, apt. #17 (℡081/747 8676), across from the main cemetery entrance. She speaks no English but is usually happy, at least on weekdays, to show visitors around, and while there's no set fee contributions are welcome. Despite the Nazis' best efforts to destroy the oldest-known Jewish cemetery in the country – literally thousands of the gravestones were used for wartime building purposes – the small groups of surviving tombstones display the full stylistic variety of Jewish monumental art. The oldest section of the cemetery, with tombstones from as early as 1541, houses the graves of many famous Jews, among them the legendary Hassidic

Following the trials of **World War I**, during which many Lublin Jews died fighting in both the Russian and Austro-Hungarian armies, Lublin Jewry flourished in the **interwar years**, developing an active web of religious and cultural associations, publishing houses, newspapers (notably the Yiddish-language daily *Lubliner Sztyme* – "Lublin Voice"), trade unions and political organizations.

Following their capture of the town in September 1939, the **Nazis** quickly set about the business of confining and eventually murdering the nearly 40,000-strong Lublin Jewry. By December 1939 transports of Jews were being brought into the city from other parts of Europe, and in early 1940 Lublin was chosen as the coordinating centre for the Nazis' efforts to liquidate the Jewish population of the Générale Gouvernement – those portions of Poland that were under German administration (but not directly incorporated into the German Reich) after September 1939. With the Stare Miasto area already filled to bursting with destitute Jews, an official **ghetto area** was established, west of the castle, in March 1941 by Governor Hans Frank.

Construction of the **Majdanek death camp** in a southern suburb of the city began in July 1941 and initially was run as a work camp, then in spring 1942 the hideous business of liquidating the ghetto population began in earnest. After initial expulsions at the end of March 1942, Jews were driven to the ghetto square, next to the modern main bus station. The old and sick were shot on the spot, and the rest taken to waiting rail wagons and transported to the death camp at **Bełżec**; in the next few months, the remaining population was either taken and shot in the **Krępiecki Forest** on the outskirts of the city or moved to a new ghetto area established close to Majdanek. The effective end of over six hundred years of traditional Jewish life in Lublin came on November 3, 1943, when the remaining 18,000 ghetto inhabitants were taken to Majdanek, its gas chambers having been set up in autumn 1942, to be exterminated after an *Aktion* (a ghetto raid followed by mass round-ups) codenamed *Erntfest* ("Harvest Festival"). Following the *Aktion*'s conclusion, the Nazis systematically demolished the buildings of Wieniawa, an outlying Jewish settlement, and the Podzamcze district.

The city was liberated by Soviet troops in July 1944, after which **Jewish partisan groups** began using Lublin as their operational base. At the end of the war several thousand Jewish refugees resettled in Lublin: as a result of **anti-Semitic outbreaks** around Poland in 1945–46, however, many of these emigrated, and others followed in the wake of the anti-Semitic purges of 1968, as in Kraków and Warsaw. The tiny remaining Jewish population keeps a low profile, many now too old to take an active role in the revival of local Jewish life encouraged by the increasing number of Western Jews visiting the city.

leader **Yaakov Yitzchak Horovitz**, one of several here regularly covered with pilgrims' candles, and **Shalom Shachna**, the renowned sixteenth-century master of the Lublin *yeshiva* (Talmudic school). Climbing to the top of the cemetery hill gives you a fine view back over the Stare Miasto.

The new Jewish cemetery and mausoleum

Leaving the cemetery and heading north along ul. Lwowska and into ul. Walecznych brings you to the entrance of the **new Jewish cemetery**. Established in 1829 in what was then the outskirts of town, the cemetery was predictably plundered and destroyed by the Nazis, who also used it for mass executions. What you see today covers a fragment of the original plot, the northern section having been cleared and levelled in the 1970s to make way for a trunk road.

Most of the precious few graves left inside date from the late nineteenth century and the postwar years, as well as a number of collective graves for Nazi wartime victims. The whole cemetery has been renovated in the past few years with financial support from the Frenkel family, whose relatives died in Majdanek.

The domed **mausoleum** (unpredictable hours, so check at the tourist office; donation), recently erected behind the cemetery entrance, houses a small but engrossing exhibition detailing the history of the Lublin Jewry.

The yeshiva and Jewish hospital

Out of the cemetery and west along ul. Unicka brings you to the corner of ul. Lubartowska, a long, straight thoroughfare running through the heart of the prewar Jewish quarter. The large classical-looking yellow building at the top corner of Lubartowska is the site of the old **yeshiva** – The School of the Sages of Lublin as it was once known – a palatial structure now occupied by the local medical academy. Built in the late 1920s using funds collected from Jewish communities around the world, the Lublin *yeshiva* was set up as an international school to train rabbis and other community functionaries. It functioned for just over nine years until 1939, when the Nazis closed it down and eventually plundered and publicly burned the contents of its huge library. Next to the *yeshiva* on the same side of Lubartowska (no. 81) is the palatial **Jewish hospital**, built in 1886. Now an obstetric clinic, a plaque outside commemorates the hospital staff and patients murdered in March 1942 in the course of a Nazi liquidation *Aktion*.

The old ghetto district

Continuing south along Lubartowska takes you through the heart of the old **ghetto district**, a grubby, lively area of shops and tenement houses west of the castle and north of the Stare Miasto. While there are no Jews left to speak of, wandering through the arched entrance ways into the back courtyards or scanning the small shops you can imagine what it must have been like here half a century ago. In the heart of the quarter a backroom at ul. Lubartowska 10 houses the city's one surviving **synagogue** (Sun 1–3pm; entrance through the gateway round the side of no. 8, and up the stairs).

Established in 1920 by the local undertakers' guild, it became the principal synagogue for the city's surviving Jews after World War II. It is still in use today and visiting Jewish tourist groups regularly hold services here. An informative collection of photos and other archival materials relating to the Lublin Jewry lines the walls, along with a small collection of ritual religious objects and some plaques dedicated to local Poles who protected Jews during World War II.

Finally, near the top of Lubartowska, on the approach to the old city, is **plac Ofiar Getta** (Ghetto Victims), a bustling square that used to be one of the main Jewish marketplaces. A simple monument to the ghetto victims stands in the square centre, engraved with the legend "Honour to the Polish citizens of Jewish nationality from the Lublin region, whose lives were bestially cut short by the Nazi fascists during World War II. The people of Lublin."

Majdanek

The proximity of **Majdanek concentration camp** (grounds 8am–dusk; Ⓦ www.majdanek.pl; free), just 4km southeast of the city centre, is a shock in itself. Established on Himmler's orders in October 1941, this was no semi-hidden location that local people could long be ignorant of – a plea more debatable at Auschwitz and Treblinka. Marked from the main road by a large monument erected in 1969 on the 25th anniversary of its liberation by the Red Army, the huge camp compound is more shocking inside. Wandering among the barbed wire and watchtowers, staring at crematoria and rows of shabby wooden barracks crammed with three-level plank beds, it's hard to take in the fact that an estimated 230,000 people, of which 40 percent were Jewish and 35 percent Polish, were murdered here, more than half through hunger, disease or exhaustion and the rest by execution or in gas chambers. Between November 3 and 5, 1943, the Nazis concluded their extermination of local Jewry by machine-gunning over 43,000 inhabitants of the nearby ghetto district; 18,000 were killed in a single day. Immediately following the war, Majdanek was used by the Soviet NKVD (secret police) to hold captured Polish resistance fighters before they were shipped to Siberian gulags (see box, pp.298–299) The **camp museum** (Tues–Sun: May–Sept 8am–4pm; Oct–April 8am–3pm; free) housed in several of the former barracks tells the terrible story in detail. At the end of the main path through the site, a domed mausoleum contains the ashes of many of those murdered here. The entrance building has a cinema showing a short documentary about Majdanek (3zł; minimum five viewers) as well as a bookshop selling maps, brochures and other publications in several languages. Guided tours are available in Polish (60zł) and English (100zł).

Bus #23 and trolleybus #156 from ul. Królewska or trolleybuses #153 and #158 from ul. Lipowa run to the monument marking the entrance to the camp (30min). For more on the concentration camps in postwar Poland, see p.446.

Eating and drinking

The **restaurant** scene in Lublin is looking up, with a range of eateries establishing themselves in the mansions of the Stare Miasto and around Krakowskie Przedmieście, which has itself emerged as the town's prime night-time promenading ground. Most restaurants and **cafés** have outdoor seating in summer, and the variety of late-night drinking establishments in the Stare Miasto provide ample opportunity for an extensive **bar**-crawl.

Restaurants and cafés

Bel Etage Krakowskie Przedmieście 56. Lublin's most formal and expensive restaurant, situated within the *Grand Hotel Lublinianka*, with fine international cuisine and an enchanting rooftop café in summer.

Espresso Bar Rynek 9. Best of the assorted pizza/ pasta options in the old town.

Gospoda Sielsko Anielsko Rynek 17. Rustic-themed place offering hearty traditional food in a dining room stuffed with rural implements. Lighter dishes like *pierogi* and omelettes at around 12zł, and main courses 18–35zł. An imitation of (but not quite matching in quality) Kraków's *Chłopskie Jadło*.

Kurcze Blade ul. Kościuszki 3. Functional little snack bar offering cheap Polish standards and good cakes. Order at the counter.

Piwnica pod Fortuną Rynek 8. Elegant restaurant occupying a series of subterranean chambers decorated with medieval-style frescoes. The usual range of Polish meat dishes augmented by a few duck and goose recipes. Slightly more expensive than the other places in the Stare Miasto.

Przez Kresy Rynek 18. Friendly, reasonably priced Stare Miasto restaurant with understated decor, serving an interesting mix of Polish and other East European cuisines. Try the Lithuanian pork chops in buttermilk (15zł) or Ukrainian ham soup (11zł).

Pueblo Desperados Rynek 5. Tiny and cheap Mexican restaurant with surprisingly tasty burritos and enchiladas.

Spiżarka ul. Kościuszki 10. An attractive, mid-priced restaurant with unusual Polish dishes like *pierogi z królika* (rabbit *pierogi*), served up in a country house atmosphere, and professional but not overly formal service.

Szeroka 28 next to the Brama Grodzka at ul. Grodzka 19 ☎081/534 4610. Stylish café/restaurant attempting to re-create the look and feel of prewar Lublin. With expensive main courses as well as affordable snacks, but watch the wine prices. There's a back terrace with a fine view onto the castle. Reservations are a good idea Friday and Saturday nights, when there are klezmer or jazz concerts at 8.30pm (5–10zł cover).

Zadora Rynek 8. Small and excellent *creperie*, good for a quick and cheap meal in the old town.

Bars, pubs and clubs

4 Pokoje ul. Rybna 13. Relaxed, student-oriented pub with old furniture and a pool table.

Café Artystyczna Hades ul. Peowiaków 12, in the Dom Kultury just round the corner from the Philharmonia. Has a restaurant, bar, pool hall and also hosts regular club nights and alternative gigs. Usually Thurs–Sun only.

Chata Zaka Club ul. Radziszewskiego 16. University cultural centre housing smoky student café, and a combined cinema and gig venue – the *Art Bis Club* – round the back.

Koniec Świata ul. Peowiaków 8. Atmospheric, rock-oriented cellar pub just off Krakowskie Przedmieście, with occasional live bands.

Magma ul. Grodzka 18. Smallish bar in the Stare Miasto whose arty-industrial decor blends rather nicely with the barrel-vaulted Baroque ceiling. An amenable place to sink a few pints.

Old Pub ul. Grodzka 8. Fancy pub-restaurant with upmarket leanings, offering a wide though pricey range of draught beers.

U Szewca ul. Grodzka 20. Relaxing pub with a range of Polish, English and Irish beers, comfy settees, and a varied, mid-price menu of bar food.

Złoty Osioł ul. Grodzka 5a. Multipurpose café, bar, restaurant and art gallery housed in a suite of medieval rooms. Lots of wicker furniture to lounge around in, and a laid-back atmosphere. Serves mid-price Polish dishes.

Entertainment

The Lublin Philharmonia, ul. Skłodowskiej 5 (☎081/743 7821), has a regular programme of high-quality **classical concerts**, and the Teatr im. Juliusz Osterwy, ul. Narutowicza 17 (☎081/532 2935, ⓦwww.teatrosterwy.pl), offers an imaginative and varied programme of modern and classical Polish **drama**. This is worth a look even if you don't speak the language, as movement and stagecraft tend to be just as important as the text. The same can be said of the internationally reputed experimental theatre group Gardzienice, based in the village of the same name 30km south of the city, which has an office in the Stare Miasto at ul. Grodzka 5a. When they're not off touring abroad they occasionally give performances out at Gardzienice or, even more rarely, in Lublin itself – an experience not to be missed if you have the chance.

Shopping

Lublin's main **market**, just west of the bus station, is a sprawling, chaotic jumble of foodstuffs, car parts and worthless heirlooms, with the regular Polish merchants supplemented by trade tourists from the Ukraine and Belarus, mostly selling contraband cigarettes. Nearer the city centre there are small **supermarkets** at pl. Wolności 1 and Rynek 5. The best place for **maps and books** in English about Lublin is the tourist office on ul. Bramowa, while there's an interesting selection of prints, old maps of Lublin and used books at the Antykwariat Staromiejski, Rynek 6. EMPiK, Krakowskie Przedmieście 61, has day-old foreign newspapers. There are a number of **art galleries** concentrated along ul. Grodzka.

Listings

Banks and exchange Exchange *kantors* and ATMs are widespread. Note that the rate posted in the window is often for $100 or €100; you may get a lower rate if changing smaller notes.

Cinemas Bajka, next to the Dom Nauczyciela at ul. Radziszewskiego 8 shows independent films; Kosmos, north of the Ogród Saski at ul. Leszczyńskiego 60, is a mainstream theatre.

Internet access Fryzjer, ul. Grodzka 36 (Mon–Sat 10am–8pm); www.café, Rynek 8 (top floor; daily 10am–10pm); enzo, Krakowskie Przedmieście 57 (Mon–Sat 10am–9pm).

Pharmacy Apteka, ul. Bramowa 8 (24hr; ring the bell 8pm–8am).

Post office Krakowskie Przedmieście 50 (24hr); ul. Grodzka 7 (Mon–Fri 8.30am–4.30pm).

Travel agents Orbis, ul. Narutowicza 31/33 (☏081/532 2256) is useful for air and rail tickets.

North from Lublin

North of the city lies the **Biała Podlaska** region, a pleasant agricultural area of ramshackle market towns and sparsely populated villages that still retains a markedly old-world Eastern feel. Like most of eastern Poland, this region has its share of grand old palaces, many of them showing the effects of decades of neglect. **Kozłówka** has one of the finest examples, and will be your main reason to visit, though further north there's **Biała Podlaska**, the regional capital, and, for horse-lovers, the breeding stables at **Janów Podlaski**, hard up by the Belarus border. In all cases, slow local **buses** are the main form of transport. For motorists heading east, the main route from Warsaw to Moscow runs across the region, reaching the border at **Terespol**, east of Biała Podlaska.

Kozłówka

Thirty-five kilometres northwest of Lublin, the **Pałac Zamojskich** (Zamoyski Palace) at **KOZŁÓWKA** is among the grandest in the region. Fully restored in the 1990s, the palace is the recipient of a good deal of tourist hype – hence the processions of day-tripper buses lined up outside the entrance gates. Kozłówka is served by about eight **buses** a day from Lublin, most bound for the village of Michów. Bear in mind that as an intermediate destination Kozłówka won't be listed on the departure board at Lublin bus station; ask at the information counter for details.

The palace

Built in the 1740s by the Bieliński family, after they inherited the local estate, the original two-storey Baroque **palace complex**, surrounded by a courtyard to the front and gardens at the back, was reconstructed and expanded in the early 1900s by its longtime owner, Count Konstanty Zamoyski, whose family took over the property in 1799 and kept it up to the beginning of World War II. Zamoyski's remodelling retained the essentials of the original Baroque design, adding a number of fine outbuildings, the iron gateway, chapel and elegant porticoed terrace leading up to the entrance to the building.

The interior

The palace **interior** (mid-March to Oct Tues–Fri 10am–4pm, Sat & Sun 10am–5pm; Nov to mid–Dec Tues–Sun 10am–3pm; ⓦ www.muzeumkozlowka .lublin.pl; 15zł) can only be visited as part of a **guided tour**, usually starting on the hour. English-language guides can be booked in advance for an extra 50zł (☏081/852 8310).

Once inside, you're immediately enveloped in a riot of artistic decor; the whole place is positively dripping in pictures, mostly family portraits and copies of Rubens, Canaletto and the like, along with a profusion of sculptures and mostly nineteenth-century furniture, every corner of the building richly ornamented in some way. First port of call is the **hallway**, the gloom partially lightened by sumptuous lamps and the delicate stuccowork of the ceiling. Past the huge Meissner stoves and up the portrait-lined marble **staircase** brings you to the main palace rooms. Upstairs in **Count Konstanty's private rooms** the procession of family portraits and genre painting continues relentlessly, the elaborate Czech porcelain toilet set in the bedroom suggesting a man of fastidious personal hygiene. After the countess's bedroom and its handsome selection of Empire furniture, the tour takes you into the voluminous **Red Salon**, an impressive ensemble with embroidered canopies enveloping the doors and a mass of heavy red velvet curtains. The portraits are at their thickest here, with emphasis on royalty, hetmans and other national figures collected by Count Konstanty during the Partition. The **Exotic Room** houses a fine selection of chinoiserie, while the **dining room** is sumptuous, heavy Baroque with a mixture of Gdańsk and Venetian furniture and enough period trinkets to keep a horde of collectors happy. As you'd expect, the **library** contains shelves full of books ranged around a classic billiard table lit by a kerosene lamp in the middle, while the **chapel**, out round the side of the palace, is a fine though rather cold place partly modelled on the royal chapel in Versailles and built in the early 1900s. Outside, the elegantly contoured **palace gardens** stretch out behind the back of the building. Refreshments are available at the **café** near the entrance gate, while the nearby **Coach House** (same hours; 3zł) holds a display of carriages, old bicycles, saddlery and vintage travel equipment.

The museum

After overdosing on opulence, the **Gallery of Socialist Art** (same hours; 5zł) housed in the one-time palace theatre makes for a real surprise. The exhibition brings together a large collection of postwar Polish Socialist Realist art and sculpture, much of which was on display in the palace itself during the 1960s. The whole pantheon of international Stalinist iconography is here: Bolesław Bierut, Mao, Ho Chi Minh, Kim Il Sung and a beaming Stalin himself. Alongside the leaders, there's a gallery of sturdy proletarian and peasant heroes building factories and joyously implementing Five-Year Plans, while playing in the background are Polish translations of important speeches by Stalin and others. More traditional themes are also given a Socialist-Realist twist, as in such paintings as Zygmunt Radricki's *Still Life with Party Journal* and *Chopin's Polonaise in A-flat Major Performed in the Kościuszko Ironworks* by Mieczysław Oracki-Serwin. There's also a selection of buttons, postcards and propagandistic matchboxes.

Biała Podlaska

The provincial capital, **BIAŁA PODLASKA**, is in a strategic position along the main high road from Warsaw to the eastern border: day and night, transit lorries thunder along the road to and from the border crossing at Terespol, forty-odd kilometres east. There's not much to see here, though the powerful Radziwiłł family, the town's fifteenth-century founders and longtime aristocratic benefactors, have left a few monuments, chiefly the **Zamek Radziwiłłów** (Radziwiłł Castle), west of the main square. Left to go to seed in the postwar era, the real damage was done earlier, with much of the original seventeenth-century complex having been destroyed by tsarist authorities in the 1870s. Today the main building is a music academy, while the old Tower House contains the well-organized regional **museum** (Tues–Sun 9/10am–3/4pm; 4zł). Exhibitions on the upper floor feature an interesting display of local ethnography, including folk tapestries and examples of the pagan-influenced "sun" crucifixes typical of the Lithuanian part of the old Commonwealth. There's also an excellent collection of eighteenth- and nineteenth-century Orthodox **icons** from the Brest (formerly Brześć) area, now in Belarus. Of a number of churches in town, the basilica-shaped **Kościół św. Anny** (St Anne's Church), just up from the palace, is the most striking, an exuberant sixteenth-century structure with twin cupolas and a richly decorated side chapel devoted to the Radziwiłłs.

Crossing the eastern border

Travel across Poland's **eastern borders** with Belarus and Ukraine is still liable to be a hassle, and you shouldn't try to cross without acquiring a visa in advance.

Behind the socialist unity rhetoric of the postwar era the reality was a strictly controlled border, at least as strongly policed at major crossing points as the former East–West Germany border. Then, as the political climate changed radically during the 1990s, Poles, Ukrainians and Belarusians were more or less free to move both ways, and cross-border trade provided a major boost to local economies, with ex-Soviet trade tourists known all over Poland as *mrówki* ("ants").

However, worries about the potential influx of illegal immigrants, drugs and cut-price goods led Brussels to demand tightened controls as a necessary condition of Polish EU membership, and Poland implemented visa requirements for citizens of Ukraine, Belarus and Russia (with the latter two erecting similar barriers for Polish citizens). With the help of EU funding border facilities were modernized, and police along the 2000km frontier armed with heat sensors, night vision goggles and other high-tech equipment. All this was predictably unpopular in the east of the country, notably in towns such as Białystok whose massive open-air bazaars flourished with cross-border trade tourism, now slowed to a trickle.

Crossing points

Heavy traffic and increased funding have led to the opening of several new crossing points, though you'll still encounter ponderous, Soviet-style customs facilities on the eastern side of the border. Two major border crossings – **Terespol–Brest** near Biała Podlaska and **Medyka** near Przemyśl – were adequate as long as few people were able to travel, but as long-distance international traffic grew these two were strained beyond capacity and amazing stories of border incidents spread: according to one recent legend, a car was stopped at customs on account of the peculiar smell emanating from the vehicle. Close examination of a back-seat passenger revealed that he had died (from a stroke) during the wait of several days; not wanting to lose their precious place in the queue, the other passengers had decided to keep the body in the car until they crossed the border. **Motorists** can still expect long waits at Terespol and Medyka, and should consider making a detour to one of the minor crossings, a full English-language list of which is maintained by Open Borders (Ⓦ www.openborders.ngo.pl), a Warsaw-based NGO. Wherever you choose to cross, keep a close watch on your vehicle at all times, as theft is always a possibility. Crossing the border **by bus** is generally faster: all PKS buses get special treatment, so unless there's trouble with customs as a result of some of the passengers' baggage you should be through the border in under three hours. By **train** you'll face a wait of roughly two hours, the time necessary to adjust wheels to the wider gauge used in former Soviet countries, a process necessary since tsarist times, when rails were widened throughout Russia out of fears of German invasion. For more information on heading east, see "On to Lithuania" (p.258) and "On to L'viv" (box, p.346).

The **train station** is on the southern side of the town, a five-minute bus ride from the centre, with the **bus station** on pl. Wojska Polskiego, a little to the east of the main Rynek along ul. Brzeska. For **accommodation**, the *Capitol*, in residential streets immediately west of the Rynek at ul. Reymonta 3 (☎083/344 2358; ❹), is a privately run venture with a good selection of rooms and one of the town's better **restaurants**. The *Sportowy*, a ten-minute walk north of the Rynek at ul. Piłsudskiego 38 (☎083/343 4550; ❸) is a basic sports hotel next to the town stadium with faded but acceptable en suites.

Janów Podlaski

Twenty kilometres north of Biała Podlaska close up by the Belarus border, formed from here southwards by the River Bug, the town of **JANÓW PODLASKI** is home to the country's most famous **stud farm**, specializing in the rearing of thoroughbred Arab horses. Located 2km east of the town centre (clearly signposted from the Rynek and served by local bus), the stables are regularly visited by luminaries of the international equestrian scene, principally during the Polish National Arabian Horse Show and Auction, held annually in mid-August.

Established by Tsar Alexander I in 1817 in order to replace horses killed during the Napoleonic wars, the farm has gone through its ups and downs: the stock was decimated by German soldiers late in World War I, and taken over by the Nazis during World War II, when the horses were transported to Germany and many died in the Allied bombing of Dresden in February 1944. The elegant stable complex you see today is essentially that designed by the Warsaw architect Marconi in the 1830s and 1840s.

Visiting the stables without an appointment – preferably made directly with the stables (☎083/341 3009; ☻www.janow.arabians.pl) – is not wildly popular, although the staff will generally let you at least walk around the grounds. Janów is easy to reach from Biała Podlaska, with frequent **buses** making the thirty-minute journey. The best option for **accommodation** is the *Wygoda* guest house (☎083/341 3060; ❷), at ul. Wygoda 2.

East of Lublin

East of Lublin stretches an expanse of the sparsely populated agricultural lowland characteristic of Poland's eastern borders. In the midst of the region lies the recently established **Polesie** national park, a scenic area of marshy swamps and ancient, largely untouched peat bogs, and the most westerly part of a huge expanse of similar terrain stretching far beyond the border into Ukraine and Belarus, known collectively as Polesie before World War II, when the majority of the region was still within Polish territory.

For those interested in the religious and cultural mix of Poles, Ukrainians and Jews historically associated with southeastern Poland, **Chełm**, the regional capital, and the border town of **Włodawa** offer the prospect of an appealing diversion off the beaten track. Further north, there's a fine Baroque church in the remote pilgrimage town of **Kodeń**.

Chełm

Sixty-five kilometres east of Lublin is the town of **CHEŁM**, a tranquil rural centre with a typically timeless eastern Polish feel to it. Like much of the surrounding area the town centre sits on a deep-running bedrock of **chalk**, providing Chełm with its best-known export. Rudely shunted into borderside oblivion by postwar frontier shifts, Chełm is currently experiencing something of a revival thanks to the growing prominence of the Poland–Ukraine border crossing at Dorohusk, 30km east of town on the main Warsaw–Kiev road. Chełm is served by frequent trains and buses from Lublin; from Zamość you can take a direct bus or change at Krasnystaw.

One of eastern Poland's oldest settlements, Chełm was established in the early tenth century to protect the borders of the nascent Piast-ruled domains. From the start the city was embroiled in a protracted contest for domination of the surrounding region between the Duchy of Kiev, the forerunner of Muscovy, and the Polish Piast monarchs. Control passed decisively to the Polish crown in 1387 and soon after the town was granted its charter by Władysław II Jagiełło. Formerly home to one of the oldest **Jewish communities** in Poland – Jews arrived here in the 1440s, possibly even earlier – they constituted roughly half of the population until 1939, enjoying legendary status in Jewish folklore as original simpletons and as such the butt of many a popular joke.

Following the local Orthodox acceptance of Rome's jurisdiction sealed in the 1596 Union of Brest (see box, p.663), Chełm also emerged as a stronghold of **Uniate** (Greek Catholic) devotion, a position it retained until the suppression of the local Uniates and their enforced reconversion to Russian Orthodoxy ordered by the tsarist authorities in the 1870s. After the town's liberation by the Red Army in summer 1944, Chełm briefly enjoyed the dubious honour of being the first base of the Soviet-appointed Polish Committee of National Liberation (PKWN) sent into Poland by Stalin to establish a new communist-led government.

The Stare Miasto

Everything worth seeing is concentrated within the relatively tight confines of the Stare Miasto, which is centred on the lively but architecturally undistinguished pl. Łuczowskiego. From here a brisk climb along the path up **Góra Zamkowa**, the hill overlooking the town from the east and the site of the original fortified settlement, brings you to the former **Uniate Cathedral** complex, a grandiose set of whitewashed buildings including the Greek Catholic cathedral turned Roman Catholic church, an imposing twin-towered Baroque structure from the 1740s with a fine high facade, as well as the Uniate bishop's former residence and a seventeenth-century Basilian monastery. Back out of the complex it's worth climbing the fifteen-metre mound, the only remains of the original Slavic settlement, rising from the northern side of the hill, for a grandstand view over the town. A short walk northwest down the slopes of Góra Zamkowa brings you to another erstwhile Uniate complex, this time comprising a former seminary and the early eighteenth-century Baroque **Kościół sw. Mikołaja** (St Nicholas's Church), these days the home of the town museum's **art collection** (Tues–Fri 10am–3.30pm, Sat & Sun 11am–3pm; 3zł), holding Uniate icons and a jumble of nineteenth-century furniture, all of which is removed from time to time for temporary exhibitions.

Back towards the centre and south down ul. Kopernika, at the corner with ul. Krzywa, stands a former **synagogue**, the only one of several that remains. Today a seedy bar, there's nothing but the building's structure to inform you of its original function. Further down the hill at ul. Młodowskiej is the **Orthodox church** (open for Sunday services), a white brick nineteenth-century *cerkiew* with an impressive iconostasis.

West of the main square down ul. Lubelska stands the **parish church**, a Piarist foundation from the 1750s, designed by Italian architect Paolo Antonio Fontana. An extravagant piece of Baroque exuberance, the walls and vaults of the interior boast a fine series of trompe l'oeil paintings and frescoes by Joseph Meyer, similar in style to the ones in Lublin's Cathedral. Just beyond is the **town museum** at no. 57 (Tues–Fri 10am–3.30pm, Sat & Sun 11am–3pm; 3zł). The ground floor displays focus on the history of Chełm, notably the Partition-era Russian occupation, while the upstairs there's a collection of regional wildlife as well as an extraordinary and presumably less local variety of molluscs.

The chalk cellars

Immediately west of the parish church at ul. Lubelska 55a is the entrance to the town's major curiosity, a labyrinthine network of **underground tunnels** hewn out of the chalk bedrock – the only such system of chalk tunnels in Europe. **Entrance** is by guided tour only (tours daily at 11am, 1pm and 4pm; ⓣ082/565 2530; ⓦwww.podziemia.website.pl; 9zł), and in English by advance appointment, though there's often an English speaker on duty. The unusual purity of the local chalk, combined with a growing appreciation of its commercial building value, resulted in the development of an amateur chalk-mining industry here as far back as the fifteenth century. Little if any control was exercised over the pattern of the mining, the result being a seemingly uncoordinated maze of tunnels and mine shafts hacked out by succeeding generations of local entrepreneurs. However, eventually much of the fifteen-kilometre network of passageways – the deepest going down fifteen metres – fell into neglect and disuse. In the 1960s, in an effort to halt the rot, the deepest sections were silted up and a two-kilometre section of tunnels twelve metres deep was cleaned up and opened to tourists.

The standard **tour** lasts about forty minutes, more than enough for most people given the temperature of the tunnels, exactly 9°C regardless of the season – bring a jacket or sweater. As you would expect, there's a stock of historical anecdotes as well as legends of spirits and demons, all of which the torchlight-bearing guide will dutifully provide.

Practicalities

The main **train** stations lie on opposite sides of the Stare Miasto. The larger of the two, Chełm Główny, is a good 2km northeast of the centre (regular buses shuttle into town), so it's preferable to alight at Chełm Miasto, a fifteen-minute walk west of pl. Łuczowskiego, the main square. The **bus station** is on ul. Lwowska, a five-minute walk south of the centre. The helpful **tourist office**, centrally located at ul. Lubelska 63 (Mon–Fri 8am–5pm, Sat & Sun 9am–2pm; ⓦwww.chelm.pl/default.htm) is well stocked with maps and other information, including a number of English-language brochures. **Internet access** is at ul. Popiełuszki 11, opposite the bus station. **Accommodation** options are limited, and you're probably better off making a day-trip from Lublin, but if you need to stay the best choice is the *Kamena*, situated halfway between Chełm Miasto train station and the town centre at ul. Armii Krajowej 50 (ⓣ082/565 6401; ⓦwww.hotelkamena.pl; ❷), a shabby but passable concrete block with a restaurant and café. Note that the more expensive rooms (❹) come with TV and breakfast but not better furnishings. The cheaper *MOSIR*, just east of the centre by the sports stadium at ul. 1 Pułku Szwoleżerów 15 (ⓣ082/563 0286; ❶), has spartan but clean en-suite doubles as well as triples and quads. The top **restaurant** is *Gęsia Szyja*, just east of the main square, which has good meat dishes and one of the only jukeboxes in Poland. A fair alternative, with an outdoor café on the square itself, is *Pizzeria Romantica*, ul. Kopernika 2.

Włodawa

Hard up by the Belarusian border, 50km north of Chełm, sits the sleepy little town of **WŁODAWA**. Situated on top of a low hill overlooking the River Bug, Włodawa gets its as yet underdeveloped tourist stars from the presence of one of the best-preserved synagogues in the country. As with many towns in this region, Jews formed a clear majority of the town population up till World War II, when virtually all of them perished in the concentration camp at Sobibór, established by the Nazis in May 1942, 12km south of town.

Built in the 1760s on the site of an earlier wooden structure, the main **synagogue** is a typically solid-looking late Baroque construction with a palatial main facade dominated by a high central section and topped by some typically Polish mansard roofing. Despite severe damage by the Nazis, and postwar conversion into a warehouse, the synagogue was thoroughly and well restored in the 1960s and has since functioned as a **museum** (Mon–Fri 9am–3pm, Sat & Sun 10am–2pm; 5zł). In the main interior room, the prayer hall, four pillars supporting the barrel-cross vaulting indicate the spot where the bema once stood. The major surviving original feature is the restored **Aron ha Kodesh**, a colourful, triple-tiered neo-Gothic structure raised in the 1930s and covered with elaborate stucco decoration. Ranged round the walls is a photo exhibition of prewar and Nazi-era Jewish life in the region, while a side room holds Torah scrolls and other Judaica. Upstairs there's a re-creation of the room where local Rabbi Melamed Menachem lived and taught, complete with tattered prayer books, worn furniture and his children's toys. Across the courtyard from the main synagogue is another smaller house of worship from the mid-nineteenth century (same opening hours), which has preserved sections of polychromy as well as Aron ha Kodesh. The upper floor here holds the local **ethnographic collection**, arranged as a *chłopskie pielgrzymowanie* ("peasant's pilgrimage"). After a captivating display featuring the contents of an old Jewish shop, handmade canoes and various traditional implements, the peasant's ultimate destination is revealed: the bleak concrete landscape of a proletarian Warsaw suburb.

There are a couple of other buildings worth seeking out elsewhere in town: north of the main square the **parish church** is a curiously squat-looking late-Baroque building dating from the mid-1700s, with some rich Rococo interior polychromy, and the nearby Orthodox church, which was built in 1842 with funds from the Zamoyski family. Here, as ever, the building is kept locked except for Sunday services.

In the unlikely event of needing **accommodation**, the *Car Polesia*, ul. Sokołowa 4 (☎082/572 4574; ❷), is a cosy small hotel, which also has a decent **restaurant**.

Kodeń

An hour north of Włodowa along the border with Belarus lies the pilgrimage town of **KODEŃ**, home to a graceful seventeenth-century **parish church** combining Renaissance and Baroque elements, and built to house an icon thought to represent Our Lady of Guadeloupe. The town's owner, powerful nobleman Mikołaj Sapieha, miraculously recovered from a serious illness after praying before the icon in Rome in 1631. Determined to possess the painting, after Pope Urban VIII refused to sell it to him Sapieha bribed a sacristan, who helped him to steal it. Sapieha was excommunicated when the crime was discovered, but, having fled with the treasure, he held his ground, building the church for the painting, and was eventually received back into the fold. Today the icon, which remains one of the most venerated in Poland, is the centrepiece of a splendid gilt altar, while the church interior is adorned with fine Renaissance stucco. The building's Baroque facade was added early in the eighteenth century. Behind the church a small **museum** (daily 8am–4pm; 2zł) displays kitschy souvenirs brought from around the world by returning missionaries, and a very complete collection of birds' eggs and nests, gathered by a local priest in boyhood and left here when he was sent to Canada. Down the dirt road leading east from the church you'll find a park containing the scant remains of a sixteenth-century fortress that belonged to the Sapiehas, and a brick church from the same period, originally Orthodox (Mikołaj himself was a convert to Catholicism).

Although only easily accessible if you're driving, Kodeń is served by two daily **buses** from Włodowa and a half-dozen from Biała Podlaska – a day-trip by bus from Lublin might be feasible with a very early start. It's possible **to stay** in the sanctuary behind the church (☎083/375 4120; ❶), while simple **meals** are available at the *Zajazd Purgatorio*, next to the church.

West to Kazimierz

The Lublin–Warsaw route has a major attraction in the town of **Kazimierz Dolny**, an ancient and highly picturesque grain-shipping centre set above the Wisła. Of all the small towns in rural Poland this is – by a long stretch – the best preserved, and continues to swallow up ever-growing numbers of tourists as a result. To reach it on public transport, the easiest approach from Warsaw is to go by train to **Puławy** and catch a connecting bus from there; from Lublin there are direct buses via the old spa town of **Nałęczów**, itself a pleasant excursion.

Nałęczów

Twenty-five kilometres west of Lublin, **NAŁĘCZÓW** (most, but not all, Kazimierz and Puławy-bound buses pass through here) saw its heyday at the end of the last century, when Polish writers and artists, including the popular novelists Bolesław Prus and Stefan Żeromski, and pianist-prime minister Ignacy Paderewski, came here, the quality of the local air and water helping establish it as one of the country's most popular resorts.

Even today the **spa** is renowned for its therapeutic waters, heart specialists and generally medicinal climate, and the town retains much of its old-time appearance and atmosphere. The local mineral water, Nałęczowianka, is one of the most popular in the country.

A leisurely stroll through the attractively landscaped spa park brings you to the Neoclassical **Pałac Małachowskiego**, an elegant Rococo structure from the 1770s, which is part health centre and part **museum** (Wed–Sun 9:30am–3pm; 3.5zł), devoted to Prus and the "Positivist" literary movement he promoted in reaction to insurrectionary Romanticism. The museum isn't especially interesting but the palace ballroom, boasting some nice stucco decoration, is impressive. A bit further into the park is the Sanatorium itself, overlooking a swan-filled lake. For an instant iron-deficiency remedy, you can taste the local waters in the nearby pavilion. Back out through the main gate, opposite the bus stop on ul. Poniatowskiego, a short way up ul. Żeromskiego is the **Żeromski villa**, a Zakopane-style residence built at the turn of the twentieth century and now housing an attractive little museum (Tues–Sun 10am–3pm; 3.5zł) with the author's original furnishings.

Better than the hotels in town, there is a wide selection of **rest homes** aimed at people here to take the cure – though you don't have to be enrolled in one to stay. The most elegant choice is the *Willa Raj*, near the park entrance at ul. Lipowa 15 (⊤081/501 4084; ⓦ www.feniks.onet.pl/osrodki.html; ❹), set in a grand villa and offering a full range of treatments as well as longer stays from around 700zł for a week with full board. There's also the modest but good-quality *Ewelina*, across the road at ul. Lipowa 16 (⊤081/501 4076; ❷), offering simple en suites and with a pleasant restaurant attached. If these are full, try the *Poniatówka*, past the bus station at ul. Poniatowskiego 24 (⊤081/501 4404; ❷), which has modern comfortable rooms and a small pizzeria.

Puławy

Sprawling over the eastern bank of the Wisła 20km northwest from Nałęczów, the featureless town of **PUŁAWY** was almost entirely rebuilt following wartime destruction. However, it remains indelibly associated with the powerful Czartoryski family, the noted aristocratic dynasty who made Puławy their base in the 1730s, and especially **Prince Adam Czartoryski** and his wife **Izabela**, passionate devotees of the arts who transformed their palace here into a cultural and intellectual centre late in the eighteenth century. Despite the advent of the Partitions, the family carried on through the early 1800s, Izabela founding a national museum here, the first of its kind in Poland, and continuing to patron-ize the arts until 1830, when the failure of that year's uprising (see "Contexts", p.667) and the Czartoryski's involvement in its planning – their son Adam had been proclaimed ruler of Poland – resulted in the confiscation of the entire family estate, the enraged tsarist authorities even going as far as to rename the town New Alexandria. Izabela retired to a country estate with their huge art collection, while her son, fleeing a death sentence, escaped to Paris, where he presided over a salon frequented by Chopin, Balzac and Liszt, among others. In 1850 he brought most of the family art collection to Paris, where it remained until the 1870s, when the city of Kraków granted the family the old arsenal inside the city walls as an exhibition space, the collection remains there today (see p.403).

The only thing worth seeking out here is the **Pałac Czartoryskich**, approached from a wide courtyard just south of the town centre. Built in the 1670s by the veteran Warsaw architect Tylman of Gameren, the main building has been remodelled several times (most recently following World War II damage), the result being the leaden Neoclassical pile you see today. The building is now an agricultural research institute, but no one seems to mind if you look around. Through the main entrance and up the grand cast-iron staircase, the arcaded **Gothic Hall** and **Music Hall** offer hints of former grandeur, while from the marble balcony there's a fine view over the palace park.

Designed and developed by the industrious Izabela over a twenty-year period (1790–1810), the meandering palace **park** is quintessentially Romantic in feel and conception. Noted for their variety of trees, the grounds are also dotted with the hotchpotch of "historical" buildings and monuments, in the manner popular with the Polish aristocracy of the period (see, for example, Arkadia, p.146). Southeast of the palace, the **Dom Gotycki** (Gothic House), a square, two-storey building with a graceful portico, was originally part of the Czartoryski museum, and the family's famous painting by Leonardo da Vinci hung inside. Opposite is the **Świątynia Sybilli** (Temple of Sibyl), consciously echoing the temple of the same name in Tivoli, near Rome. The rest of the park contains other follies, including grottoes, a Chinese pavilion, the marble family sarcophagus and assorted imitation classical statuary.

Puławy is on the major train line from Warsaw (2hr) to Lublin (1hr), with frequent connections both ways. The main **train station** (Puławy Miasto) is 2km northeast of the centre on ul. Żyrzyńska, while the **bus station**, at the junction of ul. Lubelska and ul. Wojska Polskiego, is closer; from either you can take bus #12 to the centre. There's a decent **hotel** and **restaurant**, the *Prima*, next to the train station at ul. Partyzantów 44 (☎081/886 3824; ❹).

Kazimierz Dolny and around

Tiny, riverside **KAZIMIERZ DOLNY** (Lower Kazimierz), picturesquely set between two hills and possessing one of Poland's finest architectural ensembles as well as quiet, rustic backstreets, is unquestionably established as a major tourist venue, a fact reflected in its wealth of pensions, restaurants and galleries. Artists have been drawn here since the nineteenth century, attracted by the effervescent light and ancient buildings, while in more recent decades Kazimierz has been used by film directors as a backdrop for historical thrillers and romances.

The town is closely associated with its royal namesake, **Kazimierz the Great** (1333–70), who rescued Poland from dynastic and economic chaos and transformed the country's landscape in the process. It is said of him that he "found a wooden Poland and left a Poland of stone", and Kazimierz

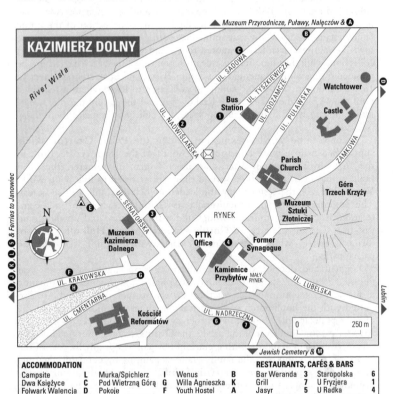

ACCOMMODATION					RESTAURANTS, CAFÉS & BARS			
Campsite	L	Murka/Spichlerz	I	Wenus	B	Bar Weranda	3	Staropolska	6
Dwa Księżyce	C	Pod Wietrzną Górą	G	Willa Agnieszka	K	Grill	7	U Fryzjera	1
Folwark Walencja	D	Pokoje	F	Youth Hostel	A	Jasyr	5	U Radka	4
Góralski	J	Strażnica Hostel	E			Pod Wietrzną		Zielona Taverna	2
Kwaskowa	M	U Góreckich	H			Gorą	G		

Dolny is perhaps the best remaining example of his ambitious town-building programme. Thanks to the king's promotion of the Wisła grain and timber trade, a minor village was transformed into a prosperous mercantile town by the end of the fourteenth century, gaining the nickname "little Danzig" in the process, on account of the goods' ultimate destination. Much of the money that poured in was used to build the ornate burghers' houses that still line the main square.

It was during this period, too, that **Jews** began to settle in Kazimierz, grateful for the legal protection proclaimed for them throughout Poland by King Kazimierz, and for the next five centuries Jewish traders and shopkeepers were integral to the character of towns like this. Jews accounted for up to fifty percent of Kazimierz's population when World War II began, but only a handful survived the war, with the result that Kazimierz entered the postwar era as a half-empty shell. However, Warsaw's elite soon rediscovered its rural charm and nowadays it is thronging with tourists over the summer and at weekends throughout the year, but it still manages to retain a relaxed, bohemian feel, and despite overcrowding during its cultural festivals (see p.316), the town never has the feel of being oppressively over-touristed.

Arrival and information

Despite lying some way off the main inter-city road routes, Kazimierz Dolny is easy to reach by **bus**, with several daily departures from Warsaw, including three fast services run by the private firm *HaloBus* – leaving from the Polski Express stop on al. Jana Pawła next to the Holiday Inn – and up to fourteen PKS services from Lublin. Alternatively you can catch a **train** to Puławy (on the Warsaw–Lublin line) and pick up a Kazimierz-bound bus there (suburban bus #12 from the train station, or one of the regular PKS services from the bus station).

There's a helpful **PTTK office** at no. 27 on the Rynek (May–Sept Mon–Fri 8am–5.30pm, Sat & Sun 10am–5.30pm; Oct–April Mon–Fri 8am–4pm, Sat & Sun 10am–4.30pm; ☎081/881 0046), with good maps and a list of **private rooms** (❶–❷). Two competing **websites**, ⓦwww.kazimierzdolny.pl and ⓦwww.kazimierz-news.com.pl have more information.

If you're taken by the idea of exploring the charming surrounding countryside, **bike rental** is widely available. The stall at ul. Nadrzeczna 48 (4zł/hr) is a good choice, and they also have scooters (30zł/hr). There's a small **Internet** café (daily 10am–9pm) at ul. Lubelska 4a. A **produce market** is held on the Rynek on Tuesday and Friday mornings.

Accommodation

There's a wide range of accommodation in Kazimierz, and you should always be able to find a cheap private room, but for all of the places listed below it's advisable to book ahead, especially at weekends. The main **youth hostel**, *Pod Wianuszkami*, ul. Puławska 64 (☎081/881 0327, ⓔwianuszki@poczta.onet.pl), 2km north of town in an old riverside granary, has dorms (30zł) as well as a few doubles (❷); it's open year-round but often full with school groups. The alternative is the newer *Strażnica Hostel*, in the fire station building at ul. Senatorska 23 (☎081/881 0427), which has doubles (❷) and dorms (28zł) but also fills up quickly. The main **campsite** is behind the *Murka/Spichlerz*, 1.5km west of the centre, at Krakowska 59/61 (May–Aug; ☎081/881 0401), but the *Strażnica Hostel* also has space, and plenty of locals rent out their lawns – try along ul. Krakowska or ul. Tyszkiewicza.

Dwa Księżyce ul. Sadowa 15 ☏081/881 0833, ✉dwa_ksiezyce@interia.pl. Medium-sized hotel in a posh-looking house on a quiet street in the town centre, offering stylish en suites. Breakfast included. ❺

Folwark Walencja ul. Góry16 ☏081/882 1165, ✉folwarkwalencja@wp.pl. In an eighteenth-century manor on the hill overlooking the town, this is a quiet pension with good rooms and an adjacent horse-riding school. ❸–❺

Góralski ul. Krakowska 47 ☏081/881 0263. Reasonable quality *górale* chalet-style *pensjonat* overlooking the river and with a good restaurant. Some rooms are en suite, others use a bathroom in the hallway. ❷

Kwaskowa ul. Czerniawy 3D ☏042/882 1330, ⓦwww.kwaskowa.pl. A ten-minute walk south-east of town on the way to the Jewish cemetery. Friendly, English-speaking pension with clean rooms and Ikea-style furnishings. En suites and rooms with shared bath ❷–❹.

Murka/Spichlerz ul. Krakowska 59/61 ☏081/881 0036. Adjacent PTTK-run hotels 1.5km west of town, both with simple but decent rooms. The former in a mansard-roofed mansion, the latter a large, refurbished granary. Restaurant, tennis courts and weight room on site. ❹

Pod Wietrzną Górą ul. Krakowska 1 ☏042/881 0543, ⓦwww.wietrznagora.pl. Smallish, centrally located *pensjonat* with cosy en suites and a good restaurant. ❹

Pokoje ul. Krakowska 14 ☏081/881 0871. One of the better of several dozen budget pensions in town, with small but modern and comfortable rooms, attractive surroundings and friendly (though not English-speaking) management. ❸

U Góreckich ul. Krakowska 23 ☏081/881 0190. Smart pension with a lovely garden and well-furnished rooms. The best choice in its price range. ❸

Wenus ul. Tyszkiewicza 25a ☏081/882 0400. Modern medium-sized hotel northeast of the centre, offering all the creature comforts. ❺

Willa Agnieszka ul. Krakowska 41a ☏081/882 0411, ✉willa_agnieszka@wp.pl. High-quality pension in a new building west of the centre, with a nice terrace and some of the best rooms in town. *Jasyr* restaurant on site (see p.316). ❹

The Town

The **Rynek**, with its solid-looking wooden well at the centre, is ringed by an engaging mixture of original buildings, the opulent town houses of rich Kazimierz merchants rubbing shoulders with more folksy structures, many boasting first-floor verandahs which jut out from underneath plunging, shingle-covered roofs. Most striking of the merchants' residences around the square – all of which were restored after the war – are the **Kamienice Przybyłów** (Przybyła Brothers' Houses), both on the southern edge. Built in 1615, they bear some striking Renaissance sculpture; the guidebooks will tell you that the largest one shows St Christopher, but his tree trunk of a staff and zodiacal entourage suggest something more like a Polish version of the Green Giant. Next door is the former **Kamienica Lustigowska** (Lustig House) – once home to a notable local Jewish mercantile dynasty. Inside its beams display the only surviving original Hebrew inscription in town, a quotation from the Psalms. On the western side of the square stands the late-eighteenth-century **Kamienica Gdańska** (Gdańsk House), a sumptuous Baroque mansion originally owned by grain merchants.

Other houses still carrying their Renaissance decorations can be seen on ul. Senatorska, which runs alongside the stream west of the square. Of these, the **Kamienica Celejowska** (Celejowski House; no. 17) has a fabulous high attic storey, a balustrade filled with the carved figures of saints and an assortment of imaginary creatures, richly ornamented windows and a fine entrance portal and hallway. It houses the town museum, the **Muzeum Kazimierza Dolnego** (May–Sept Tues–Thurs & Sun 10am–5pm, Fri–Sat 10am–7pm; Oct–April Tues–Sun 10am–5pm; 5zł), which has a small exhibition on town history and a larger gallery of paintings of Kazimierz and its surroundings. The nineteenth-century paintings focus partly on the Jews – a kind of Orientalist fascination seems to have gripped the predominantly Gentile Polish painters who formed the town's artist community. Together with the selection of works by local

Jewish artists such as Samuel Finkenstein they evoke an almost palpable atmosphere of Kazimierz in its artistic heyday. The ground floor also houses temporary exhibitions. Heading southwest up the hill from ul. Senatorska brings you to the late-sixteenth-century **Kościół Reformatów** (Reformed Franciscan Church), from where there's a nice view back down over the winding streets and tiled rooftops.

Back in the centre, just east of Rynek is the **Muzeum Sztuki Złotniczej** (Silverware Museum; Tues–Sun: May–Sept 10am–5pm; Oct–April 10am–3pm; 6zł, Thurs free), recently renovated and containing a highly impressive collection of ornamental silverwork and other decorative pieces dating back to the seventeenth century. A notable feature is the collection of Jewish ritual objects and vessels, many from the town itself. The **parish church** stands opposite the museum, a fourteenth-century building that was remodelled impressively in the early seventeenth century. The interior boasts a magnificent organ, a Renaissance font and fine stuccoed vaulting.

Further up, there's an excellent view from the ruins of the fourteenth-century **castle** (daily: May–Sept 10am–5.30pm; Oct–May 10am–dusk; 2.2zł). Built by King Kazimierz and once featuring exquisite Renaissance attics by Santi Gucci, the castle was destroyed by the marauding Swedes during their ferocious invasion of the country in the 1650s. The panorama from the top of the **watchtower** above the castle is even better, taking in the Wisła and the full sweep of the countryside. Built in the thirteenth century, during the age of the grain trade it was used as a lighthouse, with bonfires set inside. Another popular alternative is the vantage point from the top of **Góra Trzech Krzyży** (Three Crosses Hill; same hours as castle; 1zł). A steepish climb fifteen minutes east of the square (there's also a path leading directly here from the castle), the crosses were raised in memory of the early eighteenth-century plague that wiped out a large part of the local population.

Southeast of the main square, the **Mały Rynek** was the Jewish marketplace, and on its northern side you'll find the old **synagogue**. Dating from King Kazimierz's reign, the building you see today was reconstructed in the 1950s following wartime damage by the Nazis and converted into a cinema. The interior's rich polychromy didn't survive, but the octagonal wooden dome, characteristic of many Polish synagogues, was repaired, as was the women's gallery. In the centre of the square stand the former **kosher butchers' stalls**, a rough-looking wooden building from the nineteenth century. Continuing east along ul. Lubelska takes you further into the old Jewish quarter, where there are a number of fine old wooden houses.

Walking one kilometre out of town, first east along ul. Nadreczna and then south on ul. Czerniawa brings you to the Czerniawa Gorge, the site of the main **Jewish cemetery**. First mentioned in 1568, the cemetery was destroyed by the Nazis, who ripped up the tombstones and used them to pave the courtyard of their headquarters in town. In the 1980s the tombstones scattered around the area were collected here and assembled into a Wailing Wall-like monument – six hundred fragments in all – to moving and dramatic effect. A jagged split down the middle symbolizes the dismemberment of the local Jewish population, making this one of the most powerful Jewish memorials in the country. Wander up the hill behind the monument and you'll find decaying remnants of the former cemetery among the trees.

Spread out alongside the main road to Puławy northeast of town lie several of Kazimierz's sixteenth- and seventeenth-century **granaries** (*spichlerze*) – sturdy affairs with Baroque gables, they attest to the erstwhile prosperity of town merchants. One of these, a ten-minute walk from the centre, now houses the

Muzeum Przyrodnicze (Natural History Museum; Tues–Sun: May–Sept 10am–5pm; Oct–April 10am–3pm; 5zł), a didactic collection of stuffed animals from the region, while out front of the building stands the massive trunk of one of many poplar trees planted along the river around 1800 by Princess Izabela Czartoryski.

Eating and drinking

There are some excellent places to eat in Kazimierz, and your choices are not limited to Polish food. In addition to what's listed below there are open-air **bars** by the river offering fried fish and beer. For a novel **snack**, snap up some *koguty* (bread buns baked in the form of a cockerel) from the numerous stalls around the main Rynek. They're also on sale from *Piekarnia Sarzyński*, a smart patisserie at ul. Nadreczna 4 that offers numerous other pastry-snacks and **cakes**. Most **drinking** takes place in the restaurants or in the café-bars grouped around the Rynek, of which *U Radka*, with great jumble shop decor, is the best.

Bar Weranda opposite the museum on ul. Senatorska. Simple Polish milk-bar dishes like *pierogi* and *placki*, on a shady terrace coralled with pot plants.

Grill ul. Nadrzeczna 24. Despite the unassuming title and rather plain outdoor courtyard, this is a wonderful place for grilled trout, with the added attractions of a salad bar and an extensive wine list.

Jasyr ul. Krakowska 41a. Unexpected and classy Ottoman restaurant, serving vegetarian starters like hummus and carrot puree with yoghurt sauce along with high-quality meat dishes.

Pod Wietrzną Górą ul. Krakowska 1. Restaurant belonging to the pension of the same name (see p.314), offering traditional meat dishes, fresh fish

and a decent range of omelettes. Blaring pop music detracts from an otherwise attractive back patio.

Staropolska ul. Nadrzeczna 14. Long-established restaurant with a good line in mid-price traditional Polish cuisine.

U Fryzjera ul. Witkiewicza 2. One of Poland's best Jewish restaurants, with very good traditional dishes like *kugel* and *czulent*, though out of season they won't have everything on the menu.

Zielona Taverna ul. Nadwiślańska 4. Excellent but not overpriced restaurant with a relaxing country-house interior, a delightful garden, and a wider range of vegetarian choices than anywhere else in this part of Poland.

Entertainment

Although the Rynek is pressed into service as a venue for **outdoor concerts** throughout the summer, the city also hosts two very popular festivals, and if you happen into one of them without a reservation it can be almost impossible to find a bed. The **Summer Film Festival**, in late July or early August, is one of Poland's most important and increasingly international in flavour (☎022/636 7083, ⓦ www.latofilmow.pl), and is held in a 900-seat outdoor cinema by the river. Even better known is the annual **Folk Bands and Singers Festival**, a wildly popular event that takes place here in late June or early July. Now approaching its fortieth year, the festival is undoubtedly the country's premier folk music event. The festival has spearheaded something of a revival of interest in Polish roots music, particularly in regional styles that only a decade ago seemed on the verge of extinction. Highlights of the week are the rural dance parties on the main square, and the host of bizarre traditional instruments used by some bands. You'll find plenty of CDs on sale, as well as an accompanying **Handicraft Fair** on the Mały Rynek.

Around Kazimierz

There's some good **walking** territory around Kazimierz. If you really want to get the feel of the town's gentle surroundings, follow one of the marked paths from the town centre: either the five-kilometre green path that takes you southwest past the *Strażnica Hostel* and along the river cliff to **Mecmierz**; or the four-kilometre red path that heads northeast to the ruined castle of **Bochotnica**. King Kazimierz is said to have built the castle here for one of his favourite mistresses, a Jewess called Esterka, with a secret tunnel connecting the fortresses in Kazimierz and Bochotnica.

Walking two kilometres west of the centre to the end of ul. Krakowska, you'll come to a **ferry** (May–Sept 9am–7pm; every 30min; 5zł) to the village of **JANOWIEC**, known for the ruins of the Firlej family **castle**, perched on a hill a half-hour walk from the landing point. In its heyday this imposing early sixteenth-century fortress is reputed to have been one of the grandest in the country, with no fewer than eight ballrooms. Today, apart from the fine views it affords, the castle's most striking feature is its zany exterior decoration consisting of alternating red-and-white-painted stripes and occasional contorted human figures. Also of interest is the freshly cleared well in the castle courtyard, allegedly the ancient entrance to a secret passage joining this fortress to that of Kazimierz. The castle **interior** (May–Sept Mon 10am–2pm, Tues–Fri 10am–5pm, Sat–Sun 10am–7pm; Oct–April Tues–Fri 10am–3pm, Sat–Sun 10am–4pm; 8zł) holds a small exhibit on the building's history, including a nice series of photographs. To one side of the castle is a small **skansen** museum (same hours and ticket) devoted to regional folk architecture. The highlight is a wooden manor house dating from the 1770s and with period furniture inside; other displays include wooden cottages from around the region, a collection of horse carts and a nineteenth-century wooden granary. Back down in the village there's a fine Gothic **parish church** that contains the Firlej family tomb, designed by Italian Renaissance architect Santi Gucci of Kraków fame. If the ferry isn't running, you can also get to Janowiec by taking **bus** #17 from Puławy.

Sandomierz

Though not as picturesque as Kazimierz, **SANDOMIERZ**, a further 80km south along the Wisła, is a fascinating old town with a well-preserved hilltop centre and several worthy monuments. Stranded away from today's growth centres (and thus economically moribund), Sandomierz is nonetheless easy to reach, with two daily train services from Warsaw and frequent buses from Lublin. Tourist facilities have improved in the last few years, and you'll find plenty of places to stay and eat.

Like other towns in the southeast, Sandomierz rose to prominence through its position on the medieval trade route running from the Middle East, through southern Russia and the Ukraine, into central Europe. The town was sacked by the Tatars (twice) and the Lithuanians, in the thirteenth and fourteenth centuries respectively, then completely rebuilt by **Kazimierz the Great**, who gave it a castle, defensive walls, cathedral and town plan – still visible in the Stare Miasto. Subsequently, Sandomierz flourished on the timber and corn trade, with its links along the Wisła to the Baltic. It was also the scene of one of the key religious events in Polish history. In 1570, while Catholics and Protestants were slitting each other's throats in the rest of Europe, members of Poland's non-Catholic churches met here to formulate the so-called **Sandomierz Agreement**, basis for the legally enshrined freedom of conscience later established throughout the country.

Physically, Sandomierz suffered badly at the hands of the Swedes, who blew up the town castle in 1656, and it was only thanks to a minor miracle that it survived World War II intact. In August 1944, as the **Red Army** pushed the Germans back across Poland, the front line moved closer and closer to Sandomierz. A popular story in the town relates how one Colonel Skopenko, an admirer of Sandomierz, managed to steer the fighting away from the town. He was later killed further west; his last wish, duly honoured, was to be buried in the town cemetery. The statue in his honour erected after the war in front of the main city gate was recently moved to the out-of-town Soviet War Cemetery, a victim of the anti-Soviet/Russian sentiments of the present era.

The Town

The entrance to the **Stare Miasto** is the fourteenth-century **Brama Opatowska** (Opatowska Gate), part of King Kazimierz's fortifications; climbing to the top (daily 10am–6.30pm; 3zł) will get you a view over the town and surrounding area. Buses arriving in Sandomierz from the south will let you off at the gate.

From here on it's alleyways and cobblestones, as ul. Opatowska leads to the delightful, sloping **Rynek**. At its heart is the fourteenth-century **town hall**, a Gothic building which had its decorative attic, hexagonal tower and belfry added in the seventeenth and eighteenth centuries. The ground floor section

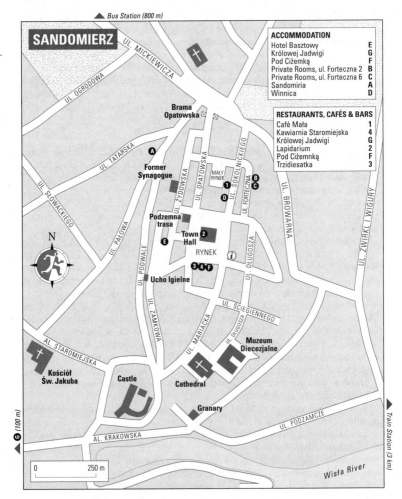

SANDOMIERZ

▲ Bus Station (800 m)

ACCOMMODATION

Hotel Basztowy	E
Królowej Jadwigi	G
Pod Ciżemką	F
Private Rooms, ul. Forteczna 2	B
Private Rooms, ul. Forteczna 6	C
Sandomiria	A
Winnica	D

RESTAURANTS, CAFÉS & BARS

Café Mała	1
Kawiarnia Staromiejska	4
Królowej Jadwigi	G
Lapidarium	2
Pod Ciżemnką	F
Trzidiesatka	3

Brama Opatowska

UL. MICKIEWICZA

UL. OGRODOWA

UL. TATARSKA

UL. SŁOWACKIEGO

Former Synagogue

UL. ŻYDOWSKA

UL. OPATOWSKA

MAŁY RYNEK

UL. SOKOLNICKIEGO

UL. FORTECZNA

UL. BROWARNA

UL. ZWIRKI I WIGURY

Podzemna trasa

N

UL. PAŁOWA

UL. PODWALE

Town Hall

RYNEK

UL. DŁUGOSZA

Ucho Igielne

UL. ZAMKOWA

UL. MARIACKA

UL. DŁUGOSZA

UL. ŚCIEGIENNEGO

AL. STAROMIEJSKA

Kościół Św. Jakuba

Castle

Cathedral

Muzeum Diecezjalne

Granary

AL. KRAKOWSKA

UL. PODZAMCZE

◀ G (100 m)

▶ Train Station (3 km)

Wisła River

0   250 m

contains a small **museum** (Tues–Fri 9am–4pm, Sat 9am–3pm, Sun 10am–3pm; 4zł) devoted to the history of the town. There's not much here other than pieces from an artful twelfth-century chess set – one of the oldest in Europe – dug up near the Church of St James (see p.320) some years back. Many of the well-preserved **burghers' houses** positively shout their prosperity: nos. 5 and 10 are particularly fine Renaissance examples.

A hidden aspect of old Sandomierz is revealed by a trip through the wine and grain **cellars** located under the Rynek – the entrance, just off the square on ul. Oleśnickich, is signposted as the *podziemna trasa* ("underground tourist route"). The forty-minute guided tour (Polish only; daily 10am–5pm; 6.50zł) takes you through thirty or so chilly, Renaissance-era cellars extending under the town hall, reaching a depth of 12m at one point. Back at ground level, the registrar's office on nearby ul. Żydowska was an eighteenth-century **synagogue**, though there is little to indicate its origins.

Continuing down either of the streets leading off the southern edge of the square will bring you to the murky **cathedral** (Tues–Sat 10am–2pm & 3–5pm, Sun 3–5pm), constructed around 1360 on the site of an earlier Romanesque church but with substantial Baroque additions. Notable features include the set of early fifteenth-century Russo-Byzantine **murals** in the presbytery, probably by the same artist who painted the Kaplica św. Trójcy in Lublin (see p.295), although these haven't been restored as sensitively. Unfortunately they're also kept roped off and unlit most of the time, so you'll probably have to crane your neck for a glimpse of them. There are no such problems with the gruesome series of eighteenth-century paintings surrounding the nave, charmingly entitled "The Torture Calendar" and depicting early church martyrs being skewered, decapitated or otherwise maimed in every conceivable way. As if this wasn't enough, there's also a group of murals underneath the organ depicting violent scenes from the town's past, including Tatars enjoying a massacre of the local populace in 1259, Swedes blowing up the castle four centuries later and, far more disturbing, an incident of supposed Jewish child sacrifice at Passover – a standard theme of anti-Semitic discourse.

Set back from the cathedral, the **Muzeum Diecezjalne** (Diocesan Museum; April–Oct Tues–Sat 9am–4pm, Sun 1.30–4pm; Nov–March Tues–Sat 9am–3pm, Sun 1.30–3pm; 5zł) and its peaceful, well-tended garden was the home of **Jan Długosz** (1415–80), author of one of the earliest Polish chronicles. The building is filled to bursting with an absorbing, well-presented collection of religious art, ceramics, glass and other curios, the latter including an early seventeenth-century portable organ that still works, a collection of Renaissance locks and keys, and a wonderful old pipe supposed to have belonged to Mickiewicz. Also look for the piece of bread left over from the Swedish invasion of 1656 and the set of seventeenth-century French playing cards illustrating the nations of the world. Among the artistic works there's a fine set of fifteenth- and sixteenth-century altarpieces, including the delicate *Three Saints* triptych from Kraków, as well as a Romanesque *Madonna and Child* stone carving and a *John the Baptist* dubiously attributed to Caravaggio.

Downhill from the cathedral is the **castle**, where the large open terrace affords good views back over the Stare Miasto. It's also used for open-air concerts and theatre performances in summer. The **museum** here (May–Sept Tues–Sun 10am–5pm; Oct–April Tues–Fri 9am–4pm, Sat 9am–3pm, Sun 10am–3pm; 5zł), occupying part of the building, holds an undistinguished permanent collection of silver, numismatics and regional folk art, although its temporary exhibitions are often more interesting. Towards the river stands a medieval **granary**; others are to be found north of town. Al. Staromiejska runs from in front of the castle to the **Kościół św. Jakuba** (St James's Church), a lime-shaded late-Romanesque building that's thought to be the first brick basilica in Poland – its restored entrance portal is particularly striking. Inside, the **Martyrs' Chapel** (Mon–Sat 10am–5pm, Sun 10.30–11.30am & 1.30–3.30pm) has a vivid painting of the martyrdom of local Dominicans by the Tatars in 1260, while in the northern nave there are glass cases said to contain the bones of the murdered monks.

The area around the church was the site of the original town, destroyed by the Tatars. Archeological digs have uncovered finds such as the twelfth-century chess set now on display in the town museum (see p.319). Since the 1960s, this whole southern district has had to be shored up, owing to subsidence caused by the network of tunnels and cellars dug for grain storage and running for hundreds of metres through the soft undersoil.

Head back down the path in front of St James and you re-enter the town walls through the **Ucho Igielne**, a narrow entrance whose name refers to the eye of the needle in the Biblical proverb.

Practicalities

The **train station** is 3km south on the far side of the river (local bus #8 to the centre), while the **bus station** is 1.5km northwest of town (walk west to the end of ul. 11 Listopada and turn left on ul. Mickiewicza). The staff at the **PTTK office** at Rynek 12 (May–Oct daily 8am–6pm; Nov–April Mon–Fri 8am–4.30pm; ☎015/832 2305, ⓦwww.pttk-sandomierz.pl) don't speak English but have a list of all **accommodation** options, including several private rooms (❶–❷). After hours you can get the list in the attached *Kordegarda* café. At the top end of the scale, the *Pod Ciżemką*, Rynek 27 (☎015/832 0550, ⓦwww.sandomierz-hotel.com.pl; ❻), is an intimate hotel offering plush en suites in a burgher's mansion. Larger, and tailored more to business travellers than tourists, is the new and well-managed *Hotel Basztowy* at pl. Poniatowskiego 2 (☎015/833 3450, ⓦwww.opiwpr.org.pl; ❻). The *Sandomiria* pension, on the north edge of the centre at ul. Podwale Górne 10 (☎015/644 5244, ⓦwww.sandomiria.pl; ❹), is a spotless new pension with kitchen facilities and a café, while the family-run *Królowej Jadwigi*, down the hill past the castle at ul. Krakowska 24 (☎015/832 2988; ❹), is another good mid-range option, with cosy and well-appointed rooms. Near the main square, the homes at ul. Forteczna 2 (☎015/832 3751; ❷) and 6 (☎015/832 2814; ❷) rent modest private rooms with shared facilities, as does the restaurant *Winnica*, ul. Mały Rynek 2 (☎015/832 3130; ❷).

There are plenty of **places to eat** and **drink** around the Rynek, many of which boast attractive outdoor terraces for people-watching. The best place for coffee is *Café Mała*, just of the Rynek at ul. Sokolnickiego, while *Kawiarna Staromiejska* on the southern side of the square doles out light Polish meals as well as coffee and cakes. Next door, *Trzidiesatka* at Rynek 30 has tasty dishes like grilled chicken with kasha. The upstairs restaurant of the *Pod Ciżemką* is the most formal in town (see above); the Italian place below, also part of the hotel, fares better with pasta than pizza. Slightly further afield, the restaurant of the *Królowej Jadwigi* offers traditional home-cooking in endearingly chintzy surroundings (see above).

For **entertainment** the *Lapidarium*, a cellar club beneath the town hall, has occasional live gigs. The town puts on an annual week-long **music festival** from late June to early July, featuring a variety of classical, folk and jazz concerts; check with the tourist office for details.

West from Sandomierz: Opatów and Krzyżtopór castle

Opatów

Some 25km west of Sandomierz on the Kielce road, the somnolent town of **OPATÓW** is worth a brief stop if you're heading towards the Świętokrzyskie region (see p.469), and is also the obvious jumping-off point for the magnificent ruins of Krzyżtopór castle (see below). A medieval market town straddling a major east–west trade route, Opatów was badly mauled during the Tatar raids (1500–1502), and owes much of its current appearance to Chancellor Krzysztof Szydłowiecki, who purchased the town soon afterwards and had the central Rynek area rebuilt along Renaissance lines.

The Rynek's most notable building, the **Kościół św. Marcina** (St Martin's Church), is a towering three-aisled Romanesque basilica raised in the mid-twelfth century and remodelled in later centuries. A few features of the original Romanesque decoration survive, notably the main doorway, the dual windows in the south tower and some frieze decoration on the facade. These aside, the thing to look out for is the group of Szydłowiecki family **tombs**, especially that of Chancellor Krzysztof. Executed, like the others in the group, in the 1530s by a duo of Italian architects from the court at Wawel, the tomb has a powerful bronze bas-relief of the citizens of Opatów mourning the chancellor's death – a moving tribute to a man whose family name had died out by the end of the century owing to a persistent failure to produce male heirs.

One section of the square is crisscrossed by a honeycomb of underground **tunnels** and **cellars**, a throwback to the town's merchant past, originally used for storing goods sold in the local market. It's now possible to visit the cellars – ask at the PTTK office on the square, which organizes guided visits underground when demand is sufficient. Ten minutes' walk away, back down the hill, through the Brama Warszawska (Warsaw Gate) and across the River Opatówka, is the **Bernardine church**, an ornate late-Baroque structure with a fine high altarpiece that replaced the earlier fifteenth-century church destroyed by Swedish troops during the invasions of the mid-1650s.

The **bus station**, in the centre of town, has good connections to Sandomierz. The **tourist office** at Obrońców Pokoju 18 (Mon–Sat 10am–6pm, Sun 11am–5pm; ☎015/868 2778) sells maps and provides local information, although with little in the way of accommodation save for a spartan seasonal hostel and an out-of-town motel, it's best to press on.

Krzyżtopór

Despite its dilapidated state, the **Krzyżtopór castle**, near the village of Ujazd, 15km southwest of Opatów, is one of the most spectacular ruins in Poland. Nothing in the surrounding landscape prepares you for the mammoth building that suddenly rears up over the skyline. Even then, it's not until you actually enter the castle compound (Tues–Sun sunrise–sunset; 4zł) that you really begin to get a handle on the scale of the place, a magnificent ruin still bearing many hallmarks of the considerable architectural ingenuity that went into designing and constructing the complex.

The **history** of the castle is a textbook case of grand aristocratic folly. Built at enormous expense for Krzysztof Ossoliński, the governor of Sandomierz province, by Italian architect Lorenzo Muretto, and completed in 1644, only a year before Ossoliński's death, the castle was thoroughly ransacked by the Swedes only a decade later, a blow from which it never really recovered, despite being inhabited by the Ossoliński family up until the 1770s. Plans for its resurrection have come and gone over time, the latest initiative being a somewhat uncertain bid to revive the place as a tourist attraction.

The basic **layout** of the castle comprises a star-shaped set of fortifications surrounding a large inner courtyard and, within this, a smaller elliptical inner area. The original architectural conception mimicked the calendar at every level: thus there were four towers, representing the seasons, twelve main walls for the months, 52 rooms for the weeks, 365 windows for the days, and even an additional window for leap years, kept bricked up when out of sync with the calendar. Ossoliński's passion for horses was accommodated by the network of stables, some 370 in all, built underneath the castle, each equipped with its own mirror and marble manger. While remnants of the stables survive, the same can't be said for the fabled dining hall in the octagonal entrance tower, originally dominated by a crystal aquarium built into the ceiling.

Carved on the entrance tower before the black marble portal are a large cross (*krzyż*) and an axe (*topór*), a punning reference to the castle's name, the former a symbol of the Catholic Church's Counter-Reformation, of which Ossoliński was a firm supporter, the latter part of the family coat of arms. Inside the complex, you're inevitably drawn to wandering around the castle's rather unstable nooks and crannies. The longer you stay, the more the sheer audacity and expanse of the place hits home – in particular, the murky ruins of the cellars, which seem to go on for ever. With the high inner walls towering above as you descend into the bowels of the building, it's easy to understand why it has generated its fair share of legends – notably that of the lady and knight said to prowl the ramparts by moonlight, the knight being Krzysztof Baldwin, the second lord of the castle killed by a Tatar archer.

The site is fairly easy to get to if you're **driving**: follow the Staszów road out of Opatów and turning east at the village of Iwaniska. By **bus**, there are five daily services to Ujazd from Opatów (fewer at weekends), although if you're coming from the Sandomierz direction you could just as easily catch a bus to Klimontów, 10km southeast of Krzyżtopór (10 daily), where you can change to an Ujazd service (7 daily).

Baranów Sandomierski

South of Sandomierz along the Wisła basin, fifteen kilometres beyond the sulphur mining centre of **Tarnobrzeg**, the castle at **BARANÓW SANDOMIERSKI** is one of the most impressive in Poland. Erected on the site of a fortified medieval structure owned by the Baranów family, the exquisitely formed and well-preserved Renaissance **castle** (Tues–Sat 9am–3pm, Sun 9am–4pm; 6zł), thought to have been designed by Santi Gucci is as fine a period piece as you'll come across anywhere, well worth a detour if you're driving. The epithet "castle" is a bit of a misnomer – the building is really an elegant palace, with fortifications added for appearance's sake. Built in the 1590s for the Leszczyński family, the castle is constructed on a rectangular plan with an inner courtyard, four towers and a gateway. The facade is crowned by an attic with a cheerful frieze decoration. In through the gateway you find yourself in a cool Italianate courtyard surrounded by two tiers of arcaded passageways, their ceilings decorated with a wealth of family emblems. To reach the upper level climb the sweeping outer staircase, a later addition. Before doing that it's worth studying the entertaining collection of grotesques, many of them animal figures, that decorate the bases of the courtyard pillars. Inside the building, you can view a section of the ground floor that has retained its ornate period furnishings.

Down in the castle basement there's a small **museum** (same hours and ticket) with temporary exhibitions, while on the south side of the building the well-tended gardens are a pleasant strolling ground.

The lavishly decorated rooms of the upper floors of the castle are occupied by a luxury **hotel**, the *Zamkowy* (℡015/811 8039, ⓦ www.baranow.com.pl) with rooms in the castle itself (❼) and an adjacent building (❺). On the south side of the castle there's a high-quality **restaurant**. The whole place is often reserved for banquets, so particularly in summer it's best to book ahead. A cheaper and perfectly acceptable alternative is the *Zajazd Wisła*, about 1km out of town, on ul. Dąbrowskiego (℡015/811 0380; ❸), with its own restaurant.

By **bus**, local services run fairly regularly from Tarnobrzeg and Mielec, accessible from Sandomierz and Rzeszów respectively. Ask the driver to drop you off at the castle (*zamek*); otherwise it's a ten-minute walk south of the bus stop at the Rynek.

Zamość

The old towns and palaces of southeast Poland often have a Latin feel to them, and none more so than **ZAMOŚĆ**, 96km southeast of Lublin. The brainchild of the dynamic sixteenth-century chancellor Jan Zamoyski, the town is a remarkable demonstration of the way the Polish intelligentsia and ruling class looked towards Italy for ideas, despite the proximity of Russia. Zamoyski, in many ways the archetypal Renaissance man, built this model town to his own ideological specifications close to his childhood village, commissioning the design from Bernardo Morando of Padua – the city where he had earlier studied. Morando produced a beautiful Italianate period piece, with a wide piazza, grid-plan streets, an academy and defensive bastions. These fortifications were obviously well thought out, as Zamość was one of the few places to withstand the seventeenth-century "Swedish Deluge" that flattened so many other Polish towns. Strategically located on the major medieval trading routes linking Kraków and Kiev from west to east, Lublin and L'viv from north to south, the town attracted an international array of merchants from early on, notably Jews, Armenians, Greeks, Scots, Hungarians and Italians, whose presence remained embedded in the diverse architecture of the city even after political changes during the Partition era brought economic decline: early in nineteenth century Zamość had sunk so far that even the Zamoyskis themselves moved on.

War returned to Zamość early in the twentieth century, when the area was the scene of an important battle during the Polish–Russian war of 1919–20. The Red Army, which only weeks before had looked set to take Warsaw, was beaten decisively near the town, forcing Lenin to sue for peace with his newly independent neighbours. Somehow, Zamość managed also to get through World War II unscathed, so what you see today is one of Europe's best-preserved Renaissance town centres, classified by UNESCO as an outstanding historical monument. Chiefly due to its off-the-beaten-track location, the town has neither assumed the prominence it deserves on the tourist trail, nor seen the sort of economic success that has revitalized Lublin and Rzeszów.

Arrival and information

There are only a handful of daily services to the **train station** located 1km southwest of the centre off ul. Akademiczka (take any bus two stops from the station side of the street), so you're more likely to arrive at the main **bus**

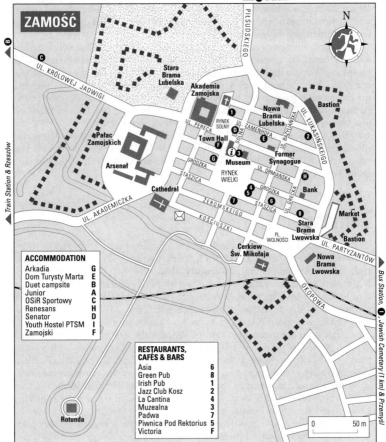

ZAMOŚĆ

ACCOMMODATION

Arkadia	G
Dom Turysty Marta	E
Duet campsite	B
Junior	A
OSiR Sportowy	C
Renesans	H
Senator	D
Youth Hostel PTSM	I
Zamojski	F

RESTAURANTS, CAFÉS & BARS

Asia	6
Green Pub	8
Irish Pub	1
Jazz Club Kosz	2
La Cantina	4
Muzealna	3
Padwa	7
Piwnica Pod Rektorius	5
Victoria	F

station, 2km east of the town centre (local buses #10, #22, #44, #47 or #59 will drop you off in the centre). Zamość's **tourist office**, understaffed but well stocked with books and maps, in the town hall at Rynek 13 (May–Sept Mon–Fri 8am–6pm, Sat 10am–4pm, Sun 10am–3pm; Oct–April Mon–Fri 8am–4pm; ☎084/639 2292, ⓦwww.osir.zamosc.pl/zoit), will provide information on accommodation possibilities as well as the small number of private rooms (❶–❷) in town. The official town website (ⓦwww.zamosc.pl) is more helpful, while the best English-language background on the web is maintained by a local high school (ⓦwww.cf2004.zamosc.pl). There's **Internet** access at Rynek 10. Advance train tickets are available at the **Orbis office** at ul. Grodzka 18 (Mon–Fri 9am–5pm; ☎084/638 5775).

Accommodation

There's a good choice of **accommodation** in Zamość, though the best budget choices are out of the centre. A decent **youth hostel**, *PTSM*, is located between the bus station and Stare Miasto at ul. Zamoyskiego 4 (July & Aug;

☎084/627 9125; 30zł per person). The *Duet* **campsite** on ul. Królowej Jadwigi (☎084/639 2499), a ten-minute walk west of the centre, has modern bungalows (❷), but they fill up quickly.

Hotels

Arkadia Rynek 9 ☎084/638 6507. Small place right on the square, but with musty, gloomy rooms that ought to be cheaper. ❸–❹

Dom Turysty Marta ul. Zamenhofa 11 ☎084/639 2639. Central pension-cum-hostel with nine rooms, most of which are dorms (45zł per person). One double without bath or breakfast (❶).

Junior ul. Gen. Sikorskiego 6 ☎084/638 6615 ⓦwww.hoteljunior.pl. Pleasant roadside hotel 2km north of the Stare Miasto (bus #3, #11 or #19) that's better value than the more central budget places. With restaurant, billiard room and weekend discounts. Breakfast 10zł extra. ❸

OSiR Sportowy ul. Królowej Jadwigi 8 ☎084/638 6011. Recently renovated athletes' hotel located in a sports complex, 500m west of the centre next to the football stadium. Roomy en suites, and breakfast for an extra 20zł. ❸

Renesans ul. Grecka 6 ☎084/639 2001. Bland and outwardly ugly but quite comfortable hotel built where long ago stood an Armenian church. Handily close to the Rynek, and with weekend discounts. ❺

Senator Rynek Solny 4 ☎084/638 9990. Small, high-quality new hotel in the old Jewish quarter, of a similar standard to the *Zamojski* but much more intimate. 25 percent weekend discounts. ❺

Zamojski ul. Kołłątaja 2/4/6 ☎084/639 2516, ⓦwww.orbis.pl. Polished Orbis-chain hotel located in a historic town house just off the Rynek. With plush rooms and a fine restaurant, this is definitely the hotel of choice if you fancy a splurge. Twenty-percent discounts at weekends. ❻

The Stare Miasto

Regulation-issue urban development surrounds Zamość's historic core, but all of the sights are within the Renaissance grid of the old town or only a few minutes' walk beyond it. Coming from the bus station you'll arrive at **plac Wolności** on the eastern edge of the centre.

The Rynek

The **Rynek Wielki**, also known as pl. Mickiewicza, is a couple of blocks in from pl. Wolności and the partly preserved circuit of walls. Ringed by a low arcade and the decorative former homes of the Zamość mercantile bourgeoisie, the geometrically designed square – exactly 100m in both width and length – is a superb example of Renaissance town architecture, a wide open space whose columned arcades, decorated facades and breezy walkways exude an upliftingly light, airy warmth. Dominating the ensemble from the north side of the square is the **town hall**, among the most photographed buildings in the country. A solid, three-storey structure topped by a soaring clock tower and spire, the original, lower construction designed by Morando acquired its present Mannerist modelling in the 1640s, with the sweeping, fan-shaped double stairway not added until the eighteenth century. The whole building has just come out of an extensive renovation, and the floodlighting used at night in summer heightens the power of the building, combining with the visual backdrop of the square to undeniably impressive effect. Occupied by local government offices, the town hall doesn't offer much to see inside.

The Dom Wilczeka and town museum

From the town hall the vaulted arcade stretching east along ul. Ormiańska features several of the finest houses on the square. Once inhabited by the Armenian merchants who moved here under special privilege in 1585, the house facades are a whirl of rich, decorative ornamentation, with a noticeable intermesh of Oriental motifs. First along is the splendid **Dom Wilczeka**

△ Town hall, Zamość

(Wilczek House), built by an early professor at the Zamość Academy, with some fine decorated bas-reliefs of Christ, Mary and the Apostles gracing the upper storey of the facade. Number 26 sports similarly exuberant decoration, this time with zoological themes. It and the adjoining mansions house the town **museum** (Tues–Sun 9am–4pm; 5zł), focusing on the Zamoyskis and local history. There are copies of portraits of the town's founder, Jan, though these are outshone by a beautiful full-sized set, dating from the 1630s, of his son Tomasz Zamoyski and daughter-in-law Katarzyna. Also on display are the original Zamość charter from 1580 and, upstairs, a re-created Armenian kitchen. The interior, retaining its early seventeenth-century wooden ceiling as well as carved portals and frescoes, is at least as captivating as the museum's contents. Back out of the museum the sumptuous facades continue, no. 24 (part of the museum) featuring a prim-looking Renaissance couple peering down from between the windows, and no. 22 next door bearing a relief of a beatific Mary trampling a fierce-looking dragon underfoot.

The Morando Kamienica

The east side of the square, another former haunt of Armenian merchants and teachers at the Academy, is similarly enjoyable; here as all around the square it's well worth wandering along the vaulted passageways and in through the doorways (many are now shops and several of them beautifully decorated), notably at no. 6, a souvenir shop, and no. 2, a 350-year-old apothecary. The southern side of the square contains some of the oldest and most obviously Italian-influenced mansions, two-storey buildings with regularly proportioned facades, several designed by Morando himself.

The **Morando Kamienica** (Morando Tenement House) at no. 25, where the great architect himself used to live, boasts an impressive facade with exuberant Mannerist friezes, while the PTTK office at no. 31, in the corner of the square, features some fine stuccowork in the vestibule and another beautifully decorated portal and surrounding vault.

West of the square

Moving west of the square, first port of call is the towering collegiate church, recently restored and upgraded to the status of **cathedral**, a magnificent Mannerist basilica designed by Morando to Zamoyski's exacting instructions and completed in 1600. A three-aisled structure with numerous side chapels and delicate pillars reaching up to the ceiling's well-proportioned Renaissance stuccowork, the whole interior is marked by a strong sense of visual and architectural harmony, a powerful expression of the self-confidence of the Polish Counter-Reformation.

The **presbytery** houses a finely wrought eighteenth-century Rococo silver tabernacle, as well as a series of paintings of scenes from the life of St Thomas attributed to Tintoretto. The Zamoyski family **chapel** topped with elegant Baroque stucco by the Italian architect, Giovanni Battista Falconi, is the grandest in the building and contains the marble tomb of Chancellor Jan. Adjoining the main building is a high **bell tower** (May–Sept Mon–Fri 10am–4pm; 3zł), the biggest of its bells, known as Jan, over three centuries old. As with the town hall the whole site is floodlit in summer.

West across the main road, ul. Akademiczka, are two buildings that played a key role in the historic life of the town. As its name implies the **Arsenal**, built by Morando in the 1580s, is where the town's ample stock of weaponry used to be kept alongside Zamoyski spoils of war. These days it houses a small **military museum** (Tues–Sun 9am–4pm; 4zł) where, among the pictures of

Polish soldiers through the ages, you can view a scale model of the seventeenth-century town, surrounded by defensive bastions arranged in the shape of a seven-pointed star. Southwest along ul. Akademiczka it's a five-minute walk to the **Wystawa Plenarna**, the military museum's outdoor branch (same hours; 4zł), where a helicopter and several post-World War II artillery pieces sit on a tiny scrap of parkland.

Back by the Arsenał, the massive **Pałac Zamojskich** (Zamoyski Palace) is a shadow of its former self, Morando's original building having undergone substantial modification early in the nineteenth century, after the Zamoyskis sold it to the Russian government for use as an army hospital. Currently occupied by the town court, the palace is a rather mournful, run-down place, with only the courtyard at the back hinting at its former grandeur.

The former Jewish quarter

Continuing north along ul. Akademiczka, west of the main street is the **Stara Brama Lubelska** (Old Lublin Gate), oldest of the entranceways dotted around the Stare Miasto fortifications, and long since bricked up. The gate, now stranded on the edge of school playing fields, is worth seeking out for the bas-relief uncovered during renovation earlier this century.

The impressive-looking former **Akademia Zamojska** (Zamoyski Academy) across the street, built in the 1630s and an important centre of learning until it was closed by the Austrian government shortly after the First Partition, is now a school, albeit on a humbler scale than originally. Beyond it, much of the northern section of the Stare Miasto belongs to the former **Jewish quarter**, centred around ul. Zamenhofa and Rynek Solny. As in so many other eastern towns, Jews made up a significant portion of the population of Zamość – some 45 percent on the eve of World War II. The first Sephardic Jews from L'viv arrived here in the 1580s, their numbers subsequently swelled by kindred settlers from Turkey, Italy and Holland, to be displaced subsequently by the powerful local Askenazi community. With much of eastern Polish Jewry in the grip of the mystical Hassidic revival, uniquely in the Lublin region Zamość developed as a centre for the progressive *Haskalah*, an Enlightenment-inspired movement originating in Germany that advocated social emancipation, the acceptance of "European" culture and scientific and educational progress within the Jewish community. Among its products were **Itzak Peretz** (1851–1915), a notable nineteenth-century Yiddish novelist born here, and **Rosa Luxemburg** (1871–1919), though it's as a radical communist rather than Jewish progressive that she's primarily known.

A few of the old Jewish merchants' houses ranged around the small square have been renovated, one of which is the smart new *Senator* hotel, and more restoration is in the works. The most impressive Jewish monument, however, is the **former synagogue** on ul. Pereca, a fine early seventeenth-century structure built as part of Zamoyski's original town scheme. Following wartime devastation by the Nazis, who used the building as a carpentry shop, the synagogue was carefully renovated in the 1960s, and since then has served as a library (Mon–Fri 8.30am–6.30pm, Sat 8.30am–3pm). Traces of the dazzling original decoration have survived too, notably the rich polychromy that once filled the interior, sections of which are still visible behind the stacks of library books filling the main body of the building, the ceiling vaulting and the stone **Aron ha Kodesh**. There are vague plans to have museum here, but for now you can look around during the library's opening hours.

The town fortifications

East across ul. Łukasińskiego takes you over onto the former town fortifications. Designed by Morando and Italian-inspired, they originally consisted of a set of seven **bastions** with three main gates. Wide moats and artificial lakes blocked the approaches to the town on every side. After holding out so impressively against the Cossacks and the Swedes, the whole defensive system went under in 1866, when the Russians ordered the upper set of battlements to be blown up and the town fortress liquidated. The interior of the bastion on the eastern edge of the old town has been renovated and now houses a **market**, while park area covers much of the rest of the battlements, leaving you free to wander along the tops and see for yourself why the marauding Swedes were checked. The ornamental **Stara Brama Lwowska** (Old Lvov Gate), another Morando construction, bricked up in the 1820s, and the **Nowa Brama Lwowska** (New Lvov Gate), added at the same time, complete the surviving elements of the fortifications.

Across pl. Wolności, the former Franciscan church, part of an old monastic complex and now an art school, is only half the building it used to be, having lost its Baroque towers in the 1870s. Into the southern section of the Stare Miasto at the bottom of ul. Bazyliańska you'll find the former Orthodox **Cerkiew św. Mikołaja** (Church of St Nicholas). A small domed building retaining some original Renaissance stucco, the church was originally used by many of the town's Eastern merchants – though not the Armenians, who had their own church on the site of today's *Renesans* hotel.

The Rotunda

The Nazis spared the buildings of Zamość, but not its residents. In the **Rotunda**, a nineteenth-century arsenal ten minutes' walk south of the Stare Miasto on ul. Wyspiańskiego, over eight thousand local people were executed by the Germans; a simple **museum** housed in its tiny cells (May–Sept Tues–Sun 9am–8pm; free) tells the harrowing story of the town's wartime trauma. In fact, Zamość (preposterously renamed "Himmlerstadt") and the surrounding area were the target of a brutal "relocation" scheme of the kind already carried out by the Nazis in Western Prussia. From 1942 to 1943 nearly three hundred villages were cleared of their Polish inhabitants and their houses taken by German settlers – all part of Hitler's plan to create an Aryan eastern bulwark of the Third Reich. The remaining villages were left alone only because the SS lacked the manpower to clear them out. Three cells are dedicated to the Soviet wartime massacre of Polish army officers at Katyń, and there's a sombre chapel in memory of local people deported to Siberia following the Soviet occupation of eastern Poland in 1939.

The Jewish cemetery

There's a tiny **Jewish cemetery** at the north end of ul. Prosta, a fifteen-minute walk east of the Stare Miasto. A monument made out of gravestones uprooted by the Nazis commemorates the many thousands of the town's Jewish population they murdered. Interestingly, the monument was erected in 1950, a good deal earlier than in many Jewish centres in Poland.

Eating, drinking and entertainment

Restaurant and bar life in the Stare Miasto is flourishing, especially around the Rynek itself, where most places combine the roles of **café** and **restaurant** in a single establishment. However, outside the summer season you may be hard-pressed to find a meal after 8pm. *La Cantina*, at Rynek 6, is the best of the pizzerias, while at Rynek 23 the appropriately named *Padwa* is more upmarket, with a wonderful original ceiling and posh cellar restaurant serving pasta and meat dishes. The other top-end choice is the *Victoria*, in the *Zamojski* hotel (see p.325), which focuses on fresh fish and game. For simple and cheap Polish dishes *Muzealna*, Rynek 30, is quite good, and has an pleasant terrace at the side of the town hall. *Asia*, south of the Rynek at ul. Staszica 10 is a standard-issue milk bar.

For **drinking**, most people opt for the al-fresco bars on the Rynek in summer. Of the indoor venues the *Piwnica Pod Rektorius*, Rynek 2, is the best of several basement beer halls around the square. *Green Pub*, a short distance east at Staszica 2, has a suave, upmarket cocktail bar feel, and also does restaurant-quality food. *Jazz Club Kosz*, ul. Zamenhofa 5 (entrance through the rear courtyard), periodically hosts live jazz and blues gigs, and is a pleasant place to sink into a dark couch on other nights. The *Irish Pub*, in the Jewish quarter at ul. Zamenhofa 20, plays a relaxed mix of blues and jazz and is the only source of draught Guinness.

If you happen to be in town at the right time there are several annual cultural happenings worth checking out. The **Zamość Jazz Na Kresach** ("Border-lands") festival, usually held in the last week of May or early June, is popular with Polish and other Slav jazzers. For the **Jarmark Hetmański** festival (second weekend in June) you'll find Polish and Ukrainian traditional music and a hand-made crafts market on the Rynek. **Theatrical Summer**, a drama festival held in the latter part of June and early July, features some excellent theatre groups from all over the country, many of whom perform on the stairway in front of the town hall. The tourist office (see p.324) will have details on all the above.

Southwest from Zamość

Southwest of Zamość lies more of the open, sparsely populated countryside characteristic of much of the country's eastern borderlands. The agricultural monotony is broken by occasional forests, the few surviving swaths of the *puszcza* that once covered the whole area. The biggest of these, now protected by the bounds of the **Roztoczański national park**, offers a glimpse of something akin to the original untamed wilderness. **Zwierzyniec**, the gateway to the park, is an enjoyable little place with good tourist facilities and a locally famous brewery, while the old town of **Szczebrzeszyn**, along the way from Zamość, is also worth a look if you're passing through.

Szczebrzeszyn

Twenty kilometres southwest of Zamość lies **SZCZEBRZESZYN**, a sleepy little town famous for its tongue-twister of a name – even Polish children have difficulty with this one. Despite the usual historical depredations – Cossacks, Swedes, Turks and Nazis have all had a go at the place – there are enough monuments to justify a quick stop. Local **buses** to Zwierzyniec call at Szczebrzeszyn's Rynek, making it an easy, low-key trip from Zamość. On the west side of the Rynek the **Kościół św. Katarzyny** (St Catherine's Church), an exuberant piece of Mannerist archi-tecture modelled on the Cathedral in Zamość (see p.327), has a fine Renaissance doorway and soothing, vaulted interior laced with rich stuccowork. **Kościół św. Mikołaja** (St Nicholas's Church), on the other side of the square, is from the same era but with rather fewer of its original fittings, a result of Cossack plundering in

1648. The town's best-known building, however, is the **former synagogue** on the northwest side of the square, an imposing early seventeenth-century brick structure – one of the country's largest – likewise ransacked by the Cossacks, which served the large Jewish population up until World War II. Turned into a cultural centre following reconstruction from the ruins left by the Nazis, elements of the original synagogue decoration are still visible in the main hall, including the bema and parts of the decorative frieze work. A recently erected tablet outside the building recalls its original use as well as the wartime slaughter of the town's 3000-strong Jewish community. A five-minute walk up the hill behind the synagogue, past the abandoned-looking Orthodox church on ul. Sądowa and then left, is the **Jewish cemetery**, as overgrown and lonely as any you'll find in this part of the country but with an unusually large number of tombstones still standing, the oldest dating back to the early 1700s.

Zwierzyniec

Eleven kilometres further south from Szczebrzeszyn is **ZWIERZYNIEC**, principal gateway to the **Roztoczański national park** (see p.332). Frequent local bus connections to and from Zamość make a day-trip a feasible option. This pleasant little town owes its existence to chancellor Jan Zamoyski, who purchased the surrounding forests in 1589 and commissioned Bernando Morando (of Zamość fame) to build him a country palace here. The palace was pulled down in the 1830s, but the village that had grown up around it remained, as did elements of the original palace complex, some of which you can still see today. Chief among these is the Zamoyski **chapel**, a delicate Baroque construction scenically located on one of a series of islands in the willow-fringed palace lake, reached by a bridge. Today, however, the town is known less for its Zamoyski connections than for the **Zwierzyniec Brewery**, beyond the lake on ul. Browara, a grand early nineteenth-century complex producing a smooth, lager-style brew that's extremely difficult to find outside the region. Though not open to the public, the brewery does have its own café-bar. Beyond the brewery, ul. Browara curves away from the lake to the national park museum, the **Ośrodek Muzealny RPN** (Tues–Sun: May–Oct 9am–5pm; Nov–April 9am–4pm; 3.50zł), which contains a display on the park's flora and fauna as well as walking maps, entrance tickets and an information desk.

Practicalities

The **bus station** is five minutes north of the lake, on the far side of an unkempt town park. There is a wealth of **pensions** (❷) around the town, though many are only accessible if you're driving. One central choice is the clean and new *Anna*, just off the main road at ul. Dębowa 1 (☎084/687 2590, ⓦwww.infofirmy.com/anna; ❷). There's also bicycle rental here. The *Karczma Młyn*, facing the lake on ul. Aleksandry Wachniewskiej, is a homely timber restaurant with a few small but decent rooms above (☎084/687 2527, ⓦwww .zwierzyniec.info.pl/karczma; ❷). Of places further out the *Zacisze*, north of the centre at ul. Rudka 5B (☎084/687 2306, ⓦwww.zacisze.zwierzyniec.com; ❷), is a tranquil and attractive pension with comfortable rooms and a good restaurant and bar.

For **eating**, *Karczma Młyn* (see above) serves a reasonable selection of pizzas and meaty Polish favourites, while further in along the lake there's a takeaway stand with great *poziomkowe* (wild strawberry) ice cream in season. The local **beer**, though available in the all of the town's bars, is ideally savoured at the brewery's own café-bar on ul. Browara.

The Roztoczański national park

The wild expanses of the **Roztoczański national park**, adjacent to Zwierzyniec, are a must for both walkers and naturalists. Part of the huge former Zamoyski family estate that used to cover much of the region, the park, created in 1974, covers an area of almost eighty square kilometres of the Roztocze district, a picturesque region of forested hills rising to 390m at their highest point. The park's existence can be traced back to Jan Zamoyski; rather than setting up a more usual aristocratic hunting ground, he turned the forest into a prototype nature reserve. His plan even included a section of enclosed game reserve: among the animals kept here were the last of the original wild ponies (tarpans; see Białowieża, p.280), who died out in the nineteenth century, only to be reintroduced in the 1980s in the genetically bred modern variant and enthusiastically promoted as an attraction by park authorities. Cutting across the heart of the park is the beautiful and uncontaminated **River Wieprz**, which has its source just east. Most of the park is forested, with flora including pine, fir and pockets of towering beeches (up to 50m high). As well as the tarpans, storks, cranes and beavers are among the creatures populating the area.

Walking in the park

Maps and detailed information about **walking routes** are available from the office located in the park museum (see p.331) where you can also buy the **ticket** (2.50zł) required for entering. The park is easily navigable with the help of a map, with several short walks branching off from the museum itself. The easiest of these leads southeast through pine forest to the reed-shrouded Echo lake (15min), the northern banks of which boast a wonderful, sloping sandy **beach**. From here, continue 200m along the road passing the lake and you'll come to an **observation deck**, from which you're likely to see tarpans. Another popular trail traces the old palace path southwest to Bukowa Góra (20min), an upland area of dense woodland where daylight is almost blotted out by the thick canopy of beech and firs. On the far side of Bukowa Góra lies an area of sandy-soiled heath and some fine views southwards: from here you can work your way eastwards towards Echo lake in about twenty minutes.

Rzeszów

Roughly 170km south of Lublin and 150km east of Kraków, **RZESZÓW** was essentially a postwar attempt to bring industry and an administrative centre to the southeast, an area that had seen the heaviest emigration for much of the previous century. The city's population of over 150,000 is evidence of some sort of success, although this expansion has come in the form of a typically soulless urban sprawl, and emigration has not altogether ceased – even today many of those you'll see waiting to apply for visas outside the US Consulate in Kraków hail from Rzeszów or around. The hinterland still consists of the small villages characteristic of this corner of Poland for centuries, which explains why in 1980 Rzeszów became a nucleus of Rural Solidarity, the independent farmers' and peasants' union formed in the wake of its better-known urban counterpart. A decade on from the fall of communism, moreover, it's a prime example of the way the new economic order is gradually penetrating those eastern reaches of the country traditionally most resistant to change: some way behind Kraków or Warsaw, perhaps, but a marked improvement nonetheless.

Although there's little reason to stay here, Rzeszów has an acceptable choice of hotels and restaurants and good bus connections to the rural towns of the Beskid Niski to the south, and the Bieszczady region to the southeast; it's also the obvious jumping-off point for the palace at **Łańcut**, 20km to the east.

Arrival and accommodation

The **bus** and **train stations** are adjacent to each other, a short walk north from the centre. Of the **hotels**, most convenient for the stations is the serviceable but overpriced *Polonia*, right across the street at ul. Grottgera 16 (☏017/852 0312, ⓦwww.hotel-polonia.com; ❹), offering 1970s furnishings and en-suite facilities. Moving up in quality, the large and business-oriented *Rzeszów*, al. Cieplińskiego 2 (☏017/853 3389, ⓦwww.hotelesemako.com.pl; ❻), offers a weekend student price for 65zł. The conveniently central *Pod Ratuszem*, off the Rynek at ul. Matejki 8 (☏017/852 9780, ⓦwww.hotelpodratuszem.rzeszow.pl; ❺) has cosy and bright en suites. The top hotel in town, and also just off the Rynek, is the *Hubertus*, ul. Mickiewicza 5 (☏017/852 6008, ⓦwww.hubertus .rzeszow.pl; ❼), a new and highly polished place with a good restaurant. The **youth hostel** (☏017/863 4430), bang in the square at Rynek 25, has a few simple doubles (❶) and dorms (18zł).

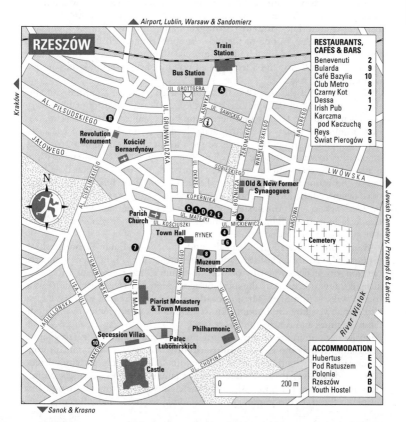

There's a regional **tourist office** near the station at ul. Asnyka 6 (Mon–Fri 9am–6pm, Sat 10am–4pm; ☎017/852 4611, ⓦwww.rcit.res.pl); the staff speak only Polish but have accommodation listings and a good selection of books and maps. The municipal **website** (ⓦwww.erzeszow.pl) has a wealth of information in English about sights and local history. **Internet** access is at the Hard Drive Café off the Rynek at ul. Kościuszki 13.

The Stare Miasto

Everything worth seeing is located within the compact confines of the **Stare Miasto** area, south of the main stations across al. Piłsudskiego. First stop are the two **former synagogues** adjacent to one another along ul. Bożnicza at the edge of pl. Ofiara Getta, the heart of the old ghetto area and all that remains of the town's formerly sizeable Jewish population. The new synagogue, a large seventeenth-century brick building designed by Italian architect Giovanni Bellotti, is now an artists' centre with a changing display of exhibitions on the ground floor and an amenable café upstairs (closed July & Aug). The old synagogue, by more than a century and gutted by the Nazis, houses the town archives as well as a recently formed research institute devoted to the history of the Rzeszów Jewry.

A short walk south brings you to the bustling Rynek. Plumped in the square centre is the **town hall**, a squat sixteenth-century edifice that was remodelled just over a hundred years ago and looks part Disney castle and part Baroque church. The **Muzeum Etnograficzne** (Tues–Fri 9am–3.30pm, Sun noon–6pm; 5.50zł), in one of the older burghers' houses on the south side of the square, contains a small and not especially compelling collection of local costumes and folk art, and a few Marian wayside shrines of the kind you find dotting country roads.

Directly west of the Rynek is the main **parish church**, a Gothic structure that was given a dull Baroque overlay in the eighteenth century, notable exceptions being the fine Renaissance decoration in the vaulted nave ceiling and the early tombstone tablets up by the altar. Heading south down ul. 3 Maja, the main shopping thoroughfare, brings you to a former Piarist monastery complex, where the **town museum** (Tues–Fri 9am–3.30pm, Sat & Sun noon–6pm; 6.50zł) is ranged around the monastery courtyard. As well as its undistinguished Polish and European paintings, the collection includes the biblical frescoes that once decorated the former cloister arcade and has changing exhibitions focused on local history. The **monastery church** next door has an elegant Baroque façade fashioned by Tylman of Gameren in the early 1700s, and a small but well-proportioned interior.

At the bottom of ul. 3 Maja, past the post office, is the **Pałac Lubomirskich** (Lubomirski Palace), another early eighteenth-century Tylman of Gameren creation; originally owned by one of the country's most powerful aristocratic clans, it's now occupied by the local music academy. From here it's a short walk to the walls of the Stare Miasto's **castle**, a huge seventeenth-century edifice also once owned by the Lubomirskis. The castle was converted into a prison in Austrian times and is now the law courts.

Finally, back up in the northwest corner of the Stare Miasto is Rzeszów's most interesting church, the **Kościół Bernardynów** (Bernardine Church), a sumptuous early seventeenth-century structure founded by the Ligęza family. Inside you'll find late-Renaissance statues of eight family members praying solemnly from niches above the choir. Also note the eighteenth-century organ and, in a chapel to the right of the transept, a late-Gothic sculpted Madonna considered to be miraculous. Considerably less attractive is the nearby **monument** to the Revolutionary Movement, a communist-era monstrosity that has thankfully been removed from the front of local tourist brochures.

Moving out of the Stare Miasto area, the large **Jewish cemetery** 1km southeast of the centre off ul. Rejtana (entrance on ul. Dołowa; the old man living next door to the car-repair workshop opposite has the key) is overgrown, having been completely destroyed by the Nazis. The three memorial chapels (*ohels*) to famed local *tzaddiks* of the past, maintained by the national Jewish monuments committee, are a regular place of pilgrimage for visiting Hassidic Jews.

Eating, drinking and entertainment

Rzeszów's **restaurant** scene is pretty good for a town of its size. The *Czarny Kot*, just off the Rynek at Mickiewicza 4, advertises itself as a pub but really functions as a plush café-restaurant with some fine Polish and international food and an English menu, while *Dessa*, ul. Matejki 2, is an upscale restaurant/gallery/antique shop with a long wine list and outdoor seating. The tiny *Café Bazylia*, ul. Lisa-Kuli 1, has an outstanding line of crepes and pastas, but closes early (Mon–Fri 6pm, Sat 2pm). *Benevenuti*, Rynek 16, serves tasty pizzas from a brick oven. Affordable Polish food is on offer in a cheerful, faux-rustic setting at the *Karczma pod Kaczuchą*, ul. Przesmyk 4, while a good bet for a **light snack** is *Świat Pierogów*, behind the town hall at ul. Słowackiego 6.

Both the Rynek and ul. 3 Maja, the main shopping street, are bustling with **cafés** and **bars**. *Club Metro*, Rynek 25, is a flash club with regular DJs and a boisterous outdoor café, while *Reys*, nearby at ul. Mickiewicza 11, is a smoky, student-oriented basement pub and cinema. The *Irish Pub*, ul. 3 Maja 8, has Guinness and other international brews, while *Bularda*, ul. 3 Maya 20, has the town's best cakes and good coffee.

Appropriately enough for a town with such a long history of emigration, the **Festival of Polonia Music and Dance Ensembles** takes place in Rzeszów in June and July every third year (next one is in 2008). It's a riotous assembly of groups from *emigracja* communities all over the world, including Britain, France, the USA, Argentina and Australia.

East from Rzeszów

From Rzeszów the main road and rail line head towards the Ukrainian borderlands. A characteristic eastern mix of villages, farmsteads and wayside shrines is the region's main feature, along with a smattering of historic towns and aristocratic palaces, notably **Łańcut**, **Leżajsk** and **Jarosław**. All are within easy travelling distance of Rzeszów, a mix of local bus and train services providing **transport** around the area.

Łańcut

First impressions of the **castle** palace complex that dominates the centre of **ŁAŃCUT** (pronounced "Winesoot"), 17km east of Rzeszów, suggest that it must have seen rather more high-society engagements than military ones. The first building on the site, constructed by the Pilecki family in the second half of the fourteenth century, was, however, burnt down in 1608 when royal troops ambushed its robber-baron owner Stanisław Stadnicki, known by his contemporaries as "The devil of Łańcut" (see box, p.336). The estate was then bought by Stanisław Lubomirski, who set about building the sturdier construction that forms the basis of today's palace. Following contemporary military theory, the four-sided palace was surrounded by a pentagonal outer defence of moat and ramparts, the outlines of which remain.

The fortifications were dismantled in 1760 by Izabela Czartoryska (see Puławy, p.311), wife of the last Lubomirski owner, who turned Łańcut into one of her artistic salons, laid out the surrounding park and built a theatre in the palace. Louis XVIII of France was among those entertained at Łańcut during this period, and the next owners, the Potocki family, carried on in the same manner, Kaiser Franz Josef being one of their guests. Oxford graduate Count Alfred Potocki, the last private owner, abandoned the place in the summer of 1944 as Soviet troops advanced across Poland. Having dispatched six hundred crates of the palace's most precious objects to liberated Vienna, Potocki himself then departed, ordering a

The devil of Łańcut

In an era replete with tales of rapacious brigands and swashbuckling proto-libertarians, the figure of **Stanisław Stadnicki** (c.1560–1616) stands out from the crowd. Brought up in a remote Carpathian outpost by independent-minded parents – his father, after whom Stanisław was named, was a staunch Arian eventually excommunicated for his religious incalcitrance. After his parents' early deaths, the young Stadnicki, together with his six brothers, inherited the family's properties. A sign of things to come was provided by his adoption of the motto *Aspettate e odiate* ("Wait and hate").

After several years in military expeditions to Hungary and Muscovy, where he received a commendation for conspicuous bravery in the field, Stadnicki returned to Poland. Angered by lack of payment for his services he seized the estate at **Łańcut**, which became his base for a life of audacious banditry. Nothing was spared his vicious attentions: passing travellers were attacked, properties inexplicably razed to the ground, and local traders and markets systematically terrorized and eventually forced to operate to his benefit through the unlicensed fair he started at nearby Rzeszów. With the help of a motley assortment of spies, torturers, thugs and mercenaries, he extended his grip on the terrorized local populace. Inevitably, Stadnicki's illicit activities eventually caught the attention of the authorities and in 1600 he was sued at the Crown Tribunal in Lublin by another magnate over his illegal Rzeszów fair, to which Stadnicki responded by leading an armed raid on his opponent's nearby estate. The conflicts surrounding Stadnicki multiplied. An active participant in the nobles' *rakosz* (rebellion) against Zygmunt III in 1605, his public denunciations of the king as a "perjurer, sodomite and card-sharper" can hardly have endeared him to the authorities.

Stadnicki's penchant for goading opponents with libellous verses, however, eventually led to his downfall. In 1608 the nobleman **Łukasz Opaliński**, the subject of a withering Stadnicki broadside entitled "A Gallows for my Guest", retaliated by storming the castle at Łańcut, where prodigious quantities of loot were discovered in the cellars, and massacring everyone there – except Stadnicki, who in characteristic fashion just managed to escape in time. Bloodied, but unbowed, Stadnicki eventually returned to the area in a bid to pick up his malevolent career once more. Things were never the same again, however: pursued relentlessly by Opaliński's Cossack guard and finally given away in the hills by his personal servant, a mortally wounded Stadnicki was at last beheaded with his own sword. Symptomatically for a country where the "Golden Freedom" was cherished so highly among the nobility, the references to Stadnicki from his contemporaries suggest that the man's claimed independence and Wild West-style championing of the spirit of liberty were at least as significant for many as his vindictive destructiveness.

Russian sign reading "Polish National Museum" to be posted on the gates. The Red Army left the place untouched, and it was opened as a museum later the same year. Today the palace looks great, but visiting can be frustrating, as management isn't really up to the task of dealing with foreign tourists.

The palace

Forty or so of the **palace**'s hundreds of rooms are open to the public (May–Sept Tues–Fri 9am–4pm, Sat & Sun 10am–5pm; Oct–April Tues–Sun 9am–3pm; closed two months in winter each year; entry by guided tour only, last tour 60min before closing; palace grounds are open daily to 11pm), and in summer they are crammed with visitors. The **ticket office** is in the gate at the western entrance to the park: tickets (18zł) are good for the Polish-speaking guided **tour**, which takes you through the palace and carriage museum. Separate tickets are needed for the icon museum and synagogue (see p.338); consider visiting one or both of these before exhausting yourself at the palace. The minimum fee for an English-speaking **guide** is 180zł (by appointment; ☎017/225 2010, ✉muzeum@zamek-lancut.pl). Most of the interesting rooms are on the **first floor** (though not all of them are always kept open – also note that the tour sequence changes frequently), reached by a staircase close to the entrance hall, which is large enough to allow horse-drawn carriages to drop off their passengers. The **corridors** are an art show in themselves: family portraits and busts, paintings by seventeenth-century Italian, Dutch and Flemish artists, and eighteenth-century classical copies commissioned by Izabela. Some of the bedrooms have beautiful inlaid wooden floors, while the bathrooms have giant old-fashioned bathtubs and enormous taps.

Moving through the **Chinese apartments**, remodelled by Izabela at the height of the vogue for chinoiserie, and the **Pompei Hall**, where genuine Roman antiquities are set in an amusing mock-ruin, you'll reach the **dining room**, its floor laid out in a curious braid pattern, and the **ballroom**, setting for concerts at the Łańcut festival (see p.338). A door here leads into the extraordinary eighty-seater **Łańcut theatre** commissioned by Izabela; as well as the ornate gallery and stalls, the romantic scenic backdrops are still there, as is the stage machinery to crank them up and down. Further on there's the **old study**, decorated in frilliest Rococo style – all mirrors and gilding – and with a fine set of eighteenth-century French furniture. In the west corner of this floor, the domed ceiling of the **Zodiac Room** still has its seventeenth-century Italian stucco. Beyond is the old **library**, where among the leather tomes you'll find bound sets of English magazines like *Country Life* and *Punch* from the 1870s – an anglophilia matched later in the carriage museum, where horse names like 'Alice' and 'Polish Princess' are still posted above the stables. On the **ground floor**, the **Turkish apartments** contain a turbaned portrait of Izabela and a suite of English eighteenth-century furniture.

Leaving the palace, the tour heads to the former **orangery**, now housing a shabby zoo featuring guinea pigs, tortoises and a pair of cockatiels. Final stop is the **Carriage Museum**, set in the 1902 coach house and including over fifty horse-drawn vehicles for every conceivable purpose, from state ceremonies to mail delivery. There are also drivers' uniforms, sepia photos from a Potocki expedition to the Sahara and a variety of hunting trophies from similar jaunts. Next door, the old stables contain the **Slavic Religious Art Museum** (May–Sept Tues–Sat 10am–4pm, Sun 10am–5pm; Oct–April Tues–Sun 10am–4pm; 6zł), housing a large and fabulous collection of Ruthenian icons and decorative art, the best in Poland after the museum in Sanok (see p.348). The bulk of the collection was removed from the Uniate and Orthodox churches of the surrounding region in the years following the notorious Operation Vistula of 1947 (see box, p.356). Only a fraction of what's here is displayed for viewing, with the rest of the icons hanging from the walls in huge, densely packed racks. Among the choice items on show there's a complete eighteenth-century iconostasis, a superb, meditative fifteenth-century *Mandilion* and a poignant, suffering *Christus Pantocrator*, reflecting the humanizing influences of Roman Catholic art on later Uniate and Orthodox iconography. In addition there's a rich collection of vestments and Old Slavonic Bibles, and a display of colour photos of some of the wooden churches from which the icons were taken.

The Town

Łańcut town has one other main point of interest: the old **synagogue**, just off the main square on ul. Zamkowa, which now houses a newly renovated **Jewish museum** (mid-June to mid-Sept Tues–Sun 10.30am–4pm; 5zł). A simple cream-coloured structure built in the 1760s on the site of an earlier wooden synagogue, the interior survived the Nazi era relatively intact, preserving an authentic and virtually unique taste of what scores of similar such synagogues throughout Poland would have looked like before the war. The walls and ceiling are a mass of rich, colourful decoration including stucco bas-reliefs, frescoes, illustrated Hebrew wall prayers, zodiacal signs and false marble ornamentation. In the centre of the building stands the bimah, its cupola decorated with some striking frescoes of biblical tales and a memorable depiction of a leviathan consuming its own tail – a symbol for the coming of the Messiah – adorning the inner canopy. In addition, there's a small collection of Torah scrolls, menorah and other religious artefacts on display. Unfortunately, outside the summer season the synagogue is kept locked due to limited demand, and you can only get in by paying the group price of 70zł (ask at the palace ticket office). The Hassidic movement that swept through Eastern Europe in the nineteenth century took strong hold among the Jews of Łańcut. The **old Jewish cemetery**, fifteen minutes' walk north of the palace complex off ul. Moniuszki, houses the recently rebuilt *ohel* (tomb) of **Reb Horovitz**, a noted nineteenth-century *tzaddik* whose grave remains a much-visited place of Hassidic pilgrimage. The key to the cemetery is kept by the family living at ul. Jagiellońska 17, round the corner from the entrance. The overgrown **new Jewish cemetery**, ten minutes south of the Rynek off ul. Armii Krajowej, is larger, but is more destroyed. A small memorial garden and monument nearby marks the spot where large numbers of local Jews were shot by the Nazis during World War II.

Practicalities

Łańcut's **train station** is a short taxi ride or a two-kilometre walk north of the centre; the **bus station**, however, is on the north edge of the castle park, just a few minutes' walk from the main entrance. The best **hotel** is the *Pałacyk*, ul. Paderewskiego 18 (☏017/225 2043, ⓦ www.palacyk.lancut.pl; ❸), offering comfortable en suites in a grand late nineteenth-century mansion. The other choice, surprisingly dilapidated considering the fact that it occupies a wing of the palace, is the *Zamkowy* (☏017/225 2671), offering en suites (❸) and rooms with shared facilities (❶). The **restaurant** of the *Zamkowy* has a decent but pricey selection of traditional Polish dishes, while the one in the *Pałacyk* offers similar fare but is a bit cheaper. There are also al-fresco **cafés** just west of the castle on Łańcut's main Rynek – *Caffe Antico* at no. 3 serves up decent coffee as well as a selection of Greek and Italian meals.

Every May, the palace hosts the prestigious **Łańcut Music Festival** (ⓦ www .festiwal.lancut.pl) now into its fourth decade an increasingly popular event on the international circuit, with a focus on chamber music – expect hotels to be booked solid at this time. Festival **tickets** are sold via the State Philharmonic Concert Office in Rzeszów in late April (℡017/862 2333), though some are available an hour before each concert, either from the office in the palace vestibule or outside the concert venue itself. Finally, in the summer international master classes for aspiring young instrumentalists are held at the palace.

Leżajsk

Thirty kilometres northeast of Rzeszów on the verges of the River San, **LEŻAJSK** is a typically sleepy provincial town known for its monastery, a pilgrimage site for both Catholics and lovers of organ music, and its brewery – long-established producer of one of the country's best beers.

From Leżajsk's combined bus and train station it's a two-kilometre walk or bus ride north to the vast Bernardine **church** and **monastery**. Built in the late 1670s inside a fortress-like defensive structure, the Baroque basilica is an established and important centre of pilgrimage thanks to an icon of the Madonna and Child placed here, venerated for centuries as a miracle-worker. On religious holidays, notably the Feast of the Assumption (Aug 15), the church draws huge crowds, but throughout the year you're likely to find buses full of schoolchildren or pensioners doing the rounds of the monastery and nearby Stations of the Cross. The cavernous church interior is a mass of Baroque decoration, with numerous side altars, religious paintings, some finely carved wooden choir stalls and a huge gilded main altarpiece.

Pride of place, however, goes to the monster Baroque **organ** filling the back of the nave, one of the finest – and most famous – in Poland. With nearly six thousand pipes, four manuals and over seventy different registers, the exquisitely decorated instrument produces a stunning sound more than capable of filling the building. Today the organ sounds better than ever following an extensive restoration programme to combat the destructive effects of wood-eating parasites.

Services apart, you can also get to hear the organ at the concerts held at the summer-long **International Organ Festival** (May–Aug; for the schedule see ⓦwww.bernardyni.ofm.pl/klasztor/lezajsk), a major musical event well worth coinciding with.

Just south of the monastery gates over ul. Klasztorna is the **Leżajsk Brewery**. You can try the tasty local brew on draught at the roadside bar along with hardened locals, or stock up on cans at the shop next door. Back into the town centre, the late Renaissance **Parish Church**, east of the square, is worth a quick look, featuring some fine early fresco work in the nave.

Practicalities

It's easy enough to get here from Łańcut, with **buses** running every hour or so; otherwise there are six buses and one train daily from Rzeszów. For **accommodation** your best choice is the small but quite comfortable *U Braci Zygmuntów*, by the monastery at ul. Klasztorna 2e (℡017/242 0469, ⓦwww .hotel-lezajsk.pl; ❸), which also has a good **restaurant**.

Jarosław

Nestled at the foot of the San river valley on the main road east to the Ukrainian border, the town of **JAROSŁAW** is one of the oldest in the country. An urban settlement is known to have been established here by the mid-twelfth century, on the site of a stronghold raised by a Ruthenian prince known as Jarosław the Wise some two centuries earlier. The town's strategic location at the nexus of major medieval international trade routes led to its rapid development as a commercial settlement.

In their medieval heyday the fairs held in Jarosław were second only to those of Frankfurt in size, drawing merchants from all over the continent. A series of raids, plagues and fires, however, eventually brought decline, and the most tangible reminder of the mercantile glory days is the old **market** complex at the centre of town, which has preserved the essentials of its medieval layout if not the buildings themselves: little of what you see predates the seventeenth century. As elsewhere in the region, Jarosław's was home to a large and dynamic **Jewish population**, who established themselves here early on. The importance of the town fairs to Jewish commercial life throughout Poland was such that the **Council of the Four Lands** (see box, pp.298–299) met regularly here during the seventeenth and eighteenth centuries. Today Jarosław is smaller and less prosperous than other old towns in the region, and the historic centre has seen very little restoration in the last fifteen years, but this neglect has endowed the town with a sense of timelessness that makes it well worth a few hours of wandering around.

The Town

The focal point is the breezy, open central square where the fairs used to be held. Filling the centre is the **town hall**, a handsome-looking building topped by a tall spire that was burnt down a in 1625 fire and subsequently remodelled in Baroque and later in neo-Renaissance style, when the raised balcony was added. On several sides the square is lined with the arcaded merchants' houses: while not as grand as those in Zamość, some of the houses are impressive, nonetheless, most notably the Renaissance **Kamienica Orsettich** (Orsetti Mansion) on the south side. Built in the 1670s by a wealthy family of Italian merchants, the building has a beautifully decorated upper attic and a typically open, airy arcade. It's also the home of the **town museum** (Wed–Fri 10am–2pm, Sat & Sun 11am–5pm; 5zł), which contains a substantial collection of Sarmatian portraits (see box, p.474), which deteriorate in quality from the seventeenth to eighteenth centuries, as well as weapons and period furniture. Looking round also gives you a chance to admire the fine original polychromy decorating several of the grand, wooden-beamed rooms.

The clearest evidence of the town's mercantile past comes from the honeycomb of **cellars** stretching beneath the town square. Originally built as storage space for the merchants trading on the square above, the network served as an effective hide-out for local people during successive assaults on the town, most notably the Tatar raids of the fourteenth century. The cellars were gradually abandoned, but a 150-metre-long section of the (by then) flooded cellars was cleared out by miners in the early 1960s and opened to visitors a decade later.

Forty-minute **tours** through the cellars are conducted on the hour by one of the staff at the museum (Mon–Fri 8am–2pm, Sat & Sun 10am–1pm; 5zł). The entrance is through a merchant's house on the eastern side of the square: from here you descend into the brick-walled passageways – many of the walls are original – and wind your way through the gloom down to a depth of twenty metres at the lowest point, eventually re-emerging where you started. The chill down below is explained by the ingeniously constructed and still-functioning ventilation system, good enough to allow meat to be kept here.

North of the square, a short walk along the bumpy, cobbled streets to pl. Skargi is the **parish church**, an imposing late sixteenth-century Renaissance construction with a grand facade but saccharine polychromy inside. A short way further north, entered up the hill on ul. Pełkińska, is the **Klasztor Sióstr Benedyktynek** (Benedictine Convent), a fine early seventeenth-century complex surrounded by its own set of fortified walls. The **Orthodox church** down ul. Sobieskiego east of the square, a colourful eighteenth-century construction now in use again by its former Uniate occupants, is also worth a look. Completing the tour of religious architecture, Jarosław's sole surviving **synagogue**, northwest off the square on the corner of ul. Opolska, dates from 1810 and is now a school building. On weekdays the town's all-purpose **market**, on ul. Grodzka leading west off the square, spills out colourfully onto the surrounding streets.

Practicalities

The combined **bus** and **train station**, at the bottom of ul. Słowackiego, is a fifteen-minute walk southwest of the Stare Miasto. There's no tourist office, but the town website (Ⓦ www.jaroslaw.pl) carries a modicum of tourist **information**. Accommodation options include the *Asticus* **hotel**, Rynek 25 (Ⓣ 016/623 1344; ❹), which offers a limited number of comfy en suites; and the modest *Turkus*, just south of the centre at ul. Sikorskiego 5a (Ⓣ 016/621 2640; ❶), most of whose rooms come with shared facilities. The **restaurant** in the *Asticus* is the best choice for Polish food, while back towards the stations *Azyl*, ul. Grunwaldzka 4, serves decent pizza. *Fantazja*, an ice-cream bar near the stations at ul. Słowackiego 19, draws crowds in summer.

Przemyśl and around

Just 10km from the Ukrainian border, overlooking the River San and with the foothills of the Carpathians in the distance, the intriguing and little-visited town of **PRZEMYŚL** is worth a side trip. Economic growth has begun to make itself felt here, but climbing the winding streets of the old quarter can still be like walking back through history to some far-flung corner of the Habsburg empire. Ideally, this is a town to see before heading across the Ukrainian border to L'viv: provincial capital before World War II and, though barely known to tourists, one of Eastern Europe's most beautiful cities. Access to Przemyśl is straightforward: this is the last stop on the main rail line running across the south of the country; buses, however, are the only public transportation option if you're coming from Sanok or the Bieszczady. Founded in the eighth century on the site of a documented prehistoric settlement, Przemyśl is the oldest town in southern Poland after Kraków, and for its first few centuries its location on the borders between Poland and Ruthenia made it a constant bone of contention. Only under Kazimierz the Great did Poles establish firm control of the town, developing it as a link in the trade routes across the Ukraine. Przemyśl maintained a commercial pre-eminence for several centuries, despite frequent invasions (notably by the Tatars), but as with many Polish towns, economic decline came in the seventeenth century, particularly after Swedish assaults in the 1650s. Much of the town's character derives from the period after the First Partition, when Przemyśl was annexed to the Austrian empire and built up to the point where it was the third largest city in the province of Galicia, after Kraków and L'viv. In 1873 the Habsburgs added a huge castle to the town's defences, and during World War I this region was the scene of some of the fiercest fighting between the Austrians and Russians: throughout the winter of 1914 Russian forces besieged the town, finally starving the city into surrender in March 1915 and then losing it again only two months later. The devastation of both town and surrounding region was even more intense then than during the Nazi onslaught 25 years later; the castle was totally destroyed and only small sections of the sturdy fortifications survived the siege. The old centre, mercifully, escaped the intense bombardments unscathed.

In more recent times Przemyśl's proximity to the Ukrainian border has made it a prime target for trade tourists from the former Soviet Union, and even now, with Poland in the EU and Ukrainians no longer able to enter without a visa, you'll find plenty congregating at the bazaar west of the train station along the river. There's more international flavour at the bus station, where crowds of Ukrainian traders wait to board buses to L'viv and beyond. Be warned that it isn't a place to hang around at night, especially if carrying luggage.

Arrival and information

Przemyśl's elegant Habsburg-era **train station** is ten minutes' walk northeast of the centre; the **bus station** is on the far side of the tracks from the train station, to which it is linked by pedestrian underpass. There are left-luggage lockers at the train station. The excellent **tourist information** office at Rynek 26 (Mon–Fri 8.30am–6pm, Sat–Sun 9am–4pm; Ⓦ www.przemysl.pl) can help with accommodation in town and elsewhere in the region, and has a good selection of maps and books. There's another branch in the train station (Mon–Fri 8.30am–3.30pm, Sat & Sun 9am–3.30pm). **Internet** access is available at the café at ul. Ratuszowa 8.

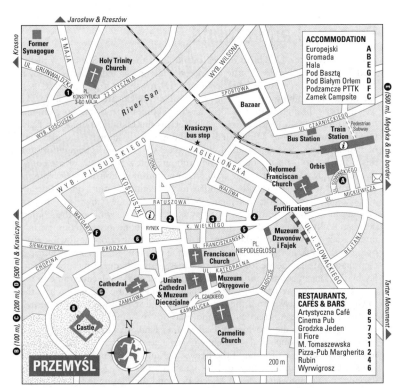

Accommodation

There's a good range of hotels and pensions in Przemyśl; in addition to what's listed below, in the streets around the bus station you'll find plenty of cheap boarding houses of dubious sanitation catering to the cross-border tourist trade. The *Zamek* **campsite**, Wybrzeże Piłsudskiego 8a (℡016/675 0265), about half a mile west of the Stare Miasto just behind the *Gromada* hotel, has bungalows (**❶**).

Europejski ul. Sowińskiego 4 (℡016/675 7100, ⓦwww.hotel-europejski.pl). Small but comfortable and clean en-suite rooms in a completely refurbished nineteenth-century building by the train station. **❸**

Gromada Wyb. J. Piłsudskiego 4 ℡016/676 1111, ⓦwww.gromada.pl. Large business-standard place just west of the town centre, on the banks of the river. Small discount at weekends. **❺**

Hala ul. Mickiewicza 30 ℡016/678 3849, ⓔhala .hotel@poczta.neostrada.pl. Basic sports hotel 500m east of the train station. Looks run-down from the outside, but the rooms (with and without bath) have been thoroughly renovated. **❶–❷**.

Pod Basztą ul. Królowej Jadwigi 4 ℡016/678 8268, ⓔhotel_baszta@poczta.onet.pl. Friendly,

six-room pension located close to the castle, offering simple but well-furnished rooms with shared facilities. **❶**

Pod Białym Orłem ul. Sanocka 13 ℡016/678 6107, ⓦwww.hotelbomba.republika.pl. Medium-sized place occupying a futuristic (in a 1980s sort of way) villa, in a peaceful location 1.5km west along the river from the centre (bus #10 or #40). Dated but tolerable en suites, and the restaurant serves good home-cooked specialities. **❸**

Podzamcze PTTK ul. Waygarta 3 ℡016/678 5374. Very basic place close to the cathedral, offering dorms (20zł per person) and sparsely furnished doubles. **❶**

The Town

Advancing into town from the train and bus stations you'll pass the recently spruced-up **Reformed Franciscan church** on the corner of ul. Mickiewicza, opposite which fragments of the Austrian **fortifications** can be seen on the approach to the Stare Miasto. First stop in the old town itself is the late Baroque bell-tower on ul. Władycze, all that remains from an abandoned Uniate Cathedral project (see box, p.344) and today home to the well-organized **Muzeum Dzwonów i Fajek** (Museum of Bells and Pipes; Tues–Sat 10.30am–5.30pm, Sun 11am–7pm; 4zł). As the name indicates, you'll pass through roomfuls of pipes and bells – both were made locally in the past – while climbing to the top of the tower, where there's a fine view of the town. From here ul. Franciszkańska brings you to the busy, sloping **Rynek**, where the mid-eighteenth-century **Franciscan church** offers a florid demonstration of unbridled Baroque, including a wealth of sumptuous interior decoration and a fine columned facade. Round the corner and slightly uphill stands the seventeenth-century former Jesuit church, now the local **Uniate Cathedral** (see box, p.344). The recent beneficiary of a pleasing custard-coloured paint job, you can admire the gilt iconostasis, displaying the full panoply of saints, from the vestibule. The Roman Catholic **Muzeum Diecezjalne** (Diocesan Museum; May–Oct daily 10am–3pm; 1zł) upstairs in the college adjacent to the church has some interesting Gothic altarpieces.

For the moment Przemyśl's **Muzeum Okręgowie** (Regional Museum; Tues & Fri 10.30am–6pm, Wed, Thurs, Sat & Sun 10am–2pm; 4zł) is still housed inside the grand old Uniate bishop's palace next to the Uniate Cathedral, but the whole collection is slated to move to a just-restored town house on the Rynek in the next few years. The museum's main attraction is the excellent collection of fifteenth- to seventeenth-century icons removed from the Uniate and Orthodox churches of the surrounding region after World War II – one of a series of such collections in the southeast of the country (see pp.337, 349 & 372).

Uniate cathedrals in Przemyśl

Przemyśl's former Jesuit church became the focus of national attention in 1991, following the Polish Catholic hierarchy's decision (approved directly by the pope) to hand the building over to the sizeable local Uniate (Greek Catholic) population, which had been deprived of a place of worship for the previous half-century. A Renaissance-era Uniate Cathedral was demolished late in the eighteenth century after Austrian Empress Maria Theresa pledged funds for a new one, but never subsequently rebuilt – at the time of her death only a new bell-tower had been erected, and the plan was dropped, with the Uniates getting the city's Carmelite church instead. They worshiped there until 1945, when the church was given back to the Carmelites by the new authorities.

After 1989 the Uniates began a campaign for restitution of the Carmelite church, but accepted the authorities' offer of the old Jesuit church as a fair compromise. Roman Catholic parishioners, however, were incensed, and blockaded the entrance, refusing to hand it over. Catholic defiance was quickly met with equally spirited opposition, and for a short time the situation looked as if it might develop into a serious confrontation with disturbing ethnic undertones. After several weeks of tense negotiations, the Roman Catholics finally agreed to give the local Uniates free use of the building, and the latter are now well established. Tempers, however, flared again in 1996, when the Carmelites, asserting sovereignty over their property, announced plans to remove the nineteenth-century cupola which had been set atop their church by the Uniates. The project went forward in the face of vigorous Uniate protests, and though the Polish Minister of Culture subsequently apologized at a press conference, the cupola was not restored.

The influence of Catholic art and theology on icon painters working in the Byzantine tradition is evident in the later works: many of the eighteenth century Madonnas and Christus Pantocrator figures are decidedly Roman in feel. Other highlights include a mystical early eighteenth-century *Assumption of Elijah*, a fabulously earthy *Day of Judgement* from the same era, which has a team of prancing black devils facing off against a beatific angelic host, and some wonderful sixteenth-century depictions of saints and holy men, including the intrepid św. Paraskeva, the patron saint of "engaged couples, happy households and commerce". The museum also has a nice collection of Habsburg-era photographs of Przemyśl street-life.

Just up the hill is the **Carmelite church** (the other half of the equation in the interdenominational controversy: see box above), a fine late-Renaissance structure designed by Gelleazo Appiani in the early 1600s, with a sumptuous Baroque interior featuring an extraordinary pulpit shaped like a ship, complete with rigging.

Heading west along ul. Katedralna, the road twists its way down towards the **cathedral** (10am–noon & 2–4pm), its sturdy 71-metre bell-tower pointing the way. Remnants of the first twelfth-century rotunda can be seen in the crypt, and there's a fine Renaissance alabaster pietà to the right of the main altar, but Baroque dominates the interior, most notably in the Fredro family chapel. Up beyond the Cathedral, a steeply climbing path leads through a park (open until sunset) to the **castle**, the remains of the fourteenth-century construction built by King Kazimierz the Great and given a thorough Renaissance remodelling a century later. The courtyard contains evidence of an eleventh-century Rotunda and adjoining palace, thought to be associated with Poland's Piast monarchs. The castle's most striking architectural feature is the pair of newly renovated Renaissance towers, tubby cylinders topped with a ring of decidedly unmilitary-looking baubles. One of them can be scaled (Tues–Sun: April–Sept 10am–6pm; Oct–March 10am–4pm; 3zł) for a panoramic view. The terrace of the *Artystyczna* café, just outside the castle walls, is particularly pleasant in summer (see below).

Fifty years ago Przemyśl had much greater ethnic diversity than today: old guidebooks indicate that the area around the Carmelite Church was the **Ruthenian district**. There are three small **Orthodox churches** still functioning in the east of the town, the main one fifteen minutes' walk east of the train station off ul. Mickiewicza. The **Jewish quarter** was more to the north of the old centre. Numbers 33 and 45 in ul. Jagiellońska were both synagogues before World War II, and there was another across the river – just off ul. 3 Maja on pl. Konstitucji, now part of a garage workshop. The decaying **Jewish cemetery**, 2km south of the centre on ul. Słowackiego, usually unlocked, still contains a couple of hundred tombs and gravestones, including a number of postwar monuments.

Przemyśl also presents some interesting **shopping** opportunities. The international **bazaar** by the bus station is not as exotic you might imagine – it focuses on food, clothes and, especially, smuggled cigarettes (in Polish, *papierosy*, a word spoken in hushed tones everywhere in the market) – but two high-end **antique** shops are worth a look. Antyki, across the pedestrian bridge from the market at ul. Kamienny Most 4 (☎016/678 6665, ⓦwww.galeria.hostings.pl) has a stunning array of icons, mostly from the nineteenth century, with prices starting at 100zł and reaching well into the thousands for larger pieces. There's a smaller selection at Antyki i Dzieła Sztuki, on the south side of the Rynek at ul. Grodzka 1 (☎016/678 5479, ⓦwww.niezgoda.pl). Keep in mind that taking anything made before 1945 out of Poland requires extensive paperwork and export duties.

Eating and drinking

For **eating** and drinking the most popular place in town is *Wyrwigrosz*, Rynek 20, a bar-restaurant with a good Polish and Chinese dishes and a large terrace overlooking the main square. A more upscale choice is *M. Tomaszewska*, pl. Konstitucji 3-go Maja, an elegant restaurant with white linen on the tables and Habsburg emperors on the walls, while *Pizza-Pub Margherita*, Rynek 4, is a trusty source of decent pizza, spaghetti and risotto in a subterranean setting. *Rubin*, ul. Kazimiera Wielkiego 10, is a small, family-run lunch place very popular with locals and with excellent *pierogi* and other Polish dishes. Aside from the *Wyrwigrosz*, good **drinking** spots include *Grodzka Jeden*, off the south end of the Rynek; the *Cinema Pub*, back towards the train station at ul. Franciszkańska 35; and the *Artystyczna Café*, just outside the castle walls, which also serves light meals. *Il Fiore*, right in the centre at ul. Kazimierza Wielkiego 17b, has what may be Poland's best *gelato* – in summer you'll have to queue.

Around Przemyśl

For an excellent view, especially towards the Carpathians, the **Kopiec Tartarski** (Tartar Monument) on the southern outskirts of Przemyśl is worth a trip; buses #28 and #28a deposit you at the bottom of the hill. Legend says the monument at the top marks the burial place of a sixteenth-century Tatar khan reputed to have died nearby. The route there takes you past a number of **World War I cemeteries**, Russian, Austrian and German included, reminders of the massive battles fought in and around the town early in the conflict. Close to the monument there are also the remnants of one of the **bastions** in an

On to L'viv

There's no better illustration of the current revival of cross-border ties in Poland than the growing tourist influx to **L'VIV**, 70km across the Ukrainian border. Alongside its cultural cousin, Vilnius, L'viv (Lwów to Poles) was long one of the main eastern centres of Poland; like the Lithuanian capital, too, traditionally this was a city characterized by a diverse, **multicultural population** – three cathedrals, Armenian, Orthodox and Catholic, are still there today. In Polish terms, the city's greatest ascendancy was during the Partitions, when, as Lemberg, capital of the Austrian province of Galicia, it became at least as important a centre as Kraków. During the interwar years, too, Polish culture flourished in the city. The postwar loss of L'viv to the Soviet Union was a cruel blow to Poles, who've always remained strongly attached to the place, as evidenced by the scores of photo albums and guidebooks you can find in Polish bookshops these days. The liberalization of border controls in the early 1990s let in a large influx of Polish visitors, thankfully unaccompanied by demands for the return to Polish control of a city that was at the forefront of the recent Ukrainian struggle for independence.

A wealth of **transport** links (currently eight buses and four trains a day – the buses, though creaky old hulks, are cheaper and usually faster – have grown up between Przemyśl and L'viv to cater for trippers on either side, and with its architectural wealth and café culture to rival Kraków, the idea of an **excursion** to L'viv is an enticing one. Be warned, however, that most people (including citizens of EU countries, Australia, New Zealand, Canada and the US) need a **visa** to enter Ukraine – they're not available at the border, but getting one at the Ukrainian Consulate in Kraków (ul. Krakowska 41; ☎012/429 6066; Mon, Wed & Fri 8am–noon) is fairly straightforward, and there's always an English speaker on duty. Tourist visas for up to six months take a week to process and cost US$40 for the nationalities listed above; express service is available for US$80. To get a visa you'll need proof of accommodation in Ukraine for at least part of your trip – your best bet is to reserve a room at L'viv's grand, Habsburg-era *George Hotel* by Internet (1 Mickiewicz Square, L'viv; ☎38/0322/725 952, ⊛www.georgehotel.com.ua; doubles US$31) and bring a printout to the consulate. The useful brochure "What to see and where to go in L'viv", published by the L'viv Tourist Board (⊛www.about.lviv.ua), is available at the tourist office in Przemyśl.

It's also possible to apply for a visa in Warsaw or in your home country; the address for the Ukrainian embassy in Warsaw is ul. Szucha 7 (☎022/625 0127, ⊛www.ukraine-poland.com); in Australia Suite 12:1, St George Centre, 60 Marcus Clarke Street, Canberra ACT 2601 (☎02/6230 5789, ⊛www.ukremb.info); in Canada, 310 Somerset St West, Ottawa, Ontario K2P OJ9 (☎1613/230 2961, ⊛www.ukremb.ca); in the UK, 60 Holland Park Rd, London W11 3SJ (☎020/7727 6312, ⊛www.ukremb.org.uk); and in the US, 3350 M St NW, Washington DC 20007 (☎202/333 7507, ⊛www.ukremb.com).

---

extensive ring of fortifications thrown up round the town by the Austrians from the 1870s onwards, consisting of an inner ring located in the immediate vicinity of the town and an outer ring pushing far out into the countryside. If you have your own transport you could have a fascinating time exploring the network of fortifications with the help of a map titled *Twierdza Przemyśl* ("Fortress of Przemyśl") available from the tourist office. One of the best preserved is at **Siedliska**, right up by the Ukrainian border – a clear indication of the size of the enterprise.

The obvious destination for a day trip is **Krasiczyn castle**, a ten-kilometre ride west of town by bus #40, which leaves every seventy minutes or so from the Jagiellońska bus stop, north of the Rynek. Built in the late sixteenth century for the Krasicki family by Italian architect Gallazzo Appiani, the castle is a fine example of Polish Renaissance architecture. Though currently in the midst of a decades-long restoration, you can take a guided tour (daily, starting on the hour from 10am to 4pm; 5.50zł) of the courtyard and three of the four cone-shaped corner towers named after the pillars of the contemporary order, to wit, the Pope, the King, the Nobility and the Almighty. There is also a tapestry collection and small portrait gallery. The surrounding **park** (daily 9am–sunset; 1zł) makes a cool, relaxing spot for a stroll. Much of the castle is now a plush **hotel**, the *Zamkowy* (☎016/671 8316, ⓦwww.krasiczyn.motronik.com.pl; ❺–❾), with its own **restaurant** and **wine bar.**

Further afield, and only easy to get to if you're driving (though a few buses do head this way; ask at the station), is the *cerkiew* in **Chotyniec**, some thirty kilometres northeast of Przemyśl. A two-domed structure dating from around 1600, this is one of the finest wooden churches in the region, with an interior that boasts a complete seventeenth-century iconostasis and, on the southern wall, a Baroque, Western-influenced *Last Judgment* painted in 1735.

The Sanok region

The main routes south from Przemyśl and Rzeszów towards the **Bieszczady** head through a rustic landscape of wooded foothills to the provincial town of **Sanok**. It's a journey that's particularly alluring in spring and autumn, the sun intensifying the green, brown and golden hues of the beech forests. If you've the time to spare, consider stopping off at picturesque little towns such as **Bircza** or **Tyrawa Wołoska** (both on the Przemyśl–Sanok road) to soak up the atmosphere; a number of villages with wooden *cerkwie* are tucked away in easy walking distance of Tyrawa. A little way to the east, close to the Ukrainian border, lies the village of **Arłamów**, site of the decommissioned army HQ where ex-president/former Solidarity leader Lech Wałęsa was imprisoned during the early days of martial law. A luxury palatial-looking complex that used to double as a Party members' hunting lodge is now a posh country hotel (☎013/461 6500, ⓦwww.arlamow.com.pl; ❹) for hunting and riding groups.

Sanok and around

Perched up on a hilltop above the San valley, **SANOK** is a sleepy sort of place. Best known within Poland for its rubber and bus factories, whose AutoSan vehicles can be seen all over the country, of late the town has begun to pick up economically, largely from increased cross-border trade. It's also becoming more popular as a tourist destination, both in its own right for its extraordinary icon collection and *skansen*, and as a staging point for trips into the Bieszczady, which loom through the mists on the horizon; once you've seen the museums, there's no real reason to stay on.

The Town

Industrial suburbs notwithstanding, Sanok's historic centre is pleasant enough, with commercial life focused on the pedestrianized section of ul. 3-go Maja leading to the Rynek and castle. There are several fine chapels in the seventeenth-century **Kościół Franciszkanów** (Franciscan Church) on the edge of the Rynek, while just to the west on pl. św. Michała the original fourteenth-century **parish church**, which was destroyed in a fire in 1782 and rebuilt a century later, hosted the 1417 wedding of King Władysław Jagiełło and Elżbieta Granowska

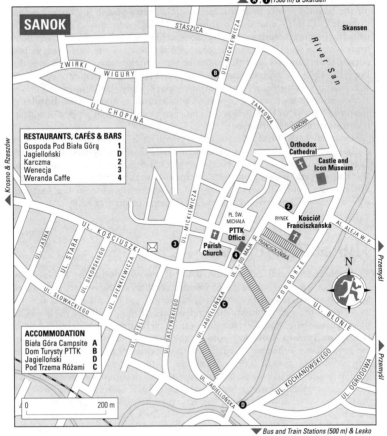

▲ **A** , **1** *(1500 m) & Skansen*

▼ *Bus and Train Stations (500 m) & Lesko*

(his third, her fourth). A short way down the hill is the **Orthodox cathedral**, an imposing late eighteenth-century edifice with a fine iconostasis (open for Sunday services at 10.30am and 5pm, but at other times you can peer in through the vestibule).

The castle and Sanok Icon Museum

Perched halfway up the hill between the two is the **castle**, a sixteenth-century construction built on the site of the original twelfth-century fortress that guarded the main highway linking the southern Carpathians to the Baltic. Though remodelled in the Habsburg era it could still pass for a Scottish laird's ancestral pile. Today the castle houses the fabulous **Sanok Icon Museum** (April to mid-June & Oct Mon 8–10am, Tues & Wed 9am–5pm, Thurs–Sun 9am–3pm; mid-June to Sept Mon 8–10am, Tues–Sun 9am–5pm; Nov–March Mon, Thurs & Fri 8am–3pm, Tues & Wed 9am–5pm, Sat & Sun 9am–3pm; 8zł; Ⓦwww .muzeum.sanok.pl), the largest collection of Ruthenian icons in the world after the Tretyakov Gallery in Moscow. Though most of the pieces date from the sixteenth and seventeenth centuries, the oldest comes from the mid-1300s, thus giving a clear impression of the development of the **Ukrainian school** of painting, which evolved in tandem with an autonomous and assertive local Church.

Unlike Russian and Byzantine iconography, however, what's on display here is little known to anyone but specialists, despite its quality. The best of the early icons have both the serenity and severity of Andrei Rublev's greatest works. In contrast, later icons manifest the increasing influence of Western Catholicism – which culminated in the formation of the Uniate Church in 1595 (see box, pp.356–357) – both in their style and subject matter, with an encroaching Renaissance approach to portraiture. In a few cases, the figures show strong Tatar influences too. Look out for a large *Icon of Hell*, a type traditionally housed in the women's section of Orthodox churches; such lurid depictions of the torments beyond the grave must have kept a few people in check. Other highlights include a three-metre-long depiction of the twelve feast days of the Orthodox Church, and two Transfigurations from the first half of the sixteenth century, both set in an unearthly mountainous landscape. After the expected Madonnas, the most common subject is St Nicholas, always clad in luxuriant robes. Upstairs you'll find more icons, as well as a rich collection of religious paraphernalia such as candle holders, wooden crosses and painted banners.

As with the related collections in Łańcut, Przemyśl and Nowy Sącz, the existence of this collection is related to postwar "resettlements". With many local villages deserted in the aftermath of Operation Vistula (see box, p.356), their wooden *cerkwie* neglected and falling apart, the oldest and most important icons were removed to museums. Genuine artistic concern prompted their removal, but now that local people are returning to the villages and using the churches again, there have been calls to hand some of the icons back. On the top floor of the castle is the **Beksiński Gallery** (same hours and ticket), displaying a selection of the imaginative canvases – part Dali-surrealist, part Lord of the Rings stage set – of Zdzisław Beksiński, the noted modern artist born here in 1929. The **archeological section** of the museum (closed for renovation at the time of writing) contains a display of finds from the excavations in progress at Trepcza, 5km northwest of Sanok.

As with most towns in the area, Jews were an integral part of local life for centuries, only to be decimated by the Nazis. Virtually all that remains is the overgrown **New Jewish cemetery**, about 1km west of the town centre on ul. Kiczury, just beyond the main Catholic cemetery.

The skansen

Sanok's other draw is the **skansen** in the Biała Góra district, well signposted 2km north of the centre (daily: May–Sept 8am–6pm; April 9am–4pm; Oct 8am–4pm; Nov–Mar 9am–2pm; 9zł; ☏013/463 1672, ⊛www.bieszczadyonline .pl/skansen); if you don't want to walk, take a bus north along ul. Mickiewicza to the bridge over the river – the *skansen* is on the other side, spread along the riverbank. This open-air museum, the largest and best in Poland, brings together examples of the different styles of all (excepting the Jews) of the region's main ethnic groups – Boyks, Łemks, Dolinianie ("Inhabitants of the Valley") and Pogórzanie ("Uplanders"). For detailed ethnography, an excellent English guidebook is available at the entrance (10zł). Many of the buildings are open only when there's a guide on hand: your options are to tag along with a larger group or hire a guide (40zł for a two-hour tour in Polish or English, but call ahead for the latter).

Specimens of every kind of country building have been (and still are being) carefully moved and reassembled here: smithies, inns, granaries, windmills, pigsties and churches, and for added verisimilitude you'll find storks, goats and other animals wandering about. Up on the hillside in the Boyk section, a couple of typical eighteenth-century *cerkwie*, one with a complete iconostasis, nestle peacefully in the shade of the trees. The neighbouring Lemk section has a good set of farmhouses, while the Dolinianie area features a quaint old fire station, complete with nineteenth-century fire engines, a church, and a fine range of rural dwellings from stately *dwór* right down to the humblest and poorest cottages. In the Pogórzanie section there's a nineteenth-century school building holding some amazing old textbooks and report cards; note too the carefully preserved maps of pre-1914 Poland, showing this area as a region of the Austro-Hungarian province of Galicia – hence the portrait of Kaiser Franz Josef behind the teacher's desk. Nearby you'll find an apiary with nineteenth-century figural beehives, carved from tree trunks into likenesses of St Francis, St Ambrose (patron of beekeepers) and others.

As if all this weren't enough, a building in the Dolinianie section displays the *skansen*'s own **icon collection** (9am–4pm; 4zł), which, if not as large as that of the Sanok Museum, is still one the country's finest. Especially noteworthy is the seventeenth-century *Last Judgment* from the village church in Paszowa, in which the damned are swallowed whole by animals and pierced by spear-wielding devils. A nearby pavilion houses excellent temporary exhibitions focusing on past and present village life.

Practicalities

The **bus station** is close to the **train station**, about fifteen minutes' walk southeast of the town centre; most buses from here will take you up to the main square. The **tourist office**, run by PTTK and with a good stock of maps, is at ul. 3-go Maja 2 (Mon–Fri 8am–4pm; ☎013/463 2171). Sanok's informative municipal website (Ⓦwww.sanok.pl) has also been fully translated into English. There's **Internet** access on ul. Jagiellońska, directly opposite the *Jagielloński* hotel. The town centre offers a small but reasonable range of **places to stay**, the most attractive being the aforementioned *Jagielloński*, ul. Jagiellońska 49 (☎013/463 1208, Ⓦwww.jagiellonski.webpark.pl; ❸), a foreigners' favourite on account of its knowledgeable, English-speaking management, the comfortable, spacious en suites and good-quality cellar restaurant – reservations are a good idea, especially in summer. Its main competitor, the *Pod Trzema Różami*, ul. Jagiellońska 13 (☎013/463 0922, Ⓦwww.ooh.pl/trzy_roze; ❸), is closer to the centre but with lower-standard rooms and monoglot staff. A budget option is provided by the *Dom Turysty PTTK*, just downhill from the town centre at ul. Mickiewicza 29 (☎013/463 1439), with frumpish but tolerable en suites (❶–❷ depending on bathroom facilities), and some hostel-style triples (25zł per person). You can pitch a tent or park a caravan at the *Biała Góra* campsite (☎013/463 2818, Ⓦwww.campsanok.hg.pl), on a hilltop overlooking the river just next to the *skansen*, where there are also bungalows (30zł per person).

The **restaurant** in the *Jagielloński* hotel has fairly good Polish standards, though its upscale pretences are deflated by over-loud pop music. A more interesting choice is *Karczma*, on the northern side of the Rynek, which offers regional specialties in a folksy atmosphere. There's also a good little snack bar attached to the *skansen*, the *Gospoda Pod Białą Górą*, with *pierogi*, *bigos* and similar fare. For pizza or pasta, try *Wenecja*, ul. Mickiewicza 3. There are plenty of **cafés** and **bars** along ul. 3-go Maja; *Weranda Caffe* at no.12 has a respectable selection of drinks and a wood-panelled interior.

Several folk music and dance events are held each summer at the *skansen*, culminating in the **Borderlands Festival** early in August (details at the *skansen*), which features bands from Poland, Ukraine and elsewhere. Lovely, hand-crafted **modern icons** (200–800zł) are sold in a workshop off ul. Franciszkańska.

Ulucz and Czerteż

If you have your own transport the *cerkiew* in **ULUCZ**, a tiny village 20km north of Sanok on the River San, is worth seeking out. Built in 1510, it's the oldest, and among the finest, of the Boyk *cerkwie* located within Polish territory (others of similar vintage are all in Ukraine). A graceful, well-proportioned building poised on a hilltop, it boasts a large bulbous dome, fine Baroque iconostasis (though sadly several icons were stolen a few years back) and mural paintings of the Passion and Crucifixion. The key is kept in a house marked by a sign at the village entrance.

At **CZERTEŻ**, immediately north of the main Krosno road, 6km west of Sanok, there's another beautiful Boyk *cerkiew* from 1742, hidden in a clump of trees up above the village. It houses another fine iconostasis, although Roman Catholics have now taken over the church as a place of worship. The free-standing belfry was added in 1887.

The Bieszczady

The valleys and slopes of the **Bieszczady** were cleared in 1947 by Operation Vistula (see box, p.356), and most of the local population, which was over eighty-percent Boyk, was forcibly displaced into the Ukraine. Today, these original inhabitants and their descendants are coming back, but the region remains sparsely populated and is largely protected as part of the **East Carpathian biosphere reserve** that was established in 1991 with support from the World Bank, which also incorporates adjacent territory in Slovakia and Ukraine. Though carefully controlled to protect wildlife, the reserves are open to the public – quite a change from communist times, when party elite maintained various sections for its own high-security hunting lodges. Ecologically, the area is of great importance, with its high grasslands and ancient forests of oak, fir and, less frequently, beech. The diverse fauna include **black storks**, far rarer than their ubiquitous white relatives, and fifty-odd **brown bears**, as well as numerous **raptors**, **wolves**, **lynx** and even **bison**, reintroduced here in the 1960s. The highest peaks in the region, at around 1300m, won't present many **hiking** problems as long as you're well equipped. Like all mountain regions, however, **weather** changes quickly, particularly on the *połonina* (alpine meadows), where terrific storms can come at a moment's notice throughout the year. The best time to visit, as in the Tatras, is late autumn, when Poles savour the delights of the "Golden October". Temperatures drop sharply in winter, bringing excellent skiing conditions.

If you're coming for serious hiking, the best place to head for is the base-camp of **Ustrzyki Górne** – direct buses run here from Rzeszów and (more frequently) Sanok, Lesko and Ustrzyki Dolne. These can get crowded in summer, but as numerous private lines have sprung up recently you should always be able to find a seat. An interesting alternative that makes an ideal base for shorter hikes (and offers a much better selection of places to stay and eat) is **Wetlina**, just west of the park and reached by bus from Sanok or Lesko.

Lesko and the foothills

East of Sanok the southbound road passes through **Zagórz**, a rail hub (and the last stop for trains from the north and west: from here you can catch an east-bound local train to Ustrzyki Dolne or a south-bound service to Nowy Łupków), and continues a further 6km to **LESKO**, a tranquil foothills town with enough sights to merit a quick stop and, if you want to stay, a sixteenth-century **castle** that's now a good and affordable hotel (see below).

As in other towns in the area, Lesko's **Jewish community** made up over half of the prewar population. Just north of the Rynek, on ul. Moniuszko, stands the **former synagogue**, a solid-looking Renaissance structure that was originally part of the town's defensive system. The vivacious, finely sculptured facade is emblazoned with a quotation from the Torah. Damaged in wartime, the building was reconstructed in the early 1960s, and is now an **art gallery** (daily 10am–5pm; 3zł). Alongside the temporary art exhibitions you can view the converted synagogue interior, including the few elements of the original decoration. A small display in the entrance hall has some prewar photos of the synagogue, records of local families murdered by the Nazis and a detailed list of the location and size of Jewish communities throughout southeastern Poland.

Head past the building and bear right at the bottom of the hill to reach the **Jewish cemetery**, one of the most beautiful and evocative in the whole country. Hidden from a distance by the trees covering the hillside cemetery, the steps up from the roadside – the Star of David on the rust-coloured gate tells you you're at the right entrance – take you up through a tangled knot of twisted tree trunks and sprawling undergrowth to the peaceful hilltop cemetery site, around which are scattered two thousand-odd gravestones, the oldest dating back to the early 1500s. As in other major surviving cemeteries there's a wealth of architectural styles in evidence, notably a number of ornately decorated Baroque tablets with seven-branched candelabra, animal motifs and often a pair of hands reaching up in prayer towards the heavens from the top of the stone. It's the setting as much as the stones that makes this cemetery so memorable, a powerful testimony to centuries of rural Jewish presence.

Lesko's **bus** station is on the Sanok road, about 1km downhill from the main Rynek. Occupying a low concrete pavilion beside the Rynek's town hall, the **tourist information office** (Mon–Sat 8am–5pm) has a wealth of leaflets on the region and details of **private rooms** in farmhouses (*agroturystyka*) in nearby villages – although you'll need your own transport to get to these. The *Zamek* **hotel** (☎013/469 6268, ✉zamek@gat.pl; ❹), in the castle, is the best place to stay, with simple but pleasant rooms as well as a terrace restaurant, fitness club and a pool table. Reservations may be necessary: conferences regularly occupy the whole place. The *Ratuszowa*, at Rynek 12 (☎013/469 8632; ❷) is serviceable as a second choice, and has the best **restaurant** after the one in the castle.

South from here the bus continues through **UHERCE**, where many Polish tourists veer off towards **Jezioro Solińskie**, a fjord-like artificial lake created in the 1970s for hydroelectric power and watersports purposes. The custom-built lakeside villages of **SOLINA**, **POLAŃCZYK** and **MYCZKÓW** have more restaurants than anywhere else in the area, but there's little else to recommend them apart from their access to the water. Polańczyk has the richest choice of **accommodation**, with dozens of new pensions (❶–❷) alongside the older workers' holiday houses. The best place here is the *Korona*, ul. Zdrójowa 29 (☎013/469 2201, ⊛www.pensjonatkorona.pl; ❹), an upmarket pension with high-quality rooms and a good restaurant. **Boat rental** is easy to arrange.

Ustrzyki Dolne

Back on the main road, **USTRZYKI DOLNE**, 25km east of Lesko, is the last sizeable town before the mountains, swarming in summer with backpacking students and youth groups. On ul. Bełzka, immediately north of the Rynek,

BIESZCZADY REGION

there's a small **museum** (Tues–Sat 9am–5pm; plus Sun July & Aug 9am–2pm; 5zł) covering the flora and fauna of the national park. There are also a couple of worthwhile hiking routes in the surrounding low hills, although you'd do better to press on towards the more inviting territory to the south. Ustrzyki Dolne's **train** and **bus stations** are a ten-minute walk east of the Rynek, where the **tourist office** at Rynek 16 (Mon–Fri 8am–4pm; ⓦwww.ustrzyki-dolne .pl) has information and hiking maps. Best bets for **accommodation** are the *Laworta*, ten minutes' walk north of the stations at ul. Nadgórna 107 (☎013/468 9000, ⓦwww.laworta.pl; ❹), the biggest place and so most likely to have a room, and the *Hotel Bieszczadzka*, on the western side of the Rynek at no. 19 (☎013/461 1071; ❷), which offers en suites with showers or rooms with shared facilities. Next to the stations, the rustic **restaurant** *Zaciszek* is a good source of simple Polish food, while *Manhattan*, on the east side of the square, has better pizza than one is wont to expect in this sort of town. The *Delikatesy ABC*, on the north side of the square, is good for stocking up on **provisions** before you head into the mountains.

Krościenko

Nine kilometres northeast of Ustrzyki Dolne is the village of **KROŚCIENKO**, last train stop before the Ukrainian border (local buses run here too) and known as a regional curiosity for its small community of Greeks – part of a little-known diaspora of **Greek communists** who fled their country following the outbreak of civil war in 1946. Only a few remain these days, the younger generation having mostly elected to return. The chief reminder of their presence is the village **cemetery**, a tranquil, wooded spot 1km east off the road to the Ukrainian border. Back in the village, there's a fine late eighteenth-century **cerkiew** over the river, while just north of Krościenko on the edge of the Przemyśl road is a **Protestant cemetery**, all that remains of an earlier generation of local German settlers, who named the area Obersdorf.

From Ustrzyki Dolne to Ustrzyki Górne

The main road south out of Ustrzyki Dolne – a section of the Bieszczady loop route built in the 1970s to open up this hitherto untouched area to tourism – winds south through the mountain valleys towards Ustrzyki Górne, an eighty-minute (50km) journey by bus. The countryside here is rich in wooden churches, and if you have time to spare and your own transport, consider a detour a few kilometres off the main road to the villages of **Jałowe**, **Równia** and **Moczary** (the first two are also reachable by bus or hiking from Ustrzyki Dolne) to see fine examples of Boyk architecture. Back on the road to Ustrzyki Górne you'll also find Boyk churches at **Hoszów**, **Czarna Górna**, **Smolnik** (one of the few remaining places of Orthodox worship in the region), and – on a road off to the east – at **Bystre** (now disused) and **Michniowiec** (bus from Czarna Górna).

Coming over the hill into the old market town of **LUTOWISKA** you'll see makeshift barracks and drilling rigs, signs of the oil industry that has developed here sporadically since the last century. Up until 1939, over half the residents of this remote area were Jews, and the abandoned Jewish cemetery east of the main road contains several hundred tombstones from the nineteenth and twentieth centuries. Near the village church a **monument** commemorates the more than 600 local Jews shot here by the Nazis in June 1942. In the centre of town the roadside café and gallery *U Biesa i Czada* has great snacks and coffee. The town is also home to the **Ośrodek Informacyno-Edukacyny BPN** (Bieszczady National Park Information and Education Centre; Mon–Fri 9am–5pm; ⊤013/461 0350, ⓔoie@oie.bdpn.pl), one of the better sources of information on the region, though there's not always an English speaker on duty. Further south, in the village of **PSZCZELINY**, there's the *Magura* (⊤013/461 0238, ⓦwww.zajazdmagura.info; ❷), a comfortable pension with three ostriches residing out front.

Ustrzyki Górne

Spread out along the bottom of a peaceful river valley and surrounded by the peaks of the Bieszczady, **USTRZYKI GÓRNE**, the final destination for most buses heading into the Bieszczady, has an end-of-the-world feel to it, being little more than a bus stop girdled by snack bars and holiday villas. There's nothing to do here but **hike**: luckily, well-marked trails start right next to the bus stop, getting you up onto the forest-carpeted hillsides within a matter of minutes. **Accommodation** choices in Ustrzyki Górne are limited, and there's a better range of places to stay on the far side of the park, in Wetlina and Cisna. First on the comfort list, but overpriced, is the PTTK-run *Hotel Górski* (⊤013/461 0614, ⓦwww.hotelgorski.webpark.pl; ❺), in a good riverside location at the north end of the village, with sparsely furnished en suites and amenities such as a sauna and a swimming pool, but a gloomy restaurant. Other options include the *Dom Biały* (⊤013/461 0641, ⓦwww.hotelik-bialy.bieszczady.info .pl; 25zł per person), run by the BPN and signposted to the southeast of the bus stop, with adequate four- and five-bed dorms. The best of several campsites is attached to the *Hotel Górski* and there are also dorms in some of the **restaurants** clustered around the bus stop, all basically similar setups specializing in the

Outdoor activities in the Bieszczady

Beyond hiking, the most accessible activity in the Bieszczady is **mountain biking**, with decent quality bikes for rent at many pensions and restaurants (5zł/hr) and plenty of gravel roads leading off into minor valleys. Another way of exploring the region is by horseback: traditionally the plateaux and high paths of the Bieszczady have been the habitat of *hucule*, an ancient and temperamental breed of **wild horses** found throughout the Carpathians. Recent years have seen a renewed interest in these captivating beasts, not least for their tourist potential – and a number of places are now offering **riding holidays** in the mountains. The best source of information is the BPN Information and Educational Centre in Lutowiska (see opposite), which responds to English-language emails and will put you on to the local stables. Best established of the riding centres is the BPN's own stable (Zachowawcza Hodowla Konia Huculskiego BPN; ☎013/461 0650) in Wołosate, 6km southeast of Ustrzyki Górne. A few pensions have their own stables, including the *Rusinowa Polana* in Dwerniczek (see below).

Although nowhere near as popular a **skiing** area as the Tatras, the Bieszczady provides some of the country's most enjoyable – and certainly uncrowded – skiing terrain. While the **slopes** are not very dramatic (the principal ones are in Lesko, Komańcza, Cisna, Dwerniczek, Polańczyk and both the Ustrzykis), the **cross-country routes** are tranquillity itself. Infrastructure is basic and the availability of **equipment** still limited – most skiers bring their own – but one place that does rent both down-hill and cross-country skis is the *Rusinowa Polana* pension (☎013/461 0848; ❷) in **Dwerniczek**, on a minor road southeast of Wetlina, and with modest but comfortable rooms and English-speaking staff. Before heading out it's always a good idea to ask at your pension or one of the park offices which areas are off limits to skiers.

local trout and with outdoor seating; *U Rzeźbiarza* (☎013/461 0629; 15zł per person) is a good choice. The main village **shop** has a basic range of food but attracts a devoted band of idlers with its plentiful supplies of Leżajsk beer.

Hiking routes in the Bieszczady

If you're making a long day trip from Sanok (only feasible if you start very early), your best choice is to alight before Ustrzyki Górne, at Przełęcz nad Berehami Górne or Przełęcz Wyźniańska, walk from one of these passes into the surrounding hills and returning via the holiday centre of Wetlina – the last bus back to Sanok from here leaves at around 5pm. You're well advised, however, to stay for a few days, either making Ustrzyki Górne, Wetlina or the more remote Muczne a base for walks, or **hiking** along the ridges and staying in mountain hostels. Both options are attractive and accessible for anyone reasonably fit; route durations given below are reckoned for an average walker's speed, including regular stops. The best **map** for hikers is the green *Bieszczady Mapa Turystczyna* (1:65,000), published by *euromapa* and available throughout the region. When first entering the **Bieszczady Park Narodowy** (Ⓦwww .bdpn.info; information in English at Ⓦwww.panparks.org) you'll need to pay an **entry fee** (3zł), collected in huts at the area's main access points.

The remoteness and rapid changes of weather here make proper **equipment** essential. Unless you stick to paths near the main road, your rucksack should hold cold clothing for cold and rain, food supplies and a good map and compass. As far as **weather conditions** go, outside the summer months (and even, sometimes including them) it is important to keep a check on things: particularly up on the *połonina*, terrific storms often appear from nowhere. It's also better not to set out alone on extended hikes, as the area's isolation reduces your chances of being spotted in an emergency.

East to Tarnica and the Ukrainian border

There are two initial routes east from Ustrzyki Górne, both leading to the high Tarnica valley (1275m). The easier is to follow the road to the hamlet of **Wołosate** (where there's a hostel and also a pension, the *Stajnia* ☎013/461 0670) then walk up via the peak of Hudow Wierszek (965m) – about four hours all in. Shorter but more strenuous is to go cross-country via the peak of Szeroki Wierch (1268m), a three-hour hike. **Tarnica** peak (1346m) is a further half-hour hike south of the valley.

From Tarnica valley you can continue east, with a stiff up-and-down hike via **Krzemien** (1335m), **Kopa Bukowska** (1320m) and **Halicz** (1333m) to **Rozsypaniec** (1280m), the last stretch taking you over the highest pass in the range. This would be a feasible day's hike from Wołosate; the really fit could do an outing from Ustrzyki to Krzemien and back in a day.

Boyks, Łemks and Uniates

Up until World War II, a large part of the population of southeast Poland was classified officially as **Ukrainian**. For the provinces of L'viv, Tarnopol and Volhynia, in the eastern part of the region (all in Ukraine today), this was accurate. However, for the western part, now Polish border country, it was seriously misrepresentative, as this region was in fact inhabited by **Boyks** (Boykowie) and **Łemks** (Łemkowie). These people, often collectively called "Rusini" in Polish, are historically close to the Ukrainians but have their own distinct identities, both groups being descendants of the nomadic shepherds who settled in the **Bieszczady** and **Beskid Niski** regions between the thirteenth and fifteenth centuries. Geographically speaking, the Boyks populated the region east of Cisna, while the Łemks inhabited the western part of the Bieszczady, the Beskid Niski and part of the Beskid Sądecki.

For centuries these farming people lived more or less peacefully. Their real troubles began at the end of World War II, when groups of every political complexion were roaming around the ruins of Poland, all determined to influence the shape of the postwar order. One such movement was the **Ukrainian Resistance Army (UPA)**, which fought against all odds for the independence of their perennially subjugated country. Initially attracted by Hitler's promises of an autonomous state in the eastern territories of the Third Reich, by 1945 the UPA were fighting under the slogan "Neither Hitler nor Stalin", and had been encircled by the Polish, Czech and Soviet armies in this corner of Poland. For almost two years small bands of partisans, using carefully concealed mountain hide-outs, held out against the Polish army, even killing the regional commander of the Polish army, General Karol Swierczewski, at Jabłonki in March 1947.

Here the story grows ambiguous: according to the official Polish account, UPA forces were fed by a local population more than happy to help the "Ukrainian fascists". The locals gave a different account, claiming they weren't involved with the UPA, except when forced to provide them with supplies at gunpoint. In no mood for fine distinctions, in April 1947 the Polish government evacuated the entire population of the Bieszczady and Beskid Niski regions in a notorious operation code-named **Operation Vistula** (Akcja Wisła). Inhabitants were given two hours to pack and leave with whatever they could carry, then were "resettled" either to the former German territories of the north and west in the case of many Łemks, or to the Soviet Union with most of the Boyks.

From the Gorlice region of the Beskids, a traditional Łemk stronghold, an estimated 120,000–150,000 were deported to the Soviet Union and a further 80,000 were scattered around Poland, of whom about 20,000 have now returned. The first arrived in

Adventurous walkers might consider trekking into the region to the north of Tarnica valley in search of the **abandoned Ukrainian villages** and tumbled-down *cerkwie* scattered along the border (delineated by the River San). Some, like Bukowiec and Tarnawa Wyznia, are marked on the *euromapa* map, but others aren't, so keep your eyes peeled. In some cases villages were razed to the ground, and only their orchards remain. The Polish **border police** who shuttle around the area in jeeps are nothing to worry about as long as you're carrying your passport. The Ukrainians who watch this area are a different proposition, though, so don't on any account wander into Ukrainian territory – police detention of hikers in L'viv has been known.

A road leading back to Ustrzyki Górne dead-ends here at **Tarnawa Niżna**, a tranquil place with a pension, the *Nad Roztoką* (☏013/461 0278, ✉tarnawa@oie .bdpn.pl; ❶). A couple of kilometres west along the road is **Muczne**, site of a secret **hunting** hotel used by the communist party leadership and international guests including French president Giscard d'Estang and Romanian leader Nicolae Ceauşescu. Now dilapidated, it is flanked on either side by a high-quality new

1957, in the wake of Prime Minister Gomułka's liberalization of previously hard-line policy. (Rumour has it that this was Gomułka's way of thanking the Łemks who had helped him personally during the war.) The trickle of returnees in the 1960s and 1970s has, since the demise of communist rule, become a flow, with Łemks and a few Boyks reclaiming the farms that belonged to their parents and grandparents. This return to the homeland brought a new level of political and cultural self-asser-tion. In the June 1989 elections, Stanisław Mokry, a Solidarity candidate from near Gorlice, openly declared himself a Łemk representative. Boyks and Łemks lost no time in pressing for official condemnation of the postwar deportations – a demand partially met by the Senate in August 1990 when it passed a resolution condemn-ing Operation Vistula, though the Sejm failed to follow suit. Like other minorities in Poland, Łemks and Boyks want their own schools, language teaching and the right to develop their own culture – although there's been little significant progress in these areas so far.

The question of self-identity in the Bieszczady is entangled by the religious divisions within the community. Like their Ukrainian neighbours, in the seventeenth century many previously Orthodox Boyks and Łemks joined the **Uniate Church**, which was created in 1595 following the Act of Union between local Orthodox metropolitans and Catholic bishops. The new church came under papal jurisdiction, but retained Ortho-dox rites and traditions – including, for example, the right of priests to marry. Today the majority of Łemks in the Bieszczady and Beskid Niski classify themselves as Uniate (or "Greek Catholic", as Poles know them). Encouraged both by the Pope's appoint-ment of a Polish Uniate bishop and political changes in Ukraine, where Uniates are finally coming into the open after years of persecution, Łemk Uniates have success-fully adopted a much higher religious profile.

The Uniates' revival in Poland is still hampered, however, by the vexed question of restitution of property confiscated in the wake of Operation Vistula, in particular the 250-odd churches in the region taken away from the Uniates and mostly given to the Roman Catholics and Orthodox, and only a few have been recovered in recent years. A further twist is added in the case of Orthodox-occupied buildings – the Church in Rzepedź (see p.362) is a good example – since like Ukrainians, the Łemk and Boyk communities are divided between the two faiths.

If you want to find out more about the Carpathian communities, the English-language ⓦwww.lemko.org and ⓦwww.carpatho-rusyn.org websites are useful sources of **information**.

pension. *Wilcza Jama* (☎013/461 0269, ⓦwww.muczne.pl) has doubles with bath and five-person bungalows (all ❹ with mandatory full board June–Aug; otherwise ❷, board optional), and an excellent bar and **restaurant**, serving game and trout and locally famous for its New Year's Eve parties. The nearby *Siedlisko Carpathia* (☎013/461 0122, ⓦwww.muczne.com; ❸) is more family-oriented, with a relaxed restaurant and a children's playground.

West to the Slovak border

From Ustrzyki Górne you can also head west to the peak of **Wielka Rawka** (1307m), flanked by woods on the Slovak border. The easier option is to go along the Cisna road and then left up the marked path to the summit (3hr). A far more strenuous choice is to head south to the bridge over the Wołosate river, turn right along a track, then follow signs to the peak of Mała Szemenowa (1071m), from where you turn right along the border to the peaks of Wielka Szemenowa (1088m) and Wielka Rawka (4hr).

Northwest of Ustrzyki

The best-known walking areas of the Bieszczady are the **połonina**, or mountain meadows. These desolate places are notoriously subject to sudden changes of weather: one moment you can be basking in autumn sunshine, the next the wind is howling to the accompaniment of a downpour. The landscape, too, is full of contrasts: there's something of the Scottish highlands in the wildness of the passes, but wading through the tall rustling grasses of the hillsides in summer you might imagine yourself in the African savannah. Walking here you can also see how Ukrainian partisans managed to hold out for so long; even for the most hardened Polish and Soviet troops, flushing partisan bands out from this remote and inhospitable landscape must have been an onerous task.

In summer, buses shuttle through the park every hour or so in both directions, running west from Ustrzyki Górne and east from Wetlina, Dołżyca and Cisna. If time is short, stop at the **Przełęc Wyzniańska** pass, from where a marked path leads up through the woods on the north side of the road to the **Połonina Caryńska** (1297m – a steep climb of roughly an hour). After a short walk along the pass to get a feel for the landscape, return to the road for the next bus. A similar hike is feasible from the next pass to the west, the **Przełęcz nad Berehami Górnymi** to the **Połonina Wetlińska** (1255m; 1hr).

For a more extended trip in this area, start in Ustrzyki Górne, taking the steep trail marked in red and green north through the woods up to the eastern edge of the Połonina Caryńska, and walk over the top to the western edge (1297m; 2.5hr). Continue down the hill to the village of Brzegi Górne, where there's a **campsite** near the road. From here you can catch a bus or continue on the red and green path up the wooded hill to the right to the all-year PTTK **hostel** on the eastern edge of the Połonina Wetlińska (1.5hr from Brzegi) – the views from this windswept corner are spectacular. Sleeping arrangements comprise mattresses in ten-person rooms; theoretically you should bring your own food, but the couple who run the place will probably be happy to feed you from the communal pot.

Beyond the hostel there's an excellent walk over the Połonina Wetlińska to **Przełęc Orłowicza** (1078m), where the path divides into three. Turning right, you'll head north on the black-marked long-distance route via Wysokie Berdo (968m), Krysowa, Jaworzec, Kiczera, Czerenina and Falowa to Dołżyca (7hr; there's a PTTK hostel here).

Straight ahead, along the middle path, you'll reach **Smerek** peak (1222m; 20min) and then continue down through the woods to Smerek village and the main road (1.5hr).

A sharp left from Przełęc Orłowicza takes you down to **WETLINA** (2hr 30min from the hostel), a scenically located and popular holiday centre with a full range of **accommodation**. The *Leśny Dwór* (☎013/468 4654, ⊛www.bieszczady.pl/dwor; ❺), a family-run *pensjonat* on the north side of the main road, is best place to stay in the Bieszczady, with carefully furnished rooms, concerts in its fine restaurant and even a library. A second good choice is the *Chata Wędrowca* (☎0502/234 501, ⊛www.chatawedrowca.pl; ❸), with three comfortable rooms above its restaurant (see below). Plenty of other houses in town offer private accommodation (❶) – there's a full list on the Cisna municipal Internet site (see below). The *Górski* hotel (☎013/468 4634, ⊛www.hotelwetlina.bieszczady.info.pl) is a reasonable, PTTK-run hotel on the southern outskirts of the village with en-suite rooms (❷) and bungalows (❶). Finally, there's a year-round PTTK hostel (dorms from 20zł) and campsite run by an extremely friendly local character. Wetlina is also the culinary capital of the Bieszczady, with two adjacent **restaurants** vying with the countryside for your attention. The larger *Chata Wędrowa* is known for its *naleśnik gigant z jagodami* (gigantic blueberry pancake) and grilled marinated meats. Next door, the small and affordable *W Starym Siole* has good Polish dishes like *pierogi z soczewicą* (*pierogi* with lentils) as well as Swiss *raclette*, great desserts and what must be the best wine list east of Kraków. There are also occasional jazz concerts here.

Cisna, Majdan and Nowy Łupków

West of Wetlina the main road passes through Smerek and sleepy Przysłup (eastern terminus of the narrow-gauge rail line – see below) before descending to Dołżca and on to **CISNA**, which saw bitter fighting during the 1945–47 civil war, when the UPA (see box on pp.356–357) had one of their main bases nearby, a struggle commemorated by the large graffiti-covered monument overlooking the village. The whole area were ruthlessly emptied during Operation Vistula; today's population of just under two thousand is only a fraction of the 60,000 or so who lived here before 1939. Cisna's pleasant, forested setting and range of **accommodation** make the town a good second choice if you can't find a place to stay in Wetlina; first try the *Przystanek Cisna* (☎013/468 6396, ⊛www.przystanek.bieszczady.info.pl; ❷), a small pension behind the town school serving good vegetarian-only meals and run by an English-speaking family. Not quite as nice, but perfectly adequate and with a few more rooms, is *Kaczmar* (☎013/468 6345; ❶), just east of the town centre. Biggest place in town is the *Perelka* (☎013/468 6325, ✉perelka@naturatour.pl), a somewhat tired workers' holiday home with rooms (❸) and family-sized bungalows (❹). The **tourist office** in the centre of town (☎013/468 6465; Tues–Fri 10am–6pm, Sat 7.30am–3.30pm) has information on other homestay and pension options, as does the town **website** (⊛www.cisna.pl; under *noclegi*), which also posts bus (under *komunikacja PKS*) and train (under *kolejka leśny/rozkład jazdy*) schedules. For **eating**, the *Niedźwiadek*, specializing in fresh trout, is the best of a smattering of snack bars in the centre; there are also a few small shops. A kilometre to the southwest is **MAJDAN**, little more than a group of houses and the main boarding point for the **narrow-gauge rail line** running from west to east through the forests along the Slovak border. In addition to carrying passengers, these days the line forms part of a network of tracks through the forest which are used by the local forestry industry. Although its dependence on subsidies makes the line economically insecure – it was temporarily forced to close down in the mid-1990s – for now, at least between April and October, it's a regular tourist attraction.

The diesel-powered train, accompanied by a couple of old passenger carriages, operates two short stretches of track: one running 20km east of Majdan to the mountain pass of Przysłup, just beyond Cisna; the other running about 30km west to Wola Michowa. **Trains** for Przysłup leave Majdan at 10am (July & Aug daily; May, June & Sept Sat, Sun & public hols), arriving in Przysłup at around 11.10am and setting off on the return leg twenty minutes later. Trains for Wola Michowa only run at weekends and on public holidays in July and August, departing from Majdan at 1pm and reaching Wola Michowa at 2.25pm. The **timetables** have been set for several years, but it's still worth checking beforehand either directly at Majdan station or on the Cisna website (see p.359). The majority of this memorable and out-of-the-way route passes through uninhabited hillside forests filled with a gloriously rich and diverse flora, the beautiful views over the valleys adding a touch of mountain thrill to the experience. The train crawls along at a snail's pace for much of the journey, which is all it can manage on the steeper hills. You can pick the train up at several points along

Wooden churches in southeastern Poland

Despite a modern history characterized by destruction and neglect, both the Bieszczady and neighbouring Beskid Niski regions still have a significant number of villages that boast the wooden churches – Orthodox, Uniate and Roman Catholic – traditional to this part of Europe.

The oldest surviving wooden **cerkwie** (singular, **cerkiew**) – as Uniate and Orthodox places of worship are known in Polish – date from the sixteenth century: there are two in Poland from this period, graceful, intricately crafted structures in the isolated villages of **Ulucz** (see p.351) and **Chotyniec** (see p.347). Later ones are more numerous and just as remarkable, especially those from the eighteenth century, when the influence of Baroque spread to the carpenter architects of the Carpathians. The simpler churches with a threesome of shingled onion domes also encountered in the Bieszczady region have their origin in later, **Boyk**-derived architectural styles. Finally, in the Łemk-inhabited districts of the Beskid Niski you'll often encounter grander, showier structures with a marked Ukrainian influence, built in the 1920s and 1930s at the height of Ukrainian self-assertion within Poland.

The dark and intimate **interior** of a Uniate church is divided into three sections from west to east: the narthex or entrance porch, the main nave and the naos or sanctuary. Even the smallest of the Uniate churches will boast a rich iconostasis all but cutting off the sanctuary, which will contain the familiar icons of (working from left to right) St Nicholas, the Madonna and Child, Christus Pantocrator and, lastly, the saint to whom the church has been dedicated. Above the central door of the iconostasis (through which only the priest may pass) is the representation of the Last Supper, while to the left are busy scenes from the great festivals of the church calendar – the Annunciation, the Assumption and so on. The top tier of icons features the Apostles (with St Paul taking the place of Judas). Typically, the Last Judgement covers the wall of the narthex. This is usually the most gruesome of all the depictions, with the damned being burned, boiled and decapitated with macabre abandon.

The current pattern of *cerkwie* ownership varies: following the expulsions of Operation Vistula, many Uniate buildings were taken over by Roman Catholics and some by Orthodox worshippers. Despite the recent upsurge in Uniate activity, Roman Catholics still retain many of these buildings. Some have been returned – grudgingly in cases – to the Uniates, others are shared by both branches of Catholicism, while a good many still remain abandoned.

the way, and the driver might be persuaded to stop en route if you want to take a longer look at the scenery. At weekends the train is liable to be joined by contingents of local drinkers, some falling off the train at regular intervals and clambering drunkenly back on again.

Heading west from Majdan by road brings you to **NOWY ŁUPKÓW**, some 20km distant, a tiny place whose name is familiar to Poles for the nearby internment camp, to which many prominent Solidarity leaders were consigned during martial law. If you have access to transport, there's an interesting Uniate **cerkiew**, now a Roman Catholic church, which is worth a visit at the village of Smolnik, just to the east.

The western Bieszczady

There is a choice of routes out of the western Bieszczady back to Sanok. The main one runs from Nowy Łupków through **Komańcza** and a series of tiny Uniate villages such as **Rzepedź**. The other is a more obscure, winding road north from Cisna, via **Jabłonki** and **Baligród**. **Buses** run along both roads, while

Throughout the region you'll also find **Roman Catholic wooden churches** (*kościoły drewniane*), the architecture of which developed simultaneously, but with more Western influences, as you might expect. A few have domes round enough to pass as *cerkwie*, but most are wooden adaptations of styles used in lowland stone churches, with sloping shingle roofs, high bell-towers and protective surrounding verandahs. Six of the oldest and best-preserved were added to UNESCO's World Heritage list in 2003 (fair or not, Polish Catholics are better poised to sponsor their monuments than the minority Uniates). Undoubtedly the most stunning are those in **Dębno** (see p.495), east of Zakopane, and **Binarowa** (see p.368), north of Biecz, both with rich polychromy and an extraordinary variety of original furnishings. East of Krosno, the fifteenth-century church in **Haczów** (see p.366) is the oldest wooden church in Poland and has another fine interior, while the one in nearby **Blizne** (see p.367) is nearly as old and has a grand Last Judgment painted on its northern wall. The other two listed by UNESCO are the elegant, fifteenth-century church of St Leonard in **Lipnica Murowana** (see p.479) and the picturesque sixteenth-century church in **Sękowa** (see p.370).

The possibility of reaching many of the churches by public transport is limited, though a few are within striking distance of several of the larger towns. If you're driving, finding the churches won't be a problem: all are clearly signposted from the road as part of the nationwide Szlak Architektury Drewnianej (Trail of Wooden Architecture; the Małopolska route can be viewed at ⓦhttp://szlak.wrotamalopolski.pl/en, while the Bieszczady section is posted at ⓦwww.sanok.pl, under The Trail of Icons). Alternatively, the easiest way of having a close look is to visit the *skansens* at Sanok or Nowy Sącz, both of which contain complete churches.

Nearly all churches, whether Uniate, Orthodox or Roman Catholic, are kept **locked**. If you can, try to arrive thirty minutes before or after mass, held daily or at least weekly during the summer in most cases. Otherwise you'll have to find the key (*klucz*), generally in the hands of the local priest (*ksiądz*). Ask politely if you can see the church – *Dzień dobry, można/możemy (may I/may we) zobaczyć kościoł?* Many village priests teach school mornings, and it's bad form to come at lunch time, so your best bet is after 2pm. The process can be frustrating, and don't be surprised if you only get to see inside every third church you visit. When you do get into one, though, it's more than worth the trouble.

two daily **trains** run from Nowy Łupków to Zagórz (there are also services to Humenne in Slovakia).

Komańcza and Rzepedź

North from Nowy Łupków, buses and PKP trains take you to the village of **KOMAŃCZA**, whose churches illustrate graphically the religious divisions of the region. West of the main Sanok road is a modern church with an attractive iconostasis constructed in the 1980s by the majority local Lemk **Uniate** population – curiously, the ethnic cleansing effected by Operation Vistula on the surrounding region seems not to have touched Komańcza itself. Round the back of the church is a **museum** of Łemk culture (ask at the presbytery if the building's not open) housed in a traditionally decorated farm building and with a small but enjoyable collection of traditional costumes, religious artefacts and farming implements. Further up the same road, hidden away in the woods on the edge of the hill is a beautiful early nineteenth-century *cerkiew*, used by the tiny local **Orthodox** community, while back on the main road, opposite the railway station, is the **Roman Catholic** church, built in the 1950s for the village's Polish settlers – a rare commodity around here up until World War II. Roughly 1km further north, on a track leading uphill to the left under the railway bridge, is the **Nazarene Sisters' Convent**, something of a shrine for Polish tourists: it was here that Cardinal Wyszyński, the redoubtable ex-primate of Poland, was kept under house arrest in the mid-1950s during the Stalinist campaign to destroy the independence of the Catholic Church. The PTTK-run *Podkowiata* (☎013/467 7013; ❶) has basic **rooms** as does the adjacent seasonal **campsite**, while plenty of locals offer private accommodation (❶). The best place for a bite to **eat** is *Kawiarenka Eden*, back in the centre on the main road.

You could have a fascinating time searching the Komańcza area for **cerkwie**: modern maps of the region mark them clearly. There's a particularly fine and typically **Łemk-style Uniate Church** – this far north is firmly outside Boyk territory – from the 1820s just beyond at **RZEPEDŹ**, roughly fifteen minutes on foot from the train station. Nestled away on a hillside surrounded by tranquil clusters of trees, the church merges into the landscape – a common quality in *cerkwie* that may explain how they escaped the destruction of Bieszczady villages in the wake of Operation Vistula. Surprisingly, this one only closed down for ten years after World War II, reopening for Uniate worship in 1956. The interior of the church gives a sense of the twin strands of Uniate worship: on the one hand Western Madonnas and oil paintings; on the other the Eastern iconostasis, the absence of an organ (in the Orthodox tradition the choir provides all the music), the pale blue Ukrainian saints, and Ukrainian-script wall inscriptions. If you're planning on **staying** here, the best option is the *Willa Grażyna*, (☎013/467 9200, ⓦwww.hellenart.com/grazyna; ❶), an amenable little place right in the town centre. At a pinch, there are also a few run-down workers' holiday centres, including the central *Pod Suliłą* (☎013/467 8066; ❶). **Turzańsk**, 1.5km east of the village along the Baligród road, has another fine *cerkiew* in the most peaceful location imaginable; built in the 1830s, its interior decoration is preserved almost intact, a fine Rococo iconostasis included.

Jabłonki and Baligród

From Cisna, buses head to Lesko and Sanok, through a region which was the scene of some of the heaviest fighting between the Polish Army and the Ukrainian resistance. At **JABŁONKI** there's a large monument to **General Karol Swierczewski**, the veteran Spanish Civil War commander whose assassination in March

1947 goaded Poland's newly established communist authorities into a decisive all-out assault on the UPA, culminating in Operation Vistula (see box, p.356). Though these days the monument's looking decidedly neglected. There's an excellent **youth hostel** here (☎013/468 4026, ⓦwww.ptsm.com.pl/jablonki) with clean doubles (❶) and dorms (20–25zł); you'll also find a few basic **snack bars**.

Continuing north is the larger village of **BALIGRÓD**, once the headquarters of the Polish Army during the Polish–Ukrainian conflict. Evidence of its prewar ethnic population group lies in the **Jewish Cemetery**, a short walk northwest of the square; around a hundred tombstones remain, the oldest dating back to 1718. Sticking to the main road north out of Baligród brings you to Lesko after about 20km, where you join the main road back to Sanok.

The Beskid Niski

West from Sanok the main road, closely tracked by the slow rail line, heads towards Gorlice through the Wisłok valley, a pleasant pastoral route, with a succession of wooden villages in the hills of the **Beskid Niski** to the south. The main stops on the way to the provincial capital of **Gorlice** are the medieval centres of **Krosno** and **Biecz**, while back roads in this area are full of surprises, with plenty of *cerkwie* and other wooden churches, as well as specialized *skansens*: south of Krosno there's one in **Bóbrka** devoted to the local oil industry's history and, closer to the Slovak border, another in **Zyndranowa** focusing on Łemk architecture. Public transportation is irregular or even nonexistent south of the Gorlice–Krosno road, making the **hiking** routes leading east into the Bieszczady all the more appealing.

Krosno and around

At the heart of the country's richest oil reserves, **KROSNO** is the **petroleum** centre of Poland and also a major glassware producer. Prior to the discovery of oil, which helped the town grow wealthy in the late 1800s, Krosno had quite a record of mercantile prosperity: a favourable position on medieval trade routes meant it rapidly became one of the wealthiest Renaissance-era towns in the country, as evidenced by the sturdy burghers' mansions lining the square. Nowadays it has come back to life after a long slump, and the sizeable historic district, bustling with activity, is as good a place as any to conjure up the spirit of Poland's distant past. With a limited but satisfactory choice of accommodation and restaurants, Krosno also makes a suitable base for exploring the surrounding countryside.

The Town

From the adjacent train and bus stations, head downhill and turn right onto the main road, which leads to the hilltop Stare Miasto after about ten minutes. Ranged around the compact-looking **Rynek** are the Italianate merchants' houses fronted by arcaded passages – reconstructed in the nineteenth century in this case – characteristic of several towns in the southeast. Notable among these is the early sixteenth-century **Kamienica Wojtówska** (Wojtówska Mansion; no. 6) on the southwest side of the square, which boasts a finely decorated Renaissance portal with four ionic columns; and no. 27, dating from the same era, which belonged to **Robert Gilbert Portius Lanxeth**, a Scottish transplant who came to Krosno around 1620, converted to Catholicism (taking the name Wojciech), and grew rich importing wine from Hungary. South of the Rynek on ul. Franciszkanska is the

BESKID NISKI & SĄDECKI

SLOVAKIA

BESKID NISKI

BESKID SĄDECKI

25 km

N

▲ Sanok

◄ Rzeszów

◄ Rzeszów

◄ Tarnów

◄ Tarnów

◄ Tarnów

◄ Kraków

► Svidník & Prešov

► Poprad, Košice & Budapest

► Stará Ľubovňa

Blizne

Haczów

Rymanów

River Wisłok

Odrzykoń

Krosno

Iwonicz-Zdrój

Tylawa

Zyndranowa

Dukla Pass (500 m)

Barwinek

Bóbrka

River Jasiołka

Dukla

Jasło

Żmigród

River Wisłoka

Krempna

Grab

Binarowa

Biecz

Wójtowa

Libusza

Zagórzany

Sękowa

Owczary

Bielanka

Gorlice

River Ropa

Gładyszów

Zydnia

Uście Gorlickie

Muszynka

Stróże

Szymbark

River Biała

Brunary Wyżne

Banica

Wojkowa

Bobowa

Grybów

Florynka

Polany

Berest

Krzyżówka

Krynica

Tylicz

Powroźnik

Muszyna

Labowa

Nowa Wieś

Złockie

Szczawnik

Żegiestów-Zdrój

Milik

Andrzejówka

Nowy Sącz

Stary Sącz

Łomnica-Zdrój

River Poprad

Rytro

Piwniczna

River Dunajec

brick-facaded late-Gothic **Kościół Franciszkanów** (Franciscan Church), where there are a few Renaissance tombstones as well as, in the north aisle, Krosno's most famous monument, the Baroque **Oświęcim family chapel**. A sumptuously ornate piece – the ceiling is especially impressive – the chapel was designed by Italian architect Falconi in 1647–48 following the death Anna of Oświęcim, whose full-sized portrait hangs on the wall, next to that of her half-brother Stanisław. As guides will point out, the placement is more befitting husband and wife than half-siblings, which helped fuel the tale of incestuous love for which the pair is known. According to legend, Stanisław's boyish affection for Anna grew into a mature passion, leading him to abandon his position as courtier in Warsaw to petition the Pope for a dispensation. When he returned, his request granted, Anna, overwhelmed with joy, expired, and Stanisław soon followed, dying of sorrow. In fact, according to Stanisław's diary, there was no trip to Rome, and he returned to court soon after his beautiful half-sister's succumbed to fever in 1647, from where he made arrangements for the raising of the chapel, "for worship and glory of God and, along with that, my beloved sister".

North from the Rynek along ul. Sienkiewicza, the main shopping street, a statue on pl. Konstytucji 3 Maja commemorates **Ignacy Łukasiewicz**, the local man who sank what's claimed to be the world's first oil well in 1854 in the village of Bóbrka, 10km south of town (see p.366). North of the square on ul. Piłsudskiego is the large Gothic **parish church**, boasting an interior that almost overflows with treasures and curiosities. Note especially the fine, late-Gothic crucifix above the spirited Baroque altar; the ceiling polychromy; the richly carved choir stalls; the massive incense burner; and, to the right of the altar, the fifteenth-century *Coronation of Our Lady*, an exquisite painting from the Kraków school. Hanging on the walls, above the Baroque side chapels – the grandest was endowed by the Scot Portius – you'll find a series of large-scale seventeenth-century paintings by the Venetian Thomas Dolabella and his work-shop, mostly after Dutch and German engravings; highlights include St George battling a many-headed dragon and a gruesome *Last Judgment*.

Further down ul. Piłsudskiego you'll come two Krosno's two museums: housed in the sixteenth-century former bishops' palace, the highlight of the **Muzeum Podkarpacie** (Subcarpathian Museum; Tues–Sun: May–Oct 10am–4pm; Nov–April 10am–2pm; 6.5zł) is a large and lovingly polished display of early kerosene lamps, the revolutionary device of which Łukasiewicz was the inventor, including an elegant set of Secessionist lamps culled from around Europe. There's also a collection of paintings, with a series of attractive studies of Krosno by Matejko pupil Seweryn Bieszczad (1852–1923), and a series of objects found in recent excavations of the Rynek, including a thirteenth-century sword and fragments of medieval-era shoes. Across the street from the main museum, the excellent **Handicraft Museum** (Mon–Fri 8am–3pm, Sat 10am–2pm; 4zł) is full of surprises, including an intact barber shop from the 1920s, still in use until a few years ago; a seventeenth-century iron chest that the staff will let you open; and a wealth of old lathes, looms and other tools.

Most of the town's thriving prewar **Jewish community** (Jews arrived here in the fifteenth century) perished in the Bełżec concentration camp during 1942. The Jewish Cemetery, northwest of the Stare Miasto, across the River Wisłok on ul. Okerzej, still contains a hundred or so gravestones and a monument to those murdered by the Nazis.

Practicalities

Krosno's helpful **tourist information** office at Rynek no. 5 (☎013/432 7707, Ⓦ www.krosno.pl; Mon–Fri 9am–5pm, Sat 9am–4pm; June–Aug also Sun

9am–3pm) publishes a detailed English-language booklet on the town (6zł) and also has maps and can help you find a place to stay. Your best bet for **accommodation** is the *Śnieżka*, ul. Lewakowskiego 22 (☎013/432 3449, ☯www .hotel.sniezka.webpark.pl; ❸), a clean and professionally run five-room hotel in an old villa two blocks north of the train station. The *Elenai* on ul. Łukasiewicza 3 (☎013/436 4334; ❸) is more basic but larger, while the concrete-and-glass palace that is *Krosno-Nafta*, southwest of town on ul. Lwowska 21 (☎013/436 6212, ☯www.hotel.nafta.pl; ❸), caters to visitors from the oil industry and offers big discounts at weekends.

The main square is lined with places to **eat** and **drink**; including two competing Italian-owned establishments, *La Piazza* at no. 5 and *San Marco* at no. 6, both serving excellent pasta and pizza. For Polish food the best choice is *Wójtowska* at Rynek 7, which has a great cellar but rather slow service. If you're feeling more adventurous, there's also an Indian option, *Bengol*, at ul. Długa 15.

Around Krosno

The area around Krosno holds a number of worthy diversions, most of which are linked to Krosno by **bus**, even if there may only be the odd service a day and none at all at weekends. Historic sites of the petroleum industry may not rank high on most people's must-see lists, but the intriguing **skansen** (Tues–Sun: May–Sept 9am–5pm; Oct–April 7am–3pm; 5zł) at **BÓBRKA**, a tiny village 10km south of Krosno, makes a good stab in that direction. Its chief claim to fame rests on the presence of what's widely reckoned to be the world's first proper oil well, sunk here in 1854 by local pioneer Ignacy Łukasiewicz. The highlight of the *skansen*, devoted to the development of the oil industry that flourished in the eastern Carpathian foothills in the latter part of the nineteenth century, is the enjoyable collection of early drilling derricks and rigs. At "Franek", the oldest specimen, built in 1860, you can see the crude oil bubbling away at the bottom of its well, while "Janina", ten years younger, is still in low-level commercial operation. Clambering up onto the platforms of some of these antiquated setups helps you appreciate the demands – and dangers – involved in extracting energy resources.

At the far end of the area, which takes a good hour to walk around, is a set of old workshops along with Łukasiewicz's former offices, converted into an informative museum; highlights include a chart of the first oil field complete with the locations of the first drill shafts, and a fine collection of Art Deco kerosene lamps, including Łukasiewicz's prototype, made in 1853. To get to the *skansen* from Krosno, you'll have to take a local bus to the village and walk the remaining 2km through the forest.

Elsewhere in the region, the ruins of the fourteenth-century **Kamieniec**, one of the oldest fortresses in the Carpathian Mountains, can be seen at **ODRZYKOŃ**, 8km north of Krosno. At **HACZÓW**, 12km east, a medieval town settled by Swedes and Germans in the fourteenth century, there's a beautiful mid-fifteenth-century Gothic **church**. The oldest wooden structure in the country, and the largest wooden framed building left from its era in all Europe, the church retains much of its original polychromy and was added to UNESCO's World Heritage list in 2003. Illuminating the walls of the nave, there's a fine sequence of scenes of the Passion of Christ and the lives of the Virgin Mary and the saints, arranged in several layers, while in a side chapel there's an early fifteenth-century wood pietà thought to be miraculous. Unusually – and a sign of things to come, it is to be hoped – the church is generally kept open and charges admission (2zł). There are, however, no set hours; if you do find it locked look for the local priest, who lives opposite. Some 25km further northeast, the church in **BLIZNE**, also listed by UNESCO, is only slightly younger than its Haczów counterpart and features a spectacular *Last Judgment*.

Dukla and around

DUKLA, 24km south of Krosno, was for centuries the main mountain crossing point on the trade route from the Baltic to Hungary and central Europe. The location has also ensured an often bloody history, the most savage episode occurring during World War II, in August 1944, when more than 60,000 Red Army soldiers and 6500 Czech and Slovak partisans died during an eventually successful attempt to capture the mountain pass from its Nazi defenders.

Today Dukla is windy, quiet and bleak, with an eerie, whitewashed square that wouldn't be out of place in Spain or Italy. There are two sights of interest: the reconstructed **parish church**, a warm, pastel-coloured Baroque edifice with a pleasing Rococo interior; and the former Mniszech family palace across the road, badly battered in 1944 and now home to a local **museum** (Tues–Sun: May–Sept 10am–5pm; Oct–April 10am–3.30pm; 5zł), focusing on the chilling story of the wartime "Valley of Death." The surrounding park is graced with a collection of Soviet and Polish artillery.

For an **overnight stay** it's a choice between the basic *Dom Wycieczkowy* at no. 18 on the main square (☏013/433 0046), which offers simple doubles (●) as well as dorm beds (20zł per person); and the *Zajazd Galicja* (☏013/433 1455; ❷), an eight-room pension on the main road heading south out of town, where there's also a modest **restaurant**. The *Tawerna pod Piratem* on the square is a good place to go for a **drink**.

Around Dukla

Twenty-five kilometres south of Dukla, off the road to Barwinek and the Slovak border, the village of **ZYNDRANOWA**, really no more than a collection of farmhouses, is the location of another of the region's diverse collection of *skansen*s. Devoted to local **Łemk culture** (Tues–Sun: May–Sept 9am–4pm; Oct–April 10.30am–3.30pm; 5zł), it was established in 1966 by Teodor Gocz, an energetic local Łemk, in a set of wooden farm buildings themselves typical of Łemk rural architecture. The *skansen* houses a vivid collection of folk religious art, traditional costumes and venerable old agricultural implements, a display detailing the results of Operation Vistula (see box, p.356), and, equally poignantly, a set of Soviet uniforms and other military leftovers from the 1944 Battle of Dukla Pass, picked up in the surrounding woods over the past few decades. Interestingly, two hundred metres down the road a recently renovated **Jewish village house** (*chata*) has now been added to the *skansen*'s collection of buildings, containing a small but informative and well-presented exhibition about rural Jewish life and culture. Getting here without your own transport isn't easy. The only option is to take a local **bus** from Dukla to the signposted turnoff from the main road, just south of **Tylawa**, and walk or thumb a lift the remaining 5km.

West of Dukla, one or two buses a day cover the backwoods route to **Gorlice**, taking you along the edge of the hills. If you have transport, or have time to **hike**, the tiny roads leading south into the Beskid Niski are well worth exploring.

Biecz and around

BIECZ is one of the oldest towns in Poland and, thanks to a royal charter, was the conduit for nearly all the wine exported north from Hungary in medieval times. This trade thrived until the middle of the seventeenth century, when the Swedish invasion flattened the economy. Much of the town, fortunately, survived, and these days it's a placid and little-known rural backwater living amidst past architectural glories. A visit to Biecz and nearby Binarowa is feasible on a day trip by bus from Kraków (changing at Gorlice), but only if you start early. Trains stop near the centre, with the Stare Miasto a short walk up on the top of the hill, while the frequent buses and minivans from Gorlice drop you off right on the **Rynek**, dominated by the fifty-metre tower of the late Renaissance **town hall**, smartly renovated over the last few years. West along ul. Węgierka is the **parish church**, a massive Gothic brick structure complete with a forty-metre fortified bell-tower, containing Renaissance and Gothic pews, a fine seventeenth-century high altar and, from the same era, a noteworthy pulpit decorated with musicians. The church is open on weekdays (Mon–Fri 10am–1pm; 4zł) and for Sunday masses, though at other times you can peer in through the vestibule. Over the road, the wide-ranging and eccentric town **museum** (May–Aug Tues–Fri 8am–5pm, Sat 8am–4pm, Sun 9am–4pm; Sept–April Mon–Sat 8am–3pm, Sun 9am–4pm; 4zł), housed in an early sixteenth-century burgher's mansion once part of the town fortifications, is a real treat. Before entering, note the 9000-litre nineteenth-century wine vat in the courtyard left of the entrance – in the sixteenth century this would have been just one of many. Inside, the exhibition starts with the entire contents of an old pharmacy – sixteenth-century medical books, herbs and prescriptions included – and then moves on to an extraordinary collection of musical instruments and early phonographs, notably a sixteenth-century *dudy* (Carpathian bagpipe), several old hurdy-gurdys, and a colourful organ handmade in 1902 by "illiterate peasant" Andrzej Wojtanowski. There's also a full-scale seventeenth-century portrait of the town *Castellan* in a room full of heavy period furniture, and a selection of eighteenth-century farming implements and carpenters' tools. For the record, a Polish-only leaflet on town history informs you that Biecz once had a school of public executioners. They were kept busy: in 1614, for example, 120 public executions took place in the square. A second section of the museum, on the other side of the church at ul. Kromera 1 (Tues–Sat 8am–3pm; May–Aug also Sun 9am–4pm; 3zł), houses temporary exhibitions, a small display of old weapons and a roomful of early editions of the works of Polish historian Marcin Kromer, born in this building in 1512. There's also a 1558 map of Poland, said to be the first accurate one of the country.

For an overnight stay there are two **hotel** options: the shabby *Grodzka*, ul. Kazimierza Wielkiego 35 (☎013/447 1121; ❷), a former synagogue just east of town on the main Krosno road; and the upmarket but excellent-value *Centennial*, a haven of luxury at Rynek 8 (☎013/447 1576) with apartments in the main building (❻), smaller rooms at ul. Węgierska 13 (❺) and twenty percent discounts at weekends. **Places to eat** include the *U Becza*, a lively restaurant and bar in a fine old beamed mansion on the Rynek, or one of the *Centennial's* three restaurants: the two within the hotel feature French and Mediterranean cuisine at high prices, while the *Ogród*, next door at Rynek 6, is an excellent and cheap pizzeria.

Around Biecz

Several villages in this area have beautiful wooden churches. If you've got time for only one sortie, go to **BINAROWA**, 5km northwest of Biecz and reached by (infrequent) local buses or by taxi (20–25zł return with 30min at the church). Constructed around 1500, the timber **church** here, which was added to the UNESCO World Heritage list in 2003, rivals the better-known one at Dębno in the Podhale (see p.495). The **polychromy** is part original, part later additions, all meriting close attention. The marvellous Passion series near the altar dates from the seventeenth century; note the devils with huge eyes and long noses cowering in the background at the Resurrection. The harrowing Last Judgement scenes on the north wall date from the same period, while the exquisite floral motifs on the ceiling are older, painted soon after the church was built. Just as interesting is the **furniture**, mostly Baroque, including ornamented pews and painted confessionals from the 1600s. The altarpieces are from the eighteenth century but hold late-Gothic and Renaissance sculpture. The church is usually open during the day, and for mass at 6pm; the village priest lives across the street.

Gorlice and around

Just 12km southeast of Biecz along the main road, the smallish industrial city of **GORLICE** has, like Krosno, been for a century associated with the oil industry, Ignacy Łukasiewicz having set up the world's first refinery here in 1853. There's no real reason to stay, but the town's decent facilities makes a good base for excursions to the surrounding countryside. The local **museum**, just south of the battered hilltop Rynek on ul. Wąska (Tues–Fri 9am–4pm, Sat & Sun 10am–2pm; 3zł), is devoted to Łukasiewicz and the petroleum industry, with some interesting paintings of early oil wells. The town's other points of interest relate to the bloody, four-month World War I battle here between Russian and Austro-Hungarian forces. The legacy of the combat, which caused over 20,000 casualties, is the series of **war cemeteries** dotted around the town. Examples can be found west of the Rynek, near ul. Krakowska; 3km south of town, off ul. Łokietka; and, largest of all, in the Korczak district, 2km northwest of the centre. In all cases you'll find tombs of soldiers from around the region: Russians, Poles, Hungarians, Czechs and others. A short walk south is the **Jewish cemetery**. A monument commemorates local Jews murdered by the Nazis in the local forests or in the death camp at Bełżec.

The **bus** station is close to the centre on the northern side of town; the main **train** station is Gorlice Zagórzany, 4km east and serviced by frequent buses. The **tourist office**, ul. Legionów 3 (Mon–Fri 8am–6pm; ☎018/353 5091, ⓦwww.it.gorlice.pl), has accommodation information, books, maps and also a nice selection of local handicrafts and art; to get there from the Rynek turn left at the end of ul. Wróblewskiego. The best places to stay are two small **hotels**, both near the Rynek. The *Dwór Karwacjanów*, at ul. Wróblewskiego 10A (☎018/353 5601, ⓦwww.gorlice.art.pl; ❷) is a reconstructed fifteenth-century mansion with three basic but clean doubles above an art gallery/café. On the other side of the Rynek, next to the town museum, the *Hotelik*, ul. Wąska 11 (☎018/352 0238, ⓦwww.hotelik.gorlice.pl; ❸) has newer furniture, and the price includes a good breakfast. As both places are small, it's worth calling in advance. Alternatively, the very basic *Dom Nauczyciela* teachers' **hostel** at ul. Wróblewskiego 10 (☎018/353 5231; ❶), just down from the *Dwór*, will do at a pinch. For **places to eat** the *Dark Pub*, below the *Hotelik* has good meat dishes and an attractive back terrace; otherwise there are a handful of bars and pizzerias around the Rynek.

South of Gorlice

The hills south of Gorlice are less dramatic than the Bieszczady, but nevertheless excellent walking country. The people, predominantly Łemks (see box, pp. 356-357), provide a warm welcome to the relatively few hikers who do get to this area, and many of their settlements have fine examples of **cerkwie**. The easiest wooden church to get to from Gorlice is the UNESCO-listed Roman Catholic one at **SĘKOWA**, 7km southeast of Gorlice, straddling the historic borderline between the ethnic Polish and Łemk populations. A graceful structure with an extraordinary, two-tiered sloping roof that forms a rounded arcade, the church was a favourite subject of Polish artists from the Młoda Polska movement (see box, p.405). What you see today dates from the 1520s but was added onto – and in the case of World War I Austro-Hungarian soldiers who pillaged it for firewood, taken away from – several times in subsequent centuries. The building is usually locked outside of mass times (4pm Sundays), but the nuns who live opposite are likely to open it for you. It's no great loss, however, if you don't get in: most of the furnishings have either been lost or removed to the Diocesan Museum in Tarnów (see p.473) and what remains is unspectacular. Local **buses** (#6, #7 and #17) run here from the ul. Biecka stop outside the Gorlice bus station, dropping you a half-kilometre from the church. The oldest *cerkiew* in the area is in the village of **OWCZARY**, a further 5km south of Sękowa (bus #7 from Gorlice). Now used by Roman Catholics, the triple-domed church dates from the 1653 and preserves a rich, seventeenth-century iconostasis. If you're in the area in early July, consider heading twenty kilometres southeast to **ZYDNIA**, a remote village near the Slovak border that hosts the annual **Łemk and Ukrainian Festival** (*Vatra*), a three-day showcase for music from all over the Carpathian region.

Finally, horse-riding enthusiasts will want to consider visiting the **stables** at **GŁADYSZÓW**, 25km or so southeast of Gorlice (the best route, via Uście Gorlickie, is slightly longer). A group of Carpathian horses (*hucule*) is bred and maintained here, and the stables (☎018/351 0097, ⓦwww.skh .horsesport.pl) organizes horse-riding excursions in the surrounding hills, starting at around 25zł/hr. Basic accommodation is available (❶), and there's a rustic restaurant.

A good local **map** will greatly increase your enjoyment of this region: the best one is *Beskid Niski i Pogórze* (1:125,000), available in local bookshops or tourist offices. The most ambitious hiking **route**, marked in blue on the map, runs some 80km from Grybów, 12km west of Gorlice, along the Slovak border to Komańcza (see p.362). **Youth hostels** (July & Aug) are strategically placed at twenty- or thirty-kilometre intervals at Uście Gorlickie and Hańczowa (day 1), Grab (day 2), Barwinek (day 3) and Rzepedź (day 4), all with **bus stops** nearby (served irregularly from Gorlice and Nowy Sącz).

The Beskid Sądecki

West from Gorlice the hills continue through a range known as the **Beskid Sądecki**, another low-lying stretch of border slopes that is one of the most picturesque areas in the country. In addition to small market towns, scattered villages and traditional peasant farms, there's a sizeable Łemk population here and – enticingly – a wealth of old wooden churches. **Nowy Sącz**, the regional capital, has a handful of attractions but isn't the best base for exploration: you'll find better tourist facilities in the spa towns further south, notably the well-known cure centre of **Krynica**. The *Beskid Sądecki: Mapa Turystyczna* (1:75,000) is widely available and particularly helpful when searching out the numerous *cerkwie* scattered in and around the hills and valleys. Finally, north of Grybów the Baroque synagogue in nearby **Bobowa** will appeal to those interested in Jewish culture.

Nowy Sącz

NOWY SĄCZ, the uninspiring main market town of the Beskid Sądecki, nestles on the banks of the River Dunajec. Long an occasional royal residence, the town's heyday came in the fifteenth century, with the birth of the **Kraków-Sącz school** of painters, the first recognizably Polish school. After a long period of decline beginning at the end of the seventeenth century, Nowy

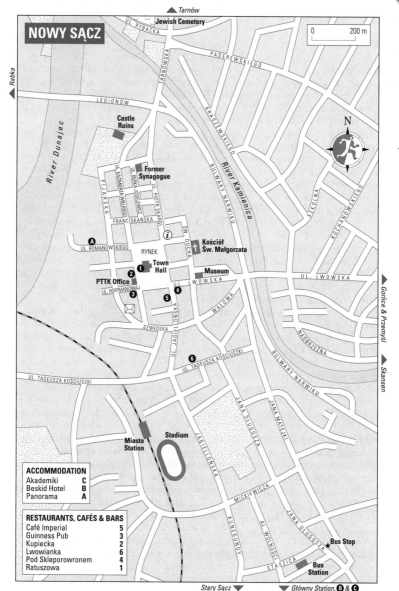

Sącz saw something of a revival late in the 1800s thanks to the development of the railways in Austrian-ruled Galicia. Then, following major damage in World War II – and the elimination of the town's Jews by the Nazis – Poland's new communist authorities invested in reconstruction and expansion, building the nondescript place you see today. As the largest town in the area, Nowy Sącz is now enjoying something of a resurgence, but for tourists the only draws are the **icon collection** in the local museum and the fine **skansen** out in the suburbs. Most of what the region has to offer can be visited on a day-trip by bus or train from Kraków.

The Town

The centre of the spacious **Rynek**, in the Stare Miasto, is occupied by the incongruous neo-Gothic **town hall** and, in summer, a collection of open-air terrace cafés and bars. Many of the surrounding burghers' houses have been renovated of late, as has the Gothic **Kościół św. Małgorzata** (St Margaret's Church) east of the square. The interior has been fully modernized, but you'll find fragments of Renaissance-era polychromy to the left of the altar.

Over the road on ul. Lwowska, the sixteenth-century Canonical House contains the town **museum** (Mon, Wed & Thurs 10am–5pm, Fri 10am–5.30pm, Sat–Sun 9am–2.30pm; 6zł, free Sun), sadly lacking pieces from the Kraków-Sącz school – look for these in the Diocesan Museum in Tarnów (see p.473) – but with a first-rate display of icons gathered from *cerkwie* in the surrounding region. The collection is not as extensive as that in Sanok, but amply demonstrates the distinctive regional style of icon painting, and includes some wonderful examples of the *Hodigitria* (Holy Virgin and Child) theme popular in Uniate iconography, as well as a seventeenth-century composite iconostasis assembled from different village churches. There's plenty of folk art on show, too, including some typically Polish *Christus Frasobliwy* sculptures, showing a seated Christ propping his mournful face on one hand. The influence of Orthodox-inspired themes is strongly evident in these locally produced works, many of which also retain the naive proportions of popular religious art.

The seventeenth-century **former synagogue** (Wed & Thurs 10am–2.30pm, Fri 10am–5.30pm, Sat & Sun 9am–2.30pm; 6zł), on ul. Bęrka Joselewicza in the former Jewish quarter north of the Rynek, where the popular nineteenth-century *tzaddik* Chaim Ben Halberstam had his base (before his even better-known son moved east to Bobowa; see p.377), houses a contemporary art gallery and a small photo exhibition of local Jewish life. An English-language brochure available here provides details of the layout of the Stare Miasto Jewish quarter; the north section of ul. Kazimierza Wielkiego alone used to have no less than four synagogues. The surrounding area was also the location of a Nazi wartime ghetto, eventually liquidated in August 1942, when its residents were either shot or transported to Bełżec concentration camp. The *ohel* of Ben Halberstam rests in the predictably overgrown **Jewish cemetery** on ul. Rybacka, over the river on the northern edge of Stare Miasto; a monument here commemorates the place where mass executions of local Jews were carried out by the Nazis. Back across the river on the northern edge of the Stare Miasto, the ruins of the **castle**, built during Kazimierz the Great's reign, give a good view over the valley below. After being used for mass executions of local civilians, the castle was blown up by the Germans in 1945.

About 3.5km east of town (bus #14 or #15 from the train station, bus station or ul. Lwowska; otherwise it's a brisk 40-minute walk or 12zł taxi ride), the **skansen** on Długoszewskiego 83 (May–Sept Tues–Sun 10am–5pm; Oct–April Mon–Fri 10am–2pm; 10zł, free Sun) has an extensive and still growing collection of regional peasant architecture. If you've already visited the *skansen* at Sanok, the buildings in the Łemk and Pogórzanie sections here will be familiar, a couple of recently erected wooden churches included. What you won't have seen before, however, are buildings like the fragments of a Carpathian Roma hamlet – realistically situated some distance from the main village – and the assortment of manor houses, including a graceful seventeenth-century specimen from Małopolska, complete with its original interior wall paintings. Other highlights include a comfortable farmstead from Zagorzyn, formerly the property of wealthy peasant Wincenty Myjak, an MP in Vienna from 1911 to 1918; and a nineteenth-century brick granary from Kicznia, featuring extravagantly carved wooden gables. The building interiors are opened only on the guided tours, which leave the entrance on the hour from 11am to 4pm; for an English tour call in advance (☎013/443 7708; no extra charge).

Practicalities

There are two **train stations**: the more central Miasto station handles only a few local trains, while all others use the Główny station, 2km south of town. Local buses shuttle from here to the town centre, via the **bus station** between al. Wolności and ul. Jana Długosza. The main **tourist office**, located at ul. Piotr Skargi 2 (Mon–Fri 8am–6pm, Sat 9am–2pm; ☎018/443 5597, ⓦ www .nowy-sacz.info), has a decent supply of maps and brochures and information about **private rooms** (❶). The PTTK office at Rynek 9 (Mon, Wed & Thurs 7am–3pm, Tues & Fri 11am–7pm; ☎018/443 7457) is useful for local **hiking** information and details of **rafting** trips in the Dunajec gorge (see p.498). There's an **Internet** café upstairs at Rynek 11.

At the top of the **accommodation** range is the professional, Orbis-run *Beskid Hotel*, a seven-storey concrete affair near the train station at Limanowskiego 1 (☎018/443 5770, ⓦ www.orbis.pl; ❺). Cheaper and more central, but not especially friendly, is the *Panorama*, offering very average rooms at ul. Romanowskiego 4a (☎018/443 7110; ⓔ poprad11@poczta.onet.pl; ❹). A good budget choice, very clean, but 3km south of the centre, is the *Akademiki* (☎018/449 9900, ⓔ osiedle@kirbud.pl; ❶), a brand new hotel catering to students but open to all.

Easily the best place to **eat** is *Ratuszowa*, offering good and inexpensive Polish dishes, including a full range of *pierogi*, in pleasant rooms underneath the town hall. More upscale, but looking rather the worse for wear, is *Kupiecka*, a cellar restaurant at Rynek 10. *Café Imperial*, ul. Jagiellońska 14, is clean and offers a bland, safe choice of pizza and meat dishes. In summer locals queue for ice cream at *Lwowianka*, ul. Tadeusza Kościuszka 9; there's also good cake and coffee here. Atmospheric spots for a **drink** include the *Guinness Pub*, at ul. Hoffmanowaj 3, with DJs at weekends; and *Pod Skleporowronem*, ul. Jagiellońska 1, an elegant underground café-bar stuffed with comfy wicker chairs, and a ground-level summer terrace.

The road around the Beskid Sądecki

The **Poprad River** – which feeds the Dunajec just south of Nowy Sącz – creates the broadest and most beautiful of the **Beskid Sądecki valleys**. A minor road runs its length to the Slovak border, which it then proceeds to trail for the best part of 25km. Meandering along this route is as good an experience of rural Poland as you could hope for, through fields where farmers still scythe the grass, with forests covering the hills above. Tracks lead off to remote hamlets, ripe for church-hunting, while along the main body of the valley you can boost your constitution at Habsburg-looking spa towns like **Krynica**. North of Krynica, the road follows another valley to Nowy Sącz, making a satisfying circuit.

Travelling into the Beskid Sądecki by public transport, there are regular **trains** plying the route from Nowy Sącz through the Poprad valley to Krynica, stopping at numerous village halts en route. Most Nowy Sącz–Krynica **buses**, however, bypass the Poprad valley entirely, taking the more direct Kamienica valley route to the north.

Stary Sącz

Nowy Sącz's smaller cousin town of **STARY SĄCZ**, 10km south (on the Krynica train line or buses #10, #11 or #43 from Nowy Sącz train station), is the oldest urban centre of the region. It grew around the convent founded by Princess Kinga, the public-spirited widow of thirteenth-century King Bolesław Wstydliwy ("the Shy"). She was long the centre of a local cult before finally being declared a saint by John Paul II in 1999. The town sits atop a hill between the Dunajec and Poprad rivers, whose confluence you pass soon after leaving Nowy Sącz.

Lined by one- and two-storey houses, mostly from the eighteenth century, Stary Sącz's ancient cobbled **Rynek** – one of the few such remaining – has an expansive feel to it. The town **museum** at Rynek 6 (Tues–Sat 10am–4pm, Sun 10am–1pm; 3zł), a fine seventeenth-century mansion, is a low-key but pleasant diversion into local history. It's also worth looking into the courtyard of the building at Rynek 21, where the walls and ceilings have been covered with murals by artists working in the characteristic local naive style, notably former owner Józef Racek, who died a few years back. The tiny town also has two noteworthy thirteenth-century churches: an imposing fortified Gothic **parish church** south of the square, subjected to the full Baroque treatment and with lovely pews and a fine organ from 1679; and the convent **Church of the Poor Clares**, to the east, its nave decorated by sixteenth-century murals depicting the life of the Blessed Kinga, who founded the convent in 1270 and subsequently entered it in 1280 following her husband's death, to whom the side chapel with a statue of her on the altar is dedicated.

The best place to **stay** is *Motel Miś*, Rynek 2 (entrance behind the square; ☎018/446 2451; ❷), a friendly little pension that also has a good **restaurant**.

The Poprad Valley

By local train or bus it's a scenic two-hour ride along the deep, winding **Poprad Valley** from Stary Sącz to Krynica, and if you're not in too much of a hurry there are a few places worth breaking your journey at before you reach the terminus.

At **RYTRO**, 16km down the line, there are ruins of a thirteenth-century castle, and lots of hiking trails up through the woods into the mountains; there's a very good PTTK hotel-cum-hostel, the *Pod Roztoką* (☎018/446 9151, ⓦwww .podroztoka.sacz.pl; ❷), offering en-suite doubles, triples and quads; as well as a number of *pensjonaty* and workers' holiday homes here too. Radziejowa summit (1262m), which is reached by following a ridge path to the southwest, is one of the more popular destinations, about two hours' walk from the village. The stretch of the river after nearby **PIWNICZNA**, where you can walk across the border into Slovakia (passport required), is one of the most attractive parts of the valley, with trout-filled water of crystalline clarity. If you're not hoping to catch the fish yourself, call in at the *Karczma Poprad* restaurant in **ZEGESTIÓW-ZDRÓJ**, a tiny spa town further down the valley, for some excellent fried trout.

MUSZYNA, next along the valley, has sixteen mineral springs, spa buildings, and the ruins of a thirteenth-century castle, just north of the train station. The town **museum** (Mon–Fri 10am–noon & 2pm–4.30pm; 4zł), installed in a seventeenth-century wooden tavern, focuses on old furniture, folk art and agricultural implements. With transport, fans of wooden churches can have a field day in this area, bearing in mind the usual caveats about access and opening hours. *Cerkwie* worth seeking out are at **Milik**, **Andrzejówka**, **Złockie** (Masses 9.30am, 11am & 4pm) – the last a characteristic three-towered Łemk structure from the 1860s with an impressive iconostasis and collection of religious art – and **Szczawnik**, now a Roman Catholic church. From Muszyna the Poprad runs south and the railway heads off to the north towards Krynica, passing through the village of **Powroźnik**, which has a low-ceilinged seventeenth-century *cerkiew* (Mass 11am; otherwise the priest is uncooperative) with a fabulous iconostasis.

Krynica

If you only ever make it to one spa town in Poland, it should be **KRYNICA**. Redolent of *fin-de-siècle* central Europe, its combination of woodland setting, rich mineral springs and moderate altitude (600m) have made it a popular resort for over two centuries. In winter the hills (and a large skating rink) keep the holiday trade coming in.

From the train and bus stations at the southern end of town, ul. Nowotarskiego heads towards the flowerbed-filled centre of the resort, where you'll come across a fine array of **sanatoria**, including pump rooms ancient and modern, assorted therapeutic centres, and mud-bath houses. The main place to try the local waters is the **Pijalnia Wód Mineralnych** (Pump Room; daily 6am–6pm; entrance free, but it costs a złoty or two to take the waters), a typically ugly 1960s building seemingly modelled on the main train station in Warsaw, boasting fountains and huge indoor plants within. Rent or buy a tankard from the desk before heading for the taps, where the regulars will urge you to try the purply-brown Zuber. Named after the professor who discovered it in 1914, it is reckoned to be the most concentrated mineral water in Europe – it's certainly the worst-smelling. Zdrój Główny, a mixture of three or four different waters, is one of the more palatable brews. Upstairs there's a concert hall that sees plenty of action during the summer season. The nearby **Stary Dom Zdrojowy**, an imposing Habsburg-era hospital, makes for a welcome change of style.

The town's other place of interest is the **Muzeum Nikifora** (Nikifor Museum; Tues–Sun 10am–1pm & 2–5pm; 6zł), occupying the bright-blue Romanówka, a nineteenth-century timber villa on Bulwary Dietla, just behind the Stary Dom Zdrojowy. The museum is devoted to the life and work of the self-taught Łemk artist Nikifor (1895–1968), a legend in Polish folk art whose style and spidery handwriting will be familiar if you've visited the *Loch Camelot* café in Kraków (see p.438). In a style reminiscent of Lowry's scenes of industrial northern England, Nikifor painted Beskid landscapes and *cerkwie* but is perhaps best known for imagining extravagant, Habsburg-style train stations in paintings of villages that were actually far from the railway line. Also look for the Fabryka Dolarów (Dollar Factory) from 1930, perhaps a wry suggestion of what was needed following the 1929 stock market crash.

At the northern end of the promenade, past a statue of Mickiewicz and a late nineteenth-century wooden church, a **funicular train** (every 20–30min daily: May–June 10am–7pm; July–Aug 10am–8pm; Sept 10am–6pm; Oct–April 10am–5pm; 5zł one way, 8zł return) ascends the nearby Góra Parkowa (741m) and drops you at the top for an enjoyable overview of town. Alternatively, a number of paths lead up the hill.

Practicalities

Tourist **information** is at the northern end of the centre, inside the Jaworzyna cinema at Piłsudskiego 8 (Mon–Fri 9am–5pm, Sat 10am–2pm, longer hours in summer; ℡018/471 6105); the staff can help you find **private rooms** (❶) and book rafting trips on the Poprad and Dunajec rivers. The town website (🌐www.krynica.pl) is also useful.

Accommodation is never a problem in Krynica: there are innumerable *pensjonaty* and old workers' rest homes as well as higher-quality hotels and villas. Cheaper places are concentrated east of the town centre, on ul. Pułaskiego or ul. Świdzinskiego, and often advertise room rates outside. One of the best is *Willa Janka*, Pułaskiego 28 (℡018/471 2057; ❶–❷), a family-run place with en suites and rooms with shared facilities surrounded by a well-tended garden. A more central choice, with similar-quality rooms but an excellent restaurant and English-speaking staff, is *Wisła*, uphill from the main sanatorium at ul. Bulwary Dietla 1 (℡018/471 5512; ❷). A more upmarket and elegant option is the grand old *Witołdówka*, ul. Bulwary Dietla 10 (℡081/471 5577, 🌐www .witoldowka.com.pl; ❺), in a fine old wooden building with comfortable en suites with TV. Nearby, at ul. Bulwary Dietla 13, the *Małopolanka* (℡018/471 5896, 🌐www.malopolanka.com.pl; ❺), is a private and professionally run spa/pension offering a full range of massages, mud baths and the like; there's also an **Internet café** you can use even if you're not staying.

For **eating and drinking**, *Lilianka*, Piłsudskiego 9, is a simple café that serves up the best pastries and cakes in town, while the restaurant in the *Wisła* pension serves Polish staples with aplomb. Nearby, the slightly smarter *Pizzeria-Kaviarnia Węgierska Korona*, ul. Bulwary Dietla 18, offers so-so pizzas, good pasta and risotto dishes, and excellent ice cream in its café section. *Pod Zieloną Górką* is a lively pizzeria and pub-style **bar** at the northern end of Nowotarskiego. Local specialties such as *oscypek* (smoked cheese) are available in the **market** running along Bulwary Dietla.

East from Krynica

The hill region **east from Krynica** towards the Slovak border is particularly rich in attractive villages and *cerkwie*, including some of the oldest in the country. Those in **Wojkowa**, which boasts a fine Rococo iconostasis, **Muszynka** and **Tylicz** are all worth a visit. Six kilometres east of Krynica, Tylicz figures in Polish history as base camp of the Confederates of the Bar (1768–72), a failed aristocrat-led revolt against growing tsarist control of the country (see "Contexts", p.665). The Tylicz *cerkiew* is adjacent to a wooden Roman Catholic church from the seventeenth century, the latter boasting an especially rich interior. Local buses run occasionally from Krynica; otherwise you could hire a taxi or walk (start from ul. K. Puławskiego in Krynica).

North from Krynica

North from Krynica buses run to Nowy Sącz and Grybów, to the west of Gorlice. For the first 6km both routes follow the main road to Krzyżówka, where the road divides. For Nowy Sącz you continue through the wooded groves of the Sącz Beskids, via villages such as Nowa Wieś and Łabowa.

The **Grybów road** is an even more attractive backroads route, due north through open countryside. The village of **BEREST**, 5km north of the main Nowy Sącz road, is a real treat. Set back from the road in pastoral surroundings, its nineteenth-century *cerkiew* (Mass 11am) is an archetype of the harmonious beauty of this region's wooden churches, with a rich iconostasis composed of seventeenth- and eighteenth-century icons. Just a couple of kilometres up the road is **POLANY**, where the village *cerkiew* (Mass 9.30am) has a Baroque pulpit and iconostasis and nineteenth-century polychromy. From here to Grybów the valley is a gorgeous riverside route; if you have a car, a brief detour south to Brunary Wyżne, then on to the border villages of Banica and Izby, is worthwhile, as all three have magnificent wooden *cerkwie*.

From **GRYBÓW**, there are buses and trains west to Nowy Sącz, east to Gorlice or north to Tarnów (see p.472). Heading north, the first stop after Grybów is **STRÓŻE**, home to the unusual *Skansen Pszczelarstwa* (Apicultural Skansen; Mon–Fri 9am–4pm, Sat & Sun 11am–4pm; 3zł), devoted to the long-standing beekeeping traditions of the Beskid Sądecki. Many of the more than a hundred whimsically carved former hives on display date from the nineteenth century or earlier; there's also a simple, hollow log that was used to keep bees as early as the thirteenth century. Uphill from the main exhibition are hundreds of real beehives, source of various honey products you'll find on sale at the entrance. Curiously, the *skansen* also boasts a dozen or so ostriches, as well as goats and ponies.

A further 8km along the Tarnów road lies the small town of **BOBOWA** (Bobover in Yiddish), an important centre of Hassidism in the nineteenth century, when the Nowy Sącz *tzaddik* Shlomo Halberstam moved his yeshiva here. His son Ben Zion carried on the tradition, establishing schools throughout Małopolska and also earning fame as a musician. During World War II he helped other Jews, including his son Solomon, flee the Nazis before being murdered in L'viv in 1942. After the war Solomon refounded the yeshiva in Brooklyn, and by his death in 2000 the Bobover community had spread to London, Toronto and elsewhere. Today, old photos of the Halberstam-dynasty rabbis hang in the entrance of the Bobowa **synagogue**, off the northeast side of the tree-lined Rynek. Built in 1756 and one of the best preserved in Poland, the building was damaged by the Nazis, then restored and used as a vocational school from 1955 to 1994, when it was given to the Kraków Jewish community. Ask the barber (*fryzjer*) next-door to unlock the building for you (Mon–Fri 10am–5pm; 10zł per individual or group). The interior, whitewashed during communist times, was originally decorated with frescoes, including a large-scale depiction of Jerusalem; a few segments have been uncovered by the current restoration project, and more may come to light. Like many synagogues, this is a "nine fields" building, with four pillars dividing the main room into nine equal sections, at the front of which stands the vivid blue **Aron ha Kodesh**, a triumph of folk Baroque. There's also a fifteenth-century **parish church** north of the Rynek, with a wooden roof, a rough stone floor and interesting primitive paintings on the walls. Frequent buses from Gorlice will drop you off right on the Rynek; coming by train alight at the Bobowa Miasto station and walk uphill to the square. There are no hotels or restaurants here, but you'll find excellent, locally made ice cream in a café on the west side of the Rynek.

Travel details

Trains

Krynica to: Nowy Sącz (12 daily; 2hr).
Lublin to: Chełm (15 daily; 1hr 15min); Gdańsk (2 daily, including 1 overnight with sleepers; 6–8hr); Kielce (4 daily; 3hr); Kraków (2 daily; 5hr); Przemyśl (1 daily; 4hr 30min); Warsaw (12 daily; 2–3hr); Zamość (1 daily; 3hr).
Nowy Sącz to: Kraków (9 daily; 2hr 30min–4hr); Krynica (12 daily; 2hr); Muszyna (13 daily; 1hr 30min); Tarnów (13 daily; 2hr).

Przemyśl to: Kraków (7 daily; 3hr); Lublin (1 daily; 4hr 30min); Rzeszów (19 daily; 1hr 15min–1hr 45min); Tarnów (11 daily; 2–3hr 15 min); Warsaw (2 daily; 6–7hr).

Rzeszów to: Kraków (15 daily; 2–2hr 30min); Krosno (2 daily; 3hr); Przemyśl (19 daily; 1hr 15min–1hr 45min); Tarnów (24 daily; 1–1hr 30min); Warsaw (4 daily; 5–7hr); Zamość (1 daily 4hr 30min).

Sandomierz to: Kielce (1 daily; 3hr); Warsaw (2 daily; 5hr); Zamość (1 daily; 3hr).

Sanok to: Kraków (1 daily; 5hr 30min); Krosno (5 daily; 1hr); Zagórz (13 daily; 15min).

Zagórz to: Nowy Łupków (2 daily; 1hr 30min); Sanok (13 daily; 15min); Ustrzyki Dolne (2 daily; 2hr 30min).

Zamość to: Kraków (2 daily; 6–8hr); Rzeszów (1 daily; 4hr 30min).

Buses

Biała Podlaska to: Białystok (3 daily; 3hr 10min); Siemiatycze (hourly; 1hr 20min).

Chełm to: Kodeń (2 daily; 3hr); Lublin (10 daily; 2hr); Włodowa (13 daily; 1hr 30min); Zamość (4 daily; 1hr 20min).

Kazimierz Dolny to: Lublin (14 daily; 1hr 40min); Rzeszów (1 daily; 4hr); Sandomierz (1 daily; 2hr); Warsaw Stadion (1 daily; 3hr); Warsaw Zachodnia (2 daily; 3hr 30min).

Krosno to: Bóbrka (Mon–Fri 10 daily; 20min); Dukla (Mon–Fri 8 daily, Sat & Sun 3 daily; 40min); Haczów (Mon–Fri 8 daily, Sat 4, Sun 2; 20min); Rzeszów (14 daily; 1hr 30min); Sanok (12 daily; 1hr); Ustrzyki Dolne (2 daily; 2hr); Ustrzyki Gorne (Jul–Aug 3 daily; 3hr 30min).

Krynica to: Nowy Sącz (every 30min; 1hr).

Lublin to: Biała Podlaska (hourly; 3hr); Chełm (10 daily; 1hr 40min); Kazimierz Dolny (14 daily; 1hr 40min); Kielce (3 daily; 4hr); Kozłówka (8 daily; 1hr); Nałęczów (24 daily; 50min); Puławy (every 30min; 1hr 30min–2hr); Przemyśl (1 daily; 5hr); Sandomierz (5 daily; 2hr 15min); Siemiatycze (hourly; 1hr 30min); Zamość (every 30min; 2hr).

Nowy Sącz to: Gorlice (10 daily; 1hr 10min); Katowice (5 daily; 3hr 20min); Kraków (hourly; 2hr 10min); Krynica (every 30min; 1hr); Lublin (4 daily; 6hr); Muszyna (5 daily; 1hr 30min); Sanok (1 daily; 3hr 15min); Rzeszów (1 daily; 3hr 30min); Szczawnica (10 daily; 1hr 20min); Warsaw (2 daily; 7hr); Zakopane (8 daily; 2hr 30min).

Przemyśl to: Jarosław (21 daily; 40min); Krosno (3 daily; 3hr); Łańcut (9 daily; 1hr 10min); Lublin (1 daily; 5hr); Rzeszów (12 daily; 1hr 40min); Sanok (5 daily; 2hr); Ustrzyki Dolne (4 daily; 3hr); Zamość (1 daily; 4hr).

Rzeszów to: Krosno (14 daily; 1hr 30min); Łańcut (Mon–Fri 24 daily, Sat 14 daily, Sun 8 daily; 30min); Krosno (12 daily; 1hr 45min); Lublin (8 daily; 4hr); Przemyśl (12 daily; 1hr 40min); Sanok (10 daily; 2hr); Ustrzyki Dolne (4 daily; 3hr 20min); Ustrzyki Górne (Mon–Fri 2 daily; Sat & Sun 1 daily; 5hr 10min); Zamość (2 daily; 4hr 15min).

Sandomierz to: Kazimierz Dolny (1 daily; 2hr); Kielce (8 daily; 2hr); Lublin (5 daily; 2hr 15min); Rzeszów (4 daily; 2hr); Warsaw Zachodnia (8 daily; 5hr 45min).

Sanok to: Cisna (July & Aug 4 daily, rest of year 2 daily; 2hr); Krosno (12 daily; 1hr); Lesko (12 daily; 25min); Przemyśl (5 daily; 2hr); Rzeszów (10 daily; 2hr); Ustrzyki Dolne (4 daily; 1hr 10min); Ustrzyki Górne (Mon–Fri 2 daily, Sat & Sun 1 daily; additional services in July & Aug; 2hr 40min).

Zamość to Lublin (every 30min; 2hr); Rzeszów (2 daily; 4hr 15min); Szczebrzeszyn (16 daily; 30min); Zwierzyniec (Mon–Fri 10 daily, Sat & Sun 6 daily; 45min).

International trains

Nowy Sącz to: Budapest (1 overnight); Košice (1 daily; 3hr 30min).

Przemyśl to: Kiev (2 daily; 12hr); L'viv (4 daily; 4hr 30min); Odessa (1 daily; 17hr).

International buses

Biała Podlaska to: Brest (3 daily; 4hr).

Przemyśl to: L'viv (8 daily; 3hr 20min).

Kraków, Małopolska and the Tatras

BALTIC SEA | KALININGRAD PROVINCE (RUSSIA) | LITHUANIA

BELARUS

GERMANY

N

CZECH REPUBLIC

AUSTRIA | SLOVAKIA

UKRAINE

CHAPTER 4 # Highlights

✳ **Krakow's Stare Miasto**
One of the most wonderfully preserved old-town complexes in Europe. See p.394

✳ **The Wawel** Kraków's hilltop castle-and-cathedral complex was for centuries the political heart of the nation. See p.409

✳ **Kazimierz** The old Jewish quarter of Kraków, now the centre of a burgeoning bar scene, is buzzing with visitors day and night. See p.417

✳ **Auschwitz-Birkenau** The infamous Nazi death camp, on the outskirts of Oświęcim, is a compelling memorial to man's inhumanity. See p.445

✳ **Ojców national park** This beautiful area of woodland makes for a great day out from Kraków. See p.454

✳ **Częstochowa** This shrine to the Black Madonna is the most popular Catholic pilgrimage site in Poland. See p.456

✳ **The Tatras** Poland's most grandiose mountain range offers all the skiing and hiking possibilities that you could ask for. See p.492

✳ **Górale folk music** The *górale* (highlanders) who live in the foothills of the Tatras have preserved folk and music traditions to a much greater extent than their lowland compatriots. See box, p.499

△ Niedzica castle

Kraków, Małopolska and the Tatras

The Kraków region attracts more visitors – Polish and foreign – than any other in the country, and the attractions are clear enough from just a glance at the map. The **Tatra mountains**, which form the border with Slovakia, are Poland's grandest and most beautiful, snowcapped for much of the year and markedly alpine in feel. Along with their foothills, the **Podhale**, and the neighbouring, more modest peaks of the **Pieniny**, they have been an established centre for hikers for the best part of a century. And with much justice, for there are few ranges in Europe where you can get so authentic a mountain experience without having to be a committed climber. The region as a whole is perfect for low-key rambling, mixing with holidaying Poles, and getting an insight into the culture of the indigenous *górale*, as the highlanders are known. Other outdoor activities are well catered for, too, with raft rides down the Dunajec Gorge in summer and some fine winter skiing on the higher Tatra slopes.

With a population of just under one million, **Kraków** itself is equally impressive: a city that ranks with Prague and Vienna as one of the architectural gems of Central Europe, with a Stare Miasto which retains an atmosphere of *fin-de-siècle* stateliness. A longtime university centre, its streets are a cavalcade of churches and aristocratic palaces, while at its heart is one of the grandest of European squares, the Rynek Główny. The city's significance for Poles goes well beyond the aesthetic though, for this was the country's ancient royal capital, and has been home to many of the nation's greatest writers, artists and thinkers, a tradition retained in its thriving cultural life. The Catholic Church in Poland has often looked to Kraków for guidance, and its influence in this sphere has never been greater – Pope John Paul II was archbishop of Kraków until his election in 1978. Equally important are the city's Jewish roots. Until the last war, this was one of the great Jewish centres in Europe, a past whose fabric remains clear in the old ghetto area of Kazimierz, and whose culmination is starkly enshrined at the death camps of **Auschwitz–Birkenau**, west of Kraków.

This chapter also takes in an area which loosely corresponds to **Małopolska** – a region with no precise boundaries, but which by any definition includes some of the historic heartlands of the Polish state. Highlights here, in country-side characterized by rolling, open landscape, market towns and farming villages, include **Tarnów**, the region's most handsome historic town after Kraków itself;

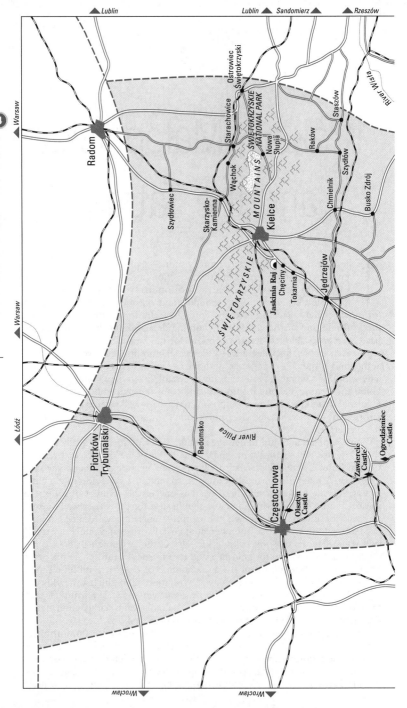

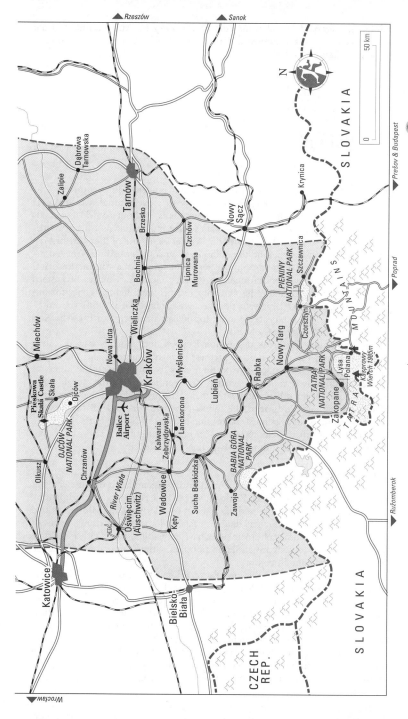

Kielce, springboard for hikes into the **Świętokrzyskie mountains**; and the pilgrim centre of **Częstochowa**, home of the Black Madonna, the country's principal religious symbol.

Kraków

KRAKÓW, the ancient capital of Poland and residence for centuries of its kings, was the only major city in the country to come through World War II essentially undamaged. Its assembly of monuments, without rival in Poland, is listed by UNESCO as one of the world's twelve most significant historic sites. The city is indeed a visual treat, with the **Wawel** being one of the most striking royal residences in Europe, and the old inner town a mass of flamboyant monuments. For Poles, these are a symbolic representation of the nation's historical continuity, and for visitors brought up on grey Cold War images of Eastern Europe they are a revelation. It's certainly a surprisingly Italianate city for this part of Europe, thanks largely to the Renaissance tastes of Poland's sixteenth-century rulers – who repeatedly lured top Italian architects north of the Alps with promises of huge bags of cash.

As a year-round city-break destination Kraków doesn't really have a tourist season, although the place is at its prettiest in spring, summer and the depths of winter. You'll need a good two to three days to do justice to the historical centre and the Wawel; much longer if you're keen to explore the city in depth – a rich and varied urban patchwork that takes in the Jewish heritage areas of **Kazimierz** and **Podgórze**, the monasteries and parklands of the western suburbs, and the gritty Stalinist-era housing projects of **Nowa Huta**. For those eager to roam further afield, Kraków is an important public transport hub and much of this chapter is within day-trip distance of the city.

Some history

The origins of Kraków are obscure. An enduring legend has it that the city was founded by the mythical ruler **Krak** on Wawel Hill, above a cave occupied by a ravenous dragon. Krak disposed of the beast by offering it animal skins stuffed with tar and sulphur, which it duly and fatally devoured. In reality, traces of human habitation from prehistoric times have been found in the city area, while the first historical records are of **Slavic peoples** settling along the banks of the Wisła here in the eighth century.

Kraków's position at the junction of several important east–west trade routes, including the long haul to Kiev and the Black Sea, facilitated commercial development. By the end of the tenth century, it was a major market centre and had been incorporated into the emerging **Polish state**, whose early **Piast** rulers made Wawel Hill the seat of a new bishopric and eventually, in 1038, the capital of the country. Subsequent development, however, was rudely halted in the mid-thirteenth century, when the Tatars left the city in ruins. But the urban layout established by **Prince Bolesław the Shy** in the wake of the Tatar invasions, a geometric pattern emanating from the market square, remains to this day.

Kraków's importance was greatly enhanced during the reign of **King Kazimierz**. In addition to founding a **university** here in 1364 – the oldest in Central Europe after Prague – Kazimierz rebuilt extensive areas of the city and, by giving Jews right of abode in Poland, paved the way for the development of a thriving **Jewish community**. The advent of the Renaissance heralded Kraków's emergence as an important European centre of learning, its most famous student (at least, according to local claims) being the young **Nicolaus Copernicus**.

King Sigismund III Waza's decision to move the capital to Warsaw in 1596, following the Union of Poland and Lithuania, was a major blow. The fact that royal coronations (and burials) continued to take place on Wawel for some time after was little compensation for a major loss of status. Kraków began to decline, a process accelerated by the pillaging of the city during the Swedish invasion of 1655–57.

Following the **Partitions**, and a brief period as capital of a tiny, notionally autonomous republic, the Free City of Kraków (1815–46), the city was incorporated into the **Austrian** province of Galicia. Habsburg rule was comparatively liberal – especially after Galicia gained a measure of autonomy in 1868 – and Kraków (in contrast to Russian-dominated Warsaw) enjoyed more or less untrammelled cultural and intellectual freedom. The city became the focus of all kinds of underground political groupings: **Józef Piłsudski** began recruiting the avowedly nationalist Polish Legion here prior to World War I, and from 1912 to 1914 Kraków was **Lenin**'s base for directing the international communist movement and for the production of *Pravda*. Artists and writers attracted by the new liberalism gathered here too. Painter **Jan Matejko** produced many of his stirring paeans to Polishness during his residency as art professor at the Jagiellonian University, and the city was centre of the **Młoda Polska** (Young Poland) movement – an Art-Nouveau-inspired flowering of the arts which drew in Stanisław Wyspiański, Stanisław Witkiewicz, and virtually every other creative spirit who happened to be around town at the time.

The brief interlude of independence following World War I ended for Kraków in September 1939 when the **Nazis** entered the city. Kraków was soon designated capital of the so-called General Government, which covered all those Polish territories not directly annexed to the Reich. Hans Frank, the notorious Nazi governor, moved into the royal castle on Wawel Hill, from where he exercised a reign of unbridled terror, presaged by the arrest and deportation to concentration camps of many professors from the Jagiellonian University in November 1939. The elimination of the **Kraków ghetto**, most of whose inhabitants were sent to nearby Auschwitz (Oświęcim), was virtually complete by 1943.

The main event of the immediate postwar years was the construction of the vast **Nowa Huta steelworks** a few miles to the east of the city, a daunting symbol of the communist government's determination to replace Kraków's Catholic, intellectually oriented past with a bright new industrial future. The plan did not succeed: the peasant population pulled in to construct and then work in the steel mills never became the loyal, antireligious proletariat the communist party hoped for. Non-communist intellectual life continued to thrive in any case, thanks in large part to the publication of *Tygodnik Powszechny*, a Kraków Catholic weekly which was then the only independent newspaper in Eastern Europe. Kraków's reputation as a centre of conservative Catholicism was enhanced by the election of **Pope John Paul II** in 1978, who until then had been archbishop of Kraków.

Nowa Huta also had an unforseen environmental impact on the city, with atmospheric **pollution** wreaking havoc on the fine old facades of the centre – prompting the Polish government to declare Kraków an "ecological disaster area" in the 1970s. A thorough clean-up operation in the 1990s gave the city's historic buildings a new sheen and reduced air pollution to negligible levels. The city centre has also been transformed by an influx of post-communist private capital – local and foreign – with Western-style shops, cafés and restaurants springing up in abundance, lending parts of the Stare Miasto a cosmopolitan, decidedly affluent feel that confirms the city's return to the place proud Kraków residents have always maintained it belonged, in the heartland of Central Europe. The historic ensemble of the square and its immediate surroundings have also benefited from a comprehensive face-lift, allowing both locals and tourists to appreciate buildings such as the Mariacki Church and the Sukiennice in all their pristine beauty.

Arrival, information and getting around

The recently modernized **Balice airport** (information on ☎012/411 1955), 15km west of the city, handles both domestic and international flights. It's a small place – so don't expect a wealth of cafés, restaurants and shopping malls. Buses #192 (to ul. Basztowa, right on the edge of the Stare Miasto) and #208 (to the central train station) connect it with the city centre (30–40min). Taxis are always available, too, and cost anything between 40 and 70zł depending on your bargaining skills and the time of day – fares rise by fifty percent between 11pm and 5am.

Kraków Główny, the central **train station**, a grand Habsburg-era building, is within walking distance of the Stare Miasto (Old Town). The **left-luggage** office at the station is open 24 hours a day. The main **bus station** (Dworzec PKS) is right outside the train station. For where to find tram and bus information and tickets, see opposite.

Arriving by car, major roads from all directions are well signposted, though once in the centre you'll need to cope with trams, narrow streets, heavy daytime traffic and, in much of the centre, heavily enforced zonal **parking restrictions**, with the risk of wheel clamps on illegally parked vehicles. The Rynek Główny and much of its immediate surroundings are now completely closed to private vehicles, and the local police no longer show much sympathy even for wayward foreigners. There's a conveniently placed **guarded car park** just behind Staro-wiślna 13, a five-minute walk southeast of the centre, but it soon fills up.

Information and maps

The **municipal tourist office** (Mon–Fri 8am–8pm, Sat & Sun 9am–5pm; ☎012/430 2646, ⓦwww.krakow.pl), occupying a circular pavilion in the Planty between the train station and the Stare Miasto, can give advice on accommodation possibilities, hands out brochures listing museum and gallery opening times, and sells maps; while the **Centrum Informacji Kulturalnej** (Cultural Information Centre; Mon–Fri 10am–7pm, Sat 11am–7pm; ☎012/421 7787, ⓦwww.karnet.krakow2000.pl), next to the Orbis office at ul. św. Jana 2, just off the Rynek, provides information on upcoming cultural events and sells *Karnet* (3zł), a small-format Polish- and English-language listings booklet. Otherwise, your best source of information is likely to be *Kraków in your Pocket* (from newsstands and bookshops;

@ www.inyourpocket.com; 5zł), a remarkably comprehensive English-language source of restaurant listings, bar recommendations and Yellow-Pages-style information that is updated five to six times a year. If you can read Polish, the Kraków edition of daily newspaper *Gazeta Wyborcza* carries local **listings** in its *Co jest grane* supplement on Fridays. For a lowdown on the bar and club scene consult the monthly, tabloid-sized *City Magazine*, or the glossier, fortnightly *Aktivist* (@ www.aktivist.pl), both of which are given away free in the trendier bars and cafés.

Copernicus, Demart and Falk publish serviceable **maps** of Kraków in various formats, all of which are available from bookshops and Ruch kiosks: Copernicus's 1:20,000 foldout version includes up-to-date public transport routes and only costs a few złoty.

Orientation and getting around

Kraków is bisected by the **River Wisła**, though virtually everything of interest is concentrated on the north bank. At the heart of things, enclosed by the **Planty** – a green belt following the course of the old ramparts – is the **Stare Miasto**, the Old Town, with its great central square, the **Rynek Główny**. Just south of the Stare Miasto, looming above the riverbank, is **Wawel**, the royal castle hill, beyond which lies the old Jewish quarter of **Kazimierz**. This whole central area is compact enough to get around **on foot**; recently introduced restrictions mean that much of the Stare Miasto – including the Rynek – is virtually car-free.

Exploring further afield, the **inner suburbs** have more character than usual thanks to the lack of wartime damage, the modern apartment blocks being interspersed with the odd villa and nineteenth-century residential area. **Trams** in and out of these areas are plentiful, start early and run till late at night – routes radiate out from the Planty to the suburbs, and useful services are detailed in the text. **Buses**, which complement the trams and keep similarly long hours (with night buses taking over from around 11pm to 5am), provide the main links with outer suburbs and nearby towns such as Wieliczka. **Tickets** are purchased at kiosks and shops displaying the MPK symbol, or from the driver for a 0.50zł surcharge. You can buy single tickets valid for one journey (2.40zł); 24-hour tickets (10zł); 48-hour tickets (18zł); or 72-hour tickets (24zł). Unless you have one of the one-, two- or three-day tickets, you'll need a separate ticket to travel on night buses (5zł). Bear in mind that public transport is subject to regular price hikes, so expect changes. Remember to punch your ticket at both ends on entering the bus or tram – if you're caught without a valid ticket, you'll be fined 40zł on the spot. Annoyingly, large pieces of luggage (including backpacks) require their own individual ticket (holders of one-, two- or three-day tickets are exempt from this); failure to follow this arcane regulation will incur another fine.

Taxis cost around 6zł initial charge, followed by 3zł per kilometre. Remember to make sure the driver turns on the meter, and that from 11pm to 5am rates go up by half. There are ranks around the centre of town at pl. św. Ducha, Mały Rynek, pl. Dominikański, pl. Szczepański, pl. Wszystkich Świętych, ul. Sienna (roughly opposite the main post office) and at the main train station. Calling a radio taxi, such as Wawel Taxi (@ 0800 666 666) or ExpresTaxi (@ 0800 111 111), can work out significantly cheaper. There's a special subsidized taxi service for people with disabilities, using a small fleet of **minibuses** adapted for **wheelchair access** (6am–10pm; @ 9633 or 644 5555).

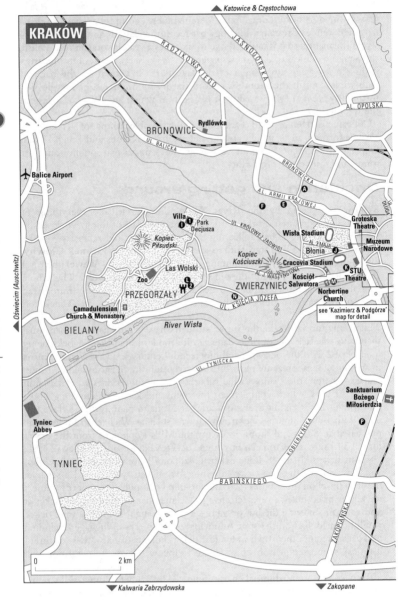

Accommodation

Kraków is becoming one of Central Europe's prime city destinations, so you're well advised to book ahead with **hotels**, particularly during the summer. **Prices** for hotel rooms are higher than in most Polish cities, especially in the Stare

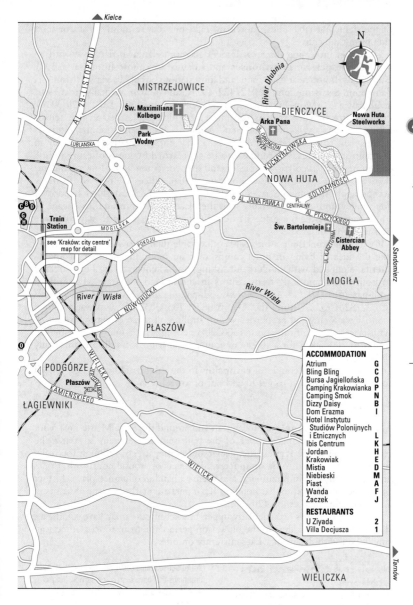

Map labels:

▲ Kielce

N

MISTRZEJOWICE

AL. 29-LISTOPADA

Św. Maximiliana Kolbego †

Park Wodny

LUBLANSKA

BIEŃCZYCE

River Dłubnia

Arka Pana †

UL. OBROŃCÓW KRZYŻA

KOCMYRZOWSKA

Nowa Huta Steelworks

NOWA HUTA

AL. JANA PAWŁA II

PL. CENTRALNY

SOLIDARNOŚCI

AL. PTASZYCKIEGO

C B D
G H

Train Station

MOGILSKA

see 'Kraków: city centre' map for detail

AL. POKOJU

Św. Bartolomieja †

UL. KLASZTORNA

Cistercian Abbey

▶ Sandomierz

MOGIŁA

River Wisła

River Wisła

UL. NOWOHUCKA

PŁASZÓW

O

PODGÓRZE

Płaszów

WIELICKA

JEROZOLIMSKA

KAMIEŃSKIEGO

ŁAGIEWNIKI

WIELICKA

▶ Tarnów

WIELICZKA

ACCOMMODATION

Atrium	G
Bling Bling	C
Bursa Jagiellońska	O
Camping Krakowianka	P
Camping Smok	N
Dizzy Daisy	B
Dom Erazma	I
Hotel Instytutu Studiów Polonijnych i Etnicznych	L
Ibis Centrum	K
Jordan	H
Krakowiak	E
Mistia	D
Niebieski	M
Piast	A
Wanda	F
Żaczek	J

RESTAURANTS

U Ziyada	2
Villa Decjusza	1

Miasto area where the top-grade places charge rates on a par with Central Europe's priciest. Price is not always an accurate guide to quality, with many of the older unrenovated hotels charging similar prices to the newer, international-style establishments. It's rare (but not entirely impossible) to find a hotel room in or around the Stare Miasto for under 300zł a double, although things are slightly cheaper in Kazimierz and other suburban areas within walking distance of the sights. Reliable cheap hotels do exist but they're mostly a bus or tram ride from the centre.

There's an increasing range of budget accommodation in Kraków, with an array of inexpensive **guesthouses** and **hostels** to choose from (see p.393). Both Waweltour, near the train and bus stations at ul. Pawia 8 (Mon–Fri 8am–8pm, Sat 8am–2pm; ☎012/422 1921), and Jordan, virtually next door at ul. Pawia 12 (Mon–Fri 8am–6pm, Sat & Sun 9am–2pm; ☎012/429 3416), can organize **private rooms** (❸), most of which are located in flats ten or fifteen minutes' walk from the Stare Miasto – ask carefully about addresses if you want to avoid being stuck a long way out. Alternatively, especially in the train station area, you're likely to be approached by locals offering rooms, sometimes at markedly lower prices (and of a correspondingly lower standard) than those quoted at the Waweltour and Jordan offices. Before you formally accept, apply the obvious rules: establish the exact location, don't hand over any money until you've actually seen the place, and be prepared to engage in some haggling over the price, particularly if you're planning to stay for more than a couple of days.

If you want something a bit more comfortable than a private room and don't like the idea of living in hotel rooms, then an increasing number of **apartments**, equipped with modern furnishings and kitchenette, are being offered to both short- and long-term visitors in and around the Stare Miasto. Both Sodispar (☎0602 247 438, ⓦwww.sodispar.pl) and Old Town Apartments (☎022/820 93227, from the UK ☎0871 733 3032, ⓦwww.warsawshotel .com) have a range of properties within strolling distance of central locations, with prices ranging from about 130–220zł per night for a one- or two-person studio to 200–600zł for a three- or four-person flat – rates drop dramatically the longer you stay.

Finally, there are a couple of **campsites** in the suburbs, although you'll need to use public transport to get in and out of town.

Hotels

Many of the city's **hotels** are located in and around the Stare Miasto area, with a cluster within striking distance of the train station. Generally speaking, the closer you get to the Rynek, the pricier and noisier it gets, although the really upmarket places tend to be on quieter side streets or around courtyards. Prices are slightly cheaper in Kazimierz, and there's a handful of choice places further out in the suburbs. Note that hotels in Kazimierz are marked on the "Kazimierz and Podgórze" map on pp.420–421.

A number of hotels – particularly upper-bracket places – may have significant **discounts** on rooms during the off-season period: the main tourist offices can supply you with details of what's currently on offer.

Near the train and bus stations

Atrium ul. Krzywa 7 ☎012/430 0203, ⓦwww .hotelatrium.com.pl. Modern, comfortable and stylish place – imagine a Scandinavian furniture showroom and you'll know what the rooms look like. Just off the bustling ul. Długa, and within minutes of both the stations and the Stare Miasto. ❽

Europejski ul. Lubicz 5 ☎012/423 2510, ⓦwww.he.pl. Undistinguished mid-range place close to the train station, and accordingly popular.

Old-fashioned rooms come with parquet floors and furnishings that have seen some service, but the bathrooms are sparkly new. En suites and rooms with shared facilities. ❻–❼

Mistia ul. Szlak 73a ☎012/633 2926, ⓦwww .mistia.org.pl. Decent budget hotel owned by a Polish local government institute ten minutes' walk north of the stations. Rooms are narrow and sparsely furnished but they're clean and well looked after throughout, and are available with en-suite shower or with shared facilities. ❹–❺

Polonia ul. Basztowa 25 ☏ 012/422 1233, ⓦ www.hotel-polonia.com.pl. Best of the hotels close to the train station, although rooms come in various stages of modernization. At least the en suites have clean bathrooms and TV; the rooms with shared bathrooms are a bit less salubrious. ❹–❻

Warszawski ul. Pawia 6 ☏ 012/424 2100. Good location right across from the train station, and thoughtfully renovated rooms with classy fittings. ❽

The Stare Miasto and around Wawel

Amadeus ul. Mikołajska 20 ☏ 012/429 6070, ⓦ www.hotel-amadeus.pl. Fairly new four-star in a fine old mansion, with orangey-pink colour schemes, chintzy fittings, and good standards of service. ❾

Campanile ul. św. Tomasza 34 ☏ 012/424 2600, ⓦ www.campanile.com.pl. Relatively new French-run place on the northeastern edge of the Stare Miasto with small but snazzy en suites – each comes with tea/coffee-making facilities. ❼

Classic ul. św. Tomasza 32 ☏ 012/424 0303, ⓦ www.hotel-classic.pl. Thoroughly modern place with bright en suites in orange and avocado colours, superbly located for the centre. ❽

Copernicus ul. Kanonicza 16 ☏ 012/424 3400, ⓦ www.hotel.com.pl. Medium-sized luxury joint in a historic building on the way to Wawel. Supreme levels of comfort and service – with the addition of a small swimming pool in the basement – though not all rooms have bathtubs, so ask. Worth the high price tag. ❾

Elektor ul. Szpitalna 28 ☏ 012/423 2317, ⓦ www .hotelelektor.com.pl. Recent addition to the city's growing stock of smart hotels. Fine central location, swish apartment-style rooms, upmarket bar and restaurant, all with prices to match. ❾

Floryan ul. Floriańska 38 ☏ 012/431 1418, ⓦ www.floryan.com.pl. Small hotel offering very stylish downtown rooms with modern furnishings. Recommended if you want a change from the faded glories on offer elsewhere. Prices depend on room size. ❻–❽

Fortuna ul. Czapskich 5 ☏ 012/422 3143, ⓦ www .hotel-fortuna.com.pl. Enjoyable, reasonably priced little hotel with simply furnished rooms in easy walking distance west of the university district. ❻

Fortuna Bis ul. Piłsudskiego 25 ☏ 012/430 1025, ⓦ www. hotel-fortuna.com.pl. Small but plush annexe of the *Fortuna*, offering en suites that wouldn't look out of place in any international three-star. The building itself has a lot of character – two houses knocked together to create a maze

of staircases and landings. Stylish pub-restaurant on site. ❻

Francuski ul. Pijarska 13 ☏ 012/422 5122, ⒺⓁ francusk@orbis.pl. Elegant, comfortable old hotel, recently renovated though still retaining some of its retro feel. A well-established favourite with upmarket travellers. ❾

Grand ul. Sławkowska 5/7 ☏ 012/421 7255, ⓦ www.grand.pl. Luxury hotel in a good central location. Habsburg-era fittings add a touch of class. ❾

Logos ul. Szujskiego 5 ☏ 012/631 6200, ⓦ www .hotel-logos.pl. Modern building aimed at business people and tourists alike, featuring fully equipped but rather sparse rooms. An easy walk west of the Stare Miasto. Weekend discounts. ❻–❽

Maltański ul. Straszewskiego 14 ☏ 012/431 0010, ⓦ www.maltanski.com. Top-quality hotel with an intimate, pension-like feel. Rooms boast a nice blend of modern and traditional furnishings and come with TV, video and minibar – and most of the bathrooms have tubs. ❽

Monopol ul. św. Gertrudy 6 ☏ 012/422 7015, ⓦ www.rthotels.com.pl. A good, well-maintained budget choice, even if the corridors are a little gloomy and the rooms come with standard issue 1970s brown furnishings. En suites as well as rooms with showers but shared WCs. ❺–❻

Pod Różą ul. Floriańska 14 ☏ 012/424 3300, ⓦ www.hotel.com.pl. Venerable, once-atmospheric place which preserves a *belle époque* sumptuousness in the reception areas and restaurant, and has largish, decent-quality rooms, each decorated in a different style. ❽

Pollera ul. Szpitalna 30 ☏ 012/422 1044, ⓦ www .pollera.com.pl. Charming, increasingly popular hotel with good central location and Art-Nouveau decor – notably the original Wyspiański stained-glass window in the foyer. Mixed bag of old-fashioned, parquet-floored rooms and modern, carpeted ones. ❽

PTTK Wyspiański ul. Westerplatte 15 ☏ 012/422 9566, ⓦ www.hotel-wyspianski.pl. Thoroughly modernized hotel with en-suite rooms decorated in warm colours. Bigger rooms with balconies cost a few extra złotys. ❼

Rezydent ul. Grodzka 9 ☏ 012/429 5495, ⓦ www .rthotels.com.pl. Newish hotel just off the Rynek Główny, offering swish modern rooms in a medieval building. ❾

Royal ul. św. Gertrudy 26–29 ☏ 012/421 5849, ⓦ www.royal.com.pl. Smart, recently renovated former army officers' hotel close to Wawel, popular with small tour groups. Rooms in the plush western wing are more expensive than the standard en suites in the eastern wing. ❻

Saski ul. Sławkowska 3 ☎012/421 4222, ⓦwww
.hotelsaski.com.pl. Art Nouveau-era building (and
featuring an old cage-lift still in working order) in
useful but noisy central location with comfy rooms
furnished with a mixture of old and new. En suites
with TV, as well as rooms with shared facilities.
⑤–⑦

Senacki ul. Grodzka 51 ☎012/421 1161 ⓦwww
.senacki.krakow.pl. Another prime location in
the heart of the Stare Miasto, offering small but
cosy en suites decked out in warm salmony
colours, although most have shower rather
than bath. ⑧

Wawel Tourist ul. Poselska 22 ☎012/424 1300,
ⓦwww.wawel-tourist.com.pl. Unspectacular
place in a central location south of the Rynek.
Simple en-suite rooms with an odd jumble of
furniture – you'll feel as if you're in either the
1960s or the 1860s depending on which room
you get. ⑤–⑥

Wentzl Rynek Główny 19 ☎012/430 2665,
ⓦwww.wentzl.pl. Intimate, twelve-room hotel above
a well-known restaurant, offering spacious rooms
with parquet floors, classy rugs and – in some cases
– direct views onto the main square. ⑦

Wit Stwosz ul. Mikołajska 28 ☎012/429 6026,
ⓦwww.wit-stwosz.com.pl. Bright, comfortable
rooms in a historic house, just off the Mały Rynek.
Good price for the quality and location. ⑦

Kazimierz

Alef ul. Szeroka 17 ☎012/421 3870, ⓦwww
.alef.pl. Tiny hotel with four rooms, all of which
are decked out in pre-World War II style,
complete with authentic furnishings and nick-
nacks. Restaurant with frequent live klezmer
music on site. ⑥–⑦

Astoria ul. Józefa 24 ☎012/432 5010, ⓦwww
.astoriahotel.pl. Serviceable modern three-star with
pinky-red furnishings, shower and TV. ⑦

Eden ul. Ciemna 15 ☎012/430 6565, ⓦwww
.hoteleden.pl. Cosy late-medieval building with
plush, tastefully decorated rooms, staff that pay
good attention to detail, and authentic Judaica
scattered around the place. ⑥

Franciszek ul. Miodowa 15 ☎012/430 6506,
ⓦwww.franciszekhotel.com.pl. Newish, medium-
sized place with pleasant pastel-shade en suites,
all with TV and tea/coffee-making facilities. Good
value for the area, and there are weekend
reductions. ⑥

Kazimierz ul. Miodowa 16 ☎012/421 6629,
ⓦwww.hk.com.pl. Recently renovated hotel
decked out in warm hues, offering newly furnished
rooms with TV, desk and minibar. Just west of the
Tempel synagogue. ⑥–⑦

The suburbs

Dom Erazma ul. 28 Lipca 17A ☎012/625 4142,
ⓦwww.erazm.pl. Unexciting but soothing pastelly
rooms in a medium-sized hotel, 5km out of the
centre in leafy suburban streets on the northeastern fringes of Las Wolski forest. Bus #152 from
Basztowa. ⑦

**Hotel Instytutu Studiów Polonijnych i
Etnicznych** ul. Jodłowa 13 ☎012/429 7110,
ⓔwieslawa@apus.filg.uj.edu.pl. The "Hotel of the
Polish and Ethnic Studies Institute", this Eighties'
vintage student accommodation is now open to all
comers. Doubles and triples with bright parquet
floors, most of which come with TV and bathtubs.
Idyllically located on the edge of Las Wolski forest,
but a 15min bus ride out of town – #209, #229,
#239 and #249 from Salwator go past the access
road. ④

Ibis Centrum ul. Syrokomli 2 ☎012/299 3300,
ⓦwww.ibishotels.com. Standards of comfort and
service that you would expect from the international chain, at a price that's just about right. As
in other Ibis hotels, all rooms come with proper
double beds. A ten-minute walk west of the
Wawel, or tram #1, #2 or #6 from pl. Wszystkich
Świętych. ⑥

Korona ul. Kalwaryjska 9/15 ☎012/656 1780,
ⓕ012/656 1566. Located south of the centre in
Podgórze (see map on pp.420–421), within walking
distance of Kazimierz. Unspectacular box-like en
suites in subdued colours, some with new furnishings and freshly tiled bathrooms. Tram #10 from
the train station. No breakfast, but plenty of cafés
nearby. ④

Krakowiak al. Armii Krajowej 9 ☎012/637 7304,
ⓦwww.wsp.krakow.pl/hotel. Modestly priced
teachers' hotel on the west side of town, lurking
below the flanks of the much more prominent
Novotel. The en-suite rooms are simple in the
extreme, but are bright and clean. Breakfast not
included, but there's a student canteen next door.
Bus #208 or #228 from the train station to the
Continental stop. ④

Niebieski ul. Flisacka 3 ☎012/431 2711, ⓦwww
.niebieski.com.pl. Pleasant Wisła-side location near
the Norbertine monastery in Zwierzyniec, offering
cosy rooms in warm colours. Go for one of the top-
floor attic rooms if you can. A twenty-minute walk
or a brief tram ride (#1, #2 or #6) from the Stare
Miasto. ⑧

Wanda ul. Armii Krajowej 15 ☎012/637 1677,
ⓔwanda@orbis.pl. Modern, functional three-star
4km west of the centre, offering a friendlier, more
intimate feel than its immediate neighbour, the
Novotel. Directions as for the *Krakowiak* (see
above). ⑧

Guesthouses

Kraków can boast a handful of informal, pension-style places where you'll get a higher level of comfort than in private rooms or hostels, but less in the way of service than you would expect in a full-blown hotel. Although they're not officially classified under any particular title, we'll call them **guesthouses** for want of a better term.

Bed & Breakfast ul. Wiślna 10 ☎012/421 9871, ✉wislna@wp.pl or ✉dziela@sztuki.com.pl. Eighteen rooms in an old-town apartment block a few steps away from the Rynek, with an eccentric assortment of old and new furnishings. Rooms either resemble a contemporary design showroom or your grandma's parlour – which one you get very much depends on luck. Most are en suite but some share facilities in the hallway. Basic breakfast. ❹–❺

Jordan ul. Długa 9 ☎012/421 2125 and 430 0292 ⓦwww.nocleg.jordan.pl. Neat rooms in a good location, with shower, TV and modern furniture – frumpy carpets being the only drawback. Breakfast in a characterful brick-lined cellar. ❺

Tournet Guest Rooms ul. Miodowa 7 ☎012/292 0088 ⓦwww.accommodation.krakow.pl. A handful of cramped but neat doubles and a triple, each with en-suite shower, located in the heart of Kazimierz (see map pp.420–421). No breakfast but there are plenty of cafés nearby. ❺

Hostels, student hostels and campsites

There's a growing number of privately owned, backpacker-oriented **hostels** in Kraków, each offering clean accommodation in a laid-back, friendly environment with – in most cases at least – free use of a washing machine. They tend to be small places that fill up quickly, and advance booking is advised whatever the season. Less intimate in style but perfectly comfortable are the **student hostels**, which are open to non-residents throughout the summer months (July & Aug) and will rent out rooms at other times if space allows. There's a reasonable choice of suburban **campsites** in Kraków and, although they're invariably several kilometres from the centre, all are well served by public transport.

Hostels

Bling Bling ul. Pędzichów 7 ☎012/634 0532, ⓦwww.blingbling.pl. In an apartment block 800m northwest of the train station, and offering spick-and-span eight- and twelve-bed dorms with modern furnishings. 45zł per person including basic breakfast.

Dizzy Daisy ul. Pędzichów 9 ☎012/292 0171, ⓦwww.hostel.pl. Bright and clean place in a courtyard next door to *Bling Bling*, with laminated floors and homely decor. Mixture of ten-bed dorms and a couple of triples. 50zł per person.

Mama's Hostel ul. Bracka 4 ☎012/429 5940, ⓦwww.mamashostel.com.pl. Superbly situated on the upper floors of an apartment house just south of the Rynek. A couple of dorm rooms and a large homely common room with kitchen. 50zł per person including bread-roll breakfast.

Nathan's Villa ul. św. Agnieszki 1 ☎012/422 3545, ⓦwww.nathansvilla.com. Welcoming place in a side street midway between the Stare Miasto and Kazimierz, offering bunk bed dorms and a couple of quads, common-room area and plenty of locker space. Breakfast included. 50–60zł per person.

Student hostels

Bursa Jagiellońska ul. Śliska 14 ☎012/656 1266, ⓦwww.bursa.krakow.pl. Clean and comfortable university student dorm south of the river on the western edge of the Podgórze district. Choice of doubles, triples and quads, with bathroom shared between every two or three rooms. Breakfast available for a few extra złotys. Discounts for ISIC holders. Tram #10 from the train station to the Smolki stop. ❸

Piast ul. Piastowska 47 ☎012/622 3100, ⓦwww.piast.bratniak.krakow.pl. A large university dormitory 3km west of the centre popular with summer language students. Lots of regular student accommodation plus some higher-grade rooms with own bathroom. There's a cafeteria on site, and a self-service laundry (open sporadically). Take tram #4 from the train station to the Wawel sports stadium stop (not to be confused with Wawel castle), followed by a 10min walk down Piastowska.

En suite doubles and rooms with shared facilities. ❸–❹
Żaczek al. 3 Maja 5 ☎012/633 1914, ⓦwww .hotele.studenckie.pl. Busy university student hostel close to the main youth hostel, and the easiest to get rooms during the summer months. Tram #15 or #18 from the train station. Simple doubles with shared facilities as well as en suites. ❷–❹

Campsites

Krakowianka ul. Żywiecka Boczna 2 ☎012/268 1133, ⓦwww.krakowianka.com.pl. Located in leafy suburbia just off the Zakopane road, 6km south of town. Includes bungalows (❸), a restaurant and outdoor swimming pool. Tram #8 from pl. Wszystkich Świętych. May–Sept.

Smok ul. Kamedulska 18 ☎012/429 7266. Privately run site 4km west of town on the main Oświęcim road, well signed in both directions. In a pleasant suburban setting with plenty of greenery round about, and within walking distance of both Las Wolski and Zwierzyniec. Buses #109, #209, #229, #239 and #249 from Salwator stop off 100m east of the campsite access road. Open all year.

The City

The heart of the city centre is the **Stare Miasto**, the Old Town, bordered by the lush, tree-shaded city park known as the **Planty**. The **Rynek Główny** is the focal point, with almost everything within half an hour's walk of it. A broad network of streets stretches south from here to the edge of **Wawel Hill**, with its royal residence, and beyond to the Jewish quarter of **Kazimierz**. Across the river, the suburb of **Podgórze** was the site of the wartime ghetto, and is within striking distance of the concentration camp at **Płaszów**. Further out to the west, the green cone of **Kopiec Kościuszki** (Kościuszko's Mound) and the attractive woodland of **Las Wolski** provide the targets for strollers and cyclists. Connoisseurs of megalomaniac urban planning will not want to miss **Nowa Huta**, the Stalinist model suburb 7km to the northeast.

Rynek Główny

The **Rynek Główny** was the largest square of medieval Europe – a huge expanse of flagstones, ringed by magnificent houses and towering spires. Long the marketplace and commercial hub of the city, it's an immediate introduction to Kraków's grandeur and stateliness. By day the square hums with crowds and commercial bustle, its size such that no matter how much is going on, you're never left feeling cramped for space. Architecturally the square is pretty much unchanged since its *fin-de-siècle* heyday, boasting as fine a collection of period buildings as any in Central Europe and beyond. This, combined with echoes of the events played out here, such as the Prussian Prince Albrecht of Hohenzollern's act of homage to Sigismund the Old in 1525, or Kościuszko's impassioned rallying call to the defence of national independence in 1794 (see box, pp.428–429), provides an endlessly renewable source of interest and inspiration. Once hooked, you'll find yourself constantly gravitating back towards the place. It's also worth exploring the stately network of passageways and recently restored Italianate courtyards leading off from the front of the square, many of them enlivened by cafés and restaurants that have colonized the area since the advent of the market economy.

The Rynek is more open today than it used to be. Until the last century, much of it was occupied by market stalls, a tradition maintained by the flower sellers and ice-cream vendors, and by the stalls in the **Sukiennice**, the medieval cloth hall at the heart of the square dividing it into west and east sections, the latter dominated by the **Kościół Mariacki** (St Mary's Church).

The Sukiennice

Dominating the Rynek from its central position, the medieval **Sukiennice** is one of the most distinctive sights in the country – a vast cloth hall built in the fourteenth century and remodelled in the 1550s, when an undulating facade topped with gargoyles was added to the upper storey by Florentine stonemason Santi Gucci (c.1530–1600). Its commercial traditions are perpetuated by a **covered market**, which bustles with tourists and street sellers at almost any time of year. Inside, the stalls of the darkened central arcade display a hotch-potch collection of tourist tat and genuine craft items from the Podhale region. Popular buys include amber jewellery, painted boxes in every shape and size and thick woollen sweaters from the mountains. Prices are inevitably inflated, so if you're travelling on to the south, it's better to wait until you get to one of the Tatra region markets, such as the one in Nowy Targ (see p.432). The colonnades on either side of the Sukiennice were added in the late nineteenth century in an attempt to smarten up the Rynek and provide a home for a brace of elegant terrace cafés, most famous of which is the **Noworolski** on the Sukiennice's eastern side. The centre of Kraków social life in the years before World War I (Lenin was one of the more famous regulars), the café boasted a series of sumptuously decorated Art-Nouveau salons, of which one – with a separate entrance from the rest – was a ladies'-only tearoom. The café was confiscated by the Nazis in 1939 and made into a German-only club, but resumed its status as Kraków's prime coffee-and-cakes venue after the war. Many of the *belle-époque* interiors were renovated in the 1990s, making it well worth a visit (see p.438) – although the locals who used to idle away the afternoon over tea and *sernik* have been almost totally replaced by tourists.

Occupying the upper floors of the Sukiennice is the **Gallery of Nineteenth-Century Polish Art** (Tues & Thurs 11am–6pm, Wed & Fri 9am–3.30pm, Sat & Sun 10am–3.30pm; 7zł, free on Sun; entrance from the eastern side), which serves up an impressive selection of the nation's artistic heavyweights, with the painter of epic patriotic themes Jan Matejko getting most of the exposure. His *Homage of Prussia*, showing Albrecht of Hohenzollern kneeling before the Polish king on this very square, occupies a whole wall of the gallery; while the nearby *Kościuszko at Racławice* celebrates the Polish peasant army's victory over the Russians in 1794 in similarly monumental style. Elsewhere in the gallery, Józef Chełmoński's *Foursome*, depicting a team of horses racing across the eastern steppe, is one of the most energy-charged (and oft-reproduced) images in the history of Polish art.

Just off the southwestern corner of the Sukiennice, a seventy-metre-high **Wieża Ratuszowa** (Town Hall Tower; May–Oct daily 9am–6pm; 4zł), capped by a Baroque spire, is all that remains of the original fourteenth-century town hall, pulled down in the 1820s by the authorities as part of a misguided improvement plan. It's worth the climb up for an excellent overview of the city.

Immediately east of the Sukiennice is a statue of national poet **Adam Mickiewicz** (see box, p.99), a facsimile of an earlier work destroyed by the Nazis, and a favourite meeting point. To its south, the copper-domed **Kościół św. Wojciecha** (St Adalbert's Church) is the oldest building in the square and the first church to be founded in Kraków. The saint was a Slav bishop, reputed to have preached here around 995 AD before heading north to convert the Prussians, at whose hands he was martyred. In the basement (reconstructed in the eighteenth century), you can see the foundations of the original tenth-century Romanesque building. Traces of an even earlier wooden building, possibly a pre-Christian temple, and an assortment of archeological finds are also on display.

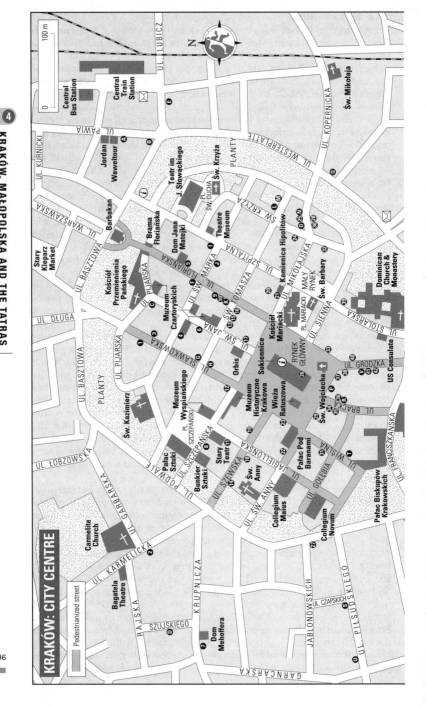

KRAKÓW: CITY CENTRE

Pedestrian street

0   100 m

N

Central Bus Station

Central Train Station

Stary Kleparz Market

Barbakan

Jordan Waweltour

Teatr im J. Słowackiego

Św. Krzyża

Theatre Museum

Brama Floriańska

Dom Jana Matejki

Kościół Przemienienia Pańskiego

Muzeum Czartoryskich

Kamienica Hipolitów

Mały Rynek

Św. Barbary

Dominican Church & Monastery

Kościół Mariacki

Sukiennice

Orbis

RYNEK GŁÓWNY

PL. MARIACKI

US Consulate

Św. Kazimierz

Muzeum Wyspiańskiego

Muzeum Historyczne Krakowa

Wieża Ratuszowa

Św. Wojciecha

Pałac Pod Baranami

Carmelite Church

Pałac Sztuki

Bunkier Sztuki

Stary Teatr

Św. Anny

Collegium Maius

Pałac Biskupów Krakowskich

Bagatela Theatre

Dom Mehoffera

Collegium Novum

Św. Mikołaja

UL. LUBICZ
UL. PAWIA
UL. KURNICKI
UL. WARSZAWSKA
UL. BASZTOWA
UL. DŁUGA
UL. PIJARSKA
UL. ŁOBZOWSKA
UL. SŁAWKOWSKA
UL. ŚW. JANA
UL. FLORIAŃSKA
UL. ŚW. MARKA
UL. ŚW. TOMASZA
UL. SZPITALNA
UL. ŚW. KRZYŻA
PLANTY
UL. MIKOŁAJSKA
UL. SIENNA
UL. STOLARSKA
UL. KOPERNICKA
UL. WESTERPLATTE
UL. GRODZKA
UL. BRACKA
UL. WIŚLNA
UL. FRANCISZKAŃSKA
UL. GOŁĘBIA
UL. JAGIELLOŃSKA
UL. ŚW. ANNY
UL. SZEWSKA
PL. SZCZEPAŃSKI
UL. PODWALE
UL. KARMELICKA
UL. GARBARSKA
RAJSKA
SZUJSKIEGO
KRUPNICZA
JABŁONOWSKICH
UL. CZAPSKICH
UL. PIŁSUDSKIEGO
GARNCARSKA
PLANTY

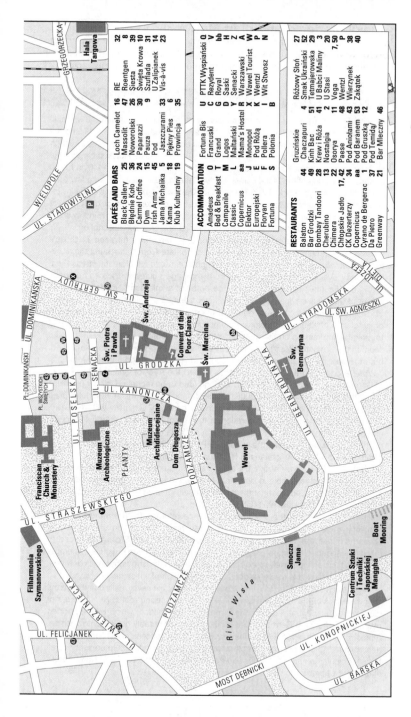

CAFÉS AND BARS

Black Gallery	25	Loch Camelot	16
Błędne Koło	36	Massolit	47
Carmel Coffee	24	Noworolski	26
Dym	15	Paparazzi	30
Irish Arms	45	Pauza	9
Jama Michalika	5	Pod	33
Kama	18	Piękny Pies	6
Klub Kulturalny	19	Prowincja	35
RE	32		
Roentgen	8		
Siesta	39		
Święta Krowa	10		
Szuflada	31		
U Zalipianek	14		
Vis-à-vis	23		

ACCOMMODATION

Amadeus	O	Fortuna Bis	Q
Bed & Breakfast	T	Francuski	V
Campanile	M	Grand	bb
Classic	D	Logos	H
Copernicus	L	Maltański	Z
Elektor	J	Mama's Hostel	aa
Europejski	E	Monopol	R
Floryan	F	Pod Różą	X
Fortuna	S	Pollera	K
		Polonia	I
PTTK Wyspiański	U	Royal	G
Rezydent	C	Saski	Y
		Senacki	A
Warszawski	W	Wentzl	N
Wawel Tourist	P	Wit Stwosz	B

RESTAURANTS

Balaton	44	Gruzińskie Chaczapuri	4
Bar Grodzki	49	Kinh Bac	51
Bombay Tandoori	28	Krewi Róża	41
Cherubino	13	Nostalgia	2
Chimera	22	Osorya	11
Chłopskie Jadło	17, 42	Paese	48
CK Dezerterzy	34	Pod Aniołami	43
Copernicus	aa	Pod Baranem	53
Cyrano de Bergerac	1	Pod Gruszką	12
Da Pietro	37	Pod Temidą/	46
Greenway	21	Różowy Słoń	27
		Smak Ukraiński	52
		Tetmajerowska	29
		U Babci Maliny	3
		U Stasi	20
		Vega	7, 50
		Wentzl	P
		Wierzynek	38
		Zakątek	40

Kościół Mariacki and plac Mariacki

Presiding haughtily over the northeastern corner of the square, the twin-towered **Kościół Mariacki** (St Mary's Church) is one of the finest Gothic structures in the country, and easily qualifies as Kraków's most instantly identifiable trademark.

Veit Stoss

As with Copernicus, the issue of the nationality of the man who carved the Mariacki altar – unquestionably the greatest work of art ever created in Poland – was long the source of a rather sterile dispute between Polish and German protagonists. Although his early career remains something of a mystery, it now seems indisputable that the sculptor's original name was **Veit Stoss**, and that he was born between 1440 and 1450 in Horb at the edge of the Black Forest, settling later in Nuremberg, where a few early works by him have been identified. He came to **Kraków** in 1477, perhaps at the invitation of the royal court (the Polish queen was an Austrian princess), though more likely at the behest of the German merchant community, a sizeable but declining minority in the city, who worshipped in the Mariacki and paid for its new altar by subscription.

Despite being his first major commission, the **Mariacki altarpiece** is Stoss's masterpiece. It triumphantly displays every facet of late-Gothic sculpture: the architectural setting, complete with its changing lights, is put to full dramatic effect; there is mastery over every possible scale, from the huge figures in the central shrine to the tiny figurines and decoration in the borders; subtle use is made of a whole gamut of technical devices, from three different depths of relief to a graded degree of gilding according to the importance of the scene; and the whole layout is based on a scheme of elaborate theological complexity that would nevertheless be bound to make an impression on the many unlettered worshippers who viewed it. It would seem that it is mostly Stoss's own work: gilders and joiners were certainly employed, but otherwise he was probably only helped by one assistant and one apprentice.

While engaged on the altarpiece, Stoss carved the relief of Christ in the Garden of Gethsemane, now in the City Art Collection (due to be reopened in new premises on ul. Kanonicza some time in 2006. Made of sandstone, a material he later used for the Mariacki crucifix, it is indicative of his exceptional versatility with materials. This is further apparent in consideration of the works he created after finishing the altarpiece: the tomb of King Kazimierz the Jagiellonian in the Wawel cathedral (see p.411) is of Salzburg marble, the epitaph to Philippus Buonaccorsi in the Dominican Church (see p.406) of Hungarian marble. These sculptures made Stoss a great Polish celebrity, and he rose far above his artisan status to engage in extensive commercial activities, and to dabble in both architecture and engineering. The forms of the Mariacki altarpiece and his monuments were widely imitated throughout Poland, and continued to be so for the next half-century.

It therefore seems all the more curious that he returned to **Nuremberg** in 1496, remaining there until his death in 1533. His homecoming was a traumatic experience: Nuremberg was well endowed with specialist craftsmen, and Stoss was forced to follow suit, concentrating on producing single, unpainted wooden figures. Attempts to maintain his previous well-to-do lifestyle led him into disastrous business dealings, which culminated in his forging a document, as a result of which he was branded on both cheeks and forbidden to venture beyond the city. He never really came to terms with the ideals of the Italian Renaissance, which took strong root in Nuremberg, nor did he show any enthusiasm for the Protestant Reformation, which was supported by nearly all the great German artists of the day, most notably his fellow townsman, Albrecht Dürer. Yet, even if Stoss never repeated the success of his Kraków years, he continued to produce memorable and highly individualistic sculptures, above all the spectacular garlanded *Annunciation* suspended from the ceiling of Nuremberg's church of St Lorenz.

Built on the site of a thirteenth-century original destroyed during the mid-century Tatar invasions, the current building was begun in 1355 and completed fifty years later. The taller of its **towers**, a late-fifteenth-century addition, is topped by an amazing ensemble of spires, elaborated with a crown and helmet. Legend has it that during one of the early Tatar raids the watchman positioned at the top of this tower saw the invaders approaching and took up his trumpet to raise the alarm; his warning was cut short by a Tatar arrow through the throat. The legend lives on, and every hour, on the hour, a lone **trumpeter** plays the sombre *hejnał* (bugle call) melody four times (from four different windows in the southernmost of the towers), on each occasion halting abruptly at the precise point the watchman was supposed to have been hit. The national radio station broadcasts the *hejnał* live at noon every day and Polish writers are still apt to wax lyrical on the symbolism of the trumpet's warning.

The tourist entrance to the church is through the south door – the square-side west door having been set aside for the local faithful. First impressions of the **church** are of a cavernous, somewhat gloomy expanse. What little light there is comes from the high windows at each end, the ancient altar window facing the stained glass of the west end, an Art-Nouveau extravaganza by Kraków artist Stanisław Wyspiański. Under arched stone vaulting enhanced in blue and gold, the walls of the nave are decorated with **friezes** by Jan Matejko, rich in brightly coloured chevrons and vegetal shapes. Separating the nave from the aisles are a succession of buttressed pillars fronted by Baroque marble altars. The aisles themselves lead off to a number of lavishly ornamented chapels, fifteenth-century additions to the main body of the building. The focal point of the nave is the huge stone **crucifix** attributed to Veit Stoss, hanging in the archway to the presbytery.

The biggest crowds are drawn by the majestic **high altar** at the far east end. Carved by the Nuremberg master craftsman **Veit Stoss** (Wit Stwosz, as he's known in Poland; see box opposite) between 1477 and 1489, the huge limewood polyptych is one of the finest examples of late-Gothic art in Europe. The outer sides of the folded polyptych feature illustrations from the life of the Holy Family executed in gilded polychromy. At 11.50am (Sundays and saints' days excluded) the altar is opened to reveal the inner panels, with their reliefs of the Annunciation, Nativity, Adoration of the Magi, Resurrection, Ascension and Pentecost; for a good view, arrive a good ten minutes before the opening. These six superb scenes are a fitting backdrop to the central panel – an exquisite **Dormition of the Virgin** in which the graceful figure of Mary is shown reclining into her final sleep in the arms of the watchful Apostles. Like most of the figures, the Apostles, several of them well over lifesize, are thought to be based on Stoss's contemporaries in Kraków. Certainly there's an uncanny mastery of human detail that leaves you feeling you'd recognize their human counterparts if you met them in the street. Other features of note in the chancel are the Gothic stained-glass windows, the Renaissance tabernacle designed by Giovanni Maria Mosca, and the exuberant early Baroque stalls.

Walking down towards the west end of the church, you'll have to pick your way past devotees kneeling in front of the fifteenth-century **Chapel of Our Lady of Częstochowa**, with its copy of the venerated image of the Black Madonna. Locals claim that this is actually older than the original.

Plac Mariacki and Kościół św. Barbary

The side door on the south side of the chancel brings you into **plac Mariacki** (St Mary's Square), a small courtyard replacing the old church cemetery closed down by the Austrians in the nineteenth century. On the far side of the courtyard stands the fourteenth-century **Kościół św. Barbary** (St Barbara's Church; rarely open except during services), among its contents a remarkable late-Gothic pietà group, sculpted in stone and attributed to the anonymous local artist known as "Master of the Beautiful Madonnas". During the Partitions, the ruling Austrians took over the Mariacki, so the locals were forced to use this tiny place for services in Polish. The back of the church looks onto the tranquil **Mały Rynek**, whose terrace cafés make an enjoyable venue for postcard sessions or a quiet beer.

Returning towards the Rynek Główny along ul. Mikołajska will take you past the **Kamienica Hipolitów** at pl. Mariacki 3 (Hippoliti House; Wed & Fri–Sun 9am–3.30pm, Thurs 11am–6pm; 5zł, free on Sat), a late-medieval structure named after one of the many families who owned it over the centuries, the Hippoliti having been cloth merchants of Italian extraction. The richly stuccoed rooms now provides the perfect home for a collection of domestic interiors through the ages: highlights include an over-the-top rococo bedroom, and a nineteenth-century bourgeois parlour which, scattered with magazines and domestic knick-knacks, looks as if the owners have just popped out and will be back any minute.

Around the square

There's a lot more in the way of historic **mansions** ranged around the Rynek Główny and in surrounding streets, many of which can boast strong historical or artistic associations. On the eastern side of the square are some of the oldest buildings in the city. The **Kamienica Szara** (Grey House; no. 6) on the corner of ul. Sienna, for example, has many of its Gothic rooms intact, despite its later appearance; its ex-residents include Poland's first elected king, Henri de Valois, and Tadeusz Kościuszko, who used the house as his headquarters during the 1794 uprising. The neighbouring **Kamienica Montelupich** (Montelupi House; no. 7), with a monumental Renaissance portal, was the site of the country's first ever post office, established by its Italian owners in King Sigismund August's reign. The Gothic **Kamienica Bonerowska** (Boner House; no. 9) was for some time the home of the Kraków writer and painter Stanisław Wyspiański; while the house at no. 15, in the southeast corner, is home to the city's oldest and most famous restaurant, the **Wierzynek** (see "Restaurants", p.437), founded in 1364 and claiming an unbroken culinary tradition. It also holds its original charter from King Kazimierz the Great. Political heavyweights who have dined here in recent years include presidents de Gaulle, Nixon, Mitterrand and Bush (the elder).

Continuing round the south section of the square, the **Pałac Potockich** (Potocki Palace; no. 20), with a small courtyard with loggias at the back, is a good example of a classical Kraków mansion, while the **Pałac Pod Baranami** (no. 27), on the western side, is another aristocratic home, constructed from four adjacent burghers' houses in the sixteenth century. Further along the western edge of the square, an orderly collection of shopfronts and restaurants added on to the old houses, ends at the **Pałac pod Krzysztofory** (Krzysztofory Palace; no. 35) on the corner of ul. Szczepańska, another well-preserved mansion created by fusing burghers' houses into a single building with a fine courtyard at the back. Today it's part of the **Muzeum Historyczne Krakowa** (Kraków History Museum; Wed & Fri–Sun 9am–3.30pm, Thurs 11am–6pm; 8zł). The first floor houses a large and varied collection relating to the historical development of the city. Interspersed among the historical exhibits is an interesting spread of paintings by artists with connections with the city, including some fine works by Witkiewicz and Malczewski. During advent, the top floor hosts a stupendous exhibition of *szopki* (the amazingly colourful and detailed Christmas cribs indigenous to Kraków; see "Festivals and events", p.442), and there's usually one on display all year round.

The rest of the Stare Miasto

Like the Rynek, the streets of the rest of the Stare Miasto still follow the medieval plan, while their **architecture** presents a rich Central European ensemble of Gothic, Renaissance and Baroque. They are a hive of commercial activity, too, with a welter of boutiques, fast-food joints and other privately owned shops that render the old state enterprise outlets almost a figment of past imagination. West of the Rynek, the atmosphere is generated by the academic buildings and student haunts of the **university district**.

South of the main square, the busy **ul. Grodzka** leads down towards **plac Dominikański**, one of the pivotal points of the Stare Miasto, and on to Wawel Hill. The historic streets combine the increasingly fast-paced bustle of the city's commercial life with the tranquillity and splendour of myriad ancient churches, palaces and mansions. Additionally, there's a brace of museums worth exploring.

Ulica Floriańska

Of the three streets leading north off the Rynek, the easternmost, **ul. Floriańska** is the busiest and most striking. In among the myriad shops, cafés and restaurants are some attractive fragments of medieval and Renaissance architecture. At no. 5, for example, a beautiful early Renaissance stone figure of the Madonna and Child sits in a niche on the facade of the Brama Floriańska (Floriańska Gate; see below). At no. 14, **Pod Różą**, the oldest hotel in Kraków (see p.391), has a Renaissance doorway inscribed in Latin, "May this house stand until an ant drinks the oceans and a tortoise circles the world" – it doesn't seem to get much attention from the moneyed revellers who flock to the hotel's reopened casino. Famous hotel guests of the past include Franz Liszt, Balzac and the occasional tsar.

Further up the street, at no. 41, is the sixteenth-century **Dom Jana Matejki** (Jan Matejko House; Tues–Thurs, Sat & Sun 10am–3.30pm, Fri 11am–6pm; 5zł, free on Sun), home of painter Jan Matejko until his death in 1893. Famous for his vast, colour-charged depictions of key events in Polish history, Matejko was out of step with an art establishment that saw him as a hysterical romantic, but was venerated as a patriotic visionary by the wider, gallery-going public. The painter's house was opened as a museum within three years of his death, and has been a national shrine ever since. Some of the rooms are like a sourcebook of nineteenth-century bourgeois interior design, retaining the fireplaces, Italian furniture, and mother-of-pearl Middle Eastern chairs that Matejko chose himself. A suite of more modern, gallery-style rooms houses paintings collected by Matejko and examples of his own work, including the sketches of the windows he designed for the Mariacki Church. There's also a rousing collection of old costumes and armour that he used as inspiration for several of his more famous pictures, notably *Sobieski at Vienna*.

The **Brama Floriańska** (Floriańska Gate), at the end of the street, marks the edge of the Stare Miasto proper. A square, robust fourteenth-century structure, it's part of a small section of fortifications saved when the old defensive walls were pulled down in the early nineteenth century. The original fortifications must have been an impressive sight – three kilometres of wall ten metres high and nearly three metres thick, interspersed with 47 towers and bastions.

Just beyond the Brama Floriańska, the **Barbakan** (Barbican; May–Oct daily 10am–6pm; 5zł) looks from a distance like the kind of castle that children

△ Hairdressers, Kraków

should be bouncing around in, but is on closer inspection a formidable addition to Kraków's medieval defences. Boasting seven spiky turrets, it was built in 1498 as an extension of the city's northern defensive wall, although the covered passage linking the Barbakan to the Brama Floriańska has long since disappeared. The Barbakan would have been pulled down by the Austrians too had it not been for locals pointing out that its removal would have subjected ul. Floriańska to chilly winds.

The Słowacki Theatre and around

Heading east from the Brama Floriańska will bring you to the northern end of **ul. Szpitalna**, another mansion-lined thoroughfare dominated by the suave, creamy form of the **Teatr im. J. Słowackiego** (Słowacki Theatre), built in 1893 on the site of the ancient Church of the Holy Ghost complex which had been demolished amid loud protests from Matejko and other local luminaries. Modelled on the Paris Opéra, the richly ornate theatre, named after the much-loved Romantic poet and playwright Juliusz Słowacki, established itself as one of Kraków's premier theatres, a position it still enjoys (see "Entertainment", p.440).

Round the back of the theatre, across pl. św. Ducha, is the **Kościół św. Krzyża** (Church of the Holy Cross) a fabulous building whose beautifully decorated Gothic vaulting is supported by a single exquisite palm-like central pillar. The graceful fifteenth- and sixteenth-century murals decorating the nave and choir were restored at the turn of the twentieth century by Wyspiański among others, who was passionately devoted to the building, regarding it as one of the city's finest.

Hogging the corner of pl. św. Ducha and ul. Szpitalna is the **Juliusz Słowacki Theatre Museum** (Tues–Sun 10am–4pm; 4zł), which traces the development of drama in Kraków with the aid of some wonderful costumes, set designs and theatre posters. There's an intriguing collection of puppets used in the satirical cabaret shows of the Młoda Polska era – one of which, for reasons which are not properly explained, features painter Jacek Malczewski with the legs of a goat. Photos of beatnik audiences stuffing themselves into cellars to watch avant-garde performances by Tadeusz Kantor's Cricot 2 Theatre remind you what an exciting time the 1960s must have been – even in communist Poland.

The Czartoryski Museum

Heading west from Brama Floriańska, ul. Pijarska runs past craft and souvenir stalls to join ul. św. Jana, at the junction of which stands the Baroque **Kościół Przemienienia Pańskiego** (Church of the Holy Transfiguration), with a facade modelled on the Gesù Church in Rome. On your left, linked to the church by an overhead passage, is the **Pałac Czartoryskich** (Czartoryski Palace), home to Kraków's finest art collection, the **Muzeum Czartoryskich** (Tues & Thurs 9am–3.30pm, Wed & Fri 11am–6pm, Sat & Sun 10am–3.30pm; 7zł, free on Sun). Its core was established by Izabela Czartoryska at the family palace in Puławy (see p.311) and was then moved to Kraków following the confiscation of the Puławy estate after the 1831 insurrection, in which the family was deeply implicated. They were legendary collectors, particularly from the Paris salons of the seventeenth and eighteenth centuries, and it shows – despite the Nazis' removal, and subsequent loss, of many precious items, including Raphael's famous *Portrait of a Young Man*, which has never been recovered.

The **ancient art** collection alone contains over a thousand exhibits, from sites in Mesopotamia, Etruria, Greece and Egypt. Another intriguing highlight is the collection of **trophies** from the Battle of Vienna (1683), which includes sumptuous Turkish carpets, scimitars, tents and other Oriental finery.

The **picture galleries** contain a rich display of art and sculpture ranging from thirteenth- to eighteenth-century works, the most famous being Rembrandt's brooding *Landscape with the Good Samaritan* and Leonardo da Vinci's *Lady with an Ermine*. A double pun identifies the rodent-handler as Cecilia Gallerani, the mistress of Leonardo's patron, Lodovico il Moro: the Greek word for this animal is *galé* – a play on the woman's name – and Lodovico's nickname was "Ermelino", meaning ermine. There is also a large collection of Dutch canvases and an outstanding array of fourteenth-century Sienese primitives, the whole thing arranged, following nineteenth-century tradition, to form distinct artistic and decorative groupings. As in all Polish museums, you may find several galleries closed off, ostensibly for lack of staff.

The Wyspiański Museum and around

Heading south from the Muzeum Czartoryskich and turning right into ul. Szczepańska will bring you to one of Kraków's newest and best-designed museums, the **Muzeum Wyspiańskiego** (Wyspiański Museum; Wed & Fri–Sun 10am–3.30pm, Thurs 10am–6pm; 5zł, free on Sun), at no. 11. Devoted to Stanisław Wyspiański (1869–1907), the writer and artist who played a crucial role in the cultural upsurge subsequently known as Młoda Polska or "Young Poland" (see box opposite), it's stuffed with an eye-pleasing array of artworks, graphics and interior design ideas. Best of the paintings are Wyspiański's touching portraits of friends and family – his wife is shown wearing traditional peasant costume in a clear reference to Młoda Polska's reverence for authentic folk traditions. Other notable exhibits include sketches of costumes and set designs intended for use in Wyspiański's plays, and some fine examples of the stained-glass windows he produced for the Dominican church (see p.406). One whole room is occupied by the models that formed the basis of Wyspiański's plan to refashion and enlarge the Wawel complex as a Polish Acropolis – a bizarre, haunting vision given full reign in his play of the same name. Proof of Wyspiański's endless inventiveness is provided by the display of wacky furniture he made for leading literary figure Tadeusz Boy Żeleński – chunky, jagged-edged stools which look like props from the set of a gothic horror film.

Immediately beyond the museum the street opens out onto pl. Szczepański, a broad square embellished by an impressive pair of *belle-époque* buildings in the Viennese Secessionist style: the decorative **Stary Teatr** to the south (see "Entertainment", p.440), the city's best known theatre, which was used by Oscar-winning cinema director Andrzej Wajda for his exemplary theatrical productions of Polish classics, and the **Pałac Sztuki** (Palace of Arts; daily 8am–8pm; price depends on what's on) to the west, a stately structure with reliefs by Malczewski and niches filled with busts of Matejko, Witkiewicz and other local artists. The latter, adorned with a mosaic frieze, features high-profile art exhibitions, often featuring major international works on loan from abroad. Just round the corner on Podwale Dunajewskiego is the **Bunkier Sztuki** (Art Bunker; daily except Mon 11am–6pm; ⓦ www.bunkier.com.pl; price depends on what's on), a brutally modernist concrete building which is the city's main venue for large-scale contemporary art shows.

The university district

Ulica Jagiellońska leads south from pl. Szczepański into Kraków's main **university district**, an assemblage of academic buildings grouped around the Gothic **Collegium Maius** on the corner of Jagiellońska and ul. św. Anny. The university was initially established on the Wawel by King Kazimierz in 1364, but it failed to outlive his death six years later and had to be

Like Art Nouveau in France and *Jugendstil* in Germany, **Młoda Polska** ("Young Poland") administered an invigorating dose of modernity and style to Polish culture in the decades prior to World War I. Młoda Polska was much wider in scope than its French and German counterparts, however, revitalizing painting, poetry and music as well as architecture and design. It was also unique in that most of its protagonists shared a sense of cultural mission: Poland was a country under foreign occupation at the time, and it was only natural that artists saw creative activity as a patriotic as well as a personal duty.

Młoda Polska was never an organized movement; the term was first coined in 1899 to describe a new generation of culturally active Poles who were united by their rejection of mainstream bourgeois taste. The cultural scene in Kraków contained plenty that was worth rebelling against, dominated as it was by the so-called Positivists, who advocated a sober realistic approach to the arts, or by romantic souls like Jan Matejko, the backward-looking painter of epic historical events. Matejko's former students at Kraków's art academy – Józef Mehoffer and Stanisław Wyspiański among them – were far more interested in exploring an alternative world of the unconscious, spiritual and symbolic. The new mood of rebellion also meant the cultivation of decadent, bohemian behaviour at the expense of good manners, and the replacement of cheery optimism with dreamy melancholia. It was a mind-set eloquently summed up by Młoda Polska poet **Kazimierz Tetmajer** in his most famous piece of verse *Nie wierzę w nic* ("I believe in nothing"), the kind of poem that finds a receptive audience among stroppy students to this day.

Kraków's position in the Austrian Empire made it an incubator of new ideas: news of cultural innovations arrived here quickly from Vienna, and the Austrian authorities were in any case fairly liberal when it came to cultural politics. Considerations like these certainly persuaded publicist Stanisław Przybyszewski to launch the periodical *Życie* ("Life") here in 1898, harnessing the young creative talent of the city and providing a focus for the anti-establishment scene. Przybyszewski held court in the (no longer standing) Turliński café on ul. Szczepańska, which soon became the unofficial headquarters of the south Polish arts world. When the landlord of the Turliński moved to Lwów, everyone decamped to the newly opened *Jama Michalika* on Floriańska. It was here that the Młoda Polska set initiated the Zielony Balonik cabaret in 1905 – many of Kraków's brightest talents were either performing on stage or being satirized in the sketches. The *Jama Michalika* (see p.438) still exists, although it's nowadays the territory of tourists rather than trendsetters.

Młoda Polska's key players also included **Tadeusz Boy Żeleńsky**, one of the main sketch-writers for Zielony Balonik, and **Feliks "Manngha" Jasieński**, the authority on Japanese art who introduced the younger generation of painters to Oriental styles. An even bigger creative impulse came from a rediscovery of Poland's indigenous folk traditions. Many Młoda Polska luminaries – notably Tetmajer, fellow poet **Jan Kasprowicz**, and architect **Stanisław Witkiewicz** – lived for much of the year in the mountain village of Zakopane (see p.482), drawing inspiration from both the natural beauty of the scenery and the age-old styles of music, dress and handicrafts cultivated by the local inhabitants. Central to the spirit of the age was the belief that Polish culture could be regenerated through renewed contact with its village roots.

After 1914 the effects of war and social upheaval opened the door to a more extreme set of aesthetics, and surviving members of the Młoda Polska generation went their separate ways. However, the era left Poland with a huge cultural legacy, exemplified more than anything by the all-embracing oeuvre of painter, dramatist and designer **Stanisław Wyspiański**. His plays, rich in national symbolism and collective soul-searching, are considered classics of Polish literature, while his work in the visual arts – above all the stained-glass windows in the Franciscan church – has helped form the visual identity of both Kraków and the country at large.

re-founded by King Władysław Jagiełło's wife Queen Jadwiga in the early fifteenth century.

Entering the Collegium through a passageway from ul. Jagiellońska, you find yourself in a quiet, arcaded **courtyard** with a marble fountain playing in the centre, an ensemble that, during the early 1960s, was stripped of neo-Gothic accretions and restored to something approaching its original form. Several first-floor rooms play host to the **Muzeum Uniwerzytecki** (University Museum; Mon–Fri 11am–2.20pm, Sat 11am–1.20pm; 16zł, although entrance is by guided tour only – the museum office will sign you up for the next English-language tour, which depart at regular intervals throughout the day). The trip begins with a series of elaborately decorated assembly halls and lecture rooms, several of which retain the mathematical and geographical murals once used for teaching, as well as an impressive library of old books. The professors' common room boasts an ornate Baroque spiral staircase guarded by wooden halberdiers, and a Gothic bay window with a replica statuette of King Kazimierz. Among the trinkets in the so-called **Treasury** (actually a glass cabinet behind a locked iron grille), the most valued possession is a tiny copper globe, constructed around 1520 as the centrepiece of a clock mechanism and featuring the earliest known illustration of America – labelled "a newly discovered land" but placed in the wrong hemisphere. The **Aula**, the grand principal assembly hall, has a Renaissance ceiling adorned with carved rosettes and portraits of Polish royalty, benefactors and professors; its Renaissance portal carries the Latin inscription *Plus Ratio Quam Vis* – "Wisdom rather than Strength".

Several other old buildings are dotted round this area. The university **Kościół św. Anny** (St Anne's Church), was designed by the ubiquitous Tylman of Gameren. A monumental Baroque extravaganza, built on a Latin cross plan with a high central dome, it's widely regarded as Gameren's most mature work, the classicism of his design neatly counterpoised by rich stucco decoration added by the Italian sculptor Baldaggare Fontana. The **Collegium Minus**, just round the corner on ul. Gołębia, is the fifteenth-century arts faculty, rebuilt two centuries later; Jan Matejko studied and later taught here. On the corner of the same street stands the outsize **Collegium Novum**, the neo-Gothic univer-sity administrative headquarters, with an interior modelled on the Collegium Maius. The **Copernicus statue**, in front of the Collegium Novum on the edge of the Planty, commemorates the university's most famous supposed student – although the only evidence that he ever studied in Kraków is a payment-book entry referring to one "Mikołaj son of Mikołaj from Toruń".

The Dominican church and monastery

Ulica Grodzka stretches south of the Rynek, crossing the tram lines circling the city centre at pl. Dominikański. East across the square stands the large brick-work basilica of the thirteenth-century **Dominican church and monastery**. Constructed on the site of an earlier church, following its destruction during the fearsome Tatar raid of 1241, the modest original Gothic brick building grew to become one of Kraków's grandest churches. Much of the accumulated splen-dour, however, was wiped out during a fire in 1850, which seriously devastated the church and much of the surrounding quarter, the Franciscan church (see opposite) included.

Today, the dominant atmosphere is one of uncluttered, tranquil contempla-tion – like most Polish churches, the main purpose of the building is worship, not display, a fact attested to by the continual stream of services held here on almost any day of the week. However, there is a wealth of architectural detail to appreciate. Adjoining the main nave, redecorated in an airy neo-Gothic style, are a succession of chapels, many of which survived the 1850 fire in better shape than the rest of the building. Oldest of them all, up a flight of steps at the end of the north aisle, is **St Hyacinth's chapel**, dedicated to the joint founder and first abbot of the monastery. Based on the design of the Sigismund Chapel in Wawel cathedral, the chapel boasts some rich stuccowork by Baldassare Fontana on the dome above the freestanding tomb. The other notable feature is a sequence of paintings portraying the life of the saint by Thomas Dolabella. The Baroque **Myszkowski family chapel**, in the southern aisle, is a fine creation from the workshop of Florentine mason Santi Gucci, the exuberantly ornamented exterior contrasting with the austere, marble-faced interior, with busts of the Myszkowski family lining the chapel dome. Similarly noteworthy is the **Rosary chapel**, built as a thanks-offering for Sobieski's victory over the Turks at Vienna in 1683, and housing a supposedly miracle-producing image of Our Lady of the Rosary. A fine series of **tombstones** survives in the chancel, notably those of the early thirteenth-century prince of Kraków Leszek, Czarny (the Black), and an impressive bronze tablet of the Italian Renaissance scholar Filippo Buonaccorsi, built to a design by Veit Stoss and cast at the Nuremberg Vischer works.

Through the Renaissance doorway, underneath the stairs leading up to St Hyacinth's chapel, are the tranquil Gothic **cloisters**, whose walls are lined with memorials to the great and good of Kraków, leading in the north wing to a fine Romanesque refectory with a vaulted crypt.

Franciscan church and monastery

West of pl. Dominikański, on the adjacent pl. Wszystkich Świętych, is the **Franciscan church and monastery**, home to the Dominicans' long-standing rivals in the tussle for the city's religious affections. Built soon after Franciscan friars first arrived from Prague in 1237, the church was completed some thirty years later. As one of Kraków's major churches it has witnessed some important events in the nation's history, notably the baptism in 1385 of the pagan Grand Duke Jogaila of Lithuania (who adopted the Polonized name Władysław Jagiełło for the occasion), prior to his assumption of the Polish throne. A plain, high, brick building, the church's somewhat murky, brooding atmosphere forms a stark contrast to its Dominican neighbour. The most striking feature is its celebrated series of Art-Nouveau **murals** and **stained-glass windows**, which were designed and executed by Stanisław Wyspiański in 1900 following the gutting of the church in the fire fifty years earlier (see opposite). An exuberant outburst of floral and geometric mural motifs extol the naturalist creed of St Francis, culminating in the magnificent stained-glass depiction of God the Creator in the large west window, the elements of the scene seemingly merging into each other in a hazy, abstract swirl of colour. By contrast, the floral motif depiction of St Francis and the Blessed Salomea in the window behind the altar conjures up an altogether more restrained, meditative atmosphere, while the **north chapel** contains a flowing set of Stations of the Cross by another Młoda Polska adherent, Józef Mehoffer. The **south chapel** contains a fine early fifteenth-century image of the Madonna of Mercy, a popular local figure. The Gothic **cloisters**, reached from the southern side of the church are worth a visit for the series of portraits of the bishops of Kraków dating back to the mid-fifteenth century and continuing up to the present day – note the portrait of Bishop Piotr Tomicki from the early 1500s. To complete the ecclesiastical picture, the archbishop of Kraków's residence, once inhabited by Karol Wojtyła, stands across from the Franciscan Church.

South from plac Dominikański

On down ul. Grodzka, past the gilded stone lion above the **Kamienica Podel-wie** (House Under the Lion) at no. 32, the oldest such stone emblem in the city, turn right into ul. Poselska to find the house, at no. 12, where novelist **Joseph Conrad** spent his childhood: a commemorative plaque in the corner carries a quotation from his work.

Further down ul. Poselska, through the garden entrance at no. 3 and past the top of ul. Senacka, is the **Muzeum Archeologiczne** (Archeological Museum; Mon–Wed 9am–2pm, Thurs 2–6pm, Fri & Sun 10am–2pm; 7zł, free on Thurs). Housed in a building with a chequered history – it was originally an early medieval stronghold, then successively a palace, monastery and Habsburg-era prison, before becoming a museum – an imaginatively mounted display features Egyptian, Greek and Roman objects alongside a large group of local finds, including an extensive set of Neolithic painted ceramics considered to be among the best in Europe. One exhibit the locals are extremely proud of is the famed figure of a pagan Slavonic god, known as **Światowit**, the only image of a Slav pagan deity ever discovered. An extraordinary carved stone idol standing 2.5m high and sporting what looks like a top hat, its crude decoration includes a face on each side (one for each of the winds, it is thought).

The route south continues down ul. Grodzka, past another run of churches before ending up at the busy crossroads in the shadow of Wawel. The first, the austere twin-domed **Kościół św. Piotra i Pawła** (Church of SS Peter and Paul), a little way back from the street, is fronted by imposing statues of the two apostles, actually copies of the pollution-scarred originals, now kept elsewhere for preservation's sake. The church's exterior recently received a thorough cleanup, the much reduced pollution levels in the inner city meaning that the distinctive statues should be able to keep their current shine for a while to come. Modelled on the Gesù in Rome, it's the earliest Baroque building in the city, commissioned by the Jesuits when they came to Kraków in the 1580s to quell Protestant agitation. A notable feature here is the **crypt** of Piotr Skarga (Mon–Fri 9am–5pm; 3zł) down the steps in front of the altar, where there are piles of slips of paper filled with the prayers of the devout. A noted Jesuit preacher and Polish champion of the Counter-Reformation, Skarga delivered anti-Protestant sermons here at the close of the sixteenth century. Fine stuccowork by Giovanni Falconi in the chapels on either side of the nave helps to relieve the severity of the place.

Immediately in front of the church stands one of Kraków's more contro-versial cultural monuments, a **statue of Skarga** erected in 2001 to provide a focal point for the recently tidied-up plaza that leads from here through to ul. Kanoniczna (see opposite). A clumsy piece of work which makes the much revered priest look more like a comic-book superhero than a spiritual leader, the sculpture is totally out of keeping with the Baroque splendours that surround it, and has proved profoundly unpopular with the Cracovian cultural elite as a consequence.

Next comes the Romanesque **Kościół św. Andrzeja** (St Andrew's Church), remodelled in familiar Polish Baroque style, where the local people are reputed to have holed themselves up and successfully fought off marauding Tatars during the invasion of 1241; it looks just about strong enough for the purpose. The early thirteenth-century mosaic icon of the Virgin from Constantinople stored in the Treasury is credited with having helped out. A little further on, **Kościół św. Marcina** (St Martin's Church), built in the seventeenth century on the site of a Romanesque foundation, now belongs to Kraków's small Lutheran community.

The route to Wawel Hill

While the most direct route from the Stare Miasto to Wawel Hill is via the pedestrianized ribbon of ul. Grodzka, there are a number of more leisurely backstreet alternatives. One of these involves heading across the plaza behind the Piotr Skarga statue and turning left into **ul. Kanoniczna**, a quiet, cobbled alleyway, unquestionably one of the most atmospheric in the city. Restoration work on the string of Gothic mansions lining the street is now almost complete, lending the ensemble a meditative aura that takes ready hold on the imagination. Almost at the bottom of the street, housed in an impressive pair of recently renovated late-fourteenth-century mansions belonging to the archbishop of Kraków (nos. 19/21), is the **Muzeum Archdiecezjalne** (Archdiocesan Museum; Tues–Fri 10am–4pm, Sat & Sun 10am–3pm; 5zł), with a wealth of religious art plucked from the churches of the surrounding Małopolska region. Highlight of the collection in the first gallery is a set of Gothic sculptures, including a wonderful sequence of Madonnas and female saints, and an exquisite relief of the Adoration of the Magi dating from the 1460s which was taken from the Mariacki Church. As with the best of Veit Stoss's work, what's most striking here is the human realism of the figures, the gentle, expressive faces reaching out across the centuries. Subsequent halls feature a notable cycle of pictures by Hans Suess of Kulmbach, illustrating the legend of St Catherine of Alexandria, painted in 1514 for the Boner family chapel in Mariacki, and a notable *Annunciation* by Jakob Mertens from 1580, alongside a wealth of assorted religious artefacts. Rounding off the exhibitions is a room dedicated to Karol Wojtyła, its one-time resident in his days as a humble priest in Kraków. As usual with Polish exhibitions devoted to the man, there's a string of papal memorabilia, much of it donated by the pope himself, including sets of his old vestments a pair of pre-papal shoes.

Back out on the street, the fifteenth-century **Dom Długosza** (Długosz House) at no. 25, named after an early resident, the historian Jan Długosz, originally served as the royal bathhouse. Local legend has it that in preparation for her marriage to Grand Duke Jogaila of Lithuania (the future King Władysław Jagiełło of Poland), Princess Jadwiga sent one of her most trusted servants to attend the duke during his ablutions and report back over rumours of the grotesque genital proportions of the pagan Lithuanians. Exactly what the servant told her is not revealed, but at any rate the queen went ahead and married the man.

At this point, most people head straight to the Wawel by heading up the access path just across the road. Before joining them, it's worth making a short detour to the left, rounding the foot if Wawel Hill as far as **Kościół św. Bernardyna** (Bernardine church). This twin-towered Baroque basilica contains a wealth of lavish period furnishings, notably a graphic depiction of the Dance of Death in the main aisle, a well-known local favourite, and a fine sculpture of St Anne with the Virgin and Child, attributed to the workshop of Veit Stoss, in one of the side chapels.

Wawel Hill: the castle, cathedral and around

For over five hundred years, the country's rulers lived and governed on **Wawel Hill**, whose main buildings stand pretty much as they have done for centuries. Even after the capital moved to Warsaw, Polish monarchs continued to be buried in the cathedral, and it's at Wawel that many of the nation's venerated poets and heroes lie in state within a set of buildings that serve as a virtual textbook of Polish history. As such, Wawel represents a potent source of national and spiritual pride, and there are often far greater crowds of Poles than foreigners looking around, many of them in large organized groups making a near-obligatory pilgrimage to the fount of national memory. In more recent times Wawel has been associated with an additional reason for making a pilgrimage here – the belief that one of the walls in the inner castle courtyard stands upon one of the world's main centres of spiritual energy. It's common for cultists and followers of the chakra come here and lean against the wall for a few minutes in order to recharge their spiritual batteries. Distaste for New Age tourism prompted the Wawel authorities to rope the area off for a while in 2001, but it seems to be accessible again – although not marked by any sign.

Visiting the Wawel

As the Wawel comprises a diverse collection of museums and sites, visiting the hill requires a modicum of pre-planning. The Wawel precinct is open to all-comers (May–Sept 8am–8pm; Oct–April 9am–5pm), and the cathedral is also easy of access despite having more limited opening hours (see opposite). All attractions, with the exception of the cathedral, require separate **tickets**: those for the State Rooms and the Treasury are sold at the main ticket office near the top of the approach path to the Wawel; entry to both is limited to ten people every ten minutes so you'll probably be given a time slot and told to wait. Entrance to the other exhibitions – the Lost Wawel, the Oriental Art Exhibition, the Cathedral Museum and the Dragon's Cave – is unrestricted, and tickets can be bought either at the main ticket office or on the door of the appropriate

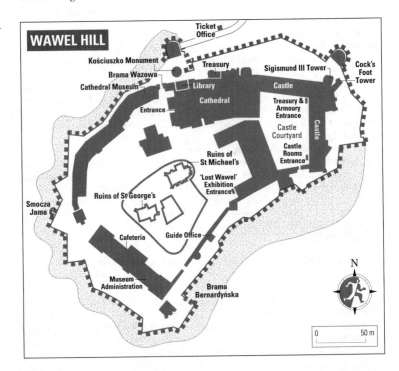

exhibition. "Doing" the Wawel can take all day, but with the judicious use of coffee breaks it's a hugely rewarding way of spending your time, and by no means as tiring as you might expect. English-speaking **guides** for small groups and individuals are available for hire from the Biuro Przewodnickie (Guide Office; ☎012/429 3336, ⓦ www.przewodnicy.krakow.pl) on the south side of the main courtyard. If there's one place where it would be worth coughing up for your own guide, this is it. With so much to see, and the crowds to navigate your way through, a reliable local hand can definitely ease the experience.

The Brama Wazowska and the main courtyard

Entrance to the Wawel is via a cobbled path that leaves Podzamcze just opposite the junction with Kanonicza. At the top of the path, a typically dramatic statue of Tadeusz Kościuszko – a copy of one destroyed by the Nazis – stands before the sixteenth-century **Brama Wazowska** (Waza Gate), protected by two huge red-brick bastions. As you emerge into the Wawel precinct the cathedral rears up to the left, with the castle and its outbuildings and courtyards beyond. Directly ahead is a huge, open **square**, once the site of a Wawel township, but cleared by the Austrians in the early nineteenth century to create a parade ground. In the middle of the square, alongside a well-tended garden, lie the remains of two Gothic churches, Kościół św. Michala (St Michael's) and Kościół św. Jerzego (St George's), both raised in the fourteenth century only to be demolished by the Austrians. Beyond the ruins, it's worth taking in the **view** over the river from the terrace at the western edge of the hill.

The Cathedral

"The sanctuary of the nation . . . cannot be entered without an inner trembling, without an awe, for here – as in few cathedrals of the world – is contained a vast greatness which speaks to us of the history of Poland, of all our past." So was the **cathedral** (Mon–Sat 9am–2.45pm, Sun 12.15–2.45pm) evoked by former Archbishop Karol Wojtyła of Kraków. As with Westminster Abbey or St Peter's, the moment you enter Wawel, you know you're in a place resonant to the core with national history.

The first cathedral was built here around 1020 when King Bolesław the Brave established the Kraków bishopric. Fragments of this building can still be seen in the west wing of the castle and the courtyard between the castle and the cathedral, while the St Leonard's crypt survives from a second Romanesque structure. The present brick and sandstone basilica is essentially Gothic, dating from the reigns of Władysław the Short (1306–33) and Kazimierz the Great (1333–70), and adorned with a mass of side chapels, endowed by just about every subsequent Polish monarch and a fair number of aristocratic families too. All bar four of Poland's 45 monarchs are buried in the cathedral, and the royal tombs and chapels, or **Groby Królewskie**, are a directory of six centuries of Central European architecture, art and sculpture.

As you enter the cathedral, look out for the bizarre collection of **prehistoric animal bones**, supposedly the remains of the Krak dragon (see p.384), but actually a mammoth's shinbone, a whale's rib and the skull of a hairy rhinoceros, in a passage near the main entrance. As long as they remain, so legend maintains, the cathedral will too.

The view down the nave of the cathedral, with its arched Gothic vaulting, is blocked by the **Mauzoleum św. Stanisława**, an overwrought seventeenth-century silver sarcophagus by the Gdańsk smith Peter van der Rennen. It commemorates the bishop who is supposed to have been murdered by King Bolesław at Skałka in Kazimierz (see p.425) in 1079 for his opposition to royal ambitions. The remains of the bishop-saint, who was canonized in 1253, were moved to Wawel the following year, and his shrine became a place of pilgrimage.

Below the shrine, on the right, is the **Sarkofag Władysława Jagiełło** (tomb of King Władysław Jagiełło), a beautiful marble creation from the mid-1400s with a fine Renaissance canopy added on by the king's grandson, Sigismund the Old (Zygmunt I Stary) a century later. Beyond stands the Baroque **high altar** and choir stalls. However, most people are drawn immediately to the outstanding array of side chapels which punctuate the entire length of the building.

To the right of the entrance, the Gothic **Kaplica Świętokrzyska** (Holy Cross Chapel) is the burial chamber of King Kazimierz IV Jagiełło (1447–92). The boldly coloured, Byzantine-looking paintings on the walls and ceiling were completed by artists from Novgorod, one of a small group of such murals in Poland, while the king's red marble tomb is the characteristically expressive work of Veit Stoss, of Mariacki fame. Two carved Gothic altars and a beautiful triptych of the Holy Trinity in the side panels round off a sumptuously elegant masterpiece.

Moving down the aisle, the next two chapels celebrate aristocratic families rather than kings: the **Potocki** (a Neoclassical creation) and **Szafraniec** (a Baroque ensemble at the foot of the Silver Bells tower). They are followed by the majestic, if gloomy, **Kaplica Wazówa** (Waza Chapel), a Baroque mausoleum to the seventeenth-century royal dynasty whose design is based on the Sigismund Chapel (see below). Protecting the chapel are some elaborately worked **bronze doors** displaying the dynastic coats of arms along with those of all their territories. The **Kaplica Zygmuntowska** (Sigismund Chapel), whose shining gilded cupola – its exterior regularly replated owing to the corrosive effects of pollution – dominates the courtyard outside. Designed for King Sigismund the Old (1506–48) by the Italian architect Bartolomeo Berrecci and completed in 1533, it's an astonishing piece of Renaissance design and ornamentation. Widely regarded as one of the artistic gems of the period, it features intricate sandstone and marble carvings, and superb sculpted figures above the sarcophagi of the king, his son Sigismund August and his wife Queen Anna. The two altarpieces are spectacular, too: the silver Altar of the Virgin was designed by craftsmen from Nuremberg and includes Passion paintings by George Pencz, a pupil of Dürer. Opposite the chapel is the modern **tomb of Queen Jadwiga**, wife of King Władysław Jagiełło and one of the country's most loved monarchs – in reality, her remains are buried nearby beneath her own favourite crucifix.

Venerable fourteenth-century bishops occupy several subsequent chapels, while the Gothic red Hungarian marble **tomb of King Kazimierz the Great**, immediately to the right of the high altar, is a dignified tribute in marble and sandstone to the revered monarch, during whose reign the cathedral was actually consecrated. The fourteenth-century **Kaplica Mariacka** (St Mary's Chapel), directly behind the altar and connected to the castle by a passage, was remodelled in the 1590s by Santi Gucci to accommodate the austere black marble and sandstone tomb of King Stefan Batory (1576–86). The **tomb of King Władysław the Short** (1306–33), on the left-hand side of the altar, is the oldest in the cathedral, completed soon after his death; the reclining, coronation-robed figure lies on a white sandstone tomb edged with expressive mourning figures.

The Wieża Zygmuntowska, the crypts and the Muzeum Katedralne

An ascent of the fourteenth-century **Wieża Zygmuntowska** (same hours as the cathedral, see p.411; 5zł), accessed through the sacristy, gives a far-reaching

4

panorama over the city and close-up views of the five medieval bells. The largest, an eight-tonne monster known as "Zygmunt", cast in 1520, is two and a half metres in diameter, eight in circumference, and famed for its deep, sonorous tone, which according to local legend scatters rain clouds and brings out the sun. These days it doesn't get too many chances to perform, as it's only rung on Easter Sunday, Christmas Eve and New Year's Eve.

Back in the cathedral, the **crypt** (in the left aisle) houses the remains of numerous Polish kings and queens, many encased in pewter sarcophagi, notably the Sigismunds and Stefan Batory. Also buried here are the poets Adam Mickiewicz and Juliusz Słowacki, while the early twelfth-century **Krypta św. Leonarda** (St Leonard's crypt), part of a long network of vaults reached from near the main entrance, contains the tombs of national heroes Prince Józef Poniatowski and Tadeusz Kościuszko. The equally sanctified prewar independence leader Józef Piłsudski lies in a separate vault nearby. Standing with the crowds filing past this pantheon, you catch the passionate intensity of Polish attachment to everything connected with past resistance and independent nationhood. The exit from the crypt takes you back out of the building and onto the main Wawel courtyard.

The highlights of the **Muzeum Katedralne** (Cathedral Museum; Tues–Sun 10am–3pm; 5zł), in a separate building opposite the cathedral's main door, includes a collection of illuminated texts and some odd items of Polish royal and ecclesiastical history – St Maurice's spear (a present to King Bolesław the Brave from Emperor Otto III when they met at Gniezno in 1000 AD), an eighth-century miniature of the four Evangelists, and King Kazimierz the Great's crown.

The castle

Entering the tiered courtyard of the **royal castle**, which occupies the eastern half of the Wawel complex, you might imagine that you'd stumbled on an opulent Italian palazzo. This is exactly the effect Sigismund the Old intended when he entrusted the conversion of King Kazimierz's Gothic castle to Florentine architect Bartolomeo Berrecci (c.1480–1537) in the early 1500s. The major difference from its Italian models lies in the response to climate: the window openings are enlarged to maximize the available light, while the overhanging wooden roof – held up by an unusually sensual set of bulbous columns – is sturdier to withstand snow. A spate of fires, and more recently the corrosive effects of Kraków's atmosphere, have taken their toll on the building, but it still exudes a palatial bravura.

After the capital moved to Warsaw, the palace started to deteriorate, and was already in a dilapidated state when the Austrians pillaged it and turned it into barracks. Reconstruction began in earnest in 1880, following Emperor Franz Josef's removal of the troops, and continued throughout the interwar years. Wawel's nadir came during World War II, when Governor Hans Frank transformed the castle into his private quarters, adding insult to injury by turning the royal apartments over to his Nazi henchmen. Luckily, many of the most valuable castle contents were spirited out of the country at the outbreak of war, eventually being returned to Wawel from Canada in 1961, after years of wrangling. Alongside many pieces donated by individual Poles at home and abroad – some of these, incidentally, items plundered by the Nazis but subsequently spotted at art auctions – they make up the core of today's ample and well-restored collection.

The castle is divided into four main sections: the **Komnaty Królewskie** (State Rooms), **Skarbiec** (Royal Treasury and Armoury), and the **Sztuka**

Wschodu (Oriental Art Exhibition) and **Wawel Zaginiony** (Lost Wawel) exhibitions – remember that tickets for the state rooms and treasury won't gain you admittance to the other two sights, for which you'll need to pay separately. The state rooms are the section to focus on if time is limited, as the best of the art collections – accumulated by the Jagiellonian and Waza dynasties – are to be found here.

The Komnaty Królewskie

The centrepiece of the art collections in the **Komnaty Królewskie** (State Rooms; April–Oct Tues, Thurs & Fri 9.30am–4pm, Wed & Sat 9.30am–3pm, Sun 10am–3pm; Nov–March Tues–Sat 9.30am–3pm, Sun 10am–3pm; 14zł) is King Sigismund August's splendid assembly of **Flanders tapestries**, scattered throughout the first and second floors. The 136 pieces – about a third of the original collection – are what remains from the depredations of tsarist, Austrian and Nazi armies. Outstanding are three series from the Brussels workshops of the "Flemish Raphael", Michel Coxie, the first and most impressive of which is a group of eighteen huge Old Testament scenes, featuring a lyrical evocation of Paradise and a wonderfully detailed tapestry of Noah and family in the aftermath of the Flood. The oldest tapestry in the castle is the mid-fifteenth-century French *Story of the Swan Knight* displayed in Sigismund the Old's first-floor bedroom.

In the northwest corner of the first floor is a remnant of the original Gothic castle, a tiny two-roomed watchtower named the **Cock's Foot Tower**. In contrast to other parts of the castle, the rooms of the north wing are in early Baroque style, the result of remodelling following a major fire in 1595. Of the luxurious apartments in this section, the **Silver Hall**, redesigned in 1786 by Domenico Merlini (of Warsaw's Łazienki Park fame), achieves a particularly harmonious blending of the old architecture with period classicism.

The state rooms on the top floor are among the finest in the building, particularly those in the **east wing** where the original wooden ceilings and wall paintings are still visible. A glance upwards at the carved ceiling of the **Audience Hall** at the southern end of the wing will tell you why it's nicknamed the "Heads Room". Created for King Sigismund in the 1530s by Sebastian Tauerbach of Wrocław and Jan Snycerz, only thirty of its original array of nearly two hundred heads remain, but it's enough to give you a feeling for the contemporary characters, from all strata of society, on which they were based. The frieze by Hans Dürer, brother of the famous Albrecht, illustrates The Life of Man, a sixteenth-century retelling of an ancient Greek legend, while the magnificent tapestries of biblical stories – the Garden of Eden, Noah and the Tower of Babel – are again from the Coxie workshop.

Back down the corridor is the **Zodiac Room**, ornamented by an astrological frieze, an ingenious 1920s reconstruction of a sixteenth-century fresco, as well as another series of biblical tapestries. The northeast corner towers contain the private royal apartments. The **chapel**, rebuilt in 1602, looks onto the king's bedchamber, while the walls of the **study**, with its fine floor and stucco decorations, are a mini-art gallery in themselves, crammed with works by Dutch and Flemish artists, among them a Rubens sketch and a painting by the younger Brueghel. The seventeenth-century **Bird Room**, named after the wooden birds that used to hang from the ceiling, leads on to the **Eagle Room**, the old court of justice, with a Rubens portrait of Prince Władysław Waza. Last comes the large **Senators' Hall**, originally used for formal meetings of the Senate in the days when Kraków was still the capital, which houses a collection of tapestries illustrating the story of Noah and the Ark, another impressive coffered ceiling and a sixteenth-century minstrel's gallery still used for the occasional concert.

The Skarbiec

If you've got the stamina, the next thing to head for is the **Skarbiec** (Royal Treasury and Armoury; same hours as Komnaty Królewskie; 14zł) in the northeast corner of the castle (entrance on the ground floor). The paucity of crown jewels on display, however, is testimony to the ravages of the past. Much of the treasury's contents had been sold off by the time of the Partitions to pay off marriage dowries and debts of state. The Prussians did most of the rest of the damage, purloining the coronation insignia in 1795, then melting down the crown and selling off its jewels. The vaulted Gothic **Kazimierz Room** contains the finest items from a haphazard display of lesser royal possessions including rings, crosses and the coronation shoes and burial crown of Sigismund August. The oldest exhibit is a fifth-century ring inscribed with the name "MARTINVS", found near Kraków.

The prize exhibit in the next-door **Jadwiga and Jagiełło Room** is the solemnly displayed Szczerbiec, a thirteenth-century copy of the weapon used by Bolesław the Brave during his triumphal capture of Kiev in 1018, used from then on in the coronation of Polish monarchs. Like other valuable items in the collection here, the sword was taken to Canada during World War II for safekeeping. The other two exhibits here are an early sixteenth-century sword belonging to Sigismund the Old, and the oldest surviving royal banner, made in 1533 for the coronation of Sigismund August's third wife, Catherine von Habsburg. In the following room are a variety of items connected with **Jan Sobieski**, most notably the regalia of the Knights of the Order of the Holy Ghost sent to him by the pope as thanks for defeating the Turks at Vienna in 1683. Things get more military from here on. The next barrel-vaulted room contains a host of finely crafted display weapons, shields and helmets, while the final **Armoury Room** is dedicated to serious warfare, with weapons captured over five centuries from Poland's host of foreign invaders, including copies of the banners seized during the epic Battle of Grunwald (1410), a fearsome selection of huge double-handed swords and a forbidding array of spears with weird and wonderful spikes on top.

The Sztuka Wschodu and Wawel Zaginiony

The **Sztuka Wschodu** (Oriental Art Exhibition; April–Oct Tues, Thurs & Fri 9.30am–4pm, Wed & Sat 9.30am–3pm, Sun 10am–3pm; Nov–March Tues–Sat 9.30am–3pm; 6zł), housed in the older west wing of the castle, focuses on Oriental influences in Polish culture. The first floor has an interesting section on early contacts with Armenia, Iran, Turkey, China and Japan, but the main "influences" displayed here seem to be war loot from the seventeenth-century campaigns against the Turks. The centrepiece is a collection of **Turkish tents and armour** captured after the Battle of Vienna, with a prize bust of Sobieski swathed in emperor-like laurels in attendance. Other second-floor rooms display an equally sumptuous assortment of Turkish and Iranian carpets, banners and weaponry seized during the fighting – the sixteenth-century **Paradise carpet** must have gone very nicely in the royal front room.

South of the cathedral is the **Wawel Zaginiony** exhibition (Lost Wawel; April–Oct Mon 9.30am–noon, Tues, Thurs & Fri 9.30am–4pm, Wed & Sat 9.30am–3pm, Sun 10am–3pm; Nov–March Tues–Sat 9.30am–3pm; 6zł), beneath the old kitchens and coach house. The route there takes you past the excavated remains of the hill's most ancient buildings, including the foundations of the tenth-century **Rotunda św. Feliksa i Adaukta** (Rotunda of SS Felix and Adauctus), the oldest known church in Poland. A diverse collection of medieval archeological finds rounds off the display.

Around Wawel

If you're feeling energetic, you could, instead of returning directly to town, clamber down the steps at the eastern end of the Wawel precinct to the **Smocza Jama** (Dragon's Cave; April–Oct Mon 9.30am–noon, Tues, Thurs & Fri 9.30am–4pm, Wed & Sat 9.30am–3pm, Sun 10am–3pm; Nov–March Tues–Sat 9.30am–3pm, Sun 10am–3pm; 3zł) at the foot of the hill. The legendary haunt of Krak (see p.384) and the medieval site of a fishermen's tavern, the den is now guarded by an aggressive-looking bronze dragon that entertains tourists by belching a brief blast of fire every couple of minutes. It's very popular with the school parties that descend here in droves from the castle, snapping up trinkets from the massed ranks of souvenir sellers. From the Dragon's Cave, a walk west along the bend of the river towards the **Dębnicki bridge** is rewarded by an excellent view back over the castle.

The Manggha Japanese Art Centre

Crossing the Dębnicki bridge to the opposite side of the Wisła will place you within five minutes' walking distance of the **Centrum Sztuki i Techniki Japońskiej Manggha** (Manggha Japanese Art Centre; Tues–Sun 10am–6pm; Ⓦ www.manggha.krakow.pl; 8zł) at Konopnickiej 26, a cool slab of modernist architecture designed by Aratolsozaki of the Los Angeles Art Gallery and Barcelona Olympic Stadium fame. Founded on the initiative of various Polish cultural figures including, among others, Oscar-winning film-maker Andrzej Wajda, the centre houses the extensive collection of Japanese art amassed by Feliks "Manggha" Jasieński, Poland's leading nineteenth-century Japanologist. Jasieński, who exerted a huge influence over the Młoda Polska generation (see box, p.405), wrote a much admired book about Eastern aesthetics entitled *Manggha* (his transliteration of the Japanese term "manga", or sketch), and subsequently adopted the term as his own literary pseudonym. Among the exhibits are ceramics, silks, samurai armour, and one of the finest collections of late eighteenth- to early nineteenth-century woodcuts you're likely to see in Europe. The centre's terrace café, a popular meeting place, offers a good view onto the river and Wawel Hill.

The Muzeum Narodowe and the Dom Mehoffera

Ten minutes west of the university district along ul. Piłsudskiego, a tawny-coloured lump of interwar architecture at al. 3 Maja 1 provides a suitably imperious-looking home for the **Muzeum Narodowe** (National Museum; Tues, Thurs, Sat & Sun 10am–3pm, Wed & Fri 11am–6pm; 8zł). There's an impressive hoard of objects relating to Polish history inside, starting with a **weapons gallery** packed with the shining breastplates and eagle-feather accessories that made the Polish hussars such a fearsome sight on the seventeenth-century battlefields of Europe. A sizeable collection of **military uniforms** takes the story up to the twentieth century – the sober grey tunic of interwar leader Marshal Piłsudski standing in stark contrast to the comic-opera kit donned by Polish uhlans serving with the Austro-Hungarian cavalry. The museum's other main strength is **decorative art**: among the highlights are brightly enamelled Romanesque crosses from Limoges (one sporting an effigy of Jesus so beady-eyed that he looks like a crucified fish), and stunning stained glass from Kraków's medieval churches. Look out too for the display of silky robes and sashes worn by local noblemen in the seventeenth and eighteenth centuries, when the quixotic belief that the Polish aristocracy was descended from an ancient eastern tribe known as the Sarmatians (see box, p.474) sparked a craze for all things Oriental.

A short walk north of the Muzeum Narodowe at Krupnicza 26, the **Dom Mehoffera** (Mehoffer House; Tues & Thurs–Sun 10am–3.30pm, Wed 11am–6pm; 5zł, free on Sun) is an essential stop off on any Młoda Polska tour of Kraków. Occupying the house where Wyspiański's friend and professional rival Józef Mehoffer lived and worked, it's stuffed with *belle-époque* furnishings, pictures of old Kraków and Mehoffer's own artworks. Portraits of contemporaries cover the walls of rooms decked out in Art-Nouveau-inspired curtains and wallpaper (most designed by Mehoffer himself), and among several larger, symbolist works, there's a stained-glass allegory of the immortality of art in which smiling muses hover fairy-like above the pale form of a dying maiden.

Kazimierz and the ghettoes

(The) Jews are gone. One can only try to preserve, maintain and fix the memory of them – not only of their struggle and death (as in Warsaw and Auschwitz), but of their life, of the values that guided their yearnings, of the international life and their unique culture. Cracow was one of the places where that life was most rich, most beautiful, most varied, and the most evidence of it has survived here.

Henryk Halkowski, a surviving Kraków Jew. Extracted from *Upon the Doorposts of Thy House* by Ruth Ellen Gruber (Wiley)

South from Wawel Hill lies the suburb of **Kazimierz**, originally a distinct town named in honour of King Kazimierz, who founded the settlement in 1335. The king's intention was to break the power of Kraków's German-dominated merchant class by establishing a rival market centre, and the granting of royal privileges to the new settlement led to its rapid development – as attested to by its huge Rynek and impressive collection of churches. Initially settled by Poles, the ethnic make-up of Kazimierz began to change with King Jan Olbracht's decision to move Kraków's significant **Jewish population** into the area from the Stare Miasto in 1495.

In tandem with Warsaw, where a **ghetto** was created around the same time, Kazimierz grew to become one of the main cultural centres of Polish Jewry. Jews were initially limited to an area around modern-day ul. Szeroka and Miodowa, and it was only in the nineteenth century that they began to spread into other parts of Kazimierz. By this time there were ghettoes all over the country, but descriptions of Kazimierz in Polish art and literature make it clear that there was something special about the headily Oriental atmosphere of this place.

The soul of the area was to perish in the gas chambers of nearby Auschwitz, but many of the buildings, synagogues included, have survived. Walking round the streets today, you feel the weight of an absent culture. Yiddish inscriptions fronting the doorways, an old pharmacy, a ruined theatre: the details make it easier to picture what has gone than wandering around the drab postwar housing estates covering the former Warsaw Ghetto.

Recent years have seen a marked **revival** of life and activity in Kazimierz. Long-neglected buildings are being renovated, many with financial assistance from the worldwide Jewish community, and the area has seen a marked increase in visitors – in part thanks to Steven Spielberg's film *Schindler's List*, much of which was filmed in and around Kazimierz. Modern Kazimierz is an invigorating mixture of gentrified tourist suburb and bohemian inner-city area: cafés, bars and clubs patronized by sassy young Cracovians have succesfully colonized Kazimierz's old tenement houses, making it Kraków's number one

One of the major Jewish communities in Poland for much of the last six centuries, the Jews of Kraków occupy a significant place in the history of the city. The first Jews settled in Kraków in the second half of the **thirteenth century**, a small community establishing itself on ul. św. Anny, then known as ul. Żydowska (Jewish Street), in today's university district, with a synagogue, baths and cemetery beyond the city walls. By the **fourteenth century**, the community still numbered no more than a couple of hundred people, but in the **fifteenth century** it was enlarged by an influx of Jews from all over Europe – notably Bohemia, Germany, Italy and Spain – fleeing growing persecution and discrimination in their homelands. Significant numbers of Jews were by now setting up home south of the Stare Miasto in Kazimierz, where they built their own ritual baths, a marketplace and a synagogue (the predecessor of the Stara Synagoga that you can still see standing today), thereby shifting the focus of community life away from the traditional areas of settlement around ul. św. Anny. It was a process completed in 1495, when a serious fire in the city was blamed on the Jews, provoking their expulsion from the Stare Miasto – thus swelling the ranks of those in Kazimierz.

Economically, the Reformation era was a time of significant growth for the city, a development in which Jews participated actively as goldsmiths, publishers, furriers and, especially, butchers. Culturally the **sixteenth century** was also something of a golden age for Jewish culture in Kraków, with local Talmudic scholars and the books produced on the printing presses of Menachim Meisler and others enjoying high international prestige. As a mark of their growing authority, rabbis and elders of the Kraków community were chosen to represent Małopolska on the Council of the Four Lands (see box, p.298) when it met for the first time in Lublin in 1581. The ghetto area was expanded in 1583, and again in 1603, attaining a considerable size which it retained for the next two centuries, with a fence and stone wall along ul. Józefa separating it from the rest of Kazimierz.

Economically, the community's heyday came to a end with the Swedish invasions (known popularly as the "Swedish Deluge") of the mid-**seventeenth century**, when Charles X's troops occupied the city and systematically destroyed large parts of it. By 1657, the ghetto population of around 4500 had declined by two-thirds, many Jews having emigrated to other parts of the country, notably the new capital Warsaw, in search of better times. Throughout the **eighteenth century**, the age-old struggle for economic ascendancy between Jewish and Gentile merchants and craftspeople continued apace, as elsewhere, culminating in the issue of an edict severely curtailing Jews' economic freedoms and even, in 1776, an order for them to leave Kazimierz altogether. The Austrian occupation of Kraków in 1776 in the wake of the First Partition temporarily put a lid on local squabbling. The Austrians' initial move was to incorporate the whole of Kraków directly into Austrian territory, abolishing the separate judicial status of Kazimierz and all other outlying districts in the process.

Under the terms of a **nineteenth-century** statute promulgated in the wake of the establishment of the Free City of Kraków (1815–46), the ghetto was officially liquidated and the walls separating it torn down, with a direct view to encouraging assimilation among the Jewish population. Jews were now permitted to live anywhere in Kazimierz, and with special permits, duly granted to merchants and craftsmen, to reside throughout the city area. It was another almost fifty years, however, before they were granted the right to vote in elections to the Austro-Hungarian Diet, eventually also benefiting from the Habsburg declaration of equal rights for all Jewish subjects of the empire.

The period following the end of **World War I** and the regaining of Polish independence was one of intense population growth in Jewish Kraków, the community rising from 45,000 people in 1921 to nearly 57,000 a decade later, and over 64,000 on the eve of the Nazi invasion of Poland. Most, but by no means all, of Kraków's Jews lived in Kazimierz. The inward-looking and mostly poor Hassidim dominated the synagogues, prayer houses and Talmudic schools of the quarter, while the more integrated, upwardly mobile sections of the community moved out into other city districts, the Stare Miasto included, and increasingly adopted the manners and educational habits of their Gentile neighbours. This was a period of rich cultural activity, notably in the Jewish Theatre, established in 1926 in southern Kazimierz, the biggest star being the legendary Ida Kamińska, still remembered today as one of the great prewar Polish actresses. Contemporary accounts make it clear that Kazimierz possessed a memorable and unique atmosphere, the predominantly poor but intensely vibrant Jewish community carrying on unchanged the traditions of its forebears, seemingly oblivious to the increasingly menacing world outside it.

Following the **Nazi invasion** of Poland, Kraków was occupied by Wehrmacht units on September 6, 1939, and within days the Nazi Security Police issued an order directing all Jewish-owned commercial enterprises to be daubed with a Star of David. A month later, the General Government was established with its capital in Kraków, and the new Nazi governor Hans Frank arrived to take over. A series of increasingly restrictive laws began to affect Jews. From the end of November 1939, all Jews were required to wear the notorious blue and white armbands, and in May 1940, Frank embarked on a drive to enforce this edict, a campaign that continued through the winter.

From here on the situation deteriorated. In March 1941, an official **ghetto** area was established. Located in the Podgórze district, south of Kazimierz across the river, the ghetto was surrounded and effectively sealed off by two-metre-high walls. As the year progressed, Jews from the area surrounding Kraków were herded into the cramped and insanitary ghetto area, and from June 1942 onwards, fearsome and bloody mass deportations from the ghetto to Bełżec concentration camp – and eventually Auschwitz-Birkenau – began. Compounding the torture and destruction, a new forced labour camp was set up in November 1942 at Płaszów, just south of the ghetto (see p.426).

A major SS operation on March 14, 1943 removed or murdered the remains of the ghetto population. Those not killed in cold blood on the streets were either marched out to Płaszów or transported to the gas chambers of Auschwitz. Thus was nearly seven hundred years of Jewish presence in Kraków uprooted and effectively destroyed. Under the ruthless rule of its notorious commander **Amon Goeth**, Płaszów was transformed into a murderous work camp where those who didn't die from hunger, disease and exhaustion were regularly finished off at whim by the twisted Goeth himself, who was later caught, tried and executed in Kraków in September 1946. In January 1945, with Soviet forces rapidly advancing west, many of the surviving camp inmates were moved to Auschwitz (the workers at Oskar Schindler's factory excepted), and the site dynamited by the camp guards.

In many ways, the **postwar history** of Kraków's Jews parallels that of other Polish cities with notable prewar Jewish communities. By the end of 1945, roughly 6000 survivors had returned to the city, about a third of whom had lived there before the war. Subsequent waves of emigration to Israel and the USA went in step with the ups and downs of domestic and international politics, the largest occurring in the wake of the post-Stalinist "thaw" (1957), the Six Day War and the semi-official anti-Semitic campaigns subsequently unleashed in Poland in 1968–69, leaving an increasingly introverted and elderly community hanging on by the 1980s. Developments since the communist demise in 1989 have been marked by a notable upsurge in interest in the city's Jewish past, symbolized by the increasingly popular annual summer **Jewish Festival** (June/July) held in Kazimierz, and a determined drive to renovate and rebuild the fading architectural glories of the quarter. The city's Jewish population can never be fully reconstituted, but the effort to ensure that their culture and memory receive due recognition continues today.

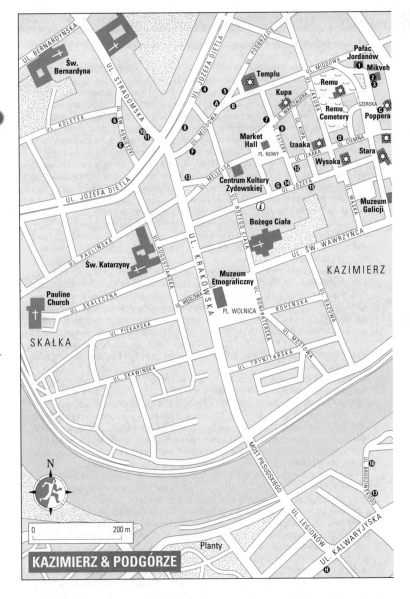

KAZIMIERZ & PODGÓRZE

area for nightlife outside the Stare Miasto itself. Above all, today's Kazimierz is a place to enjoy, as well as to ponder the more profound aspects of Poland's Jewish heritage.

There's a Kazimierz branch of the Kraków **tourist information** office at ul. Jozefa 7 (Mon–Fri 10am–4pm), and signboard-maps marked with tourist sights are planted at regular intervals throughout the district.

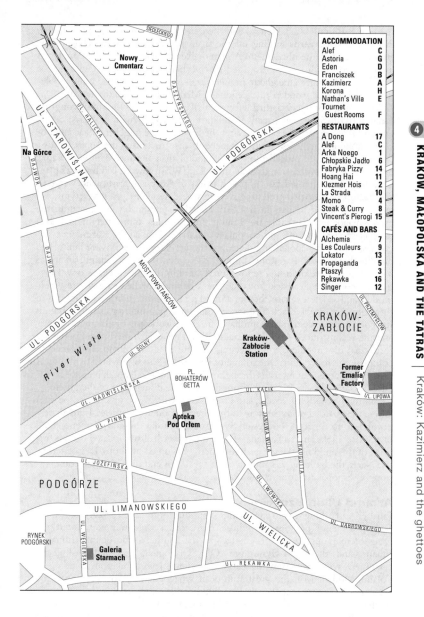

ACCOMMODATION

Alef	C
Astoria	G
Eden	D
Franciszek	B
Kazimierz	A
Korona	H
Nathan's Villa	E
Tournet Guest Rooms	F

RESTAURANTS

A Dong	17
Alef	C
Arka Noego	1
Chłopskie Jadło	6
Fabryka Pizzy	14
Hoang Hai	11
Klezmer Hois	2
La Strada	10
Momo	4
Steak & Curry	8
Vincent's Pierogi	15

CAFÉS AND BARS

Alchemia	7
Les Couleurs	9
Lokator	13
Propaganda	5
Ptaszyl	3
Rękawka	16
Singer	12

Along Ulica Józefa

Kazimierz is a ten-minute walk south of the Wawel (alternatively take tram #6, #8 or #10) along ul. Stradomska and its continuation, ul. Krakowska, which formerly separated the ghetto from the rest of the city. The obvious route into the ghetto is along **ulica Józefa**, so named following Emperor Joseph II's visit to the area during his tour of the regions of Poland annexed by the Habsburgs following the First Partition (1772). Here, as elsewhere in the area, wandering into the often dilapidated **courtyards** leading off the main street gives you a feeling of the atmosphere of the vanished ghetto. A memorable example of this is the **courtyard** linking Józefa with ul. Meiselsa, used by Spielberg for the scenes depicting the expulsion of Jews from the ghetto in *Schindler's List*, the whitewashed walls, cobblestones and arcaded wooden attics lending a Mediterranean aura to the place.

Continuing along Józefa, turn left into ul. Kupa and you'll find the **Synagoga Izaaka** (Isaac Synagogue; daily 9am–7pm, closed on Jewish holidays; 6zł), a graceful Baroque structure named after the wealthy local merchant, Isaac Jakubowicz (in Yiddish, reb Ajzyk), who financed its construction in the 1630s. Getting the building started proved more of a handful than the merchant anticipated: despite securing permission directly from King Władysław IV, Jakubowicz's plans were forcefully opposed by the parish priest of Corpus Christi, who wrote to the bishop of Kraków protesting that it would result in priests carrying the sacraments having to pass in front of, and thus presumably be contaminated by, a synagogue. Thankfully the bishop proved rather more enlightened than his ecclesiastical inferior, and building went ahead. Like all the Kazimierz synagogues, Ajzyk's was looted and destroyed by the Nazis, the surviving hull of the building being partially restored in the 1950s when it was turned into an artist's workshop. A more thorough renovation, started in the mid-1980s, is now functionally complete. Set back from the street behind a walled gate, the relatively modest and sedate exterior focuses around a raised twin staircase leading up to the main entrance. Notable features of the synagogue interior are the fabulous stuccoed **ceiling decoration**, probably from the workshop of Giovanni Falconi, and the reconstructed Aron Ha Kodesh. That said, overall the building retains a somewhat disembodied, empty feeling – more funds are obviously needed to complete the restoration. One source of revenue at least is provided by the short film, shown at regular intervals throughout the day, of local Jewish life shot by the BBC in 1936 along with scenes from the wartime dismantling of the ghetto.

Continuing along ul. Józefa, the intersection with ul. Jakuba marks the spot where the guarded main gateway to the ghetto stood for centuries. Immediately beyond, at no. 38, is the buttressed **Synagoga Wysoka** (High Synagogue), built in the late 1550s and so named because the prayer hall was located on the first floor of the building, the ground floor being occupied by shops. Devastated by the Nazis, the building was renovated in the 1960s and turned into a conservation workshop, a function it still retains.

Around Ulica Szeroka

Further east along ul. Józefa brings you out onto **ulica Szeroka** (Wide Street), a broad open space whose numerous synagogues constituted the focus of religious life in the ghetto. On the southern side of this truncated square stands the **Stara Synagoga** (Old Synagogue), the grandest of all the Kazimierz synagogues and the earliest surviving Jewish religious building in Poland. Modelled on the great European synagogues of Worms, Prague and Regensburg, the present Renaissance building was completed by Mateo Gucci in the 1570s, replacing an earlier brick building destroyed, like much of the surrounding area, by a fire in 1557. The synagogue's story is closely entwined with the country's history. It was here, for example, that Kościuszko came to rally Kraków Jews in 1794 in support of armed resistance to the Partitions, a precedent followed by the Kazimierz rabbi Ber Meissels during the uprisings of 1831 and 1863. President Ignacy Mościcki made a symbolically important state visit to the synagogue in 1931, a move designed to demonstrate official amity with the country's Jewish population. Predictably, the Nazis did a thorough job of destroying the place. Following the war, the painstaking process of refashioning the building on the lines of Gucci's graceful original structure was initiated. The rebuilt synagogue was subsequently converted into a **museum** of the history and culture of Kraków Jewry (April–Oct Mon 10am–2pm, Tues–Sun 10am–5pm; Nov–March Wed, Thurs, Sat & Sun 9am–3.30pm, Fri 10am–6pm; 5zł). Nazi destruction was thorough, so the museum's collection of art, books, manuscripts and religious objects has a slightly cobbled-together feel to it, though there's an interesting and evocative set of photos of life in the ghetto before World War II. The superb wrought-iron bimah in the centre of the main prayer hall is original, the masterful product of a sixteenth-century Kraków workshop. With the general revival of interest in Jewish Kraków, the synagogue now plays host to an increasing number of temporary exhibitions relating to the history and culture of Polish Jewry, as well as providing one of the central locations for the annual summer **Jewish Cultural Festival**.

On the east side of Szeroka, no. 22 formerly housed the **Na Górce Synagogue**, associated with Rabbi Nathan Spira, a celebrated seventeenth-century cabbalist scholar, the tercentenary of whose death was the occasion for a major commemoration in Kazimierz in 1933. This and the surrounding houses were originally owned by the Jekeles family, one of the wealthiest merchant dynasties in Kazimierz and founders of the Isaac Synagogue (see opposite). Set back from the square behind a gated yard at no. 16 is the former **Synagoga Poppera** (Popper or Stork's Synagogue), a typical brick structure raised in the 1620s by another wealthy local merchant family. These days it houses a youth cultural centre, open unpredictably, every trace of its original purpose having been erased by the Nazis. On the far northern corner of the square stands the old community bathhouse and mikveh, now the *Klezmer Hois* café-restaurant (see "Restaurants", p.437).

Moving across to the northwestern part of the square, the tiny **Synagoga Remu** (Remu'h Synagogue) at ul. Szeroka 40 (Mon–Fri 9am–4pm) is one of two still functioning in the quarter. Built in 1557 on the site of an earlier wooden synagogue, it was ransacked by the Nazis and restored after the war. It's named after Moses Isserles, also known as Rabbi Remu'h, an eminent Polish writer and philosopher and the son of the synagogue's founder. On Fridays and Saturdays, the small local congregation is regularly swelled by the increasing number of Jews visiting Poland these days. Behind the synagogue is the Remu'h **cemetery**, established twenty or so years earlier, and in use till the end of the eighteenth century, after which it was supplanted by the New Cemetery (see p.424). Many of the gravestones were unearthed in the 1950s having been covered with a layer of earth in the interwar years – a saving grace, as the rest of the cemetery was smashed up by the Nazis during the occupation. One of the finest stones is that of Rabbi Remu'h, its stele luxuriously ornamented with plant motifs. Just inside the entrance, tombstones torn up by the Nazis have been collaged together to form a high, powerful Wailing Wall.

Before leaving the ul. Szeroka area, it's worth making a short detour southeast to ul. Dajwór, where the **Muzeum Galicji** (Museum of Galicia; daily 9.30am–7pm; ⓦwww.galiciajewishmuseum.org; 7zł) at no. 18 is a privately funded enterprise located in a superbly restored brick warehouse. It's the perfect environment in which to peruse periodical exhibitions relating to southeastern Poland (which formed part of the former Austrian province of Galicia) and its Jewish heritage.

Around Ulica Miodowa

West of Szeroka along ul. Miodowa, on the corner of ul. Podbrzezie, is the **Synagoga Templu** (Tempel Synagogue; Mon–Fri 9am–5pm; 5zł), a magnificent, Neo-Renaissance construction founded in 1862 by the local Association of Progressive Jews, with whose modernist, reforming theology it was long identified. This is the second of the two synagogues in Kazimierz still used for worship today. The stunning interior presents an intoxicating blend of Moorish and Gothic influences, the large central hall surrounded by the women's gallery, erected on decorated iron supports, and graced by ornate wall decorations and lavish stuccowork on the ceiling. In the centre sits the bimah, and beyond it the white marble altar, separated from the main body of the interior by a decorated screen wall. Illuminating the whole building is a glowing set of 36 stained-glass windows, restored in the 1970s and visible only from the inside, featuring geometrical motifs alongside characteristic floral and plant designs.

Southeast of here, ul. Warszauera brings you to the **Synagoga Kupa** (Kupa Synagogue), built in the 1640s with funds collected from the local community. The first of the synagogues to be reopened as a functioning religious building after World War II, it's again not easy to view without prior arrangement. If the caretaker is around to let you in, the renovated interior shows few traces of its former character, the only surviving decoration being the zodiacal paintings covering the ceiling and beams of the gallery, and a seventeenth-century stone plaque below one of the windows. The exterior of the building stands flush against the old defensive walls of the area which you can see from around the corner on ul. Kupa.

Continuing west along ul. Warszauera brings you to pl. Nowy, the former Jewish marketplace and still referred to popularly as such. In the middle of the bustling square stands the old round covered **market hall**, little changed in appearance from its previous Jewish incarnation, when the building housed its own ritual slaughterhouse. West of the square along ul. Meiselsa, the **Centrum Kultury Żydowskiej** (Judaica Cultural Centre; Mon–Fri 10am–6pm, Sat & Sun 10am–2pm; ☎012/430 6449, ⓦ www.judaica.pl) at no. 17 hosts regular conferences and exhibitions – it's always worth looking in to see what's going on.

Finally, through the tunnel underneath the rail track at the far eastern end of ul. Miodowa, lies the **Nowy Cmentarz** (New Cemetery; Mon–Fri, Sun & Jewish holidays 9am–6pm; entrance through no. 55), a little-visited site that succeeded the Remu'h as the main Jewish burial site in the early 1800s. The contrast between the two places is striking. A quiet, brooding place of leafy, overgrown walkways and crumbling clusters of ornately carved monuments and tombstones, the cemetery is among the most powerful testaments to Jewish life in the district. In among the mausoleums of the great and good of Habsburg-era Kazimierz, for example, you'll find memorials erected after World War II by relatives of those who perished in the concentration camps, many of them simple tablets recording the names and dates of murdered family members. To the right of the entrance gate stands a memorial to local victims of the Holocaust.

Western Kazimierz

As the presence of several churches indicates, the western part of Kazimierz represents the heart of the original Christian settlement. Despite its Baroque overlay, which includes some ornately carved choir stalls and a boat-shaped pulpit complete with rigging, the interior of the Gothic **Kościół Bożego Ciała** (Church of Corpus Christi), on the corner of ul. Bożego Ciała, retains early features including stained-glass windows installed around 1420, tranquil cloisters and well-tended gardens. An additional feature is the grave of Italian architect Bartolomeo Berrecci, creator of the castle courtyard on Wawel Hill, who liked Kraków so much he settled down here – until killed in a drunken brawl in 1537. The Swedish king Carl Gustaf is supposed to have used the building as his operational base during the mid-seventeenth-century siege of the city. The high church looks onto **plac Wolnica**, the old market square of Kazimierz, now much smaller than it used to be, thanks to the houses built along the old trade route through it in the nineteenth century.

The fourteenth-century **town hall**, later rebuilt, stands in what used to be the middle of the square, its southern extension an overambitious nineteenth-century addition. It now houses the **Muzeum Etnograficzny**, the largest ethnographic museum in the country (Mon 10am–6pm, Wed–Fri 10am–3pm, Sat & Sun 10am–2pm; 4zł; free on Sun), a highly enjoyable treasure-trove of ethnic artefacts illustrating traditional lifestyles which begins with a series of re-created peasant interiors from all over Poland. Icons painted on glass occupy corners and niches in almost every room, testifying to the richness of rural craft traditions, and the exquisitely painted furniture in the Lower Silesian room will probably have you jotting down ideas for your dream cottage. An impressive collection of costumes awaits upstairs, alongside some intriguing insights into the often bizarre world of Polish folk culture – note the goat, stork and death's-head masks worn by Christmas carollers, and the alarming straw effigies burned at Shrovetide to mark the departure of winter.

Two more churches west of the square are worth looking in on. On ul. Skałeczna stands the fourteenth-century **Kościół św. Katarzyny** (St Catherine's Church), founded by King Kazimierz for Augustine monks brought from Prague. The large basilican structure, covered by an expansive roof, is a typical and structurally well-preserved example of Kraków Gothic, though the bare interior has suffered everything from earthquakes to the installation of an Austrian arsenal. The Gothic vestibule on the southern side of the church features some delicate carved stonework, while the adjoining cloisters contain some notable surviving fragments of the original Gothic murals. Further down the road is the **Pauline church and monastery**, occupying a riverbank site known as **Skałka** (the Rock). Tradition connects the church with St Stanisław, the bishop of Kraków, whose martyrdom by King Bolesław the Bold in 1079 is supposed to have happened here. Conscious of the symbolic position the canonized martyr grew to assume in the medieval tussle for power between Church and State, later kings made a point of doing ritual penance at the site following their coronation. An altar to the popular saint stands in the left aisle of the remodelled Baroque church – the piece of wood encased in glass beneath the altar is supposedly part of the block on which he was beheaded. Underneath the church is a **crypt** cut into the rock of the hill, which was turned into a mausoleum for famous Poles in the late nineteenth century. Eminent artists, writers and composers buried here include Kraków's own Stanisław Wyspiański, composer Karol Szymanowski, medieval historian Jan Długosz and most recently the Nobel-winning poet Czesław Milosz, laid to rest here in 2004.

Podgórze and Płaszów

Immediately south of Kazimierz, road and rail bridges reach across the Wisła to the suburb of **Podgórze**, another part of town with strong Jewish associations. It's a gritty, workaday place which lacks the fine buildings and post-communist affluence you'll come across elsewhere in Kraków, and you'll find a corresponding shortage of cafés, restaurants or other tourist facilities.

Long an area of mixed Polish and Jewish settlement, Podgórze owes its notoriety to the creation in March 1941 of a **ghetto** (centred on the suburb's main market square, today's pl. Bohaterów Getta), into which the entire Jewish population of the city was forcibly resettled. The area was sealed off by high walls and anyone caught entering or leaving unofficially was summarily executed. After waves of deportations to the concentration camps, the ghetto was finally liquidated in March 1943, thus ending seven centuries of Jewish life in Kraków. The story of the wartime ghetto shot to prominence in 1994 due to Steven Spielberg's film *Schindler's List*, based on Thomas Keneally's prize-winning book recounting the wartime exploits of Oskar Schindler, a German industrialist who saved the lives of hundreds of ghetto inhabitants. In search of authenticity, Spielberg shot the majority of the film in and around the area, sometimes using the original surviving buildings, as in the case of Schindler's Emalia factory, and in other cases, building locations from scratch – a prime example being the Płaszów concentration camp, re-created in an old quarry not far from the original site. The film has generated great interest in Podgórze's Jewish heritage, although the number of visitors who make their way down here is minuscule compared to the crowds descending on Kazimierz.

You can get to Podgórze by heading down either Krakowska or Starowiślna from Kazimierz and crossing over the river – the cast-iron **Most Piłsudskiego** (Piłsudski Bridge) at the southern end of Krakowska provides as fine a means of approach as any. Otherwise, trams #3 and #24 trundle from the Stare Miasto via Starowiślna to Podgórze's central pl. Bohaterów Getta.

Around Podgórze

The most obvious sign of past Jewish presence in Podgórze is the **Apteka Pod Orłem** (Pharmacy under the Eagles), the old ghetto pharmacy on the south-west corner of pl. Bohaterów Getta, now a **museum** (Tues–Fri 10am–4pm, Sat 10am–2pm; 4zł), whose recent renovation was in part financed by Kraków ghetto survivor Roman Polański. Inside lies a well-presented photographic and documentary record of life (and death) in the wartime ghetto, alongside artefacts relating to the pharmacy's wartime proprietor Dr Tadeusz Pankiewicz – the only Gentile permitted to live in the ghetto, and the prime point of contact between Jews and the world outside. The building at no. 6, on the other side of the square, was the headquarters of the Jewish Combat Organization (ŻOB) which continued operating until the ghetto's liquidation. Jews were regularly deported en masse from the square to the extermination camps of Treblinka and Auschwitz-Birkenau.

Ten minutes' walk east of the square, Oskar Schindler's **Emalia enamel factory** (these days producing electronic component parts) still stands at ul. Lipowa 4, just east of the railway tracks. Part of the factory hosts periodical exhibitions, when you'll be able to nose around the interior courtyard; at other times you'll have to be content with peering through the locked metal gate.

Although Podgórze is yet to display the signs of urban renewal so evident in nearby Kazimierz, it can still boast a relatively lively shopping street in the shape of **ul. Limanowskiego** just south and west of pl. Bohaterów Getta. There are some fine examples of nineteenth-century red-brick architecture in the surrounding streets, one of which accommodates the **Galeria Starmach** at Węgierska 5 (Mon–Fri 11am–6pm; ⓦ www.starmach.com.pl), Kraków's most adventurous contemporary art gallery.

Płaszów concentration camp

As well as imprisoning people in the ghetto, the Nazis also relocated many Jews to the **concentration camp at Płaszów**, built on the far side of an old Austrian hill fort 1.5km south of Podgórze. Levelled after the war, the site is now an empty heath bordered by concrete residential blocks. To get there, walk southeast from Podgórze along ul. Wielicka or take trams #3, #6, #9, #13, #23 or #24 (trams #3 and #24 come direct from the Stare Miasto, passing through Kazimierz on the way) to the Cmentarz Podgorski stop. Head down ul. Jerozolimska (marked by a sign reading "Podgórze: dawny obóz Płaszów" to find the camp entrance, which is marked by an unassuming signboard and a bland-looking detached house – formerly the villa occupied by camp commander Amon Goeth, it's now divided up into council flats. From here a path leads southeast through the heart of the camp. Now overrun by wild grasses and shrubs, this gently rolling landscape, punctuated by limestone outcrops, has the tranquil and untended feel of an inner-city nature reserve. After ten minutes a left fork leads up onto a verdant hill and to a monolithic concrete **monument** to the victims of the camp, erected in the 1960s. In true communist style, the inscription on its side refers simply to the "martyrs" of Hitlerism without mentioning their ethnicity. A smaller plaque placed nearby by the city's Jewish community states unequivocally who the victims of Płaszów actually were.

The Sanctuary of God's Mercy in Łagiewniki

Trams #11 and #23 head southwest from Podgórze's ul. Limanowskiego towards **Łagiewniki**, an area of housing projects, shopping centres and used car lots that wouldn't normally be worth a visit were it not for the strange, soaring form of the so-called **Sanktuarium Bożego Miłosierdzia** (Sanctuary of God's Mercy), a brand-new church located just uphill from the Łagiewniki tram stop. It was built to accommodate the growing number of pilgrims drawn to the next-door Convent of the Sisters of Mercy by its place in the cult of Sister Faustyna Kowalska (1905–38), a Catholic mystic who famously experienced visions of light emanating from the heart of Jesus Christ. Sister Faustyna's vision became a popular subject for spiritually inspired painters, one of whom donated a canvas to the Łagiewniki convent in 1940. Followers of Sister Faustyna – who call themselves the Apostles of Divine Mercy – have been flocking to this spot ever since. The new sanctuary, completed to coincide with the canonization of Sister Faustyna in 2000, is another example of the Polish Catholic Church's enthusiasm for boldly contemporary artistic statements. With a sky-piercing central spire and a curving, white exterior, it looks more like a beached ocean liner than a church. There's a remarkable sense of light and space inside, providing the perfect ambience for the seemingly continuous Masses which take place here throughout the day.

Western Kraków: Bronowice Małe, Zwierzyniec, Las Wolski and around

West of the Stare Miasto, a sequence of bustling residential quarters gradually give way to several unspoilt tracts of greenery. The largest of these is Las Wolski, a dense area of deciduous forest covered by a network of marked tracks. Architectural landmarks such as the churches of the Zwierzyniec district, the Kościuszko Mound, or the brace of monasteries at Bielany and Tyniec further west, serve as useful geographical points around which to base a leisurely suburban outing.

The area presents several good opportunities for **cycling**: potential itineraries include the trip from Zwierzyniec past the Kościuszko Mound and into Las Wolski forest; along the banks of the Rudawa stream northwest from Błonia; or along the south bank of the Wisła towards Tyniec. The gravelly tracks of the Las Wolski are perfect for a moderate burst of mountain biking.

Zwierzyniec

Moving west of Wawel along the loop of the river, you soon enter the Zwierzyniec district, one of the city's oldest suburbs and the home of several Kraków traditions, notably the custom of constructing *szopki* (cribs) at Christmas and the Lajkonik ceremony (see "Festivals and events", p.442).

Perched at the edge of the river opposite the Salwator tram stop (terminus of lines #1, #2 and #6 from the Stare Miasto), the **Norbertine church and monastery** is a fortified thirteenth-century structure with a fine Romanesque portal (all that remains of the original building) and a restful Neoclassical interior. Used by the nuns living in the complex, it's a good spot for a quiet moment away from the city bustle. The church isn't often open, though, so it's best to visit around the time of services – 5pm is generally a good bet. The annual Lajkonik pageant in June, believed to have been initiated by the nuns, starts from outside the complex.

Just up the hill from here is the **Kościół Salwatora** (Church of the Saviour), one of the oldest in the city. Built on the site of a pagan Slav temple, excavations have revealed three earlier Romanesque churches, the oldest dating back to around 1000 AD. Diagonally opposite the church is the curious octagonal **Kaplica św. Małgorzaty** (Chapel of St Margaret), an eighteenth-century wooden structure that rises out of the earth like a big brown breast. It's rarely open however, hosting a mere two Masses a month.

Tadeusz Kościuszko (1746–1817)

What Adam Mickiewicz is to the Polish literary Romantic tradition, **Tadeusz Kościuszko** is to its heroic military counterpart. Swashbuckling leader of armed national resistance in the early Partition years, Kościuszko was also a noted radical whose espousal of the republican ideals of the French Revolution did little to endear him to fellow aristocrats, but everything to win over the hearts and minds of the oppressed Polish peasantry. As the string of US towns and streets named after him testify, Kościuszko is also almost as well known in the USA as within Poland itself on account of his major role in the **American War of Independence**, in thanks for which he was made both an honorary American citizen and brigadier general in the US Army.

The bare bones of Kościuszko's life story revolve round a fabulously contorted series of battles, insurrections, revolutions and impossible love affairs. An outstanding student from the start, he fled to Paris in 1776 to escape from a general with whose daughter he had tried to elope, continuing on to America, where he joined up with the independence forces fighting the British. In the following five years he was right in the thick of things, helping to bring about the capitulation of the British forces under General Burgoyne at Saratoga (October 1778), and involved in both the important **Battle of the Ninety-Six** and the lengthy **blockade of Charleston** (1781).

Returning to Poland in 1784, he faced a lengthy period out in the political cold before finally gaining military office in 1789 – simultaneously failing (again) to win the consent of a general with whose eighteen-year-old daughter he had fallen in love. Kościuszko's finest hour came in 1792 with the tsarist army's invasion of Poland following the enactment of internal reforms intended to free the country from Russian influence. After the bloody **Battle of Dubienka** (July 1792), Kościuszko was promoted to general by King Stanisław Poniatowski, also receiving honorary French citizenship from the newly established revolutionary government in Paris. From enforced exile in Saxony, Kościuszko soon returned to Poland at the request of the expectant insurrectional army, swearing his famous **Oath of National Uprising** before a huge crowd assembled on the Rynek Główny in Kraków in March 1794.

From Salwator you can either continue west towards the Kościuszko Mound (see below), or loop back towards the centre via **Błonia**, a large green expanse twenty minutes' walk northeast. Originally a marshy bog, the area was subsequently drained and has served all manner of uses, from medieval football field to the site of the huge open-air Masses during Pope John Paul II's visits to Poland in 1979, 1983, 1987 and 2002. This last occasion attracted an estimated 2.2 million people, and is thought to be the biggest public gathering in Polish history.

The Kościuszko Mound

From the Salwator church, the tree-lined al. J. Waszyngtona heads west towards the **Kopiec Kościuszki** (Kościuszko Mound), a hundred-metre-high cone of soil erected in the 1820s in honour of Poland's greatest revolutionary hero, **Tadeusz Kościuszko** (see box below). A veteran of the American War of Independence, Kościuszko returned to Poland to lead the 1794 insurrection against the Partitions, and has served as a personification of Poland's insurrectionary tradition ever since. Kościuszko's Mound is the best known example of a uniquely Cracovian phenomenon which dates back as far as the seventh century – when man-made mounds were raised to honour chieftains or provide a platform for sky-worship. The tradition was continued with the construction of the Piłsudski Mound in the 1930s (see p.430), and current talk suggests that the next recipient of such a tribute will be Pope John Paul II.

The immediate results of Kościuszko's assumption of leadership were spectacular. A disciplined army, largely comprising scythe-bearing peasants, won a famous victory over Russian forces at the **Battle of Racławice** (April 1794). In a bid to gain more volunteer peasant recruits, Kościuszko issued the **Połaniec Manifesto** (May 1794), offering among other things to abolish serfdom, a radical move resisted by aristocratic supporters. Retreating to Warsaw, the embattled Polish forces held out for two months against the combined might of the Prussian and Russian armies, Kościuszko himself leading the bayonet charges at a couple of critical junctures. After inciting an insurrection in the Wielkopolska region that forced Prussian forces to retreat temporarily, Kościuszko was finally beaten and taken prisoner by the Russians at Maciejowice, an event that led to the collapse of the national uprising.

Imprisoned in St Petersburg and by now seriously ill, Kościuszko was freed in 1796 and returned to the USA to an enthusiastic reception in Philadelphia, soon striking up what proved to be a lasting friendship with Thomas Jefferson. The last decades of Kościuszko's life were marked by a series of further disappointments. He revisited France in 1798 in the hope that Napoleon's rise might presage a revival of Polish hopes, but refused to participate in Napoleon's plans, having failed to gain specific political commitments from Bonaparte with regard to Poland's future. Remaining studiously aloof from French advances, Kościuszko was again approached for support after Bonaparte's fall in 1814, this time from the unlikely quarter of the Russian emperor Alexander I, who attempted to gain his approval for the new Russian-ruled **Congress Kingdom** established at the Congress of Vienna (1815). Uncompromising republican to the last, the radical conditions he put forward met with no response. Embittered, Kościuszko retired to Switzerland, where he died in 1817. Two years later the legendary warrior's remains were brought to Kraków and buried among the monarchs in the vaults of Wawel. Reviving a pagan Polish burial custom, the people of the city raised the **memorial mound** to him you can still visit today.

The final approaches to the mound are dominated by a huge red-brick fort built by the city's Austrian rulers in the 1850s, and currently housing the **RMF radio station** – which explains why the fort's central courtyard bears the name of pl. Paul McCartney. Work your way round to the back of the fort to gain access to the mound itself (daily 9am–dusk; 5zł), which from this perspective looks like an enormous green pudding. An easily scaled spiral path winds its way to the top, where you can savour panoramic views back towards central Kraków, with the Wawel clearly visible in the foreground and the smokestacks of Nowa Huta further away to the northeast, even reaching as far as the Tatra mountains on really clear days.

If you're not in the mood for walking, you can catch bus #100, which runs to the mound and back from the Dębnicki stop near Rondo Grunwaldzkie, just across the river from the Wawel.

Las Wolski and the Piłsudski Mound

For a more extended bout of countryside, you could continue west from the Kościuszko Mound to the wonderful stretch of woodland known as **Las Wolski** (Wolski Forest), a popular area for picnics, hiking and cycling. Walking from the Kościuszko Mound, you can get there by continuing westward along al. J. Waszyngtona (30–40min); otherwise numerous bus routes from the centre pass nearby – #134 from the *Hotel Cracovia* being the most useful. The #134 terminates bang in the heart of the Las Wolski outside the gates of a small **zoo** (Ogród Zoologiczny) which, surrounded by snack stalls, is a good reference point on which to base your wanderings.

Ten minutes' walk northwest of the zoo stands another of Kraków's man-made mounds, this time raised in the late 1930s to honour interwar leader **Józef Piłsudski** (1867–1935). The mound was wilfully neglected during the postwar era by communist authorities uncomfortable with the man's political legacy, and in 1953 the granite memorial plaque placed on the summit was summarily removed using a tank. Calls for the mound's rehabilitation gathered pace during the 1980s, and in 1990 an ambitious restoration project received official support. After a few years of rebuilding work the mound is now in much better shape, with a newly restored granite memorial. As with its neighbour eastwards it affords some fine views over the city.

North of the zoo, the boundaries of Las Wolski are marked by **Park Decjusza** (also on the #134 bus route), built around a nineteenth-century neo-Renaissance villa (Palac Decjusza), now used for state receptions with a top-class restaurant in the cellar (see p.437). The northern edge of Park Decjusza is marked by one of Kraków's more curious galleries, the **Galeria Autorska Prof B. Chromego** (Bolesław Chromy Gallery), devoted to the work of the eponymous modern sculptor. Taking the form of a silvery dome rising out of a grassy hollow, it looks rather like a Byzantine cathedral designed by hobbits. There's an exhibition space and café inside, and a selection of sculptures scattered across the lawn outside.

Przegorzały

Marking the southeastern edge of Las Wolski is **Przegorzały**, a wooded hilltop overlooking the river Wisła, which was chosen by Hans Frank, Nazi governor of southern Poland, as the site for a modest weekend home. The red-brick, mock-medieval **Zamek w Przegorzałach** (Przegorzały Castle) was the result. Subsequently used by Kraków university as a conference centre, and currently home to the *U Ziyada* bar-restaurant (see p.437), it's popular with city folk as an out-of-town dining and drinking spot, especially during the summer. And understandably so: the main balcony offers a superb vantage point from which to take in the tranquil rural surroundings, with the Tatras visible in the distance on a really clear summer's day. A few minutes' uphill from the castle lies the modern campus (and hotel – see p.392) of the **Instytut Studiów Polonijnych i Etnicznych** (Institute of Polish and Ethnic Studies), behind which you can pick up trails back into the heart of Las Wolski. Buses #109, #209, #229, #239 and #249 from Salwator run past the access road to the centre.

The Camadulensian Hermitage at Bielany

Perched on a small hill on the southwestern edge of the Las Wolski, overlooking the settlement of Bielany, is the monumental **Camadulensian Hermitage** (Pustenia Kamedułów; gates opened at half-hour intervals between 9–11am and 3–4.30pm). It's an easy walk or cycle ride from either Las Wolski zoo or Przegorzały; otherwise take bus #109, #209, #229 or #239 from Salwator, alighting at the Srebrna Góra stop, from where it's a fifteen-minute walk up the hill. Before you decide to visit, bear in mind that **women** are not admitted to the complex except on certain religious holidays (Easter, Assumption and a smattering of other prominent Sundays throughout the year).

Only the hermitage's church and immediate forecourt are open to visitors: the monks themselves live behind the church in simple huts, devoting their days to gardening and prayer. Once through the hermitage's gate, you're confronted by the huge, crumbling facade of the **monastery church**, its high central section flanked by a pair of equally imposing square towers. The church's spacious interior consists of a soaring barrel-vaulted nave lined by a series of ornate chapels, the most notable of which, the **chapels of św. Benedykt** (St Benedict) and **św. Romuald** (St Romuald), feature a lavish series of paintings by the artist Tommaso Dolabella depicting the lives of the saints. A little behind the entrance is the tomb of the church's founder, Mikołaj Wolski, crown marshal of Poland in the early 1600s, placed here, it is said, so that churchgoers will walk over it – a stirring example of the humility the Camadolese aim to inculcate among their members. Steps lead down to the **crypt**, where the bodies of deceased hermits are stored in sealed niches for eighty years or so, after which they're taken out and buried in order to make room for the next generation of the dead.

The Camadolese Order

Of all the monastic orders present in Poland today, few could claim – or wish – to match the **Camadolese Order** for asceticism. The Order was founded in Italy in the second century AD by St Romuald (c.950–1027), and its ultra-ascetic practices include minimal contact between the monks, who live in their own separate hermitages, a vegetarian diet and little connection with the outside world. This asceticism attracted Polish champions of the Counter-Reformation, who invited them to settle in Poland, notably at **Bielany**. This they did, starting in the early 1600s, and they still retain a presence in the country, with two communities continuing to function. Well known in Polish Catholic circles for their grim motto, "Memento Mori" ("Remember that you must die"), the hermits don't actually sleep in wooden coffins, as popular rumour has it, though they do preserve the skulls of their long-deceased brethren. The Order's appeal however seems to be on the wane. Apart from the two houses in Poland, there are known to be only six other Camadolese hermitages left worldwide, four in Italy and two in Colombia.

Tyniec

Three kilometres southwest of Bielany on the opposite bank of the river, the village suburb of **Tyniec** is a popular excursion spot on summer weekends on account of its **abbey**, an eleventh-century foundation that was the Benedictines' first base in Poland. It's easy to get to from central Kraków, with bus #112 making its way here from the Dębnicki stop just across the river from the Wawel.

Perched on a white limestone cliff on the edge of the village, the abbey makes an impressive sight from the riverbank paths. The original Romanesque abbey was rebuilt after the Tatars destroyed it during the 1240 invasion, and then completely remodelled in Gothic style in the fifteenth century, when the defensive walls were also added. Most of the church's interior furnishings date from the Baroque era; particularly charming are the pulpit in the form of a ship's prow, and choir stalls individually painted with scenes from the life of St Benedict. From June to August the church holds a series of high-quality **organ concerts** during which the cloisters are opened.

Bronowice Małe

Straddling the main westbound highway 4km northwest of the centre, **Bronowice Małe** is nowadays an anonymous suburban district no different to hundreds of others around the country. However, to pre-World War I artistic folk, it was one of the most captivating places the Kraków region had to offer: an unspoiled village full of rustic buildings whose inhabitants still wore traditional costume every day. Many of the figures associated with the **Młoda Polska** period (see box, p.405) came here to sketch, scribble poems or meditate, among them the painter Włodzimierz Tetmayer (brother of the poet Kazimierz), who scandalized Kraków society by falling in love with – and marrying – local Bronowice girl Anna Mikołajczykówna in 1890. Not to be be outdone, essayist and playwright Lucjan Rydel tied the knot with Anna's sister Jadwiga ten years later. To their Młoda Polska contemporaries both Tetmayer and Rydel were living embodiments of the effort to rejuvenate Polish culture through contact with its peasant roots. Stanisław Wyspiański (himself married to peasant girl Teofila Pytko) used the weddings as real-life source material in his epoch-defining play *Wesele* ("The Wedding") – a haunting, hypnotic piece premiered in 1901 and still an unavoidable fixture in the Polish theatrical repertoire.

Still standing at ul. Tetmajera 28, the delightful house built by Tetmayer known as the **Rydlówka** (Tues, Wed, Fri & Sat 10am–2pm, Thurs 3–7pm; 3zł) contains a treasure-trove of Młoda Polska memorabilia, with cupboards and chests painted with folk motifs revealing the respect in which traditional Polish crafts were held. There are numerous photographs of the main protagonists in the Bronowice story, alongside pictures of the early productions of Wyspiański's play – with Rydel, appropriately enough, playing the groom. A display of traditional Polish wedding costumes rounds off the exhibition with a vivacious dash of colour. There's no labelling of any kind, so you really need to buy the English-language leaflet (3zł) to make any sense of the place.

Bronowice Małe can be reached by taking trams #4, #13 and #24 from Basztowa to the Bronowice terminus and walking north up Zielony Most – after passing under the railway, ul. Tetmajer is on your left. There's little else worth visiting in this part of Kraków, and precious few cafés or restaurants.

Nowa Huta and around

Raised from scratch in the late 1940s on the site of an old village, the vast industrial and residential complex of **Nowa Huta** now has a population of over

200,000, making it by far Kraków's biggest suburb, while the vast steelworks on its fringes accounts for more than fifty percent of the country's production. One of the epicentres of Solidarity-era opposition activity and all-round resistance to communist rule, it's worth visiting for the insights it offers into the working-class culture of postwar Poland. Made up of broad avenues laid out on a geometric plan, Nowa Huta is basically a gargantuan Stalinist re-working of Renaissance ideals – although the jury is still out on whether the settlement deserves be studied as an important example of urban planning or simply consigned to the dustbin of architectural history.

From Kraków city centre, it's a forty-minute tram journey (#4, #9, #15 or #22) to **plac Centralny**, a huge hexagonal space ringed by typically grey slabs of Socialist Realist architecture. From here, seemingly endless streets of residential blocks stretch out in all directions – a bigger contrast with the Stare Miasto would be hard to imagine. Two kilometres northeast along the main road, al. Solidarności, are the mills known for decades as the **Lenin Steelworks**, since renamed the Tadeusz Sendzimir Works, and still employing upwards of 10,000 people. The complex faced an uncertain future in the immediate post-communist period, due both to its role as a major environmental polluter, and its greedy reliance on government subsidues to remain in business. Such is Nowa Huta's importance as an employer, however, that it would be political suicide for any Polish government to allow it to go under.

For the time being, restructuring, and the securing of foreign loans (loans more often than not guaranteed by jittery Polish governments), have helped turn Nowa Huta into one of the more profitable steelworks in Poland – but further investment in new machinery will be needed if it is to retain this position into the future. On the pollution front, significant reductions in the steelworks' hazardous emission levels have been achieved through decreased production combined with the introduction of new smoke filters on the main chimneys.

The Arka Pana

In keeping with the antireligious policies of the postwar government, churches were not included in the original construction plans for Nowa Huta. After years of intensive lobbying, however, the ardently Catholic population eventually got permission to build one in the 1970s. The **Arka Pana** (the "Ark of the Lord", colloquial name for what is officially known as Kościół NMP, or Church of Our Lady), in the northern Bieńczyce district, is the result – an amazing ark-like concrete structure encrusted with mountain pebbles. The interior is no less revolutionary – everything you would expect to see in a Catholic church is here, but seems to have been pulled out of place: instead of a high altar there's a bronze statue of Christ on the Cross positioned halfway down the aisle, the Saviour seemingly poised to leap out Icarus-like over the congregation; while secondarily chapels are placed at mezzanine level instead of to the right and left of the nave. To get there, take tram #5 from Basztowa to al. Kocmyrzowska, then walk north up ul. Obrońców Krzyża.

The Maximilian Kolbe church

The area's other main church, the large **Kościół św. Maximiliana Kolbego** (Maximilian Kolbe Church) in the Mistrzejowice district, was consecrated by Pope John Paul II in 1983, a sign of the importance the Catholic hierarchy attached to the loyalty of Nowa Huta. Kolbe, canonized in 1982, was a priest sent to Auschwitz for giving refuge to Jews; in the camp, he took the place of a Jewish inmate in the gas chambers. Although not as striking as the Arka, the

Kolbe church is another fine example of how the contemporary arts have been put to good use by the ecclesiastical authorities, with angular concrete ribbing adorning the ceiling, and an impressively anguished Crucifixion above the main altar. Trams #1, #16 and #20 from pl. Centralny all pass by the building.

The Cistercian abbey of Mogiła

In total contrast to these recent constructions is the **Cistercian Abbey** (Opactwo Cystersów) in the semi-rural suburb of Mogiła, 2km east of pl. Centralny, just off al. Ptaszyckiego. To get there, take tram #15 or #20 from pl. Centralny (the #15 runs direct from Basztowa in the Stare Miasto) and get off at ul. Klasztorna – the monastery is five minutes' walk south. Built around 1260 on the regular Cistercian plan of a triple-aisled basilica with series of chapels in the transepts, the Abbey Church, one of the finest examples of early Gothic in the region, is a tranquil, meditative spot, the airy interior graced with a fine series of Renaissance murals. There's a serene Gothic statue of the Madonna and Child on the main altar, and some exuberant stained glass. What you won't find any longer is the late-medieval paper mill built by the Order on the banks of the nearby River Dłubnia, which exported its products all the way into Russia. Across the road from the monastery is the **Kościół św. Bartolomieja** (Church of St Bartholomew), one of the oldest wooden churches in the country, with an elaborately carved doorway from 1466 and a Baroque belfry.

Wieliczka

Fifteen kilometres southeast of Kraków is the **salt mine** at **WIELICZKA** (Kopalnia Soli Wieliczka), a unique phenomenon described by one eighteenth-century visitor as being "as remarkable as the Pyramids and more useful". Today it's listed among UNESCO's World Cultural Heritage monuments. Salt deposits were discovered here as far back as the eleventh century, and from King Kazimierz's time onwards, local mining rights, and hence income, were strictly controlled by the Crown. As mining intensified over the centuries, a huge network of pitfaces, rooms and tunnels proliferated – nine levels in all, extending to a depth of 327m with approximately 300km of tunnels stretching over an area some 10km wide. During World War II, the Germans manufactured aircraft parts in Wieliczka's subterranean chambers, using Poles and Jews as slave labour.

The future of the mine became uncertain following a serious bout of **flooding** in September 1992, when a huge river of water began pouring into the complex through an abandoned mine passageway some 170m underground. The town of Wieliczka, much of which is built over the mines, was also badly affected: walls collapsed, cracks appeared in the fabric of the local monastery, and the train tracks running through the centre of town shifted, causing Kraków–Wieliczka train services to be suspended (they didn't start up again until the middle of 2001). Active mining ceased in 1997, although salt is still extracted from water seepages and much of the salt sold in Poland still comes from here. Profitability as a tourist attraction ensures that the mine remains a major employer: indeed its popularity is such that you should be prepared for big crowds in summer.

Privately owned **minibuses** run direct to Wieliczka salt mine from outside Kraków train station – although departures may depend on how many tourists are around. Otherwise, you can take a local Kraków–Wieliczka **train** – there are plenty of them – which will drop you off a little way from the mine, but it isn't difficult to locate the pit's solitary chimney and squeaky conveyor belt; follow the "Muzeum" signs.

The mine

Entrance to the mine (mid-April to mid-Oct daily 7.30am–7.30pm; mid-Oct to mid-April Tues–Sun 8am–4pm; 50zł; ⓦ www.kopalnia.pl) is by guided **tour** only. Polish-language tours depart as soon as thirty people have assembled, while English-language tours are more strictly timetabled – there are six a day in summer (at 10am, 11.30am, 12.30pm, 1.45pm, 3pm and 5pm) and two a day in winter (10am and 12.30pm). You can always buy the English-language guidebook available at the ticket office. Be prepared for a bit of a walk – the tour takes two hours, through nearly two miles of tunnels.

The **descent** to the first of the three levels included in the tour, 65 metres down, is either by clanking lift or wooden stairway. Hewn between the seventeenth and nineteenth centuries, most of the **first-level** chambers are pure green salt, including one dedicated to Copernicus, which he is supposed to have visited.

The further you descend, the more spectacular and weird the chambers get. As well as underground lakes, carved chapels and rooms full of eerie crystalline shapes, the **second level** features a chamber full of jolly salt gnomes carved in the 1960s by the mineworkers. The star attraction, **Blessed Kinga's Chapel**, completed in the early part of the nineteenth century, comes on the **bottom level**, 135m down: everything in the ornate fifty-metre-long chapel is carved from salt, including the stairs, bannisters, altar and chandeliers. The chapel's acoustic properties – every word uttered near the altar is audible from the gallery – has led to its use as a concert venue, and even, of late, as a banquet hall: ex-US president George Bush Senior was one of the first to be feted with a feast in his honour in 1995, a token of thanks for his support for anti-pollution measures in the city. Mass is still celebrated here every Sunday. A **museum**, also down at the lowest level, reveals what a back-breaking job mining must have been – until the advent of mechanization, rock salt was laboriously crushed with hand-operated wooden machines. Pictures and manuscripts bear testimony to famous visitors such as Balzac, Emperor Franz Josef and Goethe who, as an official attached to the mining department in Weimar, found Wieliczka more impressive than the historical splendours of nearby Kraków.

Eating

Kraków's burgeoning tourist status has given rise to an ever-increasing selection of good restaurants, with new places springing up every week. There's still a number of traditional, canteen-style **milk bars** (*bar mleczny*, or *jadłodajnia* as they're more commonly known in Kraków) serving up order-at-the-counter fare to an army of eager locals – these are often the best places in which to sample a filling and cheap portion of Polish standards such as *pierogi*, *barszcz* and *placki*.

Mainstream **restaurants** concentrate on the pork, veal and poultry dishes traditional to Polish cuisine, usually with the addition of a few steaks and other international dishes. Mediterranean cuisine is common in the more style-conscious establishments, and Asian restaurants – some Arabic and Indian, but mostly Chinese and Vietnamese – are making their presence felt in and around the centre. Several eateries in the Kazimierz district concentrate on the Jewish culinary tradition, with dishes like jellied carp and various versions of gefilte fish appearing on menus. Wherever you eat you'll find **prices** somewhat cheaper than in Western Europe, even in the smart places on and around the Rynek.

Places can get crowded on busy summer weekends, when it's well worth reserving a table in advance if you've set your heart on a particular place – we've provided telephone numbers for those places where you're likely to need a **reservation**.

You'll have no trouble picking up a hamburger or **snack** in the city centre – Western-style fast-food joints have moved in on the Stare Miasto area in a major way, and there are numerous hole-in-the-wall joints doling out kebabs, pizza slices and hot dogs, often well into the early hours.

Restaurants

The Stare Miasto and around

Balaton ul. Grodzka 37. Unpromising atmosphere but fine Hungarian food and wine at very reasonable prices. The goulash – either as a dish in its own right or slopped over some Polish-style potato pancakes – is as satisfying as you would expect. Till 10pm.

Bombay Tandoori ul. Mikołajska 18. Intimate place with a menu limited to a small but well-chosen range of typical Indian restaurant classics. Standards are high, prices quite moderate, and there are a couple of vegetarian choices. Till 11pm.

Cherubino ul. św. Tomasza 15. Popular place run by the owner of *Pod Aniołami* (see below) – dependable Polish and Italian cuisine in fancy surroundings, but not wildly expensive. Till 11pm.

Chłopskie Jadło ul. św. Jana 3 ☎012/421 8520. Rootsy re-creation of an old-time Polish country inn with rooms decorated in a variety of traditional peasant styles. A fine range of calorific traditional specialities on offer, from staples like pork chop with sauerkraut to pricier items like duck, which comes with any number of sauces. Drinks include potent beers and brandies. Already a tourist-group favourite, so booking is advisable in season. Also branches at ul. św. Agnieszki 1 and ul. Grodzka 9. Till midnight.

CK Dezerterzy ul. Bracka 6. Comfortable, bistro-style place offering a quality selection of regular Polish favourites, from *pierogi*, *bigos* and the like to more substantial meat and fish dishes. Till midnight.

Copernicus ul. Kanonicza 16 ☎012/424 3421. Plush hotel restaurant offering an imaginative European-Polish mix and a wider range of meat dishes than elsewhere – hare, pheasant and venison are usually on the menu. On the formal side, and expensive with it. Till 11pm.

Cyrano de Bergerac ul. Sławkowska 26 ☎012/411 7288. Smart, high-quality new French restaurant; popular with local gastronomes, too, so booking is recommended. Expensive. Till midnight. Closed Sun.

Da Pietro Rynek Główny 17. One of the best places in town to tuck into a bowl of flavoursome pasta, in a medieval cellar below a courtyard off the main square. Reasonably priced salads too. Till midnight.

Kinh Bac ul. Zwierzyniecka 34. Quality Chinese and Vietnamese cuisine just north of the Wawel. Till 11pm.

Krew i Róża ul. Grodzka 9 ☎012/429 6187. Classic Polish cuisine with the accent on poultry and game; try roast pheasant if you're pushing the boat out. The interior decor of Bosch/Memling-style fantasy pieces is an attractive enough distraction from the stiff price tab. Till midnight.

Nostalgia ul. Karmelicka 10. Quiet, off-the-beaten-track location in which to feast on duck with apples and other classic local recipes. Handy if you've been looking round the Dom Mehoffera (see p.417) and only 5min walk west of the Stare Miasto. Till 10pm.

Osorya ul. Jagiellońska 5 ☎012/292 8020. Chintzy clutter of furnishings make for an atmospheric place to feast upon dishes such as duck breast, or sirloin rolled in bacon. Till midnight.

Paese ul. Poselska 24 ☎012/421 6273. Tastefully decorated Corsican place with beautifully prepared dishes, including the kind of Mediterranean seafood that you might not find anywhere else in the city. Popular with the Kraków smart set. Open till midnight.

Pod Aniołami ul. Grodzka 35 ☎012/421 3999. Medieval cellar restaurant with a reputation as one of the city's premium-quality Polish speciality venues, offering all manner of trout, lamb, pork, duck and grill dishes. Till midnight.

Pod Baranem ul. św. Gertrudy 21. Moderately priced pork and chicken dishes in a homely atmosphere, slightly off the well-trodden tourist route.

Pod Gruszką ul. Szczepańska 1 ☎012/422 8896. Solid town-centre upstairs restaurant attached to the Kraków Journalists Foundation: a good choice of traditional Polish dishes and very reasonable prices. Till 11pm.

Smak Ukraiński ul. Kanonicza 15. Reasonably priced and friendly place on the way to the Wawel, with tables squeezed into a folksy cellar – although there's courtyard seating up top. Filling Ukrainian peasant fare like *Tarnopolskie zrazy* (flattened dumplings stuffed with mincemeat), washed down with Ukrainian lager. Till 9pm.

Tetmajerowska Rynek Główny 34 ☎012/422 0631. Smart Polish restaurant in *fin-de-siècle* setting decorated by the artist of same name. Good food, even better service. Booking advisable in summer. Till 11pm.

Wentzl Rynek Główny 19 ☎012/429 5712. Top-quality international cuisine with a French accent, square-side seating and attentive service. Deservedly expensive. Till midnight.

Wierzynek Rynek Główny 15 ☎012/422 1035. Historic restaurant on several floors, with a refined interior and centuries of tradition, serving up the best in Polish pork, duck and trout dishes. Prices remain very reasonable at around 75–100zł a head for main course and drink. Booking is pretty essential if you want a table inside in the evening: the outside terrace has a faster turnover and you may well be lucky. Till 10.30pm.

Kazimierz, Podgórze and around

A Dong ul. Brodzińskiego 3 ☎012/656 4872. Good quality Asian food at affordable prices. Not worth making a special trip to Podgórze for, but a welcome bolt hole if you're in the area. Open till 10pm.

Alef ul. Szeroka 17 ☎012/421 3870. A well-established, cosy café-restaurant done up to look like a traditional mid-nineteenth-century Kazimierz parlour, offering a selection of Jewish and Polish cuisine. Frequent live music. Till 10pm.

Arka Noego ul. Szeroka 2. Best-value Jewish restaurant in Kazimierz, with occasional klezmer music. Its backyard terrace makes a nice place to sit out in summer.

Fabryka Pizzy ul. Józefa 34. Stylish, smoke-free and good-value pizzeria, with a tasty range of pasta dishes and salads. Very popular, so be prepared to wait. Till 10pm.

Hoang Hai ul. Stradomska 13. Vietnamese-Chinese fare and friendly service, on the road leading from the Wawel towards Kazimierz. Till 9.30pm.

Klezmer Hois ul. Szeroka 6 ☎012/411 1245. Well-regarded Polish-Jewish restaurant with yet more of the nostalgic nineteenth-century decor that seems *de rigueur* for Kazimierz eateries. Till 11pm.

La Strada ul. Stradomska 13. Relaxing, roomy Italian joint with some of the best pizzas in town, as well as a big choice of pasta dishes and more substantial meaty fare. Sun–Thurs till 10pm, Fri & Sat till midnight.

Steak & Curry ul. Dietla 33. Mixture of Argentinian steak house and Indian restaurant, which works reasonably well on both counts. The interior is on the functional side but the curries are tasty, filling and cheap, and there are plenty of spicy veggie options. Till 10pm.

West of the Stare Miasto

U Ziyada Zamek w Przegorzałach ☎012/429 7105. Occupying a cod-medieval "castle" on the southeastern edge of the Las Wolski forest, this is a moderately formal place with a good line in Polish pork and poultry dishes and a few Middle Eastern dishes thrown in for good measure. Expensive, but you do get great views from the terrace. Till 9pm.

Villa Decjusza ul. 28 Lipca 17a ☎012/425 3521, 🌐www.vd-restauracja.pl. Ultra-smart and correspondingly pricey cellar restaurant favoured by local and visiting politicians, in the cellar of the recently renovated Villa Decjusza – hence the cod Renaissance decor. Well out of town in the Wola Justowska district. Booking essential. Till midnight.

Milk bars and canteen restaurants

The Stare Miasto

Bar Grodzki ul. Grodzka 47. Trusty and cheap *jadłodajnia* midway between the Rynek and the Wawel, an excellent place to sample *placki* (potato pancakes) topped with goulash or mushrooms. Till 7pm.

Chimera ul. św. Anny 3. Expansive buffet selection in a soothing courtyard, with attractively priced main courses, a salad bar, and plenty of vegetarian choices. Till 9pm.

Greenway ul. Mikołajska 12. Cheerful order-at-the-counter restaurant offering a veggie spin on traditional Polish fare – such as cabbage leaves

(*gołąbki*) stuffed with kasha – as well as a few international dishes. Till 9pm.

Gruzińskie Chaczapuri ul. św. Marka 19. Georgian sit-down or take-out food, including *chaczapuri* (bread cake stuffed with cheese) and other Caucasian staples, liberally drenched in spicy sauces. Till 11pm.

Pod Temidą/Bar Mleczny ul. Grodzka 43. Ultra-traditional, ultra-functional and ultra-cheap milk bar serving up school-meal-style stodge to a bargain-conscious crowd of locals and students. Till 8pm.

Różowy Słoń ul. Straszewskiego 24. Café-type snack bar, with humorous comic-book decor.

Salad bar, big choice of both sweet and savoury pancakes, and excellent *pierogi*. Till 9pm.

U Babci Maliny, ul. Sławkowska. The Rolls-Royce of milk bars, housed in the basement of the Polish Academy of Sciences (PAN) building and decked out like a nineteenth-century Polish peasant's hut. Cheap range of typical home-made Polish dishes, as well as fancier options like wild boar and duck. Mon–Fri till 7pm, Sat & Sun till 5pm.

U Stasi ul. Mikołajska 18. A small, privately owned fast-food joint, east of the Rynek. Popular with students and offering home cooking including excellent *pierogi*. It's hidden from the street, but the queues are conspicuous. Mon–Fri from 12.30pm until the food runs out: definitely for lunchtimes only.

Vega ul. św. Gertrudy 7. Comfy vegetarian café-restaurant offering an excellent choice of cheap and healthy eats along with a good salad selection. Open till 9pm. Also at ul. Krupnicza 22 (till 10pm).

Zakątek ul. Grodzka 2. Excellent-quality salad and sandwich bar in a superbly central yet relaxing location, at the end of a courtyard just off the Rynek Główny. Mon–Sat till 8.30pm. Closed Sun.

Kazimierz and around

Momo ul. Dietla 47. Relaxing vegetarian diner with tasty salads, pancakes, sandwiches and soups, all at reasonable prices. Daily till 8pm.

Vincent's Pierogi ul. Józefa. Cosy corner offering all manner of *pierogi* – which come with either traditional fillings like meat or cheese, or spicier flavours with influences from around the globe.

Drinking

For relaxing over coffee and cake in between bouts of sightseeing, there's a profusion of **cafés** in and around the city centre, many of which have outdoor terraces in summer. Those ringing the Rynek Główny make nice places in which to soak up the atmosphere, with the additional distraction of the assortment of roving buskers vying for the tourist złoty. Many cafés remain open well into the night and provide comfortable venues in which to indulge in more serious imbibing, although the bulk of Kraków's drinking culture takes place in the innumerable **bars** of the Stare Miasto and Kazimierz districts. Although several establishments ape western pubs and bars in style, a far greater proportion are positively oozing with individuality and character – especially in the Stare Miasto, where Kraków's medieval cellars provide any number of uniquely atmospheric spaces. Many bars have DJs and dancing in the evening, and there isn't always a clear distinction between drinking venues and nightclubs (although see p.441 for more clubbing suggestions).

Cafés tend to close at around 10–11pm, but many of the soundproofed cellar bars keep serving until the last customer staggers home.

Cafés

Carmel Coffee ul. św. Krzyża 12. Comfy chairs, *belle-époque* furniture and good coffee. Till midnight.

Jama Michalika ul. Floriańska 45. Atmospheric old café, opened in 1895 and much patronized by artists of the Młoda Polska generation. It's worth dropping into at least once for the lovingly preserved Art-Nouveau interior, but the atmosphere of cultural ferment has long since departed.

Kama cnr Szewska and Jagiellońska. Old-fashioned order-at-the-counter ice-cream parlour serving excellent coffee and sweets, with an unintentionally groovy Sixties-meets-Eighties decor.

Loch Camelot, ul. św Tomasza 17. Upscale café with the best *szarlotka* (apple pie) in town, folk-art decor and English-language newspapers. The cellar

frequently hosts concerts and cabaret (see p.440). Till midnight.

Massolit ul. Felicjanek 4. Bookshop-cum-café owned by Americans with a Mikhail Bulgakov fixation, offering great carrot cake and 25,000 new and used English-language books. A 10min trot southwest of the Stare Miasto.

Noworolski Rynek Główny 1/3. Traditional square-side café with wonderfully restored Art-Nouveau interior that's been popular with Cracovians ever since the late nineteenth century (see also p.395). The place where elderly matrons come to nibble their way through fancy pastries. Till midnight.

Prowincja ul. Bracka 3. Cosy split-level café just off the Rynek with excellent coffee and a small but irresistible choice of cakes, served on distressed wooden tables. Till 11pm.

Rękawka ul. Brodzińskiego 4. This mellow, welcoming spot is the perfect place to recharge your batteries if you've been looking round the Podgórze and Płaszów districts. Very good coffee, plus cakes, salads and sandwiches. Till 10pm.

Siesta ul. Stolarska 6. Relaxing pastel-coloured den with comfy wicker chairs, coffee and cakes. Till midnight.

Szuflada ul. Wiślna 5. Quirky café as popular for its surrealistic design as for its drinks, with chair

people, flying zebras and the like. Reasonably priced food menu. Till 1am.

U Zalipianek ul. Szewska 24. Traditional *kawiarnia* decked out with folksy motifs based on designs from the village of Zalipie (see p.478), serving up tea, coffee and cakes to Kraków ladies of a certain age. Lovely terrace overlooking the Planty. Till 10pm.

Vis-à-vis Rynek Główny 29. Basic, functional café-bar on the main square long favoured by Polish artists, nowadays somewhat lagging behind in the style stakes. Till 10pm.

Bars

The Stare Miasto and around

Black Gallery ul. Mikołajska 24. Cellar bar with rough-hewn walls and industrial furnishings. Good vibes and a crowded dance floor downstairs, soothing shrub-enclosed patio out the back.

Błędnie Koło ul. Bracka 4. First-floor bar with plush seating in one half, DJ bar in the other. Clientele depends on who's spinning the discs.

Dym ul. św. Tomasza 11. Narrow coffee bar-cum-drinking den with artfully distressed walls and a similar-looking clientele. Jazz on the sound system and an outdoor terrace.

Irish Arms ul. Poselska 18. Guinness, football and local expats.

Klub Kulturalny ul. Szewska 25. Laid-back studenty cellar with lots of cosy nooks and a cutting-edge dance culture music policy. Try not to stare too long at the swirly floor mosaics if you've had one too many.

Paparazzi ul. Mikołajska 9. Smart pub with big cocktail menu and pictures of celebrities on the wall – and trendily dressed wannabes crowding round the bar.

Pauza ul. Floriańska 18/3. Roomy first-floor hangout with crowded bar area and loungey spaces on either side. Cool music, cool people.

Piękny Pies ul. św. Jana 18. With a tight squeeze round the bar and plush chairs stuffed into corners, the "Beautiful Dog" gets the mixture of student scruffiness and Central European chic just right.

Pod Jaszczurami Rynek Główny 8. Large student pub (the bouncers sometimes turn away people without university IDs, so have your excuses ready) with warm, salmony-pink decor and a stage at one end of the room – frequently used for concerts, literary readings and DJ events.

RE ul. Mikołajska 5. Cellar bar with mildly alternative leanings (you're unlikely to hear techno on the sound system), offering a big outdoor garden terrace and frequent live music – a schedule of what's on should be posted outside.

Roentgen pl. Szczepański 3. Deep, smoky cellar hang-out favoured by local alternative types, improbably located in the basement of a fertility clinic. Acid jazz, drum'n'bass and other non-mainstream styles on the sound system, and DJs at the weekends.

Święta Krowa ul. Floriańska 16. Set somewhere between trendy lounge and goblin's cavern, this Hindu-themed cellar bar (the name means "sacred cow") is another Kraków one-off.

Kazimierz

Alchemia ul. Estery 5. Darkly atmospheric, candle-lit café-pub in the heart of Kazimierz. You'll see bohemians, fashionably arty types and local Kazimierz drinkers lounging around in its suite of four rooms. Rock gigs, jazz and cabaret in the basement.

Les Couleurs ul. Estery 8. French-styled café-patisserie by day, a crowded and invigorating drinking joint by night, this is the perfect place to kick-start a Kazimierz bar crawl.

Lokator ul. Krakowska 10. Done up to look like a pre-World War I living room but with contemporary photographs and artworks on the walls, this is another characteristically eccentric Kazimierz location.

Propaganda ul. Miodowa 12. Relaxing corner crammed with memorabilia from the communist period and other eras – although it has the feel of a comfortable local rather than a theme pub.

Ptaszyl ul. Szeroka 10. Best of a clutch of bars on the square, with plenty of cosy nooks and crannies. Arty junk hanging from the ceiling gives it the feel of a huge, comforting bird's nest.

Singer ul. Estery 22. Classic Kazimierz café-bar whose retro style – nineteenth-century parlour furniture, lacy tablecloths and an old piano in the corner – has been mercilessly copied by its rivals. Retains a mixed clientele of laid-back locals and foreign interlopers. The name refers to the old tailors' sewing machines that serve as tables.

Entertainment, nightlife, festivals and football

There is a good deal happening on the cultural front, with a regular diet of **classical music** and **opera**, an outstanding range of challenging **theatre** and a long-established **cabaret** tradition. For local **listings** of high-brow cultural events, the monthly *Karnet* (see p.386) is invaluable, although Polish-language sources like *Gazeta Wyborcza*, *City Magazine* and *Aktivist* (see p.387) are much better sources of information on alternative culture and clubbing.

Theatre, cabaret and cinema

Ever since Stanisław Wyspiański and friends made Kraków the centre of the **Młoda Polska** movement at the beginning of the twentieth century, many of Poland's greatest actors and directors have been closely identified with the city. Until his death in December 1990, the most influential figure on the scene was avant-garde director **Tadeusz Kantor**, who used the (no longer active) Cricot 2 theatre at ul. Kanonicza 5 as the base for his visionary productions.

Theatre

Performances are invariably in the Polish language, although the traditionally strong emphasis placed on the visual aspects of the performance should make a visit to the theatre worthwhile.

Bagatela ul. Karmelicka 6 ☎012/422 4544, ⓦwww.bagatela.krakow.pl. Mainstream repertoire of popular theatre, where you might encounter anything from Ray Cooney to Anton Chekhov.
Groteska ul. Skarbowa 2 ☎012/633 3762, ⓦwww.groteska.pl. Puppet theatre known for superbly designed sets and puppets, with childrens' shows in the daytime and – occasionally – adult-oriented material in the evening. Also puts on fringe comedy and cabaret.
Stary Teatr ul. Jagiellońska 1 ☎012/422 4040, ⓦwww.stary-teatr.krakow.pl. The city's premium drama venue, with the main stage at ul. Jagiellońska 1 and studio spaces at ul.

Sławkowska 14 and Starowiślna 21. Polish and international classics from a company with strong international reputation. Box office open Tues–Sat 10am–1pm & 5–7pm.
STU al. Krasińskiego 16 ☎012/422 2744, ⓦwww.scenastu.com.pl. Specializes in the latest productions of contemporary drama.
Teatr im J. Słowackiego pl. św. Ducha ☎012/423 1700, ⓦwww.slowacki.krakow.pl. Biggest and best known of Kraków's theatres, in a splendid building modelled on the Paris Opéra. Regular diet of classical Polish drama, as well as ballet and opera.

Cabaret

Cabaret is also an established feature of Kraków entertainment, with a tradition of productions laced with thinly veiled political satire stretching back to Habsburg days, when poets and artists associated with the Młoda Polska movement established the Zielony Balonik (Green Balloon) cabaret in order to provide a showcase for satirical sketches, improvised drama and song. The tradition was revived in communist times with the creation of the Piwnica Pod Baranami in 1956, initially a student-run affair that endured to become Kraków's longest running and best-loved cabaret. The *Pod Baranami*, at Rynek Główny 27 (☎012/421 2500), is still going strong today; its main rival is *Loch Camelo*t, ul. św. Tomasza 17 (☎012/423 0638) – the latter established in 1992 in order to revive the traditions of the original Zielony Balonik. Check with the information centre (see p.386) for current details: when they are performing – usually at the weekend – tickets sell out fast, so it's best to book in advance.

Cinema

Films arrive in Kraków at around the same time as their release in Western Europe, and are usually shown in the original language with Polish subtitles. A rash of modern multiplexes has appeared over the last few years, but as these tend to be miles away from the centre we've omitted them from the list below.

Ars ul. św. Jana 6 ☎012/421 4199, ⓦwww.ars .pl. Five screens (the Aneks, Kiniarnia, Reduta, Salon and Sztuka) grouped together in one building on the corner of ul. św. Tomasza and św. Jana, bang in the heart of the Stare Miasto. Everything from commercial blockbusters to art films and cinema classics.

Kijów al. Krasińskiego 34 ☎012/422 3093, ⓦwww.kijow.pl. Current box-office hits in a big auditorium just west of the Stare Miasto.

Kino Rynek Główny 27 ☎012/423 0768. At the *Pod Baranami*, current films from outside the Hollywood mainstream.

Mikro Juliusza Lea 5 ☎012/634 2897, ⓦwww .kijow.pl. Small studio cinema showing art-house movies, west of the Stare Miasto.

Pasaż Rynek Główny 9 ☎012/422 7713. Current mainstream hits in a central location.

Classical music and opera

For classical concerts, the **Filharmonia Szymanowskiego** (box office Mon–Fri 2–7pm, Sat from 1hr before concerts; ☎012/422 9477, ⓦwww.filharmonia .krakow.pl), ul. Zwierzyniecka 1, is home of the Kraków Philharmonic, one of Poland's most highly regarded orchestras. The **Capella Cracoviensis**, the city's best-known choir, based at the Filharmonia, gives fairly regular concert performances at churches and other venues around the city – check the local listings for details. Large-scale **opera** performances – mostly, but not always in Polish – are put on fairly regularly at the **Teatr im J. Słowackiego** (see opposite).

Clubs and discos

The city's growing nightlife scene is well represented in the host of cellar bars around the Rynek and in the Stare Miasto which stay open until the early hours to accommodate a mixture of drinkers and dancers. Most of these places pull in a wide ranging hedonistic crowd by playing a mixture of current pop hits and disco oldies – for more discerning clubbing, there are a number of specialist venues around town which offer different styles of music on different nights of the week. In addition there are a number of student clubs operating around the city – unpredictable, not always easy to find but generally worth the effort. Clubs tend to be open until 4–5am, longer if enough people are still standing. Entrance fees are in the 10–25zł range, depending on what's on.

As far as live music is concerned, **jazz** has a long tradition in Kraków and is generally easier to find than rock – although it's worth checking listings or looking out for posters on the off chance that there's something going on.

Harris Piano Jazz Bar Rynek Główny 28. Upmarket Western-style piano jazz bar, popular with Kraków yuppies. Live jazz most evenings. Open till midnight, 2am at weekends.

Jazz Rock Café ul. Sławkowska 12. Not the smoky saxophone-tooting haunt the name suggests – but a disco-pub where young Cracovians bop to anything from Britney to Boney M.

Kornet al. Krasińskiego 9. Dedicated if somewhat staid jazz club near the *Cracovia* hotel. Regular live gigs.

Kredens Rynek Główny 12. Sweaty cellar hosting late-night drinking and dancing to a feel-good mixture of pop tunes old and new.

Prozac pl. Dominikański 6. For breakbeat, house and drum'n'bass, although you'll have to look the part to get past the bouncers.

Rotunda ul. Oleandry 1. Large student club/centre near the *Żaczek* hostel (see p.394). Occasional live gigs, jazz and themed club nights.

Stacja Woodstock ul. Kurniki 3. Cellar-bound rock club near the bus station which regales an easy-going crowd of local hairies with classic rock/metal discos, and frequent live gigs by local cover bands. **Stalowe Magnolia** ul. św. Jana 15. Dressy disco with live cover bands, expensive drinks. **Strefa 22** Rynek Główny 22. A young crowd parties here at weekends; several levels and good DJs.

U Muniaka ul. Floriańska 3. Long-established jazz venue with unpredictable programme: either top-quality musicians performing to a knowledgeable crowd, or mediocre stuff with tourists in mind. Always worth a try.

Festivals and events

June is the busiest month for festivities, with four major events: the **Kraków Days** (a showcase for a range of concerts, plays and other performances), the **Jewish Cultural Festival**, the **Folk Art Fair** and the **Lajkonik Pageant**. This last, based on a story about a raftsman who defeated the Tatars and made off with the khan's clothes, features a brightly dressed Tatar figure leading a procession from the Norbertine Church in the western district of Zwierzyniec to the Rynek.

Over the **Christmas** period, a Kraków speciality is the construction of intricately designed Nativity scenes or *szopki*. Unlike traditional cribs elsewhere, these amazing architectural constructions are usually in the form of a church (often based upon Mariacki), built from everyday materials – coloured tinfoil, cardboard and wood – with astounding attention to detail. A special exhibition of the best prize-winning works is displayed at the Muzeum Historyczne Krakowa on Rynek Główny (see p.400) until the end of January.

Other cultural events include the **organ concerts** at Tyniec (see p.432) from June to August, and at various of the city's churches in April. The **Graphic Art Festival**, held from May to September in even-numbered years, is a crowd-puller, too. Late May sees the **Kraków Film Festival** (Ⓦ www.cracowfilmfestival .pl), when short films (both fictional and documentary) from around the world compete for the coveted Golden Dragon awards – the main events take place in the Kijów Cinema, although other venues are used too.

Football

Wisła Kraków (Ⓦ www.wisla.krakow.pl) is one of the oldest **soccer** clubs in the country, topping the league table ten times – they were champions in 1999, 2001, 2003 and 2004. They play at the Wisła Stadium, ul. Reymonta, in the western Czarna Wieś district (a 25min walk from the Rynek; otherwise bus #144 passes close by). Their bitter rivals, Cracovia (Ⓦ www.cracovia.org.pl), were the first soccer team ever to be formed in Poland (in 1906) and were the favourite boyhood club of Pope John Paul II. Cracovia won the championship five times between 1921 and 1948, but have only just returned to the top flight after several seasons spent languishing in lower divisions. Their stadium is just beyond the *Cracovia* hotel on al. Focha.

Shopping

The city centre's inexorable return to the moneyed heart of Central Europe is eloquently expressed in the range of shops in the centre, with several commerce-oriented streets, notably ulica Floriańska, acquiring the affluent-looking **boutiques** and other consumerist hallmarks of the average Western European city. Ulica Szewska is also a good street for boutiques as well as more traditional Polish **clothes** shops. As you would expect from a university city, there are more second-hand **bookshops** (*antikwarjaty*) than you can shake a stick at in the Stare Miasto, many of which are well worth a browse for vintage guidebooks, art albums and English-language novels. There's also a fair sprinkling of **antique** shops in the narrow streets either side of the Rynek Główny – there is a lot of overpriced junk here, but the pokier establishments are always well worth a rummage.

Books

Antikwarjat Naukowy ul. św. Tomasza 8. Rare old books and prints. Mon–Fri 10am–6pm, Sat 10am–2pm.

Antikwarjat Wójtowicz ul. św. Martina 23. Good place for old maps and prints, as well as affordable second-hand books. Mon–Fri 10am–6pm, Sat 10am–2pm.

EMPiK Rynek Główny 5. Four-floor multimedia store with plenty in the way of maps, tourist-oriented books, glossy international magazines and English-language literature. Daily 10am–10pm.

Księgarnia Wydawnictwa Zielona Sowa Rynek Główny 12. All-embracing academic bookstore, and the best place for seeking out Polish literature in the original language. Mon–Fri 9am–10pm, Sat & Sun 11am–9pm.

Massolit ul. Felicjanek 4. Engagingly eccentric English-language bookstore, with a warren of stuffed shelf-lined rooms. Impressive collection of Polish literature in English translation, and titles concerning every aspect of Central European history and culture. Serves tea and cakes, too. Mon–Fri 8am–8pm, Sat 10am–8pm, Sun 12noon–8pm.

Matras Rynek Główny 23. Large mainstream bookstore with larger-than-usual collection of tourist-oriented photo albums and large format art books.

Nestor ul. Kanoniczna 5. Specialist bookstore devoted to everything to do with the Ukraine, including some beautiful coffee-table titles on old churches and icons. Small selection of handicrafts, too. Mon–Fri 10am–6pm, Sat 11am–4pm.

Food and drink

Alkohole ul. Grodzka 13. The name of this shop tells you everything you need to know. Slightly more expensive than the big supermarkets, but open longer. Daily till midnight.

Delikatesy Oczko ul. Sienna 9. Small but well-stocked shop just off the Rynek. Big choice of Polish hams and sausages. Open 24hr.

Stary Kleparz market Bustling warren of stalls five minutes' north of the Stare Miasto, with the best in fresh fruit and veg. Mon–Sat till dusk.

Music

EMPiK Rynek Główny 5. Biggest selection of Polish and international pop, jazz and classical. Daily 10am–10pm.

High Fidelity ul. Podbrzezie 6. Second-hand vinyl store in Kazimierz with plenty of intriguing Polish rock and jazz titles.

Souvenirs, gifts and collectables

Desa ul. Grodzka 8. Upmarket antique store offering fancy furniture, porcelain and folk art – for the focused collector with money to spend rather than the casual browser.

Hala Targowa Grzegórzecka. Sizeable collectors' and bric-a-brac market held on Sunday mornings, an easy five-minute trot east of the Stare Miasto. Stamps, coins, badges, crafts, genuine antiques and pure junk.

Jan Fejkiel ul. Grodzka 25 ⓦ www.fejkielgallery .com. Big collection of graphics and prints from contemporary Polish artists. Mon–Fri 11am–7pm, Sat 11am–3pm.

Made in Poland ul. Gołębia 2. Handmade crafts and souvenirs ranging from the cringeworthy to the collectable.

Poster Gallery/Galeria plakatu ul. Stolarska 8 ⓦ www.postergallery.art.pl. Dedicated to the best of Polish poster art, with rich collection of originals, reproductions and graphic art postcards. Mon–Fri 11am–6pm, Sat 11am–2pm.

Sukiennice Rynek Główny. Stalls running the length of the medieval cloth hall, selling amber jewellery, woollens, embroidery and a host of other souvenirs. A bit of a tourist trap, with prices to match.

Sukiennice ul. Bracka 11. Mainstream souvenir store with big choice of Polish crafts including wooden toys, ceramics and textiles.

Listings

Airlines Austrian Airlines, ul. Krakowska 41 ☏ 012/429 6666; BA, at the airport ☏ 00 800 441 1592; LOT, ul. Basztowa 15 ☏ 012/422 4215; Lufthansa, ul. Sienna 9 ☏ 012/422 4199.

American Express In the Orbis office (see Travel agents, below).

Banks, money and exchange ATMs are found in innumerable locations around town. The bigger banks exchange travellers' cheques and give cash advances on the major international credit cards, but both can be a slow process. For changing cash, private kantors, usually open during regular business hours, are spread throughout the Stare Miasto, although it pays to shop around – the ones around the Rynek and on ul. Floriańska do not offer the best rates.

Bike rental Wypożyczalnia Rowerów, ul. św. Anny 4 (Mon–Sat 9am–dusk).

Bus station Information is available on ☏9316 or ☏012/422 2021. Tickets for most services are sold from counters inside the bus station, although Jordan (see Travel agents, below) handles reservations for some private services to Zakopane.

Car rental Avis, ul. Lubicz 23 ☏012/629 6108, ⓦwww.avis.pl; Europcar, ul. Szlak 2 ☏012/633 7773, ⓦwww.europcar.com; Hertz, at the *Cracovia* hotel, al. Focha 1 ☏012/429 6262, ⓦwww.hertz .com.pl; Joka, ul. Starowiślna 13 ☏012/429 6630, ⓦwww.joka.com.pl.

Consulates Denmark, ul. Floriańska 37 ☏012/421 7120; Russia, ul. Biskupia 7 ☏012/422 2647; Ukraine, ul. Krakowska 41 ☏012/429 6066; UK, ul. św. Anny 1 ☏012/421 7030; USA, ul. Stolarska 9 ☏012/424 5100, ⓦkrakow.usconsulate.gov.

Dry cleaning Betty Clean, ul. Długa 17 (Mon–Fri 8am–7pm, Sat 8am–2pm).

Emergencies Ambulance ☏999; police ☏997; fire ☏998. Don't expect to get an English speaker on any of these numbers.

Hospitals Kraków lacks a central general hospital – they're mostly geared to dealing with specific complaints – so ring the information line on ☏012/422 0511 to find which one you need, or call an ambulance on ☏999.

Internet access New places are opening up all the time: try Br@cka, ul. Bracka 3–5; Pl@net, Rynek Główny 24; Nandu, ul. Wiślna 6; U Louisa, Rynek Główny 13. Places are usually open till 11pm/midnight, and prices hover between 5 and 7zł per hour.

Pharmacies Useful central pharmacies include Grodzka, ul. Grodzka 26 (Mon–Fri 8am–9pm, Sat 9am–6pm, Sun 10am–5pm) and Pod Złotą Głową, Rynek Główny 13 (Mon–Fri 9am–9pm, Sat 9am–4pm). Pharmacies stay open 24hr according to a rota; check the information posted in their windows, or call ☏012/422 0511, to find out which one is on duty.

Photographic supplies Digital Photo Express, ul. Grodzka 38 (Mon–Fri 10am–8pm, Sat 11am–8pm, Sun 11am–5pm), will print your holiday snaps as well as offering the whole range of professional processing services. Sells all kinds of film.

Post offices and mail The main post office is at ul. Westerplatte 20; it has a poste restante and offers phone and fax services (Mon–Fri 7.30am–8.30pm, Sat 8am–2pm, Sun 9–11am). The branch just outside the train station has one counter open 24hr. For express mail, try EMS in the main post office ☏012/422 6696; DHL, ul. Balicka 79 ☏012/636 8994; or TNT, ul. Pleszowska 29 ☏012/415 6030.

Swimming Park Wodny, ul. Dobrego Pasterza 126 ☏012/413 7399. The city's main aquatic indoor playground, 5km northeast of the centre. Take bus #129 from the train station. Daily 7am–11pm.

Taxis There are plenty of companies to choose from. Dependable options include Wawel Taxi ☏9666 and ☏0800 666666; Radio Taxi ☏919 and ☏0800 500919; Euro Taxi ☏9664; or Metro Taxi ☏9667.

Train station For train enquiries, call ☏9436 or ☏012/624 1436. International tickets can be bought in advance from the Orbis agency (see Travel agents, below).

Travel agents Orbis, Rynek Główny 41 (☏012/422 4035), is good for train tickets, sightseeing tours and hotel bookings; Almatur, ul. Grodzka 2 (☏012/422 4668), specializes in youth travel and sell ISIC cards; Fregata, ul. Szpitalna 32 (☏012/422 4144), deals in plane tickets and hotel reservations; and Jordan, ul. Długa 9 (☏012/421 2125), handles international bus tickets and accommodation bookings.

Małopolska

The name **Małopolska** – literally Little Poland – in fact applies to a large swathe of the country, for the most part a rolling landscape of traditionally cultivated fields and quiet villages. It's an ancient region, forming, with Wielkopolska, the early medieval Polish state, though its geographical divisions, particularly from neighbouring Silesia, are a bit nebulous. The bulk of Małopolska proper sits north of Kraków, bounded by the Świętokrzyskie mountains to the north and the broad range of hills stretching down from Częstochowa to Kraków – the so-called Szlak Orlich Gniazd (Eagles' Nest Trail) – to the west.

North of Kraków, into the Małopolska heartlands, settlements such as **Szydłów** and **Jędrzejów** offer rewarding insights into the small-town character of the region, while **Kielce**, a largish industrial centre and the regional capital, provides a good stepping-off point for forays into the **Gory Świętokrzyskie**, called mountains but really no more than high hills, though still enjoyable walking territory. Most attractive of the Małopolska towns is **Tarnów**, a historic market centre whose dainty Rynek looks like a miniaturized version of the more famous main square in Kraków. **Częstochowa** is famous as the home of the Black Madonna, drawing huge crowds for the major religious festivals and annual summer pilgrimages from all over the country. Pope John Paul II is a native of the region, too, and his birthplace at **Wadowice** has become something of a national shrine, while the Catholic trail continues to the west at **Kalwaria Zebrzydowska**, another pilgrimage site.

Due west of Kraków at **Oświęcim** is the **Auschwitz-Birkenau** concentration camp, preserved more or less as the Nazis left it.

Oświęcim: Auschwitz-Birkenau

Seventy kilometres west of Kraków, **OŚWIĘCIM** would in normal circumstances be a nondescript provincial town – a place to send visitors on their way without a moment's thought. The circumstances, however, are anything but normal here. Despite the best efforts of the local authorities to cultivate and develop a new identity, the town is indissolubly linked with the name the Nazi occupiers of Poland gave the place – Auschwitz.

Some history

Following the Nazi invasion of Poland in September 1939, Oświęcim and its surrounding region were incorporated into the domains of the Third Reich and the town's name changed to **Auschwitz**. The idea of setting up a concentration camp in the area was mooted a few months later by the Breslau (Wrocław) division of the SS, the official explanation being the overcrowding in existing prisons in Silesia combined with the political desirability of a campaign of mass arrests throughout German-occupied Poland to round up all potentially "troublesome" Poles. After surveying the region, the final choice of location fell on a disused camp for migrant workers and refugees in Oświęcim, then an unassuming provincial town, on the borders of Silesia and Małopolska. As Himmler himself was later to explain, Auschwitz was chosen on the clinically prosaic grounds that it was a "convenient location as regards communication, and because the area can be easily sealed off".

Orders to begin work on the camp were finally given in April 1940, the fearsome **Rudolf Höss** was appointed its commander, and in June of that year, the Gestapo sent the first contingent of around seven hundred prisoners, mainly Polish political detainees (most of whom were innocent students and schoolchildren arbitrarily rounded up to serve as a deterrent to others). Overworked, undernourished and subjected to beatings, the prisoners suffered from high mortality rates right from the start. Many German manufacturers – chemical giant I.G. Farben among them –relocated to Auschwitz in order to make use of this new source of forced labour.

Concentration camps in Poland

Following the country's conquest in 1939, many of the largest and most murderous of the **Nazis' concentration camps** were established in Poland. The camps described in detail in this book – Auschwitz, Majdanek, Stutthof and Treblinka – are more or less easily accessible to travellers visiting Kraków, Lublin, Gdańsk and Warsaw. Others, with no less hideous a history, are more difficult to get to. For those wanting to visit them, the other major camps are:

Bełżec Close to the Ukrainian border, some 40km southeast of Zamość. The death camp at Bełżec, a small country town with its own Jewish population, was established in January–February 1942 as an extension of a labour camp opened in May 1940. The camp rapidly began its murderous and clinically planned business, using six gas ovens to dispose of its victims at the rate of 4500 a time. By the time the Nazis began liquidating the camp in December 1942, a process completed in spring 1943 (when the whole site had been obliterated and reforested), it is estimated that some 600,000 Roma and Jews, principally from the Lublin region, Lwów (L'viv), Kraków, Germany, Austria, Hungary, Romania and Czechoslovakia, had been murdered. The monument to the Jews murdered here was built in the 1960s on the former site of the camp.

Chełmno Nad Nerem (Cumhof) Established in December 1941 on the banks of the River Ner, 50km northwest of Łódź, this was the first death camp built by the Nazis in Poland, and was liberated in 1945. An estimated 340,000 were murdered here, the majority Polish Jews. Traces of the camp remain alongside an official monument to its victims. The camp was a key subject of Claude Lanzemann's controversial documentary *Shoah*.

Rogóznica (Gross-Rosen) On the road between Legnica and Świdnica in Silesia this was one of the earliest forced labour/concentration camps, established in August 1940, and liquidated in March 1945. A monument now stands to the 40,000 people who perished here.

Sobibór Seventy kilometres east of Lublin, right up by the Belarus border, this death camp was set up in March 1942 as part of the increasingly desperate Nazi drive towards the Final Solution. It was dismantled by the Nazis in October 1943, following an inmates' revolt led by a Soviet Jewish POW officer (about 300 escaped), by which time an estimated 250,000 inmates – mostly Jews from Poland, Ukraine, Holland, France and Austria – had been murdered, most of them in the camp's gas chambers. A commemorative monument as well as a mound of ashes made from burnt corpses has been erected on the former camp site.

The construction of a huge subsidiary camp at nearby **Birkenau** was begun in autumn 1941 in order to accommodate Soviet POWs who would – it was hoped – boost the slave-driven Auschwitz economy even further. Most of the Soviet prisoners died of starvation that same winter, and Birkenau was adapted to suit a new and even more sinister purpose: the mass murder of Europe's Jews.

The decision to embark on the so-called **Final Solution** had been taken at a conference at Wannsee outside Berlin in January 1942. The technology of mass killing had already been perfected after experiments in the use of poison gas at Auschwitz, Chełmno (see box above) and other locations, and Auschwitz-Birkenau was now chosen as one of the principal venues for the forthcoming genocide.

By the end of 1942, **Jews** were beginning to be transported to Auschwitz from all over Europe, many fully believing Nazi propaganda that they were on their way to a new life of work in German factories or farms – the main reason, it appears, that so many brought their personal valuables with them. The reality, of course, couldn't have been more different. After a train journey of anything up to ten days in sealed goods wagons and cattle trucks, the dazed survivors were herded up the station ramp, whereupon they were promptly lined up for inspection and divided into two categories by the SS: those deemed "fit" or "unfit" for work. People placed in the latter category, up to 75 percent of all new arrivals, according to Höss's testimony at the Nuremberg trials, were told they would be permitted to have a bath. They were then ordered to undress, marched into the "shower room" and gassed with **Zyklon B** cyanide gas sprinkled through special ceiling attachments. In this way, up to two thousand people were killed at a time (the process took 15–30 minutes), a murderously efficient method of dispatching people, which continued relentlessly throughout the rest of the war. The greatest massacres occurred from 1944 onwards, after the special railway terminal had been installed at Birkenau to permit speedier "processing" of the victims to the gas chambers and crematoria. Compounding the hideousness of the operation, SS guards removed gold fillings, earrings, finger rings and even hair – subsequently used, amongst other things, for mattresses – from the mass of bodies before incinerating them. The cloth from their clothes was processed into material for army uniforms, their watches given to troops in recognition of special achievements or bravery.

The precise numbers of people murdered in Auschwitz-Birkenau between the camp's construction in 1940 and final liberation by Soviet forces on January 27, 1945 has long been a subject of dispute, often for reasons less to do with a concern with factual accuracy than "revisionist" neo-Nazi attempts to deny the historical reality of the Holocaust. Though the exact figure will never be known, in reputable historical circles it's now generally believed that somewhere between one and a half and two million people died in the camp, the vast majority (85–90 percent) of whom were Jews, along with sizeable contingents of Romanies (Gypsies), Poles, Soviet POWs and a host of other European nationalities.

Auschwitz and Birkenau were declared a **museum** and memorial site in 1947, although Poland's postwar leaders initially appeared ambiguous in their attitude to the true nature of the Holocaust. Central to communist thinking was the idea that Marxism-Leninism in general, and the Soviet Union in particular, were the true objects of Nazi hatred – focusing on the sufferings of a particular ethnic group, such as the Jews, was deemed politically incorrect. Recognizing the sensitivities that continue to surround these issues, Poland's post-communist authorities have shown far greater willingness than their predecessors to acknowledge the specifically anti-Semitic dimensions of Nazi devastation. Along with "revised" figures for the numbers of deaths at Auschwitz and Birkenau, official guidebooks to the camp now state clearly that the vast majority of the victims were Jews, and signs give greater prominence to the specifically Jewish aspects of the genocide practised here. Auschwitz's status as a place of both Polish and Jewish suffering has frequently led to arguments between representatives of both groups about how the site as a whole ought to be commemorated, leading to no small amount of suspicion and mistrust. Celebrations marking the sixtieth anniversary of the camp's liberation in January 2005 – attended by Poland's President Kwaśniewski and heads of state from around the world – suggested a symbolic laying to rest of many of these arguments.

Getting there and visiting the camps

To get to Auschwitz-Birkenau from Kraków by **train**, services to Oświęcim are fairly frequent (12 daily from Kraków central station). **Buses** from Kraków pick up and drop off near Oświęcim train station before continuing to Oświęcim's main bus station, which is 2km south of town. Either way, it's a ninety-minute journey. The town's **tourist office** (Mon–Fri 8am–6pm, Sat 8am–3pm; Ⓦ www.um.oswiecim.pl), in the shopping mall/restaurant complex opposite the entrance to Auschwitz camp, can help you with transport information.

Most people choose to visit Auschwitz first (the site of the main "museum" displays), before heading for Birkenau, 3km to the northwest. From Oświęcim station, it's a twenty-minute walk (turn right outside the train station and follow the signs) or a short bus ride (numerous municipal services make the journey; details are posted at the train station exit) to the gates of Auschwitz. An hourly bus service operates between Auschwitz and Birkenau (April–Sept only; 2zł); otherwise taxis are available, or you can walk there in 35 minutes. You can then catch the hourly bus back to Auschwitz, followed by a municipal bus back to the train station – or simply walk direct from Birkenau to the train station (30min). As you can appreciate from the above, **walking** the whole circuit (train station–Auschwitz–Birkenau–train station) can be time-consuming, but many people prefer to do it this way, because it gives them time to ponder the enormity of what it is they're visiting. Bear in mind, however, that you'll be walking along unshaded asphalt all the way – not particularly comfortable in high summer.

Auschwitz-Birkenau is unfathomably shocking. If you want all the specifics on the camp, you can pick up a detailed official **guidebook** (3zł; in English and other languages) with maps, photos and a horrendous array of statistics, along with other volumes detailing aspects of its history. Alternatively, you can join a **guided group**, often led by former inmates (40zł per person; apply at the clearly signed desk inside the entrance). If you want to be sure of an English-language guide, either arrive early or book in advance (☎033/844 8100 or 844 8099, ✉ museum@auschwitz.org.pl). It's important to remember that both sites are as much living memorials as museums, visited by many people – both Polish and foreign – whose relatives were murdered here, a fact testified to in the mass of candles, flowers and notes you'll find at such places as the execution wall and the crematoria.

Accommodation

In the unlikely event that you'd want a **place to stay**, you have several options. The church-run *Centrum Dialogu i Modlitwy* (Centre for Dialogue and Prayer) at ul. św. M. Kolbego 1 (☎033/843 1000, Ⓦ www.centrum-dialogu.oswiecim .pl; ❸, reductions for students), used by visiting pilgrim and tour groups, is peacefully located ten minutes' walk south of the Auschwitz site, and has a field for **camping** at the back. The *Międzynarodowy Dom Spotkań Młodzieży*, ul. Legionów 11 (☎033/843 2107, Ⓦ www.mdsm.pl; ❸), due east of the train station, and within walking distance of Auschwitz, is an International Youth Meeting Centre run by a reconciliatory German Protestant organization and offers decent accommodation in en-suite doubles, triples and quads, although it's often booked to capacity by groups. Hotels include the *Olimpijski*, opposite the main bus station at ul. Chemików 2a (☎033/842 3841; ❹), and the *Glob*, just outside the train station at ul. Powstancóv Śląskich 16 (☎033/843 3999; ❹), both of which are reasonably businesslike options with average en suites. All these places have their own **restaurants** or canteens, while the large cafeteria inside the Auschwitz camp area also provides basic meals.

Auschwitz

Most of the Auschwitz camp buildings, the barbed-wire fences, watchtowers and the entrance gate inscribed *Arbeit Macht Frei* ("Work brings freedom") have been preserved as the **Museum of Martyrdom** (daily 8am–dusk; donation requested). What you won't find here any longer, though, are the memorial stone and succession of plaques placed in front of and around the camp by the postwar communist authorities claiming that four million people died in a place officially described as an "International Monument to Victims of Fascism". In a symbolic intellectual clean-up, the inflated numerical estimates were removed and the lack of references to the central place of **Jews** in the genocide carried out in Auschwitz-Birkenau were remedied in 1990 at the orders of the International Committee set up to oversee the running of the site.

The **cinema** is a sobering starting point. The film shown was taken by the Soviet troops who liberated the camp in May 1945 – its harrowing images of the survivors and the dead aimed at confirming for future generations what really happened. The board outside lists timings for showings in different languages, although you can pay for a special showing of the English-language version (15zł). The bulk of the **camp** consists of the prison cell blocks, the first section being given over to "exhibits" found in the camp after liberation. Despite last-minute destruction of many of the 35 **storehouses** used for the possessions of murdered inmates, there are rooms full of clothes and suitcases, toothbrushes, dentures, glasses, a huge collection of shoes and a huge mound of women's hair – 70 tonnes of it. It's difficult to relate to the scale of what's shown.

Block 11, further on, is where the first experiments with Zyklon B gas were carried out on Soviet POWs and other inmates in 1941. Between two of the blocks stands the flower-strewn **Death Wall**, where thousands of prisoners were summarily executed with a bullet in the back of the head. As in the other

△ Auschwitz-Birkenau concentration camp

concentration camps, the Auschwitz victims included people from all over Europe – more than twenty nationalities in all. Many of the camp barracks are given over to **national memorials**, moving testimonies to Nazi actions throughout occupied Europe as well as the sufferings of inmates of the different countries – Poles, Russians, Czechs, Slovaks, Norwegians, Turks, French, Italians and more. This section is closed between October and April, except for those on guided tours.

Another, larger, barrack, no. 27 (open year-round), is labelled simply "**Jews**". There's a long, labyrinthine display of photographs inside, although they're left, unlabelled, to speak for themselves. The atmosphere is one of quiet reverence, in which the evils of Auschwitz are felt and remembered rather than detailed and dissected. On the second floor, there's a section devoted to Jewish resistance both inside and outside the camp, some of which was organized in tandem with the Polish AK (Armia Krajowa), or Home Army, some entirely autonomously. A simple tablet commemorates Israeli President Chaim Herzog's visit here in 1992. Despite the strength and power of this memorial, some still find it disconcerting to see it lumped in among the others, as if Jews were just another "nationality" among many to suffer at the hands of the Nazis. In contrast with other recent changes in the way events in Auschwitz are officially presented, this is one aspect of the old-style presentation of the Jewish dimension of the camp that you may feel has still not been fully addressed.

The prison blocks terminate by the **gas chambers** and the ovens where the bodies were incinerated. "No more poetry after Auschwitz", in the words of the German philosopher Theodor Adorno.

Birkenau

The **Birkenau camp** (same hours) is much less visited than Auschwitz, though it was here that the majority of captives lived and died. Covering some 170 hectares, Birkenau, at its height, comprised over three hundred buildings, of which over sixty brick and wood constructions remain; the rest were either burnt down or demolished at the end of the war, though in most instances you can still see their traces on the ground – visible along with the rest of the camp from the top of the **tower** above the entrance gate, which you can climb. Walking through the site, stretching into the distance are row upon row of barracks, fenced off by barbed wire and interspersed with watchtowers. Mostly built without foundations onto the notoriously swampy local terrain, these are the pitiful dwellings in which tens of thousands (over 100,000 at the camp's peak in August 1944) lived in unimaginably appalling conditions. Not that most prisoners lived long. Killing was the main goal of Birkenau, most of it carried out in the huge **gas chambers** at the far end of the camp, damaged but not destroyed by the fleeing Nazis in 1945. At the height of the killing, this clinically conceived machinery of destruction gassed and cremated sixty thousand people a day.

Most of the victims arrived in closed **trains**, mostly cattle trucks, to be driven directly from the rail ramp into the gas chambers. Rail line, ramp and sidings are all still there, just as the Nazis left them. In the dark, creaking huts the pitiful bare bunks would have had six or more shivering bodies crammed into each level. Wander round the barracks and you soon begin to imagine the absolute terror and degradation of the place. A monument to the dead, inscribed in ten languages, stares out over the camp from between the twisted ruins of the gas chambers and crematoria. Eerily, beyond the monument in the far northern corner of the camp area, is a pond where piles of human ashes from the crematoria were deposited, its water still a murky grey.

Oświęcim

Shuttling between the camps and the train station you're unlikely to see much of the town of Oświęcim itself, the centre of which lies 2km east of the train station on the opposite bank of the River Soła. Aside from an unassuming Rynek, ringed by cafés, and a red-brick Gothic church overlooking the river, the main focus of interest is the **Oświęcim Jewish Center** (Centrum Żydowskie w Oświęcimiu), which occupies a former synagogue on pl. ks. Jana Skarbka 3 (Ⓦwww.ajcf.pl). The beautifully restored prayer hall centres on a handsomely balustraded bimah (pulpit), while several upstairs rooms are filled with photographs of life in prewar Oświęcim – where Christians and Jews had lived perfectly harmoniously for five centuries. Banal early twentieth-century snapshots of football matches, school fetes and bathing trips to the river Soła assume a hugely poignant importance in the light of what happened to the community after 1941.

Kalwaria Zebrzydowska, Lanckorona and Wadowice

Southwest of Kraków lies an enchanting landscape of rolling hills and sleepy country towns, two of which are of great religious significance to Poles: **Kalwaria Zebrzydowska**, a centre of pilgrimage second only to Częstochowa, and **Wadowice**, birthplace of Karol Wojtyła, now Pope John Paul II. **Lanckorona**, a charming village of traditional wooden houses, is within walking distance of Kalwaria and can be covered in the same trip. Numerous local buses work the Kraków–Kalwaria–Wadowice route, ensuring that you can see all three places in the space of a long day.

Kalwaria Zebrzydowska

Nestled among hills some 30km southwest of Kraków, the town of **KALWARIA ZEBRZYDOWSKA** looks and feels like a footnote to its main attraction: a Baroque hilltop monastery whose miracle-working image of the Virgin has long been a focus for pilgrims. The charm of the place is considerably enhanced by the presence of a walkable Calvary route, linking various chapels, which winds its way from the monastery across the neighbouring hills. Whether you're spiritually inclined or simply want a nature hike, Kalwaria is a deeply rewarding place.

The Calvary came into being in the early seventeenth century, when Mikołaj Zebrzydowski, lord of nearby Lanckorona (see p.452), became convinced that the local countryside's similarity to the landscape outside Jerusalem gave it a special spiritual significance. Having decided to mark his discovery with the construction of a series of Calvary chapels, he sent an envoy to Jerusalem for drawings and models of the holy places – and many of his resulting buildings are modelled on those in the holy city – an engaging three-kilometre-long architectural tour is the result.

The area around the monastery is particularly busy during August, the traditional time of pilgrimage throughout the country, particularly during the **Festival of the Assumption** (Aug 15) and at **Easter**, when the Passion Plays are performed here on Maundy Thursday and Good Friday, with the vast accompanying crowds processing solemnly around the sequence of chapels in which the events of Holy Week are fervently re-enacted. The heady atmosphere of collective catharsis accompanying these events offers an insight into the inner workings of Polish Catholicism. With local volunteers tied on crosses and onlookers dressed as Romans, it's a powerful, even gruesome, spectacle.

The **bus station** is a twenty-minute walk east of the monastery, while the Kalwaria Zebrzydowska-Lanckorona **train station** (served by trains from Kraków to Bielsko-Biała, Sucha Beskidzka and Zakopane) is a further ten minutes' walk out in the same direction. For **eating**, the *jadłodajnia* in the monastery courtyard offers cheap, filling food and has a terrace with outstanding views.

The monastery and the Calvary chapels

Dominating the landscape from its perch, the Benedictine Monastery is reached via ul. Bernardyńska, a steep street which darts up from Kalwaria's undistinguished town centre, or by a more gently inclined road to the left which winds its way leisurely to the top, The towering main **Bazylika Matki Bożej** (Basilica of the Virgin) is a familiar Baroque effusion, with a silver-plated Italian figure of the Virgin standing over the high altar. The object that inspires the greatest devotion, however, is the **painting** of the Virgin and Child in the Zebrzydowski chapel, said to have been shedding tears at regular intervals since the 1640s. The pope (who grew up 15km away in Wadowice) used to be a regular visitor to the shrine, and you'll usually find pilgrims buzzing among the customary ranks of snack bars and trinket stalls that line the approach to the basilica. A corridor connects the church to a small cloister, where you'll find seventeenth-century portraits of the Zebrzydowski family.

The starting point for the **Calvary** begins immediately outside the monastery. It's really made up of two interlocking routes, the main Via Dolorosa (marked as "Dróżki pana Jesusa" on signboards), and a sequence of Marian Stations ("Dróżki Matki Bożej"), each of which wends its way up and down hillocks, along tree-lined avenues, through forest and in and out of rustic villages. Every few hundred metres or so you'll come across a cluster of chapels – some of which resemble insignificant huts, others magnificent domed structures which have the appearance of bonzai cathedrals. There are regular processions of schoolkids and coach parties "doing" the chapels nearest the monastery, but the further reaches of the Calvary routes are relatively crowd-free, contemplative places.

Lanckorona

Five kilometres east of Kalwaria Zebrzydowska, and reached by a minor road off the Kraków–Bielsko-Biała highway, the hillside village of **LANCKORONA** has long been noted for its traditional folk architecture and unhurried rustic feel. It served genteel Kraków folk as a health retreat in the years before World War I, although there are few relics of its time as a spa resort today. The village is served by three direct **buses** a day from Kraków, although it makes sense to combine Lanckorona with a visit to Kalwaria – the easternmost of whose Calvary chapels is only 45 minutes' walk over the hill. The Kalwaria Zebrzydowska-Lanckorona train station is about forty minutes away to the north.

At the centre of the village lies a spacious, sloping **Rynek**, lined with low, pastel-coloured houses, their broad shingle roofs hanging over wooden-pillared porches. An old granary at the bottom of the square now accommodates a small **museum** (Tues–Sat 10am–4pm; 4zł), displaying a diverting jumble of nineteenth-century agricultural implements and craft tools. Paths leave the upper end of the square towards Lanckorona's medieval **castle**, an evocative ruin shrouded in forest. As so often with such castles in Poland, there doesn't seem to be much inside save for the broken glass left by partying teenagers.

Wadowice

Fourteen kilometres west of Kalwaria Zebrzydowska is the little town of **WADOWICE**, whose rural obscurity was shattered by the election of local boy **Karol Wojtyła** to the papacy in October 1978. Almost instantly the town became a place of pilgrimage, with the souvenir industry quick to seize the opportunities.

The train and bus stations are on the eastern side of the town, from where it's a ten-minute walk to the elegantly paved and flowerbedded market square. Main point of reference here is the onion-domed **parish church**, where Karol Wojtyła was baptized in 1920. Most visitors gravitate towards the Chapel of the Virgin Mary on the left-hand side of the entrance, site of a nineteenth-century image of the Virgin to which Karol Wojtyła prayed regularly as a schoolboy. Behind the church, the old **town hall** now houses a museum (Mon–Thurs 9am–3pm, Fri 9am–4.30pm, Sat 10am–2pm, Sun 11am–3pm; 2zł) with changing exhibitions on local history. A few steps away from the museum at ul. Kościelna 7 is the **pope's birthplace**, a simple two-room apartment where he spent the first eighteen years of his life. It has now been turned into a rather tasteful and restrained **museum** (daily: May–Sept 9am–1pm & 2–6pm; Oct–April 9am–noon & 2–5pm; free), packed with photographs illustrating all stages of his life. It certainly succeeds in portraying the pontiff as a rounded personality, with pictures of him skiing, hiking, playing in goal for the school team and taking part in student drama productions. The museum is far too small to cope with the coach parties that regularly descend on the place, so be prepared for a bit of a crush.

Wadowice has one culinary claim to fame in the shape of the *Kremówka Wadowicka*, a deliciously wobbly slice of creamy custard that is sold at all the town's cafés – *Cukiernia Beskidzka*, just off the main square on ul. Jagiellońska, is one of the best places to try it. For more substantial eating, the *Piwnica* **restaurant**, also on Jagiellońska, serves up good, inexpensive pork and fish dishes in an attractive cellar. *Kawiarna Galicja*, right next to the pope's birthplace on Kościelna, is a relaxing place for civilized **drinking**.

The Ojców valley and the Szlak Orlich Gniazd

To the northwest of Kraków, the **Ojców valley** offers an easy respite from the rigours of the city. This deep limestone gorge of the River Prądnik has a unique microclimate and an astonishingly rich variety of plants and wildlife, virtually all of it now protected by the **Ojców national park** (information at ⓦ www.opn.most.org.pl), one of the country's smallest and most memorable protected regions. With an attractive and varied landscape of scenic river valley, twisted rock formations, peaceful forests and a rich and varied flora, the nineteen-square-kilometre park makes a beautiful and easily accessible area for a day's trekking, particularly in September and October, when the rich colours of the Polish autumn are at their finest. Anyone considering giving the park the attention it deserves should pick up the *Ojcówski Park Narodowy* map (1:22,500), widely available both in Kraków and on arrival in Ojców.

The valley also gives access to the most southerly of the **castles** built by King Kazimierz to defend the southwestern reaches – and, most importantly, the trade routes – of the country from the Bohemian rulers of Silesia. Known as the **Szlak Orlich Gniazd** (Eagles' Nest Trail), these fortresses are strung along the hilly ridge extending westwards from Ojców towards Częstochowa.

Ojców and into the valley

The principal point of access to the river gorge is **OJCÓW**, 25km from Kraków (and served by most – but not all – Kraków–Olkusz buses), the national park's only village and filled to bursting with local school groups in season. Developed as a low-key health resort in the mid-nineteenth century, it's a delightful village, with wooden houses straggling along a valley floor framed by deciduous forest and craggy limestone cliffs. Just beyond the car park where buses stop is a small **natural history museum** (mid-May to mid-Nov Tues–Sun 9am–4.30pm, mid-Nov to mid-May Tues–Fri 8am–3pm; 2zł), where you'll find mammoth tusks, the jaws of prehistoric cave bears, and a modest collection of stuffed local fauna. Immediately beyond is the PTTK **regional museum** (Mon–Fri 9am–3pm; 2zł), located above the Ojców post office, which contains prints of the village as it looked in the nineteenth century, and a corner stacked with local folk costumes, notable for the extravagantly embroidered and beaded women's jackets. Overlooking the village to the north is a fine, ruined **castle** (April–Oct Tues–Sun 10am–4.45pm, stays open later at the height of summer; 1.50zł), the southern extremity of the Szlak Orlich Gniazd and an evocative place in the twilight hours when it is circled by squadrons of bats. There's not much of the castle left, apart from two of the original fourteenth-century towers, the main gate entrance and the walls of the castle chapel. There are excellent views over the winding valley, and a path through the woods which leads up to the Złota Góra campsite and restaurant (see opposite). A few hundred metres north up the valley from Ojców castle is the curious spectacle of the **Kaplica na Wodzie** (Chapel on the Water), straddling the river on brick piles. This odd site neatly circumvented a nineteenth-century tsarist edict forbidding religious structures to be built "on solid ground", part of a strategy to subdue the intransigently nationalist Catholic Church. These days, it's only open for visits between Masses on Sundays.

Heading south from the village takes you through a small gorge lined with strange rock formations, most famous of which, about 15 minutes out from the village, is the **Krakowska Brama** (Kraków Gate), a pair of rocks which seem to form a huge portal leading to a side valley. Before reaching the Krakowska Brama you may well be enticed uphill to the right by a (black-waymarked) path to the **Jaskinia Łokietka** ("Shorty's Cave"; late April to mid-Nov daily 9.30am–4.30pm; 5zł), some thirty minutes' distant, the largest of a sequence of chambers burrowing into the cliffs outside Ojców. According to legend it was here that King Władysław the Short was hidden and protected by loyal local peasants following King Wenceslas of Bohemia's invasion in the early fourteenth century. Around 250m long, the rather featureless illuminated cave is a bit of a letdown if you've come expecting spectacular stone and ice formations. Individual travellers will have to wait to join a guided group before being allowed inside.

Ojców practicalities

There's a PTTK **information office** (Mon–Fri 9am–3pm; ☎012/389 2036) next to the car park which can help you find a place to stay, and a souvenir shop in the same building which sells maps. The Ojcowianin travel agency, in the same building as the PTTK museum (☎012/389 2089), also has information on rooms. Alternatively, it's usually fairly easy to rent a room in someone's house in the village by asking around, though things get pretty full up in the summer season. The only **hotel** option in easy striking distance is the basic *Zosia* (☎012/389 2008; ❷) in Złota Góra, a kilometre northwest of the castle up the hill road through the forest. There's a **campsite** a couple of hundred metres beyond the *Zosia*, as well as a **restaurant**, the *Zajazd*, which does good trout. Back down in Ojców, the *Pod Kazimierza* café-restaurant mops up many of the day-trippers.

Pieskowa Skała

If the weather's fine and you're up for walking the nine-kilometre road and footpath from Ojców, **PIESKOWA SKAŁA**, home to the region's best-known and best-preserved castle, is an enjoyable and trouble-free piece of hiking. Direct buses also run from Kraków (1hr 15min) via Ojców. If you're on foot, a trail marked with red waymarkers heads left into the woods roughly parallel with the Kaplica na Wodzie (see opposite). After 3km or so it rejoins the main road and darts uphill to the village of **Grodzisko** just to the north. The tiny late-seventeenth-century **chapel** was built on the site of a convent established here in the early fourteenth century by King Władysław the Short (1306–33) under the patronage of his saintly sister, Salomea. Figures of both founder and patroness adorn the outer walls of the courtyard. Added curiosity value is provided by the stone carving of an elephant carrying an obelisk-shaped object on its back, located round the back of the chapel.

Roughly 4km further north, the castle approach is signalled by an eighteen-metre limestone pillar known locally as **Maczuga Herkulesa** (Hercules' Club) rearing up in front of you, beyond which you can see the castle. Long the possession of the Szafraniec family, the **castle** (courtyard 7am–8pm; free) is in pretty good shape following extensive recent renovation, the fourteenth-century original having been rebuilt in the 1580s as an elegant Renaissance residence. As at Wawel, the most impressive period feature is the delicately arcaded courtyard, a photogenic construction that's a regular feature in travel brochures. Don't expect to enjoy it undisturbed, however: for most of the summer the place positively hums with tourist traffic, which can make a visit a stamina-depleting experience.

The castle **museum** (Tues–Fri 10am–3.30pm, Sat & Sun 10am–5.30pm; 7zł) offers a breathtaking sweep through several centuries of art, beginning with some fine Gothic wood-carved Madonnas, St Barbaras and St Catherines, and an exquisitely rendered sculpture of St Mary of Egypt, her entire body covered by the long tresses of her hair. A spectacular bevy of altarpieces includes a grippingly gruesome *Martyrdom of St Stanisław* with his tormentor King Bolesław looking impassively on; another panel bears a bizarre scene of punishment in which the unfaithful wives of Kraków are forced to suckle puppies while their own children are put to the teat of a bitch. A sequence of Baroque rooms feature sumptuously decorated Flemish and Dutch tapestries, the most notable among them depicting a series of heroic scenes from the life of Alexander the Great, culminating in his triumphant entry into Babylon in a chariot.

One of the fortified towers houses a **café-restaurant** with canteen food, a groovy interior arranged around a spiral staircase, and a roof terrace offering fine views over the valley.

The end of the trail

The remaining castles of the Szlak Orlich Gniazd are very ruined, but dramatic, seeming to spring straight out of the Jurassic rock formations. You really need your own vehicle to follow the whole route as, although all the castles are accessible by bus, you'll experience long waits and frequent detours, and it's unlikely you'd be able to find anywhere to stay. However, the most impressive of the other castles are also the easiest to get to. At **OGRODZIENIEC**, some 35km north of Pieskowa Skała on the main road to Olkusz (served by bus from Kraków), the ruin you see today was built during Kazimierz the Great's reign and remodelled into a magnificent Renaissance residence reputedly the equal of Wawel, before being ravaged by the Swedes in 1655. **ZAWIERCIE** preserves only the substantial shell of a frontier fortress.

The most accessible castle in the trail, after Pieskowa Skała, is at **OLSZTYN**, just a few kilometres southeast of the city boundaries of Częstochowa, to which it's linked by several buses an hour (#58 or #67 from ul. Piłsudskiego). The **castle** here, which dominates the surrounding landscape, is the one generally used to promote the route on tourist brochures and posters – understandably so, given its dramatic location on the limestone cliffs, a steepish eastwards climb from the village. Built in the mid-1300s by King Kazimierz III, like many others of its kind Olsztyn castle was laid to waste during the Swedish "Deluge" of the 1650s. Though impressive enough, the remains you see today only hint at past glories. Unusually, the castle was laid out in two parts, with a round watchtower crowning one outcrop of rock, and a keep on top of another; from the ruins of each there's a superb view over the whole upland region, the effect heightened by the winds buffeting the place most of the time. Down in the village there is a scattering of tourist-oriented **places to eat**, including the *Piccolo* and *Pod Zamkiem* restaurants, both on ul. Zamkowa – the approach road to the castle – as well as a number of more basic places on and around the Rynek. The only accommodation currently on offer is the seasonal **campsite** off ul. Zielona, 10 minutes' walk southeast of the Rynek.

Częstochowa

To get an understanding of the central role that Catholicism still holds in contemporary Poland, a visit to **CZĘSTOCHOWA** is an essential and, for many people, extraordinary experience. The hilltop monastery of **Jasna Góra** (Clear Mountain) is one of the world's greatest places of pilgrimage, and its famous icon, the **Black Madonna**, has drawn the faithful here over the past six centuries – reproductions exist in almost every Polish church.

The special position that Jasna Góra and its icon hold in the hearts and minds of the majority of Poles is the product of a rich web of history and myth. It's not a place you can react to dispassionately; indeed it's hard not to be moved as you over-hear troupes of pilgrims breaking into hymn as they shuffle between the Stations of the Cross, or watch peasants praying mutely before the icon they've waited a lifetime to see. One thing that will strike you here, as the crowds swell towards an approaching festival, is the number of excited teenagers in attendance, all treating the event with the expectation you'd find at an international rock concert.

Central to this nationwide veneration is the tenuous position Poland has held on the map of Europe; at various times the Swedes, the Russians and the Germans have sought to annihilate it as a nation. Each of these traditional and non-Catholic enemies has laid siege to Jasna Góra, yet failed to destroy it, so adding to the icon's reputation as a miracle-worker and the guarantor of Poland's very existence.

The regular influx of pilgrims to Częstochowa means that you might have problems finding somewhere to stay in town. Luckily it's an easy day-trip from

Kraków thanks to good rail connections. Buses also run daily from Katowice, Kraków, Łódź and Warsaw.

Some history

The hill known as Jasna Góra was probably used as part of the same defensive system as the castles along the Szlak Orlich Gniazd. In the **fourteenth century**, it came under the control of Ladislaus II, whose main possession was the independent duchy of Opole on the other side of the Silesian frontier. In 1382, he founded the monastery here, donating the miraculous icon a couple of years later. Ladislaus spent his final years imprisoned in his own castle, having fallen into disgrace for trying to prevent the union between Poland and Lithuania. Nevertheless, the monastery quickly attracted pilgrims from a host of nations and was granted the special protection of the Jagiellonian and Waza dynasties, though it was not until the **fifteenth century** that a shrine of stone and brick was built.

In the first half of the **seventeenth century**, the monastery was enclosed by a modern fortification system as a bulwark of Poland's frontiers – and its Catholic faith – at a time of Europe-wide political and religious conflicts. Its worth was proved in the six-week siege of 1655 by the Swedes, who failed to capture it despite having superior weapons and almost four thousand troops – ranged against just 250 defenders. This sparked off an amazing national fightback against the enemy, who had occupied the rest of the country against little resistance, and ushered in Poland's short period as a European power of the first rank.

In the early **eighteeth century**, the Black Madonna was crowned Queen of Poland in an attempt by the clergy to whip up patriotism and fill the political void created by the Russian-sponsored "Silent Sejm", which had reduced the nation to a puppet state. Jasna Góra was the scene of another heroic defence in 1770, when it was held by the Confederates of Bar against greater Russian forces, and retained by them until after the formal partitioning of Poland two years later. Częstochowa was initially annexed by Prussia, but after a few years as part of Napoleon's Duchy of Warsaw, it served as a frontier fortress of the Russian Empire for more than a century. It was incorporated into the new Polish state after **World War I**, when the icon's royal title was reaffirmed.

Towards the end of **World War II**, Soviet troops defused bombs left by the retreating Nazis that might finally have destroyed the monastery. They later had cause to regret their actions, as although Częstochowa itself developed into a model communist industrialized city, Jasna Góra became a major focus of opposition to the communist regime. The Church skilfully promoted the pilgrimage as a display of patriotism and passive resistance, a campaign that received a huge boost in 1978 with the election of Karol Wojtyła, archbishop of Kraków and a central figure in its conception, as **Pope John Paul II**. His devotion to this shrine ensured worldwide media attention for Poland's plight; as a consequence, praying at Jasna Góra has become an essential photo opportunity for the new breed of democratic politicians.

Arrival, information and accommodation

The main exit of Częstochowa's modern, Lego-like **train station** brings you out onto a neat plaza bordered by the **bus station** to the south. Turn right onto al. Wolności to reach the town's main artery, a dead straight three-kilometre-long boulevard, al. Najświętszej Marii Panny (usually abbreviated as NMP). The well-stocked and well-organized **tourist information centre** is at al. NMP

65 (Mon–Fri 9am–5pm, Sat 9am–2pm; ☎034/368 2260, ⓦwww.czestochowa
.um.gov.pl).

As you'd expect, there's a fair choice of **hostel** accommodation geared to
pilgrims, best of which is offered by the large and well-organized *Dom Pielgrzyma*
at ul. Wyszyńskiego 1 (☎034/377 7564, ⓦwww.jasnagora.pl/dom.pielgrzyma),
north of the car park on the west side of the monastery, where you can stay in
four-person dorms (20zł per person) or prim en-suite doubles (❷). Of the **hotels**,
Mercure Patria, ul. ks. J. Popiełuszki 2 (☎034/324 7001, ⓔmer.patria@orbis.pl;
❽), is a reasonably plush concrete three-star conveniently located at the foot of
Jasna Góra, and much used by foreign tour groups. The *Sekwana*, ul. Wieluńska 24
(☎034/324 8954, ⓔseine1@pro.onet.pl; ❺), is a smaller, more intimate place in
a good location immediately north of the monastery complex; while the nondescript *Sonex*, five hundred metres southeast of the train station at ul. Krakowska
45 (☎034/366 8080, ⓦwww.hotelsonex.pl; ❹), offers simple, ship-shape rooms
with shower. There's a **campsite**, *Camping Oleńka*, with a few bungalows (❶) in
an ideal spot on the west side of the monastery's car park at ul. Oleńki 22/30
(☎034/360 6066).

The Town

Other than Jasna Góra, Częstochowa has very few sights, although the broad
tree-lined boulevards at least give the heart of the city an agreeably spacious,
almost Parisian, feel. On pl. Biegańskiego, just off al. NMP, is the district
museum (Tues–Sun 11am–5pm; 3zł), which has a decent archeology section
plus the usual local history displays. If you want to continue with the ecclesiastical theme, you can visit the small Baroque **Kościół św. Barbary** (St
Barbara's Church) to the south of Jasna Góra, allegedly the place where the
Black Madonna was slashed (see box, p.460); **Kościół św. Jakuba** (St James's

Church), opposite the town hall on al. NMP, a tsarist-era Orthodox building converted into a Catholic place of worship following the attainment of independence in 1918; and the **cathedral**, east of the train station on ul. Krakowska, a vast, soulless neo-Gothic structure built – but never fully completed – in the early 1900s.

Jasna Góra

Aleja NMP, which cuts through the heart of Częstochowa, terminates at the foot of **Jasna Góra**. On most days ascending the hill is no different from taking a walk in any other public park, but the huge podium for open-air Masses gives a clue to the atmosphere here on the major Marian **festivals** – May 3, August 15, August 26, September 8 and December 8 – when up to a million pilgrims converge, often in colourful traditional dress. Many come on foot, and every year tens of thousands make the nine-day walk from Warsaw to celebrate the Feast of the Assumption.

The monastery

Jasna Góra (ⓦ www.jasnagora.pl) could hardly be called beautiful: its architecture is generally austere, while the defensive walls give the hill something of a fortress-like feel. **Entry** is still via four successive gateways, each one of which presented a formidable obstacle to any attacker. As you wander around the complex you'll notice two key components of the pilgrimage experience – redemption and commerce. At every turn you'll find confessionals at which the faithful eagerly queue, while numerous offering boxes outside key doorways and dedicated to one saint or another comfortably finance the upkeep of the spectacle. To deal with the visiting hordes there's a visitor **information centre** immediately inside the complex entrance (daily: May–Sept 7.30am–7pm; Oct–April 8am–5pm), run by nuns and usefully complete with an ATM.

The best way to begin an exploration is by ascending the hundred-metre-high **tower** (May–Sept daily 8am–4pm), a pastiche of its eighteenth-century predecessor, which was destroyed in one of the many fires which have plagued the monastery. An earlier victim was the monastic **church**, which has been transformed from a Gothic hall into a restrained Baroque basilica, now without pews, to make room for more pilgrims. Not that it's without its exuberant features, notably the colossal high altar in honour of the Virgin and the two sumptuous family chapels off the southern aisle, which parody and update their royal counterparts in the Wawel cathedral in Kraków.

Understandably, the **Kaplica Cudownego Obrazu** (Chapel of the Miraculous Image), a separate church in its own right, is the focal point of the monastery. It's also the only part to retain much of the original Gothic architecture, though its walls are so encrusted with votive offerings and discarded crutches and leg-braces that this is no longer obvious. Masses are said here almost constantly but you'll have to time it right if you want a view of the **Black Madonna** (see box, p.460), a sight that should not be missed. Part of the time the icon is shrouded by a screen, each raising and lowering of which presumably exists to add a certain dramatic tension and is accompanied by a solemn trumpet fanfare. When it's on view (Mon–Fri 6am–noon & 1–9pm, Sat & Sun 6am–1pm & 2–9pm), you only get to see the faces and hands of the actual painting (the Virgin's countenance being famously dour) as the figures of the Madonna and Child are always "dressed" in varying sets of jewel-encrusted robes that glitter all the more impressively against the black walls. Whatever your views on the validity of pilgrimages – veneration of a miraculous wonder or Church-engineered money-making device – you cannot fail to be impressed by the sheer devotion that the icon inspires in the hearts and minds of most Poles.

Other sites in the complex fail to match the resonance of the chapel, although between them they help to flesh out the site's history. To the north of the chapel, a monumental stairway leads to the **Knights' Hall**, the principal reception room, adorned with flags and paintings illustrating the history of the monastery. There are other opulent Baroque interiors, notably the **refectory**, whose vault is a real *tour de force*, and the **library**. However, you'll have to enquire at the information office by the main gateway for permission to see them, as they are normally closed to the public.

The museums

Jasna Góra's treasures are kept in three separate buildings. The most valuable liturgical items can be seen in the **Skarbiec** (Treasury; daily 9am–5pm) above the sacristy, entered from the southeastern corner of the ramparts. There's usually a long queue for entry, so be there well before it opens.

At the southwestern end of the monastery is the **Arsenał** (daily 9am–5pm), devoted to the military history of the fortress and containing a superb array of weapons, including Turkish war loot donated by King Jan Sobieski. Alongside is the **Muzeum Sześćsetlecia** (Six Hundredth Anniversary Museum; daily 9am–5pm), which tells the monastery's story from a religious standpoint. Exhibits include the seventeenth-century backing of the Black Madonna, which illustrates the history of the picture, and votive offerings from famous Poles, prominent among which is Lech Wałęsa's 1983 Nobel Peace Prize, along

The Black Madonna

According to tradition, the **Black Madonna** was painted from life by **St Luke** on a beam from the Holy Family's house in Nazareth. This explanation is accepted without question by most believers, though the official view is kept deliberately ambiguous. Scientific tests have proved the icon cannot have been executed before the sixth century, and it may even have been quite new at the time of its arrival at the monastery. Probably Italian in origin, it's a fine example of the hierarchical **Byzantine style**, which hardly changed or developed down the centuries. Incidentally, the "black" refers to the heavy shading characteristic of this style, subsequently darkened by age and exposure to incense.

What can be seen today may well be only a copy made following the picture's first great "miracle" in 1430, on the occasion of its theft. According to the official line, this was the work of followers of the Czech reformer Jan Hus, but it's more likely that political opponents of the monastery's protector, King Władysław Jagiełło, were responsible. The legend maintains that the picture increased in weight so much that the thieves were unable to carry it. In frustration, they slashed the Virgin's face, which immediately started shedding blood. The icon was taken to Kraków to be restored, but in memory of the miracle, two wounds (still visible today) were scratched into the left cheek of the Madonna.

Sceptics have pointed out that during the Swedish siege, usually cited as the supreme example of the Black Madonna's miracle-working powers, the icon had been moved to neutral Silesia for safekeeping. Yet, such was its hold over the Polish imagination that its future seemed to occasion more anguished discussion at the time of the Partitions than any other topic. In the present day, the pope's devotion to the image has helped to focus the world's attention on Poland, simultaneously supplying ample fodder for the more archaic and nationalistic strains of Polish Catholicism.

with the oversize pen he used to sign the landmark August 1980 Gdańsk Agreements (see "History" in Contexts, p.676). Completing the displays is the **Sala Maryjna** (Marian Hall; daily 9am–5pm), a collection of contemporary artists' impressions of the Black Madonna and similarly iconic representations of the pope.

Finally, it's worth strolling around the ramparts to the eastern end of the complex, which is where the big festival Masses are celebrated before the crowds of pilgrims assembled in the park below, as evidenced by the large rock stadium-style platform in place during the spring and summer.

Eating and drinking

For **eating** and drinking, there's a large choice of places along al. NMP and near the station, many of them basic snack-bar or fast-food joints. The *Dom Pielgrzyma* hostel, just outside the Jasna Góra complex, has a sizeable self-service café-restaurant catering for the needs of most day-trippers. Restaurants are gradually improving, both in range and quality. *Topolino*, al. NMP 67, offers an acceptable range of pizzas, pastas and salads, although it can't compare with *Da Vinci*, Dąbrowskiego 10, which offers a wider, more sophisticated range of Mediterranean cuisine with a few Polish favourites thrown in. The restaurant of the *Sekwana* hotel is a smartish French place that's about as good as it currently gets in the city, while *Blikle*, al. NMP 49, is the place to treat yourself to top quality pastries and cakes.

For **drinking**, *Pod Gruszką*, al. NMP 37, in a courtyard off the main street, is a decent café-bar popular with a local student crowd and also serves a small but tempting range of salads.

North of Kraków

Travelling north from Kraków on the road to Kielce and Warsaw, you soon find yourself in the heartlands of Małopolska, dominated by sleepy rural towns, villages crowded with geese, and a colourful patchwork quilt of traditional strip-farmed fields. The towns of **Jędrzejów** and **Szydłów** in particular offer a characteristic rural Polish combination of historical curiosity and comparative contemporary anonymity. If you've no need to hurry your journey north, they make an enjoyable diversion, with transport connections relatively problem-free.

Jędrzejów

Forty kilometres north of Kraków, **JĘDRZEJÓW** is, in most respects, another sleepy provincial outpost of Małopolska, a two-bit town used as a convenient stopping-off point on the main Kraków–Kielce road which bisects it. Getting in and out of the place is relatively easy, with buses and trains running to both Kraków and Kielce at fairly frequent intervals. The **bus** and **train stations** are next to each other roughly 2km west of the main square along ul. Przypkowskiego, although some buses pick up and drop off in the main Rynek, too.

Jędrzejów's main claim to tourist fame is the **Muzeum Zegarów Słonecznych** (Sundial Museum; Tues–Sun: May–Sept 9am–4pm; Oct–April 9am–3pm; compulsory guided tours on the hour every hour, last tour one hour before closing; 5zł), in an alluring, mansard-roofed mansion on the south side of the Rynek. One of the top three gnomonic collections in the world (the other two are in Chicago and Oxford), it is based on the collection of three hundred or so sundials amassed by local enthusiast Dr Tadeusz Przypkowski and left to the museum established in his house after his death in 1962. What sounds like a potentially less than thrilling proposal turns out to be well worth a visit. Dials of every shape, size and construction are gathered here, the oldest dating back to the early 1500s. Highlights of the collection include a group of attractive sixteenth- and seventeenth-century ivory pocket sundials, a set of Asian instruments and an eccentric piece from the mid-1700s that comes complete with a small cannon tuned to fire on the hour at one o'clock every afternoon. The rest of the museum is taken up with Przypkowski's more rambling collections of stuffy old furniture, books, art, clocks, watches and old bottles.

The other object of note in town is the impressive Cistercian **abbey** about 2km west of the centre – it's a short walk north of the bus and train stations. One of the group of Cistercian foundations established in the region in the early 1200s, the imposing twin-towered Romanesque basilica was remodelled a number of times over the centuries, the final product being the largely late-Baroque interior of today, featuring some ornate wall and altar paintings and lavishly carved choir stalls. Virtually the only feature reminding you of the church's architectural origins is the distinctive cross-ribbed vaulting developed by the Cistercians. Very little survives of the original monastic buildings, the main exception being sections of the Gothic cloisters, which the resident parish priest will show you on request. Among the abbey's former residents is **Wincenty Kadłubek** (1161–1223), bishop of Kraków and author of the *Chronica Polonorum*, the first written chronicle of Polish history. His remains are contained in a diminutive Baroque coffin housed in a side chapel off the abbey's southern aisle.

Szydłów

First impressions of **SZYDŁÓW**, 50km east of Jędrzejów, are less than promising. Perched atop a hill amid undulating Małopolska farmlands, this half-deserted rural backwater is certainly not a place to head for in search of action. What make a visit here worthwhile, however, are the remnants of the fortified Gothic architectural complex built by King Kazimierz the Great in the mid-fourteenth century.

Though the road takes you up around the top of the town, the principal entrance to the Stare Miasto is through the Brama Krakowska (Kraków Gate), a towering structure enhanced by the attic added in the late 1500s. Despite wartime devastation of the town, substantial sections of the **fortifications**, notably the walls, have survived essentially intact. Clambering around the chunky stone battlements, you sense that King Kazimierz, an indefatigable builder of castles, was a man who put security first. Certainly, the defences he raised here were enough to see Szydłów through the depredations and invasions that ruined many neighbouring towns in later centuries. A fair bit of the castle itself survives, too, notably a solid-looking tower that's now the town **museum** (May–Sept Tues & Thurs–Sun 8am–3.30pm, Sat & Sun 10am–2pm; Oct–April Tues–Sun 8am–3.30pm; 4zł), housing a low-key collection of local artefacts and historical finds.

West across the wide, open square, stuck out on the far edge of the medieval complex, is the **synagogue**, a large structure surrounded by heavy stone buttresses. One of the oldest synagogues in the country and built, according to local legend, at the instigation of Esterka, King Kazimierz's fabled Jewish mistress, the building is currently closed up and empty, waiting for someone to stump up the money to do something with it.

Buses serving Kielce and Jędrzejów run from the stop on the main square. There's nowhere decent to stay in town, and eating opportunities are limited to the basic café and snack-bar places on the square.

Kielce and northern Małopolska

Most people see nothing more of the northern reaches of Małopolska than the glimpses snatched from the window of a Warsaw–Kraków express train – a pity, because the gentle hills, lush valleys, strip-farmed fields and tatty villages that characterize the region are quintessential rural Poland. The main settlement is **Kielce**, a gruff workaday city halfway between Warsaw and Kraków, but the real attraction for visitors lies in rambling about in the **Góry Świętokrzyskie** – an attractive ridge of wooded, walkable hills just to the east of the city. South of Kielce, the **Jaskinia Raj** (Raj Cave), the medieval fortress of **Chęciny** and the open-air ethnographic museum at **Tokarnia** make enjoyable excursions. Heading north from Kielce along the main road to Warsaw, through the attractive Małopolska countryside, there are a couple of minor stops worth considering: the Cistercian abbey at **Wąchock** and the old *shtetl* of **Szydłowiec**, which has one of the largest remaining Jewish cemeteries in the country. All of the above are within easy striking distance of the city, making it feasible to combine several in a day's outing.

Kielce

Having undergone the standard postwar development, **KIELCE**, the regional capital, is nothing much to look at, but it has a relaxed, down-at-heel, rural atmosphere. Long the chosen summer residence of the bishops of Kraków, who furnished the city with its main architectural attractions, the town retains little more than echoes of its grander past. Its place in the postwar record is assured, as the site of the infamous **July 1946 pogrom** when over forty Jewish survivors of the Nazi terror were murdered by locals inflamed by rumours of the attempted ritual murder of a Gentile child. On a more contemporary note, the economic transformations of the post-communist era are beginning to show through – albeit much more slowly than in Kraków – in the increasing tally of new shops, cafés and restaurants in evidence in the city centre.

Arrival, information and accommodation

The town's **train** and **bus stations** – the latter a marvellously frivolous circular building resembling the kind of flying saucers imagined by 1950s sci-fi comic-book writers – are close by each other on the west side of town, a ten-minute walk down ul. Sienkiewicza into the centre. There's a 24-hour **left-luggage** office (*przechowalnia bagażu*) in the train station for those passing through.

The friendly **tourist information centre**, on the first floor of the train station's main ticket hall (Mon–Sat 10am–5pm; ☎041/367 6436), can help you to find accommodation and provides brochures. They may also have maps of Kielce and outlying regions; otherwise the bookshop on the corner of Sienkiewicza and Paderewskiego stocks a good choice.

There's a smallish selection of **accommodation** from which to choose, most of it directed towards commercial travellers and boasting prices to match. The only budget alternatives are the scattering of **private rooms**, mostly in the outskirts, on offer from the tourist office (**❷**).

Hotels

Elita ul. Równa 4b ☎ 041/344 2230. Small, privately run hotel in a residential street within walking distance south of the stations, with comfortable, well-kept rooms. Perfectly placed for ambling in Kielce's parks. ❻

Kongresowy ul. Manifestu Lipcowego 34 ☎ 041/332 6393, ⓦ www.exbud.com.pl. A towering, business-oriented place offering all the creature comforts, 2km northeast of the centre on the Warsaw road. ❼

Łysogóry ul. Sienkiewicza 78 ☎ 041/365 5000 ⓦ www.lysogory.com.pl. Ugly concrete block opposite the train station, thoroughly modernized to business standards inside. ❼

Pod Złotą Różą pl. Moniuszki 7 ☎ 041/341 5002, ⓦ www.hotel-pod-zlota-roza.pl. Elegant nineteenth-century town house at the eastern end of the main strip, offering plush rooms with Second Empire-style furniture and rich warm fabrics. ❼

Stadion ul. Ściegiennego 8 ☎ & ⓕ 041/368 7715. Utilitarian hotel aimed at visiting sports teams, 2km south of the centre but handy for the Kadzielnia reserve and the parks. Sparsely furnished rooms with shower. ❹

Tara Kościuszki 24 ☎ 041/344 2510 ⓦ www.tara.kielce.pl. Medium-sized, privately run place just east of the centre. Rooms are a little prone to over-the-top decor and colour-clash furnishings but otherwise everything is new, squeaky clean and comfortable. ❻

The City

All the monuments worth seeing are concentrated around a relatively small central area, bisected by ul. Sienkiewicza, the main city street. North of Sienkiewicza is the pleasant main **Rynek**, lined with a crumbling collection of unassuming eighteenth- and nineteenth-century mansions. South of Sienkiewicza on another square, pl. Zamkowy, you'll find the **cathedral** – Romanesque, lost in the later Baroque reconstruction. Highlights of its murky

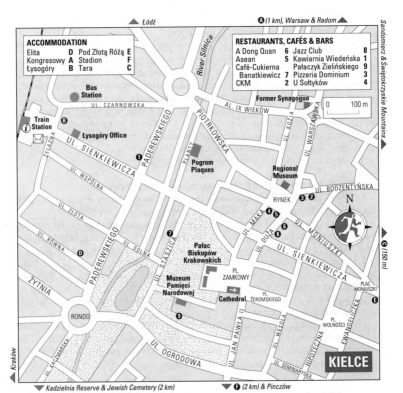

interior are a fine Renaissance monument in red marble to a female member of the local Zebrzydowski family, sculpted by Il Padovano, a sumptuous early Baroque high altarpiece from the workshops of Kraków, and some elaborate Rococo decorative carvings in the choir stalls. During major religious festivals, the square to the east of the cathedral is packed with smartly dressed locals, many in regional folk costume, processing solemnly around the square.

A short way west of the cathedral is the **Pałac Biskupów Krakowskich** (Kraków Bishop's Palace), an impressive early Baroque complex, built on a closed axial plan mimicking the layout of a period north Italian villa, supplemented – as in Wawel Castle – by features such as a sturdy-looking roof adjusted to the demands of a northern climate. Constructed in the late 1630s as a residence for the bishops of Kraków, under whose ecclesiastical jurisdiction the city and surroundings fell up until the late eighteenth century, the palace now houses another **regional museum** (Wed–Sun 9am–4pm, plus May–June & Sept–Oct Tues 10am–6pm; 5zł), this time among the country's weightier ones.

Most rooms of the **upper floor** comprise the former bishop's apartments, adorned with a sumptuous array of period furnishings, several of them still retaining their original decoration. The most notable feature here are the decorated high ceilings with intricately painted larch beams and elaborate friezes running around the tops of the walls. The finest example of this effect is in the **Great Dining Hall**, the frieze here consisting of a mammoth twin-level series of portraits of Kraków bishops and Polish monarchs. A number of apartments display some striking ceiling paintings from the workshop of Thomas Dolabella, notably the **Senatorial Hall** in the west wing, featuring the ominous *Judgement of the Polish Brethren* (the Brethren in question being a sixteenth-century Protestant sect based in nearby Raków), with a grand, sweeping depiction of scenes from the Polish–Swedish and Polish–Muscovite wars of the seventeenth century in the adjoining room.

Working your way round the back of the museum to the south brings you to ul. Zamkowa, and one of the more thought-provoking sights of Kielce, the former **prison** at no. 3, now the site of a **Museum Pamięci Narodowej** (Museum of National Remembrance; Wed, Sat & Sun 10am–5pm; donation). Used by the Gestapo in World War II and subsequently inherited by the communist security police, the prison was the site of innumerable torturings and murders between 1939 and 1956. The cells have been preserved in pretty much their original state – note the cages built over the windows to prevent notes or anything else from being passed outside to those prisoners lucky enough to be allowed some exercise in the yard.

Running southwest from Zamkowa is a spectacular swathe of parkland featuring a boating lake, ornamental flowerbeds and elegant stands of trees – all crisscrossed by paths which are thronged with locals on summer afternoons. Further south still, on the far side of Krakowska, the **Rezerwat Geologiczny Kadzielnia** (Kadzielnia Geological Reserve) is a partially submerged former limestone quarry now laid out as an (albeit scruffy) park. With its central lake surrounded by bleak crags and scrub, it's a surprise to find such a seemingly wild landscape so close to a city centre. At the far end of the reserve is an open-air concert venue, the "amphitheatre", put to good use in summer when various cultural events take place here.

Jewish Kielce

While memories of the notorious **Kielce pogrom** may have weighed heavily in wider postwar Polish–Jewish relations (see box, p.466), the same could not be

The Kielce pogrom

Kielce has achieved notoriety in postwar Poland as the site of the infamous **July 1946 pogrom**. Inflamed by rumours of the attempted ritual murder of an eight-year-old Gentile Polish child, elements of the local populace attacked buildings occupied by Jewish survivors of the Nazi terror, killing 42 people and wounding another forty over a period of hours, with no sign of intervention from the local police. Following a summary trial conducted shortly afterwards by secret police under the leadership of Edmund Kwasek, a notorious Stalinist-era butcher, nine of the twelve people rounded up and tried were found guilty of the killings and executed by firing squad. In customary communist-era fashion, all questions – concerning, for example, the precise circumstances surrounding the pogrom, or the security forces' failure to prosecute the local alcoholic whose claim that his son had been abducted sparked the killings, a story he himself later admitted to have fabricated – were met with a deafening silence. A defining moment in the development of postwar Polish–Jewish relations, the Kielce pogrom long constituted a blank spot in both local memory and official political discourse.

In symbolic terms, this has now been partially remedied by the commemorative plaque to the victims placed at the actual site of the massacre, along with a series of **official apologies** and acts of public contrition that took place on the fiftieth anniversary of the pogrom in July 1996. Politically, however, the issue continues to rankle. The report of the posthumous official commission of enquiry, released in 1997 after five years' sifting of the evidence, stopped short of pronouncing definitively on the question of ultimate responsibility for the killings. And while Kwasek has finally admitted that those brought to trial were simply picked up at random, many of the broader issues surrounding the pogrom remain unanswered. As a result, the **conspiracy theories** of various hues that have long formed the bedrock of public discussion of the event continue to hold sway. The official line during the communist era – still heard on occasion – suggests that the pogrom was the work of the armed anticommunist opposition still active in the surrounding region in 1946. By contrast, anticommunist-oriented public opinion tends toward the thesis that the Polish communist party instigated the killings in a bid to distract public opinion from the rigged summer 1946 referendum used to legitimize the party's subsequent assumption of political power, and held only a few days prior to the killings. Predictably, some more right-wing groups like to point the finger at "Zionist organizations" who are supposed to have engineered the whole thing with the intention of discrediting Poland in the outside world. On a more positive note, the commission did at least categorically reject one of the more outlandish theories, to the effect that events in Kielce were engineered by Soviet security forces as part of an attempt to encourage Holocaust survivors to emigrate to Palestine – at this stage the official Moscow line favoured the establishment of an independent Jewish state under Soviet influence. In addition, the commission asked local authorities to examine the evidence submitted to the commission with a view to prosecuting named local officials at the time for acts of gross negligence and incompetence – a valedictory admission that, whatever the remaining uncertainties, the authorities come out of the whole affair pretty appallingly.

said in the city itself, where for many years there was no effective recognition of the event in the form of an official monument or commemoration. This has now been rectified – albeit at the instigation of a private Jewish foundation, rather than the city authorities. The house where the pogrom started, at no. 7/8 Planty, is a short walk west of the square on the edge of the canal that cuts across ul. Sienkiewicza. It displays two small commemorative plaques in Polish, Hebrew and English "to the 42 Jews murdered . . . during anti-Semitic riots" – a commendably honest description of an event of which some in Poland would prefer not to be reminded. Other sites of historic Jewish interest are the former **synagogue** on al. IX Wieków Kielc, now an archive building, and the crumbling **cemetery** some way south of the centre in the Pakosz district (bus #4 passes fairly close by – get off on ul. Pakosz), where around a hundred gravestones are still standing, along with a dignified monument to local victims of the Holocaust.

Eating and drinking

The cafés and snack bars grouped around pl. Wolności, a market square just off Sienkiewicza to the south, are the best places to grab a quick bite to **eat**. For something more substantial, *U Sołtyków*, Rynek 19, is the best place to sample filling Polish meat and poultry dishes in relaxing surroundings; while *Pałaczyk Zielińskiego*, ul. Zamkowa 5, offers reasonably priced cuts of pork and veal in bone-throwing distance of the Bishop's Palace. *Pizzeria Dominium*, Rynek 7, is a basic, inexpensive source of quick nosh and nibblesome salads. *Asean*, Rynek 14, is the best of the Vietnamese restaurants, although the similar *A Dong Quan*, round the corner at ul. Duża 5, is slightly cheaper and is correspondingly popular with discerning locals.

As to cafés, the fancy, Viennese-style *Kawiarnia Wiedeńska*, just off the main strip at Paderewskiego 37/39, does a decent line in coffee and pastries, although the more down-to-earth *Café-Cukierna Banatkiewicz*, midway between Sienkiewicza and the parks at ul. Staszica 10, is the best place for cakes and ice creams. For those with a more serious evening session in mind, *CKM*, just off the Rynek at Bodzentyńska 2, is a roomy pub-like place in a covered courtyard, buzzing with revellers at the weekend. *Jazz Club*, ul. Duża 9, often features live music, although be prepared to blag your way in after 10pm, when (officially at least) it becomes a members' club.

The Jaskinia Raj

Ten kilometres southwest of Kielce, and roughly 1km west of the main Kraków road, is the **Jaskinia Raj** (Paradise Cave; mid-March to Nov Tues–Sun 9am–5pm; compulsory guided tours in Polish only; 12zł), one of the myriad underground formations dotted around southern Poland, principally in central-northern Małopolska and the Tatras. Only discovered in 1964, the cave rapidly established itself as a local favourite, and particularly in summer droves of school buses and day-trippers descend on the place. If you want to avoid the crowds, you'd be well advised to get there early. The **bus** (#31 from Kielce) drops you on the main road, from where you walk to the main car park and on along a wooded path to the ticket office-cum-café/museum at the cave entrance.

Only a stretch of 180 metres inside the caves is open to visitors, but it's a spectacular enough experience, comprising a series of **chambers** filled with a seemingly endless array of stalagmites, stalactites and other dreamlike dripstone formations. It's now been established that Neanderthals inhabited the caves as long as 50,000 years ago – these days the wintertime occupants are mainly bats – and scientific research carried out here continues to unearth archeologically significant finds, such as a recently discovered stockade constructed from reindeer antlers. Some of the finds are on display in the small museum attached to the ticket office at the cave entrance.

If you want to stop over, there's a basic **hotel**, the *Zajazd Raj* (☎041/346 5127; ❸) close to the car park, which has its own restaurant.

KRAKÓW, MAŁOPOLSKA AND THE TATRAS | The Jaskinia Raj

Chęciny

Five kilometres further south along the Kraków road (at the end of the #31 bus route), the little town of **CHĘCINY** nestles beneath a hugely impressive set of **castle ruins** (Tues–Sun 9am–6pm; 3zł), which dominate the surrounding landscape from their hilltop perch, providing the town with an instantly recognizable visual trademark. The castle is easily reached from Chęciny's Rynek, either via a path that darts straight up the hillside or by an asphalt road which curls its way more leisurely around the side. Completed in the 1310s for King Władysław I, and remodelled three centuries later following major destruction by the Swedes, this strategically significant outpost was eventually allowed to slide into ruin. All that remains today is the polygonal plan of the outer wall, the main gate and a trio of soaring towers, two of which – from a distance at least – look like the sombre chimneys of some giant hilltop factory. One of the towers – climbed via a steep spiral staircase – offers expansive views over the surrounding countryside, with Kielce, and on a clear day the Świętokrzyskie hills, visible in the distance.

There's not a great deal to see in the rest of Chęciny, although as so often in Poland, an awareness of historical context lends places like this their peculiar aura of poignancy. For centuries Chęciny was a typical Polish *shtetl*, with Jews making up more than half the population. The Jews are gone now, but the buildings they created remain – synagogue, merchant houses, cemetery – in silent testimony to their age-long presence. The former **synagogue** lies a short walk east of the Rynek along ul. Długa, a characteristically solid brick structure with a two-tiered roof built in the early seventeenth century. The building currently provides a home to various social and cultural organizations, and there's a good chance someone will allow you to take a peek inside if you arrive during normal office hours (roughly Mon–Fri 8am–3pm). A few decorative features apart, there's been little attempt to preserve anything of the original features of the building, with the main prayer hall now a featureless space occupied – at the last visit – by a table tennis table.

If you need a bite to **eat** before heading back to town, *Restauracja Pod Zamkiem* at ul. Armii Krajowej 1 runs the whole gamut of pork- and chicken-based Polish standards, but often closes on Mondays and Tuesdays.

Tokarnia

A further 7km south from Chęciny on the main Kraków road, the otherwise unremarkable village of **TOKARNIA** is the site of one of Poland's best outdoor ethnographic collections, the **Muzeum Wsi Kieleckiej** (Museum of Kielce Village Life; April–Oct Tues–Sun 10am–5pm; Nov–March Mon–Fri 9am–2pm; 10zł). It's right beside the main road and well signposted; if you're travelling by **bus** (from Kielce, take buses heading for Jędrzejów or Kraków) ask the driver for the *skansen* and you'll be dropped close by. In summer a basic café operates in the house at the entrance to the area.

With a well-laid-out collection of traditional buildings rescued from various locations in the Kielce region, the museum provides an enjoyable survey of local architectural traditions. Helpfully, there's a brief guide in each building in English, French and German outlining its traditional use, and, if your Polish is up to it, a devoted contingent of curators who can fill you in on all the details. They're justly proud of their buildings and, in customary rural fashion, in no hurry to see you move on, so be prepared to spend at least a couple of minutes paying each structure the required respect.

The thatched and shingle-roofed buildings assembled here encompass the full range of rural life, with an emphasis on traditional farmsteads, from relatively prosperous setups – the more religious pictures on display, the wealthier the family – to the dwellings of the poorest subsistence farmers. Great care and attention has been paid to re-creating the interiors as they would have been in the early part of the century and beyond, with many of the houses containing an amazing array of old wooden farm implements, kitchen utensils and tools used in traditional crafts such as ostlery, shingling, brewing, woodcarving, herbal medicinal preparations and candle-making. Additionally, there are a number of other buildings such as a wonderful old windmill, a pharmacy and a fine mid-nineteenth-century *dwór* (manor house) of the kind inhabited by relatively well-off *szchlachta* families from Chopin's generation and beyond up until World War II. The contrast between its size and opulence and the other ruder dwellings on display is striking, reflecting the grinding poverty and endemic inequalities of rural Polish society that were a major factor in the successive waves of emigration to the New World from the latter part of the last century on into the 1930s.

The Góry Świętokrzyskie and beyond

In this low-lying region, the **Góry Świętokrzyskie**, only 600m at maximum, appear surprisingly tall. Running for almost 70km east from Kielce, the mountains' long ridges and valleys are interspersed with isolated villages. The range gets its name from the **Abbey of Święty Krzyż** ("Holy Cross") right in the heart of the hills, a foundation once thought to possess a fragment of the Cross and which became a renowned pilgrimage venue as a result. It still exerts a powerful spiritual pull, and commands access to several rugged hiking trails to boot. During World War II, the area was a centre of armed resistance to the Nazis: a grim, essentially factual account of life in the resistance here is given in Primo Levi's book *If Not Now, When*. With abundant forest interspersed with twisted outcrops of broken quartzite, the whole range is encompassed within the limits of the **Świętokrzyski Park Narodowy** (Świętokrzyskie National Park), helping preserve the habitat of a range of birds and animals, including a colony of eagles.

The part of the range that most people aim for is the so-called **Łysogóry**, a scenic stretch of hilltop forest 30km east of Kielce, where the abbey, on the eastern shoulder of the ridge, provides the main focus for hikers and sightseers alike. A meagre handful of buses from Kielce head directly to the monastery,

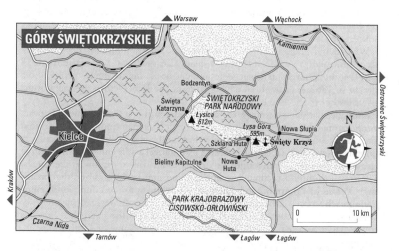

although services to the small town of Nowa Słupia, a kilometre or two down-hill, are more frequent – making this your most likely entry- and exit-point to the region.

Nowa Słupia

Just over 30km east of Kielce, **NOWA SŁUPIA** is a dusty crossroads town whose centre boasts a bus stop, a couple of cafés, and precious little else. From the town centre, ul. Świętokrzyska heads east then veers north towards the boundary of the national park. About ten minutes' out of town it passes the **Muzeum Starożytnego Hutnictwa** (Museum of Ancient Metallurgy; June–Sept daily 9am–5pm; Oct–May Tues–Sun 9am–4pm; 5zł), a concrete pavilion built to protect a second-century smelting site – when the land around Nowa Słupia made up one of Europe's biggest ironworks. The sober, Polish-language display does little to bring the site to life – although piles of ancient cinders do have a certain mystique if you stare at them for long enough.

The **tourist office** in the local government building (Urząd Gminy) at Świętokrzyska 8 (Tues–Fri 8am–3pm, Sat & Sun noon–4pm) can provide information on B&B **accommodation** in local houses; while the *Pod Skalką* **campsite**, near the museum at Świętokrzyska 57 (May–Sept; ☎041/317 7085), has dorm beds in wooden huts (❷), a grassy field for tents, and a restaurant.

On to Święty Krzyż

A short way beyond Nowa Słupia's metallurgy museum, a small car park girdled by souvenir stalls marks the end of the road and the beginning of the walking trail up onto the Łysogóry ridge. The trail starts with a small national park office charging an entrance fee (5zł) and selling maps. After a thirty-minute ascent through trees, a path marked "Miejsce pamięci narodowej" (literally "place of popular remembrance") leads off to the right, arriving after five minutes to an overgrown **Soviet war cemetery**, last resting place of POWs imprisoned by the Germans in Święty Krzyż abbey.

Back on the main track it's only a few more minutes to **ŚWIĘTY KRZYŻ** itself, an abbey established by Italian Benedictines in the early twelfth century. Legend has it that that Bolesław the Wrymouth ordered the construction of the monastery in order to house a fragment of the True Cross, brought to Kraków by Prince (later Saint) Emeric, son of King Stephen of Hungary. The abbey soon established itself as a pilgrimage centre much patronized by Polish royals – Władysław Jagiełło liked it so much he came here seven times. The Benedictine Order left Święty Krzyż after a change in diocesian boundaries in 1818 and the abbey served as a priests' retirement home before being turned into a prison in 1882. It's now back in the hands of the Benedictines, although some of its buildings are used by the national park.

Romanesque doorway apart, the abbey **church** is mostly Baroque in appearance. Lining the interior walls is a fine clutch of paintings by Neoclassicist Franciszek Smugliewicz, most impressive of which is *The Vision of St Emeric* – in which the eponymous hero is accosted by an angel while out with his hunting dogs. Working your way round the cloister from here soon brings you to the **sacristy**, beautifully decorated with Baroque ceiling paintings, and the adjoining **Oleśnicki Chapel** (Mon–Sat 9am–12.30pm & 1–5pm, Sun 12.30–5pm; 2zł), endowed in 1620 by Mikołaj Oleśnicki to hold the revered fragments of the Cross – hence the rococo reliquaries either side of the main altar. Frescoes to the right and left depict St Helena, mother of Emperor Constanine and discoverer of the Cross, and St Emeric presenting fragments of the Cross to the Bishop of Kraków. Mikołaj Oleśnicki and wife Sofia are treated to a splendid pair of funerary effigies. From the middle of the chapel, steps lead down into a small **crypt**, where a collection of open-lidded sarcophagi display the mummified remains of Mikołaj Oleśnicki and children, a nameless participant in the 1863 uprising (still wearing his black leather boots) and, most famously of all, Jeremi Wiśniowiecki (1612–51), who as Grand Hetman of the Ukraine during the Cossack revolts features strongly in the historical novels of Henryk Sienkiewicz. Wiśniowiecki left his widow with funds insufficient to finance the extravagant funerary spectacle a man of his standing was thought to deserve, and his corpse was entrusted to the monks of Święty Krzyż pending the family's financial recovery. His withered leathery form has been here ever since, wrapped in a fancy green shroud that in other circumstances would have made a fantastic pair of curtains.

The west wing of the abbey harbours the **Muzeum Świętokrzyskiego Parku Narodowego** (Museum of the Świętokrzyskie National Park; April–Oct daily 10am–5pm; Nov–March Tues–Sun 10am–3pm; 5zł), one of the country's best natural history collections, covering every aspect of the area's wildlife, with exhibits ranging from butterflies and snakes to huge deer and elk. There's a good view down into the valley below the edge of the abbey, and you can also see some of the large tracts of broken stones that are a distinctive glaciated feature of the hilltops.

Round the back of the abbey building steps lead down to a basement exhibition devoted to the abbey's period as a **prison**, particularly the 1941–45 period when, as Stalag XII C, it was used by the Germans to incarcerate Soviet POWs. Just how appalling conditions were then is indicated by photographs of camp signs (in Russian and German) forbidding cannibalism on pain of death.

Back in the cloisters, the *Jadłodajnia Benedyktyńska* **snack bar** (daily till 5pm) doles out delicious – and ridiculously cheap – portions of *bigos* and *żurek* in an attractive cellar space. A few doors away, the Stara Aptieka sells natural remedies based on traditional Benedictine recipies, and herbal teas.

From the abbey it's a twenty-minute walk westwards through the woods followed by a sharp southbound descent to the tiny settlement of **SZKLANA HUTA**, where there's another national park hut for the benefit of those entering the park from this direction, and a trio of enormous iron crosses erected in memory of Poles massacred by the Soviet authorities in 1939–40. Off to one side is the *Jodłowy Dwór* **hotel** (☎041/302 5028, ⓦ www.jodlowydwor.com.pl; ❹), a modern concrete building with small but comfy en-suite rooms and its own restaurant.

From Święty Krzyż to Święta Katarzyna

Continuing due west from Szklana Huta will take you towards the highest point of the Łysogóry, the 611-metre-high **Łysica**, 10km away at the western end of the range, a legendary witches' meeting place with an excellent viewpoint. From here the path continues for a further 2km through the woodland, past memorials to resistance fighters hunted down by the Nazis, to the village of **ŚWIĘTA KATARZYNA** – where you can catch a bus back to Kielce. In Święta Katarzyna itself, there's a **convent** that's been home to an enclosed order of Bernardine nuns since the fifteenth century. If you turn up during daylight hours you can usually peer in at the church. The *Jodelka* **hotel**, ul. Kielecka 3 (☎041/311 2111), will sort you out with a sparsely furnished room with shared bathroom (❷) or a more comfortable en suite (❹).

Tarnów and around

Though not about to step out of the shadow of its larger neighbour to the west, the regional centre of **TARNÓW**, some 80km east of Kraków, is nonetheless an interesting and ancient town in its own right, boasting a fine medieval Stare Miasto, excellent museums – including one of the Poland's best collections of Gothic art – and a haunting Jewish cemetery. As you'd expect, the background story here is essentially commercial. Founded in the 1330s, like several towns in the southeast of the country, Tarnów rapidly grew fat on the back of the lucrative trade routes running east to Ukraine and south to Hungary. Long the seat of the wealthy local Tarnowski family, it remained a privately owned town right up to the end of the eighteenth century. Under their patronage it grew to become an important Renaissance-era centre of learning within the Polish Commonwealth, a branch of the Jagiellonian University in Kraków being set up here in the mid-1500s. Later, wars and partition brought the inevitable decline, and in the twentieth century Tarnów's long-standing Jewish population was a particular target for the Nazis. Frequent and fast rail connections make it an easy and attractive day-trip from Kraków, but Tarnów can also serve as a base for trips around the region, including north to the folk art centre of **Zalipie**.

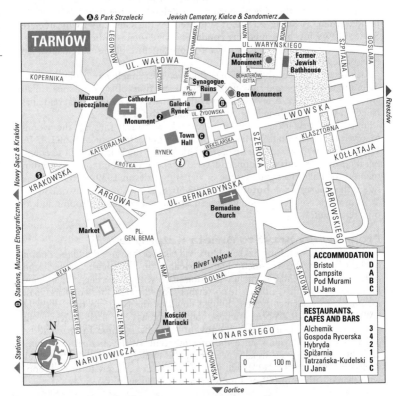

The Stare Miasto

The well-preserved central **Stare Miasto** area retains all the essentials of its original medieval layout. Oval in shape, the chequerboard network of angular streets, cobbled alleyways and open squares is ringed by the roads built over the ruins of the sturdy defensive walls that were pulled down by the Austrians in the late nineteenth century. The compact medieval ensemble retains its original two-tier layout, stone stairways connecting the lower and upper sections of the area.

The Rynek

Approached from the south side of town, steps up from the lower level lead on to the **Rynek**. Overall there's an enjoyably relaxed feel to the place, quieter and far smaller than the main square of its old rival, Kraków, but lined with historic buildings and terrace cafés. The centrepiece is the fifteenth-century **Town Hall**, a chunky, two-storey building with a roofed circular tower and an arched Renaissance brick parapet topped by a series of sculpted grotesque heads, a device suitably reminiscent of Kraków's Sukiennice. Inside you'll find the excellent permanent collection of the town **museum** (Tues & Thurs 9am–5pm, Wed & Fri–Sun 9am–3pm; 4zł or 8zł *karnet* for Town Hall, Galeria Rynek and Muzeum Etnograficzne; ⓦ www.muzeum.tarnow.pl). On the ground floor there are displays of armour and weapons, including some beautiful Persian and Turkish pieces, as well as exhibits relating to local hero Józef Bem (see box, p.475) and his military wanderings. Upstairs, the spacious Sala Pospólstwa (Commonalty Hall), retaining much of its original fresco decoration, houses a gallery of seventeenth- and eighteenth-century Sarmatian portraits (see box, p.474), remnants of a collection which once hung in Podhorce Castle, east of L'viv. At the fore are members of the wealthy Rzewuski and Sanguszko families, sporting Eastern-influenced period dress. Unusually, there's also an eighteenth-century portrait of Konik, a peasant from the Podhorce region. The hall is lined with period furniture, while adjacent rooms display *objets d'art* and curiosities like a boot from seventeenth-century China.

Back outside, the Rynek is lined with arcaded Renaissance burghers' **mansions**, notably the trio of parapeted houses on the north side, the facades adorned with their colourful original friezes. The central building of the three (no. 21) is the entrance to the **Galeria Rynek** (Tues & Thurs 10am–5pm, Wed & Fri 9am–3pm, Sat & Sun 10am–2pm; 4zł or 8zł *karnet*), where the museum's high-quality temporary exhibitions are held in impressive wood-beamed rooms and an ancient cellar.

The cathedral, diocesan museum and around

West of the Rynek on pl. Katedralny stands the **cathedral**, ostensibly dating from the fourteenth century but rebuilt in the nineteenth. The cheerful but mostly dull interior is redeemed by a sixteenth-century portal and the fine collection of Renaissance tombstones near the altar, including several executed by Italian sculptors employed at the royal court in Kraków. Particularly impressive are the grand sixteenth-century memorial to **Jan Tarnowski**, designed by Giovanni Maria Mosca and surrounded with friezes representing his military triumphs, and the Mannerist Ostrogski family monument, a sumptuous marble ensemble with sculpted representations of family members kneeling beneath a crucifix at the centre.

Behind the cathedral, a series of sixteenth-century tenements on a quiet, atmospheric side street house the **Muzeum Diecezjalne** (Diocesan Museum; Tues–Sat 10am–noon & 1–3pm, Sun 9am–noon & 1–2pm; free;

Sarmatism

The collection of seventeenth-century aristocratic portraits in Tarnów town hall is the most comprehensive pictorial record we have of the phenomenon known as **Sarmatism**, a loose system of fashions, beliefs and values that defined Polish society in the seventeenth and early eighteenth centuries. Based on the erroneous belief that the Polish nobility was directly descended from the ancient **Sarmatians** – a tribe of Iranian origin who swarmed across eastern Europe between the first and fifth centuries AD – Sarmatism engendered a fascination with all things eastern that manifested itself in the craze for caftans, sashes, topknots and moustaches so evident in the Tarnów portraits.

The idea that Poles could be descended from Sarmatians seems to have sprung from a cartographical misunderstanding. Many Renaissance map makers were unsure of what geographical label to apply to Eastern Europe, and scoured their classical history books in search of a suitable name: "Sarmatia" was what they came up with. Learned minds in Poland seized upon the beguiling idea that the Sarmatians had resided in Polish territory during antiquity, and were increasingly happy to adopt these mysterious horse-riding nomads as their ancestors.

The idea that a Slav race like the Poles could claim descent from the Sarmatians was clearly absurd; however, intellectuals got round the obvious objections by arguing that it was merely the Polish aristocracy, not the common people, who were descended from the Sarmatians, and it was precisely this unique lineage that gave them the right to rule.

Polish high society knew very little about the Sarmatians, but assumed that they were similar in appearance to other eastern races with whom they'd had more recent contact – especially the Turks and **Tatars**, who were a constant presence on Poland's southeastern borders. It was under the influence of these neighbours that wealthy Poles developed a taste for luxuriant gowns and silken sashes, and this style of dress became universally adopted by a nobility eager to demonstrate its Sarmatian credentials. Armenian merchants did a roaring trade in caravanning exotic textiles into Poland from the East, and set up wholesale depots in Zamość and Kraków to deal with the demand.

Adherence to the Sarmatian ideal was not just a matter of fine clothes. The idea that the original Sarmatians were warlike conquerors was enthusiastically taken up by Polish aristocrats who were themselves expected to spend long months in the saddle campaigning on Poland's eastern borderlands. Sarmatism became a **moral code** which placed a higher value on action and bravery than on domestic pursuits, and which cultivated a brash disregard for social niceties in preference to the courtly manners of Western Europe. Hunting, feasting and drinking were extolled as the only activities worthy of a true Sarmatian lord.

By the middle of the eighteenth century, however, Poles in Kraków and Warsaw were increasingly adopting Western – particularly French – modes of dress and behaviour, and Sarmatism was left to the more conservative-minded aristocrats of rural Poland, especially in the east. Indeed Sarmatism reached its apogee in the person of Polish-Lithuanian aristocrat **Karol Radziwiłł**, a man who deliberately played the hooligan in order to rile an increasingly etiquette-obsessed Warsaw court. He habitually subjected his peers to humiliating drinking marathons, once blew up one of his own castles in order to amuse party guests, and famously entered the royal palace in Warsaw in a carriage drawn by bears.

The Polish-Lithuanian state had ceased to exist by 1795, and what was left of Sarmatism quietly shuffled off with it. However the Sarmatist mind-set has exerted a subtle influence over Polish society ever since. Whether in the extravagant exhibitionism of today's nouveaux riches, the boorish behaviour of provincial politicians, or even in the shape and size of Lech Wałęsa's moustache, one has the feeling that the Sarmatians are yet to breathe their last.

@www.wsd.tarnow.pl/muzeum), the oldest and one of the biggest such collections in the country, and the best place to see paintings from the Kraków-Sącz artistic school, many taken from wooden village churches in the hills to the south. The setting, too, is splendid, with the paintings, sculpture and altarpieces hung gracefully in ancient rooms with original ceiling beams. Highlights include three large, fifteenth-century triptychs from St Leonard's Church in Lipnica Murowana (see p.479); a lovely painting of a white-robed St Catherine of Alexandria, from Biecz; and an elegant set of fourteenth- and fifteenth-century wooden pietà. There's also a rich collection of nineteenth-century religious folk art, but this section is not always open. Out behind the museum, as at several points around the Stare Miasto area, you can see surviving sections of the Stare Miasto walls.

South of the Stare Miasto and across ul. Bernardyńska, on the bustling market square below the main road, is the birthplace of **Józef Bem**, after whom the square is named. There's a **statue** to the man back in the Stare Miasto at the corner of ul. Wałowa and Forteczna, while his **mausoleum** is a short walk north in Park Strzelecki (see box, below).

Following ul. NMP south from pl. Gen Bema brings you after five minutes to **Kościół Mariacki** (St Mary's Church), a charming wooden structure topped with a steep shingle roof, built in the village of Przedmieście Większe in 1621 and moved to Tarnów two hundred-odd years later. Inside, much of the original polychromy has been preserved, including the lively seventeenth-century floral designs on the ceiling; the main altar is Baroque, holding a sixteenth-century Madonna. The church is normally locked, but opens for daily Mass at 6.30pm, and on Sundays also at 10.30am; if you miss these the cleaning lady usually comes by around 1pm. The free-standing bell-tower dates from 1910.

The Muzeum Etnograficzne

A ten-minute walk west of the Stare Miasto along busy ul. Krakowska brings you to the outstanding local **Muzeum Etnograficzne** (same hours and price as Galeria Rynek, see p.473). The focal point of interest here is the set of exhibits relating to Poland's **Roma** (gypsy) population, claiming to be the only one of its kind in Europe. A handy English-language booklet

---

Józef Bem

Born in Tarnów in the early Partition years, General **Józef Bem** (1794–1850) was a leading figure in the failed 1830–31 uprising against Poland's tsarist rulers, a role for which he was widely celebrated. A prototype of the dashing military figures beloved of the Polish Romantic tradition, the swashbuckling general is almost equally renowned in Hungary for his heroic part in the 1848 uprising in Vienna. Adventurer to the core, following the failure of the Hungarian revolt Bem travelled east to join Turkish forces in their struggle with Russia, assuming the name Murat following a rapid (and doubtless tactically appropriate) conversion to Islam. However, before having the chance to do much militarily for the Turks he died, in Aleppo, Syria, his cult status among resistance-minded Poles already safely assured. One of many "oppositional" figures from Polish history the country's former communist rulers were anxious to play down, in recent years Bem has been the subject of a welter of monuments that have gone up around his home town, the most recent addition being a statue of the man on the eastern edge of the Stare Miasto raised by the Polish–Hungarian Friendship Society.

produced by regional museum director Adam Bartosz, a local ethnographer and advocate for Roma rights, will fill you in on the details (the text is also available on the Tarnów museum website, see p.473). Although Roma arrived in Poland long ago, they have never settled in the country in the same way, for example, as they have in the neighbouring Czech and Slovak republics. Up to three-quarters of a population of 50,000 Polish Roma perished at the hands of the Nazis, part of the 500,000 Roma, half their entire population, murdered during the course of World War II – though these figures come with the caveat that Roma have always been difficult to count. In the 1990s, the population was swelled by influxes from nearby countries, notably Slovakia and Romania; some are still here, but most, including those who notoriously camped out for years in Warsaw train stations, have largely moved on. The Tarnów region has long been a centre for Roma in Poland, and it's this that explains the exhibition. Along with the general historical sections, there's a good collection of costumes, folk art and archival photographs, a sombre account of their treatment at the hands of the Nazis and, bravely, a section detailing contemporary ill-treatment of and prejudice against Roma in Polish society. There's also memorabilia relating to **Papusza**, a gifted Polish Roma poetess whose work was "discovered" and translated into Polish in the 1970s. To round off, there are a group of four traditional painted Roma caravans displayed in the yard at the back of the museum. Each June a traditional Roma camp is re-created in the yard as part of the **Gypsy Spring Festival**.

Park Strzelecki

Five minutes' walk north of the centre along ul. Piłsudskiego, **Park Strzelecki** (literally "Shooters' Park", a reference to the rifle associations that used to practise here in the early nineteenth century) is the town's main strolling ground, a tranquil kilometre-long stretch of flowerbeds and landscaped woodland. At its northern end stands the **mausoleum** of General Bem, an arresting Neoclassical structure built to house the relics of the hero on their return to Poland from Aleppo in 1929. The general's casket, bearing inscriptions in Hungarian and Ottoman Turkish as well as Polish, is held aloft by six Corinthian columns, the whole ensemble occupying an island in the middle of a lily pond patrolled by fat grey fish.

Jewish Tarnów

East of the Rynek takes you into what used to be the **Jewish quarter** of the town, a fact recalled in the names of streets such as ul. Żydowska and Wekslarska ("moneylenders"). Jews have a long history in Tarnów: the first settlers arrived here in the mid-fifteenth century, and right into the pre-World War II era they constituted forty percent of the town's population. The town also became an important centre of Hassidism during the nineteenth century. In 1939 the Nazis established a ghetto to the east of the Stare Miasto, filling it with local Jews as well as many transported in from elsewhere, and the population of the massively overcrowded area rose to 40,000. Between June 1942 and September 1943, virtually all the ghetto's residents were shot or deported to death camps, principally Auschwitz, and most of the area was destroyed. A few Jewish monuments, however, remain.

Architecturally the narrow streets around ul. Żydowska, all of which escaped wartime destruction, are essentially as they were before the war, with traces of the characteristic mezuzah boxes visible in a couple of doorways. The battered bimah, covered by a four-brick-pillared ceiling that stands forlornly in the middle of a small empty square north of ul. Żydowska, is what remains of the magnificent sixteenth-century **synagogue** that stood here until the Nazis gutted it in November 1939. At the corner of the street is a memorial tablet to the Jews murdered here in the course of a brutal *Aktion* carried out in June 1942. There are more Jewish buildings around the corner on ul. Goldhammer, named after a prominent local politician from the turn of the twentieth century, including the former home of the local Jewish Credit Company, at no. 5. Turning east into ul. Waryńskiego, past the corner with ul. Kupiecka, where the gate to the Nazi ghetto area stood, the corner of ul. Nowa is the former site of the New Synagogue, the biggest and most ornate in the town. Also known as the "Jubilee of Franz Joseph Synagogue" (it was consecrated on the emperor's birthday in 1908), the place burned for three days in 1939 before the Nazis blew up the remains. The bottom of ul. Nowa leads onto pl. Bohaterów Getta. Across the square is the Moorish-looking **Jewish bathhouse**, now a shabby shopping arcade-cum-office block; it was from here that a group of 728 local people were transported to Auschwitz in June 1940 to become the first inmates of the camp, a fact commemorated by the monument off the square on the corner of ul. Dibowa and Bożnica.

Final stop is the **Jewish cemetery**, a fifteen-minute walk north along ul. Nowodąbrowska. One of the largest and oldest in Poland, the cemetery was established as early as the 1580s, though the oldest surviving gravestone dates from considerably later. Surprisingly untouched by the Nazis, and still in pretty good shape, the overgrown cemetery contains a large number of tombstones, the emphasis being on the traditional type of tablet in which biblical and other illustrative reliefs are used only sparingly. Next to the entrance way on ul. Słoneczna (the cemetery's original gates are now in the Holocaust Museum in Washington), stands a monument to the Jews of Tarnów incorporating a column from the devastated New Synagogue. To get in you have to ask for the key (*klucz*), held by the owner of a small shop at ul. Widok 23 (☎014/626 3665; after hours ring the bell; donations accepted), just beyond the Julius Meinl supermarket; however, the cemetery fence is not high, and you'll be tempted to climb over if no one is around. This is also a fine place for **birdwatching**, inhabited in summer by, among others, a pair of golden orioles.

Practicalities

The main **bus and train stations** are situated next to each other on the southwest side of town, a ten-minute walk from the centre – buses #2, #9 or #41 will drop you on the edge of pl. Gen Bema at the southern side of the Stare Miasto. There's an **Internet** café in the old Jewish bathhouse off pl. Bohaterów Getta.

An extremely helpful **tourist office** at Rynek 7 (Mon–Fri 8am–6pm, Sat & Sun 9am–5pm; ☎014/627 8735, ⓦwww.turystyka.tarnow.pl) has a wealth of information on the region and sells maps and guidebooks. They also offer **accommodation** in the form of four guest rooms (❷) above the office; clean and good-value modern en suites that should be booked ahead. The other budget option is the spartan, PTTK-run *Pod Murami* hotel, ul. Żydowska 16 (☎014/621 6229), which has a mixture of bare-looking doubles (❶) and four-to five-person dorms (25zł). Several levels up in quality is *U Jana*, an elegant and well-run twelve-room hotel in the historic mansion at Rynek 14 (☎014/626 0564, ⓦwww.hotelujana.pl; ❺). Just west of the Rynek at ul. Krakowska 9 is the larger *Bristol* (☎014/621 2279, ⓦwww.bristol.tarnow.com.pl; ❻), more ostentatiously upscale but far less pleasant than *U Jana*. The town **campsite**, fifteen minutes' walk north of the centre at Piłsudskiego 28A (or bus #30 from the train station; ☏014/621 5124, ⊛www.camping.tarnow.pl), offers four-person cabins (❶), and tent and caravan pitches in an attractive apple orchard.

Given Tarnów's small size, the selection of **places to eat** around the centre is impressive. *Spiżarnia*, ul. Żydowska 12 (closed Sundays), is a bright little spot offering salads and pitta sandwiches, with some vegetarian options. For a sit-down meal the top choices are the restaurant in the *U Jana* hotel, which offers mid-priced Polish dishes in a comfortable and attractive setting; and *Tatrzańska-Kudelski*, ul. Krakowska 1, with an international menu and well-priced lunch specials – this is also the local favourite for ice cream and cakes. *Gospoda Rycerska*, just off the Rynek at Wekslarska 1, mixes pizza fare with grill food and Polish standards, served up in a cosy wooden interior. For a **drink**, *Hybryda* at Rynek 22 is the best of the outdoor cafés around the main square. *Alchemik*, nearby at ul. Żydowska 20, is a cosy subterranean café-bar with bohemian clientele.

Around Tarnów

The sprawling village of **ZALIPIE**, set in a remote agricultural region just east of the convergence of the Dunajec and Wisła rivers and 30km north of Tarnów, is a charming and little-known diversion into the folk traditions of rural Poland. Before the late nineteenth century, cottages here lacked chimneys, and before religious holidays village women used lime to cover over the soot that normally blackened their walls. When chimneys were introduced the practice lost its necessity, but survived as a novel form of decoration, with women painting **geometric and floral motifs**, first inside their houses and later on outer walls. Word of the tradition spread, and Zalipie's best painters, including Felicja Curyło (1904–74), were feted at Kraków ethnographic fairs in the 1930s. A first house painting competition was organized in 1948, and since 1965 the event has been held annually on the weekend following Corpus Christi (May/June), with around twenty of Zalipie's houses receiving a fresh array of colourful flowers and patterns each year.

From the bus stop follow the signs to the **Zagroda Felicji Curyłowej** (Felicja Curyło's Croft; Tues–Sun 10am–4pm; 3zł), site of the only house visitors can enter. The century-old building, parts of which were painted as early as 1913 – the white flowers on the ceiling above the entrance hall are oldest – is today cared for by the granddaughter of Zalipie's most famous artisan. Inside, the "black" room, so-called because it was where the family actually lived, contains a massive stove, black-and-white photographs, costumes, painted ceramics and heirlooms; while the "white" room, which was only used on Sundays and special occasions, holds the better furniture and embroideries. In the yard you'll find a painted barn, well and outhouse. The loop road that runs around the village (roughly 3km in all) leads past more painted houses before reaching the **Dom Malarek** (Painter's House; Mon–Fri 8am–4pm, Sat & Sun 11am–6pm; free), the local cultural centre, where there is a display of photographs from past competitions as well as a gallery of oil paintings by local artists and a small souvenir shop. Continuing past the Dom Malarek, turn right at the fire station to get back to the bus stop.

Getting to Zalipie from Tarnów is straightforward during the week: six daily **buses** leaving for the village of Grymboszów from gate #8 at the Tarnów bus station call at Zalipie, and the last one back to Tarnów passes through Zalipie around 6pm. On Saturdays there are fewer services, with none to Tarnów from Zalipie after 5pm. On Sundays there are no services at all. Driving from Kraków, you'll cross the Wisła on an old-fashioned river barge (5zł) at Nowy Korczyn. There's no place to stay in Zalipie, but snacks are available in the rather sparsely stocked shops near where the buses drop you off.

Lipnica Murowana

Some fifty kilometres southeast of Kraków, on a branch road running out of Wieliczka, the ancient village of **LIPNICA MUROWANA** is home to one of the region's finest wooden churches. **Buses** from Kraków (the town is an intermediate destination on several routes; ask at Kraków's bus station information desk) drop you off at the pretty, cobblestone Rynek, lined with one-storey wood houses from the nineteenth century.

The wooden **Kościół św. Leonarda** (St Leonard's Church), down the hill behind the main stone church and picturesquely set between a creek and the village cemetery, was built late in the fifteenth century on the site of an older church. The arcades date from the seventeenth century, but otherwise the building retains its original form. Most outstanding, however, and what justifies the building's 2003 inclusion on the UNESCO World Heritage list, is the fifteenth- to eighteenth-century interior polychromy. Oldest are the floral patterns decorating the ceiling, while the biblical scenes on the nave walls are mostly Baroque. The original Gothic altars are now on display in the diocesan museum in Tarnów (see p.473), but the eighteenth-century pulpit remains, as does a nice set of Baroque candlesticks. Not kept in the church, but occasionally brought out for concerts, is the *pozytyw szkatulny*, a rare portable organ from the seventeenth century. St Leonard's is open at weekends during the summer (June–Aug Sat 10am–1pm & 2pm–6pm, Sun 9am–1pm & 2pm–3.30pm; donations welcome) and there's a 4pm Sunday Mass in August, but otherwise you'll have to look for the priest, who lives next the main church and is usually available from 2 to 5pm. If he's not around, try the Dom Kultury (Cultural Centre) just north of the Rynek. The one town **restaurant**, *Łokietek*, isn't especially appealing, but there's a good country-style *Gospoda* serving tradional Polish cuisine five kilometres west. To return to Kraków, take one of the frequent buses to Bochnia and change there.

Podhale and the Tatras

Ask Poles to define their country's natural attractions and they often come up with the following simple definition: the lakes, the sea and the mountains. The mountains consist of an almost unbroken chain of ridges extending the whole length of the southern border, of which the highest, most spectacular and most revered are the **Tatras** – or **Tatry** as they're known in Polish. Eighty kilometres long, with peaks rising to over 2500m, the Polish Tatras are actually a relatively small part of the range, most of which rises across the border in Slovakia. As the estimated three million annual tourists show, however, the Polish section has enough to keep most people happy: high peaks for dedicated mountaineers, excellent trails for hikers, cable cars and creature comforts for day-trippers, and ski slopes in winter. A two-hour bus ride south of Kraków, the bustling resort

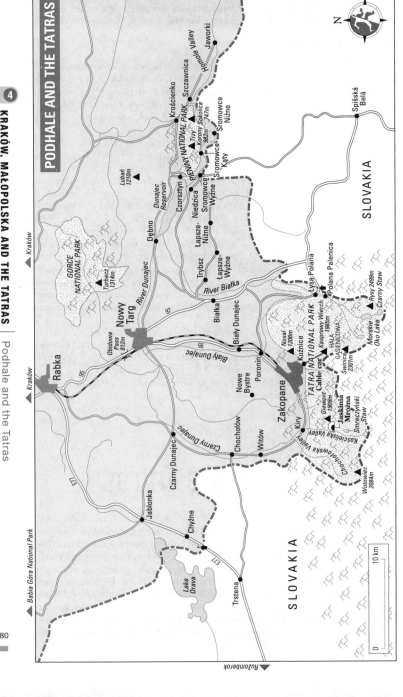

PODHALE AND THE TATRAS

of **Zakopane** is the main holiday centre, conveniently placed for access to the highest Tatra peaks and with plenty of attractive folk architecture in the immediate surroundings.

Podhale – the Tatra foothills, beginning to the south of Nowy Targ – is a sparsely populated region of lush meadows, winding valleys and old wooden villages. The inhabitants of Podhale, the **górale**, are fiercely independent mountain farmers, known throughout Poland for cultivating folk traditions which have died out elsewhere. The region was "discovered" by the Polish intelligentsia in the late nineteenth century and the *górale* tradition rapidly emerged as a symbol of an age-old, authentic Polish culture unsullied by outside influence. However, this was also an economically backward region, the poverty of rural life leading thousands of *górale* to emigrate to the United States in the 1920s and 1930s. The departures continue today, with at least one member of most households spending a year or two in Chicago, New York or other US Polish émigré centres, returning with money to support the family and, most importantly, build a house.

Despite the influx of holiday-makers, the *górale* retain a straight-talking and highly hospitable attitude to outsiders. If you're willing to venture off the beaten track away from the regular tourist attractions around Zakopane, there's a chance of real and rewarding contacts in the remoter towns and villages. The *górale* are also the guardians of one of Poland's most vibrant folk music traditions, retaining an appetite for the kind of rootsy, fiddle-driven dance music that has all but died out in the lowlands. Traditional bands regularly appear at local festivities and weddings (which are usually a high-profile component of any given Saturday), and also appear regularly in the bars and restaurants of Zakopane – which is also a good place to seek out CDs and tapes of the music.

South to Zakopane

From Kraków, the main road south heads through the foothills towards **Zakopane**, the main base for the Tatras. Approaching the mountains, the road runs through a memorable landscape of gentle valleys, undulating slopes and strip-farmed fields. Along the route you'll see plenty of houses built in the distinctive pointed Podhale style – newer houses have tin roofs, the older ones are decorated wooden structures – as well as wayside Catholic shrines and farming people dressed in the equally distinctive local costume.

Rabka and the Gorce

The climb begins as soon as you leave Kraków, following the River Raba from Myślenice to Lubień and then on, with the first glimpses of the Tatras ahead, to **RABKA**, around 60km from the city. This is a pleasant former spa resort, with a beautiful seventeenth-century **church** at the base of a hill, now housing a small **ethnographic museum** (Tues–Sun 9am–4pm; 3zł).

Surrounding Rabka is a mountainous area known as the **Gorce**, much of it national park land. It's fine, rugged hiking country, with paths clearly signposted, and offers a less-frequented and more easy-going alternative to the more demanding Tatras. There are **trails** to several mountain-top hostels: *Luboń Wielki* (1022m), *Maciejowa* (815m), *Groniki* (1027m) and – highest and best of all – *Turbacz* (1310m), a solid six-hour walk east of town. Before setting out, pick up the 1:75,000 *Beskid Makowski* **map** available locally.

Nowy Targ

From Rabka the road continues over the **Obidowa Pass** (812m), then down onto a plain crossed by the Czarny Dunajec river and towards Podhale's capital, **NOWY TARG** (New Market). The oldest town in the region, established in the thirteenth century, Nowy Targ was redeveloped as an administrative and industrial centre after World War II, and is now a dispiriting grey sprawl. The main attraction is the animated **market**, held each Thursday (and increasingly at weekends too) on a patch of ground just east of the centre. Once an authentic farmers' event, with horse-drawn carts lining the streets, it now covers a wider range of products, with agricultural produce sold alongside consumer goods and craft items. For visitors, the main shopping attractions are the chunky sweaters that are the region's hallmark – prices are lower and the quality generally better here than in either Kraków or Zakopane. Be prepared to haggle for anything you buy (wool and crafts especially), and arrive early if you want to get any sense of the real atmosphere – by 10am or so, with business done, many of the farmers retreat to local cafés for a hearty bout of eating and, especially, drinking.

There's no point in staying in Nowy Targ when a range of far more enticing mountain destinations are so close at hand, and once you've had a browse round the market, you'd be well advised to move on.

Zakopane and around

South of Nowy Targ, the road continues another 20km along the course of the Biały Dunajec before reaching the edges of **ZAKOPANE**, a major mountain resort, crowded with visitors throughout its summer **hiking** and winter **skiing** seasons. It has been an established attraction for Poles since the 1870s, when the purity of the mountain air began to attract the attention of doctors and their consumptive city patients. Within a few years, this inaccessible mountain village

The Lenin Trail

Nowy Targ marks the starting point of an unofficial **Lenin Trail**: the old prison just beyond the southeast corner of the main square is where he was briefly interned on suspicion of spying in 1914. The Bolshevik leader had already been a full-time resident of the Podhale region for over a year, renting a room in the village of Biały Dunajec, just north of Zakopane. The locality had several advantages for Lenin: it was near enough to the tsarist border for him to retain contact with his revolutionary colleagues, and the area's reputation as a rural retreat for all manner of eccentric intellectuals ensured that his presence here was unlikely to attract the unwelcome curiosity of the locals. He drank coffee and read the papers in Zakopane's main society hangout of the time, Café Trzaski on ul. Krupówki – an establishment that is sadly no more. The arty Polish types who divided their time between Kraków and Zakopane tended to regard Lenin as a kindred spirit, and the revolutionary's arrest in 1914 prompted novelist Stefan Żeromski and poet Jan Kasprowicz to intercede on his behalf, thereby speeding his release. Lenin subsequently relocated to Switzerland, from where he returned to Russia in 1917 to take command of the Revolution.

In 1947 a **Lenin Museum** was opened in the village of Poronin, between Biały Dunajec and Zakopane, but it closed its doors for good in 1990, with most of its artefacts being shunted off to the Museum of Socialist Realism in Kozłowka palace (see p.303). The house where Lenin lived in Biały Dunajec still stands, although the owners shun publicity in the hope that it won't become a target for tourists.

of sheep farmers was transformed, as the medics were followed by Kraków artists and intellectuals, many of whom lived here for several months in the year. In the years before World War I, Zakopane experienced more in the way of *belle époque* hedonism than Kraków itself, with all manner of poets, painters and composers descending on the place to get drunk, behave outrageously and steal each other's girlfriends. As well as personal liberty, Zakopane symbolized a free Poland: as Młoda Polska writer Wojciech Kossak notoriously remarked, "Austrian rule doesn't reach beyond Nowy Targ." After World War I more mainstream forms of tourism took over, Zakopane becoming Poland's premier skiing centre – a status it retains today. Nowadays its central thoroughfares have the hollow, overdeveloped feel of a major European tourist trap, although the Zakopane of old, with charming timber houses lining leafy streets, still lives on in the suburbs. Above all, the town remains the best possible place from which to access the most stunning scenery anywhere in Poland.

Arrival, information and accommodation

The **bus** and **train stations** are both a ten-minute walk east of the main street, ul. Krupówki. Some private buses to Kraków pick up and drop from a stop on

ACCOMMODATION				RESTAURANTS		Karczma		CAFÉS	
Antałówka	J	Daglezja	N	Pensjonat		Redykołka	1	AND BARS	
Api 2	A	Dom Turysty	I	Szarotka **M**	Bąkowo	Obrochtówka	14	Ampstrong	9
Belvedere	L	Giewont	G	Sabala **E**	Zohylina Nimna **13**	Pizzeria Grace	2	Café Piano	11
Camping Pod Krokwią **O**		Gromada	H	Szarotka **B**	Bar FIS **4**	Pstrąg Górski	3	Paparazzi	10
Camping Za Strugiem	D	Halny	F	Hostel **C**	Chata Zbójnicka **8**	Zbojecka	7	Rockus	6
Czarny Potok	P	Kasprowy	B		Chłopskie Jadło **5**				
		Panorama	K		Karczma Bacówka **12**				

483

ul. Kościuszki, just west of the stations. If you have your own transport, note that **parking** can be a problem in the centre. Your best bet is the big parking lot at the southern end of al. 3. Maja near the ski jump.

The **tourist office**, housed in a wooden chalet a few steps west of the stations at ul. Kościuszki 17 (daily: July, Aug & Dec–April 8am–8pm; May, June & Sept–Nov 9am–5pm; ☎018/201 2211, ⓦ www.zakopane.pl), is a helpful source of information on the whole area; ask here about anything concerning staying in Zakopane or seeing the Tatras, including maps and guides. The Tatrzański Park Narodowy, or Tatra **national park office**, at Chałubińskiego 44 (daily 8am–4pm; ☎018/206 3799, ⓔ kozica@tpn.zakopane.pl), is an essential source of expert information if you're planning a serious mountain trek. There's a well-stocked **map** shop inside the *Dom Turysty* hotel (see below).

Accommodation

Zakopane is increasingly well served with a wide range of accommodation, although it's still worth **booking** rooms well in advance in midsummer or during the skiing season. Particularly during *ferie*, the traditional two-week break for schoolchilden (usually the last week in January and first week in February), everything on offer is booked solid.

You can book **private rooms** (❷) and pensions (❹) through the tourist office (see above), and a number of private travel agents in town – the most helpful being Teresa at Kościuszki 7 (Mon–Fri 9am–5pm, Sat 9am–3pm; ☎018/201 3660, ⓦ www.teresa.zakopane.pl).

There's an HI **hostel** in the form of the *Szarotka*, downhill from the bus station at ul. Nowotarska 45 (☎018/201 3618), which offers a mixture of doubles (❸), as well as triples (40zł per person) and eight-bed dorms (20zł per person), all with bathroom attached. However, there's no breakfast. For **campers** there are two sites: *Camping Pod Krokwią* (☎018/201 2256), ul. Żeromskiego, across from the bottom of the ski jump at the south end of town; and *Za Strugiem*, ul. Za Strugiem 39 (☎018/201 4566), a thirty-minute walk west of the centre. The **hotels** listed below can be subject to considerable price hikes during high season.

Antałówka ul. Wierchowa 3 ☎018/201 3271, ⓔ antalowka@polskietatry.pl. Biggish concrete hotel with servicable en suites, ideally located a short uphill walk away from the bus station and town centre. Excellent views over the town and mountains. ❺

Api 2 Kamieniec 13a ☎018/206 2931, ⓦ www .api2.pl. Cosy pension north of the stations with smallish en suites with TV and a decent breakfast. ❹

Belvedere Droga do Białego 3 ☎018/202 1200 ⓦ www.belvederehotel.pl. Top-draw hotel 1.5km from town, with high standards of service and smart, comfortable rooms – not all have bathtubs though so ask when you book. Attic ceilings in the top-floor rooms add a bit of extra atmosphere. On-site swimming pool, gym and beauty centre make this the perfect place for a spa-style break. ❾

Czarny Potok ul. Tetmajera 20 ☎018/202 0214, ⓦ www.trip.com.pl. Medium-sized hotel on a quiet street 1km south of town, offering simple doubles decked out in warm colours, each with TV, fridge and a neat bathroom. Local rugs and tapestries in the hallways add a homely touch, and there's a sauna and pool in the basement. ❼

Daglezja ul. Piłsudskiego 14 ☎018/201 4041, ⓦ www.daglezja.com.pl. Well-equipped, medium-sized and rather swanky modern hotel 500m south of town, with sauna and solarium on site. ❼

Dom Turysty ul. Zaruskiego 5 ☎018/206 3281, ⓦ www.domturysty.z-ne.pl. Cheap central hotel in a characterful interwar building sheltering under a massive wooden-shingle roof. Gets a lot of students in season. En suites, rooms with shared facilites and some dorms (20zł per person). Breakfast costs a few złoty extra. ❸–❹

Giewont ul. Kościuszki 1 ☎018/201 2011, ⓦ www.giewont.net.pl. Orbis hotel, right in the centre. Often has rooms spare outside the high season. ❻

Gromada ul. Zaruskiego 2 ☎018/201 5011, ⓔ gromada@tatry.net.pl. Central hotel with decent quality en suites with TV, decked out in inoffensive greens and browns. Friendly staff and facilities for the disabled. ❻

Halny ul. Sienkiewicza 6a ☎018/201 2041, ⓦ www.halny.zakopane.pl or ⓦ www.mati .zakopane.pl/halny Reliable source of functional but comfortable en-suite rooms. Prone to fill up with groups as a result. ❸

Kasprowy Polana Szymaszkowa ☎018/201 4011, Ⓦwww.kasprowy.pl. Seven-storey concrete wedge perched on high ground 2km west of town, but very comfortable with it. Super views of the mountains, on-site swimming pool and tennis courts. ❼

Panorama ul. Wierchowa 6 ☎018/201 5081. A sizeable concrete neighbour to the *Antą* (see opposite), with simple unfussy en suites and good views. ❺

Pensjonat Szarotka Małe Żywczańskie 16a ☎018/201 4802 Ⓦwww.szarotka.pl. Charming

pointy-gabled suburban house in a quiet neighbourhood 1km from the centre, with a range of different shaped en-suite rooms with TV, many with quirky semi-antique furnishings. The olde-worlde theme extends to the interwar tourist posters and sepia photographs of skiing champions that decorate the hallways. Buffet breakfast available for an extra 20zł. Apartments ❻, doubles ❷–❺.

Sabala ul. Krupówki 11 ☎018/201 5092, Ⓦwww .sabala.zakopane.pl. Ultra-modern place occupying the 1894 building of one of Zakopane's first ever hotels, the Staszeczkówka. Lovely, wood-furnished en suites with TV. ❼

The Town

Zakopane's main street, **ul. Krupówki**, is a bustling pedestrian precinct given over to the traditional assortment of restaurants, cafés and souvenir shops, now spiced by the newly acquired collection of Western-style takeaway joints and billiard halls. Uphill, the street merges into **ul. Zamoyskiego**, which runs on out of town past the fashionable *fin-de-siècle* wooden villas of the outskirts, while in the other direction, it follows a rushing stream down towards Gubałówka Hill (see p.490).

The **Muzeum Tatrzanskie** (Tatra Museum; Tues–Sun 9am–3.30pm; 3zł), just off Krupówki on ul. Zaruskiego, extolls the virtues of local folk culture through a beautiful sequence of re-created peasant house interiors and some stunning costumes – note the colourfully embroidered, strutting-peacock jackets traditionally worn by *górale* menfolk. Zakopane's emergence as a society resort is remembered with pictures of Titus Chałubinski, the doctor who did more than anyone to promote the health-giving properties of the mountain air; Stanisław Witkiewicz, whose book *Na Przełęczy* ("At the Pass"; 1891) was a landmark in the propagation of Podhale culture; and the wealthy Dembowski family, who collected Podhale folk crafts and held high-society salons in their Zakopane villa.

Towards the northern end of Krupówki, ul. Kościeliska veers off towards an area liberally sprinkled with traditional buildings, kicking off with the wooden **Kościół św. Klimenta** (Church of St Clement). The low-ceilinged interior gives off an attractive piney smell, and holds several examples of a popular local form of folk art – devotional paintings on glass, in this case depicting the Stations of the Cross. Outside in the graveyard lie the tombs of many of the town's best-known writers and artists, among them that of **Stanisław Witkiewicz** (1851–1915), who developed the distinctive Zakopane architectural style based on traditional wooden building forms. The houses he built – all steep pointy roofs and jutting attic windows – went down a storm with a pre-World War I middle class who were crazy for all things rustic. Witkiewicz's memorial in the cemetery is a typical mixture of thoughtful design and woodworking craft: a smooth totem pole in which a niche bears a wooden statuette of *Christus Frasobliwy* ("Sorrowful Christ") – a pensive figure with his head in his hands – which is a traditional folk depiction of the Saviour assuming responsibilty for the world's troubles. There's also a commemorative tablet to Witkiewicz's equally famous son, **Witkacy** (see box p.486), whose body was returned to Zakopane in 1988 from its previous resting place (Jeziory in the Ukraine) by a communist regime desperate to curry favour with Poland's intelligentsia. Fifty thousand mourners turned up to pay their respects, and only later was it revealed that the

Stanisław Ignacy Witkiewicz (1885–1939) – **Witkacy** as he's commonly known – was born the son of **Stanisław Witkiewicz**, the eminent painter and art critic who created the so-called Zakopane Style of primitivist wooden architecture (see p.485). Educated at home by a father who distrusted schools, Witkacy was surrounded by the artists, poets and performers who made up the Kraków cultural elite from an early age.

As a resort town attracting all kinds of free-thinking and glamorous personalities, Zakopane functioned as a kind of artistic and personal playground for Witkacy, and his private life was rather complicated as a result. After a long affair with actress Irena Solska, ten years his senior, Witkacy got engaged to one of his mother's boarding house guests, Jadwiga Jaczewska, in 1914 – she shot herself in dramatic style (at the foot of a cliff, next to a bouquet of flowers) after learning that her fiancé was still seeing both Solska and one other lover. Eager to leave this behind Witkacy set off on a long expedition to New Guinea and Australia with family friend and celebrated anthropologist Bronisław Malinowski (with whom he also had an intimate relationship), returning home when World War I broke out. He signed up for the Russian army with some enthusiasm (born in Warsaw, he was technically a Russian citizen), and after qualifying as an officer fought with distinction on the Austrian front – he was invalided out after being wounded near Voronezh. Wartime St Petersburg was full of opportunities for a good party, however, and it was here that Witkacy first began to experiment with hallucinogenic drugs.

After 1918 Witkacy re-established himself in Zakopane and joined the Formists, a group of painters influenced by cubism and futurism, abandoning them in 1924 to set up a commercial **portrait-painting** studio – intended as an ironic statement on the position of the artist in capitalist society, it turned out to be extraordinarily successful with the interwar middle classes. Witkacy's portraits of well-heeled society figures were relatively sober and realistic, while those of his friends were wild and deranged in comparison, you'll see examples of both these styles hanging on the walls of Poland's museums and galleries. In the corner of the canvas on the wackier portraits, Witkacy habitually noted which narcotic he had been taking when painting.

The portrait company provided Witkacy with the funds he needed to finance other artistic interests. During the interwar years Witkacy produced over twenty **plays**, many of which were premiered in Zakopane by his own theatre company, formed in 1925, with several productions being staged in the epic surroundings of Morskie Oko Lake. An exponent of an avant-gardist theory of drama that extolled the virtues of "pure form" over content, Witkacy wrote dramas that are generally bizarre, almost surrealist pieces spiced up with large dollops of sex and murder. Cold-shouldered by uncomprehending 1920s Polish audiences, the Witkacy dramatic oeuvre was rediscovered in the 1950s, when Tadeusz Kantor opened the legendary Cricot 2 Theatre with a performance of Witkacy's absurdist *Cuttlefish*.

Witkacy's prose works offered similarly fantastic excursions to the far shores of the writer's consciousness. His first **novel**, *622 Downfalls of Bungo*, begun before 1914, was a surrealistic take on his own life story, with central characters based on Solska, Malinowski and himself. Later works were more doom-laden, most notably the brilliant but untranslatable *Nienasycenie* ("Insatiability"; 1930), which revolves around an epic futuristic struggle between a Poland ruled by the dictator Kocmołuchowicz ("Slovenly") and communist hordes from China hell-bent on invading Europe from the east.

In a sense, reality fulfilled Witkacy's worst apocalyptic nightmares. Following the Nazi invasion of Poland in 1939, the artist fled east. On learning that the Soviets were also advancing into Poland in the pincer movement agreed under the terms of the notorious Molotov–Ribbentrop Pact, a devastated Witkacy committed suicide, a legendary act that ensured his place in the pantheon of noble patriots, as well as that of great artists, in the eyes of the nation.

authorities had delivered the wrong body – the genuine corpse having proved impossible to locate. Alongside are the graves of old *górale* families, including well-known local figures such as the skier Helena Marusarzówna, executed by the Nazis for her part in the resistance.

Just beyond the church stands the **Willa Koliba**, Witkiewicz's first architectural experiment, and now the **Muzeum Stylu Zakopańskiego** (Museum of the Zakopane Style; Wed–Sat 9am–5pm, Sun 9am–3pm; 4zł). A must for anyone interested in Polish architecture or design, the museum starts off with a ground-floor display of the folk crafts from which Witkiewicz got his inspiration, before moving on to the kind of furniture that he set about designing – chunky chairs adorned with squiggly details in an engaging mixture of Art Nouveau and folkloric forms. There's also a scale model of Witkiewicz's greatest architectural creation, the Willa Pod Jedłami, an extraordinarily intricate wooden house which brings to mind a Scandinavian timber church redesigned as a country mansion – enjoy the model while you're here, because it's difficult to get close up to the real thing (see p.488). A biographical words-and-pictures display reveals what a rogue Witkiewicz was, using his poor health as an excuse to conduct a series of love affairs in the spas of Europe. Accompanied by long-time mistress Maria Dembowska, Witkiewicz eventually went to live full time in the Croatian resort of Lovran in 1907, leaving wife and son in Zakopane to eke a living renting out rooms to the very tourists attracted here by her husband's books. Finally there's a marvellous collection of deranged portraits by Witkiewicz's son, Witkacy, including a lot of distorted, angular depictions of the people he painted while high on one substance or another, believing that his intake of drugs would reveal the true personality of the sitter. Most of his subjects are female, members of what he called his "metaphysical harem".

Moving back towards Krupówki and turning south down ul. Kasprusie soon leads to the **Willa Atma**, a traditional-style villa and longtime home of composer **Karol Szymanowski** (see box below), now a museum dedicated to its former resident (Tues–Sun 10am–4pm; 4zł). The display is labelled in Polish

---

Karol Szymanowski

After Chopin, **Karol Szymanowski** (1882–1937) is Poland's greatest composer, forging his own distinctive style in an exotic and highly charged mix of orientalism, opulence and native folk music. Always striving to find a national voice, he feared provincialism – "Poland's national music should not be the stiffened ghost of the polonaise or mazurka . . . Let our music be national in its Polish characteristics but not falter in striving to attain universality."

From the 1920s Szymanowski spent much time in **Zakopane** and became a key member of a group of intellectuals (including the artist and playwright Witkacy) who were enthused by the folklore of the Tatras and dubbed themselves "the emergency rescue service of Tatra culture". Among Szymanowski's works that show a direct influence of Tatra music are the song cycle *Słopiewnie* (1921), the *Mazurkas for piano* (1924–25) and, above all, the ballet *Harnasie* (1931), which is stuffed full of outlaws, features a spectacular highland wedding and boasts authentic *górale* melodies in orchestral garb.

Alongside two violin concertos and his *Symphony Song of the Night*, Szymanowski's greatest work is the **Stabat Mater** (1926), which draws on the traditions of old Polish church music and is a stunning choral work of great economy and austere beauty. After many years of ill health, Szymanowski died of tuberculosis in 1937 and received an illustrious state funeral with the Obrochta family, one of the leading *górale* bands, playing around his tomb in the Skałka church in Kraków.

only, but many of the exhibits speak for themselves: look out for photographs of the *górale* folk musicians Szymanowski was inspired by, or the fantastic folk-inspired costumes featured in his ballet *Harnasie*.

East of the main drag, near the bus and train stations, a wooden building at ul. Jagiellońska 18b – it's just off the road in a side alley – houses the **Hasior Gallery** (Wed–Sat 11am–6pm, Sun 9am–3pm), presenting the work of one of the country's key postwar artists, **Władysław Hasior** (1928–99). Whether building installations from piles of junk or constructing pseudo-religious banners from pieces of metal, Hasior was typical of many Polish artists of the 1960s and 1970s in developing a quirky and often subversive form of sculpture that had little to do with the ideological dictates of either church or state – although both institutions sponsored his work at different stages. Ranging from massive landscape installations to jokey throwaway pieces, Hasior's oeuvre will leave you uncertain as to whether he was a visionary or a charlatan, but this gallery is entertaining enough to make such confusion worthwhile.

Bystre, Jaszczurówka and Swibówki

The southeastern fringes of town contain a couple of Witkiewicz's best-known creations. The **Willa Pod Jedłami** in the suburb of **Bystre**, 2km from the centre, is now in private hands and is hard to get a good look at, so you'd be well advised to press on 1.5km further east to the **wooden chapel** at **JASZCZURÓWKA** (hourly buses to Brzeziny pass by), a fairy-tale structure encrusted with folksy ornamentation. The traditional *górale* woodcraft from which Witkiewicz took his inspiration is convincingly demonstrated in the brace of wooden churches and chapels that can be seen in and around the town area. Particularly worth visiting is the **Sanktuarium Matki Bożej Fatimskiej** (Sanctuary of Our Lady of Fatima) at **SWIBÓWKI**, a thirty-minute walk west of town along ul. Kościeliska, which also has a remarkable chapel at the rear of the main church complex.

Eating, drinking and entertainment

Eating is never a problem in Zakopane. If you want a snack there are plenty of cafés, fast-food joints and streetside *zapiekanki* merchants to choose from, with many vendors along ul. Krupówki. **Restaurants** are plentiful, too, with a rash of places on the main street offering local food in faux-rustic surroundings – often with live folk music accompaniment. A local product worth trying at least once is the bun-shaped **sheep's milk cheeses** you see on sale all over town; try a small one first, because they're not to everyone's taste.

Restaurants

Bąkowo Zohylina Nimna ul. Piłsudskiego 6. Folk-style restaurant in a log building serving up hearty Polish cuisine.

Bar FIS ul. Kościuszki. Functional order-at-the-counter canteen opposite the bus station, serving up staples like *bigos*, *fasólka*, *placki* and *pierogi*, all of markedly better quality than the snack fare available on the main ul. Krupówki.

Chata Zbójnicka ul. Jagiellońska. Restaurant just uphill from the road, decked out as a mountain-smuggler's den (the name means "Robbers' Hut") complete with log fire, and serving traditional *górale* fare. The *baranina* (roast lamb) – typical of the regional cuisine – is worth a try.

Chłopskie Jadło ul. Zaruskiego. Traditional Polish eats in a place that would work equally well as an ethnographic museum, with traditional textiles and olde-worlde utensils hanging from the walls. In the same building as the *Gromada* hotel.

Karczma Bacówka ul. Krupówki 61. Standard Polish cuisine in a touristy, pine-furnished interior. Good for either a quick bowl of *bigos* or a more leisurely meal.

Karczma Redykołka corner of ul. Krupówki and ul. Kościeliska. A touristy traditional-style inn with waitresses dressed in local costume serving some *górale* specialities.

Obrochtówka ul. Kraszewskiego 10a. Reasonably priced and the best of the traditional-style restaurants – the *placki* (potato pancakes) in particular are excellent. Folk music some evenings.
Pizzeria Grace ul. Krupówki 2. Quick and easy pizzeria in fast-foodish surroundings.
Pstrąg Górski ul. Krupówki 50. Simple fish-fry place on the main drag, with alfresco seating beside a babbling brook. Grilled trout is the order of the day.
Zbojecka ul. Krupówki 30. Cellar bar-restaurant on the main strip with large wooden benches draped with sheepskins, grilled meat dishes, and live folk music (or loud pop on the sound system, depending on your luck).

Cafés, bars and clubs

Bars and nightlife are a growing feature of the town centre, though many of the venues are pretty tacky. Out of season, things are relatively quiet by 10pm. There are innumerable drinking dens on and around the main street, most of which succeed in sweeping in thirsty tourists due to their central location rather than any inherent atmosphere.

One of the nicest places to kick off an evening is *Café Piano*, hidden in a small plaza just behind Krupówki 63, which attracts a laid-back clientele with its intimate atmosphere and contemporary-design-meets-rustic-chic decor. *Paparazzi*, a smartish cellar pub just off the main street at Galicy 8, caters for the dedicated late-night beer drinkers as well as the cocktail crowd. *Rockus*, Zaruskiego 5, underneath the *Dom Turysty*, is a rock-pop disco bar popular with a teen crowd, and decorated with portraits of rock greats – and Franz Kafka. *Ampstrong*, a basement club just off Jagiellońska near the Hasior Gallery, hosts occasional live gigs and alternative DJ nights – look out for street posters.

Entertainment

Entertainment varies according to season. Founded in memory of the man who staged many of his own plays here, the **Teatr im. Stanisława Witkiewicza**, at ul. Chramcówki 15 (box office in the PTTK travel agency, open Mon–Fri 10am–4pm, Sat 10am–2pm; ☎018/206 3281, ⓦwww.witkacy .zakopane.pl), north of the train station, stages a regular variety of performances (a lot of Witkacy pieces, but also featuring twentieth-century greats like Miller and Camus) throughout the year – check with the tourist offices for current details.

The biggest cultural event, however, is the annual international **festival of mountain folklore** held since the late 1960s, and now occupying the prime mid-August tourist season spot. A week-long extravaganza of concerts, music competitions and street parades, the festival draws highlander groups from a dozen or so European countries alongside the sizeable contingent of local *górale* ensembles. The timing means that hefty crowds are guaranteed, and there's enough going on to keep most people happy. Along with the summer musical events in the Pieniny region further east you won't get a better chance to sample the tub-thumping exuberance of a *górale* choir dressed to the nines, whooping their way through a string of joyous mountain melodies. Other local cultural events of note are the **Karol Szymanowski Music Days** held every July, featuring classical concerts by Polish and guest foreign artists in and around the town, and an **art film festival**, held every other March.

Around Zakopane

If hiking in the Tatras proper sounds too energetic, there are a number of easy and enjoyable **walks** in the foothills and valleys surrounding Zakopane. A useful **map** to look out for is *Tatry i Podhale* (1:75,000).

Adventure sports around Zakopane

Poles have been enjoying the winter **ski slopes** in Zakopane for as long as there's been a resort, and in the case of the *górale*, for a good deal longer. The winter season traditionally runs from December to March, though the snow has been very unpredictable in recent years. Slopes in the area vary greatly in difficulty and quality. In accordance with international standards, they are graded black, red, blue and green in order of difficulty, with the cross-country routes marked in orange. Many otherwise closed areas of the national park are open to skiers once the snows have set in, but you must remember to avoid the avalanche (*lawina*) areas marked on signs and maps, and check conditions before leaving the marked routes.

The most popular runs are on **Nosal** and **Kasprowy Wierch**, as these are the ones with ski lifts. From the village of Kuźnice (a few minutes by bus from the centre of Zakopane) you can travel by vintage gondola (over sixty years old but still reliable) to the top of Kasprowy Wierch (1967m) and ski back down to the village (5–7km, depending which trails you use) or ski to one of the surrounding valleys, Goryczkowa or Gąsienicowa, from where you can take the lift back up again. Tickets up in the gondola cost 30zł and can be bought in advance in Zakopane. The Nosal slope is short and steep (650m with a 233m height difference), while on the other side of town Gubałówka offers a much gentler slope reached by funicular. It's south-facing, so you can rent beach chairs (even in winter) and sunbathe on its slopes. You can also get **skiing lessons** – the instructors at the Nosal ski school speak English and charge 60–70zł per hour. **Ski rental** costs about 35zł per day.

Mountain biking is a popular summertime pursuit, with legions of enthusiastic bikers heading for the slopes. Designated cycle routes within the national park area include: around Morskie Oko; up to Dolina Suchej Wody; to Hala Gąsienicowa; to Kałatówki; and along the Kościeliska and Chochołowska valleys. In addition, there are a number of cycle routes in the hills north of Zakopane – some 650km of them in total. You can **rent mountain bikes** at a number of places around town, including Wypożyczalnia, ul. Piłsudskiego 4, Rent a Bike, ul. Sienkiewicza 37 (☎018/206 4266), and the *Pod Krokwią* campsite. Bike rental costs around 50zł a day.

Paragliding is also popular, though it's confined to areas outside the national park, including the Nosal slope, Gubałówka and Wałowa Góra. If you've never tried it before, there are several instructors in town who also rent all the necessary gear. Try Air Sport, ul. Strążyska 13 (☎018/201 3311, ⊛www.air-sport.zakopane.pl).

Finally, there's a **toboggan run** (*rynna*) on the Gubałówka slope. Rides down the 750-metre-long slide reach speeds of up to 40kph, and cost around 30zł a time.

Gubałówka Hill

There's an excellent view of the Tatras from the top of **Gubałówka Hill** (1120m) to the west of town (follow ul. Krupówki out from the centre). However, it's very popular, as you'll see from the long queues for the **funicular** (July & Aug 7am–9pm; Sept–June 8am–5pm; 20zł return). Walking up is possible, though strenuous (1hr). From the summit, a good day reveals the high peaks to the south in sharp relief against clear blue mountain skies. Most people linger a while over the view, browse in the souvenir shops and head back down again, but the long wooded hill ridge is the starting point of several excellent **hikes**, taking you through characteristic Podhale landscape.

To the west, from the top of the funicular, past the refreshment stop, the **trails** begin as a single path, which soon divides. Continue south along the ridge and you gradually descend to the Czarny Dunajec valley (black route), ending up at the village of **WITÓW**, around two hours' walking in all; buses back to Zakopane take fifteen minutes. Alternatively, take the north fork and it's a four-hour hike to the village of **CHOCHOŁÓW**, with its fine wooden houses and church; you can get here by two routes, either following the track (which soon becomes a road) through the village of Dzianisz, or taking the cross-country route marked *Szlak im. Powstania Chochołowskiego* on the *Tatry i Podhale* map.

Dolina Białego and Dolina Strążyska

For some easy and accessible valley hiking, Dolina Białego and Dolina Strążyska each provide a relaxed long afternoon's walk from Zakopane; taken together they would make an enjoyable and not over-strenuous day's outing.

Leaving Zakopane to the south, along ul. Strążyska, you reach **Dolina Strążyska** after around an hour's walk. At the end of the valley (3hr) you can climb to the **Hala Strążyska**, a beautiful high mountain pasture (1303m); the **Siklawica waterfall**, on the way, makes an enjoyable rest point, a stream coursing down from the direction of Giewont. The views are excellent, too, with **Mount Giewont** (1694m) rearing up to the south, and to the north a wonderful panorama of Zakopane and the surrounding countryside. Walk east along the meadow to the top of **Dolina Białego** and you can descend the deep, stream-crossed valley, one of the gentlest and most beautiful in the region, continuing back to the outskirts of Zakopane (6–7hr in total).

Dolina Kościeliska and Dolina Chochołowska

Two of the loveliest valleys of the area are **Dolina Chochołowska** and **Dolina Kościeliska**, both a short distance west of town, either of which offers an immensely rewarding full day's hiking. **Buses** from Zakopane to Chochołów and Czarny Dunajec pass the entrances to the valleys; in addition private **minibuses** from Zakopane bus station head for the Dolina Chochołowska, terminating a few kilometres up the valley.

Six kilometres west from Zakopane on the Czarny Dunajec road, the hamlet of **KIRY** marks the entrance to the **Dolina Kościeliska**, a deep verdant valley much in evidence on postcards of the region. For around 120zł a horse-drawn cart will run you down the first section of the valley to a point known as Polana Pisana, but from here on it's walkers only. A distinctive feature of Kościeliska is the caves in its limestone cliffs – once the haunts of robbers and bandits, legend has it. Take a detour off to the left from Polana Pisana – marked *jaskinia* (caves) – and you can visit various examples, including **Jaskinia Mroźna**, where the walls are permanently encased in ice.

Beyond Polana Pisana, the narrow upper valley is a beautiful stretch of crags, gushing water, caves and greenery reminiscent of the English Lake District. The awe-inducing scenery so inspired Witkacy's fiancée Jadwiga Jaczewska (see box, p.486) that she chose this as the venue for her suicide. About 45 minutes beyond the Polana is the *Hala Ornak* **hostel** (☎018/207 0520, ⓦwww.ornak .tatrynet.pl; dorm beds from 22zł per person), a popular overnight stop with a **restaurant**. Day walkers return back down the valley to take the bus back to Zakopane, but if you want to continue, two marked paths lead beyond the hostel. The eastern route takes you the short distance to **Smreczyński Staw** (1226m), a tiny mountain lake surrounded by forest; the western route follows a high ridge over to Dolina Chochołowska – a demanding walk only for the fit.

Back on the main road, and heading northwest from Kiry, you'll pass after 2km a left turn to the **Dolina Chochołowska**, a 10km-long defile following the course of a stream deep into the hills. From the car park at the head of the valley, it's a good hour's walk to the *Chochołowska* hostel (☎018/207 0510, ⓦwww .chocholowska.zakopane.pl), beautifully situated overlooking the meadows, with the high western Tatras and the Czech border behind. A clandestine meeting between the pope and Lech Wałęsa took place here in 1983 and is commemorated by a tableau on the wall. The steep paths up the eastern side lead to ridges that separate the valley from Dolina Kościeliska – one path, from a little way beyond the car park, connects the two valleys, making the cross trip possible.

The Tatras

Poles are serious mountaineers, with an established network of climbing clubs, and it's in **the Tatras** that everyone starts and the big names train. Most of the peaks are in the 2000–2500m range, but these unimpressive statistics belie their status, and their appearance. For these are real mountains, snowbound on their heights for most of the year and supporting a good skiing season in December and January. They are as beautiful as any mountain landscape in Northern Europe, the ascents taking you on boulder-strewn paths alongside woods and streams up to the ridges, where grand, windswept peaks rise in the brilliant alpine sunshine. Wildlife thrives here: the whole area was turned into a national park in the 1950s and supports rare species such as lynx, golden eagles and brown bear, and there's a good chance of glimpsing them.

The steadily increasing volume of climbers, walkers and skiers using the slopes is having its effect on the area, though, and in a bid to generate funds for local environmental protection, the park authorities have now imposed a (nominal) entry charge on all visitors entering the park area, collected at booths at the main access points to the mountains. Groups of ten people or more must have an official guide, arranged, unless you're part of a pre-booked touring group, through the park offices in Zakopane (see p.484).

Though many of the peak and ridge climbs are for experienced climbers only, much is accessible to regular walkers, with waymarked paths which give you the top-of-the-world exhilaration of bagging a peak. For skiers, despite the relative paucity of lifts and hi-tech facilities, there are some high-quality pistes, including a dry slope running down from peaks such as **Kasprowy Wierch** and the very steep **Nosal** (see box, p.490).

Hiking in the Tatras

It is as well to remember that the Tatras are an alpine range and as such demand some respect and preparation. The most important rule is to stick to the marked paths, and to arm yourself in advance with a decent **map**. The best is the *Tatrzański Park Narodowy* (1:30,000), which has all the paths accurately marked and colour-coded. You will probably want the English version, *The Tatra National Park*. This map has all you'll need – including estimated times between various points – but an alternative is the *Polskie Tatry* **guidebook**, available in English and going into detail about the main hiking routes. All the above are available from shops in Zakopane. One book you should consider picking up before you leave home is *The High Tatras* (Cicerone Press) written jointly by an Englishman and a Slovak woman, an authentic guide to hikes in the mountains aimed at the serious enthusiast. Remember never to leave the tree line (about 2000m) unless visibility is good, and when the clouds close in, start descending immediately.

Overnighting in the PTTK-run **huts** dotted across the mountains is an experience in itself. There are seven of them in all, clearly marked on the *Tatra National Park* map (for up-to-date information on openings, check at the national park office in Zakopane). These provide dorm beds, mattress space on the floor in busy periods, and basic canteen food. Even if you don't want to lug large weights around the mountaintops, a supply of basic rations is a good idea as well as water. **Camping** isn't allowed in the national park area, and **rock-climbing** only with a permit – ask at the park offices (see p.484) for details. For anyone attempting more than a quick saunter, the right **footwear and clothing** are, of course, essential. Lastly, take a **whistle** – blow six times every minute if you need help.

The **weather** is always changeable, and you should not venture out without waterproofs and sturdy boots; most rain falls in the summer, when there may also be thunderstorms and even hail- and snow-showers. Even on a warm summer's day in the valleys, it can be below freezing at the peaks. Set out early (the weather is always better in the morning), and tell someone when and where you're going – a **weather information** service is available on ☎018/206 3019. The number of the **mountain rescue service** (Tatrzańskie Ochotnicze Pogotowie Ratunkowe) is ☎018/206 3444, though don't expect much English to be spoken.

In addition, respect the **national park rules**: don't leave any rubbish, keep to the marked paths and don't pick flowers or disturb the wild animals.

Routes

The easiest way up to the peaks is by **cable car** (July & Aug 7.30am–8pm; Sept–June 8am–5pm; 30zł return) from the hamlet of **KUŹNICE**, a three-kilometre walk or bus journey south from Zakopane along the Dolina Bystrego. In summer, the cable car is a sell-out, making advance booking at the Orbis office a virtual necessity, unless you're prepared to turn up before 8am. For the journey down, priority is always given to people who've already got tickets, but return tickets only allow you two hours at the top – this is fine if you only want to get up to Kasprowy Wierch, but no good if you're planning more extended hiking.

Kasprowy Wierch and descents to Kuźnice

The cable car ends near the summit of **Kasprowy Wierch** (1985m), where weather-beaten signs indicate the border with Slovakia. From here, many day-trippers simply walk back down to Kuźnice through the Hala Gąsienicowa (2hr). An equally popular option is to walk up and return by cable car (2hr 30min). A rather longer alternative is to strike west to the cross-topped summit of **Giewont** (1894m), the "Sleeping Knight" that overlooks Zakopane (allow 2hr for this). Watch out if it's been raining, however, as the paths here get pretty slippery and are very worn in places. The final bit of the ascent is rocky with secured chains to aid your scramble to the top. From the summit, topped with a tall cross, the views can be spectacular on a good day. For the return, head down to Kuźnice through the Dolina Kondratowa past the *Hala Kondratowa* hostel (☎018/201 9114; allow 40min to get to the hostel, then a further hour to get to the village). This downward journey is fairly easy going and the whole trip is quite feasible in a day if you start out early.

The Orła Perć and Morskie Oko

East of Kasprowy Wierch, the walking gets tougher. From **Świnica** (2301m), a strenuous ninety-minute walk, experienced hikers continue along the **Orła Perć** (Eagles' Path), a challenging, exposed ridge with spectacular views. The *Pięc Stawów* **hostel** (☎018/207 7607), occupying a lovely lakeside position in the high valley of the same name, provides overnight shelter at the end (4hr).

△ The summit of Giewont, Tatra mountains

From the hostel you can hike back down Dolina Roztoki to **Łysa Polana**, a border-crossing point with Slovakia in the valley (2hr), and get a bus back to Zakopane. An alternative is to continue east to the lake of **Morskie Oko** (Eye of the Sea; 1399m; 1hr 30min). Encircled by spectacular sheer cliff faces and alpine forest, this large glacial lake is one of the Tatras' big attractions, and one of the most popular day-trip destinations for tourists staying in Zakopane. It's particularly busy in April and May, when the area is deluged by Polish school-trip outings. Most people begin the journey by car or bus rather than on foot, following the road that loops east then south from Zakopane, passing through Poronin before climbing up into the Tatra foothills. It's a spectacular journey at times, with a road following a mountain ridge whose forest cover occasionally parts to reveal superb views of the Tatras. After descending towards the border crossing at Łysa Polana, the road continues a few more kilometres to its final destination, a large car park surrounded by snack stalls at **Polana Palenica**. From the car park, a fairly obvious track leads past a national park booth (charging the 2zł entrance fee to the park) and climbs slowly through the trees towards Morskie Oko, which is some 9km (1hr 45min) uphill. Horse-drawn carts (35zł per person) are on hand to ferry those tourists who can't face the walk.

The *Przy Morskim Oku* hostel, situated by the side of the lake, serves up decent grilled-sausage-type fare, and provides a convenient base for the ascent of **Rysy** (2499m), the highest peak in the Polish Tatras. Closer to hand, on the same red-marked route is **Czarny Staw** (1580m), a lake that if anything, appears even chillier than Morskie Oko.

East of the Tatras

East of the Tatras, the mountains scale down to a succession of lower ranges stretching along the Slovak border. The walking here is less dramatic than in the Tatras, but excellent nonetheless, and the locals are a good bunch too, including *górale* and a long-established Slovak minority. The highlights of the region are the **Pieniny**, mountains hard by the Slovak border, and a raft run through the **Dunajec Gorge** far below.

Transport in this little-known region can be a bit of a struggle, away from the immediate vicinity of **Szczawnica**, a spa town that makes the best base for exploring the Pieniny.

The Spisz region

The road east from Nowy Targ to Szczawnica is one of the most attractive in the country, following the broad valley of the Dunajec through the **Spisz**, a backwoods region whose villages are renowned for their wooden houses, churches and folk art. Annexed by Poland from the newly created Czechoslovak state in 1920, for centuries it was part of the semi-autonomous province of Spis (Slovak)/Spisz (Polish)/Zips (German) that formed part of the Hungarian kingdom. The old aura of a quiet rural backwater remains, the region's Slovak minority bearing testimony to its historic borderland position. **Buses** cover the route four or five times a day.

DĘBNO, 14km from Nowy Targ, boasts one of the best-known **wooden churches** in the country, a shingled, steep-roofed larch building, put together without using nails and surrounded by a charming wicket fence, with a profile vaguely reminiscent of a snail. Inside, the full length of walls and ceiling is covered with exuberant, brilliantly preserved fifteenth-century polychromy and **woodcarving**. The subjects are an enchanting mix of folk, national and religious motifs, including some fine hunting scenes and curiously Islamic-looking geometric patterns. In the centre of the building, fragments survive of the original rood screen, supporting a tree-like cross, while the original fifteenth-century altarpiece triptych features an unusually militant-looking St Catherine. In addition, there's a fine carved statue of St Nicholas, a medieval wooden tabernacle and some banners reputedly left by Jan Sobieski on his return from defeating the Turks in Vienna in 1683. The church is usually open during daylight hours; if not, local enquiries may reveal the whereabouts of the priest (he lives just over the road), who will probably open things up. For an overnight stay, there's a **youth hostel** (July & Aug) in the village.

Immediately east of Dębno lies the **Dunajec reservoir**, a controversial hydroelectric project which was opposed by many environmentalists before the valley – and a couple of its villages – were finally subsumed by water in 1997. The reservoir's dam saved many of the downriver settlements from floods later the same year, significantly decreasing the project's unpopularity with the locals. A minor road branches off to follow the southern banks of the river before arriving at Niedzica (see below), although most traffic sticks to the high ground north of the water. Sticking to this latter route, it's about 12km from Dębno to the hamlet of Krośnica, at the eastern end of which is a right turn to the village of **CZORSZTYN**, 2km south. The village sits on a south-facing slope overlooking the reservoir, one the banks of which sits a memorable **castle**. It's largely a ruin – struck by a thunderbolt in the 1790s, it was abandoned after the resulting fire – although a couple of towers and battlements have been made safe for visitors. From its heights you get sweeping **views** south to the castle of Niedzica across the mouth of the Dunajec Gorge. There are about six daily **buses** from Nowy Targ to Czorsztyn; otherwise catch one of the more frequent Nowy Targ–Szczawnica buses, get off in Krośnica and walk. In summer, **taxi boats** (3zł) cross the water between Czorsztyn and Niedzica every hour or so, making it possible to visit both fortresses in the space of an afternoon.

Niedzica and west along the Slovak border

NIEDZICA lies just across the gorge from Czorsztyn, but it's a roundabout trip by road, which involves heading back to Dębno, or southeast towards Sromowce. By public transport, Niedzica is served by bus from Nowy Targ.

The village occupies a strategic position at a major confluence of the Dunajec with a large tributary plunging down from Slovakia. Control of this valley and the border territory explains the presence of the **castle**, perched above the river. Originally raised in the fourteenth century as a stronghold on the Hungarian border, it was reconstructed in its current Renaissance style in the early 1600s, and today lies under threat from the hydroelectric scheme, which some experts believe will erode its rock foundations. It today houses the castle **museum** (Tues–Sun 9am–5pm; 5zł), with displays on the stronghold's history and a strong collection of local folk crafts. A Tintin-like folk tale associates the castle with the Incas. The wife of the last descendant of the Inca rulers allegedly lived here in the late eighteenth century, and left a hidden document detailing the legendary Inca treasure buried in Lake Titicaca in Peru – a document supposedly discovered in 1946. If you want a **place to stay**, there's the *Hotel Pieniny*, ul. Kanada 38 (⊕018/262 9383, ⊜pieniny@zzw-niedzica.com.pl; en suites ❸, rooms with shared facilities ❷), or the *Pensjonat Chata Spiska*, Pod Sosnami (⊕018/262 9403, ⊜niedzica@ns.onet.pl; ❺), a cosy place with folksy wooden interiors.

To the west of Niedzica, a little-frequented backroad winds its way towards Nowy Targ and Zakopane through the heart of the Spisz. Most villages here were effectively cut off from the outside world well into the nineteenth century, and serfdom was only abolished here in 1931. It still feels like another world, particularly in villages like **TRYBSZ** and **ŁAPSZE** which have Slovak populations. If you get the chance, visit on a Sunday morning, when you may catch the music of the excellent local choirs. The churches in both villages are equally enjoyable – the one in Trybsz is a wooden construction whose interior is lined with a fine sequence of mid-seventeenth-century frescoes illustrating biblical scenes and the lives of the saints in colourful, naive relief.

The Pieniny

A short range of Jurassic limestone peaks, rearing above the spectacular Dunajec Gorge, the **Pieniny** offer some stiff hillwalking, but require no serious climbing to reach the 1000-metre summits. Jagged outcrops are set off by abundant greenery, the often humid mountain microclimate supporting a rich and varied flora. Like the Tatras, the Pieniny are an officially designated national park and have a network of controlled paths. The detailed *Pieniński Park Narodowy* (1:22,500) **map** is useful and is available in most tourist offices and bookshops.

The main range, a ten-kilometre stretch between Czorsztyn and Szczawnica, is the most popular hiking territory, with the peaks of Trzy Korony (Three Crowns; 982m) the big target.

The principal southern point of access to the park is Sromowce Kąty (also the starting point for rafting trips on the Dunajec Gorge, see p.498), 10km southeast of Krośnica, where there's a tourist **information point** and a national park **ticket office** (2zł). It is served by five buses a day from Nowy Targ. Most hikers however start explorations of the Pieniny from Krościenko, which is served by the more frequent services operating the Nowy Targ–Szczawnica bus route.

Krościenko and the Trzy Korony

The town of **KROŚCIENKO**, a one-hour bus ride east of Nowy Targ, is a dusty, unexciting little place which would hardly merit a stop off were it not the main starting point for **hikes** to the Trzy Korony. The **PTTK office**, in the centre at ul. Jagiellońska 65 (☎018/262 3059), doles out private rooms (❷); and there's the *Hanka* holiday home at no. 55 in the same street (☎018/262 5528; ❷) – although Szczawnica, 4km down the road (see p.498), is a better place to stay.

From the bus stop in the middle of Krościenko you can follow the signs – and in summer the packs of hikers – south on the yellow route. The path soon begins to climb through the mountainside woods, with plenty of meadows and lush clearings on the way. Around two hours from Krościenko, you'll reach **Okrąglica**, the highest peak of the **Trzy Korony**, via some chain-bannistered steps. On a clear day there's an excellent view over the whole area: the high Tatras off to the west, the slopes of Slovakia to the south, and the Dunajec Gorge far below.

Many hikers take the same route back, but two alternatives are worth considering. One is to walk to Szczawnica (p.498), a two- or three-hour trip. Head back along the route you came as far as Bajków Groń (679m), about three-quarters of the way down, and from there follow the blue path across the mountains south to Sokolica (747m) and down to the river, where you can get a boat across to the *Orlica* **hostel**. The other, if you want to combine the walk with the Dunajec Gorge, is to descend the mountain southwest to Sromowce Kąty (3hr), one of the two starting points for the raft trip upriver (see p.498).

The Dunajec Gorge

Below the heights of the Pieniny, the fast-moving Dunajec twists and turns below great limestone rockfaces and craggy peaks. The river is a magnet for **canoeists**, who shoot fearlessly through the often powerful rapids; for the less intrepid, the two- to three-hour **raft trip** provides a gentler though thoroughly enjoyable version of the experience. Tourists have been rafting down these waters since the 1830s, a tradition derived in turn from the ancient practice of floating logs downriver to the mills and ports. Contrary to what the tourist brochures lead you to believe, this is not exactly white-water rafting – the journey is smooth-going, giving you the chance to appreciate the scenic surroundings of forest, fields and sheer limestone crags – the real pluses of the experience.

Run by the Polskie Stowarzyszenie Flisaków Pienińskich (Association of Pieniny Raftsmen; ☎018/262 9721, ⓦwww.flisacy.com.pl), the trips begin at **SROMOWCE KĄTY**, a couple of kilometres east of Sromowce Wyżne; regular buses run to Kąty from Nowy Targ.

Weather and water levels permitting, the rafting season runs from early May to late October, operating 8am to 5pm between May and August, finishing at 4pm in September and 2pm in October. In season, rafts leave as soon as they're full, and the earlier you get here the less likely it is you'll have to queue up. Rafts run to Szczawnica at the eastern end of the gorge, where a courtesy bus will bring you back to Kąty if you so desire. Individual travellers should expect to pay about 40zł per person, although it's worth bearing in mind that most of the travel agents in Zakopane offer trips, which usually include a stop off at Niedzica castle as well – excursions cost anything from 80–180zł depending on whether food is laid on.

The rafts are sturdy log constructions, made of five pontoons held together with rope and carrying up to ten passengers, plus two navigators (in traditional Pieniny costume). Here, as further east, the river forms the border with Slovakia, and at several points Slovak villages face their Polish counterparts across the banks, with their own rafters and canoeists hugging the southern side of the river. After plenty of sharp twists and spectacular cliffs, the rafts end up at Szczawnica, from where buses return to Kąty until 4pm, from a stop a few minutes' walk from the landing stage.

Szczawnica

Sited on the edge of the sparkling River Dunajec below the peaks of the Pieniny, **SZCZAWNICA** is a highly picturesque example of the small spa resorts strung out in the steep valleys east of the Tatras. Once patronized by Nobel Prize-winning novelist Henryk Sienkiewicz, it's still the most visited town in the region, crowded through the summer with all types of mountain holiday-makers: canoeists setting off down the gorge, hikers heading off to the hills or industrial workers recuperating in the sanatoria.

Buses run here from both Nowy Targ (40km) and, on a slightly roundabout route, from Zakopane (50km), dropping you in the centre of town, by the river. From here it's a short walk east to what passes for a main square, followed by a short uphill hike to the old centre of the village, where you'll find a small *pijalnia* (tap room) serving up plastic cups of Szczawnica's waters. Slightly uphill from the *pijalnia* there's a small museum (Tues–Sun 10am–1pm & 2–4pm; 5zł), with a small but engaging collection of Pieniny costumes, including the embroidered waistcoats for which the region is famous.

You can get up onto an eastern spur of the Pieniny by taking the **chairlift** (July, Aug & Dec–April), just below the main street, to the 722-metre-high

The Pieniny górale highlanders

Like the Podhale, the Pieniny region is populated by **górale highlanders** who for much of the century have been migrating to the United States in great numbers; it's not uncommon to come across broad Chicago accents in the villages. To the outsider, the main distinction between the Podhale and Pieniny clans is the colours of their **costumes** – the reds, browns and blacks of the western Podhale giving way to the purple-blues of the Pieniny decorated jackets. Like their Podhale neighbours, the *górale* of the Pieniny dress up traditionally on Sundays and for other major community events – weddings, festivals and the like. The men's costume consists of tight-fitting woollen trousers decorated with coloured strips of embroidery (*parzenice*), high leather cummerbund-type bands round the waist, decorated jackets and waistcoats and a feather-topped hat. The women wear thin woollen blouses, thickly pleated skirts festooned with flowers and brightly coloured headscarves. The men also go in for thick embossed leather shoes (*kierpce*) of the type you can pick up in the tourist shops. Besides costume, the clans have their own distinct **dialects**, and even Polish-speakers find it hard to follow a Pieniny highlander in full swing.

Music is the most accessible aspect of their culture. In summer, you may well catch vocal ensembles at open-air folk evenings held in Szczawnica or Krościenko – a good excuse for everyone to dress up and sing their hearts out. While the harmonies and vocal style are similar in both *górale* regions, the Pieniński make more use of instruments – violins and a thumping bass in particular – to create a sound that has marked similarities to Slovak and Hungarian country styles. The visiting crowds are overwhelmingly Polish at these traditional old-time romps, and for the atmosphere alone it's well worth joining them.

Góra Palenica, which provides excellent views of the valley. There's a short downhill run and a modest snowboard park here in winter, although it's nothing for the serious wintersports enthusiast to get excited about.

The chairlift terminal is also the starting point for the Dunajec Gorge **foot-** and **cycle-path**, which runs westwards along the south bank of the river, crossing over into Slovakia after 3km (the border is open to walkers and cyclists until 8pm in summer, 5pm in winter), and continuing for another 9km along the banks of the gorge as far as Cerveny Kláštor, the main Slovakian starting point for rafting trips. You can rent bikes at the chairlift terminal.

You should at least follow the path for the 2km it takes you to reach the west end of Szczawnica village; here you get excellent **views** of the sheer cliffs marking the eastern end of the Dunajec Gorge, from which the bobbing forms of rafts emerge at regular intervals.

Practicalities

Tourist information duties are currently carried out by the PTTK office, ul. Główna 1 (Mon–Fri 8am–3pm; ☎018/262 2332), which sells hiking maps and books private rooms (❶) – otherwise, just look out for *noclegi* signs or ring Anna & Michał Manowsky, ul. Szalaya 56/2 (☎018/262-1163; ❷), who offer modern en suites in a homely environment. Best of the **pensions** is the *Trzy Korony* at the western end of the village at Słoneczna 4 (☎018/262 2166; ❷–❹, depending on room size), offering en-suite rooms with TV in a modern building with a few homely traditional touches. A more down-to-earth alternative is the *Orlica* PTTK **hostel** at ul. Pienińska 12 (☎018/262 2245), which has dorm rooms (25zł per person) and some en-suite doubles (❸) right on the edge of the gorge, a kilometre south of the raft disembarkation point. You can **camp** at the *Orlica*, or at *Pole Namiotowe* (literally "tent site") nearby at Pienińska 6.

Although there are a few cafés in the village centre, the best places to **eat** are at the western end of the village where the Dunajec gorge rafts terminate; here you'll find several snack stalls selling *pierogi* and *bigos*, and the *Madejówka* restaurant, which serves up tasty, inexpensive trout.

Dolina Homole and Jaworki

A short local excursion worth considering is to the **Dolina Homole**, 8km east of Szczawnica. This is a peaceful valley of wooded glades and streams, and you can walk up to the surrounding hilltops in less than two hours. There's a PTTK **campsite** up here, too.

From Szczawnica, it's a fifteen-minute bus ride east to the village of **JAWORKI**, starting point for the walk and an interesting example of the ethnic and religious twists characterizing the eastern hill country. At first sight, the late eighteenth-century **church**, a cavernous construction with an elaborately decorated balcony, looks like a regular Catholic building, but a glance at the iconostasis behind the altar indicates a different history. Although now Roman Catholic, it was originally a Uniate *cerkiew*, in what was the western-most point of Łemk settlement in Poland (see box pp.356–357). Today only a couple of Łemk families remain. If you find the church closed, ask for the key from the house next door. A basic **bar-restaurant** (closed Mon) in the village serves fine fish dishes and Okocim beer.

Travel details

Trains

Częstochowa to: Katowice (hourly; 1–2hr); Kielce (10 daily; 2hr); Kraków (8 daily; 2–3hr); Łódź (8 daily; 2–3hr); Warsaw (8 daily; 3–4hr).

Kielce to: Częstochowa (10 daily; 2hr); Katowice (4 daily; 4hr); Kraków (7 daily; 2–3hr); Łódź (1 daily; 4hr); Lublin (4 daily; 5–6hr); Warsaw (12 daily; 3–4hr).

Kraków to: Białystok (1 daily; 10hr); Bydgoszcz (3 daily; 7–9hr); Częstochowa (8 daily; 2–4hr); Gdańsk (3 daily; 5–11hr); Jędrzejów (11 daily; 1hr 10min–1hr 45min); Katowice (15 daily; 1hr 30min–2hr); Kielce (7 daily; 2–3hr); Krynica (8 daily; 5–6hr); Lublin (3 daily; 5–7hr); Nowy Sącz (9 daily; 3–4hr; 1 express); Oświęcim-Auschwitz (12 daily, 1hr 30min); Poznań (6 daily; 7–8hr); Przemyśl (10 daily; 3–5hr; 1 express); Rzeszów (10 daily; 2–3hr); Szczecin (5 daily; 12–14hr); Tarnów (10 daily; 2hr); Warsaw (15 daily; 2hr 30min–6hr; expresses every hour 6.15am–12.15pm, every 2hrs 2.15–6.15pm); Wrocław (12 daily; 4–6hr); Zakopane (10 daily; 2–5hr; 1 express).

Nowy Sącz to: Tarnów (13 daily; 2hr).

Przemyśl to: Tarnów (11 daily; 2–3hr 15 min).

Rzeszów to: Tarnów (24 daily; 1–1hr 30min).

Tarnów to: Kraków (10 daily; 50min–1hr 20min);

Krynica (9 daily; 3hr 30min); Nowy Sącz (13 daily; 2hr); Rzeszów (every 30min; 1–1hr 30min); Warsaw (3 daily; 4hr); Zamość (2 daily; 5–7hr).

Zakopane to: Częstochowa (3 daily; 7–8hr; sleepers); Gdańsk (1 daily; 12hr; sleeper); Katowice (2–4 daily; 4–6hr); Kraków (15 daily; 3–5hr); Warsaw (2 daily; 5–12hr).

Buses

Kielce to: Chęciny (every 30min; 35min); Jędrzejów (hourly; 50min); Kraków (7 daily; 2hr 30min); Łódź (7 daily; 3hr); Nowa Słupia (hourly; 50min); Sandomierz (3 daily; 2hr); Starachowice (hourly; 2hr); Staszów (4 daily; 2hr); Święty Krzyż (Mon–Fri 4 daily, Sat 2 daily, Sun 3 daily; 1hr); Warsaw (4 daily; 4hr); Wąchock (hourly; 1hr 10min).

Kraków to: Cieszyn (7 daily; 3hr); Kalwaria Zebrzydowska (every 30min; 40min); Kielce (7 daily; 2hr 30min); Nowy Targ (12 daily; 1–2hr); Ojców (Mon–Fri 8 daily, Sat & Sun 6 daily; 45min); Oświęcim-Auschwitz (9 daily; 1hr 30min); Sandomierz (2 daily; 4–5hr); Tarnów (15 daily; 1hr 30min–2hr); Wadowice (every 30min; 1hr 20min); Zakopane (12 daily; 2hr 30min–3hr); Zamość (2 daily; 6–8hr).

Nowy Targ to Czorsztyn (Mon–Sat 6 daily, Sun 4 daily; 40min); Niedzica (5 daily; 40min); Sromowce Katy (5 daily; 1hr); Szczawnica (10 daily; 1hr).

Szczawnica to: Jawórki (7 daily; 15min).

Tarnów to: Kielce (4 daily; 2hr 45min); Kraków (15–20 daily; 1hr 30min); Krynica (5 daily; 2hr 45min); Nowy Sącz (16 daily; 1hr 45min); Sanok (4 daily; 3hr); Warsaw (4 daily; 6hr); Zakopane (3 daily; 4hr); Zalipie (Mon–Fri 6 daily, Sat 3 daily; 50min).

Wadowice to : Bielsko-Biała (hourly; 1hr 15min); Kalwaria Zebrzydowska (every 30min; 40min); Kraków (every 30min; 1hr 20min); Zawoja (2 daily; 1hr 20min).

Zakopane to: Bielsko-Biała (3 daily; 2hr 30min–4hr); Katowice (2 daily; 4hr); Kraków (12 daily; 2hr 30min–3hr); Lublin (1 daily; 8hr); Nowy Sącz (3 daily; 1–2hr); Nowy Targ (every 30min; 40min); Polana Palenica (June & Sept 12 daily, July & Aug 20 daily, Oct–May 6 daily; 45min); Rzeszów (1 daily; 3–4hr); Szczawnica (5 daily; 1hr 20min); Warsaw (1 daily; 8–9hr).

Flights

Kraków to: Gdańsk (1 daily; 2hr); Warsaw (1–3 daily; 1hr).

International trains

Kraków to: Berlin (2 daily; 9hr); Bratislava (1 daily; 8hr); Bucharest (1 daily; 25hr); Budapest (1 daily; 11hr); Kiev (1 daily; 22hr); Odessa (summer only; 1 daily; 26hr); Prague (1 daily; 8hr 30min); Vienna (2 daily; 7hr).

International buses

Kraków to: Berlin (1 daily; 12hr); Budapest (2 weekly; 10hr); London (1 daily; 28hr); Paris (1 daily; 25hr); Rome (1 daily; 25hr); Vienna (1 daily; 10hr).

5

Silesia

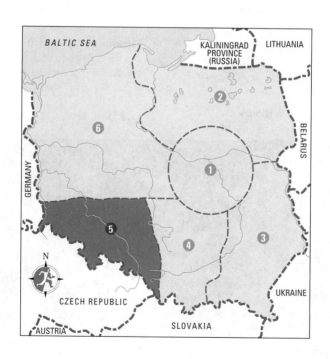

CHAPTER 5 # Highlights

* **Szczyrk** Take to the slopes at the up-and-coming skiing and hiking resort of the far south, located deep in the mountains of the Beskid Śląski. **See p.518**

* **Cieszyn** A charming historical market town straddling Poland's frontier with the Czech Republic. **See p.521**

* **Wrocław** The Rynek of this boisterous, burgeoning city ranks with any in Poland. **See p.528**

* **Ziemia Kłodzka** An enchanting area of rolling hills and fir-clad mountains, dotted with laid-back spa resorts. **See p.552**

* **Książ** One of the best-preserved castles in the country, perched fairytale-style on a hilltop above the winding River Pełcznica. **See p.566**

* **Karpacz** Snugly situated in a narrow wooded valley, this popular holiday village is the gateway to the hiking trails of the Karkonosze mountains. **See p.574**

△ Corpus Christi procession

5

Silesia

n Poland it's known as *Śląsk*, in the Czech Republic as *Slezsko*, in Germany as *Schlesien*: all three countries have at one time or another been the dominant power in the frequently disputed province that's known in English as **Silesia**. Since 1945, Poland has had the best of the argument, holding all of it except for a few of the westernmost tracts, a dominance gained as compensation for the Eastern Territories, which were incorporated into the USSR in 1939 and never returned.

Silesia presents a strange dichotomy. On the one hand it offers some of the most bewitching countryside in the whole of Poland, thanks in large part to the fir-clad mountains and rippling hills that form the province's border with the Czech Republic. On the other hand Silesia is notoriously scarred by ill-planned industrial development, its lowland regions peppered with bleak grey towns – especially the huge conurbation around **Katowice** in the southeast.

The area is traditionally divided into eastern or **Upper Silesia** and western or **Lower Silesia** – a distinction which grew out of the territorial carve-ups of the late Middle Ages and was compounded by events in the twentieth century – Upper Silesia became part of the Polish state in 1921, but Lower Silesia had to wait until 1945. Taking Upper Silesia first, the city of Katowice is your most likely entry point to the region, although it's a gritty place best treated as a gateway to more the appetizing areas beyond rather than as a destination in its own right. South of Katowice, the **Beskid mountains** fold their limbs around the up-and-coming ski resort of **Szczyrk** and the futuristic rest-cure hotels of Ustroń. Ranged around the foothills, the delightful town of Cieszyn and the Baroque palace at **Pszczyna** are the main targets for travellers.

Best place to begin exploring Lower Silesia is the region's chief city, **Wrocław**, an enticing cosmopolitan centre which combines modern commercial bustle with the attractions of a medieval Stare Miasto. The landscape around Wrocław is largely made up of level, undramatic arable terrain, although old ducal capitals like **Legnica**, **Świdnica**, **Brzeg** and **Opole** offer plenty in the way of historical interest. For more in the way of natural beauty, it's best to make a beeline for the mountains to the south and west – where the Sudeten chain contains some of the most popular recreation areas in the country. Of these, the **Karkonosze national park** is the easiest to reach from Wrocław, with the regional centre of **Jelenia Góra** providing access to the skiing and hiking resorts of **Karpacz** and **Szklarska Poreba**. Slightly further east, the **Kłodzko region**'s outlying massifs provide some of Poland's best walking country, with refined old health resorts like **Kudowa–Zdrój**, **Lądek-Zdrój** and **Międzygórze** offering everything from spa treatments to winter sports.

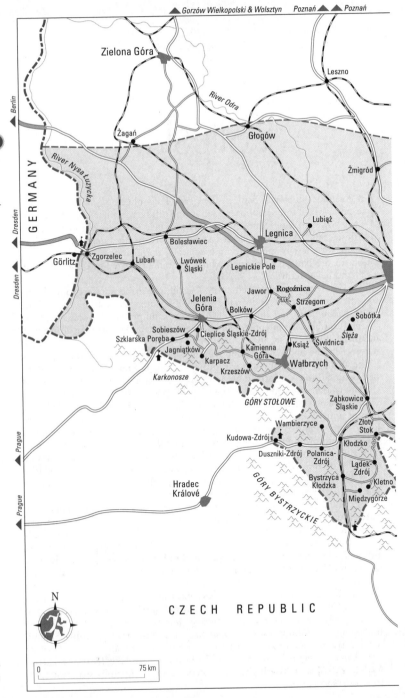

Gorzów Wielkopolski & Wolsztyn   Poznań   Poznań

Zielona Góra

Leszno

River Odra

Żagań

Głogów

Berlin

Żmigród

River Nysa Łużycka

GERMANY

Dresden

Lubiąż

Legnica

Bolesławiec

Görlitz Zgorzelec Lubań

Lwówek
Śląski

Legnickie Pole

Dresden

Jelenia
Góra

Jawor Rogoźnica

Strzegom

Sobótka

Bolków

Ślęża

Sobieszów

Cieplice Śląskie-Zdrój

Kamienna
Góra

Książ Świdnica

Szklarska Poręba

Jagniątków

Karpacz

Krzeszów

Wałbrzych

Karkonosze

GÓRY STOŁOWE

Ząbkowice
Śląskie

Wambierzyce

Złoty
Stok

Kudowa-Zdrój

Kłodzko

Duszniki-Zdrój Polanica-
Zdrój

Lądek-
Zdrój

Prague

Hradec
Králové

Bystrzyca
Kłodzka

Kletno

GÓRY BYSTRZYCKIE

Międzygórze

Prague

N

CZECH   REPUBLIC

506

0   75 km

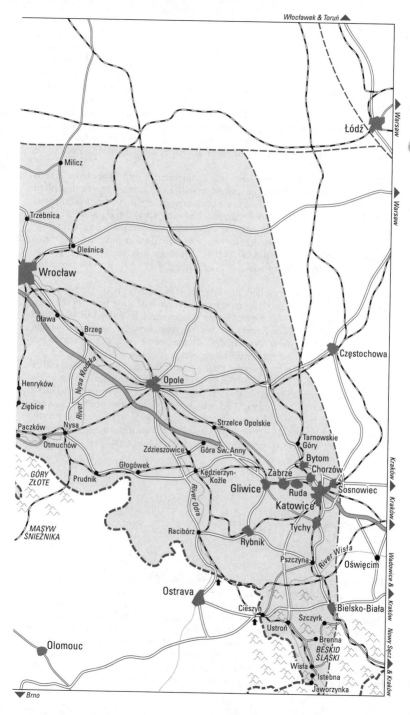

Włocławek & Toruń

Warsaw

Warsaw

Łódź

Milicz

Trzebnica

Oleśnica

Wrocław

Oława

Brzeg

Częstochowa

Nysa Kłodzka River

Henryków

Opole

Ziębice

Paczków

Nysa

Strzelce Opolskie

Tarnowskie
Góry

Otmuchów

Zdzieszowice

Góra Św. Anny

GÓRY
ZŁOTE

Głogówek

Bytom

Prudnik

Kędzierzyn-
Koźle

Zabrze

Chorzów

Gliwice

Ruda

Sosnowiec

River Odra

Katowice

MASYW
ŚNIEŻNIKA

Racibórz

Tychy

Rybnik

Kraków

Kraków

Kraków

Pszczyna

River Wisła

Oświęcim

Wadowice &

Ostrava

Cieszyn

Bielsko-Biała

Kraków

Szczyrk

Ustroń

Brenna

Nowy Sącz

Olomouc

BESKID
ŚLĄSKI

Wisła

Istebna

& Kraków

Jaworzynka

Brno

Some history

Along with Wielkopolska and Małopolska, Silesia was a key component of the early Polish nation. Following the collapse of the country's monarchical system, the duke of Silesia, a member of the Piast dynasty, sometimes served as Poland's uncrowned king. However, this system fell by the wayside in the wake of the Tatar invasions in the thirteenth century, and the duchy was divided into **Lower** and **Upper Silesia**, the northwestern and southeastern parts of the province, respectively. As the succeeding dukes divided their territory among their sons, Silesia became splintered into eighteen principalities: hence what you see today is the legacy of a series of pint-sized former capitals, each with its fair share of churches and other religious institutions as well as a few surviving castles and palaces.

As each line died out, its land was incorporated into **Bohemia**, which eventually took over the entire province when the Piasts were extinguished in 1675 – by which time it had itself become part of the Austrian-dominated **Habsburg Empire**. In 1740, Frederick the Great, king of the militaristic state of **Prussia**, launched an all-out war on Austria, his pretext being a dubious claim his ancestors had once had to one of the Silesian principalities. After changing hands several times, all but the southern part of the province was taken over by the Prussians in 1763, becoming part of Bismarck's Germany in 1871.

In 1921 a plebiscite resulted in the industrial heartlands of Upper Silesia becoming part of the recently resurrected Polish state (see box opposite on the Upper Silesia dispute). Lower Silesia was awarded to Poland in 1945, and displaced Poles from the Eastern Territories were brought in to replace the Germans who were now evacuated from the region. Yet, although postwar Silesia has developed a strongly Polish character, people are often bilingual and a small but vocal minority consider their prime loyalty to lie with Silesia rather than Poland. After the fall of the Berlin Wall some German politicians considered staking a claim to parts of Silesia, although the issue was definitively laid to rest by the treaty of November 1990, which reconfirmed the borders between the two countries. Since the fall of communism Silesia has benefited greatly from an influx of both German tourists and German investment – a process accelerated by Poland's accession to the European Union in 2004.

Upper Silesia

The northern half of Upper Silesia is dominated by an almost continuously built-up conurbation of about a dozen towns which rejoices in the collective name of **GOP** (Górnośląski Okręg Przemysłowy, or Upper Silesian Industrial District). Two million inhabitants make this the most densely populated part of the country, with the largest city, **Katowice**, serving as an important transport hub with easy onward connections to Wrocław, Kraków and Częstochowa. The gritty manufacturing city of **Bielsko–Biała** aside, the southern half of the province couldn't be more different, with the pine-cloaked mountains of the Beskid Śląski (Silesian Beskids) providing a surfeit of attractive hiking territory.

The Upper Silesia dispute of 1918–22

In the aftermath of World War I, the dispute between Poland and Germany over the ownership of **Upper Silesia** represented the first reasonably successful attempt by the international community at providing an enduring, if not permanent, solution to a potentially explosive problem by means of mediation rather than through military force.

Following Germany's wartime defeat, the Allies at first intended to transfer the whole of Upper Silesia to the newly resurrected Poland, which would otherwise have been a poor agricultural country with no industrial base. Polish spokesmen stressed their historical claim on the territory and on its demographic make-up, although the latter couldn't be quantified exactly. Strongly partisan support for the transferral of sovereignty came from France, which wished to weaken Germany as much as possible and establish a strong ally to its east. This rather unnerved the British, ever anxious about the balance of power in Europe and concerned at the potential danger of French hegemony. They gradually came to back the ferocious German backlash against the proposed change in ownership, believing that it was in Europe's best interests for industries to be left in the hands of the nation that had developed them, rather than being handed over to a new country with no business experience: Prime Minister Lloyd George went so far as to suggest that allocating Upper Silesia to Poland was like giving a clock to a monkey.

As the Allies dragged their feet on the issue, Upper Silesia remained the one unresolved question on the now much-changed map of Europe. Frustrated at the lack of progress, the Poles staged **insurrections** in 1919 and 1920. Eventually, the Allies decided to test popular feelings by means of a **plebiscite**, which was held in March 1921. This was won by the Germans by 707,000 votes to 479,000, but the result was discredited by the fact that a large number (thought to be around 182,000) of former citizens were temporarily shipped back from their new homes elsewhere in Germany. Support for continued German sovereignty was strongest in the industrial communities closest to Poland, making the solution of partition seemingly intractable, particularly as it was taken for granted that the conurbation could not be divided satisfactorily.

In May 1921, a third insurrection led to the **occupation** of the territory by the Polish army. Realizing the need for a quick solution, the Allies referred the matter to the **League of Nations**, the body newly established to promote world peace. The neutral observers who were assigned to the task decided that **partition** was the only fair solution, and used the plebiscite returns as the basis for determining the respective shares of the carve-up. By the **Geneva Convention on Upper Silesia** of 1922, which ran to 606 articles, the Germans retained two-thirds of the land and three-fifths of the population, but an international boundary was cut through the industrial conurbation, a somewhat Solomonic solution which left Poland with the vast majority of the coal mines and blast furnaces. However, in what was itself a radical and previously untried experiment, the area was kept as an economic unit, with guarantees on the movement of goods, material and labour, the provision of public services and the rights of individuals who found themselves living under an alien flag.

Despite dire predictions to the contrary, the agreement endured for the full fifteen years it was scheduled to operate. The Poles proved perfectly capable of running what had previously been German industrial concerns, and the presence of an international frontier did not impede the conurbation's productivity. Admittedly there was a persistent flow of grievances, mostly from the Germans, who conveniently forgot that they had managed to hold on to a good deal of valuable territory which they'd come close to losing. However, the country's new democratic leaders felt duty bound to stop short of calling for a return of the lost portion, and, had it not been for the advent of Hitler, the League's audacious solution might well have survived indefinitely.

5

SILESIA | Upper Silesia

Right on the Czech border, **Cieszyn** is one of southern Poland's best-preserved market towns, and serves as an excellent base if you're touring the area.

Upper Silesia's rich mineral seams have been extensively mined since the Middle Ages – nearly a tenth of the world's known coal exists here, but it wasn't until the nineteenth-century **industrial revolution** that the area became heavily urbanized. In 1800, Katowice had just 500 inhabitants. Fifty years later, its population was a still modest 4000 before Upper Silesia mushroomed into the powerhouse of the Prussian state, in tandem with the broadly similar Ruhr at the opposite end of the country.

With a population composed almost equally of Germans and Poles (and with many of mixed blood), the fate of the area became a hot political issue after World War I – and one that was to be of far more than local significance (see box, p.509, for the full story). In the communist period, the conurbation maintained its high-profile position, thanks to the ideological stress placed on heavy industry. Workers here enjoyed a privileged position; mining wages, for example, were three times the national average income. One obvious side effect of the GOP's industrial development was a catastrophically high level of atmospheric **pollution** and a correspondingly high incidence of breathing complaints among the local population. Many of the less profitable factories closed down in the 1990s, reducing environmental problems but adding to the ranks of local unemployed. However, Upper Silesia's skilled workforce and excellent communications have made it an obvious target for foreign investment, and those travellers who stop off in the GOP will find that the aura of post-industrial decay is increasingly overlaid with a palpable sense of big-city bustle.

Katowice and around

Standing at the heart of the upper-Silesian conurbation, 400,000-strong **KATOWICE** is very much the ugly duckling of Polish cities. Despite a few surviving pockets of nineteenth-century grandeur, it's a predominantly grey place grouped around a distinctly unengaging twentieth-century centre. However, thanks to its international airport and rail links, Katowice represents many peoples' first taste of southwestern Poland, and you may well find yourself spending a night or two here en route to somewhere else. With the odd museum and a spectacular park, you won't be stuck for things to do.

Arrival, information and accommodation

Katowice's **airport** is at Pyrzowice, 25km northeast of the centre. Some flights are met by direct minibuses to Kraków and other cities (contact your airline for details), meaning that you might not have to pass through Katowice at all. Otherwise, city buses (pay the driver) run from the airport 4-5 times a day to the **train station**, bang in the centre on pl. Szewczyka, a ten-minute walk southwest of the drab road junction that passes for a **Rynek**. The **bus station** is ten minutes' southwest of the Rynek on pl. Szewczyka. The Centrum Informacju o Mieście at Młyńska 2 (City Information Centre; ☎032/259 3808, ⓦwww.um.katowice.pl) is your most likely source of **information**.

Should you make an overnight stay in town, there's a handful of **hotels** in the centre, although most budget options are a short bus ride away. Katowice's rather spartan **youth hostel** is about fifteen minutes' walk north of the train station at ul. Sokolska 26 (☎032/59 6487). **Camping** in an industrial city like Katowice might sound paradoxical, but there's a reasonably tranquil, lakeside

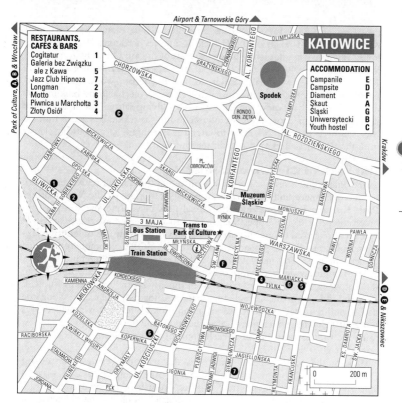

Map content (Katowice):

Airport & Tarnowskie Góry

KATOWICE

RESTAURANTS, CAFÉS & BARS
Cogitatur 1
Galeria bez Związku ale z Kawa 5
Jazz Club Hipnoza 7
Longman 2
Motto 6
Piwnica u Marchołta 3
Złoty Osiół 4

ACCOMMODATION
Campanile E
Campsite D
Diament F
Skaut A
Śląski G
Uniwersytecki B
Youth hostel C

Spodek

Street labels: OLIMPIJSKA, AL. KORFANTEGO, CZERWONKIEGO, GRAŻYŃSKIEGO, CHORZOWSKA, RONDO GEN. ZIĘTKA, AL. ROŻDZIEŃSKIEGO, MICKIEWICZA, ZABRSKA, DĄBRÓWKI, OPOLSKA, GLIWICKA, JANA III SOBIESKIEGO, UL. SOKOLSKA, CHOPINA, SKARGI, PL. OBROŃCÓW, UL. KORFANTEGO, UNIWERSYTECKA, BANKOWA, MICKIEWICZA, STAWOWA, Muzeum Śląskie, MONIUSZKI, RYNEK, TEATRALNA, SZKOLNA, 3 MAJA, Bus Station, Trams to Park of Culture ★, MŁYŃSKA, PLEBISCYTOWA, ŚW. JANA, WARSZAWSKA, PAWŁA, WODNA, GÓRNICZA, Train Station, UL. DWORCOWA, DYREKCYJNA, MIELECKIEGO, MARIACKA, TVLNA, KAMIENNA, KORDECKIEGO, MIŁOWSKA, ANDRZEJA, WOJEWÓDZKA, RACIBORSKA, ŻWIRKI I WIGURY, KOZIELSKA, BATOREGO, KOCHANOWSKIEGO, DĄBROWSKIEGO, ŁOMPY, KS. DAMROTA, ŚW. JACKA, STALMACHA, KILIŃSKIEGO, KOPERNIKA, UL. KOŚCIUSZKI, DRZYMAŁY, PLEBISCYTOWA, SIENKIEWICZA, JAGIELLOŃSKA, FRANCUSKA, JORDANA, PCK, LIGONIA, KRÓLOWEJ JADWIGI, REYMONTA

N

Park of Culture, A, B & Wrocław
Kraków
D, E & Nikiszowiec

0 — 200 m

---

site southwest of the city centre at ul. Murckowska 6 (mid-May to late Sept; ☏032/255 5388) and reached by bus #4 from al. Korfantego.

Hotels

Campanile ul. Sowińskiego 48 ☏032/205 5050, ⓦwww.campanile.com.pl. Neat, tidy, cube-shaped business hotel 2km southeast of the centre, offering en suites with TV, neutral colour schemes and tea-making facilities. Handily placed for the A4 Wrocław–Kraków highway if you're touring by car; otherwise bus #910 from the train station passes by. ⑥

Diament ul. Dworcowa 9 ☏032/253 9041, ⓦwww.hoteldiament.pl. Glitzy new three-star near to the station. ⑦

Skaut al. Harcerska 3 ☏032/241 3291, ⓔosrodek.chorzow@zhp.org.pl. Plain but nicely situated low-rise block at the northern end of the huge Park of Culture and Rest (see p.512), with functional en-suite doubles, plus a few triples and quads. Trams #6, #11, #23 or #41 from the Rynek to Stadion Śląski. ④

Śląski Mariacka 15 ☏032/253 7011. Convenient cheapie near the train station. A dingy reception area leads to lino-floored rooms with wallpaper and furniture that look like relics from the 1950s. Otherwise clean and friendly. ④

Uniwersytecki ul. Bytkowska 1a ☏032/259 9271. Functional en suites 4km northwest of the centre, on the borders of the Park of Culture and Rest (see p.512). Bus #30 or #50 from the centre. ④

The Town and around

Although central Katowice is notoriously low on sightseeing attractions, those with time to kill could do worse than peep into the **Muzeum Śląskie**

(Museum of Silesia; Tues–Fri 10am–5pm, Sat & Sun 11am–4pm; 6zł) at ul. Korfantego 3, just north of the Rynek. Inside lies a reasonable collection of Polish art, with some touching pastel portraits of the artist's family by Stanisław Wyspiański (see p.404), and a couple of canvases by Olga Boznańska (1865–1940), one of the few female painters to be active in pre-World War I Poland. North of the Rynek you can't miss also Katowice's most alluring building, the futuristic sports hall known as the **Spodek** ("flying saucer"), a dark, domed structure presiding above the road intersection to the north. Rock fans from all over southern Poland flock here to attend major gigs – numerous big names from the West have appeared here in recent years.

The Park of Culture and Rest

Three kilometres northwest of the centre, on the administrative boundary between Katowice and the neighbouring city of Chorzów, the **Wojewódzki Park Kultury i Wypoczynku** (Regional Park of Culture and Rest) is very much the pride of the Upper Silesian conurbation – an enormous expanse of greenery conceived by socialist planners in the 1950s as an area of leisure, relaxation and escape for the proletarian hordes of the GOP. Combining ornamental gardens, areas of woodland wilderness and a worthwhile ethnographic museum, the park probably deserves more of your sightseeing time than anything else in the Katowice area. It's easy to get to from the city centre, with trams #6, #11, #23 and #41 from the Rynek (destination Chorzów) all passing along the park's southern edge. A novel way of getting round the park is provided by a horizontal chairlift, which floats above the lawns and flowerbeds on a triangular route (you can get on and off at each point of the triangle; tickets cost 2zł for one stretch, 5zł for all three).

Marking the southeastern entrance to the park is **Wesołe Miasteczko** ("Happy Town"; Mon–Fri 10am–7pm, Sat & Sun 10am–9pm; 22zł), a garish amusement park offering a variety of rides. From here a central avenue leads northwest through the heart of the park, passing a boating lake, seven hectares of rose garden and a sizeable **zoo** (daily: summer 10am–7pm; winter 10am–4pm). At the northwestern end of the avenue looms the huge bowl of the **Stadion Śląski** (Silesia Stadium), the main entrance to which is decorated with an unintentionally psychedelic mosaic of frolicking footballers. The Polish national team often plays here, and English fans may wish to forget that Katowice was the scene of a famous 0–2 defeat in 1973 that helped to confirm England's decline as a footballing power – and effectively ended the international career of World Cup-winning captain Bobby Moore. The Poles, meanwhile, went on to enjoy a golden decade of international success. A kilometre beyond the stadium, the **Górnośląski Park Etnograficzny** (Upper Silesian Ethnographic Park; May–Sept: Tues–Fri 9am–5pm, Sat & Sun 11am–7pm; Oct: Tues–Sun 9am–5pm; Nov–April: Mon–Fri 9am–2pm; 4zł), presents a fascinating array of rural buildings ranged across an area of gently rolling meadowland. Jostling for attention are timber cottages from the Beskid mountains, straw-thatched farmhouses from the Pszczyna region, and – most arrestingly of all – an eighteenth-century wooden church from the village of Nieboczowy, with a wonderfully wavy shingle roof and a rash of pimply onion domes.

Nikiszowiec

Arguably the most alluring part of Katowice's industrial heritage is **Nikiszowiec** (colloquially known as "Nikisz"), a model suburb 5km southeast of the centre, built in 1908–15 to house workers employed in the nearby Wieczorek coal mine. Comprising a series of red-brick quadrangular or triangular residential blocks, each punctuated with arched gateways leading through to inner garden courtyards, the place resembles a vast system of interlocking fortifications. Presiding over the whole ensemble is the similarly red-brick **Kościół św. Anny** (St Anne's Church), a neo-Baroque structure basking beneath a fat sensual dome. It's a fascinating place for a wander – although the absence of decent cafés or food shops will probably have you scurrying back towards central Katowice after an hour or so. Nikiszowiec can be reached on bus #12 or #13 from ul. Warszawska, just east of Katowice's Rynek.

Eating, drinking and entertainment

Several quick and convenient **eating** venues can be found on two pedestrianized streets near the station; ul. Stawowa and ul. Wawelka, where you'll find numerous cafés, snack outlets and pizzerias. For something more substantial, *Piwnica u Marchołta*, Warszawska 37, offers the best in Polish pork, poultry and game dishes in elegant but not over-expensive surroundings. *Motto*, south of the railway tracks at ul. Kościuszki 18, offers mainstream meat and fish dishes in a modern, glossy-magazine interior; while *Złoty Osioł*, just east of the station at on Mariacka, is a laid-back café serving inexpensive vegetarian dishes.

As far as **drinking** is concerned, *Galeria bez Związku ale z Kawą*, Mariacka 19, is a relaxing café-bar with artworks on the walls and jazzy background music. *Longman*, a roomy pub packed with London-themed bric-a-brac at Gliwicka 10, is suitable for a raucous evening out; while the nearby *Cogitatur*, in a courtyard behind Gliwicka 9, offers worn antique-shop furnishings and an easy-going bohemian vibe. *Jazz Club Hipnoza*, south of the train station at pl. Sejmu Śląskiego 2, is the place to seek out live jazz and blues.

Tarnowskie Góry

From a tourist point of view, the only worthwhile town north of Katowice is **TARNOWSKIE GÓRY**, some 20km away on the far side of the conurbation. It's a place with a far more venerable history: silver and lead deposits were discovered in the thirteenth century and it was given an urban charter and mining rights in the sixteenth by the dukes of Opole. Some idea of its underground wealth is given in a document dated 1632 listing twenty thousand places where minerals could be exploited.

The principal reason for coming here is to see two historic **mine** sites, one of which, while not quite matching the famous salt mines of Wieliczka (see p.434), makes an intriguing excursion underground. Both sites are a walkable couple of kilometres south and west of the town centre; an inexpensive map from the PTTK office (see p.514) will make things clear, although some street names have since been changed.

The mines

The first of the sites, the **Kopalnia Zabytkowa Rud Srebrnosnych** at ul. Szczęść Boże 52 (Museum of Silver Mining; Mon–Fri 8am–2pm, Sat & Sun 9am–3pm; 15zł per person, plus 22zł for a Polish-speaking guide), is hidden away on the southwestern outskirts of town: take the main Gliwice road from the centre, go through the lights and take the second left into ul. Jedności Robotniczej and you'll find the mine a little further along on the left – altogether about thirty minutes' walk. Dating back to medieval times, the mine was formerly worked for silver, lead and copper, and in the small museum you'll see the old equipment, plus models of how the mine was operated and water levels controlled. The highlight, though, is a motorboat trip along the flooded drainage tunnels which were excavated as needs arose; dozens of kilometres of passageways undermine the entire area.

A large wall map explains the connection between the mine and the **Sztolnia Czarnego Pstrąga** (Black Trout Shaft; July & Aug: daily 10am–4pm; May, June, Sept & Oct: Sat & Sun 10am–4pm; Nov–April: Sat & Sun 11am–3pm; 12zł per person plus 20zł for a Polish-speaking guide), 3km away on the northwestern side of town. It takes its name from the eponymous fish which occasionally get into the tunnels from the rivers into which they drain. If coming from the town centre, walk west past the park along ul. Kard. S. Wyszyńskiego, cross the lights and continue down the hill. You'll see the signs to the left before a Lutheran chapel. If you have a car, leave it at the edge of the woods and walk down to the nearest of the two entrances: "Szyb Sylvester". Outside, a blackboard will indicate the times of the half-hourly excursions to the other entrance, "Szyb Ewa", 600m away through the woods. Once inside, you descend down a vertical shaft and make a spooky journey by boat along one of the former drainage channels. Passing through rock-hewn "gates", associated legends are recounted; at one point any woman wanting to find a husband within the year is invited to rap on the wall.

Practicalities

Tarnowskie Góry is reached from Katowice in about an hour by **train** with the station located a couple of minutes' walk east of the central Rynek. Best source of **information** is the Biuro Obsługi Ruch Turystycznego (Mon–Fri 7.30am–3.30pm; ☎032/285 4996), on the way towards the Silver Mine at ul. Gliwicka 2.

Accommodation really boils down to the Olimpijski at ul. Korczaka 23 (☎032/285 4524; ❺), a well-run, businesslike place formerly much used by visiting sports teams. There's a café-restaurant at the silver mine, and an excellent **restaurant**, the *Sedlaczek* on the Rynek, serving up inexpensive local food in an old-fashioned ambience.

South of Katowice

Directly south of Katowice the outstanding castle museum in the charming town of **Pszczyna** makes an unmissable stopover on the way to the hills of the **Beskid Śląski**, just south of the twin cities of **Bielsko-Biała**. Although lacking the grandeur of the nearby Tatra Mountains, the region's highlands are worth investigating, not least for the chance to experience the undeveloped charm of **Cieszyn**, which straddles Poland's border with the Czech Republic. There are regular bus and train services from Katowice to Bielsko-Biała, from where the Beskid resort of **Szczyrk** and Cieszyn are easily accessible, although the latter town can also be reached directly from Katowice by bus.

Pszczyna

About forty minutes from Katowice by train, or the same number of kilometres by road, the small town of **PSZCZYNA** is a world away from the gritty urban landscape of the conurbation. If Nysa is the "Silesian Rome" and Paczków "Poland's Carcassonne", then Pszczyna might be elevated by the same inflated logic to "Silesia's Versailles", on account of the eighteenth-century ducal palace that dominates the town centre.

Occupying the western side of a handsome Rynek lined with fine mansions, the **Museum Zamkowe** (Palace Museum; ⓦ www.zamek-pszczyna.pl;

July & Aug Mon 11am–3pm, Tues 10am–5pm, Wed 9am–4pm, Thur & Fri 9am–3pm, Sat & Sun 10am–6pm; April–June, Sept & Oct same times except Sat & Sun 10am–4pm; Nov–March Tues 11am–3pm, Wed 9am–4pm, Thur & Fri 9am–3pm, Sat & Sun 10am–3pm; 12zł) originated as a Piast hunting lodge in the twelfth century. Sold to the Promnitz family in the sixteenth century, it was transformed into an aristocratic residence in the Renaissance style before undergoing a thorough Baroque rebuild following a fire. The palace was subsequently taken over by the Hochbergs, one of Germany's richest families, who expanded the palace and added an English-style park. A museum since 1946, the palace has been stunningly refurbished, and now houses furniture and historic artefacts rescued from stately homes all over Silesia.

Begin by slipping whatever footwear you have on into the compulsory slippers in which you slide round the display. Much of the ground floor is taken up with the so-called **Royal Apartments** (Apartamenty Cezarskie), where Kaiser Wilhelm of Germany – together with much of his general staff – took up residence during World War I. His bedroom, dressing room and office have been faithfully recreated, with photographs of the likes of Ludendorff and Hindenburg recalling the strategic brainstorming sessions that took place here.

Ascending the aptly named Grand Staircase bordered by its stone balustrade, past a green serpentine vase used to hold wine at feasts, tapestries with stucco borders and marble sculptures, you reach the apartments designed for Princess Daisy von Pless, an English lady from the Cornwallis-West family who married head Hochberg Prince Hans Heinrich XV in 1891. There are some lovely portraits of Princess Daisy, and a room full of the antlers formerly belonging to beasts butchered by keen hunter Hans Heinrich. The highlight, however, comes when you have passed through the Prince's apartments and library and reach the stunning **Chamber of Mirrors**. At each end of the hall, huge mirrors in gilded brass frames create an impression of a much larger room, embellished by crystal chandeliers hung from a ceiling depicting a swirling sky. Splendidly ornate balconies look down onto the chamber from the second floor, while murals depicting the four seasons and the signs of the zodiac are squeezed in between the gilded stucco decoration. The rows of period chairs filling the chamber are used during the monthly chamber music recitals held here. Make sure you see it from the balcony above as well as from below.

Subsequent rooms include an Art Nouveau dining room, a mirror gallery, and a charming billiard-room. The final point of interest inside is the **Galeria Myśliwska** (Hunting Gallery), hung with still more antlers and half a wild boar leaping out of the wall.

Behind the castle lies an extensive landscaped park, with small lakes spanned by a sequence of gracefully arching bridges. Heading east through the park will bring you out onto ul. Dworcowa and (eventually) back to the train and bus stations, but not before first passing a small **skansen** (Tues–Sun 10am–3pm; 5zł) of reassembled rural buildings brought here from locations throughout the Beskids. There's a farmhouse filled with hand-painted furniture, and a granary containing carriages, a sleigh and an Art-Nouveau hearse.

Practicalities

You'll find the **train** and **bus stations** located a kilometre east of the town's Rynek. The helpful **tourist office**, just off the Rynek in the castle gateway (Mon–Fri 8am–4pm, Sat & Sun 10am–4pm; ☎032/210 1155, ⓦwww.pszczyna .pl), advises on accommodation as well as selling local maps and souvenirs. Best **places to stay** are the *Michalik*, midway between the stations and the palace at ul. Dworcowa 11 (☎032/210 1355, ⓦwww.umichalika.com.pl; ❹), offering small but bright rooms with contemporary furnishings, shower and satellite TV; and the *Retro*, two blocks south of the Rynek at ul. Warowna 31 (☎032/210 2245, ⓦ www.retro.pl; ❹), a family-run place where the en suites are slightly dowdier than at the *Michalik*, but offer a bit more in the way of room. Cheaper beds are on offer at the more basic PTTK **tourist hostel**, ul. Bogedaina 16 (☎032/210 3833; ❸), which occupies a fine red-brick former prison and has the customary mixture of en suites and rooms with shared bathrooms.

Café u Telemanna, in the Palace gateway, is as cosy a place as any for a quick drink and cake; its name a reminder that Baroque composer Georg Filip Telemann was once kapellmeister at Pszczyna. Best of the **restaurants** is the *Frykówka*, Rynek 3, which offers everything from wild boar to pizza in contemporary, style-conscious surroundings. *Restauracja Kasztelanska* north of the Rynek at ul. Bendarska 3, is a reliable source of traditional Polish pork and poultry dishes.

Bielsko-Biała

A further 25km south of Pszczyna, at the foot of the Beskid Śląski range, lies **BIELSKO-BIAŁA**, two formerly separate towns, united in 1951. Now forming one seamless whole around the River Biała which formerly divided them. Both towns flourished in the late nineteenth century, thanks to their high-quality textile products, and the cityscape today, like its northern English counterparts, is dominated by the imposing buildings of that period. Still overwhelmingly industrial, it's far from being one of Poland's most handsome cities, and its appeal largely lies in its proximity to the Beskid mountains, which rise suddenly from the city's southern outskirts. In addition there are easy bus connections to both the mountain resort of Szczyrk and market town of Cieszyn, either of which might make a more attractive place to stay than Bielsko-Biała itself.

The city centre

Arriving at the main bus or train stations, it's a fifteen-minute walk to **Bielsko**'s centre down ul. 3 Maja, a broad boulevard lined with the turn-of-the-twentieth-century tenements so characteristic of the city. It ends at the busy pl. Bolesława Chrobrego, above which lie the half-abandoned streets and alleys which define Bielsko's old centre. Perched on a knoll is the grey bulk of Bielsko's **Zamek** (Castle), formerly occupied by the Dukes of Cieszyn and rebuilt as a nineteenth-century office block before being taken over by the **Muzeum Okręgowe** (Regional Museum; Tues & Wed 9am–3pm, Thurs 10am–5pm, Fri 9am–5pm, Sat 10am–3pm, Sun 10am–4pm; 7zł). A varied display embraces weaponry through the ages, models of the castle as it looked in various past epochs, and a picture gallery strong on pre-World War I Polish work – Piotr Stachiewicz's dreamy *Pocałunek* ("The Kiss"; 1910) being one of the most frequently reproduced paintings of the era. Beyond the Zamek lies a small **Rynek** overlooked by the unusual **Katedra św. Mikołaja** (St Nicholas's Cathedral), its eccentric twentieth-century belfry, which could be described as an Escheresque vision of the Italian Renaissance, providing the city with its most visually striking landmark.

Just east of pl. Chrobrego, **Biała's** centre provides a complete contrast to Bielsko, its bustling streets lined with cafés and gleaming shop fronts. Just north of the coffee-and-cream coloured neo-Renaissance town hall, pl. Wojska Polskiego is a pleasant, broad square on whose northeastern corner stands the Art Nouveau-era **Kamienica Pod Żabami** (House of Frogs) – so named because of the amusing relief (best seen from ul. Targowa round the corner) in which two smartly dressed frogs puff on a pipe and strum a mandolin while two beetles scurry across the wall.

The southern suburbs

About 5km south of central Bielsko-Biała, the wooded foothills of the Beskid Śląski are girdled by a series of relaxing garden suburbs, many of which serve as the starting points for highland hikes. Most popular target for trippers is the **Szyndzielnia cable car** in the suburb of Oszówka Górna (daily 9am–5pm; 7zł each way), just above the terminus of the #8 bus. A seven-minute ascent whisks you up onto the shoulder of the 1028m **Mount Szyndzielna**, from where you can savour views back over the city, or attempt the gentle ridge-top ascent (by yellow-marked trail; 1hr 30min) to **Mount Klimczok** (1117m) – where you'll be greeted by even more impressive vistas, with Bielsko-Biała stretching out to the north and Szczyrk over to the south.

An alternative starting point for the mountains is the suburb of **Błonie**, where the extensive woodland park known as **Cygański Las** is crisscrossed by paths. From here you can pick up a trail to the low-lying, forest-covered **Kozia Góra** immediately to the south (1hr 30min), starting point for the more demanding trail to Klimczok via Szyndzielnia (2hr). To get to Błonie, take bus #12 to the Błonie terminus and continue south along ul. Czółgistów on foot.

At the extreme southeastern edge of Bielsko-Biała, in the formerly separate village of **Mikuszowice** (reached by riding bus #10 to the Mikuszowice Śląskie terminus), you'll find the **Kościół św. Barbary** (St Barbara's Church), one of the finest wooden churches in the region. Built at the end of the seventeenth century, the church is strikingly geometric, with a square tower and nave and a hexagonal chancel, while its skyline, with bulbous bell turrets and steeply pitched shingle roofs, is aggressively picturesque. The interior (no regular hours; enquire at the tourist office in Biała) was adorned a generation after its construction with a series of naive wall paintings illustrating the legend of its patron saint. There's also a lovely fifteenth-century carving of the Madonna and Child in the left aisle.

Practicalities

The main **bus** and **train stations** are in the northern part of Bielsko. The **tourist office**, opposite Biała's town hall at pl. Ratuszowy 2 (Mon–Fri 8am–6pm, Sat 8am–4pm; ☎033/819 0050, ⓦwww.um.bielsko.pl) is well supplied with accommodation listings and other local info. There are plenty of places **to stay** in town, beginning with the top-of-the-range *Park Hotel Vienna*, south of town on the Szczyrk road at ul. Bystrzańka 48 (☎033/812 0500, ⓦwww.vienna.pl; ❻). More convenient for the centre is the *Hotel Prezydent*, ul. 3 Maja 12 (☎033/822 7211, ⓦwww.prezydentbb.pl; ❼), although the well-equipped rooms are a bit on the dowdy side. Cheaper options include the *Błonie*, 5km south of the centre at ul. Pocztowa 49 (bus #12 from ul. Piastowska; ☎033/821 5452; ❸), offering frumpy but clean en suites, perfectly placed for the Cygański Las park; and the *Transportowiec*, al. Armii Krajowej 316 (bus #8 from ul. Piastowska; ☎033/812 2892; ❸), a modern block right beside the Szyndzielnia chairlift offering simple ensuites in woodland surrounds. There's a brace of decent **campsites** in the southern suburbs, with the *Ondraszek* in Błonie at ul. Pocztowa 43 (bus #12; ☎033/814 6425, ⓔkemping57ondraszek@op.pl) occupying a relaxing spot on the edge of the woods; and *Pod Dębowcem* in Olszówka Górna at Karbowa 15 (bus #8; ☎033/821 6080, ⓦwww.camping.org.pl) offering grassy pitches between neat clipped hedges, within striking distance of the Szyndzielnia cable car.

There's a wide range of places to **eat and drink**, most of them in Biała: the Sfera shopping centre, southeast of the train station on ul. Mostowa, is full of coffee bars and snack-stops. The *Farma Café*, roughly opposite the Zamek at pl. Smolki 7, is a good place to tuck into toasted sandwiches and cakes. Many of the best restaurants are along ul. Cechowa in central Biała: *Pod Jemiołami*, at no.6, serves up everything from potato pancakes to pork chops in a wood-beamed interior with herbs hanging from the rafters and traditional fireplaces; while *Vasco da Gama* at no. 8 has a more international menu, an extensive wine list, and an atmospheric basement setting. The next-door *Margerita*, also at no.8, is the best place for simple pizzas and pasta dishes; *Nirvana*, Cechowa 18, is a lounge-style café-bar that also does vegetarian food; while *Kawiarnia Papuga*, on the Bielsko side of the river at Frycza Modrzewskiego 8, is a good place for a civilized evening drink.

It's worth seeing what's on at the Banialuka theatre at ul. Mickiewicza 20 (☎033/815 0915) – it's the national **puppet theatre**, and in May during even-numbered years an international **puppet festival** is held here.

Szczyrk and the Beskid Śląski

Immediately south of Bielsko-Biała lies the small Silesian section of the **Beskid**, an archetypal central European mountain landscape characterized by fir-clad slopes reaching up towards bald summits. Within Poland, it's a popular holiday area with **SZCZYRK**, the main resort 15km southwest of Bielsko-Biała (from which there are frequent bus connections), offering an ever-widening range of places to stay. In winter the combination of guaranteed snowfall and steep slopes provides the country's most demanding **downhill skiing**, considered superior, if less varied, to its Tatran equivalents. In summer it is full of hikers moving between chalet hostels on the slopes. It is a region of wooden churches, folk costumes, occasional castles and manageable hikes. If you're heading for the hills by foot or mountain bike, the locally available *Beskid Śląski i Żywiecki* (1:75,000) **map** will come in very handy.

Fifteen minutes' walk south of the bus station (see below), an all-year-round two-stage **chairlift** (wyciąg; 8.30am–5.30pm; return 16zł) runs to the summit of **Skrzyczne** (1245m), the highest peak in the range. In summertime it's used by bucket-swinging bilberry pickers who comb the slopes and sell their produce by the roadsides on either side of town. From the summit you'll face the 1117m peak of Klinczok with the conurbation of Bielsko-Biała beyond. There's also the usual refuge and restaurant up here. The energetic alternative is to slog up either the blue or the green trail for a couple of hours from Szczyrk. The latter continues south to Barania Góra (1220m), the source of the **River Wisła**, Poland's greatest waterway, which winds a serpentine 1090km course through Kraków, Warsaw and Toruń before disgorging itself into the Baltic near Gdańsk.

Practicalities

Szczyrk is a long, straggling village with a **bus station** placed roughly at the midpoint of its single street. New arrivals should get off the bus here – otherwise they'll end up several kilometres away at the final stop, which is in Szczyrk's southernmost reaches.

As far as **information** goes, your best bet is to check out the Polish-language site ⓦ www.szczyrk.com.pl. **Accommodation** in Szczyrk, however, is easy to find. The Beskidy travel agency, just south of the bus station at ul. Myśliwska 4 (☎033/817 8878), will direct you towards private rooms (❶) and *pensjonaty*

(❸) as well as selling local hiking maps. *Pensjonat Koliba*, right by the Skrzyczne chairlift at ul. Skośna 17 (☎033/817 9930, ⓦhttp://koliba.szczyrk.com.pl; ❹), is a good-value source of simple en suites with TV and breakfast; while the *Hotel Beskidek*, ul. Górska 7A (☎033/817 8411; ⓦbeskidek.com.pl/beskidek; ❹), offers slightly plusher quarters, right next to a short slalom course. The *Meta*, Skośna 4 (☎033/817 8876, ⓦwww.meta-hotel.pl; ❻), is an attractive partly timbered building offering neat, piney en suites and a fancy international restaurant. Plusher still is the *Klimczok*, 3km west of the centre at Poziomkowa 20 (☎033/828 1400, ⓦwww.klimczok.pl; ❽), which looks like a cross between an alpine chalet and a corporate headquarters and is very much the winter resort hotel of choice, featuring restaurant, pub, swimming pool and disco. The *Skalite* **campsite** at ul. Kempingowa 4 (☎033/817 8760) is clearly visible from the roadside when entering the village from the Bielsko-Biała direction.

Plenty of snack bars line Szczyrk's main road, and there are several good **restaurants** specializing in filling Polish cuisine: notably the elegant *Senator* at ul. Myśliwska 8. *Tawerna Bałkańska*, ul. Myśliwska 42, is the place to go for Balkan-style grilled chops and meatballs. *Green Pub*, midway between the centre and the Skrzyczne chairlift, serves up decent pizza and spaghetti, and is also the best place in town to sink a pint; and the *Hacjenda Pub*, opposite the bus station, sometimes has live music gigs.

Ustroń and Brenna

Due west from Szczyrk the valley of the Wisła river provides the perfect niche for a string of highland resorts. They can be reached by car direct from Szczyrk via a scenic road that heads west from the village and zigzags its way over the hills before dropping down into Wisła. Otherwise they're best accessed by bus from Bielsko Biała or Cieszyn.

Roughly parallel with Szczyrk and 5km south of the main road from Bielso-Biała to Cieszyn, the spa resort of **USTROŃ** is at first sight a futuristic looking place, with a cluster of glass-fronted, pyramid-shaped hotels sprouting from the forested hillside on the eastern side of town. Down on the dusty main road that forms Ustroń's centre, things are a little more prosaic, with the customary gaggle of uninviting cafés and cheap shops. The park on the east side of the main road harbours the **Muzeum Hutnictwa i Kuźnictwa** (Museum of Metallurgy; Tues 9am–5pm, Wed–Fri 9am–2pm, Sat 9am–1pm, Sun 9.30am–1pm; 3zł), where ancient steam-hammers and various water-powered things provide mute testimony to Ustroń's erstwhile role as a major iron-working centre.

Hikers are drawn to Ustroń by its proximity to one of the most popular peaks in the Beskids, **Równica** (884m), just to the east. It can be reached by the red trail, well signposted from the car park-cum-bus stop in the middle of the resort, or you can try to negotiate a vehicle up the tortuous mountain road. A second recommended hike in the area is southwest from Ustroń by the blue route, which follows the main street south before darting uphill towards **Czantoria** (995m), another summit right on the Czech frontier.

The **tourist office** (Mon–Fri 8am–4pm, Sat 9am–1pm; ☎033/854 2653), right next door to the **bus station** at Rynek 2, will sort you out with a **private room** in the centre of Ustrok (❶), or send you up to one of the pyramid-shaped **hotels** (❸), which are a bit scruffier up-close than they appear to be from afar. One of the best of the latter is the *Narcyz*, ul. Zdrojowa 9 (☎033/854 3595, ⓦwww.narcyz.com.pl; ❹), which boasts en suites with TV, and also rents out mountain bikes. A swankier choice, down by the museum, is the new *Hotel Ustroń*, ul. Hutnicza 7 (☎033/854 2205, Ⓔustron@animus.pl; ❻), which also has a rather plush **restaurant**.

On the eastern side of Równica, on the bank of the River Brennica, lies **BRENNA**, the most secluded resort in the range. The course of the river has been terraced here, and there are good opportunities for bathing; there's also an open-air theatre, which is used for regional song and dance events at weekends throughout the summer. Accommodation options revolve around numerous **pensions**, including the simple, homely *Hawana*, ul. Jatny 34 (☏033/853 6729, ⓔhawana@bb.onet.pl; ❷); and the slightly more upscale *Malwa*, ul. Jatny 11 (☏033/853 6493, ⓦwww.malwa.pl; ❹), a spacious place with nice en suites.

Wisła and around

Six kilometres upriver from Ustroń, **WISŁA** is another long, thin village clinging to either side of the valley-bottom road. An unpretentious socialist-era health resort favoured by holiday-makers from the Katowice conurbation, it's main appeal to the independent traveller is as a staging-post en route to the mountain villages further south rather than as a destination in its own right. Wisła's principal modern-day claim to fame is that it's the home town of Adam Małysz, the ski jumper who won the world championship in 2001 and has been a major force in the sport ever since, becoming a national folk hero in the process – the village's shops are full of Małysz-related souvenirs.

Wisła's bus station is at the northern end of the village, just short of the long pedestrianized strip that leads to the main square, pl. B. Hoffa. The **tourist office** at pl. B. Hoffa 3 (Mon–Fri 9am–4pm, Sat & Sun 9am–1pm; ☏033/816 6566) is a good place to pick up information on the surrounding region and buy maps. Just off the opposite side of the square, the **Muzeum Beskidzkie** (Beskid Museum; Tues, Thurs & Fri 9am–3pm, Wed 9am–5pm, Sat & Sun 10am–2pm; 3zł), displays agricultural implements, folk costumes, and examples of the goatskin bagpipes on which the local herders used to tootle away. The *Wiślańska Strzecha* restaurant, in the museum yard, is a good place to catch a bite to eat before moving on.

The best **hike** from Wisła is via the yellow trail which strikes southeast from the southern end of the resort to **Stożek** (978m), a fine vantage point which forms part of the border with the Czech Republic, and which has a pleasant chalet-type **hostel** near the summit, the *Schronisko na Stożku*.

Istebna and Jaworzynka

The road south from Wisła heads up into some attractive highland terrain, with the traditional village architecture of settlements like Istebna and Jaworzynka (each of which is served by about twelve buses a day, fewer at weekends) offering an agreeable antidote to the comparative greyness of Wisła. Once beyond Wisła's southern outskirts the road winds steeply through the forested spurs of the Beskid mountains, after about 8km reaching the **Kubalonka pass** (Przełęcz Kubalonka), a popular starting point for ridge-top walks. The most popular itineraries for hikers are the well-signposted red-marked route heading east to the 1021m peak of Przysłop (1021), with the Barania Góra (1220m) just beyond; or in the other direction to Stożek (see above). The *Zajazd u Mihola*, just beyond the pass's summit, is a popular **food**-and-**drink** stop with a panoramic terrace out the back. On the south side of the pass, the roadside **Kościół św. Krzyża** (Church of the Holy Cross) is a wonderful example of local building techniques, with heavy pine logs supporting a delicately shingled roof and cluster of plump domes. Three kilometres beyond lies **ISTEBNA** (ⓦwww.ug.istebna .pl), a sleepy village spread over a sequence of pasture-filled bowls. Just east of the village centre on the Koniaków road, the timber-built **Izba Regionalna** (Regional Dwelling; enquire at the house opposite to gain admission) at Istebna

824 contains original nineteenth-century interiors and a fascinating collection of flutes, bagpipes and other instruments made by local craftsmen. Back on the main road, the *Szarotka* **hotel**, Istebna 467 (☎033/855 6018; ❹–❺), is a convenient touring base for this part of the Beskids, with comfy en-suite doubles, studio apartments and bike hire for guests.

Five kilometres south of Istebna lies **JAWORZYNKA**, a ridge-top village boasting a shop, a couple of cafés and wonderful views of pine-clad hills on either side. Lurking beside the main road, the **Muzeum na Grapie** (allegedly Mon–Sat 10am–4pm, although you might have to wait around for the curator), harbours an absorbing display of local lace, embroidery and carved wooden toys. If Jaworzynka's end-of-the road location appeals, then the *Hotel Jano* just southeast of the village in the hamlet of Kręželka (☎033/855 6320, ⓦwww .hoteljano.pl; ❺) offers chintzy rooms, on-site gym and children's play-area – all in mixed meadow and woodland surrounds. Three kilometres beyond Jaworzynka lies the Czech border, although nearest road crossing is 10km east at Mito/Zwardoń.

Cieszyn

Straddling the Czech frontier 35km west of Bielsko-Biała, the divided town of **CIESZYN** escaped wartime ruin, surviving to become the most attractive small town that Silesia has to offer. With three daily trains to Prague from the Czech side of town, it's an obvious stop-off for those heading towards the Czech Republic. Ancient Cieszyn, established nearly twelve centuries ago, was claimed by both Czechoslovakia and Poland following the break-up of the Habsburg Empire after World War I. In 1920 the Conference of Ambassadors decided on using the River Olza as the new frontier, making the eastern part of the town Polish and the opposite side (known as Český Těšín) Czech. Ignoring the fact that people of mixed ethnicity were living all over town, no attempt was made to rationalize the nationality problem and, until recently, estranged nationals could only visit their former homeland with special passes. The exception was All Saints' Day, when the border was thrown open. Nowadays the frontier at the town centre bridge flows freely in both directions.

Arrival and information

Cieszyn's **bus** and **train stations** are on the eastern side of the town centre, about ten minutes' walk downhill from the Rynek, where the well-organized **tourist office** (Miejskie Centrum Informacji; Mon 10am–6pm, Tues–Sat 8am–6pm; ☎033/852 3050, ⓦwww.um.cieszyn.pl), Rynek 1, will provide you with pretty much everything you need to know about the town. The PTTK office at Głęboka 56 (Mon–Fri 9am–3pm) sells an adequate selection of local maps.

Accommodation

There's a reasonable range of hotel accommodation in town, and an attractively situated **campsite**, the *Olza*, a 25-minute walk south of the centre at al. Łyska 13 (☎033/852 0833), beside the river Olza, and with plenty of woodland walks on the doorstep.

Akademikus ul. Paderewskiego 6 ☎033/854 6139, ⓦwww.filus.edu.pl. Student hostel-cum-hotel attached to the Silesian University campus 1km east of the bus and train stations. Simply decorated rooms with shower and TV. ❸
Dworek Cieszyński ul. Przykopa 14 ☎033/855

8401. A handful of cosy rooms above the restaurant of the same name, just below the town centre and near the riverbank. ❹
Fundacja ul. Moniuszki 4 ☎033/852 0443, ⓦwww.fundacja-hotele.com.pl. Conference centre offering sparsely furnished but agreeable rooms

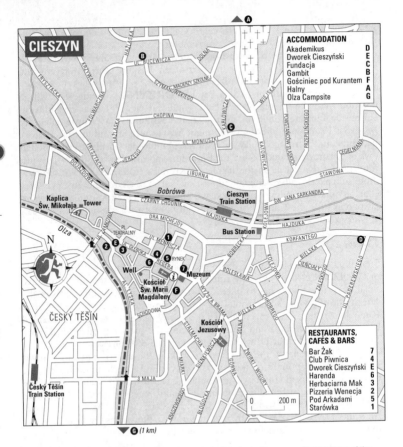

CIESZYN

ACCOMMODATION

Akademikus	D
Dworek Cieszyński	E
Fundacja	C
Gambit	B
Gościniec pod Kurantem	F
Halny	A
Olza Campsite	G

RESTAURANTS, CAFES & BARS

Bar Żak	7
Club Piwnica	4
Dworek Cieszyński	E
Harenda	6
Herbaciarna Mak	3
Pizzeria Wenecja	2
Pod Arkadami	5
Starówka	1

0   200 m

G (1 km)

(some with shared facilities, others with en-suite shower) ten minutes' north of the train and bus stations. There's no café-restaurant on site so you'll have to make your own plans for breakfast. ②–③
Gambit ul. Bucewicza 18 ℡033/852 0651, ⓦwww.hotelgambit.com.pl. Concrete lump a fifteen-minute walk north of the stations which is actually quite nice once you get inside. Simply

furnished en suites, some with nice views of the surrounding hills. ③
Gościniec pod Kurantem ul. Srebrna 7 ℡033/851 8522. A cosy guesthouse in an alley-way off the Rynek. ④
Halny ul. Motelowa 21 ℡033/852 0451. Soulless but habitable motel 2km north of town, near a main-road crossing point into the Czech Republic. ⑥

The Town

Cieszyn's central **Rynek**, with the eighteenth-century town hall, stands at the highest point of the central area. Just off the southwest corner of the square is the Gothic **Kościół św. Marii Magdaleny** (Church of St Mary Magdalene), containing a mausoleum of yet more Piast dukes who established an independent principality here in 1290. Heading east from the Rynek along Regera brings you to a handsome eighteenth-century mansion, former residence of the Princes of Cieszyn and now home to the **Muzeum Śląska Cieszyńskiego** (Museum of the Cieszyn Region; ⓦwww.muzeum-cieszyn.ox.pl; Tues–Sun 10am–2.30pm; 6zł). Inside lies an attractively laid-out assemblage of art and furniture through the ages, and one room devoted to the museum's nineteenth-century founder,

Jesuit priest Jan Leopold Szersznik, whose collection – including everything from Japanese clogs to mammoth's teeth – is laid out in the cabinet-of-curiosities style in which he left it. Among the lovingly restored period interiors are a ballroom decorated with arcadian landscape paintings and plaster cherubs riding on goat-back; and a richly decorated stable built by horse-mad aristocrat Filip Saint-Genois d'Anneaucourt (who bought the mansion in 1831) and which now serves as the museum café.

Running west from the Rynek, Cieszyn's main street, ul. Głęboka, sweeps downhill from the Rynek towards the river, passing a sequence of imposing mansions on the way. If you take ul. Sejmowa to the left and then the first turning right, you'll find yourself on ul. Trzech Braci ("Street of the Three Brothers"). Here stands the **well** associated with the legend of the town's foundation. In the year 810, the three sons of King Leszko III met at this spring after a long spell wandering the country. They were so delighted to see each other again that they founded a town named "I'm happy" (*cieszym się*). From the foot of ul. Głęboka, it's only a few paces along ul. Zamkowa to the Most Przyjazni, the **frontier post** for the crossing over to the Czech part of town, although most cars use the viaduct to the north for speedier transit avoiding the town centre. The pedestrian crossing from the Czech Republic back to Poland is about 700m upstream across Most Wolności.

On the west side of ul. Zamkowa rises a hill crowned by a fourteenth-century Gothic **tower** (daily: April–Oct 9.30am–5pm; Nov–March 9.30am–3pm), the only surviving part of the Piast palace. From the top, there's a superb view over both sides of the town and the Beskidy beyond. Alongside stands one of the oldest surviving buildings in Silesia, the **Kaplica św. Mikołaja** (Chapel of St Nicholas), a handsome Romanesque rotunda dating back to the eleventh century, with the vestiges of a contemporaneous well in front of it. Also on the hill are a Neoclassical hunting palace and a "ruined" Romantic folly among the trees. Other than that, idle ambling might lead you to the Baroque-towered Protestant **Kościół Jezusowy** (Church of Jesus), visible on the hill just east of the centre. Inside, its statues of the four Evangelists crowd over the altar and liven up the otherwise plain interior.

Eating and drinking

There are plenty of **places to eat** on and around the main square: *Bar Żak*, Rynek 20, doles out inexpensive pizzas and milk-bar-style dishes; while *Harenda*, ul. Głęboka 7, serves up cheap and tasty Polish staples in a faux-village-hut environment. Downhill towards the frontier crossing, **Dworek Cieszyński**, ul. Przykopa 14, is probably the best place to tuck into traditional meat and fish dishes in a suite of comfortable dining rooms. The nearby *Pizzeria Wenecja*, ul. Przykopa 6, is the place to go for a functional feed, and has the additional attraction of a big outdoor terrace near the river.

Among the **cafés**, *Pod Arkadami*, Rynek 4, serves up some of the best ice cream and is the perfect spot for grossing out on cakes; *Herbaciarna Mak*, ul. Głęboka 31, is a cosy refuge in which to sip speciality teas in refined surroundings; *Starówka*, ul. Mennicza 20, is an attractive cellar bar; while *Club Piwnica*, underneath the *Targowa* restaurant at Stary Targ 1, occasionally hosts live jazz.

Opole

If you're planning to spend a fair amount of time in Silesia, chances are you'll end up in **OPOLE** sooner or later. Situated in the very heart of the province, midway along the main train and road routes linking Katowice and Wrocław, it's also within easy reach of the Kłodzko region (see p.553) in Southern Silesia. Though ravaged by scores of fires throughout its history, the centre presents a well-balanced spread of old and new, ringed by a green belt and with the unsightly industrial installations banished to the outskirts.

One of Opole's main assets is its setting on the banks of the Odra. The river divides to form an island, the **Wyspa Piaseka**, which was inhabited in the ninth century by a Slavic tribe called the Opolanes. Bolesław the Brave established the island as a fortress, but it subsequently became divorced from its mother country, serving as the capital of a Piast principality from 1202 until this particular line died out in 1532.

The city and the highly productive agricultural land around were understand-ably coveted by the Polish state after World War I, but Opole voted to remain part of Germany in the plebiscite of 1921, subsequently becoming the capital of the German province of Upper Silesia. In contrast to most other places ceded to Poland after World War II, the Opole region has retained a sizeable German minority, an asset that can be admitted now that **Germany** has surrendered its territorial claims to this area.

The City

The hub of Opole has long moved from the Wyspa Piaseka to the right bank of the Odra, where the central area is laid out on a gridiron pattern. Nonethe-less, the island in many ways makes a chronologically correct place to begin an exploration.

The island

Of the four **bridges** crossing the arm of the river, look out for the second as you move northwards from the train station, one of several structures in Opole built around 1910 in Art Nouveau style. Arched like a bridge in a Japanese garden, this steel construction is known as the Most Groszowy (Groschen Bridge) after the fee that was initially charged for crossing it (the Groschen being the smallest coin then in circulation). It bears the curious coat of arms of the city, showing half an eagle and half a cross: the local Piasts allowed one side of the family's traditional blazon to be replaced by a symbol of the city's acquisition of a relic of the True Cross. Halfway across the bridge, take a glance in either direction; the thick lining of willow trees along the bank give an uncannily rural impression light years away from its urban location.

Originally occupying the middle of the island 400m north of the bridge, the medieval Piast **castle** certainly hasn't been done any favours by the city plan-ners, its surviving **round tower** now partly hidden behind ugly 1930s council offices that were built over the ruins. In summer you can climb to the top of the tower for a view of the city. The castle's grounds have been converted into a park with a large artificial lake sporting fountains and an open-air amphithea-tre, the setting for the **Festival of Polish Song** – the Polish pop industry's most important annual showcase – held each June. Continuing north along ul. Piastowska, you get a good view of the Stare Miasto on the opposite bank, lined with a jumble of riverside buildings.

The city centre

Returning across the Odra by ul. Zamkowa, you soon arrive at the Franciscan **church**, a much-altered Gothic construction chiefly remarkable for the richly decorated Chapel of St Anne, erected in 1309, off the southern side of the nave.

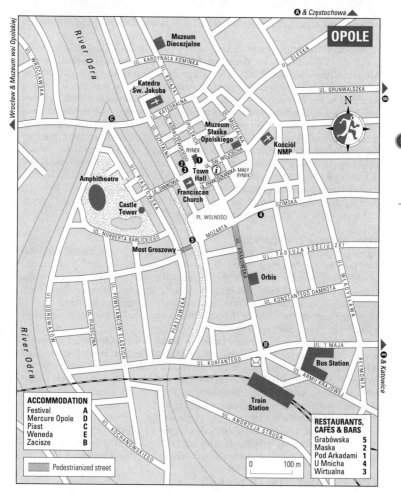

Endowed by the local Piasts to serve as their **mausoleum**, it has an exquisite star vault including keystones of the family eagle and painted with floral and heraldic motifs. The two magnificent double tombs were carved around 1380 by a member of the celebrated Parler family. Although he was still alive, an effigy of Duke Bolko III was made to accompany that of his recently deceased wife, with a similar monument created in belated memory of his two ancestral name-sakes. The retable is from a century later, and shows Bolko I offering a model of this monastery to St Anne and the Virgin, while Ladislaus II presents her with a model of the great church of Jasna Góra in Częstochowa.

Immediately beyond the Franciscan monastery is the buzzing **Rynek**, some of whose cheerful mansions were badly damaged in World War II, but which have been deftly restored. A **town hall** has stood on the square since 1308, but the fine tower you see today – a wonderful pastiche of the Palazzo Vecchio in Florence – originates from an early nineteenth-century neo-Renaissance design, being rebuilt true to form in the mid-1930s when it unexpectedly collapsed during repairs.

Housed in the former Jesuit College at ul. św.Wojciecha 13 just off the Rynek is the district museum, or **Muzeum Śląska Opolskiego** (Opole Regional Museum; Tues–Fri 9am–3.30pm, Sat 10am–3pm, Sun noon–5pm; 3zł), whose main strength is the archeology section, with exhibits from prehistoric to early medieval times. Also worth looking out for are some attractive tinted photographs from earlier this century showing the castle making way for the council offices, the town hall's tower reduced to a pile of rubble, and a chilling monochrome shot of Opole's synagogue ablaze on the Kristallnacht of 1938. Next to the museum, a broad stairway ascends to a hill where St Adalbert used to preach as bishop of Prague, Opole being part of his diocese. The **Kościół św. NMP** (Church of Our Lady), which now occupies the spot, was originally Gothic, though this is hardly apparent from the neo-Romanesque facade and Baroque interior decorations. Beyond are the tower of the fourteenth-century fortress and remains of the sixteenth-century town wall.

The cathedral quarter

From the Rynek, ul. Książąt Opolskich leads to the cathedral of **Katedra św. Jakuba** (St James's Cathedral), mixing fourteenth-century Gothic and nineteenth-century imitation with the usual Baroque excesses. Raised to the status of a cathedral only a couple of decades ago, the church, which soars with Gothic verticality, is chiefly famous for the allegedly miraculous, jewel-encrusted icon to the right of the main altar – the *Opole Madonna* crowned by a gaggle of gaily cavorting cherubs.

Occupying a block of modern buildings on ul. Książąt Opolskich (entrance round the corner on ul. Kardynała Kominka) is the **Muzeum Diecezjalne** (Diocesan Museum; Tues & Thurs 10am–noon & 2–5pm, first Sunday of the month 2–5pm; 3zł). On the ground floor are several outstanding Gothic sculptures, including an *Enthroned Madonna* in the Parler style. Upstairs, pride of place is taken by the fourteenth-century reliquary made to house Opole's fragment of the True Cross; there's also a lovely *Virgin and Child* attributed to Fra Filippo Lippi. The small room next door features gifts to adorn the *Opole Madonna* presented by worthies ranging from King Jan Sobieski to Pope John Paul II. Imaginative exhibitions of contemporary religious art are also featured.

The Muzeum Wsi Opolskiej

By the side of the main road to Wrocław, 8km west of the city centre at ul. Wrocławska 174, reached by bus #5 from the main bus station, is the excellent **Muzeum Wsi Opolskiej** (Village Museum; mid-April to mid-Oct: Tues–Sun 10am–6pm; rest of year: Mon–Fri 8am–2pm; 8zł). Some sixty examples of the wooden rural architecture of the region have been erected here, many grouped in simulation of their original environment. Particularly notable is the wooden church from Gręboszów built in 1613, a typical example of what is still the main place of worship in a few Silesian villages. Other highlights are a windmill and an eighteenth-century water mill in full working order, as well as an orchard full of beehives built in the same rustic idiom.

Practicalities

Opole's main **train** and **bus** stations are at the southern end of town close to the centre, just a few minutes along ul. Wojciecha Korfantego from the Wyspa Pasieka. It is perhaps the best-signposted town in Poland, telling you not only the names of streets but which hotels and sights lie along them. The **tourist office** at ul. Krakowska 15 (Mon–Fri 10am–6pm, Sat 10am–1pm; ☎077/451 1987, ✉promocja@um.opole.pl) will give you the low-down on local **accommodation** possibilities – although there's a shortage of budget-oriented places in town. Of the inexpensive places, the small and friendly *Zacisze*, just east of the historic quarters at Grunwaldzka 28 (☎077/453 9553, ⓌWwww.hotel-zacisze.opole.pl; ❹–❺), offers a mixture of simple decorated, smallish rooms with en-suite or shared facilities just east of the town centre; while the recently renovated *Festival*, 1km northeast of the Rynek at ul. Oleska 86 (☎077/455 6011, Ⓦwww.festival.com .pl; ❻), is already edging towards business standard. Plusher still are the *Weneda*, just east of the train and bus stations at ul. 1 Maja 77 (☎077/456 4499, Ⓦwww.hotel -weneda.opole.pl; ❻); the revamped *Mercure Opole*, conveniently located close to the train station at ul. Krakowska 59 (☎077/451 8100, ✉mer.opole@orbis.pl; ❻); and the *Piast*, ul. Piastowska 1 (☎077/454 9710, Ⓦwww.hotelpiast.com.pl; ❼), which has a pleasant terrace overlooking the river.

Opole has many excellent **restaurants**. *Wirtualna*, Rynek 2, handles a solid, well-prepared range of pork chops and steaks and has an excellent range of sweets; while *U Mnicha*, Ozimska 10, serves up a mixture of domestic and Middle Eastern grill dishes in a rough-hewn cellar done up with hi-tech fittings. The *Grabówska* creperie, next to Most Groszowy at ul. Mozarta 2, serves the best pancakes in Silesia.

In summer the Rynek is alive with people **drinking** into the early hours: try the excellent *Maska*, a lively pub-style venue at Rynek 4 which also does restaurant-quality food. *Pod Arkadami*, on the corner of the Rynek and Krakowska, is a comfy wicker-chair-furnished **café** with decent coffee and excellent cakes.

Góra Świętej Anny

Forty kilometres southeast of Opole, conspicuous on its 410-metre hill, is the village of **GÓRA ŚWIĘTEJ ANNY** (St Anne's Hill). Associated with the cult of St Anne, mother of the Virgin Mary, it's one of the most popular places of **pilgrimage** in Poland and is the scene of colourful processions on July 26 each year. Although the cult of St Anne is long established in Silesia, Góra Świętej Anny's status as a major pilgrimage shrine dates back only to the mid-seventeenth century, when a Franciscan **monastery** was built to replace a modest Gothic votive chapel. As is the case with Jasna Góra, its popularity is intimately associated with Polish nationalism, fanned by the fact that the monks have been expelled three times (as a result of the policies of Napoleon, Bismarck and Hitler). For five days in May 1921, the village was the scene of bitter fighting following the Upper Silesia plebiscite, which left it in German hands. Ill-feeling has persisted: it was only in 1989 that the outlawing of Masses in German, introduced when the monks returned in 1945 in retaliation for previous bans on Polish services, was rescinded.

The church, decorated in a restrained Baroque style, houses the source of the pilgrimage, a tiny miraculous statue of St Anne with the Virgin and Child, high above the main altar. An unassuming piece of folksy Gothic carving, it's usually decked out in gorgeous clothes. Below the monastery buildings is the mid-eighteenth century **Calvary**, an elaborate processional way with 33 chapels and shrines telling the story of the Passion. A large and less tasteful **Lourdes grotto** was added as the centrepiece in 1912.

Outside major church festivals, however, it's a moribund little place, the antithesis of the relentlessly busy Jasna Góra and not really worth the detour unless you've your own transport. Getting here by public transport is a long-winded process best done by taking a train from Opole to industrialized Zdzieszowice (on the line to Kędzierzyn-Koźle) and then covering the remaining 6km on foot or by bus. The pleasantly rustic *Alba* **restaurant** on Góra Świętej Anny's village square will sort you out with cheap and filling local food. Should you need to stay, there's a **youth hostel** at ul. Szkolna 1 (☎077/461 5484), and the *Pod Chełmską Górą* **hotel** and restaurant, half a kilometre southeast of town at ul. Leśnicka 26a (☎077/461 5484; ❸).

Lower Silesia

Despite a scattering of semi-industrial towns, **Lower Silesia** is predominantly rural, with agriculturally rich flatlands characterizing the north of the region, and the wooded heights of the Sudeten mountains rippling across its southern margins. **Wrocław**, one of Poland's most attractive cities after Kraków and Gdańsk, is undoubtedly the star attraction here, although provincial towns like **Świdnica** and **Jelenia Góra** have much to offer in the way of historical charm. Most of the other urban centres – **Legnica**, **Trzebnica** and **Brzeg** to name but three – were damaged in World War II and, postwar reconstruction notwithstanding, are places in which to seek out the odd historical curiosity rather than consider a lengthy holiday. More relaxing by far are the mountain resorts further south, with **Karpacz** and **Szklarska Poręba** serving as the main skiing and hiking centres in the Karkonosze range to the southwest, and the quaint spa towns of the **Kłodzko region** soaking up the tourists in the southeast.

Wrocław

Lower Silesia's historic capital, **WROCŁAW** is the fourth-largest city in Poland with a population of 664,000. There's an exhilarating big city feel to it, yet behind this animated appearance lies an extraordinary story of ruin and regeneration. Its special nature comes from the fact that it contains the souls of two great cities. One of these is the city that has long stood on this spot, Slav by origin but for centuries German (who knew it as Breslau). The other is Lwów (now **L'viv**), capital of the Polish Ukraine, which was annexed by the Soviets in 1939 and retained by them in 1945. After the war, its displaced population was encouraged to take over the severely depopulated Breslau, which had been confiscated from Germany and offered them a ready-made home.

Part re-creation of Lwów, part continuation of the tradition of Breslau, postwar Wrocław has a predominantly industrial character. However, there's ample compensation for this in the old city's core. The multinational influences which shaped it are graphically reflected in its architecture: the huge Germanic brick **Gothic churches** that dominate the Stare Miasto are intermingled with Flemish-style Renaissance mansions, palaces and chapels of Viennese Baroque, and boldly utilitarian public buildings from the early years of the twentieth century. The tranquillity of the parks, gardens and rivers – which are crossed by over one hundred **bridges** – offers a ready escape from the urban bustle, while the city has a vibrant cultural scene, its **theatre** tradition enjoying worldwide renown.

Some history

The origins of Wrocław are unknown. There may well have been a community here in Roman times, but the earliest documentary evidence is a ninth-century record of a Slav market town called **Wratislavia** situated on a large island at the point where the sand-banked shallows of the River Odra were easily crossed. Subsequently, this became known as **Ostrów Tumski** (Cathedral Island) in honour of the bishopric founded here in 1000 by Bolesław the Brave.

German designs on Wratislavia came to the fore in 1109, when the army of Emperor Henry V was seen off by Bolesław the Wrymouth. The site of the battlefield became known as **Psie Pole** (Dogs' Field), which today is one of the city's five administrative districts; the name supposedly arose because the Germans retreated in such chaos that they could not retrieve their dead, leaving the carcasses to the local canine population.

This proved to be only a temporary setback to German ambitions. Immediately after the creation of the duchy of Lower Silesia on the death of Bolesław the Wrymouth in 1138, German settlers were encouraged to develop a new town on the southern bank of the river. Destroyed by the Tatars in 1241, this was soon rebuilt on the grid pattern which survives to the present day. In 1259 the city, now known as **Breslau**, became the capital of an independent duchy. It joined the Hanseatic League, and its bishop became a prince of the Holy Roman Empire of Germany, ruling over a territory centred on Nysa.

The duchy lasted only until 1335, when Breslau was annexed by the **Bohemian kings**, who had sufficient clout to rebuff Kazimierz the Great's attempts to reunite it with Poland. During the two centuries of Bohemian rule the mixed population of Germans, Poles and Czechs lived in apparent harmony, and the city carried out the construction of its huge brick churches. Most of these were transferred to Protestant use at the Reformation, which managed to take root even though the Bohemian crown passed in 1526 to the staunchly Catholic **Austrian Habsburgs**. However, Breslau paid heavily for the duality of its religious make-up during the Thirty Years' War, when its economy was devastated and its population halved.

The years of Austrian rule saw Breslau become increasingly Germanized, a process accelerated when it finally fell to Frederick the Great's **Prussia** in 1763. It became Prussia's most important city after Berlin, gaining a reputation as one of the most loyal linchpins of the state during the Napoleonic wars, when the French twice occupied it, only to be driven out. In the nineteenth century it grew enormously with the Industrial Revolution, becoming one of the largest cities of the German nation.

After World War I, Breslau's **Polish community** held a series of strikes in protest at their exclusion from the plebiscite held elsewhere in Silesia to determine the boundaries of Poland. Being only twenty thousand strong and outnumbered by thirty to one, their actions made little impact. Nor did Breslau figure among the targets of Polish leaders when looking for possible gains at the expense of a defeated Nazi Germany. In the event, they gained it by default. The Nazis made the suicidal decision, on retreating from the Eastern front, to turn the entire city into a fortress. It managed to hold out for four months against the Red Army, only capitulating on May 6, the day before the unconditional surrender. However, street fighting had left seventy percent of the city in ruins, with three-quarters of the civilian population having fled west.

The subsequent **return to Poland** of this huge city, rechristened with the modern Polish version of its original name, shocked the Germans more than

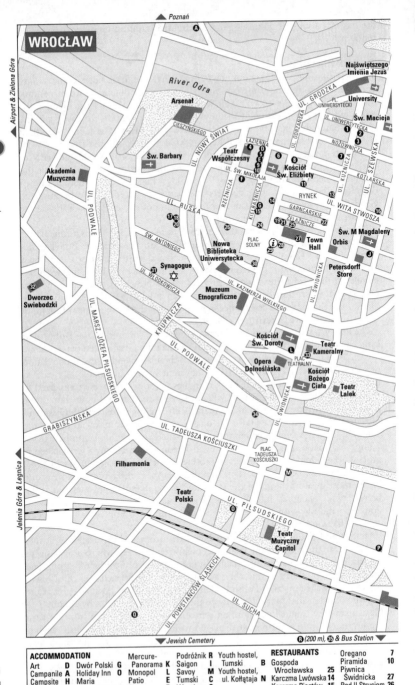

WROCŁAW

Poznań

River Odra

Arsenał

Najświętszego Imienia Jezus

University

UL. GRODZKA

PL. UNIWERSYTECKI

UL. ODRZAŃSKA

Św. Macieja

UL. UNIWERSYTECKA

CIESZYŃSKIEGO ŚWIAT

UL. NOWY ŚWIAT

Św. Barbary

Teatr Współczesny

ŁAZIENNA

UL. ŚW. MIKOŁAJA

Kościół Św. Elżbiety

NOZOWNICZA

UL. SZEWSKA

UL. KUŹNICZA

KOTLARSKA

Akademia Muzyczna

UL. RUSKA

UL. PODWALE

RZEŹNICZA

KIEŁBAŚNICA

RYNEK

GARNCARSKIE

UL. WITA STWOSZA

ŚW. ANTONIEGO

GARNCARSKIE

ŻELAŹNICZE

Św. M Magdaleny

Orbis

Nowa Biblioteka Uniwersytecka

PLAC SOLNY

Town Hall

Petersdorff Store

KRUPNICZA

UL. WŁODKOWICZA

Synagogue

Dworzec Swiebodzki

UL. MARSZ. JÓZEFA PIŁSUDSKIEGO

Muzeum Etnograficzne

UL. KAZIMERZA WIELKIEGO

UL. ŚWIDNICKA

UL. PODWALE

Kościół Św. Doroty

Teatr Kameralny

Opera Dolnośląska

PLAC TEATRALNY

Kościół Bożego Ciała

Teatr Lalek

GRABISZYŃSKA

UL. ŚWIDNICKA

UL. TADEUSZA KOŚCIUSZKI

PLAC TADEUSZA KOŚCIUSZKI

Filharmonia

Teatr Polski

UL. PIŁSUDSKIEGO

Teatr Muzyczny Capitol

UL. POWSTAŃCÓW ŚLĄSKICH

UL. SUCHA

Jelenia Góra & Legnica

Airport & Zielona Góra

Jewish Cemetery

(200 m), & Bus Station

ACCOMMODATION						RESTAURANTS			
Art	D	Dwór Polski	G	Mercure-Panorama	K	Podróżnik	R	Youth hostel, Tumski	B	Gospoda		Oregano	7
Campanile	A	Holiday Inn	O	Monopol	L	Saigon	I	Youth hostel, ul. Kołłątaja	N	Wrocławska	25	Piramida	10
Campsite	H	Maria		Patio	E	Savoy	M			Karczma Lwówska	14	Piwnica Świdnicka	27
Dorint	F	Magdalena	J	Piast	P	Tumski	C	Wrocław	Q	Karczma Piastów	15	Pod II Strusiem	26

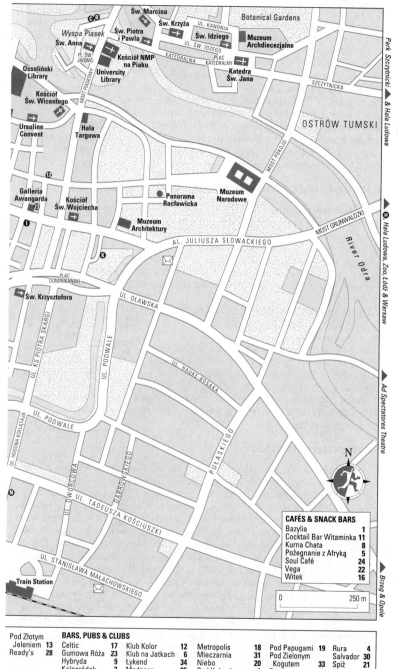

any other of their many territorial losses. Its second transformation occurred much faster than that of seven centuries earlier: over the next few years, most of the remaining German citizens were shunted westward, while the inhabitants of Lwów were transferred here across Poland, bringing many of their institutions with them.

A relatively modest amount of government aid was made available for the **restoration of the city**, much of which remained in ruins for decades. Nonetheless, a distinctive and thoroughly Polish city has gradually emerged, one whose revival finally seemed complete in the 1980s when its population level surpassed the prewar figure of 625,000. Wrocław's riverbank areas suffered serious damage in 1997, when disastrous **flooding** threatened much of south-western Poland and the Czech Republic, although the affected areas were speedily patched up, and you won't see much evidence of it today.

Arrival, information and getting around

The main **train station**, Wrocław Główny – a mock-Tudor structure that is itself one of the city's sights – faces the broad boulevard of ul. Piłsudskiego, about twenty minutes' walk south of the centre. The main **bus station** (Dworzec PKS) is on ul. Sucha, at the back of the train station. Wrocław's **airport**, which lies 10km to the west in the suburb of Strachowice, is linked to the centre by bus #406 (every 30min), which drops passengers off on ul. Podwale, near the Stare Miasto, before terminating on ul. Dworcowa just north of the train station.

The **tourist information** office at Rynek 14 (Mon–Fri 9am–8pm, Sat 10am–5pm; ☎071/344 3111, ⓦwww.wroclaw.pl) has maps and leaflets, and can advise on accommodation. Although updated less frequently than its sister publications in Warsaw and Kraków, *Wrocław in Your Pocket* (6zł; ⓦwww.inyourpocket.com), available from the tourist office and some hotels, is an indispensable guide to the city's restaurant and bar scene and includes the usual wealth of practical tips.

Trams and **buses** provide comprehensive coverage for the entire built up area of Wrocław. **Tickets** are bought in advance from newspaper kiosks and cost 2zł each; night services are 3zł.

Accommodation

Wrocław has **accommodation** to suit every taste and pocket, although the central hotels are increasingly charging Western prices, forcing budget travellers out towards the suburbs, or into the city's two hostels. There is no especially busy time of year, and most of the business-oriented hotels offer significant weekend reductions – be sure to ask when you phone. Avoid the (allegedly) three-star hotels near the train station like the *Europejski* and the *Polonia* – unless you delight in being overcharged for crummy communist-era accommodation.

The most central youth hostel is a couple of minutes' walk north of the main station at ul. Hugona Kołłątaja 20 (☎071/343 8856). It's a rather soulless place, offering mixed six-bed rooms or twenty-bed dorms for 30zł per person, but it's equipped with clean showers and toilets. However, there's a 10am–5pm lockout and a 10pm curfew. Much preferable is the new HI hostel occupying one wing of the *Hotel Tumski* (see opposite; ☎071/322 6099, ⓦwww.hotel-tumski.com.pl), which offers cramped but modern dorms for 35zł per person.

There's a **campsite** with chalets (❷) to rent on the east side of town near the Olympic Stadium at al. Paderewskiego 35 (May–Sept; ☎071/348 4651) – tram #17 (direction Sępolno) from the train station.

Around the train station

Holiday Inn ul. Piłsudskiego 49/57 ⊕071/787 0000, Ⓦ www.holiday-inn.com. The top business address in town, with the standards of comfort and service that you would expect at this price. Big weekend discounts. ❽

Piast ul. Piłsudskiego 98 ⊕071/343 0033, Ⓦ www.odratourist.pl. Conveniently situated opposite the train station, but be prepared for tired-looking musty rooms, and a certain amount of noise from the nearby main road and from other guests. Doubles with shared facilities as well as those with en-suite bathrooms. ❸–❹

Podróżnik ul. Sucha 1–11 ⊕071/373 2845. Simple no-frills place situated above the bus station's ticket hall, offering neat, if smallish, en suites. ❹

Savoy pl. Tadeusza Kościuszki 19 ⊕071/340 3219. Simple en-suite rooms located midway between the train station and the Stare Miasto. Fills up fast due to its attractive pricing, so ring in advance. ❹

Wrocław ul. Powstańców Śląskich 7 ⊕071/361 4651, Ⓦ www.orbis.pl. The most prestigious of the Orbis group of hotels in town, located a short distance southwest of the main train station. Rooms are up to international business standard, with air conditioning, minibar and satellite TV. Surrounded by residential blocks, the location is hardly picturesque, but at least you get an indoor swimming pool on site. ❼

The Stare Miasto

Art ul. Kiełbaśnicza 20 ⊕071/378 7100, Ⓦ www .arthotel.wroc.pl. Comfortable downtown hotel, offering roomy doubles with shower, TV and minibar. Probably deserves three stars rather than the four advertised (and despite the title there's not much art on display), but superbly situated nevertheless. ❻–❼

Dorint ul. św. Mikołaja 67 ⊕071/358 8300, Ⓦ www.dorint.com/wroclaw. Classy four-star hotel immediately west of the Rynek, offering fully equipped rooms decked out in calm-inducing colours. Sauna and gym on site. ❼

Dwór Polski ul. Kiełbaśnicza 2 ⊕071/372 3415, Ⓦ www.dworpolski.wroclaw.pl. Small and classy establishment offering quality service and twenty well-equipped, atmospherically old-fashioned double rooms or suites. Previous guests said to include Sigismund III of Poland, who chose the place for romantic trysts with future wife Anne of Habsburg. ❼

Maria Magdalena ul. św. Marii Magdaleny 2 ⊕071/341 0898. Spanking new and rather plush hotel with attentive service and all the creature comforts, a stone's throw from the Rynek. ❽

Mercure-Panorama pl. Dominikański 1 ⊕071/323 2700, Ⓔ panorama@orbis.pl. Flashy glass-and-steel four-star, conveniently located on the eastern side of the Stare Miasto centre. A reasonable business-standard choice. ❽

Monopol ul. Modrzejewskiej 2 ⊕071/343 7041, Ⓔ monopol@orbis.pl. Least expensive of the city's Orbis hotels, a good-looking *fin-de-siècle* establishment with a wonderful atmosphere of faded grandeur. Rooms come with creaky parquet floors, a range of olde-worlde furnishings – and satellite TV. En suites as well as rooms with shared bathrooms. ❹–❻

Patio ul. Kiełbaśnicza 24/25 ⊕071/375 0400, Ⓦ www.hotelpatio.pl. Bright, fully equipped rooms in a modern building, not too far from the main Rynek. ❽

Saigon ul. Wita Stwosza 22/23 ⊕071/344 2881, Ⓦ www.hotelsaigon.pl. Good-value if slightly careworn establishment above the eponymous Vietnamese restaurant right in the centre of the Stare Miasto. Rooms are plain but habitable and come with shower, phone and TV. ❺

North of the centre

Campanile ul. Jagiełły 7 ⊕071/326 7800, Ⓦ www.campanile.com.pl. Set uninspiringly beside a road junction 1.5km northwest of the Stare Miasto, but otherwise a relaxing comfortable place with warm colour schemes and business-standard rooms. ❻

Tumski Wyspa Słodowa 10 ⊕071/322 6088, Ⓦ www.hotel-tumski.com.pl. Newish hotel just north of the town centre enjoying a quiet riverside location on Wyspa Piasek. Pastel-coloured rooms with shower and TV. ❻

The City

Wrocław's **central area**, laid out in the usual grid pattern, is delineated by the **River Odra** to the north and by the bow-shaped **ul. Podwale** to the south – the latter following the former fortifications whose defensive moat, now bordered by a shady park, still largely survives. The main concentration of shops and places of entertainment is found at the southern end of the centre and in the streets leading south to the train station. Immediately bordering the Odra at the northern fringe of the centre is the **university quarter**. Beyond are a number of peaceful traffic-free islets, formerly sandbanks where the shallow river was once forded, and now linked to each other and to the mainland by graceful little bridges which add a great deal to the city's appeal. The southern part of the much larger island of **Ostrów Tumski**, further east, is the city's ecclesiastical heart, with half a dozen churches and its own distinctive hubbub. Further north is an area of solidly nineteenth-century tenements, while the city's main green belt lies off the eastern side of the island.

The Rynek

Fittingly, the core of the Stare Miasto's grid is occupied by the vast space of the **Rynek**, surrounded by grandly renovated town houses. Its centre taken up by the superb edifice of the **town hall**, and an accompanying ensemble of municipal buildings divided up by lateral passageways. No longer a place of commerce, the Rynek is now a leisure-oriented zone, given over mainly to restaurants, alfresco cafés, bookshops and, a telling new development, antique shops.

Of the mansions lining the main sides of the Rynek, those on the south and western sides are the most distinguished and colourful. Among several built in the self-confident style of the Flemish Renaissance, no. 2, the **Pod Gryfami** (Griffin House), is particularly notable. Number 5, with a reserved Mannerist facade, is known as the **Dwór Wazów** (Waza Court), in honour of the tradition that it was the place where King Zygmunt Waza stayed during secret negotiations for his marriage to Anna von Habsburg.

Next door, at no. 6, is the **Pod Złotym Słońcem** (House of the Golden Sun), behind whose Baroque frontage is a suite of Renaissance rooms containing the **Muzeum Sztuki Medalierskiej** (Museum of the Art of Medal Making; Wed & Fri 10am–5pm, Thurs & Sat 11am–5pm, Sun 10am–6pm; 7zł); its shop sells examples of the craft. The last striking house in the block is no. 8, again Baroque but preserving parts of its thirteenth-century predecessor; it's known as the **Pod Siedmioma Elektorami** (House of the Seven Electors), a reference to the seven grandees superbly depicted on the facade who elected the Holy Roman emperor, Leopold I. A black Habsburg eagle cowers menacingly over the building's doorway.

The town hall

The magnificent **town hall**, symbol of the city for the last seven centuries, was originally a modest one-storey structure erected in the wake of the ruinous Tatar sacking and progressively expanded down the years. Its present appearance dates largely from the fifteenth-century high point of local prosperity, when the south aisle was added and the whole decorated in an elaborate late-Gothic style. The international mix of stylistic influences reflects the city's status as a major European trading centre, creating one of the city's finest and most venerable buildings.

The **east facade** is the one which catches the eye and figures in all Wrocław's promotion material. It features an astronomical clock from 1580 and an elaborate central gable decorated with intricate terracotta patterns and exquisite pinnacles. In contrast, the west facade (the main entrance) is relatively plain, save for the octagonal Gothic belfry with its tapering Renaissance lantern. The intricate carvings embellishing the **south facade** are worthy of more protracted scrutiny, lined up between the huge Renaissance windows crowned with their spire-like roofs. Along its length are filigree friezes of animals and foliage as well as effigies of saints and knights, mostly nineteenth-century pastiches, overshadowed by an old crone and a yokel.

Relieved of its municipal duties by the adjoining nineteenth-century offices, the town hall now serves as the city museum, or **Muzeum Miejskie** (entrance from the western side; Wed–Sat 11am–5pm, Sun 10am–6pm; ⓦ www.muzeum .miejskie.wroclaw.pl; 7zł). It's largely given over to themed, seasonal exhibitions rather than a permanent display, although the chance to see the largely unaltered interior provides sufficient reason to visit.

The kernel of the town hall, dating back to the 1270s, is the twin-aisled **Hala Mieszczańska** (Burghers' Hall) on the ground floor. Not only the venue for important public meetings and receptions, the hall also did service throughout the week as a covered market, functioning as such for 450 years. A tasteless nineteenth-century marble staircase decorated with an illuminating 1927 reproduction map of the fifteenth-century island town of "Breslau" leads upstairs to the resplendent three-aisled **Sala Wielka** (Great Hall), its vaulted ceiling studded with bosses depicting all kinds of real and imaginary creatures. Even more richly decorated is the coffer-ceilinged oriel window, which gives a Renaissance flourish to the otherwise Gothic character.

At the far end of the hall are two stone portals, the one on the right (usually closed) adorned with hairy wild men. The left doorway gives access to the **Princes' Room**, a pure example of fourteenth-century Gothic with a vault resting on a single central pillar. It was originally built as a chapel, but takes its name from its later use as a meeting place for the rulers of Silesia's principalities.

West of the Rynek

The southwest corner of the Rynek leads to a second, much smaller square, **plac Solny**. Its traditional function as a market has been recently revived, with the salt from which the market takes its name now replaced by flowers. The square itself is a minor sensory delight, girdled by restored nineteenth-century town houses painted in a range of vivacious colours.

Just off the northwest corner of the Rynek are two curious Baroque houses known as **Jaś i Małgosia**, (Hänsel and Gretel), linked by a gateway giving access to the **Kościół św. Elżbiety** (St Elizabeth's Church). Proving that brick need not be an inherently dull material, this is the most impressive of Wrocław's churches. Since the mid-fifteenth century its huge ninety-metre **tower**, under construction for 150 years, has been the city's most prominent landmark. Originally a lead-sheeted spire added another 36m to the steeple's height, but this overambitious pinnacle was blown down by storms a year after completion and never rebuilt. Ill fortune has continued to dog the church, which having been destroyed by a hailstorm in 1529 was burnt out under suspicious circumstances in 1976. Restoration work has now at last been completed, and the lofty, bright interior is well worth a peek.

Facing the inner ring road just west of here is the only other block of old **burghers' houses** surviving in the city. Across the road and down ul. Antoniego Cieszynskiego is the impressive red-brick **arsenal** at no. 9, originally sixteenth-century but considerably altered by the Prussians a couple of hundred years later. It now provides a rather splendid home to both the **Muzeum Militarów** (Military Museum; Tues–Sat 11am–5pm, Sun 10am–6pm; 7zł), which displays a bristling selection of medieval swords and pikes as well as uniforms throughout the ages, and the **Muzeum Archeologiczne** (Archeology Museum; Tues–Sat 11am–5pm, Sun 10am–6pm; 7zł), with a relatively undramatic, though well-presented, collection of finds from the stone age to medieval times. Highlights include a scale model of Ostrów Tumski as it looked in the twelfth century, and the weathered tombstone of a certain Kantor David – dating from 1203, it's thought to be the oldest Jewish tombstone in Poland.

Wrocław's former **Jewish quarter** was located around ul. Włodkowicza, a ten-minute walk south of the arsenal. The Neoclassical **synagogue** (known as the "White Stork Synagogue" due to the relief above the entrance), tucked away on a tiny square off the southern side of ul. Włodkowica, is currently the subject of intensive restoration work. Another poignant reminder of the Judaic heritage is the **Jewish cemetery** (daily 8am–6pm), 3km south of the city centre at ul. Ślężna 113, where many of the imposing family memorials have been restored by the Wrocław city museum authorities. To get there take tram #9 or #16 (direction Park Południowy) from the train station.

South of the Rynek

Immediately to the east of the Jewish quarter – and southwest to the Rynek – lies a part of the city built in obvious imitation of the chilly classical grandeur of the Prussian capital, Berlin. Indeed it was Carl Gotthard Langhans, designer of the Brandenburg Gate, who built the Neoclassical palace on the northern side of ul. Kazimierza Wielkiego, now the **Nowa Biblioteka Uniwersytecka** (New University Library). He also had a hand in the monumental **Pałac Królewski** (Royal Palace) on the opposite side of the street. The central block of this is now the **Muzeum Etnograficzne** (Ethnographic Museum; Tues–Sun 10am–4pm; 5zł), which has a large collection of dolls in traditional dresses from around the world – a good place to visit if you're with children.

Further east, along ul. Świdnicka, the royal flavour of this quarter continues in a different vein with the lofty Gothic church of **Kościół św. Doroty** (St Dorothy's Church), also known as the "Church of Reconciliation". This was founded in 1351 by Charles IV, king of Bohemia and the future Holy Roman emperor, in thanks for the conclusion of his negotiations with Kazimierz the Great, which secured Bohemia's rule over Silesia in return for a renunciation of its claim to Poland. Unlike most of Wrocław's other brick churches, this stayed in Catholic hands following the Reformation, becoming a Franciscan monastery. Its interior was whitewashed and littered with gigantic altars in the Baroque period, giving it a relatively opulent appearance in comparison to its neighbours, which still bear the hallmarks of four centuries of Protestant sobriety.

Behind St Dorothy's stands the **Opera Dolnośląska** (Lower Silesian Opera House), built by Carl Ferdinand Langhans in a faithful continuation of his father's Neoclassical style. Facing it is another example of fourteenth-century Gothic, **Kościół Bożego Ciała** (Corpus Christi), distinguished by the delicate brickwork of its facade, porch and gable, and by the elaborate interior vaulting.

East of the Rynek

The first building of note moving east of the Rynek is the former **Petersdorff store** at the junction of ul. Oławska and ul. Szewska, a classic of twentieth-century design built by German Expressionist architect Erich Mendelssohn in 1927. Still in use as a shopping centre, the concrete and glass building relies for its effect on the interplay between the bold horizontals of the main street fronts and the dramatically projecting cylinder on the corner.

The twin-towered **Kościół św. Marii Magdaleny** (St Mary Magdalene's Church), a block north of here, is another illustration of the seemingly inexhaustible diversity of Wrocław's brick churches: this fourteenth-century example is unusual in having flying buttresses, giving it a French feel. A bevy of funeral plaques and epitaphs from the fifteenth to eighteenth centuries lines its exterior, though the most striking adornment is the twelfth-century Romanesque sandstone **portal** on the south side. This masterpiece of Romanesque carving, dating from 1180, (and whose tympanum has been moved for conservation to the Muzeum Narodowe) came from the demolished abbey of Ołbin in the north of the city which was dissolved in 1546 to strengthen the city's defences. The church is also notable as being the site of the first Protestant sermon to be held in Wrocław in 1523 during the earliest days of the Reformation.

Moving due east from here along ul. Wita Stwosza soon leads to the **Galeria Awangarda** at no. 32 (ⓦ www.bwa.wroc.pl; Tues–Sun 11am–6pm; 8zł), Wrocław's leading contemporary art gallery, and a good place to catch high-profile exhibitions of Polish and international art. The building itself is worth a look, incorporating the surviving Neoclassical remnants of a bombed-out nineteenth-century town house into a modern, glass-and-steel pavilion. Beyond here ul. Wita Stwosza opens out onto the broad open space of **plac Dominikański**, at the northern end of which lie the buildings of the **Dominican monastery** centred on the thirteenth-century **Kościół św. Wojciecha** (St Adalbert's Church), which is embellished with a fine brickwork gable and several lavish Gothic and Baroque chapels. A couple of blocks east, the gargantuan former **Bernardine monastery** stands in splendid isolation; there's a particularly fine view of its barn-like church from the park beyond. The last important example of Gothic brickwork in the city, the monastery was begun in the mid-fifteenth century and finished only a few years before the Reformation, whereupon it was dissolved and the church used as a Protestant parish church. Severely damaged during the war, the church and cloisters have been painstakingly reconstructed to house the somewhat misleadingly named **Muzeum Architektury** (Museum of Architecture; Tues, Wed, Fri & Sat 10am–4pm, Thurs noon–6pm, Sun 11am–5pm; ⓦ www.ma.wroc.pl; 8zł). In fact, this is a fascinating documentary record, using sculptural fragments and old photos, of the many historic buildings in the city which perished in the war.

Panorama Racławicka

Wrocław's best-loved sight, the **Panorama Racławicka** (Panorama of the Battle of Racławice; May–Sept daily 9am–6pm; Oct–April Tues–Sun 9.30am–5.30pm; 20zł) is housed in a specially designed rotunda in the park by the Museum of Architecture. Looking like a gargantuan wicker basket rendered in concrete, the building contains a truly enormous painting, 120m long and 15m high, commissioned in 1894 to celebrate the centenary of the defeat of the Russian army by the people's militia of Tadeusz Kościuszko near the village of Racławice, between Kraków and Kielce. Ultimately this triumph was in vain: the third and final Partition of Poland, which wiped it off the map altogether, occurred the following year. Nonetheless, it was viewed a century later by patriots of the still subdued nation as a supreme example of national will and self-sacrifice, which deserved a fitting memorial.

For a few decades, panorama painting created a sensation throughout Europe and North America, only to die abruptly with the advent of the cinema. In purely artistic terms, most surviving examples are of poor quality, but this one is an exception, due largely to the participation of **Wojciech Kossak**, one of the most accomplished painters Poland has produced.

The subsequent **history of the painting** is a remarkable saga which mirrors the fate of Poland itself. Despite an attempt by Polish-Americans to buy it and have it shipped across the Atlantic, it was placed on public view in Lwów, which was then part of Austria – the only one of the Partitioning powers that would have tolerated such nationalist propaganda. It remained there until 1944, when it was substantially damaged by a bomb. Although allocated to Wrocław, as the cultural heir of Lwów, it was then put into storage – officially because there were no specialists to restore it and no money to build the structure the painting would need. The truth was that it was politically unacceptable to allow Poles to glory in their ancestors' slaughter of Russians.

That all changed with the events of 1980, when the rise of Solidarity forced the Polish authorities to place more emphasis on Polish patriotic traditions. Within five years the painting had been immaculately restored and was on display in a snazzy new building, with much attention being paid to a natural foreground of soil, stones and shrubs, which greatly adds to the uncanny appearance of depth. It's one of Poland's most popular tourist attractions, an icon second only in national affection to the Black Madonna of Jasna Góra (see box, p.460). Poles flock here in their droves, and during term-time there are regular school outings to see it. Visitors are admitted at thirty-minute intervals, and are supplied with headphones with English-language commentary and appropriate sound effects. Afterwards you can study the scale model of the battlefield downstairs at leisure.

The Muzeum Narodowe

At the opposite end of the park is the ponderously Prussian neo-Renaissance home of the **Muzeum Narodowe** (National Museum; Wed, Fri & Sun 10am–4pm, Thurs 9am–4pm, Sat 10am–6pm; ⓦ www.mnwr.art.pl; 15zł, free on Sat), which unites the collections of Breslau and Lwów. An important collection of medieval stone **sculpture**, housed on the ground floor, includes the delicately linear carving *The Dormition of the Virgin*, which formed the tympanum of the portal of Kościół św. Marii Magdaleny. The other major highlight is the poignant early fourteenth-century **tomb** of Henryk IV, the armour-clad effigy of the prince surrounded by a floor-level frieze of weeping mourners.

Upstairs lies an impressive display of medieval Silesian art, kicking off with a colossal set of late-fourteenth-century saintly statues from Kościół św. Marii Magdaleny, their raw power compensating for a lack of sophistication. Several rooms of fifteenth-century altarpieces follow, with the touchingly realistic Tryptich of the Holy Virgins (made by a local artist in 1495) being one obvious high point. One of the star pieces in the comprehensive collection of **Polish paintings** on the top floor is the amazingly detailed *Entry of Chancellor Jerzy Ossolinski into Rome in 1633* by an anonymous eighteenth-century artist. The other leading exhibit here is an unfinished blockbuster by Matejko, *Vows of King Jan Kazimierz Waza*. Set in Lwów Cathedral, it illustrates the monarch's pledge to improve the lot of the peasants at the end of the war against his invading Swedish kinsmen. Other works to look out for are Piotr Michałowski's *Napoleon on Horseback*, the *Fatherland Triptych* by Jacek Malczewski and some mountainscapes by Wojciech Gerson. A number of galleries are devoted to contemporary **arts and crafts**, much of it surprisingly daring for work executed under communist rule. Władysław Hasior (see p.488) is well represented with a clutch of his often facile, often disturbing, installations from the late Sixties, and there's an impressive contingent of larger-than-life male figures, looking something like a Chinese emperor's terracotta army, courtesy of Magdalena Abakanowicz, Poland's best-known living sculptor.

The university quarter

Wrocław's academic quarter can be reached in just a few minutes from the Rynek by way of ul. Kuźnicza, but the most atmospheric approach is to walk there from the Muzeum Narodowe along the south bank of the Odra, for a series of delightful **views** of the ecclesiastical quarter opposite.

Overlooking the Piaskowski Bridge is the **Hala Targowa** (Market Hall), a preformed concrete update of the brick church idiom built in 1908, it is piled high most days with irresistible food and other commodities. From this point, the triangular-shaped university quarter, jam-packed with historic buildings, is clearly defined by two streets, ul. Uniwersytecka to the south and ul. Grodzka, which follows the Odra.

Along the northern side of the former are three religious houses. First is **Kościół św. Wincentego** (St Vincent's Church), founded as a Franciscan monastery by Henryk the Pious not long before his death at the Battle of Legnica (see p.549). One of the grandest of the city's churches, it was severely damaged in the war and rebuilt in 1991. Inside, several altarpieces by the renowned Silesian artist, Michael Willmann, have been returned to their former glory, while its Baroque monastic buildings overlooking the Odra are now used by the university. Henryk also founded the **Ursuline convent** alongside, which served as the mausoleum of the Piasts, who ruled the city during its period as an independent duchy.

Last in the row is the fourteenth-century **Kościół św. Macieja** (St Matthew's Church), containing the tomb and memorial portrait of the city's most famous literary figure, the seventeenth-century mystic poet Johann Scheffler – better known as **Angelus Silesius** ("the Silesian Angel"), the pseudonym he somewhat immodestly adopted after his conversion to Catholicism. Facing the south side of the church is the Renaissance Palace of the Piasts of Opole, while across ul. Szewska is the Baroque residence of their cousins from Brzeg-Legnica; both are now used by the university.

Behind St Matthew's stands one of Wrocław's most distinguished buildings, the domed **Ossoliński** library. Originally a hospital, it was erected in the last quarter of the seventeenth century and designed by the Burgundian architect Jean Baptiste Mathey. The library collections are another legacy from Lwów, where they were assembled by the family whose name they still bear. Among the many precious manuscripts is the original of the Polish national epic, Mickiewicz's *Pan Tadeusz*. However, you will only be able to see it during special exhibitions; the rest of the time the library is closed to visitors. The elongated pl. Uniwersytecki begins on the southern side with a dignified eighteenth-century palace, **Dom Steffensa**, again owned by the university. Facing it is one of the most obviously Austrian features of the city, the **Kościół Najświętszego Imienia Jezus** (Church of the Blessed Name of Jesus), built in the Jesuit style at the end of the seventeenth century, one of the rash of Counter-Reformation religious buildings in the Habsburg lands. Its most arresting feature is the huge allegorical ceiling fresco by the most celebrated Austrian decorative painter of the day, Johann Michael Rottmayr.

Adjoining the church is the 171-metre-long facade of the Collegium Maximum of the **university**, founded in 1702 by Emperor Leopold I. The wide entrance portal bears a balcony adorned with statues symbolizing various academic disciplines and attributes; more can be seen high above on the graceful little tower.

A frescoed staircase leads up to the main assembly hall or **Aula Leopoldina** (daily except Wed 10am–3.30pm; 4.50zł). The only historic room which remains in the huge building, it's one of the greatest secular interiors of the Baroque age, fusing the elements of architecture, painting, sculpture and ornament into one bravura whole. Lording it from above the dais is a statue of the founder, armed, bejewelled and crowned with a laurel. The huge illusionistic **ceiling frescoes** by Christoph Handke show the Apotheosis of Divine and Worldly Wisdom above the gallery and auditorium, while the scene above the dais depicts the university being entrusted to the care of Christ and the Virgin Mary. On the wall spaces between the windows are richly framed oval portraits of the leading founders of the university, while the jambs are frescoed with trompe l'oeil likenesses of the great scholars of classical antiquity and the Middle Ages.

Wyspa Piasek, Ostrów Tumski and beyond

From the Market Hall, the Piaskowski Bridge leads you out to the sandbank of **Wyspa Piasek**, with a cluster of historic buildings crammed together in the centre. The first you come to on the right-hand side is the **university library**, installed in an Augustinian monastery which was used as the Nazi military headquarters. Beside it is the fourteenth-century **Kościół NMP na Piasku** (Church of St Mary on the Sands), dull on the outside, majestically vaulted inside. The aisles have an asymmetrical tripartite rib design known as the Piast vault, which is peculiar to this region. In the south aisle is the Romanesque tympanum from the previous church on the site, illustrating the dedication by its donor, Maria Włast.

Ostrów Tumski

The two elegant little painted bridges of Most Młynski and Most Tumski connect Wyspa Piasek with **Ostrów Tumski**. For those not already sated by medieval churches, there's a concentration of five more here, beginning just beyond Most Tumski with the fifteenth-century **Kościół św. Piotra i Pawła** (Church of SS Peter and Paul), behind which is the squat hexagonal **Kościół św. Marcina** (St Martin's Church) of a couple of centuries earlier.

Far more prepossessing than these is the imperious **Kościół św. Krzyża** (Holy Cross Church), which, with its massive bulk, giant buttresses and pair of dissimilar towers, looks like some great fortified monastery of definitive Silesian Gothic. In fact, it's really two churches, one on top of the other. The lower, originally dedicated to St Bartholomew, is more spacious and extensive than an ordinary crypt, but lacks the exhilarating loftiness of its partner upstairs. The complex was founded in 1288 by Duke Henryk the Righteous as his own mausoleum, but his tomb has now been removed to the Muzeum Narodowe. A highly elaborate Baroque monument to **św. Jan Nepomuk** stands in the square outside; his life is illustrated in the column bas-reliefs.

Ulica Katedralna leads past several Baroque palaces (among which priests, monks and nuns are constantly scuttling) to the slender twin-towered **Katedra św. Jana** (Cathedral of St John). A wall mural on the right-hand side of the street, featuring the papal arms, marks the visit of Pope John Paul II to the city in 1997. Grievously damaged in 1945, the cathedral has been fully restored to its thirteenth-century form – it was Poland's first cathedral built in the Gothic style, completed in 1272. The one exterior feature of note is the elaborate **porch**, though its sculptures, with the exception of two delicate reliefs, are mostly replicas from the last century. Three chapels behind the high altar make a visit to the dank and gloomy interior worthwhile, reminiscent of the relatively unadorned English equivalents from the same era. On the southern side, **St Elizabeth's chapel** dates from the last two decades of the seventeenth century, its integrated architecture, frescoes and sculptures created by Italian followers of Bernini. Next comes the Gothic **lady chapel**, with the masterly Renaissance funerary plaque of Bishop Jan Roth by Peter Vischer of Nuremberg. Last in line is the **Corpus Christi chapel**, a perfectly proportioned and subtly decorated Baroque gem, begun in 1716 by the Viennese court architect Fischer von Erlach.

Opposite the northern side of the cathedral is the tiny thirteenth-century **Kościół św. Idziego** (St Giles's Church), the only one in the city to have escaped destruction by the Tatars, and preserving some finely patterned brickwork.

Down ul. Kanonia, the **Muzeum Archidiecezjalne** (Archdiocesan Museum; Tues–Sun 9am–3pm; 3zł) at no. 12 is a treasure trove of religious art, with late-medieval wooden sculptures from all over Silesia, and a wonderful array of altarpieces – look out for Jan Effenberger's *Deposition* (1507), which places extravagantly costumed figures of Mary and her companions against an urban backdrop that looks suspiciously like sixteenth-century Wrocław. By now you'll be craving for some relief from cultural indigestion; escape from the same street into the **botanical gardens** at ul. Sienkiewiecza 6 (April–Oct: Mon–Fri 8am–6pm; 5zł), established in the Odra's former riverbed at the beginning of the twentieth century when a municipal ornamentation programme of the city was undertaken.

Ulica Szczytnicka leads east to the elongated avenue of pl. Grunwaldzki, which gained notoriety in 1945 when it was flattened into an airstrip to allow the defeated Nazi leaders to escape. At its southern end is the most famous of the city's bridges, **Most Grundwaldzki**, built in 1910.

East of Ostrów Tumski

Wrocław's most enticing stretch of greenery is the **Park Szczytnicki**, east of Ostrów Tumski, which can be reached on trams #2 and #10 from ul. Szczytnicka or #4 and #10 from ul. Kazimierza Wielkiego in the Stare Miasto. Its focal point is the **Hala Ludowa**, a huge hall built in 1913 to celebrate the centenary of the liberation of the city from Napoleon. Designed by the innovative Max Berg, it combines traditional Prussian solidity with a modernistic dash – the unsupported 130-metre-wide dome is an audacious piece of engineering even by present-day standards, used for trade fairs and sporting events, with the occasional exhibition. Around the Hala Ludowa are a number of striking colonnaded pavilions; these were built a few years earlier by Berg's teacher Hans Poelzig, who was responsible for making the city a leading centre of the *Deutscher Werkbund*, the German equivalent of the English Arts and Crafts Movement.

In the same park is a work by a yet more famous architect: the box-like **Kindergarten** with peeling whitewash is eastern Europe's only building by Le Corbusier. Along with the huge steel needle beside the hall, this is a legacy of the Exhibition of the Regained Territories, held here in 1948. Other delights in the park include an amphitheatre, a Japanese garden and pagoda, an artificial lake and hundreds of different trees and shrubs – including oaks that are more than six hundred years old. Best of all is a sixteenth-century **wooden church**, brought here from Kędzierzyn-Koźle in Upper Silesia. Its tower is particularly striking, especially the lower storey with its highly distinctive log construction, a form normally associated with the Ukraine. Across the road lies the **Ogród Zoologiczny** (Zoo; summer 9am–6pm; winter 9am–5pm; 8zł), with the largest collection of formerly wild animals in Poland.

Eating, drinking and entertainment

Wrocław has a good selection of **places to eat**, most of which are within the old central area. Most restaurants are open until 11pm unless otherwise stated, and we've included telephone numbers of places where booking is advisable. There are plenty of cafés and snack-eating opportunities on the basement floor of the Galeria Dominikańska shopping centre (open till 8/9pm), on the eastern fringe of the Stare Miasto at pl. Dominikański 3.

Wrocław's **drinking and nightlife** scene is as vibrant as you would expect from a large university city. The area between the Rynek and the University is packed with bars, while the passageway between ul. Ruska and ul. św. Antoniego has become a key pub-crawling zone.

Note that addresses below with "Rynek-Ratusz" denote the central buildings of the market square, while those with "Rynek" refer to the periphery.

Restaurants

Gospoda Wrocławska Sukiennice 6. Fine, traditional food in an olde-worlde wooden-beamed interior. Superb fresh fish in one half; a wider menu in the other. Attentive service accompanied by very reasonable prices.

Karczma Lwówska Rynek 4. No-nonsense meat-and-potatoes fare in an interior decked out with Ukranian folk motifs and sepia photographs of old Lwów. The stuffed cabbage leaves (*goląbki*) are excellent. Reasonable prices too.

Karczma Piastów ul. Kiełbaśnicza 6/7. Located in the cellars of the Dwór Polski hotel, entered from the first street west of the Rynek. A good place for typical Polish cooking at reasonable prices.

Oregano ul. Kuźnicza 57/58. Cosy basement restaurant decorated with antique-shop bric-a-brac, and offering reliably tasty pizzas and salads. Entered from a side alley just off the street.

Piramida ul. św. Mikołaja. Cavernous place which looks like a cross between an Egyptian tomb and a deciduous forest, serving up a wide range of global fun-restaurant fare, from kebabs through to tortillas and tasty grilled steaks.

Piwnica Świdnicka Rynek-Ratusz 24. This famous old restaurant under the town hall is a city institution, serving up a filling range of meat-heavy Polish favourites and some international dishes too. It's on the formal side, and some of the furnishings look like valuable antiques, but prices aren't too steep if you order carefully.

Pod II Strusiem ul. Ruska 61. Comfortable subterranean pizza-cavern decorated with Aborigine-influenced wall friezes – it's a bit like eating on the inside of someone's sacred rock. The pizzas come with resolutely non-Italian ingredients but are well prepared and pleasantly served.

Pod Złotym Jeleniem Rynek 46. Cosy square-side restaurant with open-plan grill and dining area, herbs hanging from the ceiling and rustic-looking paintings on the walls. Grilled slabs of pork and beef form the mainstay of the menu.

Ready's Rynek 14. Quick and simple grill food from *gyros* through to beefy steaks, in a bright Greek-themed interior. Prices are very reasonable but it's a small place and fills up fast.

Cafés and snack bars

Bazylia cnr ul. Kuźnicza and ul. Univerzytetska. Modern, minimalist, order-at-the-counter place, offering a big but functional choice of canteen food from *pierogi* to pork chops. Right opposite the entrance to the main university building, and correspondingly full with snacking students. Till 7pm.

Cocktail Bar Witaminka Rynek 50. Not a cocktail bar and not particularly rich in vitamins either, this is an enjoyably old-fashioned cake and ice-cream emporium right on the main square. Till 9pm.

Kurna Chata ul. Odrzańska 7. Folksy decor, wooden tables and a choice selection of Polish staples, from *bigos* and *placki* to more substantial chicken fillets and steaks. Cheap, filling, and tends to get busy as a result. Till midnight.

Pożegnanie z Afryką ul. Kiełbaśnicza 23. Relaxing, aromatic coffee shop and café that's probably the best place in town for a reviving cup of the brown stuff – very little else on the menu save for hot chocolate and a small choice of cakes. Till 10pm.

Soul Café pl. Solny 4. Relaxing, upmarket place serving decent coffee, dainty canapés and fancy cakes. Till 10pm.

Vega Rynek-Ratusz 27a. Good, inexpensive vegetarian haunt with plant-filled interior just to the right of the town hall's famous facade. Till 7pm Mon–Fri, 5pm at weekends.

Witek ul. Wita Stwosza 41. Tiny café with tiny fast-food menu; but people queue out the door to snap up the toasted cheese-and-mushroom sandwiches. Till 7pm Mon–Fri, 6pm Sat. Closed Sun.

Bars and pubs

Celtic in the courtyard behind ul. Ruska 51. Roomy bar-cum-nightspot on two levels, with loungey furnishings, formal-ish service, a full menu of main-course food and a dance floor in the basement.

Gumowa Róża ul. Wita Stwosza 32. A cosy labyrinth in the basement of the Awangarda gallery (entrance from alley round the back), catering for an easy-going, arty clientele.

Hybryda Kiełbaśnicza 32. Lively DJ bar in a long cellar broken up into several small areas, catering for teens and early twenty-somethings eager to dance to chart hits as the night wears on.

Kalogródek ul. Kuźnicza 29b. Beer garden long popular with students from the nearby university, with outdoor tables and benches arranged on terraces overlooking a little plaza.

Klub na Jatkach Jatki. Popular drinking den that will successfully cater for at least two sides of your character, with a classy pub-like space with dark wooden tables in one half, and a minimally furnished room with DJ podium and dance floor in the other.

Mleczarnia ul. Włodkowicza. Atmospheric place characterized by antique-shop furniture, nineteenth-century knick-knacks, sepia family photographs and candle-light – although it's usually dark enough here to make any further description of the interior decor superfluous.

Niebo in the courtyard behind ul. Ruska 51. Big pub-like venue with distressed furniture, grungy vibe and a healthy mix of oblivion-seeking students crowding round the bar.

Pod Kalamburem ul. Kuźnicza 29a. Bar located between the Rynek and the university quarter, with beautiful Art-Nouveau decor and some lethal cocktails.

Pod Papugami Sukiennice 9a. Brash bar decorated in mixture of industrial and gothic styles, popular with hedonistic yuppies. Live music and dancing some nights.

Pod Zielonym Kogutem pl. Teatralny 8. Inviting bar with wooden panelling, all kinds of pub junk

on the walls, and a line of cast iron street lamps running down the middle of the room.

Ragtime pl. Solny 17. Upscale café-bar stuffed with jazz memorabilia, and featuring live jazz a couple of times per week. Also a good – if expensive – place to eat.

Rura Łazienna 4. Music club with a long bar for boozing and chatting upstairs, and a table-strewn cellar with a stage often occupied by blues or jazz bands.

Salvador ul. Szajnochy. A wall-to-ceiling image of Señor Dali hovers vigilantly over the bar area but don't let your surreal fantasies run away with you – this is a relaxing basement boozer attracting a mellow student-to-thirty-something crowd.

Spiż Rynek-Ratusz 2. Superior cellar pub incorporating Poland's first boutique brewery, with a strong dark beer, a light Pils, and a tangy wheat beer all brewed on the premises. Bread and dripping (*chleb ze smalcem*) is the traditional side order. A wider range of Polish nosh is available in the rather more formal *Spiż* restaurant next door.

Nightlife

Many of the places listed in "Bars and pubs" (see p.542) feature DJs and dancing as the night wears on. Additionally, there's a handful of dedicated music clubs with a regular programme of disc-spinning events and/or gigs by local bands. To find out what's on, look out for posters or trawl through the "Kluby" page of *Co Jest Grane* – the **listings** supplement given away free with Friday editions of the *Gazeta Wyborcza* newspaper.

Clubs

Klub Kolor pl. Nowy Targ. A vast bomb shelter of a place which offers mainstream dance music and live appearances by moderately successful Polish hip-hop or rock acts.

Łykend ul. Podwale 37/38. Relaxing cellar club that caters for specialist musical tastes (alternative rock, reggae, drum'n'bass and so on) as well as hosting regular live gigs.

Madness ul. Hubska 6. Ska-, punk- and reggae-friendly club in a red-brick warehouse decorated in the style of an alternative tropical island. Frequent

DJ sessions and live gigs but check what's on first – it's located in between factories ten minutes' east of the train and bus stations.

Metropolis in the courtyard behind ul. Ruska 51. Mainstream dance club attracting a mixture of hedonistic students and dressed-up townies, bang in the middle of a popular pub-crawling area.

Wagon pl. Orląt Lwowskich 20. Agenda-setting club located in the former Dworzec Swiebodzki train station on the western fringes of the Stare Miasto, attracting the best DJs and an enthusiastic crowd.

Entertainment and festivals

There's a good deal of high-quality **classical music** in Wrocław, with tickets for big events rarely costing more than 60zł (most performances are accessible at half the price). The city has been at the forefront of contemporary European **drama** ever since the early Sixties, when experimental director Jerzy Grotowski established the ground-breaking **Laboratory Theatre** on Wrocław's Rynek. Although the Laboratory was dissolved following Grotowski's emigration to Italy in 1982, avant-garde traditions still live on – not least in the productions organized be the Grotowski Centre (see p.544).

The tourist office on the Rynek (see p.532) can provide details of most events – otherwise *Gazeta Wyborcza's Co Jest Grane* supplement (on Fridays) is the place to look for listings.

Wrocław hosts several prestigious annual **festivals**: the renowned Jazz on the Odra (Jazz nad Odrą) in May brings together several international performers; while Wratislavia Cantans (Ⓦwww.wratislavia.art.pl), in September, is devoted to oratorios and cantatas and features choral groups from all over the world. There's also a festival of early music at the beginning of December. The city's annual **drama festivals** include one devoted to monologues in January, and a contemporary Polish play season in May and June. Details of all these events can be obtained from the tourist office.

(see p.532)

Music venues

Akademia Muzyczna (Academy of Music) pl. 1. Maja 2 ☎071/355 7276. Frequent chamber concerts, usually performed by students and very often free of charge.

Filharmonia Wrocławska ul. Piłsudskiego 19 ☎071/343 8528. Orchestral concerts and recitals, usually Fridays and Saturdays.

Opera Dolnośląska (Lower Silesian Opera) ul. Świdnicka 35 ☎071/372 4357, Ⓦwww.opera.ies .com.pl). Top-notch warbling and superb stagecraft from one of Poland's top companies.

Teatr Muzyczny Capitol ul. Piłsudskiego 72 ☎071/343 5652, Ⓦwww.teatr-muzyczny.pl. Operetta, musicals and cabaret.

Theatres

Ad Spectatores ul. Na Grobli ☎0600 830 444, Ⓦwww.adspectatores.art.pl. Imaginative, spectacular contemporary works, performed in the theatre's base (a nineteenth-century water tower) or in other venues around town.

Ośrodek Grotowskiego (Grotowski Centre) Rynek-Ratusz 27 ☎071/343 4267, Ⓦwww .grotcenter.art.pl. Keeping the traditions of Jerzy Grotowski's famous studio theatre alive in the shape of workshops, performances, and occasional concerts.

Teatr Lalek (Puppet Theatre) pl. Teatralny ☎071/344 1216. Grandiose nineteenth-century building with two auditoria, each staging superbly designed shows – some of which start at 11am or earlier. Very popular, so book early.

Teatr Polski ul. Gabrieli Zapolskiej 3 ☎071/316 0780, Ⓦwww.teatrpolski.wroc.pl. Main venue for classical drama, with performances in the main hall or in the subsidiary Teatr Kameralny at ul. Świdnicka 28 (☎071/316 0752).

Teatr Współczesny ul. Rzeźnicza 12 ☎071/358 8922, Ⓦwww.wteatrw.pl. Best place to go for contemporary Polish work as well as modern international plays in Polish translation.

Cinemas

Atom ul. Piłsudskiego 74 ☎071/347 1465. Traditional, unmodernized cinema near the train station with mix of Hollywood hits and art-house films.

Helios Kazimierza Wielkiego 19a/21 ☎071/786 6566. Modern multiplex just west of the Stare Miasto showing Hollywood films as soon as they come out.

Warszawa Piłsudskiego 64 ☎071/792 4383. Behind the *Polonia* hotel, offering a good cross-section of mainstream movies and cerebral cinema.

Listings

Airlines LOT, ul. Piłsudskiego 36 ☎0801 300 952, Ⓦwww.lot.com.

Airport information ☎071/358 1381, Ⓦwww .airport.wroclaw.pl.

Books and maps EMPiK, with stores on the north side of the Rynek and on pl. Kościuszki, has the best all-round selection of foreign magazines, maps and English-language paperbacks.

Car rental Avis, at the airport and at ul. Piłsudskiego 46 ☎071/372 3567, Ⓦwww.avis .pl; Hertz, at the airport and at ul. Powstańców Śląskich 5/7 ☎071/353 7743, Ⓦwww.hertz.com .pl; and Joka, ul. Piłsudskiego 66 ☎071/781 8188, Ⓦwww.joka.com.pl.

Internet access Internet café at Przejście Żelaznicze 4, Rynek (24hr). Expect to pay 6zł/hr.

Left luggage At bus station (daily 6am–10pm). Lockers at the train station.

Pharmacy Apteka, just off the Rynek at Wita Stwosza 3, is the most convenient for the centre. Details of 24hr duty pharmacies will be posted in the window.

Post Office Rynek 28 (24hr) and outside the train station at Piłsudskiego 12 (Mon–Fri 8am–8pm).

Taxis There are central ranks opposite *Monopol* hotel, and on ul. Wita Stwosza outside the Kościół św. Marii Magdaleny. Otherwise try Euro Taxi ☎9666 or City Radio Taxi ☎9662.

Travel Agents Orbis, Rynek 29, sells bus, train and plane tickets, as well as handling car rental.

Around Wrocław

Once outside Wrocław, the northwestern swath of Silesia is not an area of outstanding touristic interest, and you'd be best advised to move quickly towards the mountains of the south and east if time in this part of Poland is limited. Despite the lack of a real focus for visitors, a number of settlements here make worthwhile stopoffs if you're passing through the region – either because of their historical significance or due to their possession of the odd architectural monument of note. Due to the extensive **public transport** network, Wrocław itself makes a perfectly adequate touring base, though there's plenty of **accommodation** elsewhere should you prefer to stay in a more tranquil location.

Trzebnica

TRZEBNICA, 24km north of Wrocław, has a long and distinguished history, having been granted a charter in 1250 by Duke Henryk III, so making it one of Silesia's oldest recorded towns. It was his marriage to the German princess St Hedwig (known in Poland as Jadwiga) which was largely responsible for shifting Silesia towards a predominantly German culture, setting the trend for the next six centuries.

The couple established a **Cistercian convent** in the town in 1202, the sole monument of note. Built in the plain style favoured by this order – still Romanesque in shape and feel, but already with the Gothic pointed arch and ribbed vault – it was progressively remodelled and now has a predominantly Baroque appearance evident in its main feature, the **Basilica of St Jadwiga**. A survival from the original building is the **portal**, which was found during excavation work and re-erected, half-hidden, to the left of the porch. Its sculptures, showing King David playing the harp to Bathsheba attended by a maidservant, are notably refined thirteenth-century carvings. The northern doorway also survives, but is of a lower standard of workmanship.

Inside the church, every column features a sumptuous Baroque altarpiece, while, to the right of the choir, the **St Hedwig's chapel**'s resplendent gilt and silver altar almost outshines the main item. The princess, who spent her widowhood in the convent, was canonized in 1267, just 24 years after her death, whereupon this chapel was immediately built in her memory. In 1680, her simple marble and alabaster sepulchral slab was incorporated into a grandiose tomb, whose sides are lined with sacred statuary while Jadwiga clutches a model of the basilica. At the same time, a considerably less ostentatious memorial to her husband was placed in the choir, its entrance guarded by statues of St Hedwig and her even more celebrated niece, St Elizabeth of Hungary.

Served by half-hourly services from Wrocław, Trzebnica's bus station is 100m north of the convent, just below the largely modern and uninteresting town centre. On the way back, make sure you board a bus for Wrocław-Dworzec PKS (the main bus station) rather than Wrocław-Nadodrze – the latter terminate a good 2km north of the centre. The *Ratuszowa* **restaurant**, uphill from the bus station at Rynek 4, is a conveniently central place to eat; and the family-run *Hotel Pod Platanami*, just north of the convent at ul. Kilińskiego 2 (☎071/312 0980; ❹) offers comfortable **rooms** if you need to stay.

Brzeg

Half an hour east of Wrocław by train, the old ducal seat of **BRZEG** is an easily manageable market town grouped around a worthwhile castle museum. Originally a fishing village on the bank (*brzeg*) of the Odra, Brzeg became a regional capital in 1311, when it ousted Legnica as the main residence of the local branch of the Piast family. The Piasts remained here until 1675 when the male line of the family finally died out.

The Town

Starting from the adjacent bus and train stations on the south side of town, it's a short walk up ul. Piastowska to get to the centre, which focuses on a drab Rynek arranged around a much rebuilt **town hall**. Just off the eastern side of the square is the arresting red-brick bulk of the fourteenth-century **Kościół św. Mikołaja** (St Nicholas's Church), its twin towers rebuilt last century and linked by an unusual arched bridge. The interior is startlingly spacious and boasts a varied collection of finely carved memorial plaques of prominent families.

The castle

A five-minute walk west of the Rynek, Brzeg's sixteenth-century **Zamek Piastowski** (Castle of the Piasts) is fondly referred to locally as the "Silesian Wawel" (Wawel being the famous castle in Kraków; see p.409), although the results of war and reconstruction have left it looking something of a hotch-potch. The extravagantly rich **gateway** is perhaps the finest Renaissance feature, modelled on Dürer's woodcut of a triumphal arch in honour of Emperor Maximilian. Above, in a shameless piece of self-glorification, are portrait figures of Duke George II and his wife, Barbara von Brandenburg. At the same level are pairs of knights whose coats of arms include those of Brzeg, Legnica and the Jagiellonian monarchs of Poland – the last, given that Silesia had not been a part of Poland for the past three centuries, being an expression of unrequited loyalty. Two tiers of busts above the windows trace the duke's genealogy, beginning with what appears as a rather regal interpretation of the peasant Piast at the upper left-hand corner.

Through the gate lies a beautifully proportioned **courtyard** with three storeys of arcades, and the entrance to the **Muzeum Piastów Śląskich** (Museum of the Silesian Piasts; Tues & Thurs–Sun 10am–4pm, Wed 10am–6pm; 4zł). Centrepiece of the display is the burial vault of the Brzeg Piasts, which lies beneath the north wing of the castle and contains several ranks of dukes and duchesses in pewter coffins – most eye-catching of which is the casket of Duke George III (1611-64), richly decorated with scenes of fabulous animals, and a grim-faced Death hunting his victims through the Silesian countryside. Elsewhere there's a wonderful scale model of Brzeg in the eighteenth century, a suite of period function rooms, and a collection of religious art which includes an impressively monumental wooden Crucifixion from 1420, and towering eighteenth-century statues of Aaron and Moses which once stood on either side of the organ in St Nicholas's Church.

Next to the **castle** is the superbly renovated Jesuit **Kościół św. Krzyża** (Church of the Holy Cross), which dates back to the turn of the eighteenth century. Sober enough from the outside, its single interior space is encrusted with Rococo decorations with an illusionist altar replacing the usual epic construction.

Practicalities

With regular trains to Wrocław and Opole you shouldn't need to stay in Brzeg. If you do get stuck, the comfortable, family-run **Pensjonat** *Demska* at ul. Rzemieślnicza 7 (☎077/416 4688; ❺) is preferable to the run-down *Piast* **hotel**, situated near the station on the way to the town centre at ul. Piastowska

14 (☎077/416 2028; en suites ❺, rooms with shared facilities ❷). The classiest **restaurant** remains the *Ratuszowa* in the town hall cellars, which is an excellent source of good, medium-price Polish food.

In late May, Brzeg's castle, town hall and churches are put to impressive use for a four-day-long international **festival** of classical music.

Ślęża and Sobótka

The flatness of the plain southwest of Wrocław is abruptly broken some 30km out of town by an isolated outcrop of rocks with two peaks, the higher of which is known as **Ślęża** (718m). One of the most enigmatic sites in Poland, Ślęża was used for pagan worship in Celtic times, and was later settled by the Slav tribe after whom the mountain – and Silesia itself – are named.

Ślęża is normally approached from **SOBÓTKA**, a dormitory town served by half-hourly buses from Wrocław. Between the bus terminal and the train station is the Gothic parish church, outside which stands the first of several curious ancient **sculptures** to be seen in the area – consisting of one stone placed across another, it's nicknamed *The Mushroom*. On the slopes of Ślęża, there's a large and voluptuous statue of a woman with a fish, while the summit has a carved lion on it. Exactly what these carvings symbolize is not known: some certainly postdate the Christianization of the area, but that hasn't prevented their association with pagan rites. It's not exactly a place to look for quiet mystery, however, being enormously popular with day-trippers and often teeming with busloads of schoolkids.

Five separate **hiking trails** traverse the hillsides, some of them stony, so it's wise to wear sturdy shoes. More than an hour is necessary for the busiest stretch, the direct ascent from Sobótka's main street to the top of Ślęża by the route indicated by yellow signs. The summit is spoiled by a number of ugly buildings including the inevitable television tower, while the neo-Gothic chapel is a poor substitute for the castle and Augustinian monastery which once stood here. Recompense is provided in the form of an extensive panoramic view including, on a clear day, the Karkonosze and Kłodzko highlands to the south and west.

Should you wish to stay, there is one acceptable **hotel** in Sobótka, the *Pod Misiem*, ul. Mickiewicza 7/9 (☎071/316 2035; ❷), which has a small number of doubles but mostly deals in dorm-style triples (30zł per person); and a **hostel** on Ślęża itself, the Na Ślęży (☎017/344 4752; 20zł per person), which is usually occupied by groups. At Sulistrowice, 2km to the south, there's a **campsite** (☎071/316 2151) with chalets (❶). The *Pod Misiem* has a decent **restaurant**, and you'll find a couple of **snack bars** on Sobótka's main square.

Lubiąż

Set close to the north bank of the Odra, 51km west of Wrocław and signposted off the Wrocław–Legnica road, the quiet village of **LUBIĄŻ** stands in the shadow of a **Cistercian abbey** that ranks as one of the largest and most impressive former monastic complexes in central Europe. It's an easy day-trip destination if you have your own transport, but is more difficult to get to by bus, with only two services a day from Wrocław and one from Legnica.

Although resting on medieval foundations, the appearance of the complex – laid out in the ground plan of a squared-off figure 6 – is one of sober Baroque: the community flourished in the aftermath of the disastrous Thirty Years' War, and was able to build itself palatial new headquarters, with over three hundred halls and chambers. Silesia's greatest painter, **Michael Willmann** (see p.568), lived here for over four decades, carrying out a multiplicity of commissions for the province's religious houses, and was interred in the church's crypt. However, prosperity was short-lived: decline began in 1740, when Silesia came under the uncompromisingly Protestant rule of Frederick the Great's Prussia, and continued until the monastery was dissolved in 1810. Since then, the complex has served as a mental hospital, stud farm, munitions factory, labour camp and storehouse, in the process drifting into a state of semi-dereliction. After the fall of communism, the Lubiąż Fund was established to attract foreign capital to renovate the site.

What has undoubtedly the potential to become one of Poland's leading tourist attractions has the merest trickle of visitors. At present, given the continued renovation of the interior, the main reason for making a visit is to appreciate the colossal exterior – something that would stand out in any capital city let alone lost here in the Silesian countryside. Most impressive, and readily accessible by walking through the gatehouse, is the 223-metre-long **facade**, whose austere economy of ornament is interrupted only by the twin towers of the church at the point where the figure 6 plan joins back onto itself. Only parts of the rest of the abbey are open (daily: April–Sept 9am–6pm; Oct–March 10am–3pm; 6zł), but you should be able to see a number of beautifully restored rooms decorated in the Baroque style, including the refectory and the showpiece Knights' Hall (Hala Książęca).

Located in former stables next to the abbey gateway, the *Karczma Cysterska* **restaurant** offers simple meat-and-potatoes meals in relaxing surroundings.

Legnica and around

Although often ravaged by fires and badly damaged in World War II, **LEGNICA**, 75km west of Wrocław, has maintained its role as one of Silesia's most important cities, and is nowadays a busy regional centre of 110,000 inhabitants. Despite a lively town centre and a pair of rewarding churches, it's never going to be a major tourist destination, and is important primarily as a transport hub offering onward connections to prettier places to the south – notably Legnickie Pole, Jawor, Strzegom and Bolków.

The Town

If you're arriving by train or bus, the main sights can be covered by a circular walk in a clockwise direction from the stations, which are just over the road from each other at the northeastern end of town. Crossing the pedestrian bridge next to the bus station and heading straight down ul. Skarbowa will bring you after ten minutes to the huge twin-towered **Katedra św. Piotra i Pawła** (Cathedral of SS Peter and Paul), with its rich red-brick neo-Gothic exterior, stylistically matched by the arcaded turn-of-the-twentieth-century buildings facing it on the corner of the **Rynek**. Two lovely fourteenth-century portals have survived: the northern one, featuring a tympanum of the Adoration of the Magi flanked by statues of the church's two patrons, overshadows the more prominent facade doorway with its Madonna and Child. The furnishings of the interior, which largely retains its original form, range from a late-thirteenth-century font with bronze bas-reliefs to an elaborately carved Renaissance pulpit and a typically theatrical Baroque high altar.

Immediately northwest lies the elongated Rynek, which has lost much of its character save for eight arcaded Renaissance houses which still survive next to a much rebuilt town hall. These are charming narrow-gabled burgher residences, two of them with sgraffito embellishments; note in particular the lovely "Quail basket" house with its cylindrical bay window.

Leaving the northwestern corner of the Rynek by ul. św Jana will take you past a former Cistercian monastery building which now houses the **Muzeum Miedzi** (Copper Museum; Tues–Sat 11am–5pm; 7zł), a small but rewarding collection devoted to the history of copper mining and smelting in the region. Standing opposite the junction of ul. św Jana and ul. Partyzantów is the massive Baroque facade of the twin-towered **Kościół św. Jana** (St John's Church). Protruding from the eastern side of the church, its orientation and brick Gothic architecture looking wholly out of place, is the presbytery of the thirteenth-century Franciscan Monastery which formerly occupied the spot. It owes its survival to its function as the Mauzoleum Piastów Legnickich (Mausoleum of the Legnica Piasts; Tues–Sat 9.30am–6.30pm; tickets from the Muzeum Miedzi; 3zł). Inside you'll see several sarcophagi, plus Baroque frescoes illustrating the history of Poland and Silesia under the dynasty.

Heading back towards the stations along ul. Partyzantów you'll pass the **Zamek** (castle), a grim red-brick structure rebuilt in the nineteenth century and preserving few original features save for the foundations of a **Romanesque chapel**, protectively housed in a purpose-built modern pavilion inside the castle courtyard (May–Sept: Tues–Sun 9am–5pm).

Practicalities

Legnica's **hotels** boil down to the *Qubus*, a well-appointed, business-oriented establishment opposite the train and bus stations at Skarbowa 2 (☎076/866 2100, ⓦwww.qubushotel.com; ❻), and the *Kamieniczka*, Młynarska 15-16 (☎076/723 7392, ⓦwww.hotel-kamieniczka.pl; ❸–❺) a nicely restored town house just east of the Rynek with a mixture of en suites and rooms with shared facilities.

There are several moderately priced **restaurants** in town: the popular Adria, Rynek 9, includes pizzas as well as Polish specialities, and the Tivoli, southwest of the Rynek at ul. Złotoryjska 31, offers a Polish-Mediterranean culinary mixture with some passable veggie options, but closes at 9pm.

Legnickie Pole

On April 4, 1241 the Tatar hordes – having ridden five thousand miles from their Mongolian homelands and ravaged everything in their path – won a titanic battle 60km west of Wrocław against a combined army of Poles and Silesians, killing its commander, Duke Henryk the Pious. Silesia's subsequent division among Henryk's descendants into three separate duchies began a process of dismemberment which was thereafter to dog its history. Standing on the site of the battlefield today is the village of **LEGNICKIE POLE**, 11km southeast of Legnica and served by municipal bus services #9, #16, #17 and #20.

A church was erected on the spot where Henryk the Pious' body was found (according to tradition, his mother, later St. Jadwiga of Trzebnica, was only able to identify the headless corpse from his six-toed foot), and in time this became the centre of a Benedictine monastery. The church was deconsecrated after World War II, and now houses the **Muzeum Bitwy Legnickiej** (Museum of the Battle of Legnica; Wed–Sun 11am–5pm; 5zł, free on Sat), which includes diagrams and mock-ups of the conflict and a copy of Henryk's tomb (the original is in Wrocław's Muzeum Narodowe; see p.538).

The Benedictines, who were evicted during the Reformation, returned to Legnickie Pole in the early eighteenth century and constructed the large **Kościół św. Jadwigi** (St Jadwiga's Church) directly facing the museum. It was built by **Kilian Ignaz Dientzenhofer**, the creator of much of Prague's magnificent Baroque architecture. His characteristic use of varied geometric shapes and the interplay of concave and convex surfaces is well illustrated here. The interior of the church (usually closed outside Mass times; ask at the museum and they may unlock it) features an oval nave plus an elongated apse and is exceptionally bright, an effect achieved by the combination of white walls and very large windows. Complementing the architecture are the bravura **frescoes** covering the vault by the Bavarian **Cosmos Damian Asam**. Look out for the scene over the organ gallery, which shows the Tatars hoisting Henryk's head on a stake and celebrating their victory, while the duke's mother and wife mourn over his body.

Since the second dissolution of the monastery in 1810, the **monastic buildings** (currently a women's hospice) have been put to a variety of uses. For nearly a century they served as a Prussian military academy; its star graduate was Paul von Hindenburg, German commander-in-chief during World War I and president from 1925 until his death in 1934.

Jawor

Some 20km south of Legnica, on the main road to Jelenia Góra, the small town of **JAWOR** was formerly the capital of one of the independent Silesian duchies. Severely bashed up in World War II, the central **Rynek** is now fairly modern and colourless, although it has retained its arcaded style. Off to one side, the **Kościół św. Marcina** (St Martin's Church), is a fine Gothic building, with varied furnishings including Renaissance choir stalls and a Baroque high altar. Behind the church, a hole in the epitaph-laden brick wall leads to some even older, rubbish-strewn ruins.

From the Rynek, ul. Grundwalska heads northwest through pl. Wolności towards the town's most visually intriguing monument, the barn-like, timber-framed **Kościół Pokoju** (Church of Peace; April–Oct daily 10am–5pm). Its name derives from the Peace of Westphalia of 1648, which brought to an end the morass of religious and dynastic conflicts known as the Thirty Years' War, though the name could equally well apply to the tranquil setting outside the old town walls. The church was one of three (two of which survive) that Silesia's Protestant minority were allowed to build following the cessation of hostilities, and both the material used – wood and clay only, no stone or brick – and the location outside the town centre were among the conditions laid down by the ruling Habsburg emperor. Designed by an engineer, Albrecht von Säbisch, the church was cleverly laid out in such a way that an enormous congregation could be packed into a relatively modest space, an effect illustrated even more clearly in its equally charismatic counterpart in Świdnica (see p.564).

Hourly **buses** from Legnica terminate in the marketplace below Jawor's Rynek, passing the Kościół Pokoju on the way. You can catch a bite to eat at the *Ratuszowa* **restaurant** at Rynek 5: and there's a rather nice small **hotel**, the *Jawor*, just off the Rynek at Staszica 10 (☎076/871 0624, ⓦwww.hoteljawor .com.pl; ❺), offering a handful of fully equipped, pastel-coloured doubles.

Rogoźnica and Strzegom

Heading southeast from Jawor on the road to Strzegom you'll pass after about 10km signs leading towards the site of **Rogoźnica** (Gross-Rosen), established by the Nazis as a forced-labour camp in August 1940 and subsequently used as an extermination site. The partially reconstructed brick gateway serves as a memorial to the estimated 40,000 Jews, Poles and others who died here, and there's a small museum (daily 8am–5pm) telling the history of the camp.

Seven kilometres further on, straddling the main road between Wrocław and Jelenia Góra, the little town of **STRZEGOM** is regarded by some as Silesia's oldest town, and might well be among the oldest in Poland. A long-established source of granite extracted from nearby quarries, it nevertheless preserves few suggestions of its antiquity. Approaching from afar you can't miss the huge Gothic bulk of its **Bazylika św. Piotra i Pawła** (Basilica of SS Peter and Paul), built from the local stone with more readily workable sandstone tympanums illustrating the Last Judgement (with what seems like an excess of Apocalyptic Horsemen) and on the southern porch, the Dormition of the Virgin.

Bolków

The very name of **BOLKÓW**, 20km southwest of Strzegom on the road to Jelenia Góra (and served by Wrocław–Jelenia Góra buses), proclaims its foundation by the first duke of Świdnica, Bolko I. Although a ruin, his **castle** (April–Oct: Tues–Fri 9am–3pm, Sat & Sun 9am–5.30pm; 4zł) is still an impressive sight, rising imperiously above the little town. Later converted into a Renaissance palace, it passed into the control of the monks of Krzeszów (see p.567), and was finally abandoned after their Napoleonic suppression. A section of the buildings has been restored to house a small museum on the history of the town, and you can ascend the tower for a fine panoramic view.

△ Interior, Church of Peace

There's little to see in the lower town, though the gaudily painted Gothic parish church and the sloping Rynek have a certain charm. The town has two **hotels**, *Bolków*, ul. Sienkiewicza 17 (☎075/741 3341), with a mixture of refurbished en suites (❹) and simpler rooms with shared facilities (❷); and the somewhat simpler *Panorama* at ul. Mickiewicza 6 (☎075/741 3444; ❸). The *Bolków* boasts an excellent **restaurant**; and you'll find a cluster of **cafés** on the Rynek.

The Ziemia Kłodzka

Due south of Wrocław is a rural area of wooded hills, gentle valleys and curative springs that provides a timely antidote to the heavy industry which blights much of lowland Silesia. Known as the **Ziemia Kłodzka** (Kłodzko Region) after its largest town, it's surrounded on three sides by the Czech Republic with which the Sudety mountains form a natural frontier.

A popular holiday area for insolvent Silesians looking for a break from the industrial conurbations, you may not find many of the five **spa resorts** (identified by the suffix *-zdrój*) as appealing as they sound. The gracious prewar days when "taking the waters" was a fashionable indulgence are long gone, and although the spas have recently started to respond to new opportunities in tourism, a sense of faded grandeur still prevails. If you're heading for the Czech Republic then a visit to one or two and a quick swig of the effervescent local tonic won't ruin your day.

In the hills above these resorts are some fine hiking routes passing through landscapes dotted with sometimes bizarre rock outcrops. A network of marked paths covers the entire region, in which there are several separate ranges; the best are found in the southeast of the area, taken up by the Masyw Śnieżnika. This specific area is as yet little touched by the more rapacious tourist development elsewhere and is a worthwhile destination for spending a few quiet days in the hills. The red and yellow 1:90,000 Ziemia Kłodzka map, easily available from local bookshops, is an essential companion.

Accommodation throughout the Kłodzko region is plentiful, although the bigger resorts tend to fill up with partying youngsters in high summer. Nevertheless it's possible to stay here very cheaply, with the custom-built **pensions** offering particularly good value. For **getting around**, buses, which eventually get to even the smallest villages, are your best bet; picturesque rail lines hug the valleys, but train stations are usually on the outskirts of the towns.

Kłodzko

Spread out beneath the ramparts of a stolid Prussian fortress, the thousand-year-old town of **KŁODZKO** was for centuries a place of strategic importance and today its Stare Miasto still retains some of the charm of its medieval origins – a rarity in Silesia, which makes a stopover here rewarding. Situated on the main trade route between Bohemia and Poland, until the eighteenth-century Prussian takeover, Kłodzko's ownership fluctuated between the adjacent nations. Indeed at one point the town belonged to the father of Adalbert, the Czech saint who was to have a crucial impact on the development of the early Polish nation (see p.395).

Kłodzko's bus station is the main public transport hub for the whole region, linking the settlements of the Ziemia Kłodzka with Świdnica to the northwest and Paczków and Nysa to the east. However there's not a great choice of accommodation in town, so you're best advised to head for one of the spa resorts, like Kudowa-Zdrój, if you're going to be staying in this part of Silesia for any length of time.

The Town

From the main train and bus stations situated side by side in the centre of town, the best way to enjoy an exploration of the attractive **Stare Miasto** is to cross the steel-girder bridge onto ul. Grottgera. At the end of this street you'll find the main survivor of the town's medieval fortifications, the Gothic **bridge**, adorned in the Baroque period by a collection of sacred statues who still manage to look pleadingly heavenward despite centuries of weathering.

On the opposite bank, grand nineteenth-century mansions rise high above the river. Passing them, you ascend to the sloping Rynek (known as **plac Bolesława Chrobrego**) which has a number of fine old houses from various periods, an undistinguished nineteenth-century Town Hall and an ornate Baroque fountain which looks up to the fortress's walls. Greatly extended by the Prussians in the eighteenth century from earlier defensive structures built on the rocky knoll, the squat **Twierdza Kłodzka** (Kłodzko Fortress; daily 9am–6pm; 6zł) lost its reputation for impregnability when captured by the all-conquering army of Napoleon in 1807. As with other historical monuments which have suffered the vagaries of several disparate owners, the fortress nowadays has become a repository for a variety of objects from old fire engines to contemporary local glassware, and you can even learn to abseil in one of the courtyards. However, most visitors come here for the stronghold's extensive network of **tunnels** (Polish-speaking guided tours daily 9am–6pm; 6zł) which were excavated by prisoners of war during the Prussian era, and today still entail a fair amount of crawling around in semi-darkness while the guide rattles through his spiel.

During the last war the fortress was used as a prison camp and in one of the many galleries you'll find a memorial to the thousands of prisoners who perished here. Near the uppermost terrace a small chamber also houses a genuinely chilling sculpture which further commemorates the wartime dead. Nearby is the **viewpoint** over the town's roofscapes to the hills beyond; it bears a striking resemblance to the comparable, if somewhat grander, panorama from Grenoble's similar fort in southeastern France.

By the entrance of the fortress is the northern aperture of the **Podziemna Trasa**, yet another underground passage (daily 9am–6pm; 6zł), this 600-metre example making an unusual and blissfully cool way of passing under the Stare Miasto on a hot summer's day. There are various instruments of torture to see along the way, including miniature French guillotines and even more barbaric Prussian methods of execution. The exit brings you out just below a small square in which stands a church with one of the finest Baroque interiors in Poland. Kłodzko's parish **Kościół NMP** (Church of Our Lady) really should not be missed and will have avid church-spotters drooling in the aisles. Outside, the Gothic building's shell remains remarkably well preserved, but inside, two and a half centuries of Baroque ornamentation were undertaken with such zeal that you hardly know where to rest your eyes. Barely a surface is left without some kind of embellishment in gold, marble or paint, giving a busy impression that either fills you with awe or gives you a headache. One of the many things to look out for is the fourteenth-century tomb of the founder, Bishop Ernst of Pordolice, which somehow managed to survive the desecrations of the Hussites five centuries ago.

Leaving the church square to the west and following ul. Łukasiewicza to no. 4, brings you to the **Muzeum Ziemi Kłodzkiej** (Kłodzko Regional Museum; Wed–Fri 10am–4pm, Sat & Sun 11am–5pm; 5zł, free on Sun), which boasts a large collection of local glassware, and an exhaustive assembly of over four hundred **clocks** based on the fruits of the Świedbodzia and Srebrna Góra clock factories. The display features everything from ancient astronomical devices, working grandfather and irritating cuckoo clocks, to porcelain-backed kitchen clocks. One small dark room features a mirrored floor reflecting a ceiling covered in still more clocks.

Practicalities

Kłodzko Miasto **train station**, which is beside the **bus station**, is only a few minutes' walk east from the centre; this station is also the best place to catch trains heading south, and to the two spa valleys to the east and west. The main station, Kłodzko Główny, is over 2km north and only worth using if you're heading to Wrocław or Jelenia Góra. The rather excellent **tourist office**, located on the southwestern corner of the town hall at pl. Chrobrego 1 (Mon–Fri 9am–6pm, Sat 10am–2pm; ☎074/865 8970, ⓦwww.ziemiaklodzka .it.pl or ⓦwww.powiat.klodzko.pl), can fill you in on accommodation possibilities throughout the region. The PTTK office at Wita Stwosza 1 (Mon–Thur 8am–4pm, Fri 8am–6pm, Sat 9am–1pm; ☎074/867 3740) is the place to buy local hiking **maps**.

Of the **hotels**, the *Marhaba* at ul. Daszyńskiego 16 (☎074/865 9933, esnieznik@netgate.com.pl; ❸–❹), five minutes' walk west of the bus station just over the modern bridge and on the right, offers small, slightly decrepit but tolerable rooms, some of which are en suites, others just with sink. Marginally more comfortable is the *Korona* just northwest of the town centre at Nowogrudzka 1 (☎074/867 3737; ❹), with what looks like a grubby concrete building containing pleasingly bright and pastelly en suites with TV. There's a basic **youth hostel** 1km north of the centre at ul. Nadrzeczna 5 (☎074/867 2524), which will put you up for under 20zł a head – from the main square, bear right into ul. Łukasińskiego and keep going for ten minutes.

The *Romana* **restaurant** on the east side of the town hall, serves up decent pizzas as well as tasty pancakes and ice cream, and has outdoor, fountain-side seating in summer. *U Ratusza*, on the other side of the town hall at pl. Chrobrego 3, is the place to go for a slap-up Polish meal. *Tevere*, below the parish church on ul. Daszyńskiego, offers a range of authentic-ish pizzas, a palatable veggie lasagne, and sizeable salads. For **drinking**, there's a handful of beer gardens on and around the Rynek in fine weather; otherwise *AK*, Armii Krajowej 2, is a popular and atmospheric cellar bar.

Wambierzyce

Heading west from Kłodzko on the main road to Prague are a string of **spa towns**. The first of these, **Polanica-Zdrój**, is not worth the detour in its own right, but a right turn at the west end of town leads 9km to the village of **WAMBIERZYCE** (Kłodzko–Polanica–Radków buses pass through 4–5 times a day), another tiny rural settlement set out of all proportion to the huge religious institution found there.

The Baroque **basilica**, perched above a broad flight of steps above the village square has been the site of pilgrimages since 1218, when a blind man regained his sight by praying at a statue of the Virgin Mary enshrined in a lime tree.

Pilgrimages ensued over the following centuries with the shrine growing ever bigger on the donations of its visitors. The impressive monumental facade of the basilica is all that remains of the third shrine built here at the end of the seventeenth century, the main body of the building collapsing soon after completion, at which point it was rebuilt with the interior you see today. The basilica is circumvented by a broad ambulatory with a variety of chapels and grottoes representing the Stations of the Cross. The small nave of the basilica is a fairly reserved octagon hung with altarpieces by Michael Willmann, while the all-important pulpit gets the usual excess of ornamentation. On the ceiling is a fresco depicting an angel passing the design for the basilica to the local people, its anticipated form appearing as a ghostly image on the hill behind them. The oval chancel has a cupola illustrating the fifteen Mysteries of the Rosary with a magnificent silver tabernacle from Venice bearing the miraculous image, accompanied by a profusion of votive offerings encased at its side.

Found all around the town are nearly one hundred **shrines** depicting further scenes from the Passion, culminating appropriately at **Calvary**, the wooded hill facing the basilica up which lead a long series of steps lined by still more shrines. Halfway up on the left is the **Ruchoma Szopka** (Moving Crib; Tues–Sun 10am–1pm & 2–4pm), a large mechanical contraption from the early nineteenth century that presents biblical and everyday local scenes, laid out like miniature theatre sets.

There's a comfy **hotel**, the *Wambierzyce*, on the main square at pl. NMP 1 (℡074/871 9186, Ⓦwww.hotel-wambierzyce.pl; ❹), which also has a reasonable **restaurant**.

Duszniki-Zdrój

Back on the main Prague road, continuing 10km west of Polanica-Zdrój brings you to the much older spa resort of **DUSZNIKI-ZDRÓJ**, which has a little more going for it than the younger Polanica. The town is best known for its **Chopin Musical Festival** held here in the first half of August each year, an event which commemorates the concerts given by the sixteen-year-old composer during a convalescence in 1826. This, and the unusual industrial museum (see below), add to the usual charms of a spa.

Duszniki is divided by the Wrocław–Prague road with the **train station** to the north and the Stare Miasto and spa quarter located on the south side. On the **Rynek**, Renaissance and Baroque styles are mingled with less edifying postwar additions, with one of the old town houses bearing a plaque recording Chopin's stay. Leaving the market square to the east down ul. Kłodzko, you pass the parish **Kościół św. Piotra i Pawła** (Church of SS Peter and Paul), an externally bland example of early eighteenth-century Baroque with two unusually ornate pulpits inside. One is shaped like a whale, with the creature's gaping maw forming a preaching platform – a zany stylistic reference to the Jonah story which is occasionally found in other Polish churches.

At the bottom of the same street is the **Muzeum Papiernictwa** (Museum of the Paper Industry; Tues–Fri 9am–5pm, Sat & Sun 9am–3pm; 6zł), which occupies a large paper mill dating from the early seventeenth century and constitutes the town's chief curiosity. One of Poland's most precious industrial buildings, its fine half-timbering, sweeping mansard roof, novel domed entrance turret and crude gable end add up to an eye-catching if understated piece of Baroque architecture. Inside lies a worthy-but-dull history lesson on paper making through the ages, although you do get the chance to press your own carpet-thick sheets of the stuff for a few extra złoty.

The town's spa park lies over to the southwestern side of the Rynek, a long stretch of tree-shaded walkways that culminates after about 1km with an ensemble of nineteenth-century buildings including the **Chopin Palace** (Dworek Chopina) – a dinky Neoclassical pavilion that holds recitals throughout the summer season, including those connected with the Chopin Festival.

Practicalities

Buses pick up and drop off on the Wrocław–Prague road, while the **train station** is just off the road to the north. Duszniki-Zdrój is easily visited from either Kłodzko or Kudowa-Zdrój further down the road, but if you want to stay here the **tourist office**, Rynek 9 (Mon–Fri 8am–5pm, Sat 8am–2pm; ☎074/866 9413, ⓦwww.duszniki.pl), will direct you towards the town's private rooms (❶) and pensions (❸), and can provide details on the Chopin festival. Of the **hotels**, the *Sonata*, Rynek 2 (☎074/866 9504; ❹) is a centrally located source of comfortable rooms with shower and TV; while down at the far end of the spa park, the *Piastow Gród*, ul. Zdrojowa 32 (☎074/866 0770, ⓦwww.piastowgrod.pl; ❺), offers snazzy en suites in a nicely renovated *belle-époque* building. There's a rash of **bars** and **pizzerias** in the park.

West to Kudowa-Zdrój and the Góry Stołowe

Nestling at the foot of the Góry Stołowe some 16km west of Duszniki, the border town of **KUDOWA-ZDRÓJ** is one of the most popular health resorts anywhere in Poland. Patronized by the internationally rich and famous in the nineteenth century, it's nowadays a charmingly under-commercialized place which has preserved plentiful helpings of olde-worlde charm. A decent choice of accommodation and proximity to the mountains help to make Kudowa-Zdrój the most likely place to base yourself in the Ziemia Kłodza.

Arrival, information and accommodation

Buses deliver you to ul. 1 Maja on the northeastern side of the town centre, from where it's a short walk back the way you came to the centrally placed **tourist office**, ul. Zdrojowa 42 (Mon–Fri 8am–8pm, Sat 8am–6pm, Sun 9am–5pm; ☎074/866 1387, ⓦwww.kudowa.pl), which has a full list of private rooms (❷) and pensions (❸) in town. A lot of Kudowa-Zdrój's rest homes are run by the FWP (a workers' holiday association that dates back to the old regime), whose central reception desk in the *Bajka* hotel, ul. Zdrojowa 36 (☎074/866 1261), will fix you up with a simple no-frills room in one of their properties from 25zł per person. The *OSiR* sport hotel, ul. Łąkowa 12 (☎074/866 1627; ❷), is in a scruffy area 1km west of town just off the main Prague road, but it does have a **hostel** section (22zł per person) and a **camp-site** in the grounds.

Hotels

Alga ul. 1. Maja 20 ☎074/866 1460, ⓦwww.alga2.republika.pl. Modern pension diagonally opposite the bus terminal, offering comfortable rooms with shower and TV. ❹

Gwarek ul. Słowackiego 10 ☎074/866 1890. The nearest thing that Kudowa has to a package hotel, with smart but functional en suites with TV in a large modern building overlooking the centre from the north. ❸–❹

Kaprys Sikorskiego 2 ☎074/866 1663. Medium-sized place in a residential street near the bus station, with simple en-suite doubles, triples and quads. ❸

Sansouci ul. Buczka 3 ☎074/866 1350, 🌐www
.sansouci.info.pl. Upmarket place just southwest
of the centre with smart and plush rooms, all with
shower and TV. Atmospheric top-floor rooms with
attic ceilings. ❺
Scaliano Sikorskiego 6 ☎074/866 1867. Family-
run hotel in residential streets just uphill from the
bus station, offering smallish but neat en suites
with TV. ❹

Willa Diament ul. Buczka 7 ☎074/866 4156,
🌐http://willadiament.w.interia.pl. A hundred-year-
old pension in a characterful old building complete
with half-timbering and turrets, now offering
thoroughly modernized en-suite rooms with
laminate floors and TV, and a big garden out the
back. In the same part of town as the Sansouci. ❸

The Town

Grand old villas set in their own grounds give Kudowa its erstwhile aristocratic air, yet it has no obvious centre other than the **spa park**. Here the
huge domed **pijalnia** (pump room) houses the venerated marble fountain
from which issue hot and cold springs. Nearby stalls cash in on visitors'
sentimentality, selling the pipe-like *kóbki*, small flattened jugs with swan-
necked spouts, from which the surprisingly refreshing water – slightly sweet
and carbonated – is traditionally imbibed. Adjacent to the pump room is a
concert hall where a festival celebrating the music of Stanisław Moniuszko
takes place each July. Sharing the nationalist outlook of Chopin, his compa-
triot and contemporary, Moniuszko's music has never caught on abroad to
anything like the same extent, although you'll see a few bars of his music
set into the amusingly kitschy "sheet music" railings installed around town.
The spacious spa park's appeal continues with well-kept flowerbeds and over
three hundred different species of tree and shrub. Occupying a building on
the south side of the park, the **Muzeum Zabawek** (Toy Museum; daily
10am–5pm; 5zł) is an enjoyable and well-presented history of playthings
through the ages with soft toys, train sets, costumed dolls and even Javanese
shadow puppets among the exhibits – although young children might be
bemused by the hands-off nature of the display.

Eating and drinking

Most characterful place to **eat** in Kudowa is the rustic-style *W Starym Młynie*,
1km west of town along ul. nad Potokiem, where you can eat heartily on
meaty Polish staples. Similar fare can be sampled at central establishments like
Kosmiczna, ul. Zdrojowa 41; and the nearby *Piekełko*, ul. Moniuszki 2 – both of
which feature dining and dancing to an accompaniment of synthesizer-driven
easy listening tunes. *Amfora*, on the way to the bus stop at ul. 1 Maja 11, offers
a similarly Polish repertoire but without the music. *Café Domek*, ul. Zdrojowa
34, serves up decent pizzas and ice cream on a big outdoor terrace, and is also a
relaxing place for a **drink**. The other night-time drinking venues are down by
the pump house, where you'll find *Raj*, favoured by an older crowd who like to
dance to evergreen music under a mirrorball; and the next-door *Palma*, a stylish
café-bar with correspondingly trendier clientele.

The Kaplica Czaszek and the Muzeum Kultury Ludowej

Twenty minutes' walk north of town (follow ul. Moniuszki past the *Wodny Świat*
indoor swimming pool and keep going), the outlying hamlet of **Czermna** plays
host to the **Kaplica Czaszek** (Chapel of Skulls; Tues–Sun 9.30am–1pm &
2–5.30pm; 3zł), a macabre scene which threatens to undo the curative effects of
Kudowa's springs. Its walls and ceiling are decorated with over three thousand
skulls and crossed bones from the dead of various wars and epidemics. The

chapel's priest, with the help of his devoted grave-digger, amassed the collection during the last decades of the eighteenth century. Their own remains are set in a glass case by the altar and thousands more skulls are stashed in the crypt. In fact ossuaries are common in central Europe, often based on the belief that having one's bones stored in a suitably holy site will increase the chances of enjoying a favourable afterlife.

A walkable 3km north of Czermna, the village of **Pstrążna** plays host to an enjoyable open-air ethnographic collection, the **Muzeum Kultury Ludowej Pogórza Sudeckiego** (Museum of the Sudeten Foothills; May–Oct: daily 10am–6pm), with a wide-ranging collection of vernacular buildings from local villages. Among the more curious of these are the wooden, bell-topped watch-towers that used to be a feature of many a village, warning the local inhabitants of approaching fire or avalanche.

Into the Góry Stołowe

Rising above 900m and almost as flat as their name suggests, the **Góry Stołowe** (Table Mountains) are not the most enticing range in the Kłodzko region, but do have some extraordinary rock formations which can be appreciated in a full day's walk from Kudowa.

The easiest way to access the area is to continue northeastwards from Pstrążna (see above), picking up the well-signed green trail before that leads to the first of several fantastic rock formations in the range, the **Błędne Skały** (Erratic Boulders; daily 9am–6pm; 5zł), where it twists and turns, squirming through narrow gaps between gigantic rocks. It then continues via Pasterka to the village of **Karłów**, from where a climb of nearly seven hundred steps leads to the **Szczeliniec Wielki**, the highest point in the range at 919m. Here the rocks have been weathered into a series of irregular shapes nicknamed "the camel", "the elephant", "the hen", and so on. There's a small entrance fee once you get to the top where a café offers refreshments, then you follow the trail which goes down through a deep chasm, on to a viewpoint and back by a different route.

From Błędne Skały the **red trail** leads directly to Karłów continuing east 5km to the largest and most scattered group of rocks in the area, the **Skalne Grzyby** (Petrified Mushrooms), rocks whose bases were worn away by uneven erosion producing the top-heavy appearance their name suggests.

If you want to tackle either Szczeliniec Wielki or the Skalne Grzyby, without walking all the way from Kudowa, then consider catching a bus as far as Karłów (May–Sept 5 daily), and starting from there.

South of Kłodzko: Międzygórze and the Masyw Śnieżnika

At the southeastern corner of the Kłodzko region is the enticing **Masyw Śnieżnika**, the best of whose scenery can be seen in a good day's walk and which, unlike the overrun Karkonosze to the west, seems to be pleasingly ignored by the crowds. The main jumping-off point is the charming hill resort of **Międzygórze** (Among the Hills), a dead end 30km southeast of Kłodzko and well served by buses.

Midway down the valley south of Kłodzko, some 15km away, is **BYSTRZYCA KŁODZKA**, its peeling medieval core reminiscent of a charismatically decayed Mediterranean town. This impression is particularly strong if you cross over the river to get a magnificent full-frontal view of the town's tier-like layout, which on a sunny day looks more like southern

France than Poland. First appearances can be deceptive, however – the briefest of wanders around Bystrzyca's tatty streets will be enough to convince you that it was a mistake to break your journey here. Although the friendly **tourist office** at ul. Rycerska 20 (Mon–Fri 8.30am–6.30pm, Sat 10am–3pm, Sun 10am–2pm; ☎074/811 3731, ⓦwww.zgs.ta.pl) will try and persuade you otherwise, it's best to continue southwards towards Międzygórze.

Miedzygórze

Lying at the head of a wooded valley east of Bystrzyca, **MIĘDZYGÓRZE** is one of the quieter, more pleasant corners of the Kłodzko region – well worth a couple of days' stay if rustic peace and hiking opportunities are what you need. The village is characterized by the **drzewnianki** (wooden villas) built to serve as rest homes at the beginning of the nineteenth century. Ramshackle affairs with carved balustrades, neo-Gothic turrets and creaky interiors, they're still in use as tourist accommodation today.

Built around a central T-junction, the village is easy to find your way around. Five minutes' walk west of the junction, steps descend from the *Nad Wodospadem* hotel to a 27-metre-high **waterfall**, surrounded by deep forest. On the far side of the waterfall paths ascend towards the **Ogród Bajek** (Fantasy Garden) about twenty minutes away, a hilltop garden designed by local forester Izydor Kriesten before World War II, and restored by the PTTK in the 1990s. It's a charming spot consisting of huts constructed from roots, branches and cones, each of which is inhabited by an assemblage of gnomes and model animals.

Accommodation in Międzygórze's *drzewnianki* (❶) is handled by the FWP, whose central reception is just uphill from the T-junction at ul. Sanatoryjna 2 (daily 8am–6pm; ☎074/813 5109, ⓦwww.fwpmiedzygorze.ta.pl). Of the hotels, the frumpy en suites at the *Nad Wodospadem* at the western entrance to the village (☎074/813 5120; ❷) are somewhat eclipsed by the modern, avocado-coloured affairs at the central *Pensjonat Millennium*, ul. Wojska Polskiego 9 (☎074/813 5287, ⓦmillennium.maxi.pl; ❸).

Both the *Millennium* and the *Nad Wodospadem* have decent **restaurants**. A marvellously laid-back place to hang out is the **café** of the *Wilczy Dol* on the village's main T-junction, with graffiti-style decor, tasty snacks, and alternative music on the sound system – outdoor gigs are sometimes organized in summer.

Walking in the Masyw Śnieżnika

Bang in the middle of Międzygórze, there's a signpost bristling with boards indicating the many waymarked tracks in the area. One particularly good walk follows the signposted **red trail**, which rises steeply through lovely wooded countryside for about three hours, leading to the *Na Śnieżniku* **refuge** (☎074/813 5130), an isolated PTTK hostel which offers dorm beds for 15zł per person and also serves inexpensive homely meals. From here it's then a much gentler ascent to the flat summit of **Śnieżnika** (1425m), the highest point in the Kłodzko region, set right on the Czech border.

From the summit it's worth descending north by the **yellow trail** towards Kletno, which will bring you in about an hour to the Bear's Cave, or **Jaskinia Niedźwiedzia** (daily except Mon & Thurs: Feb–April & Sept–Nov 10am–4.40pm; May–Aug 9am–4.40pm). Discovered in 1966 during quarrying, the cave takes its name from the bear fossils discovered there. Bats still inhabit the cave, which boasts the usual anthropomorphically wondrous stalactites and stalagmites. Visits are by Polish-language guided tour only, with group numbers limited to fifteen people, exploring 600m of cave in about forty minutes. You can also get to the cave directly from Międzygórze in about two hours by following the red trail (see p.559) and then branching off northwards after a couple of kilometres when you see signs to the Jaskinia NiedwiedzIa and Kletno.

From the cave, another kilometre's walk brings you to the village of **KLETNO**, which has a couple of snack bars, a bus service to Kłodzko via Stronie Śląskie (see below) and Lądek-Zdrój, and a rather basic **youth hostel** at Kletno 8 (T074/814 1358; 15zł per person).

Lądek-Zdrój and beyond

Returning to Bystrzyca Kłodzka, a scenic drive winds back up into the hills directly east of town. Climbing up through forested slopes and emerging from the trees, the narrow road reaches a **pass** where it's worth stopping to appreciate the superb panorama around you. Descending down the other side, the valley unfolds revealing an isolated Lutheran chapel near the village of Sienna, and brings you to the pleasant town of **Stronie Śląskie** (terminus of the rail line from Kłodzko) whose Sudety glassworks have managed not to turn the place into the usual eyesore.

Eight kilometres further north is the spa resort of **LĄDEK-ZDRÓJ**, where, according to tradition, the waters were known for their healing properties as early as the thirteenth century, when the bathing installations were allegedly destroyed by the Tatars. They've certainly been exploited since the late fifteenth century, and in later years attracted visitors as august as Goethe and Turgenev. Today the town, strung out along the river Biała Lądecka, retains a charm that the more popular western spa resorts cannot match.

Centrepiece of the grandiose Neoclassical **spa buildings** at the east end of town is the main sanatorium, a handsome domed building evoking the heyday of the spa, and hereabouts you'll find the odd villa still surviving from that era. In the older part of town, about a kilometre to the west, a mid-sixteenth-century stone **bridge** can still be seen, decorated with statues of religious figures. The town's spacious **Rynek** features some Baroque-fronted houses, all facing the octagonal tower of the town hall.

For those dependent on public transport, the hourly **bus** from Kłodzko represents the only route in and out of town. Tourist information duties are handled by the **PTTK**, near the spa quarter at ul. Kościuszki 44 (Mon–Fri 8am–4pm; T074/814 6255, Wwww.ladek.pl). As for **accommodation**, the FWP office, ul. Kościuszki 48 (T074/814 6272), will find you a room in one of the resort's rest homes for 35zł per person. The *Hotel Lido*, ul. Kościuszki 23a (T074/814 7165; **4**), has reasonable en suites with TV; and there's a **youth hostel** (T074/814 6645; 22zł per person) in the outlying hamlet of Stojków, 3km to the south – although you'll have to walk there if you don't have your own transport. For **eating**, standard and inexpensive Polish fare is on offer at both the restaurant of the *Lido* and the *Polska Chata*, ul. Kościuszki 5.

Immediately to the east of the town, the **Góry Złote** (Golden Mountains) offer some good hiking routes. Check out the blue trail which leads southeast of the town, ascending within an hour to a ruined medieval castle near the summit of **Karpień** (776m), via a series of oddly weathered rocks so often found throughout the region.

For those with their own transport it's well worth exploring the scenic road north out of Lądek, which winds its way through forested highlands where you'll encounter soot-spewing trucks transporting rubble from the region's quarries to the processing plants. Soon the road decends swiftly to the town of

Złoty Stok, sat on the edge of the interminable plain which stretches, with only modest variations in elevation, all the way to the Baltic.

Paczków to Nysa

Heading east from the Kłodzko region, you traverse an undulating plateau peppered with small fortified towns, associated for most of their history with the bishops of Wrocław, who ruled an independent principality here from 1195 until its dissolution by Prussia in 1810. Like much of southern Silesia, it's an entrancing landscape of rolling farmland broken up by forest, largely unaffected by significant industrial development. The terrain levels out a bit towards Nysa, where most of the surrounding fields are given over to the cultivation of rapeseed, producing a blaze of bright yellow ground cover in the early summer.

Buses operating the Kłodzko–Paczków–Nysa route present your best way of **getting around**; placing the region within easy day-trip range of Kłodzko or one of the spa resorts. Should you be approaching from the north, Nysa is well connected by bus to Wrocław and Opole. Trains trundle through the region on their way from Kłodzko to Katowice, but they're both slow and infrequent.

Paczków

In contrast to its neighbours, the quiet little market town of **PACZKÓW**, 30km east of Kłodzko, has managed to preserve its medieval fortifications almost intact – hence its designation as "Poland's Carcassonne". In reality, Paczków is hardly in that league, but has the advantage of being untouched by the hands of Romantically inclined nineteenth-century restorers, as well as being generally overlooked by crowds of tourists.

Nowadays, the mid-fourteenth-century **ramparts** form a shady promenade around the centre of the Stare Miasto; their visual impact is diminished by the enveloping later buildings, though it's a wonder that the town managed to grow so much without their demolition. As it is, nineteen of the twenty-four towers survive, as does nearly all of the original 1350 metres of wall, pierced by three barbicans: the square Wrocław Gate of 1462 and the cylindrical Ząbkow and Kłodzko gates from around 1550.

The area within the walls, spread across a gentle slope, consists of just a handful of streets, but is centred on a large **Rynek**. In the familiar off-centre position is the **town hall**, so comprehensively rebuilt in the twentieth century that only the belfry of its Renaissance predecessor is left.

Rearing up behind the Rynek stands the attention-grabbing form of **Kościół św. Jana** (St John's Church), a strongly fortified part of the town's defences. With a central tower jazzed up with crenellations resembling molar teeth, it looks more like the kind of fortress the Venetians would have built in the Adriatic than a parish church in central Silesia. Inside, the box-like geometry of the design is particularly evident, with the chancel the same length as the main nave.

Practicalities

Paczków has two **hotels**. The *Korona*, ul. Wojska Polskiego 31 (☏077/431 6177; ❷), lies outside the ramparts on a street leading directly off the southeastern side of the Rynek and offers smallish, simply furnished en suites. One kilometre south of town, just off the Nysa road, the *Energopol*, ul. Chrobrego 2 (☏077/431 6298; ❷), is a former workers' hostel which makes up for its undistinguished prefabs with friendly service and good value. There's also a **campsite** on the southwestern fringes of town at ul. Jagiellońska 6 (☎077/431 6813). As far as **places to eat** are concerned, there are a number of cafés around the Rynek offering simple snacks; and a cheap, satisfying pizzeria, the *Monika*, on ul. Sienkiewicza, with outdoor seating in the shadow of the town walls.

Otmuchów

OTMUCHÓW, 14km east of Paczków, was the original capital of the prince-bishopric. In the centre of town is the **castle**, nowadays a hotel but originally twelfth-century Romanesque, which guarded an extensive fortification system now all but vanished. It was transformed into a palace in the sixteenth century, and in 1820 was sold to Wilhelm von Humboldt, founder of the university of Berlin and architect of Prussia's educational system. He lived here in retirement, the liberal views he had championed having fallen from official favour. The castle tower is sometimes open to tourists in the summer, but times are unpredictable. It's worth making your way up here however, if only to linger in the well-tended garden of the castle hotel.

On the Rynek is the Renaissance **town hall**, adorned with a beautifully elaborate, double-faced sundial mounted on a corner of the building. The square slopes upwards to a well-kept floral garden and the parish **church**, a very central-European-looking Baroque construction with a customary twin-towered facade. Recently renovated to perfection by German capital (a practice now occurring throughout the former German territories of post-communist Poland), its ample interior is richly decorated with stuccowork by Italian craftsmen and large painted altarpieces, including several by Michael Willmann.

The *Zamek* **hotel** in the castle (☎077/431 4691, ⓦwww.zamek.anonser .pl; ❺) offers rather cosy rooms furnished in a jumble of styles, although be warned that some of the singles come with shared bathroom facilities. To eat in Otmuchów, the **café-restaurant** *Herbowa* in the castle takes some beating, offering classic Polish dishes in formal, starched-napkin surroundings. The *Merkury*, facing the town hall at ul. Zamkowa 2, has a big choice of inexpensive pizzas and salads.

Nysa

The name of **NYSA**, 12km east of Otmuchów, has become synonymous with the trucks made here for export all over Eastern Europe. Yet industry is a relative newcomer to this town which, in spite of the devastation of 1945, still preserves memories of the days when it basked in the fanciful title of "the Silesian Rome", a reference to its numerous religious houses and reputation as a centre of Catholic education. It came to the fore when the adoption of the Reformation in Wrocław forced the bishops to reside outside the city; they then built up Nysa, the capital of their principality for the previous couple of centuries, as their power base. With its sprinkling of architectural monuments left stranded in a sea of postwar concrete, Nysa is a place for a brief wander rather than a protracted stay.

The Town

From both the bus and train stations, bear right along the edge of the park, then turn left into ul. Kolejowa which leads in a straight line towards the centre. On the way, you pass the fourteenth-century **Brama Wrocławska** (Wrocław Gate), an unusually graceful piece of military architecture with wrought-iron dragons' heads acting as gutter flues, left stranded by the demolition of the ramparts. It's a tantalizing reminder of Nysa's long role as a border fortress: first fortified in the twelfth century by Bolesław the Wrymouth in his struggles against his Bohemian-backed brother Zbigniew.

Having lost its town hall and all but four of its old houses during the war, Nysa's vast **Rynek** is nevertheless not as bad as you might expect, with a few flowerbeds and benches on which repose the town's idle, weary and inebriate. Particularly attractive is the jolly seventeenth-century **Waga Miejska** (Weigh House), which looks as if it belongs somewhere in the Low Countries.

Off the northeastern side of the Rynek is the **Katedra św. Jakuba i Agnieszki** (Cathedral of SS James and Agnes), which long served the exiled bishops. Put up in just six years in the 1420s, it was comprehensively flattened during World War II, and faithfully reconstructed soon afterwards. It's a fine example of the hall church style, with nave and aisles of equal height – a design much favoured in Germany but rare in Poland. Entering through the graceful double portal, it's the spareness of the lofty thirty-metre interior which makes the strongest impression. So crushing is the weight of the vault that many of the uncomfortably slender octagonal brick pillars visibly bow under the strain. The chapels provide the only intimate note: fenced off by wrought-iron grilles, they feature funerary plaques and monuments to the bishops and local notables. Outside, the church's detached stone **belfry** was abandoned after fifty years' work and further damaged during the war, after which it seems to have been left to its own devices.

South of St James's lies the well-preserved if generally deserted Baroque episcopal quarter. The **Pałac Biskupi** (Bishops' Palace), reached down ul. Jarosławka at no. 11, is now fitted out as the surprisingly good **Muzeum Nyskie** (Nisa Museum; Tues 9am–5pm, Wed–Fri 9am–3pm, Sat & Sun 10am–3pm; 4zł, free on Sat), with displays of sixteenth- to eighteenth-century engravings, several pictures of Nysa's postwar ruin, including a shrapnel-damaged 1574 weather vane, as well as fragments from irreparable buildings. There's also a model of the town as it was three hundred years ago, various secular and religious treasures and, perhaps best of all, some wonderfully chunky carved and inlaid Baroque furniture, including a few huge wardrobes it would take a crane to shift and on which you could justifiably observe "they don't make them like that anymore".

Immediately west of here lies the complex of Jesuit buildings in pl. Solny, which kick off with the white-walled **Kościół Wniebowzięcia NMP** (Church of the Ascension), its austerity is softened by some recently discovered ceiling frescoes and a beautiful eighteenth-century silver tabernacle at the high altar. Adjoining it is the famous **Carolinum College**, whose luminaries included the Polish kings Michał Korybut Wiśniowiecki and Jan Sobieski.

South of the Rynek, the only other reminder of "the Silesian Rome" is the **Klasztor Bożogrobców** (Monastery of the Hospitallers of the Holy Sepulchre). This order moved to Nysa from the Holy Land at the end of the twelfth century, but the huge complex you see today dates from the early eighteenth century. It's now a seminary, and you have to ask at the reception on ul. św. Pawła to get into the magnificent Baroque **Kościół św. Piotra i Pawła** (Church of SS Peter and Paul) on the parallel ul. Bracka. Passing a rather creepy Eye of Providence looking down on you in the courtyard, you'll soon have your efforts rewarded. The resplendent interior features gilt capitals, a multicoloured marble altar that's one of the best for miles, and a reproduction of the Holy Sepulchre in Jerusalem. There's also a cycle of highly theatrical frescoes by the brothers Christoph Thomas and Felix Anton Scheffler.

Heading northwest from the Rynek along ul. Krzywoustego brings you to the **Brama Ziębicka** (Ziębicka Gate), a plain brick tower standing in the middle of a roundabout. You can climb up its 150 steps for a couple of złoty.

Practicalities

The **bus** and **train stations** are 1km east of the Rynek at the end of Kolejowa. Nysa's one central **hotel**, the *Piast*, right by the Ziębicka Gate at ul. Krzywoustego 14 (☎077/433 4084, ✉hotelpiast@poczta.onet.pl; ➌), offers comfy en suites and Eighties decor. Otherwise, there's the *Navigator*, a friendly, upscale B&B 300m west of the Rynek at ul. Wyspiańskiego 11 (☎077/433 4170; ➌).

For **eating**, *Restauracja*, Rynek 25, is the best place to refuel on solid meat-and-potatoes fare; while the nearby *Trastevere* at Rynek 36B will sort you out with a decent pizza or salad.

Świdnica and around

In the stretch of land between Wrocław and the Karkonosze mountains to the southwest lie several historic sites, most of them connected with the former **Duchy of Świdnica**, which lasted only from 1290 to 1392 but exerted a profound influence on Silesian culture. With the exception of the sprawling industrial city of Wałbrzych, it's a delightfully rustic corner of Silesia to travel through, consisting largely of rolling arable land fringed by sizeable patches of forest. Wałbrzych is an important transport hub lying on the Wrocław–Jelenia Góra rail line, although road travellers can avoid it altogether by following the main roads to Świdnica (easily accessible by bus from Jelenia Góra, Wrocław and Kłodzko) just to the north.

Świdnica

Although visible as a collection of ever-familiar smokestacks when approached by road, **ŚWIDNICA**, 70km southwest of Wrocław and for centuries Silesia's second most important city, is blessed by the fact that it suffered little damage in World War II. Today the town still manages to preserve some of the grandeur of a former princely capital, resulting in an attractive Silesian town with a tangible self-confidence.

Although Świdnica's period of independent glory – coming soon after its twelfth-century foundation – was short-lived, the town continued to flourish under Bohemian rule. Not only was it an important centre of trade and commerce, it ranked as one of Europe's most renowned brewing centres, with its famous *Schwarze Schöps* forming the staple fare of Wrocław's best-known tavern and exported as far afield as Italy and Russia.

The lively **Rynek** is predominantly Baroque, though the core of many of the houses is often much older. Two particularly notable facades are at no. 7, known as **The Golden Cross**, and no. 8, **The Gilded Man**. In the central area of the square are two fine fountains and the handsome early eighteenth-century **town hall**, which preserves the tower and an elegant star-vaulted chamber from its Gothic predecessor. Round the back of the town hall, the **Muzeum Dawnego Kupiectwa** at Rynek 37 (Museum of Shopkeeping; Tues–Fri 10am–3pm, Sat & Sun 11am–5pm; 3zł) sheds charming light on Świdnica's mercantile past, with re-creations of traditional shop interiors, their counters bearing the cumbersome but decorous weights and measures used by the town's traders.

Kościół św. Stanisława i Wacława

Off the southeastern corner of the Rynek, the main street, ul. Długa, curves gently downhill. The view ahead stretches past a number of Baroque mansions to the majestic **belfry** – at 103m the second highest in Poland – of the Gothic parish **Kościół św. Stanisława i Wacława** (Church of SS Stanislaw and Wenceslas). Intended as one of a pair, the tower was so long under construction that its final stages were finished in 1613, long after the Reformation. This incomplete nature is visible from the strikingly unsymmetrical facade where the matching right side is conspicuous by its absence. Nevertheless, the extant facade, in front of which stands a Baroque statue of St Jan Nepomuk, is impressive enough, featuring a sublime late-Gothic relief of St Anne, the Virgin and Child. Around the early fifteenth-century portals, the two patrons occupy a privileged position in the group of Apostles framing the Madonna – notice also the relief to the right of a man being thrown from a bridge for some arcane felony.

After the Thirty Years' War the church was given to the Jesuits, who carried out a Baroque transformation of the **interior**, respecting the original architecture while embellishing it to give a richer surface effect. A massive high altar with statues of the order's favourite saints dominates the east end; the organ with its carvings of the heavenly choir provides a similar focus to the west, while the lofty walls were embellished with huge Counter-Reformation altarpieces, some of them by Michael Willmann.

The Kościół Pokoju

Set in a quiet walled close ten minutes' walk north of the Rynek (leave the northeastern corner of the square along Pulaskiego, turn left into Kościelna and keep going), the **Kościół Pokoju** (Church of Peace; April–Oct Mon–Sat 9am–1pm & 3–5pm, Sun 3–5pm; Nov–March by appointment; ☏074/852 2814; ⊛www.kosciolpokoju.pl) was built in the 1650s for the displaced Protestant congregation of SS Stanislaw and Wenceslas, according to the conditions on construction applied at Jawor (see p.550) a few years before and to plans drawn up by the same engineer. Although the smaller of the two, it is the more accomplished: indeed, it's considered by some to be the greatest timber-framed church ever built. At first sight, the rusticity of the scene, with its shady graveyard, seems to be mirrored in the architecture, but it's actually a highly sophisticated piece of design. Over 3500 worshippers could be seated inside, thanks to the double two-tiered galleries; all would be able to hear the preacher, and most could see him.

The whole appearance of the church was sharply modified in the eighteenth century, as the Protestant community increased in size and influence after Silesia came under the rule of Prussia. A domed vestibule using the hitherto banned materials was added to the west end, a baptistry to the east, while a picturesque group of **chapels and porches** was tagged on to the two long sides of the building. The latter, recognizable today by their red doorways, served as the entrances to the private boxes of the most eminent citizens whose funerary monuments are slowly crumbling away on the exterior walls. At the same time, the church was beautified inside by the addition of a rich set of furnishings – pulpit, font, reredos and the large and small organs.

Practicalities

From the **train** and **bus stations** it's a couple of minutes' walk east to the Rynek. The **tourist information centre**, right on the Rynek at ul. Wewnętrzna 2 (Mon–Fri 9am–5pm, first Sat in month 8am–4pm; ☏074/852 0290,

ⓔswidnicainftur@poczta.onet.pl), can direct you towards the town's **accommodation** possibilities, which kick off with the swish and comfortable *Hotel Park*, a short walk south of the bus and train stations at ul. Pionerów 20 (ⓣ074/853 7098; ❻). The *Piast*, situated just west of the Rynek at ul. Kotlarska 11 (ⓣ074/852 3076; ❺), also offers cosy if slightly dowdy en suites; while a cheaper option is the *Sportowy*, 1km southeast of the centre at ul. Śląska 31 (ⓣ074/852 2532), which has a mixture of functional en suites (❸) and rooms with shared facilities (❷). As for **eating**, the *Ziemiańska*, on the ground floor of the town hall building at Rynek 43, serves up superbly prepared traditional Polish food in a soothing ambience; while the *Stylowa*, a couple of blocks northwest of the Rynek at ul. ks. Bolka 14, has food with a Hungarian slant. The restaurant of the *Park* is also worth considering for slap-up Polish nosh. Best of the daytime **drinking** options is the *Café 7*, a cosy split-level place with wooden furnishings and art hanging on the walls, occupying the gatehouse of the Kościół Pokoju's graveyard on Kościelna. For an evening session, the *Czerwony Gryf*, diagonally opposite the train station on al. Niepodległości, is the liveliest of the pubs.

Książ

One of the best-preserved castles in Silesia – and the largest hilltop fortress in the country – is to be found at **KSIĄŻ**, 12km west of Świdnica just off the road to Wałbrzych. Despite its rural location the castle is easy to get to: approaching by car, the turn off is well signed a kilometre north of the Wałbrzych city limits. Coming by public transport from Świdnica, the #31 bus to Wałbrzych will drop you on the northern edge of Wałbrzych, from where it's a twenty-minute walk back towards the castle. Coming from Wrocław, your best bet is to take a Wrocław–Jelenia Góra train as far as Wałbrzych-Miasto station, where you can catch municipal bus #8 (every 30min–1hr) right to the gates of the castle. If you miss the #8, you can ride bus #12 northwards to the end of the line and walk the remaining distance (20min).

The **castle** (April & Oct Tues–Sun 10am–4pm; May–Sept Tues–Fri 10am–5pm, Sat & Sun 10am–6pm; Nov–March Tues–Sun 10am–3pm; 7zł) is well worth visiting for its surroundings alone, perched on a rocky promontory surrounded on three sides by the Pełcznica river, and tightly girdled by a belt of ornamental gardens. Despite a disparity of styles taking in practically everything from the thirteenth-century Romanesque of Duke Bolko I's original fortress to idealized twentieth-century extensions (Książ served, at various times, as an HQ for both the German Wehrmacht and the Soviet Red Army), it makes as impressive a sight as you'll get in Silesia's war- and industry-ravaged environs. At present, the four-hundred-room castle is owned by Wałbrzych town council and includes all manner of administrative offices, non-governmental associations, with an antique shop and a handful of quirky cafés stuffed into its labyrinthine lower storeys. However this lack of identity, added to the freedom to wander around the deserted corridors (possibly a result of contradictory signposting) makes for an agreeable visit. Finest of the first-floor function rooms open to the public is the **Maximilian Hall**, a piece of palatial Baroque complete with carved chimneypieces, gilded chandeliers, a fresco of Mount Parnassus and colourful marble panelling. Either side of the hall are salons which continue the ornamentation with colour-themed decor.

The castle's main **tower** (same hours; 12zł) can only be visited as part of an escorted Polish-speaking 25-minute tour, for which a minimum of six people are required – if you hang around at the ticket office for long enough you'll be able to team up with some other visitors eventually. Built over the original core of Bolko's citadel, ascending the ever-diminishing staircase to the Baroque lantern is like climbing through centuries of Książ's past. On the way the guide will point out salient details, which include Gothic elements and graffiti from the wartime and Soviet occupants. From the top, the view across the terracotta-tiled roofs and forest to the surrounding hills will absorb you while you catch your breath and gaze out at the distant hills from where V2 rockets were fired on England over fifty years ago.

Occupying some outbuildings close to the entrance gate, the *Książ* **hotel** (☎074/664 3890, ✉zamek-k@wp.pl; renovated en suites ❺, rooms with shared facilities ❸) makes an inexpensive and unusual place to spend the night. The castle's **cafés** will sort you out with refreshments; otherwise consider a coffee and cake in the **Palmarnia** (Palm House; daily till 6pm) 3km downhill on the northern outskirts of Wałbrzych, an extensive greenhouse complex stuffed with exotic plants and with a charming café at its heart.

Krzeszów

The village of **KRZESZÓW**, lies in the shade of a huge **abbey** complex which ranks, historically and certainly artistically, among the most exceptional monuments in Silesia. Situated some 30km west of Wałbrzych it's some way off the main rail and road routes, but you won't regret making the effort to visit the place – to get there by public transport, catch a bus to the grubby textile town of Kamienna Góra (hourly services from Wałbrzych, less frequently from Jelenia Góra and Wrocław) and change there.

The abbey was originally founded in 1242 by Benedictines at the instigation of Anne, widow of Henryk the Pious. However, they stayed for less than half a century; the land was bought back by Anne's grandson, Bolko I of Świdnica, who granted it to the Cistercians and made their church his family's mausoleum. Despite being devastated by the Hussites and again in the Thirty Years' War, the abbey flourished, eventually owning nearly 300 square kilometres of land, including two towns and forty villages. This economic base funded the complete rebuilding in the Baroque period, but not long afterwards the community went into irreversible decline as the result of the confiscation of its lands during the Silesian Wars.

For over a century the buildings lay abandoned, but in a nicely symmetrical turn of events they were reoccupied by Benedictine monks from Prague in 1919, with a contingent of nuns joining them after World War II. Restoration work is now largely completed, with both the main churches returned to an outstanding condition. That you should find such an architecturally impressive institution dominating this tiny Silesian village only adds to its splendour.

The two churches are very different in size and feel. The smaller and relatively plainer exterior of the two, **Kościół św. Jozefa** (St Joseph's Church), was built in the 1690s for parish use. In replacing the medieval church, its dedication was changed to reflect the Counter-Reformation cult of the Virgin Mary's husband, designed to stress a family image which was overlooked in earlier Catholic theology. Inside, the blue-veined marble and high windows give a bright impression with the newly renovated altar resplendent in the typically Baroque style. The magnificent **fresco** cycle in which Joseph – previously depicted by artists as a shambling old man – appears to be little older than his wife and is similarly transported to heaven, is a prime artistic expression of this short-lived cult. Executed with bold brushwork and warm colours, it is the masterpiece of **Michael Willmann**, an East Prussian who converted to Catholicism and spent the rest of his life carrying out commissions from Silesian religious houses. On the ceiling, Willmann continued the family theme with various biblical genealogies.

Built in the grand Baroque style, the monastic **church** was begun in 1728 and finished in just seven years – hence its great unity of design, relying for effect on a combination of monumentality and elaborate decoration. Its most striking feature is undoubtedly its imposing **facade**, with gravity-defying statues of various religious figures filling the space between the two domed towers.

Inside, the three altarpieces in the transept are all Willmann's work, but the most notable painting is a Byzantine icon which has been at Krzeszów since the fourteenth century. The nave ceiling frescoes illustrate the life of the Virgin, and thus form a sort of counterpoint to those in the parish church; that in the south transept shows the Hussites martyring the monks. From the south transept you pass into the Piast **mausoleum** behind the high altar. This is kept open when tourist groups are around (which is quite frequently in summer); at other times you'll have to persuade a monk or nun to open it up. Focal point of the chapel is the grandiose coloured marble monument to Bernard of Świdnica, to each side of which are more modest Gothic sarcophagi of Bolko I and II. The history of the abbey is told in the frescoes on the two domes.

There's a **snack bar** in the car park opposite the abbey's entrance. For an **overnight stay** the *Willmanowa Pokusa* hotel right outside the abbey complex (☎075/742 3150; ❹) offers comfortable en suites in an atmospheric old building. Alternatively the *Betlejem* pension (☎075/742 3324, ✉pensjonbetlejem@go2 .pl; ❷), signposted 2km south of town, makes an idyllic retreat: a *drzewnianka* (wooden chalet) situated in the woods, which you'll find hard to leave – reserve in advance to avoid disappointment. Adjacent to the building is the little-known Pawilion na Wodzie (Water Pavilion), a former summer house for Krzeszów's bishops, which the owners of the house will show you around for a small fee. The *Willmanowa Pokusa* has a good **restaurant** serving traditional Polish nosh; and there are a couple of other places to eat and drink around the parking lot in front of the abbey.

Jelenia Góra and around

Some 110km southwest of Wrocław, **JELENIA GÓRA** is the gateway to one of Poland's most popular holiday and recreation areas, the **Karkonosze national park**. Its name means "Deer Mountain", but the rusticity this implies is scarcely reflected in the town itself which has been a manufacturing centre for the past five centuries. Founded as a fortress in 1108 by King Bolesław the Wrymouth, Jelenia Góra came to prominence in the Middle Ages through glass and iron production, with high-quality textiles taking over as the cornerstone of its economy in the seventeenth century. With this solid base, it was hardly surprising that, after it came under Prussian control, the town was at the forefront of the German Industrial Revolution. Jelenia Góra is served from Wrocław by four or five daily trains and an equal number of buses – the latter are preferable unless you like the idea of dawdling through the Silesian countryside at walking pace.

The Town

Thankfully Jelenia Góra's present-day factories have been confined to the peripheries, leaving the traffic-free historic centre remarkably well preserved. Even in a country with plenty of prepossessing central squares, the **plac Ratuszowy** is an impressive sight. Not the least of its attractions is that it's neither a museum piece nor the main commercial centre: most of the businesses are restaurants and cafés, while the tall mansions are now subdivided into flats. Although their architectural styles range from the late Renaissance via Baroque to Neoclassical, the houses form an unusually coherent group, all having pastel-toned facades reaching down to arcaded fronts at street level. Occupying the familiar central position is the large mid-eighteenth-century **town hall**, its unpainted stonework providing an apposite foil to the colourful houses.

To the northeast of pl. Ratuszowy rises the slender belfry of the Gothic parish **church**. Epitaphs to leading local families adorn the outer walls, while the inside is chock-full of Renaissance and Baroque furnishings. Yet another eye-catching tower can be seen just to the east, at the point where the main shopping thoroughfare, ul. Marii Konopnickiej, changes its name to ul. 1 Maja. Originally part of the sixteenth-century fortifications, it was taken over a couple of centuries later to serve as the belfry of **Kaplica św. Anny** (St Anne's Chapel). The only other survivor of the town wall is the tower off ul. Jasna, the street which forms a westward continuation of pl. Ratuszowy.

Continuing down ul. 1 Maja, you come in a couple of minutes to the Baroque **Kaplica NMP** (Chapel of St Mary); it's normally kept locked, but if you happen to be here on a Sunday morning you can drop in to hear the fervent singing of its Orthodox congregation. At the end of the street, enclosed in a walled park-like cemetery, is another Baroque church, **Kościół św. Krzyża** (Holy Cross Church), built in the early eighteenth century by a Swedish architect, Martin Franze, on the model of St Catherine's in Stockholm. Though sober from the outside, the double-galleried interior is richly decorated with trompe l'oeil frescoes.

From the bustling ul. Bankowa which skirts the Stare Miasto to the south, ul. Jana Matejki leads to the **Muzeum Karkonoskie** at no. 28 (Tues, Thurs & Fri 9am–3.30pm, Wed, Sat & Sun 9am–4.30pm; 3zł, free on Wed) at its far end, just below the wooded Kościuszki Hill. Apart from temporary exhibitions, the display space here is given over to the history of **glass** from antiquity to the present day, with due emphasis on local examples and a particularly impressive twentieth-century section.

South of the centre at ul. Chałubińskiego 23, the **Muzeum Przyrodnicze Karkonoskiego Parku Narodowego** (Museum of the Karkonosze National Park; Tues, Thur & Fri 9am–3.30pm, Wed, Sat & Sun 9am–4.30pm; 4zł) draws a constant stream of Polish school parties with its didactic words-and-pictures display devoted to the flora, fauna and geology of the park.

For the best **viewpoint** in town, head west from pl. Ratuszowy along ul. Jasna, then cross ul. Podwale and continue down ul. Obrońców Pokoju into the woods and over the bridge. Several paths lead up the hill, which is crowned with an outlook tower that's permanently open. From the top there's a sweeping view of Jelenia Góra and the surrounding countryside.

Practicalities

The main **train station** is about fifteen minutes' walk from the centre, at the east end of ul. 1 Maja. Local buses plus a few services to nearby towns (notably Karpacz) leave from the bays in front, but the **bus station** for all intercity departures is at the opposite end of town, just west of the Rynek on the far side of ul. Obrońców Pokoju. The **tourist office**, just off the Rynek at ul. Grodzka 16 (Mon–Fri 9am–6pm, Sat 10am–2pm; ☎075/767 6925, ⓦwww .karkonosze.it.pl), offers a wealth of brochures and advice on tourism throughout the Karkonosze region.

Given the existence of plentiful buses to the nearby mountain resorts of Karpacz and Szklarska Poręba, it's unlikely that you'll want to stay in Jelenia Góra, although the tourist office will find you a **hotel** bed in town – or in the spa suburb of Cieplice (see below) if you do. Of the central establishments, the *Europa*, ul. 1 Maja 16 (☎075/764 649 5500, ⓦwww.ptkarkonosze.pl; ❺, rooms with shared facilities ❸) is ideally central but a little musty; preferable are the nearby *Jelonek*, ul. 1 Maja 5 (☎075/764 6541, ⓦwww.hotel-jelonek.com.pl; ❺) a welcoming, intimate place in a Baroque town house (the lower floor of which has been colonized by *Pizza Hut*); or the snazzier but equally small *Baron*, which manages to squeeze swish bright rooms into a historic building just off the main Rynek at ul. Grodzka 4 (☎075/752 3351, Ⓔhotelbaron@onet.pl; ❺). Only if the latter is full is it worth stepping up to the 180-room *Mercure Jelenia Góra*, 2km south of town on the road to Kowary and Karpacz at ul. Sudecka 63 (☎075/764 6481, ⓦwww.mercure.com; ❼). The *Park*, just short of the *Jelenia Góra* at ul. Sudecka 42 (☎075/752 6942; ❸), has clean en suites and also has year-round **camping** facilities.

Of the **snack bars** and **cafés** along the main street, *Spaghetteria al Dente*, ul. 1 Maja 33, serves up palatable pasta and risotto dishes for next to nothing; while *Bristolka* at no. 18 offers a sumptuous range of cakes. There are numerous **restaurants** grouped around the main square, most offering outdoor seating and cheap, reasonable food. *Kurna Chata* at no. 22, prides itself for inexpensive order-at-the-counter home cooking in a cosy spot underneath the arcades; while *Gospoda Biesiadna*, Rynek 39, offers a workmanlike menu of Polish pork dishes and a handful of pizzas for good measure. *Azteka*, Rynek 6/7, is a fun place to tuck into the blander side of Mexican cooking, or simply have a drink.

Cultural life centres on the Secessionist-style **Cyprian Norwid Theatre** at al. Wojska Polskiego 38 (box office Tues–Fri 3–6pm & 1hr before performances; ☎075/6428110, ⓦwww.teatr.jgora.pl); and the Filharmonia Dolnośląska, Pilsudskiego 60 (☎075/753 8160, ⓦwww.filharmonia-dolnoslaska.art.pl), while late June and early July see a **festival** of street theatre.

Cieplice Śląskie-Zdrój

The municipal boundaries of Jelenia Góra have been extended to incorporate a number of communities to the south, nearest of which is the old spa town of **CIEPLICE ŚLĄSKIE-ZDRÓJ**, 8km away. Although it has a number of modern sanatoria, along with concrete apartment blocks in the suburbs, Cieplice still manages to bask in the aura of an altogether less pressurized age. To catch this atmosphere at its most potent, attend one of the regular concerts of **Viennese music** in the spa park's delightful Neoclassical **theatre**.

The broad main street of Cieplice is designated as a square – pl. Piastowski. Its main building is the large eighteenth-century **Schaffgotsch palace**, named after the German grandees who formerly owned much of the town. There are also a couple of Baroque **parish churches** – the one for the Catholics stands in a close at the western end of the street and is generally open, whereas its Protestant counterpart to the east of the palace is locked except on Sunday mornings.

A walk south through the Park Norweski, which continues the spa park on the southern side of the River Podgórna, brings you to the small **Muzeum Przyrodnicze** (Natural History Museum; Tues 9am–6pm, Wed–Fri 9am–4pm, Sat & Sun 9am–5pm; 3zł) housed in the so-called Nordic Pavilion. Inside the wooden building, erected here last century, you'll find cases of butterflies as well as the stuffed avians in which the museum specializes.

Practicalities

Local **bus** #9 from Jelenia Góra passes through the centre of Cieplice; #7, #8 and #15 stop on the western side of town, while #4, #13 and #14 stop on the eastern side. The **tourist office**, pl. Piastowski 36 (Mon–Fri 9am–5pm, Sat 10am–2pm; ☎075/755 8844, ⓦwww.karkonosze.it.pl), will fix you up with **private rooms** (❶) in town or direct you towards the **hotels**, of which the most central is the *Cieplice*, ul. Cervi 11 (☎075/755 1041, ⓦwww .ptkarkonosze.pl; ❹), offering a mixed bag of dowdy and renovated rooms right by the spa park. The nearby *Pod Różami*, pl. Piastowski (☎075/755 1453, ⓦwww.podrozami.pl; ❹), provides a bit more in the way of intimate charm. The **campsite**, *Słoneczna Polana*, at ul. Rataja 9 (☎075/755 2566), is near the Orle train station 4km southwest of town, on the routes of buses #7 and #15.

The *Cukierna Weronika* **café** on pl. Piastowski offers some hard-to-resist home-made cakes; while the *Pod Złotym Łukiem* **restaurant**, just off pl. Piastowski at ul. Leśnica 2, serves up superb Polish cuisine in elegant surroundings.

Sobieszów

Buses #7, #9 and #15 all continue the few kilometres south to **SOBIESZÓW**. Once again, there are two Baroque **parish churches**, both located off the main ul. Cieplicka: the Protestant one is appropriately plain, while the Catholic is exuberantly decorated. In an isolated location on the southeastern outskirts is the **regional museum** (Tues–Sun 9am–4pm; 2zł), with displays on the local geology, flora and fauna.

From the centre of the village, red and black trails offer a choice of ascents to the castle of **Chojnik** (Tues–Sun 9am–4pm; 3.50zł), which sits resplend-ently astride the wooded hill of the same name. It's actually much further from town than it appears – allow about an hour for the ascent. Founded in the mid-fourteenth century, the castle is celebrated in legend as the home of a beautiful man-hating princess who insisted that any suitor had to travel through a treacherous ravine in order to win her hand. Many perished in the attempt: when one finally succeeded, the princess chose to jump into the ravine herself in preference to marriage. The castle was badly damaged in 1675, not long after the addition of its drawbridge and the Renaissance ornamentation on top of the walls. Yet, despite its ruined state, enough remains to give a good illustration of the layout of the medieval feudal stronghold it once was, with the added bonus of a magnificent **view** from the round tower.

The castle houses a **restaurant** and **tourist hostel** (☎075/755 3536) with dorm beds from 20zł per person, though the relative solitude afforded by its isolated position is the sole reason for staying.

The Karkonosze

The mountains of the **Karkonosze** are the highest and best-known part of the chain known as the Sudety, which stretches 300km northwest from the smaller

Beskid range, forming a natural border between Silesia and Bohemia. Known for its raw climate, the predominantly granite Karkonosze range rises abruptly on the Polish side, and its lower slopes are heavily forested with fir, beech, birch and pine, though these are suffering badly from the acid rain endemic in central Europe. At around 1100m, these trees give way to dwarf mountain pines and alpine plants, some of them exotic to the region.

Primarily renowned as **hiking** country, these moody, mist-shrouded mountains strongly stirred the German Romantic imagination and were hauntingly depicted by the greatest artist of the movement, Caspar David Friedrich. From the amount of German you hear spoken in the resorts, it's clear that the region offers a popular and inexpensive vacation for its former occupants – and the Polish tourist authorities certainly aren't complaining.

Lying just outside the park's boundaries, the two sprawling resorts of **Szklarska Poręba** and **Karpacz** have expanded over recent years to meet this need, and nowadays constitute well-equipped bases from which to embark on summer hiking and winter skiing expeditions. As the area is relatively compact – the total length of the Karkonosze is no more than 37km – and the public transport system good (if circuitous), there's no need to use more than one base. The upper reaches of the Karkonosze have been designated a **national park** (entry 3zł per day), but as elsewhere, this label does not guarantee an unequivocal vision of natural splendour. If you're not into extended walking or off-road biking, a **chairlift** ascent up to the summits will make an enjoyable day's excursion.

The 1:30,000 **map** of the park, available from kiosks and travel offices, shows all the paths and viewpoints and is a must if you intend doing any serious walking. Like all mountain areas, the range is notorious for its changeable weather; take warm clothing even on a sunny summer's day. **Mist** hangs around on about three hundred days in the year, so always stick to the **marked paths** and don't expect to see much.

Szklarska Poręba

SZKLARSKA PORĘBA lies 18km southwest of Jelenia Góra and just to the west of a major international road crossing into the Czech Republic. It can be reached from Jelenia Góra either by train, depositing you at the station on the northern heights of the town, or by bus, whose terminus is at the eastern entrance to the resort.

You might prefer to walk the last few kilometres of the bus route from Piechowice (which also has a train station); although not actually in the National Park, this offers some fine scenery. The road closely follows the course of the **Kamienna**, one of the main streams rising in the mountains, which is joined along this short stretch by several tributaries, in a landscape reminiscent of the less wild parts of the Scottish highlands. Many of the best vistas are to be had from the road itself, which has an intermittent lane set aside for walkers; the views from the hiking trails are obscured by trees most of the time. However, you do need to make a detour down one of the paths in order to see the **Szklarka waterfall**, situated in a beautiful canyon setting. The point to turn off is easy to find, as it's usually thronged with souvenir sellers.

The Kamienna slices Szklarska Poręba in two, with the main streets in the valley and the rest of the town rising high into the hills on each side. It's well worth following the stream all the way through the built-up part of the resort, as there follows another extremely picturesque stretch on the far side of the centre, with some striking rock formations (the **Kruce Skalny**) towering above the southern bank.

From the busy town the quickest way up to the summits is by **chairlift** (late April to mid-Oct & Dec to early April daily 9am–4.30pm; 28zł return), which goes up in two stages and terminates a short walk from the summit of **Szrenica** (1362m). Its departure point is at the southern end of town: from the bus station, follow ul. 1 Maja, then turn right into ul. Turystyczna, continuing along all the way to the end, following green then black markers. From the top of the lift, you can walk back down or, more ambitiously, follow the ridge east to the sister peak of Snieaka and the resort of Karpacz beneath it (see below), a good day's walking.

Over on the northern side of town, the **Dom Hauptmannów** at ul. 11 Listopada 23 (Hauptmann House; Tues, Thur & Fri 9am–3.30pm, Wed, Sat & Sun 9am–4.30pm; 2zł) remembers the German novelist and playwright Gerhard Hauptmann, one of the many artists and writers who spent their holidays in Szklarska at the close of the nineteenth century. It was here that Hauptmann wrote much of *The Weavers*, a drama of Silesian industrial life that helped bag the Nobel Prize for Literature in 1912. Photographs and manuscripts recall the author's career, and there's also a collection of pieces from the local Huta Julia glass works, source of the region's lead crystal.

Practicalities

As you'd expect, Szklarska Poręba has a great variety of accommodation. Online information is available at Ⓦwww.szklarskaporeba.pl, while the **tourist centre** at ul. Jedności Narodowej 3 (Mon–Fri 8am–6pm, Sat & Sun 10am–5pm; ☎075/717 2494) has access to over thirty **pensions** (❷–❹) offering good-value accommodation, often involving worthwhile half-board deals. They also have a team of **guides** if you want assistance getting up and down the misty mountains.

Good-value **hotels** include the *Eden*, ul. Okrzei 13 (☎075/717 2181; ❸) a big modern house offering en suites with TV just south of the centre; and the nearby *Husarz*, ul. Kilińskiego 18 (☎075/717 3363, Ⓦwww.husarz.wczasy.net .pl; ❺), a charming B&B run located in a half-timbered hunting lodge. *Carmen*, near the Szrenice lift at ul. Broniewskiego 8 (☎075/717 2558, Ⓦwww.carmen .info.pl; ❹), is a largish pension with well-appointed en suites; while sauna, gym and covered pool are on offer at the four-star *Hotel Bornit*, ul. Mickiewicza 21 (☎075/753 9503, Ⓦwww.bornit.hotel.pl; ❻), a glass-fronted monolith overlooking the town centre from a hillside perch just to the west. The **youth hostel** is a long way northeast of the centre at ul. Piastowska 1 (☎075/717 2141), on the wrong side of town for the best walks, but it is open all year. Most central of the **campsites** is the *Pod Mostem* at Gimnazijalna 5 (☎075/717 3062), just west of the bus station; further afield, the *Południowy Stok* on the northwest fringes of the resort at ul. Batalionów Chłopskich 12 (☎075/717 2129), is open all year and has four-person chalets for around 80zł.

There's a cluster of inexpensive snack huts at the foot of the Szrenica chairlift; otherwise the central ul. Jedności Narodowej offers the main concentration of **places to eat**. *Diavolo* at no. 26 specializes in tasty pizzas, *pierogi* and pancakes; while *Fantazija*, at no. 14, is better for more substantial meat and fish dishes – the latter also does good coffee and ice cream in the café section. *Kryształ*, ul. 1 Maja 19, is the place to go for traditional Polish nosh followed by a spot of old-time dancing.

Karpacz and around

KARPACZ, 15km south of Jelenia Góra and linked to it by at least twenty buses a day, is an even more scattered community than Szklarska Poręba, occupying an enormous area for a place with only a few thousand permanent inhabitants. It's a fairly characterless place if the centre of town is all you see, but the sheer range of easily accessible hikes in the neighbouring mountains make this the most versatile of Silesia's highland resorts.

Karpacz is a long, thin settlement built along the main road, ul. 3 Maja (ul. Karkonoska in its upper reaches), which stretches and curves uphill for some 5km. Most tourist facilities are located in **Karpacz Dolny** (Lower Karpacz), at the lower, eastern end of the resort, although **Karpacz Górny** (Upper Karpacz), up the valley to the west, has its fair share of hotels and pensions. In between lies the **Biały Jar** roundabout (named after the next-door *Biały Jar* hotel), which is the main starting point for most of the hiking trails.

Arrival, information and accommodation

Most **buses** from Jelenia Góra terminate at Biały Jar (picking up and dropping off at numerous stops along ul. 3 Maja on the way), although some continue all the way to Karpacz Górny. Bearing in mind that it can take an hour to walk from one end of the resort to the other, these buses represent a useful way of shuttling up and down the resort once you get established.

The **tourist information centre** at ul. Konstytucji 3 Maja 25a (Mon–Fri 8.30am–4.30pm; ☎075/761 9453, ⊛www.karpacz.pl) in Karpacz Dolny sells hiking maps, and will help you find a bed in one of Karpacz's innumerable **private rooms** (❷) and **pensions** (❷–❹).

Hotels

Bacówki ul. Obrońców Pokoju 6a ☎075/761 9764 Cluster of dinky wooden huts spread over a meadow just east of Karpacz Dolny, with bathrooms shared between every two or three rooms. ❸

Karkonosze ul. Wolna 4 ☎075/761 8277. Attractive alpine chalet-style building in a quiet residential street, and right next to a nursery skiing slope. Small bright rooms with shower and TV. ❺

Klub Holandia 3 Maja 67 ☎075/761 0982. Comfortable medium-sized establishment midway between Karpacz Dolny and Biały Jar offering fully equipped en suites and a good restaurant. ❻

Promyk ul. Obrońców Pokoju 7a ☎075/761 6196; ⊛www.karpacz.com.pl/promyk. Smart modern hotel whose comfortable rooms feature some odd colour schemes but plenty of wood furnishings. Gym, sauna, and a restaurant which serves Thai dishes along with the usual Polish stuff. ❺

Rezydencja ul. Parkowa 6 ☎075/761 8020. Elegant, upmarket place in Karpacz Dolny whose understated plushness makes it the cosiest place to stay in town. ❻

Skalny ul. Obrońców Pokoju 3 ☎075/752 7000, ✉skalny@orbis.pl. Orbis-run, 300-bed block that lacks the character and intimacy of the other places in town, but has reliable standards of comfort and the added bonus of a swimming pool. ❻

The Town

Located in the upper reaches of Karpacz Górny and clearly visible from the main road is the most famous, not to say curious, building in the Karkonosze – the **Świątynia Wang** (Wang Chapel; Mon–Sat 9am–6pm, Sun 11.30am–6pm; 4zł). Girdled at a discreet distance by souvenir stalls and snack bars, this twelfth-century wooden church with Romanesque touches boasts some wonderfully refined carving on its portals and capitals, as well as an exterior of tiny wooden tiles giving it a scaly, reptilian quality. It stood for nearly six hundred years in a village in southern Norway, but by 1840 it had fallen into such a state of disrepair that the parishioners sought a buyer for it. Having failed to interest any Norwegians, they sold it to one of the most enthusiastic architectural conservationists of the day, King Friedrich Wilhelm IV of Prussia. He had the church dismantled and shipped to this isolated spot, where it was meticulously reassembled over a period of two years. The stone tower added at the beginning of the twentieth century is the only feature which is not original, and looks conspicuously inappropriate. In deference to Friedrich Wilhelm's wishes, the chapel is still used on Sunday mornings for Protestant worship; there are also organ recitals on alternate Sundays in summer.

A couple of kilometres downhill from the chapel, above Biały Jar, the **Muzeum Zabawek** at ul. Karkonoska 5 (Toy Museum; Tues 9am–5.30pm, Wed–Fri 9am–3.30pm, Sat 10am–3.30pm, Sun 10am–4.30pm; 3zł) is as much a tribute to local crafts as to the history of playthings, with a host of wood-carved animals, carriages and sleds. Down in Karpacz Dolny, just east of the main strip at ul. Kopernika 2, the **Muzeum Sportu i Turystyki** (Museum of Sport and Tourism; Tues, Thurs–Sun 9am–5pm, Wed 1–5pm; 4zł), boasts an enjoyable selection of archaic bobsleighs and crampons and, upstairs, a room full of lace, carved furniture and traditional dress, as well as a model of Chojnik castle.

Eating and drinking
Karpacz is full of places where you can refuel after a hard day in the hills, with the stretch of ul. Konstitucji 3 Maja just west of the tourist office boasting a particularly generous selection of **eating** and **drinking** venues. *Bar Mieszko*, at the top end of Karpacz Dolny in what passes for a village square, is the place to go for cheap *pierogi*, *bigos* and other filling Polish staples; *Pizzeria Verdi*, a little way further down the main strip on ul. Konstitucji 3. Maja, offers a good range of thin-crust pies in stylish surroundings; and the nearby *Zagroda Goralska*, ul. Konstitucji 3 Maja 46, serves up cheap and filling cuts of roast meat in a timber hut. *Karczma Śląska*, just off the main drag at Rybacka 1, is an inexpensive source of grilled pork dishes. *Country Grill*, ul. Obrońców Pokoju 6a, is a ranch-like place next to the *Bacówki* where you can eat traditional Polish food and sink numerous beers in a vast wooden stable.

Hiking in the park
Before undertaking any day-walks in this area it's worth getting yourself a copy of the 1:30,000 Karpacz i Okolice **map**, if you haven't already got the national park map mentioned on p.572. It includes a plan of the town and is sold at the tourist information centre (see opposite).

Booths next to the Wang Chapel and the Biały Jar roundabout sell entrance **tickets** to the national park (4zł). Biały Jar is the more popular entrance point to the park, not least because it's twenty minutes' walk from the lower station of the **chairlift** (8am–5pm) which leads up towards Kopa (1375m), just twenty minutes from the Karkonosz's high point of Śnieżka (see below).

A short detour west from the lift station takes you to the upper of two **waterfalls** on the River Łomnica, which rises high in the mountains and flows all the way through Karpacz, defining much of the northern boundary of the town, as well as the course of ul. Konstytucji 3 Maja, which follows a largely parallel line. The second waterfall, below Biały Jar on a path waymarked in red, is less idyllic, having been altered to form a dam.

The most popular goal for most walks is the summit of **Śnieżka**, at 1602m the highest peak in the range and sometimes covered with snow for up to six months of the year. Lying almost due south of Karpacz, it can be reached by the

black trail in about three hours from the *Biały Jar*, or in about forty minutes if you pick up the trail at the top of the Kopa chairlift. From the chairlift you pass through the Kocioł Łomniczki, whose abundant vegetation includes Carpathian birch, cloves, alpine roses and monk's hood. Access to the actual summit is by either the steep and stony "Zigzag Way" (the red trail) which ascends by the most direct method, or the easier "Jubilee Way" (the blue route), which goes round the northern and eastern sides of the summit. At the top is a large modern weather station-cum-snack bar, where you can get cheap hot **meals**; refreshments are also available in the refuges on Kopa and *Pod Śnieżką*, and at the junction of the two trails.

The **red trail** also serves the summit. From Biały Jar it follows the stream to the chairlift terminal and then forks right near the Orlinek hotel onto an unmade track which climbs steadily for forty minutes to a junction with a yellow path and a refuge. The path continues above the tree line and after some steeper zigzags reaches the *Pod Śnieżką* refuge, another forty minutes later: the refuge is less than fifteen minutes above the Kopa chairlift terminal, following the black waymarkers. From here the side-trip east to the summit of Śnieżka takes twenty minutes by the "Zigzag Way". On a clear day, the **view** from Śnieżka stretches for 80km, embracing not only other parts of the Sudety chain in Poland and the Czech Republic, but also the Lausitz mountains in Germany.

Once at the summit, it's worth following the red trail immediately to the west above two glacial **lakes**, Mały Staw and Wielki Staw just above the tree line. Assuming you don't want to continue on to Szklarska Poręba, you can then descend by the black trail and switch to the blue, which brings you out at Karpacz Górny. If you're feeling energetic you might like to go a bit further along the red trail and check out the Słonecznik and the Pielgrzymy **rock formations** thereafter descending by the yellow and later blue trails back to Karpacz Górny. If the above routes seem too strenuous, a satisfyingly easy alternative is to take the blue trail from the Karpacz Górny to the *Samotnia* refuge on the shore of Mały Staw, a round trip taking about three hours.

Travel details

Trains

Cieszyn to: Bielsko-Biała (8 daily; 1hr).
Jelenia Góra to: Częstochowa (2 daily; 6hr); Gdańsk (1 daily; 10hr; couchettes); Katowice (3 daily; 7hr); Kielce (1 daily; 8hr; couchettes); Kłodzko (4 daily; 2hr); Kraków (2 daily; 9–10hr; couchettes); Łódź (4 daily; 6hr 30min–9hr); Opole (4 daily; 4hr–4hr 30min); Szklarska Poręba (4 daily; 1hr 30min); Wałbrzych (10 daily; 1hr); Warsaw (4 daily; 8hr 30min–9hr 30min); Wrocław (5 daily; 3–4hr).
Katowice to: Białystok (2 daily; 6–8hr; couchettes); Bielsko-Biała (every 30min; 1hr 30min–2hr 30min); Bydgoszcz (4 daily; 5–7hr); Częstochowa (26 daily; 1hr 30min–2hr); Gdańsk (6 daily; 6hr 30min–9hr; couchettes); Jelenia Góra (3 daily; 7hr); Kielce (11 daily; 2hr 30min–3hr

30min); Kołobrzeg (1 daily; 11hr 30min; couchettes); Kraków (36 daily; 1hr 30min–2hr); Legnica (7 daily; 4–7hr); Leszno (7 daily; 4hr 30min–5hr); Łódź (8 daily; 3hr 30min–5hr); Lublin (5 daily; 6–7hr); Nysa (4 daily; 4hr); Olsztyn (2 daily; 8hr 30min–11hr); Opole (23 daily; 2hr); Poznań (15 daily; 5–7hr); Przemyśl (7 daily; 5hr 30min); Pszczyna (every 30min; 1hr–1hr 30min); Rzeszów (8 daily; 4–5hr); Słupsk (1 daily; 13hr; couchettes); Szczecin (5 daily; 9–10hr); Świnoujście (3 daily; 10hr–11hr 30min); Wałbrzych (3 daily; 6hr); Warsaw (17 daily; 3hr 30min–5hr); Wrocław (21 daily; 2–3hr); Zakopane (3 daily; 5–7hr; couchettes); Zamość (2 daily; 8–10hr); Zielona Góra (4 daily; 5–6hr).
Wrocław to: Białystok (2 daily; 10hr 30min–13hr; couchettes); Bydgoszcz (6 daily; 4–5hr); Częstochowa (6 daily; 3–4hr); Gdańsk (7 daily;

6hr–7hr 30min; couchettes); Jelenia Góra (5 daily; 3–4hr); Kalisz (3 daily; 2hr–2hr 30min); Katowice (21 daily; 2–3hr); Kielce (3 daily; 5hr–6hr 30min); Kłodzko (7 daily; 2hr 30min); Kołobrzeg (2 daily; 8–10hr); Kraków (17 daily; 4–6hr); Legnica (22 daily; 1hr); Leszno (27 daily; 1hr–1hr 30min); Łódź (14 daily; 4–6hr); Lublin (3 daily; 8hr 30min–9hr 30min; couchettes); Olsztyn (2 daily; 7hr 30min–10hr; couchettes); Opole (42 daily; 1hr–1hr 30min); Poznań (26 daily; 2hr); Przemyśl (5 daily; 8hr 30min; couchettes); Rzeszów (6 daily; 7hr; couchettes); Słupsk (2 daily; 9–10hr); Szczecin (11 daily; 6hr–7hr 30min; couchettes); Świnoujście (3 daily; 7–8hr); Wałbrzych (20 daily; 1hr 30min); Warsaw (16 daily; 6–7hr; couchettes); Zakopane (1 daily; 8hr 30min; couchettes); Zielona Góra (10 daily; 2–3hr).

Buses

Bielsko-Biała to: Cieszyn (hourly; 1hr 10min); Kraków (12 daily; 3hr); Szczyrk (every 30min; 40min); Wisła (3 daily; 1hr 10min); Zakopane (3 daily; 3hr 30min).
Brzeg to: Nysa (2 daily; 2hr).
Cieszyn to Bielsko-Biała (hourly; 1hr 10min); Brenna (hourly; 1hr); Katowice (Mon–Sat 15 daily; Sun 10 daily; 1hr 30min); Kraków (6 daily; 4hr); Pszczyna (Mon–Fri 2 daily; 1hr 15min); Ustroń (every 30min; 30min); Wisła (every 30min; 45min).
Jelenia Góra to: Bolków (8 daily; 50min); Kamienna Góra (8 daily; 55min); Karpacz-Biały Jar (every 30min; 40min); Kłodzko (2 daily; 3hr 20min); Legnica (12 daily; 2hr); Świdnica (6 daily; 1hr 50min); Szklarska Poręba (hourly; 45min); Wrocław (4 daily; 2hr 20min).
Kamienna Góra to: Krzeszów (hourly; 30min).
Katowice to: Bielsko-Biała (12 daily; 1hr 45min); Cieszyn (Mon–Sat 15 daily, Sun 10 daily; 1hr

30min); Kłodzko (3 daily; 5hr); Kudowa-Zdrój (2 daily; 5hr 50min).
Kłodzko to: Duszniki Zdrój (hourly; 50min); Katowice (3 daily; 5hr); Kudowa-Zdrój (hourly; 1hr 10min); Lądek-Zdrój (hourly; 50min); Międzygórze (5 daily; 1hr 20min); Nysa (7 daily; 1hr 20min); Opole (3 daily; 3hr 40min); Packów (12 daily; 40min); Świdnica (6 daily; 1hr 50min); Wambierzyce (1 daily; 1hr).
Kudowa-Zdrój to: Duszniki Zdrój (hourly; 20min); Karłów (May–Sept: 5 daily; 20min); Katowice (1 daily; 6hr); Kłodzko (hourly; 1hr 10min).
Legnica to: Jawor (hourly; 40min); Lubiąż (1 daily; 40min); Wrocław (6 daily; 1hr 30min).
Opole to: Kłodzko (3 daily; 3hr 40min); Nysa (12 daily; 2hr 20min).
Świdnica to: Wałbrzych (every 30min; 40min); Wrocław (buses 6 daily; 1hr 30min; minibuses hourly; 1hr 15min).
Wałbrzych to: Kamienna Góra (hourly; 1hr 20min).
Wisła to: Istebna (Mon–Fri 12 daily; Sat & Sun 5 daily; 25min); Jaworzynka (Mon–Fri 12 daily; Sat & Sun 5 daily; 35min).
Wrocław to: Bolków (4 daily; 1hr 40min); Jelenia Góra (4 daily; 2hr 20min); Karpacz (2 daily; 3hr 30min); Kudowa-Zdrój (5 daily; 3hr 30min); Legnica (6 daily; 1hr 30min); Nysa (8 daily; 2hr 45min); Sobotka (hourly; 1hr); Strzegom (6 daily; 50min); Świdnica (buses 6 daily; 1hr 30min; minibuses hourly; 1hr 15min); Trzebnica (every 30min; 50min).

International trains

Katowice to: Berlin (1 daily; 8hr); Prague (3 daily; 4hr 30min); Vienna (1 daily; 9hr).
Wrocław to: Berlin (1 daily; 6hr); Budapest (1 daily; 11hr); Dresden (4 daily; 5hr); Prague (3 daily; 6hr 30min).

Wielkopolska and Pomerania

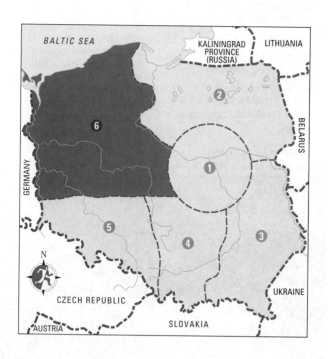

CHAPTER 6

Highlights

* **Poznań** Wielkopolska's bustling commercial and cultural capital is also home to the wonderful, leafy cathedral district of Ostrów Tumski. See p.585

* **Wielkopolska national park** This wonderfully tranquil area of forests and lakes tops the list of potential day-trips from Poznań. See p.604

* **Stalag Luft III, Żagań** A charming and dignified museum commemorates the camp – and mass break-out – that inspired the Hollywood movie *The Great Escape*. See p.609

* **Gniezno** An easy-going provincial town which was for centuries the seat of Poland's archbishops, and is still the site of a truly wonderful cathedral. See p.614

* **Biskupin** Take the narrow-gauge train from Żnin to visit this re-constructed Iron Age village, situated amid a rolling rural landscape. See p.621

* **Łeba** A characterful coastal village-cum-beach resort, right next door to the alluring dune-scapes of the Słowiński national park. See p.629

* **Międzyzdroje** A charming, old-fashioned seaside spa town, conveniently located at the edge of the thickly forested Woliński national park. See p.642

△ Old Town Square, Poznań

6

Wielkopolska and Pomerania

Wielkopolska and **Pomerania**, the two northwest regions of the country, constitute a large swathe of modern Poland. Geographically it's a fairly unified area, much of which is made up of flat arable land, although there are thick belts of forest in the north and west. However, the feel and history of the two provinces remain highly distinct. Wielkopolska formed the core of the original Polish nation and has remained identifiably Polish through subsequent centuries, despite long periods of German rule; Pomerania, by contrast, bears the imprint of the Prussians, who lorded it over this area from the early eighteenth century through to 1945 – the province only became Polish after 1945, and "Lower Pomerania", to the west of Świnoujście, remains German territory. The proximity of Germany continues to exert a strong influence over the two regions, with a steady flow of cross-border traffic and trade that will only increase now Poland is part of the EU. The impact of German investment in the area is most evident in **Poznań**, a burgeoning business centre that is also western Poland's major urban tourist draw.

Offering plenty in the way of urban sightseeing and vibrant nightlife, Poznań is also a good place from which to explore the woods of the **Wielkopolska national park** just to the south, a rare region of wilderness in this heavily agricultural belt. To the east of Poznań lies **Gniezno**, the ancient seat of Poland's first ruling dynasty, the Piasts, and still the ecclesiastical capital of Poland, full of seminaries and trainee priests. In the environs of Gniezno lie several worthwhile historical sights, notably the reconstructed Iron Age village of **Biskupin**, Poland's most ancient preserved settlement, and the Museum of the First Piasts at **Lake Lednica**.

The main focus for tourists in **Pomerania** is the string of **seaside resorts** that pull in large numbers of Poles in summer, their glorious white-sand beaches sweeping away far enough to enable you to escape the crowds. Due to the Pomeranian coast's northerly latitudes the holiday season is rather short; but in July and August hordes of tourists arrive to soak up what sun there is, with fish-and-chip stalls and beer tents springing up to service basic gastronomic needs. Although relatively quiet, spring and early autumn can be rewarding times to visit, especially if beach strolling – rather than sunbathing – is your thing. The fishing village of **Łeba**, gateway to the famed sand dunes of the **Słowiński**

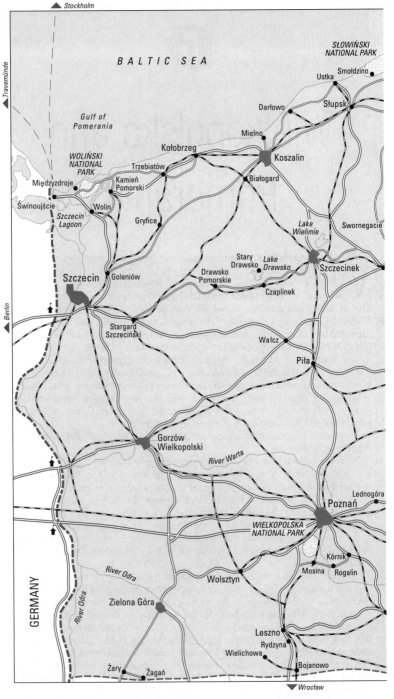

▲ Stockholm

▲ Travemünde

BALTIC SEA

SŁOWIŃSKI
NATIONAL PARK

Ustka   Smołdzino

Gulf of
Pomerania

Darłowo   Słupsk

Mielno

Kołobrzeg   Koszalin

WOLIŃSKI
NATIONAL
PARK

Trzebiatów   Białogard

Międzyzdroje   Kamień
Pomorski

Świnoujście

Wolin

Szczecin
Lagoon   Gryfice   Lake
Wielimie   Swornegacie

Stary
Drawsko   Lake
Drawsko

Drawsko
Pomorskie   Szczecinek

Szczecin   Goleniów   Czaplinek

▲ Berlin

Stargard
Szczeciński   Wałcz

Piła

GERMANY

Gorzów
Wielkopolski

River Warta

Lednogóra

Poznań

WIELKOPOLSKA
NATIONAL PARK

Kórnik

River Odra   Mosina   Rogalin

Wolsztyn

Zielona Góra

River Odra

Leszno

Rydzyna

Wielichowa   Bojanowo

Żary   Żagań

▼ Wrocław

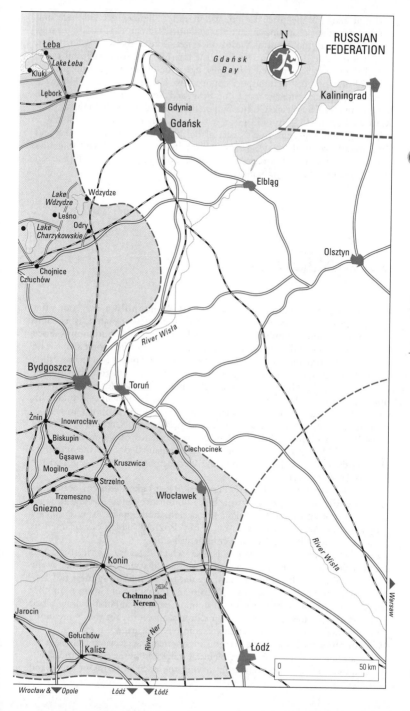

6

N

RUSSIAN
FEDERATION

*Gdańsk
Bay*

Kaliningrad

Łeba
Lake Łeba
Kluki
Lębork

Gdynia
Gdańsk

Elbląg

*Lake
Wdzydze*
Wdzydze
Leśno
Odry
*Lake
Charzykowskie*
Chojnice
Człuchów

Olsztyn

River Wisła

Bydgoszcz
Toruń

Żnin
Inowrocław
Biskupin
Gąsawa
Mogilno
Kruszwica
Strzelno
Trzemeszno
Gniezno

Ciechocinek

Włocławek

River Wisła

Konin

Chełmno nad
Nerem

River Ner

Jarocin
Gołuchów
Kalisz

Łódź

0   50 km

Wrocław & ▼ Opole   Łódź ▼   ▼ Łódź

▶ *Warsaw*

national park, is the place to aim for in eastern Pomerania, although any number of other charming beachside settlements await exploration nearby. Over to the west, the island of **Wolin** offers yet more in the way of fine sands, as well as the European bison reserve in the forested **Woliński national park**. Inland Pomerania is peppered with grey, rather downbeat towns which serve as useful nodal points for transport connections, but offer little else. However, several architectural nuggets stand out: **Stargard Szczeciński** harbours some fine examples of the brick Gothic buildings so typical of the Baltic lands, and **Kamień Pomorski** is an old lagoon settlement with a wonderful cathedral.

The big industrial cities in this part of Poland – **Szczecin** in the west and **Bydgoszcz** over to the east – are never likely to make it into Polish tourism's Top Ten, but shouldn't be overlooked entirely: both possess an appealing urban vigour, and a wealth of cultural diversions.

Wielkopolska

The ever so gently undulating landscape of **Wielkopolska** may not offer much drama, but its human story is an altogether different matter, as its name – "Greater Poland" – implies. This area has been inhabited continuously since prehistoric times, and it was here that the Polish nation first took shape. The names of the province and of Poland itself derive from a Slav tribe called the **Polonians**, whose leaders – the **Piast** family – were to rule the country for five centuries. Their embryonic state emerged under Mieszko I in the mid-tenth century, but the significant breakthrough was achieved under his son, Boleslaw the Brave, who gained control over an area similar to that of present-day Poland, and made it independent from the German-dominated Holy Roman Empire. Though relegated to the status of a border province by the mid-eleventh century, Wielkopolska remained one of the indisputably Polish parts of Poland, resisting the Germanization which swamped the nation's other western territories.

The major survival from the early Piast period is at **Lake Lednica**, located just west of **Gniezno**, the first city to achieve dominance before decline brought about the consolation role of Poland's ecclesiastical capital. It was quickly supplanted as the regional centre by nearby **Poznań**, which has retained its position as one of Poland's leading commercial cities.

Even older than either of these is **Kalisz**, which dates back at least as far as Roman times, while the region's prehistoric past is vividly represented at the Iron Age village of **Biskupin**, a halfway point on the **narrow-gauge rail line** that rattles along between the town of **Żnin** and the village of **Gąsawa**. Another town in the province which has played an important part in Polish culture, albeit at a later date, is **Leszno**, once a major Protestant centre. Yet this is predominantly a rural province, and perhaps its most typical natural attraction is the **Wielkopolska national park**, epitomizing the region's glaciated landscape.

As elsewhere in Poland, there are plentiful trains and buses, even to the smallest outpost, with the former usually having the edge in terms of speed and convenience.

Poznań

Thanks to its position on the Paris–Berlin–Moscow rail line, and as the one place where all international trains stop between the German border and Warsaw, **POZNAŃ** is many visitors' first taste of Poland. In many ways it's the ideal introduction, as no other city is more closely identified with Polish nationhood. *Posnania elegans Poloniae civitas* ("Poznań, a beautiful city in Poland"), the inscription on the oldest surviving depiction of the town, has been adopted as a local catchphrase to highlight its unswerving loyalty to the national cause over the centuries. Nowadays it's a city of great diversity, encompassing a tranquil cathedral quarter, an animated centre focused on one of Europe's finest squares and a dynamic business district whose trade fairs are the most important in the country. A brace of fine museums and a wealth of nightlife opportunities ensure that a couple of days are well spent here – it may be a big city, but most of its primary attractions are grouped in a central, walkable core that is in places free from traffic. Outside the central area the rattle of trams and tyres on cobbled streets makes it a noisy but invigorating place. It's also a good base from which to explore the region's other key attractions, with regular trains running to the Wielkopolska national park, Gniezno and beyond.

Pride of place in the Poznań **festival** calendar goes to the St John's Fair (Jarmark Świętojański), a traditional knees-up of medieval origins, with handicraft stalls and folk music performers taking over the Stary Rynek in the days leading up to St John's Day (June 24). St Martin's Day (Nov 11) is marked by the mass-consumption of *rogale świętomarcińskie*, locally produced croissant-like pastries which can be bought in bakeries and food shops.

Some history

In the ninth century the Polonians founded a castle on a strategically significant island in the River Warta, and in 968 Mieszko I made this one of the two main centres of his duchy, and the seat of its first bishop. The settlement that developed here was given the name **Ostrów Tumski** (Cathedral Island), which it still retains.

Although initially overshadowed by Gniezno, Poznań did not follow the latter's decline after the court moved to Kraków in the mid-thirteenth century. Instead, it became the undisputed capital of Wielkopolska and the main bastion of Poland's western border. The economic life of the city then shifted to the west bank of the river, adopting the familiar grid pattern around a market square which remains to this day. Poznań's prosperity soared as it profited from the fifteenth-century decline of both the Teutonic Order and the Hanseatic League, and the city became a key junction of European trade routes as well as a leading centre of learning.

Along with the rest of the country, regression inevitably set in with the ruinous Swedish Wars of the seventeenth and eighteenth centuries. Revival of sorts came during the Partitions period, when Poznań became the Prussian city of Posen; sharing in the wealth of the Industrial Revolution, it also consolidated its reputation as a rallying point for **Polish nationalism**, resisting Bismarck's Germanization policy and playing an active role in the independence movements. An uprising in December 1918 finally forced out the German occupiers, ensuring that Poznań would become part of the resurrected Polish state.

Poznań's rapid expansion during the interwar period has been followed by accelerated growth, doubling in population to its present level of almost 600,000, and spreading onto the right bank of the Warta. The city's association with the struggle against foreign hegemony – this time Russian – was again demonstrated by the **food riots** of 1956, which were crushed at a cost of 74 lives. These riots are popularly regarded as the first staging post towards the formation of Solidarity 24 years later.

As well as being a vibrant university town, modern Poznań is a brash, self-confident commercial centre revelling in its key position on the Berlin–Warsaw road and rail routes. Above all it is known for the international **trade fairs** held on the exhibition grounds just west of the train station – a tradition begun when the Great East German Exhibition was held here in 1908, restarted by the Poles in 1921, and now symbolic of the city's post-communist economic dynamism. You can check out more on this at Ⓦ www.mtp.com.pl.

Arrival, information and city transport

The main **train station**, Poznań Główny, is 2km southwest of the historic quarter; the front entrance, not immediately apparent, is situated between platforms 1 and 4, but the nearest tram station is reached from the western exit beyond platform 7 (if in doubt, follow the *McDonald's* signs) which leads out onto ul. Głogowska. Tram #5 heads from here to al. Marcinkowskiego, 300m short of the main Rynek; while tram #8 delivers you pl. Ratajskiego in the western part of the downtown area. The **bus station** is five minutes' walk to the east of the train station along ul. Towarowa. Poznań's **airport** is 7km west of the city in the suburb of Ławica – bus #78 runs towards the centre every 20–30 minutes (get off at the Baltyk stop just north of the trade fair grounds).

Visitors have the luxury of a choice of two tourist offices, both of which have a wealth of pamphlets and maps for sale and will give out information on accommodation. There's a **city information centre** (Centrum Informacji Miejskiej, or CIM; Mon–Fri 10am–7pm, Sat & Sun 10am–5pm; ☎061/851 9645 or 9431) beside the Empik store on the corner of Ratajczaka and 27 Grudnia; and a Poznań regional **tourist information centre** at Stary Rynek 59 (Mon–Fri 9am–5pm, Sat 10am–2pm; ☎061/852 6156). Both offices sell the Poznań City Card (30zł for 1 day, 35zł for 2 days, 40zł for 3 days), which provides free use of public transport and free access to museums – worthwhile if you're contemplating an exhaustive trawl of the sights.

The city is well served by a dense and efficient network of **tram** and **bus** routes, with services running from about 5.30am until 10.45pm – after which infrequent night buses run on selected routes. Tickets (bought from kiosks) cost 1.20zł for a trip of 10 minutes or under, 2.40zł for a trip of 30 minutes.

Accommodation

Poznań has a fair range of accommodation, but **hotels** tend to be overpriced for what they offer – and rates can rise by an additional fifty percent or more during trade fairs, which take place at regular intervals throughout the year except in July and August (the rates quoted below are for non-trade fair periods). There's an acute shortage of inexpensive hotel accommodation, and those on a tight budget will be dependent on the city's **youth hostels**, or on **private rooms** (❷), which are available from the 24-hour Globtour office in the main hall of the train station (private rooms available up until 10pm) or from the Biuro Zakwaterowania Przemysław (Accommodation Bureau; Mon–Fri 8am–6pm, Sat 9am–2pm; ☎061/866 3560, Ⓦ www.przemyslaw.com .pl and Ⓦ www.noclegi.poznan.pl), just across the road from the train station's western exit at Głogowska 16.

The nearest **campsite** is the *Malta* (☎061/876 6203, Ⓔ camping@malta .poznan.pl), situated 3km east of the centre at the northeastern end of the eponymous lake, although its luxury two- to four-person bungalows, complete with satellite TV (●), are more expensive than some downtown hotel rooms. Tram #8 from the train station passes along Warszawska (get off after passing the *Novotel Poznań Malta* on your right), a good 600m north of the site.

Hotels

Central

Brovaria Stary Rynek 73/74 ☎061/858 6868, ⓦwww.brovaria.pl. Boutique hotel right on the main square offering restful, cream-coloured rooms with all the creature comforts. Soon fills up so book early. ❻

Domina ul. św. Marcin 2 ☎061/859 0590, ⓦwww.dominahotels.com. Swish, fully equipped apartments in a downtown location. ❽–❾

Dom Turysty Stary Rynek 91, entrance round the side on Wroniecka ☎061/852 8893, ⓦwww.domturysty-hotel.com.pl. PTTK-run hotel occupying a reconstructed eighteenth-century palace right on the main square. The only hotel that doesn't raise its prices during trade fairs, the smallish rooms come with 1970s-era furnishings but are clean and comfortable throughout. There are some simple hostel-style triples and quads, although most rooms are doubles, which either come with en-suite facilities or with shared bathrooms. ❹–❺

Ibis ul. Kazimierza Wielkiego 23 ☎061/858 4400, ⓦwww.ibishotel.com. Reliable source of blandly functional but comfortable accommodation, a walkable 800m southeast of the Rynek. ❻

Ikar ul. Kościuszki 118 ☎061/857 6705, ⓦwww.hotelikar.com.pl. A rather soulless-looking multistorey concrete building, but the rooms are comfortable and come with fridge and satellite TV. Sizeable weekend discounts. ❻

Lech ul. św. Marcin 74 ☎061/853 0151, ⓦwww.hotel-lech.poznan.pl. One of a pair of long-established hotels right in the heart of town which claim three-star status without really delivering it. Rooms come with standard, socialist-era brown-carpet colour schemes, but the en-suite bathrooms are new. The hotel also offers a two-person apartment with a mirror above the bed, should you feel the need. ❺

Mercure ul. Roosevelta 20 ☎061/855 8000, Ⓔ mer.poznan@orbis.pl. Comfortable corporate four-star right next to the trade-fair grounds. ❽

Novotel Poznań Centrum pl. Wł. Andersa 1 ☎061/858 7000, Ⓔnov.poznan@orbis.pl. Located just 1km south of the city centre, but still well within walking distance, this high-rise building is the flagship of Orbis's concrete fleet. Ruinous rates during trade fair periods but big weekend reductions at other times of the year. ❼

Royal ul. św. Marcin 71 ☎061/858 2300, ⓦwww.hotel-royal.com.pl. Characterful, renovated place with bags of quirky charm, tucked into a quiet courtyard just off Poznań's main downtown street. The rooms (all en suite with TV) are on the small side but cosily furnished in warm colours. Many of the doubles are L-shaped, making it impossible to push the twin beds together, so you'll need to specify a double bed if that's what you want. ❼

Rzymski al. K. Marcinkowskiego 22 ☎061/852 8121, ⓦwww.rzymskihotel.com.pl. Spruced-up hotel with a good restaurant and just a couple of minutes' walk from the Stary Rynek. Uninspiring but adequate doubles with shower and TV, and some plushed-up business-class rooms. ❺–❻

Wielkopolska ul. św. Marcin 67 ☎061/852 7631. Good location directly across the street from the *Lech*, and similarly old-fashioned. Ponderously furnished but acceptably clean and comfortable. Rooms with en-suite shower and WC as well as those with shared bathrooms. ❺–❻

Out of the centre

Meridian ul. Litewska 22 ☎061/656 5353, ⓦwww.hotelmeridian.com.pl. Intimate, medium-sized hotel in a tranquil setting by a lake in Park Sołacki, 2km northwest of the centre. Rooms are en suite with minibar. Half-price weekend deals are sometimes offered if the hotel isn't full. Tram #11 from the train station passes nearby. ❼

Naramowice ul. Naramowicka 150 ☎061/822 7543, ⓦwww.naramowice.pl. Comparatively good-value two-star hotel 3km north of the Rynek, even though it looks like a factory from the outside, offering simple en-suite rooms. Reached by bus #51 from the main (northern) entrance of the train station. ❺

Novotel Poznań Malta ul. Warszawska 64/66 ☎061/654 3100, Ⓔrez.nov.malta@orbis.pl. Plush Orbis motel situated in parkland 2km east of the centre, a short walk from the northern shores of Lake Maltańskie. Off the main E30 Warsaw road. ❻–❽

Park ul. Majakowskiego 77 ☎061/874 1100, ⓦwww.hotel-park.com.pl. German-owned business hotel on the southern bank of Lake Maltańskie 2km east of the city centre. Prices for rooms and food are comparable with its Orbis

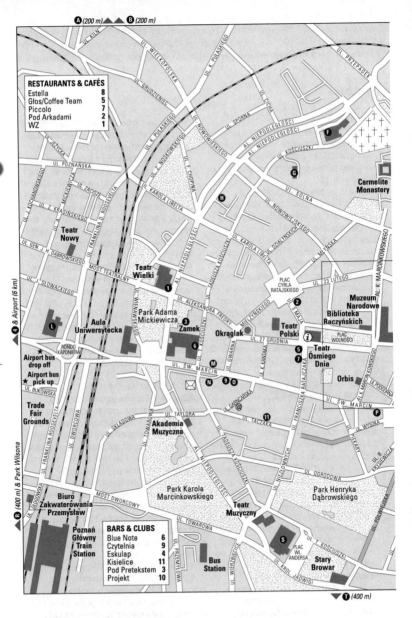

RESTAURANTS & CAFÉS

Estella	8
Głos/Coffee Team	5
Piccolo	7
Pod Arkadami	2
WZ	1

BARS & CLUBS

Blue Note	6
Czytelnia	9
Eskulap	4
Kisielice	11
Pod Pretekstem	3
Projekt	10

rivals, but it surpasses them in quality. Rooms with lakeside views are more expensive than those on the landward side. Weekend reductions. ⑧
Polonez al. Niepodległości 36 ☎ 061/864 7100, ⓔ polonez@orbis.pl. Another Orbis establishment, located to the north of the centre. It's a concrete,

expensive monster like all the others, and with the range of boutiques and services on offer it can at times look more like a shopping mall than a hotel. ⑦
Sport ul. Chwiałkowskiego 34 ☎ 061/833 0591, ⓦ www.posir.poznan.pl. Former budget hotel a

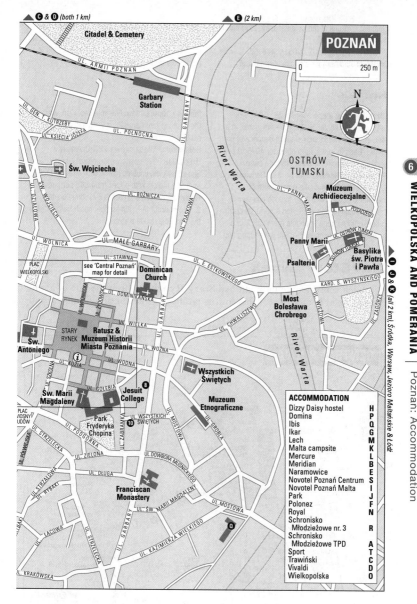

POZNAŃ

0 ————— 250 m

N

Citadel & Cemetery

UL. ARMII POZNAŃ

Garbary
Station

UL. GEN. T. KUTRZEBY

UL. KSIĘCIA JÓZEFA

UL. PÓŁNOCNA

Św. Wojciecha

UL. BOŻNICZA

OSTRÓW
TUMSKI

UL. PANNY MARII

Muzeum
Archidiecezjalne

UL. KS. I. POSADZEGO

UL. ŚW. WOJCIECHA

UL. DZIAŁOWA

UL. WOLNICA

UL. MAŁE GARBARY

UL. STAWNA

Panny Marii

UL. OSTRÓW TUMSKI

Basylika
św. Piotra
i Pawła

Psalteria

PLAC
WIELKOPOLSKI

see 'Central Poznań'
map for detail

Dominican
Church

UL. E. ESTKOWSKIEGO

KARD. S. WYSZYŃSKIEGO

UL. DOMINIKAŃSKA

UL. WRONIECKA

UL. GARBARY

UL. WIELKA

UL. CHWALISZEWO

Most
Bolesława
Chrobrego

STARY
RYNEK

Ratusz &
Muzeum Historii
Miasta Poznania

UL. WOŹNA

Św.
Antoniego

UL. KOZIA

UL. WODNA

UL. SZKOLNA

UL. GOLĘBIA

Jesuit
College

Wszystkich
Świętych

Św. Marii
Magdaleny

Muzeum
Etnograficzne

UL. CHRÓBA

ACCOMMODATION

PLAC
WIOSNY
LUDÓW

Park
Fryderyka
Chopina

UL. WSZYSTKICH
ŚWIĘTYCH

UL. ZABRAMA

UL. PODGÓRNA

UL. POWNIECKA

UL. STRZELECKA

UL. ZIELONA

UL. DOWBORA MUSNICKIEGO

UL. DŁUGA

UL. STRZAŁOWA

Franciscan
Monastery

UL. RYBAKI

UL. ŁĄCOWA

UL. GARBARY

UL. ŚW. MARII MAGDALENY

UL. MOSTOWA

UL. STRZELECKA

UL. KAZIMIERZA WIELKIEGO

UL. KRAKÓWSKA

Accommodation	
Dizzy Daisy hostel	H
Domina	P
Ibis	Q
Ikar	G
Lech	M
Malta campsite	K
Mercure	L
Meridian	B
Naramowice	E
Novotel Poznań Centrum	S
Novotel Poznań Malta	I
Park	J
Polonez	F
Royal	N
Schronisko Młodzieżowe nr. 3	R
Schronisko Młodzieżowe TPD	A
Sport	T
Trawiński	C
Vivaldi	D
Wielkopolska	O

6

WIELKOPOLSKA AND POMERANIA | Poznań: Accommodation

▲ ❶ & ❾ (all 2 4km), Środka, Warsaw, Jezioro Malańskie & Łódź

589

20min walk south of the centre, totally revamped in 2001. The management has gone for sparse modernist minimalism rather than chintzy plushness, and the results look good. All rooms are en suite with TV, and there are twenty-percent reductions at weekends. Take tram #6 or #12 from Most Dworcowy (2 stops) or the bus station (1 stop) to al. Królowej Jadwigi, then walk south past the derelict sports stadium for 5min. ❺–❻

Trawiński ul. Żniwna 2 ☎061/827 5800, ⊛www .hoteltrawinski.com.pl. Modern business-oriented four-star offering pastel coloured en suites in the

pleasant environs of the Cytadela park, 2km north-west of the Rynek. 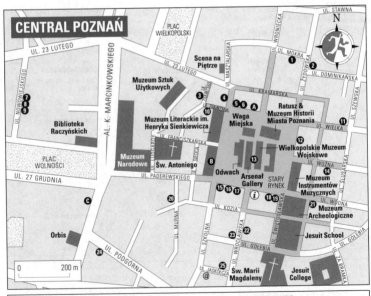❻
Vivaldi ul. Wynogrady 9 ☏061/858 8100, ⓦwww .vivaldi.pl. Another four-star establishment of

recent construction, in the same part of town as the Trawiński, boasting snazzy interiors and central Poznań's only hotel swimming pool (although it is admittedly rather small). ❽

Hostels

Dizzy Daisy al. Niepodległości 26 ☏061/829 3902, ⓦwww.hostel.pl. Summer-only hostel in a student dorm within easy walking distance of the centre. Beds in triples or doubles for 40–50zł per person. Backpacker-friendly staff; no curfew.
Schronisko Młodzieżowe nr. 3 ul. Berwińskiego 2/3 ☏061/866 4040. Like many Polish hostels this one is housed in a grim-looking nineteenth-century building, and is spartan if perfectly clean inside, offering beds in double rooms for 25zł a head. Reception is open 6–10am & 5–10pm, and

there's a 10pm curfew. Five minutes' walk west of the train station; trams #3, #5, #8 and #11 pass nearby.
Schronisko Młodzieżowe TPD Drzymały 3 ☏061/848 5836 ⓦwww.schroniskoTPD.ta.pl. Simple singles, doubles (some with en-suite facili-ties) and triples, with prices from 35zł per person. Reception is open 6–10am & 5–10pm. Located 2.5km north of the train station; catch tram #11 to the Nad Wierzbakiem stop.

The Stary Rynek

For seven centuries the distinguished **Stary Rynek** has been the hub of life in Poznań, even if these days it has lost its position as the centre of political and

ACCOMMODATION	RESTAURANTS & CAFÉS		Fripp Sarp Jazz Café	19	BARS & CLUBS		Pod Aniołem	23
Brovaria	B	Bambus	16	Herbaciarnia Chimera	2	Czarna Owca	25	Pod Minogą	8
Dom Turysty	A	Bar Przysmak	24	Kresowa	13	Czerwony		Subway	9
Rzymski	C	Bee-Jays	6	Piccolo	4	Fortepian	1	W Starym Kinie	7
		Brovaria	B	Piwnica Murna	20	Déjà Vu	14	Za Kulisami	21
		Cacao Republika	10	Ratuszowa	18	Dragon	3		
		Dom Wikingów	17	Sioux City	15	Lizard King	5		
		Dramat	12	Valpolicella	22	Piwnica 21	11		

economic power. Archetypically Polish, with the most important public buildings sited in the middle, it was badly damaged during the last war, subsequently gaining the sometimes overenthusiastic attentions of the restorers. However, only die-hard purists will be upset by this, as it's now among the most attractive of Poland's rejuvenated old city centres and makes you appreciate what a fine idea the town square is. Lined with a characterful mixture of facades – some in muted greys and browns, others in bright pastel colours – it is at its best in the spring and summer months, when pavement cafés and beer bars, basking under a forest of loudly coloured parasols, burst out onto its cobbled central area.

Outside the **town hall** (Ratusz, see p.592) stands a fine Rococo **fountain**, alongside a copy of the **pillory** in its traditional location. Still in the centre of the Rynek, running southwards from the town hall, is a colourful line of buildings, once home of the market traders, many of whom sold their wares in the arcaded passageways on either side. The present structures, each varying in height from its neighbour by a few inches, date from the sixteenth century and are thus the oldest in the square.

Immediately behind the western side of the town hall is the **Waga Miejska** (Weigh House), once the most important public building in this great trading centre; what you see today is a reproduction of the original, the work of architect, Giovanni Battista Quadro of Lugano. Adjoining it to the south is the sternly Neoclassical **Odwach** (Guardhouse), a single-storey pavilion built for the "defence and decoration" of the city in the 1780s, and surmounted by a pair of distinctly unmilitary looking female figures blowing trumpets. Closing off the southern side of the central Rynek are two low concrete buildings – ugly structures erected during the communist period, which add the only discordant notes to the square. One of them is now the **Wielkopolskie Muzeum Wojskowe** at Stary Rynek 9 (Wielkopolska Museum of Arms; Tues–Sat 9am–4pm, Sun 10am–3pm; 3.30zł), a lively display of weaponry in the province, from the Middle Ages onwards. The other houses the **Arsenał Gallery** (Tues–Sat 11am–6pm, Sun 10am–3pm; 5zł), the prime venue in the city for changing exhibitions of contemporary art.

Many a medieval and Renaissance interior lurks behind the Baroque facades of the **gabled houses** lining the outer sides of the Stary Rynek, most of them shops, restaurants, cafés or antique shops. On the eastern side, at no. 45, is the **Muzeum Instrumentów Muzycznych** (Museum of Musical Instruments; Tues–Sat 11am–5pm, Sun 10am–3pm; 5.50zł), the only collection of its kind in Poland. Its exhibits range from folk instruments from all over the world, through Chopin memorabilia to a vast array of violins. The last is a reminder that every five years the city hosts the Wieniawski International Violin Competition, one of the most prestigious events for young virtuosi (next due in 2006).

The western side of the square is almost equally imposing, above all because of the massive green and white **Działyński Palace** at no. 78, its facade topped by a monumental swan which cranes its neck down towards the square. Cultural soirées took place here in the nineteenth century, helping to keep Polish-language culture alive in what was a Prussian-governed city. Also on this side of the square, the house at no. 84 was once home to Giovanni Battista Quadro– a statue of the architect, sketchbook in hand, occupies a niche in the facade. Its interior houses the **Muzeum Literackie im. Henryka Sienkiewicza** (Henryk Sienkiewicz Literature Museum; Mon–Fri 10am–5pm; 3zł). Although Poland's most celebrated novelist (see box, pp.592–593) had only a rather tenuous connection with Poznań – he penned a couple of short stories while staying at the *Hotel Bazar* (now a clothes shop) on al. K. Marcinkowskiego – this is the most important museum dedicated to his life and works, largely due to the energies of Poznań-based Sienkiewicz enthusiast Ignacy Moś. Inside lies a straightforward words-and-pictures account of the author's life, accompanied by first editions of his works in innumerable languages.

The Ratusz

The **Ratusz** (town hall) is in every way predominant. Originally a two-storey Gothic brick structure, it was radically rebuilt in the 1550s by Quadro. The turreted facade gives it a Moorish feel. The arcaded eastern facade presents the building at its most vivacious, its lime-green pilasters framing a frieze of Polish monarchs, who are accompanied here by portraits of statesmen and poets from ancient Greece and Rome – a propagandist attempt to present Poland's rulers as the guardians of classical wisdom. Every day at noon, the effigies of two goats emerge onto the platform of the **clock** above the facade and butt their heads twelve times. This commemorates the best-known local legend in which the two animals locked horns on the steps of the town hall, and thereby drew attention to a fire which had just begun there, so saving the city from a potentially disastrous conflagration. In thanks, the goats were immortalized in the city's coat of arms, as well as in this timepiece. Other sides of the building are inscribed with the words of Polish Renaissance sages, to which post-World War II restorers were forced to add extracts from the communist constitution.

The interior is now the **Muzeum Historii Miasta Poznania** (Museum of the History of Poznań; Mon, Tues & Fri 10am–4pm, Wed noon–6pm, Sun

Henryk Sienkiewicz (1846–1916)

Outside Poland, **Henryk Sienkiewicz**'s reputation has rested largely on *Quo Vadis?*, an epic on the early Christians in the decadent days of the Roman Empire, which won him the 1905 **Nobel Prize for Literature** and quickly became a favourite subject with movie moguls. Yet the huge popular success of this led, after the author's death, to the almost total international neglect of the remainder of his colossal oeuvre, which, even in hopelessly inadequate translations, had marked him out as Poland's answer to Charles Dickens.

Born in the Podlasie region to a minor aristocratic family of Tatar origin, Sienkiewicz began his career as a **journalist** and **short story writer**, the culmination of which was a trip to the United States in 1876–77, where he worked in a short-lived Polish agricultural commune in California. Here he wrote *Letters from America* (containing vivid descriptions of such diverse subjects as New York City and the Indian campaigns), and the burlesque novella *Charcoal Sketches*, a satire on rural life in Russian Poland. On his return home, he drew on his experiences of émigré life in *American Stories*, which include his one work in this genre which frequently turns up in literary anthologies, *The Lighthouse Keeper*. These were followed by the despairing novella *Bartek the Conqueror*, the finest of a number of works set in the Poznań region – which, being under Prussian control, made a safer medium for the nationalist message of an author subject to Russian censors.

Thereafter, Sienkiewicz changed tack, reviving what was then regarded as the outmoded form of the **historical epic**. His vast trilogy *With Fire and Sword*, *The Deluge* and *Fire in the Steppe* is set against the heroic backdrop of Poland's seventeenth-century wars with the Cossacks, Swedes and Turks. It is remarkable for its sure sense of structure, employing a permanent set of characters – whose language is skilfully differentiated according to their class and culture – with plentiful genealogical digressions and romantic interludes to break the unfolding of the main plot. Historical realism, however, was sacrificed in favour of Sienkiewicz's own Catholic, nationalist, chivalrous and anti-intellectual outlook. Despite its non-Polish setting, *Quo Vadis?*, which followed the trilogy, was always regarded as a fable about the country's oppression under the

10am–3pm; 5.50zł), though this is less educational than it sounds, and the main reason for entering is to see the building itself. Surviving from the Gothic period, the vaulted **cellars** were transformed into a prison in the sixteenth century; they now contain the earliest objects in the display, notably items excavated on Ostrów Tumski and the medieval pillory. However, the most impressive room is the Renaissance **great hall** (Wielka Sień) on the first floor, dating from 1555. Its coffered vault bears polychrome bas–reliefs which embody the exemplary civic duties and virtues through scenes from the lives of Samson, King David and Hercules. The southern section by the staircase depicts astrological and bestial figures (including a rather fantastical rhino), while the marble busts of Roman emperors around the walls are reminders of the weighty tradition of municipal leadership. The top floor continues with a display of local treasures, portraits and old postcards, enlivened by temporary exhibitions on local history.

West of the Stary Rynek

Just to the west of the Stary Rynek stands a hill with remnants of the inner circle of the **medieval walls**. This particular section guarded what was once Zamek Przemysława, the castle and seat of the rulers of Wielkopolska. Modified down the centuries and almost completely destroyed in 1945, a part has been

Partitions, emphasized by the fact that two of the leading characters are Lygians – inhabitants of what subsequently became the heartlands of Poland. Ironically, it is really one of Sienkiewicz's weaker works, irredeemably marred by its maudlin sentimentality, for all its mastery of narrative, description and characterization. He showed a greater concern for historical accuracy in his final epic, *The Teutonic Knights*, in which Poland's plight was reflected in the clearest and most relevant parallel from the past.

Sienkiewicz also produced a couple of novels with contemporary settings, *Without Dogma* and *The Połłaniecki Family*. These helped to increase his cult status in nationalist circles, and political activity, boosted by the international celebrity status bestowed by *Quo Vadis?*, became increasingly important to him after the turn of the twentieth century. On the outbreak of World War I Sienkiewicz moved to Switzerland where, along with the pianist Ignacy Jan Paderewski, he was instrumental in setting up the **Polish National Committee**, which in due course came to be recognized by the Western allies as a provisional government. However, he did not live to play the direct political role that might otherwise have fallen to him when Poland was resurrected at the end of the war.

Always an important part of the curriculum in Polish schools, Sienkiewicz has made something of a comeback in recent years, with the Polish film industry turning his ouevre into a cinematic gold mine. Veteran director Jerzy Hoffman, who had already filmed creditable adaptations of *The Deluge* and *Fire in the Steppe* in the 1960s and 1970s, set the ball rolling with a lavish big-screen version of *With Fire and Sword* in 1999. It was the most expensive Polish film ever made at the time, and soon became the most succesful, garnering an incredible seven million paying viewers. The film failed to make a big impact abroad, but video and DVD versions (complete with English subtitles) are available in big-city media stores in Poland should you wish to see what all the fuss was about. A celluloid version of Sienkiewicz's *In Desert and Wilderness*, a children's adventure story set in Africa, was one of the big box office hits of 2001 (and came complete with soundtrack album and picture-book spin-offs); while a new Polish version of *Quo Vadis?* (a grandiose affair whose budget surpassed that of *With Fire and Sword*) was unleashed the following year. Sienkiewicz, it seems, is here to stay.

restored to house the **Muzeum Sztuk Użytkowych** (Museum of Decorative Arts; Tues, Wed, Fri & Sat 10am–4pm, Sun 10am–3pm; 5.50zł). This features an enjoyable collection from medieval times to the present day, while the Gothic cellars are used for exhibitions of the work of contemporary Polish artists.

Below the hill is the Baroque **Kościół św. Antoniego** (Church of St Anthony), its interior decorated by the Franciscan brothers Adam and Antonin Swach, the former a painter, the latter a sculptor and stuccoist. The church's most eye-catching corner is the sumptuous Chapel of the Virgin Mary on the left-hand side of the main altar, where a small image of the saint is buried in a dark wooden frame decorated with bold geometric designs in gold and silver. Cherubs roam across pink and golden skies in the dome above. Round by the main altar, the ornate choir stalls appear to be resting on subdued dragons.

The Muzeum Narodowe

Immediately west of St Anthony's church, Poznań's **Muzeum Narodowe** (National Museum; Tues 10am–6pm, Wed & Fri 9am–5pm, Thur 10am–4pm, Sat 10am–7pm, Sun 11am–4pm; 7zł) contains one of the best collections of Polish and international art outside Warsaw. From the entrance (located in the coolly contemporary north wing of the museum on al. K. Marcinkowskiego), steps ascend through an extensive display of Polish art, featuring examples of virtually every art movement to have impacted on the country. Nineteenth-century symbolist Jaczek Malcewski features prominently, with his distinctive spade-bearded countenance peering from numerous large-format canvases, in each of which his self-portrait is joined by a host of mystical and metaphorical characters. The Art-Nouveau-esque Młoda Polska movement (see p.405) is represented by monumental Mehoffer pastels (mostly sketches for the church murals he executed in Kraków), and touching family portraits by Stanisław Wyspiański. Further up, look out for some explosive 1950s abstract art from Maria Jarema as well as cartloads of stuff by Jerzy Nowosielski, whose enigmatic daubs have made him postwar Poland's most highly priced artist.

International art is housed in the older south wing of the museum, where an impressive Italian section includes panels from Gothic altarpieces by artists such as Bernardo Daddi and Lorenzo Monaco, and Renaissance pieces such as Bellini's *Madonna and Child with Donor* and Bassano's *At Vulcan's Forge*. Presiding haughtily over a hall-full of seventeenth-century works is Zurbarán's *Madonna of the Rosary*. This Counter-Reformation masterpiece was part of a cycle for the Carthusian monastery at Jerez, and features actual portraits of the silent monks. By the same artist is *Christ at the Column*, a sharply edged work from the very end of his career, and there are also a couple of notable works by his contemporary Ribera. Highlights of the extensive display of Flemish art include an affectionate *Madonna and Child* attributed to Massys and the regal *Adoration of the Magi* by Joos van Cleve.

Finally, the ground floor of the south wing (accessibility very much depends on whether it's being used for major touring exhibitions) contains a huge hall packed with examples of a uniquely Polish art: portraits of seventeenth-century nobles painted on sheet metal, which were then placed on the end of the deceased's coffin. Note the extravagant moustaches and partly shaven heads sported by the noblemen, a look very much in vogue during the craze for eastern-influenced fashions that went under the name of Sarmatism (see p.474).

Plac Wolności and beyond

Spreading west from the museum is the vast elongated space of pl. Wolności, which formerly bore the name of Napoleon, then Kaiser Wilhelm, and only gaining its present designation – Freedom Square – after the Wielkopolska uprising in 1918. Here stands another seminal centre of the fight to preserve Polish culture, the **Biblioteka Raczyńskich**, founded in the early nineteenth century to promote Polish-language learning and literature, and still functioning as a library. Architecturally, it's one of the most distinguished buildings in the city, erected in the 1820s in cool Neoclassical style, the elegant Corinthian pillars of its colonnaded southern facade presiding serenely over the square.

Moving into the business and shopping thoroughfares that branch out west from pl. Wolności, you shortly come to the **Teatr Polski**, a charming wedding-cake of a building at ul. 27 Grudnia. Erected in the 1870s by voluntary contributions, this was yet another major cultural institution during the Partitions period; the uphill nature of this struggle is reflected in the inscription on the facade – *Narod Sobie*, or "The Nation by Itself". Overlooking the busy junction at the end of the street is the city's most distinguished postwar building, the **Okrąglak** or "Big Log" – an imposing ten-storey cylinder built in the mid-1950s to house the city's main department store. Now given over to office space and a handful of listless shops, it's still worth popping inside to admire the hollow core and spiralling staircase.

An insight into the curious dichotomy of life during the Partitions is provided by the large buildings standing further to the west, which reflect the self-confidence of the German occupiers in the first decade of the twentieth century. Ironically, many of these cultural establishments and administration offices were taken over just a few years after they were built by an institution with very different values, the new University of Poznań. The most imposing of the group, the huge neo-Romanesque **Kaiserhaus**, had an even more dramatic change of role. Built in imitation of the style favoured by the Hohenstaufen emperors of early medieval Germany, it was intended to accommodate the Kaiser whenever he happened to be in town. Renamed the **Zamek**, it's now a vibrant cultural centre which provides an umbrella for all manner of activities – including rock concerts in the courtyard round the back. In the park beyond are two huge crucifixes bound together with heavy rope, forming a **monument** to the victims of the Poznań food riots of June 1956. The riots – and their brutal suppression by the security forces – sent shockwaves through Polish society, precipitating the return to power of the reform-minded communist Władysław Gomułka. The lesson that workers' protests could make and break regimes was not lost on future generations, helping to precipitate the rise of Solidarity in 1980. It was during Solidarity's extraordinary period of power and influence in communist Poland – before the declaration of martial law in December 1981 – that the monument was unveiled, in June 1981, marking the 25th anniversary of the riots.

West of the Zamek, ul. św. Marcin crosses the railway tracks and arrives at the roundabout known as Rondo Kaponera, just south of which lies the main entrance to the Poznań trade-fair grounds. A good reason to venture this far is provided by **Park Wilsona** (Wilson Park; named after American president Woodrow) 800m further south along ul. Głogowska, whose **Palmiarnia** (Palm House; Tues–Sun 9am–5pm; entrance 5.50zł; obligatory coat check 2zł) is one of the horticultural wonders of Poland. With banana palms, skyscraping cacti, shamelessly sensual orchids and a lot more besides, it's an inspirational place for even the least green-fingered of visitors.

South and east of the Stary Rynek

Returning to the Stary Rynek and continuing along ul. Wodna brings you to the **Pałac Górków** (Górka Palace) at no. 27, which still preserves its intricate

Renaissance portico and sober inner courtyard. The mansion now houses the **Muzeum Archeologiczne** (Archeology Museum; Tues–Fri 10am–4pm, Sat 10am–6pm, Sun 10am–3pm; ⓦwww.muzarp.poznan.pl; 5zł), which traces the history of the region in entertaining fashion, with a sequence of dioramas illustrating the daily life of Wielkopolska inhabitants from the time of the nomadic hunters who lived here between 15000 and 8000 BC, all the way to the early feudal society of the seventh century AD. The University of Poznań's archeological expeditions abroad – notably to Egypt and the Sudan – are documented with an absorbing display of artefacts, although the exhibits are periodically rearranged and it's difficult to predict what you might see at any given time.

Ulica Świętosławska ends in a cluster of gloriously salmon-coloured former Jesuit buildings, the finest examples of Baroque architecture in the city. The end of this street is closed by the facade of **Kościół Farny św. Marii Magdaleny**, understatedly known as the parish church, completed just forty years before the expulsion of the Jesuits in 1773. Its magnificently sombre interior is all fluted columns with gilded capitals, monumental sculptures, large altarpieces framed by twisted columns and rich stuccowork, in the full-blown Roman manner. Over the high altar is a painting illustrating a legendary episode from the life of St Stanisław. Then a bishop, he was accused by King Bolesław the Generous of not having paid for a village he had incorporated into his territories. In order to prove his innocence, the saint resurrected the deceased former owner of the land to testify on his behalf.

Across the road is the **Jesuit school**, now one of Poland's main ballet academies; take a peek at its miniature patio, an architectural gem. To the east of the church is the front section of the **Jesuit college**, currently the seat of the city council. The Jesuits have returned to Poznań, though they were unable to reclaim the buildings they created. Instead, they now occupy the oldest left-bank building, the **Dominican church** to the northeast of the Stary Rynek. Despite a Baroque recasing, this still preserves original Romanesque and Gothic features, as well as a stellar-vaulted Rosary chapel.

The late Baroque **Kościół Wszystkich Świętych** (All Saints' Church), almost due east of the Stary Rynek, is the epitome of a Lutheran church, with its democratic central plan layout and overall plainness. Yet although it survives as an almost complete period piece, the exodus of virtually all the Protestants this century means that it's now used for Catholic worship, as is evidenced by the jarring high altar.

At no. 25 on the adjacent ul. Grobla is the former lodge of the freemasons, now the **Muzeum Etnograficzne** (Ethnographical Museum; Tues, Wed, Fri & Sat 10am–4pm, Sun 10am–3pm; 5.5zł), with some interesting carvings, ceramics and musical instruments. Further south you'll see the twin-towered Baroque church of the **Franciscan monastery**, which has been gleamingly restored by the monks who repossessed it following its wartime use as a warehouse. Built in 1473 and destroyed by the Swedes two hundred years later, photographs in the vestibule show the church before, during and after the war, when the Franciscans completed their masterful repair. What you see now is a gleaming bright interior of white and gold with shades of ochre and Rococo flourishes.

From here a brief walk west along ul. Długa brings you to the pedestrianized **ul. Półwiejska**, the most animated of Poznań's shopping streets. It's worth following it southwards all the way to the end in order to take a look at the **Stary Browar** shopping centre, which combines restored nineteenth-century brewery buildings with modern architectural add-ons to create an eye-pleasing palace of red brick and steel. Head for the third-floor balcony for a birds'-eye view of the buzzing shoppers below.

North of the Stary Rynek

The northern quarters are best approached from pl. Wielkopolski, a large square now used for markets. From here ul. Działowa passes two churches facing each other on the brow of the hill. To the right is the Gothic **Kościół św. Wojcie-cha** (St Adalbert's Church), chiefly remarkable for its little seventeenth-century wooden belfry which somehow got left on the ground in front of the brick facade. Opposite, the handsome Baroque **Carmelite monastery** reflects a more complete image. Further uphill are the most exclusive cemeteries in Poznań, reserved for people deemed to have made a valuable contribution to the life of Wielkopolska, as well as a monument to the defenders of the city in 1939.

Beyond, al. Niepodległości heads northeast towards **Cytadela** (Citadel), a vast earthwork fortress built by the Prussians in the nineteenth century and subsequently pressed into service by the inter-war Polish state as the lynchpin of their western defences. The scene of bitter fighting in both 1939 and 1945, it is now an extensive, partly wooded park, the southern slopes of which are occupied by a **memorial garden** in honour of the six thousand Russians and Poles who lost their lives here. A stairway just off the northern end of Niepodległości leads uphill through the graves towards a huge memorial to the Red Army. A couple of hundred metres east of the stairway lies a small British and Commonwealth cemetery – interred here are POWs from both World Wars, as well as airmen shot down over Poland between 1939–45. Beyond the Red Army memorial, a crumbling red-brick bastion harbours the **Muzeum Uzbrojenia** (Armour Museum; Tues–Sat 9am–4pm, Sun 10am–4pm; 4zł), with a small but absorbing collection of tanks and armoured cars. Further north, the mid-point of the park is marked by **Nierozpoznani** ("The Undiagnozed"), a characteristically enigmatic sculptural ensemble courtesy of leading contemporary artist Magdalena Abakanowicz. Featuring a cast-iron army of 112 larger-than-life headless figures, it's a powerful piece of work up close.

Ostrów Tumski and the right bank

From the left bank the Most Bolesława Chrobrego (Great Bridge) crosses to the holy island of **Ostrów Tumski**, a world away in spirit, if not in distance, from the hustle of the city (trams #1, #4 and #8 go over the bridge.) Only a small portion of the island is built on, and a few priests and monks comprise its entire population. Lack of parishioners means that there's not the usual need for evening Masses, and after 5pm the island is a ghost town.

The first building you see is the late Gothic **psalteria**, characterized by its elaborate stepped gable. It was erected in the early sixteenth century as a residence for the cathedral choir. Immediately behind is an earlier brick structure, the **Kościół Panny Marii** (Church of Our Lady). This seemingly unfinished and unbalanced small church was given supposedly controversial stained glass and murals after the war. A couple of minutes' walk north of the cathedral is the **Muzeum Archidiecezjalne** (Archdiocesan Museum; Mon–Sat 9am–3pm; 3zł), located at ul. ks. Ignacego Posadzego 2, with a spread of sculptures, treasure and some rather fine religious art that ought to be on show somewhere more prominent.

The Basylika św. Piotra i Pawła
The streets of the island are lined with handsome eighteenth-century houses, all very much in the shadow of the **Basylika św. Piotra i Pawła** (Basilica of SS Peter and Paul), one of Poland's most venerated cathedrals. Over the centuries

the brickwork exterior succumbed to Baroque and Neoclassical remodellings, but when much of this was stripped by wartime devastation it was decided to restore as much of the Gothic original as possible. Unfortunately, the lack of documentary evidence for the eastern chapels meant that their successors had to be retained. The Baroque spires on the two facade towers and the three lanterns around the ambulatory, which give a vaguely Eastern touch, were also reconstructed. Indeed it is the view onto this end of the building which offers its most imposing, if misleading aspect.

Inside, the basilica is impressive, but not outstanding as befits its pre-eminent status among the nation's places of worship. The **crypt**, entered from below the northern tower, has been extensively excavated, uncovering the thousand-year-old foundations of the pre-Romanesque and Romanesque cathedrals which stood on the site – two models depict their probable appearance. Also extant, though isolated by grilles as if they were the Crown Jewels, are parts of the sarcophagi of the first two Polish kings, Mieszko I and Bolesław the Brave. Their remains currently rest in the **Golden Chapel** behind the altar. Miraculously unscathed during the war, this hyper-ornate creation, representing the diverse if dubious tastes of the 1830s, is the antithesis of the plain architecture all around it. Its decoration is a curious co-operation between mosaic artists from Venice (who created the patterned floor and the copy of Titian's *Assumption*) and a painter and a sculptor from the very different Neoclassical traditions of Berlin, although the untutored eye is unlikely to spot any stylistic discord.

Of the many other **funerary monuments** which form one of the key features of the cathedral, that of Bishop Benedykt Izdbieński, just to the left of the Golden chapel, is notable. This was carved by Jan Michałowicz, the one native Polish artist of the Renaissance period who was the equal of the many Italians who settled here. The other outstanding tomb is that of the Górka family, in the Holy Sacrament chapel at the northern end of the nave, sculpted just a few years later by one of these itinerant craftsmen, Hieronimo Canavesi. Other **works of art** to look out for are the late Gothic carved and gilded high altar triptych from Silesia, the choir stalls from the same period and fragments of sixteenth-century frescoes, notably a cycle of the Apostles on the south side of the ambulatory.

Śródka

Crossing Most Mieska I brings you to the right-bank suburb of **Śródka**, the second-oldest part of the city, whose name derives from the word for Wednesday – market day here in medieval times. Though there's nothing special to see, something of the atmosphere of an ancient market quarter survives in the quiet streets immediately north of the main thoroughfare. Just beyond is another distinct settlement, known as **Komandoria** after the commanders of the Knights of Saint John of Jerusalem, who settled here towards the end of the twelfth century. The late Romanesque church of this community, **Kościół św. Jana** (St John's Church), survives with Gothic and Baroque additions and now stands in splendid isolation on the far side of the **Rondo Śródka**, a busy traffic roundabout.

Jezioro Maltańskie

Immediately southeast of Rondo Śródka, paths lead down to the western end of **Jezioro Maltańskie** (Lake Malta), the city's most popular summertime playground. This two-kilometre-long stretch of water, built to accommodate rowing regattas and surrounded by footpaths, is where Poznań folk come to walk, cycle, rollerblade, and practise their pram-pushing skills. Most people gravitate towards the eastern end of the lake, where there are a couple of grassy strands equipped with concrete bathing piers, alongside children's play areas, a dry-ski slope, and an all-weather toboggan run. With a gaggle of stands doling out beer, sausage and ice cream, it's a vibrant and colourful place to spend a weekend afternoon. Just beyond the lake's eastern shore is a wooded park criss-crossed by marked walking trails. A few minutes' walk within the park lies the boundary of the sizeable, open-plan **Nowe Zoo** (New Zoo; daily 9am–7pm; 7zł), which stretches eastwards for a further 1.5km. A **narrow-gauge rail line** especially designed for children (May–Sept 10am–6pm; every 30min; 5zł) runs from Rondo Śródka to the zoo, passing alongside the northern shore of the lake on the way.

Eating, drinking and nightlife

There's a constantly growing range of restaurants, cafés and bars in what is a fast-changing city – although many new establishments go out of fashion within months of opening. Most eating and drinking takes place around the Rynek or in neighbouring alleys such as Wrocławska, Wodna and Woźna; and you'll rarely have to travel outside the walkable confines of the town centre in search of an evening out. **Restaurants** are usually open until 11pm or midnight; while **bars** are much more flexible with their opening hours, keeping going until 2 or 3am at weekends, but closing up early during the week if not enough customers show up. Many of Poznań's central bars feature DJs and dancing at the weekend. In addition there are a growing number of **clubbing** venues to choose from – look out for street posters, or consult *Gazeta Wyborcza* on Fridays, to find out what's on.

Restaurants

Bambus Stary Rynek 64/65. Central location for Chinese food, with a smart restaurant offering formal service, high standards and upscale prices in one half, and a lunchtime-oriented budget bar in the other.

Bee-Jays Stary Rynek 87. Brash modern restaurant occupying attractive barrel-vaulted rooms on the main square. Eclectic selection of ribs, Tex-Mex, and a few Indian dishes on the menu, none of which disappoints. Big outdoor terrace in summer.

Brovaria Stary Rynek. Boutique brewery with huge restaurant attached, decked out in cool post-industrial style and serving some of the best meat and fish dishes in the city. Prices are extremely reasonable, and the ales go down a treat.

Dom Wikingów Stary Rynek 62. Bringing together café, restaurant and a couple of bars all in one place, it's likely that you'll find at least one corner of this multi-purpose square-side establishment that you'll like. Danish meat and fish dishes are the house speciality, but just about everything else in the international pub-grub line crops up on the menu too.

Estella ul. Garbary 41. Probably the best pizza place in town, with a broad choice of reasonably authentic pies, plenty of pasta dishes, and comfortable slow-food surroundings.

Kresowa Rynek 3. Formal service and high standards in a traditional Polish restaurant, hidden away in one of the alleys running through the Rynek's central ensemble of buildings.

Piwnica Murna ul. Murna 3. Attractive candle-lit cellar just round the corner from the Stary Rynek with live jazz and blues some nights. A good selection of grills and salads, and a good place for a drink too.

Ratuszowa Stary Rynek 55. Expensive place offering solid Polish fare, although you pay for the atmosphere – heavy on solid furniture and dark drapes – rather than the food. Expect to pay the equivalent of £12/US$20 for a three-course meal. Open till 1am.

Sioux City corner of Stary Rynek and Szkolna. Roomy faux-Wild West saloon in ideal location. There don't seem to be any Native American dishes on the menu but there's pretty much everything else you'd expect from a downtown crowd-pleasing eatery: steaks, pizzas, kebabs, and even the odd fajita.

Valpolicella ul. Wrocławska 7. Cosy, intimate venue for a good-quality Italian meal washed down with decent wine. A good place for scampi.

WZ ul. Fredry 12. Traditional Polish pork and poultry dishes in a roomy setting – a modern building with a mock-up of a timber-built country house in the middle of the main room.

Cafés and snack bars

Bar Przysmak ul. Podgórna 2. Functional canteen serving up cheap stodge to young and old. Mon–Fri till 9pm; Sat & Sun till 7pm.

Cacao Republika Zamkowa 6. Cosy bolt-hole a stone's throw from the Rynek offering an intriguingly large menu of hot chocolate-based drinks, alongside exceedingly palatable teas and coffees. Till 11pm.

Dramat Stary Rynek 41. Uncomplicated menu of savoury pancakes and *pierogi*, in an atmospheric brick-lined dining room. Featuring table service and well-presented fare, it's a cut above the canteen-style places. Till midnight.

Fripp Sarp Jazz Café Stary Rynek 56. Pretty much what you'd expect from a café run by the Polish Architects' Association: a chic lounge bar decorated in citrus-fruit colours, with dreamy trumpets squawking away on the CD system. Good coffee and dainty desserts. Daily 11am–late.

Głos/Coffee Team corner of ul. Ratajczaka and 27 Grudnia. Genteel café on the first floor, with table service and a tempting range of cakes; more functional order-at-the-counter coffee shop at street level.

Herbaciarna Chimera ul. Dominikańska 7. Refined tea-shop-cum-restaurant with a wide range of brews, some fancy salads and snacks – such as deep-fried camembert – and a full menu of main courses. Till midnight.

Piccolo ul. Ratajczaka 37 & ul. Rynkowa 1. Functional order-at-the-counter place offering filling, cheap bowls of spaghetti and a small salad bar. Not one for the pasta purists perhaps, but outstanding value. Till 9pm.

Pod Arkadami pl. C. Ratajskiego 10. Lashings of cheap and wholesome Polish food in simple milk-bar surroundings. Mon–Fri till 9pm, Sat & Sun till 6pm.

Bars and pubs

Czytelnia ul. św. Marcin 69. ⊛www.czytelnia.iq.pl. Poky subterranean bar with bookshelves in one half and a small dance floor in the other. Filled to bursting at weekends when DJs may well be spinning discs, a quirky place for a quiet drink at other times. Hidden in a passageway between the *Royal* and *Wielkopolska* hotels.

Déjà Vu ul. Woźna 21. Several simply decorated, dimly lit rooms, each of which is perpetually full of amiable students slurping down cheap beer.

Dragon ul. Zamkowa 3. Stripped-pine tables, candlelight, and non-mainstream sounds on the CD player: this is a grungy alternative to the pack-'em-in pubs on the nearby Rynek. Worth visiting for the bat-winged lizard-type animal hanging above the bar.

Kisielice ul. Taczaka 20. Eccentric lounge bar beloved of art-academy students and their mildly bohemian hangers-on. Most nights of the week there'll be someone playing records that never featured in the Top 40.

Lizard King Stary Rynek 86. Enjoyable main-square pub decked out with pictures of Doors frontman Jim Morrison and sundry other psycho-rockers. Packed out at weekends with hedonistically inclined locals jigging to live cover bands.

Piwnica 21 ul. Wielka 21. Functional brick-and-concrete bunker that regularly fills up with live music and resident DJs. Live gigs and decent local indie bands (details on ⊛www.p21.pl).

Pod Aniołem ul. Wrocławska 8. Stylish, comfortable café-bar in an atmospheric old building. Good place for an intimate evening drink.

Pod Minogą ul. Nowowiejskiego 8. Perennial student favourite, featuring a fantastically shabby front room with trumpets hanging from the ceiling and a baby grand serving as the bar. Weekending flocks pack themselves into the club-like back room or the upstairs section where DJs are wont to spin tunes.

Pod Pretekstem ul. św. Marcin 80/82. Refined café-pub located round the back of the Zamek cultural centre, in the courtyard. Regular programme of live jazz, blues or cabaret.

W Starym Kinie ul. Nowowiejskiego 8. Dimly lit, comfy and relaxing place with moderately bohemian clientele and a soothing soul/jazz/reggae mix on the sound system.

Za Kulisami ul. Wodna 24. Cosy two-room place not far from the Stary Rynek, so stuffed with bric-a-brac that it looks like a library, stable and country cottage all rolled into one. Equally good for a daytime drink or an evening boozing session.

Nightlife

Blue Note ul. Kościuszki 76/78 ⊛www.bluenote .info.poznan.pl. Jazz club underneath the Zamek cultural centre with two tiers of seating. Frequent gigs (rock as well as jazz) and club nights, when you may have to pay a cover charge.

Czarna Owca ul. Jaskólcza 13. Welcoming warren of subterranean rooms just round the corner from the Rynek, with mainstream music and friendly fun-seeking crowd.

Czerwony Fortepian ul. Wroniecka 18 (entrance round the corner on Mokra) ⊛www.czerwony -fortepian.pl. Plush, upmarket joint with sensuous deep-red colour scheme, jazzy music and frequent live gigs.

Eskulap Przybyszewskiego 39 ⊛www .eskulapklub.pl. Agenda-setting club hosting big DJ nights (frequently hosting guest performers from abroad), and concentrating on the cutting edge of dance music rather than mainstream pop. A bit of a hike, located about 2km west of the centre near the university's medical faculty (which helps explain the reference to healing deity Esculapius in the name).

Projekt ul. Wsystkich Świętych 4a Ⓦ www .clubprojekt.pl. Classy cellar club beneath an art gallery, drawing a slightly older crowd than the other city-centre establishments, with soulful and jazzy sounds.

Subway ul. Nowowiejskiego 8 Ⓦ www.subway .alpha.pl. Small basement bar with vinyl records nailed to the wall and a regularly changing cast of DJs – expect funk and hip-hop at the weekends, more off-the-wall styles midweek.

Entertainment

There's always a great deal going on in Poznań when it comes to highbrow culture. **Tickets** to performances are easy to come by, with prices rarely exceeding 30zł even for the best seats. There are a dozen **cinemas** in town, most showing the latest international releases with Polish subtitles, so you can enjoy the film and learn a few Polish expletives along the way. Lech Poznań, once giants of Polish **football** but now struggling to retain a regular place in the top division, play at the Lech stadium, west of the centre at ul. Bułgarska 5/7 (tram #13 from Rondo Kaponera).

For details of what's on, track down a copy of *iks* (4zł), a monthly **listings** booklet whose inner pages carry an English-language calendar of events, available from newsstands or from the city information centre. A more up-to-the-minute – albeit Polish-language – source of information is the Friday edition of the *Gazeta Wyborcza* newspaper, which carries full cinema, concert and club listings in the *Co jest grane* supplement.

Music and dance

Akademia Muzyczna ul. św. Marcin 87 ☎ 061/856 8900 Regular programme of vocal and instrumental concerts, featuring students at the Poznań Musical Academy – entrance is often free.

CK Zamek ul. św. Marcin 80/82 ☎ 061/853 7699. Concerts featuring all kinds of music from classical recitals to pop.

Filharmonia Poznańska Box office (daily 1–6pm) at ul. św. Marcin 81 ☎ 061/853 6935. Concerts themselves take place at the Aula Uniwerzytecka, ul. Wienawskiego. Regular performances by the Poznań Philharmonic (usually on Fridays or Saturdays), interspersed with chamber concerts and solo recitals.

Polski Teatr Tańca ul. Kozia 4 ☎ 061/852 4241, Ⓦ www.ptt.poznan.pl. Rich diet of classical ballet and contemporary dance. Box office Tues–Sun 1–6pm.

Teatr Muzyczny ul. Niezłomnych 1e ☎ 061/852 3267. Main venue for musicals and operetta. Box office Tues–Fri 10am–7pm, Sat & Sun 2hr before performance.

Teatr Wielki ul. Aleksandra Fredry 9 ☎ 061/659 0200, Ⓦ www.opera.poznan.pl. Home of the Poznań opera. There are usually several operas running concurrently throughout the season, with performances several nights a week. Box office Mon–Sat 1–7pm, Sun 4–7pm.

Theatre

Scena na Piętrze ul. Masztalarska 8 ☎ 061/852 8833. Contemporary drama from visiting companies.

Teatr Animacji al. Niepodległości 14 ☎ 061/853 6964. Enjoyable and inventive productions from one of Poland's best-known theatres for children, located in one wing of the Zamek cultural centre. Sometimes starring live actors, sometimes featuring puppets; note that many performances start as early as 10 or 11am. Box office Tues–Sun 10am–noon & 3–5pm.

Teatr Nowy ul. Dąbrowskiego 5 ☎ 061/848 4885, Ⓦ www.teatrnowy.pl. Contemporary drama from Poland and further afield, with performances taking place in either the main auditorium or the studio-sized Scena Nowa. Box office Tues–Sat 1–7pm, Sun 4–7pm.

Teatr Ósmiego Dnia ul. Ratajczaka 44. ☎ 061/855 2086. Experimental drama from one of Poland's leading companies. Box office Mon–Fri 11am–2pm or 30 minutes prior to the performance.

Teatr Polski ul. 27 Grudnia 8/10 ☎ 061/852 5627. Drama from classical to contemporary, with a strong accent on the Polish theatrical canon. Box office Tues–Sat 10am–7pm, Sun 4–7pm.

Cinema

Apollo ul. Ratajczaka 18. Mainstream movies and comfy atmosphere in a traditional two-screen cinema, nicely renovated in 2005.

Malta ul. Filipińska 5 ☎061/877 2495. A good twenty minutes' east of the Rynek in Śródka, this has the widest range of art movies and cinema classics.
Multikino ul. Królowej Jadwigi 51 ☎061/835 3344. Handiest of the multiplexes, ten minutes'

south of the Rynek near the Stary Browar shopping centre.
Muza ul. św. Marcin 30. Mainstream films in a central location.

Listings

Airlines LOT, at the airport ☎0801 300 952, ⓦwww.lot.com.
Airport Information ☎061/849 2000, ⓦwww.airport-poznan.com.pl.
Books and maps The Empik store at ul. Ratajczaka 44 (Mon–Sat 9am–10pm, Sun 9am–4pm) has the best overall selection of maps, English-language magazines and books. Globetrotter, just off the northern side of the Rynek at ul. Żydowska 1, is a specialist store for maps and guidebooks.
Car rental Avis, at the airport ☎061/849 2335, ⓦwww.avis.com; Budget, at the airport ☎061/847 3434, ⓦwww.budget.pl; Europcar ☎061/849 2357, ⓦwww.europecar.pl; Hertz, in the Novotel at pl. Andersa 1 ☎061/853 1702, ⓦwww.hertz.com; Joka, ul. Grunwaldzka 104 ☎061/862 1171, ⓦwww.joka.com.pl.
Hospital ul. Chełmońskiego 20 ☎061/866 0066.

Internet access Internet Club, ul. Garncarska 10; and Klik, Jaskółcza.
Left luggage at the train station (24hr) and at the bus station (8am–10pm).
Libraries The British Council-supported English-language library at ul. Ratajczaka 39 (Mon–Fri 10am–6pm, Sat 10am–2pm) has a generous stock of books and periodicals.
Pharmacies There's a 24hr pharmacy just north-west of the Rynek at ul. 23 Lutego 18.
Post office Main office at ul. Kościuszki 77 (Mon–Fri 7am–9pm, Sat 8am–7pm, Sun 10am–5pm). The train station branch, just outside the western entrance at Głogowska 17, is open 24hr.
Taxis ☎919 or ☎9622.
Travel agents Orbis, ul. Marcinkowskiego 21 ☎061/853 2052, deals with international bus, train and air tickets.

Around Poznań

It's simple to escape from the big-city feel of Poznań, as its outskirts soon give way to peaceful agricultural villages set in a lake-strewn landscape. Within a 25-kilometre radius of the city is some of the finest scenery in Wielkopolska, along with two of Poland's most famous **castles**, which, if you have a car, combine to make a full day's excursion. If you're dependent on public transport, you'll probably have to devote a day to each of them.

Kórnik

Twenty-two kilometres southeast of Poznań on the main road to Katowice, the lakeside village of **KÓRNIK** is the site of one of the great castles of Wielkopolska. There are regular services from Poznań's main **bus** station; don't go by **train**, as the station is 4km from the village.

Buses pick up and drop off on the main Rynek, a well-signed five-minute walk from the **castle** (Tues–Sun: May–Sept 9am–5.30pm; Oct–March till 3.30pm; 8zł), which stands amid extensive parkland at the southern edge of the village. Originally built for the Górka family in the fourteenth century, the castle was rebuilt in neo-Gothic style in the nineteenth century by Italian and German craftsmen including Karl Friedrich Schinkel, best known for his Neoclassical public buildings in Berlin. However, his designs were considerably modified, and credit for the final shape of the castle is due to the owner, Tytus Działyński, whose aim was as much to show off his collection of arms and armour, books and *objets d'art* as to provide a luxurious home for himself.

In contrast to the affected grandeur of the exterior, with its mock defensive towers and Moorish battlements (most evident on the south side, opposite the entrance) the interior is rather more intimate. On the ground floor it's the decorative parquet flooring and Regency furniture which catch the eye. The **drawing room**, with its superb gilded ceiling and huge carved wooden portal bears Działyński's coat of arms, and none other than Chopin once ran his fingers across the keyboard of the nearby grand piano. The spacious **Black Hall**, with its slender white vaulting, gives a hint of the Moorish excesses upstairs, while next door, the **dining room** returns to a medieval European theme with its wooden coffered ceiling displaying heralds of almost the entire fifteenth-century Polish nobility. On the first floor is the one really theatrical gesture, the **Moorish Hall**, which attempts to mimic Granada's Alhambra. Here Działyński displayed his collection of antique Polish armour and weapons, including an impressive feather-peaked suit once worn by a hussar and a cannon bearing the pretentious inscription: *ultima ratio regis* (a king's last resort).

Stretching away behind the castle is Tytus Działyński's **arboretum** (May–Oct daily 9am–5pm; 3zł; in winter usually accessible during restricted hours for free), a landscaped collection of over three thousand types of tree which, judging by the crocodiles of Polish schoolchildren being marched around by enthusiastic teachers, is an even more popular day-trip destination than the castle. Originally in the formal French style, this was transformed in the seemingly arbitrary manner of a *jardin anglais*. There are over two thousand species of trees and shrubs, from all corners of the world including China, Korea and America, as well as a Gothic-Moorish view of the castle's south facade. The lakeside offers an even more pleasant stroll, particularly the western bank with its fine distant views.

Rogalin

With your own transport, it's easy to combine a visit to Kórnik with a look round the palace at **ROGALIN**, a hamlet 10km to the west on the road to Mosina. With only three buses a day from Poznań, those dependent on public transport will have to check times carefully in advance.

The **palace** (May–Sept: Tues–Sat 10am–4pm, Sun 10am–6pm; Oct–April: Tues–Sun 10am–4pm; 8zł, free on Thurs) was the seat of many Polish nobles from the eminent Poznań family, the Raczyńskis. It's one of Poland's finest mansions, a truly palatial residence forming the axis of a careful layout of buildings and gardens. Begun in 1768 and only finished 47 years later, the palace represents a remarkable and rather tasteful fusion of the Baroque and Neoclassical styles. Much of the gleaming middle block remains in the throes of long-term renovation, but there's plenty in the way of period interiors in the two bowed **wings**, which feature some fine furniture including a lovely lyre cabinet as well as portraits of illustrious Raczyńskis, most notably a sinister depiction of Roger who's buried in the chapel (see below) and a far more agreeable-looking Anna Raczyńska. Best of all is the **art gallery** (marked "Galeria Obrazów") off the southern side, a well-laid-out collection of nineteenth-century Polish and German works. Jacek Malczewski was a frequent guest at Rogalin and his works are well represented here, as are those of **Jan Matejko**, his epic *Virgin of Orleans* taking up an entire wall.

Fronting the palace courtyard is a long forecourt, to the sides of which are the stables and **coach house**, the latter now a repository of carriages once used by owners of this estate, along with the last horse-drawn cab to operate in Poznań. Passing outside the gates, a five-minute walk brings you to the unusual **chapel** which undertakes the duties of a parish church and mausoleum of the now defunct Raczyńskis. Set peacefully at the side of the road, it's a copy of one of

Europe's best-preserved Roman monuments, the Maison Carrée in Nîmes, but built in a startlingly pink sandstone.

At the back of the main palace is an enclosed and rather neglected *jardin français*. More enticing is the English-style park beyond, laid out on the site of a primeval forest. This is chiefly remarkable for its **oak trees**, three of the most ancient of which have been fenced off for protection and are known as the "Rogalin Oaks". Among the most celebrated natural wonders of Poland, they are at least one thousand years old – and thus of a similar vintage to the Polish nation itself. Following World War II they became popularly known as Lech, Czech and Rus, after the three mythical brothers who founded the Polish, Czech and Russian nations; with all due modesty, the largest is designated as Rus.

There's a **restaurant** and bar by the road, opposite the entrance to the palace, and a comfortable **hotel** (☏061/813 8480; ❹) in one of the palace outbuildings.

Wielkopolska national park

The only area of protected landscape in the province, the **Wielkopolska national park** occupies an area of some 100 square kilometres to the south of Poznań. Unspoiled by any kind of development, it's a popular day-trip destination from the regional capital. Formed in geologically recent times, it's a post-glacial landscape of low moraines, gentle ridges and lakes. Half the park is taken up by forest, predominantly pine and birch planted as replacements for the original hardwoods.

Access to the park from Poznań is fairly easy, with about twelve daily **trains** (the slow *osobowy* services from Poznań to Leszno or Wrocław) passing through a sequence of settlements on the eastern fringes of the park – Puszczykowo, Puszczykówko and Mosina – from where you can pick up hiking trails into the park itself. The western border of the park is served by the Poznań–Wolsztyn rail line (some of the five daily services are still pulled by antiquated steam engines from the Wolsztyn depot; see p.607), which passes through the trail-head town of Stęszew. Catching a train to the eastern side of the park, walking across it, and returning to Poznań from Stęszew (or vice versa), makes for a perfectly feasible day-trip. It's also increasingly popular to cross the park by bike (trails open to cyclists have orangey-red waymarks), although as yet there's nowhere in the vicinity of the park where you can actually hire one. The settlements around the park are nothing much to shout about, and it seems wise to head back to Poznań in the evening rather than opting to stay here.

Fifteen kilometres south of Poznań, the twin villages of **PUSZCZYKOWO** and **PUSZCZYKÓWKO** lie on the west bank of the snaking River Warta, both serving as the starting points for trails heading into the northern section of the park. Puszczykówko is marginally the more appealing of the two, if only because it's the site of the **Muzeum Arkadego Fiedlera** (Arkady Fiedler Museum; May–Oct: Tues–Sun 9am–5pm; 5zł), located just east of the station in the former house of the prolific Polish travel writer. Fiedler's first book was an account of a rafting trip down the River Dniester in 1926, and after a spell in the RAF, he went on to enjoy a postwar career as one of the most popular travel writers in the Eastern Bloc, churning out books on his experiences in Africa, South America and the East. The museum is full of the personal nick-nacks brought back from his sojourns abroad, while the delightful garden boasts an impressive array of replica Aztec, Olmec and other sculptures – the whole ensemble presided over by a haughty Easter Island head.

Another 2km south of Puszczykówko is **MOSINA**, a small and rather dreary town which is nevertheless the best starting point for exploring the eastern reaches of the park (see "Walking in the park", p.606).

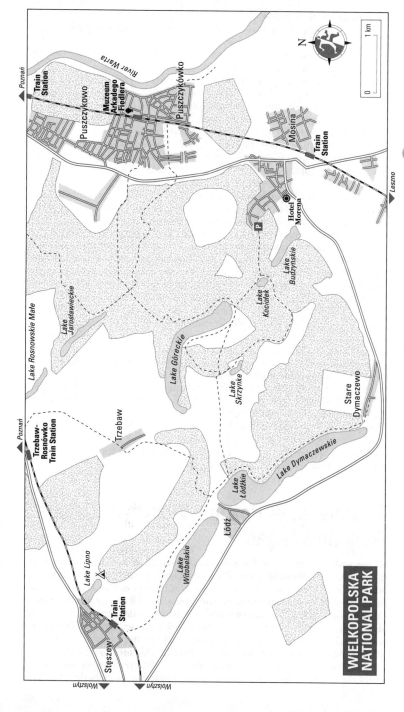

WIELKOPOLSKA NATIONAL PARK

N

0 — 1 km

Poznań

Train Station

Puszczykowo

Muzeum Arkadego Fiedlera

Puszczykówko

River Warta

Mosina

Train Station

Leszno

Hotel Morena

P

Lake Budzyńskie

Lake Kociołek

Lake Rosnowskie Małe

Lake Jarosławieckie

Lake Góreckie

Lake Skrzynka

Stare Dymaczewo

Trzebaw-Rosnówko Train Station

Trzebaw

Lake Łódzkie

Lake Dymaczewskie

Poznań

Łódź

Lake Witobelskie

Lake Lipno

Stęszew

Train Station

Wolsztyn

Wolsztyn

Walking in the park

Exploring the park, it's best to stick to the three official **hiking paths**, which are generally well marked and unstrenuous. Each takes several hours to cover its entire length, though it's easy enough to switch from one to the other – the best idea if you're restricted for time.

Walking from Mosina gets you into the best of the terrain quickly. Heading out of town on the road to Stęszew, turning right at the *Hotel Morena*, and then turning left at the top of the hill (waymarks – red for cyclists and blue for walkers – point you in the right direction), brings you to a car park and picnic site overlooking the park (and offering one of the park's few panoramic views). From here the path descends to the small heart-shaped Lake Kociołek, which is beautifully shaded by trees. If your plan is to cross the park to Stęszew, your best bet is to follow the blue trail from here, which leads north round the lake before continuing through the forest to the southern end of Lake Góreckie. It then climbs through thick woods before passing through open countryside to Lake Łódźkie, on the far side of which – off the trail but on the main road – is the hamlet of Łódź, clustered around a seventeenth-century wooden church. The route then leads along the northern shore of Lake Witobelskie to Stęszew.

The **red trail** runs south along the shore of Lake Kociołek before travelling circuitously uphill, skirting the small Lake Skrzynke just before crossing the blue trail. It arrives at the bend in the sausage-shaped Lake Góreckie, from where there's a view across to an islet with a ruined castle – a former fortress of the Działyński family, and a meeting point for the Polish insurgents of 1863. The path then leads about halfway round the perimeter of the lake as far as Jeziory, where there's another car park plus a restaurant and café. Two separate red paths proceed to Puszczykówko, while a third follows the long northerly route to Puszczykowo via Lake Jarosławieckie.

The **black trail** begins at the station of **Trzebaw-Rosnówko** (just north of Stęszew; it's also on the Poznań–Wolsztyn rail line), then traverses the fields to the hamlet of Trzebaw, before continuing through the woods to Lake Łódźkie. It then follows the eastern bank of this lake and its much longer continuation, Lake Dymaczewskie – which together make up the largest stretch of water in the park – before ending at Stare Dymaczewo on the Mosina–Stęszew road. In many ways this is the least convenient place at which to end up: buses between Mosina and Stęszew are so infrequent that you'd probably save time by back-tracking on foot and making your way out of the park by another route.

Southwest of Poznań: Wolsztyn, Zielona Góra and Żagań

Those with a nostalgia for the days of steam should make tracks for the little lakeside town of **WOLSZTYN**, 75km southwest of Poznań, the only remaining rail depot in Europe that still uses steam locomotives to haul passenger services – which currently run to Poznań, Leszno and Zbąszynek. It's something that the local railway staff are incredibly proud of, and at the time of writing there are no plans to phase out this seemingly anachronistic service. Pride of the local fleet is the green-liveried *Piękna Helena* ("Beautiful Helena"), built for the Polish state railways in 1936 and still going strong. Often seen pulling the principal morning service from Poznań to Wolsztyn (currently 8.48am but always check the timetable), she's also a much-valued showpiece, periodically trundling around Europe to represent Poland at various railway nostalgia events. Wolsztyn is a popular destination for train enthusiasts from all over Europe, and in addition to the timetabled daily services, a parade of steam locomotives is staged at Wolsztyn station every year on the first Saturday of May – extra trains are laid on from Poznań on the day. Holidays tailored to railway enthusiasts, which can include the opportunity to learn how to drive an engine, are organized by the UK-based Wolsztyn Experience, 20 Whitepit Lane, Flackwell Heath, High Wycombe, Bucks HP10 9HS (℡01628/524876, ✉trevorjones@20whitepit .freeserve.co.uk). If you want more information on the Wolsztyn-based locomotives, then websites like ⓦwww.polrail.com and ⓦwww.parowozy.com.pl are a useful resource.

Wolsztyn's main attraction is the **Parowozownia** (engine shed; daily 7am–3pm; 3zł) 1km southeast of the train and bus stations at ul. Fabryczna 1, where several working locomotives are on display. A melancholy graveyard of rusting steam engines stretches along the tracks between here and the stations. The rest of Wolsztyn, spread out to the northwest, is a drab place but boasts a couple of time-killing attractions: the **Muzeum Regionalnie** (Regional Museum; Tues–Sat 9am–4pm, Sun 10am–3pm; ⓦwww.muzea-wolsztyn.com.pl; 3zł), on the main street at ul. 5 Stycznia 34, has a collection honouring leading inter-war sculptor Marcin Rożek, sent to his death in Auschwitz after refusing to design a monument to Adolf Hitler; while the small **Robert Koch Museum**, round the corner at ul. Roberta Kocha 12 (Tues–Sat 10am–4pm; 3zł), remembers the local doctor who bagged the Nobel Prize in 1905 for his discovery of the tuberculosis bacillus.

On the northwestern side of the town centre lies the shore of Lake Wolsztyn, where there's a small sandy beach and secluded lakeside paths leading off in either direction. Walking westwards and following the shore through wooded parkland brings you after fifteen minutes or so to a **skansen** (May–Sept: Tues–Sat 9am–5pm, Sun noon–5pm; Oct–Dec & Feb–April: Tues–Fri 10am–2pm; closed Jan; 4zł), which has a small but impressive collection of sturdy traditional farm buildings, each topped by a thick thatch of reeds taken from the nearby lake.

Practicalities

Wolsztyn is best treated as a day-trip from either Poznań or Zielona Góra (see below). Should you need to stay, the *OSiR* sports **hotel** opposite the skansen (℡068/384 3320) is a utilitarian block with simple doubles with sink (❶) *and* some en suites (❷). Moving up in price, the *Kaukaska*, just west of the train station at ul. Poniatowskiego 19 (℡068/347 2852; ❹), offers smart, modern en suites with TV. There's a **campsite** next door to the *OSiR* hotel.

The al-fresco **cafés** by the beach offer the best places to grab a quick meal and a drink in summer; otherwise the **restaurant** of the *Kaukaska* offers the best range of food.

Zielona Góra

Sixty kilometres southwest of Wolsztyn, and served by regular buses from both Wolsztyn and Poznań, the medium-sized city of **ZIELONA GÓRA** straddles the border between Wielkopolska and Lower Silesia. Little damaged in World War II, it's one of Poland's more handsome provincial centres, preserving an eclectic mixture of nineteenth-century buildings. There are good public transport connections and a reasonable choice of places to stay and eat, which make it the most likely base for touring this corner of the country.

The City

Central Zielona Góra presents an engaging patchwork of turn-of-the-twentieth-century architectural styles, with quirky neo-Gothic turrets poking from the corners of some town houses, Art Nouveau decoration dripping from the facades of others. Few of the buildings around the central Rynek are of any great vintage, but their pastel colour schemes give the city a cheerful air. Most imposing of the monuments is the **Kościół Matki Boskiej Częstochowskiej** (Church of Our Lady of Częstochowa), just north of the Rynek, an eighteenth-century example of the Silesian penchant for half-timbered ecclesiastical buildings. The nearby **Muzeum Regionalnie** (Wed–Fri 11am–5pm, Sat 10am–3pm, Sun 10am–4pm; 6zł), northeast of the Rynek at al. Niepodległości 15, contains an overview of the local wine-making industry – Zielona Góra being one of the few places in Poland where this tipple was ever produced.

Practicalities

Zielona Góra's adjacent **train** and **bus stations** are on the northeastern edge of the centre, a fifteen-minute walk from the central Rynek. The **tourist information office** (mid-May to mid-Sept: Mon–Fri 9am–5pm, Sat & Sun 10am–2pm; mid-Sept to mid-May: Mon–Fri only; ☎068/323 2222, ⓦwww.zielona-gora .pl), just east of the Rynek at ul. Kupiecka 15, has information on the whole region and will direct you towards accommodation options.

Best placed of the **hotels** is the *Pod Wieżą* (☎068/327 1091; ❹), in an alleyway just east of the Rynek at ul. Kopernika 2. It's a tad gloomy but acceptable for a night or two. In a similar price range are the *Śródmiejski*, in the pedestrian area just northeast of the Rynek at Żeromskiego 23 (☎068/325 4471; ❸–❺ depending on whether you get new furniture and satellite TV or not); and the much smaller *Pod Lwem*, a functional B&B near the stations at ul. Dworcowa 14 (☎068/324 1055; ❸). In a different league entirely is the *Senator*, midway between the stations and the centre at ul. Chopina 23a (☎068/324 0436, ⓔhotelsenator@wp.pl; ❼), which offers pristine, modern rooms in an upmarket B&B environment.

There's a good choice of **restaurants** in the central area, with *Ermitaż*, a block south of the Rynek on pl. Pocztowy, offering an across-the-board range of pork, chicken and duck dishes alongside some appetizing pastas, in smart but not over-formal surroundings; while the nearby *Winnica*, pl. Pocztowy, serves up skilfully prepared and presented Polish–Ukranian standards in a neat, IKEA-ish interior. *La Gioconda*, just off the Rynek at Mariacka 5, is the place to go for pizzas, pancakes and ice cream; while *Faraon*, on the northeastern shoulder of the Rynek at Żeromskiego 1, offers a familiar Polish-meets-Middle Eastern range of grilled meats, burgers and kebabs.

Żagań

Some 50km southwest of Zielona Góra, and reachable from there by hourly bus, **ŻAGAŃ** is the kind of melancholy looking town found so often in western Poland, rendered architecturally tatty by the combined effects of wartime destruction and functional socialist-era reconstrucion. However, it has two major assets in the form of a Baroque ducal palace set in an attractive park, and a small but captivating museum commemorating the archipelago of German POW camps that once stretched southwest of town. One of these camps, **Stalag Luft III** was the scene of the real-life breakout that provided the inspiration for the film *The Great Escape*.

The Town

Standing within glowering distance of a run-of-the-mill Rynek, the most impressive of Żagań's town-centre buildings is the fourteenth-century **Kościół Wniebowzięcia NMP** (Ascension Church), a high-gabled lump of ruddy bricks surrounded by a horseshoe of former monastery buildings. Its interior, with a beautiful Renaissance altar dedicated to the Holy Trinity, was completely remodelled in the Baroque epoch. A five-minute walk southeast of the Rynek lies the **Pałac Wallensteina** (Wallenstein Palace), begun in the Renaissance period by order of Albrecht von Waldstein (aka Wallenstein), the military genius who commanded Austrian forces during the Thirty Years' War and was awarded the Duchy of Żagań (then part of Austrian-ruled Silesia) by way of recognition. Completed in Italianate Baroque style after Wallenstein's death, it was badly desecrated during World War II; it's now used as office space by the municipal authorities. However, it's monumental winged facade, facing south across parkland towards the swan-patrolled waters of the Bóbr River, is still an impressive sight. North of the palace, on the opposite side of ul. Szprotawska, stands a Neoclassical courthouse that was commandeered by French novelist Stendhal in 1813 when he was serving as a supply officer in Napoleon's Grande Armée.

Stalag Luft III and the "Great Escape"

The area of pine forest and heath immediately southwest of town was used by the Germans as the site of several POW camps during World War II. The first, Stalag VIIIC, was established in 1939 to incarcerate captured Poles; other camps were added as the war progressed and the volume of prisoners increased. Most famous of the Żagań camps was Stalag Luft III, built by the Luftwaffe in 1942 to house allied air officers – who were considered a high-risk category due to their propensity to infect rank-and-file prisoners with ideas of escape. Concentrating officers together, however, turned the camp into a veritable academy of escapology, with numerous tunnelling operations underway at any given time. One group used a wooden vaulting horse to hide their digging activities, making a succesful getaway in October 1943 – an exploit subsequently immortalized in escapee Eric Williams' best-selling account *The Wooden Horse*, which also became a hit film. A far more ambitious operation, masterminded by Squadron Leader Roger Bushell, aimed to get hundreds of prisoners out of the camp via a trio of tunnels nicknamed "Tom", "Dick" and "Harry". The first two were discovered by the Germans, but on the night of March 24, 1944, a total of 76 prisoners made their way out of Harry and into the surrounding woods. Three eventually made it to freedom; the rest were rounded up by the enraged German authorities, who decided to shoot fifty of the escapees as an example to the others. The whole extraordinary episode was first dubbed the "Great Escape" in the big-selling book of that name written by Aussie ex-POW Paul Brickhill in 1950; although it's probably thanks to John Sturges' 1963 Hollywood film of the same name that the escape occupies such a memorable and unique niche in Western popular culture.

Żagań's POW camps are remembered in the **Muzeum Martyrologii Alianckich Jeńców Wojennich** (Museum of Martyrology; daily 10am–5pm; donation requested), a small concrete building beside the Żagań–Lubań road, about 2km southwest of the town centre – a taxi from Żagań bus station (see p.610) will cost under 10zł if you don't fancy the walk. Inside there's a scale model of Stalag Luft III, a mock up of the ingenious tunnelling techniques employed by the escapees, and a words-and-pictures display devoted to the other camps established here – some 200,000 prisoners from all over the world were housed outside Żagań at one time or another, most of whom had to endure conditions far more squalid and brutal than those enjoyed by the relatively privileged air officers held at Stalag Luft III.

Outside the museum building, you're free to explore the network of paths covering the site of the camps, although little remains save for a few scraps of brickwork poking up between the pine trees. The most evocative spot is about twenty minutes' walk northeast of the museum, where an engraved boulder (placed here on the 60th anniversary of the Great Escape) marks the spot where tunnel Harry emerged – a map on the outside wall of the museum will help you find it.

Practicalities

Żagań is a feasible **day trip** from Poznań providing you don't mind changing buses in Zielona Góra. Three daily buses from Lower Silesian capital Wrocław (see p.528) ensure that it's just about do-able from there too. Żagań's **bus station** is on the west bank of the River Bóbr, five minutes' walk from the central Rynek. The **train station**, midway between the town centre and the site of the POW camps, is served by one daily Wrocław–Berlin express and precious little else.

Best value of Żagań's **hotels** is the *Młynówka*, ul. Żelazna 2a (☎068/377 3120; ❸), which offers reasonable standards of comfort at an acceptable price, and enjoys a restful riverside location just east of the palace. The best **place to eat** is the *Kepler*, Rynek 27, serving up excellent and not-too-expensive traditional Polish fare in a nicely restored town house. *Tropik*, on the opposite side of the square at no. 7–10, is a good source of cheap and filling Polish staples.

Southern Wielkopolska: Leszno and Kalisz

Leszno

Roughly midway between Poznań and Wrocław, and served by regular trains from both cities, **LESZNO** is a pleasantly low-key market town whose history is inextricably bound up with one of Poland's most remarkable dynasties, the Leszczyński family, who founded Leszno in the late fourteenth century. The last of the male line, **Stanisław Leszczyński**, deposed the hated Augustus the Strong of Saxony to become king of Poland in 1704, only to be overthrown by the same rival six years later. He briefly regained the throne in 1733, but met with far more success in exile in France, marrying his daughter to Louis XV, and himself becoming duke of Lorraine and gaining a reputation as a patron of the arts.

The Town

The handsome cobbled **Rynek** is ringed by predominantly Neoclassical buildings with the odd Baroque facade surviving the Swedish Wars that left Leszno in ruins. The colourist approach favoured by the architects – prominent among whom was the Italian Pompeo Ferrari – is shown to best effect in the salmon pink tones of the recently spruced-up **town hall**.

Just south of the Rynek, the exterior of the twin-towered **Kościół św. Mikołaja** (St Nicholas's Church) strikes a more typically sombre note. Its interior, on the other hand, displays a good example of Rococo ornamentation – the florid style of late Baroque's death throes. On each side of the altar are the huge, seemingly unpainted monuments to the Leszczyńskis. A fascinating contrast with this richness is provided by the clean, sober lines of the **Kościół św. Krzyża** (Church of Holy Cross), a couple of minutes' walk to the southwest on pl. Metziga. The church is surrounded by the ornate remains of crumbling epitaphs set in its perimeter walls, while a collection of small memorial obelisks from the late eighteenth century further commemorate the passing of Leszno's prominent families. Inside the vestibule a life-size angel bears a huge shell, an unusual vessel for holy water.

On the same square, shaded by a huge oak tree, is the regional museum, or **Muzeum Okręgowe** (Tues noon–5pm, Wed–Fri 9am–2pm, Sat & Sun 10am–2pm), a miscellaneous local collection, featuring several coffins bearing sculpted reliefs of the deceased, and a room devoted to Comenius of the Bohemian Brethren (see box below). A few streets east of here, off ul. Bolesława Chrobrego, is the brick **Kościół św. Jana** (Church of St John), aesthetically unremarkable but semi-interesting as the place where the Bohemian Brethren held their services.

Practicalities

The **train** and **bus stations** lie just west of Leszno's main street, ul. Słowiańska, which drives north to meet the Rynek. Once you've pottered around Leszno's town centre you'd be wise to move on, although the **tourist office**, Słowiańska 24 (Mon–Fri 9am–5pm, Sat 9am–3pm; ☎065/529 8191, ⓦwww.leszno.pl) will guide you towards the town's accommodation possibilities should you wish to stay.

The *Pensjonat Wienawa*, Rynek 29 (☎065/529 5058, ⓦwww.wienawa.com.pl; ❺), is a handily placed source of cosy rooms above a restaurant; although it can't compare in the comfort stakes with the *Akwawit*, ul. św. Jozefa 5 (☎065/529 3781, ⓦwww.akwavit.com.pl; ❻), at the far end of the flyover (visible from the train and bus stations) on the west side of town, which exudes an aura of plush modernity and has an adventure swimming pool next door. For a taste of the high life, try the *Hotel Zamkowy* in Rydzyna Castle (☎065/529 5040, ⓦwww.zamek-rydzyna.com.pl; ❻), a seventeenth-century stately home-cum-conference centre 12km southeast of town – the en-suite doubles with TV are quite bland but the function rooms and surrounding parks are splendid.

The Bohemian Brethren

Along with many other Polish grandees, the Leszczyńskis enthusiastically adopted the Reformation, though Stanisław, like Augustus the Strong, was forced to convert to Catholicism in order to launch his bid for the crown. In the first half of the seventeenth century Leszno became a refuge for the **Bohemian Brethren**, Czech Protestants who were forced to flee their homeland by the religious intolerance of the Thirty Years' War. The Academy these exiles founded in Leszno developed into one of Europe's great centres of learning, thanks to the leadership of Jan Amos Komenski, known as **Comenius**. Creator of the first illustrated textbook, he was called to put his educational theories into practice in England, Sweden, Hungary and Holland, and even received invitations from the Protestant-loathing Cardinal Richelieu in France and from Harvard University, which wanted him as its president. Though Comenius and his colleagues were eventually forced to leave Leszno by the Swedish Wars of the 1650s, the town remained a major educational centre into the nineteenth century. The Brethren were later transformed into the **Moravian Church**, a body which continues to have an influence out of all proportion to its size, particularly in the USA.

Back in Leszno, the *Vienawa* **restaurant** offers well-presented Polish fare at reasonable prices, and also a cosy ground-floor pub; while *Culinaria*, between the Rynek and the stations at ul. Słowiańska 35, is one of the most stylish and satisfying order-at-the-counter canteens you're likely to find in this part of Poland. Occupying the ground floor of the town hall, the *Kawiarnia Ratuszowa* is a chic place to linger over coffee and cakes.

Kalisz

At the extreme southeastern corner of Wielkopolska, midway between Poznań and Łódź, lies the industrial town of **KALISZ**. Almost universally held to be Poland's oldest recorded city, it was referred to as *Calissia* by Pliny in the first century and was described in the second century as a trading settlement on the "amber route" between the Baltic and Adriatic. Though apparently inhabited without interruption ever since, it failed to develop into a major city. Built around an attractive Rynek and its surrounding grid of cobbled alleys, Kalisz makes for a convenient stopover if you're passing through, especially if you're on the way to the palace at Gołuchów (see opposite).

The Town

As the train and bus stations are 3km from the centre of the city you'll need to catch a bus in; see "Practicalities" opposite for details. On the way in, along ul. Górnośląska and ul. Śródmiejska, you'll pass two space-age churches that shoot up from parallel boulevards – contemporary symbols of the key role of Catholicism in modern Poland.

Kalisz's pleasant if unspectacular Rynek centres on a large Neoclassical **town hall**. Down ul. Kanonicka at the northwestern end of the square is the brick Gothic **Katedra św. Mikołaja** (St Nicholas' Cathedral), which has been subject to a fair amount of neo-Gothic tinkering, though for once this is not entirely to its disadvantage. The most attention-grabbing feature is the spire, a flamboyant, flying-buttressed affair that brings to mind the kind of space rockets envisaged by 1950s comic-book artists. Inside, the prize item is *The Descent from the Cross* on the high altar, a twentieth-century copy of a seventeenth-century original, brought here from Rubens' workshop in Antwerp and lost in a fire in 1973. Located just off the southeastern corner of the Rynek is a smaller square which lies in front of the **Kościół Franciszkanów** (Franciscan Church), an older and simpler example of Gothic brickwork, but with generous Baroque interior decorations – unfortunately it's usually locked.

From here, it's just a short walk north to ul. Kolegialna, which defines the eastern perimeter of the Stare Miasto. Along it you'll pass the long facade of the **Jesuit college**, a severe Neoclassical composition incorporating a finely carved Renaissance portal. The only part of the building that visitors are allowed to enter is the church, which follows the plain Mannerist style of the Jesuits' most important church, the Gesu in Rome. Immediately beyond the college, standing beside the surviving fragment of the city's ramparts, is the single-towered **Bazylika Wniebowzięcia NMP** (Church of the Asssumption), a more adventurous example of late eighteenth-century Baroque which includes parts of its Gothic predecessor. The interior bristles with works of art, including a sixteenth-century Silesian polyptych in the left-hand aisle which displays scenes from the life of a particularly serene and beauteous Madonna. The chapel of St Joseph in the right-hand aisle is one of Wielkopolska's most popular places of pilgrimage, thanks to a miracle-working late medieval painting of the Holy Family – a charming image of Mary and Joseph leading a toddler-sized Jesus by the hand, their bodies clad in a set of decorous silver-plated robes which were added by pious locals in 1768. Ten minutes' walk southwest of the centre, across the River Prozna, the **Muzeum Okręgowe** (Regional Museum; Tues & Thurs 10am–3pm, Wed & Fri 11am–5.30pm, Sat & Sun 10am–2.30pm; 3zł), at Kościuszki 12, accommodates a small but riveting collection of locally excavated Neolithic, Celtic and Roman pottery which, beautifully displayed and lit, has the easy-on-the-eye appeal of a designer kitchenware showroom.

Practicalities

Both the **train** and **bus** stations are to be found 3km from the centre at the southwestern end of the city. To reach the centre, take buses #2, #11, #12, #15 or #19 from the stop on the main road outside the bus station – all these end up on pl. św. Jozefa just east of the main Rynek. There's a helpful **tourist office** one block northwest of the Rynek at ul. Gabarska 2 (Mon–Fri 10am–5pm, Sat 10am–2pm; ☎062/764 2184, ⓦwww.kalisz.pl).

Accommodation options include *U Bogdana*, ul. Legionów 15–17 (☎062/753 0823; ❷), which offers simple rooms with shared bathrooms in a residential block about 100m north of the train and bus stations. Moving upmarket, *Europa*, just south of the Rynek at al. Wolności 5 (☎062/767 2032, ⓦwww .hotel-europa.pl), ranges from neat simple en suites (❹) to plush rooms with thick carpets and Jacuzzis (❻); the *Calisia*, 500m southwest of the Rynek at ul. Nowy Świat 1–3 (☎062/767 9100; ❻, sizeable weekend discounts), has smart en suites with TV; while the Orbis-run *Prosna*, 2km southwest of the centre near the stations at ul. Górnośląska 53/55 (☎062/768 9100, ⓔprosna@orbis .pl; ❻), is a satisfactory if bland source of business-standard comforts.

For a quick bite to **eat** or **drink**, there are plenty of places around the Rynek. *Bar Delicije*, on the southeast corner of the square, is a comfortable order-at-the-counter place good for *pierogi*, *placki* and other snack-bar standards; *Baja Mexico*, just off the Rynek on Piskorzewska, is a relaxing place decked out in ethnic textiles and boasting a bigger and tastier range of Mex-type fare than most similarly themed places in Poland. *Marrone*, a pizzeria just over the river from the Franciscan church, has tasty pies as well as salads and spaghetti dishes. *Piwnica Ratuszowa*, Rynek 20, concentrates on stolid Polish staples in elegant surroundings. *Cukiernia Italia,* on the eastern side of the square, is the best place for cakes and ice cream.

Gołuchów

Twenty kilometres from Kalisz on the main road to Poznań, and reached by frequent Poznań-bound buses from the main bus station, the village of **GOŁUCHÓW** would be a place you'd whizz through were it not for its **palace**, the one outstanding monument in the Kalisz area.

It began as a small defensive castle, built in 1560 for Rafał Leszczyński of the famous Leszno family. Early the following century, his son Wacław completely transformed it into a palatial residence worthy of a man who had risen to be royal chancellor. Like the Polish state itself, it gradually fell into ruin. In 1853 it was bought by Tytus Działyński, the owner of Kórnik (see p.602), as a present for his son Jan, who married Izabella, daughter of the formidable Adam Czartoryski (see p.666). While her husband languished in exile for his part in the 1863 Uprising, Izabella devoted herself to re-creating the glory of the castle, eventually opening it as one of Poland's first museums. Rather than revert to the Italianate form of the original, she opted for a distinctively French touch – with its steeply pitched roofs, prominent chimneys, pointed towers and graceful arcaded terrace, the palace looks like a passable pastiche of something you might find in the Loire Valley.

The small **apartments** (Tues–Sat 10am–4pm, Sun 10am–5pm; 8zł) are crammed with paintings and *objets d'art*. The highlights of the display are some magnificent antique vases – just part of an assembly whose other items are now kept in the Muzeum Narodowe in Warsaw. After the guided tour you can wander off to the two rooms under the stairway, in which changing exhibitions from the castle's collection of engravings are held.

The landscaped **park** surrounding the palace contains a **café** and an uninspiring **Muzeum Leśnictwa** (Museum of Forestry; Tues–Sun 10am–4pm; 3.50zł). Near here you'll also come across Izabella's neo-Baroque funerary chapel, and on the northwestern outskirts of the park there's a bison farm.

If you want a **place to stay**, the *Dom Pracy Twórcej* **hotel** at ul. Borowskiego 2 (☎062/761 5044; ❸), offers plainish but adequate en-suite rooms with TV, although it's best to reserve well in advance. Otherwise there's a **campsite** (☎062/761 8281), about 2km southeast in the Kalisz direction and well signposted from the main road. The *Zamkowa* **restaurant** at ul. Kopczyńskiego 1 will sort you out with a hearty slab of pork or chicken.

Gniezno and around

Despite the competing claims of Poznań, Kruszwica and Lednica, **GNIEZNO**, 50km east of Poznań, is generally credited as the first capital of Poland, a title based on the dense web of myth and chronicled fact that constitute the story of the nation's earliest years. Nowadays Poland's ecclesiastical capital has the feel of a quiet but charming small town, but there are sufficient historical attractions

here to make Gniezno well worth a couple of days' stay. It's also an excellent base from which to visit places featured on the so-called **Szlak Piastowski** (Piast Route), a tourist trail between Poznań and Inowrocław, which highlights salient locations associated with the Piast dynasty. Most important of these is the medieval archeological site at **Lake Lednica** (also the site of a large ethnographic museum), which is only a few minutes' journey from town by bus.

Some history

Lech, the legendary founder of Poland, supposedly came across the nest (*gniazdo*) of a white eagle here; he founded a town on the spot, and made the bird the emblem of his people, a role it still maintains. Less fancifully, it's known for sure that Mieszko I had established a court here in the late tenth century, and that in the year 1000 it was the scene of a turning point in the country's history.

The catalyst for this, ironically enough, was a Czech, **św. Wojciech** (St Adalbert), the first bishop of Prague. Unable to cope with the political demands of his office, he retired to a monastery, but later bowed to pressure from Rome to take up missionary work. In 997 he set out from Gniezno to evangelize the Prussians, a fierce Baltic tribe who lived on Poland's eastern borders – and who quickly dispatched him to a martyr's death. In order to recover the body, Mieszko I's son, **Bolesław the Brave**, was forced to pay Wojciech's weight in gold, an astute investment as it turned out. At the pope's instigation, Emperor Otto III made a pilgrimage to Gniezno, bringing relics with him which would add to the site's holiness. Received in great splendour, he crowned Bolesław with his own crown, confirming Poland as a fully-fledged kingdom and one which was independent of the German-dominated Holy Roman Empire. Furthermore, Gniezno was made the seat of Poland's first archbishopric; Wojciech's brother Radim was the first to be appointed to the post.

Gniezno was soon replaced as capital by the more secure town of Kraków, and although it made a partial recovery in the Middle Ages, it never grew very big. Nevertheless, it has always been important as the official seat of the primate of Poland. Throughout the period of elected kings, the holder of this office functioned as head of state during each interregnum, and it is still one of the most prestigious positions in the land. In recent times, the Gniezno archbishopric has been coupled to that of Warsaw, with the primate tending, for obvious reasons, to spend far more time in the capital. The pressures this caused led in 1992 to Gniezno losing its historic role as the primate's seat in return for its own full-time archbishop, though it will permanently regain the honour on the retirement or death of the present incumbent, Cardinal Glemp.

Arrival, information and accommodation

The **train** and **bus** stations are side by side about 500m south of the centre – walk straight down ul. Lecha to ul. Bolesława Chrobrego, which terminates at the Rynek. The **tourist information office**, ul. Tumska 12 (Mon–Fri 9am–5pm; ☎061/428 4100, ✉turystyka@powiat-gniezno.pl), can sort you out with **B&B accommodation** with local families (❶–❷), although most of these households are in surrounding villages and you'll need your own transport to get there.

The **youth hostel**, close to the stations at ul. Pocztowa 11 (on the top floor; ☎061/424 0796, ℻426 2780), is a welcoming place with few rough edges.

Hotels

AWO ul. Warszawska 32 ☎061/426 1197, ⓦwww .hotel-awo.pl. Mid-sized hotel located in a courtyard on a lively shopping street. Comfortable en suites with TV and warm colour schemes make this a welcoming pied-à-terre. ❺

Gewert ul. Paczkowskiego 2 ☎61/428 2375, ✉gewert@02.pl. A welcoming medium-sized establishment offering bright, snazzy en suites with TV, although it's incongruously situated in an area of scruffy tower blocks 1.5km from the centre. Buses #9 or #17 from Dworcowa to Budowlanych. ❺

Lech ul. Jolenty 5 ☎61/426 2385, ⓦwww .hotel-lech.pl. Uninspiring but habitable 1970s-era hotel fifteen minutes' walk northeast of the centre, with plain en suites. Guests can use the nearby swimming pool and fitness centre. ❺

Orzeł ul. Wrzesińska 25 ☎61/426 4925. Sports

hotel situated right next to a speedway oval, offering simple but clean rooms in a frumpy part of town some twenty minutes' walk south of the centre. Cheaper doubles come with shared facilities, others are en suite. Might be noisy during race weekends. ❷–❸

Pietrak ul. Chrobrego 3 ☎61/426 1497, ⓦwww .hotel-pietrak.home.pl. Friendly, family-run place in the middle of the pedestrianized area, providing comfortable en-suite rooms with satellite TV and minibar, and a big buffet breakfast. ❺

The City

The compactness of Gniezno is immediately evident: from either the train or bus station it's only a few minutes' walk straight down ul. Lecha to ul. Bolesława Chrobrego, the quiet end of a main thoroughfare that boasts several brightly colourwashed buildings. In ten minutes you pass into the pedestrianized section of this street, which ends up at the quiet, cobbled **Rynek**.

There are three Gothic churches worth a quick look. Just off the southern side of the Rynek is the **Kościół św. Trójcy** (Church of the Holy Trinity), partly rebuilt in the Baroque style following a fire, beside which stand the only surviving remains of the city walls. Off the opposite side of the Rynek towers the Franciscan church, while further to the north is **Kościół św. Jana** (St John's Church). The latter, a foundation of the Knights Templar, preserves fourteenth-century frescoes in its chancel and has carved bosses and corbels depicting virtues and vices.

The Cathedral

Northwest from the Rynek along ul. Tumska lies Gniezno's episcopal quarter, and protruding fittingly above it is the **cathedral**, in whose forecourt stands a statue of Bolesław the Brave. Reminiscent of Poznań Cathedral, the basic brick structure was built in the fourteenth century in the severest Gothic style, but was enlivened in the Baroque period by a ring of stone chapels and by the addition of steeples to the twin facade towers. Entering the cathedral by the west door and following the ambulatory in an anticlockwise direction takes you past a sequence of richly decorated chapels, in which many of Poland's primates are buried, although most are usually only visible from behind locked grilles. Behind the high altar lies the silver **shrine of św. Wojciech**, the martyr seen here reclining on his sarcophagus. The work of Gdańsk craftsman, Peter van Rennen, the shrine is surrounded by figures representing the different social classes, along with depictions of the chief events of św. Wojciech's life. The shrine itself is housed in a huge and recently re-gilded frame flanked by arches of black and white marble. Other monuments to prominent local clerics and laymen can be seen throughout the cathedral. One which may catch your attention is that to Primate Stefan Wyszyński, in the north side of the ambulatory (see box opposite).

The cathedral's monumental highlight is the magnificent pair of bronze doors located at the entrance to southern aisle. Unfortunately the doors are frequently locked away out of sight, although a replica is housed in the Archdiocesian Museum (see p.618). Hung around 1175 and an inevitable influence on van Rennen, these are among the finest surviving examples of Romanesque decorative art, and are unique in Poland. Wojciech's life from the cradle to beyond the grave is illustrated in eighteen scenes, going up the right-hand door and

Cardinal Stefan Wyszyński (1901–81)

In the history of communist Europe, there is nothing remotely comparable to the career of **Stefan Wyszyński**, who adapted the traditional powers of the primate of Poland to act as spokesman and regent of his people.

Wyszyński's early ministry was centred in Włocławek, where he was ordained in 1924, quickly establishing a reputation in the social field. He spent the war years in the **underground resistance movement**, having been saved from the German concentration camps, which accounted for most of his colleagues in Włocławek, through the prompt action of his bishop, who had ordered him to leave the town. He returned as head of the Włocławek Seminary in 1945 before enjoying a meteoric rise through the church hierarchy, being appointed bishop of Lublin the following year, and elevated to the archdiocese of Gniezno and the title of **Primate of Poland**, in 1948.

The elimination of Poland's formerly substantial Jewish, Orthodox and Protestant minorities as a result of World War II and its aftermath meant that nearly 98 percent of the population professed **Catholicism**, as opposed to the prewar figure of 75 percent. At the same time, however, organized religion came under threat from communist atheism. Matters came to a head with the Vatican's worldwide decree of 1949, which ordered the withholding of sacraments to all communist functionaries and sympathizers: this caused particular tensions in Poland, where the new administration, particularly in rural areas, was dependent on practising Catholics. Wyszyński reached a compromise agreement with the government the following year whereby the affairs of Church and State were clearly demarcated.

This cosy relationship did not last long: a wave of Stalinist **repression** in 1952–53 led to the end of religious instruction in schools, the usurpation of most of the Church's charitable activities, and to the imprisonment and harassment of thousands of priests. As a culmination, the bishop of Kielce was sentenced to twelve years' imprisonment on charges of espionage. Wyszyński's protests led to his own **arrest**, and he was confined to the Monastery of Komańcza in the remote Bieszczady Mountains. The detention of a man widely regarded as possessing saintly qualities had the effect of alienating the regime even further from the bulk of the populace, and Wyszyński acted as the symbolic figurehead of the unrest which reached crisis proportions in 1956.

Wyszyński was released later that year as part of the package – which also included the return of Gomułka to power – forestalling the Soviet invasion that would almost certainly have ensued had a political breakdown occurred. From then on, the communists were forced to accept the **special status** of the Catholic Church in Polish society, and they were never afterwards able to suppress it: in 1957, Wyszyński was allowed to travel to Rome to receive the cardinal's hat he had been awarded five years previously. Under his leadership – which, from a theological point of view, was extremely conservative – Poland came to be regarded as the most fervently Catholic nation in the world, with the Jasna Góra pilgrimage (see p.456) promoted as the central feature of national consciousness. Wyszyński's sermons, often relayed from every pulpit in the country, became increasingly fearless and notable for such pronouncements as his celebrated claim that "Polish citizens are slaves in their own country."

Although Wyszyński did not live to see the collapse of the communist regime against which he had fought so doggedly, his last years were ones of unbridled triumph. The standing to which he had raised Poland within the Roman Catholic faith was given due reward in 1978, when his right-hand man, Karol Wojtyła – once courted by the communists as a potentially more malleable future primate – leap-frogged over him to become the first-ever Polish pope. Then, at the very end of his life, the government was forced to yield to him as a powerbroker at the heart of the **Solidarity** crisis. When Wyszyński died, he was rewarded with a **funeral** matched in postwar Europe only by those of the victorious war leaders, Churchill and de Gaulle; the country came to a standstill as even his communist opponents were prominent in paying their last respects.

then down the left, all set within a rich decorative border. Quite apart from their artistic quality, the doors are remarkable as a documentary record: even the faces of the villainous Prussians are based on accurate observation. Passing through the doorway reveals the intricate **portal** on the other side. Though its tympanum of Christ in Majesty is orthodox enough, the carvings of griffins and the prominent mask heads give it a highly idiosyncratic flavour.

Across the courtyard from the cathedral's eastern door, the **Muzeum Archidiecezjalne** (Archdiocesian Museum; Tues–Sun: summer 9am–5.30pm; winter 9am–3pm; 5zł) houses a sumptuous collection of silverware, ecclesiastical sculpture and art, the star item being a tenth-century Byzantine chalice said to have belonged to św. Wojciech.

Lake Jelonek

Just west of the cathedral is Lake Jelonek, a peaceful spot with a wonderful view of the town. Overlooking its far bank, but more easily approached via the main road, is a large modern building containing a college and the **Muzeum Pociątków Państwa Polskiego** (Museum of the Origins of the Polish State; Tues–Sun 10am–5pm; Ⓦ www.muzeum.gniezno.pl; 6zł). It's a disappointing collection, relying on copies of medieval sculptures rather than original exhibits, although there are some skilfully made modelscapes of Gniezno through the centuries. Changing art exhibitions are held upstairs, while a thirty-minute audiovisual presentation downstairs (English commentary available on request) elaborates on the development of medieval life in Wielkopolska and the significance of the Piast dynasty.

Eating and drinking

There's a cluster of pleasant **restaurants** with outdoor seating in the centre of town on the pedestrianized section of ul. Bolesława Chrobrego. The *Pietrak* hotel (see p.616), which seems to have a monopoly on the best things in central Gniezno, houses a cheap, fast and cheerful grill bar on the ground floor, and the more formal, starched-tablecloth *Restauracja Królewska* with an international menu in the cellar. *Pizzeria Pod Piątką*, ul. Tumska 5, is a trusty and cheap place for a quick bite; while *Złoty Smok*, a few steps off the west side of the Rynek at ul. Kaszarska 1a, offers good, inexpensive Chinese and Vietnamese food in unpretentious surroundings.

For **drinking**, there's a brace of outdoor bars in the Rynek in summer; although the *Pub* opposite the *Pietrak* is the most comfortable of the central bars. *Music Pub Wieża*, occupying the base of an old water tower out beyond the *Lech* hotel at ul. Żwirki i Wigury 29, has a grassy outdoor terrace and hosts occasional gigs – worth heading out for if you see fly posters around town. The *Internet Pub* on ul. Podgórna is the place to check your **emails**.

Lake Lednica

One of the most worthwhile excursions you're likely to make in this corner of Poland is to the slender **Lake Lednica**, 18km west of Gniezno and easily reached from there by taking any Poznań- or Pobiediska-bound bus. Site of a tenth-century courtly residence equal in importance to Gniezno, the lake is now the site of both an absorbing archeological site and one of the largest *skansens* in the country. The bus stop is just by the access road to the museums (you'll probably catch sight of the sign advertising the Wielkopolski Park Etnograficzny), just west of the turnoff to Dziekanowice. Driving from Poznań it's the second turn left after the three roadside windmills.

From the road end it's a ten-minute walk north to the **Wielkopolski Park Etnograficzny** (Wielkopolska Ethnographic Park; mid–Feb to mid–April: Tues–Sat 9am–3pm; mid-April to end April & Jul–Oct: Tues–Sat 9am–5pm; May–June: Tues–Sat 9am–6pm, Sun 10am–6pm; 7zł), an open-air museum consisting of about fifty traditional rural buildings from the last 250 years or so – including windmills, a Baroque cemetery chapel with all its furnishings, and several farmsteads. Some of the more eye-catching of the latter belonged to the Wielkopolska Dutch – immigrants from the Low Countries who were encouraged to settle here in the seventeenth and eighteenth centuries because of their superior knowledge of land irrigation techniques. They built solid, prosperous-looking farmhouses with red-tiled roofs, unlike their Polish neighbours, who preferred thatch. The Dutch were long ago assimilated by the Polish and German-speaking communities in the region.

From the *skansen*, continue north through the village of Dziekanowice and turn left at the T-junction to reach the disparate tourist complex known as the **Muzeum Pierwszych Piastów na Lednicy** (Museum of the First Piasts at Lednica; mid-Feb to mid-April 9am–3pm; mid-April to end April & July–Oct 9am–5pm; May–June 9am–6pm; Dec–Jan closed; ⓦwww.lednicamuzeum.pl; 8zł). Just beyond the village you'll come across the museum's cash desk and a small exhibition hall filled with replica tenth-century arms and armour. From here it's another ten-minute walk to the impressive wooden gateway (whose upper storey turns out to be a snack bar) that marks the entrance to the core of the site. Another exhibition room houses a small collection of domestic artefacts, including combs carved from animal bones and silver bowls which presumably served as the early Piasts' tableware. Once you've perused these it's a good idea to take the chained daily **ferry** (every 30min 9am–5pm) to **Ostrów Lednicki**, the largest of the three tiny islands in Lake Lednica, where it's believed that Mieszko I once held court.

This unlikely site, uninhabited for the last six centuries, was once a royal seat equal to Poznań and Gniezno in importance – **Bolesław the Brave** was born here, and it may also have been where his coronation by Emperor Otto III took place, rather than in Gniezno. It began life in the ninth century as a fortified town covering about a third of the island and linked to the mainland by a jetty. In the following century, a modest **palace** was constructed, along with a church: the excavated remains only hint at its former grandeur, but the presence of stairways prove it was probably at least two storeys high. By the landing jetty a model of the former settlement gives an idea of how it may have looked, surrounded by the still extant earth ramparts from which now flutters a Polish flag. The buildings were destroyed in 1038 by the Czech Prince Brzetysław, but the church was rebuilt soon afterwards, and then gradually fell into disuse, along with the town itself. For centuries the island served as a cemetery, until it was lulled out of its sleep by tourism.

Żnin, Biskupin and around

Forty kilometres north of Gniezno on the Bydgoszcz road (and reached by hourly buses) the small town of **Żnin** would be ordinarily unremarkable were it not for two major attributes – the ageing **narrow-gauge rail line** that meanders for 12km through the pastures south of town to the village of Gąsawa, and the reconstructed Iron Age settlement of **Biskupin** which lies along the route. In between Żnin and Biskupin, a small railway museum in the village of

Wenecja adds to the list of attractions. The narrow-gauge line still operates a limited tourist-oriented service, and presents the most enjoyable way of reaching Venecja and Biskupin in summer – otherwise, a combination of local buses and walking will enable you to see the sites and still get back to Gniezno by nightfall.

Żnin

ŻNIN is a place from which to catch services to Biskupin rather than a tourist town in its own right. Luckily, the train, bus and narrow-gauge stations are all within 100m of each other on the northeastern side of town. It's a good idea to head for the narrow-gauge station first in order to check the timetable: if there are no convenient services running that day, then consider catching a bus to Gąsawa, from where you can walk to Biskupin in about 30 minutes.

If you have time to kill in Żnin, head a block south of the train and bus stations to find ul. 700-lecia, which winds towards a neat and unassuming Rynek. At the far end of the square stands the octagonal brick **tower** of the demolished fifteenth-century town hall, whose interior has been fitted out as the local **museum** (Tues–Fri 9am–4pm, Sat 9am–3pm, Sun 10am–3pm; 3zł) displaying a far from captivating selection of local crafts and other oddments. Immediately beyond here lies the fair-sized **Lake Czaple**, the grassy shores of which make for an attractive walk.

There are a few reasonable **accommodation** options: the *Basztowy*, near the Rynek on ul. 700-lecia (☎052/302 0006, ⓦwww.hotel-basztowy.com.pl; ❸), is the most comfortable and central of the hotels; while the *Martina*, 2km north of the centre at ul. Mickiewicza 37 (☎052/302 8733; ❹), has parking facilities, a sauna and cupboard-sized rooms. The **restaurant** of the *Basztowy* offers solid Polish fare; while *Vito*, on the corner of Lewandowskiego and ul. 700-lecia, serves up snack meals, has good ice cream, and is a decent place to drink.

The Żnin–Gąsawa narrow-gauge rail line

The **Żnin–Gąsawa narrow-gauge rail line** has been running for over a century, although it has long since ceased to be a meaningful means of public transport for the locals, and now functions almost exclusively as a tourist attraction. The railway has retained one fully operational steam engine, although it only sees action on selected summer weekends, and all other services are hauled by aesthetically less appealing diesels. There are five daily Żnin–Gąsawa services between mid-June and September; two or three daily from May to mid-June and October to mid-November. Additional departures are often laid on for tour groups, and individual travellers are allowed to tag along if space allows – so it always pays to ask the station staff. The journey to Biskupin takes about fifty minutes, with trains barely exceeding walking pace, but the trip – through gently rolling countryside dotted with silver-blue lakes – is definitely worthwhile.

The train rattles noisily through hay fields and vegetable patches, its second stop, **WENECJA**, being the halfway point. This hamlet's name is the Polish word for Venice, fancifully justified by the fact that it is almost surrounded by water, lying as it does between two lakes. To the left of the station are the remains of the fourteenth-century **castle** of Mikołaj Nałęz, a notoriously cruel figure known as the "Devil of Wenecja". Only the lower parts of the walls survive. On the opposite side of the tracks is the open-air **Muzeum Kolei Wąskotorowej** (Narrow-Gauge Railway Museum; daily: mid-April to Oct 9am–6pm; Nov to mid-April 10am–2pm; 6zł), exhibiting a motley collection of undersized engines and rolling stock which once served the area.

From Wenecja the train continues along the edge of Lake Biskupin and stops right outside the entrance to the settlement a few minutes later. If you miss a train, you can walk from Wenecja to Biskupin in about 30 minutes.

Biskupin

The Iron Age village of **BISKUPIN**, 30km north of Gniezno, is one of the most evocative archeological sites in Europe. Discovered in 1933, when a schoolmaster noticed some hand-worked stakes standing in the reeds at the lakeside, excavations commenced the following year until experts from Warsaw soon pronounced that the site had been a **fortified village** of the Lusatian culture, founded around 550 BC and destroyed in tribal warfare some 150 years later. The subsequent uncovering of the settlement has thrown fresh light on the tribal life of the period, enabling the solution of many previously unresolved questions.

The site

In contrast to the overcautious approach that makes so many famous archeological sites disappointing to non-specialists, it was decided to take a guess and reconstruct the palisade, ramparts and part of the village. The price to be paid for this approach is evident at the entrance to the **archeological park** (daily: mid-April to Sept 8am–7pm; Oct to mid-April 8am till dusk; 6zł), with souvenir and snack bars lining the car park on the other side of the tracks.

From the entrance, it's best to go straight ahead past a re-erected eighteenth-century cottage and start with the **museum**, which provides a pretty good introduction to the site as a whole. Inside you'll find all manner of objects dug up here – tools, household utensils, weapons, jewellery, ornaments and objects for worship, some thought to be ten thousand years old. The exhibits are all superbly mounted and lit, and are accompanied by English-language captions. Piecing together the evidence, archeologists have been able to draw a picture of a society in which hunting had been largely superseded by arable farming and livestock breeding. Their trade patterns were surprisingly extensive – their iron seems to have come from Transylvania, and there's an intriguing group of exhibits imported from even further afield, the most exotic being some Egyptian beads. Most remarkable of all was the tribe's prowess in building, as can be seen in the model reconstruction of the entire village. Beyond the museum buildings is an enclosure for **tarpans**, miniature working horses which have evolved very little since the time of the settlement.

Backtracking to the cottage and turning right, it's only a couple of minutes' walk down the path to the **reconstructed site**. The foreground consists of the uncovered foundations of various buildings, some from as late as the thirteenth century; of more interest are re-creations of the Iron Age buildings – although only a section of each has been built, and not exactly on their former site, it requires little imagination to picture what the whole must have looked like.

The **palisade** was particularly ingenious: it originally consisted of 35,000 stakes grouped in rows up to nine deep and driven into the bed of the lake at an angle of 45 degrees. It acted both as a breakwater and as the first line of the fortifications. Immediately behind was a circular **wall** of oak logs guarded by a tall watchtower; the latter is the most conjectural part of the whole restoration project. Inside the defences were a ring road plus eleven symmetrical streets, again made of logs and filled in with earth, sand and clay; the **houses** were grouped in thirteen terraces ranged from east to west to catch the sun. An entire extended family would live in each house, so the population of the settlement probably numbered over a thousand. As you can see from the example open for inspection, each house had two chambers: pigs and cattle – the most important privately owned objects – were kept in the lobby, while the main room, where the family slept in a single bed, was also equipped with a loft for the storage of food and fuel.

The *Diabeł Wenecki* pleasure boat offers thirty-minute **cruises** on the lake (Tues–Sat 9am–5pm, Sun 9am–4pm), allowing you to view the site from the water.

In an unintentional parody of the Iron Age village, a sizeable settlement of timber-built **snack-huts** has grown up around the car park at the site's entrance; here you can feast on anything from pork chops to pancakes before moving on. If you've missed the last **train**, some (but not all) Żnin–Gąsawa **buses** pass the site entrance, although perhaps the easiest thing to do is walk uphill to Gąsawa (30min), from where you can catch regular buses plying the Gniezno–Bydgoszcz route.

Trzemeszno to Inowrocław

Once you've seen Gniezno, Lednica and Biskupin, the rest of eastern Wielkopolska is a bit of a let-down, characterized by a string of unassuming, semi-industrialized towns which have little in the way of attention-grabbing appeal. However, there's many an architectural gem hidden away in the region, together with plentiful reminders of the **Piast** dynasty – certainly enough to structure an itinerary around if you have time to spare. There's not much in the way of tourist facilities or urban thrills in the region – so it's a good idea to treat Gniezno as your most likely touring base. If you're travelling by **public transport**, you will find that Trzemeszno, Mogilno and Inowrocław are easily reached by bus and train from Gniezno; Inowrocław bus station is the most convenient jumping-off point for Strzelno and Kruszwica.

Trzemeszno

Sixteen kilometres east of Gniezno, **TRZEMESZNO** is a lightly industrialized town that was founded, according to tradition, by św. Wojciech (St Adalbert). It can be reached either by bus from Gniezno or Baltic-bound train – the latter involving a 3km walk south to the town.

The ancient church that św. Wojciech is said to have established was succeeded by a Romanesque structure, parts of which are incorporated in the town's main sight, the Baroque **basilica**. From the outside it appears merely pleasingly rotund, but once inside you'll find a revelation of light and colour that – if you've developed a taste for Baroque church interiors – is well worth the break in your journey. In this instance it's the superb **paintings** in the dome and along the transept that for once take the attention away from the central altar, under which an effigy of Wojciech reposes. The ceiling frescoes vividly depict three crucial scenes from the saint's life and death: his vicious slaying by the Prussian pagans; the retrieval of his remains for their weight in gold, with Wojciech now just a few body parts on a scale; and his eventual entombment in the basilica.

Strzelno

More artistic treasures are to be found 17km east of Mogilno in the sleepy town of **STRZELNO**. Both the **bus** and **train stations** lie at the southwestern fringe of town; from there, walk straight ahead, turning left up ul. Ducha to reach the rather unprepossessing main square. Continuing down to the right brings you to two outstanding Romanesque buildings.

The **Klasztor św. Trójcy** (Monastery of the Holy Trinity) is a typically Polish accretion: brick Gothic gables and a monumental Baroque facade sprout from a late twelfth-century Romanesque shell. After the war, some of the interior plasterwork was removed to reveal, in well-nigh perfect condition, three original nave **pillars**. Two of these, adorned with figurative carvings, are crafted with a delicacy found in few other European sculptures of the period; a third is quite plain. Another slimmer column of almost equal quality forms the sole support of the vault of the somewhat neglected chapel of St Barbara, to the right of the altar over which hangs a huge crown.

Beside the monastery church stands the slightly older little red sandstone **Kaplica św. Prokopa** (Chapel of St Procopius). In contrast to its neighbour, this has preserved the purity of its original form, its half-round tower perfectly offset against the protruding rotund apses to a most pleasing effect. It's kept locked, but you could ask in the Klasztor św. Trójcy or the buildings alongside for a look inside. Incidentally, the churches are not the earliest evidence of worship on this site: the large stone boulder in front of them is thought to have been used for pagan rites.

Kruszwica

Of the many sites associated with the Piast dynasty perhaps the oddest is in **KRUSZWICA**, a frumpy town straddling the pencil-slim **Lake Gopło**, about 16km northeast of Strzelno. Dominating a shady tree-lined peninsula just east of Kruszwica's Rynek is a thrusting brick octagon known as the **Mysia Wieża** (Mouse Tower; May–Sept daily 9am–6pm; 3zł) – allegedly the place where evil King Popiel met his doom before being replaced by the people's favourite, the good-hearted peasant who became the first of the Piast rulers (see box below for the full story). In fact the tower was built by the last of the Piast dynasty, Kazimierz the Great, although this hasn't prevented it from becoming one of the most popular – and evocative – places of historical pilgrimage in this part of Poland. During the summer season it's under constant siege from school parties, filing up the spiral staircase to savour sweeping views down the length of Lake Gopło.

Kruszwica's only other historic monument is the early twelfth-century **Kolegiata** (collegiate church), reached by heading east from the Mouse Tower, crossing the road bridge, and turning left to follow the far bank of the lake. A grim granite basilica with three apses, it has been stripped of most of its later

---

The legend of the foundation of the Piast dynasty

The legend goes that the **descendants of Lech** were ousted as the nation's rulers by the evil Popiel family. To ensure there was no competition for his succession, the last King Popiel killed all his male kin except his own children, then established himself at a castle in Kruszwica, where he subjected his people to a reign of terror. One day, SS John and Paul came in the guise of poor travellers, but the king refused them hospitality and they were forced to lodge with a peasant named **Piast**. The saints baptized him and his family, and predicted that he would be first in a long line of monarchs, whereupon they vanished. Shortly afterwards, the Poles rose up against their evil ruler. He took refuge in his castle tower, where he was eventually devoured by rats. The people then chose the worthy Piast as his successor.

accretions, except for the brick Gothic tower, and gives a good impression of what an early Christian church may have once looked like. Supposedly occupying the miraculous site of the first Piast's cottage, it served as a cathedral for the first half-century of its life, before being supplanted by Włocławek.

Kruszwica is served by frequent **buses** from Inowrocław (see below), less frequently from Bydgoszcz (see p.626), with services picking up and dropping off on the main Rynek. There's a healthy gaggle of snack stalls at the foot of the Mouse Tower, but few other inducements to make you stick around.

Inowrocław

Approaching Kruszwica by public transport, chances are you'll need to hop from train to bus at **INOWROCŁAW** 15km north, a nineteenth-century spa town subsequently blighted by twentieth-century industrialization and pollution. The town's **train station** is at the northern end of town, about fifteen minutes' walk from the centre; the **bus station** is five minutes' further in. If you've got time to kill, it's best to head straight for the Park Uzdrowiskowy or **spa park** at the western end of town (a 15min walk from the stations), a grassy expanse ringed by grand turn-of-the-twentieth-century buildings. Dominating its western extremity is the **Tężnia**, a fortress-like construction raised in the 1990s from vast piles of compacted twigs. Rather like the more famous Tężnia in Ciechocinek (see p.216), the edifice acts as a huge filter through which the local spa water is pumped, creating a recuperative salt-rich atmosphere for those who come to stroll around it.

Having had your ailments cured in the spa park the rest of Inowrocław is a severe let-down, the only rewarding monument being the **Kościół NMP** (Church of Our Lady), a contemporary of the Romanesque basilica in Kruszwica, and boasting a similarly impressive, bare-stone interior. It's located behind the much bigger, neo-Gothic **Kościół Zwiastowania NMP** (Church of the Annunciation), a few minutes' walk beyond the big roundabout which lies south of the bus and train stations.

Given Inowrocław's industrial appearance, it's unlikely to rate as an overnight stop, and there are in any case plentiful onward **train** connections to Bydgoszcz (see p.626) and Toruń (p.209).

Pomerania (Pomorze)

Pomerania's long, sandy coastline is its major attraction, and a couple of days holed up on the Baltic here is one of the most pleasant ways of unwinding that the country can offer.

On the coast there are plenty of resorts to choose from: **Łeba** manages to combine fishing-village atmosphere with fine beaches and the **Słowiński national park**; low-key resorts like **Darłówko** and **Mielno** preserve something of their genteel nineteenth-century character; while to the west many of the finest beaches are found around **Kołobrzeg** and on the islands of **Wolin** and **Uznam**. Just inland, a chain of towns from **Kamień Pomorski** to **Stargard Szczeciński** provide a modicum of architectural attractions, all of which

A brief history of Pomerania

In prehistoric times the southern Baltic coast was inhabited by the Celts, who were later displaced by a succession of Germanic tribes. By the end of the fifth century they too had been ousted by Slav people known as the **Pomorzanie**, relics of whose settlements are preserved on Wolin island in the west of the region. The lands of the Pomorzanie were in turn conquered by the Piast **King Mieszko I**, who took Szczecin in 979 – a campaign that is cited by the Poles in support of their claim to ownership of this often disputed territory. Thereafter the picture gets more complicated. Throughout the medieval era, Pomerania evolved as an essentially independent dukedom ruled by a local Slav dynasty commonly called the **Pomeranian princes**, who nonetheless owed loyalty to the Polish monarch. Eastern Pomerania was conquered by the Teutonic Knights in 1308, and was later known as Royal Prussia; this part of the region returned to the Polish sphere of influence under the terms of the 1466 Treaty of Toruń (see p.209 & p.225).

The ethnic mix of the region played a dominant part in governing its allegiances. While a Slav majority retained its hold on the countryside, heavy German colonization of the towns inexorably tilted the balance of power to the territorially ambitious Brandenburg margravate. In line with the westward drift, the Pomeranian princes finally transferred formal allegiance to the Holy Roman Empire in 1521, and the inroads of the Reformation further weakened the region's ties with Catholic Poland, which anyway was more interested in its eastern borderlands than its western terrains. In 1532, the ruling Gryfit dynasty divided into two lines, and their territory was partitioned along a line west of the Odra delta: the larger eastern duchy was henceforth known as Hinter Pomerania; the small one to the west as Lower or Hither Pomerania. None of the latter's territory has ever subsequently formed part of Poland.

Control of the region was fiercely disputed during the **Thirty Years' War**, with the Swedes taking over all of Lower Pomerania, plus some of the coastline of Hinter Pomerania. The Treaty of Westphalia of 1648 formalized the division of the latter, whose capital, Szczecin/Stettin, thereby became part of Sweden. Following the departure of the Swedes in the 1720s, the **Prussians** reunited Lower and Hinter Pomerania into a single administrative province; during the Partitions they were able to join it up with their territories to the east by annexing Royal Prussia. Their control over the region was undisturbed until after the Versailles Treaty of 1919, when a strip of Pomerania's eastern fringe was ceded to Poland, some of it forming part of the notorious "Polish Corridor". Nearly all of the territory of the old duchy of Hinter Pomerania was **allocated to Poland** in 1945, as part of the compensation deal for loss of the Eastern Territories to the Soviet Union. Mass emigration of the area's German population, which started during the final months of the war, gathered apace after the transfer of sovereignty; in their place came displaced Polish settlers, mostly from the east.

are readily accessible from the great port of **Szczecin**, Pomerania's largest city and historic capital, and today a bustling urban centre.

Bydgoszcz, a major industrial city in the east of the region, is a useful transport hub. Though it has a small historic centre, you're most likely to pass through en route for other parts of Pomerania.

Transport links within Pomerania are good: there's a reasonable train service that runs parallel to the coast on the Gdańsk–Szczecin line, including international trains to Berlin, with local connections up to the coastal resorts and buses for excursions inland into the countryside. If you're approaching the Pomeranian coast from the east, then Gdynia (see p.194) offers the best in the way of bus connections.

Bydgoszcz

BYDGOSZCZ is a sprawling industrial city, developed around a fortified medieval settlement strategically located on the River Brda, close to its confluence with the Wisła. Growth took off at the end of the eighteenth century when, as the Prussian town of Bromberg, it became the hub of an important waterway system due to the construction of a canal linking the Wisła to the Odra via the rivers Brda, Notec and Warta. Unlike much of the region to the north, it has been Polish since 1920, when it was ceded by Germany and incorporated into the province of Poznań. During World War II, the city suffered particularly badly at the hands of the Nazis: mass executions of civilians followed its fall, and by the end of the war over fifty thousand people – a quarter of the population – had been murdered, with many of the rest deported to labour and concentration camps.

Modern Bydgoszcz has the feel of a dynamic, self-confident city, and is a good place to recharge your urban batteries if you've been out in the sticks for a while. It has fast transport links with the historic city of Toruń (see p.209) to the east.

The City

As ever, the focal point of the medieval centre is the **Stary Rynek** on the south bank of the Brda, a pleasant but unexceptional square with a clutch of Baroque and Neoclassical mansions, newly done up in pastel greens and pinks. A typical communist-era **monument** to the victims of Nazism overshadows the vast bulk of the **Jesuit college**, which closes the west side of the square, with another fine frontage along ul. Jezuicka. Begun at the end of the seventeenth century, for many years this was the town's leading educational establishment. It's now used as municipal offices.

In a secluded corner just to the north is the red-brick fifteenth-century **Kościół Farny** (Parish Church). This has recently been raised to the status of a co-cathedral, though its dimensions and appearance are more modest than those of many a village church. Nonetheless, its exterior is graced by a fine Gothic gable, while inside, among the usual Baroque ornamentation, is the sixteenth-century high altar of *The Madonna with the Rose*. The church overlooks **Wyspa Mlynska**, a small island situated at the point where the River Brda separates into several little channels. Crossed by dainty bridges and overlooked by old half-timbered granaries and red-brick warehouses, these slow-flowing waterways make up an area that has been fancifully styled as the Bydgoszcz Venice. One of the warehouses, tucked away at the northern end of Wyspa Mlynska, holds the **town museum** (Tues–Fri 10am–6pm, Sat–Sun 12am–4pm; 7zł), with displays on the history of the town, including archive material on the Nazi atrocities. A couple of blocks south of the Rynek lies ul. Długa, the pedestrianized main shopping street, with a couple of interesting craft shops amongst the more ordinary stores.

Crossing over to the northern bank, you come to the former **Kościół Klarysek** (Convent Church of the Poor Clares), a curious amalgam of late Gothic and Renaissance, with later alterations. The convent buildings on ul. Gdańska house the **district museum** (Tues–Fri 10am–6pm, Sat–Sun 12am–4pm; 7zł), which displays a varied collection of twentieth-century Polish art. Gdańska is a grand thoroughfare, running on north and then east and lined with an impressive sequence of imposing nineteenth-century office blocks, many of which have been thoroughly restored in the last few years. Spinning off Gdańska

△ Bydgoszcz

towards the train station is **Dworcowa**, a narrow, cobbled street that boasts some (sadly dilapidated) Art Nouveau facades at nos. 45, 47 and 49.

Five blocks east of here is a historical curiosity that rewards the short detour – the basilica of **St Vincent de Paul** at rondo Ossolińskich, a vast circular brick church modelled on the Pantheon in Rome and capable of accommodating twelve thousand worshippers. Its construction was a direct result of the town's change in ownership from Protestant Prussia to Catholic Poland, which necessitated a much larger space for the main feast days than the existing churches were able to provide. Passing through the brick-columned portico into the basilica, the vast space beneath the dome is initially quite breathtaking, but the lack of a focal point soon makes itself felt – the circular design seems more suited to stadiums than churches. Look out for the basilica's snazzy collection of Art Deco-esque pine confessionals.

Practicalities

The **train station** is located to the northwest of the city centre: a fifteen-minute walk straight down ul. Dworcowa (or take bus #67) brings you to ul. Gdańska, from where it's a short hop over the river to the Stary Rynek. Bydgoszcz's bus station is 1km east of the centre along Jagiellońska (trams #1, #3, #5, #8 and #10 all head for the centre). There's a small **tourist office** on the first floor at Stary Rynek 15 (Mon–Fri 9am–6pm, Sat 9am–2pm; ☎052/348 2373) and online information can be found at ⓦwww.bydgoszcz .com. If you need **Internet** access, you'll find it near the train station at Dworcowa 83.

Generally speaking **accommodation** gets more expensive the further away you are from the train station. At the station itself is the *Agat* (☎052/327 5020; ❷) with basic but perfectly respectable en-suites; while the *Centralny*, at ul. Dworcowa 85 (☎052/322 8876; ❹), is marginally more salubrious but overpriced for what it offers. A little further down the road, the concrete *Brda*, ul. Dworcowa 94 (☎052/585 0100, ⓦwww.hotelbrda.com.pl; ❻) offers serviceable en suites with TV. In the heart of town just behind the Rynek, the *Hotel Ratuszowy*, ul. Długa 37 (☎052/322 8861, ⓦwww.hotelratuszowy.com.pl; ❻), is cramped but comfortable and superbly located. The Orbis-run *Pod Orłem*, al. Gdańska 14 (☎052/583 0530, ⓦwww.orbis.pl; ❽), drips with luxury and *fin-de-siècle* elegance. In complete contrast the *City Hotel*, ul. 3 Maja 6 (☎052/325 2500, ⓦwww.cityhotel.bydgoszcz.pl; ❽) is utterly contemporary. The **youth hostel** is a couple of minutes' walk from the train station at ul. Sowińskiego 5 (☎052/322 7570).

There's a wide range of **eating** possibilities: *Baalbek*, just off the Rynek at Magdzińskiego 3, serves up cheap and tasty *szaszlyk* and souvlakia takeaways; while *Pizzeria Capri*, also near the Rynek at Niedzwiedzowa 9, offers a decent range of pies in more comfortable, sit-down surroundings. *Medea*, Jezuitska 16, is the handiest central place in which to treat yourself to lashings of meat-heavy Polish food. If you're splashing out, try hotel restaurants like the *Chopin* in the *City Hotel* at ul. 3 Maja 6 (☎052/22 8841), which has an outstanding range of international cuisine and a good choice of vegetarian options – expect to pay around 150zł for a three-course meal without drinks. If you want to concentrate on dessert, *O'Lala* at Gdańska 24 does superb ice cream.

The area round the Rynek is well endowed with daytime and evening **drinking** venues. *Café Reggiano Emilia*, on the northern side of the Rynek, is a comfy place from which to watch the world go by over a coffee or a beer. The *Amsterdam* is a cosy pub-style bar on the south side of the Rynek. *Smok* at Cręta 3 just to the east of the Rynek is a little livelier and opens late. In summer, the deck of a green barge moored on the River Brda, just by the town's central bridge, is transformed into a vast beer garden. *Hysteria*, Dworcowa 13, is the main venue for Friday night pack-em-in techno **clubbing**, although a much more alternative crowd hangs out at *Mózg*, Gdańska 10 (entrance down the Parkowa side street), a rambling café-cum-music club which is one of the major venues in this corner of Poland for jazz and rock gigs.

For more high-brow **entertainment**, the Filharmonia Pomorska, just east of ul. Gdańska at ul. Karola Libelta 16 (box office daily noon–6pm), is the main **musical** venue; as well as regular concerts, it features a fortnight-long classical festival each September. The main **theatre** is the nearby Teatr Polski, al. Mickiewicza 2 (box office Tues–Fri 8am–6pm, Sat 2–6pm; ☎052/321 0530, ⓦwww.teatrpolski.pl). Opera Nova at ul. Gdańska 20 (box office Tue–Thurs & Sat 3–6.30pm, Sun 4–6.30pm; ☎052/325 1555, ⓦwww.opera.bydgoszcz.pl) is the venue for **opera**.

Łeba and around

Of all the Pomeranian seaside resorts, **ŁEBA** is the most celebrated; an attractive old fishing settlement presiding over kilometre upon kilometre of irresistible dune-backed beaches. Small enough to preserve a village-like feel, it nevertheless receives enough visitors in summer to generate an invigorating holiday bustle. The bigger of the local **dunes** (*wydmy*), just west of town in the **Słowinski national park**, form one of Poland's prime natural attractions, and attract hordes of sightseers as a result. There are plenty of unspoiled Baltic pine forests and silvery sands nearby if you want to escape the crowds.

The Village

The **village** is set a kilometre back from the sea: dunes and beaches cover the original site of the settlement, which was forced to move inland in the late sixteenth century because of shifting sands. Buses and trains drop you two blocks west of ul. Kościuszki, the main street running down the middle of the resort, which is still lined with several of the one-storey, brick-built fishermen's houses once common to the region. A little further north Kościuszki bridges a canalized branch of the River Łeba, where trawlers and pleasure boats moor, before veering eastwards and becoming Nadmorska, a shoreside avenue which leads to the bigger hotels and campsites. In summer the area is busy with cheerful holiday-makers heading for the unbroken sandy **beaches** that are widely regarded as among the cleanest on the Baltic coast. Poles aren't the only people who have enjoyed the bracing location: wandering through the park that provides the main approach to the beaches from Nadmorska, you'll pass the summer house once used by Nazi propaganda chief Josef Goebbels.

Another stretch of beach, to the west of town, can be reached by walking down ul. Turystyczna, which heads west from the train and bus stations, and passes a swanky new yachting marina and the turn-off to Rabka (see p.631) before arriving at another clutch of beachside campsites. Round the back of the PTTK campsite, just before the access to the beach, a path leads off into the forest towards the meagre ruins of **Kościół św. Mikołaja** (St Nicholas's Church), a lone reminder of the village's former location.

Practicalities

Regular **buses** and **trains** run to Łeba from the provincial town of Lębork just to the south, which stands on the main road and rail routes connecting Gdańsk in the east with Słupsk (see p.633) and Koszalin (p.635) to the west. There are also direct buses to Łeba from **Gdynia** (see p.194). Other than checking out Ⓦ www.leba.pl, you can get information just round the corner from the train and bus stations, where the public library on ul. 11 Listopada houses the local **tourist office** (summer Mon–Fri 8am–4pm, Sat & Sun 10am–1pm; winter closed Sat & Sun; ☎059/866 2565), which will help you find a **place to stay** in one of the innumerable private rooms (❸) and pensions (❸–❺). Przymorze, a travel agency based opposite the train station at Dworcowa 1 (☎059/866 1360), can also help with finding rooms. If both these are closed, many of the houses along Nadmorska and the surrounding streets display "*pokoje*" signs, indicating vacancies.

Among the handily placed **pensions**, *Pod Krokodylem*, Turystyczna 7 (☎059/866 2105; ❸), is a good source of simple rooms just west of the train and bus stations on the road to Rabka; while *Angela*, ul. Dworcowa (☎059/866 2647; ❹), is a largish place right by the station with balconied rooms and a neat garden out front. *Kowelin*, just off the main street at Nad Ujściem 6 (☎059/866 1440; ❸), is a good-value **hotel**, offering smallish en suites with TV, most of which have balconies. Closer to the beach, *Wodnik*, Nadmorska 10 (☎059/866 1366, Ⓦ www.wodnik.leba.pl; ❻) conceals very comfortable rooms behind an unattractive concrete facade. The charming *Neptun*, right on the beach among the pine trees at ul. Sosnowa 1 (☎059/866 1432, Ⓦ www.neptunhotel.pl; ❼), is a hundred-year-old villa with a mock castle-turret. After World War II it was turned into a factory-owned rest home and lost its *belle-époque* sheen, but was renovated in the 1990s and now has all mod cons including a tennis court and swimming pool.

For **campers** – and there are plenty of them in summer – there are several sites along ul. Turystyczna and ul. Nadmorska, all close to the beaches, and a number of them let chalets, too. Best of the bunch are *Ambre* on Nadmorska (☎059/866 2472), a large, well-organized place stretched out beneath birch trees, and the PTTK site at the far end of Turystyczna, right beside the beach.

There's a surfeit of **snack bars** selling locally caught fried fish (*smażona ryba*); one of the best is the canal-side *Pod Brzozkami*, just off the main street, a big shed filled with wooden tables offering excellent battered halibut alongside grilled salmon and trout. Of the **restaurants**, *Pizzeria Honotu* on Wojska Polskiego next door to the Rybak cinema has a generous range of thin-crust pies; while the more elegant *BD*, Kościuszki 35, offers a wide choice of well-presented meat and fish dishes in comfortable surroundings, and also does breakfasts. The restaurant of the *Neptun* hotel serves up international and Polish food in a formal, starched-napkin ambience.

You can **drink** in any of the fish-fry venues, although the *Skansen*, near the bridge at the beginning of the Rabka road, is the place where most of the visiting Varsovians hang out. The *Łebska Huta* on Nadmorska opposite the *Wodnik* is another popular watering hole in a building that looks a lot like a Swiss ski chalet. *Disco Mefisto*, above *Pizzeria Honotu*, is an unpretentious disco which attracts an amiable cross-section of after-hours drinkers.

Słowiński national park

West of Łeba is Jezioro Łebsko, or Lake Łebsko, the largest of several lagoons separated from the sea by a belt of mobile **sand dunes** that form the centre

Birds in the park are classified into three main groups: nesting, migratory and wintering species. Nesters include such rare species as the white-tailed eagle, crane, eagle owl and black stork. It's also a popular area for the more common white stork: in summer you're bound to encounter storks nesting atop telegraph poles. During the late autumn migration period you'll see large flocks of wild geese winging over the lakes, and in winter you'll find ducks and other fowl from the far north of Europe sheltering here on the warmer southern shores of the Baltic – velvet scoters, mergansers, auks and whooper swans included.

Mammals are numerous, too, the shores of the lakes harbouring deer and boar, with elks, racoons and badgers in the surrounding woods. Shy red squirrels are a common sight in among the trees surrounding Łeba, while foxes emerge at night to scour the village's rubbish bins.

of **Słowiński national park**, one of the country's most memorable natural attractions, special enough to be included in UNESCO's list of world Biosphere Reserves. The park gets its name from the **Slovincians**, a small ethnic group of Slav origin who, like their neighbours the Kashubians, have retained a distinctive identity despite centuries of German influence.

This area is an ornithologist's paradise, with over 250 **bird** species either permanently inhabiting the park or using it as a migratory habitat. The 600 scenic lakes attract fishing, whilst the postglacial lakes incorporated into the river systems have created excellent canoe trails. Both activities are very popular here.

Geomorphically this is an unusual region: the shallow lagoons covering the central part of the park once formed a gulf, which the deposition of sand eventually isolated from the sea. Between them a narrow spit of land emerged roughly two thousand years ago, whose dense original covering of oak and beech forests was gradually eroded by intensive animal grazing and tree felling, the forests disappearing under the dunes that overran the thirty-kilometre spit. Abandoned to the elements by its few original human inhabitants, during World War II the expanse of shifting, undulating sand provided an ideal training ground for units of the Afrika Korps, who drilled here in preparation for the rigours of Rommel's North African campaigns. In the latter stages of the war the spit west of Łeba was turned into a rocket research station; the missiles tested here were close cousins of the fearsome V1 and V2 rockets that later bombarded London.

Park access

The eastern entrance to the park is at **RABKA**, a small cluster of houses and snack bars on the shores of Lake Łebsko, one and a half kilometers west of Łeba. The shores of the lake are covered with thick reeds that provide ideal cover for birds: sanctuaries at several points protect the main breeding sites. To get to Rabka on foot or by car, go down ul. Turystyczna and take the signed left turn about 500m beyond the canal. Alternatively you can take one of the boats or tourist "trains" (electric buses, really) that leave from beside the bridge.

The **pathway to the dunes** begins on Rabka's western edge, where a kiosk sells **tickets** to the park (8am–dusk; 4zł) as well as local maps. Though walking's a very pleasant option, a multitude of alternative forms of **transport** is on offer at the park entrance: horses and carts (20zł per person), tourist trains (3zł) and chauffeured golf carts (10zł), and there are boats from Rabka's landing stage in season. By far the most popular option is to rent a bike in Rabka (4–6zł per hour). While boat passengers glide across Lake Łebsko, those going by land proceed through the birch trees down a narrow road built by the German military in World War II to serve the rocket research station – you'll see a couple of cone-headed concrete pillboxes standing guard beside the route.

Wyrzutnia

Three kilometres west of Rabka lies a small clearing known as **Wyrzutnia** ("Launchpad"), the site of the World War II base where the German military experimented with various forms of rocket between 1943 and 1945 – part of Hitler's strategy of producing terror weapons that would give Germany a psychological advantage over its adversaries. A museum (April–Oct daily 9am–5pm; 8zł) built inside one of the observation bunkers contains sepia photographs of prewar Łeba, alongside diagrams of the rockets developed here by Hitler's scientists. The first of these was the stumpy, five-and-a-half-metre-long *Rheintochter* (*Rhine Daughter*), although this was soon superseded by the much larger *Rheinbote* (*Rhine Messenger*), a sleek eleven-metre affair that closely resembles the ground-to-air missiles in use today. Despite over eighty test launches, the *Rheinbote* never saw active service, the Germans instead opting for the V2 rockets that were developed by a separate team at Peenemünde in eastern Germany. Outside the bunker is one of the launchpads themselves – a concrete pit topped by rails onto which a rocket gantry was wheeled. There are a few rusting fragments of a *Rheintocher* lying around in the nearby sands, together with a complete Soviet rocket of the 1950s, brought here from elsewhere and built to almost exactly the same design as the *Rheinbote* – an eloquent demonstration of how Nazi technology was eagerly adopted by the Cold War superpowers after 1945.

The park dunes

Passengers on boats and tourist trains (but not those in traps, golf carts or on pushbikes) disembark at Wyrzutnia and proceed to the dunes on foot, following a path which forges westwards through deep forest for a further 2km before emerging at the base of the **Biała Góra** (White Mountain), the first – and, with an altitude of 40m, the highest – of the **dunes**, which stretch westwards for about 5km.

Even a brief hike will give you the flavour of the terrain. Dried by the sun and propelled by the wind, the dunes migrate over 10m per year on average, leaving behind the broken tree stumps you see along the path. Out in the middle of the dune area, there's a desert-like feeling of desolation with the sands rippling in the wind giving an eerie sense of fluidity.

Crossing the dunes northwards will bring you down onto the seashore within a few minutes: from here you can walk back to Łeba along the beach (8km) if you don't fancy returning the way you came.

Kluki and Smołdzino

Twenty kilometres southwest of Łeba, on the southern edge of Lake Łebsko and at the end of a minor road, is the little Slovincian village of **KLUKI**, which is accessible by occasional bus from Słupsk, or by lake cruiser from Łeba in the summer months. Entirely surrounded by woods, Kluki has a charming *skansen* of Slovincian timber-framed architecture (mid-May to Sept Mon 9am–3pm; Tues–Sun 9am–6pm; Oct to mid-May Tues–Sun 9am–3pm); you'll see similar, if more dilapidated, buildings still in use in several villages all over the region.

The road to Kluki passes through **SMOŁDZINO**, home to the park headquarters and natural history museum, the **Muzeum Przyrodnicze**

Słowińskiego Parku Narodowego (daily 9am–5pm; 3zł), which contains an extensive display of the park's flora and fauna. The park offices can provide you with detailed information about the area, including advice on bird-watching around the lake. Just to the west of the village is the 115-metre-high **Rowokół Hill**, whose observation tower affords a panoramic view over the entire park area. Smołdzino has one of the nicer pensions in the area: *U Bernazkich* (☎059/811 7364; 120zł) is in a comfortable red brick villa just off the main road set in a large garden and has a good restaurant. There's a wealth of **private rooms** – although there's no accommodation bureau, so you'll have to try your luck by looking for *pokoje* signs. Finally, there's a **youth hostel** (no phone) in the summer months.

The central Pomeranian coast

West of Łeba lies a string of seaside resorts, commencing with laid-back, relatively relaxing places like **Ustka**, **Darłowo** and **Mielno**, and culminating with unwieldy **Kołobrzeg**, a major venue for mass tourism Polish style. Lying just inland are the regional administrative centres of **Słupsk** and **Koszalin** – important transport hubs, which you'll pass through en route to the coastal settlements, but hardly worthy of an overnight stop in their own right.

Słupsk

Continuing southwest through lush farming country along the back roads, the next place of any significance is **SŁUPSK**, 40km from Łeba, an early Slav settlement that was ruled by Pomeranian princes and Brandenburg margraves for much of its history. What little there is worth seeing in the town can be covered in an hour or two. By the banks of the River Słupia on the southeastern fringe of the centre, the Renaissance castle on Zamkowa houses the **Muzeum Pomorza Środkowego** (Museum of Central Pomerania; Tues–Sun: July–Aug 10am–5pm; Sept–June 10am–3pm; 4zł). Alongside displays of local ethnography, there's a large collection of modern Polish art, most notably the distorted caricatures and self-portraits of Stanisław Ignacy Witkiewicz – the avant-garde artist and playwright who committed suicide soon after the start of World War II (see box, p.486). The old castle **mill** opposite is one of the earliest specimens of its kind in the country, packed with more folksy exhibits (same times), while the reconstructed Gothic **Dominican church** has a fine Renaissance altarpiece and the tombs of the last Pomeranian princes.

Słupsk's **train station**, with the **bus station** just opposite, is at the west end of al. Wojska Polskiego, the kilometre-long boulevard leading to the centre. There are onward services to Darłowo, while buses to Ustka leave from a stop on al. Wojska Polskiego just round the corner. There's a useful **tourist information centre** at ul. Wojska Polskiego 16 (Mon–Fri 9am–5pm; ☎ & ☎059/842 0791) and a couple of reasonable downtown **hotels** if you need to stay. The *Hotel PTTK*, ul. Szarych Szeregów 1 (☎059/842 2902; ❸), is an unassuming but good-value place just across the Słupia River from the centre; while the *Zamkowy*, near the castle at ul. Dominikańska 9 (☎059/842 5294; ❺), has slightly plusher en suites with TV. Best **place to eat** in town is the *Pod Kluką*, east of the PTTK hotel at ul. Kaszubska 22, where you can enjoy moderately priced Polish fare in traditional surroundings.

Ustka

Twenty kilometres northwest of Słupsk (and accessible by bus or local train) is **USTKA**, a one-time Hansa town that's now an established member of the bucket-and-spade league. A largely modern town with shipyards straddling the mouth of the River Słupia, Ustka has beaches as good as any on the Baltic coast, but little in the way of architectural charm. It makes for a decent stopoff on a tour along the coast but it's not the best place for a longer stay.

From the **port** a seaside promenade heads eastwards along the town's principal beach. Here you'll find a few stretches of manicured park, and the usual grouping of unpretentious cafés and ice-cream stalls; further east are wilder, forest-backed stretches of beach. Behind the promenade are several half-timbered nineteenth-century **villas**, relics of the time when Ustka – then known as Stolpmünde – was a favoured watering hole of the Prussian elite.

Practicalities

Ustka's **bus station** is just off the main street, Marynarki Polskiej; the **train station** is a block to the east on ul. Dworcowa. The **tourist office** at Marynarki Polskiej 87 (July & Aug daily 8am–7pm; Sept–June Mon–Fri 10am–4pm; ☏059/814 7170) organizes accommodation in the town's many private rooms and pensions. Look for *noclegi* signs around ul. Rybacka at the eastern end of the resort if you arrive late. There's a growing number of new mid-sized **hotels**, including the *Rejs*, Marynarki Polskiej 51 (☏059/814 78 50; ●), built in imitation of the half-timbered structures that once characterized the region and boasting smart, chic ensuites; and the *Dajana*, right on the seafront promenade at Chopina 9 (☏059/814 4865; ●), where rooms come with soothing pastel colours and pine furnishings.

The usual **fried fish** stalls line the promenade. If you're looking for something more formal there's a classy **restaurant** at the *Rejs*.

Darłowo and beyond

A more attractive proposition than Ustka is **DARŁOWO**, 40km further west and a couple of kilometres inland on the River Wieprza, reached by a couple of buses a day from Ustka and more frequent services from Słupsk. The beaches north of the town, around the coastal suburb of Darłówko, are as popular as any, and Darłowo itself has an engaging historic core.

The **Rynek** here is the site of a gracefully reconstructed **town hall**, complete with its Renaissance doorway and an unusual fountain. On one side of the Rynek sits the Gothic **Kościół NMP** (St Mary's Church) an attractive brick building with a relatively restrained Baroque interior. Inside there's an eighteenth-century wooden pulpit decorated with scenes from the Last Judgement; in among a clutch of royal tombs located beneath the tower is that of the notorious King Erik VII (1397–1459), a local-born aristocrat who acceded to the thrones of Denmark, Sweden and Norway, and married Henry V of England's daughter Phillipina – whom he later tired of and banished to a nunnery. Deposed in 1439 he returned to Darłowo and lived out the last years of his life here as the Duke of Słupsk, living off piracy in the Baltic Sea.

South of the Rynek lies the well-preserved fourteenth-century **castle** of the Pomeranian princes, now home to the **Muzeum Regionalne** (daily: May–Sept 10am–4pm; Oct–April 10am–1.30pm; 8zł), which contains exhibits on local folklore as well as furnishings from the castle itself – notably the ornate seventeenth-century limewood pulpit which once graced the castle chapel.

About 400m northeast of the Rynek along ul. Ojca Damiana Tyneckiego is the extraordinary white-walled **Kaplica św. Gertrudy** (St Gertrude's Chapel), a twelve-sided seventeenth-century structure which squats beneath a tapering, inverted ice-cream cone of a roof covered in slender wooden shingles. The galleried interior is decorated with pictures of shoes and boots donated by pious tradesmen – St Gertrude being, among other things, the patron saint of cobblers.

Darłówko and Iwięcino

On the coast 3km west of Darłowo (and reached by regular shuttle service from the bus station) lies **Darłówko**, a low-rise, leafy resort straddling the mouth of the Wieprza. Clogged by fishing boats, the river is spanned by a pedestrian **drawbridge**, whose control tower – a mushroom-shaped affair resembling something out of a 1960s sci-fi movie – is very much a local attraction. There are the usual expanses of sand backed by woods, making this as restful a place as any if you're in need of a seaside breather.

If you're travelling by car it's well worth taking the backroads west from Darłowo, which pass through an attractive open landscape of fields, woods and quiet old Pomeranian villages. The sagging timber-framed farm buildings are still just about standing, as are the similarly aged brick churches. There's a charming example at **IWIĘCINO**, a tiny village halfway between Darłowo and Koszalin. The fourteenth-century structure features a faintly painted wooden ceiling and sixteenth-century pews, a delicate Renaissance altarpiece and a splendid late Baroque organ.

Practicalities

Darłowo's **bus station** is just west of the town centre: walk down Boguslawa X-ego and cross the river to reach the **Rynek**. The local **tourist office** in Darłowo's castle (see above; same hours; ☎094/314 3051) can help out with private rooms and pensions in Darłowo and Darłówko. Of Darłowo's **accommodation** options, the *Irena*, midway between the bus station and the Rynek at ul. Wojska Polskiego 64 (☎094/314 3692; ❸), and the *Hotel nad Wieprza*, just west of the centre at ul. Traugutta 6 (☎094/314 3657; ❹), are both medium-sized places that provide reasonable en-suite rooms. There's more variety in Darłówko – and you're closer to the sea. The *Albatros*, ul. Wilków Morskich 2 (☎094/314 3220; ❸), is a cosy pension, while the *Nord*, ul. Plazowa 4 (☎094/314 4351; ❹), is a holiday centre offering comfortable en suites – you may have to commit to a stay of a week or so in July and August. The *Klub Plaza*, ul. Słowiańska 3 (☎094/314 3120; ❼) is a swankier set-up with a swimming pool and outdoor bar and barbecue. There's a **campsite** midway between Darłowo and Darłówko at ul. Conrada 20 (☎094/314 2872).

Pizza Pinocchio, just off the Rynek, is one of only a few **places to eat** in Darłowo. Darłówko bristles with fish bars in season; for respite from the fish try *Pizza Papperino* on Wladyslawowa IV.

Koszalin

As even the determinedly upbeat tourist brochures tacitly admit, **KOSZALIN**, the bustling provincial capital 25km west of Darłowo, isn't the sort of place that gets the crowds shouting. The Stare Miasto was badly damaged during 1945, and much of the centre was rebuilt in utilitarian style in the years that followed. Set back some 10km from the sea, Koszalin is certainly not a holiday resort – but you're likely to pass through its bus and train stations if you're heading for the beaches at nearby Mielno, Unieście and Kołobrzeg.

There's the customary scattering of sights here if you have time to kill between connections. The modern flagstoned **Rynek** contains one of the strangest examples of Polish 1960s architecture – an orange-and-blue town hall that was considered the epitome of cool modernity when it was first built. Just south of the square is **Katedra Mariacka** (St Mary's Cathedral), an imposing, oft-remodelled Gothic structure with a few pieces of original decoration, notably a large fourteenth-century crucifix and a scattering of Gothic statuary, originally from the main altarpiece and now incorporated into the stalls, pulpit and organ loft. The nineteenth-century water mill facing the Stare Miasto walls from the corner of ul. Młyńska houses the **Muzeum Okręgowie** (Regional Museum; Tues–Sun 10am–4pm; 6zł) at no. 38, with a varied collection of folk art, archeological finds and other regional bits and pieces.

The train and bus stations are both ten minutes' walk west of the Rynek. If you get stuck in Koszalin, the choice of **accommodation** is limited, to say the least. *Arka*, between the stations and the Rynek at ul. Zwycięstwa 20 (☎094/342 7911; ❺) is a plush place mainly catering to business travellers. Other options tend to lie further afield: *Monika*, about 3km out of the centre at ul. św. Wojciecha (☎094/340 5077; ❹), offers neat motel-style rooms in a quiet garden setting.

If you need a **place to eat**, *Maredo*, Zwycięstwa 45, serves up Polish staples in a bright fast-food atmosphere, while *Bar-Pizzeria* on the northeastern corner of the Rynek serves up satisfying if unsophisticated thin-crust pies.

Mielno and Unieście

Bus #1 from Koszalin train station departs every thirty minutes or so for the resort of **MIELNO** some 12km northwest of town, a long, straggling beachside settlement that bleeds into **UNIEŚCIE** (where most buses terminate), the next village to the east. Formerly the main port for Koszalin, Mielno is now one of the quieter, more laid-back resorts on the coast, although the presence of a large saltwater lake just inland from the beach ensures a steady influx of sailors on summer weekends.

It's best to get off the bus at the western entrance to the resort, from where ul. 1 Maja leads down to a seaside promenade overlooked by a smattering of *belle-époque* holiday villas – including some attractively rickety timber constructions. It's roughly a half-hour's walk from here to Unieście, which has a comparatively sleepy, village-like feel, with wooden fishing boats parked up on the dune-fringed beach. The beach gets more unspoilt (and more deserted) the further east you go – once you've cleared Unieście, it's 10km to the next settlement.

The **tourist office**, just by the bus stop in Mielno (Mon–Fri 8am–4pm; ☎094/316 6152) has details of private rooms (❷) and pensions (❸) throughout the two villages. The *Eden* at Morska 20 in Unieście (☎094/318 9735; ❺) looks as though the builders followed the plans for a modern French ski hotel, but is well placed for the quiet, eastern end of the beach; in July and August they prefer bookings for a week or more. Midway between Mielno and Unieście, the smallish *Czarny Staw*, ul. Chrobrego 11 (☎094/318 9835; ❺), is a welcoming pension with cosy en suites. Close to the beach in the centre of Mielno, the *Willa Milenium*, at ul. 1 Maja 10 (☎094/347 1705; ❻), is a modern place aping the half-timbered style of the nearby villas, and comes with all the creature comforts.

For **camping**, *Bulaj*, at the western end of Unieście, occupies a grassy site right by the lake. For **eating**, *Café Floryn*, at the point where ul. 1 Maja meets the sea, is a bright pavilion filled with leafy houseplants and boasting a terrace both front and back – a great place for a fishy fry-up or just a drink.

Kołobrzeg

A forty-kilometre bus or train ride west of Koszalin, **KOŁOBRZEG** is Poland's largest Baltic holiday metropolis, a beach resort and health spa rolled into one that attracts over a million visitors a year. However it is also the country's most urbanized resort: most of its hotels look as if they've escaped from a big-city housing project, and the line of greying sanatoria along the seafront convey little sense of Riviera panache. **Tourism** here is organized on an industrial scale, and there's a corresponding lack of the informal, pension-style lodgings you'll find in smaller coastal places. Points in the town's favour include the beach, which is as good as any in the region, and the kind of year-round facilities (such as shops, restaurants and bars) that are often lacking in its sleepier Pomeranian neighbours.

The Stare Miasto and the beach

Much of the town centre is modern; an area of pedestrianized streets and plazas, lined with brightly painted apartments and office blocks built in imitation of the Hanseatic town houses of old. Dominating the skyline, however, is the collegiate **Kościół Mariacki** (St Mary's Church), originally built as a simple Gothic hall, but extended in the fifteenth century with the addition of star-vaulted aisles, adding to the impression of depth and spaciousness. A particularly striking effect was achieved with the facade, whose twin towers were moulded together into one imposing mass of brick. Many of the furnishings perished in the war, but some significant items remain, notably several Gothic triptychs and a fourteenth-century bronze font.

To the north stands the other key public building, the **town hall**. A castellated Romantic creation incorporating some of its fifteenth-century predecessor, it was built from designs provided by the great Berlin architect Karl Friedrich Schinkel.

However, it's the **beach** that the visitors come for, and throughout the summer you'll find throngs of Polish holiday-makers soaking up the sun on the main strand. There's 1.6km of beach to lie on, complete with deck chairs, wicker cots, parasols and rowing boats for rent. There's plenty of scope for a decent stroll, with a **promenade** running the length of the beach and a pier towards the western end. Beyond the pier stands a tall brick **lighthouse** (daily: July & Aug 10am–sunset; Sept–June 10am–5pm; 3zł) offering good views of the surroundings, and a stone monument commemorating "Poland's Reunion with the Sea", a highly symbolic event which took place here in 1945. With the German withdrawal from Kołobrzeg in March, a band of Polish patriots gathered on the beach to hurl a wedding ring into the sea, thereby marking Poland's re-marriage to a stretch of coast that had for so long been in German hands.

Practicalities

Kołobrzeg's **train** and **bus** stations are next to each other on ul. Kolejowa. The town centre lies ten minutes' walk south along ul. Dworcowa, while the seafront is an equal distance to the north.

The **tourist information** office is directly opposite the station entrance at ul. Dworcowa 1 (July & Aug daily 7am–1pm and 3pm–7pm; Sept–June Mon–Fri 8am–4pm; ☎094/355 1320). You can pick up town maps and book private **rooms** (❷) here. The *Relaks*, at ul. Kościuszki 24 (☎094/352 7735; ❻), is one of the few pleasant pensions in town, offering en-suite rooms with balconies near the eastern end of the beach, and a nice garden with kiddies' swings. Just down the road the *Mega*, ul. Kościuski 18 (☎094/352 8152; ❺), offers spa treatments and backs onto the prom; while the *Bałtyk*, ul. Rodziewiczówny 1 (℡094/352 4011; ❻), is another spa-style hotel with an all-singing and dancing swimming pool, right by the beach. The *New Skanpol*, down the road from the station at ul. Dworcowa 10 (℡094/352 8211; ❻), is the best of the downtown choices. The *Baltic* **campsite**, 1500m east of the stations at ul. IV Dywizji Wojska Polskiego 1 (℡094/352 4569, ⓦwww.baltic78.republika.pl), is beside a wooded park ten minutes' walk from the sea.

For **eating**, there are numerous excellent fish-and-chip bars along the seafront, some of which – notably *J. Rewinski* near the lighthouse – are quite swish-looking places sited in stylish plate-glass pavilions. For a more leisurely sit-down meal, the *Karczma Monte Christo*, near the sea at Morska 7c, features a faux-rustic, wooden-bench interior and succulent grilled dishes – steaks, pork chops and fish. In the modern town centre, the *Romantic*, ul. Mariacka 25, serves up good-quality traditional Polish dishes in a formal subterranean dining room. Cheap and tasty pizzas can be had at the *Bella Italia*, ul. Gierczak 27.

Kołobrzeg is not short of venues for **drinking** and evening entertainment. The hotel cafés along the seafront offer "proper" dancing to evergreen tunes. Bars tend to be located in the modern centre: *Café Mariacka*, Mariacka 27, functions as both daytime café and night-time drinking den, and has the feel of a cosy living room. *Fiddlers Green*, Dubois 16, is a smart little pub with Irish brews on tap. Otherwise, try the *Pizza Pub*, Mariacka 9, which, as the name suggests, serves as both pizzeria and pub.

Trzebiatów, Gryfice and Goleniów

Three former Hansa ports – **Trzebiatów**, **Gryfice** and **Goleniów** – lie between Kołobrzeg and Szczecin. For all their former prosperity, their churches and fortifications offer the only tangible reminder of their heyday. All three towns are now in varying stages of decline but make for an interesting stop if you want to break a journey. The road between Kołobrzeg and Kamień Pomorski passes through Trzebiatów and it's only a brief diversion to Gryfice. The train between Kołobrzeg and Szczecin stops at all three towns.

Trzebiatów

TRZEBIATÓW lies on the banks of the River Rega, about 30km from Kołobrzeg. It's a place where time seems to have gone backwards, transforming a well-heeled trading town into a straggling agricultural village. A good deal of imagination is required to visualize this sleepy backwater as it was four hundred years ago when it played a key role in the Reformation. Johannes Bugenhagen spent nearly two decades as rector of its Latin School, then left to become one of Luther's leading lieutenants. He returned in 1534 to persuade the Pomeranian Assembly to adopt the new faith throughout the province.

From many miles away, Trzebiatów's skyline is dominated by the magnificent tower of **Kościoł Mariacki** (St Mary's), one of the most accomplished Gothic churches in the region, crowned with the unusual combination of a brick octagon and a lead spire. In it hang two historic bells – one, named Gabriel, is from the late fourteenth century; the other, known as Mary, dates from the early sixteenth century. The building's interior is chiefly notable for its clear architectural lines and uncluttered appearance which, like the German epitaphs on the walls, are evidence of the four centuries it spent in Protestant hands.

Close to the church is the Rynek, in the centre of which stands the recently renovated **town hall**, constructed in the sober Baroque style favoured in northern German lands. Just off the southern side is the abandoned chapel of **św. Ducha** (the Holy Ghost), the setting for the Assembly which decided to introduce the Reformation into Pomerania. At the end of the street you can see the rotund **Kaszana** bastion and **town walls**, a significant stretch of which still survives. Much of this fortification work dates from the fifteenth century, when Trzebiatów and Gryfice were at odds over navigation rights on the Rega.

Both the **bus** and **train stations** are located outside the built-up part of town, about ten minutes' walk to the east.

Gryfice

About 20km up the Rega from Trzebiatów is **GRYFICE**, a slightly larger town with a decidedly more urban feel to it. German commentators on Pomerania are readily stirred to anger at the mere mention of its name: the town was taken undamaged by the Red Army in 1945, only to be set ablaze soon afterwards, and was later used as the site of a penal camp in which a large number of civilians was detained.

The Gothic **Kościół Mariacki** (Church of St Mary) is a copybook example of the Baltic style, notable chiefly for its sturdy single western tower and its finely detailed portals, many of which have since been bricked up. Inside you'll find some good Baroque furnishings, in particular the pulpit and the high altar. The surviving parts of the **fortifications** – the Stone Gate, the High Gate and the Powder Tower – can be seen towards the river to the east.

Goleniów

The largest and liveliest town of the three is **GOLENIÓW**, 55km southwest of Gryfice. It's an important rail junction, the meeting point of the line between Kołobrzeg and Szczecin with those to Kamień Pomorski and Świnoujście. Among its few assets is its situation in the middle of the **Puszca Goleniowska**, a vast forested area which stretches almost all the way up to Wolin – a particularly scenic journey by train.

Goleniów's main church, **Kościół św. Katarzyny** (St Catherine's Church), is imposing largely owing to extensive remodelling last century when the tower was added – today its brick columns bow visibly under the strain. Nearby are the **town walls**, whose surviving towers and gateways make a nicely varied group, with the showpiece being the **Brama Wolińska** (Wolin Gate), an elaborate building in its own right now housing a cultural centre. Also worth a look is the timber-framed **granary** standing on the banks of the River Ina.

Kamień Pomorski

Some 60km west of Kołobrzeg lies the quiet waterside town of **KAMIEŃ POMORSKI**, an atmospheric Pomeranian centre which demands a visit for its fine cathedral and agreeable setting. There are good bus connections with Kołobrzeg, Międzyzdroje, Świnoujście and Szczecin, making Kamień an easy stopoff.

The town's **history** began in the ninth century, when a port was established here on the River Dziwna, a short stretch of water connecting the huge Zalew

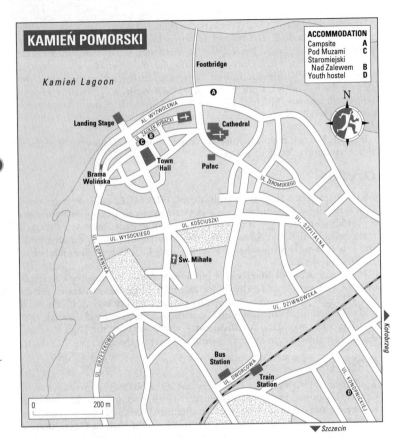

Szczeciński, or Szczecin Lagoon, with the smaller Zalew Kamieński, or Kamień Lagoon – all of which are part of the delta formed by the Odra as it nears the Gulf of Pomerania. By the late twelfth century, Kamień was significant enough to become the seat of the bishopric of West Pomerania, a position it kept for nearly four hundred years. By the late 1300s it was rich enough to join the Hanseatic League. The Swedes seized the town during the Thirty Years' War, but by the late seventeenth century it had been appropriated by the Brandenburgs and did not come under Polish control until after World War II. Despite extensive wartime damage, Kamień Pomorski seems to have come out better than most towns in the area: concrete buildings fill the huge gaps between the occasional burghers' mansions, yet there's enough of the older architecture to retain a sense of times past.

The Town

All Kamień's sights are on and around the **Rynek** whose northern edge opens onto the lagoon. The fifteenth-century **town hall** at the centre is a careful reconstruction, its brick archways rising to a stepped and curvilinear Baroque gable at each end. Parts of the walls ringing the Stare Miasto have survived, notably the **Brama Wolińska** west of the square, an imposing Gothic gateway, surrounded by apartment buildings.

East of the square stands the **cathedral**. Construction of the brick and granite basilica began in the 1170s, with many subsequent additions over the following centuries. Inside the cathedral you're enveloped by majestic Gothic vaulted arches; the presbytery is older, and covered with flowing early thirteenth-century decoration. Other sections of early polychromy are tucked away in corners around the transept, including a stern *Christ Pantocrator* and a fine *Crucifixion* that was uncovered in the 1940s. The focus of attention, though, is the superb fifteenth-century triptych gracing the altar, the most outstanding of many such Gothic pieces in the building – the rest are in the **sacristy museum**.

At the back of the cathedral stands the famous Baroque **organ**, its forest of silver pipes crowned by a procession of dreamy gilded saints. As you approach from the nave, a portrait of the instrument's creator, a local bishop by the name of Bogusław de Croy i Archot, stares down on the congregation from a cherub-encircled frame. In July the cathedral hosts an **International Organ and Chamber Music Festival**, with concerts every Friday – details from the Biuro Katedralny opposite. To complete the ensemble, across pl. Katedralny is the **Pałac Biskupski** (Bishop's Palace), a stately, late-Gothic structure with a finely carved attic.

Downhill from the cathedral lie the grassy banks of the **lagoon**. There's no real beach here, but it's a relaxing place to stretch your legs, and there's a footbridge leading over to a tranquil, reedy area on the opposite bank.

Practicalities

All Kamień's sights are a straightforward ten-minute walk north of the **bus** and **train stations**. Central Kamień offers two exceedingly cosy medium-sized **hotels**, both offering en-suite rooms with TV and standing side by side on the main square. The *Pod Muzami*, at Gryfitów 1 (☎091/382 2240; ❹), is in an old half-timbered building but has bright modern interiors; while the *Staromiejski Nad Zalewem*, Rybacka 3 (☎091/382 2644; ❹), goes for a chintzier style. There's a **campsite** by the lagoon at al. Wyzwolenia 2 (☎091/382 0076).

For **eating**, you'll find the customary gaggle of snack bars and fish-fry huts down by the water's edge. For more substantial food try the restaurant in the *Hotel Pod Muzami* or the *Ratuszowa* by the town hall.

Wolin

Across the water from Kamień Pomorski is **WOLIN**, the first of two large, heavily indented islands that separate the Szczecin Lagoon from the Gulf of Pomerania. The gap dividing Wolin from the mainland is at times so narrow that it's often described as a peninsula rather than an island; indeed, roads are built directly over the River Dziwna in two places – near its mouth at Dzwinów, some 12km from Kamień, and at **Wolin town** towards the island's southern extremity, where it is also forded by the rail line from Szczecin. From Kamień, you can choose to approach by either of these two roads, the only ones of significance on the island. They converge at the seaside town and hiking centre of **Międzyzdroje**, before continuing onwards to the western extremity of the island and **Świnoujście** – an engaging mixture of bustling port, health spa and beach resort.

The island, which is 35km long and between 8km and 20km across, offers a wonderfully contrasted landscape of sand dunes, lakes, forest, meadows and moors. The dramatic **coastline** has attracted crowds of holiday-makers since the nineteenth century but remains relatively unspoilt. A sizeable portion of the island is under protection as a national park, and you really need to take time to hike if you want to appreciate it to the full.

Wolin Town

Squatting beside the Dzwina River on the island's southeastern tip, the town of **WOLIN** occupies the site of one of the oldest Slav settlements in the country. According to early chronicles, a pagan tribe known as the Wolinians established themselves here in the eighth century, developing one of the most important early Baltic ports, and carrying on a healthy trade with the Vikings. A temple to Światowid and to Trzyglów, a triple-headed Slav deity, existed here until the early twelfth century, and was presumably destroyed by the Christian Poles only when they captured the stronghold.

Echoes of the town's pagan past are present in the totem-like reconstructed wooden figures dotted around close to the water, all depicting Slav gods. The ruins of the medieval **Kościół św. Mikołaja** (Church of St Nicholas), just up from the main square, show echoes of a Christian past too. Excavations have uncovered plentiful evidence of the Wolinian settlement: you can see their discoveries in the local **museum** (Tues–Sun 9am–4pm; 3.50zł) on the main road at the eastern end of town. The road bridge linking Wolin to the mainland provides a good vantage point from which to survey the narrow **Dziwna channel**, packed with shoals of small fishing vessels on calm days.

There's no real reason to spend the night here, especially if you're headed for the beach, but there is a leafy riverside **campsite** at ul. Slowianska 27a (☎091/326 6167). **Buses** on the Świnoujście–Szczecin route pick up and drop off on Wolin's main street; the train station is a short distance to the east.

Międzyzdroje

By far the best base for exploring the island is **MIĘDZYZDROJE**, which offers easy access to a long sandy beach and the best hiking trails in the area. A favourite Baltic resort with the prewar German middle class, it is now one of the west Baltic's busiest resorts. New hotels are springing up in the beachside areas, and the number of German and Scandinavian visitors is on the increase. However the centre of town remains a laid-back, far from overdeveloped place, its streets filled with trade union-owned sanatoria and holiday homes. It may not look all that snazzy to the outsider, but Międzyzdroje was traditionally one of the places where Polish TV and film stars spent their holidays. A modicum of showbiz glitter still exists in the shape of the **Festiwal Gwiazd** (Star Festival) at the beginning of July, when a horde of minor celebrities and their hangers-on descend on town to attend public film screenings and concerts and generally hang out.

The centre of town, 1km inland from the sea, revolves around **plac Neptuna**, a modern, pedestrianized, café-filled square which brings to mind the mall-like plazas of Mediterranean holiday resorts. Immediately to the south is the main traffic thoroughfare, ul. Niepodległości, which is overlooked by the national park museum, the **Muzeum Przyrodnice Wolińskie o Parku Narodowego** (Tues–Sat 9am–5pm; 5zł) – a well-presented display of the island's flora and fauna which is worth visiting before heading off into the park itself.

It's a ten-minute walk northwards from pl. Neptuna to ul. Bohaterów Warszawy, the **promenade** which stretches for some 4km along the shore. Its focal point is the nineteenth-century **pier**, the entrance to which is framed by an imposing pair of domed pavilions now occupied by ice-cream kiosks. The first one hundred metres or so of the pier is covered by a canopy, forming an arcade-like space filled with cafés and boutiques selling beach gear.

The bison reserve

Wolin's densely wooded national park starts right on the outskirts of Międzyzdroje, and the **bison reserve** (Tues–Sun 10am–6pm; 5zł) lies a twenty-minute walk through the park from the town centre. Head uphill from the PTTK office on ul. Niepodległości and follow the signs. You'll pass through a park gate after about five minutes, beyond which a trail leads through deep forest to the reserve itself. Bison died out here in the 1300s and the specimens on show are descended from specimens brought from Białowieża in eastern Poland (see p.277); the aim of the reserve is to breed the shaggy beasts in captivity to save them from extinction. You'll also see deer, eagles and a clutch of amusing wild boar who loll about in the mud, twitching their prodigious snouts.

Practicalities

The **train station** is at the southeastern fringe of town, five minutes' walk uphill from the centre, while **buses** pick up and drop off closer to the centre, on ul. Niepodległości.

The PTTK office at the junction of Niepodległości and Kolejowa (Mon–Fri 7am–5pm, Sat 9am–1pm; ☎091/328 0462) sells maps and gives **information** on routes into the park, and might direct you towards private rooms (❷), although you'll probably have to look round town on your own – the streets behind the seafront are the best places to start. The PTTK has a **hotel** above the office (☎091/328 0382; ❸) offering clean but plain rooms with or without bathroom; and an annexe, nearer the beach at ul. Dąbrówski 11 (☎091/328 0929; ❹). The *Marina*, Gryfa Pomorskiego 1 (☎091/328 0449, ⓦwww.marinahotel.az.pl; ❻), is a smart new building on the main road through town providing smallish but extremely cosy en-suite rooms with TV. You'll get similar standards of comfort at the *Perła*, Pomorska 7 (☎091/328 1303; ❻), a bright modern pension just off the promenade a little to the east of the pier; the *Aurora*, Bohaterów Warszawy 17 (☎091/328 1248, ⓦwww.hotelaurora.pl; ❻), whose slightly higher prices are justified by its pier-side position; and the *Slavia*, ul. Promenada Gwiazd 34 (☎091/328 0106; ❼), whose balconies have sea views. If you want to stay in unbridled comfort, the *Amber Baltic*, ul. Bohaterów Warszawy 26a (☎091/328 1000, ⓦwww.hotel-amber-baltic.pl; ❽), charges international prices for facilities that include golf, bowling and indoor and outdoor swimming pools. Best of the **campsites** is the *Gromada*, ul. Bohaterów Warszawy 1 (☎091/328 0779), at the western end of the seafront.

The *Cukierna Marczello* **café** at pl. Neptuna 3 does the best pastries and cakes in town and has decent coffee. For something more substantial, the *Carmen* **restaurant**, immediately opposite, serves up satisfying platters of Polish meat-and-potatoes cuisine. You'll find several fish-and-chip stalls along the seafront promenade, and an inexpensive Chinese fast-food joint, *Ti Li*, just west of the pier at Bohaterów Warszawy 16. For **drinking**, the café-bars on the pier (most of which also serve pizza and other snacks) fill up on summer weekends, although the best all-year-round venue is *Roza Wiatrow* at pl. Neptuna 7, a smart, cosy pub with nautical prints and model boats stashed around the place.

Woliński national park

Woliński national park is an area of outstanding natural interest: apart from its richly varied landscapes, it is the habitat of over two hundred different types of bird – the sea eagle is its emblem – and numerous animals such as red and fallow deer, wild boar, badgers, foxes and squirrels. It would take several days to cover all its many delights, but a good cross-section can be seen without venturing too far from Międzyzdroje. Alternatively, take a bus or train going in the direction of Wolin town, or a bus going towards Kamień or Kołobrzeg, and alight at any stop; you'll soon find signs enabling you to pick up one of the colour-coded trails. A good aid to walking in this region is the 1:75,000 *Zalew Szczeciński* **map** which has all the paths clearly marked; it's readily available in Międzyzdroje, notably from the national park museum (see p.642).

The trails

Some of the most impressive scenery in the park can be seen by following the **red trail** along its eastward stretch from Międzyzdroje, which passes for a while directly along the beach. You soon come to some awesome-looking tree-crowned **dunes**, where the sand has been swept up into cliff-like formations up to 95m in height – the highest to be seen anywhere on the Baltic. Quite apart from its visual impact, much of this secluded stretch is ideal for a spot of swimming or sunbathing away from the crowds. After a few kilometres, the markers point the way upwards into the forest, and you follow a path which skirts the tiny Lake Gardno before arriving at the village of **WISEŁKA**, whose setting has the best of both worlds, being by its eponymous lake, and above a popular stretch of beach. Here there's a restaurant, snack bars, and several shops. The trail continues east through the woods and past more small lakes to its terminus at **KOŁCZEWO**, set at the head of its own lake, and the only other place along the entire route with refreshment facilities. From either here or Misełka, you can pick up a bus back to Międzyzdroje.

Also terminating at Kołczewo is the **green trail**: if you're prepared to devote a very long day to it, you could combine this with the red trail in one circular trip. The trail begins in Międzyzdroje and passes by the bison reserve (see p.643) before continuing its forest course, emerging at a group of glacial lakes around the village of Warnowo (which can also be reached directly by train), where there's another reserve, this time for mute swans. Five lakeshores are then skirted en route to Kołczewo.

The third route, the **blue trail**, follows a southerly course from Międzyzdroje's train station, again passing through wooded countryside before arriving at the northern shore of the Szczecin Lagoon. Following this to the east, you traverse the heights of the Mokrzyckie Góry, then descend to the town of Wolin.

Finally, the western section of the **red trail** follows the coast for a couple of kilometres, then cuts straight down the narrow peninsula at the end of the island to the shore of the islet-strewn Lake Wicko Wielkie, before cutting inland to Świnoujście.

Świnoujście

Across the water from Wolin on the western tip of the island of Uznam, the bustling fishing port, naval base and beach resort of **ŚWINOUJŚCIE** is a popular entry point into Poland, thanks to the passenger ships which sail here from Sweden and Denmark. It's also 3km away from the land border with Germany (there's a crossing open to pedestrians and cyclists, but not cars), to whom the vast bulk of the island of Uznam belongs.

Świnoujście's international **ferry terminal**, together with both the **bus** and **train stations**, is stranded on the eastern bank of the Świna estuary – which seperates Uznam from Wolin. A half-hourly car ferry (on which pedestrians travel free) runs over to the centre of town, which lies on the western bank. The centre is fairly nondescript, and it's best to head directly to the town's superb white-sand **beach** – twenty minutes' north on the far side of the spacious **spa park**. Once you reach the shore, you'll probably be drawn in to the endless stream of strollers passing along the pedestrianized ul. Żeromskiego, which runs from east to west along the seafront, passing neat flowerbeds and stately seaside villas on the way.

The **tourist office**, just west of the ferry landing at pl. Słowiański 15 (Mon–Fri 9am–5pm, Sat 9am–3pm; ℡091/322 4999), can direct you towards private rooms (❷) and pensions (❸–❹). One of the cheapest of the **hotels** is the *Bryza* at Gdyńska 38 (℡091/321 2491), which offers fairly basic rooms with bathroom (❺) or without (❹) a ten-minute walk from the ferry landing and twenty minutes' walk from the beach. There's more choice nearer the seafront: *Senator*, Żeromskiego 15 (℡091/321 5511, ⓦwww.maxmedia.pl/dzsenator; ❹), has simple en suites in one of the finest *fin-de-siècle* villas along the prom; while the more contemporary *Villa Merry*, Żeromskiego 16 (℡091/321 2619, ⓦwww.villa-merry.uznam.net.pl), is an affordable apartment hotel offering cosy quarters with kitchenettes (❹). The *Atol*, just behind the promenade at Orkana 3 (℡091/321 3010; ❻), is one of the better new hotels in town, offering pastel-coloured en suites, a sauna, and a list of former guests that rejoices in top showbiz mastodons like Boney M and Smokie.

There's an HI **youth hostel** at Gdyńska 26 (℡091/327 0613) near the *Bryza* which has a few double rooms (❶) as well as dorms. The *Relax* **campsite** is more handily located at ul. Słowackiego 1 (℡091/321 4700), between the spa park and the beach, and has chalets (❷).

For **food**, you could do worse than head for *Gryf*, an enormous bench-filled yard on the seafront promenade serving up tasty grilled and fried fish; *Pizzeria Muszla*, about 200m further east, is a slightly more stylish sit-down venue which has some good pasta dishes. The restaurant of the *Polaris* hotel, Słowackiego 33, is a plush and formal, but affordable, place in which to feast on classic fish and meat dishes. For **drinking**, *Jazz Café Casablanca*, near the tourist office on pl. Słowiański, has a touch more style than the al-fresco beer bars on the seafront promenade. **Nightlife** centres around old-time dancing in the larger hotels, or more frenetic physical jerks in the summer-only disco-bars on the seafront.

Moving on from Świnoujście, there are regular **train** and **bus** services to Szczecin, and a summer only **hydrofoil** service that runs across the lagoon to Szczecin three times a day. In addition there are daily car ferries to Ystad, Malmö and Copenhagen, and passenger boats (intended for day-trippers, really) to the nearby German beach resorts of Ahlbeck, Bansin and Heringsdorf.

Szczecin

The largest city in northwestern Poland, with 400,000 inhabitants, **SZCZECIN** sprawls around the banks of the Odra in a tangle of bridges, cranes and dockside machinery, a city with a long maritime and shipbuilding heritage. It's a gruff, workaday place that bares few of its charms to the passing visitor. However, it's also a fast-paced, fast-changing place with a clutch of cultural diversions, not to mention an impressive collection of bars. It's also an important transport hub: the western half of Poland's Baltic coastline is served by regular buses and trains from here.

The Slav stronghold established here in the eighth century was taken by the first Piast monarch, Mieszko I, in 967 – a point much emphasized in Polish histories.

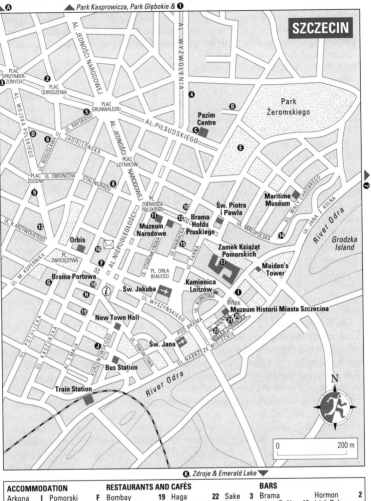

SZCZECIN

Park Kasprowicza, Park Głębokie &

Park Żeromskiego

Pazim Centre

Maritime Museum

Św. Piotra i Pawla

Brama Hołdu Pruskiego

Muzeum Narodowe

Zamek Książąt Pomorskich

Maiden's Tower

Grodzka Island

Orbis

Brama Portowa

Kamienica Loitzów

Św. Jakuba

RYNEK

Muzeum Historii Miasta Szczecina

New Town Hall

Św. Jana

Bus Station

Train Station

River Odra

0   200 m

K, Zdroje & Emerald Lake

ACCOMMODATION				RESTAURANTS AND CAFÉS						BARS			
Arkona	I	Pomorski	F	Bombay	19	Haga	22	Sake	3	Brama		Hormon	2
Elka-Sen	H	PTTK Camping	K	Café Galeria	15	Pod Muzami	11	Sphinx	9	Jazz Café	12	Irish Pub	
Gryf	D	Radisson	C	Chata	10	Restauracja		Virga	1	Café Prawda	20	Dublin	16
HI Hostel	A	Rycerski	G	Chief	5	na Kuncu				Christopher		Nautilus Pub	7
Neptun	B	Victoria	J	Cukiernia Koch	4, 13	Korytarza	17			Columbus	14	Rocker Club	18
Park	E			Duet	6	Rybarex	8			Club Kancler	21		

From the early twelfth century, Szczecin became the residence of a local branch of Piast princes, rulers of Western Pomerania, but German colonists were already present in force by the time the city joined the Hanseatic League in the mid-thirteenth century. The next key event was the port's capture by the Swedes in 1630, after which they held on to it for nearly a century. Sold to the Prussians in 1720, it remained under Prussian rule until 1945, when it became an outpost on Poland's newly established western frontier. With the border just west of the city limits and Berlin – for which Stettin/Szczecin used to be the port – only a couple of hours away by car or train, the German presence is palpable.

Wartime pummelling destroyed most of the old centre, which never received quite the same restorative attention as some less controversially Polish cities. There is no Rynek or pedestrianized town centre, although a distinctly Parisian radial pattern of streets survives in what has become the main part of the city. Despite the size and importance of the city, there isn't that much to take in – a full day is enough to cover all the main sights.

Arrival and information

The central **train station** and the nearby **bus terminal** are located near the water's edge, from where it's a fifteen-minute walk (or a quick tram ride) north up the hill to the town centre. There are **left-luggage** facilities in the pedestrian underpass beneath the train station's ticket hall (daily 6am–midnight). City maps, available from the tourist office (see below), bookstores and kiosks, give details of the comprehensive bus and tram **city transport** routes. Bus and tram tickets cost 1.90zł for twenty minutes of travel, 2.90zł for one hour. Buy them at kiosks near stops.

Szczecin **airport** – chiefly dedicated to internal flights but with some international services – is in fact located at Goleniów (℡091/182 864), 45km north of the city, with bus services to and from the LOT office at al. Wyzwolenia 17.

The municipal **tourist office**, which occupies a squat circular pavilion at al. Niepodległości 1 (Mon–Fri 9am–5pm; ℡091/434 0440, ⓦwww.szczecin.pl), gives advice on accommodation, and sells **town maps**.

Accommodation

There's a fair spread of **accommodation** in town, ranging from the most luxurious international-class hotels to a couple of post-communist fleapits, and even in high summer you shouldn't have too much trouble finding a bed for the night. Prices include breakfast unless otherwise stated.

Almatur, ul. Bohaterów Warszawy 83 (Mon–Fri 9am–5pm), will be able to tell you which **student hostels** in Szczecin are open to tourists over the summer.

Hotels

Arkona ul. Panieńska 10 ℡091/488 0261, ⓦwww.orbis.pl. Orbis concrete block with not-quite groovy 1970s furnishings. Nice location below the castle, just behind the old town hall. ⓺
Elka-Sen ul. 3 Maja 1A ℡091/433 5604. Charming little place in a converted hospital basement, handy for both the city centre and the stations. Rooms are on the cramped side but come with colourful furnishings and en-suite shower. Reserve in advance if possible. ⓹
Gryf al. Wojska Polskiego 49 ℡091/433 4030. Dowdy downtown hotel on a busy thoroughfare, with a mixture of dingy unrefurbished rooms with shared facilities (⓸), and bright modern en suites with TV. No breakfast. ⓹
Neptun ul. Matejki 18 ℡091/488 3883, ⓦwww.orbis.pl. Luxury Orbis joint on the west side of Park Żeromskiego. ⓺
Park ul. Plantowa 1 ℡094/488 1524. Newish hotel offering modern en suites attractively decorated

in pastel colours. More intimate in feel than the other business-standard hotels, and the location – right in the middle of Park Żeromskiego – is a major plus. ⓺
Pomorski pl. Brama Portowa 4 ℡091/433 6151. Ideally central, but rooms are sparsely furnished and unkempt. A short-stay bolt-hole, nothing more. En suites and rooms with shared facilities. No breakfast. ⓶
Radisson pl. Rodła 10 ℡091/359 5595. Gleaming custom-built luxury hotel with its own casino, nightclub, fitness centre and swimming pool, along with all the other upmarket facilities expected by its largely expense-account clientele. ⓼
Rycerski ul. Potulicka 2a ℡091/488 8164. Smart, fully renovated place right in the heart of town, offering tasteful en suites with TV. ⓺
Victoria pl. Batorego 2 ℡091/434 3855. Comfortable medium-sized hotel in refurbished nineteenth-century building within easy striking distance of train and bus stations. ⓸

Hostels and campsites

HI Hostel ul. Monte Cassino 19a ☎ 091/422 4761. Comfortable and friendly hostel situated just north-west of the centre, past the south end of ul. M. Kopernika. Handy for Szczecin's parks. Tram #3 to pl. Rodła, then tram #1 to the Piotra Skargi stop.

PTTK Camping ul. Przestrzenna 23 ☎ 091/460 1165. In Dąbie, 3km east of town – take the local train to Szczecin-Dąbie station, followed by bus #56, #62 or #79. Open May–Sept; tent space and chalets (❷) available.

The City

The medieval **Stare Miasto**, laid out on a slope on the left bank of the Odra, was heavily bombed in the last war. Restoration work on the showpiece build-ings went on until the 1980s, with the gaps either left vacant or filled by drab modern housing. While you're walking around you'll notice very few people and a distinct lack of shops in this area; **commercial** life shifted west a kilometre to a part of town which survived in better shape. This was laid out towards the end of the nineteenth century in the Parisian manner, with broad boulevards radiating out from pl. Grunwaldzki, the transplanted heart of Szczecin.

The commercial centre

Ascending ul. Dworcowa from the train station, you soon see some of the massive late-nineteenth- and early twentieth-century Prussian buildings so characteristic of the heart of the city. Commanding the heights is the bulky red-brick frame of the neo-Gothic new **town hall**, now the seat of the mari-time authorities. Across the street, steps lead up to the former **Savings Bank**, a Jugendstil fantasy, whose slender tower and decorative facades have a distinctly oriental flavour.

At the top of ul. Dworcowa is the traffic-engulfed square named after the **Brama Portowa** (Harbour Gate), not so much a gate as two ornate Baroque gables linked by a long hall, built by the Prussians in 1725 to mark their purchase of the city. Immediately to the west of the gateway is the largest and busiest of the squares, pl. Zwycięstwa, on which stand a couple of turn-of-the-twentieth-century churches which have successively served the local garrison. Leading off to the north is al. Niepodległości, the city's main thoroughfare, on whose western side stand two more of the big Prussian public buildings – the post office, still fulfilling its original function, and the administration building of the Pomeranian district, which has been taken over by the displaced Savings Bank.

Św. Jakuba and around

Heading east from the Brama Portowa to the river, ul. Kardynała Wyszyńskiego brings you to the **Katedra św. Jakuba** (St James's Cathedral), a massive Gothic church which was grievously damaged in 1945 and subsequently suffered over-restoration (including some concrete windows). Repairs were completed in 1982, and the church became a cathedral the following year. The oldest parts of the church date back to the fourteenth century and are the work of Hinrich Brunsberg, the finest of the specialist brickwork architects of the Baltic lands. The hall design he used here is notable for its consummate simplicity. In the middle of the following century, the single **tower** was constructed to replace the previous pair; this is now only half of its prewar height of 120m, having been rebuilt minus the spire and further trivialized with the addition of a clock. Its five-and-a-half-tonne bell now hangs in a frame outside, as does a memorial to Carl Loewe, one of the great ballad composers and singers of the nineteenth century, who was for several decades the church's organist and music director. Today the building's profile is rather plain, with its bulky exterior best appreciated coming up ul. Kardynała Wyszyńskiego from the river, although to the rear of the church you'll find a pretty little Gothic rectory.

On pl. Orła Białego, the square on the north side of the cathedral, is the Baroque **Pod Globusem Palace**, originally built for the ruler of the Prussian province of Pomerania and now used as the medical academy. Across from it, part obscured by a willow tree, stands an intriguing **fountain** adorned with the eponymous white eagle (*biały orzeł*) overlooking a group of satyrs who gurgle stoically into an enormous clam. Hidden among the trees at the cathedral end of the square is another piece of Baroque frippery, a statue of the goddess Flora.

The lower town

Down ul. Wyszyńskiego towards the river, you come on the right-hand side to the oldest surviving building in Szczecin, the Franciscan monastery of **św. Jana** (St John), part of which dates back to the thirteenth century. Its distinctive feature is its geometric inconsistency showing that medieval builders could and did get their calculations wrong. The chancel is an irregular decagon, yet has a seven-part vault, while the later nave adjoins at an oblique angle, its off-centre vaulting a vain attempt to align the bays with the aisle windows. It's a rare example of a building that was never rebuilt properly but never quite collapsed; looking inside you can see the alarmingly warped columns braced by a network of steel girders.

Immediately east of here lies the Stary Rynek, where concrete blocks and vacant lots rub shoulders with several reconstructed burghers' houses gaudily decked out in bright blue and orange colour schemes. By far the most personable of Szczecin's buildings is the gabled **old town hall** in the Rynek's centre, an artful reconstruction of the fourteenth-century original, probably designed by Hinrich Brunsberg, which was flattened in the war. The restorers opted to return it to something like its original appearance, right down to the bulging lopsided walls. These days the building serves as a small **Muzeum Historii Miasta Szczecina** (Museum of the History of Szczecin; Tues–Sun 10am–4pm; 6zł).

The only burgher's mansion still standing in Szczecin is the mid-sixteenth-century **Kamienica Loitzów** (Loitz House), just uphill at the corner of ul. Kurkowa, a tower-type residence of a prominent local banking and trading dynasty. Further down the same street are two other rare medieval survivors, a grange and the municipal weigh house. Of the once formidable fifteenth-century fortification system, almost nothing remains save the appropriately graceful **Maiden's Tower**, now stranded between the castle and a network of interchanges funnelling the city's traffic over the river.

Zamek Książąt Pomorskich

By now you'll have spotted the **Zamek Książąt Pomorskich** (Castle of the Pomeranian Princes) commanding views of the river from its hillside perch. A Slav fortified settlement on this spot was replaced in the mid-fourteenth century by a stone structure, the oldest section of the current building. The whole thing was given a Renaissance enlargement in the late sixteenth century, and again remodelled in the 1720s. Princes and dukes aside, the building has been used as a brewery, office block, barracks and anti-aircraft emplacement – the last function being the direct cause of its flattening in an air raid in 1944. Reconstruction continued into the 1980s, since when it's been turned into a museum and cultural centre. The **Muzeum Zamkowe** (Castle Museum; Tues–Sun: July–Aug 10am–6pm; Sept–June 10am–4pm; 8zł) occupies a few vaults, displaying some repaired sarcophagi as well as photographs of the castle's restoration from postwar ruin. The chapel on the ground floor of the north wing is now a concert hall. In the east wing, much of the exterior decoration has been reworked with the addition of a few more faux concrete windows and the castle's distinctive clock; most of this section is now occupied by a cinema and other cultural facilities. If you're here in summer, you might get to hear an open-air concert in the castle courtyard.

It's worth climbing the two hundred or so steps up the *wieża*, or **bell tower** (same hours as museum; 3zł) for the view over the city, port and surroundings. You'll notice a striking absence of industrial chimneys; instead church spires and dockside cranes pierce the skyline.

North of the castle

Immediately to the west of the castle is ul. Farna, where the residence of the commandant formerly stood. This was the birthplace in 1729 of Sophie von Anhalt-Zerbst, a princess of a very minor German aristocratic line who has gone down in history as **Empress Catherine the Great of Russia**. A character of extreme ruthlessness – she deposed her own husband, and was probably behind his subsequent murder – her reputation has always been a matter of controversy. Among her "achievements" was a considerable imperialistic expansion, one manifestation of which was a leading role in the three Partitions that wiped Poland off the map. That her native city is now Polish is truly ironic.

A couple of blocks further west is ul. Staromłyńska, at the corner of which rises an elegant Baroque palace, formerly the Pomeranian parliament and now home of a section of the **Muzeum Narodowe** at no. 27 (National Museum; Tues–Sun 10am–4pm; 10zł). The ground floor features several important Polish artists, most notably Waliszewski, Zofia Stryjenska and the broodingly introspective Jacek Malczewski. Upstairs there's a mushy collection of paintings by local artists on sea-based themes, although the fine Baroque-era furniture is worth an admiring look. Older works are displayed in the annexe across the street. On the ground floor here is an impressive display of medieval Pomeranian **sculpture**. Highlights include the thirteenth-century columns topped with delicately carved capitals, from the monastery of Kołbacz; a monumental wooden sacramenteum of the same period from Wolin; and several expressively carved and painted mid-fifteenth-century triptychs from Pomerania. Upstairs, later sections emphasize Polish painters, with a token German work occasionally thrown in.

Across the broad open space of pl. Żołnierza Polskiego is the Baroque **Brama Hołdu Pruskiego** (Gate of Prussian Homage), whose design, with reliefs of military trophies, echo those of the Brama Portowa. Its interior is now used for changing exhibitions of the work of contemporary painters and photographers. Facing it to the east is the beguiling fourteenth-century **Kościół św. Piotra i Pawła** (Church of SS Peter and Paul), a Gothic church built on the site of one established by Polish missionaries in the early twelfth century. In a rich ensemble of original ornamental detail the most striking elements are the seventeenth-century memorial tablets, the German inscriptions reminding you of the city's Teutonic heritage, and the unusual wooden vaulting.

On the north side of the church, ul. Małopolska leads to **Wały Chrobrego**, a leafy promenade commanding an expansive panorama of the Odra River and the industrial suburbs on the far shore. The promenade – conceived as a showpiece of muscular civic architecture by Szczecin's pre-World War I German masters – is lined with an imposing sequence of prestigous public buildings. The central sandstone edifice, fronted by a grandiose staircase leading down to the river, now houses the **Muzeum Morskie** (Maritime Museum; Tues–Sun 10am–4pm; 6zł). Inside lies a wealth of material on seafaring Slavs and Celts, with graphic displays from the Stone, Iron and Bronze ages. Huge arrow-covered maps delineate bygone migrations, while upstairs a gallery is devoted to objects from classical antiquity. Most impressive and unexpected, however, is an inspired ethnographic exhibition with detailed dioramas of villages in Mali and the Ivory Coast, along with West African statues, fetishes and carved masks, displayed with highly dramatic lighting. On the next floor, a Papuan village gets the same treatment, although the budget or the enthusiasm seems to have waned at the rather feeble rendition of a Buddhist temple.

A block to the north of the museum lies the leafy **Park Żeromskiego**, the only significant stretch of park in the centre. Over beyond the western side of the park on pl. Rodła looms the **Kompleks Pazim** (Pazim Centre), a clutch of steel-framed, blue-glass buildings that contains a hotel (the *Radisson*; see p.647), shopping centre and business complex.

The harbour

Szczecin is one of the largest ports on the Baltic, with a highly developed shipping industry, and you'll appreciate the essence of the city more fully if you take a **boat trip** round the port and harbour. Excursions, lasting just over an hour, leave from the quayside below the Maritime Museum, where you'll also find current timetables. Ask here about the boat and hydrofoil services across the vast Szczecin Lagoon to Świnoujście (see p.644).

The outskirts

Despite the patchily built-up character of its centre, Szczecin has plenty of stretches of greenery, which are ideal for a quick break from the urban bustle, particularly on summer evenings. Just to the north of the centre is the **Park Kasprowicza**, which can be reached on trams #1 or #9 or by walking up al. Jedności Narodowej from the centre. After negotiating the ornamental flowerbeds at the park's southern end, you soon reach the huge triple-eagle monument made to commemorate the fortieth anniversary of the outbreak of World War II, symbolizing the three generations of Poles who lost their lives. Proceeding northwest through the park, the **Ogród Dendrologiczny** (Dendrological Garden) on the east bank of the narrow Lake Rusałka contains over two hundred species of trees and shrubs, including a host of exotic varieties, such as Californian redwoods. Beyond the lake, tree-lined paths continue towards **Park Głębokie**, a full 5km out of the centre (and also reached by riding trams #1 and #9 to the **Głębokie** terminus), arranged around the sausage-shaped lake of the same name. This is a much wilder, less developed area, perfect for tranquil woodland walks.

The most distinctive park in the city is that in the eastern suburb of **Zdroje**, reached by a slow train or buses. Here you'll find a number of hiking trails, a couple of restaurants, and the **Jezioro Szmaragdowe** (Emerald Lake), which was created in the 1920s by flooding a former quarry; you can go for a swim here, or simply admire the play of light on its deep green waters.

Eating, drinking and entertainment

The gastronomic situation in Szczecin is as varied as in any other big Polish city, with a reasonable number of places offering good-quality Polish food, alongside a growing number of ethnic alternatives. Most restaurants stay open till 11pm, with one or two remaining open into the early hours.

Despite the rash of outdoor beer stalls that fill al. Z. Głębokie olnierza Polskiego in summer, there are no real night-time strolling areas in Szczecin, and most people aim for a particular bar rather than crawling from one to the other. Fortunately, there are loads of good **pubs** and **bars** in the main downtown area, with new ones opening up all the time – many of them also serve up good food.

Restaurants and cafés

Bombay ul. Partyzantów 1. Upmarket Indian restaurant a few steps south of the Brama Portowa, with exemplary service and a reasonably authentic menu, including some vegetarian dishes – although the spice level is on the bland side.

Café Galeria Mariacka. Stylish café-restaurant down a side street near the Brama Hołdu Pruskiego, with salads, sandwiches and a range of contemporary European mains. Also does breakfast from 10am.

Chata pl. Hołdu Pruskiego 8. Best place in town for traditional Polish food, offering roast duck, wild boar and pheasant alongside traditional porky standards. Lots of homely wooden furniture, and folksy paintings on the wall. More expensive than average but not prohibitively so. Deservedly popular with the foreign contingent.

Chief ul. Rayskiego 16. Seafood specialists. Worth a visit for the decor alone – one wall is covered in shells, another in stuffed fish heads and the window is filled by an enormous sturgeon.

Cukiernia Koch al. Wojska Polskiego 4. Prime downtown venue for relaxing over a cup of coffee or pigging out on the decadent range of pastries and cakes. There's another branch at Wyzwolenia 14.

Duet ul. Bogusława 1/2. Relaxing café with a wide choice of teas, cakes and ice creams.

Haga ul. Sienna 10. Cosy Dutch-style pancake restaurant. Good location opposite the old town hall, and excellent food.

Pod Muzami pl. Żołnierza Polskiego 2. Long-established restaurant serving mid-priced European fare in a place that looks like an old-fashioned nightclub: a basement with mauve decor, mirror ball and dance floor. DJs or show bands play golden oldies.

Restauracja na Kuncu Korytarza Inside the castle (see p.649). A mildly bohemian spot, popular with opera-goers and music students from the neighbouring academy, who come for classic Polish grub or to spend hours over coffee.

Rybarex ul. Obrońców Stalingradu 5a. Inexpensive fish bar with a wide and adventurous selection of dishes: ideal for fast lunchtime service. Closes at 7pm Mon–Fri, at 5pm on Sat. Closed Sun.

Sake ul. Piastow 1. New Japanese place serving sushi and tempura.

Sphinx ul. Wojska Polskiego 20. Part of a growing Polish chain – good-value kebabs and grills in themed Middle Eastern surroundings.

Virga Park Głębokie. Five kilometres northwest of the centre, just behind the terminus of trams #1 and #9; it's ideal stop-off after an afternoon walking in the nearby woods of Park Głębokie. Solid and not-too-expensive veal-and-pork repertoire, in a cosy room decorated with kooky ceramics and glassware.

Bars

Brama Jazz Café Inside the Brama Hołdu Pruskiego, pl. Hołdu Pruskiego 1. Chic, barrel-vaulted space, usually with art exhibits on the walls. Good choice of baguettes and salads. Frequent live jazz. Outdoor terrace in summer.

Café Prawda Wielka Odrzańska 20. Cool bar for cool people on the riverfront just behind the old town hall. Minimalist decor, cutting-edge dance music in the background, and a basement bar where DJs play at weekends.

Christopher Columbus Wały Chrobrego. Curving timber-and-glass pavilion on a leafy promenade, enjoying good views of the riverfront down below. Plenty of outdoor seating; it's a good place to spend a summer afternoon.

Club Kancler ul. Sienna 7. Noisy and cheerful bar near the old town hall with frequent gig nights showcasing a variety of local bands.

Hormon corner of pl. Odrodzenia and al. Piłsudskiego ⓦ www.hormon.pl. Spacious bare-brick cellar welcoming a trendy cross-section of teens and twenty-somethings. DJs or live bands provide entertainment at the weekends, when there's an entrance fee.

Irish Pub Dublin ul. Kaszubska 57. Prime place for a relaxing drink immediately north of the Brama Portowa, with dark wood furnishings, minimal lighting and unobtrusive music. Hearty meat dishes, and a good choice of salads on the menu.

Nautilus Pub ul. Jana z Kolna 7. Lively riverside pub with lots of outdoor seating. Turquoise colour scheme and odd bits of boat hanging from the ceiling help to hammer home the nautical theme. Extensive food menu.

Rocker Club ul. Partyzantów 2. Large, pub-style basement bar a block south of the Brama Portowa, with middle-of-the-road rock music either on tape or performed by local cover bands. Entrance fee on gig nights.

Nightlife and entertainment

For **clubbing**, *Fabryka* at Wojska Polskiego 128 is a lively weekend dance venue. *Trans*, southwest of the centre at al. Powstańców Wielkopolskich 20, is a student club with a fairly eclectic selection of DJs and gigs; *Kontrasty* at Wawrzyniaka 7 has a similarly broad range of events. Another place with regular live music is *Słowianin*, a municipally funded cultural centre just above the bus station on ul. Korzeniowskiego, which acts as an umbrella for all kinds of alternative activities and indie gigs – you'll recognize it by the psychedelic portraits of the Beatles and other idols graffitied onto the outside walls.

The Filharmonia Szczecińska, pl. Armii Krajowy 1 (☎091/422 1252), has a regular programme of **classical music** concerts, while operas and operettas are performed in the opera house at ul. Korsarzy 34 (☎091/480 0340). Szczecin's main **theatre** is the Teatr Polski, ul. Swarożyca 3 (☎091/433 0075), although the Teatr Wspólczesny, ul. Wały Chrobrego 3 (☎091/489 2323), offers a wider range of modern Polish drama. **Puppet shows** are held at the Teatr Lalek Pleciuga, ul. Kaszubska 9 (☎091/433 2821). You'll find a cluster of multiplex **cinemas** around the south end of al. Wojska Polskiego.

The Friday edition of *Gazeta Wyborcza* is the best source of **listings** information. **Annual events** include the Days of the Sea in June, which feature yacht races, parades and performances of sea shanties; a contemporary painting festival in July; and a festival of Orthodox church music in November.

Listings

Airlines LOT, ul. Wyzwolenia 17 ☎0801 300 852.
Books and Newspapers English-language press at EMPiK, on the corner of al. Wojska Polskiego and pl. Zwycięstwa.
Cinemas Colosseum, ul. 5 Lipca; Delfin, ul. Piłsudskiego 42; Kosmos, al. Wojska Polskiego 8.
Ferries Polska Żegluga Baltycka, ul. Wyszynskiego 28 (☎091/488 0238, ⓦwww.polferries.com), and Unity Line, pl. Rodła 8 (☎091/359 5692, ⓦwww.unityline.pl), sell tickets for services from Świnoujście to Denmark and Sweden.
Hospital Pomorski Akademii Medycznej, al. Unii Lubelskiej 1. Tram #1 or #9.
Internet access *Portal*, ul. Kaszubska 52, south off pl. Wycięstwa, entrance in the yard round the back of the building (daily 24 hrs).
Left luggage At the train station (see p.647).
Pharmacy There's a 24hr *apteka* at ul. Więckowskiego 12, off the north side of pl. Wycęstwa.
Post office Main office at ul. Bogurodzicy 1 (Mon–Fri 8am–8pm, Sat 9am–2pm).
Travel agents Orbis, pl. Zwycięstwa 1 (☎091/434 7563), handles international plane and bus tickets. Interglobus, at the train station (☎091/485 0422), sells in bus tickets to Germany, Britain and other European destinations.

Stargard Szczeciński

Some 35km southeast of Szczecin, on the Bydgoszcz road, lies **STARGARD SZCZECIŃSKI**. Situated on the River Ina, leading to the Odra and the Baltic, Stargard was once an important trading town and in the seventeenth century served briefly as Pomerania's capital when the Swedes occupied Szczecin. Stargard suffered severe damage in World War II, but a handful of spectacular medieval buildings survives and is definitely worth a look if you're passing through.

The Stare Miasto

From the train or bus station, it's just a few minutes' walk down ul. Kardynała Wyszyńskiego to the **Stare Miasto**, girded by substantial remains of the fifteenth-century city walls. **Park Chrobrego** stretches along the outer side of the wall and contains the longest-surviving portion of the ramparts. Following ul. Chrobrego downhill from here brings you to the river. To your left stands the most impressive survivor of the fortification system, the **Brama Młyńska** (Mill Gate), protected by a mighty pair of spire-topped octagonal towers. The gate bridges the river and was big enough for boats to pass beneath.

The **Rynek**, five minutes' walk from the Mill Gate, is a mixture of the old – handsome burghers' houses – and the new – unprepossessing 1970s concrete. At the corner stands the renovated **town hall**, a plain Renaissance structure featuring a superbly curvaceous gable adorned with colourful terracotta tracery. Next to it is the **guard house**, whose open arcades and loggia suggest the Mediterranean rather than the Baltic and the **Waga Miejska** (Weigh House). Here you'll find the local **museum** (Tues–Sun 10am–4pm; 5zł; free Sun) along with a small **tourist information** office (Mon–Fri 10am–4pm, Sat 10am–1pm).

Beside the town hall stands the magnificent **Kościół Mariacki** (Church of Our Lady), one of the most original and decorative examples of the brickwork Gothic style found in the Baltic lands, probably the work of Hinrich Brunsberg and commissioned around 1400. The two towers, with their glazed green and white ceramics, can be seen from all over the town. The southern one, flanked by a luscious coat of ivy, resembles a great tower-house; its higher northern counterpart is a truly bravura creation, topped by four chimney-like turrets and a great central octagon, itself crowned in the Baroque era with a two-storey copper lantern. The east end of the church and the protruding octagonal chapel are decorated with carved brick. The interior was impressively repainted in the nineteenth century and features an earlier and quite over-the-top illusionist altarpiece.

There's not much beyond the Rynek to keep you in Stargard, but should you need to **stay** there are two reasonable options: the *Staromiejski*, which offers plain serviceable rooms on ul. Spichrzowa 2 (☎092/577 2223; ❸); and the nearby *Hotel PTTK*, ul. Kuśnierzy 5 (☎092/578 3191; ❸). If you need a **place to eat** there's the *Ratuszowa* on the Rynek for straightforward Polish food and a café in the tourist information building.

Travel details

Trains

Bydgoszcz to: Częstochowa (5 daily; 5hr); Gdańsk (hourly; 2hr); Kołobrzeg (June–Aug only; 8 daily; 4hr); Kraków (1 daily; 8hr); Łódź Kaliska (5 daily; 3–4hr); Poznań (8 daily; 2–3hr); Toruń (hourly; 1hr); Warsaw (5 daily; 4–5hr).

Gniezno to: Bydgoszcz (7 daily; 1hr 10min–1hr 30min); Gdańsk (5 daily; 4hr); Inowrocław (14 daily; 50min–1hr); Mogilno (10 daily; 30min); Poznań (14 daily; 50min–1hr); Toruń (4 daily; 1hr 30min–2hr); Wrocław (6 daily; 3hr 10min).

Kalisz to: Łódź (7 daily; 1hr 30min–2hr); Wrocław (4 daily; 2hr–3hr 30min).

Kamień Pomorski to: Szczecin (3 daily; 1hr 30min).

Kołobrzeg to: Bydgoszcz (June–Aug only; 8 daily; 4hr); Gdańsk (2 daily; 3hr 30min); Gryfice (3 daily; 1hr); Koszalin (5 daily; 1hr); Poznań (1 daily; 4hr); Szczecin (2 daily; 3hr); Trzebiatów (3 daily; 30min); Warsaw (2 daily; 8hr).

Leszno to: Bydgoszcz (4 daily; 3hr 30min–4hr 30min); Poznań (20 daily; 50min–1hr 10min); Wrocław (16 daily; 1hr 20min–2hr).

Lębork to: Łeba (4 daily; 50min).

Międzyzdroje to: Szczecin (8 daily; 1hr 45min); Świnoujście (1 daily; 20min).

Poznań to: Bydgoszcz (6 daily; 2hr 30min–3hr); Gdańsk (5 daily; 5hr); Gniezno (14 daily; 50min–1hr); Inowrocław (13 daily; 1hr 40min–2hr); Katowice (4 daily; 5hr); Kołobrzeg (3 daily; 4–5hr); Koszalin (2 daily; 4hr); Kraków (4 daily; 6hr); Leszno (20 daily; 50min–1hr 10min); Łódź (1 daily; 3hr 15min); Lublin (1 daily; 6hr); Słupsk (2 daily; 5hr); Szczecin (9 daily; 3–4hr);

Świnoujście (3 daily; 5hr); Toruń (4 daily; 2hr 20min–3hr); Warsaw (Mon–Sat 13 daily, Sun 9 daily; 3hr–3hr 30min); Wrocław (16 daily; 2hr–2hr 40min); Zielona Góra (6 daily; 2hr 40min); Wolsztyn (5 daily; 1hr 50min).

Słupsk to: Gdańsk (10 daily; 2hr 30min); Kołobrzeg (Jul–Aug 6 daily, rest of year 2 daily; 2hr 30min); Koszalin (hourly; 50min); Szczecin (5 daily; 3hr); Ustka (6 daily; 25min).

Szczecin to: Gdańsk (5 daily; 5hr 20min); Kamień Pomorski (3 daily; 1hr 30min); Kołobrzeg (2 daily; 3hr); Koszalin (8 daily; 2hr 20min); Kraków (4 daily; 9hr); Lębork (4 daily; 4hr); Łódź (1 daily; 6hr); Poznań (12 daily; 2hr 20min); Słupsk (5 daily; 3hr); Świnoujście (8 daily; 2hr); Warsaw (5 daily; 5–6hr; couchettes).

Świnoujście to: Kraków (1 daily; 13hr; couchettes); Szczecin (8 daily; 2hr); Warsaw (1 daily; 9hr; couchettes).

Buses

Bydgoszcz to: Chełmno (1 daily; 1hr); Chojnice (12 daily; 2hr 30min); Gniezno (6 daily; 2hr 20min); Kruszwica (4 daily; 1hr 35min); Toruń (hourly; 1hr); Żnin (hourly; 1hr).

Darłowo to: Koszalin (3 daily; 1hr); Słupsk (4 daily; 1hr 20min); Ustka (1 daily; 1hr).

Gdynia to: Łeba (July & Aug 3 daily; Sept–June 1 daily; 2hr 10min); Lębork (9 daily; 1hr); Międzyzdroje (2 daily; 8hr).

Gniezno to: Bydgoszcz (6 daily; 2hr 20min); Gąsawa (10 daily; 50min); Mogilno (10 daily; 1hr); Trzemeszno (hourly; 30min); Żnin (12 daily; 1hr 5min).

Inowrocław to: Bydgoszcz (hourly; 1hr); Kruszwica (every 30min; 35min); Strzelno (hourly; 50min); Toruń (8 daily; 1hr); Żnin (Mon–Fri 8 daily, Sat & Sun 6 daily; 1hr 20min).

Kalisz to: Gołuchów (12 daily; 20min); Poznań (8 daily; 2hr 30min); Wrocław (7 daily; 2hr 40min).

Kamień Pomorski to: Kołobrzeg (4 daily; 1hr 45min); Międzyzdroje (hourly; 1hr); Stargard Szczeciński (1 daily; 1hr 30min); Szczecin (9 daily; 1hr 45min); Świnoujście (every 30 min; 1hr 15min); Wolin (12 daily; 1hr).

Kołobrzeg to: Kamień Pomorski (4 daily; 1hr 45min); Koszalin (7 daily; 1hr 10min); Poznań (5 daily; 5hr); Trzebiatów (hourly; 45–55min).

Koszalin to: Darłowo (3 daily; 1hr); Kołobrzeg (7 daily; 1hr 10min); Mielno (5 daily; 20min); Unieście (5 daily; 25min).

Łeba to: Gdynia (July–Aug 3 daily; Sept–June 1 daily; 2hr 10min); Lębork (every 30 min; 30min); Słupsk (8 daily; 1hr 30min).

Międzyzdroje to: Gdańsk (1 daily; 8hr); Gdynia (2 daily; 8hr); Kamień Pomorski (hourly; 1hr); Szczecin (July & Aug 4 daily; Sept–June 2 daily; 2hr 15min); Świnoujście (every 20min; 20min).

Poznań to: Gołuchów (8 daily; 2hr 10min); Kalisz (8 daily; 2hr 30min); Kórnik (16 daily; 30min); Wolsztyn (10 daily; 2hr); Zielona Góra (6 daily; 2hr 30min–3hr 30min).

Słupsk to: Darłowo (4 daily; 1hr 20min); Kołobrzeg (2 daily; 1hr 45min); Koszalin (9 daily; 1hr 45min); Łeba (8 daily; 1hr 30min); Ustka (every 20min; 45min).

Szczecin to: Czaplinek (3 daily; 2hr 45min); Międzyzdroje (July & Aug 4 daily; Sept–June 2 daily; 2hr 15min); Stargard Szczeciński (hourly; 50min); Szczecinek (3 daily; 3hr 40min); Świnoujście (2 daily; 2hr 35min).

Świnoujście to: Międzyzdroje (every 20min; 20min); Szczecin (2 daily; 2hr 35min).

Ustka to: Darłowo (1 daily; 1hr); Koszalin (2 daily; 2hr 5min); Słupsk (every 20min; 45min).

Wolsztyn to: Poznań (10 daily; 2hr); Zielona Góra (8 daily; 1hr–1hr 20min).

Żnin to: Bydgoszcz (8 daily; 1hr 15min); Gąsawa (every 30min; 20min); Gniezno (8 daily; 1hr 5min); Inowrocław (Mon–Fri 8 daily; Sat & Sun 6 daily; 1hr 20min).

Zielona Góra to: Poznań (6 daily; 2hr 30min–3hr 30min); Żagań (hourly; 1hr 15min).

International trains

Poznań to: Berlin (4 daily; 3hr 15min).
Szczecin to: Berlin (12 daily; 2hr 20min).

International ferries

Świnoujście to: Ahlbeck (Jun–Sept; 8 daily; 15min); Bansin (June–Sept; 3 daily; 25min); Bornholm (1 weekly; 6hr); Copenhagen (5 weekly; 10hr); Heringsdorf (June–Sept 3 daily; 20min); Malmö (1 daily; 10hr); Ystad (1 daily; 9hr).

Contexts

Contexts

History 659–682

Polish music 683–691

Books 692–704

History

Few other European countries have had so chequered a history as Poland. At its mightiest, it has been a huge commonwealth stretching deep into the Baltics, Russia and the Ukraine; at its nadir, it has been a nation that existed only as an ideal, its neighbours having on two occasions conspired to wipe it off the map. Yet, for all this, a distinctive Polish culture has survived and developed without interruption for more than a millennium.

The beginnings

The great plain that is present-day Poland, stretching from the River Odra (or Oder) in the west all the way to the Russian steppes, has been inhabited since the Stone Age. For thousands of years it was home to numerous tribes – some nomadic, others settlers – whose traces have made Poland a particularly fruitful land for archeologists. Lying beyond the frontiers of the Roman Empire, it did not sustain anything more socially advanced than a tribal culture until a relatively late date.

The exact period when this plain was first settled by Slav tribes is uncertain, but it may have been as late as the eighth century. Although diffuse, the various **Slav** groups shared a common culture – certainly to a far greater extent than is true of the Germanic tribes to the west – and the Polish language can be said to have existed before the Polish state.

It was the **Polonians** (the "people of the open fields"), based on the banks of the River Warta between Poznań and Gniezno, who were ultimately responsible for the forging of a recognizable nation, which thereafter bore their name. From the early ninth century, they were ruled by the **Piast** dynasty, whose early history is shrouded in legend but emerges into something more substantial with the beginnings of recorded history in the second half of the tenth century.

In 965, the Piast **Mieszko I** married the sister of the Duke of Bohemia and underwent public baptism, thus placing himself under the protection of the papacy. Mieszko's motives appear to have been political: Otto the Great, the Holy Roman Emperor, had extended Germany's border to the Odra and would have had little difficulty in justifying a push east against a pagan state. By 990, Mieszko had succeeded in uniting his tribal area, henceforth known as Wielkopolska (Great Poland), with that of the Vistulanian tribe, which took the name of Małopolska (Little Poland). Silesia, settled by yet another Slav tribe, became the third component of this embryonic Polish state.

Mieszko's policies were carried to their logical conclusion by his warrior son **Bolesław the Brave**. In 1000, the Emperor Otto III was dispatched by the pope to pay tribute to the relics of the Czech saint, Adalbert, which Bolesław had acquired. During his stay, the emperor crowned Bolesław with his own crown, thus renouncing German designs on Polish territory. Subsequently, Bolesław established control over Pomerania, Kujawy and Mazovia; he also gained and lost Bohemia and began Poland's own easterly drive, pushing as far as Kiev. The name "Poland" now came into general use, and its status as a fully fledged kingdom was underlined by Bolesław's decision to undergo a second coronation in 1022.

Piast Poland

By the middle of the eleventh century, Małopolska had become the centre of the nation's affairs and Kraków had replaced Gniezno as capital, owing to Wielkopolska's vulnerability to the expansionist Czechs and Germans. Political authority was in any case overshadowed by the power of the Church: when **Bishop Stanisław** of Kraków was murdered in 1079 on the orders of **Bolesław the Generous**, the clergy not only gained a national saint whose cult quickly spread, but also succeeded in dethroning the king.

In the early twelfth century, centralized monarchical power made a comeback under **Bolesław the Wrymouth**, who regained Pomerania – which had become an independent duchy – and repulsed German designs on Silesia. However, he undid his lifetime's work by a decision to divide his kingdom among his sons; for the rest of the century and beyond, Poland lacked central authority and was riven by feuds as successive members of the Piast dynasty jostled for control over the key provinces. Pomerania fell to Denmark, while Silesia began a long process of fragmentation, becoming increasingly Germanic.

In 1225 **Duke Konrad of Mazovia**, under threat from the heathen Prussians, Jacwingians and Lithuanians on his eastern border, invited the **Teutonic Knights**, a quasi-monastic German military order, to help him secure his frontiers. The knights duly based themselves in Chełmno, and by 1283 they had effectively eradicated the Prussians. Emerging as the principal military power in northern Europe, the knights built up a theocratic state defended by some of the most awesome castles ever built, ruthlessly turning on their former hosts in the process. They captured the great port of Gdańsk in 1308, renaming it Danzig and developing it into one of Europe's richest mercantile cities. At the same time, German peasants were encouraged to settle on the fertile agricultural land all along the Baltic. Poland was left cut off from the sea, with its trading routes severely weakened as a result.

If the Teutonic Knights brought nothing but disaster to the Polish nation, the effects of the **Tatar invasions** of 1241–42 were more mixed. Although the Poles were decisively defeated at the **Battle of Legnica**, the Tatars' crushing of the Kiev-based Russian empire paved the way for Polish expansion east into White and Red Ruthenia (the forerunners of Belarus and Ukraine), whose principalities were often linked to Poland by dynastic marriages. On the down side, the defeat spelt the beginning of the end for Silesia as part of Poland. It gradually split into eighteen tiny duchies under the control of Bohemia, then the most powerful part of the Holy Roman Empire.

It was only under the last Piast king, **Kazimierz the Great** (1333–70), that central political authority was firmly re-established in Poland. Kraków took on some aspects of its present appearance during his reign, being embellished with a series of magnificent buildings to substantiate its claim to be a great European capital. It was also made the seat of a university, the first in the country and before long one of the most prestigious on the continent. Kazimierz's achievements in domestic policy went far beyond the symbolic: he codified Poland's laws, created a unified administrative structure with a governor responsible for each province, and introduced a new silver currency.

With regard to Poland's frontiers, Kazimierz was a supreme pragmatist. He secured his borders with a line of stone castles and formally recognized Bohemia's control over **Silesia** in return for a renunciation of its claim to the Polish crown. More reluctantly, he accepted the existence of the independent state of the Teutonic Knights, even though that meant Poland was now landlocked. To compensate, he extended his territories east into **Red Ruthenia** and **Podolia**, which meant that, although the Catholic Church retained its prominent role, the country now had sizeable Eastern Orthodox and Armenian minorities.

Even more significant was Kazimierz's encouragement of **Jews**, who had been the victims of pogroms all over Europe, often being held responsible for the Black Death. A law of 1346 specifically protected them against persecution in Poland and was a major factor in Poland's centuries-long position as the home of the largest community of world Jewry.

The Jagiellonians

On Kazimierz's death, the crown passed to his nephew **Louis of Anjou**, king of Hungary, but this royal union was short-lived, as the Poles chose Louis' younger daughter **Jadwiga** to succeed him in 1384, while her sister ascended the Hungarian throne. This event was important for two reasons. First, it was an assertion of power on the part of the aristocracy and the beginnings of the move towards an elected monarchy. Second, it led soon afterwards to the most important and enduring alliance in Polish history – with Lithuania, whose grand duke, Jogaila (henceforth known to history by his Polish name, **Władysław Jagiełło**), married Jadwiga in 1386. Europe's last pagan nation, Lithuania had resisted the Teutonic Knights and developed into an expansionist state that now stretched from its Baltic homeland all the way to the Crimea.

After Jadwiga's death in 1399, Jagiełło reigned over the two nations alone for the next 45 years, founding the Jagiellonian dynasty – which was to remain in power until 1572 – with the offspring of his subsequent marriage. One of the first benefits of the alliance between Poland and Lithuania was a military strength capable of taking the offensive against the Teutonic Knights, and at the **Battle of Grunwald** in 1410, the order was defeated, beginning its long and slow decline. A more decisive breakthrough came as a result of the **Thirteen Years' War** of 1454–66. By the **Treaty of Toruń**, the knights' territory was partitioned: Danzig became an independent city-state, run by a merchant class of predominantly German, Dutch and Flemish origins, but accepting the Polish king as its nominal overlord; the remainder of the knights' heartlands around the Lower Wisła (Vistula) became subject to Poland under the name of Royal Prussia; and the order was left only with the eastern territory thereafter known as Ducal Prussia or East Prussia, where it established its new headquarters in the city of Königsberg.

Towards the end of the fifteenth century, Poland and Lithuania began to face new dangers from the east. First to threaten were the **Crimean Tatars**, whose menace prompted the creation of the first Polish standing army. A far more serious threat – one which endured for several hundred years – came from the **Muscovite tsars**, the self-styled protectors of the Orthodox faith who aimed to "liberate" the Ruthenian principalities and rebuild the Russian empire which had been destroyed by the Mongol Tatars. The Jagiellonians countered by building up their power in the west. The Bohemian crown was acquired by clever politicking in 1479 after the religious struggles of the Hussite Wars; that of Hungary followed in 1491. However, neither of these unions managed to last.

The Renaissance and Reformation

The spread of **Renaissance** ideas in Poland – greatly facilitated by the country's Church connections with Italy – was most visibly manifested in the large number of Italianate buildings constructed throughout the country, but science and learning also prospered under native Polish practitioners such as **Nicolaus Copernicus**.

This period saw a collective muscle-flexing exercise by the Polish nobility (*szlachta*). In 1493, the parliament, or **Sejm**, was established, gaining the sole right to enact legislation in 1505 and gradually making itself an important check on monarchical power.

The **Reformation** had a far greater impact on Poland than is often admitted by Catholic patriots. Its most telling manifestation came in 1525, with the final collapse of the Teutonic Order when the grand master, Albrecht von Hohenzollern, decided to accept the new Lutheran doctrines. Their state was converted into a secular duchy under the Polish crown but with full internal autonomy – an arrangement which removed any lingering military strength from the order. Lutheranism also took a strong hold in Danzig and the German-dominated cities of Royal Prussia, while the more radical Calvinism won many converts among the Lithuanian nobility. Poland also became home for a number of refugee sects: along with the acceptance already extended to the Jewish and Orthodox faiths, this added up to a degree of religious tolerance unparalleled elsewhere in Europe.

The Republic of Nobles

Lacking an heir, the last of the Jagiellonians, **Sigismund August**, spent his final years trying to forge an alliance strong enough to withstand the ever-growing might of Moscow. The result of his negotiations was the 1569 **Union of Lublin**, whereby Poland and Lithuania were formally merged into the **Commonwealth of the Two Nations**. Lithuania, whose aristocracy was by now almost wholly Polish-speaking, lost many of its autonomous privileges, and its huge territories in the east were integrated more closely into the Polish state. In the same year the Sejm moved to Warsaw, a more central location for the capital of this new agglomeration; its capital status became official in 1596.

On the death of Sigismund August in 1572, the royal chancellor, **Jan Zamoyski**, presided over negotiations which led to the creation of the so-called "**Republic of Nobles**" – thenceforth kings were to be elected by an assembly of the entire nobility, from the great magnates down to holders of tiny impoverished estates. On the one hand this was a major democratic advance, in that it enfranchised about ten percent of the population, by far the largest proportion of voters in any European country; but on the other hand it marked a strengthening of a feudalistic social system. Capitalism, then developing in other European countries, evolved only in those cities with a strong German or Jewish **burgher** class (predominantly in Royal Prussia), which remained isolated from the main power structures of Polish society.

In 1573, the Frenchman **Henri Valois** was chosen as the first elected monarch and, as was the case with all his successors, was forced to sign a document that reduced him to a managerial servant of the nobility. The nobles also insisted on their **Right of Resistance** – a licence to overthrow a king who had fallen from favour. The Sejm had to be convened at two-yearly intervals, while all royal taxes, declarations of war and foreign treaties were subject to ratification by the nobles.

Although candidates for the monarchy had to subscribe to Catholicism, the religious freedom that already existed was underpinned by the **Compact of Warsaw** of 1573, guaranteeing the constitutional equality of all religions. However, the Counter-Reformation left only a few Protestant strongholds in Poland: a large section of the aristocracy was reconverted, while others who had recently switched from Orthodoxy to Calvinism were persuaded to change allegiance once more. The Orthodox Church was further weakened by the schism of 1596, leading to the creation of the Uniate Church, which recognized the authority of Rome. Thus Poland gradually became a fervently Catholic nation once more.

The Republic of Nobles achieved some of its most spectacular successes early on, particularly under the second elected king, the Transylvanian prince **Stefan Bathory**. Having carried out a thorough reform of the army, he waged a brilliant campaign against the Russians between 1579 and 1582, neutralizing this particular threat to Poland's eastern borders for some time to come.

The Waza dynasty and its aftermath

The foreign policy of the next three elected monarchs, all members of the Swedish **Waza dynasty**, was less fortunate. **Sigismund August Waza**, the first of the trio, was a Catholic bigot who soon came into conflict with the almost exclusively Protestant population of his native land and was deposed from the Swedish throne in 1604. Though his ham-fistedness meant that Poland now had a new (and increasingly powerful) enemy, he continued as the Polish king for the next 28 years, having fought off a three-year-long internal rebellion.

In 1618, Ducal Prussia was inherited by the elector of Brandenburg, **John Sigismund von Hohenzollern**, who set about weakening Poland's hold on the Baltic seaboard. A couple of decades later, the Hohenzollerns inherited much of Pomerania as well, with another section being acquired by Sweden. Poland managed to remain neutral in the calamitous series of religious and dynastic conflicts known as the **Thirty Years' War**, from which Sweden emerged as Europe's leading military power.

The reign of the third of the Wazas, **Jan Kazimierz**, saw Poland's fortunes plummet. In 1648, the year of his election, the Cossacks revolted in the Ukraine, eventually allying themselves with the Russian army, which conquered eastern Poland as far as Lwów. This diversion inspired the Swedes to launch an invasion of their own, known in Polish history as the **Swedish Deluge** ("Potop"), and they soon took control of the remainder of the country. A heroic fightback was mounted, ending in stalemate in 1660 with the **Treaty of Oliwa**, in which Poland recovered its former territories except for Livonia. Three years earlier, the Hohenzollerns had wrested Ducal Prussia from the last vestiges of Polish control, merging it with their other territories to form the state of Brandenburg-Prussia (later shortened to Prussia).

As well as the territorial losses suffered, these wars had seen Poland's population reduced to four million, less than half its previous total. A further crucial development of this period had been the first use in 1652 of the **liberum veto**, whereby a single vote in the Sejm was enough to stall any piece of legislation. Once established, the practice soon became widespread in the protection of petty interests, and Poland found itself on the slippery slope towards ungovernability. This process was hastened when it was discovered that one dissenter was constitutionally empowered to object not only to any particular measure, but to dissolve the Sejm itself – and in the process repeal all the legislation it had passed. Meanwhile, the minor aristocracy gradually found themselves squeezed out of power, as a group of a hundred or so great magnates gradually established a stranglehold.

Jan Sobieski

Before repeated use of the liberum veto led to the final collapse of political authority, Poland had what was arguably its greatest moment of glory in international power politics – a consequence of the Ottoman Turks' attempt to advance from the Balkans into central Europe. They were eventually beaten back by the Poles, under the command of **Jan Sobieski**, at the **Battle of Chocim** (in southwestern Ukraine) in 1673 – as a reward for which Sobieski was elected king the following year. In 1683 he was responsible for the successful defence of Vienna, which marked the final repulse of the Turks from western Europe.

However, Poland was to pay a heavy price for the heroism of Sobieski, who had concentrated on the Turkish campaign to the exclusion of all other issues at home and abroad. His relief of Vienna exhausted Poland's military capacity while enabling Austria to recover as an imperial power; it also greatly helped the rise of the predatory state of Prussia, which he had intended to keep firmly in check. His neglect of domestic policy led to the liberum veto being used with impunity, while Poland and Lithuania grew apart as the nobility of the latter engaged in a civil war.

The decline of Poland

Known as "**Augustus the Strong**", owing to his fathering of over three hundred children, Sobieski's successor, **Augustus Wettin**, was in fact a weak ruler, unable to shake off his debts to the Russians who had secured his election. In 1701, Friedrich III of Brandenburg-Prussia openly defied him by declaring Ducal Prussia's right to be regarded as a kingdom, having himself crowned in Königsberg. From then on, the Hohenzollerns plotted to link their territories by ousting Poland from the Baltic; in this they were aided by the acquisition of most of the rest of Pomerania in 1720. Augustus's lack of talent for power politics was even more evident in his dealings with Sweden, against whom he launched a war for control of Livonia. The conflict showed the calamitous decline of Poland's military standing, and the victorious Swedes deposed Augustus in 1704, securing the election of their own favoured candidate, **Stanisław Leszczyński**, in his place.

Augustus was reinstated in 1710, courtesy of the Russians, who effectively reduced Poland to the role of a client state in the process. The "**Silent Sejm**" of 1717, which guaranteed the existing constitution, marked the end of effective parliamentary life. The Russians never hesitated to impose their authority, cynically upholding the Republic of Nobles as a means of ensuring that the liberal ideals of the Age of Reason could never take root in Poland and that the country remained a buffer against the great powers of western Europe. When Leszczyński won the election to succeed Augustus the Strong in 1733, they intervened almost immediately to have him replaced by the deceased king's son, who proved to be an even more inept custodian of Polish interests than his father. Leszczyński was forced into exile, spending the last thirty years of his life as the duke of Lorraine.

In 1740, Frederick the Great launched the **Silesian Wars**, which ended in 1763 with Prussia in control of all but a small part of the province. As a result, Prussia gained control over such parts of Poland's foreign trade as were not subject to Russia. The long-cherished ambition to acquire Royal Prussia and thus achieve uninterrupted control over the southern coast of the Baltic was Frederick's next objective.

When the younger Augustus Wettin died in 1763, the Russians again intervened to ensure the election of **Stanisław-August Poniatowski**, the former lover of their empress, Catherine the Great. However, Poniatowski proved an unwilling stooge, even espousing the cause of reform. Russian support of the Orthodox minority in Poland led to a growth of Catholic-inspired nationalism, and by obstructing the most moderately liberal measures, Russian policy led to an outbreak of revolts. By sending armies to crush these, they endangered the delicate balance of power in Eastern Europe.

The Partitions

Russia's Polish policy was finally rendered impotent by the revolt of the **Confederacy of Bar** between 1768 and 1772. A heavy-handed crackdown on these reformers would certainly have led to war with Prussia, probably in alliance with Austria; doing nothing would have allowed the Poles to reassert their national independence. As a compromise, the Russians decided to support a Prussian plan for the **Partition of Poland**. By a treaty of 1772, Poland lost almost thirty percent of its territory. White Ruthenia's eastern sectors were ceded to Russia, while Austria received Red Ruthenia plus Małopolska south of the Wisła – a province subsequently rechristened Galicia. The Prussians gained the smallest share of the carve-up in the form of most of Royal Prussia, but this was strategically and economically the most significant.

Stung by this, the Poles embarked on a radical programme of reform, including the partial emancipation of serfs and the encouragement of immigration from the three empires which had undertaken the Partition. In 1791, Poland was given the first codified **constitution** in Europe since classical antiquity and the second in the modern world, after the United States. It introduced the concept of a people's sovereignty, this time including the bourgeoisie, and adopted a separation of powers between executive, legislature and judiciary, with government by a cabinet responsible to the Sejm.

This was all too much for the Russians, who, buying off the Prussians with the promise of Danzig, invaded Poland. Despite a tenacious resistance under **Tadeusz Kościuszko**, erstwhile hero of the American War of Independence, the Poles were defeated the following year. By the **Second Partition** of 1793, the constitution was annulled; the Russians annexed the remaining parts of White and Red Ruthenia, with the Prussians gaining Wielkopolska, parts of Mazuria and Toruń in addition to the star prize of Danzig. This time the Austrians held back and missed out on the spoils.

In 1794, Kościuszko launched a national insurrection, achieving a stunning victory over the Russians at the **Battle of Racławice** with a militia largely composed of peasants armed with scythes. However, the rebellion was put down, Poniatowski forced to abdicate, and Poland wiped off the map by the **Third Partition** of 1795. This gave all lands east of the Bug and Niemen rivers to Russia, the remainder of Małopolska to Austria, and the rest of the country, including Warsaw, to Prussia. By an additional treaty of 1797, the partitioning powers agreed to abolish the very name of Poland.

Napoleon and the Congress of Vienna

Revolutionary France was naturally the country that Polish patriots looked to in their struggle to regain national independence, and Paris became the headquarters for a series of exiles and conspiratorial groups. Hopes eventually crystallized around **Napoleon Bonaparte**, who assumed power in 1799, but when three Polish legions were raised as part of the French army, Kościuszko declined to command them, regarding Napoleon as a megalomaniac who would use the Poles for his own ends.

Initially, these fears seemed unfounded: French victories over Prussia led to the creation of the **Duchy of Warsaw** in 1807 out of Polish territory annexed by the Prussians. Although no more than a buffer state, this seemed an important first step in the re-creation of Poland and encouraged the hitherto uncommitted **Józef Poniatowski**, nephew of the last king and one of the most brilliant military commanders of the day, to throw in his lot with the French dictator. As a result of his successes in Napoleon's Austrian campaign of 1809, part of Galicia was ceded to the Duchy of Warsaw.

Poniatowski again played a key role in the events of 1812, which Napoleon dubbed his "**Polish War**" and which restored the historic border of Poland-Lithuania with Russia. The failure of the advance on Moscow, leading to a humiliating retreat, was thus as disastrous for Poland as for France. Cornered by the Prussians and Russians near Leipzig, Poniatowski refused to surrender, preferring to lead his troops to a heroic, suicidal defeat. The choice faced by Poniatowski encapsulated the nation's hopeless plight, and his act of self-sacrifice was to serve as a potent symbol to Polish patriots for the rest of the century.

The **Congress of Vienna** of 1814–15, set up to organize post-Napoleonic Europe, decided against the re-establishment of an independent Poland, mainly because this was opposed by the Russians. Instead, the main part of the Duchy of Warsaw was renamed the **Congress Kingdom** and placed under the dominion of the Russian tsar. The Poznań area was detached to form the Grand Duchy of Posen, in reality no more than a dependency of Prussia. Austria was allowed to keep most of Galicia, which was governed from Lwów (renamed Lemberg). After much deliberation, it was decided to make Kraków a city-state and "symbolic capital" of the vanished nation.

The struggle against the Partitions

The most liberal part of the Russian Empire, the Congress Kingdom, enjoyed a period of relative prosperity under the governorship of **Adam Czarto-ryski**, preserving its own parliament, administration, educational system and army. However, this cosy arrangement was disrupted by the arch-autocrat

Nicholas I, who became tsar in 1825 and quickly imposed his policies on Poland. An attempted **insurrection** in November 1830, centred on a botched assassination of the tsar's brother, provoked a Russian invasion. Initially, the Polish army fared well, but it was handicapped by political divisions (notably over whether the serfs should be emancipated) and lack of foreign support, despite the supposed guarantees provided by the Vienna settlement. By the end of the following year, the Poles had been defeated; their constitution was suspended and a reign of repression began. These events led many to abandon all nationalist hopes; the first great wave of Polish **emigration**, principally to America, began soon after.

An attempted insurrection against the Austrians in 1846 also backfired, leading to the end of Kraków's independence with its reincorporation into Galicia. This setback was a factor in Poland's failure to play an active role in the European-wide revolutions of 1848–49, though by this time the country's plight had attracted the sympathy of the emergent socialist movements. Karl Marx and Friedrich Engels went so far as to declare that Polish liberation should be the single most important immediate objective of the workers' movement. The last major uprising, against the Russians in 1863–64, attracted the support of Lithuanians and Galicians but was hopelessly limited by Poland's lack of a regular army. Its failure led to the abolition of the Congress Kingdom and its formal incorporation into Russia as the province of "Vistulaland". However, it was immediately followed by the **emancipation of the serfs**, granted on more favourable terms than in any other part of the tsarist empire – in order to cause maximum ill-feeling between the Polish nobility and peasantry.

Following the crushing of the 1863–64 rebellion, the **Russian sector** of Poland entered a period of quiet stability, with the abolition of internal tariffs opening up the vast Russian market to Polish goods. For the next half-century, Polish patriots, wherever they lived, were concerned less with trying to win independence than with keeping a distinctive culture alive. In this they were handicapped by the fact that this was an era of great empires, each with many subjugated minorities whose interests often conflicted: Poles found themselves variously up against the aspirations of Lithuanians, Ukrainians and Czechs. They had the greatest success in Galicia, because they were the second largest ethnic group in the Habsburg Empire, and because the Habsburgs had a more lax attitude towards the diversity of their subjects. The province was given powers of self-government and, although economically backward and ruled by a reactionary upper class, flourished once more as a centre of learning and the arts.

Altogether different was the situation in **Prussia**, the most efficiently repressive of the three partitioning powers. It had closely followed the British lead in forging a modern industrial society, and Poles made up a large percentage of the workforce in some of its technologically most advanced areas, notably the rich minefields of Upper Silesia. The Prussians, having ousted the Austrians from their centuries-long domination of German affairs, proceeded to exclude their rivals altogether from the united Germany they created by 1871, which they attempted to mould in their own Protestant and militaristic tradition.

For the Poles living under the Prussian yoke, the price to be paid for their relative prosperity was a severe clampdown on their culture, seen at its most extreme in the **Kulturkampf**, whose main aim was to crush the power of the Catholic Church, with a secondary intention of establishing the unchallenged supremacy of the German language in the new nation's educational system. It misfired badly in Poland, giving the clergy the opportunity to whip up support for their own fervently nationalistic brand of Catholicism.

Meanwhile, an upturn in political life came with the establishment, in response to internal pressure, of representative assemblies in Berlin, Vienna and St Petersburg. Towards the end of the century, this led to the formation of various new Polish **political parties** and movements, the most important of which were: the Polish Socialist Party (PPS), active mainly in the cities of Russian Poland; the Nationalist League, whose power base was in the peripheral provinces; the Peasant Movement of Galicia; and the Christian Democrats, a dominant force among the Silesian Catholics.

The resurrection of Poland

World War I smashed the might of the Russian, German and Austrian empires and allowed Poland to rise from the dead. Desperate to rally Poles to their cause, both alliances in the conflict made increasingly tempting offers: as early as August 1914 the Russians proposed a Poland with full rights of self-government, including language, religion and government, albeit one still ultimately subject to the tsar.

When the German and Austrian armies overran Russian-occupied Poland in 1916, they felt obliged to trump this offer, promising to set up a Polish kingdom once the war was over. The foundations of this were laid immediately, with the institution of an interim administration – known as the **Regency Council** – and the official restoration of the Polish language. Even though carried out for cynical reasons, these initial steps were of crucial importance to the relaunch of a fully independent Poland, a notion which had soon gained the support of the US President Woodrow Wilson and of the new Bolshevik government in Moscow.

Meanwhile, two bitter rivals had emerged as the leading contenders for leadership of the Polish nation. **Józef Piłsudski**, an impoverished noble from Lithuania and founding member of the PPS, had long championed a military solution to Poland's problems. During the war, his legions fought on behalf of the Germans, assuming that the defeat of the Russians would allow him to create the new Polish state on his own terms. In this, he favoured a return to the great tradition of ethnic and religious diversity of centuries past. **Roman Dmowski**, leader of the Nationalist League, represented the ambitions of the new middle class and had a vision of a purely Polish and staunchly Catholic future, in which the Jews would, as far as possible, be excluded. He opted to work for independence by exclusively political means, in the hope that victory over Germany would lead the Western allies to set up a Polish state under his leadership.

In the event, Piłsudski came out on top: the Germans, having held him in internment for well over a year, released him the day before the armistice of November 11, 1918, allowing him to take command of the Regency Council. He was sworn in as head of state three days later. Dmowski had to accept the consolation prize of head delegate to the Paris Peace Conference, though his associate, the concert pianist **Ignacy Jan Paderewski**, became the country's first prime minister.

Poland redefined

The new Poland lacked a defined territory. Initially, it consisted of the German and Austrian zones of occupation, centred on Warsaw and Lublin, plus Western

Galicia. Wielkopolska was added a month later, following a revolt against the German garrison in Poznań, but the precise frontiers were only established during the following three years on an ad-hoc basis. Yet, though the Paris Conference played only a minor role in all this, it did take the key decision to give the country access to the sea by means of the **Polish Corridor**, a strip of land cut through the old Royal Prussia, which meant that East Prussia was left cut off from the rest of Germany. Despite intense lobbying, it was decided to exclude Danzig from the corridor, on the grounds that its population was over-whelmingly German; instead, it reverted to its former tradition as a city-state – an unsatisfactory compromise that was later to have tragic consequences.

The **Polish–Soviet War** of 1919–20 was the most significant of the conflicts that crucially determined the country's borders. Realizing that the Bolsheviks would want to spread their revolution to Poland and then to the industrialized West, Piłsudski aimed to create a grouping of independent nation-states stretching from Finland to Georgia to halt this new expansionist Russian empire. Taking advantage of the civil war between the Soviet "Reds" and the counter-revolutionary "Whites", his army marched deep into Belarus and the Ukraine. He was subsequently beaten back to Warsaw, but skilfully regrouped his forces to pull off a crushing victory and pursue the Russians eastwards, regaining a sizeable chunk of the old Polish-Lithuanian commonwealth's eastern territories in the process, an acquisition confirmed by the **Treaty of Riga** in 1921.

At the very end of the war, Piłsudski seized his home city of **Wilno** (Vilnius), which had a mixed Polish and Jewish population, but was claimed by the Lithuanians on the grounds that it had been their medieval capital. Other border issues were settled by plebiscites organized by the League of Nations, the new international body set up to resolve such matters. In the most significant of these, Germany and Poland competed for Upper Silesia. The Germans won, but the margin was so narrow that the League felt that the distribution of votes justified the partition of the province. Poland gained most of the Katowice conurbation, thus ensuring that the country gained a solid industrial base.

The interwar years

The fragility of the new state's political institutions became obvious when Piłsudski refused to stand in the 1922 presidential elections on the grounds that the office was insufficiently powerful. Worse, the victor, **Gabriel Narutowicz**, was hounded by the Nationalists for having won as a result of votes cast by "non-Poles", and was assassinated soon afterwards. For the next few years, Poland was governed by a series of weak governments presiding over hyperinflation, feeble attempts at agrarian reform and a contemptuous army officer class.

In May 1926, Piłsudski staged a military coup, ushering in the so-called **Sanacja** regime, named after a slogan proposing a return to political "health". Piłsudski functioned as the state's commander-in-chief until his death in 1935, though he held no formal office after an initial two-year stint as prime minister. Parliamentary life continued, but opposition was emasculated by the creation of the so-called **Non-Party Bloc for Co-operation with the Government**, and disaffected groups were brought to heel by force if necessary.

Having a country led by **Stalin** on one frontier was bad enough; when **Hitler** seized power in Germany in 1933, Poland was a sitting target for two ruthless dictators, despite managing to sign ten-year nonaggression pacts with each. Hitler had always been open about his ambition of wiping Poland off the map again, regarding the Slavs as a race who were fit for no higher role than to be slaves of the Aryans. He also wanted to unite all ethnic Germans under his rule: a foreign policy objective that was quickly put into effect by his annexation of Austria in March 1938 and of parts of Czechoslovakia – with British and French connivance – in September of the same year. As Hitler's attentions turned towards Poland, his foreign minister Joachim von Ribbentrop and his Soviet counterpart Vyacheslav Molotov concluded the notorious **Nazi–Soviet Pact** in August 1939, which allowed either side to pursue any aggressive designs without the interference of the other. It also included a secret clause which agreed on a full partition of Poland along the lines of the Narew, Wisła and San rivers.

World War II

On September 1, 1939, Hitler invaded Poland, beginning by annexing the free city of Danzig, thereby precipitating **World War II**. The Poles fought with great courage, inflicting heavy casualties, but were numerically and technologically in a hopeless position. On September 17, the Soviets invaded the eastern part of the country, claiming the share-out agreed by the Nazi–Soviet Pact. The Allies, who had guaranteed to come to Poland's defence, initially failed to do so, and by the end of the first week in October the country had capitulated. A government-in-exile was established in London under **Władysław Sikorski**.

Millions of civilians – including virtually every Jew in Poland – were to be slaughtered in the Nazi **concentration camps** that were soon being set up in the occupied territory. And as this was going on, Soviet prisoners were being transported east to the **Gulag**, while wholesale murders of the potentially troublesome elements in Polish society were being carried out, such as the massacre of **Katyń**, where 4500 officers were shot.

Nazi control of western Poland entailed further territorial dismemberment. Some parts of the country were simply swallowed up by the Reich, with north-western districts forming part of the newly created Reichgau of Danzig-West Prussia, and west-central territories around Poznań being absorbed into the Warthegau. Everything else – Warsaw and Kraków included – was placed under a German-controlled administration known as the **Gouvernement Generale**, an ad-hoc structure designed to exploit the economic and labour potential of Poland while the war lasted. Poles everywhere were subjected to dislocation and hardship. Those living in the Warthegau were forced to emigrate to the Gouvernement Generale in an attempt to Germanize the province; while those in Danzig-West Prussia fared slightly better, and were allowed to stay where they were providing they adopted German names and passports.

The Nazi invasion of the Soviet Union in June 1941 prompted Stalin to make an alliance with Sikorski, ushering in a period of uneasy co-operation between Soviet forces and the Polish resistance, which was led by the **Home Army** (AK). The Red Army's victory at Stalingrad in 1943 marked the beginning of the end for the Nazis, but it enabled Stalin to backtrack on promises made to the Polish government-in-exile. At the **Tehran Conference** in November he came to an arrangement with Britain and America with regard to future spheres of influence in Europe, making it almost inevitable that postwar Poland would be forced into the Soviet camp. He also insisted that the Soviet Union would retain the

POLAND 1938

POLAND 1945

territories it had annexed in 1939. Allied support for this was obtained by reference to the current border's virtual coincidence with the so-called Curzon Line,
which had been drawn up by a former British Foreign Secretary in 1920 in an
unsuccessful attempt at mediation in the Polish–Soviet War.

During the **liberation of Poland** in 1944, any possibility of reasserting genuine Polish control depended on the outcome of the uprising in Warsaw against

the Nazi occupiers. On July 31, with the Soviets poised on the outskirts of the city, the Home Army was forced to act. The Red Army lay in wait during the ensuing bloodbath. When the insurgents were finally defeated at the beginning of October, Hitler ordered that the city be razed before leaving the ruins to the Red Army. In early 1945, as the Soviets pushed on through Poland, the Nazis set up last-ditch strongholds in Silesia, but these were overrun by the time of the final armistice in April.

No country suffered so much from World War II as Poland. In all, around 25 percent of the population died, and the whole country lay devastated. Moreover, although the Allies had originally gone to war on its behalf, it found itself reduced in size and shifted west across the map of Europe by some 200 kilo-metres, with its western frontier fixed at the lines of the Odra and Nysa rivers. Stalin had in effect achieved his twin aims of moving his frontiers and his sphere of influence well to the west.

The losses in the east – including Lwów and Wilno, both great centres of Polish culture – were painful, and involved the transfer of millions of people across the country in the following two years. There were compensations, however: Pomerania and the industrially valuable Silesia were restored after a gap of some seven centuries; and the much-coveted city of Danzig, which had been detached since its seizure by the Teutonic Knights, was also returned – and, as Gdańsk, it was later to play a major role in postwar Polish history.

The rise of Polish communism

The Polish communists took power, not through popular revolution, as their Soviet counterparts had – nor even with significant public support, as the Czech communists had – but through the military and political dictate of an occupying force. Control was seized by the **ZPP** (Union of Polish Patriots), an organization formed by Stalin in 1943 from Polish exiles and Russian place-men with polonized names. As the Red Army drove the Germans west, the ZPP established a Committee for **National Liberation in Lublin**, under the leadership of **Bolesław Bierut**. This was to form the core of the Polish govern-ment over the next few years.

Political opposition was fragmented and ineffectual. From the government-in-exile, only a single prominent figure returned to Poland after 1945 – **Stanisław Mikołajczyk**, leader of the prewar Peasants' Party. He was to leave again in 1947, narrowly avoiding imprisonment.

The Polish communists and socialists who had remained in Poland during the war now regrouped. The communists, though suspicious of Moscow, joined the ZPP to form the **Polish Workers' Party** under general secretary **Władysław Gomułka**, as the socialists attempted to establish a separate party. Meanwhile, the Soviets ran the country as an outlying province, stripping factories of plant and materials, intimidating political opponents, and orchestrating the brutal suppression of a nationalist uprising in the western Ukraine by the Polish army, in what is referred to as the **Civil War** (1945–47).

The economic and political framework of Poland was sealed by the elec-tions of 1947. The communists and socialists, allied as the **Democratic Bloc**, won a decisive victory over their remaining opponents through an extended campaign of political harassment and manipulation. After the forcible merger of the socialists and communists in 1948 as the **PZPR** (Polish United Workers'

Party), it only remained for the external pressures of the emerging **Cold War** to lock Poland completely into the Soviet sphere of influence and the Soviet model of economic and political development. In the authoritarian climate of the era, even Polish communists were considered suspect if they failed to display unswerving loyalty to Stalin, and in 1951 First Secretary Gomułka was deposed and arrested for showing too much independence of thought. Unlike other disgraced leaders in Eastern Europe, however, Gomułka was not executed – a sign that communist rule in Poland was not as mercilessly repressive as in other satellites of the Soviet Union.

The birth of the PRL

In 1952 a new Constitution enshrined the leading role of the **PZPR** in every aspect of Polish society, designating the country as the Polish People's Republic or Polska Rzeczpospolita Ludowa – nowadays remembered by its acronym, **PRL**. Further, while the trappings of elections and a two-house parliament were retained, the other parties – the Democratic Party (SD) and the reconstituted Peasants' Party (ZSL) – were under the effective political control of the PZPR. Real power lay with the Politburo, Central Committee and the newly formed economic and administrative bureaucracies. Only the **Catholic Church**, although harassed and extensively monitored by the authorities, retained a degree of independence as a political and cultural organization – its defiance characterized by the primate, **Cardinal Wyszyński**, arrested in 1953 for "anti-state" activities and imprisoned for three years.

Nationalization continued throughout this period, accelerated through the first **Three Year Plan** (1947–50) and the first **Six Year Plan** (1950–56). Although the former retained some emphasis on the role of private ownership, the thrust of both was towards the collectivization of agriculture and the creation of a heavy industrial base. Collectivization proved impossible in the absence of the sort of force used by Stalin against the Kulaks: the programme slowed in the mid-1950s and was tacitly abandoned thereafter. Industrially the plans proved more successful: major iron and steel industries were established, mining extensively exploited in Silesia and an entire shipbuilding industry developed along the Baltic coast – most notably in Gdańsk. There were, inevitably, costs: standards of living remained almost static, food was scarce, work was long, hard and often dangerous, and unrestrained industrialization resulted in terrible pollution and despoilation of the land. Perhaps the most significant achievement of the period was the creation of an urban industrial working class for the first time in Polish history. Paradoxically, these very people proved to be the backbone of almost every political struggle against the Party in the following decades.

1956 – the Polish October

In Poland, as in Hungary, 1956 saw the first major political crisis of the communist era. Faction and dissension were already rife, with intellectuals calling for fundamental changes, splits within the Party leadership and increasing popular disenchantment with the excesses of Stalinism. In February 1956 **Khrushchev** made his famous "secret" speech to the Twentieth Congress of the Soviet

Communist Party, denouncing Stalin and his crimes; for Bolesław Bierut, president and first secretary of the PZPR, as for other Eastern European leaders, the speech was a bombshell, unmasking the lie of the absolute correctness of Stalin's every act. Reform-minded members of the Party in Poland were the first to make copies available in the West, but for Bierut and the hardline leadership it was the end: Bierut died directly after the Congress, many suspecting that he had committed suicide.

Then in June, workers in Poznań took to the streets over working conditions and wages. The protest rapidly developed into a major confrontation with the authorities, and in the ensuing street battles with the army and security police up to eighty people were killed and many hundreds of others wounded. Initial government insistence that "imperialist agents" had instigated the troubles gave way to an admission that some of the workers' grievances were justified and that the Party would try to remedy them.

The Poznań riots further divided an alarmed and weakened Party. Hardliners pushed for Defence Minister General Rokossowski to take over the leadership, but it was **Gomułka**, with his earnest promises of reform, who carried the day. In October, the Party plenum elected Gomułka as the new leader, without consulting Moscow. An enraged Khrushchev flew to Warsaw to demand an explanation of this unprecedented flouting of the Kremlin's authority. East German, Czech and Soviet troops were mobilized along Poland's borders, in response to which Polish security forces prepared to defend the capital. Poland held its breath as Gomułka and Khrushchev engaged in heated debate over the crisis. In the end, Gomułka assured Khrushchev that Poland would remain a loyal ally and maintain the essentials of communist rule. Khrushchev returned to Moscow, Soviet troops withdrew, and four days later Gomułka addressed a huge crowd in Warsaw as a national hero. The **Soviet invasion of Hungary** to crush the national uprising there in early November 1956 provided a clear reminder to Poles of how close they had come to disaster.

The **Polish October**, as it came to be known, raised high hopes of a new order, and initially those hopes seemed justified. Censorship was relaxed, Cardinal Wyszyński was released and state harassment of the Church and control over the economy eased. A **cultural thaw** encouraged an explosion of creativity in art and theatre – much of it wildly experimental – and opened the doors to "decadent" Western preoccupations such as jazz and rock and roll. But the impetus for **political reform** quickly faded, and the 1960s saw a progressive return to centralized planning, a stagnant economy and sporadic attempts to reassert some measure of control over an increasingly disaffected populace.

1970–79: from Gomułka to Gierek

The final days of the Gomułka years were marked by a contrast between triumph in foreign policy and the harsh imposition of economic constraint. Pursuing his policy of Ostpolitik, West German chancellor **Willy Brandt** visited Poland in December 1970 to sign the **Warsaw Treaty**, recognizing Poland's current borders and opening full diplomatic relations. In an emphatic symbolic gesture, Brandt knelt in penance at the monument to those killed in the Warsaw Ghetto Uprising.

A few days later, on December 12, huge food price rises were announced, provoking a simmering **discontent** that was to break out in strikes and demonstrations along the Baltic coast, centring on Gdańsk. When troops fired on demonstrators, killing many, the protests spread like wildfire, to the point of open insurrection (Gomułka's Defence Minister, a certain **Wojciech Jaruzelski**, was to be put on trial for the killings some twenty years later). A traumatized Central Committee met five days before Christmas, hurriedly bundling Gomułka into retirement and replacing him as first secretary with **Edward Gierek**, a member of the Party's reformist faction in the 1960s. Price rises were frozen and wage increases promised, but despite a Christmas calm, strikes broke out throughout January 1971, with demands for free trade unions and a free press accompanying the more usual economic demands. Peace was only restored when Gierek and Jaruzelski went to the Gdańsk shipyards by taxi to argue their case and admit their errors to the strikers.

The Gierek period marked out an alternative route to social stability. Given access to Western financial markets by Brandt's reconciliation, the Gierek government borrowed heavily throughout the **early 1970s**. Food became cheaper and more plentiful as internal subsidies were matched by purchases from the West and the Soviet Union. Standards of living rose and a wider range of consumer goods became more freely available. However, the international economic recession and oil crises of the mid-Seventies destroyed the Polish boom at a stroke. Debts became impossible to service, new loans harder to obtain, and it became apparent that earlier borrowing had been squandered in unsustainable rises in consumption or wasted in large-scale projects of limited economic value.

By **1976** the wheel had turned full circle with remarkable rapidity. The government announced food price rises of almost treble the magnitude of those proposed in the early Seventies. This time the ensuing strikes were firmly repressed and many activists imprisoned, and it is from this point that one can chart the emergence of the complex alliance between Polish workers, intellectuals and the Catholic Church. In response to the imprisonment of strikers, the KOR (Committee for the Defence of Workers) was formed. Comprising **dissident intellectuals**, it was to provide not only valuable publicity and support for the opposition through Western contacts, but also new channels of political communication through underground **samizdat** publications, plus a degree of strategic sophistication that the spontaneous uprisings had so far lacked.

But perhaps even more decisive was the election of **Karol Wojtyła**, archbishop of Kraków, as Pope John Paul II in 1978. A fierce opponent of the communist regime, he visited Poland in 1979 and was met by the greatest public gatherings that Poland had ever seen. For the Polish people he became a symbol of Polish cultural identity and international influence, and his visit provided a public demonstration of their potential power.

1980–1989: Solidarity

Gierek's announcement of 100-percent price rises on foodstuffs in July 1980 led to more strikes, centring on the **Gdańsk shipyards**. Attempts by the authorities to have a crane operator, Anna Walentynowicz, dismissed for political agitation intensified the unrest. Led by a shipyard electrician, **Lech Wałęsa**, the strikers occupied the yards and were joined by a hastily convened group of opposition intellectuals and activists, including future prime minister **Tadeusz Mazowiecki**. Together they formulated a series of demands – the **Twenty-one Points** – that were to serve not only as the principal political concerns of the Polish opposition, but to provide an intellectual template for every other oppositional movement in Eastern Europe.

Demands for popular consultation over the economic crisis, the freeing of political prisoners, freedom of the press, the right to strike, free trade unions and televised Catholic Mass were drawn up, along with demands for higher wages and an end to Party privileges. Yet the lessons of Hungary in 1956 and Czechoslovakia in 1968 had been learnt, and the opposition was careful to reiterate that they "intended neither to threaten the foundations of the Socialist Republic in our country, nor its position in international relations".

The Party caved in, after protracted negotiations, signing the historic **Gdańsk Agreements** in August 1980, after which free trade unions, covering over 75 percent of Poland's 12.5 million workforce, were formed across the country, under the name **Solidarność – Solidarity.** Gierek and his supporters were swept from office by the Party in September 1980, but the limits of Solidarity's power were signalled by an unscheduled Warsaw Pact meeting later in the year. Other Eastern European communist leaders perceptively argued that Solidarity's success would threaten not only their Polish counterparts' political futures, but their own as well. Accordingly, Soviet and Warsaw Pact units were mobilized along Poland's borders. The Poles closed ranks: the Party reaffirmed its Leninist purity, while Solidarity and the Church publicly emphasized their moderation.

Throughout 1981 deadlock ensued, while the economic crisis gathered pace. Solidarity, lacking any positive control over the economy, was only capable of bringing it to a halt, and repeatedly showed itself able to do so. **General Jaruzelski** took control of the Party in July 1981 and, in the face of threats of a general strike, continued to negotiate with Solidarity leaders, but refused to relinquish any power. A wave of strikes in late October 1981 were met by the imposition of **martial law** on December 12, 1981: occupations and strikes were broken up by troops, Solidarity was banned, civil liberties suspended and union leaders arrested. However, these measures solved nothing fundamental, and in the face of creative and determined resistance from the now underground Solidarity movement, still actively supported by large segments of the populace, martial law was lifted in the wake of Pope John Paul II's second visit to his home country in 1983.

The period 1984 to 1988 was marked by a final attempt by the Jaruzelski government to dig Poland out of its economic crisis. The country's debt had risen to an astronomical $39 billion, wages had slumped, and production was hampered by endemic labour unrest, the cutting edge of what throughout the 1980s remained Eastern Europe's most organized and broadly based opposition movement. In 1987, Jaruzelski submitted the government's programme of price rises and promised democratization to a referendum. The government lost, the real message of the vote being a rejection not merely of the programme but of the notion that the Party could lead Poland out of its crisis.

Jaruzelski finally acknowledged defeat after a devastating wave of strikes in 1988 and called for a "courageous turnaround" by the Party, accepting the need for talks with Solidarity and the prospect of real **power sharing** – an option of political capitulation only made possible by the election of Mikhail Gorbachev as secretary general in the Kremlin.

1989–90: the new Poland

The **round-table talks** ran from February to April 1989, government representatives ultimately agreeing to the opposition's demands for the legalization of Solidarity, the establishment of an independent press and the promise of what were termed "semi-free" elections. All hundred seats of a reconstituted upper chamber, the Senate, were to be freely contested; while 65 percent of seats in the lower house, the Sejm, were to be reserved for the PZPR and its allied parties, with the rest openly contested.

The communists suffered a humiliating and decisive defeat in the consequent elections held in July 1989, whereas Solidarity won almost every seat it contested. Thus while the numerical balance of the lower chamber remained with the PZPR, the unthinkable became possible – a Solidarity-led government. In the end, the parties which had previously been allied to the PZPR broke with their communist overlords and voted to establish the journalist **Tadeusz Mazowiecki** as prime minister in August 1989, installing the first non-communist government in Eastern Europe since World War II. Subsequently the PZPR rapidly disintegrated, voting to dissolve itself in January 1990 and then splitting into two notionally social democratic currents.

The tasks facing Poland's new government were formidable: economic dislocation, political volatility and a rapidly changing scene in the rest of Eastern Europe. For the most part, the government retained a high degree of support despite an austerity programme far stiffer than anything proposed under the communist regime.

President Wałęsa and the first free elections

After a long period away from the political limelight Lech Wałęsa reemerged to win the presidential elections of 1990, promising a faster pace of reform and the removal of the accumulated privileges of the communist elite. In January 1991 he appointed business-oriented liberal **Jan Krzysztof Bielecki** as prime minister. Bielecki's hard-headed finance minister Leszek Balcerowicz embarked on a tough **austerity programme**, with steadily rising prices, rocketing unemployment and continued government spending cuts making heavy inroads into the pockets and lives of ordinary Poles. These policies won the confidence of Western financial institutions, however, resulting in a landmark agreement with the **International Monetary Fund** (IMF) about the reduction of Poland's \$33 billion debt.

Elections – the first fully free ones since World War II – were held in October 1991. The campaign itself was a fairly tame affair, the most notable feature being the spectacular array of parties (nearly seventy in total) taking part, including everyone from national minorities like the Silesian Germans to the joke Beer Lovers' Party.

A total of 29 parties entered the new Sejm, the highest scorer, the Democratic Union (UD), gaining a meagre 14 percent of the alarmingly low (43 percent) turnout. Bielecki resigned, and Wałęsa called on Jan Olszewski, a lawyer and prominent former dissident, to form a new coalition government.

The new centre-right **coalition government** put together by Olszewski adopted an increasingly aggressive stance on the subject of "decommunization", pushing for the unmasking of public figures suspected of having collaborated with the security services during the communist era. The question of **lustration** – the exclusion from public life of those who had compromised themselves under the previous regime – has been a controversial issue in Poland ever since, largely because of the potentially huge number of people who could be targeted in this way. It cetainly cost Olszewski his job, ousted by a no-confidence vote in June 1992.

The Suchocka government

Olszewski's successor, **Halina Suchocka**, of the Democratic Union, proved surprisingly successful in knitting together a functioning coalition from an unruly bundle of fractious right-of-centre parties. Domestically her most important achievement was a social pact over wage increases, concluded between government and trade unions (the remnants of declining Solidarity included) in autumn 1992 following a major wave of strikes. On the darker side, the increasingly powerful role of **the Church** in Poland's political and social life came well to the fore, above all in the heated national debate sparked by government moves to criminalize abortion, a move supported strongly by the Catholic Church but opposed by many within the country, as well as by Western institutions like the Council of Europe.

The issue that caused the Suchocka government most trouble was the vexed issue of large-scale **privatization**. The Sejm threw out a bill designed to privatize over six hundred major state enterprises in March 1993, and despite the adoption of a compromise solution a month later, the whole thing was derailed by Solidarity MPs, who led a vote of no-confidence over the government's handling of economic policy.

President Wałęsa called for fresh **elections** in September 1993, which resulted in victory for a coalition between the former-communist Democratic Left Alliance (SLD) and the Peasants' Party (PSL), which won nearly 36 percent of the vote. As in many other post-communist countries, a decline in popular living standards brought about by economic reform programmes had led to a reformed-communist return to power.

1993–97: the SLD in power

The new government, led by PSL leader **Waldemar Pawlak**, affirmed its commitment to continued market reforms, but at the same time pledged to do more to address its negative social effects. However, serious outbreaks of SLD-PSL infighting weakend Pawlak's authority, and a new wave of public-sector strikes, initiated by a revived Solidarity in the early spring of 1994, damaged the government's standing still further.

Ultimately, however, the conflict that most undermined Pawlak's government was a prolonged tussle with President Lech Wałęsa. Frustrated by the left's electoral success and his own increasing political marginalization, Wałęsa engaged the government in a series of constitutional disputes. The showdown came in February 1995, when Wałęsa demanded Pawlak's resignation and threatened to dissolve parliament if he was not replaced immediately. Incensed by this blatant display of presidential arrogance, the Sejm voted to initiate **impeachment**

proceedings against Wałęsa should he make good his threats. A full-scale crisis was prevented by Pawlak's decision to quit, to be replaced in March by the SLD's Józef Oleksy, speaker of the Sejm, who proceeded to form a new government based on the same coalition of the SLD, PSL and independents.

The 1995 presidential elections

The focus of political attention now shifted towards the November presidential elections, with opinion polls suggesting that the public were weary of Wałęsa's unquenchable appetite for political intrigue. This time his main rival was the SLD's **Aleksander Kwaśniewski**, a polished, smooth-talking character who knew how to win over audiences potentially alienated by his ex-communist political record. By talking of Poland's future as a speedily modernizing country, Kwaśniewski won over both the young and the emergent middle classes, who clearly preferred consensus and stability to the divisive leadership style of Lech Wałęsa.

Following a final campaign marked by some pretty gruesome mudslinging, Kwaśniewski carried the day by a slim margin of 52 percent to Wałęsa's 48, on a 68 percent voter turnout. A chastened Wałęsa made little effort to hide his anger at the result, and the final weeks of his presidency were marked by further characteristically intemperate outbursts, notably his refusal to attend Kwaśniewski's swearing-in ceremony just before Christmas.

In December 1995 Prime Minister Józef Oleksy had to step down amid allegations that he was a former agent of the KGB, but things continued pretty much as they were under his successor and SLD colleague, former justice minister **Włodzimierz Cimoszewicz**. Needing to regroup in order to stand any chance of winning back power, the centre-right came together to form the **Solidarity Election Action** (AWS) coalition in June 1996. This was a makeshift alliance of some 25 parties, comprising such heavyweights as Solidarity, the Centre Agreement (PC) and the Christian National Union (ZChN), alongside a string of minor rightist groupings. Despite its inherent fractiousness, the AWS succeeded in making rapid political headway, not least due to the astute leadership of Solidarity chairman Marian Krzaklewski, who soon emerged as the coalition's leading figure.

The focus of national attention swung firmly away from politics following the severe **floods** that swept across southern Poland in July 1997. At least 55 people died, over 140,000 were evacuated from their homes and cities such as Wrocław suffered extensive damage, prompting the temporary adoption of emergency measures and an influx of aid from international sources. The government came in for severe criticism for what was perceived as a failure to act decisively in response to the floods, and in August it barely survived a PSL-sponsored vote of no confidence.

The return of the centre-right

The September 1997 **elections** handed victory to the Solidarity-led AWS, but with 34 percent of the vote they needed to forge a **coalition** with Leszek Balcerowicz's neo-liberal Freedom Union (UW) in order to form a government. The new prime minister was Jerzy Buzek, a veteran Solidarity activist from Silesia who owed his elevation to Krzaklewski's decision to forgo the premiership and concentrate instead on the presidential elections scheduled for 2000.

C

CONTEXTS | History

The main planks of the government's programme were little different from those of its predecessor, emphasizing integration into NATO and the EU, continuing privatization economic retrenchment. Other components, notably Buzek's pledge to promote Christian beliefs and "family values" – a familiar leitmotif of conservative Catholic agitprop – indicated real differences in ideological background and approach. In December the new Sejm accepted a **Constitutional Tribunal** ruling overturning the liberalized abortion law passed the previous year in the face of fierce Church criticism and widespread centre-right political opposition. The following month the Concordat with the Vatican regulating Church–State relations, whose formal ratification had hitherto been stalled by the SLD and its allies, was finally voted into law.

Despite the conciliatory, confidence-building style of Buzek himself, his government was ultimately hamstrung by the split between the Balcerowicz faction, which was committed to an ongoing programme of free market reforms and public spending cuts, and those closer to Solidarity, who favoured a less radical style. The economic growth of the mid-1990s was beginning to slow down by the end of the decade, unemployment was rising, and those in work were frustrated by having to put up with negligible pay rises from one year to the next. In these conditions, the SLD – guided by affable former Politburo member **Leszek Miller** – bounced back into popular affections.

Kwaśniewski wins again

The first test of the SLD's resurgent popularity came with the **presidential elections** of October 2000. The incumbent, SLD-supported **Aleksander Kwaśniewski**, had represented the interests of his country with much more dignity than his crotchety predecessor Lech Wałęsa, and possessed an accessible blokeishness that appealed strongly to the average Pole. Most importantly, he was seen as a consensus-building national figurehead who resisted the temptation to interfere too much in day-to-day politics. Even Kwaśniewski's gaffes, such as appearing to mock the pope by encouraging one of his aides to kiss the ground in papal style, failed to dent his popularity.

Kwaśniewski's subsequent **landslide victory** over AWS candidate Aleksander Krzaklewski left the government in disarray. The unpopularity brought on the government by the radical economic reform espoused by the Freedom Union prompted many prominent right-wingers to defect to a new, more moderate, centre-right political grouping called the **Civic Platform**.

The death warrant of the AWS-led government was delivered by the very organization whose interests it had been formed to promote. In May 2001, **Solidarity** finally faced up to the dilemma that had been dogging its leaders throughout the previous decade: how could a movement formed to defend workers' rights continue to participate in right-of-centre governments whose policies repeatedly conflicted with workers' interests? Desperate to retain the confidence of its core membership, Solidarity decided to withdraw from the AWS in order to concentrate on its role as a trade union.

The volatile nature of party politics throughout the post-communist period had little impact on the main strategic goals of Polish foreign policy: membership of NATO and the European Union. Initially, **membership of NATO** appeared to be the least likely of the two ambitions to be realized, but throughout the 1990s the weak international position of Russia – the country most threatened by NATO enlargement – allowed Poland unexpected freedom of manoeuvre. In January 1994, Poland signed up to the organization's newly formed Partnership for Peace Agreement, and – together with the Czech Republic and Hungary – was officially invited to join the organization three years later, despite considerable Russian grumbling. All three were formally accepted into the alliance in March 1999, one month ahead of NATO's fiftieth anniversary celebrations.

The political present

Profiting from government mistakes rather than presenting a radically different programme of its own, the SLD cruised effortlessly to victory in the **parliamentary elections** of September 2001, although with 200 of the Sejm's 460 seats it still needed the support of traditional ally the PSL in order to form a government. Both the AWS and the Freedom Union were wiped out entirely, failing to achieve the five percent of the vote necessary to win parliamentary representation, and were replaced by the Civic Platform as the main voice of right-of-centre Poland.

The new administration of Leszek Miller proved just as ineffectual as its predecessors in fulfilling the huge public expectations invested in it. Despite clear evidence that Polish economy was becoming more efficient and attracting increasing levels of foreign investment, unemployment remained high and average wages remained low.

In foreign policy the SLD remained true to the pro-Western, pro-USA line that had been a constant feature of Polish statecraft since the fall of communism, and supported the American-led **invasion of Iraq** in spring 2003 by sending several thousand troops. Poland assumed command of one of the three military zones into which Iraq was subsequently divided, although Poland's participation in the venture was increasingly questioned by a public unsure of how it served national interests.

However, it was domestic policy – and the government's commitment to free-market economics – that led to serious strains in the ruling coalition, with the PSL withdrawing its support in 2003 and a group of SDL MPs – led by speaker of the Sejm Marek Borowski – leaving to form a separate Social Democratic Party a year later. Government prestige was further tarnished by a wave of corruption scandals, culminating in the case of **Lew Rywin**, the movie producer who told top newspaper *Gazeta Wyborcza* that he could ease their entry into the satellite TV market if they paid $17.5 million to his associates in the ruling party. Rywin got two years in prison; support for the SLD went into freefall. Leszek Miller resigned as prime minister in March 2004, to be replaced by economist Marek Belka – a caretaker figure whose job it was to steady the SLD ship in preparation for the next round of parliamentary elections in 2005.

Ironically Miller resigned on the eve of what should have been his greatest triumph, Poland's entry into the **European Union** in May 2004. Poland's drive to gain membership of the EU had been far from straightforward – not least because of the existence of an **anti-EU lobby** in Poland itself – combining everyone from farmers worried about exposure to EU agricultural competition to a nationalist–religious coalition wary of the effects of secular Western values on the nation's moral fibre. A **referendum** on EU membership held in June 2003 produced a huge majority in favour, however, the result symbolizing for many Poland's extraordinary post-communist voyage from Soviet satellite to equal member of the wider European family.

The main beneficiary of the SLD's declining support was the right-of-centre Citizens' Platform. However, the lack of ideological differences between

C

CONTEXTS | History

Poland's main political groupings has encouraged the emergence of new populist parties eager to exploit those discontents which the mainstream, pro-market and pro-European politicians seem unable to face head-on. Winning their first-ever seats in the parliamentary elections of 2001 was **Samoobrona** (Self-Defence), a peasants' rights party led by **Andrzej Lepper**, a maverick populist notorious for his taste in stripy ties and his controversial and often antidemocratic outbursts. More extreme still is the **League of Polish Familes** (LPR), a much more openly anti-European, anti-liberal party which combines a left-wing social programme with a right-wing mix of nationalism and reactionary moral values. The LPR achieved 16 percent of the vote in the EU elections of June 2004 (Samoobrona got 10 percent), although the miserably low turn-out suggested that this may not have been an accurate reflection of their real support. With traditional left–right divisions also being challenged by non-ideological groupings such as Centrum, the party of middle-of-the-road technocrats led by heart surgeon Zbigniew Religa, the Polish political landscape looks set for a drawn-out process of restructuring and change.

Polish music

Traditional music in Poland isn't exactly a widespread living tradition. The country has Westernized rapidly and the memory of communist fakelore has tainted people's interest in the genuine article. But in certain pockets, Poland boasts some of the most distinctive sounds in Europe, and the experience of a *górale* (highland) wedding – fired by furious fiddling, grounded by a sawing cello and supercharged with vodka – is unforgettable. Simon Broughton, editor of *Songlines* magazine, outlines the background and highlights some of the new developments.

Roots and development

In Poland, as elsewhere in Eastern Europe, an interest in folklore emerged in the nineteenth century, allied to aspirations for national independence – folk music and politics in the region often have symbiotic links. The pioneering collector of songs and dances from all over the country was **Oskar Kolberg** (1814–90). His principal interest was in song, and it's thought that during the nineteenth century instrumental music was fairly primitive, with dramatic developments occurring only in the last one hundred and fifty years or so. From the early years of this century gramophone recordings were made, and by 1939 substantial archives had been amassed in Poznań and Warsaw. Both collections were completely destroyed during **World War II** and scholarly collecting had to begin anew in 1945. The wartime annihilation and shifting of ethnic minorities in Poland also severely disrupted the continuity of folk traditions. The postwar communist regimes throughout Eastern Europe endorsed folk culture as far as it could be portrayed as a cheerful espousal of healthy peasant labour, but each regime adopted a different approach. What survives today is sometimes in spite of, but largely a result of, those policies. At one extreme, Bulgaria strongly encouraged amateur grass-roots music; on the other, Czechoslovakia effectively sanitized its folk music to irrelevance. Poland adopted something close to the Czech approach, but allowing enough slack for a few local bands to keep some genuine traditions going.

The official face of Poland's folk culture was presented by professional folk troupes – most famously the **Mazowsze** and **Śląsk ensembles** – who gave (and still give) highly arranged and polished virtuoso performances: middle-of-the-road massed strings and highly choreographed twirls, whoops and foot-stamping. The repertoire was basically core Polish with, perhaps, a slight regional emphasis (the Mazowsze territory is around Warsaw, the Śląsk around Wrocław), but the overall effect was homogenization rather than local identity. The groups were regularly featured on radio and TV and they had their audience. Smaller, more specialized groups, like Słowianki in Kraków, were also supported and kept closer to the roots, but for the most part the real stuff withered away as the image of folk music became tarnished by the bland official ensembles.

Polish dances

Thanks to Chopin, the **mazurka** and **polonaise** (*polonez*) of central Poland are probably the best-known dance forms and are at the core of the folk repertoire. Both are in triple time, with the polonaise generally slower and more stately than the mazurka. In fact there are really three types of mazurka, the slower *kujawiak*, medium tempo *mazur* and faster *oberek*. The polonaise is particularly associated with the more ceremonial and solemn moments of a wedding party. It was taken up by the aristocracy from a slow walking dance (*chodzony*), given a French name to identify it as a dance of Polish origin and then filtered back down to the lower classes. In addition to the triple-time dances of central Poland, there are also some characteristic five-beat dances in the northeastern areas of Mazury, Kurpie and Podlasie.

As you move south, somewhere between Warsaw and Kraków, there is a transitional area where the triple-time dances of central Poland give way to the duple-time dances of the south like the **krakowiak** and **polka**. Generally speaking the music of central Poland is more restrained and sentimental than that of the south, which is wilder and more full-blooded. The *krakowiak* is named after the city of Kraków and the polka is claimed by both the Poles and the Bohemians as their own, although it was in Bohemia that it became most widely known. Of course, all these dances are not confined to their native areas, but many have become staples across the country and abroad. **Weddings** are the main occasion for traditional music, but in an agrarian country where barely eight percent of the land was collectivized, important annual events like the **harvest festival** (*dozynki*) have persisted as well.

Folk music today

Today, with the notable exception of the Tatra region and a few other pockets, traditional music has virtually ceased to function as a living tradition and has been banished to regional **folk festivals**. Several of these are very good indeed, with the Kazimierz Festival at the end of June foremost amongst them (see box opposite). But the best way to hear this music is at the sort of occasion it was designed for – for instance a **wedding** (*wesele*), where lively tunes are punched out by ad-hoc groups comprising (nowadays) clarinet, saxophone, accordion, keyboard and drums. At country weddings there is often a set of traditional dances played for the older people, even when the rest of the music is modern. In the rural areas people tend to be hospitable and welcoming and, once you've shown a keen interest, an invitation is often extended. Typically, the areas where the music has survived tend to be the remoter regions on the fringes – Kurpie and Podlasie in the northeast, around Rzeszów in the southeast (where the *cimbaly* – hammer dulcimer – is popular in the local bands), and the Podhale and highland regions in the Tatras along the southern border. But this isn't the whole story.

Podhale music

Podhale, the district around Zakopane, is home to the **górale** (highland) people and has the most vibrant musical tradition in the country. It has been one of Poland's most popular resort areas for years and is in no way remote or isolated. The Podhale musicians are familiar with music from all over the

Festivals and events

It's always worth contacting the Polish National Tourist Office (see p.40) in your home country for confirmation of the events and dates listed below: they can often provide an extensive run-down of annual festivals and cultural events. If you can navigate your way through Polish websites go to ⓦwww.independent.pl and ⓦwww .etno.serpent.pl, which frequently carry festival dates and line-ups.

Kazimierz Dolny Festival of Folk Bands and Singers (last weekend in June). Poland's biggest traditional music festival. Contact Wojewódzki Dom Kultury, ul. Dolna Panny Marii 3, 20-010 Lublin (☎081/532 4207, ⓦwww.wdk.lublin.pl).

Kraków Festival of Jewish Music & Culture. A well-established event held late every June. Draws top-line international klezmer acts as well as local bands. Contact the Centrum Informacji Kulturalnej (Cultural Information Centre), ul. św. Jana 2, 31-100 Kraków (☎012/421 7787, ⓦwww.karnet.krakow.2000).

Kraków Rozstaje Festival. Traditional music in early September, from Małopolska as well as Poland's central European neighbours. Contact the Centrum Informacji Kulturalnej (see above; ⓦwww.krakow2000.pl/rozstaje).

Lublin Mikołajke (St Nicholas' Festival). Held in early December, traditional Polish music festival that mixes serious ethnological intent with good hedonistic fun. Organized by the same people who run contemporary folk band Orkiestra św. Mikołaja. Contact Orkiestra św. Mikołaja, Chata Żaka, ul. Radziszewskiego 16, 20-031 Lublin (☎081/533 3201; ⓦwww.mikolaje.lublin.pl).

Rzeszów Festiwal Polonijnych Zespołów Folklorystycznych (World Festival of Polonia Folklore). A triennial international bash bringing together music and dance ensembles from the worldwide Polish diaspora. Next due in July 2005 and 2008. Contact Wspólnota Polska, Krakowskie Przedmieście 64, 00-071 Warsaw (☎022/635 0440, ⓦwww.wspolnota-polska.org.pl).

Warsaw Dom Tanca (Dance House). Warsaw organization that arranges folk dance evenings open to all, as well as folk concerts, in a variety of venues around the city. Check out ⓦwww.domtanca.art.pl for details.

Żywiec Międzynarodowe Spotkania Folklorystyczne (International Folk Meetings) (July–Aug), and the Festiwal Górali Polskich (Festival of Polish Highland Music). Held in July and August, both feature many of the acts who go on to appear in Zakopane (see below). Contact Żywiec tourist office, Rynek 12, 34-300 Żywiec (☎033/861 4310, ⓦwww.zywiec.pl).

Zakopane Międzynarodowy Festiwal Folkloru Ziem Gorskich (International Festival of Highland Folklore). Sizeable gathering of traditional Polish and international groups strutting their stuff in a vast marquee in the town centre during August. Details from the Zakopane tourist office at ul. Kościuszki 17, 34-500 Zakopane (☎021/201 2211, ⓦwww.zakopane.pl/festiwal).

Zydnia Vatra Festival of Łemk & Ukrainian Culture. A big event in the Łemk/Ukrainian cultural calendar, attracting thousands of people and a wide range of groups from Poland, Slovakia, Ukraine and Romania. Held in late July right out in the Beskid Niski, just southeast of Gorlice (see p.369).

Górale weddings

Górale weddings are often held in the local fire station, where there's room enough for feasting and dancing – plus it provides useful extra income for the fire brigade. It is here that the family members assemble and the couple are lectured by the leader of the band on the importance of the step they are taking – an indication of how integral the band is to the event. Then comes the departure for the church in a string of horse-drawn carriages – the band in one, the bride in another and the groom following in one behind. At the front, the **pytacy**, a pair of outriders on horseback, shout rhymes to all and sundry. The band play the couple into the wooden church and, from the gallery inside the church, keep going while communion takes place. Then it's back to the fire station for the party.

The band will keep going for hours, substituting different players from time to time to give themselves a short break. Quite unexpected until you get used to it is the way the *górale* dances and songs are superimposed, often with no relation to each other. A fast up-tempo dance will be in progress when suddenly a group of women will launch into a slow song seemingly oblivious to the other music – the tensions between the instrumental music and song are both calculated and fascinating.

Among the dances the local *ozwodne* and *krzesane* figure highly, begun by one of the men strutting over to the band and launching into the high straining vocals that cue the tune. The man then draws a girl onto the floor, dances a few steps with her before handing her over to the man on whose behalf he originally selected her. All this is part of a carefully structured form that culminates late in the evening with the ritual of the *cepiny* (or *cepowiny* as it's known in Podhale), the "capping ceremony". This is a peasant rite of passage that happens all over Poland, when the bride has a scarf tied round her head symbolizing her passage from the status of a single to a married woman.

The music whirls on throughout the night and extends well beyond the Podhale repertoire, with romantic waltzes and mazurkas, fiery polkas and *czardasz* – tunes that you might hear in northern Poland, Slovakia, Hungary or Romania, but always given a particular Podhale accent. The *górale* people are famed for keeping themselves to themselves and mistrusting outsiders, but there's no blinkered puritanism. They take and enjoy what they want from outside, confident and proud of the strength of what they have.

---

country and beyond, but choose to play in their own way. This sophisticated approach is part of a pride in Podhale identity which probably dates from the late nineteenth century, when several notable artists and intellectuals (including the composer **Karol Szymanowski**, see p.487) settled in Zakopane and enthused about the music and culture. Music, fiddlers and dancing brigands are as essential to the image of Podhale life as the traditional costumes of tight felt trousers, broad leather belts with ornate metal clasps and studs, embroidered jackets and black hats decorated with cowrie shells. This music has more in common with the peasant cultures along the Carpathians in Ukraine and Transylvania than the rest of Poland.

The typical **Podhale ensemble** is a string band (the clarinets, saxophones, accordions and drums that have crept in elsewhere in Poland are much rarer here) of a lead violin (*prym*), a couple of second violins (*sekund*) playing accompanying chords, and a three-stringed cello (*bazy*). The music is immediately identifiable by its melodies and playing style. The tunes tend to be short-winded, angular melodies in an unusual scale with a sharpened fourth. This is known to musicians as the "Lydian mode" and gives rise to the Polish word **lidyzowanie** to describe the manner of singing this augmented interval.

The fiddlers typically play these melodies with a "straight" bowing technique – giving the music a stiff, angular character as opposed to the swing and flexibility of the more usual "double" bowing technique common in Eastern Europe and typified by gypsy fiddlers. The straining high male vocals which kick off a dance tune are also typical. At the heart of the repertoire are the **ozwodna** and **krzesany** couple dances, both in duple time. The first has an unusual five-bar melodic structure and the second is faster and more energetic. Then there are the showy **zbójnicki** (Brigand's Dances) which are the popular face of Podhale culture – central to festivals and demonstrations of the music. Danced in a circle by men wielding small metal axes (sometimes hit together fiercely enough to strike sparks), they are a celebration of the *górale* traditions of brigandage, with colourful robberies, daring escapes, festivities and death on the gallows for anti-feudal heroes. "To hang on the gibbet is an honourable thing!", said the nineteenth-century *górale* musician Sabała. "They don't hang just anybody, but real men!"

The songs you are most likely to hear as a visitor to Zakopane are those about the most famous brigand of them all, **Janosik** (1688–1713). Musically they are not Podhale in style, but are lyrical ballads with a Slovakian feel, and countless tales of the region's most famous character are sung on both sides of the border. The most played songs are *Idzie Janko* and *Krywan* – and the tune for the former seems to be used for many other Janosik songs as well. The latter is not actually about the brigand, but one of the Tatra's most celebrated mountains.

The mountain regions around Podhale also have their own, if less celebrated, musical cultures. To the west there is **Orawa**, straddling the Polish–Slovak border and the Beskid Żywieckie to its north, with an annual festival in the town of Żywiec itself. To the east of Zakopane, the music of the **Spisz** region has more Slovak bounce than the Podhale style and boasts an excellent fiddle-maker and musician in Woytek Łukasz. Even if you don't make it to a highland wedding, music is relatively accessible in **Zakopane**. Many of the restaurants have good bands that play certain nights of the week; there are occasional stage shows and there's the Festival of Highland Folklore in August.

Ethnic minorities

Since the political changes of the 1980s, there's been something of a revival in the music of some of the national minorities living in Poland. There is now a more liberal climate in which to express national differences and travel is easier across the borders between related groups in Lithuania, Belarus and Ukraine. Poland's **Boyks** and **Łemks** are ethnically and culturally linked to Ukrainians and the Rusyns of Slovakia, and their music betrays its eastern Slavonic leanings in its choral and polyphonic songs. Boyk and Ukrainian groups are now a regular feature of the Kazimierz Festival. Look out for the group led by singer **Roman Kumłuk** who, with fiddler **Wołodymyr Bodnaruk**, performs music of the **Hucul** people of the Carpathian mountains. You can hear the common heritage with certain types of Romanian, Ukrainian and Jewish music. The singer **Maria Krupowes**, born in Vilnius, Lithuania, but raised in Poland, has sung Lithuanian, Belarusian, Polish and Yiddish songs exploring the connections and differences between them.

World War II saw the effective extermination of Jewish life and culture in Poland along with the exuberant and melancholy **klezmer** music for

Traditional

Gienek Wilczek's Bukowina Band *Music of the Tatra Mountains* (Nimbus, UK). Gienek is an eccentric peasant genius taught by Dziadonka, a notorious female brigand of Podhale who had learnt from Bartus Obrochta, the favoured *górale* fiddler of Szymanowski. His playing is eccentric, with a richly ornamented, raw but inspirational sound.

Sowa Family Band *Songs and Music from Rzeszów Region* (Polskie Nagrania, Poland). A wonderful disc of authentic village dances from a family band with over 150 years of recorded history. The 1970s recordings are rather harsh, but splendid all the same. Sadly, the band is no longer playing.

Trebunia Family Band *Music of the Tatra Mountains* (Nimbus, UK). A great sample of *górale* music recorded not in a cold studio session, but at an informal party to bring that special sense of spontaneity and fun. Wild playing from one of the region's best bands and well recorded. Fiddler Władysław Trebunia is the father-figure and the band includes his son Krzysztof (who often leads in his own right), daughter Hania and several other family members.

Trebunia Family *Polish Highlanders Music* (Folk, Poland). This is the Trebunia's own-label version of their *górale* music. There's terrific repertoire and playing, but it suffers from a touch too much reverb and not enough of the fun that makes the Nimbus recording so good.

Various *Polish Folk Music: Songs and Music from Various Regions* (Polskie Nagrania, Poland). An excellent cross-section of music from eight different regions all over the country, from Kashubia in the north to Podhale in the south. Recordings from Polish radio giving the perfect overview.

Various *Poland: Folk Songs and Dances* (AIMP/VDE-Gallo, Switzerland). A more "hardcore" selection of field recordings compiled by Anna Czekanowska. Includes recordings of music by ethnic minorities. Good notes.

Various *Polish Village Music: Historic Polish-American Recordings 1927–1933* (Arhoolie, US). Recordings from old 78s of Polish bands now in the US. Most still have a great down-home style. *Górale* fiddler Karol Stoch ("Last Evening in Podhale") was the most highly regarded of his day and the first to record commercially. His music sounds astonishingly similar to that which can still be heard in the region today. Not true for the bands from elsewhere in Poland. Very good notes and translations.

Various *Pologne: Danses* (Arion, France). The cover makes it look like one of those appalling "folklorique" ensembles, but this is actually a very good collection of instrumental polkas, *obereks* and other dances from southeastern Poland. Two family bands from Rzeszów district and the third, the celebrated Pudełko family, from Przeworsk. Includes several solo tracks on the *cimbały* hammer dulcimer. Excellent notes.

Various *Pologne: Instruments populaires* (Ocora, France). Predominantly instrumental music ranging from shepherds' horns and flutes, fiddles and bagpipes to small and medium-sized ensembles. A compilation, by Maria Baliszewska, of field recordings of the real thing in the best Ocora tradition. Good notes.

Various *Sources of Polish Folk Music* (Polish Radio Folk Collection, Poland). An excellent ten-volume series issued by Polish Radio, documenting Polish folk music

weddings and festivals that was part of it. The music had its distinctive Jewish elements, but drew heavily on local Polish and Ukrainian styles. Thanks to emigration and revival, the music now flourishes principally in the US and is barely heard in Poland except at the annual Festival of Jewish Culture in Kraków. The city is, though, home to a brace of highly regarded klezmer bands. **Kroke**, a trio led by violinist **Tamasz Kukurba**, started off playing with recordings from the 1960s to the mid-90s, many of them recorded at the Kazimierz Festival. Each disc focuses on a different area and comes with good notes in Polish and English on the characteristics of the region, the vocal and instrumental music and biographies of the musicians. Vol 1: Mazovia; Vol 2: Tatra Foothills; Vol 3: Lubelskie; Vol 4: Małopolska Północna; Vol 5: Wielkopolska; Vol 6: Kurpie; Vol 7: Beskidy; Vol 8: Krakowskie Tarnowskie; Vol 9: Suwalskie Podlasie; Vol 10: Rzeszowskie Pogórze. Available in the bigger Polish record shops.

Contemporary

Cracow Klezmer Band *Beresht* (Tzadik). Accomplished exercise in klezmer–jazz–contemporary fusion, combining traditionally flavoured toe-tappers with more experimental stuff – notably the moody, part-improvised title track. Also check out earlier releases *Warrior* and *De Profundis* for the same label.

Golec uOrkiestra *Golec uOrkiestra* (Program, Poland). The Golec brothers adopt a similar approach to Brathanki in writing accessible pop songs in *górale* style. However, there's something rawer, rootsier and funkier in their brass-driven sound. Massively popular but well respected with it, the uOrkiestra were paid the compliment – or indignity – of having George W. Bush quote their song lyrics during a keynote speech in Warsaw in spring 2001.

Nigel Kennedy and Kroke *East Meets East* (EMI Classical). Classical violinist and Kraków resident Kennedy teams up with one of the city's leading klezmer outfits to produce a cornucopia of cross-genre delights, with ex-Killing Joke frontman Jaz Coleman handling production duties. Kennedy/Kroke's highly individual readings of Polish, central European and Balkan tunes (Macedonian melodies looming largest) are full of surprises.

Kroke *Ten Pieces to Save the World* (Oriente). Using klezmer as a basis for further exploration rather than an end in itself, this virtuoso Kraków outfit present a shimmering instrumental set which ranges from the energizing to the contemplative, and draws on a variety of central and southern European styles for inspiration. Invesigate this first, then move on to their earlier studio albums *Time*, *Sounds of the Vanishing World*, *Eden* and *Trio* (all on Oriente).

Kwartet Jorgi *Jam* (Jam, Poland). This is the quartet's first release from 1990, featuring lots of old tunes collected by Kolberg. The Jewish-sounding *Ubinie* tune seems to tie in with the Chagall picture on the cover. Their second, eponymously titled CD (Polskie Nagrania, Poland) is a release of older material recorded in 1988. It ventures more widely into repertoire with Irish and Balkan tunes as well as excursions into what sounds like medieval jazz.

Twinkle Brothers and Trebunia Family *Twinkle Inna Polish Stylee*: *Higher Heights* and *Comeback Twinkle 2* (Ryszard Music, Poland). The intriguing sounds of "góralstafarianism".

Warsaw Village Band *Uprooting* (Jaro). This 2004 release sees the traditional music of central Poland brought thrillingly up to date, with an authentic love of ancient tunes and instruments blending nicely with anarcho-punkish attitude and energy. Their previous album *Spring of Nations* (Jaro) is equally accomplished.

schmaltzy standards, but has evolved into an inventive and exciting band who've proven their ability on tour (at the Womad festivals held worldwide, for example). The **Cracow Klezmer Band**, founded in 1997 by accordionist Jarosław Bester, has made similarly genre-bending journeys into the borderlands of klezmer, picking up a record deal with John Zorn's New York-based Tzadik label.

Revival and new music

The last two decades have seen a modest revival in Polish roots music. Not surprisingly, some of the most interesting developments have come out of Podhale and in particular the **Trebunia** family band of Poronin. Here the stern fiddler Władysław Trebunia and his son Krzysztof are both preservers of and experimenters with the tradition, as well as being leaders of one of the very best wedding bands around. In 1991 they joined up with reggae musician Norman "Twinkle" Grant to produce two albums of **Podhale reggae**, or perhaps more accurately, reggae in a Polish style. Surprising as it might seem, once you get used to the rigid beat imposed on the more flexible Polish material, the marriage works rather well and there are interesting parallels between Rasta and Podhale concerns. In 1994, the Trebunias teamed up on another project with one of Poland's leading jazz musicians, saxophonist Zbigniew Namysłowski. Here the usual *górale* ensemble meets saxophone, piano, bass and drums in an inventive romp through classic Podhale hits such as Zbójnicki tunes, Krywan and Idzie Janko.

Also making a name for themselves in the nineties were Poznań-based band **Kwartet Jorgi**, who take their music from all round Poland and beyond, with many of the tunes coming from the nineteenth-century collections of **Oskar Kolberg**. The group's leader, Maciej Rychły, plays an amazing range of ancient Polish bagpipes, whistles and flutes, which are sensitively combined with guitars, cello and drums. The music isn't purist, but is inventive and fun and shows how contemporary Polish folk music can escape the legacy of sanitized communist fakelore.

Current trends

The growing popularity of the mix-and-match approach of **world music** has had a considerable impact on the Polish folk scene, encouraging young urban Poles to dabble in traditional music from around the globe – and rediscovering their own folk heritage in the process. The tradition of experimentation pioneered by the Trebunia-Twinkle partnership was continued by other acts throughout the 1990s: Scandinavian-Polish act **De Press** produced an infectiously punky folk-rock fusion, while the more ethereal **Karpaty Magiczne** created their own genre of arty ethno chill-out music involving anything from dulcimers to digeridoos. In 1999 an album bringing together Serbian composer **Goran Bregovic** and Polish rock diva **Kayah** (entitled *Kayah and Bregovic*) was a massive hit in Poland – and even though it consisted of Balkan-inspired material rather than Polish songs, it was of inestimable importance in building an audience for folk-rock crossover music in general. The main beneficiary of this was **Brathanki**, a group from southern Poland who mixed frenetic *górale* tunes with modern pop-rock guitar riffs, and sold copies of their debut album *Ano!* by the bucketload. The success of their second album, *Pa-Ta-Taj!* (2001), seemed to confirm their status as one of the country's major pop acts. They were joined in the nation's affections by the **Golec uOrkiestra**, led by two brothers, Paweł and Lukasz (a trumpeter and trombonist) from the Żywiec region. Like Brathanki, the uOrkiestra base their repertoire on the swirling dance music of the *górale* tradition, this time adding a punchy, brass-band feel – spiced up by the occasional sonorous Latin twist.

In complete contrast to the commercialized big-label folk of the Golec brothers, Lublin-based **Orkiestra św. Mikołaja** are back-to-basics tradition-alistswhose up-beat danceable repertoire loses nothing in terms of authenticity. Working in a similar direction but with more counter-cultural attitude, the ironically named **Kapela ze wsi Warszawa** (renamed **Warsaw Village Band** for the benefit of Western consumers) combines reverence for traditional roots – and field research in Mazovian villages – with a contemporary urban taste for large-scale noise. With a conventional fiddle-and-cello string section enlivened by the addition of an archaic *suka* (a scratchy-sounding violin-like instrument of sixteenth-century origin) and a muscular rhythm section, the Warsaw Village Band is one of the most vital and original sounds to come out of Poland for a long time – a status recognized by BBC Radio 3 World Music Awards in 2004, when it picked up the gong for Best Newcomer.

With thanks to Krzysztof Cwizewicz

C

Books

A vast amount of writing both from and about Poland is available in English, and the quantity increased at an accelerated pace with the advent of the post-communist regime. Most of the books listed below are in print, and those that aren't (listed as "o.p.") should be easy enough to track down in secondhand bookshops or online at specialist websites.

Travel writing and guidebooks

Anne Applebaum *Between East and West*. Well-informed, vividly written account of British-based US journalist's travels through the eastern Polish borderlands. Starting from Kaliningrad and moving down through Lithuania, Belarus, Ukraine and Moldova, Applebaum's broad-ranging cultural-historical frame of reference means the book suffers less than others from being too close to immediate events.

Tim Burford *Hiking Guide to Poland and Ukraine* (o.p.). Thoroughly researched guide to hiking in the region.

Alfred Döblin *Journey to Poland* (o.p.). Döblin, best known for his weighty Expressionist novels, visited the newly resurrected Polish state in 1923, primarily to seek out his Jewish roots, though he himself was non-practising, and was later to convert to Catholicism. The result is a classic of travel literature, full of trenchant analysis and unnervingly prophetic predictions about the country's future, interspersed with buttonholing passages of vivid descriptive prose.

Adam Dylewski *When the Tailor was a Poet*. Polish guide to Jewish sites. Much of the book is posted on the web at ⊛www.diapozytyw.pl/en /site/slady_i_judaica.

Ruth E. Gruber *Jewish Heritage Travel: A Guide to East-Central Europe* and *Upon the Doorposts of Thy House: Jewish Life in East-Central Europe Yesterday and Today* (both o.p.). The first title is a useful country-by-country guide to Jewish culture and monuments of the region. The practical information tends to be basic, verging on the hieroglyphic, so will need supplementing for the serious searcher. The more discursive *Upon the Doorposts of Thy House* gives Gruber the space she needs to stretch out and really get into her subject. The sections on Auschwitz and Kraków's Kazimierz district are masterly, thought-provoking essays.

Eva Hoffman *Exit into History: A Journey through the New Eastern Europe*. US journalist of Polish-Jewish origin returns to her roots on a journey through the early Nineties post-communist landscape. Inevitably already dated, but the sections on Poland stand out for their combination of shrewd political insight and human warmth.

Joram Kagan *Poland's Jewish Heritage*. A useful summary of the Jewish sites of Poland, along with an outline history.

Philip Marsden *The Bronski House: A Return to the Borderlands*. Sensitively written account of the author's journey to the Polish–Belarusian borderlands in the company of Zofia Ilińska, an aristocratic former resident returning for the first time in fifty years.

Rory McLean *Stalin's Nose*. One of the best of the flurry of accounts of "epic" journeys across post-communist east-central Europe. The author's quirky brand of surrealist humour enlivens the trip, which takes in obvious Polish stopoffs, Auschwitz and Kraków, en route for Moscow.

Agata Passent *Long Live the Palace!* Sharply written history of Warsaw's Palace of Culture (see p.115), the Stalinist-era building which serves as a melancholy metaphor for communist-era Poland. Written by a young Polish journalist and published by Spis Treści in Poland, it comes in a bilingual edition available from Warsaw bookstores.

History

Chimen Abramsky, Maciej Jachimczyk and **Antony Polonsky** (eds.) *The Jews in Poland*. Historical survey of what was for centuries the largest community of world Jewry.

David Crowley *Warsaw*. Up-to-date history of the Polish capital written with enthusiasm and attitude.

Norman Davies *The Heart of Europe: A Short History of Poland*. A brilliantly original treatment of modern Polish history, beginning with the events of 1945 but looking backwards over the past millennium to illustrate the author's ideas. Scrupulously gives all points of view in disentangling the complex web of Polish history.

Norman Davies *God's Playground*. A bigger, more detailed alternative to the above, this is a masterpiece of erudition, entertainingly written and pretty much definitive for the pre-Solidarity period.

Norman Davies *White Eagle, Red Star: The Polish Soviet War, 1919–20*. Fascinating account of a little-known but critically important episode of European history, at a time when Lenin appeared ready to export the Soviet Revolution into Europe.

Colin Saunders and **Renata Narozna** *The High Tatras*. Detailed and comprehensive recent guide to the ins and outs of scaling the Tatras. For dedicated hikers and climbers.

Miriam Weiner *Jewish Roots in Poland: Pages from the Past and Archival Inventories*. Monumental coffee-table-sized guide to all aspects of Polish Jewry, the fruit of years of meticulous and painstaking trailing through archival sources – and the country itself – by its US-based author.

Norman Davies and **Roger Moorhouse** *Microcosm*. The story of the city of Wrocław, from medieval beginnings as the Slavonic settlement of Wrotizla, through life as the German-language mercantile centre of Breslau, to its current status as go-ahead capital of Poland's southwest. An exemplary exercise in urban history, and a good introduction to the history of Silesia in general.

Józef Piłsudski *Memoirs of a Polish Revolutionary and Soldier* (o.p.). Lively stuff from Lech Wałęsa's hero, who – after a dashing wartime career – was Poland's leader from 1926 to 1934.

Wacław Jedrzejewicz Piłsudski *A Life for Poland* (o.p.). Comprehensive biography of the enigmatic military strongman.

Iwo Pogonowski *Jews in Poland: A Documentary History*. Thorough if idiosyncratically presented account of Polish Jewry from the earliest times up until the present day – not too many axes to grind, either. Contains an intriguing selection of old prints from everyday life in the ghettos, shtetls and synagogues.

Anita J. Prażmowska *A History of Poland*. Intended as a handy reference work for the general reader, this is as well written, balanced and up to date as they come.

Carl Tighe *Gdańsk: National Identity in the German-Polish Border Lands.* Alternatively titled *Gdańsk: the Unauthorised Biography*, an apt description of the fascinating history of a city that Poles and Germans have tussled over for centuries. Studiously avoiding the pro- or anti-Polish–German dichotomy that bedevils many interpretations, the author sets out to capture the unique story of the Gdańsk/Danzig citizenry, arguing that claims of real Polish or German identity tell us more about the needs of latterday nationalists than the cultural complexities of the past.

Adam Zamoyski *The Polish Way.* The most accessible history of Poland, going up to the end of the communist regime. Zamoyski is an American émigré Pole, and his sympathies – as you would expect from a member of one of Poland's foremost aristocratic families – are those of a blue-blooded nationalist. His more recent *The Last King of Poland*, is a readable biography of doomed monarch Stanisław Antoni Poniatowski.

World War II and the Holocaust

Alan Adelson and **Robert Lapides** *The Łódź Ghetto – Inside a Community under Siege* (o.p.). Scrupulously detailed narrative of the 200,000-strong ghetto, with numerous personal memoirs and photographs.

Janina Bauman *Winter in the Morning*; *A Dream of Belonging* (o.p.). Bauman and her family survived the Warsaw Ghetto, eventually leaving the country following the anti-Semitic backlash of 1968. *Winter* is a delicate and moving account of life and death in the ghetto. Less dramatic but equally interesting, *Belonging*, the second volume of her autobiography, tells of life in the communist party and disillusionment in the early postwar years.

Norman Davies *Rising '44.* Impeccably researched and eminently readable piece of narrative history, published simultaneously in the UK and in Poland to coincide with the sixtieth anniversary of the ill-starred Warsaw Uprising. The question of whether the insurgents were the victims of allied betrayal is treated in balanced, meticulous fashion.

Martin Gilbert *The Holocaust.* The standard work, providing a trustworthy overview on the slaughter of European Jewry – and the crucial role of Poland, where most Nazi concentration camps were sited.

Martin Gilbert *Holocaust Journey.* Account of a study trip undertaken by Gilbert and his students in the 1990s, taking in the towns and cities where Polish Jews once lived in large numbers, as well as the key memorial sites associated with Nazi crimes. A moving and ultimately uplifting read.

Michal Grynberg *Words to Outlive Us: Voices from the Warsaw Ghetto.* History of the ghetto as seen through the eyes of those who lived through it.

Gustaw Herling-Grudziński *A World Apart* (o.p.). An account of deportation to a Soviet labour camp, based on the author's own experiences.

Rudolf Höss *Death Dealer: Memoirs of the SS Kommandant at Auschwitz.* Perhaps the most chilling record of the barbarity: a remorseless autobiography of the Auschwitz camp commandant, written in the days between his death sentence and execution at Nürnberg.

Stefan Korbonski *The Polish Underground State.* Detailed account of the history and inner workings of the many-faceted Polish wartime resistance by a leading figure of the time. Korbonski has produced a number of other books on related themes, notably *Fighting Warsaw*, an account of the 1944 Warsaw Uprising drawing on his own experience.

Dan Kurzman *The Bravest Battle* (o.p.). Detailed account of the 1943 Warsaw Ghetto Uprising, conveying the incredible courage of the Jewish combatants.

Primo Levi *If This Is a Man; The Truce; Moments of Reprieve; The Drowned and the Saved; The Periodic Table; If Not Now, When?* An Italian Jew, Levi survived Auschwitz because the Nazis made use of his training as a chemist in the death-camp factories. Most of his books, which became ever bleaker towards the end of his life, concentrate on his experiences during and soon after his incarceration in Auschwitz, analysing the psychology of survivor and torturer with extraordinary clarity. *If Not Now, When?* is the story of a group of Jewish partisans in occupied Russia and Poland; giving plenty of insights into eastern European anti-Semitism, it's a good corrective to the mythology of Jews as passive victims.

Betty Jean Lifton *Janusz Korczak: The King of the Children*. Biography of the Jewish doctor who died in Treblinka with the orphans for whom he cared. He was the eponymous subject of an Andrzej Wajda film.

Richard C. Lukas *The Forgotten Holocaust*. Detailed study of Nazi atrocities against Polish Gentiles which, in the author's view, were every bit as barbaric as against their Jewish counterparts.

Milton Nieuwsma (ed.) *Kindertransport*. Oral accounts of wartime survival from Jews who were deported to the death camps as children, collected and presented without mawkishness by a skilled and sensitive compiler.

Jan Nowak *Courier for Warsaw* (o.p.). Racily written memoir of the Polish underground resistance.

Gunnar S. Paulsson *Secret City: The Hidden Jews of Warsaw 1940–1945*. Over 11,000 Jews survived World War II in Warsaw, and this study helps explain how they did it; establishing safehouses, hunkering down in underground hideouts; disguising themselves as Gentiles and relying on the help of a significant number of Poles who were prepared to help fugitives escape. Meticulously researched, gripping stuff.

Joanna Podolska *Traces of the Litzmannstadt-Getto*. Published in Poland and on sale in bookshops in Łódź, this is an invaluable and fascinating guide to that city's wartime ghetto, with lots of black-and-white photographs, detailed maps, and quotations from ghetto survivors.

Laurence Rees *Auschwitz*. Grave, unflinching history of the Final Solution focusing on the most notorious death-camp of all. Published to accompany a BBC TV series of the same name, it contains much new research, and makes full and revealing use of interviews conducted with camp survivors, civilian witnesses and former guards.

Emmanuel Ringelblum *Polish–Jewish Relations during the Second World War*. Penetrating history of the Warsaw Ghetto focusing on the vexed issue of Polish–Jewish wartime relations. Written from the inside by the prominent prewar Jewish historian – history recorded as it was occurring. Tragically, only a portion of Ringelblum's own writings and the extensive Ghetto archives he put together were recovered after 1945.

Saul Rubinek *So Many Miracles* (o.p.). Rubinek's interviews with his parents about their early life in Poland and survival under Nazi occupation make a compelling piece of oral history, and one that paints a blacker than usual picture of Polish–Jewish relations.

Art Spiegelman *Maus*. Spiegelman, editor of the cartoon magazine *Raw*, is the son of Auschwitz survivors. *Maus* is a brilliant comic-strip exploration of the ghetto and concentration camp experiences of his father, recounted in flashbacks. The story runs through to Art's father's imprisonment at Auschwitz; subsequent chapters of the sequel – covering Auschwitz itself – have been printed in recent editions of *Raw*, now available as a separate book, *Maus II*. In 2001, *Maus* was published in Poland to great acclaim – despite the fact that the Polish characters in the book are depicted as pigs.

Sybille Steinbacher *Auschwitz: A History*. Concise, matter-of-fact account, written with the dignity and gravity that the subject deserves.

Władysław Szpilman *The Pianist*. Wartime memoirs of concert pianist and composer Szpilman (1911–2000), who miraculously survived the Warsaw Ghetto. Originally published as *Smierc Miasta* (*Death of a City*) in 1945, Szpilman's book was initially buried by a postwar Polish regime unwilling to recognize the full extent of Jewish suffering in World War II. Now available again in both Polish and English versions, *The Pianist* has already made it onto celluloid courtesy of Kraków Ghetto survivor Roman Polański.

Harold Werner *Fighting Back: A Memoir of Jewish Resistance in World War II*. Gripping, straightforwardly written account of the author's experiences as a member of a Jewish partisan unit fighting against the Nazis in wartime Poland.

Politics and society

Timothy Garton Ash *The Polish Revolution: Solidarity 1980–82* (o.p.); *The Uses of Adversity* (o.p.); *We The People: The Revolution of 89* (o.p.). Garton Ash was the most consistent and involved Western reporter on Poland during the Solidarity era, displaying an intuitive grasp of the Polish mentality. His *Polish Revolution* is a vivid record of events from the birth of Solidarity – a story extended in the climactic events of 1989, documented as an eyewitness in Warsaw, Budapest, Berlin and Prague.

Jaqueline Hayden *Poles Apart: Solidarity and the New Poland*. Personal account of political developments in Poland from August 1980 up to the election of the SLD-led government in 1993 by an Irish journalist who visited the country throughout the period. The format – a series of extended interviews with key opposition figures, tracing their lives and political development – offers an interesting overview that combines the personal with the political.

Radek Sikorski *The Polish House: An Intimate History Of Poland* (o.p.). Highly personalized and passionately penned account of modern Polish history by former Solidarity activist, UK exile and journalist who rose briefly to the heights of deputy defence minister in 1992, aged 29. The author's trenchantly anticommunist views begin to grate after a while, but overall you'd be hard put to find a better insider's introduction to contemporary realities.

Essays and memoirs

Kazimierz Brandys *Warsaw Diary 1977–81* (o.p.) and *Paris, New York: 1982–84* (o.p.). The *Warsaw Diary*, by this major Polish journalist and novelist, brilliantly captures the atmosphere of the time, and especially the effect of John Paul II's first papal visit in 1979. During martial law, possession of this book carried an automatic ten-year prison sentence. *Paris, New York* powerfully traces his early life in imposed exile while continually reflecting on developments at home.

Adam Czerniawski *Scenes from a Disturbed Childhood* (o.p.). Uplifting, entertainingly written account of a childhood spent escaping the traumas of World War II – to Turkey and an Arab school in Palestine – before ending up with his impoverished upper-class family in southeast England. A welcome addition to wartime émigré memoir literature.

Granta 30: New Europe! (o.p.). Published at the beginning of 1990, this state-of-the-continent anthology includes Neil Ascherson on the eastern Polish borderlands and a series of brief reactions to events from a dozen or so European intellectuals.

Zbigniew Herbert *Barbarian in the Garden*. Stirring, lyrical set of essays on Mediterranean themes by the noted late Polish poet, with 1960s post-Stalinist-era Poland – the period when they were written – a recurring background presence.

Eva Hoffman *Lost in Translation* (o.p.). Wise, sparklingly written autobiography of a Polish Jew centring, as the title suggests, around her experience of emigration from Kraków to North America in the 1960s. Plenty of insights into the postwar Jewish/Eastern Europe émigré experience.

Eva Hoffman *Shtetl: The Life And Death Of A Small Town and The World Of Polish Jews* (o.p.). Imaginative, well-researched reconstruction of life in a typical prewar Polish *shtetl*. Good on broader issues of Polish–Jewish relations, although her carefully balanced conclusions have come in for predictable criticism from those who say it paints too rosy a picture of the prewar period.

Ryszard Kapuściński *Shadow of the Sun*. For many years Kapuściński was the only full-time Polish foreign correspondent, and is best known for his trilogy on the dictators of Iran, Angola and Ethiopia. His latest book, a collection of sketches of African politics, offers many wry insights into his native land.

Czesław Miłosz *The Captive Mind; Native Realm; Beginning with My Streets*. The first is a penetrating analysis of the reasons so many Polish artists and intellectuals sold out to communism after 1945, with four case studies supplementing a confession of personal guilt. *Native Realm*, the unorthodox autobiography of the years before Miłosz defected to the West, is especially illuminating on the Polish–Lithuanian relationship. The last is a wide-ranging collection of essays by this Nobel Prize-winning author, including an invigorating set of pieces revolving around Wilno (Vilnius), the author's boyhood home and spiritual mentor in later life.

Toby Nobel Fluek *Memoirs of my Life in a Polish Village 1930–39* (o.p.). Touching memoir of a young Jewish girl growing up in a village near Lwów in the 1930s. Plenty of insights into the traditional prewar Polish rural way of life, enhanced by the author's simple but evocative illustrations.

Barbara Porajska *From the Steppes to the Savannah* (o.p.). Simply written yet informative memoir of one of the hundreds of Poles deported to Kazakhstan and other parts of Soviet Asia following the Soviet annexation to eastern Poland in 1939. Like many others, too, the author finally made it to Britain, via adventures in Iran and East Africa.

Theo Richmond *Konin: A Quest*. Moving account of a British Jew's tireless quest to trace his family roots in a small town in western Poland that also displays a strong feel for the broader historical and political context.

Teresa Torańska *Oni: Poland's Stalinists Cross-Examined* (o.p.). Interviews with Polish communists and Party leaders from the Stalinist era carried out during the Solidarity era by investigative journalist Torańska. The result is a fascinating insight into how Stalin established Soviet control over Eastern Europe, and Poland in particular.

Adam Zagajewski *Two Cities*. Born in Lwów, raised in the Silesian city of Gliwice and now based in Paris, contemporary poet Zagajewski's collection of essays and prose pieces roves across the themes of exile and displacement.

Culture, art and architecture

Tadeusz Budziński *In the Borderland of Cultures*. Well-presented photo album of wooden churches in southeastern Poland, published by Libra (⊛www.libra.pl) in Rzeszów. Available in both coffee-table and pocket editions.

David Buxton *The Wooden Churches of Eastern Europe* (o.p.). Wonderful illustrations of Poland's most compelling architectural style. Well worth hunting out in libraries: it will make you want to traipse around Silesia, the Bieszczady Mountains and Czech borderlands.

Jan Kott (ed.) *Four Decades of Polish Essays*. Culture-based anthology – on art, literature, drama, plus politics – that features most of the major intellectual names of postwar Poland.

Czesław Miłosz *The History of Polish Literature*. Written in the mid-1960s, this is, however, still the standard English-language work on the subject, informed by the author's consummate grasp of the furthest nooks and crannies of Polish literature.

The Polish Jewry: History and Culture Wide-ranging collection of essays and photographs on all aspects of culture – from customs and family life to theatre, music and painting. A beautiful production, published by Interpress in Warsaw.

Roman Vishniac *Polish Jews – A Pictorial Record*. Haunting selection of pictures by the legendary photographer, evoking Jewish life in the *shtetls* and ghettos of Poland immediately before the outbreak of World War II. A good introduction to the great man's work if you can't get hold of *A Vanished World* (o.p.), the acclaimed album that brings together most of the two thousand or so photos from Vishniac's travels through Jewish Poland.

Tomasz Wiśniewski *Jewish Bialystok and Surrroundings in Eastern Europe*. Encyclopedic survey of the wealth of prewar Jewish architecture in the eastern borderlands, much of it destroyed but with a significant number of buildings still surviving. Great for exploring the Białystok-Tykocin region.

Polish fiction

Shmuel Yozef Agnon *A Simple Story* and *Dwelling Place of My People* (o.p.). Agnon, Polish-born Nobel Prize-winner and father-figure of modern Hebrew literature, sets *A Simple Story* in the Jewish communities of the Polish Ukraine, belying its title by weaving an unexpected variation on the traditional Romeo-and-Juliet-type tale of crossed lovers. In *Dwelling Place* he recalls his childhood in Poland, in a series of highly refined stories and prose poems.

Jerzy Andrzejewski *Ashes and Diamonds*. Spring 1945: resistance fighters, communist ideologues and black marketeers battle it out in small-town Poland. A gripping account of the tensions and forces that shaped postwar Poland, and the basis for Andrzej Wajda's film of the same title.

Asher Barash *Pictures from a Brewery* (o.p.). Depiction of Jewish life in Galicia, told in a style very different from the mythic, romantic approach favoured by Agnon.

Tadeusz Borowski *This Way for the Gas, Ladies and Gentlemen*. These short stories based on his Auschwitz experiences marked Borowski out as the great literary hope of communist Poland, but he committed suicide soon after their publication, at the age of 29.

Joseph Conrad *A Personal Record*. An entertaining, ironic piece of "faction" about Conrad's family and his early life in the Russian part of Partition Poland, addressing the painful subjects of his loss of his own country and language.

Ida Fink *A Scrap of Time*. Haunting vignettes of Jews striving to escape the concentration camps – and of the unsung Polish Gentiles who sheltered them.

Adam Gillon (ed.) *Introduction to Modern Polish Literature*. An excellent anthology of short stories and extracts from novels, many of them (e.g. Reymont's *The Peasants*) out of print in English.

Witold Gombrowicz *Ferdydurke*; *Pornografia* and *The Possessed*. The first two experimentalist novels concentrate on humanity's infantile and juvenile obsessions, and on the tensions between urban life and the traditional ways of the countryside. *The Possessed* explores the same themes within the more easily digestible format of a Gothic thriller.

Marek Hłasko *The Eighth Day of the Week*; *Killing the Second Dog* (o.p.) and *Next Stop – Paradise & the Graveyard*. Once considered Poland's "Angry Young Man", Hłasko articulated the general disaffection of those who grew up after World War II, his bleak themes mirrored in a spare, taut prose style.

Pawel Huelle *Who Was David Weiser?*; *Moving House* and *Mercedes-Benz*. The first novel from the award-winning Gdańsk-based writer centres on an enigmatic young Jewish boy idolized by his youthful contemporaries. The author's themes and style show an obvious debt to fellow Danziger Günter Grass. Huelle's magic-realist propensities are further developed in *Moving House*, a marvellous collection of short stories, with the intersecting worlds of Polish and German/Prussian culture again providing the primary frame of reference. *Mercedes-Benz* is a hugely entertaining four-wheeled meditation on Polish history, the much-loved metal crate of the title having been requisitioned from the narrator's grandfather by the Soviets outside Lwów in 1939.

Tadeusz Konwicki *A Minor Apocalypse*; *A Dreambook for our Time*; *The*

Polish Complex (o.p.) and *Bohin Manor*. A convinced Party member in the 1950s, Konwicki eventually made the break with Stalinism; since then a series of highly respected novels, films and screenplays have established him as one of Poland's foremost writers. Describing a single day's events, *A Minor Apocalypse* is narrated by a character who constantly vacillates over his promise to set fire to himself in front of the Party headquarters. *Dreambook* is a hard-hitting wartime tale, while *The Polish Complex* is a fascinating, often elusive exploration of contemporary life in Poland. Finally, *Bohin Manor* is an elegaic novel set among the Polish-Lithuanian gentry in the wake of the 1863 anti-tsarist uprising: like Miłosz (see below) and many others who grew up in Lithuania, Konwicki betrays a yearning for a mystic homeland.

Janusz Korczak *King Matty the First*. Written by the famous Jewish doctor who died, along with his orphans, at Treblinka, this long children's novel, regarded as the Polish counterpart of *Alice in Wonderland*, appeals also to adults through its underlying sense of tragedy and gravitas.

Stanisław Lem *Solaris*; *The Futurological Congress: From the Memoirs of Ijon Tichy*; *Tales of Pirx the Pilot*; *His Master's Voice*. The only recent Polish writing to have achieved a worldwide mass-market readership, Lem's science fiction focuses on the human and social predicament in the light of technological change. An author of considerable range and invention, Lem's best-known work, *Solaris*, is a disturbing and meditative account of a spiritual quest, while *The Futurological Congress* is a sophisticated satire on the absurdity of our times.

Czesław Miłosz *The Seizure of Power* (o.p.) and *The Issa Valley*. The *Seizure of Power*, the first book by this Nobel Prize-winning writer, is a

wartime novel, while the semi-autobiographical *Issa Valley* is a wonderfully lyrical account of a boy growing up in the Lithuanian countryside.

Jan Potocki *The Manuscript Found at Saragossa: Ten Days in the Life of Alphonse von Worden*. A self-contained section of a huge unfinished Gothic novel written at the beginning of the nineteenth century by a Polish nobleman: a rich brew of picaresque adventures, dreams, hallucinations, eroticism, philosophical discourses and exotic tales.

Bolesław Prus *Pharaoh* and *The Doll*. The first, a late nineteenth-century epic, set in ancient Egypt, offers a trenchant examination of the nature of power in a society that was of more than passing relevance to Partition-era Poland. *The Doll* is probably the most famous of the "Polish Tolstoy's" lengthier works: widely regarded as one of the great nineteenth-century social novels, this is a brilliantly observed story of obsessive love against the backdrop of a crisis-ridden *fin-de-siècle* Warsaw.

R. Pynsent and **S. Kanikova** (eds.) The Everyman Companion to East European Literature. The Polish section combines thoughtful introductory essays on the place of literature and writers in the national consciousness. Includes short extracts from works by major artists (Prus, Witkiewicz, Mickiewicz), a literary itinerary through the country and a brief authors' A–Z.

Władysław Reymont *The Peasants* and *The Promised Land* (both o.p.). Reymont won the Nobel Prize for *The Peasants*, a tetralogy about village life (one for each season of the year), but its vast length has led to its neglect outside Poland. *The Promised Land*, which was filmed by Wajda, offers a comparably unromanticized view of industrial life in Łódź.

Bruno Schulz *Street of Crocodiles* and *Sanatorium under the Sign of the Hourglass*. These kaleidoscopic, dreamlike fictions, vividly evoking life in the small town of Drohobycz in the Polish Ukraine, constitute the entire literary output of their hugely influential author, who was murdered by the SS. For more on Schulz, get hold of *Regions of the Great Heresy*, a recent biography written by renowned Polish scholar Jerzy Ficowski.

Henryk Sienkiewicz *Quo Vadis?*; *Charcoal Sketches* and *Other Tales*; *With Fire and Sword*; *The Deluge* and *Fire in the Steppe*. Sienkiewicz's reputation outside Poland largely rests on *Quo Vadis?* (which won him the Nobel Prize), treating the early Christians in Nero's Rome as an allegory of Poland's plight under the Partitions. Until recently, Sienkiewicz's other blockbusters existed only in inadequate and long out-of-print translations, but the Polish–American novelist W.S. Kuniczak has recently rendered the great trilogy about Poland's seventeenth-century wars with the Swedes, Prussians, Germans and Turks into English in a manner that at last does justice to the richly crafted prose of the originals. If the sheer size of these is too daunting, a more than adequate taste of the author's style can be had from the three novellas in the *Charcoal Sketches* collection, which focus on the different classes of nineteenth-century Polish rural society with a wry wit and a sense of pathos.

Isaac Bashevis Singer *The Magician of Lublin* (o.p.); *The Family Moskat* (o.p.); *Collected Stories*; *The Slave*; *Satan in Goray*; *The King of the Fields* (o.p.). Singer, who emigrated from Poland to the US in the 1930s, wrote in Yiddish, so his reputation rests largely on the translations of his novels and short stories. Only a selection of his vast output is mentioned here. *The Magician of Lublin* and *The Family Moskat*, both novels set in the ghettos of early twentieth-century Poland, are masterly evocations of life in vanished Jewish communities. *The Slave* is a gentle yet tragic love story set in the seventeenth century, while *Satan in Goray* is a blazing evocation of religious hysteria in the same period. His penultimate work, *The King of the Fields*, re-creates the early life of the Polish state, and is his only novel without a Jewish emphasis.

Andrzej Stasiuk *White Raven* and *Tales of Galicia*. Edgy prose from a leading contemporary novelist and travel writer. The first concerns a hiking-obsessed group of Warsaw misfits whose trip to the mountains descends into gory nightmare; the second contains surreal and melancholic snatches of life from the southeastern corner of Poland, a rustic area in which city-boy Stasiuk has himself taken up residence.

Andrzej Szczypiorski *The Beautiful Mrs Seidemann*. Bestselling novel by prominent contemporary Polish writer who survived both the Warsaw Uprising and subsequently the concentration camps. The story centres around a Jewish woman who uses her wits – and beauty – to survive the Nazis. Stirringly written, though the fatalistic historical musings (he's obviously got a foreign audience in mind) become increasingly oppressive as the book progresses.

Olga Tokarczuk *House of Day, House of Night*. Award-winning novel from one of the most distinctive new voices in Polish fiction, evoking the small-town world of Nowa Ruda (a real-life mining settlement in the Polish–Czech–German borderlands) through a dream-like mixture of narrative fragments, extracts from the life of a medieval saint, and recipes for forest mushrooms.

Stanisław Ignacy Witkiewicz *Insatiability*. Explicit depiction of artistic, intellectual, religious and sexual decadence against the background of a Chinese invasion of

Europe. The enormous vocabulary, complicated syntax and philosophical diversions don't make an easy read, but this is unquestionably one of the most distinctive works of twentieth-century literature.

Polish poetry

S. Barańczak and **C. Cavanagh** (eds.) *Spoiling Cannibal's Fun: Polish Poetry of the Last Two Decades of Communist Rule*. Representative anthology of recent Polish poetry with informative introductory essay by co-editor and translator Stanisław Barańczak, one of the country's pre-eminent émigré literary figures whose poems are also featured in this volume.

Adam Czerniawski (ed.) *The Burning Forest*. Selected by one of Poland's leading contemporary poets, this anthology covers Polish poetry from the laconic nineteenth-century verses of Cyprian Norwid, through examples of Herbert, Różewicz and the editor, up to young writers of the present day.

Zbigniew Herbert *Selected Poems*; *Report from the Besieged City* (o.p.). Arguably the greatest contemporary Polish poet, with a strong line in poignant observation; intensely political but never dogmatic. The widespread international mourning occasioned by Herbert's death in 1998 confirmed the man's special place in contemporary literary affections.

Adam Mickiewicz *Pan Tadeusz*; *Konrad Wallenrod* and *Grażyna*. The first is Poland's national epic, set among the gentry of Lithuania at the time of the Napoleonic invasion – the most readable translation, that by George Rapall Noyes, has long been out of print but is available in some libraries. In contrast to the self-delusion about Polish independence shown by the characters in *Pan Tadeusz*, *Konrad Wallenrod*

Various authors *The Eagle and the Crow*. Superb short-story compilation featuring almost all the big names of twentieth-century fiction. If you're new to Polish literature, you won't find a better place to start.

demonstrates how that end can be achieved by stealth and cunning; like *Grażyna*, its setting is Poland-Lithuania's struggle with the Teutonic Knights.

Czesław Miłosz *New and Collected Poems*. A writer of massive integrity, Miłosz in all his works wrestles with the issues of spiritual and political commitment; this collection encompasses all his poetic phases, from the Surrealist of the 1930s to the émigré sage of San Francisco.

Czesław Miłosz (ed.) *Polish Postwar Poetry*. Useful anthology selected and mostly translated by Miłosz, with an emphasis on poetry written after the thaw of 1956. The closer you get to the 1980s the grittier and more acerbic they become, as befits the politics of the era.

Tadeusz Różewicz *Conversations with the Prince* (o.p.). These uncompromising verses, rooted in everyday speech, are among the most accessible examples of modern Polish poetry.

Wisława Szymborska *People on the Bridge*. For some time virtually the only volume of poems by the 1996 Nobel Prize-winning Polish author available in English. Szymborska remains one of the most distinctive modern (female) voices, translated here by fellow poet, Adam Czerniawski. Of the volumes to appear in the wake of the Nobel award, *View With a Grain of Sand* is an excellent introduction to the Szymborska oeuvre; *Poems New and Collected 1957–1997* is a large, well-translated selection of her poems spanning the last four decades; *Sounds, Feelings, Thoughts: Seventy Poems*, a reissue, covers similar territory, albeit less comprehensively.

Aleksander Wat *Selected Poems* (o.p.). Dating from Wat's middle and later years, these wide-ranging poems, with their predominant tone of despair at the century's excesses, make a fascinating contrast to the

Futurist short-story fantasies he wrote in the interwar period.

Adam Zagajewski *Without End.* Highly regarded verse from a writer following in the footsteps of Herbert and Miłosz. Drawing on Zagajewski's best-known collection *Mysticism for Beginners*, as well as other volumes, this is the best possible introduction to his work.

Polish drama

Solomon Anski *The Dybbuk*, included in *Three Great Jewish Plays*. Written by a prominent member of the Jewish socialist movement, this drama of divine justice is the masterpiece of Yiddish theatre. Also included in the anthology is a work on a similar theme, *God of Vengeance* by Scholem Asch.

Daniel Gerould (ed.) *The Witkiewicz Reader*. Painstakingly compiled and well-translated anthology of writings by the great artist/philosopher/dramatist covering the various stages of Witkiewicz's development, from the early plays via explicitly drug-induced musings through to later philosophical and literary critical pieces.

Witold Gombrowicz *The Marriage*; *Operetta* and *Princess Ivona*. Three plays exploring similar themes to those found in Gombrowicz's novels.

Tadeusz Kantor *Wielopole/Wielopole*. One of the most successful products of Poland's experimental

theatre scene, complete with a lavish record of its production plus the author and director's rehearsal notes.

Sławomir Mrożek *Tango* (o.p.); *Vatzlav* (o.p.); *Striptease, Repeat Performance and The Prophets* (o.p.). Mrożek is the sharpest and subtlest satirist Poland has produced, employing nonsensical situations to probe serious political issues.

Tadeusz Rożewicz *The Card Index*; *The Interrupted Act and Gone Out*; *Marriage Blanc and The Hunger Artist Departs*. The best works by an unremittingly inventive experimentalist.

Stanisław Ignacy Witkiewicz *The Madman and the Nun*, *The Water Hen* and *The Crazy Locomotive*. Witkiewicz created a Theatre of the Absurd twenty years before the term came into common use through the work of Ionesco and Beckett. This volume makes the ideal introduction to the versatile avant-garde painter, novelist and playwright.

Literature by foreign writers

Isaac Babel *Red Cavalry*, from *Collected Stories*. A collection of interrelated short stories about the 1919–20 invasion of Poland, narrated by the bizarrely contradictory figure of a Jewish Cossack communist,

who naturally finds himself torn by conflicting emotions.

Günter Grass *The Tin Drum*; *Dog Years* and *Cat and Mouse*. These three novels, also available in one volume as the *Danzig Trilogy*, are one of the high points of modern German literature. Set in Danzig/Gdańsk, where the author grew up, they hold up a mirror to the changing German character this century. The later *The Call of the Toad*, provides a satirical commentary on post-communist Polish and German attitudes towards the same city's past.

Gerhart Hauptmann *The Weavers* (o.p. in the UK), published as part of *Three Plays* (Waveland Press) in the US. Set against the background of a heroic but inevitably futile mid-nineteenth-century uprising by the Silesian weavers against the mill owners, this intense drama gained its reputation as the first "socialist" play by having a collective rather than a single protagonist.

E.T.A. Hoffmann *The Jesuit Chapel at G* in *Six German Romantic Tales*; *The Artushof* in *Tales of Hoffmann*. Hoffmann began writing his masterly stories of the macabre while a bored civil servant in Prussian Poland; these are two with a specifically Polish setting.

Thomas Keneally *Schindler's List*. Originally entitled *Schindler's Ark* before becoming the subject of Spielberg's film, this powerful, 1982 Booker Prize-winning novel is based on the life of Oskar Schindler, a German industrialist who used his business operations to shelter thousands of Jews.

Leon Uris *Mila 18*. Stirring tale of the Warsaw Ghetto Uprising – Mila 18 was the address of the Jewish resistance militia's HQ.

Film

Marek Haltof *The Cinema of Krzysztof Kieślowski*. Comprehensive study of the award-winning director, which also works well as an introduction to Polish cinema in general.

Krzysztof Kieślowski and **Krzysztof Piesiewicz** Decalogue. Transcripts of the internationally acclaimed series of films, set in a Warsaw housing estate, featuring tales of breaches of the Ten Commandments.

Brian McIlroy *World Cinema: Poland* (o.p.). In-depth study of the Polish

film scene including interviews, biographies and plenty of black-and-white stills.

Andrzej Wajda *Double Vision: My Life in Film* (o.p.). Autobiography of Poland's most famous director, who bagged the Lifetime Achievement Oscar in 2000; rather more rewarding than some of his later celluloid creations. The *Cinema of Andrzej Wajda*, edited by John Orr and Elzbieta Ostrowska, offers a more analytic approach to the man's four-decade-long career.

Language

Language

Pronunciation 707

Useful words and phrases 708

Food and drink 712

Glossaries 714

Language

Polish is one of the more difficult European languages for English speakers to learn. Even so, it is well worth acquiring the basics: not only is Polish beautiful and melodious, but a few words will go a long way. This is especially true away from the major cities where you won't find a lot of English spoken. Knowledge of German, however, is quite widespread.

The following features provide an indication of the problems of Polish grammar. There are three genders (masculine, feminine and neuter) and no word for "the". Prepositions (words like "to", "with", "in" and so on) take different cases, and the case changes the form of the noun. Thus, *miasto* is the Polish for "town", but "to the town" is *do miasta* and "in the town" is *w miescie*. You don't have to learn this sort of thing off by heart, but it can be useful to be able to recognize it.

Finally, a brief word on how to address people. The familiar form used among friends, relations and young people is *ty*, like French *tu* or German *du*. However, the polite form which you will usually require is *Pan* when addressing a man and *Pani* for a woman ("Sir" and "Madam"). *Always* use this form with people obviously older than yourself, and with officials.

The *Rough Guide to Polish* **phrasebook** has a more detailed selection of useful terms.

Pronunciation

While Polish may look daunting at first, with its apparently unrelieved rows of consonants, the good news is that it's a phonetic language – ie it's pronounced exactly as spelt. So once you've learnt the rules and have a little experience you'll always know how to pronounce a word correctly.

Stress

Usually on the penultimate syllable, eg *Warszawa, przyjaciel, matka*.

Vowels

a: as "a" in "cat".

e: "e" in "neck".

i: "i" in "Mick", never as in "I".

o: "o" in "lot", never as in "no" or "move".

u: "oo" in "look".

y: unknown in Standard English; cross between "e" and Polish "i", eg the "y" in the Yorkshire pronunciation of "Billy".

There are three specifically Polish vowels:

ą: nasalized – like "ong" in "long" or French "on".

ę: nasalized – like French "un" (eg Lech Wałęsa).

ó: same sound as Polish "u".

Vowel combinations include:

ie: pronounced y-e, eg *nie wiem* (I don't know): ny-e vy-em (not nee-veem).

eu: each letter pronounced separately, eg "E-u-ropa" (Europe).

ia: rather like "yah", eg *historia* (history): histor-i-yah.

Consonants

Those which look the same as English but are different:

w: as "v" in "vine", eg "wino" pronounced "vino" (wine).

r: trilled (as in Scottish pronunciation of English "r").

h: like the "ch" in Scottish "loch".

Some consonants are pronounced differently at the end of a word or syllable: "b" sounds like "p", "d" like "t", "g" like "k", "w" like "f".

Polish-specific consonants include:

ć and **ci**: "ch" as in "church".

ł: "dark l" sounding rather like a "w".

ń and **ni**: soft "n", sounding like "n-ye", eg *koń* (horse): kon-ye.

ś and **si**: "sh" as in "ship".

ź and **zi**: like the "j" of French *journal*.

ż and **rz**: as in French "g" in *gendarme*. (Note that the dot over the "z" is sometimes replaced by a bar through the letter's diagonal.)

Consonantal pairs

cz: "ch" (slightly harder than "ć" and "ci").

sz: "sh" (ditto "ś" and "si").

dz: "d" as in "day" rapidly followed by "z" as in "zoo", eg *dzwon* (bell): d-zvon. At the end of a word is pronounced like "ts" as in "cats".

dź: "d-sh", eg *dźungla* (jungle): d-shun-gla.

dż: sharper than the above; at the end of a word is pronounced like "ć" (ch).

szcz: this fearsome-looking cluster is easy to pronounce – "sh-ch" as in "pushchair", eg *szczur* (rat): sh-choor.

Useful words and phrases

Words

Tak	Yes	Ten/ta/to	This one (masc/fem/neuter)
Nie	No/not		
Proszę	Please/you're welcome	Tamten/tamta/tamto	That one (masc/fem/neuter)
Proszę bardzo	More emphatic than *proszę*	Wielki	Large
		Mały	Small
Dziekuję/dziekuję bardzo	Thank you	Więcej	More
		Mniej	Less
Gdzie	Where	Mało	A little
Kiedy	When	Dużo	A lot
Dlaczego	Why	Tani	Cheap
Ile	How much	Drogi	Expensive
Tu/tam	Here, there	Dobry	Good
Teraz	Now	Zły/niedobry	Bad
Później	Later	Gorący	Hot
Otwarty	Open	Zimny	Cold
Zamknięty	Closed/shut	Z	With
Wcześniej	Earlier	Bez	Without
Dosyć	Enough	W	In
Tam	Over there	Dla	For

Phrases

Dzień dobry	Good day; hello	Irlandczykiem/ Irlandką	Irish
Dobry wieczór	Good evening		
Dobra noc	Good night	Amerikaniem/ Amerikanką	American
Cześć!	"Hi!" or "'Bye" (like Italian *ciao*)	Kanadyjczykiem/ Kanadyjką	Canadian
Do widzenia	Goodbye		
Przepraszam	Excuse me (apology)	Australyjczykiem/ Australyjką	Australian
Proszę Pana/Pani	Excuse me (requesting information)	Mieszkam w . . .	I live in . . .
Jak się masz?	How are you? (informal)	Dzisiaj	Today
Jak się Pan/Pani ma?	How are you? (formal)	Jutro	Tomorrow
Dobrze	Fine	Pojutrze	Day after tomorrow
Czy Pan/Pani mówi po angielsku?	Do you speak English?	Wczoraj	Yesterday
		Chwileczkę	Moment!/Wait a moment
Rozumiem	I understand		
Nie rozumiem	I don't understand	Rano	In the morning
Nie wiem	I don't know	Po południu	In the afternoon
Proszę mówić trochę wolniej	Please speak a bit more slowly	Wieczorem	In the evening
		Gdzie jest . . . ?	Where is . . . ?
Nie mówię dobrze po polsku	I don't speak Polish very well	Jak dojechać do . . . ?	How do I get to . . . ?
Co to znaczy po polsku?	What's the Polish for that?	Która (jest) godzina?	What time is it?
Jestem tu na urlopie	I'm here on holiday	Jak daleko jest do . . . ?	How far is it to . . . ?
Jestem Brytyjczykiem/ Brytyjką	I'm British (male/ female)		

Accommodation

Hotel	Hotel	Z balkonem	With a balcony
Noclegi	Lodgings	Z ciepłą wodą	Hot water
Czy jest gdzieś tutaj hotel?	Is there a hotel nearby?	Z bieżącę wodą	Running water
		Ile kosztuje?	How much is it?
Czy Pan/Pani ma pokój?	Do you have a room?	To drogo	That's expensive
		To za drogo	That's too expensive
Pojedynczy pokój	Single room	Czy to obejmuje śniadanie?	Does that include breakfast?
Podwójny pokój	Double room		
Będziemy jedną dobę	For one night (*doba*: 24 hours)	Czy nie ma tańszego?	Do you have anything cheaper?
Dwie noce	Two nights	Czy mogę zobaczyć pokój?	Can I see the room?
Trzy noce	Three nights		
Tydzień	A week	Dobrze, wezmę	Good, I'll take it
Dwa tygodnie	Two weeks	Mam rezerwację	I have a booking
Pokój z łazienką	With a bath	Czy możemy tu rozbić namiot?	Can we camp here?
Z prysznicem	With a shower		

Czy jest gdzieś tutaj camping?	Is there a campsite nearby?	Schronisko młodziezowe	Youth hostel
Namiot	Tent	Proszę o jadłospis	The menu, please
Schronisko	Cabin	Proszę o rachunek	The bill, please

Travelling

Auto	Car	Kiedy odjeżdża pociąg do Warszawy?	When does the Warsaw train leave?
Samolot	Aircraft		
Rower	Bicycle		
Autobus	Bus	Czy muszę się przesiadać?	Do I have to change?
Prom	Ferry		
Pociąg	Train	Z jakiego peronu odjedzie pociąg?	Which platform does the train leave from?
Dworzec, samochód, stacja	Train station		
Autobusowy	Bus station	Ile to jest kilometrów?	How many kilometres is it?
Taksówka	Taxi	Ile czasu trwa podróż?	How long does the journey last?
Autostop	Hitchhiking		
Piechotą	On foot	Jakim autobusem do . . . ?	Which bus is it to . . . ?
Proszę bilet do . . .	A ticket to . . . , please		
Bilet powrotny	Return	Gdzie jest droga do . . . ?	Where is the road to . . . ?
W jedną stronę	Single		
Proszę z miejscówką	I'd like a seat reservation	Następny przystanek, proszę	Next stop, please

Signs

Wejście; wyjucie	Entrance; exit/way out	Peron	Platform
Wstęp wzbroniony	No entrance	Kasa	Cash desk
Toaleta	Toilet	Stop	Stop
Dla panów; męski	Men	Granica międzynarodowa	Polish state frontier
Dla pan; damski	Women		
Zajęty	Occupied	Rzeczpospolita Polska	Republic of Poland
Wolny	Free, vacant		
Przyjazd; odjazd	Arrival; departure (train, bus)	Uwaga; baczność	Beware, caution
		Uwaga; niebezpieczenstwo	Danger
Przylot; odlot	Arrival; departure (aircraft)	Policja	Police
		Informacja	Information
Remont	Closed for renovation/ stocktaking	Nie palić; palenie wzbronione	No smoking
Ciągnąć; pchać	Pull; push		
Nieczynny	Out of order; closed (ticket counters etc)	Nie dotykać	Do not touch

Driving

| Samochód, auto | Car | Na prawo | Right |
| Na lewo | Left | Prosto | Straight ahead |

Parking	Parking	Olej	Oil
Objazd	Detour	Woda	Water
Koniec	End (showing when a previous sign ceases to be valid)	Naprawić	To repair
		Wypadek	Accident
		Awaria	Breakdown
Zakaz wyprzedzania	No overtaking	Ograniczenie prędkosći	Speed limit
Benzyna	Petrol/gas		
Stacja benzynowa	Petrol/gas station		

Days, months and dates

Poniedziałek	Monday	Lipiec	July
Wtorek	Tuesday	Sierpień	August
Środa	Wednesday	Wrzesień	September
Czwartek	Thursday	Październik	October
Piątek	Friday	Listopad	November
Sobota	Saturday	Grudzień	December
Niedziela	Sunday	Wiosna	spring
Styczeń	January	Lato	summer
Luty	February	Jesień	autumn
Marzec	March	Zima	winter
Kwiecień	April	Wakacje	holidays
Maj	May	Święto	bank holiday
Czerwiec	June		

Numbers

Jeden	1	Dwadzieścia	20
Dwa	2	Trzydzieści	30
Trzy	3	Czterdzieści	40
Cztery	4	Pięćdziesiąt	50
Pięć	5	Sześćdziesiąt	60
Sześć	6	Siedemdziesiąt	70
Siedem	7	Osiemdziesiąt	80
Osiem	8	Dziewięćdziesiąt	90
Dziewięć	9	Sto	100
Dziesięć	10	Dwieście	200
Jedenaście	11	Trzysta	300
Dwanaście	12	Czterysta	400
Trzynaście	13	Pięćset	500
Czternaście	14	Sześćset	600
Piętnaście	15	Siedemset	700
Szesnaście	16	Osiemset	800
Siedemnaście	17	Dziewięćset	900
Osiemnaście	18	Tysiąc	1000
Dziewiętnaście	19	Milion	1,000,000

Food and drink

Common terms

Filiżanka	Cup	Obiad	Lunch
Gotowany	Boiled	Śniadanie	Breakfast
Grill/z rusztu	Grilled	Święzy	Fresh
Jadłospis	Menu	Słodki	Sweet
Kolacja	Dinner	Smacznego!	Bon appetit!
Kwaśny	Sour	Surowy	Raw
Łyżka	Spoon	Szklanka	Glass
Marynowany	Pickled	Sznycel	Escalope/schnitzel
Mielone	Minced	Talerz	Plate
Na zdrowie!	Cheers!	Wegetariański	Vegetarian
Nadziewany	Stuffed	Widelec	Fork
Nóż	Knife		

Basic foods

Bułka	Bread rolls	Mięso	Meat
Chleb	Bread	Ocet	Vinegar
Chrzan	Horseradish	Olej	Oil
Cukier	Sugar	Owoce	Fruit
Drób	Poultry	Pieczeń	Roast meat
Frytki	Chips/French fries	Pieprz	Pepper
Jajko	Egg	Potrawy jarskie	Vegetarian dishes
Jarzyny/warzywa	Vegetables	Ryby	Fish
Kanapka	Sandwich	Ryż	Rice
Kołduny	Ravioli-like parcels stuffed with meat	Śmietana	Cream
		Sól	Salt
Kotlet	Cutlet	Surówka	Salad
Makaron	Macaroni	Zupa	Soup
Masło	Butter		

Soups

Barszcz czerwony (z pasztecikem)	Beetroot soup (with pastry)	Żurek	Soup made from fermented rye flour and potatoes
Barszcz ukraiński	White borsch		
Bulion/rosół	Bouillon	(zupa) Cebulowa	Onion soup
Chłodnik	Sour milk and vegetable cold soup	(zupa) Fasolowa	Bean soup
		(zupa) Grochowa	Pea soup
Fasólka po bretońsku	Spicy bean soup with bacon bits	(zupa) Grzybowa	Mushroom soup
		(zupa) Jarzynowa	Vegetable soup
Kapuśniak	Cabbage soup	(zupa) Ogórkowa	Cucumber soup
Kartoflanka	Potato soup	(zupa) Owocowa	Cold fruit soup
Krupnik	Barley soup	(zupa) Pomidorowa	Tomato soup

Meat, fish and poultry

Baranina	Mutton	Kurczak	Chicken
Bażant	Pheasant	Łosoś	Salmon
Befsztyk	Steak	Makrela	Mackerel
Bekon/boczek	Bacon	Pstrąg	Trout
Cielęcina	Veal	Śledź	Herring
Dziczyzna	Game	Salami	Salami
Dzik	Wild boar	Sardynka	Sardine
Gęś	Geese	Sarnina	Elk
Golonka	Leg of pork	Szaszłyk	Shish kebab
Indyk	Turkey	Wątróbka	Liver with onion
Kaczka	Duck	Węgorz	Eel
Karp	Carp	Wierprzowe	Pork
Kiełbasa	Sausage	Wołowe	Beef
Kotlet schabowy	Pork cutlet		

Fruit and vegetables

Ananas	Pineapple	Kasza	Buckwheat
Banan	Banana	Kompot	Stewed fruit
Ćwikła/buraczki	Beetroot	Maliny	Raspberries
Cebula	Onion	Marchewka	Carrots
Cytryna	Lemon	Migdały	Almonds
Czarne jagody/ borówki	Blackberries	Morele	Apricots
		Ogórek	Cucumber
Czarne porzeczki	Blackcurrant	Ogórki	Gherkins
Czereśnie	Cherries	Orzechy włoskie	Walnuts
Czosnek	Garlic	Papryka	Paprika
Fasola	Beans	Pomarańcze	Orange
Groch	Peas	Pomidor	Tomato
Gruszka	Pears	Śliwka	Plum
Grzyby/pieczarki	Mushrooms	Szparagi	Asparagus
Jabłko	Apple	Szpinak	Spinach
Kalafior	Cauliflower	Truskawki	Strawberries
Kapusta	Cabbage	Winogrona	Grapes
Kapusta kiszona	Sauerkraut	Ziemniaki	Potatoes

Cheese

Bryndza	Sheep's cheese	(ser) Myśliwski	Smoked cheese
Oscypek	Smoked goats' cheese	(ser) Tylżycki	Hard yellow cheese
Twaróg	Cottage cheese		

Cakes and desserts

Ciastko	Cake	Czekolada	Chocolate
Ciasto drożdżowe	Yeast cake with fruit	Galaretka	Jellied fruits

Lody	Ice cream	Pączki	Doughnuts
Makowiec	Poppyseed cake	Sernik	Cheesecake
Mazurek	Shortcake	Tort	Tart

Drinks

Cocktail mleczny	Milk shake	Sok pomarańczowy	Orange juice
Gorąca czekolada	Drinking chocolate	Sok pomidorowy	Tomato juice
Herbata	Tea	Spirytus	Spirits
Kawa	Coffee	Winiak	Polish brandy
Koniak	Cognac/brandy (imported)	Wino	Wine
		Wino słodkie	Sweet wine
Miód pitny	Mead	Wino wytrawne	Dry wine
Mleko	Milk	Woda	Water
Napój	Bottled fruit drink	Woda mineralna	Mineral water
Piwo	Beer	Wódka	Vodka
Sok	Juice		

Glossaries

General terms

Aleja – Avenue (abb. al.)

Biuro Zakwaterowania – Accommodation office

Brama – Gate

Cerkiew – (pl. *cerkwie*) Orthodox church, or a church belonging to the Uniates (Greek Catholics), a tradition loyal to Rome but following Orthodox rites that dates back to the 1595 Act of Union (see box on pp.360–361)

Cmentarz – Cemetery

Dolina – Valley

Dom – House

Dom Kultury – Cultural House, a community arts and social centre

Dom Wycieczkowy – Cheap, basic type of hotel

Droga – Road

Dwór – Country house traditionally owned by member of the *szlachta* class

Dworzec – Station

Główny – Main – as in Rynek Główny, main square

Góra – (pl. *góry*) Mountain

Granica – Border

Jezioro – Lake

Kantor – Exchange office

Kaplica – Chapel

Kawiarnia – Café

Katedra – Cathedral

Klasztor – Monastery

Kościół – Church

Ksiądz – Priest

Książę – Prince, duke

Księgarnia – Bookshop

Kraj – Country

Las – Wood, forest

Masyw – Massif

Miasto – Town (Stare Miasto – Old Town; Nowe Miasto – New Town)

Most – Bridge

Naród – Nation, people

Nysa – River Neisse

Odra – River Oder

Ogród – Gardens

Pałac – Palace

Piwnica – Pub

Plac – Square (abb. pl.)

Plaża – Beach

Poczta – Post office

Pogotowie – Emergency

Pokój – (pl. *pokóje*) Room

Pole – Field

Prom – Ferry

Przedmieście – Suburb

Przystanek – Bus stop

Puszcza – Ancient forest

Ratusz – Town hall

Restauracja – Restaurant

Ruch – Chain of newpaper kiosks also selling public transport tickets

Rynek – Marketplace, commonly the main square in a town

Rzeka – River

Sejm – Parliament

Shtetl – Yiddish name for a rural town, usually with a significant Jewish population

Skała – Rock, cliff

Skansen – Open-air museum with reconstructed folk architecture and art

Stocznia – Shipyards

Święty – Saint (abb. św.)

Starowiercy – (Old Believers) Traditionalist Russian Orthodox sect, small communities of which survive in east Poland

Stary – Old

Szlachta – Term for the traditional gentry class, inheritors of status and land

Ulica – Street (Abb. ul.)

Województwo – Administrative district

Wieś – (pl. *Wsie*) Village

Wieża – Tower

Winiarnia – Wine cellar

Wisła – River Vistula

Wodospad – Waterfall

Wzgórze – Hill

Zamek – Castle

Zdrój – Spa

Ziemia – Region

Art and architecture

Aisle – Part of church to the side of the nave.

Ambulatory – Passage round the back of the altar, in continuation of the aisles.

Apse – Vaulted termination of the altar end of a church.

Aron Ha Kodesh – Place in synagogue for keeping the scrolls of the Torah (law), conventionally in the form of a niche in the eastern wall.

Baroque – Exuberant architectural style of the seventeenth and early eighteenth centuries, characterized by ornate decoration, complex spatial arrangement and grand vistas. The term is also applied to the sumptuous style of painting of the same period.

Basilica – Church in which the nave is higher than the aisles.

Bimah – Raised central platform in a synagogue containing the pulpit from which the Torah is read.

Black Madonna – National icon, an image of the Virgin and Child housed in the Jasna Góra monastery in Częstochowa.

Capital – Top of a column, usually sculpted.

Chancel – Section of the church where the altar is situated, usually the east end.

Choir – Part of church in which service is sung, usually beside the altar.

Crypt – Underground part of a church.

Fresco – Mural painting applied to wet plaster, so that colours immediately soak into the wall.

Gothic – Architectural style with an emphasis on verticality, characterized by pointed arch and ribbed vault; introduced to Poland in the thirteenth century, surviving in an increasingly decorative form until well into the sixteenth century. The term is also used of paintings and sculpture of the period.

Hall Church – Church design in which all vaults are of approximately equal height.

Iconostasis – Screen with a triple door separating the sanctuary from the nave in Uniate and Eastern Orthodox churches.

Jugendstil – German version (encountered in western Poland) of Art Nouveau, a sinuous, highly decorative style of architecture and design from the period 1900–15.

Mannerism – Deliberately over-sophisticated style of late Renaissance art and architecture.

Mansard – Curb roof in which each face has two slopes, with the lower one steeper than the upper.

Matzevah – An upright traditional Jewish tombstone adorned with inscriptions and symbolic ornamentation.

Mezuzah – Scroll containing handwritten parchment scrolls of the scriptures, traditionally placed in a small case and fixed on the righthand doorpost of a Jewish house.

Młoda Polska – (Young Poland) Turn-of-the-twentieth-century cultural movement centred on Kraków.

Nave – Main body of the church, generally forming the western part.

Neoclassical – Late eighteenth- and early nineteenth-century style of art and architecture returning to classical models as a reaction against Baroque and Rococo excesses.

Polyptych – Painting or carving on several hinged panels.

Renaissance – Italian-originated movement in art and architecture, inspired by the rediscovery of classical ideals.

Rococo – Highly florid, light and graceful style of architecture, painting and interior design, forming the last phase of Baroque.

Romanesque – Solid architectural style of the late tenth to mid-thirteenth centuries, characterized by round-headed arches and geometrical precision. The term is also used for paintings of the same period.

Romanticism – Late eighteenth- and nineteenth-century movement, rooted in adulation of the natural world and rediscovery of the country's rich historic heritage, strongly linked in Poland to the cause of national independence.

Secessionist – Style of early twentieth-century art and architecture, based in Germany and Austria, which reacted against academic establishments.

Stucco – Plaster used for decorative effects.

Transept – Arms of a cross-shaped church, placed at ninety degrees to nave and chancel.

Transitional – Architectural style between Romanesque and Gothic.

Triptych – Carved or painted altarpiece on three panels.

Trompe l'oeil – Painting designed to fool the onlooker into believing that it's actually three-dimensional.

History and politics

Arians – Radical Protestant grouping that gained a strong footing in the Reformation-era Polish-Lithuanian Commonwealth.

Austro-Jungarian Empire – Vast Habsburg-ruled domain incorporating most of central Europe, enlarged to include Polish province of Galicia during the Partition period.

Balcerowicz, Leszek – Finance minister following the 1989 elections. Responsible for introducing the country's post-communist programme of radical, free-market economic reform. Currently head of the National Bank of Poland.

Bielecki, Jan – Solidarity adviser and young technocrat, based in Gdańsk; was prime minister from December 1990 to November 1991.

Buzek, Jerzy – Prime minister in the AWS-led centre-right coalition from 1997 to 2001. Founder member of Solidarity who comes from the southwest of the country. Buzek

was the country's first non-Catholic political leader.

Commonwealth – Union of Poland, Lithuania, Royal Prussia and Livonia (Latvia); formed by Lublin Union (1569), it lasted until the Third Partition of 1795.

Congress Kingdom of Poland – Russian-ruled province of Poland established in 1815, following the Congress of Vienna.

Democratic Left Alliance (SLD) – Alliance of SdRP (Social Democracy of the Republic of Poland) and other former-communist forces. Effectively heir to the now defunct communist party (PZPR), the SLD has successfully repositioned itself as a moderate left-of-centre parliamentary party.

Democratic Union (UD) – Centrist political party which attracted strong support among former Solidarity intellectuals, now merged in the Freedom Union.

Ducal Prussia – (East Prussia) The eastern half of the territory of the Teutonic Knights, converted into a secular duchy in 1525 and divided in 1945 between Poland and the Soviet Union.

Emigracja – Commonly used Polish term for the worldwide Polish community living outside the country.

Freedom Union (UW) – Unia Wolności. Main centrist/liberal party founded as a successor to the UD when it merged with a smaller liberal party in 1994. Currently headed by a coterie of heavyweight former dissidents including Bronisław Geremek and 1995 presidential candidate manqué Jacek Kuroń.

Galicia – Southern province of Poland including Kraków incorporated into Austro-Hungarian Empire during the Partition period, granted autonomy in latter half of nineteenth century.

Gierek, Edward – Leader of the communist party in the 1970s, until removed following the strikes of summer 1980.

Habsburg – The most powerful imperial family in medieval Germany, operating from a power base in Austria. Subsequently gave their name to the agglomeration of lands, centred on Austria, known as the Habsburg Empire.

Hanseatic League – Medieval trading alliance of Baltic and Rhineland cities, numbering about a hundred at its fifteenth-century peak. Slowly died out in seventeenth century with competition from the Baltic nation-states and rise of Brandenburg-Prussia.

Hassidism – Mystical religious and social movement founded by Israel ben Elizer (1700–60) known as Baal Schem Tov. Hassidism opposed rabbinical Judaism and preached joy in life through religious ecstasy, dance and song.

Hetman – Military commander; a state officer in the Polish-Lithuanian Commonwealth era.

Holy Roman Empire – Name of the loose confederation of German states (many now part of Poland) which lasted from 800 until 1806.

Jagiellonian – Dynasty of Lithuanian origin which ruled Poland-Lithuania from 1386 to 1572.

Jaruzelski, Wojciech – General of the armed forces, called in by the Party in 1981 to institute martial law and suppress Solidarity. His subsequent flexibility and negotiating skill helped to usher in democracy and he became president after the June 1989 elections, until the election of Wałęsa in December 1990.

Kulturkampf – Campaign launched by German Chancellor Bismarck in the 1870s, aimed at suppressing Catholic culture (including the Polish language) inside German territories.

Kuroń, Jacek – Veteran opposition activist and key figure in Solidarity movement; served as minister of labour in the Mazowiecki government, returning to the same position in the Suchocka administration. Stood as the Freedom Union's official candidate in the 1995 presidential elections.

Kwaśniewski, Aleksander – Former communist government minister of sport in the 1980s, elected as president in November 1995. Cuts a confident eloquent figure, who despite political divisions over his communist background has hitherto demonstrated a deft ability to act as "president of the whole nation".

Lustration – Term applied to the controversial process of excluding from public life those supposed to have collaborated with the communist-era security services.

Mazowiecki, Tadeusz – Catholic lawyer and journalist and longtime adviser to Solidarity. Country's first post-communist prime minister who ran unsuccessfully for president against Wałęsa in December 1990.

Michnik, Adam – Warsaw academic and leading Solidarity theoretician and activist. Chief editor of *Gazeta Wyborcza*, the country's biggest-selling daily newspaper, ever since it was set up in 1989.

Nazi–Soviet Pact (or Molotov–Ribbentrop Pact) – 1939 agreement between Nazi Germany and the Soviet Union, which contained a secret clause to eliminate Poland from the map.

Oder-Neisse Line – Western limit of Polish territory set by Yalta Agreement, 1945.

Partition period – Era from 1772 to 1918, during which Poland was on three occasions divided into Prussian, Russian and Austrian territories.

Piasts – Royal dynasty which forged the Polish state in the tenth century and ruled it until 1370; branches of the family continued to hold principalities, notably in Silesia, until 1675.

Polish United Workers Party (PZPR) – Former communist party who disbanded themselves in January 1990, the majority forming a new Social Democratic Party (the SdRP, see under "Post-communists" below).

Polonians – Slav tribe which formed the embryonic Polish nation.

Post-communists – Blanket term used to describe the parties and groupings emerging from the ashes of the Polish communist party (Polish United Workers Party or PZPR), which was dissolved in January 1990. Principal successor to the PZPR is the SdRP (the full title is "Social Democracy of the Republic of Poland"), a leading force in the coalition government that ruled the country 1993–97. The post-communist label is also used to refer to the Democratic Left Alliance (see separate entry), of which the SdRP is a member.

Prussia – Originally a Slavic eastern Baltic territory, now divided between Poland and the Russian Federation. It was conquered by the Teutonic Knights in the thirteenth century and acquired in 1525 by the Hohenzollerns, who merged it with their own German possessions to form Brandenburg-Prussia (later shortened to Prussia).

Round Table Agreement – Pathbreaking bipartisan agreement between Jaruzelski's communist government and the Solidarity opposition in spring 1989, leading to the elections in June of that year.

Royal Prussia (or West Prussia) – Territory centred on the Wisła delta, originally the easternmost sector of Pomerania, renamed after its capture from the Teutonic Knights in 1466.

Ruthenia – A loose grouping of principalities, part of which formed Poland's former Eastern Territories.

Sarmatism – Seventeenth-century Polish aristocratic cult based on the erroneous notion that they were directly descended from the Sarmatians, a nomadic people who lived on the northern shores of the Black Sea during the time of the Roman Empire.

Solidarity (Solidarność) – The eastern bloc's first independent trade union, led by Lech Wałęsa, suppressed under martial law and re-legalized in 1989, before forming the core of the new democratic government. Subsequently irrevocably split into pro- and anti-Wałęsa factions, it enjoyed something of a renaissance in the mid-1990s, providing the backbone of the Solidarity Election Action (AWS), an alliance of right-wing parties formed in June 1996 to contest the 1997 parliamentary elections. Solidarity left the AWS in 2001, ostensibly to concentrate on its role as a trade union again.

Suchocka, Halina – Lawyer from Poznań chosen as Poland's first ever woman prime minister in summer 1992. A popular, if somewhat aloof figure.

Tatars – Mongol tribe who invaded Poland in the thirteenth century, some of them settling subsequently.

Teutonic Knights – Quasi-monastic German military order who conquered parts of the eastern Baltic, establishing their own independent state 1226–1525.

Tzaddik – Charismatic Hassidic religious teacher and leader belonging to hereditary dynasty.

Uniates – (also known as Greek Catholics) Eastern-rite Christians who, following the Union of Brest (1595), formally accepted the Pope's authority, though they retained many Orthodox rites. Within modern Poland, Uniates comprise a mixture of Ukrainians, Łemks and Boyks.

Wałęsa, Lech – Shipyard electrician who led strikes in the Gdańsk shipyards in 1980, leading to the establishment of the independent trade union, Solidarity, of which he became chairman. In this role, he opposed the communist government throughout the 1980s, and led negotiations in the Round Table Agreement of 1989. Following the June 1989 elections, he parted company with many of his former Solidarity allies, forcing a presidential contest, which he won in December 1990. Defeated in the next presidential elections (Nov 1995), since when he's kept a – by his standards at least – relatively low political profile. Awarded the Nobel Peace Prize in 1983.

Waza (Vasa) – Swedish royal dynasty which ruled Poland 1587–1668.

Workers' Defence Committee (KOR) – Oppositional group formed in the

LANGUAGE | Glossaries

L

mid-1970s, regarded by many as a precursor to Solidarity.

Yalta Agreement – 1945 agreement between the victorious powers that established Poland's (and Europe's) postwar borders, without necessarily consulting those it affected.

Street names

The stars from the pantheon of Polish communist iconography after whom many streets were named after **World War II** have now largely disappeared. Since the **Solidarity** election victory of 1989 a systematic renaming of streets has been carried out, though in classic Polish style it took local authorities a lot longer to agree on new names than in, say, the neighbouring Czech and Slovak republics, the whole process being held up by interminable local infighting. It's not the first time such a process has occurred either: nineteenth-century Russian and German street names were replaced by Polish ones after **World War I**, which themselves came down following the Nazi wartime occupation. Many older streets have simply reverted to their prewar names, the new ones showing a marked preference for **Catholic** identification. Remember that street names always appear in their genitive or adjectival form, eg Franciscan Street is Franciszkańska, Piłsudski Street is Piłsudskiego and Mickiewicz Street Mickiewicza.

Generał Władysław Anders (1892–1970) – Renowned military figure who led the Polish troops, was exiled to Siberia at the start of World War II and later returned to fight on the Allied side in the Middle East, then in Europe.

Armii Krajowej (AK) – The Home Army, forces of the wartime Polish resistance.

Józef Bem (1794–1850) – Swashbuckling military figure who participated in the 1848 "Springtime of the Nations" in both Austria and Hungary.

Generał Zygmunt Berling (1896–1980) – First commander-in-chief of communist-sponsored Polish forces in the Soviet Union.

Bohaterów Getta – Heroes of the Ghetto, in memory of the April 1943 Warsaw Ghetto Uprising against the Nazis.

Tadeusz Bór-Komorowski (1895–1966) – Commander of AK (Home Army) forces during the 1944 Warsaw Uprising.

Władysław Broniewski (1897–1962) – Early socialist adherent of Piłsudski's World War I Legions, revolutionary poet and famously unreformed drunkard.

Fryderyk Chopin (1810–49) (also sometimes spelt "Szopen" in Polish) – Celebrated Romantic-era composer and pianist, long a national icon (see box, pp.142–143).

Chrobrego – Refers to Bolesław Chrobry (Bolesław the Brave), first king of Poland and the man who established the country as a definite independent state.

Maria Dąbrowska (1889–1965) – Fine modern Polish writer best known for her epic novels.

Aleksander Fredro (1793–1876) – Popular dramatist, especially of comedies.

Grunwald – Landmark medieval battle (1410) where combined Polish-Lithuanian forces thrashed the Teutonic Knights.

Jan Kasprowicz (1860–1926) – Popular peasant-born neo-Romantic poet and voluminous translator of Western classics into Polish.

Jan Kochanowski (1530–84) – Renaissance-era poet, the father of the modern Polish literary canon.

Maksymilian Kolbe (1894–1941) – Catholic priest martyred in Auschwitz, canonized by Pope John Paul II.

Maria Konopnicka (1842–1910) – Children's story writer of the nineteenth century, adherent of the "Positivist" School which developed in reaction to the traditional national preference for Romanticism.

Mikołaj Kopernik (1473–1543) – Indigenous name of the great astronomer known elsewhere as Copernicus, who spent much of his life in the Baltic town of Frombork.

Tadeusz Kościuszko (1746–1817) – Dashing veteran of the American War of Independence and leader of the 1794 insurrection in Poland (see box, pp.428–429).

Józef Ignacy Krasicki (1735–1801) – Enlightenment-era poet-bishop of Warmia, dubbed the "Polish Lafontaine".

Zygmunt Krasiński (1812–59) – Author of Nieboska Komedia, one of the trio of Polish Romantic messianic greats.

Józef Kraszewski (1812–87) – Hugely popular historical novelist. His novels (over two hundred of them) cover everything from the early Piasts to the Partition era.

6 Kwietnia (6 April) – Date of the Battle of Racławice, where Kościuszko's largely peasant army defeated the tsarist forces in 1794.

11 Listopada (11 November) – Symbolically important post-World War I Polish Independence Day.

29 Listopada – Start of (failed) November 1830 uprising against the Russians.

1 Maja – Labour Day.

3 Maja – Famous democratic Constitution of 1791.

9 Maja – Polish "V" Day – the Russian-declared end of World War II – one day after Britain and other Western European countries.

Jan Matejko (1838–93) – Patriotic *fin-de-siècle* painter closely associated with Kraków, where he lived most of his life.

Adam Mickiewicz (1798–1855) – The Romantic Polish poet, a national figure considered kosher by just about everyone, former communist leaders included (see p.99).

Stanisław Moniuszko (1819–72) – Romantic composer of patriotic operas, popular in Poland but little known elsewhere.

Gabriel Narutowicz (1865–1922) – First president of the Second Polish Republic, assassinated a few days after his nomination.

Ignacy Paderewski (1860–1941) – Noted pianist and composer who became the country's first prime minister post-World War I and the country's regaining of independence.

Jan Paweł II (1920–2005) – Catholic pontiff and Polish national hero. Many streets are now renamed after Pope John Paul II.

Józef Piłsudski (1867–1935) – One of the country's most venerated military-political figures, key architect of the regaining of independence after World War I, and national leader in the late 1920s and early 1930s.

Józef Poniatowski (1767–1813) – Nephew of the last Polish king who fought in numerous Polish and Napoleonic campaigns: an archetypal Polish military-Romantic hero.

Jerzy Popiełuszko – Radical Solidarity-supporting priest murdered by the Security Forces in 1984, and since elevated to the ranks of national martyrs.

Bolesław Prus (1847–1912) – Positivist writer, best known for quasi-historical novels such as *Pharaoh* and *Lalka* ("The Doll").

Kazimierz Pułaski (1747–79) – Polish-American hero of the US War of Independence.

Mikołaj Rej (1505–69) – So-called "Father of Polish Literature", one of the first to write in the language.

Władysław Reymont (1867–1925) – Nobel Prize-winning author of *The Peasants* and *The Promised Land*.

Henryk Sienkiewicz (1846–1916) – Stirring historical novelist who won the Nobel Prize for his epic *Quo Vadis*?

15 Sierpnia – Date of the Battle of Warsaw (August 1920) that halted the Soviet offensive against Poland, popularly known as the "miracle on the Vistula".

Władysław Sikorski (1881–1943) – Prewar Polish prime minister and wartime commander-in-chief of Polish forces in the West.

Marie Skłodowska-Curie (1867–1934) – Nobel Prize-winning scientist and discoverer of the radioactive elements radium and polonium.

Juliusz Słowacki (1809–49) – Noted playwright and poet, one of the three Polish Romantic greats.

Jan Sobieski (1635–96) – Quintessentially Polish king famous for his celebrated rescue of Vienna (1683) from the Ottoman Turks.

Bohaterów Stalingradu – "Heroes of Stalingrad", a reference to the turning point in the defeat of Nazi Germany; less common than it was, but one of the few communist names to survive.

22 Styczni – Date of the start of January Uprising of 1863 against the Russians.

Karol Świerczewski (1897–1947) – One of the few communist figures to survive the post-1989 street name clearout (not everywhere though), a fact probably explained by his role in the controversial 1947 "Operation Vistula" (see box, pp.356–357).

Świętego Ducha – Holy Spirit, generally used in square names.

Świętej Trójcy – Holy Trinity – another self-explanatory Catholic favourite.

Karol Szymanowski (1882–1937) – Noted modern Polish classical composer, a long-time Zakopane resident.

Kazimierz (Przerwa) Tetmajer (1865–1940) – Turn-of-the-twentieth-century neo-Romantic poet, part of the Kraków-based Młoda Polska school.

Westerplatte – The Polish garrison the attack on whom by the Nazis in September 1939 signalled the start of World War II.

Wilsona – After US President Woodrow Wilson, who supported the cause of Polish independence at the Versailles Conference (1919).

Stanisław Ignacy Witkiewicz (1885–1939) – Maverick modernist artist and writer whose plays anticipated postwar Theatre of the Absurd.

1 Września – Start of World War II – the September 1939 Nazi invasion of Poland.

Stanisław Wyspiański (1867–1907) – Renowned Młoda Polska era poet, playwright and painter best known for his plays *Wesele* ("The Wedding") and *Wyzwolenie* ("Liberation").

Kardynał Stefan Wyszyński (1901–81) – Tenacious postwar Catholic primate of Poland, figurehead of popular resistance to communism.

Wszystkich Świętych – All Saints – a popular Catholic festival.

Stefan Żeromski (1864–1925) – One of the most renowned Polish novelists, a neo-Romantic writer best known for his historical novel *Popioły* ("The Ashes").

Town names

Because Poland's borders have changed so often, many of its towns, including virtually all which were formerly German, have gone under more than one name. What follows is a checklist of names most of which can now be regarded as historical. The letters in parenthesis identify the language of the non-Polish form: G=German, OS=Old Slav, C=Czech, R=Russian, U=Ukrainian, L=Lithuanian, E=English.

Barczewo – Wartenburg (G)
Biała – Biala (G)
Bielsko – Bielitz (G)
Bierutowice – Brückenberg (G)
Bolków – Bolkenhain (G)
Braniewo – Braunsberg (G)
Brzeg – Brieg (G)
Brześć – Brest (E), Briest (R)
Brzezinka – Birkenau (G)
Bydgoszcz – Bromberg (G)
Bystrzyca Kłodzka – Habelschwerdt (G)
Chełmno – Kulm (G)
Chmielno – Ludwigsdorf (G)
Chojnice – Kornitz (G)
Cieplice Śląskie-Zdrój – Bad Warmbrunn (G)
Cieszyn – Teschen (G)

Czaplinek – Tempelburg (G)
Dąbie – Altdamm (G)
Darłowo – Rügenwaldermünde (G)
Darłówko – Rügenwalde (G)
Dobre Miasto – Guttstadt (G)
Duszniki-Zdrój – Bad Reinerz (G)
Elbląg – Elbing (G)
Ełk – Lyck (G)
Frombork – Frauenburg (G)
Gdańsk – Gyddanyzc (OS), Danczik, Dantzig, Danzig (G), Dantsic (E)
Gdynia – Gdingen (OS), Gottenhafen (G)
Gierłoz – Görlitz (G)
Giżycko – Lötzen (G)
Głogów – Glogau (G)
Gniezno – Gnesen (G)

Goleniów – Gollnow (G)
Góra Świętej Anny – Sankt Annaberg (G)
Grudziądz – Graudenz (G)
Grunwald – Tannenberg (G), Zalgiris (L)
Gryfice – Greifenberg (G)
Hel – Hela (G)
Henryków – Heinrichau (G)
Inowrocław – Hohensalza (G)
Iwięcino – Eventin (G)
Jagniątków – Agnetendorf (G)
Jawor – Jauer (G)
Jelenia Góra – Hirschberg (G)
Kadyny – Cadinen (G)
Kamień Pomorski – Cammin (G)
Kamienna – Góra Landeshut (G)
Karłów – Karlsberg (G)
Karpacz – Krummhübel (G)
Kartuzy – Karthaus (G)
Katowice – Kattowitz (G)
Kętrzyn – Rastenburg (G)
Kłodzko – Glatz (G)
Kluki – Klucken (G)
Kołczewo – Kolzow (G)
Kołobrzeg – Kolberg (G)
Koszalin – Kösel (G)
Kraków – Cracow (E), Krakau (G)
Kruszwica – Kruschwitz (G)
Krzeszów – Grüssau (G)
Książ – Fürstenstein (G)
Kudowa-Zdrój – Bad Kudowa (G)
Kwidzyn – Marienwerder (G)
Lądek-Zdrój – Bad Landeck (G)
Łeba – Leba (G)
Legnica – Liegnitz (G)
Legnickie Pole – Wahlstatt (G)
Leszno – Lissa (G)
Lidzbark Warmiński – Heilsberg (G)
Łódź – Litzmannstadt, Lodsch (G)
Lubiąż – Leubus (G)
Lwów – Lemberg (G), Lvov (R), L'viv (U)
Malbork – Marienburg (G)
Międzygórze – Wölfesgrund (G)
Międzyzdroje – Misdroy (G)
Mikołajki – Nikolaiken (G)
Milicz – Militsch (G)
Morąg – Mohrungen (G)

Mrągowo – Sensburg (G)
Nysa – Neisse (G)
Oleśnica – Oels (G)
Oliwa – Oliva (G)
Olsztyn – Allenstein (G)
Olsztynek – Hohenstein (G)
Opole – Oppeln (G)
Orneta – Wormditt (G)
Oświęcim – Auschwitz (G)
Otmuchów – Ottmachau (G)
Paczków – Patschkau (G)
Pasłęk – Preussich Holland (G)
Polanica-Zdrój – Bad Altheide (G)
Poznań – Posen (G)
Pszczyna – Pless (G)
Reszel – Rössel (G)
Ruciane-Nida – Niedersee (G)
Słupsk – Stolp (G)
Smołdzino – Schmolsin (G)
Sobieszów – Hermsdorf (G)
Sobótka – Zobten (G)
Sopot – Zoppot (G)
Sorkwity – Sorquitten (G)
Stargard Szczeciński – Stargard (G)
Strzegom – Striegau (G)
Strzelno – Strelno (G)
Świdnica – Swidnitz, Schweidnitz (G)
Święta Lipka – Heiligelinde (G)
Świnoujście – Swinemünde (G)
Szczecin – Stettin (G)
Szczecinek – Neustettin (G)
Szklarska Poręba – Schreiberhau (G)
Sztutowo – Stutthof (G)
Tarnowskie Góry – Tarnowitz (G)
Toruń – Thorn (G)
Trzebiatów – Treptow (G)
Trzebnica – Trebnitz (G)
Trzemeszno – Tremessen (G)
Ustka – Stolpmünde (G)
Wałbrzych – Waldenburg (G)
Wambierzyce – Albendorf (G)
Warszawa – Warsaw (E), Warschau (G)
Węgorzewo – Angerburg (G)
Wilkasy – Wolfsee (G)
Wilno – Vilnius (L)
Wisełka – Neuendorf (G)

Wisła – Weichsel (G)
Włocławek – Leslau (G)
Wolin – Wollin (G)
Wrocław – Breslau (G), Wratislavia (OS), Vratislav (C)
Ząbkowice Śląskie – Frankenstein (G)

Żagań – Sagan (G)
Ziębice – Münsterberg (G)
Zielona Góra – Grünberg (G)
Żmigród – Trachenberg (G)
Żukowo – Zuchau (G)
Żywiec – Saybusch (G)

Acronyms and organizations

Almatur – Official student organization and travel office.

IT (Informator Turystyczny) – Tourist information office.

NBP (Narodowy Bank Polski) – Polish National Bank.

ORBIS – Former state travel agency, now privatized; abroad, Orbis offices are called POLORBIS in some (but not all) countries.

PKO (Polska Kasa Oszczędności) – State savings bank.

PKP (Polskie Koleje Państwowe) – State railways.

PKS (Polska Komunikacja Samochodowa) – State bus company.

PTTK (Polskie Towarzystwo Turystyczno-Krajoznawcze) – Tourist agency – Polish Tourism and Nature Lovers' Association.

PZMot (Polski Związek Motorowy) – National motorists' association.

PZPR (Polska Zjednoczona Partia Robotnicza) – Polish communist party – now defunct.

Rough
Guides
advertiser

Rough Guides travel...

...music & reference

small print and
Index

A Rough Guide to Rough Guides

In the summer of 1981, Mark Ellingham, a recent graduate from Bristol University, was travelling around Greece and couldn't find a guidebook that really met his needs. On the one hand there were the student guides, insistent on saving every last penny, and on the other the heavyweight cultural tomes whose authors seemed to have spent more time in a research library than lounging away the afternoon at a taverna or on the beach.

In a bid to avoid getting a job, Mark and a small group of writers set about creating their own guidebook. It was a guide to Greece that aimed to combine a journalistic approach to description with a thoroughly practical approach to travellers' needs – a guide that would incorporate culture, history and contemporary insights with a critical edge, together with up-to-date, value-for-money listings. Back in London, Mark and the team finished their Rough Guide, as they called it, and talked Routledge into publishing the book.

That first *Rough Guide to Greece*, published in 1982, was a student scheme that became a publishing phenomenon. The immediate success of the book – with numerous reprints and a Thomas Cook prize shortlisting – spawned a series that rapidly covered dozens of destinations. Rough Guides had a ready market among low-budget backpackers, but soon also acquired a much broader and older readership that relished Rough Guides' wit and inquisitiveness as much as their enthusiastic, critical approach. Everyone wants value for money, but not at any price.

Rough Guides soon began supplementing the "rougher" information about hostels and low-budget listings with the kind of detail on restaurants and quality hotels that independent-minded visitors on any budget might expect, whether on business in New York or trekking in Thailand.

These days the guides – distributed worldwide by the Penguin Group – offer recommendations from shoestring to luxury and cover more than 200 destinations around the globe, including almost every country in the Americas and Europe, more than half of Africa and most of Asia and Australasia. Our ever-growing team of authors and photographers is spread all over the world, particularly in Europe, the USA and Australia.

In 1994, we published the *Rough Guide to World Music* and *Rough Guide to Classical Music*; and a year later the *Rough Guide to the Internet*. All three books have become benchmark titles in their fields – which encouraged us to expand into other areas of publishing, mainly around popular culture. Rough Guides now publish:

- Travel guides to more than 200 worldwide destinations
- Dictionary phrasebooks to 22 major languages
- History guides ranging from Ireland to Islam
- Maps printed on rip-proof and waterproof Polyart™ paper
- Music guides running the gamut from Opera to Elvis
- Restaurant guides to London, New York and San Francisco
- Reference books on topics as diverse as the Weather and Shakespeare
- Sports guides from Formula 1 to Man Utd
- Pop culture books from *Lord of the Rings* to Cult TV
- World Music CDs in association with World Music Network

Visit **www.roughguides.com** to see our latest publications.

Rough Guide credits

Text editors: Edward Aves, Karoline Densley, Sarah Hudson
Layout: Jessica Subramanian
Cartography: Ed Wright, Katie Lloyd-Jones
Picture editors: Simon Bracken, Mark Thomas
Proofreader: Susannah Wight
Editorial: **London** Kate Berens, Claire Saunders, Geoff Howard, Ruth Blackmore, Gavin Thomas, Polly Thomas, Richard Lim, Clifton Wilkinson, Alison Murchie, Sally Schafer, Andy Turner, Ella O'Donnell, Keith Drew, Nikki Birrell, Chloë Thomson, Helen Marsden, Joe Staines, Duncan Clark, Peter Buckley, Matthew Milton, Daniel Crewe; **New York** Andrew Rosenberg, Richard Koss, Steven Horak, AnneLise Sorensen, Amy Hegarty, Hunter Slaton
Design & Pictures: **London** Dan May, Diana Jarvis, Jj Luck, Harriet Mills, Chloë Roberts; **Delhi** Madhulita Mohapatra, Umesh Aggarwal, Ajay Verma, Amit Verma
Production: Julia Bovis, Sophie Hewat, Katherine Owers

Cartography: **London** Maxine Repath; **Delhi** Manish Chandra, Rajesh Chhibber, Jai Prakash Mishra, Ashutosh Bharti, Rajesh Mishra, Animesh Pathak, Jasbir Sandhu, Karobi Gogoi
Online: **New York** Jennifer Gold, Suzanne Welles; **Delhi** Manik Chauhan, Narender Kumar, Shekhar Jha, Rakesh Kumar, Lalit K. Sharma
Marketing & Publicity: **London** Richard Trillo, Niki Hanmer, David Wearn, Demelza Dallow; **New York** Geoff Colquitt, Megan Kennedy, Milena Perez; **Delhi** Reem Khokhar
Custom publishing and foreign rights: Philippa Hopkins
Finance: Gary Singh
Manager India: Punita Singh
Series editor: Mark Ellingham
Reference Director: Andrew Lockett
PA to Managing and Publishing Directors: Megan McIntyre
Publishing Director: Martin Dunford
Managing Director: Kevin Fitzgerald

Publishing information

This sixth edition published July 2005 by
Rough Guides Ltd,
80 Strand, London WC2R 0RL
345 Hudson St, 4th Floor,
New York, NY 10014, USA
14 Local Shopping Centre, Panchsheel Park,
New Delhi 110017, India
Distributed by the Penguin Group
Penguin Books Ltd,
80 Strand, London WC2R 0RL
Penguin Putnam, Inc.
375 Hudson Street, NY 10014, USA
Penguin Group (Australia)
250 Camberwell Road, Camberwell
Victoria 3124, Australia
Penguin Books Canada Ltd,
10 Alcorn Avenue, Toronto, Ontario,
Canada M4V 1E4
Penguin Group (New Zealand)
Cnr Rosedale and Airborne Roads
Albany, Auckland, New Zealand

Typeset in Bembo and Helvetica to an original design by Henry Iles.

Printed and bound at Legoprint S.p.A.

© Jonathan Bousfield, Mark Salter, 2005

No part of this book may be reproduced in any form without permission from the publisher except for the quotation of brief passages in reviews.

744pp includes index
A catalogue record for this book is available from the British Library.

ISBN 1-84353-488-6

The publishers and authors have done their best to ensure the accuracy and currency of all the information in **The Rough Guide to Poland**; however, they can accept no responsibility for any loss, injury or inconvenience sustained by any traveller as a result of information or advice contained in the guide.

1   3   5   7   9   8   6   4   2

Help us update

We've gone to a lot of effort to ensure that the sixth edition of **The Rough Guide to Poland** is accurate and up to date. However, things change – places get "discovered", opening hours are notoriously fickle, restaurants and rooms raise prices or lower standards. If you feel we've got it wrong or left something out, we'd like to know, and if you can remember the address, the price, the time, the phone number, so much the better.

We'll credit all contributions, and send a copy of the next edition (or any other Rough Guide if you prefer) for the best letters. Everyone who writes to us and isn't already a subscriber will receive a copy of our full-colour thrice-yearly newsletter. Please mark letters: **"Rough Guide Poland Update"** and send to: Rough Guides, 80 Strand, London WC2R 0RL, or Rough Guides, 4th Floor, 345 Hudson St, New York, NY 10014. Or send an email to **mail@roughguides.com**

Have your questions answered and tell others about your trip at **www.roughguides.atinfopop.com**

SMALL PRINT

Acknowledgements

Jonathan Bousfield received much-appreciated advice and assistance from Thomas Brown, James Howard, Elizabeth & David Bousfield, Christina & Malcolm Martin, Artur Zyrkowski and Patrycja Wlazko in the Kraków City Tourism Department, Ewa Ambruster and the Lancaster language students, and Agnieszka Wolak & Elwira Middleton at the Polish Cultural Institute in London. He would also like to thank Edward Aves for his unflagging commitment to the cause.

Thomas Brown would like to thank Jon, Ed, Karoline and Geoff in London; Daga Hubert, for orthographical and other diverse assistance; and, for his generosity, Pan Czesław Kołodziejczyk of Wałbrzych.

Readers' letters

Many thanks to all the readers who took the time and trouble to write in with comments and updates on the fifth edition. Apologies for any omissions or misspellings:

Dr Capell Aris; V. Barber; Hans von Beers; Amanda Benstead; Martin Blackburn; Victor Blease; Michael Bourdeaux; Christina Brown; Patrick Browning; Caroline Burden; Tim Burford; Roger, Solna, Rebecca & Natasha Burnham; Dr Aris Capell; Joe Cendrowski; Jane Chesters; Katherine Courts; Ian Cowe; Kate Craddy; Edwina Currie; Mrs K Deuss; Susan Dickson; Rebecca Evans; Harry Failey; Anthony Furness; Richard Geary; Anne Gilbert; Elizabeth Gobey; Nat Gooden & Julie Dixon; Katy Hadwick; Adam Hansen; Richard Hardy; Christopher Hare; Helen Harkness; Patricia Harrison; Ken Howkins; James Hoyle; 'Janet'; Ellen Kanner; Matthias Kiener; Adam Kightley & Dagmara Gumkowska; Peter King; Martin Kochanski; Anna Lappé; little miss purple kate; Stephen Michael Lyons; S.R. McCombie; Louise McDermott; Morag M. McDonald; Alexander Macfarlane; Craig McGinn; Vincent Megaw; Espeth Morley; T. P. Murphy; Olga Muscat; Andrew Palmer; Edward Parker; Roger Parris; Hannah Pector; Anna Pestka; Carson Phillips; Joyce Ptaszek; Michaela Ranta; Roxana Reagon; E.C. Rideal; Chris Riley; Sue Ross; Amnon Shappira; Jenny Shaw; Wendy & Colin Smart; Ruth & Andrew Stuber; K. Tan; Michal Trojanowski; D.E. Wickham; Leroy Wickowski; Derek Wilde; Anna Withers; Meg Worley.

Photo credits

Cover
Main front picture: The Pieniny Mountains
© Alamy
Small front top picture: Palace statue © Alamy
Small front lower picture: Roses, Kraków © Alamy
Back top picture: Bison, Białowieża Forest
© Corbis
Back lower picture: St Mary's Church, Kraków
© Alamy

Title page
Woman painting house wall © Chris Lisle/Corbis

Full page
St Mary's Church, Kraków © Simon Crofts/Alamy

Introduction
Architectural detail, Wilanów Palace, Warsaw
© Ludovic Maisant/Corbis
Trumpeter at St Mary's Tower, Kraków © Gregory Wrona
Podhale musician © S. Broughton
Willow trees at sunset © Gregory Wrona
Old Town Square, Warsaw © Danita Delimont/Alamy
The Old Jewish Cemetery, Kraków © Michael Jenner
Near Mikołajki, Mazurian lakes © R. Petterson/Trip
Wawel © Gregory Wrona
Stall at Easter fair © Gregory Wrona

Things not to miss
01 The Tatra mountains © Danita Delimont/Alamy
02 Sand dunes, Łeba © Jerry Dennis
03 Gdańsk's ulica Długa © Danita Delimont/Alamy
04 Lublin Castle © Gregory Wrona
05 Vodka © Gregory Wrona
06 Wooden church, Haczów © Philippe Giraud/Corbis
07 Malbork Castle © Jerry Dennis
08 Smoked cheese stall, Zakopane © Gregory Wrona
09 Zamość © Gregory Wrona
10 Hel beach © Gregory Wrona
11 Palace of Culture, Warsaw © Jon Arnold
12 Milk bar, Kraków © Simon Crofts/Alamy
13 Pilgrimage during Holy Week © Bruno Barbey/Magnum

14 Białowieża national park © K. Gillham/Robert Harding Photo Library
15 Skansen, Małopolska © M. Jenkin/Trip
16 Cathedral interior, Wawel © Gregory Wrona
17 Auschwitz-Birkenau concentration camp
© Simon Bracken
18 Kazimierz Dolny © Danita Delimont/Alamy
19 Traditional dancing, Warsaw © Neil Setchfield
20 Stanisław Wyspiański, Self Portrait, 1902
© Wyspiański, Stanisław (1869–1907)/Bridgeman
21 Old Town Square, Poznań © Neil Setchfield
22 Painted house interior, Zalipie region
© SETBOUN/Corbis
23 Ornate facades, Old Town, Wrocław
© Philippe Giraud/Corbis
24 Sukiennice, Kraków © Les Polders/Alamy
25 Monastery Gate, Toruń © Paul Almasy/Corbis
26 Marina, Mazurian Lakes © Jeremy Philips/Travel Ink
27 Old Town, Warsaw © Dave G. Houser/Corbis
28 Mass at the Chapel of the Miraculous Image,
Częstochowa © Andrzej Gorzkowski/Alamy

Black and whites
p.78 View over Warsaw © Neil Setchfield
p.89 Tram, Warsaw © Neil Setchfield
p.117 Street vendor, Nowy Świat © Neil Setchfield
p.166 Gdańsk crane © Claudio Hartman/Alamy
p.182 Street market trader, Gdańsk © Neil Setchfield
p.281 Bison, Białowieża Forest © Raymond Gehman/Corbis
p.286 Castle, Kazimierz Dolny © Danita Delimont/Corbis
p.326 Town hall, Zamość © Gregory Wrona
p.380 Niedzica castle © Look Galeria/Corbis
p.402 Hairdressers, Kraków © Neil Setchfield
p.449 Auschwitz-Birkenau concentration camp
© Raymond Depardon/Magnum
p.494 The summit of Giewont, Tatra mountains
© Jeremy Philips/Travel Ink
p.504 Corpus Christi procession © Z. Harasym/Trip
p.551 Interior, Church of Peace © Bildarchiv Monheim GmbH/Alamy
p.580 Old Town Square, Poznań © Rolf Richardson/Alamy
p.627 Bydgoszcz © B&Y Photography/Alamy

SMALL PRINT

Index

Map entries are in colour.

A

Abakanowicz,
    Magdalena.........538, 597
accommodation...... 49–53
Adalbert, St....395, 615, 616
airlines, see flights
alcohol...........................57
apartments 51
Arkadia 145
Augustów 251
Augustów Canal...........252
Augustów Forest 250
Auschwitz-Birkenau....21,
    445–451

B

Baligród 363
banks............................39
Baranów
    Sandomierski............322
Belarus 276, 305
Bełżec..........................446
Bem, Józef ...473, 475, 719
Berest 376
Beskid Niski, the...363–370
Beskid Niski and
    Sądecki 364
Beskid Sądecki,
    the 370–377
Beskid Śląski 518–521
Biała Podlaska.............304
Białowieża 277
Białowieża...................278
Białowieża Forest 20,
    277–282
Białystok..............262–267
Białystok 263
Biebrzański Park
    Narodowy (Biebrza
    national park).............272
Biecz............................367
Bielsko-Biała.......516–518
Bieszczady, the... 351–363
Bieszczady Region......353
Binarowa 368
Biskupin.......................621
Black Madonna............24,
    456–460

Blizne..........................367
boat trips 244, 253
Bobowa 377
Bochotnica 316
Bohemian Brethren 611
Bohoniki 275
Bolesław the Brave 411,
    615, 619, 659, 714
Bolków.........................551
Bonaparte, Napoleon 98,
    160, 429, 666
books..................692–704
Boyks..........349, 354, 356,
    360, 687
Bóbrka.........................366
Brenna 520
Breslau, see Wrocław
Brochów 144
Brzeg 545
buses in Poland.............45
buses to Poland 31
Bydgoszcz..........626–629
Bystre 488
Bystrzyca Kłodzka........558

C

camping........................53
canoeing.........69, 236, 252
car rental 47
cerkwie 18, 360
Chełm 306–308
Chełmno 207–209
Chełmno.......................208
Chełmno nad Nerem 446
Chęciny 468
Chmielno 201
Chochołów 491
Chopin, Frédéric........114,
    116, 142–144, 311, 555,
    603, 719
Choroszcz 268
Chotyniec 347
Ciasne 268
Ciechanów...................162
Ciechocinek.................216
Cieplice Śląskie-Zdrój ... 570
Cieszyn 521–523
Cieszyn 522
cinema..........................65
Cisna 359

climate 14
consulates 36, 140
contraceptives...............73
Copernicus, Nicolaus....23,
    212, 222, 223, 228, 385,
    406, 719
costs..............................39
crime.............................70
Cumhof, see Chełmno
    nad Nerem
Curie, Marie...101, 102, 720
currency.........................39
cycling...................48, 490
Czarna Hańcza
    River 252, 257
Czartoryski, Adam.........99,
    311, 613, 666
Czermna 557
Czerteż 351
Czerwińsk nad Wisłą....156
Częstochowa 24,
    456–461
Częstochowa...............458
Czorsztyn 496

D

Danzig, see Gdańsk
Darłowko 635
Darłowo 634
Dębno 495
disabled travellers 71
Długosz,
    Jan.............319, 409, 425
Dobre Miasto...............229
Dolina Białego 491
Dolina
    Chochołowska...........491
Dolina Homole.............500
Dolina Kościeliska 491
Dolina Strążyska...........491
drinks..............56–58, 714
driving in Poland 46
driving to Poland 31
drugs 73
Dukla 367
Dunajec Gorge, the 498
Duszniki-Zdrój 555
Dziekanów Polski 142
Dzierżyński, Felix.........111,
    262, 266

E

Eagles' Nest
   Trail 453–456
East Prussia 225
eco-holidays 52
Elbląg 219
Elbląg Canal 224
electricity 73
embassies 36, 140
emergencies 73
Esperanto 265

F

festivals 20, 21,
   63, 66, 685
film 66
fishing 70
flights
   from Australia and New
      Zealand 35
   from Britain and Ireland 28
   from the US and Canada ... 32
   in Poland 46
folk music .. 9, 64, 683–691
food 54–56, 712–714
football 68, 139, 442
Frombork 222

G

Gabowe Grądy 253
gay travellers 73, 94, 135
GDAŃSK 17, 170–191
Gdańsk 177
   accommodation 173
   airport 172
   bus station 172
   Długi Targ 176
   Dom Uphagena 178
   Dwór Artusa (Arthur's
      Court) 179
   eating and
      drinking 188–190
   entertainment 190
   ferry terminal 172
   Głowne Miasto 176–183
   Historical Museum 178
   history 170–172
   information 172
   Kościół Mariacki
      (St Mary's) 180
   listings 191
   Muzeum Morskie 179
   Muzeum Narodowe
      (National Museum) 184
   Oliwa 186
   orientation 173
   post office museum 181
   public transport 173
   Roads to Freedom
      exhibition 184
   Stare Miasto 183
   Stare Przedmieście (Old
      Suburb) 184
   Stocznia Gdańska
      (Gdańsk Shipyards) 183
   Św. Mikołaja
      (St Nicholas') 181
   town hall 178
   train station 172
   Twierdza Wisłoujście
      (Wisła Fortress) 185
   ulica Długa 178
   waterfront 179
   Westerplatte 185
Gdańsk, Gdynia and
   Sopot 174
Gdynia 194–197
Gdynia 174
Gierek, Edward 675, 717
Gierłoz 241
Giewont 493
Giżycko 247
glossaries 714–723
Gładysów 370
Gniew 206
Gniezno 614–618
Gniezno 614
Gołuchów 613
Goleniów 639
Golub-Dobrzyń 215
Gomułka, Władysław ... 357,
   595, 672, 674
Goniądz 272
GOP 510
Gorce 481
Gorlice 369
górale 481, 499, 684, 686
Góra Świętej Anny 527
Góry Stołowe, the 558
Góry Świętokrzyskie,
   the 469–471
Góry Świętokrzyskie 469
Grabarka 282
Grabówka 275
Great Escape, The 609
Gross-Rosen, see
   Rogoźnica
Grunwald 232
Grybów 377
Gryfice 639
Gubałówka Hill 490
Gulbieniszki 256

H

Haczów 366
Hajnówka 275
Hańcza, Lake 257
Hasior,
   Władysław 488, 538
Hauptmann, Gerhard 573
health 38
Hel 19, 198
Herder, Johann
   Gottfried 230
hiking 69, 355, 492,
   559, 575, 606, 644
Hindenburg
   Mausoleum 232
history 659–682
holidays 62
horse riding 355
hostels 52
hotels 49–51

I

Inowrocław 624
insurance 37
Istebna 520
Iwięcino 635

J

Jabłonki 362
Jadwiga, Queen 260,
   406, 409, 412, 661
Jagiełło (see Władysław
   Jagiełło)
Janowiec 317
Janów Podlaski 306
Jarosław 339
Jaruzelski, Wojciech 675,
   676, 717
Jaskinia Raj, the 467
Jasna Góra 459
Jastrzębia Góra 198
Jaszczurówka 19, 488
Jawor 550
Jaworki 500
Jaworzynka 521
jazz 65
Jebwabne 270
Jelenia Góra 568–570
Jelonek, Lake 618
Jewish history
   Auschwitz-Birkenau ... 445–451

Baligród............................ 363
Białystok 263, 265
Bobowa............................ 377
Chełm................................ 307
Chęciny 468
Gorlice............................. 369
Jarosław 340
Jedwabne 270
Kazimierz Dolny 313–315
Kielce 465
Kraków.....................417–427
Krosno.............................. 365
Lesko 352
Lublin 297–301
Łańcut 338
Łódź........................150–154
Nowy Sącz....................... 372
Płock 160
Przemyśl 345
Rzeszów........................... 334
Siemiatycze..................... 282
Szczebrzeszyn 331
Szydłów............................ 462
Tarnów 476
Treblinka.......................... 162
Tykocin 269
Warsaw 106–110, 128
Włodawa 309
Wrocław 536
Zamość 328
Jewish tourism 12, 41
Jędrzejów 461
July Bomb Plot.............242

K

Kadyny 221
Kaliningrad (Russian
    Federation) 220
Kalisz............................ 612
Kalwaria
    Zebrzydowska 451
**Kamień
    Pomorski** 639–641
Kamień Pomorski 640
**Kampinoski Forest
    National Park** ... 141–144
Kanal Ostrodzko–
    Elblaski 224
Kantor, Tadeusz.....65, 116,
    403, 703
Karkonosze, the... 571–576
Karłów 558
Karpacz 574
Kartuzy 200
Kashubia 199–202
Kasprowicz, Jan 405,
    482, 719
Kasprowy Wierch 493
Katowice 510–513
Katowice 511

kayaking 69, 236, 252
Kazimierz Dolny........... 21,
    312–316
Kazimierz Dolny...........312
Kazimierz the Great.....313,
    316, 317, 341, 372, 385,
    411, 412, 417, 462, 528,
    660
Kąty Rybackie 218
Kętrzyn 240
Kielce 463–492
Kielce 464
Kiry 491
Kletno 560
Kluki 632
Kłodzko 552–554
Knyszyński Forest 268
Kodeń 309
Kołczewo 644
Kołobrzeg 637
Komańcza 362
Königsberg, see
    Kaliningrad
Kopiec Tartarski............345
Korczak, Janusz ...108, 700
Koszalin 635
Kościerzyna 202
Kościuszko, Tadeusz.....97,
    428, 537, 665, 666, 720
Kozłówka......................303
Kórnik 602
KRAKÓW 384–444
Kraków................. 388–389
Kraków: City
    Centre............... 396–397
Wawel Hill 410
Kazimierz and
    Podgórze........... 420–421
accommodation 388–394
airport............................. 386
Arka Pana 433
Barbakan......................... 401
Bielany 431
Błonia 429
Bronowice Małe 432
Bunkier Sztuki................. 404
bus station 386
Camadulensian
    monastery.................... 431
Centrum Japońskiej
    Manggha.................... 416
Corpus Christi Church 424
Dom Jana Matejki (Matejko
    House) 401
Dom Mehoffera 417
Dominican church............ 406
Dragon's Cave 416
eating and drinking 435–439
entertainment and
    nightlife 440–442
festivals 442
Franciscan church 407

Gallery of Nineteenth-
    Century Polish Art 395
ghetto 425
Hippoliti House 400
history 385
information 386
Jewish Cultural Centre..... 424
Jews in Kraków................ 418
Kamienica Hipolitów
    (Hippoliti House) 400
Kazimierz...................417–425
Kościół Mariacki
    (St Mary's Church)........ 398
Kościół Salvatora
    (St Saviour's Church).... 428
Kościuszko Mound 429
Las Wolski....................... 430
listings............................. 443
Łagiewniki 427
Manggha Japanese
    Cultural Centre 416
Matejko House................. 401
Maximilian Kolbe Church... 433
Mehoffer House 417
Mogiła 434
Muzeum Archeologiczne
    (Archeology Museum)... 408
Muzeum Archidiecezjalne
    (Archdiocesan
    Museum) 409
Muzeum Czartoryskich 403
Muzeum Etnograficzny
    (Ethnographic
    Museum) 425
Muzeum Historyczne
    Krakowa (Krakow
    History Museum) 400
Muzeum Narodowe
    (National Museum)........ 416
Muzeum Uniwerzytecki
    (University Museum) 406
Muzeum Wyspiańskiego ... 404
Norbertine monastery 428
Nowa Huta 432–434
orientation 387
Park Decjusza 430
parking 386
Pauline monastery 425
Piłsudski Mound 430
plac Mariacki................... 399
plac Szczepański 404
Płaszów concentration
    camp............................ 426
Podgórze......................... 425
Przegorzały 430
public transport............... 387
Rynek Główny.... 23, 394–401
Sanctuary of God's
    Mercy.......................... 427
shopping 442
Skałka 425
Smocza Jama (Dragon's
    Cave)........................... 416
Stara Synagoga 422
Stare Miasto.............394–409
Sukiennice....................... 395
Synagoga Izaaka 422

Synagoga Kupa 424
Synagoga Na Górce 423
Synagoga Poppera 423
Synagoga Remu 423
Synagoga Templu 423
Św. Andrzeja 408
Św. Katarzyny 425
Św. Krzyża 403
Św. Piotra i Pawła 408
Św. Wojciecha 395
taxis................................. 387
train station 386
Tyniec 432
ulica Floriańska 401
ulica Józefa 421
ulica Kanoniczna 409
ulica Miodowa.................. 423
ulica Szpitalna 403
university district 404–406
Wawel 20, 409–417
Wawel Castle 413
Wawel Cathedral 411
Wawel Royal Treasury 415
Wawel State Rooms 414
Wieliczka 434
Zwierzyniec 428
Kraków, Małopolska and
  the Tatras 382–383
Krasiczyn Castle........... 346
Krosno 363
Krościenko
  (Bieszczady) 353
Krościenko (Pieniny) 497
Kruszwica 623
Kruszyniamy 273
Krynica 375
Krynica Morska 218
Krzeszów 567
Krzywe 255
Krzyżtopór 321
Książ 566
Kudowa-Zdrój 556
Kuźnice......................... 493
Kwidzyn 206

L

Lanckorona................... 452
language 707–723
language courses 71
laundry............................. 73
Lądek-Zdrój.................. 560
Lednica, Lake 618
Legnica......................... 548
Legnickie Pole 549
Lenin, Vladimir Ilich 385,
  395, 482
lesbian travellers 73, 94,
  135
Lesko............................. 351

Leszczyński family....... 322,
  610, 611, 664
Leszno 610
Leżajsk 339
Lidzbark
  Warmiński 229
Lipnica Murowana 479
Lithuania 258, 260
Lower Silesia 528–577
Lubiąż........................... 547
Lublin 17, 290–303
Lublin 291
Lublin Stare Miasto 294
Lutowiska 354
L'viv (Ukraine) 346,
  528, 532

Ł

Łańcut................... 335–339
Łapsze 497
Łeba.............................. 629
Łebno 201
Łemks 349, 356,
  362, 367, 369, 687
Łowicz 145
Łódź 146–155
Łódź 148

M

magazines....................... 60
Majdan.......................... 359
Majdanek...................... 301
Malbork 18, 203–206
Malczewski, Jacek 118,
  264, 403, 404, 538, 594,
  603, 650
Małdyty......................... 224
Małopolska 444–479
Małopolska 382–383
maps.............................. 42
markets.......................... 18
Matejko, Jan..........97, 118,
  295, 385, 395, 399, 401,
  538, 603, 720
Mauzoleum
  Hindenburga 232
Mazovia 141–164
Mazovia................... 80–81
Mazurian Lakes 23,
  233–249
Mazurian Lakes ... 234–235
Mecmierz...................... 316
media............................. 60

Mehoffer, Józef 118, 407,
  417, 594
Mickiewicz, Adam 99,
  260, 395, 319, 702, 720
Mielno.................... 19, 636
Międzygórze 558
Międzyzdroje 19, 642
Mikołajki 242
milk bars................. 19, 54
Miłosz, Czesław............ 99,
  254, 256, 425, 697, 698,
  700, 702
Mirachowo................... 201
Młoda Polska........22, 118,
  159, 370, 385, 405, 417,
  432, 594
Modlin Castle 156
money............................. 39
Morąg 230
Morskie Oko 495
Mosina......................... 604
Mrągowo 237
Muczne........................ 357
music 9, 64, 683–691
Muszyna 374
Muszynka 376
Myczków 352

N

Nałęczów...................... 310
newspapers 60
Nieborów...................... 145
Niedzica....................... 496
Northeastern
  Poland 168–169
Nowa Słupia 470
Nowy Łupków 361
Nowy Sącz 371–373
Nowy Sącz 371
Nowy Targ 482
Nysa 562

O

Odrzykoń 366
Ogrodzieniec 456
Ojców........................... 454
Ojców national park 453
Ojców valley........ 453–456
Old Believers 246, 253,
  254, 256
Olsztyn (Małopolska).... 456
Olsztyn
  (Mazuria) 226–228

INDEX

739

Olsztyn 227
Olsztynek......................232
Opatów..........................321
opening hours 62
Operation Vistula.........349,
  356, 362, 363, 367
Opole 523–527
Opole............................525
Orneta..........................230
Ostpreussen 225
Ostróda........................224
Ostrzydkie Circle 201
Oświęcim 445–451
Otmuchów....................562
Owczary 370

P

Paczków.......................561
Paderewski, Ignacy
  Jan.....122, 310, 668, 720
Palmiry.........................142
pensions.........................51
phones.................. 58–60
Piast dynasty................623,
  659, 717
Pieniny, the..................497
Pieskowa Skała 455
Piłsudski, Józef 123,
  127, 385, 416, 430, 668,
  669, 720
Pisz Forest...................245
Piwniczna 374
Płock 157–160
Płock............................157
**Podhale region,
  the** 479–500
Podhale and the
  Tatras 480
Polanica-Zdrój..............554
Polany..........................377
Polańczyk 352
police.............................70
Polish cultural
  organizations 41
Pomerania 624–654
Pomerania............582–583
Pomorze, see Pomerania
Poniatowski, Stanisław
  August 97, 122,
  125, 428, 665
Pope John Paul II....7, 111,
  239, 297, 385, 407, 409,
  411, 429, 453, 457, 540,
  617, 675, 676, 720
Popiełuszko,
  Jerzy 126, 720

Poprad Valley, the 374
post offices....................58
Powroźnik.....................375
Poznań 22, 585–602
Poznań 588–589
Poznań: Centre............590
Prus, Bolesław.....113, 310,
  700, 720
Przemyśl............341–347
Przemyśl........................342
Pstrążna 558
Pszczeliny.....................354
Pszczyna 514
public holidays 62
public transport 43–46
Puck 197
Puławy.........................311
Pułtusk.........................160
Puńsk...........................258
Puszcza Białowieska ...20,
  277–282
**Puszcza
  Kampinoska** 141–144
Puszcza
  Knyszyńska 268
Puszcza Piska 245
Puszczykowo 604
Puszczykówko..............604

R

Rabka (Małopolska)......481
Rabka (Pomerania).......631
radio 61
Radziłów.......................270
Radziwiłł, Karol 146, 474
restaurants.....................55
Reszel..........................239
Rogalin 603
Rogoźnica 446, 550
rooms, private 51
Roztoczański national
  park 332
Ruciane-Nida...............245
Rytro............................374
Rzepedż 362
Rzeszów 332–335
Rzeszów.......................333

S

sailing 69
Sandomierz 317–320
Sandomierz..................318
Sanok...................347–351

Sanok 348
Sarmatism 417, 473,
  474, 594, 718
Sejny............................259
Sękowa.........................370
Siemiatycze 282
Sienkiewicz, Henryk 591,
  592, 720
Sierakowice 201
Silesia 503–577
Silesia..................506–507
skansen 20
skiing 69, 355, 490, 518
**Słowiński national
  park**.............. 17, 630–633
Słupsk..........................633
Smołdzino....................632
Smolniki.......................257
Smreczyński Staw 491
Sobibór.........................446
Sobieski, Jan.......124, 207,
  415, 563, 664, 720
Sobieszów 570
Sobótka........................547
Sochaczew 144
Solidarity
  (Solidarność).....171, 183,
  184, 676, 718
Solina...........................352
Sopot 191–194
Sopot...........................174
Sorkwity.......................236
Southeastern
  Poland 288–289
Spisz region, the 495
sports 68, 69
Sromowce Kąty............498
Stadnicki, Stanisław 335,
  336
Stanisław St 411, 425,
  594, 660
Stańczyki 257
Stargard
  Szczeciński................653
Stary Folwark 255
Stary Sącz 374
Stauffenberg, Count
  Claus Schenk von 242
Stęszew 604
Stoss, Veit 398, 399,
  407, 409, 412
Stróże 377
Strzegom......................550
Strzelno 622
student cards 73
studying in Poland..........71
Stutthof........................217
Supraśl 268
Suwalszczyzna 256–259

Suwalszczyna and the Puszcza Augustowska 250
Suwałki 254
Swibówki 488
Szczawnica 498
Szczebrzeszyn.............330
Szczecin 645–653
Szczecin...................... 646
Szczyrk 518
Szklana Huta 471
Szklarska Poręba 571
Szlak Orlich Gniazd (Eagles' Nest Trail) 453–456
Sztutowo 217
Szurpiły, Lake 256
Szydłów........................ 462
Szymanowski, Karol 487, 685, 721

Ś

Ślęża............................ 547
Św. Wojciech, see Adalbert, St
Świdnica...................... 564
Święta Katarzyna 471
Święta Lipka................. 238
Święty Krzyż................. 470
Świnoujście 644

T

Tarnobrzeg................... 322
Tarnowskie Góry........... 513
Tarnów 472–479
Tarnów 472
Tatars.................. 273, 274, 275, 549, 660, 661, 718
Tatras, the 16, 492–495
Tatras, the 480
telephones.............. 58–60
television 61
temperature................... 14
Teutonic Knights.......... 170, 204, 206, 207, 209, 225, 232, 238, 660, 661, 718
theatre 67
time................................ 73
toilets............................ 73
Tokarnia 468
Toruń 23, 209–215
Toruń 210
tourist offices................. 40

tours
from Australia and New Zealand........................... 36
from Britain and Ireland 29
from the US and Canada... 34
trains in Poland....... 43–45
trains to Poland 30
Trakiszki....................... 257
Treblinka 162
Trójmiasto (Gdańsk, Sopot and Gdynia) ... 174
Truskaw 141
Trybsz 497
Trzebaw-Rosnówko...... 606
Trzebiatów 638
Trzebnica 545
Trzemeszno 622
Trzy Korony 497
Turzańsk 362
Twierdza Osowiec 272
Tykocin 269
Tylicz........................... 376
Tylman of Gameren 102, 112, 121, 145, 311, 334

U

Uherce 352
Ukraine 305, 346
Ukrainian Resistance Army (UPA) 356, 363
Ulucz 351
Uniate Church 344, 349, 356, 360, 362, 372
Unieście....................... 636
Upper Silesia....... 508–528
Ustka 634
Ustroń.......................... 519
Ustrzyki Dolne 352
Ustrzyki Górne 354

V

Vilnius (Lithuania)......... 180, 258, 669
visas 36
vodka.................. 13, 17, 57

W

Wadowice..................... 453
Wajda, Andrzej 65, 103, 104, 147, 704

Wałbrzych.................... 566
Wałesa, Lech 183, 184, 261, 675, 677, 718
Wambierzyce............... 554
WARSAW 82–140
Warsaw 86–87
Warsaw: City Centre..... 95
Park Łazienkowski 120
Wilanów 123
    accommodation 90–94
    activities 138
    airport.............................. 84
    Barbakan.......................... 94
    bus stations 85, 139
    Church of the Holy Sacrament 102
    cinema 136
    classical music................ 135
    clubs 134
    Cmentarz Żydowski 108
    concerts and gigs 134
    eating and drinking ...128–133
    Galeria Zachęta............... 112
    gay Warsaw 94, 135
    Ghetto 107–109
    Ghetto Heroes Monument 107
    history 83
    information 85
    Jesuit Church................... 93
    Jewish cemetery.............. 108
    Jewish Historical Institute......................... 109
    Korczak Orphanage 108
    Kościół Jezuitski (Jesuit Church) 93
    Krakowskie Przedmieście 112
    listings............................. 139
    Marie Curie Museum 102
    markets 138
    Mirów 106–110
    Muranów 106–110
    Muzeum Archeologiczne (Archeological Museum)...................... 103
    Muzeum Etnograficzne (Ethnographic Museum)...................... 115
    Muzeum Fryderyka Chopina (Chopin Museum) 116
    Muzeum Historyczne Starej Warsawy (Warsaw Historical Museum)......... 98
    Muzeum Karykatury (Caricature Museum) 113
    Muzeum Kolekcji im. Jana Pawła II (John Paul II Museum)....................... 110
    Muzeum Mickiewicza (Mickiewicz Museum) ... 100
    Muzeum Narodowe (National Museum)........ 116
    Muzeum Niepodległości (Independence Museum)...................... 103

Muzeum Pawiaka (Pawiak
  Prison).............................. 103
Muzeum Warszawskego
  Powstania (Warsaw
  Uprising Museum) 109
Muzeum Wojska Polskiego
  (Army Museum) 114, 119
New Town 100–106
nightlife and
  entertainment........ 134–136
Nowe Miasto (New
  Town) 100–106
Nowy Świat...................... 116
Nożyk Synagogue............ 106
Ogród Saski 112
Old Town 24, 94–100
opera 135
orientation 84
Pałac Krasińskich (Krasiński
  Palace).......................... 102
Pałac Kultury i Nauki
  (Palace of Culture and
  Sciences) 19, 115
Pałac Łazienkowski.......... 121
Pałac Namiestnikowski.... 113
Pałac Radziwiłłow 103
Park Łazienkowski 120–123
Park Ujazdowski 120
Path of Remembrance..... 107
plac Bankowy 111
plac Krasińkich 102
plac Piłsudskiego 112
plac Teatralny 110
plac Trzech Krzyży 119
Pomnik Bohaterów Getta
  (Ghetto Heroes
  Monument) 107
Praga................................ 127
public transport.......... 88, 139
Royal Castle..................... 96
Royal Way 112
Rynek Nowego Miasta
  (New Town Square) 102
Rynek Starego Miasta
  (Old Town Square) 93
shopping 137
Stare Miasto (Old Town) .. 24,
  94–100
Śródmieście 110–119
Św. Jacka (St Jacek's).... 101
Św. Jana (St John's) 98
Św. Martina (St Martin's).... 92
taxis.................................. 90
Teatr Wielki (Grand
  Theatre)....................... 110
theatre............................. 136
train stations 84, 139
Trakt Królewski (Royal
  Way).............................. 112
ulica Freta 101
ulica Marszałkowska........ 114
ulica Miodowa................. 103
university.......................... 114

Wilanów 123–126
Zamek Królewski (Royal
  Castle)............................. 96
Zamoyski Palace.............. 116
zoo 127
Żoliborz 126
Żydowskiego Instytutu
  Historycznego (Jewish
  Historical Institute)........ 109
Warsaw and
  Mazovia................. 80–81
Warsaw Ghetto
  Uprising 107
Warsaw Uprising 102,
  103, 104, 109, 119, 127
Wdzydze
  Kiszewskie................. 202
weather............................. 14
websites 42
Wenecja........................... 620
Wetlina............................. 359
Węgorzewo 249
Wielkopolska....... 584–624
Wielkopolska and
  Pomerania........ 582–583
Wielkopolska national
  park 604–606
Wielkopolska national
  park 605
Wigry national park 255
Wilcz Tułowskie 144
Wilczy Szaniec 241
Wilkasy 248
Willmann, Michael 539,
  547, 555, 565, 568
Wilno, see Vilnius
windsurfing..................... 69
Wisełka 644
Wisła............................... 520
Wiślana Peninsula 218
Witkiewicz,
  Stanisław ..405, 485, 486,
  487
Witkiewicz, Stanisław
  Ignacy ("Witkacy") 264,
  485, 486, 487, 633, 701,
  703, 721
Witów 491
Władysław Jagiełło,
  King 158, 232, 260,
  290, 295, 296, 347, 407,
  409, 412, 661
Włodawa...................... 309
Wodziłki 256
Wojkowa 376
Wojnowo 246

Wojtyła, Karol, see Pope
  John Paul II
Wolf's Lair..................... 241
Wolin 641–645
Woliński national
  park 643
Wolsztyn 606
Wołosate....................... 356
wooden churches
  (cerkwie) 18, 360
working in Poland.......... 71
Wrocław......... 22, 528–544
Wrocław 530–531
Wyspiański,
  Stanisław 118, 159,
  399, 404, 405, 407, 417,
  425, 432, 512, 594, 721
Wyszyński, Cardinal
  Stefan 239, 297, 362,
  617, 673, 674, 721

Y

youth hostels................. 52

Z

Zakopane 21, 482–489
Zakopane 483
Zalipie....................22, 478
Zamenhof, Ludwik........ 265
Zamość.......... 19, 323–330
Zamość 324
Zamoyski, Jan 323, 327,
  328, 331, 332, 662
Zawiercie 456
Zielona Góra................. 607
Ziema Kłodzka,
  the 552–561
Zwierzyniec 331
Zydnia........................... 370
Zyndranowa................. 367

Ż

Żagań 608
Żelazowa Wola 142
Żnin............................... 620
Żukowo......................... 200

Map symbols

maps are listed in the full index using coloured text

Motorway		Post office	
Paved road		Bus stop	
Steps		Parking	
Path		Hospital	
Pedestrianized street		Metro station	
Railway		Gate	
Ferry route		Castle	
River		Lighthouse	
National boundary		Church (regional)	
Chapter division boundary		Synagogue	
Point of interest		Museum	
Mountain peak		Wall or fortifications	
Mountain range		Concentration camp	
Cave		Stadium	
Airport		Building	
Border crossing		Church (town)	
Campsite		Christian cemetery	
Accommodation		Jewish cemetery	
Restaurant		Woods or forest	
Information office		Park	
Internet access			